THE GUINNESS

19 BOOK OF 88

RECORDS

Nelson de la Rosa, the world's smallest living man
with his father. (See p. 8)

© NATIONAL ENQUIRER

Editors

Alan Russell
1986–7

Norris D. McWhirter
1955–85

GUINNESS BOOKS

The Story Behind The Guinness Book

The Rt Hon. the Earl of Iveagh

On Saturday 10 November 1951, Sir Hugh Beaver (1890–1967) was out shooting on The North Slob, by the river Slaney in County Wexford in the south-east of Ireland. Some golden plover were missed by the party. That evening at Castlebridge House it was realised that it was not possible to confirm in reference books whether or not the golden plover was Europe's fastest game bird.

In August 1954 argument arose as to whether grouse were even faster. Sir Hugh, managing director of Guinness, thought that there must be numerous other questions debated nightly in the 81,400 pubs in Britain and in Ireland, but there was no book with which to settle arguments about records.

On 12 September 1954, Sir Hugh invited Norris and Ross McWhirter to see if their fact and figure agency in London could help. An office was set up at 107 Fleet Street, London EC4 and work began on the first 198-page edition, the first copy of which was bound by the printers on 27 August 1955. Before Christmas the *Guinness Book of Records* was No 1 on the bestsellers list and it has occupied this position every year since, except in 1957 and 1959 when it was not republished.

The first US edition appeared in New York in 1956 followed by editions in French (1962) and German (1963). In 1967 there were first editions in Japanese, Spanish, Danish and Norwegian, while the following year editions were published in Swedish, Finnish and Italian. In the 'seventies there followed Dutch (1971); Portuguese (1974); Czechoslovak (1976); Hebrew, Serbo-Croat and Icelandic (all in 1977) and Slovenian (1978). In the 1980s translations into Greek, Indonesian, Chinese, Turkish, Hindi, Malay, Arabic, Thai, Tamil, Telugu, Malayalam, Kannada and Hungarian will bring the total to 262 editions in 35 languages.

In November 1974 the *Guinness Book of Records* earned its own place in the Guinness Book by becoming the top selling copyright book in publishing history with sales of 23.9 million. By 1987 global sales had risen to more than 57 million, which is equivalent to over 163 stacks each as high as Mount Everest.

Iveagh

**President
Guinness PLC
October 1987**

The Rt Hon. the Earl of Iveagh

Anna Williams, born 2 June 1873, who possesses the earliest birth certificate in the world, seen above with Norris McWhirter and Alan Russell, on her 114th birthday, and left, with her husband, Harry, whom she married in 1905 when aged 32.

A Record is . . .

A 'record' in the modern sense of 'a performance or occurrence going beyond others of the same kind' is something that represents the extremes of either animate or inanimate objects and which is measurable by the stop watch, weighing scale, measuring tape or in terms of frequency.

The oldest record of an achievement that has survived is probably that of St Simeon the Younger, a monk of the rigorous sect of the pillar-squatters known as the Stylites, who, in AD 597, near Antioch in Syria completed a sojourn on top of his stone pillar that had lasted for 45 years.

Some fourteen centuries later, the world of record breaking is as active as ever and a further six supreme achievers have been inducted as 1987 Hall of Fame members (page 4). Over the past 12 months, thousands of records have been broken.

Twins who had been separated for more than 69 years found each other, and American Richard Hoffman found he had the world's strongest bite.

Hideaki Tomoyori of Japan recited 'pi' from memory to 40,000 decimal places, and Indian S. E. Jayaraman talked non-stop for more than 8 days.

Californian Leard Wayne Woodruff balanced 242 dominoes on a single domino, and 40 members of the Brazilian Army

A Note from the Editorial Office

Military Police Force balanced on top of a motorcycle for over a kilometer.

Nelson, 'The Little Man' (see title page) was confirmed as the smallest living person at 28.3 inches (72 cm). Now twenty one years of age, he has stopped growing according to doctors in his home town of Santo Domingo.

On 2 June 1987, Anna Eliza Williams (see left) became only the third person ever to celebrate their 114th birthday and the first person to reach such an age possessing a birth certificate. She was 3 years old when General Custer died at Little Bighorn, 12 when Gordon fell at Khartoum and an old-age pensioner before the start of the Second World War.

Edwin Corley Moses (below) was beaten in the 400 metres hurdles on 4 June 1987, ending the longest unbeaten run in the history of track athletics, 122 races in 9 years 281 days.

However, not all claimants were accepted into the exclusive club of world record breakers. Some failed because they did not check for the latest record update, and others because they neglected our criteria.

The name Guinness is a registered trade mark and should not be used in publicity for, or otherwise in the context of, a record attempt without our prior written consent.

The publishers do not normally supply personnel to invigilate record attempts but reserve the right to do so.

All record attempts are undertaken at the sole risk of the (potential) claimant. The publishers cannot be held in any way responsible for any (potential) liability, howsoever arising out of any such attempt, whether to the claimant or any third party.

Regulations

Nearly every activity associated with record breaking has a set of rules. If that activity is one controlled by a recognised world or national governing body, that body should be consulted and involved in ratifying any attempt. If there is no such body, then potential claimants are advised to contact my editorial department well in advance for guidance.

In some marathon events, 5-minute rest intervals are permitted, but only AFTER each *completed* hour. These rest breaks are optional and may be accumulated. The accepted record will be the gross time, *i.e.* the total elapsed time, including rest intervals, from start to finish. However, unused accumulated rest-break time cannot be added to the final figure.

In recent years, there have been efforts to establish non-stop records in many activities and some categories, such as motionlessness, can be judged only in this way. In the very nature of record-breaking, the duration of such 'marathons' will tend to be pushed to greater and greater extremes, and it should be stressed that marathons which involve extended periods with little or no sleep are not without possible dangers.

Documentation

Signed log books should show there has been unremitting surveillance in the case of endurance or marathon events. These log books must include, in chronological order, the times of activity and the times and durations of all rest breaks taken. They must include signatures of witnesses with times of entering and leaving and at least two *independent* witnesses must be on hand at all times. Where applicable, score sheets must be kept to demonstrate a satisfactory rate of play.

Claimants should also obtain independent corroboration in the form of local or national newspaper, radio or television coverage. Newspaper clippings must be annotated with the name of the newspaper, its place of publication and the date of the issue in which the article appeared.

Colour action photographs should also be supplied. If the activity is one governed by a national or international body a signed document showing ratification by that governing body should also be supplied.

Categories

We are *likely* to publish only those records which improve upon previously published records or which are newly significant in having become the subject of widespread and, preferably, worldwide competition.

It should be stressed that unique occurrences, interesting peculiarities and the collecting of everyday objects are not themselves necessarily records. Records which are *qualified* or limited in some way—for example, by age, handicap, day of the week, etc.—cannot be accommodated in a reference work so general as the *Guinness Book of Records*.

Finally let it be said that there is no such thing as an easy record. By definition records are only on the edge of possibility. They are destined to be broken by smaller and smaller margins at longer and longer intervals in time.

OCTOBER 1987
THE GUINNESS BOOK OF RECORDS
33 LONDON ROAD
ENFIELD, MIDDLESEX EN2 6DJ
ENGLAND

1987 HALL OF FAME

Sir Edmund Hillary
NEW ZEALAND

for his outstanding achievement in being the first person to conquer Mount Everest.

Sir Donald Bradman
AUSTRALIA

whose contribution to cricket gave him the highest career and test averages in the history of the game.

Katharine Hepburn
UNITED STATES

whose contribution to the film industry for over half-a-century won her a unique four Oscars.

Valentina Tereshkova
USSR

for her outstanding achievement in being the first woman in space — successfully completing over 48 earth orbits.

— ROLL — OF HONOUR

1986 INAUGURAL MEMBERS OF THE HALL OF FAME

Joseph Kittinger

Paul McCartney

Billie-Jean King

Vesna Vulovic

Sir Ranulph Fiennes, Bt.

Vernon Craig

Sergey Bubka
USSR

whose dedication in the field of athletics enabled him to become the first pole vaulter to clear the six-metre barrier.

Charles Upham
NEW ZEALAND

whose heroism and bravery was honoured when he became the only fighting soldier to receive the Victoria Cross and Bar.

Contents

Dimensions

GIANTS

The true height of human giants is frequently obscured by exaggeration and commercial dishonesty. The only admissible evidence on the actual height of giants is that collected during this century under impartial medical supervision. Unfortunately medical authors themselves are not blameless in including fanciful, as opposed to measured, heights.

> **Tallest Living Man** ● Gabriel Estavao Monjane (b. 1944 Monjacaze, Mozambique) billed by a Portuguese circus in 1967 as 265 cm *8 ft 8.3 in.* This exaggerated height compares with an actual height of 8 ft 0¾ in *245,7 cm.* He weighs 418 lb (29 st 12 lb), *189,6 kg.*

THE HUMAN BEING

CHAPTER ONE

The assertion that Goliath of Gath (*c.* 1060 BC) stood 6 cubits and a span (9 ft 6½ in *290 cm*) suggests a confusion of units or some over-zealous exaggeration by the Hebrew chroniclers. The Jewish historian Flavius Josephus (born AD 37/38, died *c.* AD 100) and some of the manuscripts of the Septuagint (the earliest Greek translation of the Old Testament) attribute to Goliath the wholly credible height of 4 Greek cubits and a span (6 ft 10 in *208 cm*).

Giants exhibited in circuses and exhibitions are routinely under contract not to be anthropometrically assessed and are, almost traditionally, billed by their promoters at heights up to 18 in *45 cm* in excess of their true heights.

TALLEST MEN

Modern opinion is that the tallest man in medical history of whom there is irrefutable evidence was the pre-acromegalic giant Robert Pershing Wadlow, born at 6.30 a.m. on 22 Feb 1918 in Alton, Illinois, USA. Weighing 8½ lb *3,85 kg* at birth, his abnormal growth started at the age of two following a double hernia operation. On his 13th birthday he recorded a height of 7 ft 1¾ in *218 cm*, and at the age of 17 years he stood 8 ft 0½ in *245 cm*. On 27 June 1940 Dr C. M. Charles, Associate Professor of Anatomy at Washington University's School of Medicine in St. Louis, Missouri, and Dr Cyril MacBryde measured Robert Wadlow at 272 cm *8 ft 11.1 in* (arm-span 288 cm *9 ft 5¾ in*) in St. Louis. Wadlow died 18 days later at 1.30 a.m. on 15 July 1940 in an hotel in Manistee, Michigan, as a result of a septic blister on his right ankle, caused by a poorly-fitting brace. Because of his rapid growth Wadlow had limited feeling in his legs. Wadlow was still growing during his terminal illness and would probably have reached or just exceeded 9 ft *274 cm* in height if he had lived for another year. His greatest recorded weight was 491 lb (35 st 1 lb) *222,7 kg* on his 21st birthday. He scaled 439 lb (31 st 5 lb) *199 kg* at the time of his death. His shoes were size 37AA (18½ in *47 cm*) and his hands measured 12¾ in *32,4 cm* from the wrist to the tip of the middle finger (cf. the depth of this page at 11¼ in *28,5 cm*).

He was buried in Oakwood Cemetery, Alton, Illinois, in a coffin measuring 10 ft 9 in *328 cm* in length, 32 in *81 cm* wide and 30 in *76 cm* deep.

England

The tallest Englishman ever recorded was William Bradley (1787–1820), born in Market Weighton, now Humberside. He stood 7 ft 9 in *236 cm*. John Middleton (1578–1623), the famous Childe of Hale, from near Liverpool, was credited with a height of 9 ft 3 in *282 cm* but a life-size impression of his right hand (length 11½ in *29,2 cm*, cf. Wadlow's 12¾ in *32,4 cm*) painted on a panel in Brasenose College, Oxford indicates his true stature was nearer 7 ft 9 in *236 cm*. Albert Brough (1871–1919), a Nottingham publican, reached a height of 7 ft 7½ in *232 cm*. Frederick Kempster (1889–1918) of Avebury, Wiltshire, was reported to have measured 8 ft 4¼ in *255 cm* at the time of his death, but photographic evidence suggests that his height was 7 ft 8½ in *235 cm*. He measured 234 cm *7 ft 8.1 in* in 1913. Henry Daglish, who stood 7 ft 7 in *231 cm* died in Upper Stratton, Wiltshire, on 15 March 1951, aged 25. The much-publicised Edward (Ted) Evans (1924–58) of Englefield Green, Surrey, was reputed to be 9 ft 3 in *282 cm* but actually stood 7 ft 8½ in *235 cm*.

The tallest man now living in Great Britain is Christopher Paul Greener (b. New Brighton, Merseyside, 21 Nov 1943) of Hayes, Kent, who measures 7 ft 6¼ in *229 cm* (weight 364 lb *165 kg*).

Scotland

The tallest Scotsman, and the tallest recorded 'true' (non-pathological) giant, was Angus Macaskill (1823–63), born on the island of Berneray, in the Sound of Harris, in the Western Isles. He stood 7 ft 9 in *236 cm* and died in St Ann's, on Cape Breton Island, Nova Scotia, Canada.

The tallest Scotsman now living is George Gracie (b. 1938) of Forth, Lanark, Strathclyde. He stands 7 ft 3 in *221 cm* and weighs 32 st *203 kg*. His brother Hugh (b. 1941) is 7 ft 0¼ in *215 cm*.

Wales

The tallest Welshman on record was William Evans (1599–1634) of Monmouthshire, now Gwent, who was porter to King James I. He stood 7 ft 6 in *228,6 cm*.

Ireland

The tallest Irishman was the 8 ft 1 in *246 cm* tall Patrick Cotter (O'Brien) (1760–1806), born in Kinsale, County Cork. He died at Hotwells, Bristol (See table below).

TALLEST WOMEN

Giantesses are rarer than giants but their heights are still spectacular. The tallest woman in history was the acromegalic giantess Zeng Jinlian (pronounced San Chunglin) (b. 26 June 1964) of Yujiang village in the Bright Moon Commune, Hunan Province, central China who was 247 cm *8 ft 1¾ in* when she died on 13 Feb 1982. This figure, however, represented her height with assumed normal spinal curvature because she suffered from severe scoliosis and could not stand up straight. She began to grow abnormally from the age of 4 months and stood 156 cm *5 ft 1½ in* before her 4th birthday (*cf.* 162,5 cm *5 ft 4 in* for Robert Wadlow at the age of 5) and 217 cm *7 ft 1½ in* when she was 13. Her hands measured 25,5 cm *10 in* and her feet 35,5 cm *14 in* in length. Both her parents and her brother are normal in size.

Living

The tallest living woman is Sandy Allen (b. 18 June 1955, Chicago) of Niagara Falls, Ontario, Canada. On 14 July 1977 she underwent a pituitary gland operation, which inhibited further growth at 7 ft 7¼ in *231,7 cm*. A 6½ lb *2,95 kg* baby, her acromegalic growth began soon after birth. She now weighs 33 st *209,5 kg* and takes a size 16EEE American shoe (=14½ UK or 50PP Continental).

United Kingdom

The tallest British woman ever recorded and the second tallest in medical history was Jane ('Ginny') Bunford, born on 26 July 1895 at Bartley Green, Northfield, Birmingham. Her abnormal growth started at the age of 11 following a head injury, and on her 13th birthday she measured 6 ft 6 in *198 cm*. Shortly before her death on 1 April 1922 she stood 7 ft 7 in *231 cm* tall, but she had severe kyphoscoliosis and would have measured at least 7 ft 11 in *241 cm* if she had been able to stand fully erect. Her skeleton, now preserved in the Anatomical Museum in the Medical School at Birmingham University, has a mounted height of 7 ft 4 in *223,5 cm*.

Married couple

Anna Hanen Swan (1846–88) of Nova Scotia, Canada, was billed at 8 ft 1 in *246 cm* but actually measured 7 ft 5½ in *227 cm*. At St Martin's-in-the-Fields, London on 17 June 1871 she married Martin van Buren Bates (1845–1919) of Whitesburg, Letcher County, Kentucky, USA, who stood 7 ft 2½ in *219 cm*, making them the tallest married couple on record.

DWARFS

The strictures which apply to giants apply equally to dwarfs, except that exaggeration gives way to understatement. In the same way as 9 ft *274 cm* may be regarded as the limit towards which the tallest giants tend, so 23 inches *58 cm* must be regarded as the limit towards which the shortest mature dwarfs tend (*cf.* the average length of new-born babies is 18–20 in *46–50 cm*). In the case of child dwarfs their *ages* are often enhanced by their agents or managers.

There are many forms of human dwarfism, but those suffering from ateleiosis (midgets) are generally the shortest. They have essentially normal proportions but suffer from growth hormone deficiency. Such dwarfs tended to be more diminutive in the past as a result of lower nutritional standards.

Shortest

The shortest mature human of whom there is independent evidence was Pauline Musters ('Princess Pauline'), a Dutch midget. She was born at Ossendrecht, on 26 Feb 1876 and measured 30 cm *11.8 in* at birth. At the age of 9 she was 55 cm *21.65 in* tall and weighed only 1,5 kg *3 lb 5 oz*. She died on 1 Mar 1895 in New York City, at the age of 19, of pneumonia, with meningitis, her heart weakened from alcoholic excesses. Although she was billed at 48 cm *19 in*, she had earlier been medically assessed and found to be 59 cm *23.2 in* tall. A *post mortem* examination showed her to be exactly 61 cm *24 in* (there was some elongation after death). Her mature weight varied from 3,4–4 kg *7½–9 lb* and her 'vital statistics' were 47-48-43 cm *18½–19–17 in*, which suggests she was overweight.

In 1938 a height of 19 in *48 cm* was attributed to Paul Del Rio (b. Madrid, 1920) by *Life Magazine* when he visited Hollywood, but the fact that his presence created no great impression among other dwarfs in the film capital and that he weighed as much as 12 lb *5,4 kg* suggests that he was closer to 26 in *66 cm* tall.

In 1979 a height of 50 cm *19.68 in* and a weight of 4 lb 6 oz *1,98 kg* were reported for a nine-year-old Greek girl named Stamatoula (b. Sept 1969 length 15 cm *5.9 in*). When she died on 22 Aug 1985 at the Lyrion Convent, Athens, she measured 67 cm *26.4 in* and weighed 5 kg *11 lbs*. The child, believed to be the survivor of twins, suffered from Seckel's syndrome, also known as 'bird-headed dwarfism', because victims have prominent eyes and noses.

GIANTS

The only men, apart from Robert Wadlow, for whom heights of 8 ft *244 cm* or more have been reliably reported are the nine listed below. In seven cases, gigantism was followed by acromegaly, a disorder which causes an enlargement of the nose, lips, tongue, lower jaw, hands and feet, due to renewed activity by an already swollen pituitary gland, which is located at the base of the brain.

John William Rogan (1871–1905), a negro of Gallatin, Tennessee, USA [1] 8 ft 8 in *264 cm*.

John F. Carroll (1932–69) of Buffalo, New York State, USA [2] 8 ft 7¾ in *263,5 cm*.

Väinö Myllyrinne (1909–63) of Helsinki, Finland [3] 8 ft 3 in *251,4 cm*.

Don Koehler (1925–81) of Denton, Montana, USA [4] 8 ft 2 in *248,9 cm*, latterly lived in Chicago.

Bernard Coyne (1897–1921) of Anthon, Iowa USA [5] 8 ft 2 in *248,9 cm*.

Patrick Cotter (O'Brien) (1760–1806) of Kinsale, County Cork, Ireland [6] 8 ft 1 in *246 cm*.

'Constantine' (1872–1902) of Reutlingen, West Germany [7] 8 ft 0.8 in *245,8 cm*.

Gabriel Estevao Monjane (b. 1944–*fl.* 1987) of Monjacaze, Mozambique [8] *c.* 8 ft 0¾ in *245,7 cm*.

Sulaimān 'Ali Nashnush (b. 1943–*fl.* 1986) of Tripoli, Libya [9] 8 ft 0.4 in *245,0 cm*.

(1) *Measured in a sitting position. Unable to stand owing to ankylosis (stiffening of the joints through the formation of adhesions) of the knees and hips. Weighed only 175 lb 79 kg. Still growing at time of death.*

(2) *Severe kypho-scoliosis (two dimensional spinal curvature). The figure represents his height with assumed normal spinal curvature, calculated from a standing height of 8 ft 0 in 244 cm, measured on 14 Oct 1959. His standing height was 7 ft 8¼ in 234 cm shortly before his death.*

(3) *Stood 7 ft 3½ in 222 cm at the age of 21 years. Experienced a second phase of growth in his late thirties and measured 8 ft 1.2 in 246,8 cm at the time of his death.*

(4) *Abnormal growth started at the age of 10. He has a twin sister who is 5 ft 9 in 175 cm tall. His father was 6 ft 2 in 187 cm and his mother 5 ft 10 in 177 cm.*

(5) *Eunuchoidal giant (Daddy long-legs syndrome). Rejected by Army in 1918 when 7 ft 9 in 236 cm. Still growing at time of death.*

(6) *Revised height based on skeletal remeasurement after bones exhumed on 19 Dec 1972.*

(7) *Eunuchoidal. Height estimated, as both legs were amputated after they turned gangrenous. He claimed a height of 8 ft 6 in 259 cm.*

(8) *Eunuchoidal. Now walks with the aid of a stick after breaking his hip in a fall.*

(9) *Received glandular injections to check abnormal growth in Rome in 1960.*

Exaggerated heights: the following lists a number of well-known giants whose heights have been exaggerated.

NAME	DATES	COUNTRY	CLAIMED HEIGHT	ACTUAL HEIGHT
Muhammad Aalam Channa	1956–*fl.* 1987	Pakistan	8 ft 2¾ in *250,8 cm*	7 ft 10 in *238,7 cm*
Edouard Beaupre	1881–1904	Canada	8 ft 3 in *251,4 cm*	7 ft 9 in *236,2 cm*
Fernand (Atlas) Bacheland	1923–76	Belgium	9 ft 2 in *279,4 cm*	7 ft 8¼ in *234,3 cm*
Joachim Eleizegue	1822–*fl.* 1845	Spain	7 ft 10 in *238,7 cm*	7 ft 8 in *233,6 cm*
Chang Wu-Gow	1846–93	China	9 ft 2 in *279,4 cm*	7 ft 8 in *233,6 cm*
Johann Peturssen	1914–*fl.* 1986	Iceland	8 ft 8 in *264,1 cm*	7 ft 7 in *231,1 cm*
Max Palmer	1928–*fl.* 1986	USA	8 ft 0½ in *245,1 cm*	7 ft 7 in *231,1 cm*
Rigardus Riynhout	1922–*fl.* 1955	Netherlands	9 ft 1½ in *278,1 cm*	7 ft 6½ in *229,8 cm*
Baptiste Hugo	1879–1916	France	8 ft 10 in *269,2 cm*	7 ft 6½ in *239,8 cm*
Bernardo Gigli	1736–62	Italy	8 ft 0 in *243,8 cm*	7 ft 6½ in *239,8 cm*
James Toller	1795–1819	England	8 ft 6 in *259,0 cm*	7 ft 6 in *228,6 cm*
Eddie Carmel	1938–72	Israel	9 ft 0½ in *275,5 cm*	7 ft 6 in *228,6 cm*
Daniel Cajanus	1724–49	Finland	9 ft 3½ in *283,2 cm*	7 ft 3½ in *222,2 cm*
Patrick Murphy	1834–62	Ireland	8 ft 10 in *269,2 cm*	7 ft 3½ in *222,2 cm*
Jakob Loll (The Pomeranian Giant)	1783–1839	USSR	8 ft 4½ in *255,2 cm*	7 ft 3 in *220,9 cm*
Paul Henoch	1852–76	Germany	8 ft 3 in *251,4 cm*	7 ft 2 in *218,4 cm*

Note: The height of Eddie Carmel was estimated from photographs and that of Cajanus from evidence by bones. Each of the other actual heights was obtained by an independent medical authority.

The embalmed body of Beaupre in the anatomical museum of the University of Montreal measures 7 ft 1⅜ in *217 cm* in length.

Dimensions

The shortest recorded adult male dwarf was Calvin Phillips, born on 14 Jan 1791 in Bridgewater, Massachusetts, USA. He weighed 2 lb *907 g* at birth and stopped growing at the age of 5. When he was 19 he measured 26½ in *67 cm* tall and weighed 12 lb *5,4 kg* with his clothes on. He died two years later, in April 1812, from progeria, a rare disorder characterised by dwarfism and premature senility.

William E. Jackson, *alias* 'Major Mite', born on 2 Oct 1864 in Dunedin, New Zealand, measured 9 in *23 cm* long and weighed 12 oz *340 g* at birth. In November 1880 he stood 21 in *53 cm* and weighed 9 lb *4 kg*. He died in New York City on 9 Dec 1900, when he measured 27 in *69 cm*.

The most famous midget in history was Charles Sherwood Stratton, *alias* 'General Tom Thumb', born on 4 Jan 1838. When he joined up with Phineas T. Barnum, the famous American showman, his birth date was changed to 4 Jan 1832 so that when billed at 30½ in *77 cm* at the age of 18 he was in fact 12. He died in his birthplace of Bridgeport, Connecticut, USA of apoplexy on 15 July 1883 aged 45 (not 51) and was 3 ft 4 in *102 cm* (70 lb *31,7 kg*).

Living

The world's shortest known mobile living adult human is Nelson de la Rosa (b. June 1968) an ateleiotic dwarf of Santo Domingo, Dominican Republic. On 2 Apr 1987 he was examined by the Head of the Dominican Republic Medical Association who revealed that this tiny prodigy measured 72 cm *28.3 in* in height and weighed only 6,81 kg *15 lb*. (Compare 7½ lb *3,4 kg* for an average baby at birth). Other statistics include a 44,4 cm *17½ in* chest and 40,6 cm *16 in* waist. The doctor also reported that Nelson had stopped growing. The rest of his family are all of normal size.

United Kingdom

The shortest mature human ever recorded in Britain was Miss Joyce Carpenter (b. 21 Dec 1929), a rachitic dwarf of Charford, now Hereford & Worcester, who stood 29 in *74 cm* tall and weighed 30 lb *13,60 kg*. She died on 7 Aug 1973 aged 43. Hopkins Hopkins (1737–54) of Llantrisant, Mid-Glamorgan who suffered from progeria, was 31 in *79 cm* tall. He weighed 19 lb *8,62 kg* at the age of 7 and 13 lb *6 kg* at the time of his death. There are an estimated 3000 people of severely restricted growth (*i.e.* under 4 ft 8 in *142 cm*) living in Britain today.

The shortest adult living in Britain is Michael Henbury-Ballan (b. 26 Nov 1958) of Bassett, Southampton, who is 37 in *94 cm* tall and weighs 5½ st *35 kg*. A 5 lb 14 oz *2,66 kg* baby, he stopped growing at the age of 13 years. His fraternal twin brother Malcolm is 5 ft 9 in *175 cm* tall and weighs 11 st 7 lb *73 kg*. In 1981 a height of 38 in *96,5 cm* was reported for an unnamed woman (b. 1963) living in Brighton, Sussex.

Twins

The shortest twins ever recorded were the primordial dwarfs Matjus and Bela Matina (b. 1903–*fl.* 1935) of Budapest, Hungary who later became naturalised Americans. They both measured 30 in *76 cm*. The world's shortest living twins are John and Greg Rice (b. 3 Dec 1951) of West Palm Beach, Florida who both measure 34 in *86,3 cm*.

Oldest

There are only two centenarian dwarfs on record. The older was Hungarian-born Miss Susanna Bokoyni ('Princess Susanna') of Newton, New Jersey who died aged 105 years on 24 Aug 1984. She was 3 ft 4 in *101 cm* tall and weighed 37 lb *16,78 kg*. The other was Miss Anne Clowes of Matlock, Derbyshire, who died on 5 Aug 1784 aged 103 years. She was 3 ft 9 in *114 cm* tall and weighed 48 lb *21,7 kg*.

Most variable stature

Adam Rainer, born in Graz, Austria, in 1899, measured 118 cm *3 ft 10.45 in* at the age of 21. He then suddenly started growing at a rapid rate, and by 1931 he had reached 218 cm *7 ft 1¾ in*. He became so weak as a result that he was bedridden for the rest of his life. At the time of his death on 4 Mar 1950 aged 51 he measured 234 cm *7 ft 8 in* and was the only person in medical history to have been both a dwarf and a giant.

Lord Adare (4th Earl of Dunraven and Mount-Earl, b. 12 Feb 1841, d. 14 June 1926) recorded that the Scots-born medium Daniel Home (b. 1833) could elongate his body 11 in *28 cm*.

Most dissimilar couple

Nigel Wilks (6 ft 7 in *200,6 cm*) of Kingston upon Hull, Humberside married Beverly Russell (3 ft 11 in *119,3 cm*), both aged 21, on 30 June 1984. Their son Daniel, 9 lb 5 oz *4,22 kg*, was born on 22 Mar 1986.

TRIBES

Tallest

The tallest major tribes in the world are the slender Tutsi (also known as the Watussi) of Rwanda and Burundi, Central Africa, and the Dinka of the Sudan, where the average adult height (males) is just over 6 ft *183 cm*. The Tehuelches of Patagonia, long regarded as of gigantic stature (*i.e.* 7–8 ft *213–244 cm*), have in fact an average height (males) of 5 ft 10 in *177 cm*. The Montenegrins of Yugoslavia, with a male average of 5 ft 10 in *177 cm* (in the town of Trebinje the average height is 6 ft *183 cm*), compare with the men of Sutherland, at 5 ft 9½ in *176,5 cm*. In 1912 the average height of men living in Balmaclellan, in the Kircudbright district of Dumfries and Galloway was reported to be 5 ft 10.4 in *179 cm*.

Shortest

The smallest pygmies are the Mbuti, with an average height of 4 ft 6 in *137 cm* for men and 4 ft 5 in *135 cm* for women, with some groups averaging only 4 ft 4 in *132 cm* for men and 4 ft 1 in *124 cm* for women. They live in Zaïre.

WEIGHT

Heaviest men

The heaviest man in medical history was Jon Brower Minnoch (b. 29 Sept 1941) of Bainbridge Island, Washington, USA, who had suffered from obesity since childhood. The 6 ft 1 in *185 cm* tall former taxi-driver was 400 lb *181 kg* in 1963, 700 lb *317 kg* in 1966 and 975 lb *442 kg* in Sept 1976. Eighteen months later, in March 1978, Minnoch was rushed to University Hospital, Seattle, saturated with fluid and suffering from heart and respiratory failure. It took a dozen firefighters and an improvised stretcher to move him from his home to a ferry-boat. When he arrived at the hospital he was put in two beds lashed together. It took 13 people just to roll him over. By extrapolating his intake and elimination rates, consultant endocrinologist Dr Robert Schwartz calculated that Minnoch must have weighed more than 1400 lb (100 st) *635 kg* when he was admitted, a great deal of which was water accumulation due to his congestive heart failure. After nearly two years on a 1200-calories-a-day diet the choking fluid had gone, and he was discharged at 476 lb (34 st) *216 kg*. But the weight crept back again, and in Oct 1981 he had to be readmitted, after putting on 200 lb (over 14 st) *91 kg* in the previous 7 days. When he died on 10 Sept 1983 he weighed more than 800 lb (just over 57 st) *363 kg*.

Living

The heaviest living man is (or was) T. J. Albert Jackson (b. Kent Nicholson), also known as 'Fat Albert' of Canton, Mississippi, USA (see table). He recently tipped the scales at 898 lb *407 kg*. He has a 120 in *305 cm* chest, a 116 in *294 cm* waist, 70 in *178 cm* thighs and a 29½ in *75 cm* neck. Albert Pernitsch (see table below) of Grafkorn, Austria also claims to be the world's heaviest man, but the greatest weight recorded for him so far is 880 lb *399 kg*.

The greatest weight attained by a living person is 1187 lb (84 st 11 lb) *485 kg* in the case of Michael Walker (see table) of Clinton, Iowa, USA, who had reduced to 369 lb *167 kg* by February 1980.

Great Britain

The heaviest recorded man was Peter Yarnall of East Ham, London, who weighed 59 st *374 kg* and was 5 ft 10 in *177,8 cm* tall. The former docker began putting on weight at a very rapid rate in 1978 and for the last two years of his life he was completely bed-ridden. He died on 30 March 1984 aged 34. His coffin measured 7 ft 4 in *233 cm* in length, 4 ft *122 cm* across and had a depth of 2 ft 9 in *83,8 cm*.

Only two other British men had a recorded weight of more than 50 st *317,5 kg*. One of them was William Campbell (b. Glasgow 1856) who died on 16 June 1878 when a publican at High Bridge, Newcastle upon Tyne, Tyne and Wear. He was 6 ft 3 in *190 cm* tall and weighed 53 st 8 lb *340 kg* with an 85 in *216 cm* waist and a 96 in *244 cm* chest. The other was the celebrated Daniel Lambert (1770–1809) of Stamford, Lincolnshire. He stood 5 ft 11 in *180 cm* tall and weighed 52 st 11 lb *335 kg* shortly before his death and had a girth of more than 92 in *233 cm*.

SUPER HEAVYWEIGHTS

Jon Brower Minnoch (1941–83) USA (6 ft 1 in *185 cm*)
1400 lb   100 st   *635 kg*

Michael Walker *né* Francis Lang (b. 1934) USA (6 ft 2 in *188 cm*)[1]
1187 lb   84 st 11 lb   *538 kg*

Robert Earl Hughes (1926–58) USA (6 ft 0½ in *184 cm*)
1069 lb   76 st 5 lb   *485 kg*

Mills Darden (1798–1857) USA (7 ft 6 in *229 cm*)
1020 lb   72 st 12 lb   *462 kg*

'Big Tex' (1902–*fl* 1956) USA (6 ft 1½ in *186 cm*)
924 lb   66 st   *419 kg*

John Hanson Craig (1856–94) USA (6 ft 5 in *195 cm*)[2]
907 lb   64 st 11 lb   *411 kg*

Arthur Knorr (1914–60) USA (6 ft 1 in *185 cm*)[3]
900 lb   64 st 4 lb   *408 kg*

T. J. Albert Jackson (b. 1941) Canton, Mississippi, USA (6 ft 4 in *193 cm*)
898 lb   64 st 2 lb   *404 kg*

Albert Pernitsch (b. 1956) of Grafkorn, Austria (5 ft 9 in *175 cm*)[4]
880 lb   62 st 12 lb   *399 kg*

Ron High (b. 1953) of Chicago, USA
853 lb   60 st 13 lb   *387 kg*[5]

T. A. Valenzuela (1895–1937) Mexico (5 ft 11 in *180 cm*)
850 lb   60 st 10 lb   *385 kg*

Chief Wise Owl (b. 1939) USA (5 ft 4 in *163 cm*)[6]
850 lb   60 st 10 lb   *385 kg*

[1] *Reduced to 369 lb 167 kg by Feb 1980. Peak weight attained in 1971.*
[2] *Won $1000 in a 'Bonny Baby' contest in New York City in 1858.*
[3] *Gained 300 lb 136 kg in the last 6 months of his life.*
[4] *His left arm tattoo proclaims 'Nobody is perfect'. In July 1984 his girth was 200 cm 78¾ in.*
[5] *Reduced by dieting to 340 lb 154,2 kg in 16 months to Jan 1987.*
[6] *Weight not independently corroborated. Winner of National Enquirer 'Biggest Belly' contest announced 9 Sept 1986. Waist reputedly 111 in, 9 ft 3 in 2,81 m in girth.*

Twins ● The world's tallest identical twin brothers, Michael and James Lanier (b. 27 Nov 1969) from Troy, Michigan, USA who stand 7 ft 4 in *223,5 cm* seen here alongside the world's shortest identical twin sisters Dorene Williams of Oakdale, California and Darlene McGregor of Almeda, California, aged 39 and who are 4 ft 1 in *124,4 cm*.
Britain's tallest ever identical twins were the Knipe brothers (b. 1761–fl. 1780) of Magherafelt, nr Londonderry, Northern Ireland, who both measured 7 ft 2 in *218,4 cm*.
Britain's tallest living twins are Jonathan and Mark Carratt (b. 11 June 1955) of Maltby, South Yorkshire, who are 6 ft 8 in *203,3 cm* and 6 ft 9 in *205,7 cm* respectively.
(Photo: Franklin Berger)

Britain's heaviest living man is Arthur Armitage (b. 5 lb *2,3 kg* on 28 June 1929) of Knottingley, West Yorkshire, who weighed 48 st *305 kg* in Oct 1986. He had previously been billed as Britain's heaviest man in Feb 1970 when he scaled 40 st 6 lb *257 kg*, but he then went on a diet (600 calories per day), and reduced his weight to 18 st 2 lb *115 kg* by March 1972. Since then he has shot up again. The weight of the 6 ft 11 in *210,8 cm* tall professional wrestler Martin Ruane *alias* Luke McMasters ('Giant Haystacks'), who was born in Camberwell, London, in 1946, now fluctuates between 41 st *260 kg* and 43 st *273 kg*, though he once claimed to have tipped the scales at 50 st *317 kg*.

Wales

The heaviest man ever recorded in Wales was Charles Dunbar of Aberdare, Glamorgan, who died on 22 Jan 1925 aged 24 years. He weighed 44 st *279 kg* and was 6 ft 1 in *185,4 cm* tall.

Ireland

The heaviest Irishman is reputed to have been Roger Byrne, who was buried in Rosenallis, County Laoighis (Leix), on 14 Mar 1804. He died in his 54th year and his coffin and its contents weighed 52 st *330 kg*. Roly McIntyre (b. 1955) of Kesh, Fermanagh, Northern Ireland scaled a peak 41 st 4 lb *262 kg* in April 1983.

Heaviest women

The heaviest woman ever recorded was the late Mrs Percy Pearl Washington, 46 who died in hospital in Milwaukee, on 9 Oct 1972. The hospital scales registered only up to 800 lb (57 st 2 lb) *362,8 kg* but she was believed to weigh about 880 lb (62 st 12 lb) *399,1 kg*. She was 6 ft *183 cm* tall and wore a US size 62 dress. The previous feminine weight record had been set 84 years earlier at 850 lb (60 st 10 lb) *385 kg* although a wholly unsubstantiated report exists of a woman Mrs Ida Maitland (1898–1932) of Springfield, Mississippi, USA, who reputedly weighed 65 st 1 lb (911 lb) *413,2 kg*.

Great Britain and Ireland

The heaviest woman ever recorded in Britain was Mrs Muriel Hopkins (b. 1931) of Tipton, West Midlands, who weighed 43 st 11 lb *278 kg* (height 5 ft 11 in *180 cm*) in 1978. Shortly before her death on 22 April 1979 she reportedly scaled 52 st *330 kg*, but this was only an estimate, and her actual weight was found to be 47 st 7 lb *301 kg*. Her coffin measured 6 ft 3 in *190 cm* in length, 4 ft 5 in *137 cm* wide and was 3 ft 9 in *114 cm* deep.

Heaviest twins

The heaviest twins in the world were Billy Leon (•1946–79) and Benny Loyd (b. 7 Dec 1946) McCrary *alias* McGuire of Hendersonville, North Carolina, who were normal in size until the age of six when they both contracted German measles. In November 1978 they were weighed at 743 lb (53 st 1 lb) *337 kg* (Billy) and 723 lb (51 st 9 lb) *328 kg* (Benny) and had 84 in *213 cm* waists. As professional tag wrestling performers they were *billed* at weights up to 770 lb *349 kg*. Billy died at Niagara Falls, Ontario, Canada on 13 July 1979 after a mini-motorcycle accident.

Lightest
The lightest adult human on record was Lucia Zarate (b. San Carlos, Mexico 2 Jan 1863, d. October 1889), an emaciated Mexican ateleiotic dwarf of 26½ in *67 cm*, who weighed 2,125 kg *4.7 lb* at the age of 17. She 'fattened up' to 13 lb *5,9 kg* by her 20th birthday. At birth she weighed 2½ lb *1,1 kg*.

The thinnest recorded adults of normal height are those suffering from Simmonds' Disease (Hypophyseal cachexia). Losses up to 65 per cent of the original body-weight have been recorded in females, with a 'low' of 3 st 3 lb *20 kg* in the case of Emma Shaller (b. St Louis, Missouri 8 July 1868, d. 4 Oct 1890), who stood 5 ft 2 in *157 cm*. Edward C. Hagner (1892–1962), *alias* Eddie Masher (USA) is alleged to have weighed only 3 st 6 lb *22 kg* at a height of 5 ft 7 in *170 cm*. He was also known as 'the Skeleton Dude'. In August 1825 the biceps measurement of Claude-Ambroise Seurat (b. 10 Apr 1797, d. 6 Apr 1826) of Troyes, France was 4 in *10 cm* and the distance between his back and his chest was less than 3 in *7.6 cm*. According to one report he stood 5 ft 7½ in *171 cm* and weighed 5 st 8 lb *35 kg*, but in another account was described as 5 ft 4 in *163 cm* and only 2 st 8 lb *16 kg*. It was recorded that the American exhibitionist Rosa Lee Plemons (b. 1873) weighed 27 lb *12 kg* at the age of 18.

In July 1977 the death was reported of an 83-year-old woman in Mexborough, South Yorkshire who scaled only 2 st 5 lb *15 kg* (height not recorded).

Great Britain
The lightest adult ever recorded in the United Kingdom was Hopkins Hopkins (Dwarfs, see p. 7). Robert Thorn (b. 1842) of March, Cambridgeshire weighed 49 lb *22 kg* at the age of 32. He was 4 ft 6 in *137 cm* tall and had a 27 in *68 cm* chest (expanded) 4½ in *11,4 cm* biceps, and a 3 in *7,6 cm* wrist. A doctor who examined him said he had practically no muscular development, 'although he could run along the road'.

Slimming *Men*
The greatest slimming feat with published details was that of William J. Cobb (b. 1926), *alias* 'Happy Humphrey', a professional wrestler of Augusta, Georgia. It was reported in July 1965 that he had reduced from 57 st 4 lb *364 kg* to 16 st 8 lb *105 kg*, a loss of 40 st 11 lb *259 kg* in 32 months. His waist measurement declined from 101 to 44 in *256 to 112 cm*. In October 1973 it was reported that 'Happy' was back to his normal weight of 31 st or 432 lb *196 kg*. By July 1979 Jon Brower Minnoch (1941–83) (see p. 8) had reduced to 476 lb *216 kg* (34 st), thus indicating a weight loss of at least 924 lb *419 kg* (66 st) in 2 years, or an average of 8.8 lb *4 kg* per week.

Paul M. Kimelman (b. 1943) of Pittsburgh, Pennsylvania, reduced from 487 lb (34 st 11 lb) *216 kg* to 130 lb (9 st 4 lb) *59 kg* between 1 Jan 1967 and 3 Aug 1967, a loss of 357 lb *162 kg* in 215 days. Roly McIntyre (b. 1952) of Kesh, Fermanagh, N. Ireland (see heaviest men) reduced from 578 lb (41 st 4 lb) *262 kg* to 187 lb (13 st 5 lb) *84,8 kg* during the 22-month period April 1983–Feb 1985. Ron Allen (b. 1947) sweated off 21½ lb *9,7 kg* of his 250 lb *113,4 kg* in Nashville, Tennessee, in 24 hr in Aug 1984.

Women
The US circus fat lady Mrs Celesta Geyer (b. 1901), *alias* Dolly Dimples, reduced from 553 lb *251 kg* to 152 lb *69 kg* in 1950–51, a loss of 401 lb

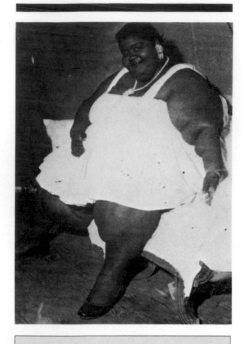

Heaviest Women ● Mrs Flora Mae Jackson (*née* King) known in show business as 'Baby Flo' was born in 1930 at Shuqualak, Mississippi. She weighed 10 lb *4,5 kg* at birth, 19 st 1 lb (267 lb) *121 kg* at the age of 11, 44 st 5 lb (621 lb) *282 kg* at 25 and 60 st (840 lb) *381 kg* shortly before her death in Meridian, Mississippi, on 9 Dec 1965 when she stood 5 ft 9 in *175 cm* tall.

182 kg in 14 months. Her vital statistics diminished *pari passu* from 79–84–84 in *200–213–213 cm* to a svelte 34–28–36 in *86–71–91 cm*. Her book 'How I lost 400 lbs' was not a best-seller because of the difficulty of would-be readers identifying themselves with the dress-making and other problems of losing more than 28 st *178 kg* when 4 ft 11 in *150 cm* tall. In December 1967 she was reportedly down to 7 st 12 lb *50 kg*. In February 1951 Mrs Gertrude Levandowski (b. 1893) of Burnips, Michigan, successfully underwent a protracted operation for the removal of a cyst which subsequently reduced her weight from 44 st *280 kg* to 22 st *140 kg* (see also p. 22).

The feminine champion in Britain was Mrs Dolly Wager (b. 1933) of Charlton, London, who, between September 1971 and 22 May 1973 reduced from 31 st 7 lb *200 kg* to 11 st *69,8 kg* so losing 20 st 7 lb *130 kg* with Weight Watchers.

Weight gaining
The reported record for gaining weight was set by Jon Minnoch (see p. 8) in October 1981 when he was readmitted to University of Washington Hospital, Seattle, Washington State, having regained 200 lb *91 kg* in 7 days. Arthur Knorr (see table p. 8) gained 300 lb *136 kg* in the last 6 months of his life. Miss Doris James of San Francisco, California, is alleged to have gained 23 st 3 lb *147 kg* in the 12 months before her death in August 1965, aged 38, at a weight of 48 st 3 lb *306 kg*. She was only 5 ft 2 in *157 cm* tall.

Greatest differential
The greatest weight differential recorded for a married couple is *c.* 1300 lb *589 kg* (92 st 12 lb) in the case of Jon Brower Minnoch (see p. 8) and his 110 lb *50 kg* (7 st 12 lb) wife Jeannette in March 1978. She bore him two sons. The UK record is held by the wrestler Martin Ruane, *alias* Giant Haystacks (see p. 8) and his 7½ st *47,6 kg* wife Rita, where their weight differential at one time may have been 42½ st *270 kg*. They have three sons.

Origins
EARLIEST MAN

Earliest *Primate*
The first primates appeared in the Palaeocene epoch about 69,000,000 years ago. The earliest members of the sub-order Anthropoidea are known from both Africa and South America in the early Oligocene, 34–30 million years ago, when the two infra-orders, Platyrrhini and Catarrhini from the New and Old Worlds respectively were already distinct.

Earliest *Hominid*
Characteristics typical of the Hominidae such as the large brain and bipedal locomotion do not appear until much later. The earliest undoubted hominid relic found is an Australopithecine jaw bone with two molars 2 in *5 cm* in length found by Kiptalam Chepboi near Lake Baringo, Kenya in Feb 1984 and dated to 4 million years by associated fossils and to 5.6–5.4 million years through rock correlation by potassium-argon dating.

The most complete of the earliest hominid skeletons is that of 'Lucy' (forty per cent complete) found by Dr Donald C. Johanson and T. Gray at Locality 162 by the Awash river, Hadar, in the Afar region of Ethiopia on 30 Nov 1974. She was estimated to be *c.* 40 years old when she died 3 million years ago, and she was 3½ ft *106 cm* tall.

Parallel tracks of hominid footprints extending over 80 ft *24 m* were discovered at Laetoli, Tanzania in 1978, first by Paul Abell, in volcanic ash dating to 3.5 million years ago. The height of the smallest of the seemingly 3 individuals was estimated to be 120 cm *4 ft 7 in.*

Earliest genus *Homo*
The earliest species of the genus *Homo* is *Homo habilis* or 'Handy Man' so named by Prof Raymond Arthur Dart (b. Brisbane 4 Feb 1893) in 1964. The greatest age attributed to fossils of this genus is 1.9 million years for the skull KNM-ER (Kenya National Museum-East Rudolf) 1470 discovered in 1972 by Bernard Ngeneo at Koobi Fora by Lake Turkana, northern Kenya. It was reconstructed by Dr Meave Leakey (*née* Epps).

The earliest stone tools are abraded core-choppers dating from *c.* 2.5 million years. They were found at Hadar, Ethiopia in Nov–Dec 1976 by Hélène Roche (France). Finger- (as opposed to fist-) held quartz slicers found by Roche and Dr John Wall (NZ) close to the Hadar site by the Gona river are also dated to *c.* 2.5 million years.

Earliest *Homo erectus*
The earliest *Homo erectus* (upright man), the species directly ancestral to *Homo sapiens*, was discovered by Kamoya Kimen on the surface at the site of Nariokotome III to the west of Lake Turkana, Kenya in 1984. The skeleton of a 12-year-old boy is the most complete of this species ever found; only a few small pieces are missing.

Great Britain

The earliest (and now less disputed) evidence for the presence of hominids in Great Britain dates from *c.* 400,000 BC. Five worked flint artefacts showing features normally attributed to human workmanship were found in cave deposits near Westbury-sub-Mendip, Somerset, and described in 1975 by Michael J. Bishop. The oldest actual human remains ever found in Britain are pieces of a brain case from a specimen of *Homo sapiens*, recovered in June 1935 and March 1936 by Dr Alvan T. Marston from the Boyn Hill terrace in the Barnfield Pit, near Swanscombe, Kent. The remains were associated with a middle Acheulian tool culture and probably date to the Holsteinian interglacial (*c.* 230,000 BC). Three hominid teeth, mandible fragments and a vertebra were found in Pontnewydd Cave, Lower Elwy Valley, North Wales from October 1980. They were dated by the Thorium/Uranium disequilibrium method to a little over 200,000 years.

Longevity

No single subject is more obscured by vanity, deceit, falsehood and deliberate fraud than the extremes of human longevity. Extreme claims are generally made on behalf of the very aged rather than *by* them.

Many hundreds of claims throughout history have been made for persons living well into their second century and some, insulting to the intelligence, for people living even into their third. Centenarians surviving beyond their 113th year are in fact of the extremest rarity and the present absolute proven limit of human longevity does not yet admit of anyone living to celebrate any birthday after their 120th.

The largest group of people in the world with reliable long pedigrees is the British peerage. After ten centuries this has produced only three centenarian peers of whom only two reached their 101st birthdays. This poor record is possibly not unconnected with the extreme draughtiness of many of their residences and the amount of lead in their game.

Several celebrated super-centenarians (over 110 years) are believed to have been double lives (father and son, relations with the same names or successive bearers of a title). The most famous example was Christian Jakobsen Drackenberg allegedly born in Stavanger, Norway on 18 Nov 1626 and died in Aarhus, Denmark aged seemingly 145 years 326 days on 9 Oct 1772. A number of instances have been commercially sponsored, while a fourth category of recent claims are those made for political ends, such as the 100 citizens of the Russian Soviet Federative Socialist Republic (population 117,494,000 at mid-1960) claimed in March 1960 to be between 120 and 156. From data on documented centenarians, actuaries have shown that only one 115-year life can be expected in 2100 million lives (*cf.* world population was estimated to be *c.* 5000 million by mid-1987).

The height of credulity was reached on 5 May 1933, when a news agency gullibly filed a story from China with a Peking date-line that Li Chungyun, the 'oldest man on Earth', born in 1680, had just died aged 256 years (*sic*).

The most extreme case of longevity recently claimed in the USSR has been 168 years for Shirali 'Baba' Muslinov of Barzavu, Azerbaijan, who died on 2 Sept 1973 and was reputedly born on 26 Mar 1805. No interview of this man was ever permitted to any Western journalist or scientist. He was even said to have celebrated in 1966 the 100th birthday of his third wife Hartun, and that of one of his grandchildren in August

1973. It was reported in 1954 that in the Abkhasian Republic of Georgia, USSR, where aged citizens are invested with an almost saint-like status, 2.58 per cent of the population was aged over 90—24 times the proportion in the USA.

Dr Zhores Aleksandrovich Medvedev (b. Tbilisi, 14 Nov 1925), the Russian gerontologist who was refused a visa to return to the USSR in 1973, referring to USSR claims in Washington DC, on 30 Apr 1974 stated 'The whole phenomenon looks like a falsification' adding 'He [Stalin] liked the idea that [other] Georgians lived to be 100 or more.' 'Local officials tried hard to find more and more cases for Stalin.' He points out (a) the *average* life-span in the regions claiming the highest incidence of centenarians is lower than that of USSR average and (b) in contradistinction to the rest of the world, the incidence of centenarians claimed in the Caucasus had declined rapidly from 8000 in 1950 to 4500 in 1970.

It was announced in February 1984 that the 1982 census in China revealed only 2450 centenarians of whom two-thirds were women. In the US the mid-1983 figure was 32,000. Birth and death

registration, however, became complete only in 1933 and was only 30.9 per cent by 1915.

Oldest living person ● Mrs Anna Eliza Williams (*née* Davies) was born on 2 June 1873 and now resides in the Tuxedo Old People's Home, Swansea, West Glamorgan. (Photo: Rex Features)

Oldest authentic centenarian

The greatest *authenticated* age to which any human has ever lived is a unique 120 years 237 days in the case of Shigechiyo Izumi of Asan on Tokunoshima, an island 820 miles *1320 km* SW of Tokyo, Japan. He was born at Asan on 29 June 1865 and recorded as a 6-year-old in Japan's first census of 1871. He died in his double-glazed bungalow at 12.15 GMT on 21 Feb 1986 after developing pneumonia.

Great Britain

The United Kingdom has an estimated population of some 4000 centenarians of whom only 22 per

AUTHENTIC NATIONAL LONGEVITY RECORDS

Oldest living man in Great Britain ● John Evans, of Llewitha, Swansea, West Glamorgan was born on 19 Aug 1877. A former miner, he had a heart pacemaker fitted on 19 Mar 1986 when he was 108 years old. He first went down the mines in 1889. (Photo: Rex Features)

	Years	Days		Born		Died	
Japan	120	237	Shigechiyo Izumi	29 June	1865	21 Feb	1986
United States[1]	114	c. 180	Martha Graham (Mrs)	Dec	1844	25 June	1959
United Kingdom[2]	114		Anna Eliza Williams (Mrs) (née Davies)	2 June	1873	fl. 2 Jun	1987
Canada[3]	113	124	Pierre Joubert	15 July	1701	16 Nov	1814
Spain[4]	112	228	Josefa Salas Mateo	14 July	1860	27 Feb	1973
France	112	66	Augustine Teissier (Sister Julia)	2 Jan	1869	9 Mar	1981
Morocco	>112		El Hadj Mohammed el Mokri (Grand Vizier)		1844	16 Sept	1957
Poland[5]	112	+	Roswlia Mielczarak (Mrs)		1868	7 Jan	1981
Ireland	111	327	The Hon. Katherine Plunket	22 Nov	1820	14 Oct	1932
Australia	111	235	Jane Piercy (Mrs)	2 Sept	1869	3 May	1981
South Africa[6]	111	151	Johanna Booyson	17 Jan	1857	16 June	1968
Sweden	111	89	Wilhelmine Sande (Mrs)	24 Oct	1874	21 Jan	1986
Czechoslovakia	111	+	Marie Bernatkova	22 Oct	1857	fl. Oct	1968
Channel Islands (Guernsey)	110	321	Margaret Ann Neve (née Harvey)	18 May	1792	4 Apr	1903
Northern Ireland	110	234	Elizabeth Watkins (Mrs)	10 Mar	1863	31 Oct	1973
Italy	110	198	Damiana Sette (Sig)	11 Aug	1874	25 Feb	1985
Yugoslavia	110	150+	Demitrius Philipovitch	9 Mar	1818	fl. Aug	1928
Netherlands[7]	110	141	Gerada Hurenkamp-Bosgoed	5 Jan	1870	25 May	1980
Greece[8]	110	+	Lambrini Tsiatoura (Mrs)		1870	19 Feb	1981
USSR[9]	110	+	Khasako Dzugayev	7 Aug	1860	fl. Aug	1970
Norway	110	+	Maren Bolette Torp	21 Dec	1876	fl. Mar	1987
Scotland[10]	109	14	Rachel MacArthur (Mrs)	26 Nov	1827	10 Dec	1936
Belgium	108	327	Mathilda Vertommen-Hellemans	12 Aug	1868	4 July	1977
Germany[11]	108	128	Luise Schwarz	27 Sept	1849	2 Feb	1958
Iceland	108	45	Halldóra Bjarndóttir	14 Oct	1873	28 Nov	1981
Portugal[12]	108	+	Maria Luisa Jorge	7 June	1859	fl. July	1967
Finland	108	198	Fanny Matilda Nyström	30 Sept	1878	fl. 16 Apr	1987
Malaysia	106	+	Hassan Bin Yusoff	14 Aug	1865	fl. Jan	1972
Luxembourg	105	228	Nicolas Wiscourt	31 Dec	1872	17 Aug	1978

[1] Ex-slave Mrs Martha Graham died at Fayetteville, North Carolina on 25 June 1959 reputedly aged 117 or 118. Census researches by Eckler show that she was seemingly born in Dec 1844 and hence aged 114 years 6 months. Mrs Rena Glover Brailsford died in Summerton, South Carolina, USA on 6 Dec 1977 reputedly aged 118 years. Mrs Rosario Reina Vasquez who died in California on 2 Sept 1980 was reputedly born in Sonora, Mexico on 3 June 1866, which would make her 114 years 93 days. The 1900 US Federal Census for Crawfish Springs Militia District of Walker County, Georgia, records an age of 77 for a Mark Thrash. If the Mark Thrash (reputedly born in Georgia in December 1822) who died near Chattanooga, Tennessee on 17 Dec 1943 was he, and the age attributed was accurate, then he would have survived for 121 years.

[2] London-born Miss Isabella Shepheard was allegedly 115 years old when she died at St Asaph, Clwyd, North Wales, on 20 Nov 1948, but her actual age was believed to have been 109 years 90 days. Charles Alfred Nunez Arnold died in Liverpool on 15 Nov 1941 reputedly aged 112 years 66 days based on a baptismal claim (London, 10 Sept 1829). Mrs Elizabeth Cornish (née Veale) who was buried at Stratton, Cornwall on 10 Mar 1691/2 was reputedly baptised on 16 Oct 1578, 113 years 4 months earlier.

[3] Mrs Ellen Carroll died in North River, Newfoundland, Canada on 8 Dec 1943, reputedly aged 115 years 49 days.

[4] Snr Benita Medrana of Avila died on 28 Jan 1979 allegedly aged 114 years 335 days.

[5] Stefania Kozlowska was reputed to have reached 114 years in Sieniawa in early Nov 1986.

[6] Mrs Susan Johanna Deporter of Port Elizabeth was reputedly 114 years old when she died on 4 Aug 1954. Mrs Sarah Lawrence, Cape Town, South Africa was reputedly 112 on 3 June 1968.

[7] Thomas Peters was recorded to have been born on 6 Apr 1745 in Leeuwarden and died aged 111 years 354 days on 26 Mar 1857 in Arnhem.

[8] The claim that Liakon Efdokia died 17 Jan 1982 aged 118 years 13 days is not substantiated by the censuses of 1971 or 1981. Birth registration before 1920 was fragmentary.

[9] There are allegedly 21,700 centenarians in USSR (cf. 7000 in USA). Of these 21,000 were ascribed to the Georgian SSR i.e. one in every 232. In July 1962 it was reported that 128, mostly male, were in the one village of Medini.

[10] Lachlen McDonald, who died 7 June 1858 in Harris, Outer Hebrides, was recorded as being '110 years' on his death certificate.

[11] West Germany: An unnamed female died in 1979 aged 112 years and an unnamed male died, aged also 112 years in 1969. The Austrian record is 108 years (female d. 1975) and the Swiss record is also 108 years (female d. 1967).

[12] Senhora Jesuina da Conceicao of Lisbon was reputedly 113 years old when she died on 10 June 1965.

Note: fl is the abbreviation for floruit, Latin for he (or she) was living at the relevant date.

---

cent are male. While husbands have a better chance than bachelors, it appears that spinsters have a better chance than wives in reaching 100 years! The only UK citizens with birth and death certificates more than 112 years apart have been Miss Alice Stevenson (1861–1973) (112 years 39 days) and Miss Janetta Jane Thomas (1869–1982) (112 years 35 days). Mrs Anna Williams is the third oldest human being on record having surpassed her 114th birthday on 2 June 1987 (see Table).

Britain's oldest proven man has been John Mosley Turner (b. 15 June 1856), who died on 22 Mar 1968 aged 111 years 281 days. In April 1706 a John Bailes was buried at All Saints Church, Northampton, having apparently been baptised on 20 Aug 1592. If these two John Bailes were the same person, he would have been 113 years 8 months.

The first recorded case in the UK of three siblings being centenarians occurred on 26 Nov 1982 when Miss Frances Adams MSc reached her 100th birthday. Her brother was Dr John Andrew Adams (1867–1967) and her sister Dr Elizabeth Hart (née Adams) (1876–1977). The family came from Omagh, Co Tyrone, Northern Ireland.

Oldest quadruplets
The world's oldest quads are the Ottman quads of Munich, West Germany—Adolf, Anne-Marie, Emma and Elisabeth. They celebrated their 75th birthday on 5 May 1987.

Oldest triplets
The longest-lived triplets on record were Faith, Hope and Charity Caughlin born at Marlboro, Massachusetts on 27 Mar 1868. The first to die was Mrs (Ellen) Hope Daniels aged 93 on 2 Mar 1962.

Oldest twins
The oldest recorded twins were Eli Shadrack and John Meshak Phipps (b. 14 Feb 1803, Affington, Virginia). Eli died at Hennessey, Oklahoma on 23 Feb 1911 aged 108 years 9 days on which day John was still living in Shenandoah, Iowa. On 17 June 1984, identical twin sisters, Mildred Widman Philippi and Mary Widman Franzini of St. Louis, Missouri celebrated their 104th birthday. Mildred died on 4 May 1985, 44 days short of the twins' would-be 105th birthday. The chances of identical twins both reaching 100 are now probably about one in 50 million.

The oldest twins on record in Great Britain have been the identical twins Isabella and Marion Weir of Longridge, West Lothian, Scotland, who were 100 on 29 Sept 1986. Marion died on 19 Mar 1987.

Most reigns
The greatest number of reigns during which any English subject could have lived is ten. A person born on the day (11 April) that Henry VI was deposed in 1471 had to live to only the comparatively modest age of 87 years 7 months and 6 days to see the accession of Elizabeth I on 17 Nov 1558. Such a person could have been Thomas Carn of London, reputedly born in 1471 and died 28 Jan 1578 in his 107th year.

Long spans
The last Briton with 18th-century paternity was Miss Alice J. Grigg of Belvedere, Kent (d. 28 Apr 1970) whose father William was born on 26 Oct 1799. The father of Baroness Elliot of Harwood (b. 15 Jan 1903), Sir-Charles Tennant Bt, was born in Glasgow in the reign of George IV on 4 Nov 1823.

Oldest mummy
Mummification (from the Persian word mām, wax) dates from 2600 BC or the 4th dynasty of the Egyptian pharaohs. The oldest surviving mummy is of Wati, a court musician of c. 2400 BC from the tomb of Nefer in Saqqâra, Egypt found in 1944.

Reproductivity

MOTHERHOOD

Most children

The greatest officially recorded number of children produced by a mother is 69 by the first of the two wives of Feodor Vassilyev (b. 1707–*fl.* 1782), a peasant from Shuya, 150 miles *241 km* east of Moscow. In 27 confinements she gave birth to 16 pairs of twins, 7 sets of triplets and 4 sets of quadruplets. The case was reported by the Monastery of Nikolskiy on 27 Feb 1782 to Moscow. At least 67 survived infancy. Empress Ekaterina II (The Great) (1762–96) was said to have evinced interest. The children, of whom almost all survived to their majority, were born in the period *c.* 1725–65.

The world's most prolific mother is currently Leontina Albina (*née* Espinosa) (b. 1925) of San Antonio, Chile, who in 1981 produced her 55th and last child. Her husband Gerardo Secunda Albina (variously Alvina) (b. 1921) states that he was married in Argentina in 1943 and they had 5 sets of triplets (all boys) before coming to Chile. 'Only' 40 (24 boys and 16 girls) survive. Eleven were lost in an earthquake, thus indicating the truth about the other children produced earlier than those born in Chile.

Great Britain

The British record is seemingly held by Elizabeth, wife of John Mott married in 1676 of Monks Kirby, Warwickshire, who produced 42 live-born children. She died in 1720, 44 years later. According to an inscription on a gravestone in Conway Church cemetery, Gwynedd, North Wales, Nicholas Hookes (d. 27 Mar 1637) was the 41st child of his mother Alice Hookes, but further details are lacking. It has not been possible to corroborate or refute this report. Mrs Elizabeth Greenhille (d. 1681) of Abbots Langley, Hertford-

shire is alleged to have produced 39 children (32 daughters, 7 sons) in a record 38 confinements. Her son Thomas was author of 'Art of Embalming' (1705). Mrs Rebecca Town (1807–51) of Keighley, Yorkshire, had 30 children, but only one survived to the age of 3. Mrs Ada Watson (b. 23 June 1886) of Cambridge gave birth to 25 children in 22 confinements, including 3 sets of twins, all of whom attained their majority, during the period 1904–31. She died in Roehampton, London, on 5 Feb 1974.

Great Britain's champion mothers of today are believed to be Mrs Margaret McNaught (b. 1923), of Balsall Heath, Birmingham (12 boys and 10 girls, all single births) and Mrs Mabel Constable (b. 1920), of Long Itchington, Warwickshire who also has had 22 children including a set of triplets and two sets of twins.

Ireland's champion is Mrs Catherine Scott (b. 4 July 1914) of Dublin, who bore an authenticated total of 24 children.

Oldest mother

Medical literature contains extreme but unauthenticated cases of septuagenarian mothers, such as Mrs Ellen Ellis, aged 72, of Four Crosses, Clwyd, who allegedly produced a still-born 13th child on 15 May 1776 in her 46th year of marriage. Many very late maternities will be cover-ups for illegitimate grandchildren. The oldest recorded mother for whom the evidence satisfied medical verification was Mrs Ruth Alice Kistler (*née* Taylor), formerly Mrs Shepard (1899–1982), of Portland, Oregon, USA. A birth certificate indicates that she gave birth to a daughter, Suzan, at Glendale, near Los Angeles, California, on 18 Oct 1956, when her age was 57 years 129 days. In the *Gazette Médicale de Liège* (1 Oct 1891) Dr E. Derasse mentioned the case of one of his patients who gave birth to a healthy baby when aged 59 years 5 months. He had managed to obtain her birth certificate. The woman already had a married daughter aged 40 years.

Great Britain

The oldest British mother reliably recorded is Mrs Winifred Wilson (*née* Stanley) of Eccles, Greater Manchester. She was born in Wolverhampton on 11 Nov 1881 or 1882 and had her tenth child, a daughter Shirley, on 14 Nov 1936, when aged 54 or 55 years and 3 days. She died aged 91 or 92 in January 1974. At Southampton, on 10 Feb 1916, Mrs Elizabeth Pearce gave birth to a son when aged 54 years 40 days. According to a report in the *Lancet* (1867) a woman reputedly 62 gave birth to triplets. She had previously had 10 children.

Ireland

The oldest Irish mother recorded was Mrs Mary Higgins of Cork, County Cork (b. 7 Jan 1876) who gave birth to a daughter, Patricia, on 17 Mar 1931 when aged 55 years 69 days.

Longest interval between twins

Mrs Mary Wright, 38, gave birth to Amy and Elizabeth 18 months apart from eggs fertilized by her husband in March 1984. Elizabeth was born at Stoke-on-Trent, Staffordshire on 22 Apr 1987 from an egg which had been in frozen storage for 29 months.

MULTIPLE BIRTHS

Lightest twins

The lightest recorded birth weight for a pair of surviving twins has been 2 lb 3 oz *992 g* in the case of Mary 16 oz *453 g* and Margaret 19 oz *538 g* born to Mrs Florence Stimson, Queens Road, Old Fletton, Peterborough, England, delivered by Dr Macaulay on 16 Aug 1931. Margaret is now Mrs M. J. Hurst.

'Siamese' twins

Conjoined twins derived the name 'Siamese' from the celebrated Chang and Eng Bunker (known in Thailand as Chan and In) born at Meklong on 11 May 1811 of Chinese parents.

Reproductivity

Multiple births ● The Walton sextuplets just prior to their third birthday. All six are girls, born to Mrs Janet Walton (b. 1952) on 18 Nov 1983 at Liverpool Maternity Hospital. From left to right, Hannah, Sarah, Kate, Lucy, Ruth and Jenny. (Photo: Camera Press)

They were joined by a cartilaginous band at the chest and married in April 1843 the Misses Sarah and Adelaide Yates of Wilkes County, North Carolina, and fathered ten and twelve children respectively. They died within three hours of each other on 17 Jan 1874, aged 62. The only known British example to reach maturity were the pygopagus twins Daisy and Violet Hilton born in Brighton, now East Sussex, on 5 Feb 1908, who were joined at the buttocks. They died in Charlotte, North Carolina, on 5 Jan 1969, aged 60, from Hong Kong flu. The earliest successful separation of Siamese twins was performed on xiphopagus girls joined at the sternum at Mt Sinai Hospital, Cleveland, Ohio by Dr Jac S. Geller on 14 Dec 1952.

The rarest form of conjoined twins is Dicephales tetrabrachius dipus (two heads, four arms and two legs). The only known examples are the pair Masha and Dasha born in the USSR on 4 Jan 1950, Nadir and Juraci Climerio de Oliverra of Santo Amaro de Purificacao, Bahia, Brazil, born on 2 June 1957, an unnamed pair separated in a 10-hour operation in Washington, DC, on 23 June 1977, Fonda Michelle and Shannon Elaine Beaver of Forest City, North Carolina, born on 9 Feb 1980, and the 'Scottish brothers', who were born near Glasgow in 1490. They were brought to the Court of King James IV of Scotland in 1491, and lived under the king's patronage for the rest of his reign. They died in 1518 aged 28 years, one brother succumbing five days before the other, who 'moaned piteously as he crept about the castle gardens, carrying with him the dead body of the brother from whom only death could

MULTIPLE BIRTHS

HIGHEST NUMBER REPORTED
AT SINGLE BIRTH *World*
10 (decaplets) (2 male, 8 female) Bacacay, Brazil, 22 Apr 1946 (also report from Spain, 1924 and China, 12 May 1936)

HIGHEST NUMBER MEDICALLY RECORDED[1] *World*
9 (nonuplets) (5 male, 4 female) to Mrs Geraldine Brodrick at Royal Hospital, Sydney, Australia on 13 June 1971. 2 males stillborn. Richard (12 oz *340 g*) survived 6 days
9 (all died) to patient at University of Pennsylvania, Philadelphia 29 May 1972
9 (all died) reported from Bagerhat, Bangladesh, *c.* 11 May 1977 to 30-year-old mother

United Kingdom
6 (sextuplets) (all female) to Mrs Janet Walton (b. 1952) at Liverpool Maternity Hospital on 18 Nov 1983. All survive. 6 (4 male, 2 female) to Mrs Jane Underhill (b. 1957) at Rosie Maternity Hospital, Cambridge, on 2 May 1985. After 9 months only 3 survived. 6 to Mrs Susan Coleman (3 male, 3 female) at Homerton, East London on 12 Nov 1986. All survive. 6 (2 male, 4 female) to Mrs Sheila Ann Thorns (*née* Manning) at New Birmingham Maternity Hospital on 2 Oct 1968. Three survive. 6 (1 male, 5 female) to Mrs Rosemary Letts (*née* Egerton) at University College Hospital, London, on 15 Dec 1969. One boy and 4 girls survive

HIGHEST NUMBER SURVIVING[2] *World*
6 out of 6 (3 males, 3 females) to Mrs Susan Jane Rosenkowitz (*née* Scoones) (b. Colombo, now Sri Lanka, 28 Oct 1947) at Mowbray, Cape Town, South Africa on 11 Jan 1974. In order of birth they were: David, Nicolette, Jason, Emma, Grant and Elizabeth. They totalled 24 lb 1 oz *10,915 kg*
6 out of 6 (4 males, 2 females) to Mrs Rosanna Giannini (b. 1952) at Careggi Hospital, Florence, Italy on 11 Jan 1980. They are Francesco, Fabrizio, Giorgio Roberto, Letizia and Linda

United Kingdom
6 out of 6 (see above): Mrs Janet Walton and Mrs Susan Coleman

QUINTUPLETS *World Heaviest*
25 lb *11,35 kg* Mrs Lui Saulien, Chekiang, China, 7 June 1953
25 lb *11,35 kg* Mrs Kamalammal, Pondicherry, India, 30 Dec 1956

World Most Sets
No recorded case of more than a single set

QUADRUPLETS *World Heaviest*
10,35 kg *22 lb 13 oz* Mrs Ayako Takeda, Tsuchihashi Maternity Hospital, Kagoshima, Japan, 4 Oct 1978 (4 girls)

World Most Sets
4 Mde Feodor Vassilyev, Shuya, Russia (d. *ante* 1770)

TRIPLETS[3] *World Heaviest*
26 lb 6 oz *11,96 kg* (unconfirmed) Iranian case (2 male, 1 female) 18 Mar 1968

UK Heaviest
24 lb 0 oz *10,886 kg* Mrs Mary McDermott, of Bearpark, Co Durham, 18 Nov 1914

World Most Sets
15 Maddalena Granata, Italy (1839–*fl.* 1886)

TWINS *World Heaviest*
27 lb 12 oz *12,590 kg* (surviving) Mrs J. P. Haskin, Fort Smith, Arkansas, USA, 20 Feb 1924

UK Heaviest
The 35 lb 8 oz, *16,1 kg* reported in the *Lancet* from Derbyshire, on 6 Dec 1884 for the Warren Case (2 males liveborn) is believed to have been a misprint for 25 lb 8 oz *11,6 kg*

World Most Sets
16 Mde Vassilyev (see above). *Note also* Mrs Barbara Zulu of Barbeton, South Africa bore 3 sets of girls and 3 mixed sets in 7 years (1967–73)

UK Most Sets
15 Mrs Mary Jonas of Chester (d. 4 Dec 1899)—all sets were boy and girl

---

[1] Mrs Edith Bonham (d. 1469) of Wishford Magna, Wiltshire reportedly had septuplets.
[2] The South African press were unable to verify the birth of 5 babies to Mrs Charmaine Craig (*née* Peterson) in Cape Town on 16 Oct 1980 and a sixth on 8 Nov. The reported names were Frank, Salome, John, Andrew, William and belatedly Deborah.
[3] Mrs Anna Steynvaalt of Johannesburg produced 2 sets within 10 months in 1960.

separate him and to whom death would again join him'.

The oldest surviving unseparated twins are the craniopagus pair Yvonne and Yvette Jones (b. 1949) of Los Angeles, California, whose heads are fused together at the crown. They have rejected an operation to separate them.

Most twins *Geographically*

In Chungchon, South Korea it was reported in September 1981 that there were unaccountably 38 pairs in only 275 families—the highest ever recorded ratio. The highest ratio of twins in Britain is to be found on the island of North Uist in the Outer Hebrides, Scotland. In June 1985 there were 36 sets aged from 82 to 2 years, a ratio of 1 to 40. (cf. the national average of 1 to 100).

Fastest triplet birth

The fastest recorded natural birth of triplets has been 2 minutes in the case of Mrs James E. Duck of Memphis, Tennessee (Bradley, Christopher and Carmon) on 21 Mar 1977.

Quindecaplets

It was announced by Dr Gennaro Montanino of Rome that he had delivered by hysterotomy at 4 months of the pregnancy the foetuses of 10 girls and 5 boys from the womb of a 35-year-old housewife on 22 July 1971. A fertility drug was responsible for this unique and unsurpassed instance of quindecaplets.

Longest and shortest pregnancy

Claims up to 413 days have been widely reported but accurate data are bedevilled by the increasing use of oral contraceptive pills which is a cause of amenorrhoea. The *US Medical Investigator* of 27 Dec 1884 reported a case of 15 months 20 days and the *Histoire de l'Académie* of 1751 the most extreme case of 36 months. In the pre-pill era English law has accepted pregnancies with extremes of 174 days (*Clark* v. *Clark*, 1939) and 349 days (*Hadlum* v. *Hadlum*, 1949). In May 1961 a Burmese woman aged 54 gave birth by caesarean in Rangoon to a 3 lb *1,3 kg* calcified baby after 25 years' gestation. She had gone into labour in 1936, but no child was born. Ernestine Hudgins was born weighing 17 oz *482 g* 18 weeks premature in San Diego, California, on 8 Feb 1983. This has been equalled by Alexander McGlade born in Middlesbrough, Cleveland, on 10 May 1986 at the same weight.

DESCENDANTS

In polygamous countries, the number of a person's descendants can become incalculable. The last Sharifian Emperor of Morocco, Moulay Ismail (1672–1727), known as 'The Bloodthirsty', was reputed to have fathered a total of 525 sons and 342 daughters by 1703 and a 700th son in 1721.

In April 1984 the death was reported of Adam Borntrager, aged 96, of Medford, Wisconsin, who had had 707 direct descendants of whom all but 32 were living. The total comprised 11 children, 115 grand, 529 great-grand and 20 great-great-grandchildren. The family is of the Amish Mennonite sect who eschew cars, telephones, electric light and higher education.

Mrs Sarah Crawshaw (d. 25 Dec 1844) left 397 descendants according to her gravestone in Stones Church, Ripponden, Halifax, West Yorkshire.

Multiple great-grandparents

The report in 1983 that Jane Kau Pung (1877–1982) had left 4 great-great-great-great-grandchildren has proved to be incorrect. She in fact proved to be one of many cases of great-great-great-grandparents. Of these cases the youngest person to learn that their great-granddaughter had become a grandmother was Mrs Ann V. Weirick (1888–1978) of Paxtonville, Pennsylva-

nia, who received news of her great-great-great-grandson Matthew Stork (b. 9 Sept 1976) when aged only 88. She died on 6 Jan 1978. Britain's youngest 3 greats grandmother was Mrs Violet Lewis (1885–1982) of Southampton.

Most living ascendants

Megan Sue Austin (b. 16 May 1982) of Bar Harbor, Maine, had a full set of grandparents and great-grandparents and five great-great-grandparents, making 19 direct ascendants.

BABIES

Heaviest

The heaviest viable babies on record, of normal parentage, were boys of 22 lb 8 oz *10,2 kg* born to Sig Carmelina Fedele of Aversa, Italy in September 1955 and by caesarian section to Mrs Christina Samane at Sipetu Hospital, Transkei, South Africa on 24 May 1982. The latter boy named Sithandive weighed 55,5 kg *8 st 10 lb* and stood 1,60 m *5 ft 3 in* on his fifth birthday. Mrs Anna Bates *née* Swan (1846–88), the 7 ft 5½ in *227 cm* Canadian giantess (see also p. 7), gave birth to a boy weighing 23 lb 12 oz *10,77 kg* (length 30 in *76 cm*) at her home in Seville, Ohio, USA on 19 Jan 1879, but the baby died 11 hours later. Her first child, an 18 lb *8,16 kg* girl (length 24 in *61 cm*) was still-born when she was delivered in 1872. On 9 Jan 1891 Mrs Florentin Ortega of Buenos Aires, Argentina produced a still-born boy weighing 25 lb *11,3 kg*. In May 1939 a deformed baby weighing 29 lb 4 oz *13,26 kg* was born in a hospital at Effingham, Illinois, USA, but died two hours later.

United Kingdom

The greatest recorded live birth weight in the United Kingdom is 21 lb *9,53 kg* for a child born on Christmas Day, 1852. It was reported in a letter to the *British Medical Journal* (1 Feb 1879) from a doctor in Torpoint, Cornwall. The only other reported birth weight in excess of 20 lb *9,07 kg* is 20 lb 2 oz *9,13 kg* for a boy with a 14¼ in *36,8 cm* chest, born to a 33-year-old schoolmistress in Crewe, Cheshire, on 12 Nov 1884. On 15 Oct 1785 the 'Irish Fairy', Mrs Catherine Kelly, who stood 34 in *86,3 cm* and weighed 22 lb *9,97 kg*, died in Norwich, Norfolk, after giving birth to a 7 lb *3,17 kg* baby which lived only 2 hours.

Most bouncing baby

The most bouncing baby on record was probably James Weir (1819–21) who, according to his headstone in Cambushnethan, Old Parish Cem-

---

Longest separated twins ● Twins Lloyd Ecre and Floyd Ellswerk Clark (b. 15 Feb 1917) in Nebraska were parted when 4 months old. Both knew they had been born twins but were not reunited until 16 June 1986 after a separation of over 69 years.

---

etery, Wishaw, Lanarks, was 8 st or 112 lb *50,8 kg* at 13 months, 3 ft 4 in *1,01 m* in height and 39 in *99 cm* in girth. T. J. Albert Jackson, the world's heaviest living man (see page 8), claimed he weighed 105 lb *47,6 kg* and stood 4 ft 1 in *124 cm* tall at the age of 12 months. Brazil's 'superbaby' Veridiano dos Santos (b. 1978) weighed 143 lb *64,8 kg* aged 5 and 187 lb *84,8 kg* aged 7 with a 43 in *109 cm* waist. Therese Parentean, who died in Rouyn, Quebec, Canada on 11 May 1936 aged 9 years, weighed 24 st 4 lb *154 kg* (cf. 27 st *171 kg* for Robert Earl Hughes at the age of ten [see table, p. 8 and Chest measurements, p. 16]).

Lightest

The lowest birth weight recorded for a surviving infant, of which there is definite evidence, is 10 oz *283 g* in the case of Mrs Marian Taggart *née* Chapman (b. 5 June 1938, d. 31 May 1983) who was born six weeks premature in South Shields, Tyne and Wear. She was born unattended (length 12¼ in *31 cm*) and was nursed by Dr D. A. Shearer, who fed her hourly for the first 30 hours with brandy, glucose and water through a fountain-pen filler. At three weeks she weighed 1 lb 13 oz *821 g* and by her first birthday 13 lb 14 oz *6,29 kg*. Her weight on her 21st birthday was 7 st 8 lb *48,08 kg*.

A weight of 8 oz *227 g* was reported on 20 Mar 1938 for a baby born prematurely to Mrs John Womack, after she had been knocked down by a lorry in East St Louis, Illinois. The baby was taken alive to St Mary's Hospital, but died a few hours later. On 23 Feb 1952 it was reported that a 6 oz *170 g* baby only 6½ in *17 cm* long lived for 12 hours in a hospital in Indianapolis, Indiana. A twin was still-born.

Coincident birthdates

The only verified example of a family producing five single children with coincident birthdays is that of Catherine (1952), Carol (1953), Charles (1956), Claudia (1961) and Cecilia (1966), born to Ralph and Carolyn Cummins of Clintwood, Virginia, all on 20 February. The random odds against five single siblings sharing a birthdate would be one in 17,797,577,730—more than 3½ times the world's population.

The three children of the Henriksen family of Andenes, Norway—Heidi (b. 1960), Olav (b. 1964) and Lief-Martin (b. 1968)—all celebrate their birthday infrequently, because these all fall on Leap Day – February 29. Ralph Bertram Williams was born on 4 July 1982 in Wilmington, North Carolina. His father, grandfather and, in 1876, his great-grandfather were also born on 4 July.

Most southerly birth

Emilio Marcos Palma (Argentina), born 7 Jan 1978 at the Sargento Cabral Base, Antarctica, is the only person alive who can claim to be the first born on any continent. The mother was flown from Argentina at governmental expense.

Test tube baby *Earliest*

Louise Brown (5 lb 12 oz *2,6 kg*) was delivered by caesarian section from Lesley Brown, 31, in Oldham General Hospital, Lancashire, at 11.47 p.m. on 25 July 1978. She was externally conceived on 10 Nov 1977.

Physiology and Anatomy

BONES

Longest

Excluding a variable number of sesamoids, there are 206 bones in the adult human body compared to 300 for children (as they grow some bones fuse together to make one). The thigh bone or

Physiology

femur is the longest. It constitutes usually 27½ per cent of a person's stature, and may be expected to be 19¾ in *50 cm* long in a 6 ft *183 cm* tall man. The longest recorded bone was the femur of the German giant Constantine, who died in Mons, Belgium, on 30 Mar 1902, aged 30 (see p. 7). It measured 76 cm *29.9 in.* The femur of Robert Wadlow, the tallest man ever recorded, measured an estimated 29½ in *75 cm*.

Smallest

The *stapes* or stirrup bone, one of the three auditory ossicles in the middle ear, is the smallest human bone, measuring from 2,6 to 3,4 mm *0.10 to 0.17 in* in length and weighing from 2,0 to 4,3 mg *0.03 to 0.065 grains*.

MUSCLES

Largest

Muscles normally account for 40 per cent of the body weight and the bulkiest of the 639 named muscles in the human body is the *gluteus maximus* or buttock muscle, which extends the thigh.

Smallest

The smallest muscle is the *stapedius*, which controls the *stapes* (see above), an auditory ossicle in the middle ear, and which is less than 1/20th of an inch *0,127 cm* long.

Largest chest measurements

The largest chest measurements are among endomorphs (those with a tendency towards globularity). In the extreme case of Hughes (see table p. 8) this was 124 in *315 cm*, and William Campbell (see p. 8), Britain's second heaviest man, had a 96 in *244 cm* chest. George Macaree (formerly Britain's heaviest man) has a chest measurement of 75 in *190,5 cm* (waist 70 in *177,8 cm*), at a bodyweight of 31 st *196,8 kg* (height 5 ft 10 in *177,8 cm*) and Martin Ruane (see p. 9) has a chest measurement of 73 in *185,4 cm* (waist 68 in *172,7 cm*).

Among muscular subjects (mesomorphs) of normal height *expanded* chest measurements above 56 in *142 cm* are extremely rare. Vasiliy Alekseyev (b. 1942), the 6 ft 1¼ in *186 cm* Russian super-heavyweight weight-lifting champion, had a 60½ in *153,6 cm* chest at his top weight of 350 lb *158,7 kg*. Arnold Schwarzenneger (b. 1948) of Graz, Austria, the 6 ft 1 in *185 cm* former Mr Universe and 'the most perfectly developed man in the history of the world', had a chest measurement of 57 in *145 cm* (bicep 22 in *55,8 cm*) at his best bodyweight of 235 lb *107 kg*.

Largest biceps ● Rick Brown (b. 4 Apr 1960) known to his friends as 'Grizzley' is armed with biceps over 25 in *63,5 cm* cold (not pumped). He has a chest measurement of 66 in *167,6 cm*, shoulders of 33 in *83,8 cm* and a 51 in *129,5 cm* waist. His weight is 367 lb *166 kg*. (Photo: Franklin Berger)

Hydrogen (63 per cent) and oxygen (25.5 per cent) constitute the commonest of the 24 elements in the human body. In 1972 four more trace elements were added—fluorine, silicon, tin and vanadium. The 'essentiality' of nickel has not yet been finally pronounced upon.

Smallest waists

Queen Catherine de Medici (1519–89) decreed a waist measurement of 13 in *33 cm* for ladies of the French Court. This was at a time when females were more diminutive. The smallest recorded waist among women of normal stature in the 20th century is a reputed 13 in *33 cm* in the cases of the French actress Mlle Polaire (1881–1939) and Mrs Ethel Granger (1905–82) of Peterborough, Cambs, who reduced from a natural 22 in *56 cm* over the period 1929–39.

Longest necks

The maximum measured extension of the neck by the successive fitting of copper coils, as practised by the women of the Padaung or Kareni tribe of Burma, is 15¾ in *40 cm*. When the rings are removed the muscles developed to support the head and neck shrink to their normal length.

BRAINS

Heaviest

The brain of an average adult male (*i.e.* 20–55 years) weighs 1424 g *3 lb 2.2 oz*, decreasing gradually to 1395 g *3 lb 1.1 oz* with advancing age. The heaviest brain ever recorded was that of a 50-year-old male which weighed 2049 g *4 lb 8.29 oz* reported by Dr Thomas F. Hegert, chief medical examiner for District 9, State of Florida, USA, on 23 Oct 1975. The brain of Ivan Sergeyvich Turgenev (1818–83), the Russian author, weighed 2012 g *4 lb 6.9 oz*. In Jan 1891 the *Edinburgh Medical Journal* reported the case of a 75-year-old man in the Royal Edinburgh Asylum whose brain weighed 1829 g *4 lb 0.5 oz*. The largest female brain on record weighed 1565 g *3 lb 7.3 oz*. It belonged to a murderess.

Human brains are getting heavier. Examination of post-mortem records shows that the average male brain weight has increased from 1372 g *3 lb 0.4 oz* in 1860 to 1424 g *3 lb 2.2 oz* today. Women's brains have also put on weight, from 1242 g *2 lb 11.8 oz* to 1265 g *2 lb 12.6 oz* and in recent years have been growing almost as fast as men's.

Prof Marian Diamond of the University of California at Berkeley announced on 13 Feb 1985 that the neuron to glial cell ratio in Section 39 of the brain of Albert Einstein (1879–1955) was 1.12 as opposed to the standard 1.936—a difference of 72.8 per cent.

Lightest

The lightest 'normal' or non-atrophied brain on record was one weighing 1096 g *2 lb 6.7 oz* reported by Dr P. Davis and Prof E. Wright of King's College Hospital, London in 1977. It belonged to a 31-year-old woman.

Most expensive skull
(excluding fossils)

On 6 March 1977 the Royal Swedish Academy of Sciences paid £5500 in London for the skull of Emanuel Swedenborg (1688–1772), the Swedish philosopher and theologian.

Highest IQ

Intelligence quotients or IQs comprise the subject's mental age divided by his chronological or actual age multiplied by 100 such that an 8-year-old more gifted than an average 16-year-old would have an IQ of $\frac{16}{8} \times 100 = 200$. The highest childhood score has been achieved by Marilyn Mach vos Savant of St Louis, Missouri, who as a 10-year-old achieved a ceiling score for 23-year-olds thus giving her an IQ of 228.

In adult high IQ clubs admission requirements are not on IQ points but are gauged in percentiles. An IQ exhibited by 1 person in 10,000 for instance coincides with 158 on the Stanford-Binet scale but 187 on the Cattell scale. The most elite ultra high IQ society is the Mega Society with 26 members with percentiles of 99.9999 or 1 in a million. The topmost scorer in the Mega admission test, devised by its founder Ronald K. Hoeflin, has been 46 out of 48 by Marilyn Mach vos Savant superseding the 43 of Jeff Ward. The three members who have scored 197 on the Stanford-Binet scale are Christopher Philip Harding (born Keynsham, England, 1944) of Rockhampton, Queensland, Australia, Dr Ferris Eugene Alger (b. Des Moines, Iowa, 1913) of New Hope, Pennsylvania, and Dr Johannes Dougles Veldhuis (b. Hamilton, Ontario, 1949) of Charlottesville, Virginia.

The highest IQ published for a national population is 111 for the Japanese. For those born in 1960–61 a figure of 115 has been published. At least 10 per cent of their whole population has an IQ > 130.

Human computer
The fastest extraction of a 13th root from a 100 digit number is in 1 min 28.8 sec by the Dutchman Willem Klein (b. 1912, k. 1 Aug 1986) on 7 Apr 1981 at the National Laboratory for High Energy Physics (KEK), Tsukuba, Japan. Mrs Shakuntala Devi of India demonstrated the multiplication of two 13-digit numbers 7,686,369,774,870 × 2,465,099,745,779 picked at random by the Computer Department of Imperial College, London on 18 June 1980, in 28 sec. Her correct answer was 18,947,668,177,995,426,462,773,730. Some experts on calculating prodigies refuse to give credence to Mrs Devi—on the grounds that it is so vastly superior to the calculating feats of any other invigilated prodigy that the invigilation must have been defective.

Memory
Bhandanta Vicitsara recited 16,000 pages of Bhuddist canonical texts in Rangoon, Burma in May 1974. Gou Yan-ling, 26, has memorized more than 15,000 telephone numbers in Harbin, China according to the Xinhua News Agency. Rare instances of eidetic memory—the ability to reproject and hence 'visually' recall material—are known to science.

Creighton Carvello (see below) memorised a random sequence of 6 separate packs (312) of cards on a single sighting with only 4 errors including an all correct straight run of 139 cards at the New Marske Institute Club, Cleveland, England on 21 Mar 1985. On 21 July 1985 on a TV programme in Japan, he achieved the rarer accomplishment of only 24 errors with 6 packs shuffled together.

The greatest number of places of π
Hideaki Tomoyori (b. 30 Sep 1932), of Yokohama, Japan, recited 'pi' from memory to 40,000 places in 17 hr 21 min including 4 hr 15 min breaks on 9–10 Mar 1987 at the Tsukuba University Club House. On a Japanese TV programme, Mr Tomoyori also demonstrated his ability to recite correctly the 20 consecutive digits following a randomly selected series of numbers. The British record is 20,013 by Creighton Carvello (see above) on 27 June 1980 in 9 hr 10 min at Saltscar Comprehensive School, Redcar, Cleveland. *Note:* It is only the *approximation* of π at $^{22}/_7$ which recurs after its sixth decimal place and can, of course, be recited *ad nauseam*. The true value is a string of random numbers fiendishly difficult to memorise. The average ability for memorizing random numbers is barely more than 8, as proved by the common inability to memorize 9 or 10 digit telephone numbers.

HANDS, FEET AND HAIR
Touch
The extreme sensitivity of the fingers is such that a vibration with a movement of 0.02 of a micron can be detected.

Most fingers and toes (Polydactylism)
At an inquest held on a baby boy at Shoreditch, East London on 16 Sept 1921 it was reported that he had 14 fingers and 15 toes.

Least toes
The two-toed syndrome exhibited by some members of the Wadomo tribe of the Zambezi Valley, Zimbabwe, and the Kalanga tribe of the eastern Kalahari Desert, Botswana, is hereditary via a single mutated gene. These 'ostrich people', as they are known, can walk great distances without discomfort.

Longest finger nails
The longest finger nails ever reported are those of Shridhar Chillal, (b. 1937) of Poona, India. The aggregate measurement, on 24 Mar 1987, was 158 in *401,3 cm* for the 5 nails on his left hand (thumb 37 in *94,0 cm*). He last cut his nails in 1952. Finger nails grow about 0.02 in *0.05 cm* a week—four times faster than toe nails.

Longest hair
Swami Pandarasannadhi, the head of the Tirudaduturai monastery, Tanjore district, Madras, India was reported in 1949 to have hair 26 ft *7,92 m* in length. In 1780 a head of hair measuring 12 ft *3,65 m* in length and dressed in a style known as the Plica Polonica (hair closely matted together) was sent to Dresden after adorning the

Longest hair ● Diane Witt, of Worcester, USA, a leading candidate for best-tressed woman. Her hair, last cut 15 years ago, has now exceeded 8½ ft *259 cm*. According to her husband it is still growing, which is rare since most people's hair will stop growing at 3 ft *91 cm*.

head of a Polish peasant woman for 52 years. The hair was a foot *30,4 cm* in circumference. The length of hair of Miss Skuldfrid Sjorgren (b. Stockholm) was reported from Toronto in 1912 to have reached twice her height at 10 ft 6 in *3,20 m*. The hair of Georgia Sabrantke (b. 10 Jan 1943) of West Germany was measured at 9 ft 9½ in *298,5 cm* on 19 Mar 1987. Human hair grows at the rate of about 0.5 in *1,27 cm* in a month. If left uncut it will usually grow to a maximum of 2–3 ft *61–91 cm*.

Strongest hair
In a test on BBC TV *Record Breakers* on 9 Sept 1984 a hair from the head of Miss Pham Thy Lan broke at a strain of 178 g *6¼ oz*.

Longest beard
The longest beard preserved was that of Hans N. Langseth (b. 1846 near Eidsroll, Norway) which measured 17½ ft *5,33 m* at the time of his burial at Kensett, Iowa in 1927 after 15 years' residence in the United States. The beard was presented to the Smithsonian Institution, Washington, DC in 1967. Richard Latter (b. Pembury, Kent, 1831) of Tunbridge Wells, Kent, who died in 1914 aged 83, reputedly had a beard 16 ft *4,87 m* long but contemporary independent corroboration is lacking and photographic evidence indicates this figure was exaggerated. The beard of the bearded lady Janice Deveree (b. Bracken Co., Kentucky, 1842) was measured at 14 in *36 cm* in 1884. The beard of Mlle Hélène Antonia of Liège, Belgium, a 17th-century exhibitionist, was said to have reached to her hips.

Longest moustache
The longest moustache on record is that of Birger Pellas (b. 21 Sept 1934) of Malmö, Sweden, grown since 1973, which reached 2,77 m *9 ft 1 in* on 2 Mar 1987. The moustache of Masuriya Din (b. 1908), a Brahmin of the Partabgarh district in Uttar Pradesh, India grew to an extended span of 8 ft 6 in *2,59 m* between 1949 and 1962. Karna Ram Bheel (b. 1928) was granted permission by a New Delhi prison governor in February 1979 to keep his 7 ft 10 in *238 cm* moustache grown since 1949 during his life sentence. He uses mustard, oil, butter and cream to keep it in trim. The longest moustache in Great Britain has been that of John Roy (b. 14 Jan 1910), of Weeley, near Clacton, Essex. It attained a peak span of 74½ in *189 cm* between 1939 and 2 Apr 1976. He accidentally sat on it in the bath in 1984 and chopped off 2 ft *61 cm*. He then took 2 ft *61 cm* off the other side to even the moustache. The current UK champion is Mike Solomons of Long Ditton, Surrey with 33 in *83,8 cm* as of 24 Mar 1987.

DENTITION
Earliest
The first deciduous or milk teeth normally appear in infants at 5–8 months, these being the mandibular and maxillary first incisors. There are many records of children born with teeth, the most distinguished example being Prince Louis Dieudonné, later Louis XIV of France, who was born with two teeth on 5 Sept 1638. Molars usually appear at 24 months, but in Pindborg's case published in Denmark in 1970, a 6-week premature baby was documented with 8 natal teeth of which 4 were in the molar region.

Most
Cases of the growth in late life of a third set of teeth have been recorded several times. A reference to a case in France of a fourth dentition, known as Lison's case, was published in 1896. A triple row of teeth was noted in 1680 by Albertus Hellwigius.

Most dedicated dentist
Brother Giovanni Battista Orsenigo of the Ospedale Fatebenefratelli, Rome, a religious dentist,

conserved all the teeth he extracted in three enormous cases during the time he exercised his profession from 1868 to 1904. In 1903 the number was counted and found to be 2,000,744 teeth, indicating an average of 185 teeth or nearly 6 total extractions a day.

Strongest bite
In August 1986, Richard Hofmann (b. 1949) of Lake City, Florida, USA, achieved a bite strength of 975 lb *442 kg* for approx. 2 seconds in a research test using a gnathodymometer at the College of Dentistry, University of Florida, USA. This figure is over 6 times normal biting strength.

Most valuable tooth
In 1816 a tooth belonging to Sir Isaac Newton (1643–1727) was sold in London for £730. It was purchased by a nobleman who had it set in a ring which he wore constantly.

Earliest false teeth
From discoveries made in Etruscan tombs, partial dentures of bridge-work type were being worn in what is now Tuscany, Italy, as early as 700 BC. Some were permanently attached to existing teeth and others were removable.

OPTICS

Smallest visible object
The resolving power of the human eye is 0.0003 of a radian or an arc of one minute ($\frac{1}{60}$th of a degree), which corresponds to 100 microns at 10 in. A micron is a thousandth of a millimetre, hence 100 microns is 0.003937, or less than four thousandths, of an inch. The human eye can, however, detect a bright light source shining through an an aperture only 3 to 4 microns across. Dentist Veronica Seider (b. 1951) of Stuttgart, West Germany, possesses a visual acuity of 20 times better than average. She can identify people at a distance of more than a mile *1,6 km*, and also specialises in microwriting without the use of artificial aids. In one test she examined what seemed to be a thread of cotton and then announced that it was actually four threads twisted tightly together. Magnification proved her right.

Colour sensitivity
The unaided human eye, under the best possible viewing conditions, comparing large areas of colour, in good illumination, using both eyes, can distinguish 10,000,000 different colour surfaces. The most accurate photo-electric spectrophotometers possess a precision probably only 40 per cent as good as this. About 7.5 per cent of men and 0.1 per cent of women are colour blind. The most extreme form, monochromatic vision, is very rare. The highest rate of red-green colour blindness is in Czechoslovakia and the lowest rate among Fijians and Brazilian Indians.

VOICE

Highest and lowest
The highest and lowest recorded notes attained by the human voice before this century were a staccato E in *alt altissimo* (e^{iv}) by Ellen Beach Yaw (US) (1869–1947) in Carnegie Hall, New York, on 19 Jan 1896, and an A$_1$ (55 Hz (cycles per sec)) by Kasper Foster (1617–73). Madeleine Marie Robin (1918–60) the French operatic coloratura could produce and sustain the B above high C in the Lucia mad scene in Donizetti's *Lucia di Lammermoor*. Since 1950 singers have achieved high and low notes far beyond the hitherto accepted extremes. However, notes at the bass and treble extremities of the register tend to lack harmonics and are of little musical value. Frl Marita Gunther, trained by Alfred Wolfsohn, has covered the range of the piano from the lowest note, A$_{II}$ to c^v. Of this range of 7$\frac{1}{4}$ octaves, six octaves were considered to be of musical value. Roy Hart, also trained by

Wolfsohn, has reached notes below the range of the piano. Barry Girard of Canton, Ohio in May 1975 reached the e (4340 Hz) above the piano's top note. The highest note put into song is G^{iv} first occurring in Mozart's *Popoli di Tessaglia*. The lowest vocal note in the classical repertoire is in Mozart's *Il Seraglio* by Osmin who descends to low D (73.4 Hz). Dan Britton reached the 4th E below middle C at 20.6 Hz at Anoka County Fair, Minnesota on 31 July 1984. Stefan Zucker sang A in *alt altissimo* for 3.8 sec in the tenor role of Salvini in the première of Bellini's *Adelson e Salvini* in New York on 12 Sept 1972.

Greatest range
The normal intelligible outdoor range of the male human voice in still air is 200 yd *180 m*. The *silbo*, the whistled language of the Spanish-speaking Canary Island of La Gomera, is intelligible across the valleys, under ideal conditions, at five miles *8 km*. There is a recorded case, under freak acoustic conditions, of the human voice being detectable at a distance of 10$\frac{1}{4}$ miles *17 km* across still water at night. It was said that Mills Darden (see table page 8) could be heard 6 miles *9 km* away when he bellowed at the top of his voice.

Because of their more optimal frequency, female screams tend to higher readings on decibel meters than male bellows. The annual World Shouting Championship record is 112.4 dBA by Anthony Fieldhouse on 9 Sept 1984 at Scarborough, North Yorkshire. The highest scientifically measured emission has been one of 123.2 dBA by the screaming of Neil Stephenson of Newcastle-upon-Tyne, Tyne and Wear on 18 May 1985.

Lowest detectable sound
The intensity of noise or sound is measured in terms of pressure. The pressure of the quietest sound that can be detected by a person of normal hearing at the most sensitive frequency of *c.* 2750 Hz is 2×10^{-5} pascal. One tenth of the logarithm to this standard provides a unit termed a decibel (dBA). A noise of 30 decibels is negligible.

Highest noise levels
Prolonged noise above 150 decibels will cause immediate permanent deafness while above 192 dBA a lethal over-pressure shock wave can be formed. Equivalent continuous sound levels (LEQ) above 90 dBA are impermissible in factories, but this compares with 125 emitted by racing cars, 130 (amplified music) and 170 (some toy guns).

Highest detectable pitch
The upper limit of hearing by the human ear is reckoned to be 20,000 Hz (cycles per sec), although it has been alleged that children with asthma can detect sounds of 30,000 Hz. Bats emit pulses at up to 90,000 Hz. It was announced in February 1964 that experiments in the USSR had conclusively proved that oscillations as high as 200,000 Hz can be detected if the oscillator is pressed against the skull.

Fastest talker
Few people are able to speak *articulately* at a sustained speed above 300 words per min. The fastest broadcaster has been regarded as Gerry Wilmot (b. Victoria, BC, Canada, 6 Oct 1914), the ice hockey commentator in the post-World War II period. Raymond Glendenning (1907–74), the BBC horseracing commentator, once spoke 176 words in 30 sec while commentating on a greyhound race. In public life the highest speed recorded is a 327 words per min burst in a speech made in December 1961 by John Fitzgerald Kennedy (1917–63), then President of the United States. Results of tests by a radio station on John Moschitta (USA) in March 1983 at a rate of 534 in 58 sec or 552 words per min were intelligible. John Helm of Yorkshire TV can recite the 92 Football League clubs in 26 sec.

BLOOD

Groups
The preponderance of one blood group varies greatly from one locality to another. On a world basis Group O is the most common (46 per cent), but in some areas, for example Norway, Group A predominates.

The full description of the commonest sub-group in Britain is O MsNs, P+, Rr, Lu(a−), K−, Le(a−b+), Fy(a+b+), Jk(a+b+), which occurs in one in every 270 people.

The rarest blood group on the ABO system, one of 14 systems, is AB, which occurs in less than 3 per cent of persons in the British Isles. The rarest type in the world is a type of Bombay blood (sub-type h-h) found so far only in a Czechoslovak nurse in 1961 and in a brother (Rh positive) and sister (Rh negative) named Jalbert in Massachusetts reported in February 1968.

Richest natural resources
Joe Thomas of Detroit, Michigan was reported in August 1970 to have the highest known count of Anti-Lewis B, the rare blood antibody. A US biological supply firm pays him $1500 per quart *1,13 l*. The Internal Revenue regard this income as a taxable liquid asset.

Donor and recipient
Since 1966 Allen Doster, a self-employed beautician, has (to April 1986) donated 1840 US pints *870,64 l* at Roswell Park Memorial Institute, New York as a plasmapheresis donor. The present-day normal limit on donations is 5 pints per annum. A 50-year-old haemophiliac Warren C. Jyrich required 2400 donor units *1080 l* of blood when undergoing open heart surgery at the Michael Reese Hospital, Chicago in December 1970.

Largest vein
The largest vein in the human body is the *inferior vena cava*, which returns most of the blood from the body below the level of the heart.

Most alcoholic subject
California University Medical School, Los Angeles reported in December 1982 the case of a confused but conscious 24-year-old female, who was shown to have a blood alcohol level of 1510 mg per 100 ml—nearly 19 times the UK driving limit and triple the normally lethal limit. After two days she discharged herself.

The United Kingdom's legal limit for motorists is 80 mg of alcohol per 100 ml of blood. The hitherto recorded highest figure in medical literature of 656 mg per 100 ml was submerged when the late Samuel Riley (b. 1922) of Sefton Park, Merseyside, was found by a disbelieving pathologist to have a level of 1220 mg on 28 Mar 1979. He had expired in his flat and had been an inspector at the plant of a well-known motor manufacturer.

BODY TEMPERATURE

Highest
Willie Jones, a 52-year-old black, was admitted to Grady Memorial Hospital, Atlanta, Georgia on 10 July 1980 with heat stroke on a day when the temperature reached 90° F *32,2° C* with 44% humidity. His temperature was found to be 46,5° C *115.7° F*. After 24 days he was discharged 'at prior baseline status'.

Lowest
There are three recorded cases of patients surviving body temperatures as low as 60.8° F *16,0° C*: Dorothy Mae Stevens (1929–74) who was found in an alley in Chicago, Illinois on 1 Feb 1951; Vickie Mary Davis aged 2 years 1 month in an unheated house in Marshalltown, Iowa on 21 Jan 1956 and 2-year-old Michael Trocle in the snow near his home in Milwaukee, Wisconsin,

Anatomy

on 19 Jan 1985, all with this temperature. People may die of hypothermia with body temperatures of 95.0° F *35,0° C*.

ILLNESS AND DISEASE

Commonest

The commonest non-contagious disease in the world is periodontal disease, such as gingivitis, which subclinically afflicts some 80 per cent of the US population. In Great Britain 13 per cent of people have lost all their teeth before they are 21 years old. During their lifetime few completely escape its effects. Infestation with pinworm (*Enterobius vermicularis*) approaches 100 per cent in some tropical areas of the world.

The commonest contagious disease in the world is coryza (acute nasopharyngitis) or the common cold. The greatest reported loss of working time in Britain is from neurotic disorders, which accounted for 28,101,200, or 8.56 per cent, of the total of 328,109,200 days lost from mid-1984 to mid-1985.

The most resistant recorded case to being infected at the Medical Research Council Common Cold Unit, Salisbury, Wiltshire is J. Brophy, who has had one mild reaction in 24 visits.

Rarest

Medical literature periodically records hitherto undescribed diseases. A disease as yet undescribed but predicted by a Norwegian doctor is podocytoma of the kidney—a tumour of the epithelial cells lining the glomerulus of the kidney.

The last case of endemic smallpox was recorded in Ali Maow Maalin in Merka, Somalia on 26 Oct 1977. Paul Braddon of Rusper, West Sussex was reported on 2 Aug 1983 to be the first case to contract malaria in Britain for more than 35 years.

Kuru, or laughing sickness, afflicts only the Fore tribe of eastern New Guinea and is 100 per cent fatal. This was formally attributed to the cannibalistic practice of eating human brains.

The rarest fatal diseases in England and Wales have been those from which the last deaths (all males) were all recorded more than 40 years ago—yellow fever (1930), cholera nostras (1928) and bubonic plague (1926).

Most infectious

The most infectious of all diseases is the pneumonic form of plague, as evidenced by the Black Death of 1347–51. It had a mortality rate of about 99.99 per cent.

The virus AIDS (acquired immune-deficiency syndrome), first recognised in 1978, was first identified in Jan 1983 at the Pasteur Institute, Paris by Luc Montagnier, Françoise Barré-Sinoussi and Jean-Claude Chermann as a Human T-lymphotrophic virus Type III (HTLV III). The US death toll from AIDS has been predicted to reach 179,000 by 1991, with care costs possibly reaching $16,000 million. Uncertainty on the percentage of sero-positive HIV carriers and the duration of incubation make it possible to assert that the toll will be of the order of 100,000 to 300,000 by this date.

Highest mortality

Rabies in humans has been regarded as uniformly fatal when associated with the hydrophobia symptom. A 25-year-old woman, Candida de Sousa Barbosa of Rio de Janeiro, Brazil, after surgery by Dr Max Karpin, was believed to be the first ever survivor of the disease in November 1968. Some sources prefer the case of Matthew Winkler, 6, who, on 10 Oct 1970, survived a bite by a rabid bat.

Leading cause of death

The leading cause of death in industrialised countries is arteriosclerosis (thickening of the arterial wall) which underlies much coronary and cerebrovascular disease. Deaths from diseases of the circulatory system totalled 278,849 in England and Wales in 1984.

Most notorious carrier

The most publicised of all typhoid carriers has been Mary Mallon (real name Maria Anna Caduff), known as Typhoid Mary, who was born in Graubunden, Switzerland, in 1855 and arrived as an immigrant in New York City, N.Y., USA, on 11 Jan 1868. In her job as a cook she was the source of 53 outbreaks, including the 1903 epidemic of 1400 cases in Ithaca, and 3 deaths. She was placed under permanent detention at Riverside Hospital on North Brother Island, East River, from 1915 until her death from bronchopneumonia on 11 Nov 1938.

Parkinson's disease

The most protracted case of Parkinson's disease (named after 'An Essay on the Shaking Palsy' of 1817 by Dr James Parkinson (1755–1824)) for which the earliest treatments were not published until 1946, is 62 years in the case of Frederick G. Humphries (d. 23 Feb 1985) of Croydon, London. His symptoms were detected in 1923.

MEDICAL EXTREMES

Heart stoppage

The longest recorded heart stoppage is a minimum of 3 hr 40 min in the case of Miss Jean Jawbone, 20, who was revived by a team of 26, using peritoneal dialysis, in the Health Sciences Centre, Winnipeg, Manitoba, Canada on 8 Jan 1977. The 'Mammalian dive effect' can be triggered in humans falling into water cooler than 70° F *21° C*. On 9 Oct 1986 Allen Smith, aged 2, fell into the swollen waters of the Stanislaus River at Oakdale, California, USA. He was spotted 90 mins later and rushed to the Modesto Memorial Hospital, but it was another two hours before his heart began beating again spontaneously.

The longest recorded interval in a *post mortem* birth was one of 84 days in the case of a baby girl delivered on 5 July 1983 from a clinically dead woman in Roanoke, Virginia, who had been kept on life support since suffering a seizure in April.

Pulse rates

A normal adult pulse rate is 70–72 beats per min at rest for males and 78–82 for females. Rates increase to 200 or more during violent exercise and drop to as low as 12 in the extreme cases of Dorothy Mae Stevens (see Lowest body temperature, column 1), and Jean Hilliard (b. 1962) of Fosston, Minnesota on 20 Dec 1980.

Longest coma

The longest recorded coma was that undergone by Elaine Esposito (b. 3 Dec 1934) of Tarpon Springs, Florida. She never stirred after an appendicectomy on 6 Aug 1941, when she was 6, in Chicago, Illinois, and died on 25 Nov 1978 aged 43 years 357 days, having been in a coma for 37 years 111 days.

Longest dream

Dreaming sleep is characterised by rapid eye movements known as REM discovered in 1953 by William Dement of the University of Chicago. The longest recorded period of REM is one of 2 hr 23 min on 15 Feb 1967 at the Department of Psychology, University of Illinois, Chicago on Bill Carskadon, who had had his previous sleep interrupted. In July 1984 The Sleep Research Centre, Haifa, Israel recorded nil REM in a 33-year-old male who had a shrapnel brain injury.

Largest stone

The largest stone or vesical calculus reported in medical literature was one of 13 lb 14 oz *6,29 kg* removed from an 80-year-old woman by Dr

Humphrey Arthure at Charing Cross Hospital, London, on 29 Dec 1952.

Longest in iron lung

The longest recorded period in an 'iron lung' is 37 years 58 days by Mrs Laurel Nisbet (b. 17 Nov 1912) of La Crescenta, California, who died on 22 Aug 1985. She had been in an 'iron lung' continuously since 25 June 1948. The longest survival in an 'iron lung' in Britain was 30 years (1949–79) by Denis Atkin in Lodge Moor Hospital, Sheffield, South Yorkshire. John Prestwich (b. 24 Nov 1938) of Kings Langley, Hertfordshire has been dependent on a negative pressure respirator since 24 Nov 1955. Paul Bates of Horsham, West Sussex, was harnessed to a mechanical positive pressure respirator on 13 Aug 1954. From continuous respiration, he has received an estimated 244,783,343 respirations via his trachea up to 1 May 1987.

Fastest reactions ● Seen here in action are Romy Müller of East Germany (above) and Wilbert Greaves of Great Britain who recorded the fastest apparent reaction times to the starting pistol for sprinters at the 1980 Olympic Games, 0.120 sec in the women's 200 metres semi-final and 0.124 sec in the 100 metre hurdles heats respectively. These compare with 0.011 sec for the cockroach *Periplaneta americana*. (Photo: All-Sport)

Motionlessness ● Voluntary: Sunardi (b. 1960), an Indonesian teacher, continuously stood motionless for 15 hr 25 sec on 21 July 1986 at the Motionlessness Festival in Semarang, Indonesia.

. . . and involuntary: Corporal Everett D Reamer (right) of the 60th Coast Artillery Regiment AA Battery F USA FFE was punished in Camp No 1, Osaka, Japan by being made to stand to attention motionless for 132 consecutive hours from 8.00 a.m. 15 Aug until 8.00 p.m. 20 Aug 1944. The above picture was taken following his release after the ordeal.

Fastest nerve impulses

The results of experiments published in 1966 have shown that the fastest messages transmitted by the human nervous system travel as fast as 180 mph *288 km/h*. With advancing age impulses are carried 15 per cent more slowly.

Hiccoughing

The longest recorded attack of hiccoughs or singultus is that afflicting Charles Osborne (b. 1894) of Anthon, Iowa, USA, for the past 65 years from 1922. He contracted it when slaughtering a hog and has hiccoughed about 430 million times in the interim period. He has been unable to find a cure, but has led a reasonably normal life in which he has had two wives and fathered eight children. He has admitted, however, that he cannot keep in his false teeth. In July 1986 he was reported to be hiccing at 20–25 per minute from his earlier high of 40.

Sneezing

The most chronic sneezing fit ever recorded is that of Donna Griffiths (b. 1969) of Pershore, Hereford & Worcester. She started sneezing on 13 Jan 1981 and surpassed the previous duration record of 194 days on 27 July 1981. She sneezed an estimated million times in the first 365 days. She achieved her first sneeze-free day on 16 Sept 1983—the 978th day. The highest speed at

which expelled particles have ever been measured to travel is 103.6 mph *167 km/h*.

Snoring

The highest measured sound level recorded by any chronic snorer is a peak of 87.5 decibels at Hever Castle, Kent in the early hours of 28 June 1984. Melvyn Switzer of Totton, Hants was 1 ft *30 cm* from the meter. His wife Julie is deaf in one ear. Research has shown that differences in lung capacity and pharynx shape account for snoring. In general the pharynx was smaller in snorers.

Yawning

In Lee's case, reported in 1888, a 15-year-old female patient yawned continuously for a period of 5 weeks.

Sleeplessness

Researches indicate that on the Circadian cycle for the majority peak efficiency is attained between 8 and 9 p.m. and the low point comes at 4 a.m. The longest recorded period for which a person has voluntarily gone without sleep is 449 hr (18 days 17 hr) by Mrs Maureen Weston of Peterborough, Cambs in a rocking chair on 14 Apr–2 May 1977 (see page 179). Though she tended to hallucinate toward the end of this surely ill-advised test, she surprisingly suffered no lasting ill-effects. Victims of the very rare condition chronic colestites (total insomnia) have been known to go without definable sleep for many years. Jesus de Frutos (b. 1925) of Segovia, Spain asserts that he has only dozed since 1954.

Most voracious fire breathers and extinguishers

Reg Morris blew a flame from his mouth to a distance of 27 ft *8,23 m* igniting a bonfire, at The

Castle Working Men's Club, Brownhills, West Midlands on 5 Nov 1983. On 17 Mar 1987 Reg Morris also extinguished 20,035 torches of flame in his mouth in 1 hr 48 min 14 sec at Cinders Night Club, Willenhall, West Midlands. On 26 July 1986 at Port Lonsdale, Victoria, Australia, Sipra Ellen Lloyd set a female record of 8357.

Human salamanders

The highest dry-air temperature endured by naked men in the US Air Force experiments in 1960 was 400° F *204,4° C* and for heavily clothed men 500° F *260° C*. Steaks require only 325° F *162,8° C*. Temperatures of 140° C *284° F* have been found quite bearable in sauna baths.

Thirty five people from the Sawau tribe on the island of Beqa in the Fijian group participated in a firewalk with the temperature over 1000° F *537° C* on 18 May 1982. There is an annual fire walk during the feast of St Constantine each May in Aghia Eleni, northern Greece.

Swallowing

The worst reported case of compulsive swallowing was an insane female Mrs H. aged 42, who complained of a 'slight abdominal pain'. She proved to have 2533 objects, including 947 bent pins, in her stomach. These were removed by Drs Chalk and Foucar in June 1927 at the Ontario

Hospital, Canada. The heaviest object extracted from a human stomach has been a 5 lb 3 oz *2,53 kg* ball of hair in Swain's case from a 20-year-old female compulsive swallower in the South Devon and East Cornwall Hospital, England on 30 Mar 1895.

Sword

Edward Benjamin 'Count Desmond' (b. 1941 of Binghamton, NY, USA) swallowed thirteen 23 in *58,4 cm* long blades to below his xiphisternum and injured himself in the process. *No further claims will be published.*

Heaviest smoker

In 1977 an English woman went to the Samaritans for help because she was afraid she was slowly committing suicide. She told astonished officials she was smoking 180 cigarettes a day, and said that during an 18-hour day she managed to light a fresh cigarette at least once every 6 minutes. It is not known whether she managed to 'kick the habit'.

Fasting

Most humans experience considerable discomfort after an abstinence from food for even 12 hr but this often passes off after 24–48 hr. Records claimed, unless there is unremitting medical surveillance, are inadmissible. The longest period for which anyone has gone without solid food is 382 days by Angus Barbieri (b. 1940) of Tayport, Fife, who lived on tea, coffee, water, soda water and vitamins in Maryfield Hospital, Dundee, Angus, from June 1965 to July 1966. His weight declined from 33 st 10 lb *214,1 kg* to 12 st 10 lb *80,74 kg*.

Hunger strike

The longest recorded hunger strike was one of 94 days by nationalist supporters John and Peter Crowley, Thomas Donovan, Michael Burke, Michael O'Reilly, Christopher Upton, John Power, Joseph Kenny and Seán Hennessy in Cork Prison, Ireland, from 11 Aug to 12 Nov 1920. These nine survivors from 12 prisoners owed their lives to expert medical attention and an appeal by the nationalist leader Arthur Griffith (1872–1922). The longest recorded hunger strike in a British gaol is 385 days from 28 June 1972 to 18 July 1973 by Denis Galer Goodwin in Wakefield Prison, West Yorkshire protesting his innocence of a rape charge. He was fed by tube orally.

The longest recorded case of survival without food *and* water is 18 days by Andreas Mihavecz, then 18, of Bregenz, Austria who was put into a holding cell on 1 Apr 1979 in a local government building in Höchst, Austria but was totally forgotten by the police. On 18 Apr 1979 he was discovered close to death having had neither food nor water. He had been a passenger in a crashed car.

Underwater

The world record for voluntarily staying underwater is 13 min 42.5 sec by Robert Foster, then aged 32, an electronics technician of Richmond, California, who stayed under 10 ft *3,05 m* of water in the swimming pool of the Bermuda Palms Motel at San Rafael, California, on 15 Mar 1959. He hyperventilated with oxygen for 30 min before his descent. (See also Heart Stoppage, p. 19.)

g forces

The acceleration g, due to gravity, is 32 ft 1.05 in per sec per sec *978,02 cm/sec²* at sea level at the Equator. A *sustained* acceleration of 25 g was withstood in a dry capsule during astronautic research by Dr Carter Collins of California. The highest g value endured on a water-braked rocket sled is 82.6 g for 0.04 of a sec by Eli L. Beeding Jr at Holloman Air Force Base, New Mexico, on 16 May 1958. He was put in hospital for 3 days. A man who fell off a 185 ft *56,39 m* cliff (before 1963) has survived a *momentary* g of 209 in decelerating from 68 mph *109 km/h* to stationary in 0.015 of a sec.

Racing driver David Purley GM (1945–1985) survived a deceleration from 108 mph *173 km/h* to zero in 26 in *66 cm* in a crash at Silverstone, Northamptonshire on 13 July 1977 which involved a force of 179.8 g. He suffered 29 fractures, 3 dislocations and 6 heart stoppages.

A land diver of Pentecost Island, New Hebrides dived from a platform 81 ft 3 in *24,76 m* high with liana vines attached to his ankles on 15 May 1982. The body speed was 50 ft *15,24 m* per sec 34 mph *54 km/h*. The jerk transmitted a momentary g force in excess of 110.

Isolation

The longest recorded period for which any volunteer has been able to withstand total deprivation of all sensory stimulation (sight, hearing and touch) is 92 hr, recorded in 1962 at Lancaster Moor Hospital, Lancashire.

Pill-taking

The highest recorded total of pills swallowed by a patient is 528,064 between 9 June 1967 and 31 Jan 1987 by C. H. A. Kilner (b. 1926) of Bindura, Zimbabwe, following a successful operation to remove a cancerous pancreas on 26 May 1966.

Most injections

A diabetic, Mrs Evelyn Ruth Winder (b. 1921) of Invercargill, New Zealand gave an estimated 58,568 insulin injections to herself over 56 years to May 1987.

Most tattoos

The seeming ultimate in being tattooed is represented by Wilfred Hardy of Huthwaite, Nottinghamshire, England. Not content with a perilous approach to within 4 per cent of totality, he has been tattooed on the inside of his cheek, his tongue, gums and eyebrows. Walter Stiglitz of North Plainfield, New Jersey, in March 1987 claimed 5465 separate tattoos by six artists. The world's most decorated woman is strip artiste Krystyne Kolorful (b. 5 Dec 1952, Alberta, Canada). Her 95% body suit took 10 years to complete and cost $15,000 £8500. Britain's most decorated woman is Rusty Field (b. 1944) of Norfolk, who after 12 years under the needle of Bill Skuse has come within 15 per cent of totality. Both the 1980 and 1981 World's Most Beautiful Tattooed Lady Contest in the US were won by Britain's Susan James (b. 1959).

OPERATIONS

Longest

The most protracted reported operation, for surgical as opposed to medical control purposes, has been one of 96 hr performed on Mrs Gertrude Levandowski (see also p. 10) during the period 4–8 Feb 1951. The patient suffered from a weak heart and surgeons had to exercise the utmost caution during the operation. The 'slowest' operation on record is one on the feet of Mrs Doreen Scott of Derby, England on 20 Nov 1981. She had been waiting since 10 March 1952—19 years 8 months.

Most

Padmabhushan Dr M. C. Modi, a pioneer of mass eye surgery in India since 1943, has performed as many as 833 cataract operations in one day, and a total of 564,834 to January 1987.

Dr Robert B. McClure (b. 1901) of Toronto performed a career total of 20,423 major operations in 1924–78.

Joseph Ascough (b. 1935) of Nottingham underwent his 337th operation (for the removal of papillomas from his wind pipe) on 9 Dec 1986.

These wart-like growths which impede breathing first formed when he was 18 months old. On 2 March 1977 Mr Jens Kjaer Jension (b. 1914) of Hoven, Denmark, was discharged from a local hospital after having 32,131 thorns removed from his body over a period of six years and 248 visits. In 1967 he had tripped and fallen into a pile of spiky berberry cuttings in his garden and was rushed unconscious to hospital. Even today he is still troubled by thorns working their way out through the skin of his legs.

Oldest subject

The greatest recorded age at which anyone has undergone an operation is 111 years 105 days in the case of James Henry Brett, Jr (b. 25 July 1849, d. 10 Feb 1961) of Houston, Texas, USA. He underwent a hip operation on 7 Nov 1960. The oldest age established in Britain was the case of Miss Mary Wright (b. 28 Feb 1862) who died during a thigh operation at Boston, Lincolnshire on 22 Apr 1971 aged 109 years 53 days.

Transplant *Heart*

The first human heart transplant operation was performed on Louis Washkansky, aged 55, at the Groote Schuur Hospital, Cape Town, South Africa, between 1.00 a.m. and 6 a.m., on 3 Dec 1967, by a team of 30 headed by Prof Christiaan Neethling Barnard (b. Beaufort West, 8 Oct 1922). The donor was Miss Denise Ann Darvall, aged 25. Washkansky lived for 18 days. The longest surviving heart transplantee was Emmanuel Vitria, of Marseilles, France (b. 24 Jan 1920) who received the heart of Pierre Ponson, 20, on 27 Nov 1968 and died on 9 May 1987. The surgeon, Edmon Herrig, died of a heart attack in 1972 aged 61. Britain's longest-surviving heart transplant patient is Nigel Olney (b. 1944) who underwent surgery at Papworth Hospital, Cambridge on 29 Jan 1980.

'Baby Moses' underwent a heart transplant at the Loma Linda Hospital, California, in November 1985 aged 4 days.

The first transplantee to give birth was Betsy Sneith, 23, with a baby girl Sierra (7 lb 10 oz *3,45 kg*) at Stanford University, California on 17 Sept 1984. She had received a donor heart in February 1980.

Heart–lung–liver

The first triple transplant took place on 17 Dec 1986 at Papworth Hospital, Cambridge, when Mrs Davina Thompson (b. 28 Feb 1951) of Rawmarsh, South Yorks, underwent surgery for 7 hours by a team of 15 headed by chest surgeon Mr John Wallwork and Prof Sir Roy Calne.

Kidney

R. H. Lawler (b. 1895) (USA) performed the first homo transplantation of the kidney in the human in 1950. The longest survival, as between identical twins, has been 20 years.

Earliest appendicectomy

The earliest recorded successful appendix operation was performed in 1736 by Claudius Amyand (1680–1740). He was Serjeant Surgeon to King George II (reigned 1727–60).

Earliest anaesthesia

The earliest recorded operation under general anaesthesia was for the removal of a cyst from the neck of James Venable by Dr Crawford Williamson Long (1815–78), using diethyl ether ($C_2H_5)_2O$, in Jefferson, Georgia, on 30 Mar 1842. The earliest amputation under an anaesthetic in Great Britain was by Dr William Scott and Dr James McLauchlan at the Dumfries and Galloway Infirmary, Scotland on 19 Dec 1846.

Most durable cancer patient

The most extreme recorded case of survival from diagnosed cancer is that of Mrs Winona

Mildred Melick (*née* Douglass) (b. 22 Oct 1876) of Long Beach, California. She had four cancer operations in 1918, 1933, 1966 and 1968 but died from pneumonia on 28 Dec 1981, 67 days after her 105th birthday.

Laryngectomy

On 24 July 1924 John I. Poole of Plymouth, Devon after diagnosis of carcinoma, then aged 33 underwent total laryngectomy in Edinburgh. He died on 19 June 1979 after surviving nearly 55 years as a 'neck-breather'. Mr F. B. Harvey of Plymouth, Devon has been a neck-breather since 1929.

Munchausen's syndrome

The most extreme recorded case of the rare and incurable condition known as 'Munchausen's syndrome' (a continual desire to have medical treatment) was William McIlroy (b. 1906), who cost the National Health Service an estimated £1 million during his 30-year career as a hospital patient. During that time he had 23 major operations, and stayed at 68 different hospitals using 22 aliases. The longest period he was ever out of hospital was for six months. In 1979 the Irishman hung up his bedpan for the last time, saying he was sick of hospitals, and retired to an old people's home in Birmingham.

Fastest amputation

The shortest time recorded for a leg amputation in the pre-anaesthetic era was 13–15 sec by Napoleon's chief surgeon Dominique Larrey. There could have been no ligation.

Largest tumour

The largest tumour ever recorded was Spohn's case of an ovarian cyst weighing 328 lb (23 st 6 lb) *148,7 kg* taken from a woman in Texas, in 1905. She made a full recovery. The most extreme case reported in Britain was of a cyst weighing 298 lb (21 st 4 lb) *135 kg* removed from a woman in England in 1846. This time the patient did not survive.

Surgical instruments

The largest surgical instruments are robot retractors used in abdominal surgery, introduced by Abbey Surgical Instruments of Chingford, Essex in 1968 and weighing 11 lb *5 kg*. Some bronchoscopic forceps measure 60 cm *23¼ in* in length. The smallest are Elliot's eye trephine, which has a blade 0.078 in *0,20 cm* in diameter and 'straight' stapes picks with a needle-type tip or blade of 0,3 mm *0.013 in* long.

PSYCHIC FORCES

Extra-sensory perception

The two most extreme published examples of ESP in scientific literature have been those of the Reiss case of a 26-year-old female at Hunter College, New York State in 1936 and of Pavel Stepánek (Czechoslovakia) in 1967–68. Any importance which might be attached to their cases was diminished by subsequent developments. The Reiss subject refused to undergo any further tests under stricter conditions. When Stepánek was retested at Edinburgh University with plastic cards he 'failed to display any clairvoyant ability'. Much smaller departures from the laws of probability have however been displayed in less extreme cases carried out under strict conditions.

Most durable ghosts

Ghosts are not immortal and seem to deteriorate after 400 years. The most outstanding exception to their normal 'half-life' would be the ghosts of Roman soldiers thrice reported still marching through the cellars of the Treasurer's House, York Minster after nearly 19 centuries. Andrew M. Green, author of *Ghost Hunting, A Practical Guide*, claims to possess the only known letter from a *poltergeist*.

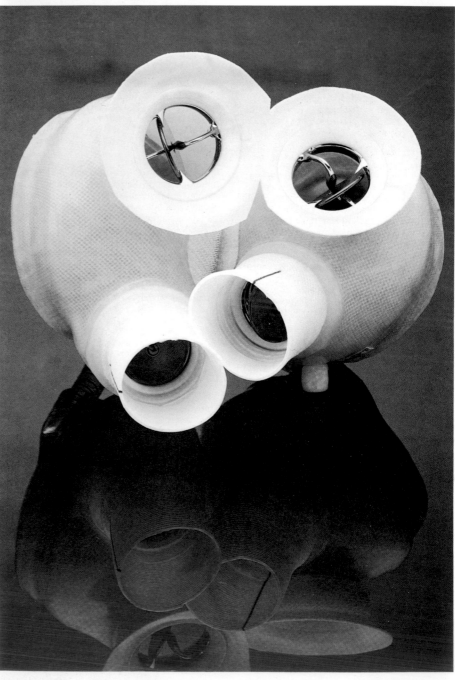

Artificial Heart ● The Jarvik Mark 7 heart, designed by Dr Robert K. Jarvik (left) in the United States. On 1–2 Dec 1982 at the Utah Medical Center, Salt Lake City, Dr Barney B. Clark, 61, of Des Moines, Wisconsin became the first recipient but died on 23 Mar 1983, 112 days later. The surgeon was Dr William C. DeVries. William J. Schroeder survived 620 days in Louisville, Kentucky from 25 Nov 1984 to 7 Aug 1986. Britain's first artificial heart patient was Raymond Cook of Hucknall, Notts who temporarily received a Jarvik Mark 7 on 2 Nov 1986 at Papworth Hospital, Cambridge.

THE LIVING WORLD

CHAPTER TWO

Animal Kingdom General Records

Fastest moving

The fastest moving living creature is the Peregrine falcon (*Falco peregrinus*) when stooping from great heights during territorial displays. In one series of experiments carried out in Germany the highest speed recorded for peregrines at a 30-degree angle of stoop was 270 km/h *168 mph*, and at 45 degrees the maximum velocity was 350 km/h *217 mph*.

Loudest sounds

The low frequency pulses made by blue whales when communicating with each other have been measured up to 188 dB, making them the loudest sounds emitted by any living source. They have been detected 850 km *530 miles* away.

Fastest burrower

The world's champion burrower is the Eurasian blind mole-rat *Spalax microphthalmus*. One burrow found in the southern USSR measured 363 m *1191 ft* in length, but this was dwarfed by another example which had a total of 114 mounds, the last two being 169 m *554 ft* apart.

Smelliest

The world's smelliest animal is the Zorilla (*Ictonyx striatus*) of Africa. It can discharge a nauseous fluid from its anal glands which can be smelt over a radius of half a mile *1,6 km*, and there is one record of a zorilla taking possession of a zebra carcass and keeping nine fully-grown lions at bay for several hours.

Longest gestation

The viviparous Alpine black salamander (*Salamandra atra*) has a gestation period of up to 38 months at altitudes above 1400 m *4600 ft* in the Swiss Alps, but this drops to 24–26 months at lower altitudes.

Fastest and slowest growth

The fastest growth in the Animal Kingdom is that of the blue whale calf. A barely visible ovum weighing a fraction of a milligramme (*0.000035 oz*) grows to a weight of *c.* 26 tons *26 tonnes* in 22¾ months, made up of 10¾ months gestation and the first 12 months of life. This is equivalent to an increase of 30,000 million-fold. The slowest growth is that of the deep-sea clam *Tindaria callistiformis* of the North Atlantic, which takes *c.* 100 years to reach a length of 8 mm *0.31 in*.

Lowest metabolism

The metabolism of the lizard-like Tuatara (*Sphenodon punctatus*) of New Zealand is so reduced that it can go as long as 60 minutes without taking breath.

Greatest size difference between sexes (dimorphism)

The largest female marine worms of the species *Bonellia viridis* are at least 100 million times heavier than the smallest males. The female is up to 100 cm *39.3 in* long against the miserable 1,0 mm *0.04 in* of the male.

Highest g force

The highest g force encountered in nature is the 400 g *averaged* by the Click beetle (*Athous haemorrhoidalis*) (a common British species) when 'jack-knifing' into the air to escape predators. One example measuring 12 mm *0.47 in* in length and weighing 40 mg *0.00014 oz* which jumped to a height of 30 cm *11¾ in* was calculated to have 'endured' a peak brain deceleration of 2300 g at the end of the movement.

Lowest internal temperatures

The lowest mammalian blood temperature is that of the Spiny anteater (Echidna) (*Tachyglossus aculeatus*), a monotreme found in Australia and New Guinea, with a normal range of 72°–87° F *22,2°–24,4° C*. The ice worm of Alaska has an internal temperature of − 10° C *14° F*.

Largest tiger ● This outsized Indian tiger (*Panthera tigris tigris*) was shot in northern Uttar Pradesh by David H. Hasinger of Philadelphia, USA in November 1967. It measures 10 ft 7 in *3,22 m*, weighed 857 lb *388,7 kg* and is on view in the US Museum of Natural History, Washington DC, USA. (Photo: Smithsonian Institution)

Largest concentration

The largest single concentration of animals ever recorded was an enormous swarm of krill (*Euphausia superba*) estimated to weigh 10 million tons/*tonnes* tracked by US scientists off Antarctica in March 1981. The swarm was so dense it equalled about one-seventh of the world's yearly catch of fish and shellfish.

Highest body temperature ● Hot dog . . . the Mexican hairless dog, or Xoloitzcuintli has the highest average blood temperature of all mammals: 104°F *40,0°C*. (Photo: Diane Pearce)

Most prodigious eater

The most phenomenal eating machine in nature is the larva of the Polyphemus moth (*Antheraea polyphemus*) of North America which, in the first 48 hours of its life, consumes an amount equal to 86,000 times its own birth weight. In human terms, this would be equivalent to a 7 lb *3,17 kg* baby taking in 269 tons *273 tonnes* of nourishment!

Slowest walker

A crab of the species *Neptunus pelagines* tagged in the Red Sea took 29 years to travel the 101.5 miles *163 km* to the Mediterranean via the Suez Canal at an average speed of 3.5 miles *5,6 km* a year.

Most valuable

The most valuable animals in cash terms are thoroughbred racehorses. It was announced in August 1983 that *Shareef Dancer* (see Chapter 12 Horseracing) had been syndicated by his owner Sheikh Maktoum al Maktoum for $40 million (*£26 million*). The most valuable zoo exhibit is the endangered Giant panda (*Ailuropoda melanoleuca*), and 'Chi-Lin' (b. Sept 1982) of Madrid Zoo, has been valued at more than £1,000,000. There are only 14 giant pandas living in captivity outside China, and the wild population may now be as low as 600–700 despite full protection. The most valuable marine exhibits are 'Orky' and 'Corky', the world's only captive breeding pair of killer whales (*Orcinus orca*) at Marineland, Palos Verdes, Los Angeles. In 1985 they were valued at $2,000,000 (*then £1,650,000*).

GUINNESS BOOKS HAVE ALSO PUBLISHED *REMARKABLE ANIMALS* AT £12.95 NET

Mammals *Mammalia*

Largest and heaviest

The longest and heaviest mammal in the world, and the largest animal ever recorded, is the Blue or Sulphur-bottom whale (*Balaenoptera musculus*), also called Sibbald's rorqual. The longest specimen ever recorded was a female landed at the Compania Argentina de Pesca, Grytviken, South Georgia, in 1909 which measured 107 Norwegian fot 33,58 m *110 ft 2¼ in* in length. Another female measuring 27,6 m *90 ft 6 in* caught in the Southern Ocean by the Soviet Slava whaling fleet on 20 Mar 1947 weighed 190 tonnes *187 tons*. Its tongue and heart weighed 4,29 tonnes *4.22 tons* and 698,5 kg *1540 lb* respectively.

The largest blue whale ever recorded in the waters of Great Britain was probably an 88 ft *26,8 m* specimen killed near the Bunaveneader station in Harris in the Western Isles, Scotland in 1904. In Dec 1851 the carcase of a blue whale measuring 94 ft 9 in *28,87 m* in length (girth 42 ft *13,7 m*) was brought into Bantry harbour, Co. Cork, after it had been found floating dead in the sea. A specimen stranded on the west coast of Lewis, Western Isles in *c.* 1870 was credited with a length of 105 ft *32 m* but the carcase was cut up by the local people before the length could be verified. The length was probably exaggerated or taken along the curve of the body instead of in a straight line from the tip of the snout to the notch in the flukes.

Blue whales inhabit the colder seas and migrate to warmer waters in the winter for breeding. Observations made in the Antarctic in 1947–8 showed that a blue whale can maintain a speed of 20 knots (23 mph *37 km/h*) for 10 min when frightened. It has been calculated that a 90 ft *27 m* blue whale travelling at 20 knots *37 km/h* would develop 520 hp *527 cv*. Newborn calves measure 6,5–8,6 m *21 ft 3¼ in–28 ft 6 in* in length and weigh up to 3000 kg *2.95 tons*.

It has been estimated that there are only about 12,000 blue whales roaming the world's oceans today as a result of over-fishing. This compares with a peak estimate of *c.* 220,000 at the turn of the century. The species has been protected *de jure* since 1967, although non-member countries of the International Whaling Commission, *e.g.* Panama and Taiwan, are not bound by this agreement. A world-wide ban on commercial whaling came into force at the start of the 1985/86 season, but South Korea, the Philippines, Iceland and Norway are still killing whales . . . although the latter country has agreed to stop after 1987.

Deepest dive

The greatest *recorded* depth to which a whale has dived is 620 fathoms (3720 ft *1134 m*) by a 47 ft *14,32 m* bull sperm whale (*Physeter macrocephalus*) found with its jaw entangled with a submarine cable running between Santa Elena, Ecuador and Chorillos, Peru, on 14 Oct 1955. At this depth the whale withstood a pressure of 1680 lb/in² *11583 kPa* of body surface. On 25 Aug 1969 another bull sperm whale was killed 100 miles *160 km* south of Durban after it had surfaced from a dive lasting 1 hr 52 min, and inside its stomach were found two small sharks which had been swallowed about an hour earlier. These were later identified as *Scymnodon* sp., a species found only on the sea floor. At this point from land the depth of water is in excess of 1646 fathoms (10,476 ft *3193 m*) for a radius of 30–40 miles *48–64 km*, which suggests that the Sperm whale sometimes descends to a depth of over 10,000 ft *3000 m* when seeking food and is limited by pressure of time rather than by pressure of pressure.

Largest Land

The largest living land animal is the African bush elephant (*Loxodonta africana*). The average adult bull stands 10 ft 6 in *3,2 m* at the shoulder and weighs 5.6 tons *5,7 tonnes*. The largest specimen ever recorded was a bull shot 25 miles *40 km* north-northeast of Mucusso, southern Angola on 7 Nov 1974. Lying on its side this elephant measured 13 ft 8 in *4,16 m* in a projected line from the highest point of the shoulder to the base of the forefoot, indicating that its standing height must have been about 13 ft *3,96 m*. Other measurements included an overall length of 35 ft *10,67 m* (tip of extended trunk to tip of extended tail) and a forefoot circumference of 5 ft 11 in *1,80 m*. The weight was computed to be 26,998 lb (12.05 tons, *12,24 tonnes*).

The largest wild mammal in the British Isles is the Red deer (*Cervus elaphus*). A full-grown stag stands 3 ft 8 in *1,11 m* at the shoulder and weighs 230–250 lb *104–113 kg*. The heaviest ever recorded was probably a stag killed at Glenfiddich, Banff in 1831, which weighed 525 lb *238 kg*. The heaviest park red deer on record was a stag weighing 476 lb *215 kg* (height at shoulder 4 ft 6 in *1,37 m*) killed at Woburn, Bedfordshire in 1836. The so-called wild pony (*Equus caballus*) may weigh up to 700 lb *320 kg* but there are no truly feral populations living today.

Largest Marine

The largest toothed mammal ever recorded is the Sperm whale, also called the Cachalot. The largest accurately measured specimen on record was a 67 ft 11 in *20,7 m* bull captured off the Kurile Islands, north-west Pacific, by a USSR whaling fleet in the summer of 1950 but bulls of much larger size were reported in the early days of whaling. The 5 m *16 ft 4¾ in* long lower jaw of a sperm whale exhibited in the British Museum (Nat. History) belongs to a bull measuring nearly 84 ft *25,6 m*, and similar lengths have been reported for other outsized individuals killed.

Thirteen cachalots have been stranded on British coasts since 1913. The largest, a bull measuring 61 ft 5 in *19 m*, was washed ashore at Birchington, Kent on 18 Oct 1914. Another bull estimated at 65 ft *19,8 m* but badly decomposed was stranded at Derryloughan, Co. Galway, Ireland on 2 Jan 1952.

Tallest

The tallest living animal is the Giraffe (*Giraffa camelopardalis*), which is now found only in the dry savannah and semi-desert areas of Africa south of the Sahara. The tallest ever recorded was a Masai bull (*G. camelopardalis tippelskirchi*) named 'George', received at Chester Zoo, England, on 8 Jan 1959 from Kenya. His 'horns' *almost* grazed the roof of the 20 ft *6,09 m* high Giraffe House when he was 9 years old. George died on 22 July 1969. Less credible heights of up to 23 ft *7 m* (between pegs) have been claimed for bulls shot in the field.

Smallest Land

The smallest recorded mammal is the endangered Kitti's hog-nosed bat (*Craseonycteris thonglongyai*), also called the Bumblebee bat, which is confined to about 20 limestone caves on the Kwae Noi River, Kanchanaburi, Thailand. Mature specimens (both sexes) have a wing span of *c.* 160 mm *6.29 in* and weigh 1,75–2 g *0.062–0.071 oz*.

The smallest mammal found in Britain is the European pygmy shrew (*Sorex minutus*). Mature specimens have a head and body length of 43–64 mm *1.69–2.5 in*, a tail length of 31–46 mm *1.22–1.81 in* and weigh between 2,4 g and 6,1 g *0.084 and 0.213 oz*.

Smallest Marine

The smallest totally marine mammal in terms of weight is probably Commerson's dolphin (*Cephalorhynchus commersoni*) also known as Le Jacobite, which is found in the waters off the southern tip of South America. In one series of six adult specimens the weights ranged from 23 kg *50.7 lb* to 35 kg *77.1 lb*. The Sea otter (*Enhydra lutris*) of the north Pacific is of comparable size (55–81.4 lb *25–38,5 kg*), but this species sometimes comes ashore during storms.

Rarest Land

A number of mammals are known only from a single or type specimen. One of these is Garrido's hutia (*Capromys garridoi*), recognised from a single individual collected on the islet of Cayo Maja off southern Cuba in April 1967. The Thylacine or Tasmanian tiger (*Thylacinus cynocephalus*), feared extinct since the last captive specimen died in Beaumaris Zoo, Hobart, on 7 Sept 1936, was rediscovered in July 1982 when a wildlife ranger saw one of these predatory marsupials in the spotlight of his parked car. Since then, however, there have been no more positive sightings.

Rarest Marine

The rarest marine mammal is Longman's beaked whale (*Indopacetus pacificus*), which is known only from two skulls. The type specimen was discovered on a beach near MacKay, Queensland, Australia, in 1922, and the second near Mogadiscio, Somalia, east Africa, in 1955.

Fastest Land

The fastest of all land animals over a short distance (*i.e.* up to 600 yd *549 m*) is the Cheetah or Hunting leopard (*Acinonyx jubatus*) of the open plains of east Africa, Iran, Turkmenia and Afghanistan, with a probable maximum speed of 60–63 mph *96–101 km/h* over suitably level ground. Speeds of 71, 84 and even 90 mph, *114, 135 and 145 km/h* have been claimed for this animal, but these figures must be considered exaggerated. Tests in London in 1937 showed that on an oval greyhound track over 345 yd *316 m* a female cheetah's average speed over three runs was 43.4 mph *69,8 km/h* (*cf.* 43.26 mph *69,6 km/h* for the fastest racehorse), but this specimen was not running flat out and had great difficulty negotiating the bends. The fastest land animal over a sustained distance (*i.e.* 1000 yd *914 m* or more) is the Pronghorn antelope (*Antilocapra americana*) of the western United States. Specimens have been observed to travel at 35 mph for 4 miles *56 km/h for 6 km*, at 42 mph for 1 mile *67 km/h for 1,6 km* and 55 mph for half a mile *88,5 km/h for 0,8 km*.

The fastest British land mammal over a sustained distance is the Roe deer (*Capreolus capreolus*), which can cruise at 25–30 mph *40–48 km/h* for more than 20 miles *32 km*, with occasional bursts of up to 40 mph *64 km/h*. On 19 Oct 1970 a frightened runaway red deer registered a speed of 42 mph *67,5 km/h* on a police radar trap as it charged through a street in Stalybridge, Manchester.

Fastest Marine

The fastest marine mammal is the Killer whale (*Orcinus orca*). On 12 Oct 1958 a bull measuring an estimated 20–25 ft *6,10–7,62 m* in length was timed at 30 knots (34.5 mph *55,5 km/h*) in the east Pacific. Speeds of up to 30 knots in short bursts have also been reported for Dall's porpoise (*Phocoenoides dalli*).

Slowest

The slowest moving land mammal is the Ai or Three-toed sloth (*Bradypus tridactylus*) of tropical America. The average ground speed is 6–8 ft *1,83–2,44 m* a minute (0.068–0.098 mph *0,109–0,158 km/h*), but in the trees it can 'accelerate' to

15 ft *4,57 m* a minute (0.17 mph *0,272 km/h*) (*cf.* these figures with the 0.03 mph *0,05 km/h* of the common garden snail and the 0.17 mph *0,27 km/h* of the giant tortoise).

Sleepiest

Some armadillos (*Dasypodidae*), opossums (*Didelphidae*) and sloths (*Bradypodidae*) spend up to 80 per cent of their lives sleeping or dozing.

Longest hibernation

The Barrow ground squirrel (*Spermophilus parryi barrowensis*) of Point Barrow, Alaska, USA, hibernates for nine months of the year. During the remaining three months it feeds, breeds and collects food for storage in its burrow.

Oldest

No other mammal can match the extreme proven 120 years attained by Man (*Homo sapiens*) (see pp. 11 and 12). It is probable that the closest approach is made by the Asiatic elephant (*Elephas maximus*). The greatest age that has been verified with absolute certainty is 78 years in the case of a cow named 'Modoc', who died at Santa Clara, California, USA, on 17 July 1975. She was imported into the USA from Germany in 1898 at the age of two years. Nepal's royal elephant 'Prem Prasad' was reportedly 81 when he died at Kasra, Chitwan, on 27 Feb 1985, but his actual age was believed to have been 65–70 years.

Highest living

The highest living wild mammal in the world is probably the Yak (*Bos grunniens*), of Tibet and the Szechwanese Alps, China, which occasionally climbs to an altitude of 20,000 ft *6100 m* when foraging.

Largest herds

The largest herds on record were those of the Springbok (*Antidorcas marsupialis*) during migration across the plains of the western parts of southern Africa in the 19th century. In 1849 John (later Sir John) Fraser observed a *trekbokken* that took three days to pass through the settlement of Beaufort West, Cape Province. Another herd seen moving near Nels Poortje, Cape Province in 1888 was estimated to contain 100,000,000 head, although 10,000,000 is probably a more realistic figure. A herd estimated to be 15 miles *24 km* wide and more than 100 miles *160 km* long was reported from Karree Kloof, Orange River, South Africa in July 1896. The largest concentration of wild mammals found living anywhere in the world today is that of the Mexican free-tailed bat (*Tadarida brasiliensis*) in Bracken Cave, San Antonio, Texas, where up to twenty million animals assemble after migration.

Britain's largest bat colony is in Greywell Canal Tunnel, Hampshire. It contains about 2000 individuals made up of six different species.

Longest and shortest gestation periods

The longest of all mammalian gestation periods is that of the Asiatic elephant (*Elephas maximus*), with an average of 609 days or just over 20 months and a maximum of 760 days—more than two and half times that of a human. By 1981 only *c.* 35,000 survived. The gestation periods of the American opossum (*Didelphis marsupialis*), also called the Virginian opossum, the rare Water opossum or Yapok (*Chironectes minimus*) of central and northern South America and the Eastern native cat (*Dasyurus viverrinus*) of Australia are all normally 12–13 days but they can be as short as 8 days.

Largest litter

The greatest number of young born to a *wild* mammal at a single birth is 31 (30 of which survived) in the case of the Tail-less tenrec (*Tenrec ecaudatus*) found in Madagascar and the

Mammals

ARTWORK: MATTHEW HILLIER FCSD

Comoro Islands. The normal litter size is 12–15, although females can suckle up to 24.

Youngest breeder

The Streaked tenrec (*Hemicentetes semispinosus*) of Madagascar is weaned after only 5 days, and females can breed 3–4 weeks after birth.

Largest living carnivore ● The Kodiak bear (*Ursus arctos middendorffi*), whose average adult male has a nose-to-tail length of 8 ft *2,44 m*, measured along the back (not the belly). He stands an average 52 in *1,32 m* at the shoulder and weighs between 1050 lb *476 kg* and 1175 lb *533 kg*. The greatest weight ever recorded is 1656 lb *751 kg* for a male shot in 1894.

This weight was exceeded by a 'cage-fat male' in the Cheyenne Mountain Zoological Park, Colorado Springs, which scaled 1670 lb *757 kg* at the time of its death on 22 Sept 1955.

It should be noted that a bear's weight will vary considerably during the course of a year. The Kodiak is found on Kodiak Island and adjacent Afognak Shuyak in the Gulf of Alaska, USA. See map below.

CARNIVORES

Largest

Unconfirmed weights in excess of 2000 lb *907 kg* have been reported for the Polar bear (*Ursus maritimus*), but the average adult male weighs 850–900 lb *386–408 kg* and measures 7¾ ft *2,4 m* nose to tail. In 1960 a polar bear allegedly weighing 2210 lb *1002 kg* before skinning was shot at the polar entrance to Kotzebue Sound, north-west Alaska, by Arthur Dubs of Medford, Oregon, USA. In April 1962 the 11 ft 1½ in *3,38 m* tall mounted specimen was put on display at the Seattle World Fair, but further details are lacking.

The largest land carnivore found in Britain is the Badger (*Meles meles*). The average adult boar (sows are slightly smaller) measures 3 ft *90 cm* in length—including a 4 in *10 cm* tail—and weighs 27 lb *12,3 kg* in the early spring and 32 lb *14,5 kg* at the end of the summer when it is in 'grease'. In December 1952 a boar weighing exactly 60 lb *27,2 kg* was killed near Rotherham, South Yorkshire.

Smallest

The smallest living member of the order Carnivora is the Least weasel (*Mustela rixosa*), also called the Dwarf weasel, which is circumpolar in distribution. Four races are recognised, the smallest of which is *M. r. pygmaea* of Siberia. Mature specimens have an overall length of 177–207 mm *6.96–8.14 in* and weigh between 35 and 70 g *1⅜–2½ oz*.

Largest feline

The largest member of the cat family (Felidae) is the protected long-furred Siberian tiger (*Panthera tigris altaica*), also called the Amur or Manchurian tiger. Adult males average 10 ft 4 in *3,15 m* in length (nose to tip of extended tail), stand 39–42 in *99–107 cm* at the shoulder and weigh about 585 lb *265 kg*. In 1950 a male weighing 384 kg *846.5 lb* was shot in the Sikhote Alin Mts, Maritime Territory, USSR. In Oct 1986 a weight of 932 lb *423 kg* was reported for a seven-year-old male Siberian tiger named 'Jaipur' owned by animal trainer Joan Byron-Marasek of Clarksburg, New Jersey, USA.

The largest 'big cat' presently in captivity is an adult male Litigon (an Indian lion/Tigon cross) named 'Cubanacan' at Alipore Zoological Gardens, Calcutta, who is believed to weigh at least 800 lb *363 kg*. This animal stands 52 in *1,32 m* at the shoulder (*cf.* 44 in *1,11 m* for the lion 'Simba') and measures a record 11 ft 6 in *2,5 m* in total length.

The average adult African lion (*Panthera leo*) measures 9 ft *2,7 m* overall, stands 36–38 in *91–97 cm* at the shoulder and weighs 400–410 lb *181–185 kg*. The heaviest wild specimen on record was one weighing 690 lb *313 kg* shot by Lennox Anderson just outside Hectorspruit in the eastern Transvaal in 1936. In July 1970 a weight of 826 lb *375 kg* was reported for a black-maned lion named 'Simba' (b. Dublin Zoo, 1959) at Colchester Zoo, Essex. He died on 16 Jan 1973 at the now defunct Knaresborough Zoo, North Yorkshire, where his stuffed body had been on display.

Smallest feline

The smallest member of the cat family is the Rusty-spotted cat (*Felis rubiginosa*) of southern India and Sri Lanka. The average adult male has an overall length of 25–28 in *64–71 cm* (tail 9–10 in *23–25 cm*) and weighs about 3 lb *1,35 kg*.

PINNIPEDS Seals, Sea-lions, Walruses

Largest

The largest of the 34 known species of pinniped is the Southern elephant seal (*Mirounga leonina*), which inhabits the sub-Antarctic islands. Adult bulls average 16½ ft *5 m* in length (tip of inflated snout to the extremities of the outstretched tail flippers), 12 ft *3,7 m* in maximum bodily girth and weigh about 5000 lb (2.18 tons *2268 kg*). The largest accurately measured specimen on record was a bull killed in Possession Bay, South Georgia on 28 Feb 1913 which measured 21 ft 4 in *6,5 m* after flensing (original length about 22½ ft *6,85 m*) and probably weighed at least 4 tons/*tonnes*. There are old records of bulls measuring 25–30 ft *7,62–9,14 m* and even 35 ft *10,66 m* but these figures must be considered exaggerated. Adult cows are much smaller, averaging 3 m *10 ft* in length and weighing about 680 kg *1500 lb*.

The largest pinniped among British fauna is the Grey seal (*Halichoerus grypus*), also called the Atlantic seal. In one sample taken during the breeding season at the Farne Islands, Northumberland the heaviest (a male) weighed 310 kg *683½ lb* (length from nose to tip of flippers 2,45 m *8 ft 0½ in*).

Smallest

The smallest pinnipeds are the Ringed seal (*Phoca hispida*) of the Arctic and the closely-related Baikal seal (*P. sibirica*) of Lake Baikal and the Caspian seal (*P. caspica*) of the Caspian Sea, USSR. Adult specimens (males) measure up to 5 ft 6 in *1,67 m* in length and reach a maximum weight of 280 lb *127 kg*. Females are about two-thirds this size.

Britain's smallest pinniped is the Common seal (*Phoca vitulina*). Adult males measure 1,5–1,85 m *4 ft 11 in–6 ft 0¾ in* in length and weigh up to 105 kg *231 lb*. Females are four-fifths this size.

Most abundant

The most abundant species of pinniped is the Crabeater seal (*Lobodon carcinophagus*) of Antarctica. In 1978 the total population was believed to be nearly 15,000,000.

Rarest

The last reliable sighting of the Caribbean or West Indian monk seal (*Monachus tropicalis*) was on Serranilla Bank off the coast of Mexico's Yucatan peninsula in 1952. In 1974 two seals were seen near Cay Verde and Cay Burro, SE Bahamas, but a search in 1979 found nothing. It has been suggested that these sightings (and others) may have been Californian sea-lions (*Zalophus californianus*) which had escaped from captivity and have been recorded in the Gulf of Mexico on several occasions.

Fastest

The highest swimming speed recorded for a pinniped is a 40 km/h *25 mph* short spurt by a Californian sea-lion. The fastest-moving pinniped on land is the crabeater seal which has been timed at speeds up to 19 km/h *11.8 mph*.

Deepest

The deepest dive recorded for a pinniped is 630 m *2067 ft* by a female northern elephant seal (*Mirounga anguistirostris*) off Ano Nuevo Point, California on 1 Mar 1983. At this depth the seal withstood a pressure of 6335 kPa *919 lb/in²* of body area. The much larger bulls of this species can probably dive even deeper.

Oldest

A female grey seal shot at Shunni Wick in the Shetland Islands on 23 Apr 1969 was believed to be 'at least 46 years old' based on a count of dentine rings. The captive record is an estimated 41 years for a bull grey seal 'Jacob' held in Skansen Zoo (1901–42).

BATS

Largest

The only flying mammals are bats (order Chiroptera), of which there are about 950 living species. That with the greatest wing span is the Bismarck flying fox (*Pteropus neohibernicus*) of the Bismarck Archipelago and New Guinea. One specimen preserved in the American Museum of Natural History has a wing spread of 165 cm *5 ft 5 in*, but some unmeasured bats probably reach 183 cm *6 ft*.

The largest bat found in Britain is the very rare large Mouse-eared bat (*Myotis myotis*). Mature specimens have a wing span of 355–450 mm *13.97–17.71 in* and weigh up to 45 g *1.58 oz* in the case of females.

Smallest

The smallest bat in the world is Kitti's hog-nosed bat. See page 25.

The smallest native British bat is the Pipistrelle (*Pipistrellus pipistrellus*). Mature specimens have a wing span of 190–250 mm *7.48–9.84 in* and weigh between 3 and 8 g *0.1–0.28 oz*.

Rarest

At least three species of bat are known only from the type specimen. They are: the Small-toothed fruit bat (*Neopteryx frosti*) from Tamalanti, West Celebes (1938/39); *Paracoelops megalotis* from Vinh, Vietnam (1945); and *Latidens salimalii* from the High Wavy Mountains, southern India (1948).

The rarest bat on the British list (15 species) is now the large Mouse-eared bat of southern England. Up until very recently the population was down to a single male which had lived in Sussex for 13 years, but in 1986 a small colony was discovered near Medbury, Dorset.

Fastest

Because of the great practical difficulties few data on bat speeds have been published. The greatest velocity attributed to a bat is 32 mph *51 km/h* in the case of a Mexican free-tailed bat but this may have been wind-assisted. In one American experiment using an artificial mine tunnel and 17 different kinds of bat, only four of them managed to exceed 13 mph *20,8 km/h* in level flight.

Oldest

The greatest age reliably reported for a bat is 31 years 5 months for an Indian flying fox (*Pteropus giganteus*) which died at London Zoo on 11 Jan 1979. The greatest reliable age reported for a banded bat is at least 24 years for a female Little brown bat (*Myotis lucifugus*) found on 30 April 1960 in a cave on Mt Aeolus, Vermont, USA. It had been banded at a summer colony in Mashpee, Massachusetts, on 22 June 1937, at which time it was already fully grown.

Highest detectable pitch

Because of their ultrasonic echolocation bats have the most acute hearing of any terrestrial animal. Vampire bats (*Desmodontidae*) and fruit bats (*Pteropodidae*) can hear frequencies as high as 120–210 kHz (*cf.* 20 kHz for the adult human limit but 280 kHz for the Common dolphin (*Delphinus delphis*)).

Deepest roost

A little brown bat has been recorded at a depth of 1160 m *3805 ft* in a zinc mine in New York State, USA. The mine serves as winter quarters for 1000 members of this species, which normally roost at a depth of 200 m *656 ft*.

PRIMATES

Largest

The largest living primate is the Eastern lowland gorilla (*Gorilla g. graueri*) of the lowland forests of eastern Zaire and south-western Uganda. The average adult male stands 5 ft 9 in *175 cm* tall and weighs 360 lb *165 kg*. The Mountain gorilla (*Gorilla g. beringei*) of the volcanic mountain ranges of western Rwanda, south-western Uganda and eastern Zaire is also of comparable size *i.e.* 5 ft 8 in *172,5 cm* and 343 lb *155 kg*, and most of the exceptionally large gorillas taken in the field have been of this race. The greatest height (top of crest to heel) recorded for a gorilla is 195 cm *6 ft 4¾ in* for a male (*Gorilla g. beringei*) collected by a German expedition at Alimbongo, north Kivu on 16 May 1938. The heaviest gorilla ever kept in captivity was a male of the mountain race named 'N'gagi', who died in San Diego Zoo, California on 12 Jan 1944 aged 18 years. He scaled 683 lb *310 kg* at his heaviest in 1943, and weighed 636 lb *288 kg* at the time of his death. He was 5 ft 7¾ in *1,72 m* tall and boasted a record chest measurement of 78 in *198 cm*.

Britain's largest captive gorilla is probably 'Djoum' (b. 1969) of Howletts Zoo, Kent, who scaled 470 lb *213 kg* in 1986. Another male example of this mountain sub-species named 'Bukhama' (b. 1960) at Dudley Zoo, West Midlands, was reportedly 500 lb *227 kg* in 1969, but this animal has not been weighed since.

Smallest

The smallest known primate is the rare Pen-tailed shrew (*Ptilocercus lowii*) of Malaysia, Sumatra and Borneo. Adult specimens have a total length of 230–330 mm *9–13 in* (head and body 100–140 mm *3.93–5.51in*, tail 130–190 mm *5.1–7.5 in*) and weigh 35–50 g *1.23–1.76 oz*. The Pygmy marmoset (*Cebuella pygmaea*) of the Upper Amazon Basin and the Lesser mouse-lemur (*Microcebus murinus*) of Madagascar are also of comparable length but heavier, adults weighing 50–75 g *1.76–2.64 oz* and 45–80 g *1.58–2.82 oz* respectively.

Rarest

The rarest living primate is the Broad-nosed gentle lemur (*Hapalemur simus*) of Madagascar, which reportedly became extinct in the early 1970s. In 1986 a group consisting of 35 animals was discovered in a remote rain forest in the south-eastern part of the island by an expedition from Duke University, Durham, North Carolina, USA.

Oldest

The greatest irrefutable age reported for a non-human primate is *c.* 59 years in the case of a male orang-utan (*Pongo pygmaeus*) named 'Guas', who died in Philadelphia Zoological Garden, Pennsylvania on 9 Feb 1977. When he was received on 1 May 1931 he was at least 13 years of age. The oldest chimpanzee (*Pan troglodytes*) on record was a male named 'Jimmy' at Seneca Zoo, Rochester, NY, who died on 17 Sept 1985 aged 55 years 6 months. The famous western lowland gorilla 'Massa' (b. July 1931) died on 30 Dec 1984 aged 53 years 5 months.

Strongest

In 1924 'Boma', a 165 lb *74,80 kg* male chimpanzee at Bronx Zoo, New York, NY, USA recorded a right-handed pull (feet braced) of 847 lb *384 kg* on a dynamometer (*cf.* 210 lb *95 kg* for a man of the same weight). On another occasion an adult female chimpanzee named 'Suzette' (estimated weight 135 lb *61 kg*) at the same zoo registered a right-handed pull of 1260 lb *572 kg* while in a rage. A record from the USA of a 100 lb *45 kg* chimpanzee achieving a two-handed dead lift of 600 lb *272 kg* with ease suggests that a male gorilla could with training raise 2000 lb *907 kg*.

MONKEYS

Largest

The only species of monkey reliably credited with weights of more than 100 lb *45 kg* is the Mandrill (*Mandrillus sphinx*) of equatorial West Africa. The greatest reliable weight recorded is 119 lb *54 kg* for a captive male but an unconfirmed weight of 130 lb *59 kg* has been reported. (Adult females are about half the size of males.)

Smallest

The smallest known monkey is the Pygmy

> **Oldest female gorilla ●** 'Carolyn' (b. 1939), of New York Zoological Park (Bronx Zoo), died on 27 Sept 1986 aged 47 years.

marmoset of the Upper Amazon Basin (see Primate Smallest).

Rarest

The rarest living monkey is the Golden-rumped tamarin (*Leontopithecus chrysopygus*), which is now restricted to two areas of forest in the State of Sao Paulo, south-east Brazil. In 1986 only 75–100 survived, and the species is now on the verge of extinction.

Oldest

The world's oldest living monkey is a male white-throated capuchin (*Cebus capucinus*) called 'Bobo' owned by Dr Raymond T. Bartus of the American Cyanamid Company in Pearl River, NY, who celebrated his 52nd birthday on 30 Oct 1986.

RODENTS

Largest

The world's largest rodent is the Capybara (*Hydrochoerus hydrochaeris*), also called the Carpincho or Water hog, which is found in tropical South America. Mature specimens have a head and body length of 3¼–4½ ft *0,99–1,4 m* and weigh up to 250 lb *113 kg* (cage-fat specimen). Britain's largest rodent is now the Coypu (*Myocastor coypus*), also known as the Nutria, which was introduced from Argentina by East Anglian fur-breeders in 1929. Three years later, the first escapes were recorded and by 1960 at least 200,000 coypus were living in East Anglia. About 80 per cent were killed by the winter of 1963 and a government campaign of extermination has since reduced the population to *c.* 1000 animals. A target date of 1990 has been set for the complete eradication of the species in Britain. Adult males measure 30–36 in *76–91 cm* in length (including short tail) and weigh up to 28 lb *13 kg* in the wild state (40 lb *18 kg* in captivity).

Smallest

The smallest known rodent is the Northern pygmy mouse (*Baiomys taylori*) of central Mexico and southern Arizona and Texas, which measures up to 109 mm *4.3 in* in total length and weighs 7–8 g *0.24–0.28 oz*.

Britain's smallest rodent is the Old World harvest mouse (*Micromys minutus*), which measures up to 135 mm *5.3 in* in total length and weighs 7–10 g *0.24–0.35 oz*.

Rarest

The rarest rodents in the world are Garrido's hutia and the Little earth hutia (*Capromys sanfelipensis*) of Juan Garcia Cay, an islet off southern Cuba. The latter species has not been recorded since its discovery in 1970.

Oldest

The greatest reliable age reported for a rodent is 27 years 3 months for a Sumatran crested porcupine (*Hystrix brachyura*) which died in National Zoological Park, Washington, DC on 12 Jan 1965.

Fastest breeder

The female Meadow vole (*Microtus agrestis*), found in Britain, can reproduce from the age of 25 days and have up to 17 litters of 6–8 young in a year.

INSECTIVORES

Largest

The largest insectivore is the Moon rat (*Echinosorex gymnurus*), also known as Raffles' gymnure, which is found in Burma, Thailand, Malaysia, Sumatra and Borneo. Mature specimens have a head and body length of 265–445 mm *10.43–17.52 in*, a tail measuring 200–210 mm *7.87–8.26 in* and weigh up to 1400 g *3.08 lb*. The European hedgehog (*Erinaceus europaeus*) is much shorter in overall length

(196–298 mm *7.71–11.73 in*), but well-fed examples have been known to scale as much as 1900 g *4.19 lb*. Although the much larger anteaters (families Tachyglossidae and Myrmecophagidae) feed on termites and other soft-bodied insects, they are not insectivores but belong to the orders Monotremata and Edentata ('without teeth').

Smallest

The smallest insectivore is Savi's white-toothed pygmy shrew (*Suncus etruscus*), also called the Etruscan shrew, which is found along the coast of the northern Mediterranean and southwards to Cape Province, South Africa. Mature specimens have a head and body length of 36–52 mm *1.32–2.04 in*, a tail length of 24–29 mm *0.94–1.14 in* and weigh between 1,5 and 2,5 g *0.052* and *0.09 oz*.

Oldest

The greatest reliable age recorded for an insectivore is 16 + years for a lesser hedgehog-tenrec (*Echinops telfairi*), which was born in Amsterdam Zoo in 1966 and was later sent to Jersey Zoo. It died on 27 Nov 1982.

ANTELOPES

Largest

The largest of all antelopes is the rare Giant eland (*Tragelaphus derbianus*), of western and central Africa, which may surpass 2000 lb *907 kg*. The Common eland (*T. oryx*) of eastern and southern Africa has the same shoulder height of up to 5 ft 10 in *1,78 m* but is not quite so massive, although there is one record of a 5 ft 5 in *1,65 m* bull shot in Nyasaland (now Malawi) in *c.* 1937 which weighed 2078 lb *943 kg*.

Smallest

The smallest known antelope is the Royal antelope (*Neotragus pygmaeus*) of western Africa. Mature specimens measure 10–12 in *25–31 cm* at the shoulder and weigh only 7–8 lb *3–3,6 kg* which is the size of a large brown hare (*Lepus europaeus*). Salt's dik-dik (*Madoqua saltina*) of north-eastern Ethiopia and Somalia weighs only 5–6 lb *2,2–2,7 kg* when adult, but this species stands about 14 in *35,5 cm* at the withers.

Rarest

The world's rarest antelope is the Arabian oryx (*Oryx leucoryx*) which, until very recently, had not been reported in the wild since 1972 when three were killed and four others captured on the Jiddat-al-Harasis plateau, South Oman. Between March 1980 and August 1983 a total of 17 antelopes from the World Herd at San Diego Zoo, California, were released into the open desert in South Oman under the protection of a nomadic tribe. Since then there have been at least 15 live births, and two antelopes born in Oman have bred. Another release has also been carried out in Jordan. In Jan 1985 the first Arabian oryx was born at London Zoo.

Oldest

The greatest reliable age recorded for an antelope is 25 years 4 months for an addax (*Addax nasomaculatus*) which died in Brookfield Zoo, Chicago, Illinois on 15 Oct 1960.

DEER

Largest

The largest deer is the Alaskan moose (*Alces alces gigas*). Adult bulls average 6 ft *1,83 m* at the shoulder and weigh *c.* 1100 lb *500 kg*. A bull standing 7 ft 8 in *2,34 m* between pegs and weighing an estimated 1800 lb *816 kg* was shot on the Yukon River in the Yukon Territory, Canada in September 1897. Unconfirmed measurements up to 8 ft 6 in *2,59 m* at the shoulder and estimated weights up to 2600 lb *1180 kg* have been claimed. The record antler spread or 'rack' is 78¼ in *199 cm* (skull and antlers 91 lb *41 kg*). They were taken from a moose killed near the headwaters of the Stewart River in the Yukon in Oct 1897 and are now on display in the Field Museum, Chicago, Illinois, USA.

Smallest

The smallest true deer (family Cervidae) is the Northern pudu (*Pudu mephistopheles*) of Ecuador and Colombia. Mature specimens measure 13–14 in *33–35 cm* at the shoulder and weigh 16–18 lb *7,2–8,1 kg*. The smallest ruminant is the Lesser Malay chevrotain (*Tragulus javanicus*) of south-east Asia, Sumatra and Borneo. Adult specimens measure 8–10 in *20–25 cm* at the shoulder and weigh 6–7 lb, *2,7–3,2 kg*.

Rarest

The rarest deer in the world is Fea's muntjac (*Muntiacus feae*) which, until recently, was known only from two specimens collected on the borders of Southern Burma and Western Thailand. In December 1977 a female was received at Dusit Zoo, Bangkok, followed by 2 females in 1981 and 3 males and 3 females from Xizang, Tibet, south-west China in Feb 1982–Apr 1983.

Oldest

The greatest reliable age recorded for a deer is 26 years 8 months for a red deer (*Cervus elaphus scoticus*) which died in Milwaukee Zoo, Wisconsin on 28 June 1954.

MARSUPIALS

Largest

The largest living marsupial is the Red kangaroo (*Macropus rufus*) of central, southern and eastern Australia. Adult males stand up to 7 ft *213 cm* tall, measure up to 8 ft ½ in *245 cm* in total length and weigh up to 187 lb *85 kg*.

Smallest

The smallest known marsupial is the rare Long-tailed planigale (*Planigale ingrami*), a flat-skulled mouse, of north-eastern and north-western Australia. Adult males have a head and body length of 55–63 mm *2.16–2.48 in*, a tail length of 57–60 mm *2.24–2.36 in* and weigh 3,9–4,5 g *0.13–0.19 oz*.

Oldest

The greatest reliable age recorded for a marsupial is 26 years 22 days for a Common wombat (*Vombatus ursinus*) which died in London Zoo on 20 Apr 1906.

Fastest speed, highest and longest jumps

The highest speed recorded for a marsupial is 40 mph *64 km/h* for a young female eastern grey kangaroo (*Macropus giganteus*). The greatest height cleared by a hunted kangaroo is 10 ft 6 in *3,20 m* over a pile of timber and during the course of a chase in January 1951 a female red kangaroo made a series of bounds which included one of 42 ft *12,80 m*. There is also an unconfirmed report of an eastern grey kangaroo jumping nearly 13,5 m *44 ft 8¼ in* on the flat.

TUSKS

Longest

The longest recorded elephant tusks (excluding prehistoric examples) are a pair from Zaïre preserved in the National Collection of Heads and Horns kept by the New York Zoological Society in Bronx Park, New York City. The right tusk measures 11 ft 5½ in *3,49 m* along the outside curve and the left 11 ft 5½ in *3,35 m*. Their combined weight is 293 lb *133 kg*. A single tusk of 11 ft 6 in *3,5 m* has been reported. Ivory rose from $2.30 to $34/lb in 1970–80.

Heaviest

The heaviest recorded tusks are a pair in the British Museum (Natural History) which were collected from an aged bull shot by an Arab with a muzzle-loading gun at the foot of Mt Kilimanjaro, Kenya in 1897. They originally weighed 240 lb *109 kg* (length 10 ft 2½ in *3,11 m*) and 225 lb *102 kg* (length 10 ft 5½ in *3,18 m*) respectively, giving a total weight of 465 lb *211 kg*, but their combined weight today is 440½ lb *200 kg*.

The greatest weight ever recorded for a single elephant tusk is 117 kg *258 lb* for a specimen collected in Benin, west Africa and exhibited at the Paris Exposition in 1900.

HORNS

Longest

The longest horns grown by any living animal are those of the Water buffalo (*Bubalus arnee* = *B. bubalis*) of India. One huge bull shot in 1955 had horns measuring 13 ft 11 in *4,24 m* from tip to tip along the outside curve across the forehead. The longest single horn on record was one measuring 81¼ in *206 cm* on the outside curve found on a specimen of domestic Ankole cattle (*Bos taurus*) near Lake Ngami, Botswana.

HORSES AND PONIES

The world's equine population is estimated to be 75,000,000.

Largest *World*

The largest horse ever recorded was a 19.2 hand (6 ft 6 in *1,98 m*) pure-bred red-roan Belgian (Brabant) stallion named 'Brooklyn Supreme' (1928–48) owned by C. G. Good of Ogden, Iowa which weighed 3200 lb 1.42 tons *1,44 tonnes* at its heaviest in 1938 and had a chest girth of 102 in *259 cm*.

In April 1973 a weight of 3218 lb *1459 kg* was reported for a 18.2-hand (6 ft 2 in *1,88 m*) Belgian (Brabant) mare named 'Wilma du Bos' (foaled 15 July 1966) shortly before she was shipped from Antwerp to her new owner, Mrs Virgie Arden of Reno, Nevada, but at the time she was heavily in foal (maximum girth 12 ft *3,65 m*). When the horse arrived in New York she scaled 3086 lb *1399 kg*, but after foaling her weight returned to her normal 2400–2500 lb *1088–1134 kg*.

The British weight record is held by the 17.2-hand (5 ft 10 in *1,78 m*) shire stallion 'Honest Tom 5123' (foaled in 1884), owned by James Forshaw of Littleport, Cambridgeshire, which scaled 2912 lb *1325 kg* in 1891.

The heaviest horse living in Britain today is the 17.2-hand (5 ft 10 in *1,78 m*) champion percheron stallion 'Pinchbeck Union Crest' (foaled 27 Jan 1964), whose weight fluctuates between 2520 lb *1143 kg* and 2632 lb *1194 kg*.

Tallest

The tallest documented horse on record was the shire gelding 'Sampson' (later renamed 'Mammoth') bred by Thomas Cleaver of Toddington Mills, Bedfordshire. This horse (foaled in 1846) measured 21.2½ hands (7 ft 2½ in *2,19 m*) in 1850 and was later said to have weighed 30 cwt 3360 lb *1524 kg*.

Britain's tallest living horses, 19.1½ hand (6 ft 5½ in *1,97 m*), are the Shires 'Goliath', foaled 1977, owned by Young & Company's Brewery, London, and 'Extra Stout', foaled 1980, owned by Samuel Smith's Brewery, Tadcaster.

Smallest

The smallest breed of horse is the Falabella of Argentina which was developed over a period of 70 years by inbreeding and crossing a small group of undersized horses originally discovered in the southern part of the country. Most

adult specimens stand less than 30 in *76 cm* and average 80–100 lb *36–45 kg*. The smallest mature horse bred by Julio Falabella of Recco de Roca before he died in 1981 was a mare which stood 15 in *38 cm* and weighed 26½ lb *11,9 kg*. On 30 Nov 1975 Dr T. H. Hamison of the Circle Veterinary Center, Spartenburg, South Carolina certified that the stallion 'Little Pumpkin' (foaled 15 Apr 1973) owned by J. C. Williams Jr of Della Terra Mini Horse Farm, Inman, South Carolina stood 14 in *35,5 cm* and weighed 20 lb *9,07 kg*.

Fastest

A Lipizzaner stallion 'Siglavy Slava I' (foaled 17 June 1970) owned by Erich Dybal of Speicher, Switzerland, ran over a half mile (880 yd *804,6 m*) course from a standing start and running free without a rider in 41.8 sec and so averaging 43.06 mph *69,3 km/h*.

Longest Texas longhorns ● The 10 ft 6 in *3,2 m* spread of a Texas longhorn steer, the largest ever recorded. They are currently on exhibition at the Hermitage Museum, Big Springs, Texas, USA. (Photo: Hermitage Museum)

Oldest
The greatest reliable age recorded for a horse is 62 years in the case of 'Old Billy' (foaled 1760), believed to be a cross between a Cleveland and eastern blood, who was bred by Mr Edward Robinson of Wild Grave Farm in Woolston, Lancashire. In 1762 or 1763 he was sold to the Mersey and Irwell Navigation Company and remained with them in a working capacity (i.e. marshalling and towing barges) until 1819 when he was retired to a farm at Latchford, near Warrington, where he died on 27 Nov 1822. The skull of this horse is preserved in the Manchester Museum, and his stuffed head, (fitted with false teeth), is now on display in Bedford Museum. The greatest reliable age recorded for a pony is 54 years for a stallion owned by a farmer in central France (fl. 1919). A moorland pony named 'Joey' owned by June and Rosie Osborne of the Glebe Equestrian Centre, Wickham Bishops, Essex, was still alive and healthy in 1987 aged 43 years. The same age has also been confirmed for a roan pony named 'Bonnie Lass' owned by twin sisters Sylvia Moore and Mrs Marion Atkinson of Old Harlow, Essex. The greatest age recorded for a thoroughbred racehorse is 42 years in the case of the chestnut gelding 'Tango Duke' (foaled 1935), owned by Mrs Carmen J. Koper of Barongarook, Victoria, Australia. The horse died on 25 Jan 1978.

Strongest
The greatest load ever hauled by a pair of draught-horses was allegedly one weighing 144 short tons (130.9 tonnes) which two shires with a combined weight of 3500 lb 1587 kg pulled on a sledge litter for a distance of 440 yd 402 m along a frozen road at the Nester Estate near Ewen, Michigan on 26 Feb 1893, but this tonnage was exaggerated. The load, which comprised 50 logs of white pine scaling 36,055 board feet, actually weighed in the region of 53 short tons 42,3 tonnes.

Top International dog ● 'Ch. Clayfield's Mon Ami', who from 1975 to 1987 won a unique ten Dog Show championships on four continents. A German Shepherd bitch whelped in 1973, she is owned by Neal, Sharon, Buffy and Holly Leas of West Des Moines, Iowa, USA.

On 23 Apr 1924 a shire gelding named 'Vulcan', owned by Liverpool Corporation, registered a pull equal to a starting load of 29 tons 29,47 tonnes on a dynamometer at the British Empire Exhibition at Wembley, and a pair of shires easily pulled a starting load of 50 tons 51 tonnes, the maximum registered on the dynamometer.

DOGS
UK canine population 6,300,000 (1987 estimate), compared with 51,600,000 for the USA.

Heaviest
The heaviest breed of domestic dog (Canis familiaris) is the St Bernard. The heaviest recorded example is 'Benedictine Jr Schwarzwald Hof', owned by Thomas and Anne Irwin of Grand Rapids, Michigan. He was whelped in 1982 and weighed 22 st 2 lb 140,6 kg on 20 Mar 1987 (height at shoulder 39 in 99 cm).

The heaviest dog ever recorded in Britain was 'Heidan Dark Blue' (whelped 23 Apr 1978) also called 'Jason', a St Bernard owned by Nicol Plummer of Skeffington, Leics. In December 1981 he reached a peak 21 st 10¾ lb 138,23 kg (shoulder height 34 in 86,3 cm) but by January 1983 he was down to 15 st 95,25 kg after being put on a diet. Shortly before his death on 4 Nov 1983 he scaled 14 st 10 lb 93,4 kg.

Tallest
The tallest breeds of dog are the Great Dane and the Irish wolfhound, both of which can exceed 39 in 99 cm at the shoulder. In the case of the Great Dane the extreme recorded example was 'Shamgret Danzas' (whelped in 1975), owned by Mr and Mrs Peter Comley of Milton Keynes, Bucks. He stood 41½ in 105,4 cm or 42 in 106,6 cm when his hackles went up and weighed up to 17 st 108 kg. He died on 16 Oct 1984. The Irish wolfhound 'Broadbridge Michael' (1920–29),

owned by Mrs Mary Beynon of Sutton-at-Hone, Kent, stood 39½ in 100,3 cm at the age of 2 years.

Smallest
The world's smallest breeds of dog are the Yorkshire terrier, the Chihuahua and the Toy poodle, miniature versions of which have been known to weigh less than 16 oz 453 g when adult.

The smallest mature dog on record was a matchbox-sized Yorkshire terrier owned by Mr Arthur F. Marples of Blackburn, Lancs, a former editor of Our Dogs. This tiny atom, which died in 1945 aged nearly two years, stood 2¼ in 6,3 cm at the shoulder and measured 3¾ in 9,5 cm from the tip of its nose to the root of its tail. Its weight was an incredible 4 oz 113 g!

Oldest
Most dogs live between 8 and 15 years, and authentic records of dogs living over 20 years are rare. The greatest reliable age recorded for a dog is 29 years 5 months for an Australian cattle-dog named 'Bluey', owned by Mr Les Hall of Rochester, Victoria, Australia. The dog was obtained as a puppy in 1910 and worked among cattle and sheep for nearly 20 years. He was put to sleep on 14 Nov 1939.

The British record is 27 years 313 days for a Welsh collie named 'Taffy' owned by Mrs Evelyn Brown of Forge Farm, West Bromwich, West Midlands. He was whelped on 2 Apr 1952 and died on 9 Feb 1980.

Strength and endurance
The greatest load ever shifted by a dog was 6400¼ lb 2905 kg of railroad steel pulled by a 176 lb 80 kg St Bernard named 'Ryettes Brandy Bear' at Bothell, Washington, USA on 21 July 1978. The 4-year-old dog, owned by Douglas Alexander of Monroe, Washington, pulled the weight on a four-wheeled carrier across a concrete surface for a distance of 15 ft 4,57 m in less than 90 sec. Ten days earlier the same dog had moved 6600 lb 2993 kg, but was 5 in 12,7 cm short of the 15 ft 4,5 m minimum distance when the 90 seconds were up. The strongest dog in the world in terms of most proportionate weight hauled is 'Barbara-Allen's Dark Hans', a 97 lb 44 kg Newfoundland, who pulled 5045½ lb 2289 kg (= 52 lb 23,5 kg per lb 0,45 kg body weight) across a cement surface at Bothell on 20 July 1979. The dog, owned by Miss Terri Dickinson of Kenmore, Washington, was only 12 months old when he made the attempt. The record time for the annual 1049 mile 1688 km Iditarod Trail sled dog race from Anchorage to Nome, Alaska (inaugurated 1973) is 11 days 2 hours 5 mins 13 secs by Susan Butcher's team of dogs in the 1987 race. It was her second consecutive win.

Rarest
The world's rarest breed of dog is the Chinook, which was developed originally in New Hampshire in the early 1900s for use as a sled dog. Even at the height of its popularity this breed numbered less than 300, and by 1966 the population had dropped to 125. Twelve years later there were only 28 Chinooks left, but since then the population has more than doubled thanks to the efforts of the Chinook Owners' Association. In September 1985 a litter of six puppies was born in New York, bringing the total to 76, all of them in the USA.

Guide dog
The longest period of active service reported for a guide dog is 13 years 2 months in the case of a Labrador-retriever bitch named 'Polly' (whelped 10 Oct 1956), owned by Miss Rose Resnick of San Rafael, California. The dog was put to sleep on 15 Dec 1971.

Largest litter
The largest recorded litter of puppies is one of

23 thrown on 19 June 1944 by 'Lena', an American foxhound bitch owned by Commander W. N. Ely of Ambler, Pennsylvania. All survived. On 6–7 Feb 1975 'Careless Ann', a St Bernard, owned by Robert and Alice Rodden of Lebanon, Missouri also produced a litter of 23, 14 of which survived.

The British record is held by 'Settrina Baroness Medina', (d. 1983) an Irish red setter owned by Mgr M. J. Buckley, Director of the Wood Hall Centre, Wetherby, West Yorkshire. The bitch gave birth to 22 puppies, 15 of which survived, on 10 Jan 1974.

Most prolific

The greatest sire of all time was the champion greyhound 'Low Pressure', nicknamed 'Timmy', whelped in September 1957 and owned by Mrs Bruna Amhurst of Regent's Park, London. From December 1961 until his death on 27 Nov 1969 he fathered 2414 registered puppies, with at least 600 others unregistered.

Most valuable

In 1907 Mrs Clarice Ashton Cross of Ascot, Berkshire turned down an offer of £32,000 (equivalent to £865,000 today!) from the American financier and industrialist J. Pierpont Morgan for her famous Pekingese 'Ch. Ch'êrh of Alderbourne' (1904–fl. 1914). Mr Morgan then came back with an 'open' cheque, but again she turned him down. The largest legacy devoted to a dog was by Miss Ella Wendel of New York who 'left' her standard poodle 'Toby' £15 million in 1931.

Highest and longest jump

The canine 'high jump' record for a leap and a scramble over a smooth wooden wall (without any ribs or other aids) is held by a German shepherd dog named 'Max of Pangoula', who scaled an 11 ft 5¼ in *3,48 m* wall, at Chikurubi prison's dog training school near Harare, Zimbabwe on 18 Mar 1980. His trainer was Chief Prison Officer Alec Mann. 'Duke', a three-year-old German shepherd dog, handled by Cpl Graham Urry of RAF Newton, Nottinghamshire, scaled a ribbed wall with regulation shallow slats to a height of 11 ft 9 in *3,58 m* on the BBC *Record Breakers* TV programme on 11 Nov 1986. The longest recorded canine long jump was one of 30 ft *9,14 m* by a greyhound named 'Bang' whilst coursing a hare at Brecon Lodge, Gloucestershire in 1849. He cleared a 4 ft 6 in *1,4 m* gate and landed on a hard road.

Ratting

The greatest ratter of all time was a 26 lb *11,8 kg* 'bull and terrier' dog named 'Billy'. During the five-year period 1820–24 he despatched 4000 rats in 17 hr in matches, a remarkable feat considering that he was blind in one eye. His most notable feat was the killing of 100 rats in 5 min 30 sec at the cockpit in Tufton Street, Westminster, London on 23 Apr 1825. He died on 23 Feb 1829 aged 13 yrs. James Searle's famous 'bull and terrier' bitch 'Jenny Lind' was another outstanding ratter. On 12 July 1853 she was backed to kill 500 rats in under 3 hr at 'The Beehive' in Old Crosshall Street, Liverpool, and completed the job in 1 hr 36 min.

Tracking

The greatest tracking feat on record was performed by a Dobermann Pinscher named 'Sauer', trained by Detective-Sergeant Herbert Kruger. In 1925 he tracked a stock-thief 100 miles *160 km* across the Great Karroo, South Africa by scent alone. In 1923 a collie dog named 'Bobbie', lost by his owners while they were on holiday in Wolcott, Indiana, USA, turned up at the family home in Silverton, Oregon 6 months later, after covering a distance of some 2000 miles *3200 km*. The dog, later identified by householders who had looked over him along the route, had apparently travelled back through the states of Illinois, Iowa, Nebraska and Colorado, before crossing the Rocky Mountains in the depths of winter.

Top show dogs

The greatest number of Challenge Certificates won by a dog is the 78 compiled by the famous chow chow 'Ch. U'Kwong King Solomon' (whelped 21 June 1968). Owned and bred by Mrs Joan Egerton of Bramhall, Cheshire, 'Solly' won his first CC at the Cheshire Agricultural Society Championship Show on 4 June 1969, and his 78th CC was awarded at the City of Birmingham Championship Show on 4 Sept 1976. He died on 3 April 1978. The greatest number of 'Best-in-Show' awards won by any dog in all-breed shows is the career-total of 203 compiled by the Scottish terrier bitch 'Ch. Braeburn's Close Encounter' (whelped 22 Oct 1978) up to 10 Mar 1985. She is owned by Sonnie Novick of Plantation Acres, Florida, USA.

Largest show

At the Ladies' Kennel Association Show (LKA) held at the Birmingham National Exhibition Centre on 14–15 Dec 1984 there were 21,212 entries and a total of 14,611 dogs exhibited.

Top trainer

The most successful dog trainer in the world is Mrs Barbara Woodhouse of Rickmansworth, Hertfordshire, who trained 19,000 dogs to obey the basic commands during the period 1951 to her retirement in 1985. The fastest is Mr Armand Rabuttinio of Aston, Pennsylvania, USA. His highest total for a single day (9 a.m.–6 p.m.) is 132 dogs at a training marathon held at Upland, Pennsylvania on 12 June 1982.

Drug sniffing

The greatest drug-sniffing dog on record was a golden retriever named 'Trep' (whelped 1969), owned by former policeman Tom Kazo of Dade County, Miami, Florida. During the 5-year period 1973–77 'Agent K9–3', as he was also known, sniffed out $63 million (then £36 million) worth of narcotics. His owner said he would retire his pet, who could detect 16 different drugs, when he reached the magic $100 million (then £57 million) mark, but it is not known whether Trep achieved this target. The only drug-sniffing dog with a 100 per cent arrest record was a German shepherd of the US Army called 'General'. During the period April 1974 to March 1976 this canine detective and his handler, SP4 Michael R. Harris of the 591st Military Police Company in Fort Bliss, Texas, carried out 220 searches for narcotics, arrested 220 people for possession and uncovered 330 caches of drugs. The German shepherd 'Blue' of the Los Angeles Police Department was reported in January 1986 to have assisted in apprehending 253 suspected felons.

CATS

UK feline population 6,100,000 (1987 estimate), compared with 56,200,000 for the USA.

Largest

The largest of the 330 breeds of cat is the ragdoll with males weighing 15–20 lb *6,8–9,07 kg*. In the majority of domestic cats (*Felis catus*), the average weight of the male (tom) at maturity is 6.2 lb *2,81 kg*, compared to 5.4 lb *2,45 kg* for the adult female or queen. Neuters and spays average out somewhat heavier. The heaviest domestic cat on record was a neutered male tabby named 'Himmy', owned by Thomas Vyse of Redlynch, Cairns, Queensland, Australia. At the time of his death on 12 Mar 1986 aged 10 years 4 months he weighed 21,3 kg *46 lb 15¼ oz* (neck 38,1 cm *15 in*, waist 83,8 cm *33 in*, length 96,5 cm *38 in*).

The heaviest cat ever recorded in Britain was an 11-year-old male tabby called 'Poppa' owned by Miss Gwladys Cooper of Newport, Gwent, South Wales. He scaled 44½ lb *20,19 kg* in Nov 1984 and died on 25 June 1985.

Smallest

The smallest breed of domestic cat is the Singapura or 'Drain Cat' of Singapore. Adult males average 6 lb *2,72 kg* in weight and adult females 4 lb *1,81 kg*. A male Siamese cross named 'Ebony-Eb-Honey Cat' owned by Miss Angelina Johnston of Boise, Idaho, USA tipped the scales at only 1 lb 12 oz *0,79 kg* in February 1984 when aged 23 months.

Oldest

Cats are generally longer-lived than dogs. Information on this subject is often obscured by two or more cats bearing the same nickname in succession. The oldest cat ever recorded was probably the tabby 'Puss', owned by Mrs T. Holway of Clayhidon, Devon, who celebrated his 36th birthday on 28 Nov 1939 and died the next day. A more recent and better-documented case was that of the female tabby 'Ma', owned by Mrs Alice St George Moore of Drewsteignton, Devon. This cat was put to sleep on 5 Nov 1957 aged 34.

Largest kindle

The largest litter ever recorded was one of 19 kittens (4 stillborn) delivered by caesarean section to 'Tarawood Antigone', a 4-year-old brown Burmese, on 7 Aug 1970. Her owner, Mrs Valerie Gane of Church Westcote, Kingham, Oxfordshire, said the result was a mis-mating with a half-Siamese. Of the 15 survivors, 14 were males and one female.

The largest live litter (all of which survived) was one of 14 kittens born in December 1974 to a Persian cat named 'Bluebell', owned by Mrs Elenore Dawson of Wellington, Cape Province, South Africa.

Most prolific

The greatest number of kittens produced by a cat during her breeding life was 420 in the case of a tabby named 'Dusty' (b. 1935) living in Bonham, Texas. She gave birth to her last kindle (a single kitten) on 12 June 1952.

Most valuable

In 1967 Miss Elspeth Sellar of Grafham, Surrey turned down an offer of 2000 guineas (£2100) from an American breeder for her international champion copper-eyed white Persian tom 'Coylum Marcus' (b. 28 Mar 1965) who died on 14 Apr 1978. When Mrs Grace Alma Patterson of Joplin, Missouri died in January 1978 she left her entire estate worth $250,000 (then £131,000) to her 18 lb 8,16 kg white alley cat 'Charlie Chan'. When the cat dies the estate, which includes a three-bedroom house, a 7 acre *2,9 ha* pet cemetery and a collection of valuable antiques, will be auctioned off and the proceeds donated to local and national humane societies.

Best climber

On 6 Sept 1950 a four-month-old kitten belonging to Josephine Aufdenblatten of Geneva, Switzerland, followed a group of climbers up to the top of the 14,691 ft *4,478 m* Matterhorn in the Alps.

Mousing champion

The greatest mouser on record was a female tortoiseshell named 'Towser' (b. 21 Apr 1963) owned by Glenturret Distillery Ltd near Crieff, Tayside, Scotland who notched up an estimated life-time score of 28,899. She averaged three mice per day until her death on 20 Mar 1987.

RABBITS AND HARES

Largest

The largest breed of domestic rabbit (*Oryctola-*

CAGED PET LONGEVITY

Animal/Species	Name, Owner etc.	Years	Months
HAMSTER *Golden*	...Reported 1984 Cambridge, England	19	—
RABBIT	*Flopsy* caught 6 Aug 1964 d. 29 June 1983 (owner Mrs L. B. Walker) Longford, Tasmania	18	10¾
GUINEA PIG	*Snowball* Died: 14 Feb 1979 (owner, M. A. Wall) Bingham, Notts.	14	10½
GERBIL *Mongolian*	*Sahara* 21 May 1973–4 Oct 1981 (owner Aaron Milstone) Lathrup Village, Michigan, USA	8	4½
MOUSE *House*	*Fritzy* 11 Sept 1977–24 April 1985 (owner Mrs Bridget Beard) West House School, Edgbaston, Birmingham	7	7
RAT *Common*	...Died: c. 1924 Philadelphia, Pennsylvania, USA.	5	8

LARGEST PET LITTERS

Animal/Breed	Date	No.	Owner
CAT *Burmese/Siamese*	7.8.1970	15[1]	Mrs Valerie Gane, Church Westcote, Kingham, Oxfordshire.
DOG *American Foxhound*	19.6.1944	23[2]	Cdr W. N. Ely, Ambler, Pennsylvania, USA.
DOG *St Bernard*	6/7.2.1975	23[3]	R. and A. Rodden, Lebanon, Missouri, USA.
RABBIT *New Zealand White*	1978	24	Joseph Filek, Sydney, Cape Breton, Nova Scotia, Canada.
GUINEA PIG (CAVY)	1972	12	Laboratory Specimen.
HAMSTER *Golden*	28.2.1974	26[4]	L. and S. Miller, Baton Rouge, Louisiana, USA.
MOUSE *House*	12.2.1982	34[5]	Marion Ogilvie, Blackpool, Lancs.
GERBIL *Mongolian*	5.1983	14	Sharon Kirkman, Bulwell, Nottingham.
GERBIL *Mongolian*	1960's	15[6]	George Meares, geneticist-owner gerbil breeding farm, St Petersburg, Florida, USA.

[1] 4 still born [2] all survived [3] 14 survived [4] 18 killed by mother [5] 33 survived [6] Uses special food formula

Largest wingspan ● A Wandering albatross (*Diomedea exulans*) being handled to reveal its wingspan. This species has the largest spread of any living bird averaging 10 ft 4 in *3,15 m*. A specimen with a span of 11 ft 11 in *3,63 m* was caught in the Tasman Sea on 18 Sept 1965. (Photo: Robert Burton/Bruce Coleman)

gus cuniculus) is the Flemish giant. Adults weigh 7–8,5 kg *15.4–18.7 lb* (average toe to toe length when fully stretched 36 in *91 cm*), but weights up to 25 lb *11,3 kg* have been reliably reported for this breed. In April 1980 a five-month-old French lop doe weighing 12 kg *26.45 lb* was exhibited at the Reus Fair, north-east Spain. The heaviest recorded wild rabbit (av. weight 3½ lb *1,58 kg*) was one of 8 lb 4 oz *3,74 kg*, killed by Norman Wilkie of Markinch, Fife, Scotland while ferreting on 20 Nov 1982.

Smallest

The smallest breeds of domestic rabbit are the Netherland dwarf and the Polish, both of which have a weight range of 2–2½ lb *0,9–1,13 kg* when fully grown. In 1975 Jacques Bouloc of Coulommière, France, announced a new cross of the above breeds which weighed 396 g *14 oz*.

Most prolific

The most prolific domestic breeds are the New Zealand white and the Californian. Does produce 5–6 litters a year, each containing 8–12 kittens during their breeding life (*cf.* five litters and three to seven young for the wild rabbit).

Longest ears

The longest ears are found in the Lop family where measurements exceeding 30 in *76 cm* have been recorded for the British variety.

Largest hare

In November 1956 a brown hare weighing 15 lb 1 oz *6,83 kg* was shot near Welford, Northamptonshire. The average adult weight is 8 lb *3,62 kg*

Birds *Aves*

Largest *Ratite*

The largest living bird is the North African ostrich (*Struthio c. camelus*), which is found in reduced numbers south of the Atlas mountains from Upper Senegal and Niger across to the Sudan and central Ethiopia. Male examples (adult hens are smaller) of this flightless or ratite sub-species have been recorded up to 9 ft *2,74 m* in height and 345 lb *156,5 kg* in weight.

Largest *Carinate*

The heaviest flying bird or carinate is the Kori bustard or Paauw (*Otis kori*) of East and South Africa. Weights up to 40 lb *18 kg* have been reliably reported for cock birds shot in South Africa. The Mute swan (*Cygnus olor*), which is resident in Britain, can also reach 40 lb *18 kg* on occasion, and there is a record from Poland of a cob weighing 22,5 kg *49.5 lb* which could not fly.

Smallest

The smallest bird in the world is the Bee hummingbird (*Mellisuga helenae*) of Cuba and the Isle of Pines. Adult males (females are slightly larger) measure 57 mm *2.24 in* in total length, half of which is taken up by the bill and tail. It weighs 1,6 g *0.056 oz* which means it is lighter than a Privet hawk-moth (2,4 g *0.084 oz*). The smallest bird of prey is the 35 g *1.23 oz* White-fronted falconet (*Microhierax latifrons*) of north-western Borneo which is sparrow-sized. The smallest sea bird is the Least storm petrel (*Halocyptena microsoma*), which breeds on many of the small islands in the Gulf of California, north-western Mexico. Adult specimens average 140 mm *5¾ in* in total length and weigh *c.* 28 g *1 oz*.

The smallest regularly-breeding British bird is the Goldcrest (*Regulus regulus*), also known as the Golden crested wren or Kinglet. Adult specimens measure 90 mm *3.5 in* total length and weigh between 3,8 and 4,5 g *0.108* and *0.127 oz*.

Most abundant

The most abundant species of wild bird is the Red-billed quelea (*Quelea quelea*) of the drier parts of Africa south of the Sahara with a population estimated at 10,000,000,000. The most abundant sea bird is probably Wilson's storm-petrel (*Oceanites oceanicus*) of the Antarctic. No population estimates have been published, but the numbers run into hundreds of millions.

The most abundant species of domesticated bird is the Chicken, the tame version of the wild Red jungle fowl (*Gallus gallus*) of south-east Asia. In 1982 there was a total of 6,500,000,000 fowl in the world, or 1.4 birds for every member of the human race.

The most common nesting bird found in Britain is now the Blackbird (*Turdus merula*), with a peak breeding population of 15 million. It is followed by the Wren (*Troglodytes troglodytes*) and the Robin (*Erithacus rubecula*) at 10.5 million and 10 million respectively. Britain's most abundant sea bird is the Common guillemot (*Uria aalge*), with an estimated 577,000 breeding pairs nesting along the coastlines, 80 per cent of them in Scotland, in 1969–70. It was estimated in 1984 that 250,000 pigeon fanciers owned an average of 40 racing pigeons per loft, making a population of *c.* 10 million in Great Britain.

Rarest

Because of the practical difficulties in assessing bird populations in the wild, it is virtually impossible to establish the identity of the world's rarest living bird. The strongest contender, however, must be the Dusky seaside sparrow (*Ammospiza nigrescens*), formerly of Titusville Marshes, Florida, USA, with only a solitary captive male remaining at Discovery Island, Disney World, Orlando in March 1987. (The last female was sighted in 1975.) Despite the fact that this bird is aged between 10 and 15 years of age, blind in one eye and afflicted with gout, scientists think he may be good for another year or two. In March 1987 one of the last two Californian condors (*Gymnogyps californianus*) still living in the wild was captured in an effort to save the species (total population 27) from extinction by breeding them in captivity. The rarest sea bird is the Fiji petrel (*Pseudobulweria macgillivraya*). It is known only from three specimens, the last of which was collected on 3 July 1985 but died a week later.

According to the British Ornithologists' Union there are more than 40 species of birds which have been recorded only once in the British Isles—most of them since the end of the Second World War in 1945. That which has not recurred for the longest period is the Black-capped petrel (*Pterodroma hasitata*), of the West Indies. A specimen was caught alive on a heath at Southacre, near Swaffham, Norfolk in March or April 1850. On 28–29 May 1979 an Aleutian tern (*Sterna aleutica*) was sighted on the Farne Islands, Northumberland. This bird breeds on the coasts of Alaska and eastern Siberia, and until then had never been recorded outside the N. Pacific. In August 1986 thousands of bird-watchers descended on Blackcroft Sands Nature Reserve on Humberside for a sighting of a Red-necked stint (*Calidris ruficollis*) from Siberia, the first ever recorded in Britain. The most tenuously established British bird is the Snowy owl (*Nyctea scandiaca*). During the period 1967–75 one pair bred regularly on Fetlar, Shetland Isles and reared a total of 21 young, but soon afterwards the old male took off for an unknown destination, having driven off all the young males, and left the females without a mate. On 19–22 April 1979 an adult male was seen on Fair Isle some 80 miles *129 km* further south, but it did not find its way to Fetlar. In 1984 four females were seen on Fetlar, but once again no males were in evidence. In 1916 an English vicar stole the eggs of the last White-tailed sea eagle (*Haliaeetus albicilla*) on Skye in the Inner Hebrides, Scotland. During the

GUINNESS HAS PUBLISHED *WORLD BIRDS* AT £12.95

period 1975–7 an attempt to re-introduce this magnificent bird on the island of Rhum was made, and 13 eaglets from Norway were released. In the summer of 1985 the first specimen raised in the wild in Britain for more than 70 years took to the air, and it bred again successfully the following year.

Britain's rarest bird-of-prey is Montagu's harrier (*Circus pygargus*), which is confined to heathland and moorland areas of southern and eastern England. In 1974 there were no confirmed breeding pairs, but now they have re-established themselves, and in 1986 there were seven pairs, six of which raised 13 chicks.

Fastest and slowest flying

The fastest fliers are found among the ducks and geese (*Anatidae*), and some powerful species like the Red-breasted merganser (*Mergus serrator*), the Eider (*Somateria mollissima*), the Canvasback (*Aythya valisineria*) and the Spur-winged goose (*Plectropterus gambiensis*) can probably reach 80 mph *108 km/h* in an escape-dive. The White-throated spinetail swift (*Hirundapus caudacutus*) of Asia and the Alpine swift (*Apus melba*) are also extremely fast during courtship display flights, and the former has been timed at speeds up to 170 km/h *105,6 mph* in tests carried out in the USSR.

Probably at least 50 per cent of the world's flying birds cannot exceed an air speed of 40 mph *64 km/h* in level flight.

The slowest flying bird is the American woodcock (*Scolopax minor*), which has been timed at 5 mph *8 km/h* without sinking.

Fastest and slowest wing beat

The fastest recorded wing beat of any bird is that of the Horned sungem (*Heliactin cornuta*) of tropical South America with a rate of 90 beats a second. Large vultures (*Vulturidae*) sometimes exhibit a flapping rate as low as one beat per sec, and condors can cruise on air currents for up to 60 miles *96 km* without beating their wings once.

Longest lived

The greatest irrefutable age reported for any bird is 80+ years for a male Sulphur-crested cockatoo (*Cacatua galerita*) named 'Cocky', who died at London Zoo in 1982. He was presented to the Zoo in 1925, and had been with his previous owner since 1902 when he was already fully mature.

In 1987 an unconfirmed age of *c.* 82 years was reported for a male Siberian white crane (*Grus leucogeranus*) named 'Wolfe' at the International Crane Foundation, Baraboo, Wisconsin, USA. The bird was said to have hatched out in a zoo in Switzerland *c.* 1905.

In 1964 the death was reported of a male Andean Condor called 'Kuzya' at Moscow Zoo, aged 70+ years. This bird was already fully grown when it was received in 1892.

The oldest ringed bird on record is 'Blue White', a 58-year-old female Royal albatross (*Diomedea epomophora*), which nests annually at Taiaroa Head, Otago, New Zealand. Her mate 'Green White Green' is 45.

Longest flights

The greatest distance covered by a ringed bird is 14,000 miles *22 530 km* by an Arctic tern (*Sterna paradisea*), which was banded as a nestling on 5 July 1955 in the Kandalaksha Sanctuary on the White Sea coast and was captured alive by a fisherman 8 miles *13 km* south of Fremantle, Western Australia on 16 May 1956. The bird had

flown south via the Atlantic Ocean and then circled Africa before crossing the Indian Ocean. It did not survive to make the return journey.

Highest flying

The highest acceptable altitude recorded for a bird is just over 27,000 ft *8230 m* for 30 Whooper swans (*Cygnus cygnus*) flying in from Iceland to winter at Lough Foyle, Northern Ireland. They were spotted by an airline pilot over the Outer Hebrides on 9 Dec 1967, and the height was also confirmed on radar by air traffic control in Northern Ireland.

Most airborne

The most aerial of all birds is the Sooty tern (*Sterna fuscata*) which, after leaving the nesting grounds, remains continuously aloft for 3 or 4 years in a permanent state of insomnia before returning to the breeding grounds. The most aerial land bird is the Common swift (*Apus apus*) which remains airborne for 2–3 years until it is mature enough to breed.

Fastest swimmer

The fastest swimming bird is the Gentoo penguin (*Pygoscelis papua*) which has a maximum burst speed of *c.* 17 mph *27,4 km/h*. The deepest diving bird is the Emperor penguin (*Aptenodytes forsteri*) of the Antarctic which can reach a depth of 265 m *870 ft* and remain submerged for up to 18 minutes.

Vision

Birds of prey (*Falconiformes*) have the keenest eyesight in the avian world, and their visual acuity is at least 8–10 times stronger than that of human vision. The Golden eagle (*Aquila chrysaetos*) can detect an 18 in *46 cm* long hare at a range of 2 miles *3,2 km* in good light and against a contrasting background, and a Peregrine falcon can spot a pigeon at a range of over 5 miles *8 km*.

Bird—Largest ● The Andean condor (*Vultur gryphus*), the heaviest bird of prey, averages 20–25 lbs *9,09–11,3 kg*. (Photo: Gunter Ziesler/Bruce Coleman)

g force

American scientific experiments have revealed that the beak of the Red-headed woodpecker (*Melanerpes erythrocephalus*) hits the bark of a tree with an impact velocity of 13 mph *20,9 km/h*. This means that when the head snaps back the brain is subject to a deceleration of about 10 g.

Longest feathers

The longest feathers grown by any bird are those of the Phoenix fowl or Onagadori (a strain of Red junglefowl *Gallus gallus*) which has been bred in south-western Japan since the mid-17th century. In 1972 a tail covert measuring 10,6 m *34 ft 9¼ in* was reported for a rooster owned by Masasha Kubota of Kochi, Shikoku. Among flying birds the two central pairs of tail feathers of Reeve's pheasant (*Syrmaticus reevesi*) of central and northern China can exceed 8 ft *2,43 m*. They serve as an escape brake.

Most feathers

In a series of 'feather counts' on various species of bird a Whistling swan (*Cygnus columbianus*) was found to have 25,216 feathers, 20,177 of which were on the head and neck. The Ruby-throated hummingbird (*Archilochus colubris*) has only 940.

Smallest egg

The smallest egg laid by any bird is that of the Vervain hummingbird (*Mellisuga minima*) of Jamaica. Two specimens measuring less than 10 mm *0.39 in* in length weighed 0,365 g *0.0128 oz* and 0,375 g *0.0132 oz* respectively (*cf.* 0,5 g *0.017 oz* for the Bee hummingbird).

The smallest egg laid by a bird on the British list is that of the Goldcrest, which measures 12,2–14,5 mm *0.48–0.57 in* in length and between 9,4 and 9,9 mm *0.37* and *0.39 in* in diameter with a weight of 0,6 g *0.021 oz*. Eggs emitted from the oviduct before maturity, known as 'sports', are not reckoned to be of significance.

Incubation

The longest normal incubation period is that of the Wandering albatross, with a normal range of 75–82 days. There is an isolated case of an egg of the Mallee fowl (*Leipoa ocellata*) of Australia taking 90 days to hatch against its normal incubation of 62 days. The shortest incubation period is the 10 days of the Great spotted woodpecker (*Dendrocopus major*) and the Blackbilled cuckoo (*Coccyzus erythropthalmus*). The idlest of cock birds include hummingbirds (family Trochilidae), Eider duck (*Somateria mollissima*) and Golden pheasant (*Chrysolophus pictus*) among whom the hen bird does 100 per cent of the incubation, whereas the female Common kiwi (*Apteryx australis*) leaves this to the male for 75–80 days.

Bills

The largest bill or beak grown by any bird in relation to its body size is that of the male Toco toucan (*Rhamphastos toco*) of eastern S. America. It measures 20 cm *7.87 in* in length and almost equals the body in bulk. The longest bill grown by any bird in terms of relative size is that of the Swordbill hummingbird (*Ensifera ensifera*) of the Andes from Venezuela to Bolivia. It measures 10,2 cm *4 in* in length and is longer than the bird's actual body if the tail is excluded.

Cuckoos

It is unlikely that the Cuckoo (*Culculus canorus*) has ever been *heard and seen* in Britain earlier than 2 Mar, on which date one was observed under acceptable conditions by Mr William A. Haynes of Trinder Road, Wantage, Oxfordshire in 1972. The two latest dates are 16 Dec 1912 at Anstey's Cove, Torquay, Devon and 26 Dec 1897 or 1898 in Cheshire.

Bird-spotter

The world's leading bird-spotter or 'twitcher' is Norman Chesterfield (b. 8 Mar 1913) of Wheatley, Ontario. By March 1987 he had logged exactly 6220 of the 9016 known species.

The British life list record is 450 by Ron Johns of Slough, Bucks, and the British year list record is 329 by Stephen Webb of Chelmsford, Essex in 1980 who drove 40,000 miles *64 000 km* and spent about 150 days in the field to achieve his record. The greatest number of species spotted in a 24-hr period is 342 by Terry Stevenson, John Fanshawe and Andy Roberts (Block Hotels) at the Birdwatch Kenya '86 event held on 29–30 November. The 48-hour record is held by Don Turner, David Pearson and Alan Root (Brewery Birders) who spotted 494 species at the same event.

Largest egg ● A chick preparing to break its way out of the 1/16 in *1,5 mm* thick shell of the largest egg, that of the ostrich (*Struthio camelus*). Some minutes later the chick begins to emerge.
Around 2 dozen hens eggs in volume, the average ostrich egg requires about 40 mins to boil, measures 6–8 in *15–20 cm* in length, 4–6 in *10–15 cm* in diameter and weighs 3.63–3.88 lb *1,65–1,78 kg*.

The largest egg laid by any British bird, that of the Mute swan (*Cygnus olor*), measures 4.3–4.9 in *109–124 mm* in length, 2.8–3.1 in *71–78,5 mm* in diameter and weighs 12–13 oz *340–368 g*. (Photo: Des Bartlett and Christian Zuber/Bruce Coleman)

Smallest nest

The smallest nests are built by hummingbirds (*Trochilidae*). That of the Vervain hummingbird (*Mellisuga minima*) is about half the size of a walnut, while the deeper one of the Bee hummingbird is thimble-sized.

DOMESTICATED BIRDS

Heaviest chicken

The heaviest breed of chicken is the White Sully, which Mr Grant Sullens of West Point, California, developed over a period of 7 years by crossing and re-crossing large Rhode Island Reds with other varieties. One monstrous rooster named 'Weirdo' reportedly weighed 22 lb *10 kg* in January 1973, and was so aggressive that he had already killed two cats and crippled a dog which came too close.

The heaviest chicken reported in Britain was a 5-month-old 17 lb 3 oz *7,78 kg* Cobb capon bred by Mr Henry Ransom of Brancaster Staithe, Kings Lynn, Norfolk and weighed in December 1975 before ending up on the Christmas table.

Chicken flying

The record distance flown by a chicken is 310 ft 6 in *94,64 m* by *Shorisha*, owned by Morimitzu Meura, at Hammatzu, Japan on 8 Mar 1981. Hens are better fliers than cocks.

Heaviest turkey

The greatest dressed weight recorded for a turkey (*Meleagris gallapavo*) is 81 lb 0¼ oz *36,75 kg* for a stag reared by British United Turkeys of Chester, Cheshire. It won the annual 'heaviest turkey' competition held in London on 9 Dec 1986. Turkeys were introduced into Britain via Spain from Mexico in 1549.

Most expensive turkey

The highest price reached at auction for a turkey was the £3600 paid by Dewhurst, the butchers, for the 81 lb 0¼ oz *36,75 kg* stag (see above) at Smithfield Market, London on 9 Dec 1986.

Oldest

The longest-lived domesticated bird (excluding the ostrich) is the domestic goose (*Anser anser domesticus*) which normally lives about 25 years. On 16 Dec 1976 a gander named 'George' owned by Mrs Florence Hull of Thornton, Lancashire, died aged 49 years 8 months. He was hatched out in April 1927. The longest-lived small cage-bird is the canary (*Serinus canaria*). The oldest example on record was a 34-year-old cock bird named 'Joey' owned by Mrs K. Ross of Hull. The bird was purchased in Calabar, Nigeria in 1941 and died on 8 Apr 1975. The oldest budgerigar (*Melopsittacus undulatus*) was a hen bird named 'Charlie' owned by Miss J. Dinsey of Stonebridge, London which died on 20 June 1977 aged 29 years 2 months.

Most talkative

The world's most talkative bird is a female African grey parrot (*Psittacus erythacus*) named 'Prudle', owned by Mrs Lyn Logue of Seaford, East Sussex, which won the 'Best talking parrot-like bird' title at the National Cage and Aviary Bird Show in London each December for 12 consecutive years (1965–76). Prudle, who has a vocabulary of nearly 800 words, was taken from a nest at Jinja, Uganda in 1958. She retired undefeated.

Reptiles *Reptilia*

(Crocodiles, snakes, turtles, tortoises, lizards.)

CROCODILIANS

Largest

The largest reptile in the world is the Estuarine or Saltwater crocodile (*Crocodylus porosus*) of south-east Asia, the Malay Archipelago, Indonesia, northern Australia, Papua New Guinea, Vietnam and the Philippines. Adult males average 14–16 ft *4,2–4,8 m* in length and scale about 900–1150 lb *408–520 kg*. The longest recorded is a 20 ft 4 in *6,20 m* male which drowned after getting entangled in a fisherman's net at Obo on the Fly River, Papua New Guinea, in 1979. In July 1957 an unconfirmed length of 28 ft 4 in *8,63 m* was reported for an estuarine crocodile shot by Mrs Kris Pawlowski on MacArthur Bank in the Norman River, Queensland, Australia.

Smallest

The smallest living crocodilian is Osborn's dwarf crocodile (*Osteolaemus osborni*), found in the upper region of the Congo River, West Africa. It rarely exceeds 1,2 m *3 ft 11 in* in length.

Oldest

The greatest age authenticated for a crocodilian is 66 years for a female American alligator (*Alligator mississipiensis*), which arrived at Adelaide Zoo, South Australia, on 5 June 1914 as a two-year-old, and died there on 26 Sept 1978 aged 66 years. Another female of this species at the Maritime Museum Aquarium, Gothenburg, Sweden, died on 10 Feb 1987 aged 65 years after the electricity heating its pool was accidentally cut off.

Rarest

The world's rarest crocodilian is the protected Chinese alligator (*Alligator sinensis*) of the lower Chang Jiang (Yangtse Kiang) River of Anhui, Zhejiang and Jiangsu Provinces. The total population is currently estimated at 700–1000 individuals.

LIZARDS

Largest

The largest of all lizards is the Komodo monitor or Ora (*Varanus komodoensis*), a dragonlike reptile found on the Indonesian islands of Komodo, Rintja, Padar and Flores. Adult males average 225 cm *7 ft 5 in* in length and weigh about 59 kg *130 lb*. Lengths up to 30 ft *9,14 m* (sic) have been claimed for this species, but the largest specimen to be accurately measured was a male presented to an American zoologist in 1928 by the Sultan of Bima which taped 3,05 m *10 ft 0.8 in*. In 1937 this animal was put on display in St Louis Zoological Gardens, Missouri for a short period. It then measured 10 ft 2 in *3,10 m* in length and weighed 365 lb *166 kg*. The longest lizard in the world is the slender Salvadori monitor (*Varanus salvadori*) of New Guinea which has been reliably measured up to 15 ft 7 in *4,75 m*.

Smallest

The smallest lizard in the world is believed to be *Sphaerodactylus parthenopion*, a tiny gecko indigenous to the island of Virgin Gorda, one of the British Virgin Islands. It is known only from 15 specimens, including some gravid females found between 10 and 16 Aug 1964. The three largest females measured 18 mm *0.71 in* from snout to vent, with a tail of approximately the same length. It is possible that another gecko, *S. elasmorhynchus*, may be even smaller. The only known specimen was an apparently mature female with a snout-vent length of 17 mm *0.67 in* and a tail of the same measurement. It was found on 15 Mar 1966 among the roots of a tree in the western part of the Massif de la Hotte in Haiti.

Oldest

The greatest age recorded for a lizard is more than 54 years for a male Slow worm (*Anguis fragilis*) kept in the Zoological Museum in Copenhagen, Denmark from 1892 until 1946.

Heaviest nest ● The heaviest birds' nests are built by Bald eagles (*Haliaeetus leucocephalus*). The most extreme example, reported near St Petersburg, Florida, USA in 1963, was 9½ ft *2,9 m* wide, 20 ft *6 m* deep and weighed more than 3 tons. (Photo: Bruce Coleman)

Fastest

The highest speed measured for any reptile on land is 18 mph *29 km/h* for a Six-lined race runner (*Cnemidophorus sixlineatus*) near McCormick, South Carolina, USA, in 1941.

CHELONIANS

Largest

The largest chelonian found in the waters around Britain is the Atlantic leatherback turtle (*Dermochelys coriacea coriacea*). On 8 Sept 1983 a specimen weighing 1130 lb *512 kg* was caught off the Rosbeg coast, Co. Donegal, Ireland. It measured 6 ft 7 in *200,6 cm* in total length and 7 ft *213 cm* across the flippers. This turtle was later mounted and is now on display in Ardara.

The largest living tortoise is *Geochelone gigantea* of the Indian Ocean islands of Aldabra, Mauritius, and the Seychelles (introduced 1874). A male named 'Marmaduke' received at London Zoo in 1951 recorded a peak weight of 616 lb *279 kg* before his death on 27 Jan 1963.

Smallest

The smallest marine turtle in the world is the Atlantic ridley (*Lepidochelys kempii*), which has a shell length of 50–70 cm *19.7–27.6 in* and does not exceed 36 kg *80 lb*.

Longest lived

The greatest authentic age recorded for a tortoise is over 152 years for a male Marion's tortoise (*Testudo sumeirii*) brought from the Seychelles to Mauritius in 1766 by the Chevalier de Fresne, who presented it to the Port Louis army garrison. This specimen (it went blind in 1908) was accidentally killed in 1918. The greatest proven age of a continuously observed tortoise is more than 116 years for a Mediterranean spur-thighed tortoise (*Testudo graeca*). The oldest turtle on record was an Alligator snapping turtle (*Macrochelys temminckii*) at Philadelphia Zoo, Pennsylvania, USA. When it was accidentally killed on 7 Feb 1949 it was 58 years 9 months 1 day.

Fastest and slowest

The highest speed claimed for any reptile in water is 22 mph *35 km/h* by a frightened Pacific leatherback turtle. In a recent 'speed' test carried out in the Seychelles a male giant tortoise (*Geochelone gigantea*) could only cover 5 yd *4,57 m* in 43.5 sec (0.23 mph *0,37 km/h*) despite the enticement of a female. The National Tortoise Championship record is 18 ft *5,48 m* up a 1:12 gradient in 43.7 sec (0.28 mph *0,45 km/h*) by 'Charlie' at Tickhill, South Yorkshire on 2 July 1977.

Rarest

The world's rarest chelonian is the protected short-necked swamp tortoise (*Pseudemydura umbrina*), which is confined to Ellen Brook and Twin reserves near Perth, Western Australia. The total wild population is now only 20–25, with another 22 held at Perth Zoo.

SNAKES

Longest

The longest of all snakes (average adult length) is the Reticulated python (*Python reticulatus*) of south-east Asia, Indonesia and the Philippines, which regularly exceeds 20 ft 6 in *6,24 m*. In 1912 a specimen measuring 10 m *32 ft 9½ in* was shot near a mining camp on the north coast of Celebes in the Malay Archipelago.

The longest snake found in Britain is the Grass snake (*Natrix natrix*), which is found throughout southern England, parts of Wales and in Dumfries and Galloway. The longest accurately measured specimen was probably a female killed in South Wales in 1887 which measured 1775 mm *5 ft 10 in*. In Sept 1816 a 7 ft *213 cm* female with a maximum girth of 22 in *55,8 cm* (*sic*) was allegedly killed by a labourer at Trebun, Anglesey, N. Wales and 'left for public curiosity at Llangefni', but further details are lacking.

In captivity

The longest (and heaviest) snake ever held in captivity was a female Reticulated python named 'Colossus' who died in Highland Park Zoo, Pennsylvania, USA on 15 Apr 1963. She measured 28 ft 6 in *8,68 m* in length, and scaled 320 lb *145 kg* at her heaviest.

Shortest

The shortest known snake is the Thread snake (*Leptotyphlops bilineata*), which is found on the islands of Martinique, Barbados and St Lucia in the West Indies.

Heaviest

The heaviest snake is the Anaconda (*Eunectes murinus*), which is nearly twice as heavy as a Reticulated python (*Python reticulatus*) of the same length. A female shot in Brazil *c.* 1960 was not weighed, but it measured 27 ft 9 in *8,45 m* in length with a girth of 44 in *111 cm* which implies it must have scaled nearly 500 lb *227 kg*.

The heaviest venomous snake is the Eastern diamond-back rattlesnake (*Crotalus adamanteus*) of the south-eastern United States. One specimen measuring 7 ft 9 in *2,36 m* in length weighed 34 lb *15 kg*. In February 1973 a posthumous weight of 28 lb *12,75 kg* was reported for a 14 ft 5 in *4,39 m* long King cobra (*Ophiophagus hannah*) at New York Zoological Park (Bronx Zoo).

Oldest

The greatest irrefutable age recorded for a snake is 40 years 3 months and 14 days for a male Common boa (*Boa constrictor constrictor*).

Fastest

The fastest-moving land snake is probably the slender Black mamba (*Dendroaspis polylepis*). A speed of 10–12 mph *16–19 km/h* may be possible for short bursts over level ground. The

---

> **Largest chelonian** ● Pacific leatherback turtles, the world's largest living chelonians, have recorded weights of up to 1908 lb *865 kg*. This female of the species is seen egglaying at night in Malaysia. (Photo: Jane Burton/Bruce Coleman)

British grass snake has a maximum speed of 4.2 mph *6,8 km/h*.

Most venomous

The world's most venomous snake is the Sea snake (*Hydrophis belcheri*) which has a venom a hundred times as toxic as that of the Australian taipan (*Oxyuranus scutellatus*). The snake abounds round Ashmore Reef in the Timor Sea, off the coast of north-west Australia. The most venomous land snake is the 2 m *6 ft 6 in* long Inland taipan (*Oxyuranus microlepidotus*) of the Diamantina River and Cooper's Creek drainage bases in Channel County, Queensland which has a venom nine times as toxic as that of the Tiger snake (*Notechis scutatus*) of South Australia and Tasmania. One specimen yielded 110 mg *0.00385 oz* of venom after milking, a quantity sufficient to kill 218,000 mice. More people die of snakebite in Sri Lanka than any comparable area in the world. An average of 800 people are killed annually on the island by snakes, and 97 per cent of the fatalities are caused by the Common krait (*Bungarus ceylonicus*), Russell's viper (*Vipera russelli*) and the Asiatic cobra (*Naja naja*).

The only venomous snake in Britain is the adder (*Vipera berus*). Since 1890 ten people have died after being bitten by this snake, including six children. The most recent recorded death was on 1 July 1975 when a 5-year-old was bitten at Callander, Perthshire and died 44 hr later. The longest recorded specimen was a female measuring 43½ in *110,5 cm* which was killed by Graham Perkins of Paradise Farm, Pontrilas, Hereford & Worcester in August 1977.

Longest and shortest venomous

The longest venomous snake in the world is the King cobra (*Ophiophagus hannah*), also called the Hamadryad, of south-east Asia and the Philippines. An 18 ft 2 in *5,54 m* specimen, captured alive near Fort Dickson in the state of Negri Sembilan, Malaya, in April 1937, later grew to 18 ft 9 in *5,71 m* in London Zoo. It was destroyed at the outbreak of war in 1939. The shortest venomous snake is the Spotted dwarf adder (*Bitis paucisquamata*) of Little Namaqua-

land, South West Africa (Namibia), with adults averaging 9 in *228 mm* in length.

Longest fangs

The longest fangs of any snake are those of the highly venomous Gaboon viper (*Bitis gabonica*) of tropical Africa. In a 6 ft *1,83 m* long specimen they measured 50 mm *1.96 in*. On 12 Feb 1963 a Gaboon viper bit itself to death in the Philadelphia Zoological Gardens, Philadelphia, Pennsylvania, USA. Keepers found the dead snake with its fangs deeply embedded in its own back.

Rarest

The rarest snake in the world is the Keel-scaled boa (*Casarea dussumieri*) of Round Island, western Indian Ocean, with a total wild population of 58 in 1982.

The rarest snake of Britain's three indigenous species is the Smooth snake (*Coronella austriaca*) of southern England.

Amphibians *Amphibia*

Largest

The largest species of amphibian is the Chinese giant salamander (*Andrias davidianus*), which lives in north-eastern, central and southern China. The average adult measures 3 ft 9 in *114 cm* in length and weighs 55–66 lb *25–30 kg*. One species collected in Hunan Province measured 5 ft 11 in *180 cm* in length and scaled 143 lb *65 kg*.

The largest British amphibian is the Common toad (*Bufo bufo*). A female collected from Marlpit Pond, Boxley, Kent, measured 99 mm *3.89 in* snout to vent and weighed 118 g *4.16 oz*.

Smallest

The smallest known amphibian is the frog *Sminthillus limbatus*, found only in Cuba. Adult specimens have a snout-vent length of 8,5–12,4 mm *0.44–0.48 in*.

The smallest found in Britain is the Palmate newt (*Triturus helveticus*). Adult specimens measure 7,5–9,2 cm *2.95–3.62 in* in length and weigh up to 2,39 g *0.083 oz*. The Natterjack or Running toad (*Bufo calamita*) has a maximum snout-vent length of only 80 mm *3.14 in* (female) but it is a bulkier animal.

Oldest

The greatest authentic age recorded for an amphibian is 55 years for a Japanese giant salamander which died in Amsterdam Zoo, Netherlands, in 1881.

Rarest

The rarest amphibian in the world is the Israel painted frog (*Discoglossus nigriventer*) of Lake Huleh. Only five have been reported since 1940.

Britain's rarest amphibian is the introduced Green tree frog (*Hyla arborea*), which is now confined to a single site on the outskirts of London.

Highest and lowest

The greatest altitude at which an amphibian has been found is 8000 m *26,246 ft* for a Common toad collected in the Himalayas. This species has also been found at a depth of 340 m *1115 ft* in a coal mine.

Most poisonous

The most active known poison is the batrachotoxin derived from the skin secretions of the Golden dart-poison frog (*Phyllobates terribilis*) of western Colombia, South America, which is at least 20 times more toxic than that of any other known dart-poison frog. An average adult specimen contains enough poison (1100 mg *0.038 oz*) to kill 2200 people.

Largest frog

The largest known frog is the rare Goliath frog (*Conraua goliath*) of Cameroun and Equatorial Guinea. A female weighing 3306 g *7 lb 4.5 oz* was caught in the River Mbia, Equatorial Guinea on 23 Aug 1960. It had a snout-vent length of 34 cm *13.38 in* and measured 81,5 cm *32.08 in* overall with legs extended. A slightly longer female (35,6 cm *14 in*) collected in the same river in December 1966 weighed 3100 g *6 lb 13¼ oz*.

The largest frog found in Britain is the *introduced* Marsh frog (*Rana r. ridibunda*). Adult males have been measured up to 96 mm *3.77 in* snout-vent, and adult females up to 133 mm *5.25 in*, the weight ranging from 60 to 95 g *1.7–3 oz*.

The largest captive frog living in Britain today is a male African bull frog (*Pyxicephalus adspersus*) named 'Colossus' (b. 1978) owned by Mr Steve Crabtree of Southsea, Hants. It has a snout-vent length of 8¾ in *22,2 cm*, a girth of 18 in *45,7 cm* and weighs 4 lb 3 oz *1,89 kg*.

Longest jump

(*Competition frog jumps are invariably the aggregate of three consecutive leaps.*)

The greatest distance covered by a frog in a triple jump is 10,3 m *33 ft 5½ in* by a South African Sharp-nosed frog (*Rana oxyrhyncha*) named 'Santjie' at a Frog Derby held at Larula Natal Spa, Paulpietersburg, Natal, on 21 May 1977. At the famous annual Calaveras Jumping Jubilee held at Angels Camp, California, USA, on 18 May 1986 an American bullfrog (*Rana catesbeiana*) called 'Rosie the Ribeter', owned and trained by Lee Giudicci of Santa Clara, California, leapt 21 ft 5¾ in *6,55 m*. 'Santjie' would have been ineligible for this contest because entrants must measure at least 4 in *10,16 cm* 'stem to stern'.

Largest toad

The most massive toad is probably the Marine toad (*Bufo marinus*) of tropical South America. An enormous female collected on 24 Nov 1965 at Miraflores Vaupes, Colombia and later exhibited in the Reptile House at Bronx Zoo, New York City had a snout-vent length of 23,8 cm *9.37 in* and weighed 1302 g *2 lb 11¼ oz* at the time of its death in 1967.

The largest toad and heaviest amphibian found in Britain is the Common toad. An outsized female collected in Kent with a snout-vent length 99 mm *3.89 in* weighed 118 g *4.16 oz*.

Smallest toad

The smallest toad in the world is *Bufo beiranus*, first discovered *c.* 1906 near Beira, Mozambique, East Africa. Adult specimens have a maximum recorded snout-vent length of 24 mm *0.94 in*.

Fishes
Agnatha, Gnathostomata

Largest marine

The largest fish in the world is the rare plankton-feeding Whale shark (*Rhincodon typus*), which is found in the warmer areas of the Atlantic, Pacific and Indian Oceans. The longest scientifically-measured one on record was a 41½ ft *12,65 m* specimen captured off Baba Island near Karachi, Pakistan, on 11 Nov 1949. It measured 23 ft *7 m* round the thickest part of the body and weighed an estimated 15 tonnes/*tons*.

The largest carnivorous fish (excluding plankton-eaters) is the comparatively rare Great white shark (*Carcharodon carcharias*), also called the 'Man-eater'. Adult specimens (females are larger than males) average 14–15 ft *4,3–4,6 m* in length and generally scale between 1150–1700 lb *522–771 kg*, but larger individuals have been recorded. The length record is 6,4 m *21 ft* for a female caught off Castillo de Cojimar, Cuba, in May 1945. She weighed 7302 lb *3312 kg*.

The longest of the bony or 'true' fishes (Pisces) is the Oarfish (*Regalecus glesne*), also called the 'King of the Herrings', which has a worldwide distribution. In *c.* 1885 a 25 ft *7,6 m* long example weighing 600 lb *272 kg* was caught by fishermen off Pemaquid Point, Maine. Another oarfish, seen swimming off Asbury Park, New Jersey by a team of scientists from the Sandy Hook Marine Laboratory on 18 July 1963, was estimated to measure 50 ft *15,2 m* in length. The heaviest bony fish in the world is the Ocean sunfish (*Mola mola*), which is found in all tropical, sub-tropical and temperate waters. On 18 Sept 1908 a specimen was accidentally struck by the SS *Fiona* off Bird Island about 40 miles *65 km* from Sydney, New South Wales and towed to Port Jackson. It measured 14 ft *4,26 m* between the anal and dorsal fins and weighed 4927 lb *2235 kg*.

The largest fish ever recorded in the waters of the British Isles was a 36 ft 6 in *11,12 m* Basking shark (*Cetorhinus maximus*) washed ashore at Brighton, East Sussex in 1806. It weighed an estimated 8 tons/*tonnes*. The largest bony fish found in British waters is the Ocean sunfish. A specimen weighing 800 lb *363 kg* stranded near Montrose, Angus on 14 Dec 1960 was sent to the Marine Research Institute in Aberdeen.

Largest freshwater

The largest fish which spends its whole life in fresh or brackish water is the rare Pa beuk or Pla buk (*Pangasianodon gigas*). This *was* exceeded by the European catfish or Wels (*Silurus glanis*) in earlier times (in the 19th century lengths up to 15 ft *4,57 m* and weights up to 720 lb *336,3 kg* were reported for Russian specimens), but today anything over 6 ft *1,83 m* and 200 lb *91 kg* is considered large. The Arapaima (*Arapaima glanis*), also called the Pirarucu, found in the Amazon and other South American rivers and often claimed to be the largest freshwater fish, averages 6½ ft *2 m* and 150 lb *68 kg*. The largest 'authentically recorded' measured 8 ft 1½ in *2,48 m* in length and weighed 325 lb *147 kg*. It was caught in the Rio Negro, Brazil in 1836. In September 1978, a Nile perch (*Lates niloticus*) weighing 416 lb *188,6 kg* was netted in the eastern part of Lake Victoria, Kenya.

The largest fish ever caught in a British river was a Common sturgeon (*Acipenser sturio*) weighing 507½ lb *230 kg* and measuring 9 ft *2,74 m*, which was accidentally netted in the Severn at Lydney, Gloucestershire on 1 June 1937. Larger specimens have been taken at sea—notably one weighing 700 lb *317 kg* and 10 ft 5 in *3,18 m* long netted by the trawler *Ben Urie* off Orkney and landed on 18 Oct 1956.

Smallest

The shortest and lightest freshwater fish is the Dwarf pygmy goby (*Pandaka pygmaea*). The shortest recorded marine fish—and the shortest known vertebrate—is the Dwarf goby (*Trimmatom nanus*) of the Chagos Archipelago, central Indian Ocean. In one series of 92 specimens collected by the 1978–9 Joint Services Chagos Research Expedition of the British Armed Forces the adult males averaged 8,6 mm *0.338 in* in length and the adult females 8,9 mm *0.35 in*. The lightest of all vertebrates and the smallest catch possible for any fisherman is the Dwarf goby (*Schindleria praematurus*) from Samoa which measures 12–19 mm *0.47–0.74 in*. Mature specimens have been known to weigh only 2 mg, which is equivalent to *17,750 to the oz*. The smallest known shark is the Long-faced dwarf shark (*Squaliolus laticaudus*) of the western Pacific which does not exceed 150 mm *5.9 in*.

The world's smallest commercial fish is the now endangered Sinarapan (*Mistichthys luzonensis*), a goby found only in Lake Buhi, Luzon, Philippines. Adult males measure 10–13 mm *0.39–0.51 in* in length, and a dried 1 lb *454 g* fish cake contains about 70,000 of them!

The smallest British marine fish is Guillet's goby (*Lebetus guilleti*) which does not exceed 24 mm *0.94 in*. It has been recorded in the English Channel, off the west coast of Ireland and the Irish Sea.

Fastest

The Cosmopolitan sailfish (*Istiophorus platypterus*) is considered to be the fastest species of fish, although the practical difficulties of measurement make data extremely difficult to secure. A figure of 68 mph *109 km/h* (100 yd *91 m* in 3 sec) has been cited for one off Long Key, Florida. The swordfish (*Xiphias gladius*) has also been credited with very high speeds, but the evidence is based mainly on bills that have been found deeply embedded in ships' timbers. A speed of 50 knots (57.6 mph *92,7 km/h*) has been calculated from a penetration of 22 in *56 cm* by a bill into a piece of timber, but 30–35 knots (35–40 mph *56–64 km/h*) is the most conceded by some experts. A Wahoo (*Acanthocybium solandri*), 1,1 m *43 in* in length is capable of attaining a speed of 77 km/h *47.8 mph*.

Oldest

Aquaria are of too recent origin to be able to establish with certainty which species of fish can be regarded as being the longest lived. Early indications are, however, that it may be the Lake sturgeon (*Acipenser fulvescens*) of North America. In one study of the growth rings (annuli) of 966 specimens caught in the Lake Winnebago region, Wisconsin, USA, between 1951 and 1954 the oldest sturgeon was found to be a male (length 2,01 m *6 ft 7 in*), which gave a reading of 82 years and was still growing. In July 1974 a growth ring count of 228 years (*sic*) was reported for a female Koi fish, a form of fancy carp, named 'Hanako' living in a pond in Higashi Shirakawa, Gifu Prefecture, Japan, but the greatest authoritatively accepted age for this species is 'more than 50 years'. In 1948 the death was reported of an 88-year-old female European eel (*Anguilla anguilla*) named 'Putte' in the aquarium at Halsingborg Museum, southern Sweden. She was allegedly born in the Sargasso Sea, in the North Atlantic in 1860, and was caught in a river as a three-year-old elver.

Oldest goldfish

Goldfish (*Carassius auratus*) have been reported to live for over 40 years in China. The British record is held by a specimen named 'Fred' owned by Mr A. R. Wilson of Worthing, West Sussex, which died on 1 Aug 1980, aged 41 years.

Shortest lived

The shortest-lived fishes are probably certain species of the sub-order Cyprinodontei (Killifish) found in Africa and South America which normally live about eight months.

Most abundant

The most abundant species is probably the 3 in *76 mm* long deep-sea Bristlemouth (*Cyclothone elongata*) which has a worldwide distribution.

Deepest

The greatest depth from which a fish has been recovered is 8300 m *27,230 ft* in the Puerto Rico Trench (27,488 ft *8366 m*) in the Atlantic by Dr Gilbert L. Voss of the US research vessel *John Elliott* who took a 6½ in *16,5 cm* long *Bassogigas profundissimus* in April 1970. It was only the fifth such brotulid ever caught. Dr Jacques Piccard and Lieutenant Don Walsh, US Navy, reported they saw a sole-like fish about 1 ft *33 cm* long (tentatively identified as *Chascanopsetta lugubris*) from the bathyscaphe *Trieste* at a depth of 35,820 ft *10 917 m* in the Challenger Deep (Mari-

anas Trench) in the western Pacific on 24 Jan 1960. This sighting, however, has been questioned by some authorities, who still regard the brotulids of the genus *Bassogigas* as the deepest-living vertebrates.

Most and least eggs

The Ocean sunfish *Mola mola* produces up to 300,000,000 eggs, each of them measuring about 0.05 in *1,3 mm* in diameter, at a single spawning. The egg yield of the Tooth carp (*Jordanella floridae*) of Florida is only *c.* 20 over several days.

Most valuable

The world's most valuable fish is the Russian sturgeon (*Huso huso*). One 2706 lb *1227 kg* female caught in the Tikhaya Sosna River in 1924 yielded 541 lb *245 kg* of best quality caviare which would be worth £123,000 on today's market.

A fancy carp which won supreme champion classes in nationwide Japanese koi shows in 1976, 1977, 1979 and 1980 was sold two years later for 17,000,000 yen (£75,000). In March 1986 the fish was acquired by Mr Derry Evans, owner of the Kent Koi Centre at Sevenoaks, Kent, England, for an undisclosed sum, but this much-prized specimen died five months later.

Most venomous

The most venomous fish in the world are the Stonefish (Synanceidae) of the tropical waters of the Indo-Pacific, and in particular *Synanceja horrida* which has the largest venom glands of any known fish. Direct contact with the spines of its fins, which contain a strong neurotoxic poison, often proves fatal.

Most electric

The most powerful electric fish is the Electric eel (*Electrophorus electricus*), which is found in the rivers of Brazil, Colombia, Venezuela and Peru. An average sized specimen can discharge 400 volts at 1 ampere, but measurements up to 650 volts have been recorded.

Starfishes *Asteroidea*

Largest

The largest of the 1600 known species of starfish in terms of total arm span is the very fragile brisingid *Midgardia xandaros*. A specimen collected by the Texas A & M University research vessel *Alaminos* in the southern part of the Gulf of Mexico in the late summer of 1968 measured 1380 mm *54.33 in* tip to tip, but the diameter of its disc was only 26 mm *1.02 in*. Its dry weight was 70 g *2.46 oz*. The heaviest species of starfish is the five-armed *Thromidia catalai* of the Western Pacific. One specimen collected off Ilot Amedee, New Caledonia on 14 Sept 1969 and later deposited in Noumea Aquarium weighed an estimated 6 kg *13.2 lb* (total arm span 630 mm *24.8 in*).

The largest starfish found in British waters is the Spiny starfish (*Marthasterias glacialis*). In January 1979 Jonathon MacNeil from Isle of Barra, Western Isles, found a specimen on the beach which originally spanned 30 in *76,2 cm*.

Smallest

The smallest known starfish is the Asterinid sea star (*Patiriella parvivipara*) discovered by Wolfgang Zeidler on the west coast of the Eyre peninsula, South Australia in 1975. It has a maximum radius of only 4,7 mm *0.18 in* and a diameter of less than 9 mm *0.35 in*.

Most destructive

The most destructive starfish in the world is the Crown of Thorns (*Acanthaster planci*) of the Indo-Pacific region and the Red Sea. It can destroy 300–400 cm² *46.5–62 in²* of coral a day.

Deepest

The greatest depth from which a starfish has been recovered is 7584 m *24,881 ft* for a specimen of *Porcellanaster ivanovi* collected by the USSR research ship *Vityaz* in the Marianas Trench, in the West Pacific *c.* 1962.

Crustaceans *Crustacea*

(Crabs, lobsters, shrimps, prawns, crayfish, barnacles, water fleas, fish lice, woodlice, sandhoppers, krill, etc.)

Largest

The largest of all crustaceans (although not the heaviest) is the Taka-ashi-gani or Giant spider crab (*Macrocheira kaempferi*), also called the Stilt crab, which is found in deep waters off the south-eastern coast of Japan. Mature specimens usually have a body measuring 10 × 12 in *254 × 305 mm* and a claw-span of 8–9 ft *2,43–2,74 m*, but unconfirmed measurements up to 19 ft *5,79 m* have been reported. A specimen with a claw-span of 12 ft 1½ in *3,69 m* weighed 41 lb *18,6 kg*.

The largest species of lobster, and the heaviest of all crustaceans, is the American or North Atlantic lobster (*Homarus americanus*). On 11 Feb 1977 a specimen weighing 44 lb 6 oz *20,14 kg* and measuring 3 ft 6 in *1,06 m* from the end of the tail-fan to the tip of the largest claw was caught off Nova Scotia, Canada, and later sold to a New York restaurant owner.

The largest crustacean found in British waters is the Common or European lobster (*Homarus vulgaris*), which averages 2–3 lb *900–1360 g*. In June 1931 an outsized specimen weighing 20¼ lb *5,80 kg* and measuring 4 ft 1½ in *1,26 m* in total length was caught in a caisson during the construction of No 3 jetty at Fowey, Cornwall. Its crushing claw weighed 2 lb 10 oz *1188 g* after the meat had been removed. The largest crab found in British waters is the Edible or Great crab (*Cancer pagurus*). In 1895 a crab measuring 11 in *279 mm* across the shell and weighing 14 lb *6,35 kg* was caught off the coast of Cornwall.

Smallest

The smallest known crustaceans are water fleas of the genus *Alonella*, which may measure less than 0,25 mm *0.0098 in* in length. They are found in British waters. The smallest known lobster is the Cape lobster (*Homarus capensis*) of South Africa, which measures 10–12 cm *3.9–4.7 in* in total length. The smallest crabs in the world are the aptly named Pea crabs (family Pinnotheridae). Some species have a shell diameter of only 6,3 mm *0.25 in*, including *Pinnotheres pisum* which is found in British waters.

Oldest

The longest lived of all crustaceans is the American lobster (*Homarus americanus*). Very large specimens may be as much as 50 years old.

Deepest

The greatest depth from which a crustacean has been recovered is 10 500 m *34,450 ft* for *live* amphipods from the Challenger Deep, Marianas Trench, West Pacific by the US research vessel *Thomas Washington* in November 1980. Amphipods and isopods have also been collected in the Ecuadorean Andes at a height of 13,300 ft *4053 m*.

Arachnids *Arachnida*

SPIDERS (order Araneae)

Largest

The world's largest known spider is the Goliath bird-eating spider (*Theraphosa leblondi*) of the coastal rain-forests of Surinam, Guyana (formerly British Guyana) and French Guiana, north-eastern South America; isolated specimens have also been reported from Venezuela and Brazil. In Feb 1985 Charles J Seiderman of New York City, captured a huge female just north of Paramarido, Surinam. This spider had a maximum leg span of 266,7 mm *10¼ in* (total body length 102 mm *4 in*), 25 mm *1 in* long fangs and weighed a peak 122,2 g *4.3 oz* before its death from moulting problems in Jan 1986. An outsized male example collected by members of the Pablo San Martin Expedition at Rio Cavro, Venezuela in April 1965 had a leg span of 280 mm *11.02 in*, but the female is built on much heavier lines.

Of the 617 known species of British spider covering an estimated population of over 500,000,000,000, the Cardinal spider (*Tegenaria gigantea*) of southern England has the greatest leg span. In October 1985 Mrs Lyndsay Jarrett of Marston Meysey, Wiltshire collected an outsized female in her home with a span of 5.5 in *139 mm*.

The well-known 'Daddy Longlegs' spider (*Pholcus phalangioides*) rarely exceeds 4½ in *114 mm* in leg span, but one outsized specimen collected in England measured 6 in *15,2 cm* across. The heaviest spider found in Britain is the Orb weaver (*Araneus quadratus*). On 10 Sept 1979 a female weighing 2,25 g *0.079 oz* was collected at Lavington, West Sussex by J. R. Parker.

Smallest

The smallest known spider is *Patu marplesi* (family Symphytognathidae) of Western Samoa.

Britain's smallest spider is the extremely rare Money spider (*Glyphesis cottonae*) found only in a swamp near Beaulieu Road Station, Hampshire and on Thursley Common, Surrey. Adult specimens of both sexes have a body length of 1 mm *0.039 in*.

Rarest

The most elusive of all spiders are the rare Trapdoor spiders of the genus *Liphistius*, which are found in south-east Asia.

The most elusive spiders in Britain are the four species which are known only from the holotype specimen. These are the jumping spiders *Salticus mutabilis* (1 male Bloxworth, Dorset, 1860) and *Heliophanus melinus* (1 female Bloxworth, 1870); the Crab spider *Philodromus buxi* (1 female Bloxworth pre-1879); and the Cobweb spider *Robertus insignis* (1 male Norwich, 1906).

Oldest

The longest lived of all spiders are the primitive *Mygalomorphae* (tarantulas and allied species). One female therasophid collected in Mexico in 1935 lived for an estimated 26–28 years. The longest-lived British spider is probably the Purse web spider (*Atypus affinis*). One specimen was kept in a greenhouse for nine years.

Fastest

The fastest-moving arachnids are the long-legged Sun-spiders of the genus *Solpuga*, which live in the arid semi-desert regions of Africa and the Middle East. Some species probably have a burst sprint capability of at least 10 mph *16 km/h*.

Webs

The largest webs are aerial ones spun by the Tropical orb weavers of the genus *Nephila*, which have been measured up to 18 ft 9¾ in *573 cm* in circumference. The smallest webs are spun by spiders such as *Glyphesis cottonae* (see above) which cover about 0.75 in² *480 mm²*.

Most venomous

The most venomous spiders in the world are the Brazilian wandering spiders of the genus *Phoneutria*, and particularly *P. fera*, which has the

most active neurotoxic venom of any living spider. These large and highly aggressive creatures frequently enter human dwellings and hide in clothing or shoes. When disturbed they bite furiously several times, and hundreds of accidents involving these species are reported annually. Fortunately an effective antivenin is available, and when deaths do occur they are usually among children under the age of seven.

Insects *Insecta*

Heaviest

The heaviest living insects are the Goliath beetles (family Scarabaeidae) of Equatorial Africa. The largest members of the group are *Goliathus regius* and *G. goliathus* (= *G. giganteus*), and in one series of fully-grown males (females are smaller) the weight ranged from 70 to 100 g *2.5–3.5 oz*.

The heaviest insect found in Britain is the Stag beetle (*Lucanus cervus*) which is widely distributed over southern England. The largest specimen on record was a male collected at Sheerness, Kent, in 1871 and now preserved in the British Museum (Natural History), which measures 87,4 mm *3.04 in* in length (body plus mandibles) and probably weighed over 6 g *0.21 oz* when alive.

Longest

The longest insect in the world is the Giant stick-insect (*Pharnacia serratipes*) of Indonesia, females of which have been measured up to 330 mm *13 in*. The longest known beetle (excluding antennae) is the Hercules beetle (*Dynastes hercules*) of Central and South America, which has been measured up to 190 mm *7.48 in*. More than half the length however, is taken up by the prothoracic horn.

Smallest

The smallest insects recorded so far are the 'Hairy-winged' beetles of the family Ptiliidae (= Trichopterygidae) and the 'Battledore-wing fairy flies' (parasitic wasps) of the family Myrmaridae. They are smaller than some of the protozoa (single-celled animals). The male Bloodsucking banded louse *Enderleinellus zonatus*, ungorged, and the parasitic wasp *Caraphractus cinctus* may each weigh as little as

0,005 mg, or *5,670,000 to an oz*. Eggs of the latter each weigh 0,0002 mg, *or 141,750,000 to an oz*.

Rarest

It has recently been estimated that there may be as many as 30 million species of insect—more than all other phylums and classes put together—but thousands are known only from a single or type specimen.

Fastest flying

Experiments have proved that the widely publicised claim by an American scientist in 1926 that the Deer bot-fly (*Cephenemyia pratti*) could attain a speed of 818 mph *1316 km/h* (*sic*) at an altitude of 12,000 ft *3657 m* was wildly exaggerated. If true the fly would have had to develop the equivalent of 1.5 hp *1.1 kW* and consume 1½ times its own weight in food per second to acquire the energy that would be needed, and even if this were possible it would still be crushed by the air pressure and incinerated by the friction. Acceptable modern experiments have now established that the highest maintainable air speed of any insect including the Deer bot-fly is 24 mph *39 km/h* rising to a maximum of 36 mph *58 km/h* for short bursts.

Oldest

The longest-lived insects are the Splendour beetles (Buprestidae). On 27 May 1983 a *Buprestis aurulenta* appeared from the staircase timber in the home of Mr W. Euston of Prittlewell, Southend-on-Sea, Essex after 47 years as a larva.

Loudest

The loudest of all insects is the male cicada (family Cicadidae). At 7400 pulses/min its tymbal organs produce a noise (officially described by the United States Department of Agriculture as 'Tsh-ee-EEEE-e-ou') detectable more than a quarter of a mile *400 m* distant.

The only British species is the very rare Mountain cicada (*Cicadetta montana*), which is confined to the New Forest area in Hampshire.

Toughest

According to experiments carried out by Prof H. E. Hinton at Bristol University, the larva of the Chironomid fly (*Polypedilum vanderplanki*) can tolerate temperatures ranging from −270°C to 102°C *−454°F to 215.6°F*, and is the most advanced organism so far known that can be totally dehydrated.

Largest cockroach

The largest cockroach in the world is the Giant burrowing cockroach (*Macropanesthia rhinoceros*) of tropical northern Queensland, Australia. A female measuring 79 mm *3.11 in* in length, 35 mm *1.49 in* across and weighing 21,9 g *0.77 oz* was collected at Agnes Water, Queensland, in Dec 1986.

Largest locust swarm

The greatest swarm of Desert locusts (*Schistocera gregaria*) ever recorded was one covering an estimated 2000 miles² *5180 km²* observed crossing the Red Sea in 1889. Such a swarm must have contained about 250,000,000,000 insects weighing about 500,000 tons *508 000 tonnes*. In 1958 in Somalia a swarm of *c.* 60,000 million covering a measured 1000 km² *400 miles²* was estimated to be devouring *c.* 120,000 tons of biomass daily.

Fastest wing beat

The fastest wing beat of any insect under natural conditions is 62,760 per min by a tiny midge of the genus *Forcipomyia*. In experiments with truncated wings at a temperature of 37° C *98.6° F* the rate increased to 133,080 beats/min. The muscular contraction–expansion cycle in 0.00045 or 1/2218th of a sec further represents the fastest muscle movement ever measured.

Slowest wing beat

The slowest wing beat of any insect is 300 per min by the Swallowtail butterfly (*Popilio machaon*). The average is 460–636 per min.

Hive yield

The greatest reported amount of wild honey ever extracted from a single hive is 549 lb *249,02 kg* recorded by A. D. Wilkes of Cairns, Queensland, Australia in the 11 months Feb–Dec 1983.

Dragonflies

The largest dragonfly in the world is *Megaloprepus caeruleata* of Central and South America, which has been measured up to 191 mm *7.52 in* across the wings and 120 mm *4.72 in* in body length.

The largest dragonfly found in Britain is *Anax imperator*, which has a wing span measurement of up to 106 mm *4.17 in*. The smallest is *Lestes dryas*, which has a wing span of 20–25 mm *0.78–0.98 in*.

Largest flea

Siphonapterologists recognise 1830 varieties, of which the largest known is *Hystrichopsylla schefferi*, described from a single specimen taken from the nest of a Mountain beaver (*Aplodontia rufa*) at Puyallup, Washington, USA in 1913. Females measure up to 8 mm *0.31 in* in length, which is the diameter of a pencil.

The largest flea (61 species) found in Britain is the Mole and Vole flea (*H. talpae*)—females have been measured up to 6 mm *0.23 in.*

The champion jumper among fleas is the Common flea (*Pulex irritans*). In one American experiment carried out in 1910 a specimen allowed to leap at will performed a long jump of 13 in *330 mm* and a high jump of 7¾ in *197 mm*. In jumping 130 times its own height a flea subjects itself to a force of 200 g.

BUTTERFLIES AND MOTHS (order Lepidoptera)

Largest

The largest known butterfly is the protected Queen Alexandra's birdwing (*Ornithoptera alexandrae*) which is restricted to the Popondetta Plain in Papua New Guinea. Females may have a wing span exceeding 280 mm *11.02 in* and weigh over 25 g *0.88 oz*. The largest moth in the world (although not the heaviest) is the Hercules moth (*Cosdinoscera hercules*) of tropical Australia and New Guinea. A wing area of up to 40.8 in² *263,2 cm²* and a wing span of 280 mm *11 in* have been recorded. In 1948 an unconfirmed measurement of 360 mm *14.17 in* was reported for a female captured near the post office of the coastal town of Innisfail, Queensland, Australia, now in the Oberthur collection. The rare Owlet moth (*Thysania agrippina*) of Brazil has been measured up to 12.16 in *308 mm* wing span in the case of a female taken in 1934 and now in the collection of John G. Powers in Ontario, Canada.

The largest butterfly found in Britain is the Monarch butterfly (*Danaus plexippus*), also called the Milkweed or Black-veined brown butterfly, a rare vagrant which breeds in the southern United States and Central America. It has a wing span of up to 5 in *127 mm* and weighs about 1 g *0.04 oz*. The largest *native* butterfly is the Swallowtail (*Papilio machaon britannicus*), females of which have a wing span up to 100 mm *3.93 in*. This species is now confined to fens in Suffolk, Cambridgeshire and the Norfolk Broads.

The largest (but not the heaviest) of the 21,000 species of insect found in Britain is the very rare Death's head hawkmoth (*Acherontia atropos*). One female found dead in a garden at Tiverton, Devon, in 1931 had a wing span of 5.75 in *145 mm* and weighed nearly 3 g *0.10 oz.*

Smallest

The world's smallest known butterfly is the recently discovered *Micropsyche ariana*, which has a wing span of 7 mm *0.275 in*. The type specimen was collected on Mt Khwajaghar in the Koh-i-Baba range, Afghanistan. The smallest of the 140,000 known species of Lepidoptera are the moths *Johanssonia acetosea* found in Britain, and *Stigmella ridiculosa* from the Canary Islands, which have a wing span of *c.* 2 mm *0.08 in* with a similar body length.

The smallest butterfly found in Britain is the Small blue (*Cupido minimus*), which has a wing span of 19–25 mm *0.75–1.0 in*.

Rarest

The birdwing butterfly *Ornithopteria* (= *Troides*) *allottei* of Bougainville, Solomon Islands is known from less than a dozen specimens. A male from the collection of C. Rousseau Decelle was auctioned for £750 in Paris on 24 Oct 1966.

Britain's rarest butterfly (59 species) is the Large tortoiseshell (*Nymphalis polychloros*). There have been isolated sightings on the Isle of Wight, Wiltshire, Suffolk and South Wales but this species no longer breeds in this country. The Large blue (*Maculinea arion*) was officially declared extinct in 1979, but it was successfully reintroduced in the West Country when larvae were imported from Sweden in 1983 and 1986.

Most acute sense of smell

The most acute sense of smell exhibited in nature is that of the male Emperor moth (*Eudia pavonia*) which, according to German experiments in 1961, can detect the sex attractant of the virgin female at the almost unbelievable range of 11 km

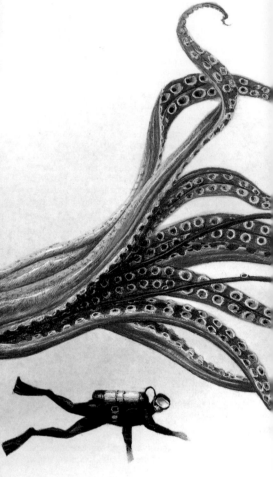

6.8 *miles* upwind. This scent has been identified as one of the higher alcohols ($C_{16}H_{29}OH$), of which the female carries less than 0,0001 mg.

Largest butterfly farm

Stratford-upon-Avon Butterfly Farm has a main flight area of 6338 ft² *582 m²* which can accommodate 2,000 exotic butterflies in authentic rain forest conditions. The total of all flight areas at the butterfly farm, which opened on 15 June 1985, is 8789 ft² *807 m²*.

Centipedes *Chilopoda*

Longest

The longest known species of centipede is a large variant of the widely distributed *Scolopendra morsitans*, found on the Andaman Islands in the Bay of Bengal. Specimens have been measured up to 13 in *330 mm* in length and 1½ in *38 mm* in breadth.

The longest centipede found in Britain is *Haplophilus subterraneus*, which has been measured up to 70 mm *2.75 in* in length and 1,4 mm *0.05 in* across the body.

Shortest

The shortest recorded centipede is an unidentified species which measures only 5 mm *0.19 in.*

The shortest centipede found in Britain is *Lithobius dubosequi*, which measures up to 9,5 mm *0.374 in* in length.

Molluscs

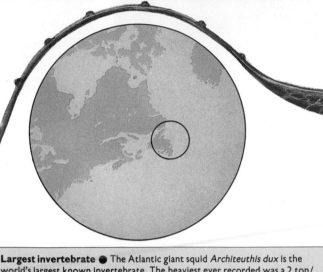

Largest invertebrate ● The Atlantic giant squid *Architeuthis dux* is the world's largest known invertebrate. The heaviest ever recorded was a 2 ton/tonne monster which ran aground in Thimble Tickle Bay, Newfoundland on 2 Nov 1878. There are numerous types of 10-armed cephalopods ranging in size from 1,5 cm *0.75 in* to the longest ever recorded—a 57 ft *17,37 m* giant *Architeuthis longimanus* which was washed up on Lyall Bay, Cook Strait, New Zealand in October 1887. Its long slender tentacles with four rows of suckers each measured 49 ft 3 in *15,01 m*.

The Atlantic Giant squid has the largest eye of any animal—living or extinct. It has been estimated that the one recorded at Thimble Tickle Bay had eyes 400 mm *15.75 in* in diameter—almost the width of this open book!

The largest squid ever recorded in British waters was an *Architeuthis monachus* found at the head of Whalefirth Voe, Shetland on 2 Oct 1959 which measured 24 ft *7,31 m* in total length.   Artwork: Matthew Hillier F.C.S.D.

Millipedes *Diplopoda*

Longest
The longest known species of millipede are *Graphidostreptus gigas* of Africa and *Scaphistostreptus seychellarum* of the Seychelles in the Indian Ocean, both of which have been measured up to 280 mm *11.02 in* in length and 20 mm *0.78 in* in diameter.

The longest millipede found in Britain is *Cylindroiulus londinensis* which measures up to 50 mm *1.96 in.*

Shortest
The shortest millipede in the world is the British species *Polyxenus lagurus*, which measures 2,1–4,0 mm *0.082–0.15 in.*

Most legs
The greatest number of legs reported for a millipede is 375 pairs (750 legs) for *Illacme plenipes* of California.

Segmented Worms *Annelida*

Longest
The longest known species of earthworm is *Microchaetus rappi* (= *M. microchaetus*) of South Africa. In *c.* 1937 a giant measuring 22 ft *6,70 m* in length when naturally extended and 0.78 in *20 mm* in diameter was collected in the Transvaal.

The longest segmented worm found in Britain is the King rag worm (*Nereis virens*). On 19 Oct 1975 a specimen measuring 44 in *111,7 cm* when fully extended was collected by Mr James Sawyer in Hauxley Bay, Northumberland.

Most legs
The centipede with the greatest number of legs is *Himantarum gabrielis* found in southern Europe which has 171–177 pairs when adult.

Fastest
The fastest centipede is probably *Scrutigera coleoptrata* of southern Europe which can travel at 1.1 mph *1,8 km/h.*

Shortest
The shortest known segmented worm is *Chaetogaster annandalei*, which measures less than 0,5 mm *0.019 in* in length.

Worm charming
At the third international Worm Charming Championship held in Blackawton, Devon, on 22 Mar 1986, a Round Table team led by Bob Benn of Dartmouth coaxed 149 worms from a square metre of soil in 15 minutes.

Molluscs *Mollusca*
(Squids, octopuses, shellfish, snails, etc.)

Largest octopus
The largest octopus known to science is *Octopus apollyon* of the coastal waters of the North Pacific. One huge individual caught single-handed by skin-diver Donald E. Hagen in Lower Hoods Canal, Puget Sound, Washington on 18 Feb 1973 had a relaxed radial spread of 23 ft *7,01 m* and weighed 118 lb 10 oz *53,8 kg.*

The largest octopus found in British waters is the Common octopus (*Octopus vulgaris*). It may span 7 ft *2,13 m* and weigh more than 10 lb *4,5 kg.*

Oldest mollusc
The longest-lived mollusc is the Ocean quahog (*Arctica islandica*), a thick-shelled clam found in mid-Atlantic. A specimen with 220 annual growth rings was collected in 1982.

SHELLS

Largest
The largest of all existing bivalve shells is the marine giant clam *Tridacna gigas*, found on the Indo-Pacific coral reefs. A specimen measuring 110 cm *43.3 in* in length and weighing 333 kg *734 lb* collected off Ishigaki Island, Okinawa, Japan, was found in 1956 but not formally measured until Aug 1984 by Dr Shohei Shirai.

The largest bivalve shell found in British waters is the Fan mussel (*Pinna fragilis*). One specimen found at Tor Bay, Devon measured 37 cm *14.56 in* in length and 20 cm *7.87 in* in breadth at the hind end.

Smallest
The smallest known shell-bearing species is the gastropod *Ammonicera rota*, which is found in British waters. It measures 0,5 mm *0.02 in* in diameter. The smallest bivalve shell is the Coinshell *Neolepton sykesi*, which is known only from a few examples collected off Guernsey, Channel Islands and western Ireland. It has an average diameter of 1,2 mm *0.047 in.*

Most expensive
The value of a sea-shell does not necessarily depend on its rarity or its prevalence. The most sought-after shell at the moment is probably *Conus lamberti sowerbie* from New Caledonia in the Pacific, which could fetch $10,000 (£6250) on the open market.

GASTROPODS

Largest
The largest known gastropod is the Trumpet or Baler conch (*Syrinx aruanus*) of Australia. One outsized specimen collected off Western Australia in 1979 and now owned by Don Pisor (who bought it from a fisherman in Kaoh-siung, Taiwan in November 1979) of San Diego, California measures 77,2 cm *30.39 in* in length and has a maximum girth of 101 cm *39.76 in.* It weighed nearly 40 lb *18,14 kg* when alive.

The largest known land gastropod is the African giant snail (*Achatina* sp.). A specimen named 'Gee Geronimo' owned by Christopher Hudson (1955–79) of Hove, E. Sussex, measured 15¼ in

39,3 cm from snout to tail when fully extended (shell length 10¾ in *27,3 cm*) in December 1978 and weighed exactly 2 lb *900 g*. The snail was collected in Sierra Leone, West Africa, in June 1976.

The largest land snail found in Britain is the Roman or Edible snail (*Helix pomatia*), which measures up to 4 in *10 cm* in overall length and weighs up to 3 oz *85 g*.

Fastest

The fastest-moving species of land snail is probably the Common garden snail (*Helix aspersa*). According to tests carried out in the United States the absolute top speed for this species is 0.0313 mph *0,05 km/h* (or 55 yd *50,3 m* per hr).

Ribbon Worms
Nemertina

Longest

The longest of the 550 recorded species of ribbon worm, also called nemertines (or nemerteans), is the 'Boot-lace' worm (*Lineus longissimus*), which is found in the shallow waters of the North Sea. A specimen washed ashore at St Andrews, Fife, Scotland, in 1864 after a severe storm measured more than 180 ft *55 m* in length.

Immolation
Some ribbon worms (nemertines) absorb themselves when food is scarce. One specimen under observation digested 95 per cent of its own body in a few months without apparently suffering any ill-effects. As soon as food became available the lost tissue was restored.

Jellyfishes and Corals *Cnidaria*

Largest jellyfish

The largest jellyfish is the Arctic giant jellyfish (*Cyanea capillata arctica*) of the north-western Atlantic. One washed up in Massachusetts Bay had a bell diameter of 7 ft 6 in *2,28 m* and tentacles stretching 120 ft *36,5 m*.

The largest cnidarian found in British waters is the rare 'Lion's mane' jellyfish (*Cyanea capillata*), also known as the Common sea blubber. One specimen measured at St Andrew's Marine Laboratory, Fife, had a bell diameter of 91 cm *35.8 in* and tentacles stretching over 13,7 m *45 ft*.

Coral

The world's greatest stony coral structure is the Great Barrier Reef off Queensland, north-east Australia. It stretches 1260 miles *2028 km* and covers 80,000 miles² *207 000 km²*.

The world's largest reported discrete coral is a stony colony of *Galaxea fascicularis* found in Sakiyama Bay off Irimote Island, Okinawa on 7 Aug 1982 by Dr Shohei Shirai. It measured more than 16 m *52⅓ ft* overall.

Sponges *Porifera*

Largest

The largest known sponge is the barrel-shaped Loggerhead sponge (*Spheciospongia vesparium*) of the West Indies and the waters off Florida.

Individuals measure up to 3 ft 6 in *105 cm* in height and 3 ft *91 cm* in diameter. Neptune's cup or goblet (*Poterion patera*) of Indonesia grows to 4 ft *120 cm* in height, but it is a less bulky animal. In 1909 a Wool sponge (*Hippospongia canaliculatta*) measuring 6 ft *183 cm* in circumference was collected off the Bahamas. When first taken from the water it weighed between 80 and 90 lb *36* and *41 kg* but after it had been dried and relieved of all excrescences it scaled 12 lb *5,44 kg* (this sponge is now preserved in the US National Museum, Washington, DC).

Smallest

The smallest known sponge is the widely distributed *Leucosolenia blanca*, which measures 3 mm *0.11 in* in height when fully grown.

Deepest

Sponges have been recovered from depths of up to 18,500 ft *5637 m*.

Extinct Animals

The first dinosaur to be scientifically described was *Megalosaurus bucklandi* ('great fossil lizard') in 1824. The remains of this 30 ft *9,1 m* long bipedal flesh-eater had been found by workmen before 1818 in a slate quarry near Woodstock, Oxfordshire, England and were later placed in the University Museum, Oxford.

Largest

The largest land vertebrates of all time were probably the brachiosaurids ('arm lizards') of the Late Jurassic (160 million years BP) of Tanzania, South Africa, Algeria, Portugal, Laos, Korea and the south-western USA. Weights up to 187 tonnes/*190 tons* have been claimed for the biggest members of this family by extrapolation from bone material, but palaeophysiologists (people who study the physical make-up of extinct animals) now believe that the actual tonnages of *Brachiosaurus brancai* (total length 25 m *82 ft*) and others are an estimated 45–50 tonnes/*tons* based on the mid-shaft circumferences of their long bones. In 1985 the remains of a diplodocid said to be 'the largest dinosaur ever known' were excavated from a site near Albuquerque, New Mexico, USA. According to the New Mexico Museum of Natural History this animal, named *Seismosaurus* ('earthshaker'), measured an estimated 100–120 ft *30–36 m* in total length and weighed at least 80 tonnes/*tons*.

Britain's largest known dinosaur was probably the diplodocid *Cetiosaurus oxoniensis* ('whale lizard'), which roamed across southern England about 150 million years ago. It measured up to 21 m *69 ft* in total length and weighed an estimated 27 tonnes/*tons*.

Smallest

The smallest dinosaurs so far recorded are the chicken-sized *Compsognathus* ('pretty jaw') of southern West Germany and south-east France, and an undescribed plant-eating fabrosaurid from Colorado. Both measured 75 cm *29.5 in* from the snout to the tip of the tail and weighed about 6,8 kg *15 lbs*.

Longest trackway

In 1983 a series of four *Apatosaurus* (= *Brontosaurus*) trackways which ran parallel for a distance of over 215 m *705 ft* were recorded from 145-million-year-old Jurassic strata in south-east Colorado.

Fastest

Trackways can be used to estimate dinosaur speeds, and one from the Lower Cretaceous of Texas discovered in 1981 indicated that a carnivorous dinosaur had been moving at 40 km/h *25 mph*. Some of the ornithomimids (ostrich dinosaurs) were even faster, and the large-brained 220 lb *100 kg* *Dromiceiomimus* ('emu mimic') of the Late Cretaceous of southern Alberta, Canada, could probably outsprint an ostrich, which has a top speed of 45 mph *72 km/h*.

Largest footprints

In 1932 the gigantic footprints of a large bipedal hadrosaurid (duckbill) measuring 1,36 m *53.5 in* in length and 81 cm *31.8 in* in diameter were discovered at Salt Lake City, Utah, and other reports from Colorado and Utah refer to footprints 95–100 cm *37.4–39.4 in* in diameter. Footprints attributed to the largest brachiosaurids also range up to 100 cm *39.3 in* in diameter for the hind feet, and the Korean *Ultrasaurus tabriensis* has yielded prints measuring 115 cm *45.28 in* in diameter.

Earliest

The earliest known dinosaur is a yet unnamed plant-eating prosauropod which lived 230,000,000 years ago. In 1984 a partial skeleton of this animal, which measured 2,4 m *8 ft* in length and weighed 67 kg *147 lb* when alive, was discovered in the Petrified Forest National Park, eastern

Arizona, USA by a team from the University of California.

Most brainless

Stegosaurus ('plated reptile'), which measured up to 30 ft *9 m* in total length had a walnut-sized brain weighing only 2½ oz *70g*, which represented 0.004 of 1 per cent of its computed body weight of 1¾ tons/*tonnes* (*cf.* 0.074 of 1 per cent for an elephant and 1.88 per cent for a human). It roamed across the states of Colorado, Oklahoma, Utah and Wyoming, USA, about 150,000,000 years ago.

Largest eggs

The largest known dinosaur eggs are those of *Hypselosaurus priscus*, ('high ridge lizard'), a 40 ft *12,19 m* long titanosaurid which lived about 80,000,000 years ago. Some examples found in the valley of the Durance near Aix-en-Provence, southern France in October 1961 would have had, uncrushed, a length of 12 in *300 mm* and a diameter of 10 in *255 mm* (capacity 5.8 pints *3,3 l*).

Largest land predator ● The largest flesh-eating dinosaur recorded so far is *Tyrannosaurus rex* ('king tyrant lizard'), which stalked across what are now the states of Montana, Wyoming and Texas in the USA, Alberta and Saskatchewan in Canada, and also Shandung province in China, during the Late Cretaceous. No complete skeleton of this carnosaur has ever been discovered, but the upper jaw bone (maxilla) in the Museum of Comparative Zoology at the University of California, Berkeley, is 900 mm *35.4 in* in length. It has been calculated that the owner of this jaw must have measured 44 ft *13,4 m* in total length and weighed 8.5 tonnes/ *tons*.

Map: Eddie Botchway

Artwork: Matthew Hillier FCSD.

Largest claws

The therizinosaurids ('scythe lizards') from the Late Cretaceous of the Nemegt Basin, southern Mongolia, had the largest claws of any known animal, and in the case of *Therizinosaurus cheloniformis* measured up to 36 in *91,4 cm* round the outer curve. (*cf.* 8 in *20,3 cm* for *T. rex*). It has been suggested that these suckle claws were designed for grasping and tearing apart large victims, but this creature had a feeble skull partially or entirely lacking teeth and probably lived on termites.

In January 1982, amateur fossil collector William Walker found a 30 cm *11,8 in* long clawbone in a clay pit in Surrey. Further excavations by a team from the Natural History Museum revealed that the owner of this huge claw measured more than 6 m *19 ft 8 in* in total length (estimated weight 2 tonnes/tons) and had a bipedal height of 3–4 m *9 ft 10 in–13 ft*. The dinosaur was subsequently named *Baryonyx walkeri* after its discoverer.

Largest flying creature

The largest flying creature was the pterosaur *Quetzalcoatlus northropi* ('feathered serpent') which glided over what is now Texas, and Alberta, Canada about 65 million years ago. Partial remains discovered in Big Bend National Park, western Texas in 1971 indicate that this reptile must have had a wing span of 11–12 m *36–39 ft* and weighed about *86 kg* 190 lb.

Britain's largest known flying reptile was *Ornithodesmus latidens*, which soared over what is now Hampshire and the Isle of Wight about 90,000,000 years ago. It had a wing expanse of *c.* 5 m *16 ft 4¼ in* allowing for the natural curve.

Largest marine reptile

The largest marine reptile ever recorded was *Kronosaurus queenslandicus*, a short-necked pliosaur from the Early Cretaceous (135 million years BP) of Australia. It had a 10 ft *3,04 m* long skull containing 80 massive teeth and measured up to 50 ft *15,2 m* in length.

Largest crocodile

The largest known crocodile was the euschian *Deinosuchus riograndensis*, which lived in the lakes and swamps of what is now the state of Texas, USA about 75 million years ago. Fragmentary remains discovered in Big Bend National Park, western Texas, indicate a hypothetical length of 16 m *52 ft 6 in*, compared with the 50 ft *15,2 m* of the huge gharial *Rhamphosuchus* of northern India (2 million years BP) and the 46 ft *14 m* of *Sarcosuchus imperator* of Niger.

Largest chelonians

The largest prehistoric chelonian was *Stupendemys geographicus*, a pelomedusid turtle which lived about 5 million years ago. Fossil remains discovered by Harvard University palaeontologists in northern Venezuela in 1972 indicate that this turtle had a carapace (shell) 218–230 cm *7 ft 2 in–7 ft 6¼ in* in mid-line length and measured 3 m *9 ft 10 in* in overall length. It had a computed weight of 4500 lb *2041 kg* in life.

Largest tortoise

The largest prehistoric tortoise was probably *Geochelone* (= *Colossochelys*) *atlas*, which lived in what is now northern India, Burma, Java, the Celebes and Timor, about 2 million years ago. In 1923 the fossil remains of a specimen with a carapace 5 ft 11 in *180 cm* long (7 ft 4 in *223 cm* over the curve) and 2 ft 11 in *89 cm* high were discovered near Chandigarh in the Siwalik Hills, India. This animal had a total length of 8 ft *2,44 m* and is computed to have weighed 2100 lb *852 kg* when it was alive.

Longest snake

The longest prehistoric snake was the python-like *Gigantophis garstini*, which inhabited what

is now Egypt about 55 million years ago. Parts of a spinal column and a small piece of jaw discovered at Fayum in the Western Desert indicate a length of *c.* 37 ft *11 m*.

Largest amphibian

The largest amphibian ever recorded was the gharial-like *Prionosuchus plummeri* which lived 230 million years ago. In 1972 the fragmented remains of a specimen measuring an estimated 9 m *30 ft* in life were discovered in northern Brazil.

Largest insect

The largest prehistoric insect was the dragonfly *Meganeura monyi*, which lived about 280 million years ago. Fossil remains (*i.e.* impressions of wings) discovered at Commentry, central France, indicate a wing extending up to 70 cm *27.5 in*.

Britain's largest dragonfly was *Pupus diluculum* (family Meganeuridae), which is known only from a wing impression found on a lump of coal in Bolsover colliery, Derbyshire in July 1978. It had an estimated wing span of 50–60 cm *19.68–23.62 in* and lived about 300 million years ago, making it the oldest flying creature so far recorded.

Largest bird

The largest prehistoric true bird was the flightless *Dromornis stirtoni*, a huge emu-like creature which lived in central Australia 11 million years ago. Fossil leg bones found near Alice Springs in 1974 indicate that the bird must have stood *c.* 10 ft *3 m* in height and weighed *c.* 1100 lb *500 kg*. The giant moa *Dinornis maximus* of New Zealand was even taller, attaining a maximum height of 12 ft *3,6 m*, but it weighed only about 500 lb *227 kg*.

The largest known flying bird was the Giant teratorn (*Argentavis magnificens*) which lived in Argentina about 6 million years ago. Fossil remains discovered at a site 100 miles *160 km* west of Buenos Aires in 1979 indicate that this gigantic vulture had a wing span of 7,0–7,6 m *23–25 ft* and weighed about 120 kg *265 lb*.

Largest mammal

The largest land mammal ever recorded was *Paraceratherium* (= *Baluchitherium*), a long-necked hornless rhinocerotid which roamed across western Asia and Europe (Yugoslavia) about 35 million years ago. A restoration in the American Museum of Natural History, New York

measures 17 ft 9 in *5,41 m* to the top of the shoulder hump and 37 ft *11,27 m* in total length, and this particular specimen must have weighed about 20 tonnes/tons. The bones of this gigantic browser were first discovered in the Bugti Hills in east Baluchistan, Pakistan in 1907–8.

The largest marine mammal was the serpentine *Basilosaurus* (*Zeuglodon*) *cetoides*, which swam in the seas over modern-day Arkansas and Alabama 50 million years ago. It measured up to 70 ft *21,3 m* in length.

Largest mammoth

The largest prehistoric elephant was the Steppe mammoth *Mammuthus* (*Parelephas*) *trogontherii*, which roamed over what is now central Europe a million years ago. A fragmentary skeleton found in Mosbach, West Germany indicates a shoulder height of 4,5 m *14 ft 9 in*.

Largest primate

The largest known primate was *Gigantopithecus*, which lived in Asia about 7 million years ago. The only remains that have been discovered so far are partial lower jaws and single teeth, but if this giant ape's body was in proportion to its massive jaw then it would have stood about 9 ft *2,74 m* tall when erect and weighed at least 600 lb *272 kg*.

Antlers

The prehistoric Giant deer (*Megaceros giganteus*), which lived in northern Europe and northern Asia as recently as 8000 BC, had the longest horns of any known animal. One specimen recovered from an Irish bog had greatly palmated antlers measuring 14 ft *4,3 m* across.

Tusks

The longest tusks of any prehistoric animal were those of the Straight-tusked elephant *Palaeoloxodon antiquus germanicus*, which lived in northern Germany about 300,000 years ago. The average length in adult bulls was 5 m *16 ft 5 in*. A single tusk of a Woolly mammoth (*Mammuthus primigenius*) preserved in the Franzens Museum at Brno, Czechoslovakia measures 5,02 m *16 ft 5¼ in* along the outside curve. In *c.* August 1933, a single tusk of an Imperial mammoth (*Mammuthus imperator*) measuring 16 + ft *4,87 + m* (anterior end missing) was unearthed near Post, Gorza County, in Texas. In 1934 this tusk was presented to the American Museum of Natural History in New York City.

The heaviest single fossil tusk on record is one weighing 150 kg *330 lb* with a maximum circum-

EARLIEST OF THEIR TYPES

Type	Scientific name and year of discovery	Location	Estimated years before present
Primate	Unnamed ape (May 1979)	Padaung Hills, Burma	40,000,000
Primate	Lemur	Madagascar	70,000,000
Primate	Tarsier-like	Indonesia	70,000,000
Insect	*Sphecomyrma freyi* (1967)	New Jersey, USA	110,000,000
Insect	*Archaeolepis* (1985) (moth)	Dorset coast, England	180,000,000
Mammal	*Megazostrodon* (1966)	Thaba-ea-Litau, Lesotho	190,000,000
Bird	*Protoavia* (1984)	Post, Texas, USA	225,000,000
Reptile	Unnamed (insectivorous) (1972)	Kentucky, USA	310,000,000
Amphibian	*Ichthyostega* (first quadruped)	Greenland	350,000,000
Arachnid	*Palaeostenzia crassipes*	Tayside, Scotland	370,000,000
Insect	*Rhyniella procursor*	Tayside, Scotland	370,000,000
Fish	*Branchiostoma*	Canada	550,000,000
Crustacean	*Karagassiema* (12-legged)	Sayan Mts, USSR	*c.* 650,000,000
Metazoans	Bore hole tracks	Zambia	1,000,000,000
Eukaryotes	(*c.* Sept 1983)	Tianjin, China	1,800,000,000
Microfossils	*Kakabekia barghoorniana* (1964–86)	Harlech, Gwnedd, Wales	4,000,000,000

Note: Free Oxygen began forming in the Earth's atmosphere about 2300 million years ago.

ference of 35 in *89 cm* now preserved in the Museo Civico di Storia Naturale in Milan. The specimen (in two pieces) measures 11 ft 9 in *3,58 m* in length.

The heaviest recorded fossil tusks are a pair belonging to a 13 ft 4 in *4,06 m* tall Columbian mammoth (*Mammuthus columbi*) in the State Museum, Lincoln, Nebraska, which have a combined weight of 498 lb *226 kg* and measure 13 ft 9 in *4,21 m* and 13 ft 7 in *4,14 m* respectively. They were found near Campbell, Nebraska in April 1915.

Plant Kingdom *Plantea*

PLANTS

The medicinal value of plants was known to Neanderthal man in Iraq *c.* 60,000 BC. The earliest evidence for a garden is a relief of proto-dynastic age *c.* 3000 BC in Egypt depicting a specimen palm in a protective enclosure amid irrigation or decorative waterways. Though the Romans had gardens in England from AD 43 the earliest surviving garden is at Romsey Abbey, Hampshire laid out *c.* 1092.

Oldest

'King Clone', the oldest known clone of the Creosote plant (*Larrea tridentata*), found in southwest California, was estimated in February 1980 by Prof Frank C. Vasek to be 11,700 years old. It is possible that crustose lichens in excess of 500 mm *19.6 in* in diameter may be as old. In 1981 it was estimated that Antarctic lichens of more than 100 mm *3.9 in* in diameter are at least 10,000 years old.

Rarest

Plants thought to be extinct are rediscovered each year and there are thus many plants of which specimens are known in but a single locality. Cuttings from a Cafe marron tree (*Ramsomania heterophylla*), a single specimen growing on Rodriguez Island, Indian Ocean, reported in April 1986 were flown to the Royal Botanical Gardens, Kew, west London in an attempt to propagate it and preserve the species. *Pennantia baylisiana*, a tree found in 1945 on Three Kings Island, off New Zealand, only exists as a female and cannot fruit. In May 1983 it was reported that there was a sole surviving specimen of the Lady's slipper orchid (*Cypripedium calceolus*).

Northernmost

The Yellow poppy (*Papaver radicatum*) and the Arctic willow (*Salix arctica*) survive, the latter in an extremely stunted form, on the northernmost land (83° N).

Southernmost

Lichens resembling *Rhinodina frigida* have been found in Moraine Canyon in 86°09′S 157°30′W in 1971 and in the Horlick Mountain area, Antarctica in 86°09′S 131°14′W in 1965. The southernmost recorded flowering plant is the Antarctic hair grass (*Deschampsia antarctica*) which was found in latitude 68°21′S on Refuge Island, Antarctica on 11 Mar 1981.

Highest

The greatest certain altitude at which any flowering plants have been found is 21,000 ft *6400 m* on Kamet (25,447 ft *7756 m*) by N. D. Jayal in 1955. They were *Ermania himalayensis* and *Ranunculus lobatus*.

Roots

The greatest reported depth to which roots have penetrated is a calculated 400 ft *120 m* in the case of a wild fig tree at Echo Caves, near Ohrigstad, eastern Transvaal, South Africa. An elm tree root of at least 360 ft *110 m* was reported

'It's the Biggest Aspidistra in the World' (*pace* Gracie Fields) ● It belongs to Cliff Evans of Kiora, Moruya, New South Wales, Australia and measures 56 in *142 cm.*

from Auchencraig, Largs, Ayrshire *c.* 1950. A single Winter rye plant (*Secale cereale*) has been shown to produce 387 miles *622,8 km* of roots in 1.83 ft³ *0,051 m³* of earth.

Worst weeds

The most intransigent weed is the mat-forming Water weed *Salvinia auriculata*, found in Africa. It was detected on the filling of Kariba Lake in May 1959 and within 11 months had choked an area of 77 miles² *199 km²* rising by 1963 to 387 miles² *1002 km²*. The world's worst land weeds are regarded as Purple nut sedge, Bermuda grass, Barnyard grass, Jungle-rice, Goose grass, Johnson grass, Guinea grass, Cogon grass and lantana.

The most damaging and widespread cereal weeds in Britain are the wild oats *Avena fatua* and *A. ludoviciana*. Their seeds can withstand temperatures of 240° F *115,6° C* for 15 min and remain viable. The largest weed in Britain is the Giant hogweed (*Heracleum manteggazzianum*) which established itself from seeds brought from the Caucasus before 1862. It reaches 12 ft *3,65 m*.

Most spreading

The greatest area covered by a single clonal growth is that of the wild Box huckleberry (*Gaylussacia brachyera*), a mat-forming evergreen shrub first reported in 1796. A colony covering about 100 acres *40 ha* was found on 18 July 1920 near the Juniata River, Pennsylvania. It has been estimated that this colony began 13,000 years ago.

Smallest flowering and fruiting

The floating flowering Aquatic duckweed (*Wolffia angusta*) of Australia, described in 1980, is only 0,6 mm $\frac{1}{42}$ *of an inch* in length and 0,33 mm $\frac{1}{85}$ *of an inch* in width. It weighs about 0,00015 g *1/190,000 of an oz*, its fruit resembling a miniscule fig weighs 0,00007 g or 400,000 to the oz.

The smallest land plant regularly flowering in Britain is the chaffweed (*Cetunculus minimus*), a single seed of which weighs 0,00003 of a gramme.

Fastest growing

The case of a *Hesperogucca whipplei* of the family Liliaceae growing 12 ft *3,65 m* in 14 days was reported from Tresco Abbey, Isles of Scilly in July 1978.

Slowest flowering

The slowest flowering of all plants is the rare *Puya raimondii*, the largest of all herbs, discovered at 13,000 ft *3960 m* in Bolivia in 1870. The panicle usually emerges after about 80–150 years of the plant's life. One planted near sea level at the University of California's Botanical Garden, Berkeley, in 1958 bloomed as early as August 1986 after only 28 years. It then dies. (See also below under Largest bloom.)

Oldest pot plant

The oldest known pot plant is the succulent *Fockea crispa* potted by Baron Jacquin (1728–1817) at the Schönbrunn gardens, Vienna *c.* 1801.

Biggest collection

Dr Julian A. Steyermark of the Herbario Nacional, Caracas, Venezuela, had by September 1985 made an unrivalled total of 137,000 collections of which 132,000 were solo.

Largest aspidistra

The aspidistra (*Aspidistra elatior*) was introduced to Britain as a parlour palm from Japan and China in 1822.

The biggest aspidistra known in Britain is one 50 in *127 cm* tall with more than 500 leaves spanning 5 ft *1,52 m* grown by Gertie James in Staveley, Chesterfield.

Earliest flower

The oldest fossil of a flowering plant with palm-like imprints was found in Colorado in 1953 and dated about 65,000,000 years old.

Largest cactus

The largest of all cacti is the Saguaro (*Cereus giganteus* or *Carnegiea gigantea*), found in Arizona, south-eastern California and Sonora, Mexico. The green fluted column is surmounted by candelabra-like branches rising to a height of 16 m *52 ft 6 in* in the case of a specimen measured on the boundary of the Saguaro National Monument, Arizona. They have waxy white blooms which are followed by edible crimson fruit. An armless cactus 78 ft *24 m* in height was measured in April 1978 by Hube Yates in Cave Creek, Arizona. It was toppled in a windstorm in July 1986 at an estimated age of 150 years.

Mosses

The smallest of mosses is the microscopic Pygmy moss (*Ephemerum*) and the longest is the Brook moss (*Fontinalis*), which forms streamers up to 3 ft *91 cm* long in flowing water.

SEAWEED

Longest

The longest species of seaweed is the Pacific giant kelp (*Macrocystis pyrifera*), which, although it does not exceed 196 ft *60 m* in length, can grow 45 cm *18 in* in a day.

The longest of the 700 species of British seaweed is the Brown seaweed *Chorda filum* which grows up to a length of 20 ft *6,10 m*. The Japanese *Sargassum muticum* introduced *c.* 1970 can grow to 30 ft *9,0 m*.

Deepest

The greatest depth at which plant life has been found is 884 ft *269 m* by Mark and Diane Littler (USA) off San Salvadore Island, Bahamas in October 1984. These maroon-coloured algae survived though 99.9995 per cent of sunlight was filtered out.

VINES AND VINEYARDS

Largest

This was planted in 1842 at Carpinteria, California. By 1900 it was yielding more than 9 tons/*tonnes* of grapes in some years, and averaging 7 tons/*tonnes* per year. It died in 1920. A single bunch of grapes (Red Thomson seedless) weighing 9400 grammes *20 lb 11½ oz* was weighed in Santiago, Chile in May 1984.

Britain's largest vine (1898–1964) was at Kippen, Stirling with a girth, measured in 1956, of 5 ft *1,52 m*. England's largest vine is the Great Vine, planted in 1768 at Hampton Court, London. Its girth is 85 in *215,9 cm* with branches up to 114 ft *34,7 m* long and an average yield of 703 lb *318,8 kg*. In 1986 Leslie Stringer of Dartford, Kent obtained a yield of 2241 lb *1016,5 kg* from a vine from Banstead, Surrey planted in 1962.

Most northerly and southerly

A vineyard at Sabile, Latvia, USSR is just north of Lat. 57° N. The most southerly commercial vineyards are to be found in central Otago, South Island, New Zealand south of Lat. 45° S.

The most northerly commercial vineyard in Britain is that at Renishaw Hall, Nr Chesterfield, Derbyshire with 2600 vines at Lat. 53° 18′ N.

BLOOMS AND FLOWERS

Largest

The largest known inflorescence as distinct from the largest of all blooms is that of *Puya raimondii*, a rare Bolivian monocarpic member of the Bromeliaceae family with an erect panicle (diameter 8 ft *2,4 m*) which emerges to a height of 35 ft *10,7 m*. Each of these bears up to 8000 white blooms (see also Slowest flowering plant above). The flower-spike of an agave was in 1974 measured to be 52 ft *15,8 m* long in Berkeley, California.

The world's largest blossoming plant is the giant Chinese wisteria (*wisteria sinensis*) at Sierra Madre, California. It was planted in 1892 and now has branches 500 ft *152 m* long. It covers nearly an acre, weighs 225 tons *228 tonnes* and has an estimated 1,500,000 blossoms during its blossoming period of five weeks, when up to 30,000 people pay admission to visit it.

The largest bloom of any indigenous British flowering plant is that of the Wild white water lily (*Nymphaea alba*), which measures 6 in *15 cm* across.

Most valuable

The Burpee Co $10,000 prize offered in 1954 for the first all-white marigold was won on 12 Aug 1975 by Alice Vonk of Sully, Iowa, USA.

Largest arrangement

The largest arrangement of a single variety of flower was made by Johan Weisz, floral designer of Amsterdam, and 15 assistants at the City Hall, Aalsmeer, Netherlands on 23–5 Sept 1986. It consisted of 35,000 'Zurella' roses and measured 21,8 m *71 ft 6 in* in length, 7,68 m *25 ft 2 in* in width and 7,59 m *24 ft 11 in* high.

Largest wreath

The largest wreath constructed was the wreath built by The Farm Stand, wholesale nurserymen of Walworth, New York, USA in November 1985 measuring 100 ft 8 in *30,68 m* in diameter and weighing 9840 lb *4463 kg*.

Longest daisy chain

The longest daisy chain, made in 7 hr, was one of 6980 ft 7 in *2,12 km* by villagers of Good Easter, Chelmsford, Essex on 27 May 1985. The team is limited to 16.

Largest rhododendron

The largest species of rhododendron is the scarlet *Rhododendron arboreum*, examples of which reach a height of 65 ft *19,8 m* on Mt Japfu, Nagaland, India. The cross-section of the trunk of a *Rhododendron giganteum*, reputedly 90 ft *27,43 m* high from Yunnan, China is preserved at Inverewe Gardens, Highland.

The largest in the United Kingdom is one 25 ft *7,60 m* tall and 272 ft *82,90 m* in circumference at Government House, Hillsborough, Co. Down. A specimen 35 ft *10,65 m* high and 3 ft 3 in *99 cm* in circumference has been measured at Tregothan, Truro.

Longest Philodendron

A Philodendron 1114 ft *339,5 m* in length was grown by Prof F. J. Francis of the University of Massachusetts, USA. It is now 32 years old.

Largest rose tree

A 'Lady Banks' rose tree at Tombstone, Arizona, has a trunk 40 in *101 cm* thick, stands 9 ft *2,74 m* high and covers an area of 5380 ft² *499 m²* supported by 68 posts and several thousand feet of piping. This enables 150 people to be seated under the arbour. The cutting came from Scotland in 1884.

ORCHIDS

Tallest

The largest of all orchids is *Grammatophyllum speciosum*, native to Malaysia. Specimens have been recorded up to 25 ft *7,62 m* in height.

Largest flower

The largest orchid flower is that of *Phragmipedium caudatum*, found in tropical areas of America. Its petals grow up to 18 in *46 cm* long, giving it a maximum outstretched diameter of 3 ft *91 cm*. The flower is, however, much less bulky than that of the Stinking corpse lily (see left). *Galeola foliata,* a saprophyte of the Vanilla family, has been recorded at a height of 49 ft *15 m*. It grows in the decaying rain forests of Queensland, Australia but is not free-standing.

The first flowering in Britain of *Grammatophyllum wallisii* from Mindanao, Philippines at Burnham Nurseries, Kingsteignton, Devon in 1982 produced 557 flowers.

Smallest

The smallest orchid is *Platystele jungermannnoides*, found in Central America. Its flowers are 1 mm *0.04 in* across.

Most expensive

The highest price ever paid for an orchid is 1150 guineas (£1,207.50), paid by Baron Schröder to Sanders of St Albans for an *Odontoglossum crispum* (variety *pittianum*) at an auction held by

Largest bloom ● The largest of all blooms, the parasitic Stinking corpse lily (*Rafflesia arnoldii*). They attach themselves to the cissus vines of the jungle in south-east Africa and measure up to 3 ft *91 cm* across and ¾ in *1,9 cm* thick, and attain a weight of 15 lb *7 kg*. True to name, the plant is extremely offensive in scent.

Protheroe & Morris of Bow Lane, London, on 22 Mar 1906. A Cymbidium orchid called Rosanna Pinkie was sold in the United States for $4500 (*then £1600*) in 1952.

FRUITS AND VEGETABLES

Most and least nutritive

An analysis of the 38 commonly eaten raw (as opposed to dried) fruits shows that the one with the highest calorific value is avocado (*Persea americana*), with 741 calories per edible pound or *163 cals per 100 gr*. That with the lowest value is cucumber with 73 calories per pound *16 cals per 100 gr*. Avocados probably originated in Central and South America and also contain vitamins A, C and E and 2.2 per cent protein.

Chilli

The tallest chilli plant was one of 6,6 m *21 ft 7 in* grown by Shri Kishan Joshi of Almora, India in 1985–6.

Peach

The largest peach reported in Britain is one of $14\frac{1}{2}$ oz *411 g*, 12 in *30,4 cm* in August 1984 from a 26-year-old Italian tree grown by Mrs Jean Bird of London SW6.

Pineapple

A pineapple weighing 17 lb 8 oz *7,96 kg* was harvested by Dole Philippines Inc at South Cotabato, Philippines in November 1984. Pineapples up to 13 kg *28.6 lb* were reported in 1978 from Tarauaca, Brazil.

Smallest sunflower ● A fully-mature sunflower 5,6 cm *2.2 in* tall grown by Michael Lenke in Lake Oswego, Oregon in 1985 using a patented 'Bonsai' technique.

UNITED KINGDOM FRUIT, VEGETABLES, FLOWERS

Many data subsequent to 1958 come from the annual *Garden News* and Phostrogen Ltd Giant Vegetable and Fruit Contest and the Super Sunflower Contest.

APPLE	3 lb 1 oz	*1,357 kg*	V. Loveridge	Ross-on-Wye, Hereford & Worcester	1965
ARTICHOKE	8 lb	*3,625 kg*	A. R. Lawson	Tollerton, North Yorkshire	1964
BEETROOT	29 lb	*13,154 kg*	F. A. Pulley	Maidstone, Kent	1964
BROAD BEAN	$23\frac{3}{8}$ in	*59,3 cm*	T. Currie	Jedburgh, Borders	1963
	$23\frac{3}{8}$ in	*59,3 cm*	Mrs M. Adrian	Irvine, Strathclyde	1982
BROCCOLI	28 lb $14\frac{3}{4}$ oz	*13,100 kg*	J. T. Cooke	Funtington, W. Sussex	1964
BRUSSELS SPROUT[1]	16 lb 1 oz	*7,285 kg*	E. E. Jenkins	Shipston-on-Stour, Warwickshire	1974
CABBAGE	114 lb 3 oz	*51,8 kg*	P. G. Barton	Cleckheaton, W. Yorkshire	1977
CABBAGE, RED[2]	42 lb	*19,05 kg*	R. Straw	Staveley, Derbyshire	1925
CARROT[3]	10 lb 4 oz	*4,649 kg*	E. Stone	East Woodyates, Wiltshire	1984
CAULIFLOWER	52 lb $11\frac{1}{2}$ oz	*23,900 kg*	J. T. Cooke	Funtington, W. Sussex	1966
CELERY	35 lb 8 oz	*16,1 kg*	E. Stone	East Woodyates, Wiltshire	1986
CUCUMBER[4]	13 lb $10\frac{3}{4}$ oz (indoor)	*6,201 kg*	A. Emery	Rochester, Kent	1984
	8 lb 4 oz (outdoor)	*3,740 kg*	C. Bowcock	Willaston, Merseyside	1973
	$43\frac{1}{2}$ in	*110 cm*	A. C. Rayment	Chelmsford, Essex	1984–6
DAHLIA[5]	10 ft 5 in	*3,17 m*	R. Lond	Diss, Norfolk	1985
DWARF BEAN	$17\frac{1}{2}$ in	*43,4 cm*	C. Bowcock	Willaston, Merseyside	1973
GLADIOLUS	8 ft $4\frac{1}{2}$ in	*2,55 m*	A. Breed	Melrose, Roxburgh, Borders	1981
GOOSEBERRY	2.06 oz	*58,5 g*	A. Dingle	Macclesfield, Cheshire	1978
GOURD	196 lb	*88,900 kg*	J. Leathes	Herringfleet Hall, Suffolk	1846
GRAPEFRUIT*[6]	3 lb 11 oz	*1,673 kg*	Willington G.C.	Willington, Bedfordshire	1986
HOLLYHOCK	24 ft 3 in	*7,39 m*	W. P. Walshe	Eastbourne, E. Sussex	1961
KALE[7]	12 ft tall	*3,65 m*	B. T. Newton	Mullion, Cornwall	1950
LEEK, BLANCH	9 lb $5\frac{1}{2}$ oz	*4,235 kg*	C. Bowcock	Willaston, Merseyside	1973
LEEK, POT	9 lb $9\frac{1}{8}$ oz	*4,34 kg*	R. Hankey	Bishop Auckland, Durham	1983
LEMON[8]	4 lb 11 oz	*2,13 kg*	Pershore College	Pershore, Worcestershire	1986
LETTUCE	25 lb	*11,335 kg*	C. Bowcock	Willaston, Merseyside	1974
LUPIN*	6 ft $0\frac{1}{2}$ in	*1,84 m*	J. Lawlor	New Malden, Surrey	1971
MANGOLD	$54\frac{1}{2}$ lb	*24,720 kg*	P. F. Scott	Sutton, Humberside	1971
MARROW	105 lb 8 oz	*47,85 kg*	D. C. Payne	Tewkesbury, Glos.	1982
MELON[9]	14 lb $2\frac{3}{4}$ oz	*6,42 kg*	R. D. Sainsbury	Paull, Hull, Humberside	1985
MUSHROOM[10]	54 in circum.	*1,37 m*	—	Hasketon, Suffolk	1957
ONION[11]	7 lb $11\frac{3}{4}$ oz	*3,508 kg*	W. Rodger	Crail, Fife	1984
PARSNIP[12]	$142\frac{3}{4}$ in	*3,62 m*	K. Lloyd	Kydwelly, Dyfed	1984
PEAPOD[13]	$10\frac{1}{8}$ in	*25,7 cm*	T. Currie	Jedburgh, Borders	1964
PEAR[14]	2 lb $10\frac{1}{2}$ oz	*1,200 kg*	Mrs. K. Loines	Hythe, Hampshire	1973
PETUNIA*[15]	8 ft 4 in	*2,53 m*	G. A. Warner	Dunfermline, Fife	1978
POTATO[16]	7 lb 1 oz	*3,200 kg*	J. H. East	Spalding, Lincolnshire	1963
	7 lb 1 oz	*3,200 kg*	J. P. Busby	Atherstone, Warwickshire	1982
PUMPKIN[17]	444 lb	*201,4 kg*	R. A. Butcher	Stockbridge, Hampshire	1984
RADISH[18]	17 lb	*7,711 kg*	K. Ayliffe	Brecon, Powys	1976
RHUBARB	5 lb 14 oz	*2,665 kg*	E. Stone	East Woodyates, Wiltshire	1985
RUNNER BEAN	$39\frac{1}{2}$ in	*100,3 cm*	J. Taylor	Shifnal, Shropshire	1986
SAVOY CABBAGE	38 lb 8 oz	*17,450 kg*	W. H. Neil	Retford, Nottinghamshire	1966
SHALLOT*	2 lb 12 oz (47 bulbs)	*1,245 kg*	M. Silverstoff	Falmouth, Cornwall	1977
STRAWBERRY	8.17 oz	*231 g*	G. Anderson	Folkestone, Kent	1983
SUGAR BEET[19]	30 lb 10 oz	*13,9 kg*	K. McLean	Meldreth, Hertfordshire	1984
SUNFLOWER[20]	23 ft $6\frac{1}{2}$ in tall	*7,17 m*	F. Kelland	Exeter, Devon	1976
SWEDE	48 lb 12 oz	*22,11 kg*	A. Foster	Alnwick, Northumberland	1980
TOMATO[21]	4 lb $5\frac{1}{2}$ oz	*1,970 kg*	R. G. Burrows	Huddersfield, Yorkshire	1985
TOMATO PLANT[22]	45 ft $9\frac{1}{2}$ in (length)	*13,96 m*	Chosen Hill School	Gloucester, Glos.	1981
TOMATO TRUSS	20 lb 4 oz	*9,175 kg*	C. Bowcock	Willaston, Merseyside	1973
TURNIP[23]	35 lb 4 oz	*15,975 kg*	C. W. Butler	Nafferton, Humberside	1972

Footnotes on these categories

1 *A Brussels Sprout plant measuring 11 ft 8 in* 3,55 m *was grown by Ralph G. Sadler of Watchbury Farm, Barford, Warwickshire on 6 July 1978.*

2 *The Swalwell, County Durham Red Cabbage of 1865 grown by William Collingwood (d. 8 Oct 1867) reputedly weighed 123 lb* 55,7 kg *and was 259 in* 6,57 m *in circumference.*

3 *A specimen of 7 kg* 15 lb 7 oz *was grown by Miss I. G. Scott of Nelson, New Zealand in October 1978. A 118 in* 2,99 m *specimen grown by Ken Ayliffe of Brecon, Powys was recorded in September 1986.*

4 *A Vietnamese variety 6 ft* 1,83 m *long was reported by L. Szabo of Debrecen, Hungary in September 1976.*

5 *A 16 ft 5 in* 5,0 m *dahlia was grown by Sam and Pat Barnes of Chattahoochee, Florida, USA in 1982.*

6 *A 6 lb $8\frac{1}{2}$ oz* 2,966 kg *specimen was weighed for Joshua and Allison Sosnow in Tucson, Arizona, USA on 21 Dec 1984.*

7 *F. Doven of Mt Lawley, Australia grew a kale measuring 4,16 m* 13 ft $7\frac{1}{2}$ in *in 1982.*

8 *An 8 lb 8 oz* 3,88 kg *lemon with a $29\frac{1}{2}$ in* 74,9 cm *girth was grown by Charlotte and Donald Knutzen of Whittier, California in August 1983.*

9 *Jason Bright, 10, of Hope, Arkansas, USA, grew a watermelon reported by Grace's Gardens in September 1985 to weigh 260 lb* 118 kg *and overtaking the joint record set by his father and grandfather.*

10 *Same size reported by J. Coombes at Mark, Somerset on 28 July 1965. In September 1968 one weighing 18 lb 10 oz* 8,425 kg *was reported from Whidbey I., Washington, USA. A specimen of the edible* Termitomyces titanicus *found near Kitwe, Zambia on 18 Dec 1978 measured 26 in* 63 cm *in diameter and weighed 5.5 lb* 2,5 kg. *A mushroom of 'nearly 100 lb' and 20 in* 51 cm *thick was reported from Potenza, Italy on 30 Oct 1985.*

11 *An onion of $7\frac{1}{2}$ lb* 3,4 kg *was grown by Nelson W. Hope of Cardiff, California in 1965 with a girth of 26 in* 66 cm. *Its original gross weight was reputedly 8 lb* 3,62 kg.

12 *One 60 in* 152 cm *long was reported by M. Zaninovich of Waneroo W. Australia.*

13 *A 25-inch* 63,5 cm *peapod was grown by Chad McInville in July 1986.*

14 *A specimen weighing 1,405 kg* 3.09 lb *was harvested on 10 May 1979 at Messrs K. & R. Yeomans, Arding, Armidale, New South Wales.*

15 *Bert Lawrence of Windham, New York, USA grew a petunia plant measured on 19 Sept 1985 at 13 ft 8 in* 4,16 m.

16 *One weighing 18 lb 4 oz* 8,275 kg *reported dug up by Thomas Siddal in his garden in Chester on 17 Feb 1795. A yield of 515 lb* 233,5 kg *from a $2\frac{1}{2}$ lb parent seed by Bowcock planted in April 1977. Six tubers weighing 54 lb 8 oz* 24,72 kg *by Alan Nunn of Rhodes, Greater Manchester were reported on 18 Sept 1949.*

17 *A pumpkin (*C. maxima*) of 671 lb* 304,3 kg *($143\frac{1}{4}$ in* 3,63 m *girth) grown by Robert Gancanz of Jacobstown, New Jersey won the World Pumpkin Federation contest at Collins, New York, on 13 Oct 1986.*

18 *A radish of 27 lb* 12,25 kg *and $27\frac{1}{2}$ in* 69,8 cm *long was grown by Ron Whitford in Wollongong, Australia in Nov 1985.*

19 *One weighing $45\frac{1}{2}$ lb* 20,63 kg *was grown by R. Meyer of Brawley, California in 1974.*

20 *A sunflower of 7,38 m* 24 ft $2\frac{1}{2}$ in *was grown by Martien Heijms of Oirschot, The Netherlands in 1983. A sunflower with a head measuring $32\frac{1}{4}$ in* 82 cm *in diameter was grown by Mrs Emily Martin of Maple Ridge, British Columbia, Canada in September 1983.*

21 *Gordon Graham of Edmond, Oklahoma, has grown a tomato of 7 lb 12 oz* 3,51 kg *in 1986.*

22 *Gordon Graham of Edmond, Oklahoma, has grown a tomato plant of 53 ft 6 in* 16,3 m *in 1985. Charles H. Wilber grew a cherry tomato plant with a height of 28 ft 7 in* 8,71 m *recorded in November 1985. It was reported at the Tsukuba Science Expo, Japan on 16 Sept 1985 that a single plant produced 12,312 tomatoes in 347 days.*

23 *A 73 lb* 33,1 kg *turnip was reported in Dec. 1768 and one of 51 lb* 23,1 kg *from Alaska in 1981.*

* *Not in official contest.*

The heaviest orange ever reported is one weighing 5 lb 8 oz 2,50 kg *exhibited in Nelspruit, South Africa on 19 June 1981. It was the size of a human head, but was stolen.*

Largest cucumber ● Mrs Eileen Chappel of Bowen Hills, Queensland, Australia, holding the cucumber which she grew. On 13 May 1986 it weighed in at 22 kg *48.5 lb*. (See also p. 47.)

Potato

A record display of 369 varieties of potato (*Solanum tuberosum*) was mounted on *BBC Record Breakers* by Donald MacLean on 16 Sept 1984.

HERBS

Herbs are not botanically defined but consist of plants whose leaves or roots are of culinary or medicinal value. The most heavily consumed is coriander (*Coriandrum sativum*). It is used in curry powder, confectionery, in bread and in gin.

FERNS

Largest

The largest of all the more than 6000 species of fern is the Tree fern (*Alsophila excelsa*) of Norfolk Island, in the South Pacific, which attains a height of up to 60 ft *18,28 m*.

The highest in Britain is bracken *Pteridium aquilinum* measuring over 16 ft *4,8 m* in Ruislip, Middlesex in 1970.

Smallest

The world's smallest ferns are *Hecistopteris pumila*, found in Central America, and *Azolla caroliniana*, which is native to the United States and has fronds down to ½ in *12 mm*.

GRASSES

Commonest

The world's commonest grass is *Cynodon dactylon* or Bermuda grass. The 'Callie' hybrid, selected in 1966, grows as much as 6 in *15,2 cm* a day and stolons reach 18 ft *5,5 m* in length.

Fastest growing

Some species of the 45 genera of bamboo have been measured to grow at up to 36 in *91 cm* per day (0.00002 mph *0,00003 km/h*).

Tallest

A Thorney bamboo culm (*Bambusa arundinacea*) felled at Pattazhi, Travancore, India in November 1904 measured 121½ ft *37,0 m*. The tallest of the

160 grasses found in Great Britain is the Common reed (*Phragmites communis*), which reaches a height of 9 ft 9 in *2,97 m*.

Shortest

The shortest grass native to Great Britain is the very rare sand bent (*Mibora minima*) from Anglesey which has a maximum growing height of under 6 in *15 cm*.

LEAVES

Largest

The largest leaves of any plant belong to the Raffia palm (*Raphia raffia*) of the Mascarene Islands, in the Indian Ocean, and the Amazonian bamboo palm (*R. toedigera*) of South America, whose leaf blades may measure up to 65 ft *19,81 m* in length with petioles up to 13 ft *3,96 m*.

The largest undivided leaf is that of *Alocasia macrorrhiza*, found in Sabah, East Malaysia. One found in 1966 was 9 ft 11 in *3,02 m* long and 6 ft 3½ in *1,92 m* wide, with a unilateral area of 34.2 ft² *3,17 m²*.

The largest leaves to be found in outdoor plants in Great Britain are those of *Gunnera manicata* from Brazil with leaves 6–10 ft *1,82–3,04 m* across on prickly stems 5–8 ft *1,52–2,43 m* long.

Fourteen-leafed clover

A fourteen-leafed white clover (*Trifolium repens*) was found by Randy Farland near Sioux Falls, South Dakota on 16 June 1975.

SEEDS

Largest

The largest seed in the world is that of the double coconut or Coco de Mer (*Lodoicea seychellarum*), the single-seeded fruit of which may weigh 40 lb *18 kg*. This grows only in the Seychelles, in the Indian Ocean.

Smallest

The smallest seeds are those of epiphytic orchids, at 35,000,000 to the oz (*cf.* grass pollens at up to 6,000,000,000 grains/oz). A single plant of the American ragweed can generate 8,000,000,000 pollen grains in five hours.

Most viable

The most protracted claim for the viability of seeds is that made for the Arctic lupin (*Lupinus arcticus*) found in frozen silt at Miller Creek in the Yukon, Canada in July 1954 by Harold Schmidt. The seeds were germinated in 1966 and were dated by the radiocarbon method of associated material to at least 8000 BC and more probably to 13,000 BC.

Most conquering conker

The highest recorded battle honours for an untreated conker (fruit of the Common horse-chestnut or *Aesculus hippocastanum*) is a 'five thousander plus', which won the BBC Conker Conquest in 1954. A professor of botany has however opined that this heroic specimen might well have been a 'ringer', probably an ivory or tagua nut (*Phytelephas macrocarpa*). The *Guinness Book of Records* will not publish any category for the largest collection of conkers for fear that trees might suffer wholesale damage.

HEDGES

Tallest

The world's tallest hedge is the Meikleour beech hedge in Perthshire. It was planted in 1746 and has now attained a trimmed height of 85 ft *26 m*. It is 600 yd *550 m* long. Some of its trees now exceed 105 ft *32 m*.

Tallest yew

The tallest yew hedge in the world is in Earl Bathurst's Park, Cirencester, Gloucestershire. It was planted in 1720, runs for 170 yd *155 m*, reaches 36 ft *11 m*, is 15 ft *4,5 m* thick at its base and takes 20 man-days to trim.

Tallest box

The tallest box hedge is 35 ft *10,7 m* in height at Birr Castle, Offaly, Ireland dating from the 18th century.

TREES AND WOOD

Most massive

The most massive living thing on Earth is the biggest known Giant Sequoia (*Sequoiadendron giganteum*) named the 'General Sherman', standing 274.9 ft *83,8 m* tall, in the Sequoia National Park, California, USA. It has a true girth of 114.6 ft *34,9 m* (1980) (at 5 ft *1,52 m* above the ground). The 'General Sherman' has been estimated to contain the equivalent of 600,120 board feet of timber, sufficient to make 5,000,000,000 matches. The foliage is blue-green, and the red-brown tan bark may be up to 24 in *61 cm* thick in parts. Estimates place its weight, including its root system, at 2500 tons/*tonnes* but the timber is light (18 lb/ft³ *288,3 kg/m³*). This 2500-year-old monster has an annual growth rate of almost a millimetre ($\frac{1}{25}$ *in*)—the volume contained in a tree 15 m *49.2 ft* tall and 30 cm *1 ft* in diameter. The largest known petrified tree is one of this species with a 295 ft *89,9 m* trunk near Coaldale, Nevada.

The seed of a 'big tree' weighs only 1/6000th of an oz *4,7 mg*. Its growth at maturity may therefore represent an increase in weight of 1,300,000 million-fold.

The tree canopy covering the greatest area is the great Banyan *Ficus benghalensis* in the Indian Botanical Garden, Calcutta with 1775 prop or supporting roots and a circumference of 1350 ft *412 m*. It covers overall some 3 acres *1,2 ha* and dates from *ante* 1787.

Greatest girth

'El Arbol del Tule', in the state of Oaxaca, in Mexico is a 135 ft *41 m* tall Montezuma cypress (*Taxodium mucronatum*) with a girth of 117.6 ft *35,8 m* at a height of 5 ft *1,52 m* above the ground in 1982. A figure of 167 ft *51 m* in circumference was reported for the pollarded European chestnut (*Castanea sativa*) known as the 'Tree of the 100 Horses' (Castagno di Cento Cavalli) on Mount Etna, Sicily in 1972 and measurements up to 180 ft *54,5 m* have been attributed to Baobab trees (*Adansonia digitata*).

The tree of greatest girth in Britain is a sweet ('Spanish') chestnut (*Castanea sativa*) in the grounds of Canford School, nr Wimborne, Dorset, with a bole 43 ft 9 in *13,33 m* in circumference. The largest-girthed living British oak is one at Bowthorpe Farm near Bourne, south Lincolnshire, measured in September 1973 to be 39 ft 1 in *11,91 m*. The largest 'maiden' (*i.e.* not pollarded) oak is the Majesty Oak at Fredville Park, near Nonington, Kent, with a girth of 38 ft 1 in *11,60 m* (1973). The largest yew with a clear bole at 5 ft *1,52 m* is 35 ft 5 in *10,79 m* at Ulcombe Church, Kent.

Fastest growing

Discounting bamboo, which is not botanically classified as a tree, but as a woody grass, the fastest rate of growth recorded is 35 ft 3 in *10,74 m* in 13 months by an *Albizzia falcata* planted on 17 June 1974 in Sabah, Malaysia. The youngest recorded age for a tree to reach 100 ft *30,48 m* is 64 months for one of the species planted on 24 Feb 1975, also in Sabah.

Slowest growing

The speed of growth of trees depends largely upon conditions, although some species, such as box and yew, are always slow-growing. The extreme is represented by a specimen of Sitka spruce which required 98 years to grow to 11 in *28 cm* tall with a diameter of less than 1 in *2,5 cm* on the Arctic tree-line. The growing of miniature trees or *bonsai* is an oriental cult mentioned as early as *c.* 1320.

Tallest

The tallest tree ever measured was a Douglas Fir *Pseudotsuga menziesii* in Lynn Valley, British Columbia, in 1902. It stood 415 ft *126,5 m*. According to the researches of Dr A. C. Carder (Canada) the closest measured rivals to this champion have been:

ft	m	
393	*119,7*	The Mineral Douglas fir *Pseudotsuga menziesii*, Washington State, 1905
380	*115,8*	Nisqually fir *Pseudotsuga menziesii*, Nisqually River, Washington State, 1899
375	*114,3*	Cornthwaite Mountain ash *Eucalyptus regnans*, Thorpdale, Victoria, Australia, 1880
*367.8	*112,1*	'Tallest Tree', Redwood Creek *Sequoia sempervirens*, Humboldt County, California, 1963
367.6	*112*	Coast redwood *Sequoia sempervirens*, Guerneville, California, 1873

* Tallest standing tree in the world. Crown dying back. Height last re-estimated at 362 ft *110,3 m* in 1972.

Currently the tallest standing broadleaf tree is a mountain ash in the Styx Valley, Tasmania at 325 ft *99 m*.

The tallest trees in Great Britain are a Grand fir (*Abies grandis*) at Strone, Cairndow, Argyllshire and Douglas firs at The Hermitage, Perth, and in Moniac Glen, Inverness. In June 1985 all were 200–203 ft *61–62 m*. Only the Strone grand fir can be measured from both sides. At 203 ft *62 m* and still making visible annual increase, this is the best claimant. The tallest in England is a Douglas fir (*Pseudotsuga taxifolia*) measured at 174 ft *53,0 m* at Broadwood, Dunster, Somerset. The tallest measured in Northern Ireland is a Giant Sequoia (*Sequoiadendron giganteum*), measured in 1983 to be 164 ft *50 m* tall at Caledon Castle, County Tyrone. The tallest in Wales is a grand fir at Leighton Park, Powys (pl. 1886) measured in 1982 to be 190 ft *58 m*.

The tallest tree in Ireland is a Sitka spruce (*Picea sitchensis*) 166 ft *50,59 m* tall at Curraghmore, Waterford, measured in March 1974.

Christmas

The world's tallest cut Christmas tree was a 221 ft *67,36 m* tall Douglas fir (*Pseudotsuga taxifolia*) erected at Northgate Shopping Center, Seattle, Washington in December 1950.

The tallest Christmas tree erected in Britain was an 85 ft 3¼ in *25,98 m* long spruce from Norway erected for the Canterbury Cathedral appeal on the South Bank, London on 20 Nov 1975.

Oldest

The oldest recorded tree was a Bristlecone pine (*Pinus longaeva*) designated WPN-114, which grew at 10,750 ft *3275 m* above sea level on the north-east face of Mt Wheeler, eastern Nevada. It was found to be 5100 years old. The oldest known *living* tree is the Bristlecone pine named 'Methuselah' at 10,000 ft *3050 m* in the California side of the White Mountains confirmed as 4600 years old. In March 1974 it was reported that this tree had produced 48 live seedlings. Dendrochronologists estimate the *potential* life-span of a bristlecone pine at nearly 5500 years, but that of a California big tree (*Sequoia giganteum*) at perhaps 6000 years. No single cell lives more than 30 years.

Of all British trees that with the longest life is the Yew (*Taxus baccata*), for which a maximum age well in excess of 1000 years is usually conceded. The oldest known is the Fortingall Yew near Aberfeldy, Perthshire, part of which still grows. In 1777 this tree was over 50 ft *15,24 m* in girth and it cannot be much less than 2500 years old today.

Earliest species

The earliest species of tree still surviving is the Maiden-hair tree (*Ginkgo biloba*) of Zhekiang, China, which first appeared about 160,000,000 years ago, during the Jurassic era. It was 'rediscovered' by Kaempfer (Netherlands) in 1690 and reached England *c.* 1754. It has been grown in Japan since *c.* 1100 where it was known as *ginkyō* ('silver apricot') and is now known as *icho*.

Most leaves

Little work has been done on the laborious task of establishing which species has most leaves. A large oak has perhaps 250,000 but a cypress may have some 45–50 million leaf scales.

Remotest

The tree believed to be the remotest from any other is a Norwegian spruce, the only one on Campbell Island, Antarctica. Its nearest companion would be over 120 miles *145 km* away on the Auckland Islands.

Most expensive

The highest price ever paid for a tree is $51,000 (then £18,214) for a single Starkspur Golden Delicious apple tree from near Yakima, Washington, USA, bought by a nursery in Missouri in 1959.

Largest forest

The largest afforested areas in the world are the vast coniferous forests of the northern USSR, lying between latitude 55° N and the Arctic Circle. The total wooded area amounts to 2,700,000,000 acres *1100 million ha* (25 per cent of the world's forests), of which 38 per cent is Siberian larch. The USSR is 34 per cent afforested.

The largest forest in England is Kielder Forest (72,336 acres *29 273 ha*), in Northumberland. The largest in Wales is the Coed Morgannwg (Forest of Glamorgan) (42,555 acres *17 221 ha*). Scotland's most extensive forest is the Glen Trool Forest (51,376 acres *20 791 ha*) in Kirkcudbright, Dumfries & Galloway. The United Kingdom is 7 per cent afforested.

Longest avenue

The longest avenue of trees has been the now partly-felled private avenue of 1750 beeches in Savernake Forest near Marlborough, Wiltshire. It measured 3.25 miles *5,23 km*.

Heaviest wood

The heaviest of all woods is Black ironwood (*Olea laurifolia*), also called South African ironwood, with a specific gravity of up to 1.49, and weighing up to 93 lb/ft³ *1490 kg/m³*.

The heaviest British wood is boxwood (*Buxus sempervirens*) with an extreme of 64 lb/ft³ *1025 kg/m³*.

Lightest wood

The lightest wood is *Aeschynomene hispida*, found in Cuba, which has a specific gravity of 0.044 and a weight of only 2¾ lb/ft³ *44 kg/m³*. The wood of the Balsa tree (*Ochroma pyramidale*) is of very variable density—between 2½ and 24 lb/ft³ *40* and *384 kg/m³*. The density of cork is 15 lb/ft³ *240 kg/m³*.

Kingdom Protista

Protista were first discovered in 1676 by Antonie van Leeuwenhoek of Delft (1632–1723), a Dutch microscopist. Among Protista are characteristics common to both plants and animals. The more plant-like are termed Protophyta (protophytes), including unicellular algae, and the more animal-like are placed in the phylum Protozoa (protozoans), including amoeba and flagellates.

Largest

The largest protozoans in terms of volume which are known to have existed were calcareous foraminifera (Foraminiferida) belonging to the genus *Nummulites*, a species of which, in the Middle Eocene rocks of Turkey, attained 22 cm *8.6 in* in diameter. The largest existing protozoan, a species of the fan-shaped *Stannophyllum* (Xenophyophorida), can exceed this in length (25 cm *9.8 in* has been recorded) but not in volume.

Smallest

The smallest of all protophytes is the marine microflagellate alga *Micromonas pusilla*, with a diameter of less than 2 microns or micrometres $(2 \times 10^{-6}$ m) or *0.00008 in*.

Fastest

The protozoan *Monas stigmatica* has been measured to move a distance equivalent to 40 times its own length in a second. No human can cover even seven times his own length in a second.

Fastest reproduction

The protozoan *Glaucoma*, which reproduces by binary fission, divides as frequently as every three hours. Thus in the course of a day it could become a 'six greats grandparent' and the progenitor of 510 descendants.

Kingdom Fungi

Largest

Martin Mortenson, a science teacher at Dodgeland Junior High, Reeseville, Wisconsin, found a Puff ball (*Calvatia gigantea*) 76½ in *194,3 cm* in circumference in 1985. A 72 lb *32,6 kg* example of the edible mushroom (*Polyporus frondosus*) was reported by Joseph Opple near Solon, Ohio in September 1976. The largest officially recorded tree fungus was a specimen of *Oxyporus* (*Fomes*) *nobilissimus*, measuring 56 in *142 cm* by 37 in *94 cm* and weighing at least 300 lb *136 kg* found by J. Hisey in Washington State, USA, in 1946.

The largest recorded in the United Kingdom is an Ash fungus (*Fomes fraxineus*) measuring 50 in by 15 in *127 cm* by *38 cm* wide, found by the forester A. D. C. LeSueur on a tree at Waddesdon, Buckinghamshire, in 1954.

Most poisonous toadstool

The yellowish-olive Death cap (*Amanita phalloides*) is regarded as the world's most poisonous fungus. It is found in England. From six to fifteen hours after tasting, the effects are vomiting, delirium, collapse and death. Among its victims was Cardinal Giulio de' Medici, Pope Clement VII (b. 1478) on 25 Sept 1534.

In the United Kingdom there were 39 fatalities from fungus poisoning between 1920 and 1950. As the poisonous types are mostly *Amanita* varieties, it is reasonable to assume that the deaths were predominantly due to *Amanita phalloides*. The most recent fatality was probably in 1960.

Aeroflora

Fungi were once classified in the subkingdom Protophyta of the Kingdom Protista. The highest total fungal spore count was 161,037 per m³ near Cardiff on 21 July 1971. A plane tree pollen count of 2160 per m³ was recorded near London on 9 May 1971. The lowest counts of airborne allergens are nil.

The highest recorded grass pollen count in Britain was one of 2824 per m³ recorded at Aberystwyth on 29 June 1961.

Kingdom Procaryota

Earliest

The earliest life form reported from Britain is *Kakabekia barghoorniana*, a micro-organism similar in form to an orange slice, found near Harlech, Gwynedd, Wales in 1964 and dated to 4000 million years ago in July 1986.

BACTERIA

Antonie van Leeuwenhoek (1632–1723) was the first to observe bacteria, in 1675. The largest of the bacteria is the sulphur bacterium *Beggiatoa mirabilis*, which is from 16 to 45 microns in width and which may form filaments several millimetres long.

The bacteria *Thermoactinomyces vulgaris* have been found alive in cores of mud taken from the bottom of Windermere, Cumbria, England and have been dated to 1500 years before the present.

Smallest free-living entity

The smallest of all free-living organisms are pleuro-pneumonia-like organisms (PPLO) of the *Mycoplasma*. One of these, *Mycoplasma laidlawii*, first discovered in sewage in 1936, has a diameter during its early existence of only 100 millimicrons, or 0.000004 in. Examples of the strain known as H.39 have a maximum diameter of 300 millimicrons and weigh an estimated 1.0×10^{-16} gramme. Thus a 190-tonne blue whale would weigh 1.9×10^{24} or 1.9 quadrillion times as much.

Highest

In April 1967 the US National Aeronautics and Space Administration (NASA) reported that bacteria had been discovered at an altitude of 135,000 ft (25.56 miles) *41 100 m*.

Oldest

The oldest deposits from which living bacteria are claimed to have been extracted are salt layers near Irkutsk, USSR, dating from about 600,000,000 years ago, but the discovery was not accepted internationally. The US Dry Valley Drilling Project in Antarctica claimed resuscitated rod-shaped bacteria from caves up to a million years old.

Fastest

The rod-shaped bacillus *Bdellovibrio bacteriovorus*, by means of a polar flagellum rotating 100 times/sec, can move 50 times its own length of 2 μm per second. This would be the equivalent of a human sprinter reaching 200 mph *320 km/h* or a swimmer crossing the English Channel in 6 min.

Toughest

The bacterium *Micrococcus radiodurans* can withstand atomic radiation of 6.5 million röntgens or 10,000 times that fatal to the average man. In March 1983 John Barras (University of Oregon) reported bacteria from sulfurous sea bed vents thriving at 306°C *583°F* in the East Pacific Rise at Lat. 21°N.

VIRUSES

Largest

Dmitriy Ivanovsky (1864–1920) first reported filterable objects in 1892 but Martinus Willem Beijerink (1851–1931) first confirmed the nature of viruses in 1898. These are now defined as aggregates of two or more types of chemical (including either DNA or RNA) which are infectious and potentially pathogenic. The longest known is the rod-shaped *Citrus tristeza* virus with particles measuring 200×10 nm (1 nanometre = 1×10^{-9} m).

Smallest

The smallest known viruses are the nucleoprotein plant viruses such as the satellite of tobacco *Necrosis virus* with spherical particles 17 nm in diameter. A putative new infectious submicroscopic organism but without nucleic acid, named a 'prion', was announced from the University of California in February 1982. Viroids (RNA cores without protein coating) are much smaller than viruses. They were discovered by Theodor O. Diener (USA) in February 1972. Dr Rohwer of Bethesda, Maryland, stated in September 1984 that scrapie-specific protein was smaller than the concept of a 'yet to be identified prion'.

Parks, Zoos, Oceanaria, Aquaria

PARKS

Largest

The world's largest park is the Wood Buffalo National Park in Alberta, Canada (established 1922), which has an area of 11,172,000 acres (17,560 miles² *45 480 km²*).

The largest national park in Great Britain is the Lake District National Park which has an area of 866 miles² *2240 km²*. The largest private park in the United Kingdom is Woburn Park (3000 acres *1200 ha*), near Woburn Abbey, the seat of the Dukes of Bedford.

ZOOS

It has been estimated that throughout the world there are some 500 zoos with an estimated annual attendance of 330,000,000.

Oldest

The earliest known collection of animals was that set up by Shulgi, a 3rd-dynasty ruler of Ur in 2094–2097 BC at Puzurish in south-east Iraq. The oldest known zoo is that at Schönbrunn, Vienna, built in 1752 by the Holy Roman Emperor Franz I for his wife Maria Theresa. The oldest existing privately-owned zoo in the world is that of the Zoological Society of London, founded in 1826. Its collection, housed partly in Regent's Park, London (36 acres *14,5 ha*) and partly at Whipsnade Park, Bedfordshire (541 acres *219 ha*) (opened 23 May 1931), is the most comprehensive in the United Kingdom. The stocktaking on 1 Jan 1987 accounted for a total of 10,538 specimens. These comprised 2628 mammals, 1916 birds, 664 reptiles and amphibians, an estimated total of 2290 fish and an estimated total of 3040 invertebrates excluding some common species. The record annual attendances are 3,031,571 in 1950 for Regent's Park and 756,758 in 1961 for Whipsnade.

OCEANARIA

Earliest

The world's first oceanarium is Marineland of Florida, opened in 1938 at a site 18 miles *29 km* south of St Augustine, Florida. Up to 5,800,000 gal *26,3 million litres* of sea-water are pumped daily through two major tanks, one rectangular (100 ft *30,48 m* long by 40 ft *12,19 m* wide by 18 ft *5,48 m* deep) containing 375,000 gal *1,7 million litres*, and one circular (233 ft *71 m* in circumference and 12 ft *3,65 m* deep) containing 330,000 gal *1,5 million litres*. The tanks are seascaped, including coral reefs and even a shipwreck.

AQUARIA

Largest aquarium

The world's largest aquarium, as opposed to fish farm, is the $40 million Monterey Bay Aquarium, California opened on 20 Oct 1984. The two biggest tanks hold 335,000 and 326,000 US gallons.

Largest game reserve ● A herd of African elephants, the largest living land animals, in the Etosha National Park, Namibia, the world's largest zoological reserve. Established in 1907, its area has grown to 38,427 square miles *99,525 km²*. (Photo: Jen and Des Bartlett/Bruce Coleman)

THE
NATURAL
WORLD

CHAPTER THREE

Tallest Mountain ● Mauna Kea on the Island
of Hawaii measures 33,476 ft *10 203 m* from its
submarine base to its peak which is 13,796 ft
4205 m above sea-level. On top among some
small remaining pockets of snow sit four
astronomical observatories. (Photo: Colorific)

THE EARTH

The Earth is not a true sphere, but flattened at the poles and hence an oblate spheroid. The polar diameter of the Earth (7899.806 miles *12 713,505 km*) is 26.575 miles *42,769 km* less than the equatorial diameter (7926.381 miles *12 756,274 km*). The Earth has a pear-shaped asymmetry with the north polar radius being 148 ft *45 m* longer than the south polar radius. There is also a slight ellipticity of the equator since its long axis (about longitude 37° W) is 522 ft *159 m* greater than the short axis. The greatest departures from the reference ellipsoid are a protuberance of 240 ft *73 m* in the area of Papua New Guinea and a depression of 344 ft *105 m* south of Sri Lanka, in the Indian Ocean.

The greatest circumference of the Earth, at the equator, is 24,901.46 miles *40 075,02 km*, compared with 24,859.73 miles *40 007,86 km* at the meridian. The area of the surface is estimated to be 196,937,400 miles^2 *510 065 600 km²*. The period of axial rotation, *i.e.* the true sidereal day, is 23 hr 56 min 4.0996 sec, mean time.

The mass of the Earth was first assessed by Dr Nevil Maskelyne (1732–1811) in Perthshire, Scotland in 1774. The modern value is 5,879,000,000,000,000,000,000,000 tons *5,937 × 10²¹ tonnes* and its density is 5.515 times that of water. The volume is an estimated 259,875,300,000 miles^3 *1 083 207 000 000 km³*. The Earth picks up cosmic dust but estimates vary widely with 30,000 tons/*tonnes* a year being the upper limit. Modern theory is that the Earth has an outer shell or lithosphere 50 miles *80 km* thick, then an outer and inner rock layer or mantle extending 1745 miles *2809 km* deep, beneath which there is an iron-rich core of radius 2164 miles *3482 km*. If the iron-rich core theory is correct, iron would be the most abundant element in the Earth. At the centre of the core the estimated density is 13,09 g/cm³, the temperature 4500°C and the pressure 23,600 tons f/in² or 364 GPa.

Structure and Dimensions

OCEANS

Deepest

The deepest part of the ocean was first pinpointed in 1951 by HM Survey Ship *Challenger* in the Marianas Trench in the Pacific Ocean. The depth was measured by wide-band sounding at 5940 fathoms (35,640 ft *10 863 m*). Subsequent visits have resulted in slightly deeper measurements by multi-beam sonar now refined to 6034 fathoms (36,204 ft *11 034 m*) or 6.85 miles made by the Soviet research ship *Vityaz* in 1959. On 23 Jan 1960 the US Navy bathyscaphe *Trieste* descended to the bottom at 5970 fathoms (35,820 ft *10 917 m*).

A metal object, say a pound ball of steel, dropped into water above this trench would take nearly 64 min to fall to the sea bed, where hydrostatic pressure is over 18,000 lb/in² *1250 bars*.

The deepest point in the territorial waters of the United Kingdom is an area 6 cables (*1100 m*) off the island of Raasay, off Skye, in the Inner Sound at Lat. 57° 30′ 33″ N, Long. 5° 57′ 27″ W.

Largest sea

The largest of the world's seas is the South China Sea, with an area of 1,148,500 miles^2 *2 974 600 km²*.

Largest gulf

The largest gulf in the world is the Gulf of Mexico, with an area of 580,000 miles^2 *1 500 000 km²* and a shoreline of 3100 miles *4990 km* from Cape Sable, Florida, to Cabo Catoche, Mexico.

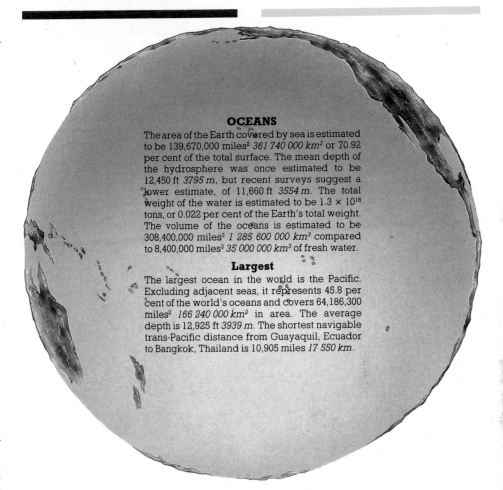

OCEANS

The area of the Earth covered by sea is estimated to be 139,670,000 miles^2 *361 740 000 km²* or 70.92 per cent of the total surface. The mean depth of the hydrosphere was once estimated to be 12,450 ft *3795 m*, but recent surveys suggest a lower estimate, of 11,660 ft *3554 m*. The total weight of the water is estimated to be 1.3 × 10¹⁸ tons, or 0.022 per cent of the Earth's total weight. The volume of the oceans is estimated to be 308,400,000 miles^3 *1 285 600 000 km³* compared to 8,400,000 miles^3 *35 000 000 km³* of fresh water.

Largest

The largest ocean in the world is the Pacific. Excluding adjacent seas, it represents 45.8 per cent of the world's oceans and covers 64,186,300 miles^2 *166 240 000 km²* in area. The average depth is 12,925 ft *3939 m*. The shortest navigable trans-Pacific distance from Guayaquil, Ecuador to Bangkok, Thailand is 10,905 miles *17 550 km*.

Largest bay

The largest bay in the world measured by shoreline length is Hudson Bay, northern Canada, with a shoreline of 7623 miles *12 268 km* and with an area of 317,500 miles^2 *822 300 km²*. The area of the Bay of Bengal is however 839,000 miles^2 *2 172 000 km²*.

Great Britain's largest bay is Cardigan Bay which has a 140 mile *225 km* long shoreline and measures 72 miles *116 km* across from the Lleyn Peninsula, Gwynedd to St David's Head, Dyfed in Wales.

Longest fjord

The world's longest fjord is the Nordvest Fjord arm of the Scoresby Sund in eastern Greenland, which extends inland 195 miles *313 km* from the sea. The longest Norwegian fjord is the Sogne Fjord, which extends 183 km *113.7 miles* inland from Sygnefest to the head of the Lusterfjord arm at Skjolden. It averages barely 4,75 km *3 miles* in width and has a deepest point of 1245 m *4085 ft*. If measured from Huglo along the Bømlafjord to the head of the Sørfjord arm at Odda, Hardangerfjorden can also be said to extend 183 km *113.7 miles*. The longest Danish fjord is Limfjorden (100 miles *160 km*).

Longest sea loch

Loch Fyne, Scotland, extends 42 miles *67,5 km* inland into Strathclyde.

Highest seamount

The highest known submarine mountain, or seamount, is one discovered in 1953 near the Tonga Trench, between Samoa and New Zealand. It rises 28,500 ft *8690 m* from the sea bed, with its summit 1200 ft *365 m* below the surface.

Remotest spot from land

The world's most distant point from land is a spot in the South Pacific, approximately 48° 30′ S, 125° 30′ W, which is about 1660 miles *2670 km* from the nearest points of land, namely Pitcairn Island, Ducie Island and Cape Dart, Antarctica. Centred on this spot, therefore, is a circle of water with an area of about 8,657,000 miles^2 *22 421 500 km²*—about 7000 miles^2 *18 000 km²* larger than the USSR, the world's largest country.

Most southerly

The most southerly part of the oceans is 85° 34′ S, 154° W, at the snout of the Robert Scott Glacier, 305 miles *490 km* from the South Pole.

Temperature

The temperature of the water at the surface of the sea varies from −2° C *28.5° F* in the White Sea to 35,6° C *96° F* in the shallow areas of the Persian Gulf in summer. Ice-focused solar rays have been known to heat lake water to nearly 80°F *26,8° C*. The normal Red Sea temperature is 22° C *71.6° F*. The highest temperature recorded in the ocean is 759°F *404°C*, for a spring measured by an American research submarine some 300 miles *480 km* off the American west coast, in an expedition under the direction of Prof Jack Diamond of Oregon State University. Remote probes measured the temperature of the spring which was kept from vaporising by the weight of water above it.

Clearest

The Weddell Sea, 71° S 15° W off Antarctica, has the clearest water of any sea. A 'Secchi' disc was visible to a depth of 80 m *262 ft* on 13 Oct 1986, as measured by Dutch researchers of the German Alfred-Wegener Institute. Such clarity corresponds to what scientists consider attainable in distilled water.

STRAITS

Longest

The longest straits in the world are the Tatarskiy Proliv or Tartar Straits between Sakhalin Island and the USSR mainland running from the Sea of

Japan to Sakhalinsky Zaliv: 800 km *497 miles*, thus marginally longer than the Malacca Straits.

Broadest
The broadest named straits in the world are the Davis Straits between Greenland and Baffin Island with a minimum width of 210 miles *338 km*. The Drake Passage between the Diego Ramirez Islands, Chile and the South Shetland Islands is 710 miles *1140 km* across.

Narrowest
The narrowest navigable straits are those between the Aegean island of Euboea and the mainland of Greece. The gap is only 45 yd *40 m* wide at Khalkis. The Seil Sound, Inner Hebrides, Scotland, narrows to a point only 20 ft *6 m* wide where the Clachan bridge joins the island of Seil to the mainland and is said to span the Atlantic.

WAVES

Highest
The highest officially-recorded sea-wave was calculated at 112 ft *34 m* from trough to crest; it was measured by Lt Frederic Margraff USN from the USS *Ramapo* proceeding from Manila, Philippines, to San Diego, California, on the night of 6–7 Feb 1933, during a 68-knot (78.3 mph *126 km/h*) hurricane. The highest instrumentally-measured wave was one 86 ft *26,2 m* high, recorded by the British ship *Weather Reporter*, in the North Atlantic on 30 Dec 1972 in Lat. 59° N, Long. 19° W. It has been calculated on the statistics of the Stationary Random Theory that one wave in more than 300,000 may exceed the average by a factor of 4.

On 9 July 1958 a landslip caused a 100 mph *160 km/h* wave to wash 1720 ft *524 m* high along the fjord-like Lituya Bay in Alaska.

Highest seismic
The highest estimated height of a *tsunami* (often wrongly called a tidal wave) was one of 85 m *278 ft*, which appeared off Ishigaki Island, Ryukyu Chain on 24 Apr 1771. It tossed a 750-ton block of coral more than 2,5 km *1.3 miles*. *Tsunami* (a Japanese word meaning *nami*, a wave; *tsu*, overflowing) have been observed to travel at 490 mph *790 km/h*.

Evidence for a 1000 ft *300 m* ocean wave breaking on the southern shore of Lanai, Hawaiian Islands was reported on 4 Dec 1984. This occurred about 100,000 years ago due to a meteorite, a volcanic eruption or a submarine landslide.

CURRENTS

Greatest
The greatest current in the oceans is the Antarctic Circumpolar Current or West Wind Drift Current which was measured in 1969 in the Drake Passage between South America and Antarctica to be flowing at a rate of 9500 million ft³ *270 000 000 m³* per sec—nearly treble that of the Gulf Stream. Its width ranges from 185 to 1240 miles *300–2000 km* and has a proven surface flow rate of $\frac{4}{10}$ of a knot *0,75 km/h*.

Strongest
The world's strongest currents are the Nakwakto Rapids, Slingsby Channel, British Columbia, Canada (Lat. 51° 05′ N, Long. 127° 30′ W) where the flow rate may reach 16.0 knots *29,6 km/h*.

The fastest current in British territorial waters is 10.7 knots *19,8 km/h* in the Pentland Firth between the Orkney Islands and Caithness.

TIDES

Extreme tides are due to lunar and solar gravitational forces affected by their perigee, perihelion and syzygies. Barometric and wind effects can superimpose an added 'surge' element. Coastal and sea-floor configurations can accentuate these forces. The normal interval between tides is 12 hr 25 min.

Greatest
The greatest tides occur in the Bay of Fundy, which divides the peninsula of Nova Scotia, Canada, from the United States' north-easternmost state of Maine and the Canadian province of New Brunswick. Burncoat Head in the Minas Basin, Nova Scotia, has the greatest mean spring range with 47.5 ft *14,50 m*. A range of 54½ ft *16,6 m* was recorded at springs in Leaf Basin in 1953. Tahiti experiences virtually no tide.

The place with the greatest mean spring range in Great Britain is Beachley, on the Severn, with a range of 40.7 ft *12,40 m*, compared with the British Isles' average of 15 ft *4,57 m*. Prior to 1933 tides as high as 28.9 ft *8,80 m* above and 22.3 ft *6,80 m* below datum (total range 51.2 ft *15,60 m*) were recorded at Avonmouth though an extreme range of 52.2 ft *15,90 m* for Beachley was officially accepted. In 1883 a freak tide of greater range was reported from Chepstow, Gwent.

ICEBERGS

Largest and tallest
The largest iceberg on record was an antarctic tabular 'berg of over 12,000 miles² *31 000 km²* (208 miles *335 km* long and 60 miles *97 km* wide and thus larger than Belgium) sighted 150 miles *240 km* west of Scott Island, in the South Pacific Ocean, by the USS *Glacier* on 12 Nov 1956. The 200 ft *61 m* thick arctic ice island T.1 (140 miles² *360 km²*), discovered in 1946, was tracked for 17 years. The tallest iceberg measured was one of 550 ft *167 m* reported off western Greenland by the US icebreaker *East Wind* in 1958.

Most southerly arctic
The most southerly arctic iceberg was sighted in the Atlantic by a USN weather patrol in Lat. 28° 44′ N, Long. 48° 42′ W in April 1935. The southernmost iceberg reported in British home waters was sighted 60 miles *96 km* from Smith's Knoll, on the Dogger Bank, in the North Sea.

Most northerly antarctic
The most northerly antarctic iceberg was a remnant sighted in the Atlantic by the ship *Dochra* in Lat. 26° 30′ S, Long. 25° 40′ W, on 30 Apr 1894.

LAND

There is satisfactory evidence that at one time the Earth's land surface comprised a single primeval continent of 80 million miles² *2 × 10⁸ km²*, now termed Pangaea, and that this split about 190 million years ago, during the Jurassic period, into two super-continents, termed Laurasia (Eurasia, Greenland and Northern America) and Gondwanaland (Africa, Arabia, India, South America, Oceania and Antarctica) and named after Gondwana, India, which itself split 120 million years ago. The South Pole was apparently in the area of the Sahara as recently as the Ordovician period of *c.* 450 million years ago.

ROCKS

The age of the Earth is generally considered to be within the range of 4430 ± 20 million years, by analogy with directly-measured ages of meteorites and of the moon. However, no rocks of this great age have yet been found on the Earth since geological processes have presumably destroyed them.

Oldest
The greatest reported age for any scientifically-dated rock is 4300 million years in the case of zircon crystals found by Bob Pidgeon and Simon Wilde 700 km *935 miles* in the Jack Hills, north-

east of Perth, Western Australia. The find was reported in July 1986.

The oldest in Great Britain are the original volcanic products from which were formed the gneiss and granulite rocks of the Scourian complex in the north-west Highlands and the Western Isles which were crystallised 2800 million years ago.

Largest
The largest isolated monolith in the world is the 1237 ft *377 m* high Mount Augustus (3627 ft *1105 m* above sea level), discovered on 3 June 1858, 200 miles *320 km* east of Carnarvon, Western Australia. It is an upfaulted monoclinal gritty conglomerate 5 miles *8 km* long and 2 miles *3 km* across and thus twice the size of the celebrated monolithic arkose Ayer's Rock (1100 ft *335 m*), 250 miles *400 km* south-west of Alice Springs, in Northern Territory, Australia. It was estimated in 1940 that La Gran Piedra, a volcanic plug in the Sierra Maestra, Cuba weighs 61,355 tons/*tonnes*.

CONTINENTS

Largest
Of the Earth's surface 41.25% or 81,200,000 miles² *210 400 000 km²* is covered by continental masses of which only about two-thirds or 29.08% of the Earth's surface (57,270,000 miles² *148 328 000 km²*) is land above water, with a mean height of 2480 ft *756 m* above sea level. The Eurasian land mass is the largest, with an area (including islands) of 20,733,000 miles² *53 698 000 km²*. The Afro-Eurasian land mass, separated artificially only by the Suez Canal, covers an area of 32,704,000 miles² *84 702 000 km²* or 57.1% of the Earth's land mass.

Smallest
The smallest is the Australian mainland, with an area of 2,941,526 miles² *7 618 493 km²*, which, together with Tasmania, New Zealand, New Guinea and the Pacific Islands, is described sometimes as Oceania.

Land remotest from the sea
The point of land remotest from the sea is at Lat. 46° 16.8′ N, Long. 86° 40.2′ E. It is in the Dzoosotoyn Elisen (desert), northern Xinjiang Uygur Zizhiqu (Sin Kiang), China's most north-westerly province. It was visited by Dr Richard Crane (GB) on 27 June 1986 and is at a straight-line distance of 2648 km *1645 miles* from the nearest open sea.

The point furthest from the sea in Great Britain is a point near Meriden, West Midlands, England, which is 72½ miles *117 km* equidistant from the Severn Bridge, the Dee and Mersey estuaries and the Welland estuary in the Wash. The equivalent point in Scotland is in the Forest of Atholl, north-west Tayside, 40½ miles *65 km* equidistant from the head of Loch Leven, Inverness Firth and the Firth of Tay.

Peninsula
The world's largest peninsula is Arabia, with an area of about 1,250,000 miles² *3 250 000 km²*.

ISLANDS

Largest
Discounting Australia, which is usually regarded as a continental land mass, the largest island in the world is Greenland (renamed Kalaatdlit Nunaat 1 May 1979), with an area of about 840,000 miles² *2 175 000 km²*. There is evidence that Greenland is in fact several islands overlaid by an ice cap without which it would have an area of 650,000 miles² *1 680 000 km²*. The largest sand island in the world is Fraser Island, New South Wales with a 75 mile *120 km* long sand dune.

The mainland of Great Britain is the eighth largest island in the world, with an area of 84,186

miles² *218 024 km²*. It stretches 603½ miles *971 km* from Dunnet Head in the north to Lizard Point in the south and 287½ miles *463 km* across from Porthaflod, Dyfed to Lowestoft, Suffolk. The island of Ireland (32,594 miles² *84 418 km²*) is the 20th largest in the world.

Freshwater

The largest island surrounded by fresh water is the Ilha de Marajó (18,500 miles² *48 000 km²*), in the mouth of the River Amazon, Brazil. The world's largest inland island (*i.e.* land surrounded by rivers) is Ilha do Bananal, Brazil (7000 miles² *18 130 km²*). The largest island in a lake is Manitoulin Island (1068 miles² *2766 km²*) in the Canadian (Ontario) section of Lake Huron.

The largest lake island in Great Britain is Inchmurrin in Loch Lomond, Dunbarton/Stirling, Scotland with an area of 284 acres *115 ha.*

Remotest

The remotest island in the world is Bouvet Øya (formerly Liverpool Island), discovered in the South Atlantic by J. B. C. Bouvet de Lozier on 1 Jan 1739, and first landed on by Capt George Norris on 16 Dec 1825. Its position is 54° 26′ S, 3° 24′ E. This *uninhabited* Norwegian dependency is about 1050 miles *1700 km* from the nearest land—the uninhabited Queen Maud Land coast of eastern Antarctica.

The remotest *inhabited* island in the world is Tristan da Cunha, discovered in the South Atlantic by Tristão da Cunha, a Portuguese admiral, in March 1506. It has an area of 38 miles² *98 km²* (habitable area 12 miles² *31 km²*). The first permanent inhabitant was Thomas Currie, who landed in 1810. The island was annexed by the United Kingdom on 14 Aug 1816. After evacuation in 1961 (due to volcanic activity), 198 islanders returned in November 1963. The nearest *inhabited* land to the group is the island of St Helena,

---

Highest mountain ● Mount Everest's status as the world's highest mountain, maintained for 135 years (1852–1987), was finally challenged by K2 (formerly Godwin-Austin), also known as Chogori, in Pakistan in an announcement on 6 Mar 1987 by the US K2 Expedition. Their satellite transit surveyor yielded altitudes of between 29,064 and 29,228 ft *8858–8908 m* as against the hitherto official 19th-century figure of 28,250 ft *8610 m*, and the 20th-century proposed height of 28,740 ft *8760 m*. These compare with Everest's latest altitude of 8848,1 m *29,029 ft* announced by the Chinese on 25 July 1973. K2 was first climbed 14 months after Everest on 31 July 1954 by A. Campagnoni and L. Lacedelli of Italy.

1320 miles *2120 km* to the north-east. The nearest continent, Africa, is 1700 miles *2735 km* away.

The remotest of the British islets is Rockall, 191 miles *307 km* west of St Kilda, Western Isles. This 70 ft *21 m* high rock measuring 83 ft *25 m* across was not formally annexed until 18 Sept 1955. It was 'occupied' by Tom McClean for 38 days 22 hr 52 min on 25 May–4 July 1985. The remotest British island which has ever been inhabited is North Rona which is 44 miles *70,8 km* from the next nearest land at Cape Wrath and the Butt of Lewis. It was evacuated c. 1844. Muckle Flugga, off Unst, in the Shetlands, is the northernmost inhabited with a population of 3 (1971) and is in a latitude north of southern Greenland. Just to the north of it is the rock of Out Stack in Lat. 60° 51′ 35.7″ N.

Greatest archipelago

The world's greatest archipelago is the 3500 mile *5600 km* long crescent of more than 13,000 islands which forms Indonesia.

Highest rock pinnacle

The world's highest rock pinnacle is Ball's Pyramid near Lord Howe Island in the Pacific, which is 1843 ft *561 m* high, but has a base axis of only 200 m *220 yd*. It was first scaled in 1965.

Northernmost land

On 26 July 1978 Uffe Petersen of the Danish Geodetic Institute observed the islet of OOdaq Ø 30 m *100 ft* across, 1,36 km *1478 yd* north of Kaffeklubben Ø off Pearyland, Greenland in Lat. 83° 40′ 32.5″ N, Long. 30° 40′ 10.1″ W. It is 706,4 km *438.9 miles* from the North Pole.

Southernmost land

The South Pole, unlike the North Pole, is on land. The Amundsen–Scott South Polar station was built there at an altitude of 9370 ft *2855 m* in 1957. It is drifting bodily with the ice cap 27–30 ft *8–9 m* per annum in the direction 43° W and was replaced by a new structure in 1975.

Newest

The world's newest island is the lava islet of Fukuto Kuokanoba near Iwo Jima in the Pacific reported in Jan 1986. It measures 650 × 450 m *2132 × 1476 ft* and is 12 m *40 ft* above sea level.

Largest atoll

The largest atoll in the world is Kwajalein in the Marshall Islands, in the central Pacific Ocean. Its slender 176 mile *283 km* long coral reef encloses a lagoon of 1100 miles² *2850 km²*. The atoll with the largest land area is Christmas Atoll, in the Line Islands, in the central Pacific Ocean. It has an area of 248 miles² *642 km²* of which 125 miles² *323 km²* is land. Its principal settlement, London, is only 2½ miles *4,0 km* distant from another settlement, Paris.

Longest reef

The Great Barrier Reef off Queensland, north-eastern Australia, is 1260 statute miles *2027 km* in length. Between 1959 and 1971 a large section between Cooktown and Townsville was destroyed by the proliferation of the Crown of Thorns starfish (*Acanthaster planci*).

DEPRESSIONS

Deepest

The deepest depression so far discovered is the bed rock in the Bentley sub-glacial trench, Antarctica at 2538 m *8326 ft* below sea level. The greatest submarine depression is an area of the north-west Pacific floor which has an average depth of 15,000 ft *4570 m*. The deepest exposed depression on land is the shore surrounding the Dead Sea, now 400 m *1312 ft* below sea level. The deepest point on the bed of this saltiest of all lakes is 728 m *2388 ft* below sea level. The deepest part of the bed of Lake Baykal in Siberia, USSR, is 4872 ft *1485 m* below sea level.

The lowest-lying area in Great Britain is in the Holme Fen area of the Great Ouse, in Cambridgeshire, at 9 ft *2,75 m* below sea level. The deepest depression in England is the bed of part of Lake Windermere, 94 ft *28,65 m* below sea level, and in Scotland the bed of Loch Morar, Inverness 987 ft *300,8 m* below sea level.

Largest

The largest exposed depression in the world is the Caspian Sea basin in the Azerbaydzhani, Russian, Kazakh and Turkmen Republics of the USSR and northern Iran (Persia). It is more than 200,000 miles² *518 000 km²* of which 143,550 miles² *371 800 km²* is lake area. The preponderant land area of the depression is the Prikaspiyskaya Nizmennost, lying around the northern third of the lake and stretching inland for a distance of up to 280 miles *450 km*.

CAVES

Longest

The most extensive cave system in the world is that under the Mammoth Cave National Park, Kentucky, first discovered in 1799. On 9 Sept 1972 an exploration group led by Dr John P. Wilcox completed a connection, pioneered by Mrs Patricia Crowther on 30 Aug, between the Flint Ridge Cave system and the Mammoth Cave system, so making a combined system with a total mapped passageway length which is now over 530 km *330 miles*.

The longest cave system in Great Britain is the Ease Gill system, West Yorkshire which now has 52,4 km *32.5 miles* of explored passage.

Largest

The world's largest cave chamber is the Sarawak Chamber, Lubang Nasib Bagus, in the Gunung Mulu National Park, Sarawak, discovered and surveyed by the 1980 British–Malaysian Mulu Expedition. Its length is 700 m *2300 ft* and its average width is 300 m *980 ft* and it is nowhere less than 70 m *230 ft* high. It would be large enough to garage 7500 buses.

Longest stalactite

The longest known stalactite in the world is a wall-supported column extending 195 ft *59 m* from roof to floor in the Cueva de Nerja, near Málaga, Spain. Probably the longest free-hanging stalactite is one of 7 m *23 ft* in the Poll, an Ionian cave in County Clare, Ireland. The tallest cave column is probably the 128 ft *39 m* high Flying Dragon Pillar in Nine Dragons Cave (Daji Dong), Guizhou, China.

Tallest stalagmite

The tallest known stalagmite in the world is La Grande Stalagmite in the Aven Armand cave, Lozère, France, which has attained a height of 98 ft *29 m* from the cave floor. It was found in September 1897.

DEEPEST CAVES

Depth			
m	ft		
1535	5036	Réseau Jean Bernard	France
1370	4495	Snieznaja Piezcziera	USSR
1338	4390	Puerta de Illamina	Spain
1252	4108	Sistema Huautla	Mexico
1219	3999	Schwersystem	Austria
1208	3964	Complesso Fighiera Carchia	Italy
1007	3304	Anou Ifflis	Algeria
912	2993	Siebenhengste System	Switzerland
897	2944	Jama u Vjetrena brda	Yugoslavia
870	2854	Nettlebed System	New Zealand
775	2543	Jaskinia Sniezna	Poland
751	2464	Ghar Parau, Zagros	Iran

308	1010	Ogof Ffynnon Ddu	Wales
214	702	Giant's Hole System	England
179	587	Reyfad Pot	N Ireland
140	459	Carrowmore Cavern	Rep. of Ireland
76	250	Cnoc nan Uamh	Scotland

MOUNTAINS

Highest

The mountain whose summit is farthest from the Earth's centre is the Andean peak of Chimborazo (20,561 ft *6267 m*), 98 miles *158 km* south of the equator in Ecuador, South America. Its summit is 7057 ft *2150 m* further from the Earth's centre than the summit of Mt Everest (see p. 55). The highest mountain on the equator is Volcán Cayambe (19,285 ft *5878 m*), Ecuador, in Long. 77° 58′ W. A mountaineer atop the summit would be moving at 1671 km/h *1038 mph* relative to the Earth's centre due to the Earth's rotation.

The highest insular mountain in the world is Puncak Jayak (formerly Puncak Sukarno, formerly Carstensz Pyramide) in Irian Jaya, Indonesia. A survey by the Australian Universities' Expedition in 1973 yielded a height of 4884 m *16,023 ft*. Ngga Pula, now 4861 m *15,950 ft*, was in 1936 possibly c. 4910 m c. *16,110 ft* before the melting of its snow cap.

The highest mountain in the United Kingdom is Ben Nevis (4406 ft *1343 m* excluding the 12 ft *3,65 m* cairn), 4¼ miles *6,85 km* south-east of Fort William, Argyll, Scotland. It was climbed before 1720 but though acclaimed the highest in 1790 was not confirmed to be higher than Ben Macdhui (4300 ft *1310 m*) until 1847. In 1834 Ben Macdhui and Ben Nevis (Gaelic, *Beinn Nibheis*) (first reference, 1778) were respectively quoted as 4570 ft *1393 m* and 4370 ft *1332 m*. The highest mountain in England is Scafell Pike (3210 ft *978 m*), in Wales is Snowdon (*Yr Wyddfa*) (3560 ft *1085 m*) in Gwynedd; and in the island of Ireland is Carrauntual (3414 ft *1041 m*) in County Kerry.

There is some evidence that, before being ground down by the ice cap, mountains in the Loch Bà area of the Isle of Mull, Strathclyde were 15,000 ft *4575 m* above sea level. There are 577 peaks and tops over 3000 ft *915 m* in the whole British Isles and 165 peaks and 136 tops in Scotland higher than England's highest point, Scafell Pike. The highest mountain off the mainland is Sgùrr Alasdair (3309 ft *1008 m*) on Skye, named after Alexander (Gaelic, *Alasdair*) Nicolson, who made the first ascent in 1873.

Unclimbed

The highest unclimbed mountain is now only the 31st highest—Zemu Gap Peak (25,526 ft *7780 m*) in the Sikkim Himalaya.

Tallest

The world's tallest mountain measured from its submarine base (3280 fathoms *6000 m*) in the Hawaiian Trough to its peak is Mauna Kea (Mountain White) on the island of Hawaii, with a combined height of 33,476 ft *10 203 m* of which 13,796 ft *4205 m* are above sea level. Another mountain whose dimensions, but not height, exceed those of Mount Everest is the volcanic Hawaiian peak of Mauna Loa (Mountain Long) at 13,680 ft *4170 m*. The axes of its elliptical base, 16,322 ft *4975 m* below sea level, have been estimated at 74 miles *119 m* and 53 miles *85 km*. It should be noted that Cerro Aconcagua (22,834 ft *6960 m*) is more than 38,800 ft *11 826 m* above the 16,000 ft *4875 m* deep Pacific abyssal plain or 42,834 ft *13 055 m* above the Peru-Chile Trench which is 180 miles *290 km* distant in the South Pacific.

Greatest ranges

The world's greatest land mountain range is the Himalaya-Karakoram, which contains 96 of the world's 109 peaks of over 24,000 ft *7315 m*. Himalaya derives from the sanskrit *him*, snow; *alaya*, home. The greatest of all mountain ranges is, however, the submarine Indian/East Pacific Oceans Cordillera extending 19,200 miles *30 900 km* from the Gulf of Aden to the Gulf of California by way of the seabed between Australia and Antarctica with an average height of 8000 ft *2430 km* above the base ocean depth.

Longest lines of sight

Vatnajökull (6952 ft *2118 m*), Iceland has been seen by refracted light from the Faeroe Islands 340 miles *550 km* distant. In Alaska Mt McKinley (20,320 ft *6193 m*) has been sighted from Mt Sanford (16,237 ft *4949 m*) from a distance of 230 miles *370 km*. McKinley, so named in 1896, was called Denali (Great One) in the Athabascan language of North American Indians and is the highest mountain in the United States.

Greatest plateau

The most extensive high plateau in the world is the Tibetan Plateau in Central Asia. The average altitude is 16,000 ft *4875 m* and the area is 77,000 miles² *200 000 km²*.

Sheerest wall

Mount Rakaposhi (25,498 ft *7772 m*) rises 5,99 vertical kilometres *3.72 miles* from the Hunza Valley, Pakistan in 10 horizontal kilometres *6.21 miles* with an overall gradient of 31°.

The 3200 ft *975 m* wide north-west face of Half Dome, Yosemite, California is 2200 ft *670 m* high but nowhere departs more than 7 degrees from the vertical. It was first climbed (Class VI) in 5 days in July 1957 by Royal Robbins, Jerry Gallwas and Mike Sherrick.

Highest halites

Along the northern shores of the Gulf of Mexico for 725 miles *1160 km* there exist 330 subterranean 'mountains' of salt, some of which rise more than 60,000 ft *18 300 m* from bed rock and appear as the low salt domes first discovered in 1862.

Lowest hill

Official maps of Seria, Brunei show an artificial hillock named Bukit Thompson by the 13th hole on the Panaga Golf Course at 15 ft *4,5 m*.

WATERFALLS

Highest

The highest waterfall (as opposed to vaporised 'Bridal Veil') in the world is the Salto Angel in Venezuela, on a branch of the River Carrao, an upper tributary of the Caroni with a total drop of 3212 ft *979 m*—the longest single drop is 2648 ft *807 m*. The 'Angel Falls' were named after the United States pilot Jimmy Angel (died 8 Dec 1956), who recorded them in his log book on 14 Nov 1933. The falls, known by the Indians as Cherun-Meru, were first reported by Ernesto Sanchez La Cruz in 1910.

The tallest waterfall in the United Kingdom is Eas a'Chùal Aluinn, from Glas Bheinn (2541 ft

774 m), Sutherland, Scotland, with a drop of 658 ft 200 m. England's highest fall above ground is Caldron (or Cauldron) Snout, on the Tees, with a fall of 200 ft 60 m in 450 ft 135 m of cataracts, but no sheer leap. It is on the border of Durham and Cumbria. The cascade in the Gaping Gill Cave descends 365 ft 111 m. The highest Welsh waterfall is the Pistyll-y-Llyn on the Powys-Dyfed border which exceeds 300 ft 90 m in descent. The highest falls in Ireland are the Powerscourt Falls (350 ft 106 m), on the River Dargle, County Wicklow.

Greatest

On the basis of the average annual flow, the greatest waterfalls in the world are the Boyoma (formerly Stanley) Falls in Zaïre with 600,000 cusec 17 000 m³/sec. The peak flow of the Guaíra (Salto das Sete Quedas) on the Alto Paraná river between Brazil and Paraguay at times attained a peak flow rate of 1,750,000 cusec 50 000 m³/sec.

It has been calculated that, when some 5,500,000 years ago the Mediterranean basins began to be filled from the Atlantic through the Straits of Gibraltar, a waterfall 26 times greater than the Guairá and perhaps 800 m 2625 ft high was formed.

Widest

The widest waterfalls in the world are the Khône Falls (50–70 ft 15–21 m high) in Laos, with a width of 6.7 miles 10,8 km and a flood flow of 1,500,000 cusec 42 500 m³/sec.

RIVERS

Longest

The two longest rivers in the world are the Nile (Bahr-el-Nil) flowing into the Mediterranean, and the Amazon (Amazonas), flowing into the South Atlantic. Which is the longer is more a matter of definition than simple measurement.

The length of the Nile watercourse, as surveyed by M. Devroey (Belgium) before the loss of a few miles of meanders due to the formation of Lake Nasser, behind the Aswan High Dam, was 4145 miles 6670 km. This course is unitary from a hydrological standpoint and runs from the source in Burundi of the Luvironza branch of the Kagera feeder of the Victoria Nyanza via the White Nile (Bahrel-Jebel) to the delta in the Mediterranean.

The true source of the Amazon was discovered in 1953 to be a stream named Huarco, deriving from the Misuie Glacier (5400 m 17,715 ft) in the Arequipa Andes of Peru. This stream progressively becomes the Toro then the Santiago then the Apurimac, which in turn is known as the Ene and then the Tambo before its confluence with the Amazon prime tributary the Ucayali. The length of the Amazon from this source to the South Atlantic via the Canal do Norte was measured in 1969 and found to be 4007 miles 6448 km (usually quoted to the rounded-off figure of 4000 miles 6437 km).

If, however, a vessel navigating down the river follows the 'arm' (carrying 10% of the river's water) to the south of Ilha de Marajó through the Furo Tajapuru and Furo dos Macacos into the Pará, the total length of the water-course becomes 4195 miles 6750 km. The Rio Pará is not however a tributary of the Amazon, being hydrologically part of the basin of the Tocantins which itself however flows into the Bahia de Marajó and out into the South Atlantic.

The longest river in Great Britain is the Severn, which empties into the Bristol Channel and is 220 miles 354 km long. Its basin extends over 4409 miles² 11 419 km². It rises in north-western Powys, Wales, and flows through Shropshire, Hereford & Worcester, Gloucestershire and Avon and has a record 17 tributaries. The longest river wholly in England is the Thames, which is 215 miles, 346 km long to the Nore. Its remotest source is at Seven Springs, Gloucestershire, whence the River Churn joins the other head waters. The source of the Thames proper is Trewsbury Mead, Coates, Cirencester, Gloucestershire. The basin measures 3841 miles² 9948 km². The Yorkshire Ouse's 11 tributaries aggregate 629 miles 1012 km.

The longest river wholly in Wales is the Usk, with a length of 65 miles 104,5 km. It rises on the border of Dyfed and Powys and flows out via Gwent into the Severn Estuary. The longest river in Scotland is the Tay, with Dundee, Tayside, on the shore of the estuary. It is 117 miles 188 km long from the source of its remotest head-stream, the River Tummel, Tayside and has the greatest volume of any river in Great Britain, with a flow of up to 49,000 cusecs 1387 m³/sec. Of Scottish rivers the Tweed and the Clyde have most tributaries with 11 each.

The longest river in Ireland is the Shannon, which is longer than any river in Great Britain. It rises 258 ft 78,6 m above sea level, in County Cavan, and flows through a series of loughs to Limerick. It is 240 miles 386 km long, including the 56 mile 90 km long estuary to Loop Head. The basin area is 6060 miles² 15 695 km².

Shortest

The world's shortest named river is the D River, Lincoln City, Oregon which connects Devil's Lake to the Pacific Ocean and is 440 ft 134 m long at low tide.

Largest basin

The largest river basin in the world is that drained by the Amazon (4007 miles 6448 km). It covers about 2,720,000 miles² 7 045 000 km². It has about 15,000 tributaries and subtributaries, of which four are more than 1000 miles 1609 km long. These include the Madeira, the longest of all tributaries, with a length of 2100 miles 3380 km, which is surpassed by only 14 rivers in the whole world.

Longest sub-tributary

The longest sub-tributary is the Pilcomayo (1000 miles 1609 km) in South America. It is a tributary of the Paraguay (1500 miles 2415 km long), which is itself a tributary of the Paraña (2500 miles 4025 km).

Longest estuary

The world's longest estuary is that of the often frozen Ob', in the northern USSR, at 550 miles 885 km. It is up to 50 miles 80 km wide.

Largest delta

The world's largest delta is that created by the Ganges (Ganga) and Brahmaputra in Bangla Desh (formerly East Pakistan) and West Bengal, India. It covers an area of 30,000 miles² 75 000 km².

Greatest flow

The greatest flow of any river in the world is that of the Amazon, which discharges an average of 4,200,000 cusec 120 000 m³/sec into the Atlantic Ocean, rising to more than 7,000,000 cusec 200 000 m³/sec in full flood. The lowest 900 miles 1450 km of the Amazon average 300 ft 90 m in depth.

Submarine

In 1952 a submarine river 250 miles 400 km wide, known as the Cromwell current, was discovered flowing eastward 300 ft 90 m below the surface of the Pacific for 3500 miles 5625 km along the equator. Its volume is 1000 times that of the Mississippi.

Subterranean

In August 1958 a crypto-river was tracked by radio isotopes flowing under the Nile with 6 times its mean annual flow or 500,000 million m³ 20 million million ft³.

Largest swamp

The world's largest tract of swamp is in the basin of the Pripet or Pripyat River—a tributary of the Dnieper in the USSR. These swamps cover an estimated area of 18,125 miles² 46 950 km².

RIVER BORES

The bore on the Ch'ient'ang'kian (Hang-chou-fe) in eastern China is the most remarkable of the 60 in the world. At spring tides the wave attains a height of up to 25 ft 7,5 m and a speed of 13–15 knots 24–27 km/h. It is heard advancing at a range of 14 miles 22 km. The annual downstream flood wave on the Mekong sometimes reaches a height of 46 ft 14 m. The greatest volume of any tidal bore is that of the Canal do Norte (10 miles 16 km wide) in the mouth of the Amazon.

> **World's wettest place** ● By average annual rainfall, the wettest place in the world is Tutunendo in Colombia, South America, which experiences 11770 mm 463.4 in per annum. Its average of 32,24 mm 1.27 in per day is nearly 2¾ times as much as its British counterpart. (Photo: Al Gentry/Missouri Botanical Gardens)

The most notable of the 8 river bores in the United Kingdom is that on the Severn, which attained a measured height of 9¼ ft *2,8 m* on 15 Oct 1966 downstream of Stonebench, and a speed of 13 mph *20 km/h*. It travels from Framilode towards Gloucester.

LAKES AND INLAND SEAS

Largest

The largest inland sea or lake in the world is the Kaspiskoye More (Caspian Sea) in the southern USSR and Iran (Persia). It is 760 miles *1225 km* long and its total area is 139,000 miles² *360 700 km²*. Of the total area some 55,280 miles² *143 200 km²* (38.6 per cent) are in Iran, where it is named the Darya-ye-Khazar. Its maximum depth is 1025 m *3360 ft* and its surface is 28,5 m *93 ft* below sea level. Its estimated volume is 21,500 miles³ *89 600 km³* of saline water. Its surface has varied between 32 m *105 ft* (11th century) and 22 m *72 ft* (early 19th century) below sea level.

Deepest

The deepest lake in the world is Ozero (Lake) Baykal in central Siberia, USSR. It is 385 miles *620 km* long and between 20 and 46 miles *32–74 km* wide. In 1957 the lake's Olkhon Crevice was measured to be 1940 m *6365 ft* deep and hence 1485 m *4872 ft* below sea level.

The deepest lake in Great Britain is the 10.30 mile *16,57 km* long Loch Morar, in Inverness. Its surface is 30 ft *9 m* above sea level and its extreme depth 1017 ft *310 m*. England's deepest lake is Wast Water (258 ft *78 m*), in Cumbria. The lake with the greatest mean depth is Loch Ness with *c.* 426 ft *130 m*.

Highest

The highest steam-navigated lake in the world is Lake Titicaca (maximum depth 1214 ft *370 m*), with an area of about 3200 miles² *8285 km²* (1850 miles² *4790 km²* in Peru, 1350 miles² *3495 km²* in Bolivia), in South America. It is 130 miles *209 km* long and is situated at 12,506 ft *3811 m* above sea level. There is an unnamed glacial lake near Everest at 19,300 ft *5880 m*. Tibet's largest lake Nam Tso of 722 miles² *1956 km²* is at 15,060 ft *4578 m*.

The highest lake in the United Kingdom is the 1.9 acre *0,76 ha* Lochan Buidhe at 3600 ft *1097 m* above sea level in the Cairngorm Mountains, Scotland. England's highest is Broad Crag Tarn (2746 ft *837 m* above sea level) on Scafell Pike, Cumbria and the highest named freshwater lake in Wales is The Frogs Pool, a tarn near the summit of Carnedd Llywelyn, Gwynedd at *c.* 2725 ft *830 m*.

Freshwater

The freshwater lake with the greatest surface area is Lake Superior, one of the Great Lakes of North America. The total area is 31,800 miles² *82 350 km²*, of which 20,700 miles² *53 600 km²* are in Minnesota, Wisconsin and Michigan, USA and 11,100 miles² *27 750 km²* in Ontario, Canada. It is 600 ft *182 m* above sea level. The freshwater lake with the greatest volume is Lake Baykal in Siberia, USSR with an estimated volume of 5520 miles³ *23 000 km³*.

The largest lake in the United Kingdom is Lough Neagh (48 ft *14,60 m* above sea level) in Northern Ireland. It is 18 miles *28,9 km* long and 11 miles *17,7 km* wide and has an area of 147.39 miles² *381,73 km²*. Its extreme depth is 102 ft *31 m*.

Freshwater loch

The largest lake in Great Britain, and the largest inland loch in Scotland is Loch Lomond (23 ft *7,0 m* above sea level), which is 22.64 miles *36,44 km* long and has a surface area of 27.45 miles² *70,04 km²*. It is situated in the Strathclyde and Central regions and its greatest depth is 623 ft *190 m*. The lake or loch with the greatest volume is, however, Loch Ness with 262,845,000,000 ft³ *7 443 000 000 m³*. The longest lake or loch is Loch Ness which measures 24.23 miles *38,99 km*. The three arms of the Y-shaped Loch Awe, Argyll, aggregate, however, 25.47 miles *40,99 km*. The largest lake in England is Windermere, in Cumbria. It is 10½ miles *17 km* long and has a surface area of 5.69 miles² *14,74 km²*. Its greatest depth is 219 ft *66,75 m* in the northern half. The largest *natural* lake in Wales is Llyn Tegid, with an area of 1.69 miles² *4,38 km²*, although the largest lake in Wales is that formed by the reservoir at Lake Vyrnwy, where the total surface area is 1120 acres *453,25 ha*.

Freshwater loughs

The largest lough in the Republic of Ireland is Lough Corrib in Mayo and Galway. It measures 27 miles *43,5 km* in length and is 7 miles *11,25 km* across at its widest point with a total surface area of 41,616 acres (65.0 miles² *168 km²*).

Lake in a lake

The largest lake in a lake is Manitou Lake (41.09 miles² *106,42 km²*) on the world's largest lake island Manitoulin Island (1068 miles² *2766 km²*) in the Canadian part of Lake Huron. It contains itself a number of islands.

Underground

Reputedly the world's largest underground lake is the Lost Sea 300 ft *91 m* subterranean in the Craighead Caverns, Sweetwater, Tennessee, USA measuring 4½ acres *1,8 ha* and discovered in 1905.

Largest lagoon

Lagoa dos Patos in southernmost Brazil is 158 miles *254 km* long and extends over 4110 miles² *10 645 km²*.

OTHER FEATURES

Desert

Nearly an eighth of the world's land surface is arid with a rainfall of less than 25 cm *9.8 in* per annum. The Sahara in North Africa is the largest in the world. At its greatest length it is 3200 miles *5150 km* from east to west. From north to south it is between 800 and 1400 miles *1275 and 2250 km*. The area covered by the desert is about 3,250,000 miles² *8 400 000 km²*. The land level varies from 436 ft *132 m* below sea level in the Qattâra Depression, Egypt, to the mountain Emi Koussi (11,204 ft *3415 m*) in Chad. The diurnal temperature range in the western Sahara may be more than 80° F or *45° C*.

Sand dunes

The world's highest measured sand dunes are those in the Saharan sand sea of Isaouane-n-Tifernine of east central Algeria in Lat. 26° 42′ N, Long. 6° 43′ E. They have a wave-length of *c.* 3 miles *5 km* and attain a height of 1410 ft *430 m*.

Largest gorge

The largest land gorge in the world is the Grand Canyon on the Colorado River in north-central Arizona. It extends from Marble Gorge to the Grand Wash Cliffs, over a distance of 217 miles

349 km. It varies in width from 4 to 13 miles 6–20 km and is some 5300 ft 1615 m deep. The submarine Labrador Basin canyon is c. 2150 miles 3440 km long.

Deepest canyon

The deepest canyon is El Cañón de Colca, Peru reported in 1929 which is 3223 m 10,574 ft deep. It was first traversed by the Polish Expedition CANOANDES' 79-kayak team from 12 May–14 June 1981. A stretch of the Kali River in central Nepal flows 18,000 ft 5485 m below its flanking summits of the Dhaulagiri and Annapurna groups. The deepest submarine canyon yet discovered is one 25 miles 40 km south of Esperance, Western Australia, which is 6000 ft 1800 m deep and 20 miles 32 km wide.

Cliffs

The highest sea cliffs yet pinpointed anywhere in the world are those on the north coast of east Moloka'i, Hawaii near Umilehi Point, which descend 3300 ft 1005 m to the sea at an average gradient of >55°.

The highest cliffs in north-west Europe are those on the north coast of Achill Island, in County Mayo, Ireland, which are 2192 ft 668 m sheer above the sea at Croaghan. The highest cliffs in the United Kingdom are the 1300 ft 396 m Conachair cliffs on St Kilda, Western Isles (1397 ft 425 m). The highest sheer sea cliffs on the mainland of Great Britain are at Clo Mor, 3 miles 4,8 km south-east of Cape Wrath, Sutherland, Scotland which drop 921 ft 280,7 m. England's highest cliff (gradient >45°) is Great Hangman Hill, near Combe Martin, in north Devon, which descends from 1043 ft 318 m to the sea in 984 ft 300 m, the last 700 ft 213 m of which is sheer.

Natural arches

The longest natural arch in the world is the Landscape Arch in the Arches National Park, 25 miles 40 km north of Moab in Utah, USA. This natural sandstone arch spans 291 ft 88 m and is set about 100 ft 30 m above the canyon floor. In one place erosion has narrowed its section to 6 ft 1,82 m. Larger, however, is the Rainbow Bridge, Utah discovered on 14 Aug 1909 with a span of 278 ft 84,7 m but more than 22 ft 6,7 m wide. The highest natural arch is the sandstone arch 25 miles 40 km west-north-west of K'ashih, Sinkiang, China, estimated in 1947 to be nearly 1000 ft 312 m tall with a span of about 150 ft 45 m.

Longest glaciers

It is estimated that 6,020,000 miles^2 15 600 000 km^2, or 10½ per cent of the Earth's land surface, is permanently glaciated. The world's longest known glacier is the Lambert Glacier, discovered by an Australian aircraft crew in Australian Antarctic Territory in 1956–7. It is up to 40 miles 64 km wide and, with its upper section, known as the Mellor Glacier, it measures at least 250 miles 402 km in length. With the Fisher Glacier limb, the Lambert forms a continuous ice passage about 320 miles 514 km long. The longest Himalayan glacier is the Siachen (47 miles 75,6 km) in the Karakoram range, though the Hispar and Biafo combine to form an ice passage 76 miles 122 km long. The fastest-moving major glacier is the Quarayaq in Greenland flowing 20–24 m 65–80 ft per day.

Greatest avalanches

The greatest natural avalanches, though rarely observed, occur in the Himalayas but no estimates of their volume have been published. It was estimated that 3,500,000 m^3 120 000 000 ft^3 of snow fell in an avalanche in the Italian Alps in 1885. The 250 mph 400 km/h avalanche triggered by the Mount St Helens eruption in Washington, USA on 18 May 1979 was estimated to measure 2800 million m^3 96,000 million ft^3 (see Disasters, Chapter 11).

GREAT BRITAIN AND IRELAND WEATHER RECORDS

MAXIMUM AND MINIMUM SUNSHINE

78.3 per cent of maximum possible in one month (382 hours from 488), Pendennis Castle, Falmouth, Cornwall, June 1925.
Nil in a month at Westminster, London, Dec 1890; while the south-eastern end of the village of Lochranga, Isle of Arran, Strathclyde is in shadow of mountains 18 Nov–8 Feb each winter.

HIGHEST SHADE TEMPERATURE 98.2° F
36,77° C Raunds, Northants; Epsom, Surrey and Canterbury, Kent, 9 Aug 1911.

HOTTEST PLACE (Annual mean) 52.7° F
11,5° C average 1931–60, Penzance, Cornwall, and Isles of Scilly.

GREATEST RAINFALL

24 hours—11.00 in 279 mm, Martinstown, Dorset, 18–19 July 1955.
Calendar month—56.54 in 1436 mm, Llyn Llydau, Snowdon, Gwynedd, Oct 1909. 12 months—257.0 in 6527 mm, Sprinkling Tarn, Cumbria, in 1954.

MOST INTENSE RAINFALL 2.0 in 51 mm
in 12 min at Wisbech, Cambridgeshire on 27 June 1970, the most intense recorded in modern standards.

MOST RAINY DAYS (One year) 309—
Ballynahinch, Galway, 1923.

LONGEST FREEZE

40 days (unremitting) at Great Dun Fell radio station, Appleby, Cumbria, 23 Jan–3 Mar 1986. Less rigorous data includes a frost from 5 Dec 1607–14 Feb 1608 and a 91-day frost on Dartmoor, Devon in 1854–5. By contrast, no temperature lower than 1° C 34° F has ever been recorded on Bishop Rock, Isles of Scilly.

GREATEST SNOWFALL (12 months) 60 in
1524 mm Upper Teesdale and Denbighshire Hills, Clwyd, 1947.

EARLIEST AND LATEST SNOWFALL
London's earliest recorded snow—25 Sept 1885, and latest—27 May 1821. Less reliable reports suggest snow on 12 Sept 1658 (Old Style) and 12 June 1791.

HEAVIEST HAILSTONES 5 oz 141 g,
Horsham, W. Sussex, 5 Sept 1958.

WINDIEST PLACE (Annual average) 20.6
mph 33,1 km/h Fair Isle 1974–8.

HIGHEST SURFACE WIND SPEED 172
mph 278 km/h (150 knots), Caingorm Summit (4084 ft 1245 m), 20 Mar 1986.

THUNDER DAYS (Year) 38—Stonyhurst,
Lancs, 1912 and Huddersfield, West Yorks, 1967.

EARLIEST SUMMER AND WINTER The
earliest reliably known hot summer was in AD 664 during our driest-ever century and the earliest known severe winter was that of AD 763–4.

GREATEST TEMPERATURE VARIATION IN A DAY 52.2° F 29°C
Tummel Bridge, Perthshire, from −7° C 19.4° F to 22° C 71.6° F, on 9 May 1978.

Best British summers
According to Prof. Gordon Manley's survey over the period 1728–1978 the best (i.e. driest and hottest) British summer was that of 1976. Temperatures of >32° C (89.8° F) were recorded on 13 consecutive days (25 June–7 July) within Great Britain including 35,9° C 96.6° F at Cheltenham on 3 July. In 1983 there were 40 days >80° F 26,6° C in Britain between 3 July–31 Aug including 17 consecutively (3–19 July). London experienced its hottest month (July) since records began in 1840.

DRIEST PLACE Annual mean—20.2 in 513
mm St Osyth, Lee Wick Farm, Essex, 1964–82. One year—9.29 in 236 mm weather station in Margate, Kent, 1921.

LONGEST DROUGHT 73 days, Mile End,
London, 4 Mar–15 May 1893.

Falsest St. Swithin's Days
The legend that the weather on St. Swithin's Day, celebrated on 15 July (Old and New Style) since AD 912, determines the rainfall for the next 40 days is one which has long persisted. There was a brilliant 13½ hr sunshine in London on 15 July 1924, but 30 of the next 40 days were wet. On 15 July 1913 there was a 15-hr downpour, yet it rained on only 9 of the subsequent 40 days in London.

WETTEST PLACE (Annual mean) 172.9 in
4391 mm Styhead Tarn, Cumbria, (1600 ft 487 m).

White Christmases
London has experienced seven 'White' or snowing Christmas Days since 1900. These have been 1906, 1917 (slight), 1923 (slight), 1927, 1938, 1956 (slight) and 1970. These were more frequent in the 19th century and even more so before the change of the calendar, which, by removing 3–13 Sept brought forward all dates subsequent to 2 Sept 1752 by 11 days.
The last of the nine recorded Frost Fairs held on the Thames since 1564–5 was from Dec 1813 to 26 Jan 1814.

LOWEST SCREEN TEMPERATURE
−17° F −27,2° C, recorded twice at Braemar, Aberdeenshire, Scotland, 11 Feb 1895 and 10 Jan 1982.

COLDEST PLACE (Extrapolated annual
mean) 43.41° F 6,34° C, Braemar, Aberdeenshire, Scotland, 1952–81.

FROSTS In 1863–4 there was frost in London
from November to April. Frosts during August were recorded in the period 1668–89.

BAROMETRIC PRESSURE Highest—1054.7
mb (31.15 in), Aberdeen, 31 Jan 1902. Lowest—925.5 mb (27.33 in), Ochtertyre, Near Crieff, Tayside, 26 Jan 1884.

LONGEST SEA LEVEL FOG (visibility
<1000 yd 914.4 m), London record—4 days 18 hr, 26 Nov–1 Dec 1948 and 5–9 Dec 1952.

Tornadoes
(see also Accidents and Disasters, Chap 11)
Britain's strongest tornado was at Southsea, Portsmouth on 14 Dec 1810 (Force 8 on the Meaden-TORRO scale). The Newmarket tornado (Force 6) of 3 Jan 1978 caused property damage estimated at up to £1,000,000. On 23 Nov 1981, 58 tornadoes were reported in one day from Anglesey to eastern England.
A height of c. 1600 m was measured (by sextant) for the Spithead waterspout off Ryde, Isle of Wight on 21 Aug 1878.

Weather

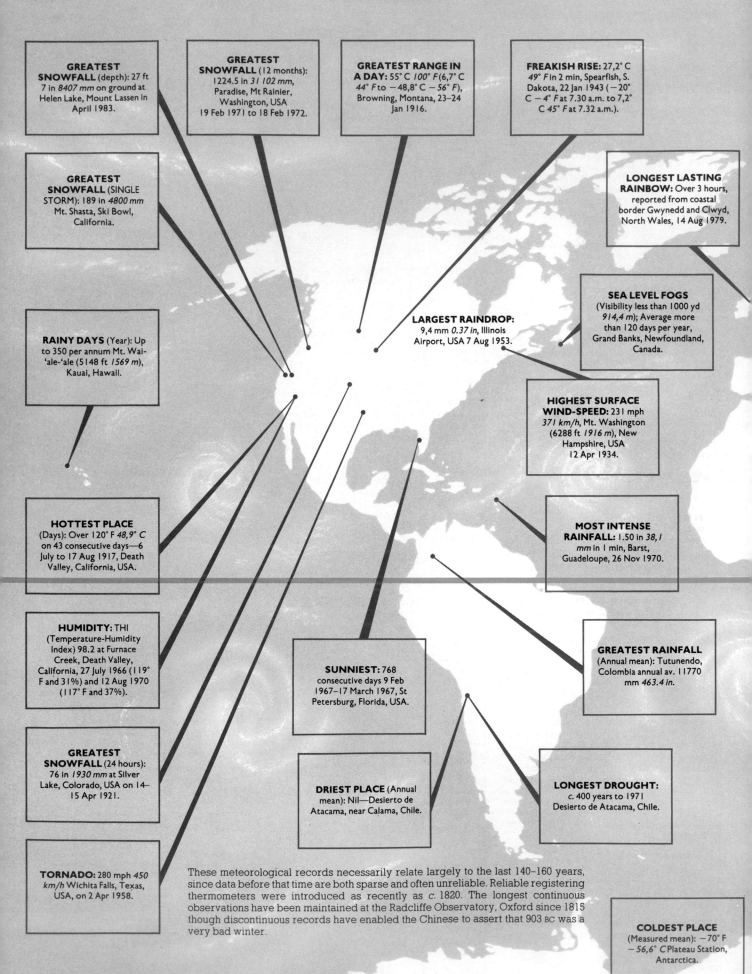

GREATEST SNOWFALL (depth): 27 ft 7 in *8407 mm* on ground at Helen Lake, Mount Lassen in April 1983.

GREATEST SNOWFALL (12 months): 1224.5 in *31 102 mm*, Paradise, Mt Rainier, Washington, USA 19 Feb 1971 to 18 Feb 1972.

GREATEST RANGE IN A DAY: 55° C *100° F* (6,7° C *44° F* to −48,8° C *− 56° F*), Browning, Montana, 23–24 Jan 1916.

FREAKISH RISE: 27,2° C *49° F* in 2 min, Spearfish, S. Dakota, 22 Jan 1943 (−20° C −4° F at 7.30 a.m. to 7,2° C *45° F* at 7.32 a.m.).

LONGEST LASTING RAINBOW: Over 3 hours, reported from coastal border Gwynedd and Clwyd, North Wales, 14 Aug 1979.

GREATEST SNOWFALL (SINGLE STORM): 189 in *4800 mm* Mt. Shasta, Ski Bowl, California.

SEA LEVEL FOGS (Visibility less than 1000 yd *914,4 m*); Average more than 120 days per year, Grand Banks, Newfoundland, Canada.

LARGEST RAINDROP: 9,4 mm *0.37 in*, Illinois Airport, USA 7 Aug 1953.

RAINY DAYS (Year): Up to 350 per annum Mt. Wai-'ale-'ale (5148 ft *1569 m*), Kauai, Hawaii.

HIGHEST SURFACE WIND-SPEED: 231 mph *371 km/h*, Mt. Washington (6288 ft *1916 m*), New Hampshire, USA 12 Apr 1934.

HOTTEST PLACE (Days): Over 120° F *48,9° C* on 43 consecutive days—6 July to 17 Aug 1917, Death Valley, California, USA.

MOST INTENSE RAINFALL: 1.50 in *38,1 mm* in 1 min, Barst, Guadeloupe, 26 Nov 1970.

HUMIDITY: THI (Temperature-Humidity Index) 98.2 at Furnace Creek, Death Valley, California, 27 July 1966 (119° F and 31%) and 12 Aug 1970 (117° F and 37%).

SUNNIEST: 768 consecutive days 9 Feb 1967–17 March 1967, St Petersburg, Florida, USA.

GREATEST RAINFALL (Annual mean): Tutunendo, Colombia annual av. 11770 mm *463.4 in*.

GREATEST SNOWFALL (24 hours): 76 in *1930 mm* at Silver Lake, Colorado, USA on 14–15 Apr 1921.

DRIEST PLACE (Annual mean): Nil—Desierto de Atacama, near Calama, Chile.

LONGEST DROUGHT: c. 400 years to 1971 Desierto de Atacama, Chile.

TORNADO: 280 mph *450 km/h* Wichita Falls, Texas, USA, on 2 Apr 1958.

These meteorological records necessarily relate largely to the last 140–160 years, since data before that time are both sparse and often unreliable. Reliable registering thermometers were introduced as recently as *c.* 1820. The longest continuous observations have been maintained at the Radcliffe Observatory, Oxford since 1815 though discontinuous records have enabled the Chinese to assert that 903 BC was a very bad winter.

COLDEST PLACE (Measured mean): −70° F *− 56,6° C* Plateau Station, Antarctica.

Records

MINIMUM SUNSHINE: Nil at North Pole—for winter stretches of 186 days.

BAROMETRIC PRESSURE (Highest): 1083.8 mb. (*32.00 in*), Agata (alt. 862 ft *262 m*), Siberia, USSR, 31 Dec 1968.

DEEPEST PERMAFROST: More than 4500 ft *1370 m* reported from the upper reaches of the Viluy River, Siberia, USSR in February 1982.

GREATEST TEMPERATURE RANGE: 106,7° C *192° F* (−70° C − *94° F* to 36,7° C *98° F*), Verkhoyansk, USSR.

HIGHEST SHADE TEMPERATURE: 136.4° F *58° C* al'Azīzīyah, Libya, (alt. 367 ft *111 m*) 13 Sep 1922.

COLDEST PERMANENTLY INHABITED: −96°F − *71,1° C* Oymyakon (pop. 600) (63° 16'N; 143° 15'E.), (alt. 2300 ft *700 m*) Siberia, USSR, 1964.

GREATEST RAINFALL (Calendar Month): 366.14 in *9299 mm*, Cherrapunji, Meghalaya, India, July 1861.

GREATEST RAINFALL (12 months): 1041.78 in *26 461 mm*, Cherrapunji, Meghalaya, 1 Aug 1860–31 July 1861.

HEAVIEST HAILSTONES: 2¼ lb *1,02 kg*, reported to have killed 92 people in the Gopalganj district of Bangladesh on 14 Apr 1986.

MOST EQUABLE TEMPERATURE: Extreme range 11,8° C *21.2° F*, Saipan, Mariana Islands, 1927–35 (19,6° C *67.3° F*–31,4° C *88.5° F*).

MAXIMUM SUNSHINE: > 97 per cent (over 4300 hours), eastern Sahara.

BAROMETRIC PRESSURE (Lowest): 870 mb (*25.69 in*), 300 miles *482 km* west of Guam, Pacific Ocean, in Lat. 16°44' N, Long. 137°46' E. 12 Oct 1979.

HOTTEST PLACE (Annual mean): Dallol, Ethiopia, 94° F *34,4° C* (1960–66).

THUNDER-DAYS (Year): 322 days, Bogor (formerly Buitenzorg), Java, Indonesia (average, 1916–19).

HOTTEST PLACE (Days): At Marble Bar, Western Australia (maximum 121° F, *49,4° C*) 160 consecutive days over 100° F *37,8° C*, 31 Oct 1923 to 7 Apr 1924.

HOTTEST PLACE (Days): The temperature reached 90° F *32,2°C* on 333 days in 1946, Wyndham, Western Australia.

GREATEST RAINFALL (24 hours): 73.62 in *1870 mm*, Cilaos, (alt. 3937 ft *1200 m*) La Réunion, Indian Ocean, 15–16 Mar 1952 (equal to 7435 tons *7554 tonnes*/acre).

WINDIEST: The Commonwealth Bay, George V Coast, Antarctica, where gales reach 200 mph *320 km/h.*

COLDEST PLACE (Extrapolated annual mean): −72° F − *57,8° C* Polus Nedostupnosti, Pole of Cold (78° S., 96° E.), Antarctica.

LOWEST SCREEN TEMPERATURE: −128.6° F − *89,2° C* Vostok (alt. 11,220 ft *3,419 m*), Antarctica, 21 July 1983.

THICKEST ICE: 2.97 miles (15,670 ft) *4776 m* 69° 9' 38" S 135° 20' 25" E 400 km *250 miles* from the coast in Wilkes Land on 4 Jan 1975.

HIGHEST WATERSPOUT: 1528 m *5014 ft* (diameter 3 m *10 ft*) off Eden, NSW, Australia, 16 May 1898.

Natural Phenomena

EARTHQUAKES

(Seismologists record all dates with the year *first*, based not on local time but on Greenwich Mean Time).

Greatest

It is estimated that each year there are some 500,000 detectable seismic or micro-seismic disturbances of which 100,000 can be felt and 1000 cause damage. The deepest recorded hypocentres are of 720 km *447 miles* in Indonesia in 1933, 1934 and 1943.

An inherent limitation in the widely-used Gutenberg–Richter scale (published in 1954) precludes its usefulness when extended to the relative strengths of the strongest earthquakes ever recorded. The scale was named after Dr Beno Gutenberg (1889–1960) and Dr Charles Robert Richter (1900–1985). Its use of surface-wave magnitudes, based on amplitudes of waves of a period of 20 sec, results in the 'damping' of any increase in amplitude where fault ruptures break over a length much above 60 km *37 miles*. These, however, provenly may reach a length of 800 to 1000 km *500–620 miles*.

This 'overload' or 'saturation effect' has resulted in the adoption since 1977 of the Kanamori scale for comparing the most massive earthquakes. Magnitudes are there defined in terms of energy release using the concept of the seismic moment, devised by K-Aki in 1966. Thus the most massive instrumentally-recorded earthquake has been the cataclysmic Lebu shock south of Concepción, Chile on 1960 May 22 estimated at 10^{26} ergs. While this uniquely rates a magnitude of 9.5 on the Kanamori scale, it ranks in only equal 4th place (with the 1922 Chilean earthquake) at Magnitude 8.3 on the Gutenberg–Richter scale.

Worst death roll

The greatest chronicled loss of life occurred in the earthquake which rocked every city of the Near East and eastern Mediterranean *c.* July 1201. Contemporary accounts estimate the loss of life at 1,100,000. Less uncertain is the figure of 830,000 fatalities in a prolonged quake (*ti chen*) in the Shensi, Shansi and Honan provinces of China, of 1556 Feb 2, (new style) (Jan 23 os). The highest death toll in modern times has been the Tangshan 'quake (Mag. 8.2) in eastern China on 1976 July 27 (local time was 3 a.m. July 28). A first figure published on 4 Jan 1977 revealed 655,237 killed, later adjusted to 750,000. On 22 Nov 1979 the New China News Agency unaccountably reduced the death toll to 242,000. As late as Jan 1982 the site of the city was still a prohibited area.

Material damage

The greatest physical devastation was in the 'quake on the Kwanto plain, Japan, of 1923 Sept 1 (Mag. 8.2, epicentre in Lat. 35° 15′ N, Long. 139° 30′ E); in Sagami Bay the sea bottom in one area sank 400 m *1310 ft*. The official total of persons killed and missing in this *Shinsai* or great 'quake and the resultant fires was 142,807. In Tōkyō and Yokohama 575,000 dwellings were destroyed. The cost of the damage was estimated at £1000 million (now £17,000 million).

Great Britain and Ireland

The total of the undisputed death roll for Great Britain is two—an apprentice, Thomas Grey, struck by falling masonry from Christ's Hospital Church, near Newgate, London at 6 p.m. on 6 Apr 1580, and another youth, Mabel Everet, who died of injuries 4 days later.

The East Anglian or Colchester earthquake of 1884 Apr 22 (9.18 a.m.) (epicentres Lat. 51° 48′ N, Long. 0° 53′ E, and Lat. 51° 51′ N, Long. 0° 55′ E) caused damage estimated at more than £12,000 to 1250 buildings. Langenhoe Church was wrecked. Windows and doors were rattled over an area of 53,000 miles² *137 250 km²* and the shock was felt in Exeter and Ostend, Belgium. It has been estimated to have been of magnitude 5.2 on the Richter scale.

The highest instrumentally-measured magnitude is 6.0 for the Dogger Bank event of 1931 June 7. The strongest Scottish tremor occurred at Inverness at 10.45 p.m. on 1816 Aug 13, and was felt over an area of 50,000 miles² *130 000 km²*. The strongest Welsh tremor occurred in Swansea at 9.45 a.m. on 1906 June 27 (epicentre Lat. 51° 38′ N, Long. 4° W). It was felt over an area of 37,800 miles² *97 900 km²*.

No earthquake with its epicentre in Ireland has ever been instrumentally measured, though the effects of the North Wales shock of 1984 July 19 (Mag. 5 to 5.5) dislocated traffic lights in Dublin. However, there was a shock in August 1734 which damaged 100 dwellings and five churches.

VOLCANOES

The total number of known active volcanoes in the world is 850 of which many are submarine. The greatest active concentration is in Indonesia, where 77 of its 167 volcanoes have erupted within historic times. The name volcano derives from the now dormant Vulcano Island (from the God of fire Vulcanus) in the Mediterranean.

Greatest explosion

The greatest explosion (possibly since Santoriní in the Aegean Sea 1626 ± 1 BC) occurred at *c.* 10 a.m. (local time), or 3.00 a.m. GMT, on 27 Aug 1883, with an eruption of Krakatoa, an island (then 18 miles² *47 km²*) in the Sunda Strait, between Sumatra and Java, in Indonesia—163 villages were wiped out, and 36,380 people killed by the wave it caused. Rocks were thrown 34 miles *55 km* high and dust fell 3313 miles *5330 km* away 10 days later. The explosion was recorded four hours later on the island of Rodrigues, 2968 miles *4776 km* away, as 'the roar of heavy guns' and was heard over 1/13th part of the surface of the globe. This explosion, estimated to have had about 26 times the power of the greatest H-bomb test (by the USSR), was still only a fifth part of the Santoriní cataclysm.

Greatest eruption

The total volume of matter discharged in the eruption of Tambora, a volcano on the island of Sumbawa, in Indonesia, 5–7 Apr 1815, was 150–180 km³. The energy of this 1395 mph *2245 km/h* eruption, which lowered the height of the island by 4100 ft *1250 m* from 13,450 ft *4100 m* to 9350 ft *2850 m*, was 8.4 × 10^{19} joules. A crater seven miles *11 km* in diameter was formed. Some 90,000 were killed or died of famine. This compares with a probable 60–65 km³ ejected by Santoriní (see below) and 20 km³ ejected by Krakatoa (see above). The internal pressure at Tambora has been estimated at 3270 kg/cm² or *20.76 tons/in².*

The ejecta in the Taupo eruption in New Zealand *c.* AD 130 has been estimated at 30,000 million tonnes/*tons* of pumice moving at one time at 400 mph *700 km/h*. It flattened 16 000 km² *6180 miles²* (over 26 times the devastated area of Mt St Helens which erupted in Washington State on 18 May 1979). Less than 20 per cent of the 14 × 10^9 tonnes of pumice ejected in this most violent of all documented volcanic events fell within 200 km *125 miles* of the vent.

Longest lava flow

The longest lava flow in historic times, known as *pahoehoe* (twisted cord-like solidifications), is that from the eruption of Laki in 1783 in southeast Iceland which flowed 65–70 km *40.5–43.5 miles*. The largest known prehistoric flow is the Roza basalt flow in North America *c.* 15 million years ago, which had an unsurpassed length (480 km *300 miles*), area (40 000 km² *15,400 miles²*) and volume (1250 km³ *300 miles³*).

Largest active

Mauna Loa (meaning 'long mountain') in Hawaii has a dome 75 miles *120 km* long and 64 miles *103 km* wide with a lava flow that occupies more than 2000 miles² *5180 km²* of the island. Its pit crater, Mokuaweoweo, measures 4 miles² *10,4 km²* and is 500–600 ft *150–180 m* deep. It rises 13,677 ft *4168 m* and has averaged one eruption every 3½ years since 1832, most recently in April 1984.

Highest extinct

The highest extinct volcano in the world is Cerro Aconcagua (stone sentinel) (22,834 ft *6960 m*) on the Argentine side of the Andes. It was first climbed on 14 Jan 1897 by Mathias Zurbriggen; the highest summit climbed until 12 June 1907.

Highest dormant

The highest dormant volcano is Volcán Llullaillaco (22,057 ft *6723 m*), on the frontier between Chile and Argentina.

Highest active

The highest volcano regarded as active is Volcán Antofalla (21,162 ft *6450 m*), in Argentina, though a more definite claim is made for Volcán Guayatiri or Guallatiri (19,882 ft *6060 m*), in Chile, which erupted in 1959.

Northernmost and southernmost

The northernmost volcano is Beeren Berg (7470 ft *2276 m*) on the island of Jan Mayen (71° 05′ N) in the Greenland Sea. It erupted on 20 Sept 1970 and the island's 39 inhabitants (all male) had to be evacuated. It was possibly discovered by Henry Hudson the English navigator and explorer (d. 1611) in 1607 or 1608, but was definitely visited by Jan Jacobsz Mayen (Netherlands) in 1614. It was annexed by Norway on 8 May 1929. The Ostenso seamount (5825 ft *1775 m*) 346 miles *556 km* from the North Pole in Lat. 85° 10′ N, Long. 133° W was volcanic. The most southerly known active volcano is Mount Erebus (12,450 ft *3795 m*) on Ross Island (77° 35′ S), in Antarctica. It was discovered on 28 Jan 1841 by the expedition of Captain (later Rear-Admiral Sir) James Clark Ross, RN (1800–62), and first climbed at 10 a.m. on 10 Mar 1908 by a British party of five, led by Professor (later Lieut-Col Sir) Tannatt William Edgeworth David (1858–1934).

Largest crater

The world's largest *caldera* or volcano crater is that of Toba, north-central Sumatra, Indonesia covering 685 miles² *1775 km²*.

GEYSERS

Tallest

The Waimangu (Maori, *black water*) geyser, in New Zealand, erupted to a height in excess of 1500 ft *457 m* in 1904, but has not been active since it erupted violently at 6.20 a.m. on 1 Apr 1917 and killed 4 people. Currently the world's tallest active geyser is the US National Parks' Service Steamboat Geyser, in Yellowstone National Park, Wyoming which from 1962 to 1969 erupted with intervals ranging from 5 days to 10 months to a height of 250–380 ft *76–115 m*. The greatest measured water discharge has been 825,000 gal *37 850 hl* by the Giant Geyser, also in Yellowstone National Park, which has been dormant since 1955. The *Geysir* ('gusher') near Mount Hekla in south-central Iceland, from which all others have been named, spurts, on occasions, to 180 ft *55 m*, while the adjacent Strokkur, reactivated by drilling in 1963, spurts at 10–15 min intervals.

THE
UNIVERSE
& SPACE

CHAPTER FOUR

Most frequent aurorae ● A flush of the polar
lights over the snow-capped volcano Mt Ranier
in the Cascade Range, Washington, USA. Known
since 1560 as Aurora Borealis or Northern
Lights in the northern hemisphere and since
1773 as Aurora Australis in the southern
hemisphere, polar lights are caused by electrical
solar discharges in the upper atmosphere and
occur most frequently in high latitudes. Aurorae
are visible at some time on *every* clear dark
night in the polar areas within 20 degrees of the
magnetic poles. The extreme height of aurorae
has been measured at 1000 km *620 miles*, while
the lowest may descend to 72,5 km *45 miles*.
Reliable figures exist only from 1952, since
when the record high and low numbers of nights
of auroral displays in Shetland (geomagnetic Lat.
63°) have been 203 (1957) and 58 (1965). The
most recent great display in north-west Europe
was that of 4–5 Sept 1958. (Photo: Jim Grace/
Science Photo Library)

LIGHT-YEAR—that distance travelled by light (speed 186,282.397 miles/sec *299 792,458 km/s* or 670,616,629.2 mph *1 079 252 848,8 km/h in vacuo*) in one tropical year (365.24219878 mean solar days at January 0,12 hours Ephemeris time in AD 1900) and is 5,878,499,814,000 miles *9 460 528 405 000 km*. The unit was first used in March 1888 and fixed at this constant in October 1983.

MAGNITUDE—a measure of stellar brightness such that the light of a star of any magnitude bears a ratio of 2.511886 to that of a star of the next magnitude. Thus a fifth magnitude star is 2.511886 times as bright, while one of the first magnitude is exactly 100 (or 2.511886^5) times as bright, as a sixth magnitude star. In the case of such exceptionally bright bodies as Sirius, Venus, the Moon (magnitude −12.71) or the Sun (magnitude −26.78), the magnitude is expressed as a minus quantity.

PROPER MOTION—that component of a star's motion in space which, at right angles to the line of sight, constitutes an apparent change of position of the star in the celestial sphere.

The universe is the entirety of space, matter and anti-matter. An appreciation of its magnitude is best grasped by working outward from the Earth, through the Solar System which is revolving around the centre of the Milky Way once in each 237,000,000 years, at a speed of 492,000 mph *792 000 km/h* and has a velocity of 44,700 mph *72 000 km/h* relative to stars in our immediate region and then on to the remotest extra-galactic nebulae and quasars.

METEOROIDS

Meteoroids are of cometary or asteroidal origin. A meteor is the light phenomenon caused by the entry of a meteoroid into the Earth's atmosphere.

Meteor shower

The greatest meteor 'shower' on record occurred on the night of 16–17 Nov 1966, when the Leonid meteors (which recur every $33\frac{1}{4}$ years) were visible between western North America and eastern USSR. It was calculated that meteors passed over Arizona, USA, at a rate of 2300 per min for a period of 20 min from 5 a.m. on 17 Nov 1966.

METEORITES

When a meteoroid penetrates to the Earth's surface, the remnant which could be either aerolite (stony) or siderite (metallic) is described as a meteorite. This occurs about 150 times per year over the whole land surface of the Earth. The most anxious time of day for meteorophobes should be 3 p.m. In historic times, the only recorded person injured by a meteorite has been Mrs E. H. Hodges of Sylacauga, Alabama, USA. On 30 Nov 1954 a 9 lb *4 kg* stone went through her roof.

Oldest

The oldest dated meteorites are from the fall in Allende, Coahuila, Mexico on 8 Feb 1969 dating back 4610 million years.

It was reported in August 1978 that dust grains in the Murchison meteorite which fell in Australia in September 1969 also pre-date the formation of the Solar System 4600 million years ago.

Largest

There was a mysterious explosion of $12\frac{1}{2}$ megatons in Lat. 60° 55′ N, Long. 101° 57′ E, in the basin of the Podkamennaya Tunguska river, 40 miles north of Vanavar, in Siberia, USSR, at 00 hrs 17 min 11 sec UT on 30 June 1908. The cause was variously attributed to a meteorite (1927), a comet (1930), a nuclear explosion (1961) and to anti-matter (1965). This devastated an area of about 1500 miles² *3885 km²* and the shock was felt as far as 1000 km (more than *600 miles*) away. The theory is now favoured that this was the terminal flare of stony debris from a comet, possibly Encke's comet, at an altitude of only 6 km or less than *20,000 ft*. A similar event may have occurred over the Isle of Axholm, Humberside, England a few thousand years before. A stony meteorite with a diameter of 10 km *6.2 miles* striking the Earth at 25 km/sec *55,925 mph* would generate an explosive energy equivalent to 100 million megatons. Such events should not be expected to recur more than once in 75 million years.

The largest known meteorite is one found in 1920 at Hoba West, near Grootfontein in south-west Africa. This is a block 9 ft *2,75 m* long by 8 ft *2,43 m* broad, estimated to be 132,000 lb (59 tons/ *tonnes*). The largest meteorite exhibited by any museum is the 'Tent' meteorite, weighing 68,085 lb (30.39 tons *30 883 kg*) found in 1897 near Cape York, on the west coast of Greenland, by the expedition of Commander (later Rear-Admiral) Robert Edwin Peary (1856–1920). It was known to the Eskimos as the Abnighito and is now exhibited in the Hayden Planetarium in New York City, NY, USA. The largest piece of stony meteorite recovered is a piece of 1770 kg *3902 lb*, part of a 4 tonne shower which struck Jilin (formerly Kirin), China on 8 Mar 1976.

The heaviest of the 22 meteorites known to have fallen on the British Isles since 1623 was one weighing at least 102 lb *46,25 kg* (largest piece 17 lb 6 oz *7,88 kg*), which fell at 4.12 p.m. on 24 Dec 1965 at Barwell, Leicestershire. Scotland's largest recorded meteorite fell in Strathmore, Tayside on 3 Dec 1917. It weighed 22¼ lb *10,09 kg* and was the largest of four stones totalling 29 lb 6 oz *13,324 kg*. The largest recorded meteorite to fall in Ireland was the Limerick Stone of 65 lb *29,5 kg*, part of a shower weighing more than 106 lb *48 kg* which fell near Adare, County Limerick, on 10 Sept 1813. The larger of the two recorded meteorites to land in Wales was one weighing 28 oz *794 g* of which a piece weighing 25¼ oz *723 g* went through the roof of the Prince Llewellyn Hotel in Beddgelert, Gwynedd, shortly before 3.15 a.m. on 21 Sept 1949. Debris from the Bovedy Fall in Northern Ireland in 1969 spread over 50 miles *80 km*.

Craters *Largest*
It has been estimated that some 2000 asteroid-Earth collisions have occurred in the last 600 million years. 102 collision sites or astroblemes have been recognised. A crater 150 miles *241 km* in diameter and ¼ mile *805 m* deep was postulated in 1962 in Wilkes Land, Antarctica. It would be caused by a 13,000 million ton meteorite striking at 44,000 mph *70 811 km/h*. Soviet scientists reported in December 1970 an astrobleme with a 60 mile *95 km* diameter and a maximum depth of 1300 ft *400 m* in the basin of the River Popigai. There is a crater-like formation or astrobleme 275 miles *442,5 km* in diameter on the eastern shore of the Hudson Bay, Canada, where the Nastapoka Islands are just off the coast.

The largest proven crater is the Coon Butte or Barringer crater, discovered in 1891 near Canyon Diablo, Winslow, northern Arizona. It is 4150 ft *1265 m* in diameter and now about 575 ft *175 m* deep, with a parapet rising 130–155 ft *40–48 m* above the surrounding plain. It has been estimated that an iron-nickel mass with a diameter of 200–260 ft *61–79 m* and weighing about 2,000,000 tons/*tonnes* gouged this crater in *c.* 25,000 BC. Evidence was published in 1963 discounting a meteoric origin for the crypto-volcanic Vredefort Ring (diameter 26 miles *41,8 km*), to the south-west of Johannesburg, South Africa, but this has now been re-asserted. The New Quebec (formerly the Chubb) 'Crater', first sighted on 20 June 1943 in northern Ungava, Canada, is 1325 ft *404 m* deep and measures 6.8 miles *10,9 km* round its rim.

Tektites
The largest tektite of which details have been published has been of 3,2 kg *7.04 lb* found in 1932 at Muong Nong, Saravane Province, Laos and now in the Paris Museum. Eight SNC meteorites named after their find sites at Shergotty, India; Nakla, Egypt and Chassigny, France, are believed to have emanated from Mars.

Fireball *Brightest*
The brightest fireball ever photographically recorded was by Dr Zdenek Ceplecha over Sumava, Czechoslovakia on 4 Dec 1974 with a momentary magnitude of −22 or 10,000 times brighter than a full Moon.

AURORAE
Most frequent
Polar lights, known since 1560 as Aurora Borealis or Northern Lights in the northern hemisphere and since 1773 as Aurora Australis in the southern hemisphere, are caused by electrical solar discharges in the upper atmosphere and occur most frequently in high latitudes. Aurorae are visible at some time on *every* clear dark night in the polar areas within 20 degrees of the magnetic poles. The extreme height of aurorae has been measured at 1000 km *620 miles*, while the lowest may descend to 72,5 km *45 miles*. Reliable figures exist only from 1952, since when the record high and low number of nights of auroral displays in Shetland (geomagnetic Lat. 63°) has been 203 (1957) and 58 (1965). The most recent great display in north-west Europe was that of 4–5 Sept 1958.

Lowest latitudes
Extreme cases of displays in very low latitudes are Cuzco, Peru (2 Aug 1744); Honolulu, Hawaii (1 Sept 1859) and, questionably, Singapore (25 Sept 1909).

Noctilucent clouds
Regular observations (at heights of *c.* 52 miles *85 km*) in Western Europe date only from 1964, since when the record high and low number of nights on which these phenomena have been observed have been 41 (1974) and 15 (1970).

THE MOON
The Earth's closest neighbour in space and only natural satellite is the Moon, at a mean distance of 238,855 statute miles *384 400 km* centre-to-centre or 233,812 miles *376 284 km* surface-to-surface. The average orbital speed is 2287 mph *3680 km/h*. In the present century the closest approach (smallest perigee) was 216,398 miles *348 259 km* surface-to-surface or 221,441 miles *356 375 km* centre-to-centre on 4 January 1912, and the farthest distance (largest apogee) was 247,675 miles *398 598 km* surface-to-surface or 252,718 miles *406 711 km* centre-to-centre on 2 March 1984. The Moon was only a few Earth radii distant during the 'Gerstenkorn period' 3900 million years ago. It has a diameter of 2159.3 miles *3475,1 km* and has a mass of 7.232 × 10^{19} tons *7,348 × 10^{19} tonnes* with a mean density of 3.344. The first direct hit on the Moon was achieved at 2 min 24 sec after midnight (Moscow time) on 14 Sept 1959, by the Soviet space probe *Luna II* near the *Mare Serenitatis*. The first photographic images of the hidden side were collected by the USSR's *Luna III* from 6.30 a.m. on 7 Oct 1959, from a range of up to 43,750 miles *70 400 km* and transmitted to the Earth from a distance of 470 000 km *292,000 miles*. The oldest of the Moon material brought back to Earth by the *Apollo* programme crews has been soil dated to 4720 million years.

Crater *Largest and deepest*
Only 59 per cent of the Moon's surface is directly visible from the Earth because it is in 'captured rotation', *i.e.* the period of rotation is equal to the period of orbit. The largest wholly visible crater is the walled plain Bailly, towards the Moon's South Pole, which is 183 miles *295 km* across, with walls rising to 14,000 ft *4250 m*. The Orientale Basin, partly on the averted side, measures more than 600 miles *965 km* in diameter. The deepest crater is the Newton crater, with a floor estimated to be between 23,000 and 29,000 ft

7000–8850 m below its rim and 14,000 ft *2250 m* below the level of the plain outside. The brightest directly visible spot on the Moon is *Aristarchus*.

Highest mountains
In the absence of a sea level, lunar altitudes are measured relative to an adopted reference sphere of radius 1 738,000 km *1079.943 miles*. Thus the greatest elevation attained on this basis by any of the 12 US astronauts has been 7830 m *25,688 ft* on the Descartes Highlands by Capt John Watts Young USN and Major Charles M. Duke Jr on 27 Apr 1972.

Temperature extremes
When the Sun is overhead the temperature on the lunar equator reaches 243°F *117,2°C* (31 deg F *17,2 deg C* above the boiling point of water). By sunset the temperature is 58°F *14,4°C* but after nightfall it sinks to −261°F *−162,7°C*.

THE SUN
Distance extremes
The Earth's 66,620 mph *107 210 km/h* orbit of 584,017,800 miles *939 885 500 km* around the Sun is elliptical, hence our distance from the Sun varies. The orbital speed varies between 65,520 mph *105 450 km/h* (minimum) and 67,750 mph *109 030 km/h*. The average distance of the Sun is 1.000 000 230 astronomical units or 92,955,829 miles *149 597 906 km*.

Our closest approach (perihelion) is 91,402,000 miles *147 097 000 km* and our farthest departure (aphelion) is 94,510,000 miles *152 099 000 km*.

Temperature and dimensions
The Sun has a central temperature of about 15 400 000 K, a core pressure of 1,650,000,000 tons/in^2 *25,4 PPa* and uses up 4,000,000 tons/ *tonnes* of hydrogen per sec, thus providing a luminosity of 3 × 10^{27} candlepower, with an intensity of 1,500,000 candles/in^2 *1 530 000 candelas*. The Sun has the stellar classification of a 'yellow dwarf' and, although its density is only 1.407 times that of water, its mass is 332,946 times as much as that of the Earth. It has a mean diameter of 865,270 miles *1 392 520 km*. The Sun with a mass of 1.9575 × 10^{27} tons *1,9889 × 10^{27} tonnes* represents more than 99 per cent of the total mass of the Solar System but will exhaust its energy in 10,000 million years.

Sunspots
To be visible to the *protected* naked eye, a sunspot must cover about one two-thousandth part of the Sun's disc and thus have an area of about 500,000,000 miles^2 *1300 million km^2*. The largest sunspot ever noted was in the Sun's southern hemisphere on 8 Apr 1947. Its area was about 7000 million miles^2 *18 000 million km^2* with an extreme longitude of 187,000 miles *300 000 km* and an extreme latitude of 90,000 miles *145 000 km*. Sunspots appear darker because they are more than 1500 deg C cooler than the rest of the Sun's surface temperature of 5525° C. The largest observed solar prominence was one protruding 365,000 miles *588 000 km*, photographed on 19 Dec 1973 during the 3rd and final manned Skylab mission. In October 1957 a smoothed sunspot count showed 263, the highest recorded sunspot index since records started in 1755 (*cf.* previous record of 239 in May 1778). In 1943 one sunspot lasted for 200 days from June to December.

ECLIPSES
Earliest recorded
For the Middle East, lunar eclipses have been extrapolated to 3450 BC and solar ones to 4200 BC. No centre of the path of totality for a solar eclipse crossed London for the 575 years from 20 Mar 1140 to 3 May 1715. On 14 June 2151 at 18.25 GMT

the eclipse will be 99 per cent total in central London but total in Sheffield and Norfolk. The most recent occasion when a line of totality of a solar eclipse crossed Great Britain was on 29 June 1927 for 24.5 sec at 6.23 a.m. at West Hartlepool, Cleveland and the next instance will clip the coast at St Just, Cornwall at 10.10 a.m. on Wednesday 11 Aug 1999. On 30 June 1954 a total eclipse was witnessed from Unst, Shetland Islands but the centre of the path of totality was to its north.

Longest duration

The maximum *possible* duration of an eclipse of the Sun is 7 min 31 sec. The longest actually *measured* was on 20 June 1955 (7 min 8 sec), seen from the Philippines. One of 7 min 29 sec should occur in mid-Atlantic on 16 July 2186, which will then be the longest for 1469 years. The longest possible in the British Isles is 5 min 30 sec. That of 15 June 885 lasted nearly 5 min, as will that of 20 July 2381 in the Borders area. Durations can be extended by observers being airborne as on 30 June 1973 when an eclipse was 'extended' to 72 min aboard *Concorde*. An annular eclipse may last for 12 min 24 sec. The longest totality of any lunar eclipse is 104 minutes and has occurred many times.

Most and least frequent

The highest number of eclipses possible in a year is seven, as in 1935, when there were five solar and two lunar eclipses; or four solar and three lunar eclipses, as occurred in 1982. The lowest possible number in a year is two, both of which must be solar, as in 1944 and 1969.

COMETS

Earliest recorded

The earliest records of comets date from the 7th century BC. The speeds of the estimated 2,000,000 comets vary from 700 mph *1125 km/h* in outer space to 1,250,000 mph *2 000 000 km/h* when near the Sun. The successive appearances of Halley's Comet have been traced back to 467 BC. It was first depicted in the Nuremberg Chronicle of AD 684. The first prediction of its return by Edmund Halley (1656–1742) proved true on Christmas Day 1758, 16 years after his death. On 13–14 Mar 1986, the European satellite *Giotto* (launched 2 July 1985) penetrated to within 335 miles *540 km* of the nucleus of Halley's Comet. It was established that this was 9.3 miles *15 km* in length and velvet black in colour.

Closest approach

On 1 July 1770, Lexell's Comet, travelling at a speed of 23.9 miles/sec *38,5 km/sec* (relative to the Sun), came within 745,000 miles *1 200 000 km* of the Earth. However, the Earth is believed to have passed through the tail of Halley's Comet, most recently on 19 May 1910.

Largest

The tail of the brightest of all comets, the Great Comet of 1843, trailed for 205,000,000 miles *330 million km*. The bow shock of Holmes Comet of 1892 once measured 1,500,000 miles *2 400 000 km* in diameter.

Shortest period

Of all the recorded periodic comets (these are members of the Solar System), the one which most frequently returns is Encke's Comet, first identified in 1786. Its period of 1206 days (3.3 years) is the shortest established. Not one of its 53 returns (including 1983) has been missed by astronomers. Now increasingly faint, it is expected to 'die' by February 1994. The most frequently observed comets are Schwassmann–Wachmann I, Kopff and Oterma which can be observed every year between Mars and Jupiter.

Longest period

At the other extreme is Delavan's Comet of 1914,

whose path was not accurately determined. It is not expected to return for perhaps 24 million years.

PLANETS

Largest

The nine major planets (including the Earth) are bodies within the Solar System and which revolve round the Sun in definite orbits. The search for Planet X continues. Jupiter, with an equatorial diameter of 88,846 miles *142 984 km* and a polar diameter of 83,082 miles *133 708 km* is the largest of the nine major planets, with a mass 317.83 times, and a volume 1321.4 times that of the Earth. It also has the shortest period of rotation resulting in a Jovian day of only 9 hr 50 min 30.003 sec in the equatorial zone.

Smallest, coldest and outermost

Pluto was first recorded by Clyde William Tombaugh (b. 4 Feb 1906) at Lowell Observatory, Flagstaff, Arizona, USA on 18 Feb 1930 from photographs he took on 23 and 29 Jan. His find was announced on 13 March. Pluto's companion Charon was announced on 22 June 1978 from the US Naval Observatory, Flagstaff, Arizona. Pluto has a diameter of 2200 $\pm$ 140 km *1365 $\pm$ 87 miles* and Charon 1160 km *720 miles*. Their surface temperature is an estimated $-220°C$ *$-360°F$*. Their mean distance from the Sun is 3,674,488,000 miles *5 913 514 000 km* with a period of revolution of 248.54 years. Because of their orbital eccentricity they will have been temporarily closer to the Sun than Neptune in the period from 23 Jan 1979 to 15 Mar 1999.

Fastest

Mercury, which orbits the Sun at an average distance of 35,983,100 miles *57 909 200 km*, has a period of revolution of 87.9686 days, so giving the highest average speed in orbit of 107,030 mph *172 248 km/h*.

Hottest

For Venus a surface temperature of 462° C *864°F* has been estimated from measurements made from the USSR *Venera* and US Pioneer Cytherean surface probes.

Nearest

The fellow planet closest to the Earth is Venus, which is, at times, only 25,700,000 miles *41 360 000 km* inside the Earth's orbit, compared with Mars's closest approach of 34,600,000 miles *55 680 000 km* outside the Earth's orbit. Mars, known since 1965 to be cratered, has temperatures ranging from 85° F *29,4° C* to $-190°$ F *$-123°$ C*.

Surface features

By far the highest and most spectacular is Olympus Mons (formerly Nix Olympica) in the Tharsis region of Mars with a diameter of 500–600 km *310–370 miles* and a height of 26 $\pm$ 3 km *75,450–95,150 ft* above the surrounding plain. Venus has a canyon some 1000 miles *1600 km* south of Venusian equator 21,000 ft *6,4 km* deep and 250 miles *400 km* long. The ice cliff on the Uranian moon Miranda is 65,000 ft *5,20 km* high.

Brightest and faintest

Viewed from the Earth, by far the brightest of the five planets visible to the naked eye is Venus, with a maximum magnitude of -4.4. Uranus, the first to be discovered by telescope when it was sighted by Sir William Herschel from his garden at 19, New King St., Bath on 13 Mar 1781, is only marginally visible with a magnitude 5.5. The faintest is Pluto, with a magnitude of 15.0.

Densest and least dense

Earth is the densest planet with an average figure of 5.515 times that of water, whilst Saturn has an average density only about one-eighth of this value or 0.687 times that of water.

Conjunctions

The most dramatic recorded conjunction (coming together) of the other seven principal members of the Solar System (Sun, Moon, Mercury, Venus, Mars, Jupiter and Saturn) occurred on 5 Feb 1962, when 16° covered all seven during an eclipse in the Pacific area. It is possible that the seven-fold conjunction of September 1186 spanned only 12°. The next notable conjunction will take place on 5 May 2000.

Largest scale model

The largest scale model of the Solar System was inaugurated by the Futures' Museum, Falun, Sweden on 29 Nov 1986. A model of the Earth of diameter 13 mm *0.5 in* was placed in the museum. The Sun 1.5 m *5 ft* and the planets which ranged from 3.5 mm *0.13 in* to 140 mm *5.5 in* were positioned in the nearby city of Borlänge some 16,2 km *10 miles* away. *Proxima Centauri* was positioned at the Museum of Victoria, Melbourne.

SATELLITES

Most

Of the nine major planets, all but Venus and Mercury have satellites. The planet with the most is Saturn with at least 18 satellites. The Earth and Pluto are the only planets with a single satellite. The distance from their parent planets varies from the 5827 miles *9377 km* of *Phobos* from the centre of Mars to the 14,700,000 miles *23 700 000 km* of Jupiter's outer satellite *Sinope* (Jupiter IX). The Solar System has a total of 63 established satellites.

Largest and smallest

The largest and heaviest satellite is *Ganymede* (Jupiter III), which is 2.017 times heavier than our own Moon and has a diameter of 5262 km *3270 miles*. The smallest satellite is *Leda* (Jupiter XIII) with a diameter of less than 15 km *9.3 miles*.

Largest asteroids

In the belt which lies between Mars and Jupiter, there are some 45,000 (3700 numbered to April 1987) minor planets or asteroids which are, for the most part, too small to yield to diameter measurement. The largest and first discovered (by G. Piazzi at Palermo, Sicily on 1 Jan 1801) of these is *Ceres*, which has a diameter of 588 miles *946 km*. The only one visible to the naked eye is asteroid 4 *Vesta* (diameter 318 miles *512 km*) discovered on 29 Mar 1807 by Dr Heinrich Wilhelm Olbers (1758–1840), a German amateur astronomer. The closest measured approach to the Earth by an asteroid was 485,000 miles *780 000 km* in the case of *Hermes* on 30 Oct 1937 (asteroid now lost). The most distant detected is 2060 *Chiron*, found between Saturn and Uranus on 18–19 Oct 1977, by Charles T. Kowal from the Hale Observatory, California.

STARS

Largest and most massive

The variable star *Eta Carinae*, which is 9100 light-years distant in the Carina Nebula in our own galaxy, has a mass at least 200 times greater than our own Sun. *Betelgeux* (top left star of Orion) has a diameter of 700 million km *400 million miles* or about 500 times greater than the Sun. In 1978 it was found to be surrounded not only by a dust 'shell' but also an outer tenuous gas halo up to 5.3×10^{11} miles *$8,5 \times 10^{11}$ km* in diameter, that is over 1100 times the diameter of the star. The light left *Betelgeux* in AD 1680.

Smallest and lightest

A mass of 0.014 that of the Sun is estimated for the very faint star RG 0058.8-2807 which was discovered by I. Neill Reid and Gerard Gilmore using the UK Schmidt telescope and was announced in April 1983. The white dwarf star L362-81 has an estimated diameter of 3500 miles *5600 km* or only 0.0040 that of the Sun.

Smallest and coldest planet ● Clyde
Tombaugh (above) discovered Pluto using a
thirteen-inch refractor telescope in Flagstaff,
Arizona. He made the find by systematically
photographing regions of the sky days apart and
comparing the results using a blink-comparator.
The picture on the left was taken on 23 Jan and
the one on the right on 29 Jan 1930. The relative
positions of Pluto are circled. With an estimated
surface temperature of −360°F −220°C, its
diameter is approximately 3000 km *1860 miles*
and the mass about 1/470th that of the Earth.
(Science Photo Library)

Brightest

Sirius A (*Alpha Canis Majoris*), also known as
the Dog Star, is apparently the brightest star of
the 5776 stars of naked eye visibility in the
heavens, with an apparent magnitude of
−1.46. It is in the constellation *Canis Major* and
is visible in the winter months of the northern
hemisphere, being due south at midnight on the
last day of the year. The Sirius system is 8.64
light-years distant and has a luminosity 26 times
as much as that of the Sun. It has a diameter of
1,450,000 miles *2,33 million km* and a mass of
4.20×10^{27} tons *$4,26 \times 10^{27}$ tonnes*. The faint white
dwarf companion Sirius B has a diameter of only
6000 miles *10 000 km* but is 350,000 times heavier
than the Earth. The magnitude of Sirius should
rise to a maximum of −1.67 by *c.* AD 61,000.

Farthest

The Solar System, with its Sun's nine principal
planets, 63 satellites, asteroids and comets, was

estimated in 1982 to be 28,000 light-years from the centre of the lens-shaped Milky Way galaxy (diameter 70,000 light-years) so that the most distant stars in our galaxy are estimated to be 63,000 light-years distant.

Nearest

Excepting the special case of our own Sun (*q.v.* above) the nearest star is the very faint *Proxima Centauri*, discovered in 1915, which is 4.22 light-years (24,800,000,000,000 miles $4,00 \times 10^{13}$ km) away. The nearest 'star' visible to the naked eye is the southern hemisphere binary *Alpha Centauri*, or *Rigel Kentaurus* (4.35 light-years distant), with an apparent magnitude of −0.29. It was discovered by Nicolas L. da Lacaille (1713–62) in *c.* 1752. In AD 29,700 this binary will reach a minimum distance of 2.84 light-years and should then be the second brightest 'star' with an apparent magnitude of −1.20.

Most and least luminous

If all the stars could be viewed at the same distance the most luminous would be the variable *Eta Carinae* (see Most Massive Star), which now has a total luminosity 6,500,000 times that of the Sun but at its peak brightness in 1843 was at least ten times more luminous than this. The visually brightest star is the hypergiant *Cygnus*, 5900 light-years distant, which has an absolute visual magnitude of ¯−9.9 and is therefore visually 810,000 times more luminous than the Sun. This brightness may be matched by the supergiant IV b 59 in the nearby galaxy Messier 101 but this would depend on the distance adopted for this galaxy (estimates varying between 15,600,000 and 19,700,000 light-years). The variable η *Carinae* in *c.* 1840 had an absolute luminosity 4 million times that of the Sun. The faintest star detected is the recently discovered RG 0058.8–2807 (see Lightest Star) which has a total luminosity only 0.00021 that of the Sun and an absolute visual magnitude of 20.2 so that the visual brightness is less than one millionth that of the Sun.

Brightest and latest supernova

The brightest supernova ever seen by historic man is believed to be SN 1006 in April 1006 near *Beta Lupi*, which flared for 2 years and attained a magnitude of −9 to −10. The remnant is believed to be the radio source G.327.6 + 14.5 nearly 3000 light-years distant. Others have occurred in 1054, 1604, 1885 and most recently on 23 Feb 1987 when Ian Shelton sighted that in the Large Magellanec Cloud 170,000 light-years distant.

Constellations

The largest of the 89 constellations is *Hydra* (the Sea Serpent), which covers 1,302.844 deg^2 or 6.3 per cent of the hemisphere and contains at least 68 stars visible to the naked eye (to 5.5 mag.). The constellation *Centaurus* (Centaur), ranking ninth in area embraces however at least 94 such stars. The smallest constellation is *Crux Australis* (Southern Cross) with an area of only 0.16 per cent of the whole sky *viz* 68.477 deg^2 compared with the 41,252.96 deg^2 of the whole sky.

Stellar planets

The first direct evidence of a planet-like companion was announced in Jan 1985 by D. McCarthy Jr, F. J. Law and R. G. Probst (US). It is an object in orbit 1000 million km *600 million miles* from the very faint red dwarf star *Van Biesbroeck 8* (VB8), 21 light-years distant in Ophiuchus. In 1983 Brad Smith and Rick Tervile announced that *Beta Pictoris* exhibited a curious disc formation.

Longest name

The longest name for any star is *Shurnarkabtishashutu*, the Arabic for 'under the southern horn of the bull'.

Black Holes

The concept of superdense bodies was first adumbrated by the Marquis de LaPlace (1749–1827).

This term for a star that has undergone complete gravitational collapse was first used by Prof John Archibald Wheeler at an Institute for Space Studies meeting in New York City on 29 Dec 1967.

The first tentative identification of a Black Hole was announced in December 1972 in the binary-star X-ray source Cygnus X-1. The best candidate is LMC X-3 of 10 solar masses and 180,000 light-years distant reported in Jan 1983. The critical size has been estimated to be as low as a diameter of 3.67 miles *5,90 km*. One at the centre of the Seyfert galaxy, NGC 4151 in *Canes Venatici*, was estimated by Michael Preston (GB) in Oct 1983 to be of between 50–100 million solar masses or up to 2×10^{35} tonnes.

THE UNIVERSE

Outside the Milky Way galaxy, which is part of the so-called Local Group of galaxies moving at a speed of 1,400,000 mph *2 300 000 km/h* relative to the microwave background radiation in a direction offset 44° from the centre of the Virgo cluster, there exist 10,000 million other galaxies. In March 1985 David J. Batuski and Jack O. Burns of the University of New Mexico, Albuquerque, announced the discovery of the largest discrete object in the Universe—a filamentary arrangement of Abell clusters stretching across the South Galactic Cap and measuring 1,000 million light-years, 5.88×10^{21} miles *9,46 $\times 10^{21}$ km* in length.

Farthest visible object

The remotest heavenly body visible with the *naked eye* is the Great Galaxy in *Andromeda* (mag. 3.47), known as Messier 31. It was first noted by the German Simon Marius (1570–1624). This is a rotating nebula in spiral form, and its distance from the Earth is about 2,150,000 light-years, or *c.* 12,600,000,000,000,000,000 miles $20,3 \times 10^{18}$ km and is moving towards us. It is just possible however that, under ideal seeing conditions, Messier 33, the Spiral in Triangulum (mag. 5.79), can be glimpsed by the naked eye of keen-sighted people at a distance of 2,360,000 light-years.

THE MOST DISTANT MEASURED HEAVENLY BODIES

The possible existence of galaxies external to our own Milky Way system was mooted in 1789 by Sir William Herschel (1738–1822). These extra-galactic nebulae were first termed 'island universes'. Sir John Herschel (1792–1871) opined as early as 1835 that some might be more than 250,000,000,000 million miles distant. The first direct measurement of any body outside our Solar System was in 1838. Distances in the table below are based on a Hubble *constant* of 60 km/s^{-1} Mpc^{-1} and assume that the edge of the observable Universe is at a distance of 16,300 million light-years.

Estimated Distance in Light-years[1]	Object	Method	Astronomers	Observatory	Date
about 6 (now 11.08)	61 Cygni	Parallax	F. Bessel	Königsberg, Germany	1838
> 20 (now 26)	Vega	Parallax	F. G. W. Struve	Dorpat (now Tartu), Estonia	1840
c. 200	Limit	Parallax			by 1900
750,000 (now 2.15 m)[2]	Galaxy M31	Cepheid variable	E. P. Hubble (1889–1953)	Mt. Wilson, Cal., USA	1923
900,000 (now 2.15 m)[2]	Galaxy M31	Cepheid variable	E. P. Hubble	Mt. Wilson, Cal., USA	1924

Millions of Light-years	Recession Speed % of c	Red shift[3]		Astronomers	Observatory	Date
c. 200	1.3		NGC 7619	M. L. Humason	Mt. Wilson, Cal., USA	early 1928
> 2100	13.3		Ursa Major No. 2	Humason & E. P. Hubble	Mt. Wilson, Cal., USA	by 1936[4]
5300	32.6	0.403	Cluster 1448	R. Minkowski	Palomar, Cal., USA	1956
5900	36.2	0.461	3C 295 in Boötes	R. Minkowski	Palomar, Cal., USA	June 1960
6700	41.0	0.545	QSO 3C 147	M. Schmidt & T. A. Matthews	Palomar, Cal., USA	Feb 1964[5]
13,100	80.1	2.01	QSO 3C 9	M. Schmidt	Palomar, Cal., USA	April 1965
c. 13,200	81.3	2.11	QSO 0106 × 01	E. M. Burbridge et al.	Palomar, Cal., USA	Dec 1965
13,300	81.4	2.12	QSO 1116 + 12	C. R. Lynds & A. N. Stockton	Steward, Ariz., USA	March 1966
				M. Schmidt	Palomar, Cal., USA	March 1966
13,400	82.4	2.22	QSO Pks 0237−23	H. C. Arp et al.	Palomar, Cal., USA	Dec 1966
13,600	83.7	2.36	QSO 4C 25.05	E. T. Olsen & M. Schmidt	Palomar, Cal., USA	Dec 1967[6]
14,300	87.5	2.88	QSO 4C 05.34	R. Lynds & D. Wills	Kitt Peak, Ariz., USA	March 1970
14,700	90.2	3.40	QSO OH 471	R. F. Carswell & P. A. Strittmatter	Steward, Ariz., USA	March 1973
14,800	90.7	3.53	QSO OQ 172	E. J. Wampler et al.	Lick, Cal., USA	May 1973
14,900	91.6	3.78	QSO Pks 2000−330	B. A. Peterson et al.	Siding Spring, NSW, Australia	April 1982
14,900	91.7	3.80	QSO Pks 1208+1011	C. Hazard et al.	Siding Spring, NSW, Australia	Feb 1986[7]
15,000	92.3	4.01	QSO 0046−293	P. Hewett & S. J. Warren et al.	Siding Spring, NSW, Australia	Sept 1986[8]

Note: c is the notation for the speed of light. (see p. 64). [1] *Term first utilised in March 1888.* [2] *Re-estimate by G. de Vaucouleurs in Dec 1983.* [3] *Discovered by Vesto Slipher (1875–1969) from Flagstaff, Arizona, USA 1920. Red shift, denoted by z, is the measure of the speed of recession indicated by the ratio resulting from the subtraction of the rest wavelength of an emission line from the observed wavelength divided by the rest wavelength.* [4] *In 1934 Hubble opined that the observable horizon would be 3000 m light-years.* [5] *In Dec 1963 Dr I. S. Shklovsky's (USSR) suggestion that QSO 3C2 was more distant was subsequently confirmed with a value of 0.612 c.* [6] *In Oct 1968 Dr Margaret Burbidge (GB) published a tentative red shift of 2.38 for QSO 5C 2.56.* [7] *Anglo-Australian telescope.* [8] *UK Schmidt telescope.*

Rockets

Quasars

An occultation of 3C-273, observed from Australia on 5 Aug 1962, enabled the existence of quasi-stellar radio sources ('quasars' or QSOs) to be announced by Maarten Schmidt (b. Netherlands 1929). The red shift proved to be z = 0.158. Quasars have immensely high luminosity for bodies so distant and of such small diameter. It was announced in May 1983 that the quasar S5 0014 + 81 had a visual luminosity 1.1×10^{15} times greater than that of the Sun. The first double quasar (0957 + 56) among 1500 known quasars, was announced in May 1980.

Pulsars

The earliest observation of a pulsating radio source or 'pulsar' CP 1919 (now PSR 1919 + 21) by Dr Jocelyn Burnell (née Bell, 1943) was announced from the Mullard Radio Astronomy Observatory, Cambridgeshire, England, on 24 Feb 1968. It had been detected on 28 Nov 1967. The fastest spinning is pulsar 1937 + 214 which is in the region of the minor constellation Vulpecula (The Fox) 16,000 light-years distant. It has a pulse period of 1.557806449 milli-sec and a spin-down rate of 1.0511×10^{-19} sec/sec. However, the most *accurate* stellar clock is the pulsar PSR 1855 + 09 which has a spin-down rate of only 2.1×10^{-20} sec/sec.

Remotest object

Both the interpretation of the very large red shifts exhibited by quasars and the estimation of equivalent distances remain controversial. The record red shift of z = 4.01 for quasar 0046–293 (see Table) was announced by Stephen Warren *et al* on 8 Jan 1987 from analyses from plates from the UK Schmidt Telescope, Siding Spring, NSW. Assuming an 'observable horizon', where the speed of recession very closely approaches the speed of light *c*. to be at 16,300 million light-years or 96,000,000,000,000,000,000,000 miles *$1,54 \times 10^{23}$ km*, this quasar would be more than 15,000 million light-years distant. The 3 K background radiation

or primordial hiss discovered in 1965 by Arno Penzias and Robert Wilson of Bell Laboratories appears to be moving at a velocity of 99.9998 per cent of the speed of light.

Age of the Universe

For the age of the Universe a value of 16.3 ± 2 aeons or gigayears (an aeon or gigayear being 1000 million years) is obtained from cosmochronology and nucleochronology. Based on the presently accepted Friedman models of the Universe with zero cosmological constant then the equivalent Hubble ratio is about 60 km/s/Mpc which compares to the most likely experimental value of 80 km s⁻¹ Mpc⁻¹. In 1973 an *ex nihilo* creation was postulated by Edward P. Tryon (US). Modified versions of the Inflationary Model, originally introduced by Alan Guth (US) in 1981, now rival the 'Big Bang' theory of creation.

ROCKETRY AND MISSILES

Earliest uses

War rockets, propelled by a charcoal-saltpetre-sulfur gun-powder, were described by Tseng Kung Liang of China in 1042. This early form of rocket became known in Europe by 1258.

The pioneer of military rocketry in Britain was Col Sir William Congreve, Bt, MP (1772–1828),

Comptroller of the Royal Laboratory, Woolwich, London and Inspector of Military Machines. His 'six-pound (*2,72 kg*) rocket' was developed to a range of 2000 yd *1825m* by 1805 and first used by the Royal Navy against Boulogne, France on 8 Oct 1806.

The first launching of a liquid-fuelled rocket (patented 14 July 1914) was by Dr Robert Hutchings Goddard (1882–1945) of the United States, at Auburn, Massachusetts, on 16 Mar 1926, when his rocket reached an altitude of 41 ft *12,5 m* and travelled a distance of 184 ft *56 m*. The USSR's earliest rocket was the semi-liquid fuelled GIRD-IX (Gruppa Izucheniya Reaktivnogo Dvizheniya) begun in 1931 and tested on 17 Aug 1933.

Longest ranges

On 16 Mar 1962, Nikita Khrushchev, then Prime Minister of the USSR, claimed in Moscow that the USSR possessed a 'global rocket' with a range of 30 000 km (*about 19,000 miles*) *i.e.* more than the Earth's semi-circumference and therefore capable of hitting any target from either direction.

Most powerful

It has been suggested that the USSR lunar booster which blew up on the pad at Tyuratam on 3 July 1969 had a thrust of 10–14 million lb *4,5–6,35 million kg*.

The most powerful rocket yet launched has been the Saturn V, used for the Project Apollo and Skylab programmes on which development began in January 1962, at the John F. Kennedy Space Center, Merritt Island, Florida. The rocket was 363 ft 8 in *110,85 m* tall, with a payload of 74 783 kg *73.60 tons* in the case of *Skylab 1*, and gulped 13.4 tons *13,6 tonnes* of propellant per sec for 2½ min (2010 tons *2042 tonnes*). The whole assembly generated 175,600,000 hp and weighed up to 7,600,000 lb (3393 tons *3447 tonnes*) fully loaded in the case of *Apollo 17*. It was first launched on 9 Nov 1967, from the Kennedy Space Center, Florida.

Highest velocity

The first space vehicle to achieve the Third Cosmic velocity sufficient to break out of the Solar System was *Pioneer 10* (see table p. 70). The Atlas SLV-3C launcher with a modified Centaur D second stage and a Thiokol Te-364-4 third stage left the Earth at an unprecedented 32,114 mph *51 682 km/h* on 2 Mar 1972. The highest recorded velocity of any space vehicle has been 240 000 km/h *149,125 mph* in the case of the US-German solar probe *Helios B* launched on 15 Jan 1976.

Remotest man-made object

Pioneer 10, launched from Kennedy Space Center, Cape Canaveral, Florida, crossed the mean orbit of Pluto on 17 Oct 1986 being then at a distance of 3670 million miles *5900 million km*. It will be beyond the furthest extension of Pluto's orbit by April 1989 and will continue into space at 49 000 km/h *30,450 mph*. In AD 34,593 it will make its nearest approach to the *Star Ross* 248, 10.3 light-years distant. Before 1991, *Voyager 1*, travelling faster, will surpass *Pioneer 10* in remoteness from the Earth.

The spacecraft carries a plaque designed to communicate with any possible interstellar humanoids. This shows a man and a woman and, diagramatically, where the spacecraft comes from in our Solar System and how our Sun relates to the pulsars whose rates are given in digital code.

SPACE FLIGHT

The physical laws controlling the flight of artificial satellites were first propounded by Sir Isaac Newton (1642–1727) in his *Philosophiae Naturalis Principia Mathematica* ('Mathematical Principles of Natural Philosophy'), begun in March 1686 and first published in the summer of 1687. The first artificial satellite was successfully put into orbit at an altitude of 142/588 miles *228,5/946 km* and a velocity of more than 17,750 mph *28 565 km/h* from Baikonar, north of Tyuratam, 170 miles *275 km* east of the Aral Sea on the night of 4 Oct 1957. This spherical satellite *Sputnik* ('Fellow Traveller') *1*, officially designated 'Satellite 1957 Alpha 2', weighed 83,6 kg *184.3 lb*, with a diameter of 58 cm *22.8 in*, and its lifetime is believed to have been 92 days, ending on 4 Jan 1958. The 29,5 m *96 ft 8 in* SL-1 launcher was designed under the direction of former Gulag prisoner Dr Sergey Pavlovich Korolyov (1907–66).

Earliest manned satellite

The earliest manned space flight ratified by the world governing body, La Fédération Internationale Aéronautique (founded 1905), was by Cosmonaut Flight Major (later Colonel) Yuriy Alekseyevich Gagarin (b. 9 Mar 1934) in *Vostok 1* on 12 Apr 1961.

Details filed showed take-off to be from Baikonar at 6.07 a.m. GMT and the landing near Smelovka, near Engels, in the Saratov region, USSR, 108 minutes later. The maximum altitude during *Vostok 1*'s 40 868,6 km *25,394.5 miles* flight was listed at 327 km *203.2 miles* with a maximum speed of 17,560 mph *28 260 km/h*.

Colonel Gagarin, invested a Hero of the Soviet Union and awarded the Order of Lenin and the Gold Star Medal, was killed in a low level jet plane crash near Moscow on 27 Mar 1968.

First woman in space

The first woman to orbit the Earth was Junior Lieutenant (now Lt-Col Eng) Valentina Vladimirovna Tereshkova (b. 6 Mar 1937), who was launched in *Vostok 6* from Tyuratam, USSR, at 9.30 a.m. GMT on 16 June 1963, and landed at 8.16 a.m. on 19 June, after a flight of 2 days 22 hr 50 min, during which she completed over 48 orbits (1,225,000 miles *1 971 000 km*) and passed momentarily within 3 miles *4,8 km* of *Vostok 5*.

Space fatalities

The greatest published number to perish in any of the 117 attempted space flights to date is seven (five men and two women) aboard the ill-fated *Challenger* 51L on 28 Jan 1986 when an explosion occurred 73 sec after lift off, at a height of 14 326 m *47,000 ft*. The number killed in the launcher explosions at Baikonar, USSR has never been revealed.

First 'walk' in space

Lt-Col (now Maj-Gen) Aleksey A. Leonov (b. 20 May 1934) from *Voskhod 2* was the first person to engage in 'extra-vehicular activity' on 18 Mar 1965. Capt Bruce McCandless II (b. 8 Jun 1937) USN, from the space shuttle *Challenger*, was the first to engage in untethered EVA, at an altitude of 164 miles *264 km* above Hawaii, on 7 Feb 1984. His MMU (Manned Manoeuvring Unit) back-pack cost $15 million to develop.

Longest manned space flight

The longest time spent in space is 236 days 22 hr 49 min, by Dr Oleg Y. Atkov (b. 9 May 1949), Leonid D. Kizim (b. 5 Aug 1941) and Vladimir A. Solovyev (b. 11 Nov 1946) on board *Soyuz T10*. They were launched on 8 Feb 1984. Yuri Romanenko and Aleksandr Laveikin were launched in *Soyuz TM2* on 5 Feb 1987 to dock with the space station *Mir* with the intention of prolonging the record on 9 Jan 1988.

Astronaut *Oldest and youngest*

The oldest of the 200 people in space has been Karl G. Henize (US), aged 58 while on the 19th Space Shuttle mission aboard the *Challenger* on 29 Jul 1985. The youngest has been Major (later Lt-Gen) Gherman Stepanovich Titov (b. 11 Sept 1935), who was aged 25 years 329 days when launched in *Vostok 2* on 6 Aug 1961.

Most journeys

Capt John Watts Young (b. 24 Sept 1930) (USN ret) completed his sixth space flight on 8 Dec 1983 when he relinquished command of *Columbia* STS 9/Spacelab after a space career of 34 days 19 hr 42 min 13 sec.

Duration record on the Moon

The crew of *Apollo 17* collected a record 253 lb *114,8 kg* of rock and soil during their 22 hr 5 min 'extra-vehicular activity'. They were Capt Eugene A. Cernan, USN (b. Chicago, 14 Mar 1934) and Dr Harrison H. (Jack) Schmitt (b. Santa Rosa, New Mexico, 3 July 1935) who became the 12th man on the Moon. The crew were on the lunar surface for 74 hr 59 min during this longest of lunar missions which took 12 days 13 hr 51 min on 7–19 Dec 1972.

First extra-terrestrial vehicle

The first wheeled vehicle landed on the Moon was *Lunakhod I* which began its Earth-controlled travels on 17 Nov 1970. It moved a total of 10,54 km *6.54 miles* on gradients up to 30° in the Mare Imbrium and did not become non-functioning until 4 Oct 1971. The lunar speed and distance record was set by the *Apollo 16* Rover with 11.2 mph *18km/h* downhill and 22.4 miles *33,8 km*.

Closest approach to the Sun by a rocket

The research spacecraft *Helios B* approached within 27 million miles *43,4 million km* of the Sun, carrying both US and West German instrumentation on 16 Apr 1976.

Heaviest and largest space object

The heaviest object orbited is the Saturn V third stage with *Apollo 15* (spacecraft) which, prior to trans-lunar injection in parking orbit, weighed 140 512 kg *138.29 tons*. The 442 lb *200 kg* US RAE (Radio Astronomy Explorer) B or *Explorer 49* launched on 10 June 1973 had, however, antennae 1500 ft *415 m* from tip to tip.

Most expensive project

The total cost of the US manned space programme up to and including the lunar mission of *Apollo 17* has been estimated to be $25,541,400,000 (*then £9,823,150,000*). The first 15 years of the USSR space programme from 1958 to September 1973 have been estimated to have cost $45,000 million. The cost of the NASA Shuttle programme was $9.9 billion (£4350 million) to the launch of *Columbia* on 12 Apr 1981.

ROCKET ALTITUDE RECORDS

Height in miles	Height in km	Rocket	Place	Launch	Date
0.71	1,14	A 3 in *7,62 cm* rocket	near London, England	April	1750
1.24	2	Reinhold Tiling[1] (Germany) solid fuel rocket	Osnabruck, Germany	April	1931
3.1	5	GIRD-X liquid fuel (USSR)	USSR	25 Nov	1933
8.1	13	USSR 'Stratosphere' rocket	USSR		1935
52.46	84,42	A.4 rocket (Germany)[2]	Peenemünde, Germany	3 Oct	1942
c. 85	c. 136	A.4 rocket (Germany)[2]	Heidelager, Poland	early	1944
118	190	A.4 rocket (Germany)[2]	Heidelager, Poland	mid	1944
244	392,6	V-2/W.A.C. Corporal (2-stage) Bumper No. 5 (USA)	White Sands, NM, USA	24 Feb	1949
318	512	Geophysical rocket V-5-V (USSR)	Tyuratam, USSR		1950–52
682	1097	Jupiter C (USA)	Cape Canaveral, Florida, USA	20 Sept	1956
>800	>1300	ICBM test flight R-7 (USSR)	Tyuratam, USSR	Aug	1957
>2700	>4345	Farside No. 5 (4-stage) (USA)	Eniwetok Atoll	20 Oct	1957
70,700	113 770	Pioneer 1-B Lunar Probe (USA)	Cape Canaveral, Florida, USA	11 Oct	1958
215,300,000*	346 480 000	Luna I or Mechta (USSR)	Tyuratam, USSR	2 Jan	1959
242,000,000*	389 450 000	Mars I (USSR)	USSR	1 Nov	1962
3,666,000,000[3]	5 900 000 000	Pioneer 10 (USA) (see page 70)	Kennedy Space Center, Cape Canaveral, Florida, USA	2 Mar	1972

* Apogee in solar orbit. [1] There is some evidence that Tiling may shortly after have reached 9500 m (5.90 miles) with a solid fuel rocket at Wangerooge, East Friesian Islands, W. Germany.
[2] The A4 was latterly referred to as the V2 rocket, a code for second revenge weapon (vergeltungswaffe) following upon the V1 'flying bomb'. [3] Distance on crossing Pluto's mean orbit on 17 Oct 1986.

THE
SCIENTIFIC
WORLD
CHAPTER FIVE

The largest radio telescopic installation ●
Part of the array of antennae that spans the San
Augustin Plains in New Mexico (see page 75).

Elements

All known matter in, on and beyond the Earth is made up of chemical elements. It is estimated that there are 10^{87} electrons in the known Universe. The total of naturally-occurring elements is 94, comprising, at ordinary temperatures, two liquids, 11 gases and 81 solids. The so-called 'fourth state' of matter is plasma, when negatively-charged electrons and positively-charged ions are in flux.

Lightest and heaviest sub-nuclear particles

By April 1986 the existence was accepted of 29 'stable' particles, 56 meson resonance multiplets, and 48 baryon resonance multiplets, representing the eventual discovery of 224 particles and an equal number of anti-particles. The heaviest stable particle fully accepted is the neutral weak gauge boson, the Z°, of mass 92.6 GeV which was first detected in May 1983 by the UA1 Collaboration, CERN, Geneva, Switzerland using the 540 GeV Super Proton Synchrotron proton-anti-

Enrico Fermi 1901–54 ● This Italian-born US physicist, who designed the first nuclear reactor in 1942, gave his name to the 100th element, fermium. (Photo: Argonne National Laboratory)

proton beam collider. The heaviest hadron accepted is the upsilon (6S) meson resonance of mass 11.02 GeV and lifetime 8.3×10^{-24} sec, which consists of a bottom or beauty quark and its anti-quark, and which was first identified in October 1984 by two groups using the electron storage ring facilities at Cornell University, Ithaca, New York, USA. Sub-atomic concepts require that the masses of the graviton, photon, and neutrino should all be zero. Based on the sensitivities of various cosmological theories, upper limits for the masses of these particles are $7,6 \times 10^{-67}$ g for the graviton, $3,0 \times 10^{-53}$ g for the photon, and $1,4 \times 10^{-32}$ g for the neutrino (cf. electron mass $9,10939 \times 10^{-28}$ g).

Newest particles

The discovery in July 1984 by the Crystal Ball Collaboration, Hamburg, West Germany of a particle of mass 8.32 GeV known as the 'zeta', and which was associated with the existence of the important theoretical particle known as the Higgs boson, has not been confirmed. It was named after Prof Peter Higgs (b. 29 May 1929) of the University of Edinburgh.

THE 109 ELEMENTS

There are 94 naturally-occurring elements comprising, at ordinary temperatures, two liquids, 11 gases, 72 metals and nine other solids.
To date the discovery of a further 15 transuranic elements (Elements 95 to 109) has been claimed of which 10 are undisputed.

CATEGORY	NAME	SYMBOL	DISCOVERY OF ELEMENT	RECORD
COMMONEST (LITHOSPHERE)	OXYGEN	O	1771 Scheele (Germany-Sweden)	46.60% by weight
COMMONEST (ATMOSPHERE)	NITROGEN	N	1772 Rutherford (GB)	78.09% by volume
COMMONEST (EXTRA-TERRESTRIAL)	HYDROGEN	H	1776 Cavendish (GB)	90% of all matter
RAREST (OF THE 94)[1]	ASTATINE	At	1940 Corson (US) et al.	1/176th oz *0,16 g* in Earth's crust
LIGHTEST	HYDROGEN	H	1776 Cavendish (GB)	0.005612 lb/ft³ *0,00008989 g/cm³*
LIGHTEST (METAL)	LITHIUM	Li	1817 Arfwedson (Sweden)	33.30 lb/ft³ *0,5334 g/cm³*
DENSEST	OSMIUM	Os	1804 Tennant (GB)	1410 lb/ft³ *22,59 g/cm³*
HEAVIEST (GAS)	RADON	Rn	1900 Dorn (Germany)	0.6274 lb/ft³ *0,01005 g/cm³* at 0° C
NEWEST[2]	UNNILOCTIUM	Uno	1984 G. Munzenberg et al. (W. Germany) and at Dubna Research Institute, Moscow	Element 108
PUREST[3]	HELIUM	⁴He	1868 Lockyer (GB) & Janssen (France)	2 parts in 10^{15} (1978)
HARDEST	CARBON	C	prehistoric	Diamond allotrope, Knoop value 8400
MOST EXPENSIVE	CALIFORNIUM	Cf	1950 Seaborg (US) et al.	Sold in 1970 for $10 per µg
MOST STABLE[4]	TELLURIUM	¹²⁸Te	1782 von Reichenstein (Austria)	Half-life of 1.5×10^{24} years
LEAST STABLE	LITHIUM (ISOTOPE 5)	Li 5	1817 Arfwedson (Sweden)	Lifetime of 4.4×10^{-22} sec.
MOST ISOTOPES	XENON	Xe	1898 Ramsay & Travers (GB)	36
	CAESIUM	Cs	1860 Bunsen & Kirchoff (Germany)	36
LEAST ISOTOPES	HYDROGEN	H	1776 Cavendish (GB)	3 (confirmed)
MOST DUCTILE	GOLD	Au	prehistoric	1 oz drawn to 43 miles *1 g/2,4 km*
HIGHEST TENSILE STRENGTH	BORON	B	1808 Gay-Lussac & Thenard (France) & H. Davy (GB)	3.9×10^6 lb f/in² *26,8 GPa*
LOWEST MELTING/BOILING POINT (NON-METALLIC)[3,5]	HELIUM	⁴He	1868 Lockyer (GB) & Janssen (France)	−272,375° C under pressure 24.985 atm (*2,532 MPa*) and −268,928° C
LOWEST MELTING/BOILING POINT (METALLIC)	MERCURY	Hg	protohistoric	−38,836° C/356,661° C
HIGHEST MELTING/BOILING POINT (NON-METALLIC)	CARBON (CARBYNE 6)	C	prehistoric[4]	3530° C/3870° C
HIGHEST MELTING/BOILING POINT (METALLIC)[6]	TUNGSTEN	W	1783 J. J. & F. d'Elhuyar (Spain)	3420° C and 5730° C
LARGEST EXPANSION (NEGATIVE)	PLUTONIUM	Pu	1940 Seaborg (US) et al.	$-5,8 \times 10^{-5}$ cm/cm/deg C between 450–480° C (Delta prime allotrope disc. 1953)
LOWEST EXPANSION (POSITIVE)	CARBON (DIAMOND)	C	prehistoric	$1,0 \times 10^{-6}$ cm/cm/deg C (at 20° C)
HIGHEST EXPANSION (METAL)	CAESIUM	Cs	1860 Bunsen & Kirchoff (Germany)	$9,7 \times 10^{-5}$ cm/cm/deg C (at 20° C)
HIGHEST EXPANSION (SOLID)	NEON	Ne	1898 Ramsay & Travers (GB)	$1,94 \times 10^{-3}$ cm/cm/deg C at −248,59° C
MOST TOXIC	RADIUM	²²⁴Ra	1898 The Curies & Bemont (France)	Naturally occurring isotope 17,000 × more toxic than plutonium 239

[1] The naturally-occurring isotope astatine 215 occurs only to the extent of 1.6×10^{-10} oz *4,5 nanograms*.

[2] Provisional IUPAC name. A single atom of unnilennium Une (Element 109) was created by bombardment of bismuth by iron ions at the GSI laboratory, Dormstadt, W. Germany on 29 Aug 1982. It had the highest atomic number (element 109) and the highest atomic mass (266).

[3] Identified on Earth by Ramsay (GB) in 1895.

[4] Double beta decay estimate. Alpha particle record is Samarium 148 at 8×10^{15} years and Beta particle record is Cadmium 113 at 9×10^{15} years.

[5] Monatomic hydrogen H is expected to be a non-liquefiable superfluid gas.

[6] The carbyne forms of carbon were discovered by A. E. Goresy and G. Donnay (USA) and A. M. Sladkov and Yu. P. Koudrayatsev (USSR) in 1968.

Most and least stable

Experiments from 1982 to 1985 have finally confirmed that the proton has a lifetime in excess of 1×10^{30} years compared to theoretical predictions based on the 'grand unified theory' which suggests that the lifetime may be less than 1×10^{34} years. The least stable or shortest-lived particles are the two baryon resonances N(2220) and N(2600), both with 1.6×10^{-24} sec although the *predicted* lifetimes of both the weak gauge bosons, the $W^{\pm}$ and Z°, are 2.4×10^{-25} sec.

Smelliest substance

The most evil-smelling substance, of the 17,000 smells so far classified, must be a matter of opinion but ethyl mercaptan (C_2H_5SH) and butyl seleno-mercaptan (C_4H_9SeH) are powerful claimants, each with a smell reminiscent of a combination of rotting cabbage, garlic, onions and sewer gas.

Most expensive perfume

The retail prices of the most expensive perfumes tend to be fixed with an eye to public relations rather than at levels solely dictated by the cost of ingredients and packaging. The Chicago-based firm Jōvan marketed from March 1984 a cologne called Andron which contains a trace of the attractant pheromone androstenol which has a cost of $2750 (*£2381*) per oz $97 (*£84*) per gramme.

Most potent poison

The rickettsial disease, Q-fever, can be instituted by a *single* organism though it is only fatal in 1 in 1000 cases. About 10 organisms of *Francisella tularenesis* (formerly *Pasteurella tularenesis*) can institute tularaemia variously called alkali disease, Francis disease or deerfly fever. This is fatal in upwards of 10 cases in 1000.

Most powerful nerve gas

VX, 300 times more toxic than phosgene $(COCl_2)$ used in World War I, was developed at the Chemical Defence Experimental Establishment, Porton Down, Wiltshire in 1952. Patents were applied for in 1962 and published in February 1974 showing it to be Ethyl S-2-diisopropyl-aminoethylmethylphosphonothiolate. The lethal dosage is 10 mg-minute/m³ airborne or 0,3 mg orally.

Most absorbent substance

The US Department of Agriculture Research Service announced on 18 Aug 1974 that 'H-span' or Super Slurper composed of one half starch derivative and one fourth each of acrylamide and acrylic acid can, when treated with iron, retain water 1300 times its own weight.

Finest powder

The ultimate in fine powder is solid helium which was first postulated to be a monatomic powder as early as 1964.

Drink and Drugs

As from 1 Jan 1981 the strength of spirits has been expressed only in terms of percentage volume of alcohol at 20° C. Absolute or '100% vol' alcohol was formerly expressed to be 75.35 degrees over proof or 75.35° OP. In the USA proof is double the actual percentage of alcohol by volume at 60° F *15,6° C* such that absolute alcohol is 200 per cent proof spirit. 'Hangovers' are said to be aggravated by the presence of such toxic congenerics as amyl alcohol $(C_5H_{11}OH)$.

Most alcoholic

During independence (1918–40) the Estonian Liquor Monopoly marketed 98 per cent potato alcohol (196 proof US). In 31 US states *Everclear*, 190 proof or 95% vol alcohol, is marketed by the American Distilling Co 'primarily as a base for

Most expensive white wine ● A bottle of white wine—Château d'Yquem of 1784—was sold at auction by Christie's, London on 4 Dec 1986 for £39,600 to Iyad Shiblaq, Jordan, a teetotaller.

home-made cordials'. Royal Navy rum, introduced in 1655, was 40° OP (79% vol) before 1948, but was reduced to 4.5° UP (under proof) or 46% vol before its abolition on 31 July 1970. Full strength Pusser's naval rum was again sold by E. D. & F. Man from 1984.

Strongest beer

The strongest beer as measured by original gravity is the German EKU Kulminatur Urtyp Hell 28 with 1131.7° and 13.52% alcohol by volume. The most alcoholic beer is Samichlaus Bier brewed by Brauerei Hürlimann of Zürich, Switzerland. It is 13.94 per cent alcohol by volume at 20° C with an original gravity of 1107.6°.

The strongest regularly-brewed beer in Britain is Thomas Hardy's brewed by Eldridge Pope & Co at their Dorchester Brewery, Dorset. It has an alcoholic content of 12.48 per cent by volume at 60° F and an original gravity of 1125.8°.

Weakest beer

The weakest liquid ever marketed as beer was a sweet ersatz beer which was brewed in Germany by Sunner, Colne-Kalk, in 1918. It had an original gravity of 1000.96° and a strength 1/30th that of the weakest beer now obtainable in the U.K.

Oldest wine

The oldest datable wine ever found were two bottles from Xinyang, Hunan, China in 1980 from a tomb dated to 1300 BC. A wine jar recovered in Rome has been found to bear the label 'Q. Lutatio C. Mario Cos' meaning that it was produced in the consulship of Q. Lutatius and C. Marius *i.e.* in 102 BC. A bottle of 1748 Rudesheimer Rosewein was auctioned at Christie's, London for £260 on 6 Dec 1979.

Most expensive wine

The highest price paid for any bottle has been £105,000 for a 1787 Château Lafite claret sold to Christopher Forbes (USA) at Christie's, London on 5 Dec 1985. The price was affected insofar as the bottle was initialled by Thomas Jefferson (1743–1826), 3rd President of the United States. In Nov 1986 its cork, dried out by exhibition lights, slipped thus making the wine undrinkable.

Wine auction

The largest single sale of wine was conducted by Christie's of King Street, St James's, London on 10–11 July 1974 at Quaglino's Ballroom, London when 2325 lots comprising 432,000 bottles realised £962,190.

Wine tasting

The largest ever reported wine tasting was that staged by the Wine Institute at St Francis Hotel,

Smallest bottle ● The smallest and meanest bottles of liquor now sold are bottles of White Horse Scotch Whisky standing just over 2 in *5 cm* tall and containing 1,3 millilitres *22 minims*. A mini case of 12 bottles is available measuring 1.84 × 1.31 × 1.06 in *4,67 × 3,33 × 2,69 cm* and costs £5.15 + VAT. (Photo: Rex Features)

San Francisco, California on 17 July 1980 with 125 pourers, 90 openers and a consumption of 3000 bottles.

Most expensive spirits

The most expensive bottle of spirits at auction was £1265 for Lot 402, 'The Macallan Over 50 Years Old', a single malt whisky distilled in 1928, to a Scottish wine merchant, Christopher Lynas, at Christie's, Glasgow, Scotland on 17 June 1986. *Grande Fine Champagne Cognac, Biscuit du Boucher 1811* retails at 18,000 F (*now £1667*) a bottle at Fauchon. In Britain *Hennessy Private Reserve Grande Champagne* retails for £120 (including VAT) for a standard bottle.

Largest bottles

The largest bottle ever built was unveiled at the *Guinness World of Records*, Piccadilly, London on 31 Mar 1987 measuring 6 ft *1,83 m* tall and 4 ft 9½ in *1,46 m* in circumference. It contained 185 litres *40.7 galls* of William Grant's Family Reserve Finest Scotch Whisky.

The largest bottle normally used in the wine and spirit trade is the Jeroboam (equal to 4 bottles of champagne or, rarely, of brandy and from 5 to 6½ bottles of claret according to whether blown or moulded) and the double magnum (equal, since *c.* 1934 to 4 bottles of claret or, more rarely, red Burgundy). A complete set of champagne bottles would consist of a ¼ bottle, through the ½ bottle, bottle, magnum, Jeroboam, Rehoboam, Methuselah, Salmanazer and Balthazar, to the Nebuchadnezzar, which has a capacity of 16 litres *28.14 pt*, and is equivalent to 20 bottles. Martell Cognac is available in a range of 21 bottle sizes from 3 cl *0.05 pt* to 3.78 l *6.6 pt*.

Bottle collections

David L. Maund of Upham, Hampshire, has a collection of unduplicated miniature Scotch Whisky bottles amounting to 6792. Over the past 30 years he has also collected 323 miniature Guinness bottles.

The largest reported collection of distilled spirits or liqueurs in any bar is 1722 unduplicated labels by Ian Boasman at Bistro French, Preston, Lancashire audited in May 1986.

The world's greatest collection of whisky bottles is one of 3100 unduplicated labels assembled by Sig Edward Giaccone at his Whiskyteca, Salo, Lake Garda, Italy.

Champagne cork flight

The longest distance for a champagne cork to fly from an untreated and unheated bottle 4 ft *1,22 m* from level ground is 105 ft 9 in *32,23 m* by Peter Kirby at Idlewild Park, Reno, Nevada, on 4 July 1981.

Most powerful drugs

The most powerful commonly available drug is d-Lysergic Acid Diethylamide tartrate (LSD-25, $C_{20}H_{25}N_3O$) first produced in 1938 for common cold research and as a hallucinogen by Dr Albert Hoffman (Swiss) on 16–19 Apr 1943. The most potent analgesic drug is the morphine-like R33799 confirmed in 1978 to have almost 12,000 times the potency of morphine. Interferon was reported available for $10 per millionth of a microgramme.

Most prescribed drug

The world's top-selling prescription drug is the anti-ulcer drug Zantac, manufactured by Glaxo Holdings plc. Worldwide sales in 1986 exceeded $1 billion. Zantac is also the top-seller in the UK, with sales of more than £70 million in the prescribed drug market.

Most lethal man-made chemical

TCDD (2,3,7,8-tetrachlorodibenzo-p-dioxin), discovered in 1872, is admitted to be 150,000 times more deadly than cyanide at $3{,}1 \times 10^{-9}$ moles/kg.

CAMERAS

Earliest

The earliest veiled reference to a photograph on glass taken in a camera was in a letter dated 19 July 1822 from Joseph Nicéphore Niépce (1765–1833), a French scientist. It was a photograph of a copper engraving of Pope Pius VII taken at Gras, near Chalon-sur-Saône and it was rediscovered in London in Feb 1952 by the photo-historian Helmut Gernsheim after six years' research. The earliest photograph taken in England was one of a diamond-paned window in Laycock (or Lacock) Abbey, Wiltshire, taken in August 1835 by William Henry Fox Talbot, MP (1800–77), the inventor of the negative-positive process. The negative of this was donated to the Science Museum, London in 1937 by his grand-daughter Matilda. The world's earliest aerial photograph was taken in 1858 by Gaspard Félix Tournachon (1820–1910), *alias* Nadar, from a balloon near Villacoublay, on the outskirts of Paris.

Largest

The largest and most expensive industrial camera ever built is the 27 ton/*tonne* Rolls Royce camera now owned by BPCC Graphics Ltd of Derby, England commissioned in 1956. It measures 8 ft 10 in *2,69 m* high, 8 ft 3 in *2,51 m* wide and 46 ft *14,02 m* in length. The lens is a 63 in *160 cm* f 16 Cooke Apochromatic. In 1987 it was still in full use.

Smallest

Apart from cameras built for intra-cardiac surgery and espionage, the smallest camera that has been marketed is the circular Japanese 'Petal' camera with a diameter of 1.14 in *2,9 cm* and a thickness of 0.65 in *1,65 cm*. It has a focal length of 12 mm *0.47 in*. The BBC TV programme *Record Breakers* showed prints from this camera on 3 Dec 1974.

Fastest

A camera built for research into high-power lasers by The Blackett Laboratory of Imperial College of Science and Technology, London, registers images at a rate of 33,000 million per sec.

Most expensive

The most expensive complete range of camera equipment in the world is that of Nikon of Tokyo, Japan, who marketed in April 1985 their complete range of 24 cameras with 72 lenses and 553 accessories. Shadow Photographic Ltd of London quoted £218,167.50 excluding VAT. The highest auction price for an antique camera is £21,000 for a J. B. Dancer stereo camera, patented in 1856 and sold at Christie's, South Kensington on 12 Oct 1977.

Longest negative

On 22 June 1985 Robert J. Paluzzi using a 16 in *40,6 cm* Century Cirkut camera captured a 200 degree view of Las Vegas in a single shot. The resulting negative measured 9 ft *274 cm* by 16 in *40,6 cm*.

Telescopes

Earliest

Although there is evidence that early Arabian scientists understood something of the magnifying power of lenses, their first use to form a telescope has been attributed to Roger Bacon (*c.* 1214–92) in England. The prototype of modern refracting telescopes was completed by Johannes Lippershey for the Netherlands government on 2 Oct 1608.

Largest reflector

The largest telescope in the world is the alt-azimuth mounted 6 m *236.2 in* telescope sited on Mount Semirodriki, near Zelenchukskaya in the Caucasus Mountains, USSR, at an altitude of 6830 ft *2080 m*. Work on the mirror, weighing 70 tons/*tonnes*, was not completed until the summer of 1974. Regular observations were begun on 7 Feb 1976 after 16 years' work. The weight of the 42 m *138 ft* high assembly is 840 tonnes *827 tons*. Being the most powerful of all telescopes its range, which includes the location of objects down to the 25th magnitude, represents the limits of the observable Universe. Its light-gathering power would enable it to detect the light from a candle at a distance of 15,000 miles *24 000 km*.

On 12 Sept 1985, work started on the W. M. Keck 10 metre *393.7 inch* reflector for Caltech and the University of California on Mauna Kea, Hawaii. It is due to be completed by 1989 and will comprise 36 independently-controlled fitting hexagonal mirrors.

Note: The attachment of an electronic charge-coupled device (CCD) increases the 'light-grasp' of a telescope by a factor up to 100 fold. Thus a 200 in *508 cm* telescope achieves the light-gathering capacity of a 1000 inch *25,4 m* telescope.

Largest refractor

The largest refracting (*i.e.* magnification by lenses) telescope in the world is the 62 ft *18,90 m* long 40 in *101,6 cm* telescope completed in 1897 at the Yerkes Observatory, Williams Bay, Wisconsin, and belonging to the University of Chicago, Illinois, USA. In 1900 a 125 cm *49.2 in* refractor 54,85 m *180 ft* in length was built for the Paris Exposition but its optical performance was too poor to justify attempts to use it.

Largest radio dish

Radio waves of extra-terrestrial origin were first detected by Karl Jansky of Bell Telephone Laboratories, Holmdel, New Jersey using a 100 ft *30,48 m* long shortwave rotatable antenna in 1932. The world's largest dish radio telescope is the partially-steerable ionospheric assembly built over a natural bowl at Arecibo, Puerto Rico, completed in November 1963 at a cost of about $9,000,000 (*then £3.75 million*). The dish has a diameter of 1000 ft *304,8 m* and covers 18½ acres *7,48 ha*. Its sensitivity was raised by a factor of 1000 and its range to the edge of the observable Universe at some 15,000 million light-years by the fitting of new aluminium plates at a cost of $8.8 million. Rededication was on 16 Nov 1974.

The world's largest trainable dish-type radio telescope is the 100 m *328 ft* diameter, 3000 ton *3048 tonnes* assembly at the Max Planck Institute for Radio Astronomy of Bonn in the Effelsberger Valley, West Germany; it became operative in May 1971. The cost of the installation, begun in November 1967, was 36,920,000 DM (*then £6,150,000*).

Largest radio installation

The world's largest radio-telescopic installation is the US National Science Foundation VLA (Very Large Array). It is Y-shaped with each arm 13 miles *20,9 km* long with 27 mobile antennae (each of 25 m *82 ft* diameter) on rails. It is 50 miles *80 km* west of Socorro in the Plains of San Augustin, New Mexico, and was dedicated on 10 Oct 1980 at a cost of $78 million (*now £41 million*).

A computer-linked very long base-line array of 25 m *82 ft* radio telescopes stretched over 4200 km *2600 miles* on Latitude 49.3° N has been planned by the Canadian Astronomical Society.

Oldest observatory

The oldest astronomical observatory building extant in the world is 'Tower of the Winds' used by Andronichus of Cyrrhos in Athens, Greece *c.* 70 BC, and equipped with sundials and clepsydra.

Highest observatory

The highest observatory in the world is the University of Denver's High Altitude Observatory at 14,100 ft *4297 m*, opened in 1973. The principal instrument is a 24 in *60,48 cm* Ealing Beck reflecting telescope.

Planetaria

The ancestor of the planetarium is the rotatable Gottorp Globe, built by Andreas Busch in Denmark between 1654 and 1664 to the orders of Olearius, court mathematician to Duke Frederick III of Holstein. It is 34.6 ft *10,54 m* in circumference, weighs nearly 3½ tons/*tonnes* and is now preserved in Leningrad. The stars were painted on the inside. The earliest optical installation was not until 1923 in the Deutsches Museum, Munich, by Zeiss of Jena, East Germany. The world's largest planetarium is in Moscow, USSR, and has a diameter of 82½ ft *25,15 m*.

Space telescope

The first space observatory was the Orbiting Solar observatory 0504 launched on 18 Oct 1967. The largest will be the $1.2 billion NASA Space Telescope of 11 tonnes *10.8 tons* and 13,1 m *43 ft* in overall length with a 94.5 inch *240 cm* reflector eventually to be placed in orbit at *c.* 480 km *300 miles* altitude aboard a US Space Shuttle.

The largest radio-telescopic installation ● Two US National Science Foundation engineers standing in one of the 27 mobile antennae (each 25 m *82 ft* diameter) that make up the Y-shaped VLA (Very Large Array) in the Plains of San Augustin, New Mexico. Each arm is 13 miles *20,9 km* long and the installation costing $78 million (£41 million) was dedicated on 10 Oct 1980. (Photo: Rex Features)

Gems, Jewels and Precious Stones

OPAL

Largest. 220 troy oz. The 17,700 carat *Olympic Australis* (SiO_2nH_2O) found in Coober Pedy, South Australia in August 1956 owned by Altmann and Cherny Pty Ltd, is on public display in Melbourne and valued at $1.8 million (US).

DIAMOND

Largest. 3106 carats. Found on 25 January 1905 in the Premier Mine, Pretoria, South Africa and named *The Cullinan* after the mine's discoverer Sir Thomas Cullinan. Presented to King Edward VII in 1907.

Rarest colour. Blood red. The largest is a 5.05 carat flawless stone found in Tichtenburg, South Africa in 1927 and now in a private collection in the United States.

Smallest cut. 0.00063 carats. Gebroeders van den Wouwer of Antwerp, Belgium, produced a 57 facet stone 0,53 mm *0.02 in* in diameter.

Highest priced. £2,100,000. The *Polar Star* was bought in Geneva on 21 November 1980 by Mr Razeen Salih. The value of this 41.3 carat gem is calculated at over £50,847 per carat.

Largest cut. 530.2 carats. A 74-facet pear-shaped gem named *The Star of Africa*, cleaved from *The Cullinan* by Jak Asscher and polished by Henri Koe in Amsterdam in 1908. Now in the Royal Sceptre. The uncut 890 carat Zale Corporation stone may yield a larger cut stone

Largest amber ● The 'Burma Amber', largest in the world at 33 lb 10 oz *15,25 kg*, which is located in the Natural History Museum, London. Amber is a fossil resin derived from extinct coniferous trees, and often contains trapped insects. (Photo: Natural History Museum, London)

JADE

Largest. 143 tons/tonnes. On 17 September 1978 it was reported that a boulder of nephrite jade $Ca_2(Mg, Fe)_5(Si_4O_{11})_2(OH)_2$ of 21,300 ft³ *603 m³* was found in China.

TOPAZ

Largest. 21,327 carats. The light blue *Brazilian Princess* is cut from a 75 lb *334 kg* crystal and has resided in the American Museum of Natural History, New York, from 10 December 1985. Valued at $1,066,350 and with 221 facets, this is the world's largest faceted stone.

GOLD

Largest nugget. 7560 oz *214,32 kg*. The *Holtermann Nugget* found on 19 October 1872 in the Beyers & Holtermann Star of Hope mine, Hill End, New South Wales, Australia, contained some 220 lb *99,8 kg* of gold in a 630 lb *285,7 kg* slab of slate.

Largest pure nugget. The *Welcome Stranger* found at Moliagul, Victoria, Australia in 1869 yielded 2248 troy oz *69,92 kg* of pure gold from 2280¼ oz *70,92 kg*.

Numerals

In dealing with large numbers, scientists use the notation of 10 raised to various powers to eliminate a profusion of noughts. For example, 19,160,000,000,000 miles would be written 1.916×10^{13} miles. Similarly, a very small number, for example 0,0000154324 of a gram, would be written $1,54324 \times 10^{-5}$. Of the prefixes used before numbers the smallest is 'tredo' from the Danish *tredyvo* for 30, indicating 10^{-30} of a unit, and the highest is 'dea' (Greek, *deca*, ten); symbol *D*, indicating ten groups of 3 zeros 10^{30} or a quintillion (UK) or a nonillion (US).

Highest numbers

The highest lexicographically accepted named number in the system of successive powers of ten is the centillion, first recorded in 1852. It is the hundredth power of a million, or one followed by 600 noughts. The highest named number outside the decimal notation is the Buddhist *asankhyeya*, which is equal to 10^{140}.

The number 10^{100} is designated a Googol. The term was devised by Dr Edward Kasner (US) (d. 1955). Ten raised to the power of a Googol is described as a Googolplex. Some conception of the magnitude of such numbers can be gained when it is said that the number of electrons in some models of the observable Universe does not exceed 10^{87}.

The highest number ever used in a mathematical proof is a bounding value published in 1977 and known as Graham's number. It concerns bi-chromatic hypercubes and is inexpressible without the special 'arrow' notation, devised by Knuth in 1976, extended to 64 layers. Mr Candelaria ('the only man infinity fears') of Loma Linda, California has devised a Large Number Denomination System concluding with a milli-decilli-fiveillionillion.

Prime numbers

A prime number is any positive integer (excluding 1) having no integral factors other than itself and unity, *e.g.* 2, 3, 5, 7 or 11. The lowest prime number is thus 2. The highest known prime number is $2^{216,091} - 1$, discovered in Sept 1985 by analysts using a Cray X-MP/24 computer at Chevron Geosciences Co in Houston, Texas. It is the 30th known Marsenne prime, and contains

EMERALD

Largest cut. 86,136 carats. This natural beryl Gleim [$Be_3Al_2(SiO_3)_6$] was found in Carnaiba, Brazil in August 1974. It was carved by Richard Chan in Hong Kong and valued at £718,000 in 1982.

RUBY

Largest star. 2475 carats. *Rajarathna*, India, displays an animated star of six lines and is cut as a cabochon.

Largest double star. 1370 carats. A cabochon cut gem, *Neelanjahi* owned by G. Vidyaraj, Bangalore, India, displays twelve star lines and measures 3 inches *7,62 cm* in height and 2 inches *5,08 cm* in diameter.

Largest. 8500 carats. In July 1985 jeweller James Kazanjian of Beverly Hills, California, displayed a 5½ inch *14 cm* tall red corundum (Al_2O_3) carved into the Liberty Bell.

PEARL

Largest. 14 lb 1 oz *6,37 kg*. The *Pearl of Laotze* was found at Palawan, Philippines on 7 May 1934 in the shell of a giant clam. The property of Wilburn Dowell Cobb until his death, this 9½ in *24 cm* long by 5½ in *14 cm* diameter *molluscan consecretion* was bought at auction on 15 May 1980 in San Francisco by Peter Hoffman and Victor Barbish for $200,000 £85,000. An appraisal by the San Francisco Gem Laboratory in May 1982 suggested a value of $32,640,000.

SAPPHIRE

Largest. 2,302 carats. Found at Anakie, Queensland, Australia in *c.* 1935, this corundum (Al_2O_3) was carved into a 1318 carat head of Abraham Lincoln and is now in the custody of the Kazanjian Foundation of Los Angeles, California.

Largest cut. 1444 carats. A bust of General Dwight David Eisenhower that was carved in 1953–5 from a 2097-carat black star stone.

Highest priced. £579,300. A step-cut single stone of 66.03 carats from the Rockefeller Collection was sold by auction on 8 May 1980 at Sotheby's, Zurich.

65,050 digits. The lowest non-prime or composite number (excluding 1) is 4.

Perfect numbers

A number is said to be perfect if it is equal to the sum of its divisors other than itself, *e.g.* $1 + 2 + 4 + 7 + 14 = 28$. The lowest perfect number is 6 ($= 1 + 2 + 3$). The highest known and the 30th so far discovered, is $(2^{216,091} - 1) \times 2^{216,090}$. It is a consequence of the highest known prime (see above).

Most innumerate

The most innumerate people are the Nambiquara of the north west Matto Grosso of Brazil who lack any system of numbers. They do, however, have a verb which means 'they are alike'.

Most accurate and most inaccurate version of 'pi'

The greatest number of decimal places to which *pi* (π) has been calculated is 133,554,000 on 13 Jan 1987 by Yasumasa Kanada (Japan), at the NEC Fuchu Factory, Tokyo. The printout was almost 20,000 pages long. In 1897 the General Assembly of Indiana enacted in House Bill No. 246 that *pi* was *de jure* 4.

Earliest measures

The earliest known measure of weight is the *beqa* of the Amratian period of Egyptian civilisation *c.* 3800 BC found at Naqada, Egypt. The weights are cylindrical with rounded ends from 188,7 to 211,2 g *6.65–7.45 oz*. The unit of length used by the megalithic tomb-builders in north western Europe *c.* 3500 BC appears to have been 2.72 ± 0.003 ft *82,90 cm ± 0,09 cm*. This was deduced by Prof Alexander Thom (1894–1985) in 1966.

Time measure

Owing to variations in the length of a day, which is estimated to be increasing irregularly at the average rate of about a millisecond per century due to the Moon's tidal drag, the second has been redefined. Instead of being 1/86,400th part of a mean solar day, it has, since 1960, been reckoned as 1/31,556,925,9747th part of the solar (or tropical) year at AD 1900, January 0.12 hr, Ephemeris time. In 1958 the second of Ephemeris time was computed to be equivalent to 9,192,631,770 ± 20 cycles of the radiation corresponding to the transition of caesium 133 atoms when unperturbed by exterior fields. The greatest diurnal change recorded has been 10 milliseconds on 8 Aug 1972 due to the most violent solar storm recorded in 370 years of observations.

The accuracy of the caesium beam frequency standard approaches 8 parts in 10^{14} compared to 2 parts in 10^{13} for the methane-stabilised helium-neon laser and 6 parts in 10^{13} for the hydrogen maser.

The longest measure of time is the *kalpa* in Hindu chronology. It is equivalent to 4320 million years. In astronomy a cosmic year is the period of rotation of the Sun around the centre of the Milky Way galaxy, *i.e.* 225 million years. In the Late Cretaceous Period of *c.* 85 million years ago the Earth rotated faster so resulting in 370.3 days per year while in Cambrian times some 600 million years ago there is evidence that the year extended over 425 days.

Physical Extremes

Highest temperature

The highest man-made temperatures yet attained are those produced in the centre of a thermonuclear fusion bomb, which are of the order of 300 000 000 – 400 000 000° C. Of controllable temperatures the highest effective laboratory figure reported is 230 million degrees C achieved in the Tokamak Fusion Test Reactor at the Princeton Plasma Physics Laboratory, USA, in June 1986. A figure of 3000 million degrees C was reportedly achieved in the USSR with Ogra injection-mirror equipment *c.* 1962.

Lowest temperature

The lowest temperature reached is 3×10^{-8} Kelvin above absolute zero attained in a two-stage nuclear demagnetisation cryostat at Espoo, Finland by the team led by Prof Olli V. Loúnasmaa (b. 1930) and announced in June 1984. Absolute or thermodynamic temperatures are defined in terms of ratios rather than as differences reckoned from the unattainable absolute zero, which on the Kelvin scale is $-273,15°$ C or

$-459.67°$ F. Thus the lowest temperature ever attained is 1 in 9.1×10^9 of the melting point of ice (0° C or 273.15 K or 32° F). Tokyo University's Institute of Solid State Physics announced on 15 Feb 1983 that a team led by Prof Kazuo Ono had attained a temperature within 0.00003 of a degree of absolute zero at which molecular motion ceases.

Smallest thermometer

Dr Frederick Sachs, a biophysicist at the State University of New York at Buffalo, has developed an ultra-microthermometer for measuring the temperature of single living cells. The tip is one micron in diameter, about one fiftieth the diameter of a human hair.

Largest barometer

A water barometer 12 m *39 ft* in height was constructed by Bert Bolle, Curator of the Barometer Museum, Maartensdijk, Netherlands where the instrument is situated.

Highest pressures

The highest sustained laboratory pressures yet reported are of 1.70 megabars (11,000 tons force/in² *170 GPa*) achieved in the giant hydraulic diamond-faced press at the Carnegie Institution's Geophysical Laboratory, Washington DC reported in June 1978. This laboratory announced solid hydrogen achieved at 57 kilobars pressure on 2 Mar 1979. If created, metallic hydrogen is expected to be silvery, white but soft with a density of 1,1 g/cm³. The pressure required for the transition is estimated by H. K. Mao and P. M. Bell to be 1 megabar at 25°C. Using dynamic methods and impact speeds of up to 18,000 mph *29 000 km/h*, momentary pressures of 75,000,000 atmospheres (490,000 tons/in² *7000 GPa*) were reported from the United States in 1958.

Highest velocity

The highest velocity at which any solid visible object has been projected is 150 km/sec *335,000 mph* in the case of a plastic disc at the Naval Research Laboratory, Washington DC, reported in August 1980.

Finest balance

The most accurate balance in the world is the Sartorius Model 4108 manufactured in Göttingen, West Germany, which can weigh objects of up to 0,5 g to an accuracy of 0,01 µg or 0,00000001 g, equivalent to little more than one sixtieth of the weight of the ink on this full stop.

Largest bubble chamber

The largest bubble chamber in the world is the $7 million (*then £2.5 million*) installation completed in October 1973 at Weston, Illinois. It is 15 ft *4,57 m* in diameter and contains 7259 gal *33 000 litres* of liquid hydrogen at a temperature of −247°C with a super conducting magnet of 3 tesla.

Fastest centrifuge

Ultra-centrifuges were invented by Theodor Svedberg (b. 30 Aug 1884) (Sweden) in 1923. The highest man-made rotary speed ever achieved and the fastest speed of any earth-bound object is 4500 mph *7250 km/h* by a swirling tapered 6 in *15,2 cm* carbon fibre rod in a vacuum at Birmingham University, England reported on 24 Jan 1975.

Finest cut

The $13 million Large Optics Diamond Turning Machine at the Lawrence Livermore National Laboratory, California was reported in June 1983 to be able to sever a human hair 3000 times lengthwise.

Longest echo

The longest recorded echo in any building is one of 15 sec following the closing of the door of the Chapel of the Mausoleum, Hamilton, Lanarkshire built 1840–55.

Physical Extremes

Most powerful electric current
The most powerful electric current generated is that from the Zeus capacitor at the Los Alamos Scientific Laboratory, New Mexico. If fired simultaneously the 4032 capacitors would produce, for a few microseconds, twice as much current as that generated elsewhere on Earth.

Hottest flame
The hottest flame that can be produced is from carbon subnitride (C_4N_2) which at one atmosphere pressure is calculated to reach 5261 K.

Highest measured frequency
The highest *directly* measured frequency is a visible yellow-green light at 520.2068085 terahertz (a terahertz being a million million hertz or cycles per second) for the o-component of the 17–1 P(62) transition line of iodine 127. The highest measured frequency determined by precision metrology is a green light at 582.491703 terahertz for the b_{21} component of the R(15) 43–0 transition line of iodine 127. However, with the decision on 20 October 1983 by the Conférence Générale des Poids et Mesures (CGPM) to define exactly the metre (m) in terms of the velocity of light (c) such that 'the metre is the length of the path travelled by light in vacuum during a time interval of 1/299,792,458 of a second' then frequency (f) and wavelength (λ) are exactly interchangeable through the relationship $f\lambda = c$.

Lowest friction
The lowest coefficient of static and dynamic friction of any solid is 0.02, in the case of polytetrafluoroethylene ($[C_2F_4]_n$), called PTFE —equivalent to wet ice on wet ice. It was first manufactured in quantity by E. I. du Pont de Nemours & Co Inc in 1943, and is marketed from the USA as Teflon. In the United Kingdom it is marketed by ICI as Fluon. In the centrifuge at the University of Virginia a 30 lb *13,60 kg* rotor magnetically supported has been spun at 1000 rev/sec in a vacuum of 10^{-6} mm of mercury pressure. It loses only one revolution per second per day, thus spinning for years.

Smallest hole
A hole of 40 Å (4×10^{-6} mm) was shown visually using a JEM 100C electron microscope and Quantel Electronics devices at the Dept of Metallurgy, Oxford on 28 Oct 1979. To find such a hole is equivalent to finding a pinhead in a haystack with sides of 1.2 miles *1,93 km*. An electron microscope beam on a sample of sodium beta-alumina at the University of Illinois, USA, in May 1983 accidentally bored a hole 2×10^{-9} m in diameter.

Most powerful laser beams
The first illumination of another celestial body was achieved on 9 May 1962, when a beam of light was successfully reflected from the Moon by the use of a laser (light amplification by stimulated emission of radiation) attached to a 48 in *121,9 cm* telescope at Massachusetts Institute of Technology, Cambridge, Massachusetts. The spot was estimated to be 4 miles *6,4 km* in diameter on the Moon. The device was propounded in 1958 by the American Dr Charles Hard Townes (born 1915). Such a flash for 1/5000th of a second can bore a hole through a diamond by vaporisation at 10,000°C, produced by 2×10^{23} photons. The 'Shiva' laser was reported at the Lawrence Livermore Laboratory, California to be concentrating 2.6×10^{13} watts into a pinhead-sized target for 9.5×10^{-11} sec in a test on 18 May 1978.

Brightest light
The brightest artificial light sources are 'laser' pulses generated at the US Los Alamos National Laboratory, New Mexico announced in March 1987 by Dr Robert Graham. An ultra-violet flash lasting 1 picosecond (1×10^{-12} sec) is intensified to an energy of 5×10^{15} watts. Of continuously burning sources, the most powerful is a 313 kW high-pressure argon arc lamp of 1,200,000 candle-power, completed by Vortek Industries Ltd of Vancouver, BC, Canada in March 1984.

The most powerful searchlight ever developed was one produced during the 1939–45 war by the General Electric Company Ltd at the Hirst Research Centre in Wembley, London. It had a consumption of 600 kW and gave an arc luminance of 300,000 candles/in² *46 500 candelas/cm²* and a maximum beam intensity of 2,700,000,000 candles from its parabolic mirror (diameter 10 ft *3,04 m*).

Shortest light pulse
Charles Z. Shank and colleagues of the AT & T Laboratories in New Jersey achieved a light pulse of 8 femtoseconds (8×10^{-15} sec) announced in April 1985. The pulse comprised only 4 or 5 wavelengths of visible light or 2,4 micrometres long.

Most durable light
The average bulb lasts for 750–1000 hr. There is some evidence that a 5 watt carbide filament bulb made by the Shelby Electric Co and presented by Mr Bernell in the Fire Department, Livermore, south Alameda County, California was first shedding light in 1901.

Heaviest magnet
The heaviest magnet in the world is one measuring 60 m *196 ft* in diameter, with a weight of 36,000 tons/*tonnes* for the 10 GeV synchrophasotron in the Joint Institute for Nuclear Research at Dubna, near Moscow.

Magnetic fields
The strongest continuous magnetic field strength achieved has been one of 33,6 teslas at the Francis Bitter National Magnet Laboratory, Massachusetts Institute of Technology, on 20 March 1986 employing a hybrid magnet with holmium pole pieces which enhanced the central field.

The weakest magnetic field measured is one of 8×10^{-15} tesla in the heavily shielded room at the same laboratory. It is used by Dr David Cohen for research into the very weak magnetic field generated in the heart and brain.

Most powerful microscope
The world's most powerful microscope is the scanning tunnelling microscope invented at the IBM Zürich research laboratory in 1981. It has the magnifying ability of 100 million and is capable of resolving down to one hundredth the diameter of an atom (3×10^{-10} m). The fourth generation of the scanning tunnelling microscope now being developed is said to be 'about the size of a finger tip'.

By using field ion microscopy the tips of probes of scanning tunnelling microscopes have been shaped to end in a single atom—the last three layers constituting the world's smallest manmade pyramid consisting of seven, three and one atoms. It was announced in July 1986 from AT & T Bell Laboratories, Murray Hill, New Jersey that they had successfully deposited a single atom (probably of germanium) from the tungsten tip of a scanning tunnelling microscope back on to a germanium surface.

Loudest noise
The loudest noise created in a laboratory has been 210 decibels or 400,000 acoustic watts reported by NASA from a 48 ft *14,63 m* steel and concrete test bed for the Saturn V rocket static with 60 ft *18,3 m* deep foundations at Marshall Space Flight Center, Huntsville, Alabama in October 1965. Holes could be bored in solid material by this means and the audible range was in excess of 100 miles *161 km*.

Smallest microphone
Prof Ibrahim Kavrak of Bogazici University, Istanbul, Turkey, developed a microphone for a new technique of pressure measurement in fluid flow in 1967. It has a frequency response of 10 Hz to 10 KHz and measures 1,5 mm × 0,76 mm *0.06 in × 0.03 in*.

Highest note
The highest note yet attained is one of 60 gigahertz, generated by a 'laser' beam striking a sapphire crystal at the Massachusetts Institute of Technology in September 1964.

Most powerful particle accelerator
The 2 kilometre *6562 ft* diameter proton synchrotron at the Fermi National Accelerator Laboratory east of Batavia, Illinois, is the highest energy 'atom-smasher' in the world. On 14 May 1976 an energy of 500 giga electron volts (5×10^{11}) was achieved for the first time. On 13 Oct 1985 a centre of mass energy of 1.6 tera electron volts (1.6×10^{12} electron volts) was achieved by colliding beams of protons and anti-protons. This involves 1000 super-conducting magnets maintained at a temperature of −452°F *−268,8° C* by means of the world's largest 4500 litre *990 gal* per hour helium liquefying plant which began operating on 18 Apr 1980.

The aim of CERN (*Conseil Européen pour la Recherche Nucléaire*) to collide beams of protons and anti-protons in their Super Proton Synchrotron (SPS) near Geneva at 270 GeV × 2 = 540 GeV was achieved at 4.55 a.m. on 10 July 1981. This was the equivalent of striking a fixed target with protons at 150 TeV or 150 000 GeV.

The US Department of Energy set up a study for a $6 billion Super Superconductivity Collider (SSC) 1995 with two 20 TeV proton and anti-próton colliding beams on 16 Aug 1983 with a diameter of 52 miles *83,6 km*. White House approval was announced on 30 Jan 1987.

Quietest place
The 'dead room', measuring 35 ft by 28 ft *10,67 × 8,50 m* in the Bell Telephone System laboratory at Murray Hill, New Jersey, USA, is the most anechoic room in the world, eliminating 99.98 per cent of reflected sound.

Sharpest objects and smallest tubes
The sharpest objects yet made are glass micropipette tubes used in intracellular work on living cells. Techniques developed and applied by Prof Kenneth T. Brown and Dale G. Flaming of the Department of Physiology, University of California, San Francisco achieved by 1977 bevelled tips with an outer diameter of 0.02 μm and 0.01 μm inner diameter. The latter is smaller than the smallest known nickel tubing by a factor of 340 and is 6500 times thinner than human hair.

Highest vacuum
The highest (or 'hardest') vacuums obtained in scientific research are of the order of 10^{-14} torr at the IBM Thomas J. Watson Research Center, Yorktown Heights, New York in October 1976 in a cryogenic system with temperatures down to −269°C *−452°F*. This is equivalent to depopulating (baseball-sized) molecules from 1 metre apart to 80 km apart or from 1 yard to 50 miles.

Lowest viscosity
The California Institute of Technology announced on 1 Dec 1957 that there was no measurable viscosity, *i.e.* perfect flow, in liquid helium II, which exists at temperatures close to absolute zero (−273,15° C *−459.67° F*).

Highest voltage
The highest potential difference ever obtained in a laboratory has been 32±1.5 million volts by the National Electrostatics Corporation at Oak Ridge, Tennessee on 17 May 1979.

THE
ARTS
& ENTERTAINMENT
CHAPTER SIX

Most theatrical roles ● Kanzaburo
Nakamura (b. 29 July 1909) of Tokyo, seen here
in the title role from *Ichijo Okura Monogatari*
(The Tale of Lord Ichijo Okura), has performed
in 806 different Kabuki titles from November
1926 to January 1987. As each title in this
classical Japanese theatrical form lasts 25 days,
he has therefore played 20,150 performances.

Painting

Oldest

Evidence of Palaeolithic art was first found in 1833 at Veyrier, 3 miles *5 km* south-west of Geneva, Switzerland when François Mayor (1779–1854) found two harpoon-like objects decorated with geometric figures. The oldest known dated examples come from La Ferrassie, near Les Eyzies in the Périgord, France, in layers dated to *c.* 25,000 BC. Blocks of stone were found with engraved animals and female symbols; some of the blocks also had symbols painted in red ochre. Pieces of ochre with ground facets have been found at Lake Mungo, NSW, Australia, in a context *ante* 30,000 BC but there is no evidence whether these were used for body-painting or art.

Largest

Panorama of the Mississippi, completed by John Banvard (1815–91) in 1846, showing the river for 1200 miles *1930 km* in a strip probably 5000 ft *1524 m* long and 12 ft *3,66 m* wide, was the largest painting in the world, with an area of more than 60,000 ft² *5575 m²*. The painting is believed to have been destroyed when the rolls of canvas, stored in a barn at Cold Spring Harbor, Long Island, New York State, USA, caught fire shortly before Banvard's death on 16 May 1891.

The Battle of Gettysburg, completed in 1883, after 2½ years of work, by Paul Philippoteaux (France) and 16 assistants, was 410 ft *125 m* long, 70 ft *21,3 m* high and weighed 5.36 tons *5,45 tonnes*. It depicts the climax of the battle, in southern Pennsylvania, USA, on 3 July 1863. In 1964 it was bought by Joe King of Winston-Salem, North Carolina, after being stored by E. W. McConnell in a Chicago warehouse since 1933 but, owing to deterioration, the sky was trimmed so decreasing the area.

Jackson Bailey's *Life of Christ* exhibited by Religious Art Institute of America Inc of Atlanta, Georgia comprises 50 panels 11 × 20 ft *3,35 × 6,09 m* and was complete by 1971 with an area of 11,000 ft² *1022 m²*.

Kimiko Hibino (b. 1942) painted over 800 species of the Animal Kingdom on a canvas 3 km *1.86 miles* long and 2,2 m *7.2 ft* wide. On 27 Oct 1985, it was unveiled with the help of 3000 volunteers along the bank of the Tamagawa River in Tokyo, Japan.

The largest 'Old Master' is *Il Paradiso*, by Jacopo Robusti, *alias* Tintoretto (1518–94), and his son Domenico (1565–1637) on the east wall of the Sala del Maggior Consiglio in the Palazzo Ducale (Doge's Palace) in Venice, Italy between 1587 and 1590. The work is 22 m *72 ft 2 in* long and 7 m *22 ft 11¼ in* high and contains some 350 human figures.

The largest painting in Great Britain is the oval *Triumph of Peace and Liberty* by Sir James Thornhill (1676–1734), on the ceiling of the Painted Hall in the Royal Naval College, Greenwich. It measures 106 ft *32,3 m* by 51 ft *15,4 m* and took 20 years (1707–1727) to complete.

Most valuable

The 'Mona Lisa' (*La Gioconda*) by Leonardo da Vinci (1452–1519) in the Louvre, Paris, was assessed for insurance purposes at $100,000,000 (*then £35.7 million*) for its move to Washington, DC, and New York City, NY, USA, for exhibition from 14 Dec 1962 to 12 Mar 1963. However, insurance was not concluded because the cost of the closest security precautions was less than that of the premiums. It was painted in *c.* 1503–7 and measures 77 × 53 cm *30.5 × 20.9 in.* It is believed to portray either Mona (short for Madonna) Lisa Gherardini, the wife of Francesco del Giocondo of Florence, or Constanza d'Avalos, coincidentally nicknamed La Gioconda, mistress of Giuliano de' Medici. Francis I, King of France, bought the painting for his bathroom in 1517 for 4000 gold florins or 92 oz *15,30 kg* of gold.

Most prolific painter

Picasso was the most prolific of all painters in a career which lasted 78 years. It has been estimated that Picasso produced about 13,500 paintings or designs, 100,000 prints or engravings, 34,000 book illustrations and 300 sculptures or ceramics. His life-time *oeuvre* has been valued at £500 million. Morris Katz (b. 1932) of Greenwich Village, New York City is the most prolific painter of saleable portraits in the world. His sales total as of 5 Mar 1986 was 153,629. Described as the 'King of Schlock Art', he sells his paintings 'cheap and often'. On the NBC 'Today' TV programme in Nov 1985 Katz demonstrated he could paint at a rate of 2.64 ft² *0,25 m²* per min.

Most repetitious painter

Antonio Bin of Paris has painted the *Mona Lisa* on some 300 occasions. These sell for up to £1000 apiece.

Oldest and youngest RA

The oldest ever Royal Academician has been (Thomas) Sidney Cooper CVO, who died on 8 Feb 1902 aged 98 yr 136 days, having exhibited 266 paintings over the record span of 69 consecutive years (1833–1902). The youngest ever RA has been Mary Moser (1744–1819) (later Mrs Hugh Lloyd), who was elected on the foundation of the Royal Academy in 1768 when aged 24.

Youngest exhibitor

The youngest ever exhibitor at the Royal Academy of Arts Annual Summer Exhibition has been Lewis Melville 'Gino' Lyons (b. 30 Apr 1962). His *Trees and Monkeys* was painted on 4 June 1965, submitted on 17 Mar 1967 and exhibited to the public on 29 Apr 1967.

Largest galleries

The world's largest art gallery is the Winter Palace and the neighbouring Hermitage in Leningrad, USSR. One has to walk 15 miles *24 km* to visit each of the 322 galleries, which house nearly 3,000,000 works of art and objects of archaeological interest. The world's largest modern art museum is the Georges Pompidou National Centre for Art and Culture, Beauborg, opened in Paris in 1977 with 17 700 m² *183,000 ft²* of floor space. The most heavily endowed is the J. Paul Getty Museum, Malibu, California with an initial £700,000,000 in Jan 1974 and now £104 million p.a. for acquisitions. It has 38 galleries.

Finest brush

The finest standard brush sold is the 000 in Series 7 by Winsor and Newton known as a 'triple goose'. It is made of 150–200 Kolinsky sable hairs weighing 15 mg *0.000529 oz.*

MURALS

Earliest

The earliest known murals on man-made walls are the clay relief leopards at Çatal Hüyük in southern Anatolia, Turkey, discovered by James Malaart at level VII in 1961 and dating from *c.* 6200 BC.

Largest

The world's largest 'mural' was unveiled in 44 colours on the 30 storey Villa Regina condominium, Biscayne Bay, Miami, Florida on 14 Mar 1984 covering 300,000 ft² *27 870 m²*. The longest recorded continuous mural is one stretching 1633 ft *497,7 m* on the walls of the Royal Liverpool Children's Hospital, Alder Hey. It covers an area of 17,963 ft² *1668,7 m²*. *Future entries for this category will be assessed on overall area only.*

Largest mosaic

The world's largest mosaic is on the walls of the central library of the Universidad Nacional Autónoma de Mexico, Mexico City. There are four walls, the two largest measuring 12,949 ft² *1203 m²* each representing the pre-Hispanic past.

The largest Roman mosaic in Britain is the Woodchester Pavement, Gloucestershire of *c.* AD 325, excavated in 1793, now re-covered with protective earth. It measures 47 ft *14,3 m* square comprising 1½ million tesserae. A brilliant total reconstruction was carried out by Robert and John Woodward from 1973-1982.

Largest poster
The largest recorded poster was one measuring 40,24 × 51,47 m *132 ft × 168 ft 10 in* (2071 m² *22,292 ft²*) constructed by students of Osaka Gakun University, Osaka, Japan on 7 Oct 1984.

'WORK OF ART'

Largest
The largest work of art ever perpetrated was the wrapping in 1983 of 11 islands in Biscayne Bay, Florida, USA in flamingo pink plastic tutus for Christo's work entitled *Surrounded Islands*. The amount of plastic sheeting used was 6,500,000 ft² *603 000 m²*.

HIGHEST PRICE

Abstract
The auction record for an abstract painting is $5.06 million *£3,489,155* for *Composition in a Square with Red Corner* painted in 1938 by Piet Mondrian (1872-1944) at Sotheby's, New York on 18 Nov 1986. The purchaser was an anonymous Japanese businessman.

Miniature portrait
The highest price ever paid is the £75,000 given by an anonymous buyer at a sale held by Sotheby's, London on 24 Mar 1980 for a miniature of Jane Broughton, aged 21, painted on vellum by Nicholas Hilliard (1547-1619) in 1574. The painted surface measures 1.65 in *42 mm* in diameter.

Modern painting
The record bid at auction for an impressionist painting is $9,900,000 *£7.9 million* for *Landscape with Rising Sun* by Van Gogh (1853-1890) from the estate of the late Mrs Florence J. Gould (d. 1983) by an anonymous private collector at Sotheby Parke Bernet, New York City on 25 Apr 1985. The hammer price was $9 million and the buyer's premium was 10 per cent of that.

Living artist
The highest price at auction for a work by a living artist is $3,630,000 *£2,420,000* for *Out of the Window* by Jasper Johns at Sotheby's, New York on 10 Nov 1986. The $1,950,000 paid for the two canvasses *Two Brothers* (1905) and *Seated Harlequin* (1922) by Pablo Diego José Francisco de Paula Juan Nepomuceno Crispín Crispiano de la Santisima Trinidad Ruiz y Picasso (1881-1973) of Spain, bought by the Basle City Government from the Staechelin Foundation in Dec 1967, would be even more if inflation is allowed for.

The highest price for any painting by a living United Kingdom-born artist is £1,035,294 for *Study for Portrait II* by Francis Bacon (b. Dublin, Ireland, 1909, then part of the United Kingdom) sold on 6 May 1987 at Christie's, New York.

Print
The record price for a print at auction was £561,600 for a 1655 print of *Christ Presented to the People* by Rembrandt at Christie's, London on 5 Dec 1985 sold by Chatsworth Settlement Trustees.

Drawing
The highest price ever paid for any drawing is £3,546,000 for a study of an apostle's head and hand for the Transfiguration in the Vatican by Raphael (Raffaello Santi 1483-1520) and sold for the 11th Duke of Devonshire (b. 1920) at Christie's, London on 3 July 1984.

Poster
The record price for a poster is £62,000 for an advertisement for the 1902 Vienna Exhibition by Koloman Moser (b. Vienna 30 Mar 1868—d. 18 Oct 1918) sold at Christie's, South Kensington, London on 1 April 1985.

Most expensive painting ● *Sunflowers*, Les Tournisol, one of a series of seven paintings by Vincent van Gogh (b. 30 Mar 1853, Zundert, Netherlands—d. 29 July 1890, Auvers-sur-Oise, France) was sold at auction by Christie's on 30 Mar 1987 in London for £22,500,000 (£24,750,000 including buyer's premium of £2,250,000). The auctioneer was the Hon. Charles Allsopp and the purchaser the Yasuda Fire and Marine Insurance Co, of Tokyo. The record price paid for the 39 × 30 in *99 × 76 cm* painting implies a value of £1,500,000 per sunflower or £19,230 per square inch, *£2900 per square centimetre.*

Sculpture

Earliest
A piece of ox rib found in 1973 at Pech de l'Aze, Dordogne, France in an early Middle Palaeolithic layer of the Riss glaciation *c.* 105,000 BC has several engraved lines on one side, thought to be possibly intentional. A churinga or curved ivory plaque rubbed with red ochre from the Middle Palaeolithic Mousterian site at Tata, Hungary has been dated to 100,000 BC by the thorium/uranium method. The earliest known examples of sculpture date from the Aurignacian culture *c.* 28,000-22,000 BC and include the so-called Venus figurines from Austria and the numerous figurines from northern Italy and central France. A carving in mammoth ivory of a horse 2½ in *6,3 cm* long was found in the Vogelherd cave in south-west Germany.

The earliest example of an engraving found in Britain is of a horse's head on a piece of rib-bone from Robin Hood Cave, Creswell Crag, Derbyshire. It dates from the Upper Palaeolithic period (*c.* 15,000 to 10,000 BC). The earliest Scottish rock carving from Lagalochan, Argyll dates from *c.* 3000 BC.

Most expensive
The highest price for a sculpture is $3,900,000 (*£2,400,000*) paid by private treaty in London in early 1977 by the J. Paul Getty Museum, Malibu, California for a 4th century BC bronze statue of a youth attributed to the school of Lysippus. It was found by fishermen on the seabed off Faro, Italy in 1963.

The highest price paid for the work of a sculptor during his lifetime is the $1,265,000 (*then £702,780*) given at Sotheby Parke Bernet, New York on 21 May 1982 for the 75 in *190,5 cm* long elmwood *Reclining Figure* by Henry Moore, OM, CH, (b. 30 July 1898, d. 31 Aug 1986).

Largest
The world's largest sculptures are the mounted figures of Jefferson Davis (1808-89), Gen Robert Edward Lee (1807-70) and Gen Thomas Jonathan ('Stonewall') Jackson (1824-63), covering 1.33

acres *0,5 ha* on the face of Stone Mountain, near Atlanta, Georgia. They are 90 ft *27,4 m* high. Roy Faulkner was on the mountain face for 8 years 174 days with a thermo-jet torch working with the sculptor Walker Kirtland Hancock and other helpers from 12 Sept 1963 to 3 Mar 1972.

If completed, the world's largest sculpture will be that of the Indian chief Tashunca-Uitco (*c.* 1849–77), known as Crazy Horse, of the Oglala tribe of the Dakota or Nadowessioux (Sioux) group. The sculpture was begun on 3 June 1948 near Mount Rushmore, South Dakota, USA. A projected 563 ft *171,6 m* high and 641 ft *195 m* long, it was the uncompleted life work of one man, Korczak Ziólkowski (1908–82). The horse's nostril is 50 ft *15,2 m* deep and 35 ft *10,7 m* in diameter. In 1985–86 another 400,000 tons of granite blasted off the mountain face brought the total to 8.2 million tons.

Hill figures

In August 1968, a 330 ft *100 m* tall figure was found on a hill above Tarapacá, Chile.

The largest human hill carving in Britain is the 'Long Man' of Wilmington, East Sussex, 226 ft *68 m* in length. The oldest of all White Horses in Britain is the Uffington White Horse in Oxfordshire, dating from the late Iron Age (*c.* 150 BC) and measuring 374 ft *114 m* from nose to tail and 120 ft *36 m* high.

> **Ground figures ●** In the Nazca Desert, 300 km *185 miles* south of Lima, Peru there are straight lines (one more than 7 miles *11,2 km* long), geometric shapes and shapes of plants and animals drawn on the ground some time between 100 BC and AD 600 for an uncertain but probably religious, astronomical, or even economic, purpose by an imprecisely identified civilisation. They were first detected from the air *c.* 1928 and have also been described as the world's longest works of art. (Photo: Servicio Aerofotografico Nacional)

Most massive mobile

The most massive mobile is *White Cascade* weighing 8 tons/*tonnes* and measuring 100 ft *30,48 m* from top to bottom installed on 24–25 May 1976 at the Federal Reserve Bank of Philadelphia, Pennsylvania, USA. It was designed by Alexander Calder (1898–1976), whose first mobiles were exhibited in Paris in 1932 and whose *Big Crinkley* sold for a record £555,572 at Sotheby's, New York on 10 May 1984.

Language and Literature

Earliest

The ability to speak is believed to be dependent upon physiological changes in the height of the larynx between *Homo erectus* and *Homo sapiens sapiens* as developed *c.* 45,000 BC. The earliest written language discovered has been on Yangshao culture pottery from Paa-t'o, near Xi'an (Sian) in the Shanxi (Shensi) province of China found in 1962. This bears proto-characters for the numbers 5, 7 and 8 and has been dated to 5000–4000 BC. The earliest dated pictographs are on clay tablets from Nippur, southern Iraq from a level equivalent to Uruk V/VI and dated in 1979 to *c.* 3400 BC. Tokens or tallies from Tepe Asiab and Ganji-I-Dareh Tepe in Iran have however been dated to 8500 BC. The earliest known piece of English writing (*c.* 630 AD) is a fragment of Irish uncial script in an ecclesiastical history sold for £75,000 by the Folger Shakespeare Library, Washington DC to the British Rail Pension Fund at Sotheby's, London on 25 June 1985.

Fragments of Roman wooden writing tablets found in the 1970s at Vindolandia near Newcastle-upon-Tyne have been shown to make up the earliest known substantial written records in British history. These contain letters and a quotation from the Roman poet Virgil and are dated to *c.* AD 100.

Oldest

The written language with the longest continuous history is Chinese, extending over more than 6000 years (see above) to the Yangshao culture (see above) to the present day.

Oldest English words

It was first suggested in 1979 that languages ancestral to English and to Latvian (both Indo-European) split *c.* 3500 BC. Research shortly to be published will indicate that about 40 words of a pre-Indo-European substrate survive in English *e.g.* apple (apal), bad (bad), gold (gol) and tin (tin).

Commonest language

Today's world total of languages and dialects still spoken is about 5000 of which some 845 come from India. The language spoken by more people than any other is Northern Chinese, or Mandarin, by an estimated 68 per cent of the population, hence 709 million people in 1985. The so-called national language (*Guóyǔ*) is a standardised form of Northern Chinese (*Běifānghuà*) as spoken in the Peking area. This was alphabetised into *zhùyīn fúhào* of 37 letters in 1913 by Wa Chih-hui (1865–1953). On 11 Feb 1938 the *Hanyu-Pinyin-Fang'an* system, which is a phonetic pronunciation guide, was introduced. The next most commonly spoken language, and the most widespread, is English, by an estimated 400,000,000 in mid-1986.

In Great Britain and Ireland there are six indigenous tongues: English, Cornish, Scots Gaelic, Welsh, Irish Gaelic and Romany (Gipsy). Mr Edward (Ned) Maddrell (1877–1974) of Glen Chass, Port St Mary, Isle of Man, died as the last islander whose professed tongue was Manx. Cornish, of which there are now some 300 students, came within an ace of extinction. A dictionary was published in 1887, four years before the death of the then last fluent speaker John Davey. A novel by Melville and Kitty Bennetto, *An Gurun Wosek a Geltya*, was published in Nov 1984. In the Channel Islands, apart from Jersey and Guernsey *normand*, there survive words of Sarkese or *Sèrtchais* in which the Parable of the Sower, as recited by some fishermen, was noted and published by Prince Louis Lucien Bonaparte (1813–91) in 1862.

Most complex

The following extremes of complexity have been noted: Chippewa, the North American Indian language of Minnesota, has the most verb forms with up to 6000; Haida, the North American Indian language, has the most prefixes with 70; Tabassaran, a language in Daghestan, USSR, uses the most noun cases with 37, while Eskimos use 63 forms of the present tense and simple nouns have as many as 252 inflections. In Chinese the 40 volume *Chung-wén Tà Tz'u-tiěn* dictionary lists 49,905 characters. *The Dictionary of Chinese Characters* (Sichuan and Huber) in 8 volumes will contain 20 million characters when completed in 1989. The fourth tone of 'i' has 84 meanings, varying as widely as 'dress', 'hiccough' and 'licentious'. The written language provides 92 different characters of 'i⁴'. The most complex written character in Chinese is that representing *xiè* consisting of 64 strokes, meaning 'talkative'. The most complex in current use is *yù* with 32 strokes meaning to urge or implore.

Most and least irregular verbs

Esperanto was first published by its inventor Dr Ludwig Zamenhof (1859–1917) of Warsaw in 1887 without irregular verbs and is now estimated (by text book sales) to have a million speakers. The even earlier interlanguage Volapük, invented by Johann Martin Schleyer (1831–1912), also has absolutely regular configuration. The Turkish language has a single irregular verb—*olmak*, to be. According to *The Morphology and*

Syntax of Present-day English by Prof Olu Tomori, English has 283 irregular verbs of which 30 are merely formed with prefixes.

Rarest and commonest sounds

The rarest speech sound is probably the sound written ř in Czech which occurs in very few languages and is the last sound mastered by Czech children. In the southern Bushman language !xo there is a click articulated with both lips, which is written⊙. The *l* sound in the Arabic word *Allah*, in some contexts, is pronounced uniquely in that language. The commonest sound is the vowel *a* (as in the English father); no language is known to be without it.

Vocabulary

The English language contains about 490,000 words plus another 300,000 technical terms, the most in any language, but it is doubtful if any individual uses more than 60,000. Those in Great Britain who have undergone a full 16 years of education use perhaps 5000 words in speech and up to 10,000 words in written communications. The membership of the International Society for Philosophical Enquiry (no admission for IQs below 148) have an average vocabulary of 36,250 words. Shakespeare employed a vocabulary of *c.* 33,000 words.

Greatest linguist

If the yardstick of ability to speak with fluency and reasonable accuracy is adhered to, it is doubtful whether any human could maintain fluency in more than 20–25 languages concurrently or achieve fluency in more than 40 in a lifetime.

Historically the greatest linguists have been proclaimed as Cardinal Mezzofanti (1774–1849) (fluent in 26 or 27), Professor Rask (1787–1832), Sir John Bowring (1792–1872) and Dr Harold Williams of New Zealand (1876–1928), who were all fluent in 28 languages.

The most multi-lingual living person is Georges Henri Schmidt (b. Strasbourg, France, 28 Dec 1914), the Chief of the UN Terminology Section in 1965–71. The 1975 edition of *Who's Who in the United Nations* listed 'only' 19 languages because he was then unable to find time to 'revive' his former fluency in 12 others. Powell Alexander Janulus (b. 1939) has worked with 41 languages in the Provincial Court of British Columbia, Vancouver, Canada.

Britain's greatest linguist is George Campbell (b. 9 Aug 1912), who is retired from the BBC Overseas Service where he *worked* with 54 languages.

ALPHABET

Earliest

The earliest example of alphabetic writing has been found at Ugarit (now Ras Sharma), Syria dated to *c.* 1450 BC. It comprised a tablet of 32 cuneiform letters.

The oldest letter is 'O', unchanged in shape since its adoption in the Phoenician alphabet *c.* 1300 BC. The newest letters added to the English alphabet are 'j' and 'v' which are of post-Shakespearean use *c.* 1630. Formerly they were used only as variants of 'i' and 'u'. There are 65 alphabets now in use.

Longest and shortest

The language with most letters is Cambodian with 72 (including useless ones) and Rotokas in central Bougainville Island has least with 11 (just a, b, e, g, i, k, o, p, ř, t and u).

Most and least consonants and vowels

The language with most distinct consonantal sounds is that of the Ubykhs in the Caucasus, with 80–85, and that with least is Rotokas, which has only 6 consonants. The language with the most vowels is Sedang, a central Vietnamese language with 55 distinguishable vowel sounds and that with the least is the Caucasian language Abkhazian with two. The record in written English for consecutive vowels is 6 in the musical term *euouae*. The Estonian word jäääärne, meaning the edge of the ice, has the same 4 consecutively. The name of a language in Pará State, Brazil consists solely of 7 vowels—uoiauai. The English word 'latchstring' has 6 consecutive letters which are consonants, but the Georgian word gvprtskvnis (he is feeling us) has 8 separately pronounced consonants.

Largest letters

The largest permanent letters in the world are giant 600 ft *183 m* letters spelling READYMIX on the ground in the Nullarbor near East Balladonia, Western Australia. These were constructed in December 1971.

Smallest letters

The 16 letters MOLECULAR DEVICES have been etched into a salt crystal by an electron beam so that the strokes were only 2 to 3 nm (10^{-9}) wide—the width of 20 hydrogen atoms. This was done by Michael Isaacson at Cornell University, Ithaca, New York in February 1982.

WORDS

Longest

Lengthy concatenations and some compound or agglutinative words are or have been written in the closed up style of a single word e.g. the 182 letter fricassee of 17 sweet and sour ingredients in Aristophanes' comedy *The Ecclesiazusae* in the 4th century BC. A compound 'word' of 195 sanskrit characters (which transliterates into 428 letters in the Roman alphabet) describing the region near Kanci, Tamil Nadu, India appears in a 16th century work by Tirumalāmbā, Queen of Vijayanagara.

The longest word in the Oxford English Dictionary is floccipaucinihilipilification (alternatively spelt in hyphenated form with 'n' in seventh place), with 29 letters, meaning 'the action of estimating as worthless', first used in 1741, and later by Sir Walter Scott (1771–1832). Webster's Third International Dictionary lists among its 450,000 entries: pneumonoultramicroscopicsilicovolcanoconiosises (47 letters), the plural of a lung disease contracted by some miners.

The longest regularly-formed English word is praetertranssubstantiationalistically (37 letters), used by Mark McShane in his 1963 novel *Untimely Ripped*. The medical term hepaticocholangiocholecystenterostomies (39 letters) refers to the surgical creations of new communications between gallbladders and hepatic ducts and between intestines and gallbladders. The longest words in common use are disproportionableness and incomprehensibilities (21 letters). Interdenominationalism (22 letters) is found in Webster's Dictionary and hence perhaps interdenominationalistically (28 letters) is permissible. Simon Proctor of Maidstone, Kent has compiled 15,592 lesser words (excluding plurals) from its 28 letters.

Longest palindromes

The longest known palindromic word is *saippuakivikauppias* (19 letters), Finnish for a dealer in lye (*i.e.* caustic soda). The longest in the English language is *redivider* (9 letters). The nine-letter word, *Malayalam*, is a proper noun given to the language of the Malayali people in Kerala, southern India while *Kanakanak* near Dillingham, Alaska is a nine-lettered palindromic placename. The contrived chemical term *detartrated* has 11 letters. Some baptismal fonts in Greece and Turkey bear the circular 25 letter inscription NIΨON ANOMHMATA MH MONAN OΨIN meaning 'wash (my) sins not only (my) face'. This appears at St Mary's Church, Nottingham, St Paul's, Woldingham, Surrey and other churches. The longest palindromic composition devised is one of 66,666 words by Edward Benbow of Bewdley, Hereford & Worcs in April 1987. It begins 'Al, sign it, "Lover"! . . .' and hence predictably ends '. . . . revolting, Isla'. The longest palindromic novel, *Dr Awkward and Olson in Oslo*, contains 31,594 words and was written by Lawrence Levine, New York, in 1986.

Longest scientific name

The systematic name for deoxyribonucleic acid of the human mitochondria contains 16,569 nucleotide residues and is thus *c.* 207,000 letters long. It was published in key form in *Nature* on 9 Apr 1981.

Longest anagrams

The longest non-scientific English words which can form anagrams are the 18-letter transpositions 'conservationalists' and 'conversationalists'. The longest scientific transposals are cholecystoduodenostomy / duodenocholecystostomy and hydropneumopericardium/pneumohydropericardium, each of 22 letters.

Longest abbreviation

The longest known abbreviation is S.K.O.M.K.-H.P.K.J.C.D.P.W.B., the initials of the Syarikat Kerjasama Orang-orang Melayu Kerajaan Hilir Perak Kerana Jimat Cermat Dan Pinjam-meminjam Wang Berhad. This is the Malay name for The Cooperative Company of the Lower State of Perak Government's Malay People for Money Savings and Loans Ltd, in Teluk Anson, Perak, West Malaysia (formerly Malaya). The abbreviation for this abbreviation is Skomk. The 55-letter full name of Los Angeles (El Pueblo de Nuestra Señora la Reina de los Angeles de Porciuncula) is abbreviated to LA or 3.63 per cent of its length.

Longest acronym

The longest acronym is NIIOMTPLABOPARM-BETZHELBETRABSBOMONIMONKONOTDTEK-HSTROMONT with 56 letters (54 in Cyrillic) in the *Concise Dictionary of Soviet Terminology* meaning: The laboratory for shuttering, reinforcement, concrete and ferroconcrete operations for composite-monolithic and monolithic constructions of the Department of the Technology of Building—assembly operations of the Scientific Research Institute of the Organisation for building mechanisation and technical aid of the Academy of Building and Architecture of the USSR.

Commonest words and letters

In written English the most frequently used words are, in order: the, of, and, to, a, in, that, is, I, it, for *and* as. The most used in conversation is I. The commonest letter is 'e' and the commonest initial letter is 'T'.

Most meanings

The most over-worked word in English is the word *set* which has 58 noun uses, 126 verbal uses and 10 as a participial adjective.

Most succinct word

The most challenging word for any lexicographer to define briefly is the Fuegian (southernmost Argentina and Chile) word 'mamihlapinatapai' meaning 'looking at each other hoping that either will offer to do something which both parties desire but are unwilling to do'.

Most synonyms

The condition of being inebriated has more synonyms than any other condition or object. Delacourt Press of New York City, USA has published a selection of 1224 from 2241 compiled by Paul Dickson of Garrett Park, Maryland, USA.

Most homophones

The most homophonous sounds in English are *air* and *sol* which, according to the researches of

Dora Newhouse of Los Angeles, both have 38 homonyms. The homonym with most variant spellings is *air* with Aire, are, Ayer, Ayr, Ayre, err, e'er, ere, eyre and heir.

Most accents

Accents were introduced in French in the reign of Louis XIII (1601–43). The word with most accents is újjáépítésére, the Hungarian word meaning 'for its reconstruction'. Two runners up each with 5 accents are the French *hétérogénéité*, meaning heterogeneity and an atoll in the Pacific Ocean 320 miles *516 km* east-south-east of Tahiti which is named Héréhérétué.

Shortest pangram (holoalphabetic sentence)

Pangrammists who endeavour to produce meaningful sentences of minimal length utilizing all the letters in the alphabet have now attained the ultimate of 26-letter brevity. Michael Jones of Chicago, Illinois, compiled in 1984 the sentence to describe the situation in which a wryneck woodpecker from the grasslands of Africa climbed up the side of a male bovid which is grazing on sacred Muslim-owned land, *viz:* 'Veldt jynx grimps waqf zho buck'. The number of ways 26 letters can be combined is 4.0329×10^{26}.

PERSONAL NAMES

Earliest

The earliest personal name which has survived is seemingly that of a predynastic king of Upper Egypt *ante* 3050 BC, who is indicated by the hieroglyphic sign for a scorpion. It has been suggested that the name should be read as Sekhen. The earliest known name of any resident of Britain is Divitiacus, King of the Suessiones, the Gaulish ruler of the Kent area *c.* 100 BC under the name Prydhain. Scotland, unlike England, was never fully conquered by the Roman occupiers (AD 43–410). Calgācus (b. *c.* AD 40), who led the final resistance in Scotland, was the earliest native whose name has been recorded.

Longest pedigree

The only non-royal English pedigree that can with certainty show a clear pre-Conquest descent is that of the Arden family. Shakespeare's mother was a Mary Arden. It is claimed on behalf of the Clan Mackay that their clan can be traced to Loarn, the Irish invader of south west Pictland, now Argyll, *c.* AD 501.

Longest single name

The longest Christian or given name on record is one of 622 letters given by Mr Scott Roaul Sör-Lökken of Missoula, Montana, to his daughter Miss S. Ellen Georgianna Sör-Lökken (b. 1979). The 'S' stands for a 598-letter name designed to throw a monkey wrench into the computers of federal bureaucracy. She is known as 'Snow Owl' for short or 'Oli' for shorter.

Longest personal name

The longest name appearing on a birth certificate is that of Rhoshandiatellyneshiaunneveshenk Koyaanfsquatsiuty Williams born to Mr and Mrs James L. Williams in Beaumont, Texas, on 12 Sept 1984. On 5 Oct 1984 the father filed an amendment which expanded his daughter's first name to 1,019 letters and the middle name to 36 letters.

The longest surname in the United Kingdom was the six-barrelled one borne by the late Major L.S.D.O.F. (Leone Sextus Denys Oswolf Fraudatifilius) Tollemache-Tollemache-de Orellana-Plantagenet-Tollemache-Tollemache, who was born on 12 June 1884 and died of pneumonia in France on 20 Feb 1917. Of non-repetitious surnames, the last example of a five-barrelled one was that of the Lady Caroline Jemima Temple-Nugent - Chandos - Brydges - Grenville (1858–1946). The longest single English surname is Featherstonehaugh (17 letters), correctly pro-

---

LONGEST WORDS

JAPANESE[1]
Chi-n-chi-ku-ri-n (12 letters)
a very short person (slang)

SPANISH
Superextraordinarisimo (22 letters)
extraordinary

FRENCH
Anticonstitutionnellement (25 letters)
anticonstitutionally.

CROATIAN
Prijestolonasljednikovica (25 letters)
wife of an heir apparent.

ITALIAN
Precipitevolissimevolmente (26 letters)
as fast as possible.

PORTUGUESE
Inconstitucionalissimamente (27 letters)
with the highest degree of unconstitutionality.

ICELANDIC
Hæstaréttarmálaflutningsmaður (29 letters)
supreme court barrister

RUSSIAN
Ryentgyenoelyektrokardiografichyeskogo
(33 Cyrillic letters, transliterating as 38)
of the radioelectrocardiographic.

HUNGARIAN
Megszentségtelenithetetlenségeskedéseitekért
(44 letters)
for your unprofaneable actions.

TURKISH[4]
Cekoslovakyalılastıramadıklarımızdanmıymıssınız (47 letters)
'are you not of that group of persons that we were said to be unable to Czechoslovakianise?'

DUTCH[4]
Kindercarnavalsoptochtvoorbereidingswerkzaamheden (49 letters)
preparation activities for a children's carnival procession

MOHAWK[2]
Tkanuhstasrihsranuhwe'tsraaksahsrakaratattsrayeri' (50 letters)
the praising of the evil of the liking of the finding of the house is right.

GERMAN[3,4]
Donaudampfschiffahrtselectrizitaetenhauptbetriebswerkbauunterbeamtengesellschaft (80 letters)
The club for subordinate officials of the head office management of the Danube steamboat electrical services (Name of a pre-war club in Vienna).

SWEDISH[4]
Nordöstersjökustartilleriflygspaningssimulatoranläggningsmaterielunderhållsuppföljningssystemdiskussionsinläggsförberedelsearbeten (130 letters)
Preparatory work on the contribution to the discussion on the maintaining system of support of the material of the aviation survey simulator device within the north-east part of the coast artillery of the Baltic.

[1] Patent applications sometimes harbour long compound 'words'. An extreme example is the 40-letter Kyūkitsūrohekimenfuchakunenryōsekisanryō which transliterates the 13 kana meaning 'the accumulated amount of fuel condensed on the wall face of the air intake passage'.

[2] Lengthy concatenations are a feature of Mohawk. Above is an example.

[3] The longest dictionary word in everyday usage is Kraftfahrzeugreparaturwerkstätten (33 letters or 34 if the ä is written as ae) meaning motor vehicle repair shops (or service garages).

[4] Agglutinative words are limited only by imagination and are not found in standard dictionaries. The first 100-letter such word was published in 1975 by the late Eric Rosenthal in Afrikaans.

---

nounced on occasions (but improbably on the correct occasion) Featherstonehaw or Festonhaw or Fessonhay or Freestonhugh or Feerstonhaw or Fanshaw. In Scotland the surname Nin (feminine of Mac) Achinmacdholicachinskerray (29 letters) was recorded in an 18th-century parish register.

Most Christian names

The great-great-grandson of Carlos III of Spain, Don Alfonso de Borbón y Borbón (1866–1934) had 94 Christian names of which several were lengthened by hyphenation.

John and Margaret Nelson of Chesterfield, Derbyshire, gave their daughter Tracy Nelson (b. 31 Dec 1985) a total of 139 other Christian names. ´

Shortest

The commonest single-letter surname is O, prevalent in Korea, but with 52 examples in US phone books (1973–81) and 12 in Belgium. This name causes most distress to those concerned with the prevention of cruelty to computers. Every other letter, except Q, has been traced in US phone books (used as a surname) by A. Ross Eckler. There are two one-lettered Burmese names: E (calm), pronounced aye and U (egg), pronounced Oo. U *before* the name means 'uncle'.

There exist among the 47,000,000 names on the Dept of Health & Social Security index 6 examples of a one-lettered surname. Their identity has not been disclosed, but they are 'A', 'B', 'J', 'N', 'O' and 'X'. Two-letter British surnames include By and On and have recently been joined by Oy, Za and others. The Christian name 'A' has been used for 5 generations in the Lincoln Taber family of Fingringhoe, Essex.

Commonest family name

The commonest family name in the world is the Chinese name Chang which is borne, according to estimates, by between 9.7 and 12.1 per cent of the Chinese population, so indicating even on the lower estimate that there are at least some 104 million Changs—more than the entire population of all but 7 of the 170 other sovereign countries of the world.

The commonest surname in the English-speaking world is Smith. The most recent published count showed 659,050 nationally-insured Smiths in Great Britain, of whom 10,102 were plain John Smith and another 19,502 were John (plus one or more given names) Smith. Including uninsured persons there were over 800,000 Smiths in England and Wales alone, of whom 81,493 were called A. Smith. There were an estimated 2,382,509 Smiths in the USA in 1973. It is no secret that by 1984 there were some 90,000 Singhs in Britain—the name means 'in secret'.

'Macs'

There are estimated to be 1,600,000 persons in Britain with M', Mc or Mac (Gaelic genitive of 'son') as part of their surnames. The commonest of these is Macdonald which accounts for about 55,000 of the Scottish population.

Most versions

Mr Edward A. Nedelcov of Regina, Saskatchewan, Canada has collected 1050 versions of the spelling of his family name since January 1960. Mzilikazi of Zululand (b. *c.* 1795) had his name chronicled in 325 spellings, according to researches by Dr R. Kent Rasmussen.

Most changed

Excluding members of the royal family the living monogamous woman who has most times changed her name is Lady Home of the Hirsel formerly Lady Douglas-Home; Countess of Home; Lady Dunglass and originally Miss Elizabeth Alington.

Most contrived

In the United States the determination to derive commercial or other benefit from being the last listing in the local telephone book has resulted in self-given names, starting with up to 9 Z's—an extreme example being Zachary Zzzzzzzzzzra in the San Francisco book. The alpha and omega of Britain's 82 directories are Mrs Maude E. Aab of Hull, Humberside and the Zzzzzz Coffee Shop in Gray's Inn Road, London WC1.

PLACE-NAMES

Earliest

The world's earliest place-names are pre-Sumerian e.g. Kish, Ur and Attara. The earliest recorded British place-name is Belerion, the Penwith peninsula of Cornwall, referred to as such by Pytheas of Massilia in *c.* 308 BC. The name Salakee on St Mary's, Isles of Scilly is however arguably of a pre Indo-European substrate meaning *tin island*. There are reasons to contend that Leicester (Roman, Ligora Castrum) contains an element reflecting its founding by the Western Mediterranean navigators, the Ligurians, as early as *c.* 1200 BC. The earliest distinctive name for what is now Great Britain was Albion by Himilco *c.* 500 BC. The oldest name among England's 46 counties is Kent, first mentioned in its Roman form of Cantium (from the Celtic *canto,* meaning a rim, *i.e.* a coastal district), from the same circumnavigation by Pytheas. The earliest mention of England is the form *Angelcymn,* which appeared in the Anglo-Saxon Chronicle in AD 880.

Longest

The official name for Bangkok, the capital city of Thailand, is Krungthep Mahanakhon. The full name is however: Krungthep Mahanakhon Bovorn Ratanakosin Mahintharayutthaya Mahadilokpop Noparatratchathani Burirom Udomratchanivetmahasathan Amornpiman Avatarnsathit Sakkathattiyavisnukarmprasit (167 letters) which in its most scholarly transliteration emerges with 175 letters.

Great Britain

The longest place-name in the United Kingdom is the concocted 58-letter version of Llanfairpwllgwyngyll/gogerychwyrndrobwllllantysiliogogogoch, which is translated: 'St Mary's Church by the pool of the white hazel trees, near the rapid whirlpool, by the red cave of the Church of St Tysilio'. This is the name used for the reopened (April 1973) village railway station in Anglesey, Gwynedd, Wales, and was coined by a local bard, Y Bardd Cocos—John Evans (1827–95) as a hoax. The *official* name consists of only the first 20 letters. The longest Welsh place-name listed in the Ordnance Survey Gazetteer is Lower Llanfihangel-y-Creuddyn (26 letters), a village near Aberystwyth, Dyfed. For commercial rather than toponymic reasons the proprietors of the Fairbourne Steam Railway, near Barmouth, North Wales have posted a 67-letter long name on a station board 64 ft *19,5 m* long. It reads Gorsafawddachaidraigddanheddogleddollonpenrhynarevrdraethceredigion though the 'll' should read 'l' making 66 letters or 65 if 'ch' is regarded as a single letter.

England

The longest single-word (unhyphenated) place-name in England is Blakehopeburnhaugh, a hamlet between Byrness and Rochester in Northumberland, of 18 letters. The nearby Cottonshopeburnfoot (19 letters) is locally rendered as one word though not by the Ordnance Survey. The hyphenated Sutton-under-Whitestonecliffe, North Yorkshire has 27 letters on the Ordnance Survey but with the insertion of 'the' and the dropping of the final 'e' it has 29 letters in the Post Office List. The longest parish name is Saint

Mary le More and All Hallows with Saint Leonard and Saint Peter, Wallingford (68 letters) in Oxfordshire formed on 5 Apr 1971.

Scotland

The longest single-word place-name in Scotland is Coignafeuinternich in Inverness-shire. Kirkcudbrightshire (also 18 letters) became merged into Dumfries and Galloway on 16 May 1975. A 12-acre *5 ha* loch 9 miles *14 km* west of Stornoway on Lewis, Western Isles is named Loch Airidh Mhic Fhionnlaidh Dhuibh (31 letters).

Ireland

The longest place-name in Ireland is Muckanaghederdauhaulia (22 letters), 4 miles *6 km* from Costello in Camus Bay, County Galway. The name means 'soft place between two seas'.

Shortest

The shortest place-names in the world are the French village of Y (population 143), so named since 1241, the Danish village Å on the island Fyn, the Norwegian village of Å (pronounced 'Aw'), the Swedish place Å in Vikholandet, U in the Caroline Islands, Pacific Ocean; and the Japanese town of Sosei which is alternatively called Aioi or O. There was once a '6' in West Virginia, USA. The shortest place-names in Great Britain are the two-lettered places of Ae (population 199 in 1961), Dumfries and Galloway; Oa on the island of Islay, Strathclyde and Bu on Wyre, Orkney Islands. In the Shetland Islands there are skerries called Ve and two stacks called Aa. The island of Iona was originally I. The River E flows into the southern end of Loch Mhór, Inverness-shire, and O Brook flows on Dartmoor, Devon. The shortest place-name in Ireland is Ta (or Lady's Island) Lough, a sea inlet on the coast of County Wexford. Tievelough, in County Donegal, is also called Ea.

Most spellings

The spelling of the Dutch town of Leeuwarden has been recorded in 225 versions since AD 1046. Bromesberrow, Hereford and Worcester, is recorded in 161 spellings since the 10th century as reported by local historian Lester Steynor.

Literature

Oldest

The oldest surviving printed work is the Dharani scroll or *sutra* from wooden printing blocks found in the foundations of the Pulguk Sa pagoda, Kyŏngju, South Korea, on 14 Oct 1966. It has been dated to no later than AD 704. It was claimed in November 1973 that a 28-page book of Tang dynasty poems at Yonsei University, Korea was printed from metal type *c.* 1160.

Oldest mechanically printed

It is widely accepted that the earliest mechanically printed full length book was the 42-line Gutenberg Bible, printed in Mainz, West Germany, in *c.* 1454 by Johann Henne zum Gensfleisch zur Laden, called 'zu Gutenberg' (*c.* 1398–*c.* 1468). Work on water marks published in 1967 indicates a copy of a surviving printed 'Donatus' Latin grammar was made from paper in *c.* 1450. The earliest exactly dated printed work is the Psalter completed on 14 Aug 1457 by Johann Fust (*c.* 1400–66) and Peter Schöffer (1425–1502), who had been Gutenberg's chief assistant. The earliest printing by William Caxton (*c.* 1422–1491) though undated would appear to be *The Recuyel of the Historyes of Troye* in Cologne in late 1473 to spring 1474.

Largest book

The largest book in the world is the *Super Book* measuring 9 ft × 10 ft 2¼ in *2,74 × 3,07 m* weighing 557 lb *252,6 kg* consisting of 300 pages published in Denver, Colorado, USA in 1976.

Largest publication

The largest publication in the world is the 1112-volume set of *British Parliamentary Papers* published by the Irish University Press in 1968–72. A complete set weighs 3¼ tons *3,3 tonnes*, costs £50,000 and would take 6 years to read at 10 hours per day. The production involved the death of 34,000 Indian goats, and the use of £15,000 worth of gold ingots. The total print is 500 sets and the price per set in 1987 was £49,500.

Largest dictionary

Deutches Wörterbuch started by Jacob and Wilhelm Grimm in 1854 was completed in 34,519 pages and 33 volumes in 1971. Today's price is DM5456.97 (*now £1428*). The largest English language dictionary is the 12-volume Royal quarto *The Oxford English Dictionary* of 15,487 pages published between 1884 and 1928 with a first supplement of 963 pages in 1933. Of the 4-volume supplement, edited by R. W. Burchfield, the final (Se-Z) volume and the Bibliography were published in 1986. The work contains 414,825 words, 1,827,306 illustrative quotations and reputedly 227,779,589 letters and figures, 63.8 times more than the Bible. The greatest outside contributor has been Marghanita Laski (b. 1915) with 175,000 quotations since 1958.

The *New Grove Dictionary of Music and Musicians* edited by Stanley Sadie CBE (b. 30 Oct 1930), published in 20 volumes by Macmillan in February 1981, contains over 22 million words and 4500 illustrations and is the largest specialist dictionary. The price in 1987 is £1100.

Smallest book

The smallest marketed bound printed book with cursive material is one printed on 22 gsm paper measuring 1 mm × 1 mm $\frac{1}{25} \times \frac{1}{25}$ *in*, comprising the children's story *Old King Cole!* and published in 85 copies in March 1985 by The Gleniffer Press of Paisley, Renfrew, Scotland. The pages can only be turned (with care) by the use of a needle.

Longest novel

The longest important novel ever published is *Les hommes de bonne volonté* by Louis Henri Jean Farigoule (1885–1972), *alias* Jules Romains, of France, in 27 volumes in 1932–46. The English version *Men of Good Will* was published in 14 volumes in 1933–46 as a 'novel-cycle'. The 4959-page edition published by Peter Davies Ltd has an estimated 2,070,000 words excluding a 100-page index. The novel *Tokuga-Wa Ieyasu* by Sohachi Yamaoka has been serialised in Japanese daily newspapers since 1951. Now completed, it will require nearly 40 volumes.

Earliest encyclopaedias

The earliest known encyclopaedia was compiled by Speusippus (*post* 408–c. 338 BC), a nephew of Plato, in Athens c. 370 BC. The earliest encyclopaedia compiled by a Briton was *Liber exerptionum* by the Scottish monk Richard (d. 1173) at St Victor's Abbey, Paris c. 1140.

Largest encyclopaedia

The largest encyclopaedia is *La Enciclopedia Universal Ilustrada Europeo-Americana* (J. Espasa & Sons, Madrid and Barcelona) totalling 105,000 pages and an annual supplement since 1935 comprising 165,200,000 words. The number of volumes in the set in August 1983 was 104, and the price $2325 (*£1660*).

Most comprehensive encyclopaedia

The most comprehensive English language encyclopaedia is the *Encyclopaedia Britannica*, first published in Edinburgh, Scotland, in December 1768–1771. A group of booksellers in the United States acquired reprint rights in 1898 and completed ownership in 1899. In 1943 the *Britannica* was given to the University of Chicago, Illinois, USA. The current 30-volume 15th edition contains 33,141 pages and 43,000,000 words from 4277 contributors. It is now edited in Chicago and in London.

Longest index

The Tenth Collective Index of *Chemical Abstracts* completed in June 1983 contains 23,948,253

entries in 131,445 pages and 75 volumes, and weighs 380 lb *172,3 kg*.

MAPS

The oldest known map of any kind is a clay tablet depicting the river Euphrates flowing through northern Mesopotamia, Iraq, dated c. 3800 BC. The earliest surviving product of English map-making is the Anglo-Saxon *mappa mundi*, known as the Cottonian manuscript from the late 10th century. The earliest printed map in the world is one of western China dated to 1115. The earliest printed map of Britain was Ptolemy's outline printed in Bologna, Italy in 1477.

A *Giant Relief Map of California*, by Reuben Hall, weighing 38.4 tons *39 tonnes*, was displayed in the Ferry Building, San Francisco from 1924 until 1962. Now in storage in Hamilton Air Force Base, Novato, California, it measures 450 × 18 ft *137,1 × 5,48 m*.

HIGHEST PRICES

Most expensive book

The highest price paid for any book was £8,140,000 for the 226-leaf manuscript *The Gospel Book of Henry the Lion, Duke of Saxony* at Sotheby's, London on 6 Dec 1983. The book, 13½ × 10 in *34,3 × 25,4 cm*, was illuminated by the monk Herimann in c. 1170 at Helmershansen Abbey with 41 full-page illustrations, and was bought by Hans Kraus for the Hermann Abs consortium.

Printed book

The highest price ever paid for a printed book is $2,400,000 (*then £1,265,000*) for one of the only 21 complete known copies of the Gutenberg Bible, printed in Mainz, West Germany c. 1454. It was bought from the Carl and Lily Pforzheimer Foundation by Texas University in a sale by Quaritch of London in New York on 9 June 1978. The most expensive new book is the reproduction of the full set of ornithological prints *The Birds of America* by John James Audubon (1785–1851) by Abbeville Press, at $15,000.

Broadsheet

The highest price ever paid for a broadsheet has been $412,500 (*then £264,500*) for one of the 22 known copies of *The Declaration of Independence*, printed in Philadelphia in 1776 by Samuel T. Freeman & Co, and sold to the Chapin Library, Williams College, Williamstown, Massachusetts, USA at Christie's, New York City on 22 Apr 1983.

Manuscript

The highest price ever paid for a complete manuscript is £2.2 million by Armand Hammer at Christie's, London on 12 Dec 1980 for Leonardo da Vinci's 36-page Codex Leicester illustrated manuscript on cosmology compiled in c. 1507. It was sold by the trustees of the Holkham estate.

The highest price for a British manuscript is £1,375,000 paid by John Paul Getty II at Sother-by's, London on 29 June 1986 for 4 leaves of the only known illustrated life of St Thomas à Becket (1119–1170).

The auction record for a musical manuscript is £330,000 for *The Rite of Spring* by Igor F. Stravinsky (1882–1971), by Otto Haas for the Paul Sacher Collection in Basel, Switzerland at Sotheby's, London on 11 Nov 1982.

Atlas

The highest price paid for an atlas is £340,000 for a Gerardus Mercator atlas of c. 1571 of Europe, sold at Sotheby's, London, on 13 Mar 1979.

BIBLE

Oldest

The earliest biblical texts are from two silver amulets found under the Scottish Church, Jeru-

salem in 1983 bearing Numbers Ch. 6 v. 22–27 dated to c. 587 BC. The oldest known bible is the *Codex Vaticanus* written in Greek *ante* AD 350 and preserved in the Vatican Museum, Rome. The earliest complete Bible *printed* in English was one edited by Miles Coverdale, Bishop of Exeter (c. 1488–1569), while living in Antwerp, and printed in 1535. William Tyndale's New Testament in English had, however, been printed in Cologne and in Worms, Germany in 1525 while John Wycliffe's first manuscript translation dates from 1382.

Longest and shortest books

The longest book in the Authorized version of the Bible is the Book of Psalms, while the longest book including prose is the Book of the Prophet Isaiah, with 66 chapters. The shortest is the Third Epistle of John, with 294 words in 14 verses. The Second Epistle of John has only 13 verses but 298 words.

Longest and shortest psalm and verse

Of the 150 psalms, the longest is the 119th, with 176 verses, and the shortest is the 117th, with two verses. The shortest verse in the Authorised Version (King James) of the Bible is verse 35 of Chapter XI of the Gospel according to St John, consisting of the two words 'Jesus wept'. The longest is verse 9 of Chapter VIII of the Book of Esther, which extends to a 90-word description of the Persian empire.

Total letters and words, longest name

The total number of letters in the Bible is 3,566,480. The total number of words depends on the method of counting hyphenated words, but is usually given as between 773,692 and 773,746. The word 'and' according to Colin McKay Wilson of the Salvation Army appears 46,227 times. The longest personal name in the Bible is the 18-letter Maher-shalal-hash-baz, the symbolic name of the second son of Isaiah (Isaiah, Chapter VIII, verses 1 and 3). The caption of Psalm 22, however, contains a Hebrew title sometimes rendered Al-'Ayyeleth Hash-Shahar (20 letters).

DIARIES AND LETTERS

Longest diary

Col Ernest Loftus CBE of Harare, Zimbabwe began his daily diary on 4 May 1896 at the age of 12 and has thus completed 91 years.

George C. Edler (b. 13 Dec 1889) of Bethesda, Maryland, USA, has kept a diary with no breaks since 1 Jan 1912.

Longest and most letters

The longest personal letter based on a word count is one of 1,402,344 words started on 3 Jan 1982 by Alan Foreman of Erith, Kent, England and posted to his wife Janet on 25 Jan 1984.

Vichi Noda, former Vice Minister of Treasury and Minister of Construction in Japan, from July 1961 until his bedridden wife Mitsu's death in March 1985, wrote her 1307 letters amounting to 50,000 characters during his overseas trips. These letters have been published in 25 volumes totalling 12,404 pages.

Longest letter to an editor

The *Upper Dauphin Sentinel* of Pennsylvania published a letter of 25,513 words over 8 issues from August to November 1979, written by John Sultzbaugh of Lykens, Pennsylvania.

Most letters to an editor

David Green, a solicitor, of Castle Morris, Dyfed had 114 letters published in the main correspondence columns of *The Times* by May 1987. His record year was 1972 with 12.

Shortest correspondence

The shortest correspondence on record was that between Victor Marie Hugo (1802–85) and his publisher Hurst and Blackett in 1862. The author was on holiday and anxious to know how his new novel *Les Misérables* was selling. He wrote '?'. The reply was '!'.

The shortest letter to *The Times* comprised the single abbreviated symbol 'Dr^2?' in the interrogative from R. S. Cookson of London NW11, on 30 July 1984, in a correspondence on the correct form of recording a plurality of academic doctorates. On 8 Jan 1986 a letter was sent by a 7-year-old girl from the Isle of Man, responding to an appeal for any survivor bearing a particularly rare name. It read 'Sir, Yours faithfully Caroline Sophia Kerenhappuch Parkes'.

Most personal mail

The highest confirmed mail received by any private citizen in a year is 900,000 letters by the baseball star Hank Aaron (b. 1934) reported by the US Postal Department in June 1974. About a third were letters of hate engendered by his bettering of 'Babe' Ruth's career record for 'home runs' set in 1927. (See Chapter 12.)

Pen pals

The longest sustained correspondence on record is one of 75 years from 11 Nov 1904 between Mrs Ida McDougall of Tasmania, Australia and Miss R. Norton of Sevenoaks, Kent until Mrs McDougall's death on 24 Dec 1979.

Birthday card

Mrs Amelia Finch (b. 18 Apr 1912) of Lakehurst, New Jersey, USA and Mr Paul E. Warburgh (1902–80) of Huntington, New York exchanged the same card from 1 Feb 1927 to 18 Apr 1980.

Christmas cards

The greatest number of personal Christmas cards sent out is believed to be 62,824 by Mrs Werner Erhard of San Francisco, California in December 1975. Many must have been to unilateral acquaintances. The earliest known Christmas card was sent out by Sir Henry Cole (1808–82) in 1843 but did not become an annual ritual until 1862.

AUTOGRAPHS AND SIGNATURES

Earliest

The earliest surviving examples of an autograph are those made by scribes on cuneiform clay tablets from Tell Abu Ṣalābīkh, Iraq dated to the early Dynastic III A *c.* 2600 BC. A scribe named 'a-du' has added 'dub-sar' after his name thus translating to 'Adu, scribe'. The earliest surviving signature is that of the scribe Amen-'aa dated to the Egyptian middle kingdom which began in *c.* 2130 BC and which is in the Leningrad Museum, USSR. A signum exists for William I (the Conqueror) *c.* 1070. The earliest English sovereign whose handwriting is known to have survived is Edward III (1327–77). The earliest full signature extant is that of Richard II (dated 26 July 1386). The Magna Carta does not bear even the mark of King John (reigned 1199–1216), but carries only his seal affixed on 19 June 1215.

Most expensive

The highest price ever paid on the open market for a single autograph letter signed is $360,000 paid on 29 Oct 1986 at Sotheby's, New York, for a letter by Thomas Jefferson condemning prejudice against Jews in 1818. It was sold by Charles Rosenbloom of Pittsburgh.

The highest price paid for an autograph letter signed by a living person is $12,500 (*then £5430*) at the Hamilton Galleries on 22 Jan 1981 for a letter from President Ronald Reagan praising Frank Sinatra.

A record $4250 (*then £2500*) was paid at a Hamilton sale on 12 Aug 1982 by Barry D Hoffman for the signed portrait of Al Capone (1899–1947).

Rarest and most valuable

Only one example of the signature of Christopher Marlowe (1564–93) is known. It is in the Kent County Archives on a Will of 1583. It is estimated that a seventh Shakespearean signature, should it ever come to light, might realise at least £1 million at auction.

AUTHORS

Most prolific

The champion of the goose quill era was Józef Ignacy Kraszewski (1812–87) of Poland who produced more than 600 volumes of novels and historical works. Until recently very high productivity had been attributed to Charles Hamilton, *alias* Frank Richards (1875–1961) with up to 80,000 words a week in 1913 including the whole of the periodicals *Gem* (founded 1907) and *Magnet* (1908–40). In 1984 George Samways (b. 1894) asserted that Hamilton used him and others as 'ghost-writers'.

Soho Tokutomi (1863–1957) wrote the history *Kinsei Nippon Kokuminshi* in 100 volumes of 42,468 pages and 19,452,952 letters in 35 years.

Most novels

The greatest number of novels published by an authoress is 904 by Kathleen Lindsay (Mrs Mary

Faulkner) (1903–73) of Somerset West, Cape Province, South Africa. She wrote under two other married names and 8 pen names. Baboorao Arnalkar (b. 9 June 1907) of Maharashtra State, India between 1936 and 1984 has published 1092 short mystery stories in book form and several non-fiction books.

After receiving a probable record 743 rejection slips the British novelist John Creasey MBE (1908–73), under his own name and 25 noms de plume had 564 books totalling more than 40,000,000 words published from 1932 to his death. The British authoress with the greatest total of full-length titles was Ursula Harvey Bloom (Mrs A. C. G. Robinson, formerly Mrs Denham-Cookes 1892–1984), who reached 560 in 1976, starting in 1924 with *The Great Beginning* and including the best sellers *The Ring Tree* (novel) and *The Rose of Norfolk* (non-fiction). Enid Mary Blyton (1898–1968) (Mrs Darrell Waters) completed 600 titles of children's stories, many of them brief, with 59 in 1955. She was translated into a record 128 languages.

Most text books

Britain's most successful writer of text books is the ex-schoolmaster Ronald Ridout (b. 23 July 1916) who between 1948 and April 1987 had 505 titles published with sales of 86,900,000. His *The First English Workbook* has sold 5,200,000.

Highest paid

In 1958 Mrs Deborah Schneider of Minneapolis, Minnesota, wrote 25 words to complete a sentence in a competition for the best blurb for Plymouth cars. She won from about 1,400,000 entrants the prize of $500 (then £178) every month for life. On normal life expectations she would have collected $12,000 (£4285) per word. No known anthology includes Mrs Schneider's deathless prose but it is in her deed box at her bank 'Only to be opened after death'. She passed $6000 a word by 1983.

Greatest advance

The greatest advance paid for any book is $5,000,000 (then £3,430,000) for *Whirlwind* to James Clavell at auction in New York City on 11 Jan 1986 by William Morrow & Co and Avon Books.

Top-selling

It was announced on 13 Mar 1953 that 672,058,000 copies of the works of Generalissimo Stalin (born Yózef Vissarionovich Dzhugashvili) (1879–1953), had been sold or distributed in 101 languages.

Currently the top-selling authoress is Barbara Cartland with global sales of over 450,000,000 for 450 titles in 21 languages. She has averaged 23 titles per year for the last decade.

The all-time estimate of book sales by Erle Stanley Gardner (1889–1970) (US) to 1 Jan 1987 is 319,034,707 copies in 37 languages. The top-selling lady crime writer has been Dame Agatha Christie (née Miller) (later Lady Mallowan) (1890–1976) whose 87 crime novels sold an estimated 500,000,000 in 103 languages. *Sleeping Murder* was published posthumously in 1977.

Longest biography

The longest biography in publishing history is that of Sir Winston Churchill by his son Randolph (4832 pages) and Martin Gilbert (15,268 pages) to date comprising some 8,684,000 words. George Simenon (b. 1903) wrote 22 autobiographical books from 1972.

Most rejections

The greatest recorded number of publishers' rejections for a manuscript is 238 (by January 1987) for the 130,000-word manuscript *World Government Crusade* written in 1966 by Gilbert Young (b. 1906) of Bath, England. The record for rejections before publication (and wide acclaim)

is 69 from 55 publishers in the case of Prof Steven Goldberg's *The Inevitability of Patriarchy*.

Oldest authoress

The oldest authoress in the world was Mrs Alice Pollock (née Wykeham-Martin) (1868–1971), of Haslemere, Surrey, whose book *Portrait of My Victorian Youth* (Johnson Publications) was published in March 1971 when she was aged 102 years 8 months.

Literary luncheons

Literary luncheons were inaugurated by Christina Foyle (Mrs Ronald Batty) in Oct 1930 at the Old Holborn Restaurant, London. Attendances were over 1500 at the Grosvenor House, Park Lane, London at lunches for Mistinguett (1873–1956) and Dr Edvard Benes (1884–1948) both in 1938.

Longest literary gestation

The standard German dictionary *Deutsches Wörterbuch*, begun by the brothers Grimm in 1854, was finished in 1971. *Acta Sanctorum* begun by Jean Bolland in 1643, arranged according to saints' days, reached the month of November 1925 and an introduction for December was published in 1940. Oxford University Press received back their proofs of *Constable's Presentments* from the Dugdale Society in Dec 1984. They had been sent out for correction 35 years earlier in Dec 1949.

Youngest and oldest Poet Laureate

The youngest Poet Laureate was Laurence Eusden (1688–1730), who 'received the bays' on 24 Dec 1718 at the age of 30 years and 3 months. The greatest age at which a poet has succeeded is 73 in the case of William Wordsworth (1770–1850) on 6 Apr 1843. The longest lived Laureate was John Masefield, OM, who died on 12 May 1967, aged 88 years 345 days. The longest any poet has worn the laurel is 41 years 322 days, in the case of Alfred (later the 1st Lord) Tennyson (1809–92), who was appointed on 19 Nov 1850 and died in office on 6 Oct 1892.

Longest poem

The lengthiest poem ever published has been the Kirghiz folk epic *Manas*, which appeared in printed form in 1958 but which has never been translated into English. It runs to 'more than 500,000 lines'. Short translated passages appear in *The Elek Book of Oriental Verse*.

The longest poem ever written in the English language is one on the life of King Alfred by John Fitchett (1766–1838) of Liverpool which ran to 129,807 lines and took 40 years to write. His editor Robert Riscoe added the concluding 2585 lines.

Roger Brien's (b. Montreal, 1910) *Prométhée—dialogue des vivants et des morts* runs to 456,047 lines written in 1964–81. Brien has written another 497,000 lines of French poetry in over 90 published works.

Most successful poem

If by Joseph Rudyard Kipling (1865–1936), first published in 1910, has been translated into 27 languages and, according to Kipling, 'anthologised to weariness'.

HIGHEST PRINTINGS

The world's most widely distributed book is the Bible, which has been translated into 286 languages and portions of it into a further 1522 languages. This compares with 222 languages for Lenin. It has been estimated that between 1815 and 1975 some 2,500,000,000 copies were printed of which 1,500,000,000 were handled by Bible Societies. *The English Good News Bible*, translation of the New Testament (which is copyright of The Bible Society), sold 80,000,000 copies in the period 1976–80.

The King James version is not copyright but at least 14 copyrights exist on other versions. The oldest publisher of Bibles is the Cambridge University Press which began with the Geneva version in 1591.

It has been reported that 800,000,000 copies of the red-covered booklet *Quotations from the Works of Mao Tse-tung* were sold or distributed between June 1966, when possession became virtually mandatory in China, and September 1971 when its promoter Marshal Lin Piao died in an air crash.

It is believed that in the USA Van Antwerp Bragg and Co printed some 60 million copies of the 1879 edition of *The McGuffey Reader*, compiled by Henry Vail in the pre-copyright era for distribution to public schools.

The total disposal through non-commercial channels by Jehovah's Witnesses of *The Truth That Leads to Eternal Life* published by the Watchtower Bible and Tract Society of Brooklyn, New York, on 8 May 1968, reached 106,486,735 in 116 languages by April 1987.

BEST-SELLING BOOKS

Excluding versions of the Bible, the world's all-time best-selling copyright book is *The Guinness Book of Records* first published in September 1955 by the Guinness Brewery and edited by Norris Dewar McWhirter (b. 12 Aug 1925) and his twin brother Alan Ross McWhirter (k. 27 Nov 1975). Sales to May 1987 were 57.0 million.

Best-seller lists

The longest duration on the *New York Times* best-seller list (founded 1935) is *A Light in the Attic* by Shelby Silverstein (b. 1932) which on 10 Jan 1985 had its 112th week on the lists.

Fiction

The novel with the highest sales has been *Valley of the Dolls* (first published March 1966) by Jacqueline Susann (Mrs Irving Mansfield) (1921–74) with a worldwide total of 28,712,000 to 30 March 1987. In the first 6 months Bantam sold 6.8 million. In the United Kingdom the highest print order has been 3,000,000 by Penguin Books Ltd for their paperback edition of *Lady Chatterley's Lover*, by D. H. (David Herbert) Lawrence (1885–1930). The total sales to May 1987 were 4,735,000. Alistair Stuart MacLean (1922–87) wrote 30 books of which 28 each sold over a million in the United Kingdom alone. His books have been translated into 28 languages and 13 have been filmed. It has been estimated that a 'MacLean' novel is purchased every 18 seconds. *The Cruel Sea* by Nicholas Monsarrat (1910–79), published in 1951 by Cassell, reached sales of 1,200,000 in its *original* edition.

Fastest publisher

The fastest time in which a hardback book has been published is 43 hr 15 min in the case of *The ITN Book of the Royal Wedding*, published by Michael O'Mara. Typesetting began at 2.00 p.m. on 24 July 1986 and the books were on sale at 9.15 a.m. two days later.

Slowest seller

The accolade for the world's slowest selling book (known in US publishing as slooow-sellers) probably belongs to David Wilkins's Translation of the New Testament from Coptic into Latin published by Oxford University Press in 1716 in 500 copies. Selling an average of one each 139 days, it remained in print for 191 years.

PUBLISHERS AND PRINTERS

Oldest publisher

Cambridge University Press has a continuous history of printing and publishing since 1584.

Literature

The University received Royal Letters Patent to print and sell all manner of books on 20 July 1534.

In 1978 the Oxford University Press celebrated the 500th anniversary of the printing of the first book in the City of Oxford in 1478. This was before OUP was itself in existence.

Most prolific publisher

In terms of new titles per annum Britain's most prolific publisher in 1986 was Oxford University Press with 956. The UK published a record 57,845 book titles in 1986 of which a record 13,671 were reprints.

Largest printer

The largest printers in the world are R. R. Donnelley & Sons Co of Chicago, Illinois. The company, founded in 1864, has plants in 15 main centres, turning out $2,233,000,000 (£1440.6 million) worth of work per year. More than 140,000 tons of inks and 1,725,000 tons of paper and board are consumed every year. The largest printer under one roof is the United States Government Printing Office (founded 1861) in Washington, DC. Encompassing 33 acres *13,35 ha* of floor spacing the central office processes an average of 1500 print orders daily, and consumes 100 million lb *45 360 tonne* of paper annually. The Superintendent of Documents sells almost $60 million (£40 million) worth of US governmental publications every year and maintains an inventory of over 17,200 titles in print, receiving 6500 mail orders each day.

Largest print order

The initial print order for the 54th Automobile Association *Members' Handbook* (1986–7) was 4,800,000 copies—stacked one on top of each other, 33 times the height of Ben Nevis. The total print since 1908 has been 86,700,000. It is currently printed by web offset by Petty & Sons of Leeds. The aggregate print of *The Highway Code* (instituted 1931) reached 90,000,000 after 50 years in mid-1981.

LIBRARIES

Earliest

One of the earliest known collections of archival material was that of King Ashurbanipal at Nineveh, *c* 7th century BC. He had day tablets referring to events and personages as far back as the Dynasty of Agade *c.* 23rd century BC.

Largest

The largest library in the world is the United States Library of Congress (founded on 24 Apr 1800), on Capitol Hill, Washington, DC. By 1987 it contained 85 million items, including 22 million volumes and pamphlets. The buildings contain 64.6 acres *26,14 ha* of floor space and contain 532 miles *856 km* of shelving. The James Madison Memorial Building was dedicated in April 1980 and has 34.5 acres *14 ha* of floor space.

The largest non-statutory library in the world is the New York Public Library (founded 1895) on Fifth Avenue with a floor space of 525,276 ft² *48 800 m²* and 88 miles *141,6 km* of shelving. Its collection including 81 branch libraries embraces 11,907,217 volumes, 14,466,478 manuscripts and 363,679 maps.

The greatest personal library ever amassed was that of Sir Thomas Phillipps. Dispersal began in 1886. The residue was bought largely unseen by the brothers Lionel Robinson CBE MC and Philip Robinson for £100,000. Sales began on 1 July 1946.

The largest library in the United Kingdom is the British Library, dispersed among more than 20 buildings in London and a 60 acre *24,3 ha* site at Boston Spa, West Yorkshire, with a total staff of some 2500. The Library contains over 15.5 million volumes. Stock increases involve over 8 miles *12,8 km* of new shelving annually. The News-

paper Library at Colindale, North London, opened in 1932, has 562,300 volumes and parcels comprising 70,000 different titles on 22 miles *35,4 km* of shelving. The Document Supply Centre in West Yorkshire (shelf capacity 98 miles *157,7 km*) runs the largest library interlending operation in the world; it handles annually nearly 3 million requests from other libraries (UK and overseas) for items they do not hold in stock. The National Sound Archive holds 1,000,000 discs and 50,000 hours of recorded tape. The largest public library in Europe is the extended Mitchell Library, North Street, Glasgow with a floor area of 538,200 ft² *50 000 m²* or 12.3 acres *4,9 ha* and an ultimate capacity for 4,000,000 volumes. The Mitchell also houses Europe's largest public reference library.

Overdue books

The most overdue book taken out by a known borrower was one reported in December 1986. This was a book on British laws enacted in 1656–1667 entitled Townsend's Collection. It was returned in a plain envelope by an unknown person to avoid a fine of 'thousands of dollars' by Pennsylvania State Library.

Oldest museum

The oldest museum still extant in the world is the Ashmolean Museum in Oxford built from 1679–83 and named after the collector Elias Ashmole (1617–1692). Since 1924 it has housed an exhibition of historic scientific instruments.

Largest museum

The world's largest complex of museums is the Smithsonian Institution comprising 13 museums with 5600 employees. The largest and most visited museum in the United Kingdom is the British Museum (founded in 1753), which was opened to the public in 1759. The main building in Bloomsbury, London, was built in 1823 and has a total floor area of 17.57 acres *7,11 ha*. In 1986, 3,869,639 people passed through its doors.

Most popular

The highest attendance for any museum is that at the Smithsonian Air and Space Museum, Washington DC opened in July 1976. The record-setting day in 1984 at 118,437 required the doors to be temporarily closed.

Literature

NEWSPAPERS

Oldest

A copy has survived of a news pamphlet published in Cologne, West Germany in 1470. The oldest existing newspaper in the world is the Swedish official journal *Post och Inrikes Tidningar*, founded in 1645. It is published by the Royal Swedish Academy of Letters. The oldest existing commercial newspaper is the *Haarlems Dagblad/Oprechte Haarlemsche Courant*, published in Haarlem in the Netherlands. First issued as the *Weeckelycke Courante van Europa* on 8 Jan 1656, a copy of issue No 1 survives.

The newspaper with the earliest origins in the United Kingdom is *Berrow's Worcester Journal* (originally the *Worcester Post Man*), published in Worcester. It was traditionally founded in 1690 and has appeared weekly since June 1709. No complete file exists. The earliest date of foundation for any British newspaper published under the same title is the *Stamford Mercury*, printed since 1712 and traditionally even 1695. The *London Gazette* (originally the *Oxford Gazette*) was first published on 16 Nov 1665. The oldest Sunday newspaper is *The Observer*, first issued on 4 Dec 1791. The earliest known edition of the Belfast-based *News Letter* was dated 6 Mar 1738 and has been a daily since 1855. *The Daily Universal Register* was founded in 1785 and changed its name to *The Times* in 1788.

Largest newspapers

The most massive single issue of a newspaper was the 7½ lb *3,40 kg New York Times* of Sunday 17 Oct 1965. It comprised 15 sections with a total of 946 pages, including about 1,200,000 lines of advertising. The largest page size ever used has been 51 in × 35 in *130 cm × 89 cm* for *The Constellation*, printed in 1859 by George Roberts as part of the Fourth of July celebrations in New York City, NY, USA. The *Worcestershire Chronicle* was the largest British newspaper. A surviving issue of 16 Feb 1859 measures 32¼ in × 22½ in *82 cm × 57 cm*.

Smallest newspapers

The smallest original page size has been 3 × 3½ in *7,6 × 9,5 cm* of the *Daily Banner* (25 cents per month) of Roseberg, Oregon, USA, issues of which, dated 1 and 2 Feb 1876, survive. The *Answers to Correspondents* published by Messrs Carr & Co, Paternoster Square, London in 1888 was 3½ × 4½ in *9 × 11 cm*. The British Library Newspaper Library has the *Watford News and Advertiser* of 1 Apr 1899 measuring 2.9 × 3.9 in *7,5 × 10 cm*.

Most expensive

Britain's most expensive papers are *The Observer* and *The Sunday Times* at 50p, or double the price of the original 1955 fully bound edition of the *Guinness Book of Records*.

The United States had 1692 English-language daily newspapers at 1 May 1985 with a combined net paid circulation of 62,000,000 copies per day. The peak year for US newspapers was 1910, when there were 2202. The leading newspaper readers in the world are the people of Sweden, where 580 newspapers are sold for each 1000 compared with the UK figure of 410.

Longest editorship

Sir Etienne Dupuch OBE (b. 16 Feb 1899) of Nassau, Bahamas, editor of the *Tribune* since 1 Apr 1919, entered his 69th year in the chair on 1 Apr 1987. The longest editorship of any United Kingdom national newspaper has been more than 59 years by C. P. Scott (1846–1932) of the *Manchester Guardian*, who was appointed, aged 25, in 1877 and who died on 1 Jan 1932.

Most durable feature

The longest lasting feature in the British national press from one pen was *Your Stars* by Edward Lyndoe. It ran from Oct 1933 to 1982 in *The Sunday People*. Frank Lowe contributed a weekly natural history column to the *Bolton Evening News* every week from 4 Feb 1926 to his death on 26 Oct 1985. Albert E. Pool (b. 1909) was a part-time journalist for the *Lincolnshire and South Humberside* (formerly *Hull*) *Times* since March 1923 until the demise of the paper on 26 July 1985.

Most syndicated columnist

The world's most syndicated columnist is Ann Landers (*née* Eppie Lederer), 67, whose number of newspapers in 30 years has surpassed 1,100 with an estimated readership of 85 million. In Feb 1987 she switched after 32 years from the *Chicago Sun-Times* to the *Chicago Tribune*.

Longest-lived strip

The most durable newspaper comic strip has been the 'Katzenjammer Kids' (Hans and Fritz) created by Rudolph Dirks and first published in the *New York Journal* on 12 Dec 1897, and perpetuated by his son John. The earliest strip was 'The Yellow Kid', which first appeared in the *New York Journal* on 18 Oct 1896. The most widely syndicated is 'Peanuts' by Charlie Schulz of Santa Rosa, California, appearing in more than 2,000 newspapers in 68 countries in 26 languages starting in October 1950. In 1986 his income was estimated at $1 million per month.

Most misprints

The record for misprints in *The Times* was set on 22 Aug 1978 when on page 19 there were 97 in 5½ single column inches. The passage concerned 'Pop' (Pope) Paul VI.

Most durable advertiser

The Jos Neel Co, a clothing store in Macon, Georgia (founded 1880) has run an 'ad' in the *Macon Telegraph* every day in the upper left corner of page 2 since 22 Feb 1889 or 35,760 times to March 1987.

CIRCULATION

Earliest 1,000,000

The first newspaper to achieve a circulation of 1,000,000 was *Le Petit Journal*, published in Paris, France, which reached this figure in 1886, when selling at 5 centimes. The *Daily Mail* first reached a million on 2 Mar 1900.

Highest

The highest circulation for any newspaper in the world is that for the *Yomiuri Shimbun* (founded 1874) of Japan which attained a figure of 14,247,132 copies on 1 April 1987. This is achieved by totalling the figures for editions published in various centres with a morning figure of 9,278,686 and an evening figure of 4,968,446. It reaches 38 per cent of Japan's 34 million households. It has a staff of 3060 and 436 bureaux. In Japan 569 newspapers are printed for each 1000 people. *Trud*, the Soviet trade union daily, is printed in 53 cities in 15.4 million copies of which only 70,000 are bought at newsstands.

The highest circulation of any single newspaper in Britain is that of the *News of the World*, printed at Wapping, London E1. Single issues have attained a sale of 9,000,000 copies with an estimated readership of more than 19,000,000. The paper first appeared on 1 Oct 1843, and surpassed the million mark in 1905. The latest sales figure is 4,954,416 copies per issue (average for 1 July to 31 Dec 1986), with an estimated readership of 12,690,000.

The highest net sale of any daily newspaper in the United Kingdom is that of *The Sun*, founded in London in 1964. The latest sales figure is 4,049,991 (1 July to 31 Dec 1986), with an estimated readership of 11,221,000.

Most read

The national newspaper which achieves the closest to a saturation circulation is *The Sunday Post*, established in Glasgow in 1914. In 1986 its estimated readership in Scotland of 2,510,000 represented 61 per cent of the entire population aged 15 and over. The *Arran Banner* (founded March 1974) has a readership of 97+ per cent on Britain's seventh largest off-shore island.

PERIODICALS

Oldest

The oldest continuing periodical in the world is *Philosophical Transactions of the Royal Society*, published in London, which first appeared on 6 Mar 1665.

The bi-monthly *Gospel Magazine* has been published since 1766. Curtis's *Botanical Magazine* has been in continuous publication since 1 Feb 1787, as several 'parts' a year forming a series of continuously numbered volumes. Britain's oldest weekly periodical is *The Lancet*, first published in 1823. The *Scots Magazine* began in 1739 and ran until 1826, and with three breaks has been produced continuously since 1924.

Largest circulations

The largest circulation of any weekly periodical is that of *TV Guide* (USA) which in 1974 became the first magazine in history to sell a billion (1000 million) copies in a year. The weekly average for July–December 1986 was 16,800,441. In its 39 basic international editions *Reader's Digest* (established February 1922) circulates 28,000,000 copies monthly in 15 languages, including a United States edition of more than 16,250,000 copies and a United Kingdom edition (established 1939) of 1,558,073 copies (ABC January–December 1986).

Parade, the American syndicated Sunday newspaper colour magazine, is distributed with 135 newspapers every Sunday. The current circulation is 25,153,000 (April 1985).

The highest circulation of any periodical in Great Britain is that of the *Radio Times* (instituted on 28 Sept 1923). The average weekly sale for July–December 1986 was 3,235,977 copies with a readership of 9,171,000. The highest sale of any issue was 10,617,421 copies for the Christmas issue of 1986. *TV Times* averaged sales of 3,185,705 in the period July–December 1986 with an estimated readership of 9,487,000 (January–December 1986).

Annual

Old Moore's Almanack has been published annually since 1697, when it first appeared as a broadsheet by Dr Francis Moore (1657–1715) of Southwark, London to advertise his 'physiks'. The annual sale certified by its publishers W. Foulsham & Co Ltd of Slough, England is one million copies and its aggregate sale is estimated to be in excess of 108 million.

CROSSWORDS

First

The earliest known crossword was a 9 by 9 Double Diamond published in *St Nicholas* for September 1875 in New York City. This was discovered by Dr Kenneth Miller of Newcastle-upon-Tyne, England, inventor of the colour crossword in 1983. The first crossword published in a British newspaper was one furnished by C. W. Shepherd in the *Sunday Express* of 2 Nov 1924. However, a 25-letter acrostic of Roman provenance was discovered on a wall in Cirencester, Gloucestershire in 1868.

Largest

The world's largest published crossword has been one compiled in July 1982 by Robert Turcot of Québec, Canada. It comprised 82,951 squares,

Longest alphorn ● The longest alphorn is one of 118 ft *35,96 m* (excluding mouthpiece) weighing 83 kg *183 lb* built by Swiss-born Peter Wutherich, of Boise, Idaho. The sound takes 105,7 milliseconds to emerge from the bowl after entry into the mouthpiece.

contained 12,489 clues across and 13,125 down and covered 38.28 ft² *3,55 m²*.

Fastest and slowest solution

The fastest recorded time for completing *The Times* crossword under test conditions is 3 min 45.0 sec by Roy Dean, 43 of Bromley, London in the BBC 'Today' radio studio on 19 Dec 1970. Dr John Sykes won *The Times* championship 8 times between 1972 and 1985. In May 1966 *The Times* of London received an announcement from a Fijian woman that she had just succeeded in completing their crossword No 673 in the issue of 4 Apr 1932.

Most durable compilers

Adrian Bell (1901–1980) of Barsham, Suffolk contributed a record 4520 crosswords to *The Times* from 2 Jan 1930 until his death. R. J. Baddock of Plymouth (b. 30 Oct 1894) has been a regular contributor to national newspapers since 13 Aug 1926. The most prolific compiler is Roger F. Squires of Ironbridge, Shropshire, who compiles 35 published puzzles single-handedly each week. His total output to August 1986 was over 27,388.

ADVERTISING RATES

The highest ever price for a single page has been $327,230 (*£218,155*) for a four-colour back cover in *Parade* (circulation 25.2 million per week) in April 1985 (see above). The record for a four-colour inside page is $284,560 (*£189,705*) in *Parade* (in April 1985). The advertising revenue from the November 1982 US edition of *The Reader's Digest* was a peak $14,716,551 (*then £9,811,035*).

The highest expenditure ever incurred on a single advertisement in a periodical is $3,200,000

(*£2,135,000*) by Gulf and Western Industries on 5 Feb 1979 for insertions in *Time* Magazine (US and selected overseas editions).

The British record is some £100,000 for a 20-page colour supplement by Woolworths in the *Radio Times* of 16 Nov 1972. The rate for a single page in the *News of the World SunDay* magazine is £28,500, and £57,000 for a centre spread (April 1987). The world's highest newspaper advertising rate is 39,210,000 yen (*£163,375*) for a full page in the morning edition and 32,205,000 yen (*£134,188*) for the evening edition of the *Yomiuri Shimbun* of Tokyo (October 1986).

The highest rate in Britain is a full page in *The Sunday Express* at £40,000 (April 1987).

Music

Whistles and flutes made from perforated phalange bones have been found at Upper Palaeolithic sites of the Aurignacian period (*c.* 25,000–22,000 BC) *e.g.* at Istallóskö, Hungary and in Molodova, USSR. The world's earliest surviving musical notation dates from *c.* 1800 BC. A heptatonic scale deciphered from a clay tablet by Dr Duchesne-Guillemin in 1966–7 was found at a site in Nippur, Sumer, now Iraq. An Assyrian love song also *c.* 1800 BC to an Ugaritic god from a tablet of notation and lyric was reconstructed for an 11-string lyre at the University of California, Berkeley on 6 Mar 1974. Musical history can, however, be traced back to the 3rd millennium BC, when the yellow bell (*huang chung*) had a recognised standard musical tone in Chinese temple music.

INSTRUMENTS

Earliest piano

The earliest pianoforte in existence is one built in Florence, Italy, in 1720 by Bartolommeo Cristofori (1655–1731) of Padua, and now preserved in the Metropolitan Museum of Art, New York City.

Grandest piano

The grandest grand piano was one of 1¼ tons/ *tonnes* 11 ft 8 in *3,55 m* in length made by Chas. H. Challen & Son Ltd of London in 1935. The longest bass string measured 9 ft 11 in *3,02 m* with a tensile of 30 tons/*tonnes*.

Most expensive piano

The highest price ever paid for a piano is $390,000 (*then £177,273*) at Sotheby Parke Bernet, New York on 26 Mar 1980 for a Steinway grand of *c.* 1888 sold by the Martin Beck Theatre. It was bought by a non-pianist.

Smallest piano

The smallest playable piano is a ⅛th scale model of a 1910 Knabe. It measures 7½ × 3⅜ × 6½ in *19,05 × 8,57 × 16,5 cm* and was built by Emil J. Cost.

Largest organ

The largest and loudest musical instrument ever constructed is the now only partially functional Auditorium Organ in Atlantic City, New Jersey. Completed in 1930, this heroic instrument had two consoles (one with seven manuals and another movable one with five), 1477 stop controls and 33,112 pipes ranging in tone from 1/16 of an inch *4,7 mm* to the 64 ft *19,5 m* tone. It had the volume of 25 brass bands, with a range of seven octaves. The world's largest fully functional organ is the six manual 30,067 pipe Grand

Largest drum kit ● Professional Rock Star Luis Cardenas 'inside' his 'Status cymbal'—a 75-piece (excluding the stool) custom-made drum kit. Drummer with the Los Angeles-based group *Renegade* as well as a solo artiste, Luis' kit includes two suspended overhead toms, two Agogo percussion bells, fifteen finger cymbals and a 1948 Black Beauty snare drum. (Photo: Michael Jacobs)

Court Organ installed in the Wanamaker Store, Philadelphia, Pennsylvania in 1911 and enlarged between then and 1930. It has a 64 ft *19,5 m* tone gravissima pipe. The world's largest church organ is that in Passau Cathedral, West Germany. It was completed in 1928 by D. F. Steinmeyer & Co and has 16,000 pipes and five manuals. The world's most powerful electronic organ is the 5000 watt Royal V. Rodgers organ, designed by Virgil Fox with 465 speakers installed by Orient Shoji Co in Chuo-ku, Tokyo, Japan in June 1983. The chapel organ at West Point US Military Academy, NY has, since 1911, been expanded from 2406 to 18,200 pipes.

The largest organ in Great Britain is that completed in Liverpool Anglican Cathedral on 18 Oct 1926, with two five-manual consoles of which only one is now in use, and 9704 speaking pipes (originally 10,936) ranging from tones ¾ in to 32 ft *1,9 cm to 9,75 m*.

Loudest organ stop

The loudest organ stop in the world is the Ophicleide stop of the Grand Great in the Solo Organ in the Atlantic City Auditorium (see above). It is operated by a pressure of 100 in *254 cm* of water (3½ lb/in² *24 kPa*) and has a pure trumpet note of ear-splitting volume, more than six times the volume of the loudest locomotive whistles.

Most durable musicians

Elsie Maude Stanley Hall (1877–1976) gave piano recitals for 90 years, giving her final concert in Rustenburg, Transvaal, South Africa aged 97. Charles Bridgeman (1779–1873) of All Saints Parish Church, Hertford, England, who was appointed organist in 1792, was still playing 81 years later in 1873. Norwegian pianist Reidar Thommesen (1889–1986) played over 30 hours a week in theatre cafés when a nonagenarian.

Largest brass instrument

The largest recorded brass instrument is a tuba standing 7½ ft *2,28 m* tall, with 39 ft *11,8 m* of tubing and a bell 3 ft 4 in *1 m* across. This contrabass tuba was constructed for a world tour by the band of American composer John Philip Sousa (1854–1932), in *c*. 1896–8. It is now owned by a circus promoter in South Africa.

Largest stringed instrument

The largest movable stringed instrument ever constructed was a pantaleon with 270 strings stretched over 50 ft² *4,6 m²* used by George Noel in 1767. The greatest number of musicians required to operate a single instrument was the six required to play the gigantic orchestrion, known as the Apollonican, built in 1816 and played until 1840.

Largest and most expensive guitar

The largest and presumably also the loudest playable guitar in the world is one 14 ft 3¼ in *4,35 m* tall, and 309 lb *140 kg* in weight, built by Joe Kovacic of Lado Musical Inc, Scarborough, Ontario, Canada. The most expensive standard sized guitar is the German chittara battente by Jacob Stadler, dated 1624, which was sold for £10,500 at Christie's, London on 12 June 1974.

Largest double bass

The largest double bass ever constructed was one 14 ft *4,26 m* tall, built in 1924 in Ironia, New Jersey by Arthur K. Ferris, allegedly on orders from the Archangel Gabriel. It weighed 11.6 cwt *590 kg* with a sound box 8 ft *2,43 m* across, and had leathern strings totalling 104 ft *31,7 m*. Its low notes could be felt rather than heard. On 27 June 1984 5 members of 'Bass Ten' from Bournemouth, Dorset bowed and six-fingered a double bass simultaneously in a rendition of Monti's *Czardas* at Hever Castle, Kent.

Most valuable 'cello

The highest ever auction price for a violoncello is £145,000 at Sotheby's, London on 8 Nov 1978 for a Stradivari made in Cremona, Italy in 1710.

Most valuable violin

The Lady Blunt Stradivarius violin of 1721 failed at £820,000 to reach its undisclosed 'reserve' at Sotheby's, London on 14 Nov 1985. The highest price ever *paid* at auction for a violin or any musical instrument is £440,000 for 'The Colossus' Stradivari dated 1716 at Christie's, London on 29 Apr 1987. Some 700 of the 1116 violins by Stradivarius (1644–1737) have survived. His Alard violin was confirmed by Jacques Français to have been sold by private treaty by W. E. Hill for $1.2 million (*then* £600,000) to a Singaporean.

Underwater violinist

The pioneer violinist to surmount the problems of playing the violin underwater was Mark Gottlieb. Submerged in Evergreen State College swimming bath in Olympia, Washington State in March 1975 he gave a submarine rendition of Handel's Water Music. His most intractable problem was his underwater *détaché*. On 7 Oct 1979 the first underwater quartet performed in the *Challenge the Guinness* TV show on Channel 7 in Tokyo, Japan.

Most durable fiddlers

Rolland S. Tapley retired as a violinist from the Boston Symphony Orchestra after reputedly playing for an unrivalled 58 years from February 1920 to 27 Aug 1978. Otto E. Funk, 62, walked 4165 miles *6702 km* from New York City to San Francisco, California playing his Hopf violin every step of the way westward. He arrived on 16 June 1929 after 183 days on the road.

Largest drum

The largest drum ever constructed was one 12 ft *3,65 m* in diameter weighing 600 lb *272 kg* for the Boston World Peace Jubilee of 1872.

Highest and lowest notes

The extremes of orchestral instruments (excluding the organ) range between a handbell tuned to g^v (6272 cycles/sec) and the sub-contrabass clarinet, which can reach C_{11} or 16.4 cycles/sec. The highest note on a standard pianoforte is c^v (4186 cycles/sec), which is also the violinist's limit. In 1873 a sub double bassoon able to reach $B_{111}\sharp$ or 14.6 cycles/sec was constructed but no surviving specimen is known. The extremes for the organ are g^{vi} (the sixth G above middle C) (12,544 cycles/sec) and C_{111} (8.12 cycles/sec) obtainable from ¾ in *1,9 cm* and 64 ft *19,5 m* pipes respectively.

Easiest and most difficult instruments

The American Music Conference announced in September 1977 that the easiest instrument is the ukulele, and the most difficult are the French horn and the oboe, which latter has been described as 'the ill woodwind that no-one blows good'.

ORCHESTRAS

Largest orchestra

On 17 June 1872, Johann Strauss the younger (1825–99) conducted an orchestra of 987 pieces supported by a choir of 20,000, at the World Peace Jubilee in Boston, Massachusetts, USA. The number of first violinists was 400.

Largest band

The most massive band ever assembled was one of 20,100 bandsmen at the Ullevaal Stadium, Oslo, from Norges Musikkorps Forbund bands from all Norway on 28 June 1964. On 17 Apr 1982, 6179 'musicians' congregated at Bay Shore Mall, Milwaukee, Wisconsin, USA, for a rendering of Sousa's 'Stars and Stripes Forever'. According to one music critic, the 'instruments' included 'kazoos, 7-Up bottles, one-man-band contraptions, coffee cans, bongo drums and anything-you-can-thump-on. At times' the report concludes, 'you could almost tell what they were playing'.

Largest marching band

The largest marching band was one of 4524 including 1342 majorettes under direction of Danny Kaye (1913–87) at Dodger Stadium, Los Angeles on 15 Apr 1985. The longest recorded musical march is one of 61 km *37.9 miles* from Lillehammer to Hamar, Norway in 15 hours when, on 10 May 1980, 26 of 35 members of the Trondheim Brass Band survived the playing of 135 marches.

Most durable conductor

The Cork Symphony Orchestra has performed under the baton of Dr Aloys Fleischmann for 52 seasons (1935–86).

Most successful bands

Most British Open Brass Band Championship titles (inst. 1853) have been won by the Black

Dyke Mills Band which has won 22 times from 1862 to 1974 including three consecutive wins in 1972–4. The most successful pipe band is the Shotts & Dykehead Caledonian Pipe Band with their 10th world title in August 1980.

ATTENDANCES

Classical

The greatest attendance at any classical concert was an estimated 800,000 at a free open-air concert by the NY Philharmonic conducted by Zubin Mehta, on the Great Lawn of Central Park, New York, on 5 July 1986, as part of the Statue of Liberty Weekend.

Pop festival

The greatest claimed attendance has been 600,000 for the 'Summer Jam' at Watkins Glen, New York, on Sunday 29 July 1973 of whom about 150,000 actually paid. There were 12 'sound towers'. The attendance at the third Pop Festival at East Afton Farm, Freshwater, Isle of Wight, England on 30 Aug 1970 was claimed by its promoters, Fiery Creations, to be 400,000.

Solo performer

The largest paying audience ever attracted by a solo performer was an estimated 175,000 in the Maracaña Stadium, Rio de Janeiro, Brazil to hear Frank Sinatra (b. 1915) on 26 Jan 1980. Jean-Michel Jarre entertained an estimated 1.3 million at downtown Houston, Texas at a free concert on 5 Apr 1986.

Greatest choir

Excluding 'sing alongs' by stadium crowds, the greatest choir was one of 60,000 which sang in unison as a finale of a choral contest among 160,000 participants in Breslau, Germany on 2 Aug 1937.

COMPOSERS

Most prolific

The most prolific composer of all time was probably Georg Philipp Telemann (1681–1767) of Germany. He composed 12 complete sets of services (one cantata every Sunday) for a year, 78 services for special occasions, 40 operas, 600 to 700 orchestral suites, 44 Passions, plus concertos and chamber music. The most prolific symphonist was Johann Melchior Molter (*c.* 1695–1765) of Germany who wrote 169. Joseph Haydn (1732–1809) of Austria wrote 108 numbered symphonies many of which are regularly played today.

Most rapid

Among composers of the classical period the most prolific was Wolfgang Amadeus Mozart (1756–91) of Austria, who wrote *c.* 1000 operas, operettas, symphonies, violin sonatas, divertimenti, serenades, motets, concertos for piano and many other instruments, string quartets, other chamber music, masses and litanies, of which only 70 were published before he died aged 35. His opera *La Clemenza di Tito* (1791) was written in 18 days, and three symphonic masterpieces, *Symphony No 39 in E flat major*, *Symphony No 40 in G minor* and the *Jupiter Symphony No 41 in C major*, were reputedly written in the space of 42 days in 1788. His overture *Don Giovanni* was written in full score at one sitting in Prague in 1787 and finished on the day of its opening performance.

Longest symphony

The longest of all single classical symphonies is the orchestral symphony No 3 in D minor by Gustav Mahler (1860–1911) of Austria. This work, composed in 1896, requires a contralto, a women's and a boys' choir in addition to a full

Most successful concert tour ● Bruce Springsteen's tour which began in April 1984 grossed an estimated $117 million. He played 158 dates in 61 cities spread over 11 countries and was seen by 4,767,854 people. (Photo: LFI)

orchestra. A full performance requires 1 hr 40 min, of which the first movement alone takes between 30 and 36 min. The Symphony No 2 (the Gothic), composed in 1919–22 by William Havergal Brian (1876–1972) was played by over 800 performers (4 brass bands) in the Victoria Hall, Hanley, Staffordshire on 21 May 1978 (conductor Trevor Stokes). A recent broadcast required 1 hr 45½ min. Brian wrote an even vaster work based on Shelley's 'Prometheus Unbound' lasting 4 hr 11 min but the full score has been missing since 1961. The symphony *Victory at Sea* written by Richard Rodgers and arranged by Robert Russell Bennett for NBC TV in 1952 lasted for 13 hours.

Longest piano composition

The longest continuous non-repetitious piano piece ever published has been *The Well-Tuned Piano* by La Monte Young first presented by the Dia Art Foundation at the Concert Hall, Harrison St, New York on 28 Feb 1980. The piece lasted 4 hr 12 min 10 sec. *Symphonic Variations,* composed in the 1930s by Kaikhosru Shapurji Sorabji (b. 1892) on 500 pages of close manuscript in 3 volumes would last for 6 hours at the prescribed tempo.

Longest silence

The longest interval between the known composition of a major composer and its performance in the manner intended is from 3 Mar 1791 until 9 Oct 1982 (over 191 years), in the case of Mozart's *Organ Piece for a Clock,* a fugue fantasy in F minor (K 608), arranged by the organ builders Wm Hill & Son and Norman & Beard Ltd at Glyndebourne, East Sussex.

PERFORMERS

Highest-paid pianist
Wladziu Valentino Liberace (1917–87) earned more than $2 million each 26-week season with a peak of $138,000 (then £49,285) for a single night's performance at Madison Square Garden, New York in 1954. The highest paid classical concert pianist was Ignace Jan Paderewski (1860–1941), Prime Minister of Poland (1919–20), who accumulated a fortune estimated at $5,000,000, of which $500,000 (then £110,000) was earned in a single season in 1922–23. The *nouveau riche* wife of a US industrialist once required him to play in her house behind a curtain. For concerts Artur Rubinstein (1887–1982), between 1937 and 1976, commanded 70 per cent of the gross.

Greatest span
Sergei Vassilievitch Rachmaninov (1873–1943) had a span of 12 white notes and could play a left hand chord of C, E♭, G, C, G.

Most successful singer
Of great fortunes earned by singers, the highest on record are those of Enrico Caruso (1873–1921), the Italian tenor, whose estate was about $9,000,000 (then £1,875,000) and the Italian-Span-

Singer's pulling power ● Portrait of Johanna ('Jenny') Maria Lind (1820–87), the 'Swedish nightingale'. In 1850, up to $653 was paid for a single seat at her concerts in the United States. She had a range from g to e^{III} of which the middle register is still regarded as unrivalled. (Photo: Mary Evans Picture Library)

ish coloratura soprano Amelita Galli-Curci (1889–1963), who received about $3,000,000 (£750,000). The Irish tenor Count John Francis McCormack (1884–1945) gave up to 10 concerts to capacity audiences in a single season in New York.

David Bowie drew a fee of $1.5 million (then £960,000) for a single show at the US Festival in Glen Helen Regional Park, San Bernardino County, California on 26 May 1983. The 4-man Van Halen rock band attracted a matching fee. The total attendance at Michael Jackson's 'Victory Tour' in the United States, July–Dec 1984, brought in a tour gross revenue of $81 million (then £67.5 million).

Worst singer
While no agreement exists as to the identity of history's greatest singer, there is unanimity on the worst. The excursions of the soprano Florence Foster Jenkins (1868–1944) into lieder and even high coloratura culminated on 25 Oct 1944 in her sell-out concert at the Carnegie Hall, New York. The diva's (already high) high F was said to have been made higher in 1943 by a crash in a taxi. It is one of the tragedies of musicology that Madame Jenkins' *Clavelitos*, accompanied by Cosme McMoon, was never recorded for posterity.

OPERA

Longest
The longest of commonly performed operas is *Die Meistersinger von Nürnberg* by Wilhelm Richard Wagner (1813–83) of Germany. A normal uncut performance of this opera as performed by the Sadler's Wells company between 24 Aug and 19 Sept 1968 entailed 5 hr 15 min of music. *The Heretics* by Gabriel von Wayditch (1888–1969), a Hungarian-American, is orchestrated for 110 pieces and lasts 8½ hr.

Shortest
The shortest opera published was *The Deliverance of Theseus* by Darius Milhaud (1892–1972), first performed in 1928, which lasted for 7 min 27 sec.

Longest aria
The longest single aria, in the sense of an operatic solo, is Brünnhilde's immolation scene in Wagner's *Gotterdammerung* A well-known recording of this has been precisely timed at 14 min 46 sec.

Largest opera houses
The largest opera house in the world is the Metropolitan Opera House, Lincoln Center, New York, completed in September 1966 at a cost of $45,700,000 (then £16,320,000). It has a capacity of 3800 seats in an auditorium 451 ft *137 m* deep. The stage is 234 ft *71 m* wide and 146 ft *44,5 m* deep. The tallest opera house is one housed in a 42-storey building on Wacker Drive in Chicago, Illinois. The Teatro della Scala (La Scala) in Milan, Italy, shares with the Bolshoi Theatre in Moscow the distinction of having the greatest number of tiers. Each has six, with the topmost being nicknamed the *Galiorka* by Russians.

Youngest and oldest opera singers
The youngest opera singer in the world has been Ginetta Gloria La Bianca, born in Buffalo, New York on 12 May 1934, who sang Rosina in *The Barber of Seville* at the Teatro dell'Opera, Rome, on 8 May 1950 aged 15 years 361 days, having appeared as Gilda in *Rigoletto* at Velletri 45 days earlier. Ginetta La Bianca was taught by Lucia Carlino and managed by Angelo Carlino. The tenor Giovanni Martinelli sang Emperor Altoum in *Turandot* in Seattle, Washington on 4 Feb 1967 when aged 81.

Danshi Toyotake (b. 1 Aug 1891) has been singing *Musume Gidayu* for 91 years.

Most curtain calls ● The show must go on . . . it was reported on 5 July 1983 that Placido Domingo received 83 curtain calls and was applauded for 1 hr 30 min after singing the lead in Puccini's *La Bohème* at the State Opera House in Vienna, Austria. (Photo: S Ward)

Longest encore
The longest operatic encore, listed in the *Concise Oxford Dictionary of Opera*, was of the entire opera Cimarosa's *Il Matrimonio Segreto* at its première in 1792. This was at the command of the Austro-Hungarian Emperor Leopold II (1790–92).

SONG

Oldest
The oldest known song is the *shaduf* chant, which has been sung since time immemorial by irrigation workers on the man-powered pivoted-rod bucket raisers of the Nile water mills (or *saqiyas*) in Egypt. The oldest known harmonised music performed today is the English song *Sumer is icumen in* which dates from *c.* 1240.

National anthems
The oldest national anthem is the *Kimigayo* of Japan, in which the words date from the 9th century. The anthem of Greece constitutes the first four verses of the Solomos poem, which has 158 stanzas. The shortest anthems are those of Japan, Jordan and San Marino, each with only four lines. Of the 23 wordless national anthems the oldest is that of Spain dating from 1770.

Longest rendering
'God Save the King' was played non-stop 16 or 17 times by a German military band on the platform of Rathenau railway station, Brandenburg, Germany on the morning of 9 Feb 1909. The reason was that King Edward VII was struggling inside the train with the uniform of a German Field-Marshal before he could emerge.

Top songs
The most frequently sung songs in English are *Happy Birthday to You* (based on the original *Good Morning to All*), by Mildred and Patty S. Hill of New York (published in 1935 and in copyright until 2010); *For He's a Jolly Good Fellow* (originally the French *Malbrouk*), known at least as early as 1781, and *Auld Lang Syne* (originally the Strathspey *I fee'd a Lad at Michaelmass*), some words of which were written by Robert Burns (1759–96). *Happy Birthday* was sung in space by the Apollo IX astronauts on 8 Mar 1969.

Top-selling sheet music
Sales of three non-copyright pieces are known to have exceeded 20,000,000, namely *The Old Folks at Home* by Stephen Foster (1855), *Listen to the Mocking Bird* (1855) and *The Blue Danube* (1867). Of copyright material the two top sellers are *Let Me Call You Sweetheart* (1910, by Whitson and Friedman) and *Till We Meet Again* (1918, by Egan and Whiting) each with some 6,000,000 by 1967. Other huge sellers have been *St Louis Blues*, *Stardust* and *Tea for Two*.

Most successful songwriters
The songwriters responsible for the most number one singles are John Lennon and Paul McCartney. In America McCartney is credited as writer on 32 number one hits, 6 more than Lennon. In Britain Lennon authored 27 number ones, McCartney 26. In both countries 23 of their number ones were jointly written. After Lennon/McCartney the most successful songwriters in terms of number one hits in Britain are Benny Anderson and Bjorn Ulvaeus of the group ABBA, who have written ten. In America Barry Gibb of the Bee Gees has written or co-written 16 number ones. The most successful female songwriter in America is Carole King with 8 number ones—in Britain it is Madonna with 4.

HYMNS

Earliest
There are more than 950,000 Christian hymns in existence. The music and parts of the text of a hymn in the *Oxyrhynchus Papyri* from the 2nd century are the earliest known hymnody. The earliest exactly datable hymn is the *Heyr Himna Smiður* (*Hear, the maker of heaven*) from 1208 by the Icelandic bard and chieftain Kolbeinn Tumason (1173–1208).

Longest and shortest
The longest hymn is *Hora novissima tempora pessima sunt; vigilemus* by Bernard of Cluny (12th century), which runs to 2966 lines. In English the longest is *The Sands of Time are Sinking* by Mrs Anne Ross Cousin, *née* Cundell (1824–1906), which is in full 152 lines, though only 32 lines in the Methodist Hymn Book. The shortest hymn is the single verse in long metre *Be Present at our Table Lord*, anon., but attributed to 'J. Leland'.

Most prolific hymnists
Mrs Frances (Fanny) Jane van Alstyne *née* Crosby (1820–1915) (USA) wrote 8500 hymns although she had been blinded at the age of 6 weeks. She is reputed to have knocked off one hymn in 15 minutes. Charles Wesley (1707–88) wrote about 6000 hymns. In the seventh (1950) edition of *Hymns Ancient and Modern* the works of John Mason Neale (1818–66) appear 56 times.

BELLS

Oldest
The oldest bell in the world is the tintinnabulum found in the Babylonian Palace of Nimrod in 1849 by Mr (later Sir) Austen Henry Layard (1817–94) dating from *c.* 1100 BC. The oldest known tower bell is one in Pisa, Italy dated MCVI (1106).

The fragile hand bell known as the Black or Iron Bell of St Patrick is dated *c.* AD 450. The oldest tower bell in Great Britain is one of 1 cwt *50 kg* at St Botolph, Hardham, Sussex still in use but dated *ante* 1100. The oldest inscribed bell is the Gargate bell at Caversfield church, Oxfordshire and is dated *c.* 1200–1210. The oldest *dated* bell in England is one hanging in Lissett church, near Bridlington, Humberside discovered in October 1972 to bear the date MCCLIIII (1254).

Heaviest
The heaviest bell in the world is the Tsar Kolokol, cast on 25 Nov 1735 in Moscow. It weighs 193 tons *196 tonnes*, measures 5,9 m *19 ft 4¼ in* in diameter and 5,87 m *19 ft 3 in* high, and its greatest thickness is 24 in *60 cm*. The bell is cracked, and a fragment, weighing about 11 tons/*tonnes* was broken from it. The bell has stood, unrung, on a platform in the Kremlin in Moscow since 1836.

The heaviest bell in use is the Mingun bell, weighing 55,555 viss or *90.52 tons* with a diameter of 16 ft 8½ in *5,09 m* at the lip, in Mandalay, Burma, which is struck by a teak boom from the outside. It was cast at Mingun late in the reign of King Bodawpaya (1782–1819). The heaviest swinging bell in the world is the Petersglocke in the south-west tower of Cologne Cathedral, West Germany, cast in 1923 with a diameter of 3,40 m *11 ft 1¾ in* weighing 25,4 tonnes *25.0 tons*.

The heaviest bell hung in Great Britain is 'Great Paul' in the south-west tower of St Paul's Cathedral, London, cast in 1881. It weighs 16 tons 14 cwt 2 qrs 19 lb net *17 002 kg*, has a diameter of 9 ft 6½ in *2,90 m* and sounds note E-flat. 'Big Ben', the hour bell in the clock tower of the House of Commons, was cast in 1858 and weighs 13 tons 10 cwt 3 qrs 15 lb *13 761 kg*. It is the most broadcast bell in the world and is note E.

Peals
A ringing peal is defined as a diatonic 'ring' of five or more bells hung for full-circle change ringing. Of 5500 rings so hung only 70 are outside the United Kingdom and Ireland. The heaviest ring in the world is that of 13 bells cast in 1938–39 for the Anglican Cathedral, Liverpool. The total bell weight is 16½ tons *16,76 tonnes* of which Emmanuel, the tenor bell note A, weighs 82 cwt 11 lb *4170,8 kg*.

Largest carillon
The largest carillon (minimum of 23 bells) in the world is the Laura Spelman Rockefeller Memorial Carillon in Riverside Church, New York with 74 bells weighing 102 tons. The bourdon, giving the note lower C, weighs 40,926 lb *18 563 kg*. This 18.27 ton bell, cast in England, with a diameter of 10 ft 2 in *3,09 cm* is the largest *tuned* bell in the world.

The heaviest carillon in Great Britain is in St Nicholas Church, Aberdeen. It consists of 48 bells, the total weight of which is 25 tons 8 cwt 2 qrs 13 lb *25 838 kg*. The bourdon bell weighs 4 tons 9 cwt 3 qrs 26 lb *4571 kg* and is the note G-sharp.

Bell ringing
Eight bells have been rung to their full 'extent' (40,320 unrepeated changes of Plain Bob Major) only once without relays. This took place in a bell foundry at Loughborough, Leicestershire, beginning at 6.52 a.m. on 27 July 1963 and ending at 12.50 a.m. on 28 July, after 17 hr 58 min. The peal was composed by Kenneth Lewis of Altrincham, Manchester, and the eight ringers were conducted by Robert B. Smith, aged 25, of Marple, Manchester. Theoretically it would take 37 years 355 days to ring 12 bells (maximus) to their full extent of 479,001,600 changes. The greatest number of peals (minimum of 5040 changes, all in tower bells) rung in a year is 209 by Mark William Marshall of Ashford, Kent in 1973. The late George E. Fearn rang 2666 peals from 1928 to May 1974. Matthew Lakin (1801–1899) was a regular bell-ringer at Tetney Church near Grimsby for 84 years.

Theatre

Oldest
Theatre in Europe has its origins in Greek drama performed in honour of a god, usually Dionysus. The earliest amphitheatres date from the 5th century BC. The first stone-built theatre in Rome erected in 55 BC could accommodate 40,000 spectators.

Oldest indoor theatre
The oldest indoor theatre in the world is the Teatro Olimpico in Vicenza, Italy. Designed in the Roman style by Andrea di Pietro, *alias* Palladio (1508–80), it was begun three months before his death and finished by his pupil Vicenzo Scamozzi (1552–1616) in 1583. It is preserved today in its original form.

The earliest London theatre was James Burbage's 'The Theatre', built in 1576 near Finsbury Fields. The oldest theatre still in use in Great Britain is The Royal, Bristol. The foundation stone was laid on 30 Nov 1764, and the theatre was opened on 30 May 1766 with a 'Concert of Music and a Specimen of Rhetorick'. The City Varieties Music Hall, Leeds was a singing room in 1762 and so claims to outdate the Theatre Royal. Actors had the legal status of rogues and vagabonds until the passing of the Vagrancy Act in 1824. The oldest amateur dramatic society is the Old Stagers inaugurated in Canterbury, Kent in 1841. They have performed in every year except the years of World Wars I and II.

Largest
The world's largest building used for theatre is the National People's Congress Building (*Ren min da hui tang*) on the west side of Tian an men Square, Peking, China. It was completed in 1959 and covers an area of 12.9 acres *5,2 ha*. The theatre seats 10,000 and is occasionally used as such as in 1964 for the play *The East is Red*. The highest capacity purpose-built theatre is the Perth Entertainment Centre, Western Australia completed at a cost of $A 8.3 million (*then £4.2 million*) in November 1976 with 8003 seats. The stage area is 12,000 ft² *1148 m²*.

The highest capacity theatre is the Odeon, Hammersmith, London, with 3483 seats. The largest theatre stage in Great Britain is the Opera House in Blackpool, Lancashire. It was rebuilt in July 1939 and has seats for 2975 people. Behind the 45 ft *14 m* wide proscenium arch, the stage is 110 ft *33 m* high, 60 ft *18 m* deep and 100 ft *30 m* wide, and there is dressing-room accommodation for 200 artistes.

Smallest
The smallest regularly operated professional theatre in the world is the Piccolo in Juliusstrasse, Hamburg, West Germany. It was founded in 1970 and has a maximum capacity of 30 seats.

Largest amphitheatre
The largest amphitheatre ever built is the Flavian amphitheatre or Colosseum of Rome, Italy, completed in AD 80. Covering 5 acres *2 ha* and with a capacity of 87,000, it has a maximum length of 612 ft *187 m* and maximum width of 515 ft *175 m*.

Largest stage
The largest stage in the world is in the Ziegfeld Room Reno, Nevada with 176 ft *53,6 m* passerelle, three main lifts each capable of raising 1200 show girls (64½ tons *65,3 tonnes*), two 62½ ft *19,1 m* circumference turntables and 800 spotlights.

Longest runs
Plays

The longest continuous run of any show in the world is *The Mousetrap* by Dame Agatha Mary Clarissa Christie, DBE (*née* Miller, later Lady

Mallowan) (1890–1976). This thriller opened on 25 Nov 1952, at the Ambassadors Theatre (capacity 453) and moved after 8862 performances 'down the road' to St Martin's Theatre on 25 Mar 1974. The 30th anniversary performance on 25 Nov 1982 was the 12,481st and the total is now over 14,250. The Vicksburg Theater Guild, Mississippi, USA have been playing the melodrama *Gold in the Hills* by J. Frank Davis discontinuously but every season since 1936.

Revue

The greatest number of performances of any theatrical presentation is 47,250 (to April 1986) in the case of *The Golden Horseshoe Revue*—a show staged at Disneyland Park, Anaheim, California, USA. It started on 16 July 1955, closed on 12 Oct 1986 and has been seen by 16 million people. The three main performers were Fulton Burley, Dick Hardwick and Betty Taylor who played as many as five houses a day in a routine that lasted 45 minutes.

Broadway

The long-run record for any Broadway show was set on 29 Sept 1983 with the 3389th performance of *A Chorus Line*. It opened on 25 July 1975 and had been seen by an estimated 22,300,000 people with a box office receipt of $260 million.

The off-Broadway musical show *The Fantasticks* by Tom Jones and Harvey Schmidt opened on 3 May 1960 and closed on 8 June 1986 after 10,864 performances at the Sullivan Street Playhouse, Greenwich Village, New York.

Musical shows

The longest-running musical show ever performed in Britain was *The Black and White Minstrel Show* later *Magic of the Minstrels*. The aggregate but discontinuous number of performances was 6464 with a total attendance of 7,794,552. The show opened at the Victoria Palace, London on 25 May 1962 and closed on 4 Nov 1972. It re-opened for a season in June 1973 at the New Victoria and finally closed on 8 Dec 1973.

Jesus Christ Superstar, which opened at Palace Theatre, London on 8 Aug 1972, closed on 23 Aug 1980 after 3357 performances having played to 2 million people with box office receipts of £7 million. By 1984 it had been produced in 37 other countries.

Shortest runs

The shortest run on record was that of *The Intimate Revue* at the Duchess Theatre, London, on 11 Mar 1930. Anything which could go wrong did. With scene changes taking up to 20 min apiece, the management scrapped seven scenes to get the finale on before midnight. The run was described as 'half a performance'.

The opening and closing nights of many Broadway shows have coincided. Spectacular failures are known as 'turkeys' of which there were 11 in 1978–79. *Frankenstein*, which opened and closed on Broadway on 4 Jan 1981, lost an estimated $2 million but *A Doll's Life* (23–26 Sept 1982) lost close to $4 million.

Lowest attendance

The ultimate in low attendances was in December 1983 when the comedy *Bag* in Grantham, Lincolnshire opened to a nil attendance.

Youngest Broadway producer

Margo Feiden (Margo Eden) (b. New York, 2 Dec 1944) produced the musical *Peter Pan*, which opened on 3 Apr 1961 when she was 16 years 5 months old. She wrote *Out Brief Candle*, which opened on 18 Aug 1962. She is now a leading art dealer.

One-man shows

The longest run of one-man shows is 849 by Victor Borge (b. Copenhagen, 3 Jan 1909) in his

"NO SEX" IS THE ALL TIME *CHAMP*
EVENING STANDARD 17.8.78

ON 21st FEBRUARY 1979 "NO SEX, PLEASE, WERE BRITISH" REACHED 3214 PERFORMANCES AND BECAME THE LONGEST RUNNING COMEDY IN THE WORLD

BEATING THESE OTHER FAMOUS LONG RUNNING COMEDIES

"NO SEX PLEASE WERE BRITISH"	3214 Performances ON 21.2.1979
"LIFE WITH FATHER"	3213
"THERES A GIRL IN MY SOUP"	2517
"BOEING-BOEING"	2035
"BLITHE SPIRIT"	1997
"WORM'S EYE VIEW"	1745
"RELUCTANT HEROES"	1610

Now over 6615 performances

Longest running comedy ● *No Sex Please We're British* entered its 16th year in 1987, having opened at The Strand Theatre on 3 June 1971 and transferred to the Duchess Theatre on 2 Sept 1986. Its director Allan Davis has had his name in lights from the start.

Comedy in Music from 2 Oct 1953 to 21 Jan 1956 at the Golden Theater, Broadway, New York City. The world aggregate record for one-man shows is 1700 performances of *Brief Lives* by Roy Dotrice (b. Guernsey, 26 May 1923) including 400 straight at the Mayfair Theatre, London ending on 20 July 1974. He was on stage for more than 2½ hr per performance of this 17th-century monologue and required 3 hr for make up and 1 hr for removal of make-up so aggregating 40 weeks in the chair.

Most durable actors and actresses

Kanmi Fujiyama (b. 1929) played the lead role in 10,288 performances by the comedy company Sochiku Shikigeki from Nov 1966 to June 1983. Dame Anna Neagle, DBE (1904–86) played the lead role in *Charlie Girl* at the Adelphi Theatre, London for 2062 of 2202 performances between 15 Dec 1965 and 27 Mar 1971. She played the role a further 327 times in 327 performances in Australasia. Frances Etheridge has played Lizzie, the housekeeper, in *Gold in the Hills* (see Longest Runs) more than 660 times over a span of 47 years since 1936. David Raven played Major Metcalfe in *The Mousetrap* on 4575 occasions between 22 July 1957 and 23 Nov 1968. Jack Howarth MBE (1896–1984) was an actor on the stage and in television for 76 years from 1907 until his last appearance after 23 years as Albert Tatlock in *Coronation Street* on 25 Jan 1984.

Least insecure

Ben Vereen was given a 20-week guarantee of $52,500 per week plus a cut of the 'box office' in the Broadway production *Pippin* in 1986.

Most roles

The greatest recorded number of theatrical, film and television roles is 3371 from 1951 to May 1987 by Jan Leighton (US).

Longest play

The longest recorded theatrical production has been *The Acting Life* staged in the Tom Mann Theatre, Sydney, Australia on 17–18 Mar 1984 with a cast of 10. The production required 19¼ hours or 21 hours with intervals.

Shakespeare

The first all-amateur company to have staged all 37 plays was The Southsea Shakespeare Actors, Hampshire (founded 1947) in October 1966 when, under K. Edmonds Gateley MBE, they presented *Cymbeline*. The longest is *Hamlet* with 4042 lines and 29,551 words. Of Shakespeare's 1277 speaking parts the longest is Hamlet with 11,610 words.

Longest chorus line

The longest chorus line in performing history numbered up to 120 in some of the early Ziegfeld's Follies. In the finale of *A Chorus Line* on the night of 29 Sept 1983 when it broke the record as the longest-running Broadway show ever, 332 top-hatted 'strutters' performed on stage.

Highest cabaret fee

Dolly Parton received up to $400,000 (£333,000) per live concert. Johnny Carson's fee for the non-televised Sears Roebuck Centenary Gala in Oct 1984 was set at 1 million dollars (£833,000).

Ice shows

Holiday on Ice Production Inc, founded by Morris Chalfen in 1945, stages the world's most costly live entertainment with up to seven productions playing simultaneously in several of 75 countries drawing 20,000,000 spectators paying $40 million (£33.3 million) in a year. The total skating and other staff exceeds 900. The most prolific producer of ice shows was Gerald Palmer (1908–83) with 137 since 1945 including 34 consecutive shows at the Empire Pool, Wembley, London with attendances up to 850,000. Hazel Wendy Jolly (b. 1933) has appeared in the Wembley Winter Pantomime for 27 years.

Most ardent theatre-goers

Dr H. Howard Hughes (b. 1902), Professor Emeritus of Texas Wesleyan College, Fort Worth, Texas, has attended 5512 shows in the period 1956–83. Britain's leading 'first nighter' Edward Sutro MC (1900–78) saw 3000 first night productions in 1916–56 and possibly more than 5000 in his 60 years of theatre-going. The highest precisely recorded number of theatre attendances in Britain is 3687 shows in 33 years from 28 Mar 1953 to his death on 10 Sept 1986 by John Iles of Salisbury, Wiltshire.

Arts festival

The world's largest arts festival is the annual Edinburgh Festival Fringe (instituted in 1959). In 1983, 454 groups gave 6886 performances of 875 shows between 21 Aug and 10 Sept. Prof Gerald Berkowitz of Northern Illinois University attended a record 145 separate performances at the 1979 Festival from 15 Aug–8 Sept.

Fashion shows

The most prolific producer of fashion shows is Adalene Ross of San Francisco, California with totals over 4711 to mid-1987.

Professional wrestling

The professional wrestler who has received most for a single bout has been Kanii Antonio Inoki of

on 19 Feb 1878. The horizontal disc was introduced by Emile Berliner (1851–1929).

Earliest recordings

The earliest birthdate of anyone whose voice is recorded is that of Lajos Kossuth (b. 9 Sept 1802 d. 24 Mar 1894), former Governor of Hungary whose speech in Torino, Italy on 20 Sept 1890 is still preserved on a wax cylinder in the National Széchényi Library in Budapest. The earliest-born recorded singer was Peter Schram, the Danish baritone of whom a cylinder was made in the role of Don Giovanni on his 70th birthday on 5 Sept 1889.

Tape recording

Magnetic recording was invented by Valdemar Poulsen (1869–1942) of Denmark with his steel wire Telegraphone in 1898 (US Pat. No 661619). Fritz Pfleumer (German Patent 500900) introduced tape in 1928. Tapes were first used at the Blattner Studios, Elstree, Hertfordshire in 1929. Plastic tapes were devised by BASF of Germany in 1932–35, but were not marketed until 1950 by Recording Associates of New York. In April 1983 Olympic Optical Industry Co of Japan marketed a micro-cassette recorder 10,7 × 5,1 × 1,4 cm *4.2 × 2 × 0.55 in* weighing 125 g *4.4 oz.*

Oldest records

The BBC record library contains over 1,000,000 records, including 5250 with no known matrix. The oldest records in the library are white wax cylinders dating from 1888. The earliest commercial disc recording was manufactured in 1895. The world's largest private collection is believed to be that of Stan Kilarr (b. 1915) of Klamath Falls, Oregon with some 500,000.

Smallest record

The smallest functional gramophone record is one 1⅜ in *3,5 cm* in diameter of 'God Save the King' of which 250 were made by HMV Record Co in 1924.

Phonographic identification

Dr Arthur B. Lintgen (b. 1932) of Rydal, Pennsylvania has an as yet unique and proven ability to identify the music on phonograph records purely by visual inspection without hearing a note.

Earliest jazz records

The earliest jazz record made was *Indiana* and *The Dark Town Strutters Ball*, recorded for the Columbia label in New York on or about 30 Jan 1917, by the Original Dixieland Jazz Band, led by Dominick (Nick) James La Rocca (1889–1961). This was released on 31 May 1917. The first jazz record to be released was the ODJB's *Livery Stable Blues* (recorded 24 Feb), backed by *The Dixie Jass Band One-Step* (recorded 26 Feb), released by Victor on 7 Mar 1917.

Most successful solo recording artists

No independently audited figures have ever been published for Elvis Aron Presley (1935–77). In view of Presley's worldwide tally of over 170 major hits on singles and over 80 top-selling albums from 1956 continuing after his death, it may be assumed that it was he who must have succeeded Bing Crosby as the top-selling solo artist of all time. CBS Records reported in August 1983 that sales of albums by Julio Iglesias (b. 1943) in 6 languages had surpassed 100,000,000.

On 9 June 1960 the Hollywood Chamber of Commerce presented Harry Lillis (*alias* Bing) Crosby, Jr (1904–77) with a platinum disc to commemorate the alleged sale of 200,000,000 records from the 2600 singles and 125 albums he had recorded. On 15 Sept 1970 he received a second platinum disc when Decca claimed a sale of 300,650,000 discs. No independently audited figures of his global life-time sales have ever been published and figures as high are considered exaggerated.

Japan on 26 June 1976. He received $2 million for the drawn wrestler *v* boxer bout against Muhammad Ali in the Budokan Arena, Tokyo. Lou Thesz has won 7 of wrestling's many 'world' titles. 'Fabulous' Moolah won major US women's alliance titles over the longest span starting in 1956. The heaviest ever wrestler has been William J. Cobb of Macon, Georgia (b. 1926), who was billed in 1962 as the 802 lb *363 kg* (57 st 4 lb) 'Happy' Humphrey. Ed 'Strangler' Lewis (1890–1966) *né* Robert H. Friedrich fought 6200 bouts in 44 years losing only 33 matches. He won world titles in 1921, 1922, 1928 and 1931–32. (See also Chapter 12 Heaviest Sportsmen.)

Most successful singer ● Madonna whose album *True Blue*, with sales of over 11 million, was a number one LP in 28 countries—a totally unprecedented achievement. Up to May 1987 she had a total of 14 British Top Ten hits, with record sales of over 6 million copies. Her first three albums together sold 3 million copies in Britain. In 1986 she became the first woman ever to top the annual sales tabulations for both singles and albums, massively outselling all other recording artists. Each of her last two albums, *Like A Virgin* (1985), and *True Blue* (1986) have contained 5 Top Five singles. (Photo: Rex Features)

Recorded Sound

Origins

The gramophone (phonograph) was first *conceived* by Charles Cros (1842–88), a French poet and scientist, who described his idea in sealed papers deposited in the French Academy of Sciences on 30 Apr 1877. However the realisation of a practical device was first *achieved* by Thomas Alva Edison (1847–1931) of the USA. The first successful wax cylinder machine was constructed by his mechanic, John Kruesi on 4–6 Dec 1877, demonstrated on 7 Dec and patented

Most successful group

The singers with the greatest sales of any group have been The Beatles. This group from Liverpool, Merseyside, comprised George Harrison, MBE (b. 25 Feb 1943), John Ono (formerly John Winston) Lennon, MBE (b. 9 Oct 1940–k. 8 Dec 1980), James Paul McCartney, MBE (b. 18 June 1942) and Richard Starkey, MBE alias Ringo Starr (b. 7 July 1940). The all-time Beatles sales by May 1985 have been estimated by EMI at over 1000 million discs and tapes.

All 4 ex-Beatles sold many million further records as solo artists. Since their break-up in 1970, it is estimated that the most successful group in the world in terms of record sales is the Swedish foursome ABBA (Agnetha Faltskog, Anni-Frid Lyngstad, Bjorn Ulvaeus and Benny Andersson) with total sales of 215 million discs and tapes by May 1985.

Earliest golden discs

The earliest recorded piece eventually to aggregate a total sale of a million copies was performances by Enrico Caruso (b. Naples, Italy, 1873, d. 2 Aug 1921) of the aria 'Vesti la giubba' ('On with the Motley') from the opera I Pagliacci by Ruggiero Leoncavallo (1858–1919), the earliest version of which was recorded with piano on 12 Nov 1902.

The first single recording to surpass the million mark was Alma Gluck's Carry Me Back to Old Virginny on the Red Seal Victor label on the 12-inch 30, 48 cm single faced (later backed) record 74420.

The first actual golden disc was one sprayed by RCA Victor for the US trombonist and bandleader Alton 'Glenn' Miller (1904–44) for his Chattanooga Choo Choo on 10 Feb 1942.

Most golden discs

The only audited measure of gold, platinum and multiplatinum singles and albums within the United States is certification by the Recording Industry Association of America introduced 14 Mar 1958. Out of the 2,582 RIAA awards made to 1 Jan 1985, The Beatles with 47 (plus one with Billy Preston) have most for a group. McCartney has 27 more awards outside the group and with Wings (including one with Stevie Wonder and one with Michael Jackson).

The most awards to an individual is 51 to Elvis Presley (1935–77) spanning the period 1958 to 1 Jan 1986. Globally, however, Presley's total of million-selling singles has been authoritatively placed at 'approaching 80'.

Most recordings

Miss Lata Mangeshker (b. 1928) between 1948 and 1987 has reportedly recorded not less than 30,000 solo, duet and chorus-backed songs in 20 Indian languages. She frequently had five sessions in a day and has 'backed' in excess of 2000 films.

Biggest sellers Singles

The greatest seller of any gramophone record to date is White Christmas by Irving Berlin (b. Israel Bailin, at Tyumen, Russia, 11 May 1888) with 30,000,000 for the Crosby single (recorded 29 May 1942) (and more than 100,000,000 in other versions).

The highest claim for any 'pop' record is an unaudited 25,000,000 for Rock Around The Clock, copyrighted in 1953 by James E. Myers under the name Jimmy DeKnight and the late Max C. Freedmann and recorded on 12 Apr 1954 by Bill Haley (1927–1981) and the Comets.

The top-selling British record of all time is I Want To Hold Your Hand by The Beatles, released in 1963, with world sales of over 13,000,000.

The top selling single of all time in the United Kingdom is Do They Know It's Christmas written and produced by Bob Geldof and Midge Ure with 36 million by May 1987 with a further 8.1 million worldwide. The profits were in aid of the Ethiopian Famine Relief Fund and are now estimated to be over £90 million.

The only female solo artist to have a million-selling single in the UK is Jennifer Rush, whose single The Power Of Love was certified in 1985. Forty-five other singles by groups, duos or male soloists have sold a million copies in the UK. The best selling female duet in the UK is I Know Him So Well by Elaine Paige and Barbara Dickson with sales of over 820,000 to May 1987.

Biggest sellers Albums

The best selling album of all time is Thriller by Michael Jackson (b. Gary, Indiana, 29 Aug 1958) with global sales of 38.5 million copies by 1 Aug 1987.

The best selling album by a group is Fleetwood Mac's Rumours with over 20 million sales to May 1987.

The best selling album by a British group is Dark Side Of The Moon by Pink Floyd with sales audited at 19.5 million to December 1986.

The best selling album in Britain is Dire Straits' Brothers In Arms, with 2.6 million sold by May 1987.

The best selling album by a woman is Whitney Houston by Whitney Houston released in 1985. It had sold over 14 million copies by May 1987, including over 9 million in America, one million in the UK, and a further million in Canada. This is also the 'best selling debut album of all time'.

The best selling movie soundtrack is Saturday Night Fever with sales of over 26.5 million to May 1987.

The charts—US Singles

Singles record charts were first published by Billboard on 20 July 1940 when the No 1 was I'll Never Smile Again by Tommy Dorsey (b. 19 Nov 1905, d. 26 Nov 1956). Three discs have stayed top for a record 13 consecutive weeks—Frenesi by Artie Shaw from December 1940; I've Heard That Song Before by Harry James from February 1943 and Goodnight Irene by Gordon Jenkins and the Weavers from August 1950. Tainted Love by Soft Cell stayed on the chart for 43 consecutive weeks from January 1982.

The Beatles have had the most No 1s (20), Conway Twitty the most Country No 1s (35) and Aretha Franklin the most Black No 1s (20). Aretha Franklin is also the female solo artist with the most million-selling singles with 14 between 1967 and 1973. Elvis Presley has had the most hit singles on Billboard's Hot 100—149 from 1956 to May 1987.

US Albums

Billboard first published an album chart on 15 Mar 1945 when the No 1 was King Cole Trio featuring Nat 'King' Cole (b. 17 Mar 1919, d. 15 Feb 1965). South Pacific was No 1 for 69 weeks (non-consecutive) from May 1949. Dark Side Of The Moon by Pink Floyd (see above) enjoyed its 674th week on the Billboard charts in May 1987.

The Beatles had the most No 1s (15), Elvis Presley was the most successful male soloist (9), and Simon and Garfunkel the top duo with 3. Elvis Presley had the most albums (93 from 1956–May 1987).

The woman with the most No 1 albums (6), and most hit albums in total (39 between 1963 and June 1987), is Barbra Streisand, 29 of which have been certified gold (500,000 sales) or platinum (1 million sales) by the RIAA making Streisand the best selling female singer of all time.

UK Singles

Singles record charts were first published in Britain on 14 Nov 1952 by New Musical Express. I Believe by Frankie Laine (b. 30 Mar 1913) held No 1 position for 18 weeks (non-consecutive) from April 1953, with Rose Marie by Slim Whitman (b. 20 Jan 1924) the consecutive record holder with 11 weeks from July 1955.

The longest stay has been the 122 weeks of My Way by Francis Albert Sinatra (b. 12 Dec 1915) in 10 separate runs from 2 Apr 1969 into 1984.

The record for an uninterrupted stay is 56 weeks for Engelbert Humperdinck's Release Me from 26 Jan 1967. The Beatles and Presley hold the record for most No 1 hits with 17 each, with Presley having an overall record of 106 hits in the UK singles chart from 1956 to May 1987.

UK Albums

The first British album chart was published on 8 Nov 1958 by Melody Maker. The first No 1 LP was the film soundtrack South Pacific which held the position for a record 70 consecutive weeks and eventually achieved a record 115 weeks at No 1.

The album with the most total weeks on chart is Bat Out Of Hell by Meat Loaf with 391 weeks by early 1987. The Beatles have had most No 1 albums—12; and Elvis Presley the most hit albums—90.

Fastest selling albums

The fastest selling record of all time is John Fitzgerald Kennedy—A Memorial Album (Pre-

---

TOP 10 BEST SELLING SINGLES IN THE UK

as at 26 Nov 1986

Figures supplied by Gallup

1 **Do They Know It's Christmas**
BAND AID

2 **Mull Of Kintyre**
WINGS

3 **Rivers Of Babylon/Brown Girl In The Ring**
BONEY M

4 **You're The One That I Want**
JOHN TRAVOLTA & OLIVIA NEWTON JOHN

5 **She Loves You**
THE BEATLES

6 **A Hard Day's Night**
THE BEATLES

7 **I Want To Hold Your Hand**
THE BEATLES

8 **Mary's Boy Child**
BONEY M

9 **Relax**
FRANKIE GOES TO HOLLYWOOD

10 **Tears**
KEN DODD

Number 12 in this chart would be White Christmas by BING CROSBY. Sales figures from its release until the inception of the Singles charts in 1952 are not recorded, therefore not expressing accurately the popularity of this single.

Cinema

mium Albums), recorded on 22 Nov 1963, the day of Mr Kennedy's assassination, which sold 4,000,000 copies at 99 cents (*then 35 p*) in six days (7–12 Dec 1963), thus ironically beating the previous speed record set by the satirical LP *The First Family* in 1962–3.

The fastest selling British record is the Beatles' double album *The Beatles* (Apple) with 'nearly 2 million' in its first week in November 1968.

Advance sales
The greatest advance sale for a single worldwide is 2,100,000 for *Can't Buy Me Love* by the Beatles. Released 21 Mar 1964, it also holds the British record of 1 million jointly with another Beatles single, *I Want To Hold Your Hand*, released 29 Nov 1963. The UK record for advance sales of an album is 1,100,000 for *Welcome To The Pleasure Dome*, the debut album by Frankie Goes To Hollywood from 1984.

Compact discs
Announced by Philips in 1978, and introduced by the same company in 1982, the compact disc (CD) increasingly challenges the LP and cassette as a recording medium. By 1986 the CD represented 7 per cent of all albums sold in the UK, 10 per cent in America and 20 per cent in Japan.

The first CD to sell a million copies worldwide was Dire Straits' *Brothers In Arms* in 1986. It subsequently topped a million sales in Europe alone including over 250,000 in Britain—both records.

FILMS
The earliest motion pictures ever taken were by Louis Aimé Augustin Le Prince (1842–1890). He was attested to have achieved dim moving outlines on a whitewashed wall at the Institute for the Deaf, Washington Heights, New York, USA as early as 1885–87. The earliest surviving film (sensitised 2⅛ in *53,9 mm* wide paper roll) is from his camera, patented in Britain on 16 Nov 1888, taken in early October 1888 of the garden of his father-in-law, Joseph Whitley in Roundhay, Leeds, West Yorkshire at 10 to 12 frames per second. The first commercial presentation of *motion pictures* was at Holland Bros' Kinetoscope Parlor at 1155 Broadway, New York City on 14 April 1894. Viewers could see 5 films for 25 cents or 10 for 50 cents from a double row of Kinetoscopes developed by William Kennedy Laurie Dickson (1860–1935), assistant to Thomas Alva Edison (1847–1931) in 1889–91. The earliest publicly presented film on a *screen* was *La Sortie des Ouvriers de l'Usine Lumière* probably shot in August or September 1894 in Lyon, France. It was exhibited at 44 rue de Rennes, Paris on 22 Mar 1895 by the Lumière Brothers, Auguste Marie Louis Nicholas (1862–1954) and Louis Jean (1864–1948).

Earliest 'Talkie'
The earliest sound-on-film motion picture was achieved by Eugene Augustin Lauste (1857–1935) who patented his process on 11 Aug 1906 and produced a workable system using a string galvanometer in 1910 at Benedict Road, Stockwell, London. The earliest public presentation of sound on film was by the Tri-ergon process at the Alhambra cinema, Berlin, Germany on 17 Sept 1922.

Most expensive film
The highest ever budgeted film has been *Star Trek* which received its world première in Washington DC on 6 Dec 1979. Paramount Studios stated that the cost of this space epic, directed by Robert Wise and produced by Gene Roddenberry, was $46 million (*then £21 million*). A figure of $60 million has been attributed to *Superman II* but never substantiated.

Least expensive film
Cecil Hepworth's highly successful release of 1905 *Rescued by Rover* cost £7.69 (*then $37.40*).

Most expensive film rights
The highest price ever paid for film rights was $9,500,000 (*then £4,950,000*) announced on 20 Jan 1978 by Columbia for *Annie*, the Broadway musical by Charles Strouse starring Andrea McCardle, Dorothy Loudon and Reid Shelton.

Longest film
The longest film ever premièred was the 48-hr-long *The Longest Most Meaningless Movie in the World* in 1970. It was British made and later compassionately cut to 90 minutes.

Longest running film
One Flew Over The Cuckoo's Nest opened on 26 Feb 1976 in Stockholm, Sweden. It has played continuously since—a total of over 11 years.

Highest box office gross
The box office gross championship for films is highly vulnerable to inflated ticket prices. Calculations based on the 1983 value of the dollar show that *Gone with the Wind* with Clark Gable (1901–1960) and Vivien Leigh (1913–1967) released in 1939 is unsurpassed at $312 million. The highest numerical (as opposed to value) dollar champion is Steven Spielberg's *ET: The Extra-Terrestrial*, released on 11 June 1982, and which by 2 Jan 1983 had grossed $322 million (*then £208 million*). On 29 May 1983 *The Return of the Jedi* (20th Century Fox) grossed $8,440,105 (*£5,445,200*) for a single day record, and a record $6,219,929 (*£4,013,000*) for its opening day on 25 May 1985.

Largest loss
Michael Cimino's 1980 production *Heaven's Gate* absorbed $35,190,718 (*then £16,750,000*) causing United Artists to write the film off at a final cost of $44,000,000 (*£21,000,000*).

Most violent
A study on the portrayal of violence showed the worst film on record was *Red Dawn*, released in the US in 1984, with acts of violence occurring at the rate of 134 per hour (2.23 per min).

Highest earnings
The highest rate of pay in cinema history is that paid to Sylvester Stallone (b. New York, 6 July 1946). He received $12 million for *Rocky IV* and for *Over the Top* plus as yet uncomputed shares of box office. In January 1986 Hollywood sources predicted that his salary plus profit share from *Rambo* would reach $20 million. The highest paid actress in 1985 was Meryl Streep (b. Summit, N.J., 1949) with $3 million in *Out of Africa*.

Stuntman Dar Robinson was paid $100,000 (*then £45,500*) for the 1100 ft *335 m* leap from the CN Tower, Toronto in Nov 1979 for *High Point*. His parachute opened just 300 ft *91 m* above ground. He died 21 Nov 1986 (aged 39).

Longest series
Japan's *Tora-San* films have now stretched from *Tora-San I* in August 1968 to *Tora-San XXXII* in 1983 with Kiyoshi Atsumi (b. 1929) starring in each for Shochiku Co.

Most portrayed character
The character most frequently recurring on the screen is Sherlock Holmes, created by Sir Arthur Conan Doyle (1859–1930). Sixty-eight actors portrayed him in 187 films in 1900–1986.

Largest studios
The largest complex of film studios in the world is that at Universal City, Los Angeles, California. The Back Lot contains 561 buildings and there are 34 sound stages on the 420 acre *170 ha* site.

Most prolific director
Allan Dwan (1885–1981), the Canadian-born pioneer, directed, from 1909 to the early 'sixties, more than 400 films.

Most Oscars
Walter (Walt) Elias Disney (1901–66) won more 'Oscars'—the awards of the United States Academy of Motion Picture Arts and Sciences, instituted on 16 May 1929 and named after Mr Oscar Pierce of Texas, USA—than any other person. The physical count comprises 20 statuettes and 12 other plaques and certificates including posthumous awards. The only person to win four Oscars in a starring role has been Miss Katharine Hepburn, formerly Mrs Ludlow Ogden Smith (b. Hartford, Conn., 9 Nov 1909) in *Morning Glory* (1932–3), *Guess Who's Coming to Dinner* (1967), *The Lion in Winter* (1968) and *On Golden Pond* (1981). She has been nominated 12 times. Only 4 actors have won two Oscars in starring roles—Frederic March in 1931/32 and 1946, Spencer Tracy in 1937 and 1938, Gary Cooper in 1941 and 1952, and Marlon Brando in 1954 and 1972. Edith Head (Mrs Wiard B. Ihnen) (1907–81) won 8 individual awards for costume design. The film with most awards has been *Ben Hur* (1959) with 11. That with the highest number of nominations was *All About Eve* (1950) with 14. It won six. The youngest ever winner was Shirley Temple (b. 24 Apr 1928) aged 5 with her honorary Oscar, and the oldest George Burns (b. 20 Jan 1896) aged 80 for *The Sunshine Boys* in 1976. Acceptance speeches are now limited to 45 sec. In 1942 Greer Garson (b. County Down, N.I. 29 Sept 1908) took over 1½ hours to say 'Thank you' for *Mrs Miniver*.

Versatility showbusiness awards
The only 3 performers to have won Oscar, Emmy, Tony and Grammy awards have been Helen Hayes (b. 1900) in 1932 1970, Richard Rodgers

DARRYL F. ZANUCK *presents*

ETTE
AVIS · ANNE
BAXTER · GEORGE
SANDERS · CELESTE
HOLM in "ALL ABOUT EVE"
ARY MERRILL · HUGH MARLOWE

Produced by Darryl F. Zanuck
Written for the Screen and Directed by Joseph L. Mankiewicz

Twentieth Century-Fox
Picture

Cert. "A"

Oscar nominations ● *All About Eve* recorded 14 in 1950 and won six: Best film; Best director—Joseph L. Mankiewicz; Best cinematography—Milton Krasner; Best supporting actor—George Sanders; Best supporting actress—Celeste Holm; and Best screenplay—Joseph Mankiewicz. (Photo: Cinema Bookshop)

(1902–1979), composer of musicals, and Rita Moreno (b. 1931) in 1961–1977. Barbra Streisand (b. 24 Apr 1942 in Brooklyn, NY) received Oscar, Grammy and Emmy awards in addition to a special 'Star of the Decade' Tony award.

CINEMAS

Earliest

The earliest structure designed and exclusively used for exhibiting projected films is believed to be one erected at the Atlanta Show, Georgia, USA in October 1895 to exhibit C. F. Jenkins' phantoscope. The earliest cinema constructed in Great Britain was built without permission at Olympia, London, to house the 'Theatregraph' promoted by Robert William Paul (1869–1943). This was completed by 16 Apr 1896.

Largest

The largest cinema in the world is the Radio City Music Hall, New York City, opened on 27 Dec 1932 with 5945 (now 5882) seats. The Roxy, opened in New York City on 11 March 1927 had 6214 (later 5869) seats but was closed on 29 Mar

1960. Cineplex, opened at the Toronto Eaton Centre, Canada on 19 Apr 1979 has 18 separate theatres with an aggregate capacity of 1700.

The world's largest drive-in cinema is Loew's Open Air at Lynn, Mass., USA with a capacity of 5000 cars. The earliest, at Wilson Boulevard, Camden, New Jersey opened on 6 June 1933.

Great Britain's largest cinema is the Odeon Theatre, Hammersmith, London, with 3483 seats. The Playhouse, Glasgow had 4235 seats.

Most and least cinemas

Saudi Arabia (population 8.4 million) has no cinemas. Ascension Island has a record 733 cinema seats for a population of 971. The USA has most cinemas with 20,200. The UK had 1250 screens in 1986.

Highest cinema going

The Chinese ministry of culture reported in September 1984 that there were 27,000 million cinema attendances in 1983—or nearly 27 per person per annum.

Biggest screen

The permanently installed cinema screen with the largest area is one of 92 ft 9 in × 70 ft 6 in *28,28 × 21,48 m* installed in the Keong Emas Imax Theatre, Taman Mini Park, Jakarta, Indonesia opened on 20 Apr 1984. It was made by Harkness Screens Ltd at Borehamwood, Herts. A temporary screen 297 ft × 33 ft *90,5 × 10 m* was used at the 1937 Paris Exposition.

Most films seen

Albert E. van Schmus (b. 1921) saw 16,945 films in 32 years (1949–1982) as a rater for Motion Picture Association of America Inc.

Radio

The earliest patent for telegraphy without wires (wireless) was received by Dr Mahlon Loomis (USA) (1826–86). It was entitled 'Improvement in Telegraphing' and was dated 20 July 1872 (US Pat. No 129,971). He in fact demonstrated only potential differences on a galvanometer between two kites 14 miles *22 km* apart in Loudoun County, Virginia in October 1866.

Earliest patent

The first patent for a system of communication by means of electro-magnetic waves, numbered No 12039, was granted on 2 June 1896 to the Italian-Irish Marchese Guglielmo Marconi (1874–1937). A public demonstration of wireless transmission of speech was, however, given in the town square of Murray, Kentucky, USA in 1892 by Nathan B. Stubblefield. He died destitute on 28 March 1928. The first permanent wireless installation was at The Needles on the Isle of Wight, by Marconi's Wireless Telegraph Co Ltd, in November 1897.

Earliest broadcast

The world's first advertised broadcast was made on 24 Dec 1906 by the Canadian-born Prof Reginald Aubrey Fessenden (1868–1932) from the 420 ft *128 m* mast of the National Electric Signalling Company at Brant Rock, Massachusetts, USA. The transmission included Handel's *Largo*. Fessenden had achieved the broadcast of speech as early as November 1900 but this was highly distorted.

The first experimental broadcasting transmitter in Great Britain was set up at the Marconi Works in Chelmsford, Essex, in December 1919, and broadcast a news service in February 1920. The earliest regular broadcast was made from the Marconi transmitter '2MT' at Writtle, Essex, on 14 Feb 1922.

Transatlantic transmissions

The earliest claim to have received wireless signals (the letter S in Morse Code) across the Atlantic was made by Marconi, George Stephen Kemp and Percy Paget from a 10 kW station at Poldhu, Cornwall, at Signal Hill, St John's, Newfoundland, Canada, at 12.30 p.m. on 12 Dec 1901. Human speech was first heard across the Atlantic in November 1915 when a transmission from the US Navy station at Arlington, Virginia, was received by US radio-telephone engineers on the Eiffel Tower.

Earliest radio-microphones

The radio-microphone, which was in essence also the first 'bug', was devised by Reg Moores (GB) in 1947 and first used on 76 MHz in the ice show *Aladdin* at Brighton Sports Stadium, East Sussex in September 1949.

Longest BBC national broadcast

The longest BBC national broadcast was the reporting of the Coronation of Queen Elizabeth II on 2 June 1953. It began at 10.15 a.m. and finished at 5.30 p.m., after 7 hr 15 min.

Longest continuous broadcast

The longest continuous broadcast (excluding disc-jockeying) has been one of 484 hr (20 days 4 hr) by Larry Norton of WGRQ FM Buffalo, New York, USA on 19 Mar–8 Apr 1981. *No further claims for the above category will be entertained.* Radio Telefís Éireann transmitted an unedited reading of *Ulysses* by James Joyce (1882–1941) for 29 hr 38 min 47 sec on 16–17 July 1982.

Topmost prize

Mary Buchanan, 15, on WKRQ, Cincinnati, USA won a prize of $25,000 for 40 years (viz $1 million) on 21 Nov 1980.

Brain of Britain Quiz

The youngest person to become 'Brain of Britain' on BBC radio was Anthony Carr, 16, of Anglesey in 1956. The oldest contestant has been the author and translator Hugh Merrick (1898–1980) in his 80th year in August 1977. The record score is 35 by the 1981 winner Peter Barlow of Richmond, Surrey and Peter Bates of Taunton who won the title in 1984.

Most durable programmes *BBC*

The longest running BBC radio series is *The Week's Good Cause* which began on 24 Jan 1926. The St Martin-in-the-Fields Christmas appeal by Canon Geoffrey Brown on 14 Dec 1986 raised a record £138,039. The longest running record programme is *Desert Island Discs* which began on 29 Jan 1942 and on which programme only one guest, Arthur Askey CBE (1900–82), has been stranded a fourth time (on the 1572nd show on 20 Dec 1980). The programme was originally presented by its creator, Roy Plomley OBE, who died on 28 May 1985 having presented 1791 editions. The longest running solo radio feature is *Letter from America* by (Alfred) Alistair Cooke, Hon KBE (b. Salford 20 Nov 1908), first broadcast on 24

Mar 1946. The longest running radio serial is *The Archers* which was created by Godfrey Baseley and was first broadcast on 29 May 1950. Up to May 1987 the signature tune *Barwick Green* had been played over 38,680 times. The only role which has been played without interruption from the start has been that of Philip Archer by Norman Painting OBE (b. Leamington Spa, 23 Apr 1924).

Most heard broadcaster

Larry King has broadcast on network for 27½ hours a week since 30 Jan 1978 from Washington DC on Mutual Broadcasting Systems to all 50 US States (now on 272 stations).

Earliest antipodal reception

Frank Henry Alfred Walker (b. 11 Nov 1904) on the night of 12 Nov 1924 at Crown Farm, Cuttimore Lane, Walton-on-Thames, Surrey, received on his home-made 2-valve receiver on 75 metres, signals from Marconi's yacht *Electra* (call sign ICCM) in Australian waters.

Most assiduous radio ham

The late Richard C. Spenceley of KV4AA at St Thomas, Virgin Islands built his contacts (QSOs) to a record level of 48,100 in 365 days in 1978.

Most stations

The country with the greatest number of radio broadcasting stations is the United States, where there were 9512 authorised broadcast stations as at April 1985 made up of both AM (amplitude modulation) and FM (frequency modulation).

Highest listening

The peak recorded listenership on BBC Radio was 30,000,000 adults on 6 June 1950 for the boxing match between Lee Savold (US) and Bruce Woodcock (GB) (b. Doncaster, S. Yorks, 1921).

Highest response

The highest recorded response from a radio show occurred on 27 Nov 1974 when, on a 5-hr talk show on WCAU, Philadelphia, USA, astrologer Howard Sheldon registered a call count of 388,299 on the 'Bill Corsair Show'.

Smallest set

The Toshiba AM-FM RP-1070 with inbuilt loudspeaker measures 9,0 × 5,4 × 1,3 cm *3.5 × 2.1 × 0.5 in* and with battery weighs 70 g *2.5 oz*.

Television

Invention

The invention of television, the instantaneous viewing of distant objects by electrical transmissions, was not an act but a process of successive and interdependent discoveries. The first commercial cathode ray tube was introduced in 1897 by Karl Ferdinand Braun (1850–1918), but was not linked to 'electric vision' until 1907 by Prof Boris Rosing (disappeared 1918) of Russia in St Petersburg (Leningrad). A. A. Campbell Swinton FRS (1863–1930) published the fundamentals of television transmission on 18 June 1908 in a brief letter to *Nature* entitled 'Distant Electric Vision'. The earliest public demonstration of television was given on 27 Jan 1926 by John Logie Baird (1888–1946) of Scotland, using a development of the mechanical scanning system patented by Paul Gottlieb Nipkow (1860–1940) on 6 Jan 1884. He had achieved the transmission of a Maltese Cross over 10 ft *3,05 m* at 8, Queen's Arcade, Hastings, East Sussex by February 1924 and the first facial image (of William Taynton, 15) at 22, Frith Street, London on 30 Oct 1925. Taynton had to be bribed with 2s 6d. A patent application for the Iconoscope had been filed on 29 Dec 1923 by Dr Vladimir Kosma Zworykin (1889–1982) but was not issued until 20 Dec 1938. Kenjiro Takayanagi (b. 20 Jan 1899) succeeded in

transmitting a 40-line electronic picture on 25 Dec 1926 with a Braun cathode ray tube and a Nipkow disc at Hamamatsu Technical College, Japan. Baird launched his first television 'service' via a BBC transmitter on 30 Sept 1929 and marketed the first sets, Baird Televisors, at £26.25 in May 1930. Public transmissions on 30 lines were made from 22 Aug 1932 until 11 Sept 1935.

Earliest service

The world's first high definition (*i.e.* 405 lines) television broadcasting service was opened from Alexandra Palace, north London, on 2 Nov 1936, when there were about 100 sets in the United Kingdom. The Chief Engineer was Mr Douglas Birkinshaw. A television station in Berlin, Germany, made a low definition (180-line) transmission from 22 Mar 1935 but the transmitter burnt out in August that year.

Transatlantic transmission

On 9 Feb 1928 the image of J. L. Baird and of a Mrs Howe was transmitted from Station 2 KZ at Coulsdon, Surrey, England to Station 2 CVJ, Hartsdale, NY, USA. The earliest transatlantic transmission by satellite was achieved at 1 a.m. on 11 July 1962, via the active satellite *Telstar 1* from Andover, Maine, USA, to Pleumeur Bodou, France. The picture was of Frederick R. Kappell, chairman of the American Telephone and Telegraph Company, which owned the satellite. The first 'live' broadcast was made on 23 July 1962 and the first woman to appear was the *haute couturière* Ginette Spanier, directrice of Balmain, the next day.

Longest telecast

The longest pre-scheduled telecast on record was a continuous transmission for 163 hr 18 min by GTV 9 of Melbourne, Australia covering the Apollo XI moon mission on 19–26 July 1969. The longest continuous TV transmission under a single director was the ECTV 25-A-Thon television production transmitted on Channel 25 in Portland, Oregon, USA, on 27–28 Sept 1985 for 25 hours under the direction of Rick Ray. The programme was hosted by Deb Williams who was carried off the set on a stretcher to an awaiting ambulance with the cameras still rolling.

Earliest video-tape recording

Alexander M. Poniatoff first demonstrated video-tape recording known as Ampex (his initials plus 'ex' for excellence) in 1956. The earliest demonstration of a home video recorder was on 24 June 1963 at the BBC News Studio at Alexandra Palace, London of the Telcan developed by Norman Rutherford and Michael Turner of the Nottingham Electronic Valve Co.

Fastest video production

Tapes of the Royal Wedding of HRH Prince Andrew and Miss Sarah Ferguson on 23 July 1986 were produced by Thames Video Collection. Live filming ended with the departure of the honeymoon couple from Chelsea Hospital by helicopter at 4.42 p.m. The first fully edited and packaged VHS tapes were purchased 5 hr 41 min later by Fenella Lee and Lucinda Burland of West Kensington at the Virgin Megastore in Oxford Street, London at 10.23 p.m.

Most durable shows

The world's most durable TV show is NBC's *Meet the Press* first transmitted on 6 Nov 1947 and weekly since 12 Sept 1948, originated by Lawrence E. Spivak, who appeared weekly as either moderator or panel member until 1975. On 1 June 1986 Joe Franklin presented the 21,700th version of his show started in 1951. The greatest number of hours on camera on US national commercial television is 10,000 by the TV personality Hugh Downs in over 42 years to 1 Jan 1987.

Great Britain

Andy Pandy was first transmitted on 11 July 1950 but consisted of repeats of a cycle of 26 shows until 1970. *Come Dancing* was first transmitted on 29 Sept 1950 but is seasonal. *Sooty* was first presented on BBC by its deviser Harry Corbett (born 1918) from 1952 to 1967 and is continued by his son Matthew on ITV. *The Good Old Days* ran from 20 July 1953 to 31 Dec 1983. Barney Colehan MBE produced all 244 programmes. The *BBC News* was inaugurated in vision on 5 July 1954. Richard Baker OBE read the news from 1954 to Christmas 1982. Of current affairs programmes BBC's weekly *Panorama* was first transmitted on 11 Nov 1953 but has summer breaks, whereas Granada's *What The Papers Say* has been transmitted every week since 5 Nov 1956. The monthly *Sky at Night* has been presented by Patrick Moore OBE without a break or a miss since 24 Apr 1957. The BBC's *Farming* programme has been transmitted weekly since 3 Oct 1957. The longest serving TV quizmaster is Bamber Gascoigne of Granada's *University Challenge* which has run since 21 Sept 1962. The longest running domestic drama serial is Granada's *Coronation Street* which has run twice weekly since 9 Dec 1960. William Roache had played Ken Barlow without a break since the outset for 26 years by 9 Dec 1986.

Above: TV producer ● Cynthia Felgate (b. 8 Oct 1935) has produced children's programmes for the BBC since January 1965. During her 22-year career, she has been responsible for 5433 programmes totalling 1826 hours and, with repeats, has recorded over 10,000 screen credits.

Right: Fastest video production ● Fenella Lee and Lucinda Burland, purchasers of the first Royal Wedding video to go on sale to the public—less than 6 hours after the event. (Photo: Andy Phillips)

Most sets

The US had, by January 1986, 87.59 million TV households, with 40.38 million on cable TV. The number of homes with colour sets was 80,100,000 (91%) by January 1986. More than 50 per cent of the total homes own more than one TV set. The number of licences current in the United Kingdom was 18,953,161 on 1 Apr 1987 of which 16,538,665 (87.2 per cent) were for colour sets. Black and white licences became less commonplace than colour in 1976.

TV watching

The National Coalition on TV Violence published an estimate in June 1985 that, by its 16th birthday, the *average* American child will have seen 50,000 TV murders or attempted murders and 200,000 acts of violence. Between the ages of 2 and 11 the average viewing time is 28.0 hours per week. The global total of homes with television surpassed 500 million in 1986 led by the USA with 85.9 million. There are 8250 TV transmitting stations worldwide of which 1194 are in the US. There are 364 TV sets per 1000 people in the USA compared with 348 in Sweden and 330 in Britain. In Britain in winter the average male views 26 hr 4 min and the average female 30 hr 38 min per week.

Greatest audience

The greatest estimated number of viewers worldwide for a televised event is 2500 million for the live and recorded transmissions of the XXIIIrd Olympic Games in Los Angeles, California from 27 July to 13 Aug 1984. The American Broadcasting Co airing schedule comprised 187½ hours of coverage on 56 cameras. The estimated viewership for the 'Live Aid' concerts organised by Bob Geldof and Bill Graham, via a record 12 satellites, was 1.6 billion or nearly one third of the world's population.

The programme which attracted the highest ever viewership was the *Goodbye, Farewell and Amen* final episode of M*A*S*H (the acronym for Mobile Army Surgical Hospital 4077) transmitted by CBS on 28 Feb 1983 to 60.3 per cent of all households in the United States. It was estimated that some 125 million people tuned in, taking a 77 per cent share of all viewing. The UK record is 39 million for the wedding of TRH the Prince and Princess of Wales in London on 29 July 1981.

Most expensive production

The Winds of War, a seven-part Paramount World War II saga aired by ABC was the most expensive ever TV production costing $42 million over 14 months' shooting. The final episode on 13 Feb 1983 attracted a rating of 41.0 per cent (% of total number of viewers), and a share of 56 per cent (% of total sets turned on that were tuned in).

Largest contracts

Currently television's highest-paid performer is John William Carson (b. 23 Oct 1925), the host of *The Tonight Show*. His current NBC contract reportedly calls for annual payment of $5,000,000 (*now £2,275,000*) for his one-hour evening show aired four times weekly. The highest-paid current affairs or news performer is Dan Rather of CBS who reportedly signed an $8 million (*then £4.7 million*) contract for five years from 1982.

Great Britain

The largest contract in British television was one of a reported £9,000,000, inclusive of production expenses, signed by Tom Jones (b. Thomas Jones Woodward, 7 June 1940) of Treforest, Mid Glamorgan, Wales in June 1968 with ABC-TV of the United States and ATV in London for 17 one-hour shows per annum from January 1969 to January 1974.

Highest-paid TV performers

Carroll O'Connor, star of *Archie Bunker's Place*, received $275,000 (*£182,500*) for each of 22

Largest TV contract ● Marie Osmond signed a contract worth $7 million (*then £3,100,000*) for 7 hours of transmission, paid by NBC on 9 Mar 1981. The figure includes talent and production costs. (Photo: Loftus/LFI)

episodes in the 1982/83 season totalling $6,050,000 (*£4 million*). Peter Falk (b. 16 Sept 1927), the disarmingly persistent detective *Columbo*, was paid from $300,000 to $350,000 for a single episode of his series of six. Singer Kenny Rogers was reported in February 1983 to have been paid $2 million (*then £1,280,000*) for a single taping of a concert for HBO (Home Box Office) TV channel. The highest paid newscaster and journalist is Dan Rather of the CBS' *Nightly News* reported in February 1986 to be paid $2,500,000 (*then £1,785,000*) per annum.

Largest TV prizes

On 24 July 1975 WABC-TV, New York City transmitted the first televised Grand Tier draw of the State Lottery in which the winner took the grand prize of $1,000,000 (*now £454,545*). This was, however, taxable.

Most successful Telethon

The Jerry Lewis Labor Day Telethon on 2 Sept 1984 raised $32,074,566 (*then £26,700,000*) in pledges for the Muscular Dystrophy Association. The Victims of Famine in East Africa and the Sahel appeal raised a record £9,518,736 from 17 July 1984 to 6 Feb 1985.

Biggest sale

The greatest number of episodes of any TV programme ever sold has been 1144 episodes of *Coronation Street* by Granada Television to CBKST Saskatoon, Saskatchewan, Canada, on 31 May 1971. This constituted 20 days 15 hr 44 min continuous viewing. A further 728 episodes (Jan 1974–Jan 1981) were sold to CBC in August 1982.

Most prolific scriptwriter

The most prolific television writer in the world is the Rt Hon Lord Willis known as Ted Willis (b. 13 Jan 1918), who in the period 1949–87 has created 33 series, including the first seven years and 2,250,000 words of *Dixon of Dock Green* which ran from 1955 to 1976, 29 stage plays and 33 feature films. He has had 24 plays produced. His total output since 1942 can be estimated at 18,750,000 words.

'Mastermind' records

Mrs Jennifer Keaveney (on 'The life and work of E. Nesbit') scored a record 40 points in a 1986 semi-final and equalled her semi-final score of 40 points when she won the 1986 final (with 'The life and works of Elizabeth Gaskell') of this BBC TV series which began on 11 Sept 1972. Sir David Hunt KCMG, OBE won the 'Mastermind Champions' contest on 3 May 1982.

TV producer

Aaron Spelling (b. 1928) has produced more than 1770 TV episodes totalling 2250 hours of air time, as well as 207½ hours of TV movies and 8 feature films. The total 2467 broadcast hours is equal to 13.7 million feet *3688 km* of film and, projected 24 hours a day, it would take 103.9 days—just over 3½ months— to screen it all. The average American TV is turned on 6 hours per day. At that rate, Spelling has produced enough film to last 374 days.

Highest TV advertising rates

The highest TV advertising rate has been $600,000 per ½ min (*then £6,580 per sec*) for NBC network prime time during the transmission of Super Bowl XXI on 25 Jan 1987, watched by a record 127 million viewers. In Great Britain the peak time weekday 60-sec spot rate (5.40–10.40 p.m.) for Thames Television is £67,375 + VAT (May 1986). The longest run was 7 min 10 sec by Great Universal Stores on *Good Morning Britain* for £100,000 on 20 Jan 1985.

Most takes

The highest number of 'takes' for a TV commercial is 28 in 1973 by Pat Coombs, the comedienne. Her explanation was 'Every time we came to the punch line I just could not remember the name of the product.'

Commercial records

The highest fee for a 30-sec commercial is $1.5 million paid by Japanese television to 'Boy' George for promoting gin—reported in December 1985.

Largest and smallest sets

The Sony Jumbo Tron colour TV screen at the Tsukuba International Exposition '85 near Tokyo in March 1985 measured 80 ft × 150 ft *24,3 m × 45,7 m*.

The largest cathode ray tubes for colour sets are 37 in *94 cm* models manufactured by Mitsubishi Electric of Japan.

The Seiko TV-Wrist Watch launched on 23 Dec 1982 in Japan has a 1.2 in *30,5 mm* screen and weighs only 80 g *2.8 oz*. Together with the receiver unit and the headphone set the entire black and white system, costing 108,000 yen (*then £260*), weighs only 320 g *11.3 oz*. The smallest single-piece set is the Casio-Keisanki TV-10 weighing 338 g *11.9 oz* with a 2.7 in *6,85 cm* screen, launched in Tokyo in July 1983. The smallest colour set is the liquid crystal display (LCD) Japanese Epson launched in 1985 with dimensions of 3 × 6¾ × 1¼ in *7,6 × 17,1 × 2,8 cm* weighing, with batteries and its 52,800 crystals, only 16 oz *453 g*.

Highest definition

A system with a 1125-line definition was demonstrated by NHK (Nippon Hoso Kyokai) built by Hitachi and Sony at Brighton, East Sussex on 19 Sept 1982.

THE WORLD'S STRUCTURES

CHAPTER SEVEN

Tallest tower in the world ● The $44-million CN Tower seen here dominating the Toronto, Canada, skyline. At 1822 ft 1 in *555,33 m* it is the tallest self-supporting tower. Excavations began on 12 Feb 1973 and the 130,000-ton reinforced, post-tensioned concrete structure was topped out on 2 Apr 1975. The 416-seat restaurant revolves in the Sky Pod at 1140 ft *347,5 m* from which visibility extends to hills 74½ miles *120 km* distant. Lightning strikes the top about 200 times in 30 storms each year. (See also page 112.) (Photo: *Daily Telegraph*)

EARLIEST STRUCTURES

World

The earliest known human structure is a rough circle of loosely piled lava blocks found on the lowest cultural level at the Lower Palaeolithic site at Olduvai Gorge in Tanzania revealed by Dr Mary Leakey in January 1960. The structure was associated with artifacts and bones on a work-floor, dating from c. 1,750,000 BC. The earliest evidence of *buildings* yet discovered is that of 21 huts with hearths or pebble-lined pits and delimited by stake-holes found in October 1965 at the Terra Amata site in Nice, France, thought to belong to the Acheulian culture of c. 400,000 years ago. Excavation carried out between 28 June and 5 July 1966 revealed one hut with palisaded walls with axes of 49 ft *15 m* and 20 ft *6 m*. The remains of a stone tower 20 ft *6,1 m* high originally built into the walls of Jericho have been excavated and are dated to 5000 BC. The foundations of the walls themselves have been dated to as early as 8350 BC. The oldest free-standing structures in the world are now believed to be the megalithic temples at Mgarr and Skorba in Malta and Ggantija in Gozo dating from c. 3250 BC.

Great Britain

Twelve small stone clusters, associated with broken bones and charcoal in stratum C of the early Palaeolithic site at Hoxne, near Eye, Suffolk may be regarded as Britain's earliest structural remains, dated c. 250,000 BC. Remains of the earliest dated stone shelter and cooking pit were discovered in 1967 at Culver Well, Isle of Portland, Dorset (mesolithic, 5200 BC ± 135). On the Isle of Jura, Argyll, a hearth consisting of three linked stone circles has been dated to the Mesolithic period 6013 ± 200 BC. The earliest surviving piece of Roman building is the bottom 14 ft *4,25 m* of their beacon at Dover, Kent, dating from the 1st century AD.

Ireland

The earliest known evidence of human occupation in Ireland dates from the Mesolithic period c. 7500 at the Carrowmore site in County Sligo. Ireland became enisled or separated from Great Britain c. 9050 BC. Nearby there are megalithic burials dated to 3800 ± 80 BC.

Buildings for Working

LARGEST

Construction project

The Madinat Al-Jubail Al-Sinaiyah project in Saudi Arabia (1976–1996) covering 230,412.8 acres *932,43 km²* is the largest in history. The work force on the city and industrial port complex is increasing to a peak of 33,187 from the mid-1982 figure of 17,200. The total earth moving and dredging volume will reach 345 million m³ or *0.82 of a cubic mile*.

Industrial

The largest industrial plant in the world is the Nizhniy Tagil Railroad Car and Tank Plant, 85 miles *136 km* north-west of Sverdlovsk, USSR which has 827 000 m² *204.3 acres* of floor space. It has an annual capacity to produce 2500 T-72 tanks.

Commercial

The greatest ground area covered by any commercial building in the world under one roof is the flower auction building of the Co-operative VBA (Verenigde Bloemenveilingen Aalsmeer), Aalsmeer, Netherlands, which was built with dimensions of 776 × 547 m *2546 × 1794 ft*. The floor surface of 343 277 m² *84.82 acres* was ex-

tended in 1986 to 368 477 m² *91.05 acres*. The building with the largest cubic capacity in the world is the Boeing Company's main assembly plant at Everett, Washington State, USA completed in 1968 with a capacity of 200 million ft³ *5,6 million m³*.

The largest building in Britain is the Ford Parts Centre at Daventry, Northamptonshire, which measures 1978 × 780 ft *602 × 237 m* and 1.6 million ft² or 36.7 acres *14,86 ha*. It was opened on 6 Sept 1972 and cost nearly £8 million. It employs 1600 people and is fitted with 14,000 fluorescent lights.

Scientific

The most capacious scientific building in the world is the Vehicle Assembly Building (VAB) at Complex 39, the selected site for the final assembly and launching of the Apollo moon spacecraft on the Saturn V rocket, at the John F. Kennedy Space Center (KSC) on Merritt Island, Cape Canaveral, Florida. Construction began in April 1963 by the Ursum Consortium. It is a steel-framed building measuring 716 ft *218 m* in length, 518 ft *158 m* in width and 525 ft *160 m* high. The building contains four bays, each with its own door 460 ft *140 m* high. Its floor area is 343,500 ft² (7.87 acres *3,18 ha*) and its capacity is 129,482,000 ft³ *3 666 500 m³*. The building was 'topped out' on 14 Apr 1965 at a cost of $108,700,000 (*then £38.8 million*).

Administrative

The largest ground area covered by any office building is that of the Pentagon, in Arlington, Virginia, USA. Built to house the US Defense Department's offices it was completed on 15 Jan 1943 and cost an estimated $83,000,000 (*then £20,595,000*). Each of the outermost sides is 921 ft *281 m* long and the perimeter of the building is about 1500 yd *1370 m*. Its five storeys enclose a floor area of 6,500,000 ft² *604 000 m²* (149.2 acres *60,3 ha*). The corridors measure 17 miles *27 km* in length and there are 7748 windows to be cleaned. Twenty-nine thousand people work in the building which has over 44,000 telephones connected by 160,000 miles *257 500 km* of cable. Two hundred and twenty staff handle 280,000 calls a day. Two restaurants, six cafeterias and ten snack bars and a staff of 675 form the catering department.

Office

The office buildings with the largest rentable space in the world are The World Trade Center in New York, with a total of 4,370,000 ft² *406 000 m²* (100.32 acres *40,6 ha*) in each of the twin towers of which the taller Tower Two (formerly B) is 1362 ft 3¼ in *415,22 m*. The tip of the TV antenna on Tower One is 1710 ft *521,2 m* above street level and is thus 151 ft *46 m* taller than the antennae atop the Sears Tower (see below).

The largest single open plan office in the United Kingdom is that of British Gas West Midlands at Solihull, built by Spooners (Hull) Ltd in 1962. It now measures 753 ft by 160 ft *230 by 49 m* (2.77 acres *1,12 ha*), accommodating 2125 clerical and managerial staff.

TALLEST

The tallest office building in the world is the Sears Tower, national headquarters of Sears, Roebuck & Co in Wacker Drive, Chicago, Illinois with 110 storeys rising to 1454 ft *443 m* and begun in August 1970. Its gross area is 4,400,000 ft² (101.0 acres *40,8 ha*). It was 'topped out' on 4 May 1973, having surpassed the World Trade Center in New York in height at 2.35 p.m. on 6 Mar 1973 with the first steel column reaching to the 104th storey. The addition of two TV antennae brought the total height to 1559 ft *475,18 m*. The building's population is 16,700 served by 103 elevators and 18 escalators. It has 16,000 windows. Tentative

plans for a 169-storey 2300 ft *701 m* tall building, projected to cost $1250 million, for the Chicago Loop, Illinois, were published on 27 Oct 1981.

The tallest office block in Britain and the tallest cantilevered building in the world is the £72 million National Westminster tower block in Bishopsgate, City of London completed in 1979. It has 49 storeys and 3 basement levels, serviced by 21 lifts, and is 600 ft 4 in *183 m* tall. The gross floor area is 636,373 ft² *59,121 m²* (14.6 acres *5,9 ha*). The Canary Wharf development plans in London Docklands include three office towers of up to 850 ft *259 m*.

HABITATIONS

Greatest altitude

The highest inhabited buildings in the world are those in the Indo–Tibetan border fort of Bāsisi by the Māna Pass (Lat. 31° 04' N; Long. 79° 24' E) at c. 19,700 ft *5988 m*. In April 1961, however, a 3-room dwelling was discovered at 21,650 ft *6600 m* on Cerro Llullaillaco (22,058 ft *6723 m*), on the Argentine–Chilean border, believed to date from the late pre-Columbian period c. 1480. A settlement on the T'e-li-mo trail in southern Tibet is sited at an apparent altitude of 19,800 ft *6019 m*.

Northernmost

The most northerly habitation in the world is the Danish Scientific station set up in 1952 in Pearyland, northern Greenland (Kalaalit Nunaat), over 900 miles *1450 km* north of the Arctic Circle. Eskimo hearths dated to before 1000 BC were discovered in Pearyland in 1969. Polar Eskimos were discovered in Inglefield Land, NW Greenland in 1818. The USSR's drifting research station 'North Pole 15' passed within 1¼ miles *2,8 km* of the North Pole in December 1967. The most northerly continuously inhabited place is the Canadian Department of National Defense outpost at Alert on Ellesmere Island, Northwest Territories in Lat. 82° 30' N, Long. 62° W, set up in 1950.

Southernmost

The most southerly permanent human habitation is the United States' Amundsen–Scott South Polar Station (see Chapter 10) completed in 1957 and replaced in 1975.

EMBASSIES AND CIVIC BUILDINGS

Largest

The largest embassy in the world is the USSR embassy on Bei Xiao Jie, Beijing, China, in the north-eastern corner of the northern walled city. The whole 45 acre *18,2 ha* area of the old Orthodox Church Mission (established 1728), now known as the *Bei guan*, was handed over to the USSR in 1949.

The largest in Great Britain is the United States of America embassy in Grosvenor Square, London. The Chancery Building alone, completed in 1960, has 600 rooms for a staff of 700 on seven floors with a usable floor area of 255,000 ft² (5.85 acres *2,37 ha*).

EXHIBITION CENTRES

Largest *Great Britain*

Britain's largest exhibition centre is the National Exhibition Centre, Birmingham opened in February 1976. Five halls which inter-connect cover 87 180 m² *938,397 ft²* or 21.54 acres with a volume of 1 168 466 m³ or *41.26 million ft³*.

INDUSTRIAL STRUCTURES

Tallest chimneys

The world's tallest chimney is the $5.5 million International Nickel Company's stack 1245 ft 8 in *379,6 m* tall at Copper Cliff, Sudbury, Ontario, Canada, completed in 1970. It was built by

Canadian Kellogg Ltd in 60 days and the diameter tapers from 116.4 ft *35,4 m* at the base to 51.8 ft *15,8 m* at the top. It weighs 38,390 tons *39 006 tonnes* and became operational in 1971. The world's most massive chimney is one of 1148 ft *350 m* at Puentes de Garcia Rodriguez, north-west Spain, built by M. W. Kellogg Co. It contains 20,600 yd³ *15 750 m³* of concrete and 2.9 million lb *1315 tonnes* of steel and has an internal volume of 6.7 million ft³ *189 720 m³*. Europe's tallest chimney serves the Zasavje thermo-power plant in Trboulje, Yugoslavia and was completed to 350 metres *1181 ft* on 1 June 1976.

The tallest chimney in Great Britain is one of 850 ft *259 m* at Drax Power Station, North Yorkshire, begun in 1966 and topped out on 16 May 1969. It has an untapered diameter of 87 ft 9 in *26 m* and has the greatest capacity of any chimney. The architects were Clifford Tee & Gale of London. The oldest known industrial chimney in Britain is the Stone Edge Chimney, near Chesterfield, Derbyshire built to a height of 55 ft *16,76 m ante* 1771.

Cooling towers

The largest cooling tower in the world is that adjacent to the nuclear power plant at Uentrop, West Germany which is 590 ft *179,8 m* tall, completed in 1976. The largest in the United Kingdom are of the Ferrybridge and Didcot type and measure 375 ft *114 m* tall and 300 ft *91 m* across the base.

HANGARS

Largest

The world's largest hanger is Hangar 375 ('Big Texas') at Kelly Air Force Base, San Antonio, Texas, completed on 15 Feb 1956. It has 4 doors each 250 ft *76,2 m* wide and 60 ft *18,28 m* high weighing 598 tons *608 tonnes*. The high bay area measures 2000 × 300 × 90 ft *609,6 × 91,4 × 27,4 m* and is surrounded by a 44 acre *17,8 ha* concrete apron. Delta Airlines' jet base on a 140 acre *56,6 ha* site at Hartsfield International Airport, Atlanta, Georgia, has 36 acres *14,5 ha* under roof.

The largest hangar building in the United Kingdom is the Britannia assembly hall at the former Bristol Aeroplane Company's works at Filton, Avon, now part of British Aerospace. The overall width of the hall is 1054 ft *321 m* and the overall depth of the centre bay is 420 ft *128 m*. It encloses a floor area of 7½ acres *3,0 ha*. The cubic capacity of the hall is 33,000,000 ft³ *934 000 m³*. The building was begun in April 1946 and completed by September 1949 (see also Largest Doors).

GLASSHOUSE

Largest *Great Britain*

The largest glasshouse in the United Kingdom is one covering 22.5 acres *9,10 ha* owned by van Heyningen Bros at Waterham, Herne Bay, Kent completed in October 1982. A crop of 160,000 tomato plants is grown under 1155 tons of glass.

GRAIN ELEVATOR

Largest

The world's largest single-unit grain elevator is operated by the C-G-F Grain Company at Wichita, Kansas. Consisting of a triple row of storage tanks, 123 on each side of the central loading tower or 'head house', the unit is 2,717 ft *828 m* long and 100 ft *30 m* wide. Each tank is 120 ft *37 m* high, with an inside diameter of 30 ft *9 m* giving a total storage capacity of 20,000,000 bushels *7,3 million hl* of wheat. The largest collection of elevators in the world are the 23 at City of Thunder Bay, Ontario, Canada, on Lake Superior with a total capacity of 103.9 million bushels *37,4 million hl*.

SEWAGE WORKS

Largest

The largest single full treatment sewage works in the world is the West-Southwest Treatment Plant, opened in 1940 on a site of 501 acres *203 ha* in Chicago, Illinois. It serves an area containing 2,940,000 people and it treated an average of 835,000,000 US gal *3160 million litres* of wastes per day in 1973. The capacity of its sedimentation and aeration tanks is 1 280 000 m³ *1.6 million yd³*.

The largest full treatment works in Britain and probably in Europe is the Beckton Works, East London, which serves a 2,966,000 population and handles a daily flow of 207 million gal *941 million litres* in a tank capacity of 757,000 ft³ *21 400 m³*.

WOODEN BUILDING

Largest

The world's largest buildings in timber are the two US Navy airship hangers built in 1942–3 at Tillamook, Oregon. Now used by the Louisiana-Pacific Corporation as a sawmill they measure 1000 ft long, 170 ft high at the crown and 296 ft wide at the base (*304,8 m × 51,8 m × 90,22 m*).

What is believed to be the oldest complete wooden building in England was discovered in December 1986 in the Fenlands, Cambridgeshire. It measures 8 m *26.2 ft* × 2 m *6.65 ft* and was a burial chamber of the Neolithic period c. 5000 years ago.

AIR-SUPPORTED BUILDING

Largest

The world's largest air-supported roof has been that of the 80,600 capacity octagonal Pontiac Silverdome Stadium, Michigan, 522 ft *159 m* wide and 722 ft *220 m* long. The air pressure was 5 lb/in² *34,4 kPa* supporting the 10 acre *4 ha* translucent 'Fiberglas' roofing. The structural engineers were Geiger-Berger Associates of New York City. The largest standard size air hall was one 860 ft *262 m* long, 140 ft *42,6 m* wide and 65 ft *19,8 m* high. One was first sited at Lima, Ohio, made by Irvin Industries of Stamford, Connecticut.

Buildings for Living

WOODEN BUILDINGS

Oldest

The oldest extant wooden buildings in the world are those comprising the Pagoda, Chumanar Gate and the Temple of Horyu (Horyu-ji), at Nara, Japan, dating from *c.* AD 670 and completed in 715. The nearby Daibutsuden, built in 1704–11, once measured 285.4 ft long, 167.3 ft wide and 153.3 ft tall *87 × 51 × 46,75 m*. The present dimensions are 188 × 165.3 × 159.4 ft *57,3 × 50,4 × 48,6 m*.

CASTLES

Earliest

The oldest castle in the world is at Gomdan, in the Yemen, which originally had 20 storeys and dates from before AD 100.

The oldest stone castle extant in Great Britain is Richmond Castle, Yorkshire, built *c.* 1075. The oldest Irish castle is Ferrycarrig near Wexford dating from *c.* 1180. The oldest castle in Northern Ireland is Carrickfergus Castle, County Antrim, Northern Ireland, which dates from before 1210.

Largest

The largest inhabited castle in the world is the royal residence of Windsor Castle at New Windsor, Berkshire. It is primarily of 12th-century construction and is in the form of a waisted parallelogram 1890 by 540 ft *576 by 164 m*.

The total area of Dover Castle, however, covers 34 acres *13,75 ha* with a width of 1100 ft *335,2 m* and a curtain wall of 1800 ft *550 m* or if underground works are taken in, 2300 ft *700 m*. The overall dimensions of Carisbrooke Castle (450 ft by 360 ft *110 by 137 m*), Isle of Wight, if its earthworks are included, are 1350 ft by 825 ft *411 m by 251 m*. The largest castle in Scotland is Edinburgh Castle with a major axis of 1320 ft *402 m* and measuring 3360 ft *1025 m* along its perimeter wall including the Esplanade. The most capacious of all Irish castles is Carrickfergus (see above) but that with the most extensive fortifications is Trim Castle, County Meath, built *c.* 1205 with a curtain wall 1455 ft *443 m* long.

Forts

The largest ancient castle in the world is Hradčany Castle, Prague, Czechoslovakia, originating in the 9th century. It is an oblong irregular polygon with an axis of 570 m *1870 ft* and an average traverse diameter of 128 m *420 ft* with a surface area of 7,28 ha *18 acres*. Fort George, Ardersier, Inverness-shire, built in 1748–69 measures 2100 ft *640 m* in length and has an average width of 620 ft *189 m*. The total site covers 42½ acres *17,2 ha*.

Thickest walls

Urnammu's city walls at Ur (now Muqayyar, Iraq), destroyed by the Elamites in 2006 BC, were 27 m *88⅓ ft* thick in mud brick. The walls of the Great Tower or Donjon of Flint Castle, built in 1277–80, are 23 ft *7,01 m* thick.

PALACES

Largest

The largest palace in the world is the Imperial Palace (Gu gong) in the centre of Peking (Beijing, the northern capital), China, which covers a rectangle 1050 yd by 820 yd *960 by 750 m*, an area of 177.9 acres *72 ha*. The outline survives from the construction of the third Ming Emperor, Yung Lo of 1402–24, but due to constant rearrangements most of the intra-mural buildings are 18th-century. These consist of 5 halls and 17 palaces of which the last occupied by the last Empress until 1924 was the Palace of Accumulated Elegance (*Chu xia gong*).

The Palace of Versailles, 23 km *14 miles* southwest of Paris has a facade with 375 windows, 634 yards *580 m* in length. The building, completed in 1682 for Louis XIV occupied over 30,000 workmen under Jules Hardouin-Mansert (1646–1708).

Residential

The palace (Istana Nurul Iman) of H.M. the Sultan of Brunei in the capital Bandar Seri Begawan, completed in January 1984 at a reported cost of £300 million, is the largest in the world with 1788 rooms. The underground garage accommodates the Sultan's 110 cars.

The largest palace in the United Kingdom in royal use is Buckingham Palace, London, so named after its site, bought in 1703 by John Sheffield, the 1st Duke of Buckingham and Normanby (1648–1721). Buckingham House was reconstructed in the Palladian style between 1835 and 1836, following the design of John Nash (1752–1835). The 610 ft *186 m* long East Front was built in 1846 and refaced in 1912. The Palace, which stands in 39 acres *15,8 ha* of garden, has 600 rooms including a ballroom 111 ft *34 m* long. The largest ever royal palace has been Hampton Court, Middlesex, acquired by Henry VIII from Cardinal Wolsey in 1525 and greatly enlarged by him and later by William III, Anne and George I, whose son George II was its last resident monarch. It covers 4 acres *1,6 ha* of a 669 acre *270,7 ha* site.

Largest moat

The world's largest moats are those which surround the Imperial Palace in Beijing (see above). From plans drawn by French sources it appears to measure 54 yd *49 m* wide and have a total length of 3600 yd *3290 m*. The city's moats total in all 23½ miles *38 km*.

HOTELS

Largest

The world's largest hotel is the Las Vegas Hilton, Nevada, USA built on a 63 acre *25,5 ha* site in 1974–81 with 3174 rooms, 13 international restaurants and a staff of 3600. It has a 10 acre *2,47 ha* rooftop recreation deck, a 48,000 ft² *4460 m²* pillar-free ballroom and 125,000 ft² *11 600 m²* of convention space.

The Hotel Rossiya in Moscow opened in 1967 with 3200 rooms but, owing to its proportion of dormitory accommodation, is not now internationally listed among the largest hotels. The Izmailovo Hotel complex opened in July 1980 for the XXIInd Olympic Games in Moscow was designed to accommodate 9500 people.

The greatest sleeping capacity of any hotel in Great Britain is 1859 in the London Forum Hotel, Cromwell Road, London which has a staff of 419 and was opened in 1973. The Regent Palace Hotel, Piccadilly Circus, London, opened 20 May 1915, has, however, 225 more rooms totalling 1140. The largest hotel is the Grosvenor House Hotel, Park Lane, London, which was opened in 1929. It is 8 storeys high covering 2½ acres *1 ha* and caters for more than 100,000 visitors per year in 470 rooms. The Great Room is the largest single hotel room measuring 181 ft by 131 ft *55 by 40 m* with a height of 23 ft *7 m*. Banquets for 1500 are frequently handled.

The Regent Hotel, Royal Leamington Spa, Warwickshire, when first opened in 1819 with 100 bedrooms and one bathroom was acclaimed to be the largest in the world.

Tallest

The tallest hotel in the world, measured from the street level of its main entrance to the top, is the 741.9 ft *226,1 m* tall 73-storey Westin Stamford in Raffles City, Singapore topped out in March 1985. The $235 million (*£156.66 million*) hotel is operated by Westin Hotel Company and owned by Raffles City Pte Ltd. Their Detroit Plaza measuring from the rear entrance level is however 748 ft *227,9 m* tall.

Britain's tallest hotel is the 27-storey 380 ft *132,24 m* tall 907-bedroom London Forum Hotel (see above).

Most remote

Garvault Hotel, by Kinbrace, Sutherland, is claimed to be the most isolated in mainland Britain being some 16 miles *25,7 km* from its nearest competitor at Forsinard, also in Sutherland.

Most expensive

The world's costliest hotel accommodation is the roof-top Royal Suite at $3000 (*£2000*) per day for a minimum term of 6 months in the Marbella

> **Narrowest hotel** ● The Star Hotel in Moffat, Dumfries & Galloway, Scotland, the narrowest detached hotel is only 20 ft *6,1 m* in width. The 8-bedroom hotel has two bars and is owned by Douglas and Monica House and Tim and Allison Leighfield.

Dinamar, Spain. It has 2 halls, 2 dining rooms, 5 double bedrooms, 7 bathrooms, a kitchen, a service area, a study/library/office, a lounge, an 8 metre heated swimming pool with a massage system, 2 solariums, a sauna and an 18-hole putting green.

The most expensive hotel suite in Britain is the Wellington Suite on the 8th floor of the Hotel Inter-Continental, London, at £810 per day (incl. VAT) (May 1986).

Mobile

The 3-storey brick Hotel Fairmount (built 1906) in San Antonio, Texas, which weighed 3,200,000 lb, was moved on 36 dollies with pneumatic tyres over city streets approximately 5 blocks, and over a bridge, which had to be reinforced. The move by Emmert International of Portland, Oregon, took 4 days, 30 Mar–2 Apr 1985, and cost $650,000.

Spas

The largest spa in the world measured by number of available hotel rooms is Vichy, Allier, France, with 14,000 rooms. Spas are named after the watering place in the Liège province of Belgium where hydropathy was developed from 1626. The highest French spa is Barèges, Hautes-Pyrénées, at 4068 ft *1240 m* above sea level.

HOUSING

Largest estate

The largest housing estate in the United Kingdom is the 1670 acre *675 ha* Becontree Estate, on a site of 3000 acres *1214 ha* in Barking and Redbridge, London, built between 1921 and 1929. The total number of homes is 26,822, with an estimated population of nearly 90,000.

New towns

Of the 32 new towns set up in Great Britain, that with the largest eventual planned population is Milton Keynes, Buckinghamshire, with a projected 210,000 for 1992.

Largest house

The most expensive private house ever built is the Hearst Ranch at San Simeon, California. It was built from 1922–39 for William Randolph Hearst (1863–1951), at a total cost of more than $30,000,000 (*then £6,120,000*). It has more than 100 rooms, a 104 ft *32 m* long heated swimming pool, an 83 ft *25 m* long assembly hall and a garage for 25 limousines. The house required 60 servants to maintain it.

The largest house in Great Britain is Wentworth Woodhouse, near Rotherham, South Yorkshire, formerly the seat of the Earls Fitzwilliam and now a teachers' training college. The main part of the house, built over 300 years ago, has more than 240 rooms with over 1000 windows, and its

Largest house ● Aptly-named Biltmore House, in Asheville, North Carolina, USA is the largest private house in the world. It comprises 250 rooms, and was built between 1890 and 1895 in an estate of 119,000 acres. Owned by George and William Cecil, grandsons of George Washington Vanderbilt II (1862–1914), it cost $4,100,000 and is now valued at $55,000,000 with just 12,000 acres. (Photo: Biltmore Estate)

principal façade is 600 ft *183 m* long. The royal residence Sandringham House, Norfolk, has been reported to have had 365 rooms before the demolition of 73 surplus rooms in 1975. The largest house in Ireland is Castletown in County Kildare, owned by the Hon. Desmond Guinness and is the headquarters of the Irish Georgian Society. Scotland's largest house is Hopetoun House, West Lothian, built between 1696 and 1756 with a west façade 675 ft *206 m* long.

Smallest

The smallest house in Britain is the 19th-century fisherman's cottage at The Quay, Conway, Gwynedd. It has a 72 in *182 cm* frontage, is 122 in *309 cm* high, 100 in *254 cm* front to back and has two tiny rooms and a staircase. The narrowest known house frontage is of 47 inches *1,19 m* at 50 Stuart Street, Millport on Great Cumbrae, Bute.

Most expensive

The most expensive private house is The Kenstead Hall with the adjoining Beechwood property in The Bishop's Avenue, Hampstead, London, residence of the late King of Saudi Arabia. It was put on the market for £16 million in August 1982.

Oldest

The oldest house in Britain is Eastry Court near Sandwich, Kent dating from AD 603. Some of the original timbers and stone infill still survive behind its present Georgian façade.

Barracks

The oldest purpose-built barracks are believed to be Collins Barracks, formerly the Royal

Barracks, Dublin, completed in 1704 and still in use.

FLATS

Tallest

The tallest blocks of flats in the world are Lake Point Towers of 70 storeys, and 645 ft *197 m* in Chicago, Illinois.

Largest

The largest blocks of private flats in Britain form the Barbican Estate, in the City of London with 2011 flats on a 40 acre *16 ha* site with covered parking space for 2000 cars. The architects were Chamberlain, Powell and Bon.

The tallest residential block in Great Britain is Shakespeare Tower in the Barbican in the City of London, which has 116 flats on 44 storeys and rises to a height of 419 ft 2½ in *127,77 m* above the street. The first of the three Barbican towers was 'topped out' in May 1971.

Most expensive

The largest of the four flats at Rutland Gate, Kensington, London designed by YRM Architects for occupation in 1988 is reputed to be worth around £6 million. The flat has a private swimming pool, five bedrooms, and overlooks Hyde Park.

Mobile

The Cudecom Building, an eight-storey apartment block in Bogota, Colombia, South America weighing 7700 tons/*tonnes* was moved intact 95 ft *28,95 m* on 6 Oct 1974 to make way for a road.

Buildings for Entertainment

STADIUM

Largest

The world's largest stadium is the open Strahov Stadium in Prague (Praha), Czechoslovakia. It was completed in 1934 and can accommodate 240,000 spectators for mass displays of up to 40,000 Sokol gymnasts.

Football

The largest football stadium in the world is the Maracaña Municipal Stadium in Rio de Janeiro, Brazil, where the football ground has a normal capacity of 205,000, of whom 155,000 may be seated. A crowd of 199,854 was accommodated for the World Cup final between Brazil and Uruguay on 16 July 1950. A dry moat, 7ft *2,13 m* wide and more than 5 ft *1,5 m* deep, protects players from spectators and *vice versa*. Britain's most capacious football stadium is Hampden Park, Glasgow, opened on 31 Oct 1903 and once surveyed to accommodate 184,000 compared

with a record attendance of 149,547 on 17 Apr 1937 and the present licensed limit of 74,400.

Covered

The Azteca Stadium, Mexico City, Mexico, opened in 1968, has a capacity of 107,000 of whom nearly all are under cover. The world's largest retractable roof is being constructed to cover the 60,000-capacity Toronto Blue Jays new stadium near the CN Tower for completion by August 1988. The diameter will be 207 m *679 ft*.

The largest covered stadium in Britain is the Empire Stadium, Wembley, Middlesex, opened in April 1923. It was the scene of the 1948 Olympic Games and the final of the 1966 World Cup. In 1962-3 the capacity under cover was increased to 100,000 of whom 45,000 may be seated. The original cost was £1,250,000.

Largest roof

The transparent acryl glass 'tent' roof over the Munich Olympic Stadium, West Germany measures 914,940 ft² (21.0 acres *8,5 ha*) in area resting on a steel net supported by masts. The roof of longest span in the world is the 680 ft *207,2 m* diameter of the Louisiana Superdome (see below). The major axis of the elliptical Texas Stadium completed in 1971 at Irving, Texas is, however, 240 m *787 ft 4 in*.

Indoor

The world's largest indoor stadium is the 13 acre

Buildings for Entertainment

5,26 ha $173 million (then £75 million) 273 ft 83,2 m tall Superdome in New Orleans, Louisiana, completed in May 1975. Its maximum seating capacity for conventions is 97,365 or 76,791 for football. Box suites rent for $35,000 excluding the price of admission. A gondola with six 312 in 7,92 m TV screens produces instant replay.

Ballroom

The dance floor used for championships at Earl's Court Exhibition Hall, London extends 256 ft 78 m in length.

Largest pleasure beach

The largest pleasure beach in the world is Virginia Beach, Virginia, USA. It has 28 miles 45 km of beach front on the Atlantic and 10 miles 16 km of estuary frontage. The area embraces 255 miles² 600 km² and 134 hotels and motels. The most visited pleasure beach in Britain is at Blackpool, Lancashire which attracts 6½ million visitors annually.

Piers

A pleasure pier was completed at Great Yarmouth, Norfolk in 1808 but was washed away in 1953. The Old Pier, Weymouth, Dorset dates back to 1812. The longest pleasure pier in the world is Southend Pier at Southend-on-Sea in Essex. It is 1.34 miles 2,15 km in length and was first opened in August 1889 with final extensions made in 1929. In 1949–50 the pier had a peak 5,750,000 visitors. The pier railway closed in October 1978, and reopened on 2 May 1986.

The resort with most piers is Atlantic City, New Jersey with 6 pre-war and 5 currently. In Britain only Blackpool has as many as three—North, Central and South.

Earliest fair

The earliest major international fair was the Great Exhibition of 1851 in the Crystal Palace, Hyde Park, London which in 141 days attracted 6,039,195 admissions.

Largest fair

The largest ever International Fair site was that for the St Louis, Missouri, Louisiana Purchase Exposition which covered 1271.76 acres 514,66 ha. It also staged the 1904 Olympic Games and drew an attendance of 19,694,855.

Record fair attendance

The record attendance for any fair was 64,218,770 for Expo 70 held on an 815 acre 330 ha site at Osaka, Japan from March to 13 Sept 1970. It made a profit of 19,439,402,017 yen (then £22.6 million).

Big wheel

The original Ferris Wheel, named after its constructor, George W. Ferris (1859–96), was erected in 1893 at the Midway, Chicago, Illinois, at a cost of $385,000 (then £79,218). It was 250 ft 76 m in diameter, 790 ft 240 m in circumference, weighed 1070 tons 1087 tonnes and carried 36 cars each seating 60 people, making a total of 2160 passengers. The structure was removed in 1904 to St Louis, Missouri, and was eventually sold as scrap for $1800 (then £370). In 1897 a Ferris Wheel with a diameter of 284 ft 86,5 m was erected for the Earl's Court Exhibition, London. It had ten 1st-class and 30 2nd-class cars. The largest diameter wheels now operating are 'The Giant Peter' at Himeji Central Park, Himeji City, Hyogo, and that at the city of Tsukuba, both in Japan and with a height of 85 m 278 ft 10 in. The latter has a capacity for 384 riders.

Fastest switchbacks

The maximum speeds claimed for switchbacks, scenic railways or roller coasters have in the past been exaggerated for commercial reasons. The twin-track triple-helix American Eagle at Six Flags Great America, Gurnee, Illinois,

Largest amusement resort ● The 180 ft 54,8 m high Cinderella Castle dominates the skyline at Disney World, the largest amusement resort in the world. Occupying 28,000 acres 11,322 ha near Orlando, Florida, USA this $400-million investment was opened on 1 Oct 1971 and the annual attendance now exceeds 20 million.
The most attended resort is Disneyland, Anaheim, California (opened 1955), which received its 250-millionth visitor on 24 Aug 1985 at 9.52 a.m. (Photo: K J A Brookes)

opened on 23 May 1981, has a vertical drop of 147.4 ft 44,92 m on which a speed of 66.31 mph 106,73 km/h is reached. The longest roller coaster in the world is The Beast at Kings Island near Cincinnati, Ohio. Measurements at the bottom of its 141 ft 42,98 m high drop returned a speed of 64.77 mph 104,23 km/h on 5 Apr 1980.

The run of 7400 ft or 1.40 miles 2,25 km incorporates 800 ft 243,8 m of tunnels and a 540-degree banked helix. The tallest is the Moonsault Scramble at the Fujikyu Highland Park, near Kawaguchi Lake, Japan opened on 24 June 1983. It is 75 m 246 ft tall (with a speed of 105 km/h 65.2 mph).

Longest slide

The longest dry slide in the world is the Bromley Alpine Slide on Route 11 in Peru, Vermont. This has a length of 4600 ft 1402 m (0.87 mile) and a vertical drop of 820 ft 250 m.

Largest harem

The world's most capacious harem is the Winter Harem of the Grand Seraglio at Topaki, Istanbul, Turkey completed in 1589 with 400 rooms. By the time of the deposing of Abdul Hamid II in 1909 the number of carge (those who serve) had dwindled from 1200 to 370 odalisques with 127 eunuchs.

Night club *Oldest*

The earliest night club (*boîte de nuit*) was 'Le Bal des Anglais' at 6 rue des Anglais, Paris 5e, France. Founded in 1843, it closed *c.* 1960.

Largest

The largest night club in the world is 'Gilley's Club' (formerly 'Shelly's') built in 1955 and extended in 1971 on Spencer Highway, Houston, Texas, with a seating capacity of 6000 under one roof covering 4 acres *1,6 ha*. In the more classical sense the largest night club in the world is 'The Mikado' in the Akasaka district of Tokyo, with a seating capacity of 2000. It is 'manned' by 1250 hostesses. Binoculars are essential to an appreciation of the floor show.

Lowest

The lowest night club is the 'Minus 206' in Tiberias, Israel on the shores of the Sea of Galilee. It is 206 m *676 ft* below sea level. An alternative candidate is the oft-raided 'Outer Limits', opposite the Cow Palace, San Francisco, California. It has been called 'The Most Busted Joint' and 'The Slowest to Get the Message'.

Restaurants

The earliest restaurant, named 'Casa Botin', was opened in 1725 in calle de Cuchilleros 17, Madrid. The 'Tump Nak' Thai restaurant in Bangkok consists of 65 adjoining houses built on 10 acres *4 hectares*. A thousand waiters are available to serve the 3000 potential customers. The highest restaurant in the world is at the Chacaltaya ski resort, Bolivia at 5340 m *17,519 ft*. The highest in Great Britain is the 'Ptarmigan Observation Restaurant' at 3650 ft *1112 m* above sea level on Cairngorm (4084 ft *1244 m*) near Aviemore, Inverness-shire.

PUBLIC HOUSES

Oldest

There are various claimants to the title of the United Kingdom's oldest inn. A foremost claimant is 'The Fighting Cocks', St Albans, Hertfordshire (an 11th-century structure on an 8th-century site). The timber frame of The Royalist Hotel, Digbeth Street, Stow-on-the-Wold, Gloucestershire has been dated to even earlier. It was the inn 'The Eagle and the Child' in the 13th century and known to exist in AD 947. An origin as early as AD 560 has been claimed for 'Ye Olde Ferry Boat Inn' at Holywell, Cambridgeshire. There is some evidence that it antedates the local church, built in 980, but the earliest documents are not dated earlier than 1100. There is evidence that the 'Bingley Arms', Bardsey, near Leeds, West Yorkshire, restored and extended in 1738, existed as the 'Priest's Inn', according to Bardsey Church records, dated 905.

The oldest pub in Northern Ireland is 'Grace Neill's Bar', Donaghadee, County Down built in 1611. An inn has stood on the site of the 'Brazen Head Inn', Lower Bridge Street, Dublin since the late 12th century. The present structure dates from 1668.

Largest *World*

The largest beer-selling establishment in the world is the 'Mathäser', Bayerstrasse 5, Munich, West Germany, where the daily sale reaches 84,470 pts *48 000 litres*. It was established in 1829, was demolished in World War II and rebuilt by 1955, and now seats 5500 people. The throughput at the Dube beer halls in the Bantu township of Soweto, Johannesburg may, however, be higher on some Saturdays when the average daily consumption of 6000 gal (48,000 pts *27 280 litres*) is far exceeded.

Great Britain

The largest public house in Great Britain is the 'Courage' house, Downham Tavern, Downham Way, Bromley, Kent built in 1930. Two large bars (counter length 45 ft *13,7 m*) accommodate 1000 customers with 18–20 staff.

Smallest

The pub with the smallest bar room is the 'Earl Grey', Quenington, Gloucestershire, measuring 12 ft 3 in × 9 ft 6 in *3,73 m × 2,89 m*.

Longest bars

The world's longest permanent bar is the 340 ft *103,6 m* long bar in 'Lulu's Roadhouse', Kitchener, Ontario, Canada opened on 3 Apr 1984. The 'Bar at Erickson's', on Burnside Street, Portland, Oregon, in its heyday (1883–1920) possessed a bar which ran continuously around and across the main saloon measuring 684 ft *208,48 m*. The chief bouncer Edward 'Spider' Johnson had an assistant named 'Jumbo' Reilly who weighed 23 stone and was said to resemble 'an ill-natured orang-utan'. Beer was 5 cents for 16 fluid ounces. Temporary bars have been erected of greater length.

The longest bar in the United Kingdom with beer pumps is the Long Bar at The Cornwall Coliseum Auditorium at Carlyon Bay, St Austell, Cornwall measuring 104 ft 4 in *31,8 m* and having 34 dispensers (beer and lager). The longest bar in a pub is of 104 ft 3 in *31,77 m* in 'The Horse Shoe', Drury Street, Glasgow. The Grand Stand Bar at Galway Racecourse, Ireland, completed in 1955, measures 210 ft *64 m*.

Longest name

The pub with the longest name is the 49-letter 'Henry J. Bean's But His Friends All Call Him Hank Bar and Grill', Raphael Street, Knightsbridge, London.

Shortest name

The public house in the United Kingdom with the shortest name was the 'X' at Westcott, Cullompton, Devon but in October 1983 the name was changed to the 'Merry Harriers'.

Commonest name

The commonest pub name in Britain is 'Red Lion' of which there are probably about 630. Arthur Amos of Bury St Edmunds, Suffolk, has recorded 21,516 differently-named pubs. On his death in June 1986 his son John took over the collection which now numbers 22,622.

Highest

The highest public house in the United Kingdom is the 'Tan Hill Inn'. It is 1732 ft *528 m* above sea level just in Co. Durham, on the moorland road between Reeth, North Yorkshire and Brough, Cumbria. The 'Snowdon Summit' licensed bar and cafeteria is, when open, the highest at 3560 ft *1085 m*.

Most visits

Stanley House of Totterdown, Bristol has visited 3308 differently-named pubs in Britain by way of public transport only, from 1969 to 1987. Jimmy Young GM, BEM, of Better Pubs Ltd, claims to have visited 23,733 different pubs.

Towers and Masts

TALLEST STRUCTURES

World

The tallest structure in the world is the guyed Warszawa Radio mast at Konstantynow near Gabin and Plock 60 miles *96 km* north-west of the capital of Poland. It is 646,38 m *2120 ft 8 in* tall or more than four-tenths of a mile. It was completed on 18 July 1974 and put into operation on 22 July 1974. It was designed by Jan Polak and weighs 550 tons/*tonnes*. The mast is so high that anyone falling off the top would reach their terminal velocity and hence cease to be accelerating before hitting the ground. Work was begun in July 1970 on this tubular steel construction, with its 15 steel guy ropes. It recaptured for Europe, after 45 years, a record held in the USA since the Chrysler Building surpassed the Eiffel Tower in 1929.

The tallest structure in the United Kingdom is the Independent Broadcasting Authority's mast north of Horncastle, Lincolnshire completed in 1965 to a height of 1265 ft *385 m* with 7 ft *2,13 m* added by meteorological equipment installed in September 1967. It serves Yorkshire TV and weighs 210 tons *tonnes*.

TALLEST TOWERS

The tallest self-supporting tower (as opposed to a guyed mast) in the world is the $44-million CN Tower in Metro Center, Toronto, Canada, which rises to 1822 ft 1 in *555,33 m*. Excavation began on 12 Feb 1973 for the 130,000 ton/*tonne* structure of reinforced, post-tensioned concrete topped out on 2 Apr 1975. The 416-seat restaurant revolves in the Sky Pod at 1140 ft *347,5 m* from which the visibility extends to hills 74¼ miles *120 km* distant. Lightning strikes the top about 200 times (30 storms) per annum.

The tallest tower built before the era of television masts is the Eiffel Tower in Paris, designed by Alexandre Gustav Eiffel (1832–1923) for the Paris Exhibition and completed on 31 Mar 1889. It was 300,51 m *985 ft 11 in* tall, now extended by a TV antenna to 320,75 m *1052 ft 4 in* and weighs 7340 tonnes *7224 tons*. The maximum sway in high winds is 12,7 cm *5 in*. The whole iron edifice, which has 1792 steps, took 2 years, 2 months and 2 days to build and cost 7,799,401 francs 31 centimes.

The tallest self-supported tower in Great Britain is the 1080 ft *329,18 m* tall Independent Broadcasting Authority transmitter at Emley Moor, West Yorkshire, completed in September 1971. The structure, which cost £900,000, has an enclosed room at the 865 ft *263,65 m* level and weighs with its foundations more than 15,000 tons/*tonnes*. The tallest tower of the pre-television era was the New Brighton Tower of 562 ft *171,29 m* built on Merseyside in 1897–1900 and dismantled in 1919–21.

Bridges

Oldest

Arch construction was understood by the Sumerians as early as 3200 BC and a reference exists to a Nile bridge in 2650 BC. The oldest surviving datable bridge in the world is the slab stone single arch bridge over the River Meles in Smyrna (now Izmir), Turkey, which dates from *c.* 850 BC.

The clapper bridges of Dartmoor and Exmoor (*e.g.* the Tarr Steps over the River Barle, Exmoor, Somerset) are thought to be of prehistoric types although none of the existing examples can be certainly dated. They are made of large slabs of stone placed over boulders. The Romans built stone bridges in England and remains of these have been found at Corbridge (Roman, Corstopitum), Northumberland dating to the 2nd century AD; Chesters, Northumberland; and Willowford, Cumbria. Remains of a very early wooden bridge have been found at Aldwinkle, Northamptonshire.

LONGEST

Cable suspension

The world's longest bridge span is the main span of the Humber Estuary Bridge, England at 4626 ft

1410 m. Work began on 27 July 1972, after a decision announced on 22 Jan 1966. The towers are 162,5 m *533 ft 1⅞ in* tall from datum and are 1⅜ in *36 mm* out of parallel, to allow for the curvature of the Earth. Including the Hessle and the Barton side spans, the bridge stretches 2220 m or *1.37 miles.* It was structurally completed on 18 July 1980 at a cost of £96 million and was opened by HM the Queen on 17 July 1981. Tolls, ranging between 60 pence for motorcycles and £8 for heavy vehicles, as at April 1987, are the highest in Britain. By 1995 the debt is expected to grow to £500 million.

The double-deck road-rail Akashi-Kaikyo bridge linking Honshū and Shikoku, Japan is planned to be completed in 1998. The main span will be 6496 ft *1980 m* in length with an overall suspended length with side spans totalling 11,680 ft *3560 m.* Work began on the approaches in October 1978 and the cost is expected to exceed £3.7 billion on completion in 1998.

Plans for a Messina Bridge linking Sicily with the Italian mainland are dependent upon EEC budgets. One preliminary study calls for towers 405 m *1329 ft* tall and a span of 3500 m *11 483 ft* (*2.17 miles*). The escalating cost of such a project was estimated by 1982 already to have passed the £10,250 million mark.

Cantilever
The Quebec Bridge (Pont de Québec) over the St Lawrence River in Canada has the longest cantilever truss span of any in the world—1800 ft *549 m* between the piers and 3239 ft *987 m* overall. It carries a railway track and 2 carriageways. Begun in 1899, it was finally opened to traffic on 3 Dec 1917 at a cost of 87 lives, and $Can.22,500,000 (*then £4,623,000*).

The longest cantilever bridge in Great Britain is the Forth Bridge. Its two main spans are 1710 ft *521 m* long. It carries a double railway track over the Firth of Forth 156 ft *47,5 m* above the water level. Work commenced in November 1882 and the first test trains crossed on 22 Jan 1890 after an expenditure of £3 million. It was officially opened on 4 Mar 1890. Of the 4500 workers who built it, 57 were killed in various accidents.

Steel arch
The longest steel arch bridge in the world is the New River Gorge Bridge, near Fayetteville, West Virginia, completed in 1977 with a span of 1700 ft *518,2 m.*

The longest steel arch bridge in Great Britain is the Runcorn–Widnes Bridge, Cheshire opened on 21 July 1961. It has a span of 1082 ft *329,8 m.*

Floating bridge
The longest floating bridge in the world is the Second Lake Washington Bridge, Evergreen, Seattle, Washington State. Its total length is 12,596 ft *3839 m* and its floating section measures 7518 ft *2291 m* (1.42 miles *2,29 km*). It was built at a total cost of $15,000,000 (*then £5,357,000*) and completed in August 1963.

Covered bridge
The longest covered bridge in the world is that at Hartland, New Brunswick, Canada measuring 1282 ft *390,8 m* overall, completed in 1899.

Railway bridge
The longest railway bridge in the world is the Huey P. Long Bridge, Metairie, Louisiana, with a railway section 22,996 ft *7009 m* (4.35 miles *7 km*) long. It was completed on 16 Dec 1935 with a longest span of 790 ft *241 m.* The Yangtse River Bridge, completed in 1968 in Nanking, China is the world's longest combined highway and railway bridge. The rail deck is 6772 m *4.20 miles* and the road deck is 4589 m *2.85 miles.*

The longest railway bridge in Britain is the second Tay Bridge (11,653 ft *3552 m*), across the

Firth of Tay at Dundee opened on 20 June 1887. Of the 85 spans, 74 (length 10,289 ft *3136 m*) are over the waterway. The 878 brick arches of the London Bridge to Deptford Creek viaduct built in 1836 extend for 3¾ miles *6,0 km.*

Longest bridging
The world's longest bridging is the Second Lake Pontchartrain Causeway, completed on 23 Mar 1969, joining Lewisburg and Metairie, Louisiana. It has a length of 126,055 ft *38 422 m* (23.87 miles). It cost $29,900,000 (*then £12.45 million*) and is 228 ft *69 m* longer than the adjoining First Causeway completed in 1956. The longest railway viaduct in the world is the rock-filled Great Salt Lake Railroad Trestle, carrying the Southern Pacific Railroad 11.85 miles *19 km* across the Great Salt Lake, Utah. It was opened as a pile and trestle bridge on 8 Mar 1904, but converted to rock fill in 1955–60.

The longest stone arch bridging is the 3810 ft *1161 m* long Rockville Bridge north of Harrisburg, Pennsylvania, with 48 spans containing 196,000 tons/*tonnes* of stone and completed in 1901.

Bridge building
A ten-man team of the 26th Regiment of Royal Engineers constructed a bridge across a nine-metre gap using a 5-bay MGB in 16 min 17 sec at Chattenden Barracks, Rochester, Kent on 15 Sep 1986.

Widest bridge
The world's widest long-span bridge is the 1650 ft *502,9 m* span Sydney Harbour Bridge, Australia (160 ft *48,8 m* wide). It carries two electric overhead railway tracks, 8 lanes of roadway and a cycle and footway. It was officially opened on 19 Mar 1932. The Crawford Street Bridge in Providence, Rhode Island, has a width of 1147 ft *350 m.* The River Roch is bridged for a distance of 1460 ft *445 m* where the culvert passes through the centre of Rochdale, Manchester and this is sometimes claimed to be a breadth.

HIGHEST
The highest bridge in the world is the bridge over the Royal Gorge of the Arkansas River in Colorado which is 1053 ft *321 m* above the water

level. It is a suspension bridge with a main span of 880 ft *268 m* and was constructed in 6 months, ending on 6 Dec 1929. The highest railway bridge in the world is the single-track span at Fades, outside Clermont-Ferrand, France. It was built in 1901–9 with a span of 472 ft *144 m* and is 435 ft *132,5 m* above the River Sioule. The road bridge at the highest altitude in the world, 18,380 ft *5602 m,* is the 30 m *98.4 ft* long Bailey Bridge built by the Indian Army in Aug 1982 near Khardung La, in Ladakh, India.

The highest railway bridge in Great Britain is the Ballochmyle viaduct over the River Ayr, Ayrshire built 169 ft *51,5 m* over the river bed in 1846–8 with the then world's longest masonry arch span of 181 ft *55,16 m.*

AQUEDUCTS

Longest ancient
The greatest of ancient aqueducts was the Aqueduct of Carthage in Tunisia, which ran 87.6 miles *141 km* from the springs of Zaghouan to Djebel Djougar. It was built by the Romans during the reign of Publius Aelius Hadrianus (AD 117–138). By 1895, 344 arches still survived. Its original capacity has been calculated at 7,000,000 gal *31,8 million litres* per day. The triple-tiered aqueduct Pont du Gard, built in AD 19 near Nîmes, France, is 160 ft *48 m* high. The tallest of the 14 arches of Aguas Livres Aqueduct, built in Lisbon, Portugal, in 1784 is 213 ft 3 in *65 m.*

Longest modern
The world's longest aqueduct, in the non-classical sense of any water conduit, excluding irrigation canals, is the California State Water Project aqueduct, completed in 1974, to a length of 826 miles *1329 km* of which 385 miles *619 km* is canalised.

The longest bridged aqueduct in Britain is the Pont Cysylltau in Clwyd on the Frankton to Llantisilio branch of the Shropshire Union Canal. It is 1007 ft *307 m* long, has 19 arches up to 121 ft *36 m* high above low water on the Dee. Designed by Thomas Telford (1757–1834) it was opened in 1805. The oldest is the Dundas aqueduct on the Kennet and Avon canal near Bath. It was built in 1810 and restored in 1984.

Canals

Earliest
Relics of the oldest canals in the world, dated by archaeologists *c.* 4000 BC, were discovered near Mandali, Iraq early in 1968.

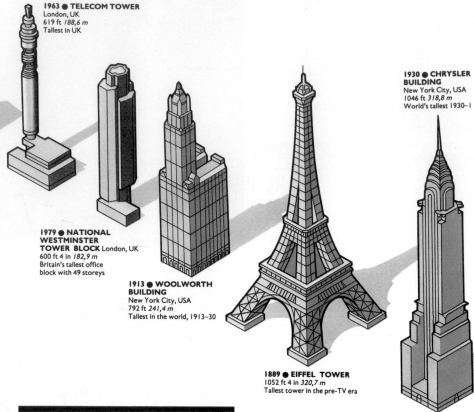

c. **2580 BC ● GREAT PYRAMID OF CHEOPS**
El Gîza, Egypt
480 ft 11 in *146,5 m*
One of the Seven Wonders of the Ancient World

1902 ● 'FLAT-IRON'
New York City, USA
285 ft *86,8 m*
An early skyscraper

1963 ● TELECOM TOWER
London, UK
619 ft *188,6 m*
Tallest in UK

1979 ● NATIONAL WESTMINSTER TOWER BLOCK London, UK
600 ft 4 in *182,9 m*
Britain's tallest office block with 49 storeys

1913 ● WOOLWORTH BUILDING
New York City, USA
792 ft *241,4 m*
Tallest in the world, 1913–30

1889 ● EIFFEL TOWER
1052 ft 4 in *320,7 m*
Tallest tower in the pre-TV era

1930 ● CHRYSLER BUILDING
New York City, USA
1046 ft *318,8 m*
World's tallest 1930–1

The earliest canals in Britain were first cut by the Romans. In the Midlands the 11 mile *17 km* long Fossdyke Canal between Lincoln and the River Trent at Torksey was built in about AD 65 and was scoured in 1122. Part of it is still in use today. Though the Exeter Canal was cut as early as 1564–6, the first wholly artificial major navigation canal in the United Kingdom was the 18½ mile *29,7 km* long canal with 14 locks from Whitecoat Point to Newry, Northern Ireland opened on 28 Mar 1742. The Sankey Navigation Canal in Lancashire, 8 miles *12,8 km* in length, with 10 locks, was opened in November 1757.

Longest

The longest canalised system in the world is the Volga–Baltic Canal opened in April 1965. It runs 1850 miles *2300 km* from Astrakhan up the Volga, via Kuybyshev, Gor'kiy and Lake Ladoga, to Leningrad. The longest canal of the ancient world has been the Grand Canal of China from Peking (Beijing) to Hangchou. It was begun in 540 BC and not completed until 1327 by which time it extended (including canalised river sections) for 1107 miles *1781 km*. The estimated work force *c.* AD 600 reached 5,000,000 on the Pien section. Having been allowed by 1950 to silt up to the point that it was nowhere more than 6 ft *1,8 m* deep, it is now, however, plied by vessels of up to 2000 tons/*tonnes*.

The Beloye More (White Sea) Baltic Canal from Belomorsk to Povenets, in the USSR, is 141 miles *227 km* long with 19 locks. It was completed with the use of forced labour in 1933. It cannot accommodate ships of more than 16 ft *5 m* in draught.

The world's longest big ship canal is the Suez Canal linking the Red and Mediterranean Seas, opened on 16 Nov 1869 but inoperative from June 1967 to June 1975. The canal was planned by the French diplomatist Comte Ferdinand de Lesseps (1805–94) and work began on 25 Apr 1859. It is 100.6 miles *161,9 km* in length from Port Said lighthouse to Suez Roads and 197 ft *60 m* wide. The work force consisted of 8213 men and 368 camels. The largest vessel to transit has been SS *Settebello* of 322 446 tonnes dwt (length 338,43 m *1110.3 ft*; beam 57,35 m *188.1 ft* at a maximum draft of 22,35 m *73.3 ft*). This was southbound in ballast on 6 Aug 1986. USS *Shreveport* transited southbound on 15–16 Aug 1984 in a record 7 hr 45 min.

Canals and river navigations in Great Britain amount to approximately 3500 miles *5630 km* with 150 miles *290 km* being restored. Of this total 2500 miles *4000 km* are inter-linked.

The geographical north–south extreme is Ripon, North Yorks, to Godalming, Surrey at 415 miles *670 km*.

Busiest

The busiest big ship canal is the Panama, first transited on 15 Aug 1914. In 1974 there were a record 14,304 ocean-going transits. The largest liner to transit is *Queen Elizabeth 2* (66,851 gross tons) on 25 Jan 1980 for a toll of $89,154.62 (*then £38,760*). The ships with the greatest beam to transit the Panama Canal have been four Iowa class battleships of the US Navy with beams of 108 ft 2 in *33 m*. The lowest toll was 36 US cents by the swimmer Richard Halliburton in 1928. The fastest transit has been 2 hr 41 min by the US Navy hydrofoil *Pegasus* on 20 June 1979.

Longest seaway

The world's longest artificial seaway is the St Lawrence Seaway (189 miles *304 km* long) along the New York State–Ontario border from Montreal to Lake Ontario, which enables ships up to 222 m *728 ft* long and 8 m *26.2 ft* draught, some of which are of 26,000 tons *26 400 tonnes*, to sail 2342 miles *3769 km* from the North Atlantic up the St Lawrence estuary and across the Great Lakes to Duluth, Minnesota, on Lake Superior (602 ft *183 m* above sea level). The project, begun in 1954, cost $470,000,000 (*then £168 million*) and was opened on 25 Apr 1959.

Irrigation canal

The longest irrigation canal in the world is the Karakumskiy Kanal, stretching 528 miles *850 km* from Haun-Khan to Ashkhabad, Turkmenistan, USSR. In September 1971 the 'navigable' length reached 280 miles *450 km*. The length of the £370-million project will reach 930 miles *1300 km*.

LOCKS

Largest

The world's largest single lock is the sea lock at Zeebrugge, Belgium measuring 500 × 57 × 23 m *1640 × 187 × 75.4 ft* giving a volume of 655 300 m³ *857,066 yd³*. The Berendrecht Lock, Antwerp planned for completion in 1986 will have the same length but a width of 68 m *223 ft* at a depth of 21,5 m *70.5 ft* giving a volume of 731 000 m³ *956,000 yd³*.

The largest and deepest lock in the United Kingdom is the Royal Portbury Entrance Lock, Bristol which measures 1200 × 140 ft *366 × 42,7 m* and has a depth of 66 ft *20,2 m*. It was opened in August 1977.

Deepest

The world's deepest lock is the John Day dam lock on the Columbia river, Oregon and Washington, USA completed in 1963. It can raise or lower barges 113 ft *34,4 m* and is served by a 982 ton *998 tonne* gate.

Highest rise and longest flight

The world's highest lock elevator overcomes a head of 68,58 m *225 ft* at Ronquières on the Charleroi-Brussels Canal, Belgium. The two 236-wheeled caissons, each able to carry 1350 tons, take 22 min to cover the 1432 m *4698 ft* long ramp. The highest rise of any boat-carrying plane in Britain was the 225 ft *68,6 m* of the 935 ft *285 m* long Hobbacott Down plane on the Bude Canal, Cornwall.

The longest flight of locks in the United Kingdom is on the Worcester and Birmingham Canal at Tardebigge, Hereford and Worcester, where in a 2½ mile *4 km* stretch there are the Tardebigge (30 locks) and Stoke (6 locks) flights which together drop the canal 259 ft *78,9 m*. The flight of locks on the Huddersfield Canal, closed in 1944, on the 7¼ mile *11,6 km* stretch to Marsden numbered 42.

Largest cut

The Gaillard Cut (known as 'the Ditch') on the Panama Canal is 270 ft *82 m* deep between Gold

A Progressive Record of the World's Tallest Structures

Artwork: Peter Harper and *The Times*

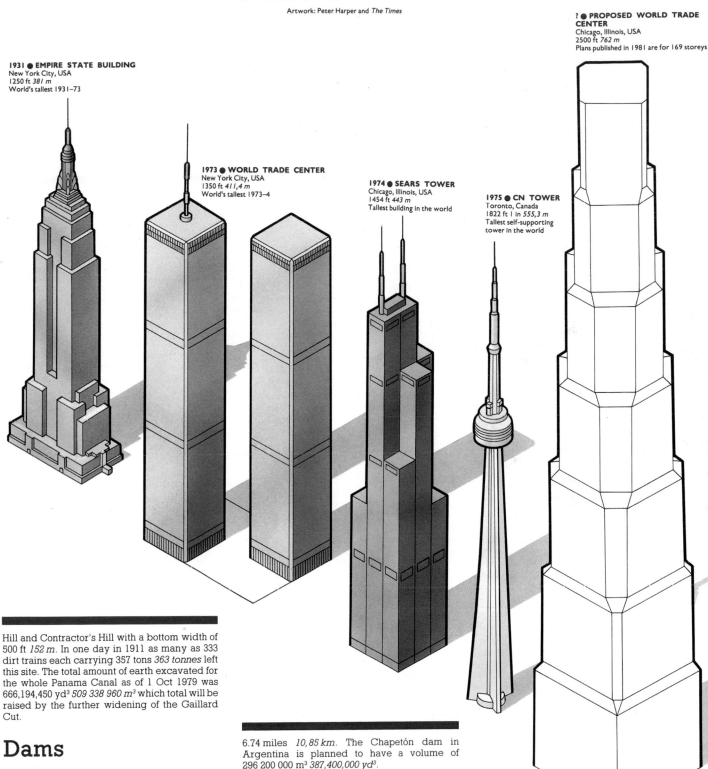

1931 ● EMPIRE STATE BUILDING
New York City, USA
1250 ft *381 m*
World's tallest 1931–73

1973 ● WORLD TRADE CENTER
New York City, USA
1350 ft *411,4 m*
World's tallest 1973–4

1974 ● SEARS TOWER
Chicago, Illinois, USA
1454 ft *443 m*
Tallest building in the world

1975 ● CN TOWER
Toronto, Canada
1822 ft 1 in *555,3 m*
Tallest self-supporting
tower in the world

? ● PROPOSED WORLD TRADE CENTER
Chicago, Illinois, USA
2500 ft *762 m*
Plans published in 1981 are for 169 storeys

Hill and Contractor's Hill with a bottom width of 500 ft *152 m*. In one day in 1911 as many as 333 dirt trains each carrying 357 tons *363 tonnes* left this site. The total amount of earth excavated for the whole Panama Canal as of 1 Oct 1979 was 666,194,450 yd³ *509 338 960 m³* which total will be raised by the further widening of the Gaillard Cut.

Dams

Earliest

The earliest known dams were those uncovered by the British School of Archaeology in Jerusalem in 1974 at Jawa in Jordan. These stone-faced earth dams are dated to *c.* 3200 BC.

Most massive

Measured by volume, the largest dam in the world is the 98 ft *29,8 m* high New Cornelia Tailings earth-fill dam, on the Ten Mile Wash, Arizona, with a volume of 274,015,735 yd³ *209 501 000 m³* completed in 1973 to a length of

6.74 miles *10,85 km*. The Chapetón dam in Argentina is planned to have a volume of 296 200 000 m³ *387,400,000 yd³*.

Largest concrete

The world's largest concrete dam, and the largest concrete structure in the world, is the Grand Coulee Dam on the Columbia River, Washington State, USA. Work on the dam was begun in 1933, it began working on 22 Mar 1941, and was completed in 1942 at a cost of $56 million. It has a crest length of 4173 ft *1272 m* and is 550 ft *167 m* high. It contains 10,585,000 yd³ *8 092 000 m³* of concrete and weighs about 19,285,000 tons *19 595 000 tonnes*.

Highest

The highest dam in the world will be the 335 m *1098 ft* high Rogunsky earth-fill dam across the Vakhsh river, Tadzhikistan, USSR with a crest length of only 2165 ft *660 m* and a volume of 75,5 million m^3. Building since 1973, the completion date is still unconfirmed. Meanwhile the tallest completed is the 300 m *984 ft* high Nurek dam, USSR of 58 million m^3 volume.

Longest

The 41 m *134.5 ft* high Yacyreta–Apipe dam across the Paraná on the Paraguay–Argentina borders extends for 72 km *44.7 miles*. In the early 17th century an impounding dam of moderate height was built in Lake Hungtze, Kiangsu, China, to a reputed length of 100 km *62 miles*.

The longest sea dam in the world is the Afsluitdijk stretching 20.195 miles *32,5 km* across the mouth of the Zuider Zee in two sections of 1.553 miles *2,499 km* (mainland of North Holland to the Isle of Wieringen) and 18.641 miles *30 km* from Wieringen to Friesland. It has a sea-level width of 293 ft *89 m* and a height of 24 ft 7 in *7,5 m*.

Strongest

The world's strongest structure will be the 242 m *793 ft* high Sayano-Shusenskaya dam on the River Yenisey, USSR which is designed to bear a load of 18 000 000 tonnes/*tons* from a fully-filled reservoir of 31,300 million m^3 *41,000 million* yd^3 capacity.

The most massive dam in Britain is the Northumbrian Water Authority's Kielder Dam, a 52 m *170 ft* high earth embankment measuring 1140 m *3740 ft* in length and 5 300 000 m^3 *6,932,000* yd^3. There are longer low dams or barrages of the valley cut-off type, notably the Hanningfield Dam, Essex, built from July 1952 to August 1956 to a length of 6850 ft *2088 m* and a height of 64.5 ft *19,7 m*. The rock-fill Llyn Brianne Dam, Dyfed is Britain's highest dam reaching 298½ ft *91 m* in Nov 1971. It became operational on 20 July 1972.

Largest reservoir

The most voluminous man-made reservoir is the Kahkovskaya Reservoir, USSR, with a volume of 182 km^3 *147,550,000 acre-feet*. The world's largest artificial lake measured by surface area is Lake Volta, Ghana, formed by the Akosombo Dam completed in 1965. By 1969 the lake had filled to an area of 3275 $miles^2$ *8482* km^2 with a shoreline 4500 miles *7250 km* in length.

The completion in 1954 of the Owen Falls Dam near Jinja, Uganda, across the northern exit of the White Nile from the Victoria Nyanza marginally raised the level of that *natural* lake by adding 270 km^3 *218,900,000 acre-feet*, and technically turned it into a reservoir with a surface area of 17,169,920 acres *6,9 million ha* (26,828 $miles^2$ *69 484* km^2).

The $4-billion Tucurui Dam in Brazil of 64,3 million m^3 had, by 1984, converted the Tocantins River into a 1900 km *1180 mile* long chain of lakes.

The most capacious reservoir in Britain is Kielder Water in the North Tyne Valley, Northumberland, which filled to 44,000 million gallons *2000 million hl* from 15 Dec 1980 to mid-1982, and which acquired a surface area of 2684 acres *1086 ha* and a perimeter of 27 miles *43,4 km* to become England's second largest lake. Rutland Water has a lesser capacity (27,300 million gallons *124 106 million l*) and a lesser perimeter (24 miles *38,6 km*) but a greater surface area of 3100 acres *1254 ha*. The deepest reservoir in Europe is Loch Morar, Inverness-shire, with a maximum depth of 1017 ft *310 m* (see also page 58).

The largest wholly artificial reservoir in Great Britain is the Queen Mary Reservoir, built from August 1914 to June 1925, at Littleton, near Staines, Surrey, with an available storage capacity of 8130 million gal *369,6 million hl* and a water area of 707 acres *286 ha*. The length of the perimeter embankment is 20,766 ft *6329 m* (3.93 miles *6,32 km*).

Largest polder *(Reclaimed land)*

The largest of the five great polders in the old Zuider Zee, Netherlands, will be the 149,000 acre *60 300 ha* (232.8 $miles^2$ *603* km^2) Markerwaard. Work on the 66 mile *106 km* long surrounding dyke was begun in 1957. The water area remaining after the erection of the 1927–32 dam (20 miles *32 km* in length) is called IJsselmeer, which will have a final area of 487.5 $miles^2$ *1262,6* km^2.

Largest levees

The most massive levees ever built are the Mississippi levees begun in 1717 but vastly augmented by the US Federal Government after the disastrous floods of 1927. These extend for 1732 miles *2787 km* along the main river from Cape Girardeau, Missouri, to the Gulf of Mexico and comprise more than 1000 million yd^3 *765 million* m^3 of earthworks. Levees on the tributaries comprise an additional 2000 miles *3200 km*. The Pine Bluff, Arkansas to Venice, Louisiana segment of 650 miles *1046 km* is continuous.

Tunnels

LONGEST

Water supply

The world's longest tunnel of any kind is the New York City West Delaware water-supply tunnel, begun in 1937 and completed in 1944. It has a diameter of 13 ft 6 in *4,1 m* and runs for 105 miles *168,9 km* from the Rondout Reservoir into the Hillview Reservoir, on the border of Yonkers and New York City.

The longest water-supply tunnel in the United Kingdom is the Kielder Water tunnel system. These tunnels have been driven through the rock to link the Tyne Valley with the Wear Valley. A pipe then passes under the River Wear and the tunnel then proceeds to link up with the Tees Valley. The system is 20.2 miles *32,18 km* in length.

Vehicular *(Rail)*

The 33.46 mile *53,85 km* long Seikan Rail Tunnel has been bored 240 m *787 ft* beneath sea level and 100 m *328 ft* below the sea bed of the Tsugaru Strait between Tappi Saki, Honshū, and Fukushima, Hokkaidō, Japan. Tests started on the subaqueous section (14.5 miles *23,3 km*) in 1964 and construction in June 1972. It was holed through on 27 Jan 1983 after a loss of 34 lives. The cost by the finish of tunnelling after 20 years 10 months in March 1985 and subsequent maintenance to Feb 1987 was 800,000 million yen (£3,700 million).

Great Britain's longest main-line railway tunnel is the Severn Tunnel (4 miles 628 yd *6 km*), linking Avon and Gwent completed with 76,400,000 bricks between 1873 and 1886.

Subway

The world's longest continuous subway tunnel is the Moscow Metro underground railway line from Belyaevo to Medvedkovo. It is *c.* 30,7 km *19.07 miles* long and was completed in 1978/9.

Road

The longest road tunnel is the 10.14 mile *16,32 km* long two-lane St Gotthard Road Tunnel from Göschenen to Airolo, Switzerland, opened to traffic on 5 Sept 1980. Nineteen lives were lost during the construction, begun in autumn 1969, at a cost of SF 686 million (*then £173.6 million*).

The longest road tunnel in the United Kingdom is the Mersey Tunnel, joining Liverpool and Birkenhead, Merseyside. It is 2.13 miles *3,43 km* long, or 2.87 miles *4,62 km* including branch tunnels. Work was begun in December 1925 and it was opened by HM King George V on 18 July 1934. The total cost was £7¾ million. The 36 ft *11 m* wide 4-lane roadway carries nearly 7½ million vehicles a year. The first tube of the second Mersey Tunnel was opened on 24 June 1971.

Excavation of the projected £6000-million Eurotunnel under the English Channel between Cherton near Folkestone, Kent and Sargatte by Calais, France was due to begin in late 1987 and to be completed by 1993. The length of the twin rail tunnels of 7,6 m *24 ft 11 in* diameter will be 31.03 miles *49,94 km*.

Largest

The largest diameter road tunnel in the world is that blasted through Yerba Buena Island, San Francisco, California. It is 76 ft *23 m* wide, 58 ft *17 m* high and 540 ft *165 m* long. More than 80,000,000 vehicles pass through on its two decks every year.

Hydro-electric, irrigation or sewerage

The longest irrigation tunnel in the world is the 51.5 mile *82,9 km* long Orange-Fish Rivers Tunnel, South Africa, begun in 1967 at an estimated cost of £60 million. The boring was completed in April 1973. The lining to a minimum thickness of 9 inches *23 cm* will give a completed diameter of 17 ft 6 in *5,33 m*.

The Majes project in Peru involves 98 km *60.9 miles* of tunnels for hydro-electric and water-supply purposes. The dam is at 4200 m *13,780 ft* altitude. The Chicago TARP (Tunnels and Reservoir Plan) in Illinois involves 120 miles *193 km* of sewerage tunnelling.

Bridge

The world's longest bridge-tunnel system is the Chesapeake Bay Bridge-Tunnel, extending 17.65 miles *28,40 km* from Eastern Shore, Virginia Peninsula to Virginia Beach, Virginia, USA. It cost $200,000,000 (*then £71,4 million*) and was completed after 42 months and opened to traffic on 15 Apr 1964. The longest bridged section is Trestle C (4.56 miles *7,34 km* long) and the longest tunnel is the Thimble Shoal Channel Tunnel (1.09 miles *1,75 km*).

Canal

The world's longest canal tunnel is that on the Rove canal between the port of Marseilles and the river Rhône, built in 1912–27. It is 4.53 miles *7,29 km* long, 72 ft *22 m* wide and 50 ft *15 m* high, involving 2¼ million yd^3 *1,7 million* m^3 of excavation.

The longest canal tunnel in Great Britain is the Standedge (more properly Stanedge) Tunnel in West Yorkshire on the Huddersfield Narrow Canal built from 1794 to 4 Apr 1811. It measures 3 miles 418 yd *5,21 km* in length and was closed on 21 Dec 1944.

The British canal system has contained 84 tunnels exceeding 30 yd *27,4 m* of which 48 are still open. The longest of these is the 3056 yd *2,79 km* long Blisworth Tunnel on the Grand Union in Northamptonshire.

The now closed Huddersfield Narrow Canal is the highest in the United Kingdom, at 638 ft *194 m* above sea level.

Tunnelling

The longest unsupported example of a machine-bored tunnel is the Three Rivers Water Tunnel driven 30,769 linear feet *9,37 km* with a 10.5 ft *3,2 m* diameter for the city of Atlanta, Georgia, from April 1980 to February 1982.

S & M Constructors Inc of Cleveland, Ohio achieved 179 ft *54,5 m* in a day through the granite, schist and gneiss.

The NCB record of 251,4 m *824.8 ft* for a 3,80 m *12½ ft* wide, 2 m *6½ ft* high roadway by a team of 35 pitmen in 5 days was set at West Cannock, Staffordshire No 5 Colliery from 30 Mar–3 Apr 1981.

Specialised Structures

Highest advertising sign

The highest advertising signs in the world are the four Bank of Montreal logos atop the 72-storey 935 ft *285 m* tall First Canadian Place, Toronto. Each sign, built by Claude Neon Industries Ltd, measures 20 × 22 ft *6,09 × 6,70 m* and was lifted by helicopter.

Largest

The most conspicuous sign ever erected was the electric Citroën sign on the Eiffel Tower, Paris. It was switched on on 4 July 1925, and could be seen 24 miles *38 km* away. It was in six colours with 250,000 lamps and 56 miles *90 km* of electric cables. The letter 'N' which terminated the name 'Citroën' between the second and third levels measured 68 ft 5 in *20,8 m* in height. The whole apparatus was taken down after 11 years in 1936. For the largest ground sign see Chapter 6, page 83—Largest letter.

The world's largest neon sign measures 210 × 55 ft *64 × 16,7 m* built for Marlboro cigarettes at Hung Hom, Kowloon, Hong Kong in May 1986. It contains 35,000 ft *10 668 m* of neon tubing and weighs approximately 113 tons *114,7 tonnes*. The world's largest reported hoarding is one 44,5 m *146 ft* long and 17,5 m *57 ft 5 in* tall erected by Propaganda Campanella on Route N9, Buenos Aires, Argentina. The largest 'hoarding' in Britain measures 226 ft *68,9 m* by 54 ft *16,5 m* and was produced by Forwardair Ltd. The site is the roof of the Brentford Football Club stand, at its Griffin Park, Middlesex ground which is on the flight path of London, Heathrow airport. Britain's largest illuminated sign is the name NEI NUCLEAR SYSTEMS LTD extending 170 ft 6 in *52 m* installed at their factory in Gateshead, Tyne and Wear, in June 1983. It can be seen from the air at a distance of 20 miles *32 km*.

An interior lit fascia advertising sign in Clearwater, Florida, completed by Adco Sign Corp in April 1983 measures 1168 ft 6½ in *356,17 m* in length.

The world's most massive animated sign is reputed to be that outside the Circus Circus Hotel, Reno, Nevada named Topsy, the Clown. It is 127 ft *38,7 m* tall and weighs over 40 tons *40,8 tonnes* with 1.4 miles *2,25 km* of neon tubing. His smile measures 14 ft *4,26 m* across.

Barn

The largest barn in Britain is one at Frindsbury, Kent. Its length is 219 ft *66,7 m* and it is still wholly roofed. The Ipsden Barn, Oxfordshire, is 385½ ft *117 m* long but 30 ft *9 m* wide (11,565 ft² *1074 m²*). The longest tithe barn in Britain is one measuring 268 ft *81 m* long at Wyke Farm, near Sherborne, Dorset.

Bonfire

The largest recorded bonfire constructed in Britain was the Coronation bonfire atop Arrowthwaite Brows, Whitehaven, Cumbria, lit in 1902 with 800 tons *812 tonnes* of timber, and 1000 gal *4546 litres* each of petroleum and tar. It was octagonal in shape and built to a height of 120 ft *36,67 m* with a base circumference of 155 ft *47,2 m* tapering to 20 ft *6,1 m*.

Longest breakwater

The world's longest breakwater is that which protects the Port of Galveston, Texas. The granite South Breakwater is 6.74 miles *10,85 km* in length.

The longest breakwater in Great Britain is the North Breakwater at Holyhead, Anglesey, which is 7860 ft (1.48 miles *2395 m*) in length and was completed in 1873.

Most cremations ● The Golders Green Crematorium, London, has performed 264,312 cremations since 1902, including a record 7509 in 1957.

Buildings demolished by explosives

The largest building demolished by explosives has been the 21-storey Traymore Hotel, Atlantic City, New Jersey, on 26 May 1972 by Controlled Demolition Inc of Towson, Maryland. This 600-room hotel had a cubic capacity of 6,495,500 ft³ *181 340 m³*. The tallest chimney ever demolished by explosives was the Matla Power Station chimney, Kriel, South Africa on 19 July 1981. It stood 275 m *902 ft* and was brought down by The Santon (Steeplejack) Co Ltd of Manchester, England.

Cemetery

The world's largest cemetery is that in Leningrad, which contains over 500,000 of the 1,300,000 victims of the German army's siege of 1941-3. The largest cemetery in the United Kingdom is Brookwood Cemetery, Brookwood, Surrey. It is owned by the London Necropolis Co and is 500 acres *200 ha* in extent with more than 225,000 interments.

Column

The tallest columns (as opposed to obelisks) in the world are the 36 fluted pillars 90 ft *27,43 m* tall, of Vermont marble in the colonnade of the Education Building, Albany, New York. Their base diameter is 6½ ft *1,98 m*. The tallest load-bearing stone columns in the world are those measuring 69 ft *21 m* in the Hall of Columns of the Temple of Amun at Karnak, opposite Thebes on the Nile, the ancient capital of Upper Egypt. They were built in the 19th dynasty in the reign of Rameses II *c.* 1270 BC.

Crematorium

The oldest crematorium in Britain was built in 1879 at Woking, Surrey. The first cremation took place there on 26 Mar 1885, the practice having been found legal after the cremation of Iesu Grist Price on Caerlan Fields, Powys, on 13 Jan 1884. The total number of people cremated in Britain since has been 11,172,452 (to 31 Dec 1985), and the percentage is now 68%. The percentage in Japan is 93.4%.

The largest crematorium in the world is at the Nikolo-Arkhangelskoye Cemetery, East Moscow, with 7 twin cremators of British design, completed in March 1972. It has several Halls of Farewell for atheists. Currently, Britain's largest is the City of London Crematorium, E.12, which performed 5395 cremations in 1979.

Dome

The world's largest dome is the Louisiana Superdome, New Orleans. It has a diameter of 680 ft *207,26 m*. (See pages 110-11 for further details.) The largest dome of ancient architecture is that of the Pantheon, built in Rome in AD 112, with a diameter of 142½ ft *43 m*.

The largest dome in Britain is that of the Bell Sports Centre, Perth, with a diameter of 222 ft *67 m* designed by D. B. Cockburn and constructed in Baltic whitewood by Muirhead & Sons Ltd of Grangemouth.

Door

The largest doors in the world are the four in the Vehicle Assembly Building near Cape Canaveral, Florida, with a height of 460 ft *140 m* (see page 106). The world's heaviest door is that leading to the laser target room at Lawrence Livermore National Laboratory, California. It weighs 321.4 tons *326,5 tonnes*, is up to 8 ft *2,43 m* thick and was installed by Overly.

The largest doors in Great Britain are those to the Britannia Assembly Hall, at Filton airfield, Avon. The doors are 1035 ft *315 m* in length and 67 ft *20 m* high, divided into three bays each 345 ft *105 m* across. The largest simple hinged door in Britain is that of Ye Old Bull's Head, Beaumaris, Anglesey, which is 11 ft *3,35 m* wide and 13 ft *3,96 m* high.

The oldest doors in Britain are those of Hadstock Church, near Saffron Walden, Essex, which date from *c.* 1040 AD and exhibit evidence of Danish workmanship.

Dry dock

The largest dry dock in the world with a maximum shipbuilding capacity of 1,200,000 tons deadweight is the Okpo No 1 Dry Dock, Chojé Island in South Korea. It measures 525 m *1722.4 ft* long by 131 m *430 ft* wide and was completed in 1979. The dock gates 14 m *46 ft* high and 10 m *32.8 ft* thick at the base are the world's largest.

The largest shipbuilding dry dock in the UK is the Belfast Harbour Commission and Harland and Wolff building dock in Belfast. It was excavated by Wimpey to a length of 1825 ft *556 m* and a width of 305 ft *93 m* and can accommodate tankers of 1,000,000 tons deadweight. Work was begun on 26 Jan 1968 and completed on 30 Nov 1969 and involved the excavation of 400,000 yd³ *306 000 m³*.

Earthworks

The largest earthworks in the world carried out prior to the mechanical era were the Linear Earth Boundaries of the Benin Empire in the Bendel state of Nigeria. These were first reported in 1900 and partially surveyed in 1967. In April 1973 it was estimated by Patrick Darling that the total length of the earthworks was probably between 4000 and 8000 miles *6400–12 800 km* with the amount of earth moved estimated at from 500 to 600 million yd³ *380–460 million m³*.

The greatest prehistoric earthwork in Britain is Wansdyke, originally Wodensdic, which ran 86 miles *138 km* from Portishead, Avon to Inkpen Beacon and Ludgershall, south of Hungerford, Berkshire. It was built by the Belgae as their north boundary. The most extensive single site earthwork is the Dorset Cursus near Gussage St Michael, 5 miles *8 km* SW of Cranborne, dating from c. 1900 BC. The workings are 6 miles *9,7 km* in length, involving an estimated 250,000 yd³ *191 000 m³* of excavations. The largest of the Celtic hill-forts is that known as Mew Dun, or Maiden Castle, 2 miles *3 km* SW of Dorchester, Dorset. It covers 115 acres *46,5 ha* and was abandoned shortly after AD 43.

Fence

The longest fence in the world is the dingo-proof fence enclosing the main sheep areas of Australia. The wire fence is 6 ft *1,8 m* high, 1 ft *30 cm* underground and stretches for 3437 miles *5531 km*. The Queensland State Government discontinued full maintenance in 1982 but 500 km *310 miles* is now being repaired.

The world's tallest fences are security screens 20 m *65.6 ft* high erected by Harrop-Allin of Pretoria in November 1981 to protect fuel depots and refineries at Sasolburg, South Africa.

Flagstaff

The tallest flagstaff ever erected was that outside the Oregon Building at the 1915 Panama-Pacific International Exposition in San Francisco, California. Trimmed from a Douglas fir, it stood 299 ft 7 in *91 m* in height and weighed 45 tons *47 tonnes*. The tallest unsupported flag pole in the world is the 282 ft 4 in *86 m* tall steel pole weighing 120,000 lb *54430 kg* erected on 22 Aug 1985 at the Canadian Expo 86 exhibition in Vancouver, British Columbia. It supports a gigantic ice hockey stick 205 ft *62,5 m* in length.

The tallest flagstaff in Great Britain is a 225 ft *68 m* tall Douglas fir staff at Kew, Richmond upon Thames. Cut in Canada, it was shipped across the Atlantic and towed up the River Thames on 7 May 1958, to replace the old 214 ft *65 m* tall staff of 1919.

Fountain

The world's tallest fountain is the Fountain at Fountain Hills, Arizona built at a cost of $1,500,000 for McCulloch Properties Inc. At full pressure of 375 lb/in² *26,3 kg/cm²* and at a rate of 5828 imp. gal/min *26 500 litres/min* the 560 ft *170 m* tall column of water weighs more than 8 tons/*tonnes*. The nozzle speed achieved by the three 600-hp pumps is 146.7 mph *236 km/h*.

Britain's tallest fountain is the Emperor Fountain at Chatsworth, Bakewell, Derbyshire. When first tested on 1 June 1844, it attained the then unprecedented height of 260 ft *79 m*. Since the war it has not been played to more than 250 ft *76 m* and rarely beyond 180 ft *55 m*.

Garbage dump

Reclamation Plant No 1, Fresh Kills, Staten Island, New York, opened in March 1974, is the world's largest sanitary landfill. In its first 4 months 450,000 tons *457 000 tonnes* of refuse from New York City was dumped on the site by 700 barges.

Gasholder

The world's largest gasholder is that at Fontaine l'Eveque, Belgium, where disused mines have been adapted to store up to 500 million m³ *17,650 million ft³* of gas at ordinary pressure. Probably the largest conventional gasholder is that at Wien-Simmering, Vienna, completed in 1968, with a height of 274 ft 8 in *84 m* and a capacity of 10.59 million ft³ *300 000 m³*.

The largest gasholder ever constructed in Great Britain is the East Greenwich Gas Works No 2 Holder built in 1891 with an original capacity for 12,200,000 ft³ *346 000 m³*. As constructed its capacity is 8.9 million ft³ *252 000 m³* with a water tank 303 ft *92 m* in diameter and a full inflated height of 148 ft *45 m*. The No 1 holder (capacity 8.6 million ft³ *243 500 m³*) has a height of 200 ft *61 m*. The River Tees Northern Gas Board's

---

1186 ft *361 m* deep underground storage in use since January 1959 has a capacity of 330,000 ft³ *9300 m³*.

Globe

The world's largest revolving globe is the 21½ ton/*tonne* 27 ft 11 in *8,50 m* diameter sphere in Babson College Wellesley, Massachusetts, completed at a cost of $200,000 (then £71,425) in 1956.

Jetty

The longest deep-water jetty in the world is the Quai Hermann du Pasquier at Le Havre, France, with a length of 5000 ft *1524 m*. Part of an enclosed basin, it has a constant depth of water of 32 ft *9,8 m* on both sides.

Kitchen

The largest kitchen ever set up has been an Indian government field kitchen set up in April 1973 at Ahmadnagar, Maharashtra, a famine area, which daily provided 1.2 million subsistence meals.

Lamppost

The tallest lighting columns ever erected are four of 63,5 m *208 ft 4 in* made by Petitjean & Cie of Troyes, France, and installed by Taylor Woodrow at Sultan Qaboos Sports Complex, Muscat, Oman.

Lighthouse

The £18½ million 100 m *328 ft* tall rock lighthouse built in 1983–85 40 km *24.8 miles* SW of l'Ile d'Ouessant is visible at 40 nautical miles *74 km*. With reflective clouds at optimal altitude the loom is detectable in the Isles of Scilly 105 miles *169 km* distant. The lights with the greatest range are those 1092 ft *332 m* above the ground on the Empire State Building, New York City. Each of the four-arc mercury bulbs has a rated candle-power of 450,000,000, visible 80 miles *130 km* away on the ground and 300 miles *490 km* away from aircraft. They were switched on on 31 Mar 1956.

The most remote Trinity House lighthouse is The Smalls, about 16 sea miles (18.4 statute miles *29,6 km*) off the Dyfed coast. The most remote Scottish lighthouse is Sule Skerry, 35 miles *56 km* off shore and 45 miles *72 km* north-west of Dunnet Head, Caithness. The most remote Irish light is Blackrock, 9 miles *14 km* off the Mayo coast.

Bishop Rock, Isles of Scilly measures 47,8 m *156.8 ft* high to its helipad. The tallest Scottish lighthouse is the 139 ft *42,3 m* tall North Ronaldsay lighthouse, Orkney Islands.

The lighthouse in Great Britain with the most powerful light is the shorelight at Strumble Head, near Fishguard, Dyfed. It has an intensity of 6,000,000 candelas. The Irish light with the greatest intensity is Aranmore on Rinrawros Point, County Donegal.

Largest marquee

The largest tent ever erected was one covering an area of 188,368 ft² *17 500 m²* (4.32 acres *1,7 ha*) put up by the firm of Deuter from Augsburg, West Germany, for the 1958 'Welcome Expo' in Brussels.

The largest single-unit tent in Britain covers a ground area of more than 12000 m² *129,170 ft²* and was manufactured by Clyde Canvas Ltd of Edinburgh, Scotland.

The largest marquee in Britain was one made by Piggot Brothers in 1951 and used by the Royal Horticultural Society at their annual show (first held in 1913) in the grounds of the Royal Hospital in Chelsea, London. The marquee is 310 ft *94 m* long by 480 ft *146 m* wide and consists of 18¾ miles *30 km* of 36 in *91 cm* wide canvas covering a ground area of 148,800 ft² *13 820 m²*. A tent

435 ft *132,5 m* long was erected in one lift by thirty-five men of the Military Corrective Training Centre, Colchester on 23 July 1980.

The Offshore Europe 1983 exhibition at Bridge of Don, Aberdeenshire was housed in 15 contiguous air tents covering 28 400 m² *6.91 acres.*

Maypole
The tallest reported Maypole erected in England was one of Sitka spruce 105 ft 7 in *32,12 m* tall put up in Pelynt, Cornwall on 1 May 1974. The permanent pole at Paganhill, near Stroud, Gloucestershire is 90 ft *27,43 m* tall.

Maze
The oldest datable representation of a labyrinth is that on a clay tablet from Pylos, Greece from *c.* 1200 BC.

The world's largest hedge maze is that at Longleat, near Warminster, Wilts, with 1.69 miles *2,72 km* of paths flanked by 16,180 yew trees. It was opened on 6 June 1978 and measures 381 × 187 ft *116 × 57 m.* 'Il Labirinto' at Villa Pisani, Stra, Italy, in which Napoleon was 'lost' in 1807, had 4 miles *6,4 km* of pathways.

Menhir
The tallest menhir found is the 380 tons/*tonnes* Grand Menhir Brisé, now in 4 pieces, which originally stood 69 ft *22 m* high at Locmariaquer, Britanny, France. Britain's tallest is one of 25 ft *7,6 m* at Rudston, Humberside.

Monument
Britain's largest megalithic prehistoric monument and largest existing henge are the 28¼ acre *11,5 ha* earthworks and stone circles of Avebury, Wiltshire, 'rediscovered' in 1646. The earliest calibrated date in the area of this Neolithic site is *c.* 4200 BC. The work is 1200 ft *365 m* in diameter with a 40 ft *12 m* ditch around the perimeter and required an estimated 15 million man-hours of work. The henge of Durrington Walls, Wiltshire, obliterated by road building, had a diameter of 1550 ft *472 m.* It was built from *c.* 2500 BC and required some 900,000 man-hours.

The largest trilithons exist at Stonehenge, to the south of Salisbury Plain, Wiltshire, with single sarsen blocks weighing over 45 tons/*tonnes* and requiring over 550 men to drag them up a 9° gradient. The earliest stage of the construction of the ditch has been dated to 2800 BC. Whether Stonehenge, which required some 30 million man-years, was a lunar calendar, a temple, an eclipse-predictor or a navigation school is still debated.

The tallest monumental column commemorates the battle of San Jacinto (21 Apr 1836), on the bank of the San Jacinto River near Houston, Texas. General Sam Houston (1793–1863) and his force of 743 Texan troops killed 630 Mexicans (out of a total force of 1600) and captured 700 others, for the loss of nine men killed and 30 wounded. Constructed from 1936–9, at a cost of $1,500,000 (*then £372,000*), the tapering column is 570 ft *173 m* tall, 47 ft *14 m* square at the base, and 30 ft *9 m* square at the observation tower, which is surmounted by a star weighing 196.4 tons *199,6 tonnes.* It is built of concrete, faced with buff limestone, and weighs 31,384 tons *31 888 tonnes.*

The newest scheduled ancient monuments are a hexagonal pill box and 48 concrete tank traps south of Christchurch, Dorset built in World War II and protected since 1973.

Mound
The gravel mound built as a memorial to the Seleucid King Antiochus I (reigned 69–34 BC) on the summit of Nemrud Dagi (8205 ft *2494 m*) south-east of Malatya, eastern Turkey measures 197 ft *59,8 m* tall and covers 7.5 acres *3 ha.*

The largest artificial mound in Europe is Silbury Hill, 6 miles *9,7 km* west of Marlborough, Wiltshire, which involved the moving of an estimated 670,000 tons *681,000 tonnes* of chalk, at a cost of 18 million man-hours to make a cone 130 ft *39 m* high with a base of 5¼ acres *2 ha.* Prof Richard Atkinson, in charge of the 1968 excavations, showed that it is based on an innermost central mound, similar to contemporary round barrows, and is now dated to 2745 ± 185 BC. The largest long barrow in England is that inside the hill-fort at Maiden Castle near Dorchester (see Earthworks). It originally had a length of 1800 ft *548 m* and had several enigmatic features such as a ritual pit with pottery, limpet shells and animal bones, but the date of these is not certain. The longest long barrow containing a megalithic chamber is that at West Kennet (*c.* 2200 BC), near Silbury, measuring 385 ft *117 m* in length.

Naturist resorts
The oldest resort is Der Freilichtpark, Klingberg, West Germany established in 1903. The largest

in area in the world is the Beau Valley Country Club, Warmbaths, South Africa extending over 4 million m² *988 acres* with up to 20,000 visitors a year. However, 100,000 people visit the smaller centre Helio-Marin at Cap d'Agde, southern France, which covers 90 ha *222 acres.* The appellation 'nudist camp' is deplored by naturists.

Obelisk (monolithic)
The largest standing obelisk (from the Gk *obeliskos,* skewer or spit) in the world is the obelisk of Tuthmosis III brought from Aswan, Egypt by Emperor Constantius in the spring of AD 357. It was repositioned in the Piazza San Giovanni in Laterane, Rome on 3 Aug 1588. Once 36 m *118.1 ft* tall, it now stands 32,81 m *107.6 ft* and weighs 455 tonnes. The unfinished obelisk, probably commissioned by Queen Hatshepsut *c.* 1490 BC, at Aswan, is 41,75 m *136.8 ft* in length and weighs 1168 tonnes/*tons.* The largest obelisk in the United Kingdom is Cleopatra's Needle on the Embankment, London, which at 68 ft 5 in *20,88 m* is the world's 11th tallest. It weighs 186.3 tons *189,35 tonnes* and was towed up the Thames from Egypt on 21 Jan 1878 and positioned on 13 Sept. The longest an obelisk has remained *in situ* is that still at Heliopolis, near Cairo, erected by Senusret I *c.* 1750 BC.

Pier
The world's longest pier was the Dammam Pier, Saudi Arabia, on the Persian Gulf with an overall length of 6.79 miles *10,93 km.* The work was begun in July 1948 and completed on 15 Mar

1950. The area was subsequently developed by 1980 into the King Abdul Aziz Port with 39 deep-water berths.

The longest pier in Great Britain is the Bee Ness Jetty, completed in 1930, which stretches 8200 ft *2500 m* along the west bank of the River Medway, 5 to 6 miles *8 to 9,6 km* below Rochester, at Kingsnorth, Kent.

Largest pyramid

The largest pyramid, and the largest monument ever constructed, is the Quetzacóatl at Cholula de Rivadabia, 63 miles *101 km* south-east of Mexico City. It is 177 ft *54 m* tall and its base covers an area of nearly 45 acres *18,2 ha*. Its total volume has been estimated at 4,300,000 yd³ *3 300 000 m³* compared with 3,360,000 yd³ *2,5 million m³* for the Pyramid of Cheops (see Seven Wonders of the World). The pyramid-building era here was between the 2nd and 6th centuries AD.

Oldest pyramid

The oldest known pyramid is the Djoser step pyramid at Saqqâra, Egypt constructed by Imhotep to a height of 204 ft *62 m* originally with a Tura limestone casing *c.* 2650 BC. The largest known single block comes from the Third Pyramid (the pyramid of Mycerinus) and weighs 290 tonnes *285 tons*. The oldest New World pyramid is that on the island of La Venta in south-eastern Mexico built by the Olmec people *c.* 800 BC. It stands 100 ft *30 m* tall with a base dimension of 420 ft *128 m*.

Snow construction

The world's largest snow construction is the Ice Palace built in January 1986 using 9,000 blocks of ice at St Paul, Minnesota, during the Winter Carnival. Designed by Ellerbe Associates Inc, it stood 128 ft 9 in *39,24 m* high—the equivalent of a 13-storey building.

The biggest snowman was one built by students of Dartmouth College, New Hampshire, USA during January/February 1987. It stood 47 ft 6 in *14,47 m* and was estimated by the Thayer School of Engineering to weigh 183 tons/*tonnes*.

Stairs

The world's longest stairway is the service staircase for the Niesenbahn funicular which rises to 2365 m *7759 ft* near Spiez, Switzerland. It has 11,674 steps and a bannister. The stone-cut T'ai Chan temple stairs of 6600 steps in the Shantung Mountains, China ascend 4700 feet in 5 miles *1428 m* in *8 km*. The longest spiral staircase is one 1103 ft *336,2 m* deep with 1520 steps installed in the Mapco-White County Coal Mine, Carmi, Illinois by Systems Control Inc in May 1981.

The longest stairs in Britain are those from the transformer gallery to the surface 1065 ft *324 m* in the Cruachan Power Station, Argyll. They have 1420 steps and the plant's work study unit allows 27 min 41.4 sec for the ascent.

Longest statue

Near Bamiyan, Afghanistan there are the remains of the recumbent Sakya Buddha, built of plastered rubble, which was 'about 1000 ft' *305 m* long and is believed to date from the 3rd or 4th century AD.

Tallest statue

The tallest full-figure statue in the world is that of 'Motherland', an enormous pre-stressed concrete female figure on Mamayev Hill, outside Volgograd, USSR, designed in 1967 by Yevgenyi Vuchetich, to commemorate victory in the Battle of Stalingrad (1942–3). The statue from its base to the tip of the sword clenched in her right hand measures 270 ft *82,30 m*.

7 WONDERS

The Seven Wonders of the World were first designated by Antipater of Sidon in the 2nd century BC. They included the Pyramids of Giza, built by three Fourth Dynasty Egyptian Pharaohs, Khwfw (Khufu or Cheops), Khaf-Ra (Khafre, Khefren or Chepren) and Menkaure (Mycerinus) near El Giza (El Gizeh), south-west of El Qâhira (Cairo) in Egypt.

THE GREAT PYRAMID

The 'Horizon of Khufu' was finished under Rededef *c.* 2580 BC. Its original height was 480 ft 11 in *146,5 m* (now, since the loss of its topmost stones and the pyramidion, reduced to 449 ft 6 in *137 m*) with a base line of 756 ft *230 m* and thus covering slightly more than 13 acres *5 ha*. It has been estimated that a permanent work force of 4000 required 30 years to manoeuvre into position the 2,300,000 limestone blocks averaging 2½ tons/*tonnes* each, totalling about 5,750,000 tons *5 840 000 tonnes* and a volume of 90,700,000 ft³ *2 568 000 m³*. Some blocks weigh 15 tons. A costing exercise published in December 1974 indicated that it would require 405 men 6 years at a cost of $1.13 billion (*then £500 million*).

FRAGMENTS REMAIN OF:

The Temple of Artemis (Diana) of the Ephesians, built *c.* 350 BC. at Ephesus, Turkey (destroyed by the Goths in AD 262);

The Tomb of King Mausolus of Caria, at Halicarnassus, now Bodrum, Turkey, *c.* 325 BC.

NO TRACE REMAINS OF:

The Hanging Gardens of Semiramis, at Babylon, Iraq *c.* 600 BC;

The statue of Zeus (Jupiter), by Phidias (5th century BC) at Olympia, Greece (lost in a fire at Istanbul) in marble, gold and ivory and 40 ft *12 m* tall;

The figure of the god Helios (Apollo), the 117 ft *35 m* tall statue by Chares of Lindus called the Colossus of Rhodes (sculptured 292–280 BC, destroyed by an earthquake in 224 BC);

The 400 ft *122 m* tall world's earliest lighthouse, built by Sostratus of Cnidus (*c.* 270 BC) as a pyramidically-shaped tower of white marble (destroyed by earthquake in AD 1375), on the island of Pharos (Greek, *pharos* = lighthouse), off the coast of El Iskandariya (Alexandria), Egypt.

Swing

The tallest swing is a glider swing 30 ft *9,14 m* high and was constructed by Kenneth R. Mack, Langenburg, Saskatchewan, Canada for Uncle Herb's Amusements. The swing is capable of taking its 4 riders 25 ft *7,62 m* off the ground.

Tidal river barrier

The largest tidal river barrier in the world is the £90 million Thames Flood Barrier at Woolwich, London. It has 9 piers and 10 gates. There are 6 rising sector gates 61 m *200 ft 1½ in* wide and 4 falling radial gates 31,5 m *103 ft 4 in* wide. The site was chosen in 1971. It was opened by HM Queen on 8 May 1984.

Tomb

The largest tomb yet discovered is that of Emperor Nintoku (died *c.* AD 428) south of Osaka, Japan. It measures 1594 ft *485 m* long by 1000 ft *305 m* wide by 150 ft *45 m* high.

Totem pole

A totem pole 173 ft *52,73 m* tall was raised on 6 June 1973 at Alert Bay, British Columbia, Canada. It tells the story of the Kwakiutl and took 36 man-weeks to carve.

Vats

The largest vat in the world is named 'Strongbow', and used by H.P. Bulmer Ltd, the English cider makers of Hereford. It measures 64½ ft *19,65 m* in height and 75½ ft *23,0 m* in diameter with a capacity of 1,630,000 gallons *74 099 hl*.

The largest wooden wine cask in the world is the Heidelberg Tun completed in 1751 in the cellar of the Friedrichsbau Heidelberg, West Germany. Its capacity is 1855 hl *40,790 gal*. The world's oldest is that in use since 1715 at Hugelet Fils (founded 1639) Riquewihr, Haut-Rhin by the most recent of the 12 generations of the family.

Wall

The longest of the Roman walls in Britain was the 15–20 ft *4,5–6 m* tall Hadrian's Wall, built AD 122–126. It crossed the Tyne-Solway isthmus for 73½ miles *118 km* from Bowness-on-Solway, Cumbria, to Wallsend-on-Tyne, Tyne and Wear, being abandoned in AD 383.

Water tower

The world's tallest water tower is that at Union, New Jersey, built in 1965 to a height of 210 ft *64 m* with a capacity of 250,000 gal *9462 hl*. The tower is owned and operated by the Elizabethtown Water Company.

Waterwheel

The largest waterwheel in the world is the Mohammadieh Noria wheel at Hamah, Syria with a diameter of 131 ft *40 m* dating from Roman times.

The Lady Isabella wheel at Laxey, Isle of Man is the largest in the British Isles and was built for draining a lead mine. It was completed on 27 Sept 1854, and has been disused since 1929. It has a circumference of 228 ft *69 m*, a diameter of 72½ ft *22 m* and an axle weighing 9 tons/*tonnes*. The largest waterwheel in Britain is the 50 ft 5 in *15,36 m* diameter wheel built in 1870 at Caernarfon, Gwynedd. It worked until 1925 and is 5 ft *1,52 m* in width. It is exhibited and can be seen working at the Welsh Slate Museum, Dinorwic, Llanberis, Gwynedd.

Window

The largest sheet of glass ever manufactured was one of 50 m² *538.2 ft²*, or 20 m *65 ft 7 in* by 2,5 m *8 ft 2½ in*, exhibited by the Saint Gobin Company in France at the *Journées Internationales de Miroiterie* in March 1958. The largest single windows in the world are those in the Palace of Industry and Technology at Rondpoint de la Défense, Paris, with an extreme width of 218 m 715.2 ft and a maximum height of 50 m *164 ft*.

The record for Pilkington of St Helens, Merseyside is a sheet of 2,5 × 15,2 m *8 ft 2¼ × 49 ft 10½ in* made for the Festival of Britain in 1951.

Wine cellar

The largest wine cellars in the world are at Paarl, those of the Ko-operative Wijnbouwers Vereeniging, known as KWV, near Cape Town, in the centre of the wine-growing district of South Africa. They cover an area of 25 acres *10 ha* and have a capacity of 30 million gal *136 million litres*. The Cienega Winery of the Almaden Vineyards in Hollister, California covers 4 acres *1,6 ha* and can house 37,300 oak barrels containing 1.83 million gallons of wine.

Ziggurat

The largest ziggurat ever built was by the Elamite King Untash *c.* 1250 BC known as the

Ziggurat of Choga Zanbil, 30 km *18.6 miles* from Haft Tepe, Iran. The outer base was 105 × 105 m *344 ft* and the fifth 'box' 28 × 28 m *91.8 ft* nearly 50 m *164 ft* above. The largest surviving ziggurat (from the verb *zaqaru*, to build high) or stage-tower is the Ziggurat of Ur (now Muquyyar, Iraq) with a base 61 × 45,7 m *200 × 150 ft* built to three storeys surmounted by a summit temple. The first and part of the second storeys now survive to a height of 60 ft *18 m*. It was built in the reign of Ur-nammu (*c.* 2113–2096 BC).

Borings and Mines

Deepest

Man's deepest penetration into the Earth's crust is a geological exploratory drilling near Zapolarny, Kola peninsula, USSR begun in 1970. By 1987 a depth of 13 km *8.07 miles* or *42,650 ft* was surpassed. Progress has understandably greatly slowed to 500 m *1640 ft* per annum as the eventual target of 15 000 m *49,212 ft* in 1989–90 is neared. The drill bit is mounted on a turbine driven by a mud pump. The temperature at 11 km *6.83 miles* was already 200° C *392° F*.

Ocean drilling

The deepest recorded drilling into the sea bed by the *Glomar Challenger* of the US Deep Sea Drilling Project is one of 5709 ft *1740 m* off northwest Spain in 1976. The deepest site is now 7034 m *23,077 ft* below the surface on the western wall of the Marianas Trench (see page 53) in May 1978.

Oil fields

The world's largest oil field is the Ghawar field, Saudi Arabia developed by ARAMCO which measures 150 miles by 22 miles *240 km by 35 km*.

The area of the designated parts of the UK Continental shelf as at mid 1987 was 651,650 km² *252,000 miles²* with proven and probable reserves of 1330 million tonnes of oil and 634,000 million m³ *22,400,000 million ft³* of gas. Gas was first discovered in the West Sole Field in October 1965 and oil in commercial quantities in the Forties Field (Block 22/17) at 11,000 ft *3352 m* from the drilling barge *Sea Quest* on 18 Sept 1970, though a small gas field was detected near Whitby, North Yorkshire in 1937. The most productive field is BP's Forties Field with 224.7 million tonnes. Production peaked for the UK's 32 oil fields at 127.5 million tonnes. The deepest drilling in British waters is 2400 ft *731 m* in Block 206, west of Shetland by Shell using the drill ship *Petrel* in April 1980.

Gas deposits

The largest gas deposit in the world is at Urengoi, USSR with an eventual production of 200,000 million m³ *261,600 million yd³* per year through 6 pipelines from proved reserves of 7,000,000 million m³ *9,155,600 million yd³*. The trillionth (10¹²) cubic metre was produced on 23 Apr 1986.

Oil platforms

The world's most massive oil platform is the *Statfjord B* concrete gravity-base platform built at Stavanger, Norway owned by the Statfjord Group and operated by Mobil Exploration Norway Inc until 31 Dec 1986. Tow-out to its permanent field took place between 1 and 5 Aug 1981 and it was the heaviest object ever moved— 816,000 tonnes or 803,000 long tons ballasted weight. The £1.1 billion structure was towed by

EARLIEST SEA-GOING BOATS

Aborigines are thought to have been able to cross the Torres Strait from New Guinea to Australia, then at least 70 km *43½ miles* across, at least as early as 40,000 BC. They are believed to have used double canoes. The earliest *surviving* 'vessel' is a pinewood dug-out found in Pesse, Netherlands and dated to *c.* 6315 ± 275 BC and now in the Provincial Museum, Assen. The earliest representation of a boat is disputed between possible rock art outlines of Mesolithic skin-boats in Høgnipen, Norway (*c.* 8000–7000 BC); Minateda, Spain (7000–3000 BC) and Kobystan, USSR (8000–6000 BC). An 18 in *45 cm* long paddle was found at the Star Carr, North Yorkshire site, described in 1948. It has been dated to *c.* 7600 BC and is now in the Cambridge Museum of Archaeology.

The oldest surviving boat is a 27 ft *8,2 m* long 2.5 ft *0,76 m* wide wooden eel-catching canoe discovered at Tybrind Vig on the Baltic Island of Fünen which is dated to *c.* 4490 BC.

The oldest shipwreck ever found is one of a Cycladic trading vessel located off the islet of Dhókós, near the Greek island of Hydra, reported in May 1975 and dated to 2450 BC ± 250.

Earliest power

Propulsion by steam engine was first achieved when in 1783 the Marquis Jouffroy d'Abbans (1751–1832) ascended a reach of the river Saône near Lyon, France, in the 180-tonne paddle steamer *Pyroscaphe*.

The tug *Charlotte Dundas* was the first successful power-driven vessel. She was a stern paddle-wheel steamer built for the Forth and Clyde Canal, Scotland in 1801–2 by William Symington (1763–1831), using a double-acting condensing engine constructed by James Watt (1736–1819). The screw propeller was invented and patented by a Kent farmer, Sir Francis Pettit Smith (1808–71) on 31 May 1836 (Brit. Pat. No 7104).

Oldest vessels

The oldest mechanically-propelled boat in the world of certain date is the 48-ton Bristol-built steam-driven dredger or drag-boat *Bertha* of 50 ft *15,42 m*, designed by I. K. Brunel (1806–59) in 1844 and afloat in the custody of Exeter Maritime Museum, Devon, England. Mr G. H. Pattinson's 40 ft *12,20 m* steam launch *Dolly*, which was raised after 67 years from Ullswater, Cumbria, in 1962, and now on Lake Windermere, also probably dates from the 1840s. The world's oldest active steam ship is the paddle steamer *Skibladner*, which has plied Lake Mjøsa, Norway since 1856. She was built in Motala, Sweden and has had two major refits. The oldest motor vessel afloat in British waters is the *Proven* on the run from the Clyde to the Inner Hebrides. She was built in Norway in 1866. The oldest vessel on *Lloyd's Yacht Register* is the twin-screw steam yacht *Esperance* built on the Clyde in 1869 and salvaged from Windermere in 1941.

The future of the sail training ship HMS *Foudroyant*, built in Bombay in 1857, was forced into 'mothballs' in Portsmouth Harbour in 1987 due to repair costs.

Earliest turbine

The first turbine ship was the *Turbinia*, built in 1894 at Wallsend-on-Tyne, Tyne and Wear, to the design of the Hon. Sir Charles Parsons OM, KCB (1854–1931). The *Turbinia* was 100 ft *30,48 m* long and of 44½ tons *45,2 tonnes* displacement with machinery consisting of three steam turbines totalling about 2000 shaft horsepower. At her first public demonstration in 1897 she reached 34.5 knots (39.7 mph *63,9 km/h*) and is now preserved at Newcastle-upon-Tyne.

PASSENGER LINERS

Largest

The world's largest and the world's longest ever liner is the *Norway* of 70,202.19 grt and 315,66 m *1035 ft 7½ in* in overall length with a capacity of 2400 passengers. She was built as the *France* in 1961 and renamed after purchase in June 1979 by Knut Kloster of Norway. Her second maiden voyage was from Southampton on 7 May 1980. Britain's largest liner is RMS *Queen Elizabeth 2* at 67,140 gross tons and with an overall length of 963 ft *293 m*, completed for Cunard Line in 1969. She set a 'turn round' record of 5 hr 47 min at New York on 21 Nov 1983. Her original steam turbine machinery was replaced with diesel electric units in April 1987.

The RMS *Queen Elizabeth* (finally 82,998 but formerly 83,673 gross tons), of the Cunard fleet, was the largest passenger vessel ever built and had the largest displacement of any liner in the world. She had an overall length of 1031 ft *314 m*, was 118 ft 7 in *36 m* in breadth and was powered by steam turbines which developed 168,000 hp. Her last passenger voyage ended on 15 Nov 1968. In 1970 she was removed to Hong Kong to serve as a floating marine university and renamed *Seawise University*. She was burnt out on 9 Jan 1972 when 3 *simultaneous* outbreaks of fire strongly pointed to arson. The gutted hull had been cut up and removed by 1978. *Seawise* was a pun on the owner's initials—C. Y. Tung (1911–1982).

WARSHIPS

Largest battleships

The largest battleship in service in the world is the 887 ft 9 in *270,6 m* long USS *New Jersey* with a full load displacement of 58,000 tons *58 000 tonnes*. She was the last fire support ship on active service off the Lebanon coast with her nine 16-in guns from 14 Dec 1983 to 26 Feb 1984. The $405-million refit of USS *Iowa* was completed in May 1984. USS *Missouri* and USS *Wisconsin* have also been re-activated. The 16-inch projectiles of 2700 lb *1225 kg* can be fired 23 miles *39 km*.

The Japanese battleships *Yamato* (completed on 16 Dec 1941 and sunk south-west of Kyūshū, Japan, by US planes on 7 Apr 1945) and *Musashi* (sunk in the Philippine Sea by 11 bombs and 16 torpedoes on 24 Oct 1944) were the largest battleships ever commissioned, each with a full load displacement of 72,809 tons *73 977 tonnes*. With an overall length of 863 ft *263 m*, a beam of 127 ft *38,7 m* and a full load draught of 35½ ft *10,8 m* they mounted nine 460 mm *18.1 in* guns in three triple turrets. Each gun weighed 162 tons *164,6 tonnes* and was 75 ft *22,8 m* in length firing a 3200 lb *1451 kg* projectile.

Britain's largest ever and last battleship was HMS *Vanguard* (1944–1960) with a full load displacement of 51,420 tons *52 245 tonnes* and an overall length of 814 ft *248,1 m*. She mounted eight 15 in *38 cm* guns.

Guns and armour

The largest guns ever mounted in any of HM ships were the 18 in *45 cm* pieces in the light battle cruiser (later aircraft carrier) HMS *Furious* in 1917. In 1918 they were transferred to the monitors HMS *Lord Clive* and *General Wolfe*. The thickest armour ever carried was in HMS *Inflexible* (completed 1881), measuring 24 in *60 cm* backed by teak up to a maximum thickness of 42 in *106,6 cm*.

Fastest destroyer

The highest speed attained by a destroyer was 45.25 knots (51.84 mph *83,42 km/h*) by the 2830 ton/*tonne* French destroyer *Le Terrible* in 1935. She was built in Blainville and powered by four Yarrow small tube boilers and two Rateau geared turbines giving 100,000 shaft horsepower. She was removed from the active list at the end of 1957.

AIRCRAFT CARRIERS

Largest

The warships with the largest full load displacement in the world are the Nimitz class US Navy aircraft carriers USS *Nimitz, Dwight D. Eisenhower, Carl Vinson, Theodore Roosevelt* and *Abraham Lincoln* at 91,487 tons. They are 1092 ft *322,9 m* in length overall with 4½ acres *1,82 ha* of flight deck and have a speed well in excess of 30 knots *56 km/h* from their 4 nuclear-powered 260,000 shp geared steam turbines. They have to be refuelled after about 900,000 miles *1 450 000 km* steaming. Their complement is 5,684. The total cost of the *Abraham Lincoln*, laid down at Newport News on 3 Nov 1984, will exceed, together with the *George Washington*, $3½ billion (*£2.6 billion*), excluding the 90-plus aircraft carried. USS *Enterprise* is, however, 1102 ft *335,8 m* long and thus still the longest warship ever built.

The Royal Navy's largest fighting ship is the aircraft carrier HMS *Ark Royal*, commissioned 1 Nov 1983. She has a 550 ft *167,6 m* long flight deck and is 685.8 ft *209,03 m* long overall, and has a top speed of 28 knots being powered by 4 Rolls Royce Olympus TM3B gas turbines delivering 94,000 shp.

Most landings

The greatest number of landings on an aircraft carrier in one day was 602 achieved by Marine Air Group 6 of the United States Pacific Fleet Air Force aboard the USS *Matanikau* on 25 May 1945 between 8 a.m. and 5 p.m.

SUBMARINES

Largest

The world's largest submarines are of the USSR Typhoon class code named Oscar. The launch of the first at the secret covered shipyard at Severodvinsk in the White Sea was announced by NATO on 23 Sept 1980. They are believed to have a dived displacement of 25,000 tonnes, measure 170 m *557.6 ft* overall and be armed with twenty SS NX 20 missiles with a 4,800 nautical mile *8895 km* range, each with 7 warheads. By late 1987 two others built in Leningrad are expected to be operational, each deploying 140 warheads.

The largest submarines ever built for the Royal Navy are the four atomic-powered nuclear missile R class boats with a surface displacement of 7500 tons *7620 tonnes* and 8400 tons *8534 tonnes* submerged, a length of 425 ft *129,5 m*, a beam of 33 ft *10 m* and a draught of 30 ft *9,1 m*. The longest submarine patrol ever spent dived and unsupported is 111 days by HM Submarine *Warspite* (Cdr J. G. F. Cooke RN) in the South Atlantic from 25 Nov 1982 to 15 Mar 1983. She sailed 30,804 nautical miles *57 085 km*.

Fastest

The Russian Alfa-class nuclear-powered submarines have a reported maximum speed of 42 knots *77,8 km/h* plus. With use of titanium alloy they are believed to be able to dive to 2500 ft *762 m*. A US spy satellite over Leningrad's naval yard on 8 June 1983 showed they were being lengthened and are now 79.3 m *260.1 ft* long.

Deepest

The two USN vessels able to descend 12,000 ft *3650 m* are the 3-man *Trieste II* (DSV I) of 303 tons (recommissioned in November 1973) and the DSV 2 (deep submergence vessel) USS *Alvin*.

The *Trieste II* was reconstructed from the record-breaking bathyscaphe *Trieste* but without the Krupp-built sphere, which enabled it to descend to 35,820 ft *10 917 m.* (See Chapter 10, Greatest ocean descent.)

TANKERS

Largest

The world's largest tanker and ship of any kind is the 564,739-tonne deadweight *Seawise Giant* completed for C. Y. Tung in 1976. She is 458,45 m *1504 ft* long overall with a beam of 68,86 m *225 ft 11 in* and has a draught of 24,61 m *80 ft 9 in.* She had been lengthened by Nippon Kokan in 1980 by adding an 81 m *265 ft 8 in* midship section.

CARGO VESSELS

Largest

The largest vessel in the world capable of carrying dry cargo is the Norwegian ore carrier *Berge Stahl,* of 364,767 dwt, built in South Korea for the Norwegian owner Sig Bergesen. It has a length of 342 m *1122 ft,* a beam measuring 63,5 m *208 ft* and was launched on 5 Nov 1986. The largest British ore/oil carriers are Lombard North Central Leasing's *Rapana* and *Rimula* built in Sweden in 1973 and 1974 of 121,164 grt, *227,412 dwt* with lengths of 332,77 m *1091 ft 9 in.*

Whale factory

The largest whale factory ship is the USSR's *Sovietskaya Ukraina* (32,034 gross tons), with a summer deadweight of 46,000 tons *46 738 tonnes* completed in October 1959. She is 217,8 m *714 ft 6 in* in length and 25,8 m *84 ft 7 in* in the beam.

Barges

The world's largest RoRo (roll-on, roll-off) ships are four *El Rey* class barges of 16,700 tons and 580 ft *176,78 m* in length. They were built by the FMC Corp of Portland, Oregon, and are operated by Crowley Maritime Corp of San Francisco between Florida and Puerto Rico with tri-level lodging of up to 376 truck-trailers.

Container ship

Shipborne containerisation began in 1955 when the tanker *Ideal X* was converted by Malcom McLean (US). She carried containers only on deck.

The world's largest container ships are the twelve built for United States Lines in Korea in 1984–5. They are capable of carrying 4482 TEU (20ft equivalent units—20 ft *6,1 m* containers) and have a gross tonnage of 57,075. They are named *American Alabama, American California, Illinois, Kentucky,* etc.

Tugs

The world's most powerful tug is the *Smit Singapore* commissioned in April 1984 by Smit Tak International, of 22,000 horsepower and 189 tons bollard pull at full power. It is 75,2 m *246.72 ft* long and 15,68 m *51.44 ft* wide.

Car ferry

The world's largest car and passenger ferry is the 37,800 grt M/S *Olympia* which entered service across the Baltic between Helsinki and Stockholm on 28 Apr 1986. Built in Åbo, Finland for the Viking Line, she is 177,10 m *581 ft* long, 29 m *95 ft* in the beam and can carry 2500 passengers and 600 cars.

The 9700-dwt 21-knot *Railship II* went into service on the Baltic run in November 1984. She can carry 88 20 m *65 ft 7 in* long rail cars, is 186,5 m *611 ft 10 in* overall and was built for HM Gehrckens of Hamburg.

Propeller

The world's largest ship propeller is the triple-bladed screw of 11,0 m *36 ft 1 in* diameter made by Kawasaki Heavy Industries on 17 Mar 1982 for the 208,000-ton bulk carrier *Hoei Maru.*

Hydrofoil

The world's largest naval hydrofoil is the 212 ft *64,6 m* long *Plainview* (310 tons *314 tonnes* full load), launched by the Lockheed Shipbuilding and Construction Co at Seattle, Washington State on 28 June 1965. She has a service speed of 50 knots (57 mph *92 km/h*). Three 165-ton Supramar PTS 150 Mk III hydrofoils carry 250 passengers at 40 knots *74 km/h* across the Öre Sound between Malmö and Copenhagen. They were built by Westermoen Hydrofoil Ltd of Mandal, Norway. A 500-ton wing ground effect vehicle capable of carrying 900 tons has been reported in the USSR.

River boat

The world's largest inland river boat is the 378 ft *115,2 m* long SS *Admiral* now undergoing a 6-year $26.7 million renovation at St Louis, Missouri as a Mississippi river 'floating entertainment centre'.

Building

The fastest times in which complete ships of more than 10,000 tons were ever built were achieved at Kaiser's Yard, Portland during the war-time programme for building 2,742 Liberty ships in 18 yards from 27 Sept 1941. In 1942 No 440, named *Robert E. Peary,* had her keel laid on 8 Nov, was launched on 12 Nov, and was operational after 4 days 15 hrs on 15 November. She was broken up in 1963.

Largest and most powerful icebreakers

A 61,000 ton/*tonne* nuclear-powered barge-carrying merchantman designed for work along the USSR's arctic coast was completed in early 1982 and is known to be designed to break ice. The longest purpose-built icebreaker is the 25,000-ton 460 ft *140 m* long *Rossiya*, powered by 75,000 hp nuclear engines built in Leningrad and completed in 1985. A new $Can500-million, 100,000-hp, 194 m *636 ft* long icebreaker of the Polar Class 8 was ordered by the Canadian Government in October 1985.

The largest *converted* icebreaker has been the 1007 ft *306,9 m* long SS *Manhattan* (43,000 shp), which was converted by the Humble Oil Co into a 150,000 ton *152 407 tonne* icebreaker with an armoured prow 69 ft 2 in long. She made a double voyage through the North-West Passage in arctic Canada from 24 Aug to 12 Nov 1969. The Passage was first navigated by Roald Engebereth Gravning Amundsen (Norway) (1872–1928) in the sealing sloop *Gjöa* on 11 July 1906.

Yacht

The fitting out of the £20-million 470 foot *143,2 m* Saudi Arabian royal yacht *Abdul Aziz*, built in Denmark, was completed on 22 June 1984 at Vospers Yard, Southampton at a cost of £9 million. The longest private yacht is the 282 ft *85,9 m Nabila* originally cost some $29 million.

Dredger

The world's most powerful dredger is the 468.4 ft *142,7 m* long *Prins der Nederlanden* of 10,586 grt.

Ships

She can dredge 20,000 tonnes/tons of sand from a depth of 35 m *115 ft* via two suction tubes in less than an hour.

Wooden ship

The heaviest wooden ship ever built was the *Richelieu*, 333 ft 8 in *101,70 m* long and of 8534 tons launched in Toulon, France on 3 Dec 1873. HM battleship *Lord Warden*, completed in 1869, displaced 7940 tons *8060 tonnes*. The longest modern wooden ship ever built was the New York-built *Rochambeau* (1867–72) formerly *Dunderberg*. She measured 377 ft 4 in *115 m* overall. *It should be noted that the biblical length of Noah's Ark was 300 cubits or, at 18 in 45,7 cm to a cubit, 450 ft 137 m.*

Human powered

The largest human-powered ship was the giant *Tessarakonteres* 3-banked catamaran galley with 4000 rowers built for Ptolemy IV *c.* 210 BC in Alexandria, Egypt. It measured 128 m *420 ft* with up to 8 men to an oar of 38 cubits (17,5 m *57 ft*) in length. The world's longest canoe is the 117 ft *35,7 m* long 20-ton Kauri wood Maori war canoe *Nga Toki Matawhaorua* built by adzes at Kerikeri Inlet, New Zealand in 1940 for a crew of 70 or more. The 'Snake Boat' *Nadubhagóm*, 135 ft *41,1 m* long from Kerala, southern India has a crew of 109 rowers and 9 'encouragers'.

Light vessels

The earliest station still marked by a light vessel is the Newarp in the North Sea, off Great Yarmouth in 1791. A Nore light vessel was first placed in the Thames estuary in 1732.

SAILING SHIPS

Largest

The largest vessel ever built in the era of sail was the *France II* (5806 gross tons), launched at Bordeaux in 1911. The *France II* was a steel-hulled, five-masted barque (square-rigged on four masts and fore and aft rigged on the aftermost mast). Her hull measured 418 ft *127,4 m* overall. Although principally designed as a sailing vessel with a stump topgallant rig, she was also fitted with two steam engines. She was wrecked off New Caledonia on 13 July 1922. The only seven-masted sailing schooner ever built was the 375.6 ft *114,4 m* long *Thomas W. Lawson* (5218 gross tons) built at Quincy, Massachusetts in 1902 and lost off the Isles of Scilly on 15 Dec 1907.

The world's only surviving First Rate Ship-of-the-Line is the Royal Navy's 104-gun battleship HMS *Victory* laid down at Chatham, Kent on 23 July 1759 and constructed from the wood of some 2200 oak trees. She bore the body of Admiral Nelson from Gibraltar to Portsmouth arriving 44 days after serving as his victorious flagship at the Battle of Trafalgar of 21 Oct 1805. In 1922 she was moved to No 2 dock, Portsmouth—site of the world's oldest graving dock. The length of her cordage (both standing and running rigging) is 100,962 ft (19.12 miles *30,77 km*).

Largest junks

The largest junk on record was the sea-going *Cheng Ho*, flagship of Admiral Cheng Ho's 62 treasure ships, of *c.* 1420, with a displacement of 3100 tons *3150 tonnes* and a length variously estimated up to 538 ft *164 m* and believed to have had 9 masts. A river junk 361 ft *110 m* long, with treadmill-operated paddle-wheels, was recorded in AD 1161. In *c.* AD 280 a floating fortress 600 ft *182,8 m* square, built by Wang Chün on the Yangtze, took part in the Chin-Wu river war. Present-day junks do not, even in the case of the Chiangsu traders, exceed 170 ft *51,8 m* in length.

Longest day's run under sail

The longest day's run calculated for any commercial vessel under sail was one of 462 nautical miles (532.0 statute miles *856,16 km*) by the clipper *Champion of the Seas* (2722 registered tons) of the Liverpool Black Ball Line running before a north-westerly gale in the south Indian Ocean under the command of Capt Alex Newlands in 1854. The elapsed time between the fixes was 23 hr 17 min giving an average of 19.97 knots *37,00 km/h* (see Chapter 12 Yachting for sporting record).

Largest sails

Sails are known to have been used for marine propulsion since 3500 BC. The largest spars ever carried were those in HM battleship *Temeraire*, completed at Chatham, Kent, on 31 Aug 1877. She was broken up in 1921. The fore and main yards measured 115 ft *35 m* in length. The foresail contained 5100 ft² of canvas, weighing 2 tons *2,03 tonnes* and the total sail area was 25,000 ft² *2322 m²*. HM battleship *Sultan* was ship-rigged when completed at Chatham, Kent on 10 Oct 1871 and carried 34,100 ft² *3168 m²* of sails plus 15,300 ft² *1421 m²* of stunsails. She was broken up in 1946.

Largest wreck

The largest ship ever wrecked has been the 312,186-dwt VLCC (Very Large Crude Carrier) *Energy Determination* which blew up and broke in two in the Straits of Hormuz on 12 Dec 1979. Her full value was $58 million (*then £26.3 million*). The largest wreck removal was carried out in 1979 by Smit Tak International who removed the remains of the French tanker *Betelguese*, 120,000 tons, from Bantry Bay, Ireland, within 20 months.

Most massive collision

The closest approach to an irresistible force striking an immovable object occurred on 16 Dec 1977, 22 miles *35 km* off the coast of southern Africa when the tanker *Venoil* (330,954 dwt) struck her sister ship *Venpet* (330,869 dwt).

OCEAN CROSSINGS

Atlantic *Earliest*

The earliest crossing of the Atlantic by a power vessel, as opposed to an auxiliary-engined sailing ship, was a 22-day voyage begun in April 1827, from Rotterdam to the West Indies by the *Curaçao*. She was a 127 ft *38,7 m* wooden paddle boat of 438 tons, built as the *Calpe* in Dover in 1826 and purchased by the Dutch Government for the West Indian mail service. The earliest Atlantic crossing entirely under steam (with intervals for desalting the boilers) was by HMS *Rhadamanthus* from Plymouth to Barbados in 1832. The earliest crossing under continuous steam power was by the condenser-fitted packet ship *Sirius* (703 tons *714 tonnes*) from Queenstown (now Cóbh), Ireland, to Sandy Hook, New Jersey in 18 days 10 hr on 4–22 Apr 1838.

Atlantic *Fastest*

The fastest Atlantic crossing was made by the *United States* (then 51,988, now 38,216 gross tons), former flagship of the United States Lines. On her maiden voyage between 3 and 7 July 1952 from New York to Le Havre and Southampton, she averaged 35.39 knots, or 40.98 mph *65,95 km/h* for 3 days 10 hr 40 min (6.36 p.m. GMT, 3 July to 5.16 a.m., 7 July) on a route of 2949 nautical miles *5465 km* from the Ambrose Light Vessel to the Bishop Rock Light, Isles of Scilly. During this run, on 6–7 July 1952, she steamed the greatest distance ever covered by any ship in a day's run (24 hr)—868 nautical miles *1609 km*, hence averaging 36.17 knots (41.65 mph *67,02 km/h*). The maximum speed attained from her 240,000-shp engines was 38.32 knots (44.12 mph *71,01 km/h*) in trials on 9–10 June 1952.

Pacific *Fastest*

The fastest crossing of the Pacific Ocean from Yokohama to Long Beach, California (4840 nautical miles *8960 km*) was 6 days 1 hr 27 min (30 June–6 July 1973) by the container ship *Sea-Land Commerce* (50,315 tons) at an average of 33.27 knots (38.31 mph *61,65 km/h*).

Channel crossing *Fastest*

The fastest crossing of the English Channel by a commercial ferry is 52 min 49 sec from Dover to Calais by Townsend Thoresen's *Pride of Free Enterprise* in a near gale of Force 7 on 9 Feb 1982.

HOVERCRAFT (skirted air-cushion vehicles)

Earliest

The ACV (air-cushion vehicle) was first made a practical proposition by Sir Christopher Sydney Cockerell CBE, FRS (b. 4 June 1910), a British engineer who had the idea in 1954, published his Ripplecraft report 1/55 on 25 Oct 1955 and patented it on 12 Dec 1955. The earliest patent relating to air-cushion craft was applied for in 1877 by John I. Thornycroft (1843–1928) of Chiswick, London and the Finn Toivo Kaario developed the idea in 1935. The first flight by a hovercraft was made by the 4 ton/*tonne* Saunders-Roe SR-N1 at Cowes on 30 May 1959. With a 1500 lb *680 kg* thrust Viper turbojet engine, this craft reached 68 knots *126 km/h* in June 1961. The first hovercraft public service was run across the Dee estuary by the 60 knot *111 km/h* 24-passenger Vickers-Armstrong VA-3 between July and September 1962.

Largest

The world's largest civil hovercraft is the 305-ton British-built SRN4 Mk III. It has a capacity of 418 passengers and 60 cars. It is 185 ft *56,38 m* in length, is powered by 4 Bristol Siddeley Marine Proteus engines giving a maximum speed in excess of the permitted cross-Channel operating speed of 65 knots.

Fastest warship

The world's fastest warship is the 78 ft *23,7 m* long 100 ton/*tonne* US Navy test vehicle SES-100B. She attained a world record 91.9 knots *105.8 mph* on 25 Jan 1980 on the Chesapeake Bay Test Range, Maryland. The 3000-ton US Navy Large Surface Effect Ship (LSES) was built by Bell Aerospace under contract from the Department of Defense in 1977–81.

Longest flight

The longest hovercraft journey was one of 5000 miles *8047 km* through eight West African countries between 15 Oct 1969 and 3 Jan 1970 by the British Trans-African Hovercraft Expedition.

Cross channel

The fastest crossing of the Channel was achieved by an SRN4 Mk II Mountbatten Class Hovercraft operated by Hoverspeed on 1 Sep 1984 when *The Swift* completed the Dover–Calais run in 24 min 8.4 secs.

Highest

The greatest altitude at which a hovercraft is operating is on Lake Titicaca, Peru, where since 1975 an HM2 Hoverferry has been hovering 12,506 ft *3811 m* above sea level.

Road Vehicles

COACHING

Before the widespread use of tarred road surfaces from 1845 coaching was slow and hazardous. The zenith was reached on 13 July 1888 when J. Selby Esq. drove the *Old Times* coach 108 miles *173 km* from London to Brighton and back with 8 teams and 14 changes in 7 hr 50 min to average 13.79 mph *22,19 km/h*. Four-horse carriages could maintain a speed of 21¼ mph *34 km/h* for nearly an hour. The *Border Union* stage coach, built *c.* 1825, ran 4 in hand

from Edinburgh to London (393 miles *632 km*). When it ceased in 1842, due to competition from railways, the allowed schedule was 42 hr 23 min to average better than 9¼ mph *14,9 km/h*.

John Parker (b. July 1939) drove a mail coach and four horses 136 miles *218,8 km* from Bristol to London in 17 hr 30 mins on 1–2 Aug 1984. Norwich Union's six teams of greys were changed 11 times while an estimated 1 million people lined the route.

The record for changing a team of four horses by a team of 12 ostlers is 25.02 sec set at Wingfield, Norfolk on 29 July 1986, by the Norwich Union Mercury Mail Coach team led by driver John Parker.

MOTOR CARS

Most cars

For 1984 it was estimated that the United States, with 168,607,000 vehicles, passed 37.9 per cent of the total world stock of 411,113,000. In 1986 the American automobile industry sold an all-time record 16.3 million vehicles including 8,214,671 domestically-built cars retail. Of the latter General Motors sold 4,532,798.

Earliest automobiles *Model*

The earliest automobile of which there is record is a two-foot-long steam-powered model constructed by Ferdinand Verbiest (d. 1687), a Belgian Jesuit priest, and described in his *Astronomia Europaea*. His model of 1668 was possibly inspired either by Giovanni Branca's description of a steam turbine, published in his *La Macchina* in 1629, or by writings on 'fire carts' or *Nan Huai-Jen* in the Chu dynasty (*c.* 800 BC).

Passenger-carrying

The earliest full-scale automobile was the first of two military steam tractors, completed at the

Longest horse-drawn procession ● 'Nose to tail' this cavalcade of 68 carriages measured 920 m *3018 ft*. Organised by the Spies Travelling Company of Denmark, on 7 May 1986 it carried 810 people through the woods around Copenhagen to celebrate the coming of spring.

Paris Arsenal in 1769 by Nicolas-Joseph Cugnot (1725–1804). This reached 2¼ mph *3,6 km/h*. Cugnot's second, larger tractor, completed in May 1771, today survives in the *Conservatoire nationale des arts et métiers* in Paris. The world's first passenger-carrying automobile was a steam-powered road vehicle carrying eight passengers and built by Richard Trevithick (1771–1833). It first ran on 24 Dec 1801 in Camborne, Cornwall.

Internal combustion

The Swiss Isaac de Rivaz (d. 1828) built a carriage powered by his 'explosion engine' in 1805. The first practical internal-combustion-engined vehicle was that built by the Londoner Samuel Brown (Patent 5350, 25 Apr 1826) whose 4 hp *4,05 cv* two-cylinder atmospheric gas 88-litre engined carriage climbed Shooters Hill, Blackheath, Kent in May 1826. Britain's continuous motoring history started in November 1894 when Henry Hewetson drove his imported Benz Velo in the south-eastern suburbs of London. The first successful petrol-driven car, the Motorwagen, built by Karl-Friedrich Benz (1844–1929) of Karlsruhe, ran at Mannheim, Germany, in late 1885. It was a 5 cwt *250 kg* 3-wheeler reaching 8–10 mph *13–16 km/h*. Its single-cylinder 4-stroke chain-drive engine (bore 91,4 mm, stroke 160 mm) delivered 0.85 hp *0,86 cv* at 200 rpm. It was patented on 29 Jan 1886. Its first 1-km road test was reported in the local newspaper, the *Neue Badische Landeszeitung*, of 4 June 1886, under the heading 'Miscellaneous'. Two were built in 1885 of which one has been preserved in

'running order' at the Deutsches Museum, Munich.

Registrations *Earliest and most expensive*
The world's first plates were probably introduced by the Parisian police in 1893. Registration plates were introduced in Britain in 1903. The original A1 plate was secured by the 2nd Earl Russell (1865–1931) for his 12 hp *12,1 cv* Napier. This plate, willed in September 1950 to Trevor T. Laker of Leicester, was sold in August 1959 for £2500 in aid of charity. By April 1986, prices for plates reached £25,000. Licence plate No 3 was reported in Jan 1984 to have been sold at a Hong Kong government auction for £94,000.

FASTEST CARS

Diesel engined

The prototype 230-hp 3-litre Mercedes C 111/3 attained 327,3 km/h *203.3 mph* in tests on the Nardo Circuit, southern Italy on 5–15 Oct 1978, and in April 1978 averaged 195.398 mph *314,462 km/h* for 12 hours, so covering a world record 2399.76 miles *3773,55 km*.

Rocket-powered sleds

The highest speed recorded on ice is 247.93 mph *399,00 km/h* by *Oxygen* driven by Sammy Miller (b. 15 Apr 1945) on Lake George, NY, on 15 Feb 1981.

Steam car

On 19 Aug 1985 Robert E. Barber broke the 79-year-old record for a steam car driving No 744 *Steamin' Demon*, built by the Barber-Nichols Engineering Co, 145.607 mph *234,33 km/h* at Bonneville Salt Flats, Utah.

Road cars

Various detuned track cars have been licensed for road use but are not for-sale production models. Manufacturers of very fast and very

FASTEST CARS FASTEST CARS FASTEST CARS FASTEST CARS FASTEST CARS

CATEGORY	MPH	KM/H	CAR	DRIVER	PLACE	DATE
Jet Engined (*official*)	633.468	1019,4	Thrust 2	Richard Noble (UK)	Black Rock Desert Nevada, USA	4 Oct 1983
Rocket Engined (*official*)	622.287	1001,473	Blue Flame	Gary Gabelich (US)	Bonneville, Utah, USA	23 Oct 1970
Wheel Driven (*turbine*)	429.311	690,909	Bluebird	Donald Campbell (UK)	Lake Eyre, Australia	17 July 1964
Wheel Driven (*multi-piston engine*)	418.504	673,516	Goldenrod	Robert Summers (US)	Bonneville, Utah, USA	12 Nov 1965
Wheel Driven (*single-piston engine*)	357.391	575,149	Herda-Knapp-Milodon	Bob Herda (US)	Bonneville, Utah, USA	2 Nov 1967
Rocket Engined (*unofficial*)*	739.666	1190,377	Budweiser Rocket	Stan Barrett (US)	Edwards Air Force Base, California, USA	17 Dec 1979

* This published speed of Mach 1.0106 is *not* officially sanctioned by the USAF whose Digital Instrumented Radar was not calibrated or certified. The radar information was *not* generated by the vehicle directly but by an operator aiming the dish by means of a TV screen. To claim a speed to 6 significant figures appears quite unsustainable.

expensive models understandably limit speed tests to stipulated engine revs. The fastest current manufacturer's *claim* (as opposed to an independent road test) for any road car is the Porsche 959, a limited edition road car announced in April 1986 with a top speed of 205 mph at 7500 rpm. The highest road-tested acceleration reported is 0–60 mph *0–96,5 km/h* in 4.1 sec for an MG Metro 6R4 International Rally Car in 1986.

LARGEST CARS

Of cars produced for private road use, the largest has been the Bugatti 'Royale' type 41, known in Britain as the 'Golden Bugatti', of which only six (not seven) were made at Molsheim, France by the Italian Ettore Bugatti, and all survive. First built in 1927, this machine has an 8-cylinder engine of 12,7 litres capacity, and measures over 22 ft *6,7 m* in length. The bonnet is over 7 ft *2 m* long.

Of custom-built cars the longest is the 16-wheeled 60 ft *18,3 m* long Cadillac limousine 'American Dream' created by Jay Ohrberg Show Cars of Newport Beach, California. It features a swimming pool, hot tub, helipad, satellite dish, crystal chandelier and has 'ample luggage space'.

Largest engines

The world's most powerful piston engine car is 'Quad Al'. It was designed and built in 1964 by Jim Lytle and was first shown in May 1965 at the Los Angeles Sports Arena. The car featured four Allison V12 aircraft engines with a total of 6840 in³ *112 087 cc* displacement and 12,000 hp. It has 4-wheel drive, 8 wheels and tyres, and dual 6-disc clutch assemblies. The wheelbase is 160 in *406,4 cm*, and weighs 5860 lb *2658 kg*. It also has 96 spark plugs and 96 exhaust pipes.

The largest car ever used was the 'White Triplex', sponsored by J. H. White of Philadelphia, Pennsylvania. Completed early in 1928, after two years' work, the car weighed about 4 tons *4,06 tonnes* and was powered by three Liberty V12 aircraft engines with a total capacity of 81 188 cc, developing 1500 bhp at 2000 rpm. It was used to break the world speed record but crashed at Daytona, Florida on 13 Mar 1929.

Currently the most powerful car on the road is the 6-wheeled Jameson-Merlin, powered by a 27 000 cc 1760 hp Rolls Royce V12 Merlin aero-

engine, governed down to a maximum speed of 185 mph *298 km/h*. It has a range of 300 miles *480 km* with tanks of 60 gal *272 litres* capacity. The vehicle weighs 2.65 tons *2,69 tonnes* overall.

Production car

The highest engine capacity of a production car was 13½ litres *824 in³*, for the US Pierce-Arrow 6-66 Raceabout of 1912–18, the US Peerless 6–60 of 1912–14 and the Fageol of 1918. The most powerful current production car is the Lamborghini Countach 5000S quattro-valvole with a 5167 cc V12 engine developing 455 bhp.

Engine change

The fastest time recorded for removing a car engine and replacing it is 42 sec for a Ford Escort by a Royal Marine team of five from Portsmouth, on 21 Nov 1985 on the BBC *Record Breakers* programme.

Petrol consumption

On 29 May 1986 at the Shell Oakville Research Center test track at Ontario, Canada, Tim Leier of the University of Saskatchewan, Saskatoon covered a distance of 5691 miles *9158 km* on one gallon *4,54 litre* although subsequently figures of 5107 mpg and 5691 mpg have been reported from Australia and Canada respectively.

> **Fastest car** ● The highest road-tested speed for a production car is 190.1 mph *305,8 km/h* for the Lamborghini Countach QV 5000 S. (Photo: Courtesy of Cliff Barron)

Longest fuel range

The greatest distance driven without refuelling on a tankful of fuel (19.4 l galls *88,12 l*) is 1150.3 miles *1851,2 km* by an Audi 100 turbo diesel driven by Stuart Bladon with his son Bruce (navigator) and Bob Proctor (RAC observer) from Land's End to John O'Groats and back to West Falkirk in 22 hrs 28 min in July 1984. The average speed was 51.17 mph *82,33 km/h* giving 59.27 mpg *4,77 l/100 km*.

Most durable car

The highest recorded mileage for a car was 1,184,880 authenticated miles *1 906 879 km* by August 1978 for a 1957 Mercedes 180 D owned by Robert O'Reilly of Olympia, Washington State. Its subsequent fate is unknown. R. L. Bender of Madison, Wisconsin claimed 1,021,041 miles *1 643 206 km* by 9 June 1984 for his car which he had been driving since 1958.

Taxis

The largest taxi fleet is that in Mexico City, with 60,000 'normal' taxis, pesaros (communal fixed route taxis) and settas (airport taxis) in mid-1984. On 31 Dec 1986 there were 14,218 taxis and 19,186 drivers in London. The longest fare on record is one of 7533 miles *12 133 km* through 10 countries from Marble Arch, London from 19 Sept–18 Oct 1981. The trip was sponsored for charity and the driver was Stephen Tillyer. Francis Edward Kenyon (b. 1904) was continuously licensed as a taxi driver in Manchester for 57 years 36 days from 1924–81.

MOST EXPENSIVE CARS

Special

The most expensive car to build has been the US Presidential 1969 Lincoln Continental Executive delivered to the US Secret Service on 14 Oct 1968. It has an overall length of 21 ft 6.3 in *6,56 m* with a 13 ft 4 in *4,06 m* wheel base and with the addition of 2 tons *2,03 tonnes* of armour plate, weighs 5.35 tons *5,43 tonnes* (12,000 lb *5443 kg*). The estimated cost of research, development and manufacture was $500,000 (*then £208,000*) but it is rented at $5000 (*now £2300*) per annum. Even if all four tyres were shot out it can travel at 50 mph *80 km/h* on inner rubber-edged steel discs. Carriage House Motor Cars of New York in March 1978 completed 4 years' work on converting a 1973 Rolls Royce including lengthening it by 30 in *76,2 cm*. The price tag was $500,000 (*then £263,157*).

Standard

The most expensive British standard car is the Rolls-Royce 8-cylinder 6750 cc Phantom VI quoted in 1987 at £195,596 (including tax). More expensive are custom-built models. Jack Barclay Ltd of Berkeley Square, London quote £350,000 for an armour-plated Rolls-Royce Phantom VI.

The unrivalled collector of Rolls-Royces was Bhagwan Shri Rajneesh (b. 1931), the Indian mystic lately of Rajneeshpuram, Oregon. His disciples bestowed 93 of these upon him before his deportation in November 1985.

Used

The greatest price paid for any used car is $8.1 million (*then £5,700,000*) for the 1931 Berline de Voyage Royale, one of six Bugatti Royales, by Thomas Monaghan of Ann Arbor, Michigan. The car, formerly part of the William F. Harrah collection, was first sold to property developer Jerry Moore for $6.5 million when the collection was cut down from 1700 to 300 cars in June 1986, then on to Mr Monaghan some months later. In Great Britain £440,000 was paid at auction at Sotheby's for a Bugatti Type 55 roadster on 9 Sept 1985 by an anonymous overseas buyer.

Most inexpensive

The cheapest car of all time was the 1922 Red Bug Buckboard, built by Briggs and Stratton Co of Milwaukee, Wisconsin listed at $150–$125. It had a 62 in *1,57 m* wheel base and weighed 245 lb *111 kg*. Early models of the King Midget cars were sold in kit form for self-assembly for as little as $100 (*then £24 16s*) as late as 1948. By May 1987 the cheapest quoted new car price in Britain was £2431 for a Fiat 126, 652-cc 2-door car.

Longest in production

The longest any car has been in mass production is 49 years (1938 to date), including wartime interruptions, for the Volkswagen 'Beetle' series, originally designed by Ferdinand Porsche. The 20-millionth car came off the final production line in Mexico on 15 May 1981, and more than 21 million had been built by January 1987. Residual production continues in South America. Britain's all-time champion is the Morgan series 4/4 from 27 Dec 1935 from the Morgan Motor Car Co of Malvern (founded 1910). Britain's champion seller has been the Mini which originally sold for £496 19s 2d in August 1959. Sales reached 5,000,000 on 19 Feb 1986. Bernard Ferriman, 83, sold his own pre-production model, the first ever built, for £2500 on 5 Aug 1985. The off-white vehicle, which he bought for £296 in 1962, went to car distributors Penta of Reading.

DRIVING

Round the world

The fastest circumnavigation embracing more than an equator's length of driving (24,901.47 road miles *40 075,0 km*) is one of 74 days 1 hr 11 min by Garry Sowerby (driver) and Ken Langley (navigator) of Canada from 6 Sept to 19 Nov 1980 in a Volvo 245 DL westwards from Toronto, through 4 continents and 23 countries. The distance covered was 43 030 km *26,738 miles* (see below for their Cape to Cape record). Between 30 Mar 1964 and 23 Apr 1984 the folk-singers Manfred Müller and Paul-Ernst Luhrs drove round the world covering 78 countries and 250 000 km *174,000 miles*. They started and finished in Bremerhaven, West Germany.

Cape to Cape

The first traverse of the world's greatest land mass (Afro-Eurasia) was achieved by Richard Pape, who left the North Cape in an Austin A90 on 28 July and arrived in Cape Town on 22 Oct 1955 with the milometer recording 17,500 miles *28 160 km* after 86 days. The speed record was set by Ken Langley and Garry Sowerby of Canada driving north in 28 days 13 hr 10 min for 12,531 miles *20 166 km* from 4 Apr—2 May 1984.

Round Britain economy

John Bloxham, Toney Cox and Ian Hughes assisted by Wolverhampton Rotary Club drove the Round Britain course from 14–18 June 1986 in a diesel-powered Peugeot 205 GRD. The overall fuel consumption for the 3623 mile *5830,6 km* run was 64.376 mpg *22,79 km/litre*.

Mountain driving

Cars have been driven up Ben Nevis, Inverness-shire, Scotland (4406 ft *1343 m*) on five occasions. The record times are 7 hr 23 min (ascent) and 1 hr 55 min (descent) by George F. Simpson in an Austin 7 on 6 Oct 1928. Henry Alexander accomplished the feat twice in May 1911 (Model T Ford) and on 13 Sept 1928 (Model A Ford). The most recent ascent was on 5 June 1984 in a 33-year-old Land Rover.

Driving in reverse

Charles Creighton (1908–70) and James Hargis of Maplewood, Missouri, drove their Ford Model A 1929 roadster in reverse from New York 3340 miles *5375 km* to Los Angeles, from 26 July–13 Aug 1930 without once stopping the engine. They arrived back in New York in reverse on 5 Sept so completing 7180 miles *11 555 km* in 42 days. The highest average speed attained in any non-stop reverse drive exceeding 500 miles *800 km* was achieved by Gerald Hoagland who drove a 1969 Chevrolet Impala 501 miles *806, 2 km* in 17 hr 38 min at Chemung Speed Drome, New York, on 9–10 July 1976 to average 28.41 mph *45,72 km/h*.

Brian 'Cub' Keene and James 'Wilbur' Wright drove their Chevrolet Blazer 9,031 miles *14 533 km* in 37 days (1 Aug–6 Sept 1984) through 15 US states and Canada. Though it was prominently named 'Stuck in Reverse' law enforcement officers in Oklahoma refused to believe it and insisted they drove in reverse reverse, *i.e.* forwards, out of the state.

Battery-powered vehicle

John W. Owen and Roy Harvey travelled 919 miles *1479 km* from John O'Groats to Land's End in a Sinclair C5 in 103 hr 15 min from 30 Apr–4 May 1985. David Turner and Tim Pickhard of Turners of Boscastle Ltd, Cornwall, travelled 875 miles *1408 km* from Land's End to John O'Groats in 63 hours in a Freight Rover Leyland Sherpa powered by a Lucas electric motor from 21–23 Dec 1985. Joe Schwarzkopf-Bowers, 37, of Watford, Herts drove his modified battery-powered Bond Equipe from Heathrow Airport, London to Crewkerne, Somerset on 16 May 1986, a distance of 132 miles *212,4 km* on a single charge costing an estimated 60p.

Two-side-wheel driving

Gilbert Bataille of Paris drove a Leyland T45 Road Runner Truck on two wheels for 2.864 miles *4,60 km* at the British Truck Grand Prix, Silverstone, Northants on 17 Aug 1986.

Göran Eliason (b. 7 Dec 1946) of Boras, Sweden achieved 134,9 km/h *83.8 mph* on the two wheels of a standard Volvo 760 at Anderstrop, Sweden on 18 May 1986.

Wheelie

Steve Murty drove a Multi-Part Skytrain truck on its rear wheels for 319,8 m *1049 ft* at the British Truck Grand Prix, Silverstone, Northants on 17 Aug 1986. The 60 tonne/ton truck was powered by a 500-bhp Cummins turbo-charged 14-litre engine and had a ZF-Ecomat hp 600 5-speed automatic gearbox.

Oldest driver

Roy M. Rawlins (b. 10 July 1870) of Stockton, California, was warned for driving at 95 mph *152 km/h* in a 55 mph *88,5 km/h* zone in June 1974. On 25 Aug 1974 he was awarded a California State licence valid till 1978 by Mr John Burrafato, but Mr Rawlins died on 9 July 1975, one day short of his 105th birthday. Mrs Maude Tull of Inglewood, California, who took to driving aged 91 after her husband died, was issued a renewal on 5 Feb 1976 when aged 104. Britain's oldest known driver has been Benjamin Kagan of Leeds (b. Nov 1878). Major Geoffrey Chance CBE (b. 16 Dec 1893) of Braydon, Wiltshire, who began driving in 1908, successfully took a driving test to re-qualify after a 'minor bump' when aged 90 years 90 days at Swindon, Wiltshire on 15 March 1984. The oldest age at which a man has passed the Department of Transport driving test has been 89 years 2 months by David Coupar (b. 9 Feb 1898) on 4 Mar 1987 in Perth, Perthshire. The oldest woman to pass was Mrs Harriet Emma Jack (née Morse) (b. 9 Dec 1887) on 18 May 1976 in Bognor Regis, West Sussex. She was aged 88 years 5 months.

The holder of the earliest driving licence to be issued in Britain is Reginald 'Gerry' Bond (b. 16 July 1889) of Bournemouth, Dorset whose first licence is dated Oct 1907.

Youngest driver

Instances of drivers have been recorded in HM Armed Forces much under 17 years. Mrs P. L.

M. Williams (b. 3 Feb 1926), now of Risca, Gwent, as Private Patterson in the ATS, drove a 5-ton truck in 1941 aged 15. Mark Blackbourn of Lincoln, having passed his driving test the day after his 17th birthday, went on to pass the advanced test less than 48 hours later on 7 Aug 1985. Mark Collins Hall of Otley, West Yorkshire passed his test on 24 July 1985 aged 16 years 103 days.

Most durable

The Goodyear Tire and Rubber Co test driver Weldon C. Kocich drove 3,141,946 miles *5 056 470 km* from 5 Feb 1953 to 28 Feb 1986 so averaging 95,210 miles *153 226 km* per year.

Driving tests

The record for persistence in taking the Ministry of Transport's Learner's Test is held by Mrs Miriam Hargrave (b. 3 Apr 1908) of Wakefield, West Yorkshire, who failed her 39th driving test in eight years on 29 Apr 1970 after 'crashing' a set of red lights. She triumphed at her 40th attempt after 212 lessons on 3 Aug 1970. The examiner was alleged not to have known about her previous 39 tests. In 1978 she was reported still to disdain right-hand turns. The world's easiest tests have been those in Egypt in which the ability to drive 6 m *19.64 ft* forward and the same in reverse has been deemed sufficient. In 1979 it was reported that accurate reversing had been added between two rubber traffic cones. 'High cone attrition' soon led to the substitution of white lines. Mrs Fannie Turner (b. 1903) of Little Rock, Arkansas passed the *written* test for drivers on her 104th attempt in October 1978.

SERVICES

Car parks

The world's largest car park is at the West Edmonton Mall, Edmonton, Alberta, Canada, which can hold 20,000 vehicles. There are overflow facilities on an adjoining lot for 10,000 more cars.

The largest parking area in Great Britain is that for 15,000 cars and 200 coaches at the National Exhibition Centre, Birmingham (see p. 106).

Britain's highest capacity underground car park is under the Victoria Centre, Nottingham with a capacity of 1650 cars, opened in June 1972.

The largest private garage is one of two storeys built outside Bombay for the private collection of 176 cars owned by Pranlal Bhogilal (b. 1939).

Filling stations

Little America, west of Cheyenne, Wyoming, at the junction of Interstate Routes 80 and 25 claims to be the world's biggest gas station with 52 diesel and gas pumps—none self-service. The largest filling station of the 36,000 in the United Kingdom is the Esso service area on the M4 at Leigh Delamere, Wiltshire, opened on 3 Jan 1972. It has 48 petrol and diesel pumps and extends over 43 acres *17,4 ha*. The highest in the world is at Leh, Ladakh, India at 3658 m *12,001 ft*, operated by Indiaoil.

Unleaded petrol

The first unleaded petrol to be available in the United Kingdom went on sale on 24 June 1986. The Minister of State for the Environment, William Waldegrave, made the first fill at Esso's Stamford Bridge Service Station, London.

Largest garage

The KMB Overhaul Centre operated by the Kowloon Motor Bus Co (1933) Ltd, Hong Kong, is the world's largest multi-storeyed service centre. Purpose built for double deck buses, its 4 floors occupy in excess of 47,000 m² *11.6 acres.*

Tow

The longest tow on record was one of 4759 miles *7658 km* from Halifax, Nova Scotia to Canada's Pacific coast, when Frank J. Elliott and George A. Scott of Amherst, Nova Scotia, Canada, persuaded 168 passing motorists in 89 days to tow their Model T Ford (in fact engineless) to win a $1000 bet on 15 Oct 1927.

Tyres

The world's largest tyres ever manufactured were by the Goodyear Tire & Rubber Co for

---

Most illuminated truck ● 'Midnight Bandit' is the creation of Todd Pellegrini of Hummelstown, Pennsylvania. He spent over 5 years equipping his 1971 F-250 Ford Explorer camper truck with 1900 practical lights which are connected by over 5000 ft *1524 m* of wire and 45 togel switches to three 150 ampere alternators and five 12-volt batteries.

---

giant dumper trucks. They measure 12 ft *3,65 m* in diameter, weigh 12,500 lb *5670 kg* and cost $74,000 (£49,000). A tyre 17 ft *5,18 m* in diameter is believed to be the limitation of what is practical.

Skid marks

The longest recorded skid marks on a public road have been those 950 ft *290 m* long left by a Jaguar car involved in an accident on the M1 near Luton, Bedfordshire, on 30 June 1960. Evidence given in the subsequent High Court case *Hurlock* v. *Inglis* et al. indicated a speed 'in excess of 100 mph *160 km/h* before the application of the brakes'. The skid marks made by the jet-powered *Spirit of America*, driven by Norman Craig Breedlove, after the car went out of control at Bonneville Salt Flats, Utah, USA, on 15 Oct 1964, were nearly 6 miles *9,6 km* long.

VEHICLES

Crawler

The most massive vehicle ever constructed is the Marion eight-caterpillar crawler used for conveying *Saturn V* rockets to their launching pads at Cape Canaveral, Florida (see Chapter 4, Most powerful rocket). It measures 131 ft 4 in *40 m* by 114 ft *34,7 m* and the two built cost $12,300,000 (then £5,125,000). The loaded train weight is 8036 tons *8165 tonnes*. The windscreen wipers were 42 in *106 cm* blades and were the world's largest.

Land

The most massive automotive land vehicle is 'Big Muskie' the 10,700 ton *10 890 tonne* mechanical shovel built by Bucyrus Erie for the Musk mine. It is 487 ft *148,43 m* long, 151 ft *46,02 m* wide and 222 ft *67,66 m* high with a grab capacity of 325 tons.

Longest

The longest vehicle ever built is the Arctic Snow Train owned by the world-famous wire-walker Steve McPeak (US). This 54-wheeled 572 ft *174,3 m* long vehicle was built by R. G. Le Tourneau Inc of Longview, Texas for the US Army. Its gross train weight was 400 tons with a top speed of 20 mph *32 km/h* and it was driven by a crew of 6 when used as an 'overland train' for the military. McPeak repaired it and every punctured wheel single-handed in often sub-zero temperatures in Alaska. It generates 4680 shp and has a capacity of 6522 imperial gallons *29 648 litres*.

Ambulance *Largest*

The world's largest ambulances are the 18 m *59 ft 0¼ in* long articulated Alligator Jumbulances Mark VI, VII and VIII, operated by The Across Trust to convey the sick and handicapped on holidays and pilgrimages to Europe. They are built by Van Hool of Belgium with Fiat engines, cost £176,000 and convey 44 patients and staff.

Amphibious circumnavigation

The only circumnavigation by an amphibious vehicle was achieved by Ben Carlin (Australia) (d. 7 Mar 1981) in an amphibious jeep *Half-Safe*. He completed the last leg of the Atlantic crossing (the English Channel) on 24 Aug 1951. He arrived back in Montreal, Canada on 8 May 1958 having completed a circumnavigation of 39,000 miles *62 765 km* over land and 9600 miles *15 450 km* by sea and river. He was accompanied on the trans-Atlantic stage by his ex-wife Elinore (US) and on the long trans-Pacific stage (Tokyo to Anchorage) by Broye Lafayette De-Mente (b. Missouri, 1928).

Buses *Earliest*

The first municipal motor omnibus service in the world was inaugurated on 12 Apr 1903 between Eastbourne railway station and Meads, East Sussex, England. A steam-powered bus named *Royal Patent* ran between Gloucester and Cheltenham for 4 months in 1831.

MIDNIGHT BANDIT

Largest fleet

In 1983 the world's largest bus fleet were the 6580 single-deck buses in Rio de Janeiro, Brazil. Of London Regional Transport's 5,100 fleet, 4,550 are double-deckers.

Longest

The longest buses in the world are the 10.72 ton *10 870 kg*, 76 ft *23,16 m* articulated buses, with 121 passenger seats and room also for 66 'straphangers', built by the Wayne Corporation of Richmond, Indiana for use in the Middle East.

Longest route

The longest regularly-scheduled bus route is by 'Across Australia Coach Lines', who inaugurated a regular scheduled service between Perth and Brisbane on 9 Apr 1980. The route is 5455 km *3389 miles* taking 75 hr 55 min. The longest bus service in Great Britain is 669 miles *1076 km* between Plymouth and Aberdeen operated by National Express.

Trolleybuses

The last trolleybus in Britain, owned by Bradford Corporation, ran in 1972. Plans have been made to reintroduce trolleybuses by both West Yorkshire and South Yorkshire Passenger Transport Executives.

Caravans *Longest journey*

The longest continuous motor caravan journey is one of 143,716 miles *231 288 km* by Harry B. Coleman and Peggy Larson in a Volkswagen Camper from 20 Aug 1976 to 20 Apr 1978 through 113 countries. Saburo Ouchi (b. 7 Feb 1942) of Tokyo, Japan drove 270 000 km *167,770 miles* in 91 countries from 2 Dec 1969 to 10 Feb 1978.

Largest

The largest caravans built in Britain are the £300,000 'State Super Caravans', 18 m *59 ft 0¼ in* in length and 3,5 m *11 ft 5¾ in* wide built since 1977 by Coventry Steel Caravans of Newport Pagnell, Buckinghamshire.

Fastest

The world speed record for a caravan is 124.91 mph *201,02 km/h* by an Alpha 14 towed by a Le Mans Aston Martin V8 saloon driven by Robin Hamilton at RAF Elvington, North Yorkshire on 14 Oct 1980.

Dumper truck

The world's largest dumper truck is the Terex Titan 33–19 manufactured by the Terex Division of General Motors Corporation. It has a loaded weight of 539.9 tons *548,6 tonnes* and a capacity of 312½ tons *317,5 tonnes*. When tipping its height is 56 ft *17,06 m*. The 16-cylinder engine delivers 3300 hp. The fuel tank holds 1300 imperial gallons *5904,6 litres*. It went into service in November 1974.

Earth mover

The world's largest earth mover is the 100-tonne T-800 built at the Lenin Tractor Works in Chelyabinsk, USSR, announced in Sept 1984.

Fire engine

The world's most powerful fire appliance is the 860-hp 8-wheel Oshkosh firetruck used for aircraft fires. It can discharge 41,600 gal *190 000 l* of foam through two turrets in just 150 sec. It weighs 59 tons *60 tonnes*. The fastest on record is the Jaguar XJ12 – 'Chubb Firefighter', which, in Nov 1982, attained a speed of 130.57 mph *210,13 km/h* in tests when servicing the *Thrust 2* land speed record trials (see pp. 128 & 160).

Go-karting

The highest mileage recorded in 24 hours on a closed twisting circuit for go-karts driven by a 4-man team is 1018 laps of a mile *1638,3 km* at Erbsville Kartway, Waterloo, Ontario, Canada. The 5-hp 140-cc Honda-engined kart was driven

Longest lawnmower drive ● Ben Garcia drove a rebuilt AMF lawnmower powered by an 8-horse-power Briggs and Stratton engine (he replaced it twice) 2801 miles *4507 km* across the United States from Old Orchard Beach, Portland, Maine to Los Angeles, California in 38 days from 6 Oct–13 Nov 1986.

by Owen Nimmo, Gary Ruddock, Jim Timmins and Danny Upshaw on 4–5 Sept 1983.

The highest mileage for the 100-cc non-gearbox solo six-hour record is 313,51 km *194.81 miles* by Emily Newman at Rye House Raceway, Hoddesdon, Hertfordshire on 25 July 1986.

Lawn mowers

The widest gang mower in the world is the 5-ton 60 ft *18,28 m* wide 27-unit 'Big Green Machine' used by the sod farmer Jay Edgar Frick of Monroe, Ohio. It mows an acre in 60 sec. The greatest distance covered in the annual 12-hour Lawn Mower Race (under the rules of the BLMRA, the British Lawn Mower Racing Association) is 276 miles *444,1 km* by Tony Hazelwood, Derek Bell, Tony Smith and Ray Kilminster at Wisborough Green, W. Sussex on 21–22 June 1980. A 12-hour run-behind record of 101.15 miles *162,7 km* was set at Wisborough Green on 8–9 July 1984 by the 'Super Gnome' team.

Snowmobiles

Richard and Raymond Moore and Loren Matthews drove their snowmobile 5876 miles *9456 km* from Fairbanks, Alaska to Fenton, Michigan, USA, in 39 days from 3 Feb–13 Mar 1980. Tony Lenzini of Duluth, Minnesota, USA, drove a 1986 Arctic Cat Cougar snowmobile a total of 7211 miles *11 604,6 km* in 60 riding days between 28 Dec 1985 and 20 Mar 1986.

Solar-powered

The highest speed attained under IHPVA (International Human Powered Vehicle Association) rules by a solely solar-powered vehicle is 24.74 mph *39,81 km/h* at Bellflower, California on 1 July 1984 by *Sunrunner*, designed by Joel Davidson and Greg Johanson of Photovoltaic Power Systems.

Tractor

The world's largest tractor is the $459,000 (*then £285,000*) US Department of Agriculture Wide Tractive Frame Vehicle completed by Ag West of Sacramento, California in June 1982. It meas-

ures 33 ft *10,05 m* between its wheels which are designed to run on permanent paths and weighs 21.87 tons *22,22 tonnes*.

The sport of tractor-pulling was put on a national US championship basis in 1967 at Bowling Green, Ohio where the winner was 'The Purple Monster' built and driven by Roger E. Varns. Today there are 12 classes ranging up to '12,200 lb unlimited'.

Wrecker

The world's most powerful wrecker is the Twin City Garage and Body Shop's 21 ton *20.6 tonne* 36 ft *10,9 m* long 1969 International M6-23 'Hulk' stationed at Scott City, Missouri. It can lift in excess of 300 tons *295 tonnes* on its short boom.

ROAD LOADS

Heaviest road load

On 14–15 July 1984 John Brown Engineers & Contractors BV moved the Conoco Kotter Field production deck with a roll-out weight of 3805 tonnes for the Continental Netherlands Oil Company of Leidsenhage, Netherlands.

The heaviest road load moved in the United Kingdom has been a 1305 tonne *1284 ton* module for the semi-submersible drilling rig *Ocean Alliance 2002*. It measured 70 ft *21 m* high by 100 ft *30,5 m* long by 90 ft *27,4 m* wide and was drawn by four tractor units developing a total of 1625 hp over half a mile *0,8 km* of public road on its journey from the River Tees to the River Clyde on 5 Nov 1985. The longest item moved has been a 275 ft *83,8 m* long high-pressure steel gas storage vessel weighing 233 tonnes *229 tons* transported to a new site at Beckton gasworks in east London on 10 July 1985. The overall train length was 325 ft *99 m*.

MOTORCYCLES (see Chapter 12)

Earliest

The earliest internal combustion-engined motorised bicycle was a wooden-framed machine built at Bad Cannstatt in Oct–Nov 1885 by Gottlieb Daimler (1834–1900) of Germany and first ridden by Wilhelm Maybach (1846–1929). It had a top speed of 12 mph *19 km/h* and developed one-half of one horsepower from its single-cylinder 264-cc four-stroke engine at 700 rpm. Known as the 'Einspur', it was lost in a fire in 1903. The first motorcycles of entirely British production were the 1046-cc Holden flat-four and the 2¾-hp Clyde single both produced in 1898. The earliest factory which made motorcycles in quantity was opened

Wheelie

Doug Domokos on the Alabama International Speedway, Talladega, USA on 27 June 1984 covered 145 miles *233,34 km* non-stop on the rear wheel of his Honda XR 500. He stopped only when the gas ran out. The highest speed attained on a back wheel is 137.6 mph *221,43 km/h* by Richard Almet (France) on 15 Aug 1986 at the Multi-Part British Truck Grand Prix, Silverstone, Northants.

Round Britain

Richard Parkhouse of Gwynedd covered all 62 mainland counties of Great Britain by motor cycle (Suzuki 6SX 750 EFE) on a 1634-mile *2629 km* route on 11–12 June 1984 in 28 hours 52 min, averaging 56.6 mph *91,0 km/h.*

BICYCLES

Earliest

The first design for a machine propelled by cranks and pedals with connecting rods has been attributed to Leonardo da Vinci (1452–1519), or one of his pupils, dated *c.* 1493. The earliest such design actually built was in 1839–40 by Kirkpatrick Macmillan (1810–78) of Dumfries, Scotland. It is now in the Science Museum, Kensington and Chelsea, London. The first practical bicycle was the *vélocipède* built in March 1861 by Pierre and his son Ernest Michaux of rue de Verneuil, Paris. In 1870, James Starley, in Coventry, constructed the first 'penny-farthing' or Ordinary bicycle. It had wire-spoked wheels for lightness and was available with an optional speed gear.

Trishaw

The longest trishaw parade on record was when 177 trishaw pedlars rode in single convoy in Penang, Malaysia on 23 Nov 1986.

Longest

The longest true tandem bicycle ever built (*i.e.* without a third stabilising wheel) is one of 20,4 m

> **Most on one motorcycle ●** Forty members of the Brazilian Army Military Police drove on this 1976 Harley Davidson 1200 cc for 1 mile *1,6 km* on 8 Feb 1986.

> **Most expensive motorcycle ●** The Harley Davidson FLHTC Electra Glide Classic, with a four-stroke 45-degree V-Twin engine of 1340 cubic capacity, a sound system with handlebar controls, adjustable three-position rider floorboards, a seat with a 'floating' rubber-mounted backrest and a choice of five two-tone colours, costs £8860 including tax and VAT.

in 1894 by Heinrich and Wilhelm Hildebrand and Alois Wolfmüller at Munich, West Germany. In its first two years this factory produced over 1000 machines, each having a water-cooled 1488-cc twin-cylinder four-stroke engine developing about 2.5 bhp at 600 rpm—the highest capacity motor cycle engine ever put into production.

Fastest road machine

The 115-bhp Japanese Honda V65 Magna with a liquid-cooled, in-line V-4, 16-valve DoHC engine of 1098-cc capacity has a design speed of 173 mph *278,4 km/h.*

Fastest racing machine

There is no satisfactory answer to the identity of the fastest track machine other than to say that the current Kawasaki, Suzuki and Yamaha machines have all been geared to attain speeds marginally in excess of 300 km/h *186.4 mph* under race conditions.

Duration

The longest time a solo motorcycle has been kept in non-stop motion is 560 hr by Norberto Naummi, Foppiani Maurizio and Roberto Ghillani who covered 30 370 km *18,000 miles* at an average speed of 54.23 km/h *33.69 mph* in Varano de Melegari, Italy from 16 Aug–8 Sep 1986.

Biggest fan

The White Helmets, the Royal Air Force Motorcycle Display Team, successfully achieved an 8-bike, 36-man pyramid for 300 m *328 yds* on 2 Sep 1986 at Catterick, North Yorkshire.

66 ft 11 in for 35 riders built by the Pedaalstompers Westmalle of Belgium. They rode c. 60 m 195 ft in practice on 20 Apr 1979. The machine weighs 1100 kg 2425 lb.

Smallest
The world's smallest wheeled ridable bicycle is one with 3,5 cm 1.37 in wheels weighing 700 g 24.6 oz built and ridden by Jacques Puyoou of Pau, Pyrénées-Atlantiques, France in 1983. He has also built a tandem 36 cm 14.1 in long to accommodate Madame Puyoou.

Largest
A classic Ordinary bicycle with wheels of 65¼ in 165,7 cm diameter front and 18 in 45,7 cm back was constructed by the Coventry Machinists Co in 1881. It is now owned by Paul Foulkes-Halbard of Crowborough, Sussex.

A bicycle with an 8 ft 2½ in 2,50 m front wheel with pedal extenders was built in 1878 for circus demonstrations.

Fastest HPV's
The world speed records for human-powered vehicles (HPVs) are 61.94 mph 99,68 km/h (single rider) by John Seibert at La Garita, Colorado on 27 Oct 1980; and 62.92 mph 101,25 km/h (multiple riders) by Dave Grylls and Leigh Barczewski at the Ontario Speedway, California on 4 May 1980.

A British 200-m record was set by S. Poulter in Poppy Flyer, in 9.10 sec at Greenham Common, Berkshire on 2 Aug 1981.

Endurance
From 10–21 July 1983, 24 City and Guilds College, London, students drove an HPV round Great Britain on a 3675 mile 5914 km route to average 14.41 mph 23,19 km/h.

Unicycles
The tallest unicycle ever mastered is one 101 ft 9 in 31,01 m tall ridden by Steve McPeak (with a safety wire or mechanic suspended to an overhead crane) for a distance of 376 ft 114,6 m in Las Vegas in October 1980. The freestyle riding of ever taller unicycles (i.e. without any safety harness) must inevitably lead to serious injury or fatality. Deepak Lele of Maharashtra, India unicycled 3963 miles 6378 km from New York to Los Angeles from 6 June–25 Sept 1984. Brian Davis, 33 of Tillicoultry, Clackmannan, Scotland rode 901 miles 1450 km from Land's End to John O'Groats from 16 May to 4 June 1980 in 19 days 1 hr 45 min. Floyd Beattie of Athens, Ohio set a record for 100 miles 160,9 km in 7 hr 18 min 55 sec on 11 Oct 1986. The sprint record from a standing start over 100 metres is 14.89 sec by Floyd Grandall of Pontiac, Michigan, USA, in Tokyo, Japan on 24 Mar 1980.

Wheelie
A world duration record of 4 hr 21 min 1 sec was set by Robert Hurd at the Recreation Centre, Winchester, Hants on 18 Nov 1986.

Penny-farthing
The record for riding from Land's End to John O'Groats on Ordinary bicycles, more commonly known in the 1870s as Penny-farthings, is 9 days 6 hr 52 min by police officer Clive Flint, 31 of Manchester from 2–10 June 1984. G. P. Mills (Anfield BC) rode this course in 5 days 1 hr 45 min on a 53-inch Humber from 4–10 July 1886.

Underwater cycling
Thirty-two certified Scuba divers in 60 hours from 27–29 Nov 1981 rode a submarine tricycle 64.96 miles 104,54 km on the bottom of Amphi High School pool, Tucson, Arizona, USA, in a scheme devised by Lucian Spataro to raise money for the Casa De Los Niños Nursery.

A team of 32 in 72 underwater hours achieved 87.81 miles 141,322 km in Narvik, Norway from 28–31 Mar 1984.

Highest railway line ● At 15,806 ft 4817 m above sea level this standard-gauge (4 ft 8½ in 1435 mm) train on the Morococha branch of the Peruvian State Railways at La Cima is the highest in the world. (Photo: Alex Hansen)

Railways

TRAINS

Earliest
Wagons running on wooden rails were used for mining as early as 1550 at Leberthal, Alsace, and in Britain for conveying coal at Wollaton near Nottingham from 1603–15 and at Broseley Colliery, Shropshire, in October 1605. The earliest commercially successful steam locomotives worked on the Middleton Colliery Railway to Leeds, Yorkshire, authorised by Britain's first Railway Act on 9 June 1758. Richard Trevithick (1771–1883) built his first steam locomotive for the 3 ft 914 mm gauge iron plateway at Coalbrookdale, Shropshire, in 1803, but there is no evidence that it ran. His second locomotive drew wagons in which men rode on a demonstration run at Penydarren, Mid-Glamorgan, Wales, on 22 Feb 1804, but it broke the plate rails. The first permanent public railway to use steam traction was the Stockton & Darlington, from its opening on 27 Sept 1825 from Shildon to Stockton via Darlington, in Cleveland. The 7 ton/tonne Locomotion could pull 48 tons/tonnes at a speed of 15 mph 24 km/h. It was designed and driven by George Stephenson (1781–1848). The first regular steam passenger service was inaugurated over a one-mile section (between Bogshole Farm and South Street in Whitstable) on the 6¼ mile 10,05 km Canterbury & Whitstable Railway in Kent on 3 May 1830, hauled by the engine Invicta. The first practical electric railway was Werner von Siemens' oval metre-gauge demonstration track about 300 m 328 yd long at the Berlin Trades Exhibition on 31 May 1879.

Fastest
The highest speed attained by a railed vehicle is 6121 mph 9851 km/h or Mach 8 by an unmanned rocket sled over the 9¼ mile 15,2 km long rail track at White Sands Missile Range, New Mexico, USA on 5 Oct 1982. The world's fastest rail speed with passengers is 400,7 km/h 249 mph by the Maglev (magnetic levitation) ML-500 test train over the 7 km 4.3 mile long JNR experimental track at Miyazaki, Japan on 4 Feb 1987. The highest speed recorded on any national rail system is 236 mph 380 km/h by the French SNCF high-speed train TGV-PSE on trial near Tonnerre on 26 Feb 1981. The TGV (Train à Grande Vitesse) inaugurated on 27 Sept 1981 by September 1983 had reduced its scheduled time for the Paris–Lyon run of 425 km 264 miles to 2 hr exactly, so averaging 212,5 km/h 132 mph. The peak speed attained is 270 km/h 168 mph.

British Rail inaugurated their HST (High Speed Train) daily services between London–Bristol and South Wales on 4 Oct 1976. The electric British Rail APT-P (Advanced Passenger Train-Prototype) attained 162 mph 261 km/h between Glasgow and Carlisle on its first revenue-earning run on 7 Dec 1981. It covered the 400 miles 644 km from Glasgow to London in 4¼ hr.

A British Rail test train powered by two InterCity 125 power cars achieved a speed of 144.7 mph 232,8 km/h over a measured mile between York and Darlington, Durham on 9 Nov 1986. This was a world record speed for diesel power.

Longest non-stop
The longest run on British Rail without any advertised stop is the Night Motorail Service from Inverness to Euston. The distance is 567.75 miles 913,7 km and the time taken is 11 hr 4 min. The longest passenger journey without a stop is the re-inaugurated Flying Scotsman's 268.5 mile 432,1 km run from King's Cross to Newcastle en route to Edinburgh.

Most powerful
The world's most powerful steam locomotive, measured by tractive effort, was No 700, a triple-articulated or triplex 2-8-8-8-4, 6-cylinder engine built by the Baldwin Locomotive Works in 1916 for the Virginian Railroad. It had a tractive force of 166,300 lb 75 434 kg working compound and 199,560 lb 90 520 kg working simple.

Probably the heaviest train ever hauled by a single engine was one of 15,300 tons 15 545 tonnes made up of 250 freight cars stretching 1.6 miles 2,5 km by the Matt H. Shay (No 5014), a 2-8-8-8-2 engine which ran on the Erie Railroad from May 1914 until 1929.

Railways

On 16 Feb 1986, a single locomotive, No 59001, one of four diesels built by General Motors and privately owned by quarry company Foster Yeoman of Minehead, Somerset, hauled a 4639 tonne *4565 ton* train, the heaviest on record, during trials at Savernake Bank, Wiltshire.

Greatest load

The heaviest single pieces of freight ever conveyed by rail are limited by the capacity of the rolling stock. The world's strongest rail carrier with a capacity of 807 tonnes is the 336-tonne 36 axle 92 m *301 ft 10 in* long 'Schnabel' built for a US railway by Krupp, West Germany, in March 1981.

The heaviest load carried by British Rail was a 122 ft *37,1 m* long boiler drum, weighing 275 tons *279 tonnes* which was carried from Immingham Dock to Killingholme, Humberside, in September 1968.

The heaviest load ever moved on rails is the 10,700-ton Church of the Virgin Mary built in 1548 in the village of Most, Czechoslovakia, in October–November 1975 because it was in the way of coal workings. It was moved 800 yd *730 m* at 0.0013 mph *0,002 km/h* over 4 weeks at a cost of £9 million.

Freight trains

The longest and heaviest freight train on record was about 4 miles *6 km* in length. It comprised 500 coal cars with three 3600-hp diesels pulling and three more in the middle, on the Iaeger, West Virginia, to Portsmouth, Ohio stretch of 157 miles *252 km* on the Norfolk and Western Railway on 15 Nov 1967. The total weight was nearly 42,000 tons *42 674 tonnes*.

British Rail's heaviest freight train began its regular run on 16 Sept 1983 from Merehead Quarry, Somerset, to Acton, west London, with 3300 tonnes of limestone in 43 wagons and 2 engines stretching nearly ¼ mile *800 m*.

TRACKS

Longest

The world's longest run is one of 9438 km *5864¼ miles* on the Trans-Siberian line from Moscow to Nakhodka, USSR, in the Soviet Far East. There are 97 stops on the journey which takes 8 days 4 hr 25 min. The 3145 km *1954 mile* Baykal-Amur northern main line (BAM), begun with forced labour in 1938, was restarted in 1974 and put into service on 27 Oct 1984. A total of 13,500 million ft³ *382 million m³* of earth had to be moved and 3,901 bridges built in this £8000 million project.

Longest straight

The longest straight in the world is on the Commonwealth Railways Trans-Australian line over the Nullarbor Plain from Mile 496 between Nurina and Loongana, Western Australia, to Mile 793 between Ooldea and Watson, South Australia, 297 miles *478 km* dead straight although not level. The longest straight on British Rail is the 18 miles *29 km* between Barlby Junction and Brough on the 'down' line on the Selby, North Yorkshire, to Kingston-upon-Hull, Humberside, line.

Widest and narrowest

The widest gauge in standard use is 5 ft 6 in *1,676 m*. This width is used in Spain, Portugal, India, Pakistan, Bangladesh, Sri Lanka, Argentina and Chile. The narrowest gauge on which public services are operated is 10¼ in *260 mm* on the Wells Harbour (0.7 mile *1,12 km*) and the Wells–Walsingham Railways (4 miles *6,5 km*) in Norfolk, England.

Highest line

The highest point on the British Rail system is at the pass of Drumochter on the Perthshire–Inverness border, where the track reaches an altitude of 1484 ft *452 m* above sea level. The highest railway in Britain is the Snowdon Mountain Railway, which rises from Llanberis, Gwynedd to 3493 ft *1064 m* above sea level, just below the summit of Snowdon (*Yr Wyddfa*). It has a gauge of 2 ft 7½ in *800 mm*.

Lowest

The lowest point on British Rail is in the Severn Tunnel—144 ft *43,8 m* below sea level.

Steepest gradient

The world's steepest standard-gauge gradient by adhesion is 1:11 between Chedde and Servoz on the metre gauge SNCF Chamonix line, France.

Fastest steam locomotive ● *Mallard*, seen here in its original LNER livery achieved the highest ratified speed of 125 mph *201 km/h* over 440 yd *402 m* on 31 July 1938. Seven coaches weighing 240 tons *243 tonnes* were hauled down Stoke Bank, near Essendine, Leicestershire. During the run the engine suffered some damage. (Photo: National Railway Museum)

BRITAIN'S FASTEST EVER EXPRESS DOES 125 MILES AN HOUR!

The steepest sustained adhesion-worked gradient on main line in the United Kingdom is the 2 mile *3,2 km* Lickey incline of 1:37.7 just south-west of Birmingham. From the tunnel bottom to James Street, Liverpool, on the former Mersey Railway, there is a stretch of 1:27; and between Folkestone Junction and Harbour a mile *1,6 km* of 1:30.

Slightest gradient

The slightest gradient posted on the British Rail system is one indicated as 1 in 14,400 between Pirbright Junction and Farnborough, Hampshire. This could be described alternatively as England's most obtuse summit.

Busiest system

The world's most crowded rail system is Japanese National Railways, which in 1986 carried 19,017,419 passengers daily. Among articles lost in 1986 were 572,700 umbrellas, 285,092 clothing items, 217,968 books and stationery items, 5913 accessories and 201,170 purses.

RAIL TRAVEL

Calling All Stations

Alan M. Witton (b. 1943) of Chorlton, Manchester visited every open British Rail station (2362) in a continuous tour for charity of 16,592¾ miles *26 703 km* in 27,136 minutes from 13 July–28 Aug 1980.

Colin M. Mulvany and Seth N. Vafiadis of west London visited every British Rail station (2,378) embracing also the Tyne and Wear, Glasgow and London underground systems (333 stations) for charity in 31 days 5 hr 8 min 58 sec over 15,527¾ miles *24 989 km* to average 38.05 mph *61,2 km/h* from 4 June–5 July 1984.

John E. Ballenger of Dunedin, Florida has logged 76,485 miles *123 090 km* of unduplicated rail routes in North and South America. Using Amtrak's All Aboard America $299 ticket, valid for a month, James J. Brady of Wilmington, Ohio travelled through 442 (out of 498) stations over 21,485 unduplicated miles of track (out of 23,000) from 11 Feb–11 Mar 1984.

Carl Lombardelli of Romford, Essex traversed the extreme points of the compass for stations in Great Britain—Thurso (north), Lowestoft (east), Penzance (south) and Arisaig (west) in 48 hrs 15 mins from 8–10 Sept 1985.

Most countries in 24 hours

The record number of countries travelled through entirely by train in 24 hours is 10 by Aaron Kitchen on 16–17 Feb 1987. His route started in Yugoslavia and continued through Austria, Italy, Liechtenstein, Switzerland, France, Luxembourg, Belgium, Netherlands arriving in West Germany 22 hr 42 min later.

Handpumped railcars

A speed of 20 mph for a 300 m *984 ft* course was first surpassed at Port Moody, British Columbia, Canada by the 5-man team (1 pusher, 4 pumpers) from Port Moody Motors with 33.54 sec on 27 June 1982. They averaged 20.008 mph *32,20 km/h*.

Longest journey

The longest journey on the British Rail system is from Penzance, Cornwall to Wick, Caithness. A round trip of 2229½ miles *3587,6 km*, it was travelled by John Shaw of Huddersfield for charity from 22–24 Sept 1983 in 50 hr 20 mins via London, Glasgow, Aberdeen and Inverness.

The highest mileage on British Rail within 24 hours is 1716 miles *2761,5 km* on 29–30 Apr 1987 by Paul Boskett of Crewe, Cheshire.

In the course of some 73 years commuting on British Rail from Kent to London, Ralph Ransome of Birchington travelled an equivalent of an estimated 39 times round the world. He retired early, aged 93, on 5 Feb 1986.

STATIONS

Largest

The world's largest railway station is Grand Central Terminal, Park Avenue and 43rd Street, New York City, built 1903–13. It covers 48 acres *19 ha* on two levels with 41 tracks on the upper level and 26 on the lower. On average more than 550 trains and 180,000 people per day use it, with a peak of 252,288 on 3 July 1947.

The largest railway station in extent on the British Rail system is the 17-platform Clapham Junction, London, extending over 27¾ acres *11,22 ha* with a total face of 11,185 ft *3409 m*. The station with the largest number of platforms is London Waterloo (24½ acres *9,9 ha*), with 21 main and two Waterloo and City Line platforms, with a total face of 15,352 ft *4679 m*. Victoria Station (21¾ acres *8,80 ha*) has, however, a total face length of 18,412 ft *5611 m* for its 17 platforms.

Oldest

The oldest station in the world is Liverpool Road Station, Manchester, England first used on 15 Sept 1830 and now partly turned into a museum.

Busiest

The busiest railway junction in Great Britain is Clapham Junction, London, on the Southern Region of British Rail, with an average of 2200 trains passing through each 24 hr.

Highest

The highest station in the world is Condor, Bolivia at 15,705 ft *4786 m* on the metre-gauge Rio Mulato to Potosi line. The highest passenger station on British Rail is Corrour, Inverness-shire, at an altitude of 1347 ft *410,5 m* above sea level.

Waiting rooms

The world's largest waiting rooms are the four in Peking Station, Chang'an Boulevard, Peking, China, opened in September 1959, with a total standing capacity of 14,000.

Platform

The longest railway platform in the world is the Khargpur platform, West Bengal, India, which measures 2733 ft *833 m* in length. The State Street Center subway platform staging on 'The Loop' in Chicago, Illinois measures 3500 ft *1066 m* in length.

The longest in the British Rail system is the 1977 ft 4 in *602,69 m* long platform at Gloucester.

The two platforms comprising the New Nisato railway station on the Musashino line, Saitama, Japan are 300 m *984 ft 3 in* apart and are connected by a bridge.

UNDERGROUND RAILWAYS

Most extensive

The earliest (first section between Farringdon St and Edgware Road, opened 10 Jan 1863) and one of the most extensive underground or rapid transit railway systems of the 67 in the world is the London Underground with 254 miles *408 km* of route, of which 85 miles *135 km* is bored tunnel and 20 miles *32 km* is 'cut and cover'. The whole system is operated by a staff of 22,000 serving 273 stations. The 457 trains comprising 3875 cars carried 750,000,000 passengers in 1985/6. The greatest depth is 221 ft *67,3 m* near Hampstead on the Northern Line. The longest journey without a change is Epping to West Ruislip—34.1 miles *54,8 km*.

The record for touring the 272 stations including Heathrow Terminal 4 station opened 12 Apr 1986 is 18 hr 41 min 41 sec set by a team of five: Robert A. Robinson, Peter D. Robinson, Timothy J. Robinson, Timothy J. Clark and Richard J. Harris on 30 July 1986. Peter Robinson (b. 19 July 1974) was the youngest to tour all stations on 22 July 1982 aged 8.

The subway with most stations in the world is the New York City Transport Authority subway (first section opened on 27 Oct 1904) with a total of 231.73 route miles *372,93 km* and 1,096,006,529 passengers in 1979. The 458 stations are closer set than London's. The record for travelling the whole system is 21 hr 8½ min set by Mayer Wiesen and Charles Emerson on 8 Oct 1973.

Busiest

The world's busiest metro system is that in Greater Moscow with as many as 6½ million passengers per day. To mid-1985 it had 123 stations and 198 km *123 miles* of track. The record transit (with 18 changes) in 1982 (115 stations) was 8 hr 10 min 22 sec by Eric Rudkin of Chaddesden, Derbyshire.

MODEL RAILWAYS

The non-stop duration record for a model train (loco plus 6 coaches) is 864 hr 30 min from 1 June–7 July 1978, covering 678 miles *1091 km*, organised by Roy Catton at 'Pastimes' Toy Store, Mexborough, S. Yorkshire.

The longest recorded run by a model *steam* locomotive is 144 miles *231,7 km* in 27 hr 18 min by the 7¼ inch *18,4 cm* gauge 'Winifred', built in 1974 by Wilf Grove at Thames Ditton, Surrey, on 8–9 Sept 1979. 'Winifred' works on 80 lb/in² *5,6 kg/cm²* pressure and is coal fired with cylinders 2⅛ in *54 mm* in diameter and 3⅛ in *79 mm* stroke.

The most miniature model railway ever built is one of 1:1000 scale by Jean Damery (b. 1923) of Paris. The engine ran on a 4½-volt battery and measures 5/16 in *7,9 mm* overall.

TRAMS

Longest journey

The longest tramway journey now possible is from Krefeld St Tönis to Witten Annen Nord, West Germany. With luck at the 8 inter-connections the 105,5 km *65.5 mile* trip can be achieved in 5½ hr. By late 1987 there were more than 320 tramway systems surviving of which the most extensive is that of Leningrad, USSR with 2500 cars on 53 routes. The only system in Great Britain, until Manchester re-opens, is at Blackpool, Lancashire.

Oldest

The oldest trams in revenue service in the world are motor cars 1 and 2 of the Manx Electric Railway dating from 1893.

Aircraft

Note—The use of the Mach scale for aircraft speeds was introduced by Prof Ackeret of Zürich, Switzerland. The Mach number is the ratio of the velocity of a moving body to the local velocity of sound. This ratio was first employed by Dr Ernst Mach (1838–1916) of Vienna in 1887. Thus Mach 1.0 equals 760.98 mph *1224,67 km/h* at sea level at 15°C, and is assumed, for convenience, to fall to a constant 659.78 mph *1061,81 km/h* in the stratosphere, *i.e.* above 11 000 m *36,089 ft*. In 1986 the speed of sound was revised to 741.07 mph *1192,64 km/h*.

EARLIEST FLIGHTS

The first controlled and sustained power-driven flight occurred near the Kill Devil Hill, Kitty Hawk, North Carolina, USA, at 10.35 a.m. on 17 Dec 1903, when Orville Wright (1871–1948) flew the 12-hp chain-driven *Flyer I* for a distance of 120 ft *36,5 m* at an air speed of 30 mph *48 km/h*, a ground speed of 6.8 mph *10,9 km/h* and an altitude of 8–12 ft *2,5–3,5 m* for about 12 sec watched by his brother Wilbur (1867–1912), 4 men and a boy. Both brothers, from Dayton, Ohio, were bachelors because, as Orville put it, they had not the means to 'support a wife as well as an aeroplane'. The *Flyer* is now in the National Air and Space Museum at the Smithsonian Institution, Washington DC.

The first hop by a man-carrying aeroplane entirely under its own power was made when Clément Ader (1841–1925) of France flew in his *Eole* for about 50 m *164 ft* at Armainvilliers, France, on 9 Oct 1890. It was powered by a lightweight steam engine of his own design which developed about 20 hp (15 kW). The earliest 'rational design' for a flying machine, according to the Royal Aeronautical Society, was that published by Emanuel Swedenborg (1688–1772) in Sweden in 1717.

The first officially recognised flight in the British Isles was made by the US citizen Samuel Franklin Cody (1861–1913) who flew 1390 ft *423 m* in his own biplane at Farnborough, Hampshire, on 16 Oct 1908. Horatio Frederick Phillips (1845–1924) almost certainly covered 500 ft *152 m* in his Phillips II '*Venetian blind*' aeroplane at Streatham, in 1907.

The first Briton to fly was George Pearson Dickin (1881–1909), a journalist from Southport, Lancashire as a passenger to Wilbur Wright at Auvóur, France on 3 Oct 1908. The first resident British citizen to fly in Britain was J. T. C. Moore-Brabazon (later Lord Brabazon of Tara PC, GBE, MC) (1884–1964) with 3 short but sustained flights from 30 Apr–2 May 1909.

Cross-Channel

The earliest cross-Channel flight by an aeroplane was made on Sunday, 25 July 1909 when Louis Blériot (1872–1936) of France flew his *Blériot XI* monoplane, powered by a 23-hp Anzani engine, 26 miles *41,8 km* from Les Baraques, France, to Northfall Meadow near Dover Castle, England, in 36½ min, after taking off at 4.41 a.m.

Jet-engined

Proposals for jet propulsion date back to Captain Marconnet (1909) of France, and Henri Coanda (1886–1972) of Romania, and to the turbojet proposals of Maxime Guillaume in 1921. The earliest tested run was that of the British Power Jets Ltd's experimental WU (Whittle Unit) on 12 Apr 1937, invented by Flying Officer (later Air Commodore Sir) Frank Whittle OM, KBE (b. Coventry, 1 June 1907), who had applied for a patent on jet propulsion in 1930. The first flight by an aeroplane powered by a turbojet engine was made by the Heinkel He 178, piloted by Flug Kapitan Erich Warsitz, at Marienehe, Germany,

on 27 Aug 1939. It was powered by a Heinkel He S3b engine (834 lb *378 kg* as installed with long tailpipe) designed by Dr Hans 'Pabst' von Ohain and first tested in August 1937.

The first British jet flight occurred when Fl-Lt P. E. G. 'Jerry' Sayer OBE (k. 1942) flew the Gloster-Whittle E.28/39 (wing span 29 ft *8,84 m*, length 25 ft 3 in *7,70 m*) fitted with an 860 lb *390 kg* s. t. Whittle W-1 engine for 17 min at Cranwell, Lincolnshire, on 15 May 1941. The maximum speed was c. 350 mph *560 km/h.*

Supersonic flight

The first supersonic flight was achieved on 14 Oct 1947 by Capt (later Brig Gen) Charles ('Chuck') Elwood Yeager (b. 13 Feb 1923), over Edwards Air Force Base, Muroc, California, in a Bell XS-1 rocket plane ('Glamorous Glennis') with Mach 1.015 (670 mph *1078 km/h*) at an altitude of 42,000 ft *12 800 m.* The first British aircraft to attain Mach 1 in a dive was the de Havilland D. H. 108 tail-less research aircraft on 6 Sept 1948, piloted by John Derry.

Trans-Atlantic

The first crossing of the North Atlantic by air was made by Lt-Cdr (later Rear Admiral) Albert Cushion Read (1887–1967) and his crew (Stone, Hinton, Rodd, Rhoads and Breese) in the 84 knot *155 km/h* US Navy/Curtiss flying-boat NC-4 from Trepassey Harbor, Newfoundland, via the Azores, to Lisbon, Portugal, from 16–27 May 1919. The whole flight of 4717 miles *7591 km*, originating from Rockaway Air Station, Long Island, NY on 8 May, required 53 hr 58 min, terminating at Plymouth, England, on 31 May. The Newfoundland–Azores flight of 1200 miles *1930 km* took 15 hr 18 min at 81.7 knots *151,4 km/h.*

Non-stop

The first non-stop trans-Atlantic flight was achieved 18 days later from 4.13 p.m. GMT on 14 June 1919, from Lester's Field, St John's, Newfoundland, 1960 miles *3154 km* to Derrygimla bog near Clifden, County Galway, Ireland, at 8.40 a.m. GMT, 15 June, when the pilot, Capt John William Alcock DSC (1892–1919), and the navigator Lt Arthur Whitten Brown (1886–1948) flew across in a Vickers *Vimy*, powered by two 360-hp Rolls-Royce *Eagle VIII* engines. Both men were created civil KBE's on 21 June 1919 when Alcock was aged 26 years 227 days, and they shared a *Daily Mail* prize of £10,000.

Most flights

Between March 1948 and his retirement on 1 Sept 1984 Flight Service manager Charles M. Schimpf logged a total of 2,880 Atlantic crossings—a rate of 6.4 per month.

Trans-Pacific

The first non-stop trans-Pacific flight was by Major Clyde Pangborn and Hugh Herndon in the Bellanca cabin plane *Miss Veedol* from Sabishiro Beach, Japan 4558 miles *7335 km* to Wenatchee, Washington in 41 hr 13 min from 3–5 Oct 1931. (For earliest crossing see Circumnavigational flights below.)

Circumnavigational flights

Strict circumnavigation requires passing through two antipodal points thus with a minimum distance of 24,859.75 miles *40 007,89 km.* The FAI permits flights which exceed the length of the Tropic of Cancer or Capricorn *viz* 22,858.754 miles *36 787,599 km.*

The earliest such flight of 26,345 miles *42 398 km* was by two US Army Douglas DWC amphibians in 57 'hops'. The *Chicago* was piloted by Lt Lowell H. Smith and Lt Leslie P. Arnold and the *New Orleans* by Lt Erik H. Nelson and Lt John Harding between 6 Apr and 28 Sept 1924 beginning and ending at Seattle, Washington.

The earliest solo claim was by Wiley Hardemann Post (1898–1935) (US) in the Lockheed Vega 'Winnie Mae' starting and finishing at Floyd Bennett Field, New York City on 15–22 July 1933 in 10 'hops'. The distance of 15,596 miles *25 099 km* with a flying time of 115 hr 36 min was, however, at too high a latitude to qualify.

The fastest flight was the non-stop eastabout flight of 45 hr 19 min by three flight-refuelled USAF B-52s led by Maj-Gen Archie J. Old, Jr. They covered 24,325 miles *39 147 km* from 16–18 Jan 1957 finishing at March Air Force Base, Riverside, California, having averaged 525 mph *845 km/h* with four in-flight refuellings by KC-97 aerial tankers.

The first circum-polar flight was solo by Capt Elgen M. Long, 44, in a Piper Navajo from 5 Nov–3 Dec 1971. He covered 38,896 miles *62 597 km* in 215 flying hours. The cabin temperature sank to − 40°F *− 40°C* over Antarctica.

Solo trans-Atlantic crossing ● The *Spirit of St Louis*, in which the first solo trans-Atlantic flight was made by Charles Augustus Lindbergh (1902–74). He took off in the 220-hp Ryan monoplane at 12.52 p.m. GMT on 20 May 1927 from Roosevelt Field, Long Island, NY, USA and landed at Le Bourget airfield, Paris, after 3610 miles *5810 km* and 33 hr 9½ min. His prize was $25,000 (*then £5300*). (Photo: K J A Brookes)

A circum-polar flight in a single-engined aircraft was attempted unsuccessfully in January 1987. Richard Norton, an American airline captain, and Calin Rosetti, head of satellite navigation systems at the European Space Agency, planned to fly a Piper Malibu beginning and finishing at Le Bourget airport, Paris. The so-called Arctic Tern expedition also aimed to set a number of point-to-point records. It ended when the aircraft could not continue north beyond Mould Bay in northern Canada. It was hoped that the aircraft would be able to continue over the North Pole to complete the flight at the 1987 Paris Air Show.

Largest wing span

The aircraft with the largest ever wing span is the $40-million Hughes H.4 Hercules flying-boat ('Spruce Goose'), which was raised 70 ft *21,3 m* into the air in a test run of 1000 yd *914 m*, piloted by Howard Hughes (1905–76) off Long Beach Harbor, California, on 2 Nov 1947. The eight-engined 190 ton *193 tonne* aircraft had a wing span of 319 ft 11 in *97,51 m* and a length of 218 ft 8 in *66,64 m*, and never flew again. In a brilliant engineering feat she was moved bodily by Goldcoast Corp aided by the US Navy barge crane YD-171 on 22 Feb 1982 to her final resting place 6 miles *9,6 km* across the harbour under a 700 ft *213,4 m* diameter dome.

The $34-million Piasecki Heli-Stat, comprising a framework of light-alloy and composite materials to mount four Sikorsky SH-34J helicopters and the envelope of a Goodyear ZPG-2 patrol airship, was exhibited on 26 Jan 1984 at Lakehurst, New Jersey. Designed for use by the US Forest Service and designated Model 94-37J Logger, it has an overall length of 343 ft *104,55 m* and was intended to carry a payload of 21.4 tons. It crashed on 1 July 1986.

> **Circumnavigation without refuelling** ●
> Dick Rutan, 48, and Jeana Yeager, 34, flew non-stop round the world without refuelling their specially constructed aircraft *Voyager* from Edwards Air Force Base, California, USA, from 14–23 Dec 1986 in 9 days 3 min 44 sec, a distance of 25,012 miles *40 253 km* and averaging 115.8 mph *186,36 km/h*. Designed by Dick's brother, Burt Rutan, *Voyager*, with a wing span of 110.8 ft *33,77 m* and capable of carrying 1240 gal *5636 litres* of fuel weighing 8934 lb *4052 kg*, took over 2 years and 22,000 man-hours to construct.
>
> The pilot flew the plane from a cockpit measuring 5.6 × 1.8 ft *1,7 × 0,54 m* and the off-duty crew member occupied a cabin 7.5 × 2.0 ft *2,3 × 0,6 m*.
> (Photos: Colorific)

Heaviest

The highest recorded gross take-off weight has been 379.9 tons *386,0 tonnes* in the case of a Boeing 747-200B 'Jumbo' jet during certification tests of its Pratt & Whitney JT9D-7Q engines on 23 May 1979. Some versions are certified for standard airline operation at a maximum take-off weight of 371.9 tons *377,9 tonnes*.

Solar powered

The solar-powered *Solar Challenger*, designed by a team led by Dr Paul MacCready, was flown for the first time entirely under solar power on 20 Nov 1980. On 7 July 1981, piloted by Steve Ptacek (USA), the *Solar Challenger* became the first aircraft of this category to achieve a crossing of the English Channel. Taking off from Pontois-Cormeilles, Paris, the 163 mile *262,3 km* journey to Manston, Kent was completed in 5 hr 23 min at a maximum altitude of 3353 m *11,000 ft*. The aircraft has a wing span of 47 ft *14,3 m*.

Ultralight

On 3 Aug 1985 Anthony A. Cafaro (b. 30 Nov 1951) flew a ULA (max weight 245 lb *111 kg*, max speed 65 mph *104,6 km/h*, capacity 5 US gal *18,93 l*) single-seater Gypsey Skycycle for 7 hr 31 min at Dart Field, Detroit, Michigan. Nine fuel 'pick-ups' were completed during the flight.

Smallest

The smallest aeroplane ever flown is the *Baby Bird*, designed and built by Donald R. Stits. It is 11 ft *3,35 m* long, with a wing span of 6 ft 3 in *1,91 m*, and weighs 252 lb *114,3 kg* empty. It is powered by a 55-hp 2-cylinder Hirth engine, giving a top speed of 110 mph *177 km/h*. It was first flown by Harold Nemer on 4 Aug 1984 at Camarillo, California. The smallest jet is the 280 mph *450 km/h Silver Bullet* weighing 432 lb *196 kg* with a 17 ft *5,18 m* wing span built by Bob Bishop (USA).

Bombers *Heaviest*

The world's heaviest bomber is the eight-jet swept-wing Boeing B-52H Stratofortress, which has a maximum take-off weight of 488,000 lb (217.86 tons *221,35 tonnes*). It is 185 ft *56,38 m* and is 157 ft 6¾ in *48,02 m* in length, with a speed of over 650 mph *1046 km/h*. The B-52 can carry twelve SRAM thermonuclear short-range attack missiles or twenty-four 750 lb *340 kg* bombs under its wings and eight more SRAMs or eighty-four 500 lb *226 kg* bombs in the fuselage. The ten-engined Convair B-36J, weighing 183 tons *185 tonnes*, had a greater wing span, at 230 ft *70,10 m* but it is no longer in service. Its top speed was 435 mph *700 km/h*.

Fastest

The world's fastest operational bombers are the French Dassault Mirage IV, which can fly at Mach 2.2 (1450 mph *2333 km/h*) at 36,000 ft *11 000 m*. The American General Dynamics FB-111A has a maximum speed of Mach 2.5; and the Soviet swing-wing Tupolev Tu-22M known to NATO as 'Backfire' has an estimated over-target speed of Mach 2.0 but which may be as fast as Mach 2.5.

Largest airliner

The highest capacity jet airliner is the Boeing 747 'Jumbo Jet', first flown on 9 Feb 1969 (see Heaviest aircraft) and has a capacity of from 385 to more than 500 passengers with a maximum speed of 602 mph *969 km/h*. Its wing span is 195.7 ft *59,64m* and its length 231.8ft *70,7m*. It entered service on 22 Jan 1970. The Boeing 747-300 with lengthened upper deck, allowing an extra 37 passengers, entered service in March 1983.

The greatest passenger load recorded was one of 306 adults, 328 children and 40 babies (total 674) from the cyclone-devastated Darwin to Sydney, New South Wales, Australia on 29 Dec 1974.

The largest ever British aircraft was the experimental Bristol Type 167 Brabazon, which had a maximum take-off weight of 129.4 tons *131,4 tonnes*, a wing span of 230 ft *70,10 m* and a length of 177 ft *53,94 m*. This eight-engined aircraft first flew on 4 Sept 1949. Concorde (see below) has a maximum take-off weight of 408,000 lb *185 065 kg* (182.14 tons).

Fastest airliner

The supersonic BAC/Aérospatiale Concorde, first flown on 2 Mar 1969, with a capacity of 128 passengers, cruises at up to Mach 2.2 (1450 mph *2333 km/h*). It flew at Mach 1.05 on 10 Oct 1969, exceeded Mach 2 for the first time on 4 Nov 1970 and became the first supersonic airliner used on passenger services on 21 Jan 1976 when Air France and British Airways opened services simultaneously between, respectively, Paris–Rio de Janeiro and London–Bahrain. Services between London–New York and Paris–New York began on 22 Nov 1977. The New York–London record is 2 hr 56 min 35 sec set on 1 Jan 1983.

Most capacious

The Aero Spacelines Super Guppy has a cargo hold with a usable volume of 49,790 ft³ *1410 m³* and a maximum take-off weight of 78.12 tons *79,38 tonnes*. Wing span is 156.2 ft *47,63 m*, length 141 ft 3 in *43,05 m*. Its cargo compartment measures 108 ft 10 in *33,17 m* in length with a cylindrical section of 25 ft *7,62 m* in diameter. The Soviet Antonov AN-124 Ruslan has a cargo hold with a usable volume of 35,800 ft³ *1014 m³* and a maximum take-off weight of 398.6 tons *405 tonnes*. It is powered by four Lotarev D-18T turbofans giving a cruising speed of up to 528 mph *850 km/h* at 39,370 ft *12 000 m* and a range of 2796 miles *4500 km*.

Largest propeller

The largest aircraft propeller ever used was the 22 ft 7½ in *6,9 m* diameter Garuda propeller, fitted to the Linke-Hofmann R II built in Breslau, Germany (now Wroclaw, Poland), which flew in 1919. It was driven by four 260-hp Mercedes engines and turned at only 545 rpm.

Scheduled flights *Longest*

The longest scheduled non-stop flight is the weekly Pan-Am Sydney–San Francisco non-stop 13 hr 25 min Flight 816, in a Boeing 747 SP, opened in December 1976, over 7475 statute miles *12 030 km*. The longest delivery flight by a commercial jet is 8936 nautical miles or 10,290 statute miles *16 560 km* from Seattle, Washington to Cape Town, South Africa by the South African Airways' Boeing 747 SP (Special Performance) 'Matroosberg' using 178 400 kg *175.5 tons* of pre-cooled fuel in 17 hr 22½ min on 23–24 Mar 1976.

Shortest

The shortest scheduled flight in the world is that by Loganair between the Orkney Islands of Westray and Papa Westray which has been flown with Britten-Norman Islander twin-engined 10-seat transports since September 1967. Though scheduled for 2 min, in favourable wind conditions it has been accomplished in 58 sec by Capt Andrew D. Alsop.

United Airlines provide the shortest scheduled flight by jet, a Boeing 727, between San Francisco and Oakland, California. There are three flights daily and return, the flight time averaging 5 minutes for the 12 mile *19,3 km* journey.

Gary W. Rovetto of Island Air on 21 Mar 1980 flew on the scheduled flight from Center Island to Decatur Island, Washington, USA in 41 sec.

Fastest intercontinental scheduled airline

GB Airways have, since 1931, been operating a scheduled service from Gibraltar in Europe to Tangier in Africa on an almost daily basis. The flight by Vickers Viscount averages 15 minutes and covers a distance of 37 miles *60 km*.

Paris–London

The fastest time to travel the 214 miles *344 km* from central Paris to central London (BBC TV centre) is 38 min 58 sec by David Boyce of Stewart Wrightson (Aviation) Ltd on 24 Sept 1983 by motorcycle–helicopter to Le Bourget; Hawker Hunter jet (piloted by the late Michael Carlton) to Biggin Hill, Kent; helicopter to the TV centre car park.

London–New York

The record for central London to downtown New York City by helicopter and Concorde is 3 hr 59 min 44 sec and the return in 3 hr 40 min 40 sec both by David J. Springbett, 1981 Salesman of the Year, and David Boyce (see above) on 8 and 9 Feb 1982.

HIGHEST SPEED

Official record

The official air speed record is 2193.167 mph *3529,56 km/h* by Capt Eldon W. Joersz and Maj George T. Morgan, Jr, in a Lockheed SR-71A near Beale Air Force Base, California over a 15 to 25 km *9.3 to 15.5 mile* course on 28 July 1976.

Air-launched record

The fastest fixed-wing aircraft in the world was the US North American Aviation X-15A-2, which flew for the first time (after modification from X-15A) on 25 June 1964 powered by a liquid oxygen and ammonia rocket propulsion system. Ablative materials on the airframe once enabled a temperature of 3000°F to be withstood. The landing speed was momentarily 210 knots (242 mph *389,1 km/h*). The highest speed attained was 4520 mph *7274 km/h* (Mach 6.7) when piloted by Maj William J. Knight, USAF (b. 1930), on 3 Oct 1967. An earlier version piloted by Joseph A. Walker (1920–66) reached 354,200 ft *107 960 m* (67.08 miles) also over Edwards Air Force Base, California, on 22 Aug 1963. The programme was suspended after the final flight of 24 Oct 1968.

The US NASA Rockwell International Space Shuttle Orbiter *Columbia* was launched from the Kennedy Space Center, Cape Canaveral, Florida commanded by Cdr John W. Young USN and piloted by Robert L. Crippen on 12 Apr 1981 after expenditure of $9900 million since 1972. *Columbia* broke all records for space by a fixed-wing craft with 16,600 mph *26 715 km/h* at main engine cut-off. After re-entry from 400,000 ft *122 km*, experiencing temperatures of 2160°C *3920°F*, she glided home weighing 97 tonnes/ tons with the highest ever landing speed of 216 mph *347 km/h* on Rogers Dry Lake, California on 14 Apr 1981. Under a new FAI Category P for Aerospacecraft, the *Columbia* is holder of the current absolute world record for duration of 8 days 4 min 45 sec, with two astronauts, but *Challenger* (launched 18 June 1983) set a duration record of 6 days 2 hr 23 min 59 sec with five astronauts including Sally K. Ride, the first female Space Shuttle astronaut. On a previous mission it set a new record altitude of 206.36 miles *332,1 km*. *Columbia* also holds the current absolute world record for the greatest mass lifted to altitude, a figure of 235,634 lb *106 882 kg* or 105.2 tons. *Challenger* was destroyed soon after launch from Cape Canaveral on 28 January 1986 (see Chapter 4).

Fastest combat jet

The fastest combat aircraft in the world is the USSR Mikoyan MiG-25 fighter (code name 'Foxbat'). The reconnaissance 'Foxbat-B' has been tracked by radar at about Mach 3.2 (2110 mph *3395 km/h*). When armed with four large underwing air-to-air missiles known to NATO as 'Acrid', the fighter 'Foxbat-A' is limited to Mach 2.8 (1845 mph *2969 km/h*). The single-seat 'Foxbat-A' spans 45 ft 9 in *13,95 m*, is 78 ft 2 in *23,82 m* long and has an estimated maximum take-off weight of 82,500 lb *37 421 kg*.

Fastest jet ● The USAF Lockheed SR-71, a reconnaissance aircraft that is the world's fastest jet (see official record opposite). First flown on 22 Dec 1964, it is reportedly capable of attaining an altitude ceiling of close to 100,000 ft *30480 m*. The SR-71 has a wing span of 55.6 ft *16,94 m* and a length of 107.4 ft *32,73 m* and weighs 170,000 lb (75.9 tons) at take-off. Its reported range is 2982 miles *4800 km* at Mach 3 at 78,750 ft *24000 m*. At least 30 are believed to have been built. (Photo: K J A Brookes)

Fastest biplane

The fastest recorded biplane was the Italian Fiat C.R.42B, with a 1010-hp Daimler-Benz DB601A engine, which attained 323 mph *520 km/h* in 1941. Only one was built.

Fastest piston-engined aircraft

The fastest speed for a piston-engined aeroplane is for a cut-down privately-owned Hawker Sea Fury which attained 520 mph *836 km/h* in level flight over Texas, USA, in August 1966. It was piloted by Mike Carroll (k. 1969) of Los Angeles. The FAI accredited record for a piston-engined aircraft is 517.055 mph *832,12 km/h* over Mojave, California by Frank Taylor (US) in a modified North American P-51D Mustang powered by a 3000-hp Packard Merlin, over a 15 to 25 km *9.3 to 15.5 mile* course, on 30 July 1983.

Fastest propeller-driven aircraft

The Soviet Tu-114 turboprop transport achieved a recorded speed of 545.076 mph *877,212 km/h* carrying heavy payloads over measured circuits. It is developed from the Tupolev Tu-95 bomber, known in the West as the 'Bear', and has four 14,795-hp engines. The turboprop-powered Republic XF-84H prototype US Navy fighter which flew on 22 July 1955 had a top *design* speed of 670 mph *1078 km/h* but was abandoned.

Fastest trans-Atlantic flight

The trans-Atlantic flight record is 1 hr 54 min 56.4 sec by Maj James V. Sullivan, 37, and Maj Noel F. Widdifield, 33, flying a Lockheed SR-71A eastwards on 1 Sept 1974. The average speed, slowed by refuelling by a KC-135 tanker aircraft, for the New York–London stage of 3461.53 miles *5570,80 km* was 1806.963 mph *2908,026 km/h*. The solo record (Gander to Gatwick) is 8 hr 47 min 32 sec by Capt John J. A. Smith in a Rockwell 685 on 12 Mar 1978.

Altitude

The official world altitude record by an aircraft taking off from the ground under its own power is 123,524 ft (23.39 miles *37 650 m*) by Aleksandr Fedotov (USSR) in a Mikoyan E.266M (MiG-25) aircraft, powered by two 30,865 lb *14 000 kg* thrust turbojet engines, on 31 Aug 1977. In the same aircraft he established the fastest climb record on 17 May 1975 reaching 30 000 m *98,425 ft* in 4 min 11.7 sec after take off.

Duration

The flight duration record is 64 days 22 hr 19 min and 5 sec, set up by Robert Timm and John Cook in a Cessna 172 'Hacienda'. They took off from McCarran Airfield, Las Vegas, Nevada, just before 3.53 p.m. local time on 4 Dec 1958, and landed at the same airfield just before 2.12 p.m. on 7 Feb 1959. They covered a distance equivalent to six times round the world with continued refuellings, without landing.

AIRPORTS

Largest

The world's largest airport is the £2100-million King Khalid International Airport outside Riyadh, Saudi Arabia covering an area of 86 miles[2] *221 km[2]*, opened on 14 Nov 1983. It also has the world's largest control tower, 243 ft *74 m* in height. The Hajj Terminal at the £2800-million King Abdul-Aziz airport near Jeddah is the world's largest roofed structure covering 1,5 km[2] *370 acres*. The present 6 runways and 5 terminal buildings of Dallas/Fort Worth Airport, Texas are planned to be extended to 9 runways and 13 terminals with 260 gates with an ultimate capacity for 150 million passengers. The world's largest airport terminal is Hartsfield Atlanta International Airport, Georgia, USA, opened on 21 Sept 1980 with floor space covering 50.50 acres *20,43 ha*. It has 138 gates handling nearly 50 million passengers a year but has a capacity for 75 million.

Sixty-nine airline companies from 60 countries operate scheduled services into Heathrow Airport, London (2958 acres *1197 ha*), and during 1985 there was a total of 315,860 air transport movements, including 282,423 passenger flights, handled by a staff of 47,201 employed by the various companies and Heathrow Airport Ltd, a subsidiary of the British Airports Authority. The total number of passengers, both incoming and outgoing, was 31,315,348. The most flights yet handled by Heathrow in a day was 1,041 on 5 Sept 1986 and the largest number of passengers yet handled in a day was 122,177 on 31 August 1986, including 11,302 passengers in one hour. Aircraft fly to 218 destinations direct in 80 countries. Heathrow Airport is now Britain's busiest port, handling £21,000 million worth of cargo. This represents some 13 per cent of total UK trade annually. The airport's busiest single hour for aircraft movements was 0800–0900 hr GMT on 20 July 1984 when 81 flights were handled using two active runways.

Busiest

The world's busiest airport is Chicago International Airport, O'Hare Field, Illinois, with a total of 795,026 movements and 54,770,673 passengers in the year 1986. This represents a take-off or landing every 39.66 sec round the clock. Heathrow Airport, London handles more *international* traffic than any other. The busiest landing area ever has been Bien Hoa Air Base, South Vietnam, which handled more than 1,000,000 take-offs and landings in 1970. The world's largest 'helipad' was An Khe, South Vietnam.

The heliport at Morgan City, Louisiana, USA, one of a string used by helicopters flying energy-related offshore operations into the Gulf of Mexico, has pads for 46 helicopters.

Highest and lowest

The highest airport in the world is La Sa (Lhasa) Airport, Tibet at 14,315 ft *4363 m*.

The highest landing ever made by a fixed-wing plane is 19,947 ft *6080 m* on Dhaulagiri, Himalaya by a Pilatus Porter named 'Yeti', supplying the 1960 Swiss expedition. The lowest landing field is El Lisan on the east shore of the Dead Sea, 1180 ft *360 m* below sea level, but during World War II BOAC Short C-class flying boats operated from the surface of the Dead Sea 1292 ft *394 m* below sea level. The lowest international airport is Schiphol, Amsterdam, at 13 ft *3,9 m* below sea level. Rotterdam's airport is fractionally lower at 15 ft *4,5 m*.

Farthest and nearest to city or capital centres

The airport farthest from the city centre it allegedly serves is Viracopos, Brazil, which is 60 miles *96 km* from São Paulo. Gibraltar airport is 880 yd *800 m* from the centre.

Longest runway

The longest runway in the world is one of 7 miles *11 km* in length (of which 15,000 ft *4572 m* is concreted) at Edwards Air Force Base on the bed of Rogers Dry Lake at Muroc, California, USA. The whole test centre airfield extends over 65 miles² *168 km²*. In an emergency an auxiliary 12 mile *19 km* strip is available along the bed of the Dry Lake. The world's longest civil airport runway is one of 16,076 ft (3.04 miles *4,89 km*) at Pierre van Ryneveld Airport, Upington, South Africa constructed in five months from August 1975 to January 1976. A paved runway 20,500 ft (3.88 miles *6,24 km*) long appears on maps of Jordan at Abu Husayn. The longest runway normally available to civil aircraft in the United Kingdom is No 1 at Heathrow Airport, London, measuring 12,800 ft (2.42 miles *3,90 km*). The most southerly major runway (1.6 miles *2,57 km*) in the world is at Mount Pleasant, East Falkland (Lat 51° 50′S) built in 16 months to May 1985.

HELICOPTERS

Fastest

Trevor Eggington, 53, averaged 249.10 mph *400,87 km/h* over Somerset on 11 Aug 1986 in a Westland Lynx Company demonstrator helicopter.

Largest

The world's largest helicopter is the Soviet Mil Mi-12 ('Homer'), also known as the V-12. It is powered by four 6500-hp turboshaft engines and has a span of 219 ft 10 in *67 m* over its rotor tips with a length of 121 ft 4½ in *37,00 m* and it weighs 103.3 tons *105 tonnes*.

Greatest load

On 3 Feb 1982 at Podmoscovnoé in the Soviet Union, a Mil Mi-26 heavy-lift helicopter, crewed by G. V. Alfeurov and L. A. Indeev (co-pilot), lifted a total mass of 125,153.8 lb *56 768,8 kg* (55.87 tons *56,77 tonnes*) to 2000 m *6560 ft*.

Smallest

The Aerospace General Co one-man rocket-assisted minicopter weighs about 160 lb *72,5 kg* cruising 250 miles *400 km* at 85 mph *137 km/h*.

Highest

The altitude record for helicopters is 40,820 ft *12 442 m* by an Aérospatiale SA315B *Lama*, over France on 21 June 1972. The highest recorded landing has been at 23,000 ft *7000 m* below the south-east face of Everest in a rescue sortie in May 1971. The South Tower of the World Trade Center helipad is 1385 ft *422 m* above street level in New York City.

Circumnavigation

H. Ross Perot and Jay Coburn, both of Dallas, Texas made the first helicopter circumnavigation in 'Spirit of Texas' on 1–30 Sept 1982. The first solo round-the-world flight in a helicopter was completed by Dick Smith (Australia) on 22 July 1983. Flown from and to the Bell helicopter facility at Fort Worth, Texas, in a Bell Model 206L *Long Ranger III*, his unhurried flight began on 5 Aug 1982 and covered a distance of 35,258 miles *56 742 km*.

AUTOGYROS

Earliest

The autogyro or gyroplane, a rotorcraft with an unpowered rotor turned by the airflow in flight, preceded the practical helicopter with engine-driven rotor. Juan de la Cierva (Spain) made the

> **Trans-Atlantic ballooning** ● Ex-USAF Colonel Joe Kittinger became the first man to complete a solo trans-Atlantic crossing by balloon. Accomplished in the 3000-m³ helium-filled balloon *Rosie O'Grady* between 14–18 Sept 1984, Kittinger lifted off from Caribou, Maine and completed a distance of approximately 3543 miles *5701 km* before landing at Montenotte, Italy after 86 hr.

first successful autogyro flight with his model C.4 (commercially named an *Autogiro*) at Getafe, Spain, on 9 Jan 1923.

Speed, altitude and distance records

Wing-Cdr Kenneth H. Wallis (GB) holds the straight-line distance record of 543.27 miles *874,32 km* set in his WA-116F autogyro on 28 Sept 1975 non-stop from Lydd, Kent to Wick, Caithness. Wing-Cdr Wallis flew his WA-116, with a 72-hp McCulloch engine, to a record speed of 120.5 mph *193,9 km/h* over a 3 km *1.86 mile* straight course on 18 Sept 1986. On 20 July 1982, flying from Boscombe Down, Wiltshire, he established a new autogyro altitude record of 18,516 ft *5643,7 m* in his WA-121/Mc. It was reported that on 8 Apr 1931 Amelia Earhart (US) reached a height in excess of 19,000 ft *5791 m* at Pitcairn Aviation Field, Pennsylvania.

FLYING-BOAT

Fastest

The fastest flying-boat ever built has been the Martin XP6M-1 Seamaster, the US Navy 4-jet-engined minelayer flown in 1955–9 with a top speed of 646 mph *1040 km/h*. In September 1946 the Martin JRM-2 Mars flying-boat set a payload record of 68,327 lb *30 992 kg*. The official flying-boat speed record is 566.69 mph *912 km/h*, set up by Nikolay Andreyevskiy and crew of two in a Soviet Beriev M-10, powered by two AL-7 turbojets, over a 15 to 25 km *9.3 to 15.5 mile* course on 7 Aug 1961. The M-10 holds all 12 records listed for jet-powered flying-boats, including an altitude of 49,088 ft *14 962 m* set by Georgiy Buryanov and crew over the Sea of Azov on 9 Sept 1961.

AIRSHIPS

Earliest

The earliest flight in an airship was by Henri Giffard from Paris in his steam-powered coal-gas 88,300 ft³ *2500 m³* 144 ft *43,8 m* long airship on 24 Sept 1852. The earliest British airship was a 20,000 ft³ *566 m³* 75 ft *22,8 m* long craft built by Stanley Spencer whose maiden flight was from Crystal Palace, London on 22 Sept 1902. The latest airship to be built in Britain is the 235,400 ft³ *6666 m³* 193.6 ft *59 m* long Skyship 600 designed and built by Airship Industries. This 20-passenger dirigible (G-SKSC) was flown for the first time at RAE Cardington, Bedfordshire on 6 Mar 1984.

Largest *Rigid*

The largest rigid airship ever built was the 210.5 ton *213,9 tonne* German *Graf Zeppelin II* (LZ 130), with a length of 245 m *803.8 ft* and a capacity of 7,062,100 ft³ *199 981 m³*. She made her maiden flight on 14 Sept 1938 and in May and August 1939 made radar spying missions in British air space. She was dismantled in April 1940. Her sister ship *Hindenburg* was 5.6 ft *1,70 m* longer.

The largest British airship was the R101 built by the Royal Airship Works, Cardington, Bedfordshire, which first flew on 14 Oct 1929. She was 777 ft *236,8 m* in length and had a capacity of 5,508,800 ft³ *155 995 m³*. She crashed near Beauvais, France, killing 48 aboard on 5 Oct 1930.

Non-rigid

The largest non-rigid airship ever constructed was the US Navy ZPG 3-W which had a capacity of 1,516,300 ft³ *42 937 m³*, was 403.4 ft *122,9 m* long and 85.1 ft *25,93 m* in diameter, with a crew of 21. She first flew on 21 July 1958, but crashed into the sea in June 1960.

Hot-air

The world altitude, duration and distance records, of 10,365 ft *3159 m*, 1 hr 26 min 52 sec, and 23.03 miles *37,07 km* respectively, are held by the Cameron D-38 hot-air airship flown at Cunderdin, Western Australia on 27 Aug 1982 by R. W. Taaffe (Australia).

Greatest passenger load

The most people ever carried in an airship was 207 in the US Navy *Akron* in 1931. The trans-Atlantic record is 117 by the German *Hindenburg* in 1937.

Distance records

The FAI accredited straight-line distance record for airships is 3967.1 miles *6384,5 km*, set up by the German *Graf Zeppelin*, captained by Dr Hugo Eckener, between 29 Oct and 1 Nov 1928. The German Zeppelin L59 flew from Yambol, Bulgaria to south of Khartoum, Sudan and returned from 21–25 Nov 1917 to cover a minimum of 4500 miles *7250 km*.

Duration record

The longest recorded flight by a non-rigid airship (without refuelling) is 264 hr 12 min by a US Navy Goodyear-built ZPG-2 class ship (Cdr J. R. Hunt USN) from South Weymouth NAS, Massachusetts from 4–15 Mar 1957 landing back at Key West, Florida having flown 9448 miles *15 205 km*.

BALLOONING

Earliest

I. William Deiches (b. 1934) of Brentwood, Essex, has adduced that the 'mace-head' of the Scorpion King *c.* 3100 BC found at Hierakonpolis, Egypt is in reality a depiction of a panelled hot-air balloon of papyrus construction. The earliest recorded ascent was by a model hot-air balloon invented by Father Bartolomeu de Gusmão (né Lourenço) (1685–1724), which was flown indoors at the Casa da India, Terreiro do Paço, Portugal on 8 Aug 1709.

Distance record (*Great-circle distance between take-off and first landing point*)

The record distance travelled by a balloon is 5208.68 miles *8382,54 km* by the Raven experimental helium-filled balloon *Double Eagle V* (capacity 11 300 m³ *399,053 ft³*) from 9–12 Nov 1981, from Nagashima, Japan to Covello, California. The crew for this first manned balloon crossing of the Pacific Ocean were Ben L. Abruzzo, 51, Rocky Aoki, 43 (Japan), Ron Clark, 41 and Larry M. Newman, 34.

The first balloon crossing of the North Atlantic had been made during 12–17 Aug 1978 in the gas balloon *Double Eagle II* crewed by Ben L. Abruzzo, Maxie L. Anderson and Larry M. Newman.

The first crossing of the United States was by the helium-filled balloon *Super Chicken III* (pilots Fred Gorell and John Shoecraft) from Costa Mesa, California, 2515 miles *4047 km* to Blackbeard's Island, Georgia from 9–12 Oct 1981.

Highest *Unmanned*

The highest altitude attained by an unmanned balloon was 170,000 ft *51 815 m* by a Winzen balloon of 47.8 million ft³ *1,35 million m³* launched at Chico, California in October 1972.

Manned

The greatest altitude reached in a manned balloon is an unofficial 123,800 ft (23.45 miles *37 735 m*) by Nicholas Piantanida (1933–66) of Bricktown, New Jersey, from Sioux Falls, South Dakota, on 1 Feb 1966. He landed in a cornfield in Iowa but did not survive. The official record is 113,740 ft *34 668 m* by Cdr Malcolm D. Ross, USNR and the late Lt-Cdr Victor A. Prother, USN in an ascent from the deck of USS *Antietam* on 4 May 1961, over the Gulf of Mexico.

Owing to a miscalculation, Harold Froelich and Keith Lang, scientists from Minneapolis, ascended in an open gondola and without the protection of pressure suits to a height of 42,150 ft *12,84 km*, just under 8 miles, on 26 Sept 1956. During their 6½-hour flight, the temperature fell to −72°F *−57,7°C*.

Largest

The largest balloon built is one with an inflatable volume of 70 million ft³ *2 million m³* by Winzen Research Inc, Minnesota.

Hot-air

(Modern revival began in the USA in 1961. First World Championships 10–17 Feb 1973 at Albuquerque, New Mexico, USA.)

Richard Branson (GB) with his pilot Per Linstrand (Sweden), the first to cross the Atlantic in a hot-air balloon, flew on 2–3 July 1987 from Sugarloaf, Maine, USA, to Limavady, Co Londonderry, N Ireland, a distance of 3075 miles *4947 km*. Their balloon, *Virgin Atlantic Flyer*, of 2.3 million ft³ *65 000 m³* capacity was the largest ever flown and reached speeds in excess of 130 mph *209 km/h*. The duration record of 40 hr 12 min 5 sec was established by the French pair Hélène Dorigny and her co-pilot Michel Arnould on 6–7 July 1984 in the balloon *Le Primagaz* flying from Germaine to Le Mele-sur-Sarthe, France. On 31 Oct 1980 Julian Nott (GB) attained an altitude of 55,137 ft *16 805 m*, taking off from Longmont, near Denver, Colorado in the Cameron-built ICI balloon *Innovation*. The open-basket altitude record using a pressure suit is 53,000 ft *16 154,4 m* established by Chauncey M. Dunn (US) on 1 Aug 1979. Donald Allan Cameron (GB) and Major Christopher Davey set endurance and distance records in their gas and hot-air balloon *Zanussi* of 96 hr 24 min and 2074.817 miles *3339,086 km* on 30 July 1978.

PERSONAL AVIATION RECORDS

Oldest and youngest passengers

Airborne births are reported every year. The oldest person to fly has been Mrs Jessica S. Swift (b. Anna Stewart 17 Sept 1871) aged 110 yrs 3 months, from Vermont to Florida in Dec 1981. The oldest Briton to fly was probably Mrs Julia Caroline Black (b. 24 Feb 1874 d. 12 May 1980) on a British Caledonian flight from Abbotsinch to Gatwick on 17 Nov 1978 when aged 104 years 8 months.

Youngest and oldest pilots

The youngest age at which anyone has ever qualified as a military pilot is 15 years 5 months in the case of Sgt Thomas Dobney (b. 6 May 1926) of the RAF. He had overstated his age (14 years) on entry. The youngest solo pilot has been Cody A. Locke in a Cessna 150 aircraft near Mexicali, Mexico on 24 Feb 1983, when aged 9 years 316 days. A wholly untutored James A. Stoodley aged 14 years 5 months took his 13-year-old brother John on a 29-minute joy ride in an unattended US Piper Cub trainer aircraft near Ludgershall, Wiltshire in December 1942.

The world's oldest pilot is Ed McCarty (b. 18 Sept 1885) of Kimberly, Idaho who in 1979 was flying his rebuilt 30-year-old Ercoupe, aged 94. The oldest British pilot is Air Commodore Harold 'Daddy' Probyn (b. 8 Dec 1891), who first flew with the RFC in 1916 and was flying in Kenya on his 92nd birthday 67 years later in 1983.

Most flying hours

Max Conrad (1903–79) (USA) between 1928 and mid-1974 totalled 52,929 hr 40 min logged flight —more than 6 years airborne. He completed 150 trans-Atlantic crossings in light aircraft. The record as a supersonic passenger is held by Fred Finn who made his 604th Concorde crossing in June 1986.

Most take-offs and landings from airports

Al Yates and Bob Phoenix of Texas made 193 take-offs and daylight landings at unduplicated airfields in 14 hr 57 min in a Piper Seminole, on 15 June 1979.

E. K. Coventry (pilot) and D. Bullen (navigator) made full-stop landings in a Piper Arrow in all of England's 45 counties between dawn and dusk on 24 July 1984.

Human-powered flight

The first man-powered crossing was achieved on 12 June 1979 by Bryan Allen (US) in the *Gossamer Albatross*, designed by Dr Paul MacCready. The 22.26 mile *35,82 km* flight from Folkestone to Cap Gris Nez set the duration record of 2 hr 49 min.

MODEL AIRCRAFT

Altitude, speed and duration

Maynard L. Hill (US) flying radio-controlled models established the world record for altitude of 26,929 ft *8208 m* on 6 Sept 1970 and on 4 July 1983 set a closed-circuit distance record of 1231 miles *765 km*. The free-flight speed record is 213.70 mph *343,92 km/h* by V. Goukoune and V. Myakinin (both USSR) with a radio-controlled model at Klementyeva, USSR, on 21 Sept 1971. The record duration flight is one of 32 hr 7 min 40 sec by Eduard Svoboda (Czechoslovakia), flying a radio-controlled glider on 23–24 Aug 1980. An indoor model with a rubber motor designed by J. Richmond (USA) set a duration record of 52 min 14 sec on 31 Aug 1979.

Cross-Channel

The first cross-Channel model helicopter flight was achieved by an 11 lb *5 kg* model Bell 212 radio controlled by Dieter Zeigler for 32 miles *52 km* between Ashford, Kent and Ambleteuse, France on 17 July 1974.

Smallest

The smallest model aircraft to fly is one weighing 0.004 oz *0,1 g* powered by attaching a horsefly and designed by insectonaut Don Emmick of Seattle, Washington on 24 July 1979. One flew for 5 minutes at Kirkland, Washington.

Paper aircraft

The flight duration record for a paper aircraft is 16.89 sec by Ken Blackburn in the Reynolds Coliseum, North Carolina State University, on 29 Nov 1983. The indoor record with a 12 ft *3,65 m* ceiling is 1 min 33 sec set in the Fuji TV studios, Tōkyō, Japan on 21 Sept 1980. A paper plane was reported and witnessed to have flown 1¼ miles *2,0 km* by 'Chick' C. O. Reinhart from a 10th-storey office window at 60 Beaver Street, New York across the East River to Brooklyn in August 1933, helped by a thermal from a coffee-roasting plant. An indoor distance of 193 ft *58,82 m* was recorded by Tony Felch at the La Crosse Center, Wisconsin on 21 May 1985.

The largest flying paper aeroplane was constructed on 26 Apr 1986 by Grahame Foster, David Broom and Andrew Barnes at the Old Warden Aerodrome, Biggleswade, Bedfordshire. It was launched from a platform of height 10 ft *3,04 m* and flew for 54 ft *16,4 m* during the course of the BBC television programme *The Great Egg Race*.

Power

Steam engines

The oldest steam engine in working order is the 1812 Boulton & Watt 26-hp 42 in *1066 mm* bore beam engine on the Kennet & Avon Canal at Great Bedwyn, Wiltshire. It was restored by the Crofton Society in 1971 and still runs periodically.

The largest single-cylinder steam engine ever built was that designed by Matthew Loam of Cornwall and made by the Hayle Foundry Co in 1849 for installation for land draining at Haarlem, Netherlands. The cylinder was 12 ft *3,65 m* in diameter such that each stroke, also of 12 ft *3,65 m*, lifted 13,440 gallons *61 096 l* or 60 tons of water.

The most efficient steam engine recorded was Taylor's engine built by Michael Loam for United Mines, Gwennap, Cornwall in 1840. It registered only 1.7 lb of coal per horsepower per hour.

Earliest atomic pile

The world's first atomic pile was built in a disused squash court at Stagg Field, University of Chicago, Illinois. It went 'critical' at 3.25 p.m. on 2 Dec 1942.

Largest power plant

Currently, the world's most powerful installed power station is the Grand Coulee, Washington State, USA with 9.7 million kilowatt hours (ultimately 10,080 MW) which began operating in 1942.

The $11-billion Itaipu power station on the Paraná river by the Brazil-Paraguay border began generating power formally on 25 Oct 1984 and will by 1988/89 attain 12,600,000 kW from 18 turbines. Construction began in 1975 with a work force reaching 28,000. A 20,000-MW power station project on the Tunguska River, USSR was announced in February 1982.

The world's largest coal-fired power complex at Ekibastuz, Kazakhstan, USSR began generating in May 1982.

The power station with the greatest installed capacity in Great Britain is Drax, North Yorkshire, with 5 of its 6660-MW sets yielding 3300 MW in mid-1985. The sixth set became operational in early 1986. A 3300-MW oil-fired installation is under construction on the Isle of Grain, Kent.

The largest hydroelectric plant in the UK is the North of Scotland Hydroelectricity Board's Power Station at Loch Sloy, Dumbartonshire. The installed capacity of this station is 130 MW. The Ben Cruachan pumped storage scheme was opened on 15 Oct 1965 at Loch Awe, Argyllshire. It has a capacity of 400 MW and cost £24,000,000.

The 1880-MW underground pumped storage scheme at Dinorwig, Gwynedd is the largest in

---

Human-powered flight ● *Michelob Light Eagle* set a world distance record for human-powered flight of 37.2 miles *59,8 km* on 22 Jan 1987 at Edwards Air Force Base, California, USA. The 90 lb *40,8 kg* craft with a 114 ft *34,7 m* wing span was piloted by Glenn Tremml of New Haven, Connecticut and covered the distance in 2 hr 13 min 14 sec averaging 16.7 mph *26,9 km/h*. The flight was part of the Daedalus Project, centred on the Massachusetts Institute of Technology, whose goal is to make, by human power, the flight from Crete to mainland Greece, a distance of about 70 miles *112,6 km.* (Photo: Colorific)

Europe with a head of 1739 ft *530 m* and a capacity of 13,770 ft³/sec *390 m³/sec.* The £425-million plant was completed in 1984 with a capacity of 1681 MW.

Nuclear power station

The first nuclear power station producing electricity was the ERR-1 in the USA on 20 Dec 1951. Britain's earliest was Calder Hall (Unit 1), Cumbria on 27 Aug 1956.

The world's largest nuclear power station with 10 reactors and an output of 9096 MW is the station in Fukushima, Japan.

Nuclear reactor

The largest single nuclear reactor in the world is the 1450-MW (net) reactor at the Ignalina station, Lithuania, USSR, put on full power in January 1984. The largest under construction is the CHOOZ-B1 reactor in France which is scheduled for operation in 1991 and will have a net capacity of 1457 MW.

Fusion power

Tokamak-7, the experimental thermonuclear apparatus, was declared in January 1982 by USSR academician Velikhov to be operating 'reliably for months on end'. An economically functional thermonuclear reactor is not anticipated in the near future.

Solar power plant

The largest solar furnace in the world is the $141-million 10-megawatt 'Solar I', 12 miles *19,3 km* south-east of Barstow, California, first tested in April 1982. It comprises 1818 mirrors in concentric circles focused on a boiler atop a 255 ft *77,7 m* high tower. Sunlight from 222 heliostats is concentrated on a target 114 ft *34,7 m* up in the power tower. The $30-million thermal solar energy system at Pakerland Packing Co, Bellevue Plant, Green Bay, Wisconsin completed in January 1984 comprises 9750 4 × 8 ft *1,21 × 2,43 m* collectors covering 7.16 acres *28 985 m².* It will yield up to 8000 million BTUs a month.

Tidal power station

The world's first major tidal power station is the *Usine marémotrice de la Rance*, officially opened on 26 Nov 1966 at the Rance estuary in the Golfe de St Malo, Brittany, France. It was built in five years at a cost of 420,000,000 francs (*£34,685,000*), and has a net annual output of 544,000,000 kWh. The 880 yd *804 m* barrage contains 24 turbo alternators. The $1000-million (*£540 million*) Passamaquoddy project for the Bay of Fundy in Maine, USA, and New Brunswick, Canada, remains a project. A $46-million (*then £25.5 million*) pilot Annapolis River project for the Bay of Fundy was begun in 1981.

Largest boiler

The largest boilers ever designed are those ordered in the United States from Babcock & Wilcox (USA) with a capacity of 1330 MW so involving the evaporation of 9,330,000 lb *4 232 000 kg* of steam per hour. The largest boilers being installed in the United Kingdom are five 660-MW units for the Drax Power Station, designed and constructed by Babcock & Wilcox.

Largest generator

Generators in the 2,000,000-kW (or 2000-MW) range are now in the planning stages both in the UK and the USA. The largest operational is a turbo-generator of 1450 MW (net) being installed at the Ignalina Atomic Power Station in Lithuania (see column 2).

Largest turbines

The largest hydraulic turbines are those rated at 815,000 kW (equivalent to 1.1 million hp), 32 ft *9,7 m* in diameter with a 401 ton *407 tonne* runner and a 312½ ton *317,5 tonne* shaft installed by Allis-Chalmers at the Grand Coulee 'Third Powerplant', Washington, USA.

Pump

The world's largest reversible pump-turbine is that made by Allis-Chalmers for the Bath County project, Virginia, USA. It has a maximum rating of 457 MW as a turbine and maximum operating head of 393 m *1289 ft*. The impeller/runner diameter is 6349 mm *20 ft 9 in* with a synchronous speed of 257.1 rpm.

Longest-lasting battery

The zinc foil and sulfur dry-pile batteries made by Watlin and Hill of London in 1840 have powered ceaseless tintinnabulation inside a bell jar at the Clarendon Laboratory, Oxford since that year.

Largest gasworks

The flow of natural gas from the North Sea is diminishing the manufacture of gas by the carbonisation of coal and the reforming process using petroleum derivatives. Britain's largest ever gasworks, 300 acres *120 ha*, were at Beckton, Newham, east London. Currently, the largest gasworks in the UK are the Breakwater Works at Oreston, Plymouth, Devon which opened in 1966–7 and cover an area of 19 acres *7,6 ha*. They convert complex hydrocarbons into methane and produce 50 million ft³ *1 415 850 m³* per day.

Biggest black-out

The greatest power failure in history struck seven north-eastern US states and Ontario, Canada, on 9–10 Nov 1965. About 30,000,000 people in 80,000 miles² *207 200 km²* were plunged into darkness. Only two were killed. In New York the power failed at 5.27 p.m. and was not fully restored for 13½ hr. The total consequential losses in the 52-min New York City power failure of 13 July 1977 including looting was put at $1 billion (*then £580 million*).

Windmill

Earliest

The earliest recorded windmills are those used for grinding corn in Iran (Persia) in the 7th century AD.

The earliest date attributed to a windmill in England is 1185 for one at Weedley, near Hull, Humberside. The oldest Dutch mill is the tower-mill at Zeddam, Gelderland built in *c*. 1450. The oldest working mill in England is the post-mill at Outwood, near Redhill, Surrey, built in 1665, though the Ivinghoe Mill in Pitstone Green Farm, Buckinghamshire, dating from 1627, has been restored. The post-mill in North Ronaldsay, Orkney Islands operated until 1905.

Largest

The world's most powerful wind generator is the 3000-kW 150 m *492 ft* tall turbine, built by Grosse Windenergie-Anlage which was set up in 1982 on the Friesian coast of West Germany. A £10.5-million 3000-kW aerogenerator with 60 m *196 ft 10 in* blades on Burgar Hill, Evie, Orkney built by Taylor Woodrow will be operational by autumn 1987. It should yield 9 million kW/h per annum. The $14.2-million GEC MOD-5A installation on the north shore of Oahu, Hawaii will produce 7300 kW when the wind reaches 32 mph *51,5 km/h* with 400 ft *122 m* rotors. Installation started in March 1984.

The largest Dutch windmill is the Dijkpolder in Maasland built in 1718. The sails measure 95¾ ft *29 m* from tip to tip. De Noord windmill in Schiedam, Netherlands at 33,33 m *109 ft 4 in* is the tallest in Europe. The tallest windmill still standing in Britain is the 9-storey Sutton mill, Norfolk built in 1853 which, before being struck by lightning in 1941, had sails 73 ft *22,2 m* in diameter with 216 shutters.

Water mill

There has been a water-powered corn-mill at Priston Mill near Bath, Avon since pre-Norman times. The earliest recorded is dated AD 931.

Engineering

Oldest machinery

The earliest machinery still in use is the *dâlu*—a water-raising instrument known to have been in use in the Sumerian civilisation which originated *c*. 3500 BC in lower Iraq thus even earlier than the *Saqiyas* on the Nile.

The oldest piece of machinery (excluding clocks) operating in the United Kingdom is the snuff mill driven by a water wheel at Messrs Wilson & Co's Sharrow Mill in Sheffield, South Yorkshire. It is known to have been operating in 1797 and more probably since 1730.

Blast furnace

The world's largest blast furnace is one with an inner volume of 5070 m³ *179,040 ft³* and a 14,8 m *48 ft 6½ in* diameter hearth at the Oita Works, Kyūshū, Japan completed in October 1976 with an annual capacity of 4,380,000 tons *4 451 500 tonnes*.

Cat cracker

The world's largest catalyst cracker is Exxon's Bayway Refinery plant at Linden, New Jersey, with a fresh feed rate of 5,040,000 US gal *19 077 000 litres* per day.

Conveyor belt

The world's longest single-flight conveyor belt is one of 18 miles *29 km* in Western Australia installed by Cable Belt Ltd of Camberley, Surrey. The longest in Great Britain is also by Cable Belt and of 5½ miles *8,9 km* underground at Longannet Power Station, Fife. The world's longest multi-flight conveyor is one of 100 km *62 miles* between the phosphate mine near Bucraa and the port of El Aaiun, Morocco, built by Krupps and completed in 1972. It has 11 flights of between 9 and 11 km *5.6–6.8 miles* and was driven at 4,5 m/sec *10.06 mph* but has since been closed down.

Most powerful crane

The world's most powerful cranes are those aboard the semi-submersible vessel *Balder* (105 000-tonnes displacement) operated by Heerema Marine Contractors, Switzerland. Each has one 3000- and one 2000-tonne capacity crane which, working in tandem, could raise a 4000-tonne piece. The *Balder* set a record with a 3412-tonne lift in August 1983 and in March 1984 was refitted to raise her capacity to close to 6000 tonnes. The American company Brown & Root announced the building of a 140 000-tonne crane-ship with lifting capacity of 6500 tonnes in December 1983.

Gantry crane

The 92.3 ft *28,14 m* wide Rahco (R. A. Hanson Disc. Ltd) gantry crane at the Grand Coulee Dam Third Powerplant was tested to lift a load of 2232 long tons *2268 tonnes* in 1975. It lowered a 3,944,000 lb *1789 tonne* generator rotor with an accuracy of 1/32 in *0,8 mm*.

Tallest mobile crane

The tallest mobile crane in the world is the 810-tonne Rosenkranz K10001 with a lifting capacity of 1000 tonnes *984 tons*, and a combined boom and jib height of 202 m *663 ft*. It is carried on 10 trucks each limited to 75 ft 8 in *23,06 m* and an axle weight of 118 tonnes *116 tons*. It can lift 30 tonnes *29.5 tons* to a height of 160 m *525 ft*.

Dragline (see also p. 131)

The Ural Engineering Works at Ordzhonikdze, USSR, completed in March 1962, has a dragline known as the ES-25(100) with a boom of 100 m *328 ft* and a bucket with a capacity of 31.5 yd³ *24 m³*. The world's largest walking dragline is 'Big Muskie', the Bucyrus-Erie 4250W with an all-up weight of 12,000 tons *12 192 tonnes* and a bucket capacity of 220 yd³ *168 m³* on a 310 ft *94,4 m* boom. This machine, the world's largest mobile land machine, is now operating on the Central Ohio Coal Company's Muskingum site in Ohio.

The largest dragline excavator in Britain is 'Big Geordie', the Bucyrus-Erie 1550W 6250 gross hp, weighing 3000 tons *3048 tonnes* with a forward mast 160 ft *48,7 m* high. On open-cast coal workings at Butterwell, Northumberland in September 1975 it proved able to strip 100 tons *101 tonnes* of overburden in 65 sec with its 65 yd³ *49,7 m³* bucket on a 265 ft *80,7 m* boom. It is owned by Derek Crouch (Contractors) Ltd of Peterborough, Cambridgeshire.

Escalator

The term was registered in the US on 28 May 1900 but the earliest 'Inclined Escalator' was installed by Jesse W. Reno on the pier at Coney Island, New York in 1896. The first installation in Britain was at Harrods department store, London in November 1898. The escalators on the Leningrad underground at Lenin Square have 729 steps and a vertical rise of 59,68 m *195 ft 9½ in*.

The longest escalators in Britain are four in the Tyne Tunnel, Tyne and Wear installed in 1951. They measure 192 ft 8 in *58,7 m* between combs with a vertical lift of 85 ft *25,9 m* and a step speed of up to 1.7 mph *2,7 km/h*. The world's longest 'moving sidewalks' are those installed in 1970 in the Neue Messe Centre, Dusseldorf, West Germany which measure 225 m *738 ft* between comb plates. The longest in Great Britain is the 375 ft *114,3 m* long Dunlop Starglide at London's Heathrow Airport Terminal 3, installed in March-May 1970.

The world's longest *ride* is on the 4-section outdoor escalator at Ocean Park, Hong Kong which has an overall length of 745 ft *227 m* and a total vertical rise of 377 ft *115 m*.

Excavator

The world's largest excavator is the 13,000-tonne bucket wheel excavator being assembled at the open-cast lignite mine of Hambach, West Germany with a rating of 200 000 m³ *260,000 yd³* per 20-hr working day. It is 210 m *690 ft* in length and 82 m *269 ft* tall. The wheel is 67,88 m *222 ft* in circumference with 5 m³ *6.5 yd³* buckets.

Forging

The largest forging on record is one of a 450,600 lb *204,4 tonne* 55 ft *16,76 m* long generator shaft for Japan, forged by the Bethlehem Steel Corp of Pennsylvania in October 1973.

Fork lift truck

Kalmar LMV of Sweden manufactured in 1985 ten counterbalanced fork lift trucks capable of lifting loads up to 80 tonnes *78.7 tons* at a load centre of 2300 mm *90.5 in*. They were built to handle the large-diameter pipeline in the Libyan Great Man-made River Project.

Lathe

The world's largest lathe is the 126 ft *38,4 m* long 416,2 tonne giant lathe built by Waldrich Siegen of West Germany in 1973 for the South African Electricity Supply Commission at Rosherville. It has a capacity for 300 tonne work pieces and a swing-over bed of 5 m *16 ft 5 in* in diameter.

Greatest lift

The heaviest lifting operation in engineering history was the 41,000 short ton (36,607 long ton

37 194 tonne) roof of the Velodrome in Montreal, Canada in 1975. It was raised by jacks some 4 in *10 cm* to strike its centring.

Slowest machine

A nuclear environmental machine for testing stress corrosion has been developed by Nene Instruments of Wellingborough, Northants that can be controlled at a speed as slow as one million millionth of a millimetre per minute, or one metre *3,28 ft* in about 2000 million years.

Nut

The largest nuts ever made weigh 4,74 tonnes *93.4 cwt* each with an outside diameter of 52 in *132 cm* and a 25 in *63,5 cm* thread. Known as 'Pilgrim Nuts', they are manufactured by Pilgrim Moorside Ltd of Oldham, Lancashire for use on the columns of a large forging press.

Oil tank

The largest oil tanks ever constructed are the five Aramco 1½-million-barrel storage tanks at Ju'aymah, Saudi Arabia. They are 72 ft *21,94 m* tall with a diameter of 386 ft *117,6 m* and were completed in March 1980.

Passenger lift

The fastest domestic passenger lifts in the world are the express lifts to the 60th floor of the 240 m *787.4 ft* tall 'Sunshine 60' building, Ikebukuro in Tōkyō completed 5 Apr 1978. They were built by Mitsubishi Corp and operate at a speed of 2000 ft/min *609,6 m/min* or 22.72 mph *36,56 km/h*. Much higher speeds are achieved in the winding cages of mine shafts. A hoisting shaft 6800 ft *2072 m* deep, owned by Western Deep Levels Ltd in South Africa, winds at speeds of up to 40.9 mph *65,8 km/h* (3595 ft *1095 m* per min). Otitis-media (popping of the ears) presents problems much above even 10 mph *16 km/h*.

The longest lift in the United Kingdom is one 930 ft long inside the BBC Television Tower at Bilsdale, West Moor, North Yorkshire, built by J. L. Eve Construction. It runs at 130 ft/min *39,6 m/min*. The longest fast lifts are the two 15-passenger cars in the British Telecom Tower, London which travel 540 ft *164 m* at up to 1000 ft/min *304 m/min*.

Graham Coates established an involuntary duration record when trapped in a lift for 62 hr in Brighton, East Sussex on 24–26 May 1986.

Pipelines *Oil*

The world's earliest pipeline of 2 in *5 cm* cast iron, laid at Oil Creek, Pennsylvania in 1863 was torn up by Luddites.

The longest crude oil pipeline in the world is the Interprovincial Pipe Line Company's installation from Edmonton, Alberta, Canada to Buffalo, New York State, USA, a distance of 1775 miles *2856 km*. Along the length of the pipe 13 pumping stations maintain a flow of 6,900,000 gal *31 367 145 litres* of oil per day. The eventual length of the Trans-Siberian Pipeline will be 2319 miles *3732 km*, running from Tuimazy through Omsk and Novosibirsk to Irkutsk. The first 30 mile *48 km* section was opened in July 1957.

Submarine

The world's longest submarine pipeline is that of 425 km *264 miles* for natural gas from the Union Oil Platform to Rayong, Thailand opened on 12 Sept 1981. The longest North Sea pipeline is the Ekofisk–Emden line stretching 260 miles *418 km* and completed in July 1975. The deepest North Sea pipeline is that from the Cormorant Field to Firths Voe, Shetland at 530 ft *162 m*.

Natural gas

The longest natural gas pipeline in the world is the Trans-Canada Pipeline which by 1974 had 5654 miles *9099 km* of pipe up to 42 in *106,6 cm* in diameter. The Tyumen–Chelyabinsk–Mos-

cow–Brandenburg gasline stretches 4330 km *2690 miles*.

The large-calibre Urengoi-Uzhgorod line to Western Europe, begun in November 1982, stretches 4451 km *2765 miles* and was completed on 25 July 1983. It has a capacity of 32,000 million m³ *42,000 million yd³* per annum.

Water

The world's longest water pipeline runs a distance of 350 miles *563 km* to the Kalgoorlie gold fields from near Perth in Western Australia. Engineered in 1903, the system has since been extended five-fold by branches.

Most expensive

The world's most expensive pipeline is the Alaska Pipeline running 798 miles *1284 km* from Prudhoe Bay to Valdez. By completion of the first phase in 1977 it had cost at least $6000 million (*£3250 million*). The pipe is 48 in *1,21 m* in diameter and will eventually carry up to 2 million barrels of crude oil per day.

Press

The world's two most powerful production machines are forging presses in the USA. The Loewy closed-die forging press, in a plant leased from the US Air Force by the Wyman-Gordon Company at North Grafton, Massachusetts weighs 9469 tons *9620 tonnes* and stands 114 ft 2 in *34,79 m*, of which 66 ft *20,1 m* is sunk below the operating floor. It has a rated capacity of 44,600 tons *45 315 tonnes*, and became operational in October 1955. The other similar press is at the plant of the Aluminum Company of America in Cleveland, Ohio. There has been a report of a press in the USSR with a capacity of 75 000 tonnes *73,800 tons* at Novo Kramatorsk. The Bêché and Grohs counter-blow forging hammer, manufactured in West Germany, is rated at 60,000 tonnes/*tons*. The most powerful press in Great Britain is the closed-die forging and extruding press installed in 1967 at the Cameron Iron Works, Livingston, West Lothian. The press is 92 ft *28 m* tall (27 ft *8,2 m* below ground) and exerts a force of 30,000 tons *30 481 tonnes*.

Printer

The world's fastest printer is the Radiation Inc electro-sensitive system at the Lawrence Radiation Laboratory, Livermore, California. High-speed recording of up to 30,000 lines, each containing 120 alphanumeric characters, per minute is attained by controlling electronic

pulses through chemically-impregnated recording paper which is rapidly moving under closely-spaced fixed styli. It can thus print the wordage of the whole Bible (773,692 words) in 65 seconds—3306 times as fast as the world's fastest typist.

Radar installation

The largest of the three installations in the US Ballistic Missile Early Warning System (BMEWS) is that near Thule, in Kalaatdlit Nunaat (Greenland), 931 miles *1498 km* from the North Pole. It was completed in 1960 at a cost of $500,000,000 (then *£178.5 million*). Its sister stations are one at Cape Clear, Alaska, completed in 1961, and a $115,000,000 (then *£41.07 million*) installation at Fylingdales Moor, North Yorkshire, completed in June 1963. The largest scientific radar installation is the 21 acre *84 000 m²* ground array at Jicamarca, Peru.

Ropeway or téléphérique

The longest ropeway in the world is the Compagnie Minière de l'Ogooué or COMILOG installation built in 1959–62 for the Moanda manganese mine in Gabon which extends 76 km *47.2 miles*. It has 858 towers and 2800 buckets with 155 km *96.3 miles* of wire rope running over 6000 idler pulleys.

The highest and longest passenger-carrying aerial ropeway in the world is the Teleférico Mérida (Mérida téléphérique) in Venezuela, from Mérida City (5379 ft *1639,5 m*) to the summit of Pico Espejo (15,629 ft *4763,7 m*), a rise of 10,250 ft *3124 m*. The ropeway is in four sections, involving 3 car changes in the 8 mile *12,8 km* ascent in 1 hr. The fourth span is 10,070 ft *3069 m* in length. The two cars work on the pendulum system—the carrier rope is locked and the cars are hauled by means of three pull ropes powered by a 230 hp *233 cv* motor. They have a maximum capacity of 45 persons and travel at 32 ft *9,7 m* per sec (21.8 mph *35,08 km/h*). The longest single-span ropeway is the 13,500 ft *4114 m* span from the Coachella Valley to Mt San Jacinto (10,821 ft *3298 m*), California, USA, inaugurated on 12 Sept 1963.

Britain's longest cabin lift is that at Llandudno, Gwynedd, opened in June 1969. It has 42 cabins with a capacity of 1000 people per hour and is 5320 ft *1621 m* in length.

Transformer

The world's largest single-phase transformers are rated at 1,500,000 kVA of which eight are in service with the American Electric Power Service Corporation. Of these, five stepdown from 765 to 345 kV.

Britain's largest transformers are those rated at 1,000,000 kVA 400/275 kV built by Hackbridge & Hewittic, Walton-on-Thames, Surrey first commissioned for the CEGB in October 1968.

Transmission lines *Longest*

The longest span between pylons of any power line in the world is that across the Sogne Fjord, Norway, between Rabnaberg and Fatlaberg. Supplied in 1955 by Whitecross of Warrington, Cheshire, and projected and erected by A. S. Betonmast of Oslo as part of the high-tension power cable from Refsdal power station at Vik, it has a span of 16,040 ft *4888 m* and a weight of 12 tons/*tonnes*. In 1967 two further high-tensile steel/aluminium lines 16,006 ft *4878 m* long, and weighing 33 tons *33,5 tonnes*, manufactured by Whitecross and BICC were erected here. The longest in Britain are the 5310 ft *1618 m* lines built by J. L. Eve across the Severn with main towers each 488 ft *148 m* high.

Highest

The world's highest are those across the Straits of Messina, with towers of 675 ft *205 m* (Sicily side) and 735 ft *224 m* (Calabria) and 11,900 ft *3627 m* apart. The highest lines in Britain are those made by BICC at West Thurrock, Essex, which cross the Thames estuary suspended from 630 ft *192 m* tall towers at a minimum height of 250 ft *76 m*, with a 130 ton *132 tonne* breaking load. They are 4500 ft *1371 m* in length.

Highest voltages

The highest voltages now carried are 1,330,000 volts 1224 miles *1970 km* on the DC Pacific Intertie in the United States. The Ekibastuz DC transmission lines in Kazakhstan, USSR are planned to be 2400 km *1490 miles* long with 1,500,000 volt capacity.

Valve

The world's largest valve is the 32 ft *9,75 m* diameter, 170 ton/*tonne* butterfly valve designed by Boving & Co Ltd of London for use at the Arnold Airforce Base engine test facility in Tennessee.

Wire ropes

The longest wire ropes in the world are the 4 made at British Ropes Ltd, Wallsend, Tyne and Wear each measuring 24 000 m *14.9 miles*. The ropes are 35 mm *1.3 in* in diameter, weigh 108,5 tonnes *106.8 tons* each and were ordered by the CEGB for use in the construction of the 2000-MW cross-Channel power cable. The thickest ever made are spliced crane strops from wire ropes 28,2 cm *11¼ in* thick made of 2392 individual wires in March 1979 by British Ropes Ltd of Doncaster at Willington Quay, also Tyne and Wear, designed to lift loads of up to 3000 tons/*tonnes*. The heaviest ever wire ropes (4 in number) are each of 130 tonnes/*tons*, made for the twin shaft system of Western Deep Levels Gold Mine, South Africa, by Haggie Rand Ltd of Johannesburg.

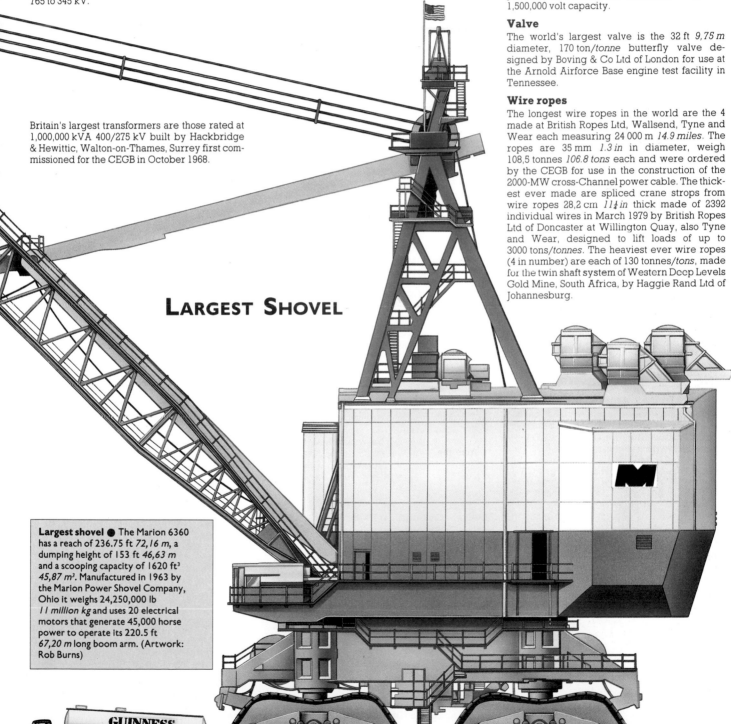

LARGEST SHOVEL

Largest shovel ● The Marion 6360 has a reach of 236.75 ft *72,16 m*, a dumping height of 153 ft *46,63 m* and a scooping capacity of 1620 ft³ *45,87 m³*. Manufactured in 1963 by the Marion Power Shovel Company, Ohio it weighs 24,250,000 lb *11 million kg* and uses 20 electrical motors that generate 45,000 horse power to operate its 220.5 ft *67,20 m* long boom arm. (Artwork: Rob Burns)

Engineering

TIME PIECES

Clock

Oldest

The earliest mechanical clock, that is, one with an escapement, was completed in China in AD 725 by I Hsing and Liang Lingtsan.

The oldest surviving working clock in the world is the faceless clock dating from 1386, or possibly earlier, at Salisbury Cathedral, Wiltshire, which was restored in 1956 having struck the hours for 498 years and ticked more than 500 million times. Earlier dates, ranging back to c. 1335, have been attributed to the weight-driven clock in Wells Cathedral, Somerset, but only the iron frame is original. A model of Giovanni de Dondi's heptagonal astronomical clock of 1348–64 was completed in 1962.

Largest

The world's most massive clock is the Astronomical Clock in the Cathedral of St Pierre, Beauvais, France, constructed between 1865 and 1868. It contains 90,000 parts and measures 40 ft *12,1 m* high, 20 ft *6,09 m* wide and 9 ft *2,7 m* deep. The Su Sung Clock, built in China at K'aifeng in 1088–92, had a 20 ton *20,3 tonne* bronze armillary sphere for 1½ tons *1,52 tonnes* of water. It was removed to Beijing in 1126 and was last known to be working in its 40 ft *12,1 m* high tower in 1136.

The world's largest clock face is that of the floral clock at Tokachigaoka Park, Otofuke, Hokkaido, Japan, completed on 1 Aug 1982 with a diameter of 18 m *59 ft 0⅜ in.*

The largest four-faced clock in the world is that on the building of the Allen-Bradley Company of Milwaukee, Wisconsin. Each face has a diameter of 40 ft 3½ in *12,28 m* with a minute hand 20 ft *6,09 m* in overall length. The largest single-faced clock is the octagonal Colgate Clock in Jersey, New Jersey with a diameter of 15,24 m *50 ft* and a minute hand 8,31 m *27 ft 3 in* in length. The tallest four-faced clock in the world is that of the Williamsburgh Savings Bank in Brooklyn, New York City. It is 430 ft *131 m* above street level.

The largest clock in the United Kingdom is that on the Royal Liver Building, Liverpool (built 1908–11) with dials 25 ft *7,62 m* in diameter and the 4 minute hands each 14 ft *4,26 m* long. The

mechanism and dials weigh 22 tons and are 220 ft *67 m* above street level.

Most accurate

The most accurate and complicated clockwork in the world is the Olsen Clock, completed for Copenhagen Town Hall, Denmark in December 1955. The clock, which has more than 14,000 units, took 10 years to make and the mechanism functions in 570,000 different ways. The celestial pole motion will take 25,753 years to complete a full circle and is the slowest-moving designed mechanism in the world. The clock is accurate to 0.5 sec in 300 years—50 times more accurate than the previous record.

Most expensive

The highest price paid for any clock is £500,000 for a Thomas Tompion (1639–1713) bracket clock bought by the British Museum by private treaty on 15 July 1982.

Longest stoppage 'Big Ben'

The longest stoppage of the clock in the House of Commons clock tower since the first tick on 31 May 1859 has been 13 days from noon on 4 Apr to noon on 17 Apr 1977. In 1945 a host of starlings slowed the minute hand by 5 minutes.

Pendulum

Longest

The longest pendulum in the world is 22,5 m *73 ft 9¾ in* on the water-mill clock installed by Hattori Tokeiten Co in the Shinjuku NS building in Tokyo in 1983.

Watch

Oldest

The oldest watch (portable clockwork timekeeper) is one made of iron by Peter Henlein in Nürnberg (Nüremberg), Bavaria, Germany, c. 1504. The earliest wrist watches were those of Jacquet-Droz and Leschot of Geneva, Switzerland, dating from 1790.

Largest

A facsimile 'Swatch' watch was draped from the roof of the Comme Bank building, Frankfurt, West Germany in December 1985. It was 469 ft *143 m* long, weighed 13 tonnes and had a face 54 ft *16,45 m* in diameter. A 'Swatch' 162 m *531 ft 6 in* long and 20 m *65 ft 7½ in* in diameter, made by D. Tomas Feliu, was set up on the Bank of Bilbao building, Madrid, Spain from 7–12 Dec 1985.

The Eta 'watch' on the Swiss pavilion at Expo 86 in Vancouver, British Columbia from May–Oct weighed 34.4 tons *35 tonnes* and stood 80 ft *24,3 m* high.

Smallest

The smallest watches in the world are produced by Jaeger le Coultre of Switzerland. Equipped with a 15-jewelled movement they measure just over ½ in *1,2 cm* long and 3/16 in *0,476 cm* in width. Movement and case weigh under 0,25 oz *7 g.*

Thinnest

The world's thinnest wrist watch is the Swiss Concord Delirium IV. It measures 0,98 mm *0.0385 in* thick and retailed for $16,000 *£6800* (including 18-carat gold strap) in June 1980.

Most expensive

The record price for an antique watch is SwFr1,870,000 (*£670,250*) paid at Christie's, Geneva on 13 May 1986 by a European collector for a gold-enamelled and diamond-set pocket watch with a movement c.1650 by the Parisian maker Jehan Cremfdorff.

Most accurate time measurer

The most accurate time-keeping devices are the twin atomic hydrogen masers installed in 1964 in the US Naval Research Laboratory, Washing-

ton, DC. They are based on the frequency of the hydrogen atom's transition period of 1,420,450,751,694 cycles/sec. This enables an accuracy to within 1 sec in 1,700,000 years.

Largest sundial

The world's largest sundial is the Samrat Yantra with a gnomon height of 27 m *88.5 ft* and a vertical height of 36 m *118 ft* built in 1724 at Jaipur, India.

COMPUTERS

A geared calculator dated c. 80 BC was found in the sea by Antikythera Island off north-west Crete in April 1900.

The earliest programmable electronic computer was the 1500-valve Colossus formulated by Prof Max H. A. Newman FRS (1897–1985) and built by T. H. Flowers MBE. It was run in December 1943 at Bletchley Park, Buckinghamshire to break the German coding machine Enigma. It arose from a concept published in 1936 by Dr Alan Mathison Turing OBE, FRS (1912–54) in his paper *On Computable Numbers with an Application to the Entscheidungsproblem.* Colossus was declassified on 25 Oct 1975. The world's first stored-program computer was the Manchester University Mark I which incorporated the Williams storage cathode ray tube (pat. 11 Dec 1946). It ran its first program, by Prof Tom Kilburn CBE FRS (b. 1921) for 52 min on 21 June 1948.

Computers were greatly advanced by the invention of the point-contact transistor by John Bardeen and Walter Brattain announced in July 1948, and the junction transistor by R. L. Wallace, Morgan Sparks and Dr William Bradford Shockley (b. 1910) in early 1951. The concept of the integrated circuit, which has enabled microminiaturisation, was first published on 7 May 1952 by Geoffrey W. A. Dummer MBE (b. 1909) in Washington, DC. The microcomputer was achieved in 1969–73 by M. E. Hoff Jr of Intel Corporation with the production of the microprocessor chip '4004'.

Most powerful and fastest

The world's most powerful and fastest computer is the liquid-cooled CRAY-2, named after Seymour R. Cray of Cray Research, Inc, Minneapolis, Minnesota. Its memory has a capacity of 256 million 64-bit words, resulting in a capacity of 32 million bytes of main memory. (NB a 'byte' is a unit of storage compressing 8 'bits' collectively equivalent to one alphabetic symbol or two numericals.) It attains speeds of 250 million floating point operations per second. The cost of a mid-range system was quoted in October 1985 at $17 million. The most powerful British computer is the International Computer's Distribution Array Processor—the ICL DAP.

Smallest word processor

The world's smallest word processor, the Easi-Text 1350, was introduced by Minimicro of Huntington, North Yorkshire, in April 1986. It is based on the Sharp PC-1350 computer which measures 182 × 72 × 16 mm *7.2 × 2.8 × 0.6 in* and the entire system including an A4-size Epson P-80 printer fits into an executive briefcase.

Megabits

The megabit barrier was broken in February 1984, with the manufacture of a 1024K-bit integrated circuit the size of a drawing pin head and as thin as a human hair, by 4 Japanese companies, Hitachi, NEC, NTT Atsugi Electrical Communications and Toshiba. Toshiba announced that manufacture of an 80-picosecond LSI (large scale integration) chip of gallium arsenide would start in 1985–86.

Fastest transistor

A transistor capable of switching 230,000 million times per second was announced by Illinois State University on 5 Oct 1986.

THE BUSINESS WORLD

CHAPTER NINE

Commerce

The $(US) has in this chapter been converted to £ sterling at the exchange rate appropriate to the relevant date *viz.* $1.53 at mid-1986; $1.48 at 31 Dec 1986 and $1.60 at 31 Mar 1987.

Oldest industry

The oldest known industry is flint knapping, involving the production of chopping tools and hand axes, dating from 2.4 million years ago in Ethiopia. The earliest evidence of trading in exotic stone and amber dates from *c.* 28,000 BC in Europe. Agriculture is often described as 'the oldest industry in the world', whereas in fact there is no firm evidence yet that it was practised before *c.* 11,000 BC.

Oldest company

The oldest company in the world is the Faversham Oyster Fishery Co, referred to in the Faversham Oyster Fishing Act 1930 as existing 'from time immemorial', *i.e.* in English law, from before 1189.

The Royal Mint has origins going back to AD 287. The Oxford University Press celebrated a 500th anniversary in 1978 not of itself but of the earliest origin of printing in Oxford in 1478. The Shore Porters' Society of Aberdeen, a haulier, shipping and warehouse partnership, is known to have been established before 4 June 1498. The White-chapel Bell Foundry of Whitechapel Road, east London, has been in business since *c.* 1570. It has, through Master Founder Thomas Mears II, indirect successions, since 1810, via Rudhalls of Gloucester back to 1270. The retail business in Britain with the oldest history is the Oxford

Largest restaurant chain ● McDonald's Corporation of Oak Brook, Illinois was founded on 15 Apr 1955 in Des Plaines, Chicago by Ray A. Kroc BH (Bachelor of Hamburgerology) (1902–1984). 'Mac' McDonald, who with his brother Dick opened his first fast food drive-in outlet in Pasadena, California in 1937 (above), died in 1971. By 31 Dec 1986 the number of McDonald's restaurants licensed and owned in 45 countries and territories around the world reached 9401, with an aggregate throughput of 60 billion 100 per cent pure beef hamburgers. Sales systemwide in 1986 surpassed $12,400 billion (*£8386 million*). The top photograph is the *Drive-Thru* at Neasden, London which opened in 1986.

ironmonger Gill & Co of 127–8, High Street founded by Abel Smythe *c.* 1530. R. Durtnell & Sons, builders, of Brasted, Kent, has been run by the same family since 1591. Mr Richard Durtnell is of the 12th generation. The first bill of adventure signed by the English East India Co was dated 21 Mar 1601.

Greatest assets

The business with the greatest amount in physical assets has been the Bell System, which comprised the American Telephone and Telegraph Company and its subsidiaries. The Bell System's total assets on the consolidated balance sheet at the time of its divestiture and break-up into 8 companies on 31 Dec 1983 reached $149,529 million (*then £106,800 m*). The plant involved included more than 142 million telephones. The number of employees was 1,036,000. The company's market value of $47,989 million (*then £30,960 million*) was held among 3,055,000 share-holders. A total of 20,109 shareholders had attended the Annual Meeting in April 1961, thereby setting a world record.

Currently the largest assets of any manufacturing corporation are the $72,593,000,000 (*then £49,050 million*) of Exxon Corporation, the world's largest oil company, on 1 Jan 1987. They have 102,000 employees. The first company to have assets in excess of $1 billion was the United States Steel Corporation with $1400 million (*then £287.73 million*) at the time of its creation by merger in 1917.

The net assets of The Shell Transport and Trading Company plc at 31 Dec 1986 were £10,002 million, comprising mainly its 40 per cent share in the net assets of the Royal Dutch/Shell Group

Commerce

of Companies which stood at £25,006 million. Group companies employ some 138,000. Shell Transport was formed in 1897 by Marcus Samuel (1853–1927), later the 1st Viscount Bearsted.

The biggest British manufacturing company is Imperial Chemical Industries plc with assets employed of £8686 million as at 1 Jan 1987. Its staff and payroll averaged 121,800 during the year. The company, which has more than 300 UK and overseas subsidiaries, was formed on 7 Dec 1926 by the merger of four concerns—British Dyestuffs Corporation Ltd; Brunner, Mond & Co Ltd; Nobel Industries Ltd and United Alkali Co Ltd. The first chairman was Sir Alfred Moritz Mond (1868–1930), later the 1st Lord Melchett.

Greatest profit and loss
The greatest net profit ever made by any corporation in 12 months is $7647 million (£4933 million) by American Telephone and Telegraph Co from 1 Oct 1981 to 30 Sept 1982. The Argentine petroleum company YPF (Yacimientos Petrolíferos) (government owned) made a trading record loss of US $4,643,995,000 in 1983. The loss for the National Coal Board (now British Coal) in the tax year ending on 31 Mar 1985 was £2225 million.

Largest employer
The world's largest employer is Indian Railways with 1,613,280 staff in 1985/6. Europe's largest employer is Britain's National Health Service with 1,130,777 staff in 1986.

Greatest sales
The first company to surpass the $1 billion (US) mark in annual sales was the United States Steel Corporation in 1917. Now there are 570 corporations with sales exceeding £1000 million including 272 from the United States. The *Fortune 500 List* of April 1987 is headed by the General Motor Corporation of Detroit with $102,813,700,000 (£69,468 million) for 1986. The world's largest private company is Cargill Inc, the Minneapolis, Minnesota grain-trading company, with sales of $32,000 million (£20.9 billion) in 1985/86.

The top gross profits in the United Kingdom in *The Times 1000 1986–87* were those of British Petroleum with £7053 million.

Largest take-over
The largest corporate take-over agreement in commercial history is by Chevron (formerly Standard Oil Co of California) which on 15 June 1984 bought Gulf Oil Corporation for $13,231,253,000 (then £9450 million). The fees of the financial intermediaries were estimated by *Fortune* to be $63.9 million.

The greatest acquisition by a British company was that achieved in stages by British Petroleum of American Standard Oil (formerly Sohio). BP offered $7.7 billion for the unacquired 45% of shares by 13 May 1987. The Guinness PLC takeover of the Distillers Company PLC on 18 Apr 1986 was £2.695 billion.

Greatest bankruptcy
Rajendra Sethia (b. 1950) was arrested in New Delhi on 2 Mar 1985 on charges including criminal conspiracy and forgery. He had been declared bankrupt by the High Court in London on 18 Jan 1985 when Esal Commodities was stated to be in debt for a record £170 million. His personal debts were estimated at £140 million. William G. Stern (b. Hungary, 1936) of Golders Green, north London, a US citizen since 1957, who set up Wilstar Group Holding Co in the London property market in 1971, was declared bankrupt for £104,390,248 in February 1979. This figure rose to £142,978,413 by February 1983. He was discharged for £500,000 suspended for 2½ years on 28 Mar 1983.

Companies
The number of companies on the register in Great Britain at 31 Dec 1986 was 1,065,600 of which 4601 were public and the balance private companies.

Most directorships
The record for directorships was set in 1961 by Hugh T. Nicholson (1914–1985), formerly senior partner of Harmood Banner & Sons, London who, as a liquidating chartered accountant, became director of all 451 companies of the Jasper group in 1961 and had 7 other directorships.

Accountancy firm
The largest firm of accountants worldwide is that resulting from the merger of Peat Marwick International and Klynveld Main Goerdeler of the Netherlands announced on 3 Sept 1986 with a combined annual revenue of $2700 million (£1.8 billion) and a total of 58,000 employees.

Advertising agency
The largest advertising agency group in the world is Saatchi & Saatchi plc of London. *Advertising Age* lists the group's billings at about $8255.4 million (£5503 million).

Biggest advertiser
The world's biggest advertiser is Sears, Roebuck and Co, with $1,129,800,000 (£753.2 million) in 1986 excluding its catalogue.

Aerospace company
The world's largest aerospace company is Boeing with 1986 sales of $16,341,000,000 (£11,041 million) and a work force of 118,500. Cessna Aircraft Company of Wichita, Kansas, USA, in the year 1986, had total sales of $539,500,000 (£359.6 million). The company has produced more than 176,300 aircraft since Clyde Cessna's first was built in 1911.

Airline
The largest airline in the world is the USSR state airline 'Aeroflot', so named since 1932. This was instituted on 9 Feb 1923, with the title of Civil Air Fleet of the Council of Ministers of the USSR, abbreviated to 'Dobrolet'. It operates 1650 aircraft over more than 620,000 miles *1 000 000 km* of routes, employs 500,000 people and carried 112 million passengers in 1986. Seventy per cent of its routes are international and it serves 122 towns or cities in 97 countries. Its domestic network covers 3600 towns. The commercial airline carrying the greatest number of passengers (Dec 1984) was United Airlines Inc of Illinois, with 41,273,000 passengers. The company had 47,900 employees and a fleet of 319 jet planes. On 1 Apr 1987 British Airways operated a fleet of 165 aircraft. Staff employed on airline activities totalled 39,000 and 19,681,000 passengers were carried in 1986-7 on 341,754 miles *550 000 km* of unduplicated routes.

The oldest existing national airline is Koninklijke-Luchtvaart-Maatschappij NV (KLM) of the Netherlands, which opened its first scheduled service (Amsterdam–London) on 17 May 1920, having been established on 7 Oct 1919. One of the original constituents of BOAC, Handley-Page Transport Ltd, was founded in May 1919 and merged into Imperial Airways in 1924. Delag (Deutsche Luftschiffahrt AG) was founded at Frankfurt am Main on 16 Nov 1909 and started a scheduled airship service in June 1910. Chalk's International Airline has been flying amphibians from Miami, Florida to the Bahamas since July 1919. Albert 'Pappy' Chalk flew from 1911 to 1975.

Aluminium producer
The world's largest producer of primary aluminium is Alcan Aluminum Ltd of Montreal, Canada with its affiliated companies. The company had an output of 2 119 000 tonnes *2,085,000 tons* in 1986.

Art auctioneering
The largest and oldest firm of art auctioneers in the world is the Sotheby Group of London and New York, founded in 1744. The turnover in 1985–86 was $691,485,000 (£473,317,000). The total realised at the sale of Impressionist Modern Paintings and Sculpture at Sotheby's, London on 2 Dec 1986 was a world record £40,159,900 ($57,800,000).

Bank
The International Bank for Reconstruction and Development (founded 27 Dec 1945), the 'World Bank', the world's largest multilateral development bank, at 1818 H Street NW, Washington, DC, has an authorised share capital of $92.6 billion (£61,733 million). There were 150 members with a subscribed capital of $77,527 million (£51,684 million) at 30 June 1986. The International Monetary Fund also in Washington, DC had 151 members with total quotas of SDR 89,987.6 million ($114,068.28 million or £74,578.12 million) at April 1987.

The world's biggest commercial bank is Dai-Ichi Kango Bank Ltd of Japan with assets in March 1986 of $207,000 million.

The world's oldest bank is C. Hoare & Co started in 1633 by Lawrence Hoare, a goldsmith, in London. The bank with most branches is The State Bank of India with 11,171 on 1 Jan 1987 with assets of $26,340 million £17,800 million. The bank with the largest network in the United Kingdom is the National Westminster with consolidated total assets of £83,325,000,000 and 3200 branches as at 31 Dec 1986.

Banquet
It was estimated that some 30,000 attended a military feast at Radewitz, Poland on 25 June 1730 thrown by King August II (1709–33).

The greatest number of people served indoors at a single sitting was 18,000 municipal leaders at the Palais de l'Industrie, Paris on 18 Aug 1889. At the wedding of cousins Menachem Teitelbaum and Brucha Sima Melsels, both 18, conducted by their grandfather Grand Rabbi Moses at Uniondale, Long Island, New York on 5 Dec 1984 the attendance of the Satmar sect of Hasidic Jews was estimated at between 17,000 and 20,000. Meal Mart of Brooklyn, a kosher caterer, provided the food including 2 tons of gefilte fish.

The most expensive menu ever served was for the main 5½-hr banquet at the Imperial Iranian 2500th Anniversary gathering at Persepolis in October 1971. It comprised quail eggs stuffed with Iranian caviar, a mousse of crayfish tails in Nantua sauce, stuffed rack of roast lamb, with a main course of roast peacock stuffed with *foie gras*, fig rings and raspberry sweet champagne sherbet, with wines including *Château Lafite-Rothschild* 1945 at £40 (now £235) per bottle from Maxime's, Paris.

Bicycle manufacturers
The world's biggest manufacturer of bicycles is Hero Cycles of Ladhiana, Punjab, India founded in 1956 by the Munjal brothers. In 1986 they turned out 2,220,000 units. China is estimated to have 210 million bicycles.

Book shop
The book shop with most titles and the longest shelving (30 miles *48 km*) in the world is W. & G. Foyle Ltd, London. First established in 1904 in a small shop in Islington, the company is now at 113–119 Charing Cross Road. The area on one site is 75,825 ft² *7044 m²*. The most capacious individual bookstore in the world measured by square footage is Barnes & Noble Bookstore of Fifth Ave at 18th Street, New York City, USA with 154,250 ft² *14 330 m²* and with 12.87 miles *20,71 km* of shelving.

Brewer

The oldest brewery in the world is the Weihenstephan Brewery, Freising, near Munich, West Germany, founded in AD 1040.

The largest single brewing organisation in the world is Anheuser-Busch Inc of St Louis, Missouri, USA, with 12 breweries in the US. In 1986 the company sold 72,300,000 US barrels, equivalent to *14,930 million imp. pints (8482,7 million litres)*, the greatest annual volume ever produced by a brewing company. The company's St Louis plant covers 100 acres *40,5 ha* and after completion of current modernisation projects will have an annual capacity in excess of 13,000,000 US barrels *2684 million imp. pints (1525,183 million litres)*. The largest brewery on a single site is Adolph Coors Co of Golden, Colorado where 15,238,000 barrels *3146 million imp. pints (1787,8 million litres)* were sold in 1985.

The largest brewing company in the United Kingdom based on its 7337 public houses, 709 off-licences and over 100 hotels, is Bass plc. With net assets of £1,799,700,000, it controls 13 breweries and has 76,922 employees. Its sales figure for the year ending 30 Sept 1986 was £2,709,700,000.

Brickworks

The largest brickworks in the world is the London Brick Company Limited plant at Stewartby, Bedfordshire. The works, established in 1898, now cover 221 acres *90 ha* and have a production capacity of 10.5 million bricks and brick equivalent each week.

Building contractors'

The largest construction company in the United Kingdom is George Wimpey plc (founded 1880), of London, which undertakes building, civil, offshore, process and marine engineering work worldwide employing 23,000 staff. The turnover of work was £1461 million in more than 20 countries in 1986.

Building societies

The world's biggest lender is the Japanese government-controlled House Loan Corporation. The biggest building society in the world is the Halifax Building Society of Halifax, West Yorkshire. It was established in 1853 and has total assets exceeding £28,690,000,000. Lending during 1986 was £7,165,000,000. It has 13,391 employees and over 3250 offices.

Chocolate factory

The largest chocolate and confectionery factory is that built by Hershey Chocolate Company in Hershey, Pennsylvania in 1903–5. It has 2,000,000 ft² *185 800 m²* of floor space.

Computer company

The world's largest computer firm is International Business Machines (IBM) Corporation of New York. In Dec 1986 assets were $57,814,000 *(£37,230,000)* and gross income was $51,250,000 *(£33,065,000)*. In Oct 1979 it made the largest borrowing in corporate history with $1 billion. Its worldwide employees number 403,508 and there are 792,689 stockholders.

Department stores

The largest department store in the United Kingdom is Harrods Ltd of Knightsbridge, London named after Henry Charles Harrod (1800–85), who opened a grocery in Knightsbridge Village in 1849. It has a total selling floor space of 20 acres *80 940 m²*, employs 4000 people and achieved record sales of £312 million for the year ending 1 Feb 1987. The record for a day is £6.7 million. The record time from the opening of the doors to the crockery counter is 43 secs.

Highest sales per unit area

The department store with the fastest-moving stock in the world is the Marks & Spencer

Jewellery auction ● The world's largest which included the Van Cleef and Arpels 1939 ruby and diamond necklace, above, brought £31,380,197 ($50.2 million) on 3 Apr 1987 when the Duchess of Windsor's (1896–1986) collection was auctioned at Sotheby's, Geneva.

premier branch, known as 'Marble Arch' at 458 Oxford Street, London. The figure of £1600-worth of goods per square foot of selling space per year is believed to be an understatement. The selling area is 129,300 ft² *12 025 m²*. The company has 274 branches in the UK and operates on over 7.1 million ft² *660 300 m²* of selling space and has stores on the Continent, Canada and the United States.

Distillery

The world's largest distilling company is The Seagram Company Ltd, of Canada. Its sales in the year ending 31 Jan 1987 totalled US $3,344,820,000 *(£2260 million)*. The group employs about 14,400 people, including some 4600 in the United States.

The largest establishment for blending and bottling Scotch whisky is the United Distillers Group plant at Kilmarnock, Ayrshire, where there is a capacity to fill over 3 million bottles of Johnnie Walker each week. This brand is the world's largest-selling brand of Scotch whisky. The world's largest-selling brand of gin is Gordon's. Old Bushmills Distillery, County Antrim, Northern Ireland, licensed in 1608, claims to have been in production since 1276.

Fisheries

The greatest catch ever recorded with a single throw is 2471 tonnes by the purse seine-net boat M/S *Flømann* from Hareide, Norway in the Barents Sea on 28 Aug 1982. It was estimated that more than 120 million fish were caught in this shoal.

Grocery stores

The largest grocery chain in the world is Safeway Stores, Inc of Oakland, California with sales in 1986 of $20,311,480,000 *(£13,541 million)* and total current assets valued at $2,181,699,000 *(£1454 million)* as at 3 Jan 1987. The company operates 2284 stores. The total number of employees is 172,412.

Hotelier

The top revenue-earning hotel business is the Holiday Inn hotel system, with a 1986 total revenue of $4.6 billion *(£3067 million)*, from 1633 hotels (316,776 rooms) at 31 Dec 1986, in 53 countries. The business was founded by Charles Kemmons Wilson with his first Holiday Inn hotel on Summer Avenue, Memphis, Tennessee in 1952.

Insurance

The company with the highest volume of insurance in force in the world is the Prudential Insurance Company of America of Newark, New Jersey with $638.9 billion *(£431.6 billion)* at 31 Dec 1986, which is more than 2½ times the UK National Debt figure. The admitted assets are $104,496 million *(£70,605 million)*.

The largest single association in the world is the Blue Cross and Blue Shield Association, the US-based hospital insurance organisation with a membership of 77,000,000 on 31 Dec 1986. Benefits paid out in 1986 totalled $40,600 million *(£27,000 million)*.

The largest life-assurance group in the United Kingdom is the Prudential Corporation plc. At 1 Jan 1987 the tangible assets were £25,787,400,000.

The largest life-assurance policy ever written was one for $44 million *(£24.4 million)* for a

Chemist shop chain ● The largest chain of chemist shops in the world is Boots The Chemists, which has 1025 retail branches. The firm was founded by Jesse Boot (b. Nottingham, 1850), later the 1st Baron Trent, who died in 1931.

Largest flotation

The largest ever flotation in stock-market history has been that of British Gas plc with an equity offering producing proceeds of £7750 million to 4½ million shareholders. Allotment letters were dispatched on 15 Dec 1986.

Largest investment house

The largest securities company in the US, and once the world's largest partnership with 124 partners, before becoming a corporation in 1959, is Merrill, Lynch, Pierce, Fenner & Smith Inc (founded 6 Jan 1914) of New York. Its parent, Merrill, Lynch and Co, has assets of $53 billion (*£33 billion*), approximately 47,000 employees, more than 1000 offices and 5 million customer accounts.

Names

The longest name on the British Index of Company Names is The Australian Academy of the Humanities for the Advancement of Scholarship in Language, Literature, History, Philosophy and the Fine Arts, a company incorporated by Royal Charter. The longest name on the Index registered under the Companies Acts is The Liverpool and Glasgow Association for the Protection of Commercial Interest as Respects Wrecked and Damaged Property Ltd, company number 15147. The shortest names on the Index are G Ltd, company number 1656906 and U Ltd, company number 1910886.

Manufactured Articles

Antique

The largest antique ever sold was London Bridge in March 1968. The sale was made by Ivan F. Luckin of the Court of Common Council of the Corporation of London to the McCulloch Oil Corporation of Los Angeles, California for $2,460,000 (*then £1,029,000*). The 10,000 tons/*tonnes* of façade stonework were re-assembled, at a cost of £3 million, at Lake Havasu City, Arizona and 're-dedicated' on 10 Oct 1971.

Armour

The highest auction price paid for a suit of armour is £1,925,000 by B. H. Trupin (US) on 5 May 1983 at Sotheby's, London for a suit made in Milan by Giovanni Negroli in 1545 for Henri II of France. It came from the Hever Castle Collection in Kent.

Astrolabe

The Astrolabium Galileo Galilei wristwatch, made by Ulysse Nardin, is the only wristwatch that indicates the time of the day, local time, month, zodiac, length of the day and night, moon phases and sun and moon eclipses. The mechanism for indicating the tropical year is accurate to one day in 144,000 years. The retail price is £17,850.

> **Most expensive toy soldiers** ● A rare British Camel Corps trooper, one of nine in a boxed set of soldiers comprising 251 pieces which sold for £11,000 at Phillips auctioneers, London on 14 Jan 1987. The lead soldiers formed the largest boxed set made by the firm Britain's, and date to 1905.

Basket

The biggest basket ever made was 15 ft *4,57 m* tall, woven by Nineteenth Century Basket Company, Warren, Ohio in 1986.

ANTIQUE PRICE RECORDS

ANCIENT SCULPTURE

An eight-inch 6000-year-old Neolithic sculpture of a seated goddess from the estate of James Johnson Sweeney was sold for $1.32 million (*£891,890*) at auction by Sotheby's, New York on 24 Nov 1986. The purchaser was Mrs Shelby White Levy, a New York financial writer.

ART NOUVEAU

The highest auction price for any piece of art nouveau is $360,000 (*then £163,600*) for a spider-web leaded glass mosaic and bronze table lamp by L. C. Tiffany at Christie's, New York on 8 Apr 1980.

BED

A 1930 black lacquer kingsize bed made by Jean Durand was auctioned at Christie's, New York on 2 Oct 1983 for £49,668.

BLANKET

The most expensive blanket was a Navajo Churro hand-spun serape of c. 1852 sold for $115,500 (*then £79,500*) with premium at Sotheby's, New York on 22 Oct 1983.

CARPET

In 1946 the Metropolitan Museum, New York, privately paid $1 million (*then £248,138*) for the 26.5 × 13.6 ft *807 × 414 cm* Anhalt Medallion carpet made in Tabriz or Kashan, Persia c. 1590. The highest price ever paid at auction for a carpet is £231,000 for a 17th-century 'Polonaise' silk and metal thread carpet at Sotheby's, London on 13 Oct 1982.

CERAMICS

The Greek urn painted by Euphronios and thrown by Euxitheos c. 530 was bought by private treaty by the Metropolitan Museum of Art, New York, for $1.3 million (*then £541,666*) in August 1972.

CHAMBER POT

A 33 oz *935 g* silver pot, made by David Willaume and engraved for the 2nd Earl of Warrington, made £9500 at Sotheby's, London on 14 June 1984.

CIGARETTE CARD

The most valuable card is one of the 6 known baseball series cards of Honus Wagner, who was a non-smoker, which was sold in New York in December 1981 for $25,000 (*then £13,900*).

DOLLS

The highest price at auction for a doll is £67,100 for a 14-inch wooden 17th-century doll of c. 1690 at Sotheby's, London on 24 Mar 1987. It was purchased by Mme Didi Vierny for a planned doll museum in Paris, France.

FURNITURE

The highest price ever paid for a single piece of furniture is $2.75 million (*then £1,758,000*) at Sotheby's, New York on 31 Jan 1987 for a Chippendale carved mahogany wing armchair, made by Philadelphia cabinetmaker Thomas Affleck for General John Cadwalader by New York dealer Leigh Keno.

The English furniture record was set by a black-japanned bureau-bookcase of c. 1705. Formerly owned by Queen Mary, it made $860,000 (*then £463,366*) at Christie's, New York on 18 Oct 1981. The record in

the UK was set on 10 Apr 1986 when twin silver Chippendale mirrors were sold at Christie's, London for £280,000 to Roy Miles, the London dealer.

GLASS

The auction record is £520,000 for a Roman glass cage-cup of c. AD 300 measuring 7 in *17,78 cm* in diameter and 4 in *10,16 cm* in height, sold at Sotheby's, London, on 4 June 1979 to Robin Symes.

GOLD PLATE

The highest price for any gold artefact is £950,400 for the 22-carat font made by Paul Storr to the design of Humphrey Repton in 1797. It was sold at Christie's by Lady Anne Cavendish-Bentinck and bought by Armitage of London on 11 July 1985.

GUNS

The highest price ever paid for a single gun is £125,000 given by the London dealers F. Partridge for a French flintlock fowling piece made for Louis XIII c. 1615 and attributed to Pierre le Bourgeoys of Lisieux, France (d. 1627). This piece was included in the collection of the late William Goodwin Renwick of the United States sold by Sotheby's, London on 21 Nov 1972 (see also Pistol). It is now in the Metropolitan Museum of Art, New York.

HAT

The highest price ever paid for a hat is $66,000 (*then £34,750*) by the Alaska State Museum at a New York auction in November 1981 for a Tlingit Kiksadi ceremonial frog helmet from c. 1600.

ICON

The record auction price for an icon is $150,000 (*then £67,500*) paid at Christie's, New York on 17 Apr 1980 for the *Last Judgement* (from the George R. Hann

Beds

In Bruges, Belgium, Philip, Duke of Burgundy had a bed 12½ ft wide and 19 ft long *3,81 × 5,79 m* erected for the perfunctory *coucher officiel* ceremony with Princess Isabella of Portugal in 1430.

The largest bed in Great Britain is the Great Bed of Ware, dating from *c*. 1580, from the Crown Inn, Ware, Hertfordshire, now preserved in the Victoria and Albert Museum, London. It is 10 ft 8½ in wide, 11 ft 1 in long and 8 ft 9 in tall *3,26 × 3,37 × 2,66 m*. The largest bed currently marketed in the United Kingdom is a Super Size Diplomat bed, 9 ft wide by 9 ft long, *2,74 m × 2,74 m* from The London Bedding Centre, Sloane Street. It costs more than £4000. A promotional 1½ ton *1500 kg* bed 6 m × 4,40 m *19 ft 8 in × 14 ft 5 in* in pinewood bed accommodating 39 people was exhibited by a French company in August 1986.

Beer cans

Beer cans date from a test marketing by Krueger Beer of Newark, New Jersey at Richmond, Virginia in 1935. The largest collection has been made by John F. Ahrens of Mount Laurel, New Jersey, with nearly 15,000 different cans. A Rosalie Pilsner can sold for $6000 (*then £2700*) in the US in April 1981.

Beer labels *(Labology)*

Jan Solberg of Oslo, Norway has amassed 218,600 different labels from around the world.

The greatest collection of different British beer labels is 30,722 (to April 1987) by Keith Osborne, Hon. Sec. of The Labologists' Society (founded by Guinness Exports Ltd in 1958). His oldest is one from A. B. Walker & Co, Warrington of *c*. 1846.

Beer mats *(Tegestology)*

The world's largest collection of beer mats is owned by Leo Pisker of Vienna, who had collected over 118,300 different mats from 149 countries by April 1987. The largest collection of purely British mats is 36,150 formed by Timothy J. Stannard of Birmingham.

Silver ● (above) £770,000 for an epergne by de Lamerie sold at Christie's, London by the Earl of Portarlington and bought by Jacques Koopman on 17 Dec 1986.

Sword ● (below) The highest price paid for a sword is the £823,045 for the Duke of Windsor's Royal Navy Officer's sword (presented to him by King George V in 1913) at Sotheby's in Geneva on 3 Apr 1987.

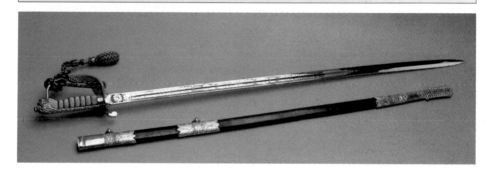

collection, Pittsburgh, USA) made in Novgorod in the 16th century.

JADE

The highest price ever paid for an item in jade is $396,000 (£270,307) (with premium) at Sotheby's, New York on 6 Dec 1983 for a mottled brownish-yellow belt-hook and pendant mask of the Warring States Period of Chinese history.

JEWELS

The highest auction price for any jewels is £2,825,000 (or £3.1 million with the buyer's premium) for two pear-shaped diamond drop earrings of 58.6 and 61 carats at Sotheby's, Geneva on 14 Nov 1980. Neither the buyer nor seller was disclosed.

MECHANICAL TOY

The auction record for a toy is £25,500 for a model train set of Stephenson's *Rocket* made by Marklin of Germany in tin plate in 1909 sold at Sotheby's, London on 29 May 1984.

MUSICAL BOX

The highest price paid for a musical box is £20,900 (with premium) for a Swiss-made example made for a Persian prince in 1901, sold at Sotheby's, London on 23 Jan 1985.

PAPERWEIGHT

The highest price ever paid for a glass paperweight is $143,000 (£97,278) (with premium) at Sotheby's, New York on 2 Dec 1983 for a blue glass weight made at Pantin, Paris *post* 1850.

PISTOL

The highest price paid at auction for a pistol is £110,000 at Christie's London on 8 July 1980 for a Sadeler wheel-lock holster pistol from Munich dated *c*. 1600.

PLAYING CARDS

The highest price paid for a deck of playing cards is $143,352 (£98,850) (with premium) by the New York Metropolitan Museum of Art at Sotheby's, London on 6 Dec 1983.

PORCELAIN AND POTTERY

The highest auction price for any ceramic or any Chinese work of art is £792,000 (with premium) for a blue and white Ming vase of 1426–35 bought by Hirano of Japan at Sotheby's, London on 15 Dec 1981.

POT LID

The highest price paid for a pot lid is £3960 for one depicting 'Eastern Lady with Black Attendant', sold at Phillips, London on 7 Jan 1987.

SNUFF BOX

The highest price ever paid for a snuff box is £764,826 in a sale at Christie's, Geneva on 11 Nov 1986 for a jade-green chrysoprase and diamond gold box once owned by Frederick the Great of Prussia. It was purchased by a London dealer.

SPOONS

A Wiener werkstaffe spoon by Josef Hoffmann, Austria *c*. 1905 was sold at Sotheby's, London for £17,600 (with premium) on 28 Apr 1983. A set of 13 Henry VIII Apostle spoons owned by Lord Astor of Hever was sold for £120,000 on 24 June 1981 at Christie's, London.

STUFFED BIRD

The highest price ever paid for a stuffed bird is £9000. This was given on 4 Mar 1971 at Sotheby's, London by the Iceland Natural History Museum for a specimen of the Great Auk (*Alca impennis*) in summer plumage, which was taken in Iceland *c*. 1821; it stood 22½ in *57 cm* high. The Great Auk was a flightless north Atlantic seabird which was finally exterminated on Eldey, Iceland in 1844, becoming extinct through hunting. The last British sightings were at Co. Waterford in 1834 and St Kilda, Western Isles *c*. 1840.

TAPESTRY

The highest price ever paid for a tapestry is £550,000 for a Swiss Medieval tapestry frieze in two parts dated 1468–1476 at Sotheby's, Geneva, on 10 Apr 1981 by the Basle Historische Museum.

THIMBLE

The record auction price for a thimble is £8000 paid by London dealer Winifred Williams at Christie's, London on 3 Dec 1979 for a Meissen dentil-shaped porcelain piece of *c*. 1740.

TYPEWRITER

The highest price paid for an antique machine is £3000 for an 1886 Daw and Tait machine auctioned at Sotheby's, London on 12 Dec 1980.

WALKING STICK

The highest auction price for a walking stick has been $24,200 (*then £17,285*) at Sotheby Parke Bernet, New York in 1983 for an octagonal whale ivory nobbed stick decorated by Scrimshanders in 1845.

Beer tankard

The largest tankard was made by the Selangor Pewter Co, Kuala Lumpur, Malaysia and unveiled on 30 Nov 1985. It measures 198,7 cm *6 ft 6 in* in height and has a capacity of 2796 litres *615 gals*.

Blanket

The largest blanket measured 68 × 100 ft *20,7 × 30,48 m* weighing 600 lb *272 kg*. It was knitted in 20,160 squares in 10 months (October 1977–July 1978) by *Woman's Weekly* readers for Action Research for the Crippled Child. It was shown on BBC TV *Record Breakers* in October 1978.

Bottle caps

Since 1950 Helge Friholm (b. 1910) of Søborg, Denmark has amassed 38,570 different bottle caps (to April 1986) from 145 countries.

Cans

A pyramid consisting of 210,479 empty beverage cans was built in 28 hr at Maizuru Playground, Nagoya, Japan on 4 Nov 1985 to celebrate the International Youth Year.

Candle

A candle 80 ft *24,38 m* high and 8½ ft *2,59 m* in diameter was exhibited at the 1897 Stockholm Exhibition by the firm of Lindahls. The overall height was 127 ft *38,70 m*. Currently the largest is that made by the Atletiek-en Trimvereniging Tegelen Sportsclub of Tegelen, Netherlands on 1 June 1986. It stands 27,15 m *89 ft 1 in* high.

Carpets and rugs

The earliest carpet known is a Scythian woollen pile-knotted carpet measuring 6 ft by 6 ft *(1,8 m × 1,8 m)* and dating from the 4th–3rd centuries BC. It was discovered by the Russian archaeologist Sergey Ivanovich Rudenko in 1947 in the Pazyryk Valley in southern Siberia and is now presented in the Hermitage, Leningrad.

Of ancient carpets the largest was a gold-enriched silk carpet of Hashim (dated AD 743) of the Abbasid caliphate in Baghdad, Iraq. It is reputed to have measured 180 by 300 ft *54,86 × 91,44 m*. A 52,225 ft² *4851 m²* or 1.23-acre 28-ton red carpet was laid on 13 Feb 1982, by the Allied Corporation, from Radio City Music Hall to the New York Hilton along the Avenue of the Americas.

The most finely woven old carpet known is one having more than 2600 knots per in² *403 per cm²* produced in March 1985 by the Bikaner Woollen Mills of Varanasi, Uttar Pradesh, India. The carpet was displayed at the 1986 *Heimtextil* International Trade Fair in Frankfurt, West Germany, where a consensus of expert opinion declared the 'knottage' to be close to 3000 per in² *465 per cm²*. The most magnificent carpet ever made was the Spring carpet of Khusraw made for the audience hall of the Sassanian palace at Ctesiphon, Iraq. It was about 7000 ft² *650 m²* of silk and gold thread, and encrusted with emeralds. It was cut up as booty by looters in AD 635 and from the known realisation value of the pieces must have had an original value of some £100,000,000.

Chair

The largest chair is the 2000 lb *907 kg* 33 ft 1 in *10,08 m* tall, 19 ft 7 in *5,96 m* wide chair constructed by Anniston Steel & Plumbing Co Inc for Miller Office Furniture in Anniston, Alabama and completed in May 1981.

Chandelier

The largest set of chandeliers (ten) was built for the palace of HM Sir Muda Hassanal Bolkiah of Brunei in 1983. His palace or Istana Nurul Iman is in the capital Bandar Seri Begawan. Britain's largest chandelier measures 30 ft *9,1 m* in the Chinese Room at the Royal Pavilion, Brighton. It was made in 1818 and weighs 1 ton/*tonne*.

Christmas cracker

The largest functional cracker ever constructed was one measuring 24,384 m *80 ft* long by 3 m *9 ft 10 in* diameter built by Markson Sparks, Sydney for Christmas 1986.

Cigars

The largest cigar ever made measures 5,095 m *16 ft 8½ in* in length and weighs 262 kg *577 lb 9 oz* (over ¼ ton) taking 243 hours and using 3330 full tobacco leaves. It was made by Tinus Vinke and Jan Weijmer in Feb 1983 and is in the Tobacco Museum in Kampen, Netherlands. The largest marketed cigar in the world is the 14 in *35,5 cm* Valdez Emperado by San Andres Cigars.

The most expensive standard cigar in the world is the 9¼ in *23,5 cm* long Montecristo 'A', which retails in Britain at £13.50.

Joseph Hruby of Lyndhurst, Ohio has the largest known collection of cigar bands with 175,391 different examples dating from *c.* 1895 onwards.

Cigarettes

World production in 1985 was 9873 billion cigarettes. The people of China were estimated to consume 1180 million in 1985. In Senegal 80 per cent of urban males smoke. The peak consumption in the United Kingdom was 3230 cigarettes per adult in 1973. The peak volume was 243,100,000 lb *110,2 million kg* in 1961, compared with 79,8 million kg *176 million lb* in 1986 when 95,500 million cigarettes were sold. In the United Kingdom in 1986 36 per cent of males smoked, averaging 115 cigarettes a week each. Of women 32 per cent smoked.

Of the 140 brands most recently analysed for the Dept of Health and Social Security, the one with highest tar/nicotine content is *Capstan Full Strength* with 25/2,6 mg per cigarette. *Silk Cut Ultra Low King Size*, *Embassy Ultra Mild King Size* and *John Player King Size Ultra Mild* with < 4/0,3 are at the lower risk end of the league table. In the Philippines there is a brand with 71 mg nicotine per cigarette.

The world's most popular cigarette is *Marlboro*, a filter cigarette made by Philip Morris, which sold 237,000 million units in 1982. The largest-selling British cigarette in 1986 was *Benson and Hedges Special Filter*. The oldest brand still available on the British market is Wills Woodbine, introduced in 1888.

The longest cigarettes ever marketed were *Head Plays*, each 11 in *27,9 cm* long and sold in packets of 5 in the United States in about 1930, to save tax. The shortest were *Lilliput* cigarettes, each 1¼ in *31,7 mm* long and ⅛ in *3 mm* in diameter, made in Great Britain in 1956.

The world's largest collection of cigarettes is that of Robert E. Kaufman MD, of 950 Park Avenue, New York City 10028, USA. In April 1987 he had 8017 different cigarettes made in 172 countries. The oldest brand represented is *Lone Jack*, made in the USA *c.* 1885. Both the longest and shortest (see above) are represented.

Cigarette cards

The earliest known tobacco card is 'Vanity Fair' dated 1876, issued by Wm S. Kimball & Co, Rochester, New York. The earliest British example appeared *c.* 1883 in the form of a calendar issued by Allen & Ginter, of Richmond, Virginia, trading from Holborn Viaduct, City of London. The largest known collection is that of Mr Edward Wharton-Tigar MBE (b. 1913) of London with a collection of more than 1,000,000 cigarette and trade cards in about 45,000 sets.

Cigarette lighter

The Leader Lighthouse Table Lighter is made in 18-ct gold—designed in the shape of a lighthouse set on an island base of amethyst which alone weighs 1 cwt *50 kg*. It weighs 51.4 oz troy *1600 g* and the windows on the lighthouse stem are amethyst. Priced at £37,500, it was sold by Alfred Dunhill, St James's, London in 1986.

Cigarette packets

The earliest surviving cigarette packet is a Finnish *Petit Canon* packet for 25, made by Tollander & Klärich in 1860, from the Ventegodt Collection. The rarest is the Latvian 700-year anniversary (1201–1901) *Riga* packet, believed to be unique, from the same collection. The largest verified private collection is one of 60,955 from over 150 countries owned by Vernon Young of Farnham, England.

Credit card collection

The largest collection of valid credit cards at April 1986 is one of 1196 (all different) by Walter Cavanagh (b. 1943) of Santa Clara, California, USA. The cost of acquisition to 'Mr Plastic Fantastick' was nil, and he keeps them in the world's longest wallet—250 ft *76,2 m* long weighing 35 lb *15,87 kg* and worth more than $1.30 million in credit.

Curtain

The largest curtain ever built was a bright orange-red 4 ton *4064 kg* 185 ft *56 m* high curtain suspended 1350 ft *411 m* across the Rifle Gap, Grand Hogback, Colorado by Bulgarian-born sculptor Christo, (né Javacheff) on 10 Aug 1971. It blew apart in a 50 mph *80 km/h* gust 27 hr later. The total cost involved in displaying this work of art was $750,000 (*then £312,500*).

The world's largest functional curtain is one 550 ft long × 65 ft high *167,6 × 19,8 m* in the Brabazon hangar at British Aerospace Filton, Bristol used to enclose aircraft in the paint-spraying bay. It is electrically drawn.

Dress

EVA suits for extra-vehicular activity worn by Space Shuttle crews from 1982 had a unit cost of $2.3 million (*then £1,437,000*).

The dress with the highest price tag ever exhibited by a Paris fashion house was one in the Schiaparelli spring/summer collection on 23 Jan 1977. 'The Birth of Venus' designed by Serge Lepage with 512 diamonds was priced at Fr. 7,500,000 (*then £880,000*).

A robe for Emperor Field-Marshal Jean-Bédel Bokassa with a 39 ft *11,8 m* long train was encrusted with 785,000 pearls and 1,220,000 crystal beads by Guiselin of Paris for £77,125. It was worn for his coronation at Bangui, Central African Empire (now Republic) on 4 Dec 1977 (see also Shoes).

Fabrics

The oldest surviving fabric discovered from Level VI A at Çatal Hüyük, Turkey has been radio-carbon dated to 5900 BC.

The most expensive fabric is Vicuña cloth manufactured by Fuji Keori Ltd of Osaka, Japan at US$3235 (*£2087*) per metre in July 1983. The most expensive evening wear fabric was that designed by Alan Hershman of Duke Street, London at £775 per metre. Each square metre, despite 155,000 hand-sewn sequins, weighs less than 7 oz *198 g*.

The most expensive cloth, the brown-grey throat hair of Indian goats, is Shatoosh (or Shatusa), finer and more expensive than Vicuña. It was sold jby Neiman-Marcus of Dallas, Texas, at $1000 (*£555*) per yard but supplies have now dried up.

Firework

The largest firework ever produced has been *Universe I* exploded for the Lake Toya Festival, Hokkaido, Japan on 28 Aug 1983. The 421 kg *928 lb* shell was 108 cm *42.5 in* in diameter and burst to a diameter of 860 m *2830 ft*, with a 5-

colour display. The longest firework 'waterfall' was produced for the Yonago-Gaina Festival in Tottori, Japan and ignited at 8.55 p.m. on 24 Aug 1986. It measured 1710 m *5610 ft* in length and 37 m *120 ft* in height.

Flags

The oldest known flag is one dated to *c.* 3000 BC found in 1972 at Khablis, Iran. It is of metal and measures 23 × 23 cm *9 × 9 in* and depicts an eagle, lions and goddesses. The oldest national flags are claimed by Austria, Denmark, Malta, Japan, Sri Lanka and Mali.

The largest flag in the world, the 'Great American Flag', was displayed at Evansville, Indiana on 22 Mar 1980 measuring 411 ft *125 m* by 210 ft *64 m* with a weight of 7 tons/tonnes. It was donated to the White House and was the brainchild of Len Silverfine. The largest Union Flag (or Union Jack) was one 240 × 108 ft *73,15 × 32,91 m* displayed at the Royal Tournament, Earl's Court, London in July 1976. It weighed more than a ton and was made by Form 4Y at Bradley Rowe School, Exeter, Devon. The largest flag *flown* from a flagstaff is a Brazilian national flag measuring 70 × 100 m *229 ft 8 in × 328 ft 1 in* in Brasilia. The study of flags is known as vexillology from Latin *vexillum*, a flag, and was coined by Dr Whitney Smith of Winchester, Massachusetts.

Float

The largest float was the 155 ft *47,24 m* long, 24 ft *7,32 m* wide 'Merry Christmas America' float bearing 3 double arches, a 17 ft *5,18 m* Christmas tree, two 15 ft *4,57 m* peppermint candy sticks and 5380 ft² *500 m²* of wrapping paper, used at the 40th Annual Christmas Parade, Baton Rouge, Louisiana on 5 Dec 1986.

Furniture

The largest item of furniture in the world is a wooden bench in Green Park, Obihiro, Hokkaido, Japan which seats 1282 people and measures 400 m *1312 ft 4 in* long. It was completed by a team of 770 on 19 July 1981.

Garden gnome

The earliest recorded garden gnome was one placed in the rockery at Lamport Hall, near Northampton, by Sir Charles Isham Bt (1819–1903).

Glass

The most priceless example of the art of glass-making is usually regarded as the glass Portland Vase which dates from late in the 1st century BC or 1st century AD. It was made in Italy, and was in the possession of the Barberini family in Rome from at least 1642. It was eventually bought by the Duchess of Portland in 1792 but smashed while in the British Museum by William Lloyd on 7 Feb 1845. The thinnest glass made is 0.003 in *0,076 mm* thick for liquid crystal display (LCD) watches by Corning Glass Works, New York.

Gold

The gold coffin of the 14th-century BC Pharaoh Tutankhamun discovered by Howard Carter on 16 Feb 1923 in the Valley of the Kings, western Thebes, Egypt weighed 110,4 kg *243 lb*. The exhibition at the British Museum from 30 Mar to 30 Dec 1972 attracted 1,656,151 people (of whom 45.7 per cent bought catalogues) resulting in a profit of £657,731.22.

Grill

A 100,2 m *328.7 ft* long grill was made for a barbecue at Esplugnes de Llobregat, Barcelona, Spain on 22 Sep 1986. A single *butifarra* (sausage) 1803,6 m *5,917 ft* in length was cooked on it.

Jigsaw

The earliest jigsaws were made as 'dissected maps' by John Spilsbury (1739–69) in Russell Court off Drury Lane, London *c.* 1762. The largest jigsaw ever made is one measuring 84 ft 10½ in ×

Largest dress ● The largest 'dress' ever made was one 100 ft *30,48 m* long made of 2500 yds *2286 m* of aqua and pink dacron weighing 1000 lbs *453,6 kg* for the 'engagement' between Miss Liberty (US) and Christopher Columbus (Spain). It was created by Antoni Miraldi in October 1986. (Photo: Marta Sentis)

55 ft 2½ in *25,87 × 16,83 m* with 15,520 pieces constructed by the Monadnock United Way of Keene, New Hampshire from 21–23 Sept 1985. Fujisankei Communications Group of Japan commissioned Yanoman Co to produce a puzzle 3,24 × 5,88 m *10.63 × 19.29 ft* with 61,752 pieces. Each piece was sold for charity. Custom-made Stave puzzles made by Steve Richardson of Vermont, USA of 2300 pieces cost $3700 (*then £2430*) in Jan 1983.

Kettle

The largest antique copper kettle was one standing 3 ft *0,9 m* high with a 6 ft *1,8 m* girth and a 20 gal *90 l* capacity, built in Taunton, Somerset for the hardware merchants Fisher and Son *c.* 1800.

Lamp

The smallest electric bulb is one 3 mm *0.12 in* long by 0,5 mm *0.02 in* in diameter made by the Hamai Electric Lamp Co, Tokyo, Japan.

Matchbox labels

The oldest match label of accepted provenance is that of Samuel Jones *c.* 1830. The finest collection of trade mark labels (excluding any bar or other advertising labels) is some 280,000 pieces collected by the phillumenist Robert Jones of Indianapolis, USA. The greatest British prize is a Lucifer & Congreve label of *c.* 1835.

Needles

Needles made of bone have been found in sites of the Upper Palaeolithic Aurignacian period in France dated *c.* 28,000–24,000 BC. The longest is one 6 ft 1 in *185,5 cm* made by George Davies of Thomas Somerfield, Bloxwich for stitching mattress buttons lengthways. One is preserved in the National Needle Museum at Forge Mill, Redditch, Worcestershire.

Nylon

The lowest denier nylon yarn ever produced is the 6 denier used for stockings exhibited at the

Nylon Fair in London in February 1956. The sheerest stockings normally available are 9 denier. A hair from the average human head is about 50 denier.

Penknife

The penknife with the greatest number of blades is the Year Knife made by cutlers Joseph Rodgers & Sons, of Sheffield, England, whose trade mark was granted in 1682. The knife was made in 1822 with 1822 blades and a blade was added every year until 1973 when there was no further space. It was acquired by Britain's largest hand tool manufacturers, Stanley Works (Great Britain) Ltd of Sheffield, South Yorkshire in 1970.

Pens

The most expensive writing pens were the 18-carat pair of pens (one fibre-tipped and one ballpoint) capped by diamonds of 3.88 carats sold by Alfred Dunhill of London for £9943 the pair (incl. VAT). The most expensive fountain pen was the Mont Blanc 18-carat gold and platinum nibbed Meisterstück made by Dunhill in Hamburg, West Germany and which retailed in 1984 for $4250 (then £3035).

Pistol

In December 1983 it was reported that Ray Bily (US) owned an initialled gold pistol made for Hitler which was valued for insurance at $375,000 (£267,850).

The pistol with the largest magazine capacity is the .22LR M.100P with 103 rounds of continuous firepower, manufactured by Calico, Bakersfield, California.

Postcards

Deltiology is claimed to be the third largest collecting hobby next only to stamps and coins. Austria issued the first cards in 1869 followed by Britain in 1872. The highest price paid for a postcard was $4400 (£3143) for one of the five known Mucha Waverly Cycle postcards. It was sold by Susan Brown Nicholson of Lisle, Illinois, USA in Sept 1984.

Quilting

The world's largest quilt, designed by A. Platteau, was made by the people of Kortrijk-Rollegem, Belgium. It comprises 16,240 squares measuring 21,24 × 30,35 m *69.6 × 99.5 ft*. On 28 Aug 1982 it was hoisted by two cranes.

Ropes

The largest rope ever made was a coir fibre launching rope with a circumference of 47 in *119 cm* made in 1858 for the British liner *Great Eastern* by John and Edwin Wright of Birmingham. It consisted of four strands, each of 3780 yarns. The longest fibre rope ever made without a splice was one of 10,000 fathoms or 11.36 miles *18 288 m* of 6½ in *16,5 cm* circumference manila by Frost Brothers (now British Ropes Ltd) in London in 1874. (See Wire ropes, Chapter 8.)

The world's largest shoe ● This Spanish-made giant was cobbled together by Antonio Alonso de la Prieta of Madrid. It measures 1,3 m *4.26 ft* in length, weighs 72 kg *158 lb* and took the skins of two cows.

The strongest cable-laid wire rope strop made is one 282 mm *11.1 in* in diameter with a breaking strain of 3250 tonnes.

Shoes

James Smith, founder of James Southall & Co of Norwich, introduced sized shoes in 1792. The firm began making 'Start-rite' children's shoes in 1923.

Emperor Bokassa of the Central African Empire (now Republic) commissioned pearl-studded shoes from the House of Berluti, Paris for his self-coronation on 4 Dec 1977 at a cost of $85,000 (£38,800).

The most expensive shoes are mink-lined golf shoes with 18-carat gold embellishments and ruby-tipped spikes made by Stylo Matchmakers International, of Northampton, England, which retail for £8580, or *$13,700* per pair in the USA.

Excluding cases of elephantiasis, the largest shoes ever sold are a pair size 42 built for the giant Harley Davidson of Avon Park, Florida. The normal limit is size 14. For advertising and display purposes facsimiles of shoes weighing up to 1,5 tonnes have been constructed.

Silver

The largest single pieces of silver are a pair of water jugs of 10,408 troy oz 4.77 cwt *242,7 kg* made in 1902 for the Maharaja of Jaipur (1861–1922). They are 160 cm *5 ft 3 in* tall, with a circumference of 2,48 m *8 ft 1¼ in*, and have a capacity of 1800 gallons *8182 litres*. They are now in the City Palace, Jaipur, India. The silversmith was Gorind Narain.

Snuff

The most expensive snuff obtainable in Britain is 'Café Royale' sold by G. Smith and Sons (est. 1869) of 74, Charing Cross Road, London. The price was £2.18 per oz in April 1987.

Sofa

The longest standard sofa manufactured for market is the King Talmage Sofa, 12 ft 2 in *3,7 m* in length made by the Talmageville Furniture Manufacturers of California. Barton Grange Hotel, near Preston, Lancashire bought a 14 ft *4,26 m* long pink leather settee for £3250 on 4 Oct 1984.

Table

The longest table was set up from La Punta to The Terramar, Sitges, Spain on 4 Oct 1986. It was 2410,6 m *2636.2 yds* in length and was used to seat 6,400 people.

Table cloth

The world's largest table cloth is one 219 yd *200 m* long by 2 yd *1,8 m* wide double damask made by John S. Brown & Sons of Belfast in 1972 and shipped to a royal palace in the Middle East. There was also an order for matching napkins for 450 places.

Tapestry

The earliest known examples of tapestry woven linen are three pieces from the tomb of the Egyptian pharaoh Thutmose IV and dated to 1483–1411 BC.

The largest tapestry ever woven is the 'History of Irak', with an area of 13,370.7 ft² *1242,1 m²*. Designed by the Yugoslavian artist Frane Delale and completed in 1986, it adorns the wall of an amphitheatre in Baghdad.

Britain's largest single piece of tapestry is 'Christ in His Majesty', measuring 72 ft by 39 ft *21,94 × 11,88 m* designed by Graham Vivian Sutherland OM (1903–80) as an altar hanging in Coventry Cathedral. It cost £10,500, weighs ¾ ton *760 kg* and was delivered from Pinton Frères of Felletin, France on 1 Mar 1962.

The famous Bayeux *Telle du Conquest, dite tapisserie de la reine Mathilde*, a hanging 19½ in *49,5 cm* wide by 231 ft *70,40 m* in length depicts events of 1064–6 in 72 scenes and was probably worked in Canterbury, Kent, *c.* 1086. It was 'lost' for 2½ centuries from 1476 until 1724.

The Overlord Embroidery of 34 panels each 8 × 3 ft *2,43 × 0,91 m*, commissioned by Lord Dulverton CBE, TD (b. 1915) from the Royal School of Needlework in London, was completed in 1979 after 100 man-years of work and is 41 ft *12,49 m* longer than the Bayeux and has the largest area of any embroidery with 816 ft² *75,8 m²*.

An uncompleted 8 in *20,3 cm* deep 1280 ft *390,14 m* long embroidery of scenes from C. S. Lewis's Narnia children's stories has been worked by Mrs Margaret S. Pollard of Truro, Cornwall to the order of Michael Maine.

Tartan
The earliest evidence of tartan is the so-called Falkirk tartan, found stuffed in a jar of coins in Bells Meadow, Falkirk, Stirlingshire. It is of a dark and light plaid pattern and dates from *c.* AD 245. The earliest reference to a specific named tartan is to a Murray tartan in 1618 although Mackay tartan was probably worn earlier. There are 1300 tartans known to the Museum of Scottish Tartans at Comrie, Perthshire. HRH Prince of Wales is eligible to wear 11 including the Balmoral which has been exclusive to the Royal Family since 1852.

Tea towels
The largest reported collection of unduplicated tea towels was 5967 formed by Tony Judkin of Luton, Bedfordshire. In April 1986 a fire destroyed 'over a thousand' of them.

Time capsule
The world's largest time capsule is the Tropico Time Tunnel of 10,000 ft³ *283 m³* in a cave in Rosamond, California, sealed by the Kern Antelope Historical Society on 20 Nov 1966 and intended for opening in AD 2866.

Typewriters
The first patent for a typewriter was by Henry Mill in 1714 but the earliest known working machine was made by Pellegrine Turri (Italy) in 1808.

Vase
The largest vase on record is one 8 ft *2,78 m* in height, weighing 650 lb *294,8 kg*, thrown by Sebastiano Maglio at Haeger Potteries of Dundee, Illinois (founded 1872) during August 1976. The Chinese ceramic authority Chingwah Lee of San Francisco was reported in August 1978 to have appraised a unique 39 in *99 cm* Kang Hsi 4-sided vase then in a bank vault in Phoenix, Arizona at '$60 million' (*then £30 million*).

Wallet
The most expensive wallet ever made is a platinum-cornered, diamond-studded crocodile creation made by Louis Quatorze of Paris and Mikimoto of Tokyo selling in September 1984 at £56,000.

Wreath
The most expensive wreath on record was that presented to Sri Chinmoy in New York on 11 July 1983 by Ashrita Furman and Pahar Meltzer. It was handled by the Garland of Divinity's Love Florist, contained 10,000 flowers, and cost $3500 (*£2260*).

Zip-fastener
The world's longest zip-fastener is 632,45 m *2074 ft* long made for covers of aquatic cables by RIRI of Mendrisio, Italy in January 1985. It has 119,007 nylon teeth.

Origins
It has been estimated that only 21 per cent of the world's land surface is cultivable and that only 7.6 per cent is actually under cultivation. Evidence adduced in 1971 from Nok Nok Tha and Spirit Cave, Thailand tends to confirm that plant cultivation and animal domestication were part of the Hoabinhian culture *c.* 11,000 BC. Goats were herded on Mount Carmel, Palestine as early as 16,000 BC.

Goat was domesticated at Asiab, Iran by *c.* 8050 BC and dog at Star Carr, North Yorkshire by *c.* 7700 BC; the earliest definite date for sheep is *c.* 7200 BC at Argissa-Magula, Thessaly, Greece and for pig and cattle *c.* 7000 BC at the same site. The earliest date for horse is *c.* 4350 BC from Dereivka, Ukraine, USSR.

FARMS

Earliest
The earliest dated British farming site is Neolithic and is enclosed within the Iron-Age hill-fort at Hembury, Devon, excavated during 1934–5 and now dated to 4210–3990 BC. Pollen analysis from two sites, Oakhanger, Hampshire and Winfrith Heath, Dorset (Mesolithic *c.* 5000 BC) indicates that Mesolithic man may have had deer herds which were fed on ivy during the winter months.

Largest
The largest farms in the world are collective farms (*sovkhozes*) in the USSR. These have been reduced in number from 235,500 in 1940 to only 18,000 in 1980 and have been increased in size so that units of over 60,000 acres *25 000 ha* are not uncommon. The pioneer farm owned by Laucidio Coelho near Campo Grande, Mato Grosso, Brazil *c.* 1901 was 3358 miles² *8700 km²* or 2.15 million acres with 250,000 head of cattle at the time of his death in 1975.

The largest farms in the British Isles are Scottish hill farms in the Grampians. The largest arable farm is that at Elveden, Suffolk, farmed by the Earl of Iveagh. Here 11,207 acres *4535 ha* are farmed on an estate of 22,918 acres *9275 ha*, the greater part of which was formerly derelict land. The 1986 production included 9340 tonnes *9173 tons* of grain and 60 392 tonnes *61,493 tons* of sugar beet. The livestock includes 316 beef cattle, 1030 ewes and 6118 pigs.

Cattle station
The world's largest cattle station is the Anna Creek station of 30 113,5 km² *11,626.8 miles²*, South Australia owned by the Kidman family. It is thus 23 per cent of the size of England. The biggest component is Strangway at 14 114 km² *5449 miles²*. Until 1915 the Victoria River Downs Station, Northern Territory had an area of 22,400,000 acres (35,000 miles² *90 650 km²*), the same as England's 20 largest counties put together.

Sheep station
The largest sheep station in the world is Commonwealth Hill, in the north-west of South Australia. It grazes between 60,000 and 70,000 sheep, *c.* 700 cattle and 54,000 uninvited kangaroos in an area of 4080 miles² *10 567 km²*, i.e. larger than the combined area of Norfolk and Suffolk. The head count on Sir William Stevenson's 30,000 acre *12 140 ha* Lochinver Station in New Zealand was 117,500 on 1 Jan 1983 on 21,000 acres *8500 ha*. The largest sheep move on record occurred when 27 horsemen moved a mob of 43,000 sheep 40 miles *64 km* from Barcaldine to Beaconsfield Station, Queensland, in 1886.

Rice farming
The largest contiguous wild rice (*Zizania aquatica*) farm in the world is Clearwater Rice Inc at Clearbrook, Minnesota, USA with 2000 acres *809 ha*. In 1986 it yielded 577,000 lb *261 727 kg*, the largest to date.

Turkey farm
The world's largest turkey farm is that of Bernard Matthews plc, centred at Great Witchingham, Norfolk, with 2600 staff tending 8,000,000 turkeys.

Chicken ranch
The world's largest chicken ranch is the Croton Egg Farm in Ohio, which has 4.8 million hens laying some 3.7 million eggs daily.

Piggery
The world's largest piggery is the Sljeme pig unit in Yugoslavia which is able to process 300,000 pigs in a year.

Cow shed
The longest cow shed in Britain is that of the Yorkshire Agricultural Society at Harrogate, North Yorkshire. It is 456 ft *139 m* in length with a capacity of 686 cows. The National Agricultural Centre, Kenilworth, Warwickshire, completed in 1967, has, however, capacity for 782 animals.

Foot-and-mouth disease
The worst outbreak of foot-and-mouth disease in Great Britain was that from Shropshire on 25 Oct 1967 to 25 June 1968 in which there were 2364 outbreaks and 429,632 animals slaughtered at a direct and consequential loss of £150,000,000. The outbreak of 1871, when farms were much smaller, affected 42,531 farms. The disease first appeared in Britain at Stratford, east London in August 1839.

Sheep shearing
The highest speed for sheep shearing in a working day was that recorded for John Fagan who machine-sheared 804 lambs (average 89.3 per hour) in 9 hr at Hautora Rd, Pio Pio, New Zealand on 8 Dec 1980. Peter Casserly of Christchurch, New Zealand, achieved a solo blade (*i.e.* hand-shearing) record of 353 lambs in 9 hours on 13 Feb 1976. In a shearing marathon, four men machine-shore 2519 sheep in 29 hr at Stewarts Trust, Waikia, Southland, New Zealand on 11 Feb 1982.

Mr Lavor Taylor (b. 27 Feb 1896) of Ephraim, Utah claims to have sheared 515,000 sheep to May 1984.

British records for 9 hr have been set at 555 by Roger Poyntz-Roberts (300) and John Savery (255) on 9 June 1971 (sheep caught *by* shearers), and 610 by the same pair (sheep caught *for* shearers) in July 1970.

Sheep survival
The longest recorded survival by a sheep buried in snow is 50 days when Alex Maclennan uncovered 15 dead and 1 live sheep near the River Skinsdale on Mrs Tyser's Gordonbush Estate, Sutherland on 24 Mar 1978 during the great January blizzard.

Mushroom farm
The largest single mushroom farm in the world is that of the Moonlight Mushroom Inc, founded in 1937 in a disused limestone mine near West Winfield, Pennsylvania. It employs over 900 in a maze of underground galleries 110 miles *177 km* long, producing over 22,000 short tons *21 770 tonnes* of mushrooms per year. The French annual consumption is unrivalled at 7 lb *3,17 kg* per caput.

Wheat field
The largest single fenced field sown with wheat was one of 35,000 acres *14 160 ha* sown in 1951 south-west of Lethbridge, Alberta, Canada.

Vineyard
The world's largest vineyard extends over the Mediterranean façade between the Rhône and the Pyrenees in the *départements* Hérault, Gard, Aude, and Pyrénées-Orientales in an area of 840 000 ha *2,075,685 acres* of which 52.3 per cent is *monoculture viticole*.

Hop field

The largest is one of 1863 acres *753,9 ha* near Toppenish, Washington State. It is owned by John I. Haas Inc, the world's largest hop growers, with hop farms in Idaho, Oregon and Washington, with a total net area of 3700 acres *1497,4 ha*.

Community garden

The largest such project is that operated by the City Beautiful Council, and the Benjamin Wegerzyn Garden Center at Dayton, Ohio. It comprises 1173 allotments each of 812¼ ft² *74,45 m²*.

CROP YIELDS

Wheat

Crop yields for highly tended small areas are of little significance. The British record is 111.4 cwt/acre *13,99 tonnes/ha* at 15.5 per cent moisture on a field of 43.24 acres *17,49 ha* by Gordon Rennie of Clifton Mains, Newbridge, Midlothian.

Barley

A yield of 93.7 cwt/acre *11 762 kg/ha* of Gerbel Winter Barley was achieved in August 1984 by the Brewster family farm at Kirknewton, Midlothian from a 20.48 acre *8,29 ha* field.

Potato

The greatest number of US barrels picked in a 9¼ hr day is 235 by Walter Sirois (b. 1917) of Caribou, Maine on 30 Sept 1950.

Corn

A yield of 352.64 US bushels (15¼ per cent moisture) from an acre, using De Kalb XL-54, was achieved by Roy Lynn, Jr near Kalamazoo, Michigan on 30 Sept 1977.

Sugar beet

The highest recorded yield for sugar beet is 62.4 short tons (55.71 long tons) per acre *139,9 tonnes/ha* by Andy Christensen and Jon Giannini in the Salinas Valley, California.

Field-to-loaf

The fastest time for producing loaves from growing wheat is 40 min 44 sec at O. S. North's Bakery at Heydon, near Royston, Hertfordshire on 10 Sept 1983.

Two one-pound loaves (1 white, 1 wholemeal) and 115 g *4.05 oz* of butter (from 9 litres *15.8 pints* of milk produced by 'Daffodil') were produced in 29 min 37 sec at Thriplow Farm, Cambs on 18 April 1986.

Ploughing

The world championship (instituted 1953) has been staged in 18 countries and won by ploughmen of 11 nationalities of which the United Kingdom has been most successful with 8 championships. The only man to take the title three times has been Hugh B. Barr of Northern Ireland in 1954–5–6. The 1984 champion was Desmond Wright, 48 (Northern Ireland).

The fastest recorded time for ploughing an acre *0,404 ha* (minimum 32 right-hand turns and depth 9 in *22 cm*) is 11 min 21.8 sec by Robert Dee using a Fiat 180-90 DT tractor at Hodstock Priory Farm, Blythe, Nottinghamshire on 1 Nov 1984. Frank Allinson of Leyburn, North Yorkshire, ploughed for 250 hr 9 min 50 sec from 14–24 Nov 1981. DMI Inc of Goodfield, Illinois marketed a 'Hydrawide' plough with 21 furrows in 1978.

Rick

A rick of 40,400 bales of straw was completed from 22 July to 3 Sept 1982 by Nick and Tom Parsons with a gang of 8 at Cuckoo-pen Barn Farm, Birdlip, Gloucestershire. It measured 150 × 30 × 60 ft *45,7 × 9,1 × 18,2 m* high and weighed some 700 tons *711 tonnes*. They baled, hauled and ricked 24,200 bales in 7 consecutive days from 22–29 July.

LIVESTOCK

Note: Some exceptionally high livestock auction prices are believed to result from collusion between buyer and seller to raise the ostensible price levels of the breed concerned. Others are marketing and publicity exercises with little relation to true market prices.

Highest priced *Bull*

The highest price has been $2,500,000 (*then £1,087,000*) for the beefalo (a ⅜ bison, ⅜ charolais, ¼ Hereford) 'Joe's Pride' sold by D. C. Basalo of Burlingame, California to the Beefalo Cattle Co of Canada, of Calgary on 9 Sept 1974. A young 14-month-old Canadian Holstein bull 'Pickland Elevation B. ET' was bought by Premier Breeders of Stamfordham, Northumberland for £233,000.

The highest price in Britain has been 60,000 guineas (£63,000), paid on 5 Feb 1963 at Perth, Scotland, by James R. Dick (1928–74) co-manager of Black Watch Farms, for 'Lindertis Evulse', an Aberdeen-Angus owned by Sir Torquil and Lady Munro of Lindertis, Kirriemuir, Angus. This bull failed a fertility test in August 1963, thus becoming the world's most expensive piece of beef.

Cow

The highest price for a cow has been $1,300,000 (*then £1 million*) for a Holstein at auction in East Monpelier, Vermont in 1985. The British record is £33,600 for 'Ullswater Beatexus 8th', a British Friesian sold to The British Livestock Embryo Syndicate of Royston, Hertfordshire by Sir Keith and Lady Showering of West Horrington, Wells, Somerset on 9 May 1981 (auctioneers: Hobsons).

Sheep

The highest price ever paid for a ram is $A79,000 (*£49,500*) by the Gnowangerup Animal Breeding Centre, Western Australia for a Merino ram from the Collinsville Stud, South Australia at the Royal Adelaide Show on 10 Sept 1981.

The British auction record is £21,000 paid by Mr W. Sheddon of Brighouse, Kirkcudbrightshire for A. W. Carswell & Son's Blackface ram on 4 Oct 1978.

The highest price ever paid for wool is $A280 per kg greasy for a bale of Tasmania superfine from the Launceston, Tasmania sales on 11 Dec 1986 by Fujii Keori Ltd of Osaka, Japan—top bidders since 1973.

Pig

The highest price ever paid for a pig is $56,000 (*then £38,356*) for a cross-bred barrow named 'Bud' owned by Jeffrey Roemisch of Hermleigh, Texas and bought by E. A. 'Bud' Olson and Phil Bonzio on 5 Mar 1981. The UK• record is 3300 guineas (£3465), paid by Malvern Farms for a Swedish Landrace gilt 'Bluegate Ally 33rd' owned by Davidson Trust in a draft sale at Reading, Berkshire on 2 Mar 1955.

Horse

The highest price for a draught horse is $47,500 (*£9970*) paid for the 7-year-old Belgian stallion 'Farceur' by E. G. Good at Cedar Falls, Iowa on 16 Oct 1917. A Welsh mountain pony stallion 'Coed Cock Bari' was sold to an Australian builder in Wales in September 1978 for 21,000 guineas (*then £22,050*).

Donkey

The lowest ever price for livestock was at a sale at Kuruman, Cape Province, South Africa in 1934 where donkeys were sold for less than 2p each.

Heaviest *Cattle*

The heaviest on record was a Holstein-Durham cross named 'Mount Katahdin' exhibited by A. S. Rand of Maine, USA from 1906–10 and frequently weighed at an even 5000 lb *2267 kg*. He was 6 ft

2 in *1,88 m* at the shoulder with a 13 ft *3,96 m* girth and died in a barn fire *c.* 1923. The British record is the 4480 lb *2032 kg* of 'The Bradwell Ox' owned by William Spurgin of Bradwell, Essex. He was 15 ft *4,57 m* from nose to tail and had a girth of 11 ft *3,35 m* when 6 years old in 1830. The largest breed of heavyweight cattle is the Chianini, brought to Italy from the Middle East in pre-Roman times. Mature bulls average 5 ft 8 in *1,73 m* at the forequarters and weigh 2865 lb *1300 kg*. The Airedale Heifer of East Riddlesdon, near Keighley, South Yorkshire *c.* 1820 was 11 ft 10.6 in *3,62 m* long and weighed 2640 lb *1197,5 kg*.

The highest recorded birthweight for a calf is 225 lb *102 kg* from a British Friesian cow at Rockhouse Farm, Bishopston, Swansea, West Glamorgan, in 1961.

Pigs

The heaviest hog recorded was a Poland-China hog 'Big Bill' of 2552 lb or 22¾ cwt *1157,5 kg* measuring 9 ft *2,75 m* long with a belly on the ground, owned by Burford Butler of Jackson, Tennessee and chloroformed in 1933. Raised by W. J. Chappall he was mounted and displayed in Weekly County, Tennessee until 1946. The British record is held by the now extinct Rudgewick boar. In 1805 a weight of 1456 lb *660,4 kg* was recorded for an individual bred at Godstone, Surrey. The highest recorded weight for a piglet at weaning (8 weeks) is 81 lb *36,7 kg* for a boar, one of nine piglets farrowed on 6 July 1962 by the Landrace gilt 'Manorport Ballerina 53rd', *alias* 'Mary', and sired by a Large White named 'Johnny' at Kettle Lane Farm, West Ashton, Trowbridge, Wiltshire.

Sheep

The highest recorded birthweight for a lamb is 38 lb *17,2 kg* at Clearwater, Sedgwick County, Kansas in 1975, but neither lamb nor ewe survived. Another lamb of the same weight was born on 7 April 1975 in Howard, South Dakota, but died soon after.

Broiler growth

The record for growth for flocks of at least 2400 at 56 days is 2,901 kg *6.396 lb* with a conversion rate of 2.17 by D. B. Marshall (Newbridge) Ltd of Newbridge, Midlothian reported in October 1981.

Prolificacy *Cattle*

On 25 Apr 1964 it was reported that a cow named 'Lyubik' had given birth to seven calves at Mogilev, USSR. Five live and one dead calf were recorded from a Friesian at Te Puke, North Island, New Zealand on 27 July 1980 but none survived. A case of five live calves at one birth was reported in 1928 by T. G. Yarwood of Manchester. The lifetime prolificacy record is 39 in the case of 'Big Bertha', a Dremon owned by Jerome O'Leary of Blackwatersbridge, Co. Kerry, Ireland.

'Soender Jylland's Jens', a Danish black and white bull, left 220,000 surviving progeny by artificial insemination when he was put down aged 11 in Copenhagen in September 1978. 'Bendalls Adema', a Friesian bull, died aged 14 at Clondalkin, County Dublin, Ireland on 8 Nov 1978 having sired an estimated 212,000 progeny by artificial insemination.

Pigs

The highest recorded number of piglets in one litter is 34, thrown on 25–26 June 1961 by a sow owned by Aksel Egedee of Denmark. In February 1955 a Wessex sow owned by Mrs E. C. Goodwin of Paul's Farm, Leigh, near Tonbridge, Kent, had a litter of 34, of which 30 were born dead. The highest number of live births in Britain is 30 reported by W. Ives of Dane End Fruit Farm, near Ware, Hertfordshire from a white Welsh sow in September 1979. A sow, 'Gertie' (Large White × Landrace), owned by John Caley of Selby, North Yorkshire farrowed 3 litters of 19, 19 and 23 in under 12 months (18 July 1982–20 May 1983) of which 55 were live born.

Sheep

A case of eight lambs at a birth was reported by D. T. Jones of Priory Farm, Gwent, in June 1956 and by Ken Towse of Buckton near Bridlington in March 1981 but none lived. A Border Leicester-Merino cross-bred sheep owned by Roger Saunders gave birth to 4 ram and 3 ewe live lambs at Strathdownie, Victoria, Australia on 19 June 1984. A case of a sheep living to 26 years was recorded in flock book records by H. Poole, Wexford, Ireland.

Egg-laying

The highest authenticated rate of egg-laying is by a White Leghorn chicken hen, No 2988 at the College of Agriculture, University of Missouri, USA, with 371 eggs in 364 days in an official test conducted by Professor Harold V. Biellier ending on 29 Aug 1979. The UK record is 353 eggs in 365 days in a National Laying Test at Milford, Surrey in 1957 by a Rhode Island Red 'Wonderful Lady' owned by W. Lawson of Welham Grange, Retford, Nottinghamshire.

The heaviest egg reported is one of 16 oz *454 g*, with double yolk and double shell, laid by a white Leghorn at Vineland, New Jersey on 25 Feb 1956. The largest recorded was one of 'nearly 12 oz' for a 5-yolked egg 12¼ in *31 cm* around the long axis and 9 in *22,8 cm* around the short, laid by a Black Minorca at Mr Stafford's Damsteads Farm, Mellor, Lancs in 1896.

An egg of 1,47 g *0.05 oz* (27 × 22 mm *1.06 × 0.86 in*) was laid by a Leghorn/Ranger cross named 'Obedience' owned by Miss Verity Nicholson of Adstock Fields Farm House, Buckingham, Bucks on 12 Mar 1986.

The highest recorded annual average for a flock is 313 eggs in 52 weeks from a flock of 1000 Warren-Stadler SSL layers (from 21 weeks of age) by Eric Savage, White Lane Farm, Albury, Surrey in 1974–5.

Most yolks

The highest claim for the number of yolks in a chicken's egg is 9 reported by Mrs Diane Hainsworth of Hainsworth Poultry Farms, Mount Morris, New York in July 1971 and also from a hen in Kirgizya, USSR in August 1977.

Goose egg

The white goose 'Speckle' owned by Donny Brandenberg, of Goshen, Ohio on 3 May 1977 laid a 24 oz *680 g* egg measuring 13½ × 9½ in *34 × 24 cm* in circumferences.

Duck

An Aylesbury duck belonging to Annette and Angela Butler of Princes Risborough, Bucks laid 457 eggs in 463 days including an unbroken run of 375 in as many days. The duck died on 7 Feb 1986.

Milk yields *Cows*

The highest recorded world lifetime yield of milk is 465,224 lb (207.68 tons *211 025 kg*) by the unglamorously named cow No 289 owned by M. G. Maciel & Son of Hanford, California to 1 May 1984. The greatest yield of any British cow was that given by 'Winton Pel Eva 2' owned by John Waring of Glebe House, Kilnwick near Pocklington, Humberside with 165 tonnes. The greatest recorded yield for one lactation (maximum 365 days) is 55,661 lb *25 247 kg* by the Holstein 'Beecher Arlinda Ellen' owned by Mr and Mrs Harold L. Beecher of Rochester, Indiana in 1975. The British lactation record (305 days) was set by 'Michaelwood Holm Emoselle 25' (b. 1 Aug 1973), a Friesian, owned by Mr & Mrs M. T. Holder of Aylesmore Farm, Newent, Gloucestershire with 19 400 kg *42,769 lb* in 1984–5. The highest reported milk yield in a day is 241 lb *109,3 kg* by 'Urbe Blanca' in Cuba on or about 23 June 1982.

Hand milking

Andy Faust at Collinsville, Oklahoma, USA in 1937 achieved 120 US gal *99.92 UK gal* in 12 hr.

Goats

The highest recorded milk yield for any goat is 7714 lb *3499 kg* in 365 days by 'Osory Snow-Goose' owned by Mr and Mrs G. Jameson of Leppington, NSW, Australia in 1977. A 15-year-old goat owned by Mrs Nanbui Meghani of Bhuj, Gujarat, India was reported in November 1984 to have lactated continuously for 12 years.

Butter fat yield

The world record lifetime yield is 16,370 lb *7425 kg* by the US Holstein 'Breezewood Patsy Bar Pontiac' in 3979 days. Her lactation record for 365 days of 2230 lb *1011 kg* was reported on 8 Oct 1976. The British record butter fat yield in a lifetime is 12,166 lb *5518 kg* by the Ayrshire cow 'Craighead Welma' owned by W. Watson Steele from 273,072 lb at 4.45 per cent. The British record for 365 days is 761 kg *1677.7 lb* by 'Crookgate Aylwinia 7', a Friesian, owned by J. V. Machin of Hill Farm, Penley, near Wrexham, Clwyd, set on 5 May 1973. The United Kingdom record for butter fat in one day is 9.30 lb *4,218 kg* (79 lb *35,8 kg* milk at 11.8 per cent) by Queens Letch Farms' Guernsey cow 'Thisbe's Bronwen of Trewollack'.

Cheese

The most active cheese-eaters are the people of France, with an annual average in 1983 of 19,8 kg *43.6 lb* per person. The world's biggest producer is the United States with a factory production of 4,773,500,000 lbs (2,165,000 tons *2 200 000 tonnes*) in 1980. The UK cheese consumption in 1985 was 7,2 kg *15.87 lb* per head.

The oldest and most primitive cheeses are the Arabian *kishk*, made of dried curd of goats' milk. There are today 450 named cheeses in 18 major varieties, but many are merely named after different towns and differ only in shape or the method of packing. France has 240 varieties.

The world's most expensive cheese in its home market is Le Leruns made from ewes' milk at 90 francs per kilo (*now £3.40 per lb*). Cheese made to the Liederkranz formula in Van Wert, Ohio retails for $2.25 per 4 oz; equivalent to $9.00 (*£6.40*) per lb. Britain's most costly cheese is Lanark Blue which is obtainable from some shops for £5.50 per lb.

CHICKEN PLUCKING

Ernest Hausen (1877–1955) of Fort Atkinson, Wisconsin died undefeated after 33 years as champion. On 19 Jan 1939 he was timed at 4.4 sec and reputedly twice did 3.5 sec a few years later.

The record time for plucking 12 chickens clean by a team of 4 women at the annual Chicken Plucking Championship at Masaryktown, Florida is 32.9 sec set on 9 Oct 1976 by Doreena Cary, Diane Grieb, Kathy Roads and Dorothy McCarthy.

TURKEY PLUCKING

Vincent Pilkington of Cootehill, County Cavan, Ireland killed and plucked 100 turkeys in 7 hr 32 min on 15 Dec 1978. His record for a single turkey is 1 min 30 sec on RTE television in Dublin on 17 Nov 1980.

On 23 May 1983 Joe Glaub (USA) killed 7300 turkeys in a 'working' day. Mrs Madge Colenso gutted 94 turkeys in 60 mins at Rivington Farm, Burstow, Horley, Surrey on 20 Dec 1984.

Endurance and Endeavour

Lunar conquest

Neil Alden Armstrong (b. Wapakoneta, Ohio, of Scottish [via Ireland] and German ancestry), on 5 Aug 1930), command pilot of the *Apollo 11* mission, became the first man to set foot on the Moon, on the Sea of Tranquility, at 02.56 and 15 sec GMT on 21 July 1969. He was followed out of the Lunar Module *Eagle* by Col Edwin Eugene Aldren, Jr, USAF (b. Glen Ridge, New Jersey, of Swedish, Dutch and British ancestry, on 20 Jan 1930), while the Command Module *Columbia* piloted by Lt Col Michael Collins, USAF (b. Rome, Italy, of Irish and pre-Revolutionary American ancestry, on 31 Oct 1930) orbited above.

Eagle landed at 20.17 and 42 sec GMT on 20 July and lifted off at 17.54 GMT on 21 July, after a stay of 21 hr 36 min. *Apollo 11* had blasted off from Cape Canaveral, Florida at 13.32 GMT on 16 July and was a culmination of the US space programme which, at its peak, employed 376,600 people and attained in 1966–7 a peak budget of $5,900,000,000 (*then £2460 million*).

There is evidence that Pavel Belyayev was the cosmonaut selected by the USSR for a manned circumlunar flight in *Zond 7* on 9 Dec 1968, 12 days before the *Apollo 8* flight, but no launch took place.

Altitude

The greatest altitude attained by man was when the crew of the ill-fated *Apollo 13* were at apocynthion (*i.e.* their furthest point) 158 miles *254 km* above the lunar surface and 248,655 miles *400 187 km* above the Earth's surface at 1.21 a.m. BST on 15 Apr 1970. The crew were Capt James Arthur Lovell, Jr, USN (b. Cleveland, Ohio, 25 Mar 1928), Fred Wallace Haise, Jr (b. Biloxi, Miss., 14 Nov 1933) and the late John L. Swigert (1931–82).

The greatest altitude attained by a woman is 340 km *211 miles* by Pilot-Cosmonaut of the USSR Svetlana Savitskaya (b. 1948) during her flight in *Soyuz T7* on 19–27 Aug 1982. The record in an

> **Tallest parachute stack** ● The Royal Marines Free Fall Parachute Display Team completed a stack of 24 men-high over Dunkerswell, Honiton, Devon on 20 August 1986. The 'base and pin' jumped from 15,000 ft *4570 m* and the team was led by Capt Rod Boswell. (Photo: Simon Ward)

aircraft is 24 336 m *79,842 ft* by Natalia Prokhanova (USSR) (b. 1940) in an E-33 jet, on 22 May 1965.

Speed

The fastest speed at which humans have travelled is 24,791 mph *39 897 km/h* when the Command Module of *Apollo 10* carrying Col (now Brig Gen) Thomas Patten Stafford, USAF (b. Weatherford, Okla. 17 Sept 1930), and Cdr Eugene Andrew Cernan (b. Chicago, 14 Mar 1934) and Cdr (now Capt) John Watts Young, USN (b. San Francisco, 24 Sept 1930), reached this maximum value at the 400,000 ft *121,9 km* altitude interface on its trans-Earth return flight on 26 May 1969.

The highest speed ever attained by a woman is 28 115 km/h *17,470 mph* by Jnr Lt (now Lt Col) Valentina Vladimirovna Tereshkova-Nikolayev (b. 6 Mar 1937) of the USSR in *Vostok 6* on 16 June 1963. The highest speed ever achieved by a woman aircraft pilot is 2687,42 km/h *1669.89 mph* by Svetlana Savitskaya (USSR) reported on 2 June 1975.

Land speed

The highest reputed land speed is 739.666 mph *1190,377 km/h* or Mach 1.0106 by Stan Barrett (US) in *The Budweiser Rocket*, a rocket-engined 3-wheeled car at Edwards Air Force Base, California on 17 Dec 1979 (see also p. 128).

The *official* one-mile land-speed record is 633.468 mph *1019,467 km/h* set by Richard Noble OBE (b. 1946) on 4 Oct 1983 over the Black Rock

MILESTONES IN ABSOLUTE HUMAN ALTITUDE RECORDS

Altitude ft	m	Pilot	Vehicle	Place	Date	
80*	24	Jean François Pilâtre de Rozier (1757–1785) (France)	Hot Air Balloon (tethered)	Fauxbourg, Paris	15 & 17 Oct	1783
c.330	c.100	de Rozier and the Marquis d'Arlandes (1742–1809) (France)	Hot Air Balloon (free flight)	LaMuette, Paris[1]	21 Nov	1783
c.3000	c.900	Dr Jacques-Alexandre-César Charles (1746–1823) and Aîné Robert (France)	Charlière Hydrogen Balloon	Tuileries, Paris	1 Dec	1783
c.9000	c.2750	Dr J.-A.-C. Charles (France)	Hydrogen Balloon	Nesles, France	1 Dec	1783
c.13,000	c.4000	James Sadler (GB)	Hydrogen Balloon	Manchester	May	1785
25,400[2]	7740	James Glaisher (1809–1903) (UK)	Hydrogen Balloon	Wolverhampton	17 July	1862
31,500	9615	Prof A. Berson (Germany)	Hydrogen Balloon Phoenix	Strasbourg, France	4 Dec	1894
36,565	11 145	Sadi Lecointe (France)	Nieuport Aircraft	Issy-les-Moulineaux, France	30 Oct	1923
51,961	15 837	Prof Auguste Piccard and Paul Kipfer (Switzerland)	FNRS 1 Balloon	Augsburg, Germany	27 May	1931
72,395	22 066	Capts Orvill A. Anderson and Albert W. Stevens (US Army Air Corps)	US Explorer II Helium Balloon	Rapid City, South Dakota, USA	11 Nov	1935
79,600	24 262	William Barton Bridgeman (USA)	US Douglas D558—11 Skyrocket	California, USA	15 Aug	1951
126,200	38 465	Capt Iven C. Kincheloe, Jr (USAF)	US Bell X-2 Rocket plane	California, USA	7 Sept	1956
169,600	51 694	Joseph A. Walker (USA)	US X-15 Rocket plane	California, USA	30 Mar	1961
Statute miles	**Km**					
203.2	327	Flt-Major Yuriy A. Gagarin (USSR) (1934–68)	USSR Vostok I Capsule	Orbital flight	12 Apr	1961
234,672		Col Frank Borman, USAF, Capt James Arthur Lovell, Jr, USN and Major William A. Anders, USAF	US Apollo VIII Command Module	Circum-lunar flight	25 Dec	1968
248,655	400 171	Capt James Arthur Lovell Jr, USN, Frederick Wallace Haise Jr and John L. Swigert Jr (1931–82)	US Apollo XIII	Abortive lunar landing mission	15 Apr	1970

* There is some evidence that Father Bartolomeu de Gusmo flew in his hot-air balloon in his 4th experiment post August 1709 in Portugal.
[1] Duration c.1.54 to 2.16 pm from Château de LaMuette to Butte aux Cailles, Paris 13º. Volume of the 70 ft 21,3 m high balloon was 60 000 'piedcubes' c.1700 m³.
[2] Glaisher, with Henry Tracey Coxwell (1819–1900) claimed 37,000 ft 11 275 m from Wolverhampton on 5 Sept 1862. Some writers accept 30,000 ft 9145 m.
Note: A complete progressive table comprising entries from 1783 to date was published in the 23rd edition of 1977.

Desert, Nevada in his 17,000 lb thrust Rolls Royce Avon 302 jet-powered *Thrust 2*, designed by John Ackroyd.

The highest land speed attained in Britain is 263.92 mph *424,74 km/h* by Richard Noble in *Thrust 2* at Greenham Common, Berkshire on 25 Sept 1980.

The highest land speed recorded by a woman is 524.016 mph *843,323 km/h* by Mrs Kitty Hambleton *née* O'Neil (US) in the 48,000-hp rocket-powered 3-wheeled S.M.1 *Motivator* over the Alvard Desert, Oregon, USA on 6 Dec 1976. Her official two-way record was 512.710 mph *825,126 km/h* and she probably touched 600 mph *965 km/h* momentarily.

Water speed

The highest speed ever achieved on water is an estimated 300 knots (345 mph *556 km/h*) by Kenneth Peter Warby MBE, (b. 9 May 1939) on the Blowering Dam Lake, NSW, Australia on 20 Nov 1977 in his unlimited hydroplane *Spirit of Australia*. The official world water speed record is 514,389 km/h *319.627 mph 277.57 knots* set on 8 Oct 1978 by Warby on Blowering Dam Lake.

The fastest woman on water is Mary Rife (USA), who has driven her drag boat *Proud Mary* at more than 190 mph *305 km/h*.

The highest speed recorded by a propeller-driven boat is 229.00 mph *368,54 km/h* by *The Texan*, a Kurtis top fuel hydro drag boat, driven by Eddie Hill on 5 Sept 1982 at Chowchilla, California.

Most travelled

The man who visited more countries than anyone was Jesse Hart Rosdail (1914–77) of Elmhurst, Illinois, a 5th-grade teacher. Of all the separately administered countries and territories listed in the *UN Population Report*, he had visited all excepting only North Korea and French Antarctic Territories. He estimated his mileage to visit 215 countries was 1,626,605 statute miles *2 617 766 km*.

Giorgio Ricatto (b. 1934, Italy) has visited all 170 sovereign countries and all the non-sovereign territories except 4.

The most travelled member of the Travellers Century Club of Los Angeles (limited to those who have visited 100 or more countries) is G.

Parke Thompson of Akron, Ohio. His blanket coverage of the world lacks only four Antarctic territories.

The most travelled man in the horseback era was probably the Methodist preacher Francis Asbury (b. Birmingham, England), who travelled 264,000 miles *424 850 km* in North America from 1771 to 1815 preaching 16,000 sermons.

Most isolated

The farthest any human has been removed from his nearest living fellow man is 2233.2 miles *3596,4 km* in the case of the Command Service Module pilot Alfred M. Worden on the US *Apollo 15* lunar mission of 30 July–1 Aug 1971.

Round the world

The fastest time for a round-the-world trip on scheduled flights for a circumnavigation is 44 hr 6 min by David J. Springbett (b. 2 May 1938) of Taplow, Buckinghamshire. His route took him from Los Angeles eastabout via London, Bahrain, Singapore, Bangkok, Manila, Tokyo and Honolulu from 8–10 Jan 1980 over a 23,068 mile *37 124 km* course.

PROGRESSIVE SPEED RECORDS

Speed mph	km/h	Person and Vehicle	Place	Date	
25	40	Sledging	Heinola, Finland	c.6500 BC	
35	55	Horse-riding	Anatolia, Turkey	c.1400 BC	
45	70	Mountain Sledging	Island of Hawaii (now USA)	ante AD	1500
50	80	Ice Yachts (earliest patent)	Netherlands	AD	1600
56.75	95	Grand Junction Railway 2–2–2: *Lucifer*	Madeley Banks, Staffs, England	13 Nov	1830
87.8	141,3	Tommy Todd, downhill skier	La Porte, California, USA	Mar	1873
90.0	144,8	Midland Railway 4–2–2 7 ft 9 in 2,36 m single	Ampthill, Bedford, England	Mar	1897
130.61	210,2	Siemens and Halske electric engine	Marienfeld-Zossen, near Berlin	27 Oct	1903
c.150	c.257,5	Frederick H. Marriott (fl. 1957) Stanley Steamer *Wogglebug*	Ormond Beach, Florida, USA	26 Jan	1907
210.64	339	Sadi Lecointe (France) Nieuport-Delage 29	Villesauvage, France	25 Sept	1921
415.2	668,2	Flt Lt (Later Wing Cdr) George Hedley Stainforth AFC *Supermarine S.6B*	Lee-on-Solent, England	29 Sept	1931
623.85	1004	Flugkapitan Heinz Dittmar *Me. 163V–1*	Peenemunde, Germany	2 Oct	1941
670	1078	Capt Charles Elwood Yeager, USAF *Bell XS-1*	Muroc Dry Lake, California, USA	14 Oct	1947
967	1556	Capt Charles Elwood Yeager, USAF *Bell XS-1*	Muroc Dry Lake, California, USA	26 Mar	1948
2905	4675,1	Major Robert M. White, North American *X-15*	Muroc Dry Lake, California, USA	7 Mar	1961
c.17,560	c.28 260	Flt Maj Yuriy Alekseyevich Gagarin, *Vostok I*	Earth orbit	12 Apr	1961
24,226	38 988	Col Frank Borman, USAF, Capt James Arthur Lovell, Jr, USN, Major William A. Anders, USAF *Apollo VIII*	Trans-lunar injection	21 Dec	1968
24,790.8	39 897,0	Cdrs Eugene Andrew Cernan and John Watts Young, USN and Col Thomas P. Stafford, USAF *Apollo X*	Re-entry after lunar orbit	26 May	1969

Note: A complete progressive table comprising entries from prehistoric times to date was published in the 23rd edition of 1977.

Long-distance walking ● Steven Newman of Bethal, Ohio, USA spent 4 years walking 22,500 miles *36 200 km* around the world, covering 20 countries and all 5 continents. Having left on 1 Apr 1983, he made over 40,000,000 steps in 1460 days on the road, and reckons to have met 73,000 people before his return on 1 Apr 1987. While tramping through jungles, over snow-covered mountains and in arid deserts, Newman was variously chased by wild boars in Algeria (spending the night up a tree), attacked by bandits in Thailand, and arrested and accused of being a spy in Turkey. Despite such hazards, he described the world as 'ever friendlier and more special than I had imagined'. His favourite country was Australia, while the best dish he came across was Goanna Lizard, a six-foot-long reptile roasted by Australian aborigines. Sponsored by an American shoe company, the most common question he was asked was how many pairs he had got through. The total, four, is itself a record.

Longest walk in Britain ● Helen Krasner (b. 12 Aug 1948) of Croydon, Surrey set a record for the longest continuous feminine walk by walking round the coastline of Britain. She set off from Brighton on 1 Mar 1986 and returned on 31 Jan 1987, having completed a clockwise walk of more than 4922 miles *7921 km*.

LONGEST WALKS

The first person reported to have 'walked round the world' is George Matthew Schilling (USA) from 3 Aug 1897 to 1904, but the first verified achievement was by David Kunst (b. 1939, USA) from 10 June 1970 to 5 Oct 1974. Tomas Carlos Pereira (b. Argentine, 16 Nov 1942) spent ten years, 6 Apr 1968–8 Apr 1978, walking 29,825 miles *48,000 km* around all five continents. George Meegan (b. 2 Oct 1952) from Rainham, Kent walked 19,019 miles *30 431 km* from Usuaia, the southern tip of South America to Prudhoe Bay in northern Alaska, taking 2426 days from 26 Jan 1977 to 18 Sept 1983, and thus completed the first traverse of the Western Hemisphere. Sean Eugene Maguire (b. USA 15 Sept 1956) walked 7327 miles *11 791 km* from the Yukon River, north of Livengood, Alaska, to Key West, Florida, in 307 days, 6 June 1978–9 Apr 1979. The trans-Canada (Halifax to Vancouver) record walk of 3764 miles *6057 km* is 96 days by Clyde McRae, 23, from 1 May to 4 Aug 1973. John Lees (b. 23 Feb 1945) of Brighton, East Sussex, between 11 Apr and 3 June 1972 walked 2876 miles *4628 km* across the USA from City Hall, Los Angeles to City Hall, New York in 53 days 12 hr 15 min (average 53.75 miles *86,49 km* a day).

The longest continuous walk in Britain is one of 6824 miles *10 982 km*, around the British coast by John N. Merrill (b. 19 Aug 1943), from 3 Jan to 8 Nov 1978.

North Pole conquest

The claim of neither of the two US Arctic explorers, Dr Frederick Albert Cook (1865–1940) and Cdr (later Rear Ad) Robert Edwin Peary (1856–1920), of the US Naval Civil Engineering branch in reaching the North Pole is subject to positive proof. Cook, accompanied by the Eskimos, Ah-pellah and Etukishook, two sledges and 26 dogs, struck north from a point 60 miles *96,5 km* north of Svartevoeg, on Axel Heiberg I., Canada, 460 miles *740 km* from the Pole on 21 Mar 1908, allegedly reaching Lat. 89° 31′ N on 19 Apr and the Pole on 21 Apr. Peary, accompanied by his assistant, Matthew Alexander Henson (1866–1955, USA) and the four Eskimos, Ooqueah, Eginwah, Seegloo and Ootah (1875–1955), struck north from his Camp Bartlett (Lat. 87° 44′ N) at 5 a.m. on 2 Apr 1909. After travelling another 134 miles *215 km*, he allegedly established his final camp, Camp Jessup, in the proximity of the Pole at 10 a.m. on 6 Apr and marched a further 42 miles *67,5 km* quartering the sea-ice before turning south at 4 p.m. on 7 Apr. On excellent pack ice and modern sledges Wally Herbert's 1968–9 expedition (see below) attained a best day's route mileage of 23 miles *37 km* in 15 hr. Cook claimed 26 miles *41,8 km* twice while Peary claimed a surely unsustainable average of 38 miles *61 km* over 8 consecutive days.

The earliest indisputable attainment of the North Pole over the sea-ice was at 3 p.m. (Central Standard Time) on 19 Apr 1968 by Ralph Plaisted (US) and three companions after a 42-day trek in four Skidoos (snow-mobiles). Their arrival was independently verified 18 hr later by a US Air Force weather aircraft. The sea bed is 13,410 ft *4087 m* below the North Pole.

Naomi Uemura (1941–1984), the Japanese explorer and mountaineer, became the first person to reach the North Pole in a solo trek across the Arctic ice cap at 4.45 a.m. GMT on 1 May 1978. He had travelled 450 miles *725 km* setting out on 7 Mar from Cape Edward, Ellesmere Island in northern Canada. He averaged nearly 8 miles *13 km* per day with his sled 'Aurora' drawn by 17 huskies.

Dr Jean-Louis Etienne, 39, was the first to reach the Pole solo and without dogs, on 11 May 1986 after 63 days. On 20 Apr 1987 Fukashi Kazami, 36, of Tokyo reached the North Pole from Ward Hunt Island, northern Canada in 44 days having started on his 250-cc motorcycle on 8 March.

The first woman to set foot on the North Pole was Mrs Fran Phipps, wife of Canadian bush pilot Weldy Phipps, on 5 Apr 1971. Galina Aleksandrovna Lastovskaya (b. 1941) and Lilia Vladislavovna Minina (b. 1959) were crew members of the USSR atomic icebreaker *Arktika* which reached the Pole on 17 Aug 1977.

The Soviet scientist Dr Pavel A. Gordienko and 3 companions were arguably the first ever to stand on the exact point Lat. 90° 00′ 00″ N (+300 metres) on 23 Apr 1948.

South Pole conquest

The first men to cross the Antarctic circle (Lat. 66° 33′ S) were the 193 crew of the *Resolution* (462 tons/tonnes) (Capt James Cook, RN (1728–79)) and *Adventure* (336 tons/tonnes) (Lt T. Furneaux) on 17 Jan 1773 in 39° E. The first person known to have sighted the Antarctic ice shelf

was Capt F. F. Bellinghausen (USSR) (1778–1852) on 27 Jan 1820 from the vessels *Vostock* and *Mirnyi*. The first known to have sighted the mainland of the continent was Capt William Smith (1790–1847) and Master Edward Bransfield, RN, in the brig *Williams*. They saw the peaks of Trinity Land 3 days later on 30 Jan 1820.

The South Pole (alt. 9186 ft *2779 m* on ice and 336 ft *102 m* bed rock) was first reached at 11 a.m. on 16 Dec 1911 by a Norwegian party led by Capt Roald Engebereth Gravning Amundsen

MARINE CIRCUMNAVIGATION RECORDS

(Compiled by Sq Ldr D. H. Clarke DFC, AFC)

A true circumnavigation entails passing through two antipodal points which are at least 12,429 statute miles *20 000 km* apart. A non-stop circumnavigation is entirely self-maintained; no water supplies, provisions, equipment or replacements of any sort may be taken aboard en route. Vessel may anchor, but no physical help accepted apart from passing mail or messages.

CATEGORY	VESSEL	NAME	START	FINISH
Earliest	*Vittoria* Expedition of Fernão de Magalhães, c. 1480–k. 1521	Juan Sebastián de Elcano or del Cano (d. 1526) and 17 crew	Seville, Spain 20 Sept 1519	San Lucar, 6 Sept 1522 30,700 miles *49 400 km*
Earliest British	*Golden Hind* (ex *Pelican*) 100 tons/tonnes	Francis Drake (c. 1540–96) (Knighted 4 April 1581)	Plymouth, 13 Dec 1577	26 Sept 1580
Earliest Woman	*Etoile* (Storeship for Bougainville's *La Boudeuse*)	Crypto-female valet of M. de Commerson, named Baré	St Malo, 1766	1769
Earliest Fore-and-aft Rigged Vessel	*Union* 98 tons (Sloop)	John Boit Junior, 19–21, (US) and 22 crew	Newport, RI 1794 (via Cape Horn westabout)	Newport, RI 1796
Earliest Yacht	*Sunbeam* 170 ft *51,8 m* 3 Mast Topsail schooner	Lord and Lady Brassey (GB) passengers and crew	Cowes, Isle of Wight 1876	Cowes, Isle of Wight 1877
Earliest Solo Owners	*Spray* 36¾ ft *11,20 m* Gaff yawl	Capt Joshua Slocum, 51, (US) (a non-swimmer) (No 1 solo circum)	Newport, RI, via Magellan Straits, 24 Apr 1895	3 July 1898 46,000 miles *74 000 km*
Earliest Motor Boat	*Speejacks* 98 ft *29,87 m*	Albert Y. Gowen (US) wife and crew	New York City 1921	New York City 1922
Earliest Motor Boat (Solo)	*Mabel E. Holland* 42 ft *12,8 m* (no sails)	David Scott Cowper (GB)	Plymouth 1984 (via Panama Canal)	Plymouth 170 days 2 hr 15 min (165.7 mpd)
Earliest Woman Solo	*Mazurek* 31 ft 2 in *9,5 m* Bermudan sloop	Krystyna Chojnowska-Liskiewicz (Poland) (No 58 solo circum)	Las Palmas 28 Mar 1976 (westabout via Panama)	Tied knot 21 Mar 1978
Earliest Woman Solo (via Cape Horn)	*Express Crusader* 53 ft *16,15 m* Bermudan sloop	Naomi James (NZ/GB) (later DBE) (No 59 solo circum)	Dartmouth 9 Sept 1977 (Cape Horn 19 Mar 1978)	Dartmouth 8 June 1978 (266 days 19 hr)
Smallest Boat	*Super Shrimp* 18 ft 4 in *5,58 m* Bermudan sloop	Shane Acton (GB) Iris Derungs (Swiss)	Cambridge, England August 1972	Cambridge, England August 1980
Smallest Boat (solo)	*Glory* 19 ft 8 in *6 m* Junk sloop	Sir Henry Pigott Bt (1st solo knight to circumnavigate)	Poole June, 1983	Poole Feb, 1986
Earliest Submerged	US Submarine *Triton*	Capt Edward L. Beach USN plus 182 crew	New London, Connecticut 16 Feb 1960	10 May 1960 39,708 miles *49 422 km*
Earliest Non-stop Solo (Port to Port)	*Suhaili* 32.4 ft *9,87 m* Bermudan ketch	Robin Knox Johnston CBE (b. 1939) (No 25 solo circum)	Falmouth, 14 June 1968	22 Apr 1969 (312 days)
Longest Non-stop Alone at Sea	*Dar Przemysla* 46 ft 7 in *14,2 m* Ketch	Henryk Jaskula (Poland) (No 68 solo circum)	Gdynia 1979 (W–E via Cape Horn)	Gdynia 1980 (344 days)
Fastest Solo (speed) (multihull)	*Kriter Brut de Brut* 77 ft *23,5 m* Trimaran	Philippe Monnet (Fr) (No 120 solo circum)	Brest 1986 (via Cape Town)	Brest 1987 127 days 12 hr 11 min (210.4 mpd)
Earliest Solo in Both Directions	*Solitaire* 34 ft *10,36 m* Bermudan sloop	Leslie Thomas Powles (GB) (Nos 62 & 71 solo circum)	Falmouth 1975 (E–W) Lymington 1980 (W–E)	(via Panamá) Lymington 1978 (via Horn) Lymington 1981
Earliest Solo in Both Directions (via Horn)	*Ocean Bound* 41 ft 1 in *12,52 m* Bermudan sloop	David Scott Cowper (GB) (Nos 66 & 78 solo circum)	Plymouth 1979 (W–E) Plymouth 1981 (E–W)	Plymouth 1980 Plymouth 1982 (see below)
Fastest Solo Non-stop (time and speed)	*American Promise* 60 ft *18,3 m* Bermudan sloop	Dodge Morgan (US)	Bermuda 12 Nov 1985 (W–E via Horn)	Bermuda 11 Apr 1986 25,671 miles *41 312 km* in 150 days 1 hr 6 min = 171.1 mpd
Fastest Time and Fastest Speed (yacht)	UB5 *Switzerland* 80 ft *24,38 m* Bermudan sloop	Pierre Fehlmann (Swiss) and crew	Portsmouth 1985	Portsmouth 1986 117 days 14 hr 31 min (238 mpd)
Fastest (clipper)	*James Baines* 266 ft *81,07 m*	Capt C. McDonald (GB) and crew	Liverpool to Melbourne (58 days) 1854	Melbourne to Liverpool (69 days) 1855
Fastest Solo Westabout (via Cape Horn)	*Ocean Bound* 41 ft 1 in *12,52 m* Bermudan sloop	David Scott Cowper (GB) (No 78 solo circum)	Plymouth 22 Sept 1981 (south of 5 capes)	Plymouth 17 May 1982 221 days (141.85 mpd)
Fastest-ever Time (yacht) (short circumnavigation)	*Awahnee II* 53 ft *16,15 m* Bermudan cutter	Bob Griffith (US) (5 crew)	Bluff, NZ 1970 (W–E via Horn)	Bluff, NZ, 1971 (88 sailing days plus 23 days stopovers)
Fastest-ever Time (clipper)	*Red Jacket* 260 ft *79,24 m*	Capt S. Reid (GB) and crew	From/to Lat 26° 25′ W (via Horn)	62 days 22 hr 1854
Earliest Solo Double Circumnavigation	*Perie Banou* 33 ft 7 in *10,24 m* Bermudan sloop	Jon Sanders (Australia) (Nos 75 & 81 solo circum)	Fremantle 1981 (W–E) (continuously at sea but not non-stop)	(via Horn) Fremantle 1982 (via Plymouth) 420 days 1982
Most Circumnavigations Alone by Husband/Wife	*Myonie* 36 ft *11 m* Gaff ketch	Al Gehrman (US) Helen (wife)	Florida 1961, 1966, 1972, 1979	Florida 1964, 1970, 1976, 1983

* Eduard Roditi, author of *Magellan of the Pacific*, advances the view that Magellan's slave, Enrique, was the first circumnavigator. He had been purchased in Malacca and it was shown that he already understood the Filipino dialect Vizayan, when he reached the Philippines from the east. He 'tied the knot' off Limasawa on 28 Mar 1521. The first to circumnavigate in both directions was Capt Tobias Furneaux, RN (1735–81) as second lieutenant aboard the *Dolphin* from/to Plymouth east to west via the Magellan Straits from 1766–68 and as captain of the *Adventure* from/to Plymouth west to east via Cape Horn from 1772–4.

Endurance and Endeavour

(1872–1928), after a 53-day march with dog sledges from the Bay of Whales, to which he had penetrated in the *Fram*. Subsequent calculations showed that Olav Olavson Bjaaland (the last survivor, dying in June 1961, aged 88) and Helmer Hanssen probably passed within 400–600 m *1310–1970 ft* of the exact pole. The other two members were Sverre H. Hassell (d. 1928) and Oskar Wisting (d. 1936).

The first woman to set foot on Antarctica was Mrs Karoline Mikkelsen on 20 Feb 1935. No woman stood on the South Pole until 11 Nov 1969. On that day Lois Jones, Eileen McSaveney, Jean Pearson, Terry Lee Tickhill (all US), Kay Lindsay (Australia) and Pam Young (NZ) arrived by air.

First on both Poles

Dr Albert P. Crary (USA) reached the North Pole in a Dakota aircraft on 3 May 1952. On 12 Feb 1961 he arrived at the South Pole by Sno Cat on a scientific traverse party from the McMurdo Station. He thus pre-empted David Porter by 18 years.

Arctic crossing

The first crossing of the Arctic sea-ice was achieved by the British Trans-Arctic Expedition which left Point Barrow, Alaska on 21 Feb 1968 and arrived at the Seven Island archipelago north-east of Spitzbergen 464 days later on 29 May 1969 after a haul of 2920 statute miles *4699 km* and a drift of 700 miles *1126 km* com-

pared with the straight-line distance of 1662 miles *2674 km*. The team comprised Wally Herbert (leader), 34, Major Ken Hedges, 34, RAMC, Allan Gill, 38, and Dr Roy Koerner, 36 (glaciologist), and 40 huskies. The only crossing achieved in a single season was that by Fiennes and Burton (see below) from Alert via the North Pole to the Greenland Sea in open snowmobiles.

Antarctic crossing

The first surface crossing of the Antarctic continent was completed at 1.47 p.m. on 2 Mar 1958, after a trek of 2158 miles *3473 km* lasting 99 days from 24 Nov 1957, from Shackleton Base to Scott Base via the Pole. The crossing party of twelve was led by Dr (now Sir) Vivian Ernest

TRANS-ATLANTIC MARINE RECORDS

(Compiled by Sq Ldr D. H. Clarke, DFC, AFC)

CATEGORY	NAME	VESSEL	START	FINISH	DURATION	DATE
Earliest Rowing (Fastest crew row)	John Brown + 5 British deserters from garrison	Ship's boat c. 20 ft 6,1 m	St Helena (10 June)	Belmonte, Brazil (fastest ever row)	28 days (83 mpd) (see 2-crew row)	1799
Earliest Crossing (2 men)	C. R. Webb + 1 crew (US)	Charter Oak 43 ft 13,1 m	New York	Liverpool	35 days 15 hr	1857
Earliest Trimaran (Raft)	John Mikes + 2 crew (US)	Non Pareil 25 ft 7,62 m	New York	Southampton	51 days	1868
Earliest Solo Sailing (E–W)	Josiah Shackford (US)	15-ton Gaff sloop	Bordeaux, France	Surinam (Dutch Guiana)	35 days	1786
Earliest Solo Sailing (W–E)	Alfred Johnson (US)	Centennial 20 ft 6,09 m	Glos., Mass	Wales	46 days	1876
Earliest Woman (with US husband)	Mrs Joanna Crapo (b. Scotland) (Thomas Crapo)	New Bedford 20 ft 6,09 m (Bermudan ketch)	Chatham, Mass.	Newlyn, Cornwall	51 days (earliest with Bermudan rig)	1877
Earliest Single-handed Race	J. W. Lawlor (US) (winner)	Sea Serpent 15 ft 4,57 m	Boston (21 June)	Coverack, Cornwall	45 days	1891
Earliest Rowing by 2 men (Fastest 2-crew)	Georg Harboe and Frank Samuelsen (Nor)	Fox 18⅓ ft 5,58 m	New York City (6 June)	Isles of Scilly (1 Aug)	55 days (56 mpd) (see solo rows)	1897
Fastest Solo Sailing (W–E)	J. V. T. McDonald (GB)	Inverarity 38 ft 11,58 m	Nova Scotia	Ireland	16 days (147 mpd)	1922
Earliest Canoe (with sail)	Franz Romer (Germany)	Deutscher Sport 21½ ft 6,55 m	Las Palmas	St Thomas	58 days (47 mpd)	1928
Earliest Woman Solo (East–West)	Ann Davison (GB)	Felicity Ann 23 ft 7,01 m	Portsmouth Las Palmas	Dominica (20 Nov 1952)	65 days	1952–3
Earliest Woman Solo (W–E)	Gladys Gradeley (US)	Lugger 18 ft 5,5 m	Nova Scotia	Hope Cove, Devon	60 days	1903
Earliest Woman Solo (across 2 oceans)	Anna Woolf (SA)	Zama Zulu 43 ft 13,1 m (Ferroconcrete)	Cape Town	Bowling, Scotland	8920 miles in 109 days	1976
Fastest Woman Solo	Naomi James DBE (GB)	Kriter Lady 53 ft 16,15 m	Plymouth	Newport, R.I.	25 days 19 hr 12 min	1980
Fastest 2-woman crew	Annick Martin (Fr) Annie Cordelle (Fr)	Super Marches Bravo 45 ft 13,7 m	Plymouth	Newport, R.I.	21 days 4 hr 28 min	1981
Smallest West–East	Wayne Dickinson (US)	God's Tear 8 ft 11 in 2,71 m	Allerton, Mass. (30 Oct)	Aranmore Is. NW Eire (20 Mar)	142 days	1982–3
Smallest (East–West) (Southern)	Eric Peters (GB)	Toniky-Nou 5 ft 10½ in 1,79 m (barrel)	Las Palmas (25 Dec)	St Françoise, Guadaloupe (8 Feb)	46 days	1982–3
Fastest Crossing Sailing (multihull) (East–West)	Eric Tabarly (France) + 2 crew	Pen Duick IV 67 ft 20,42 m	Tenerife	Martinique	251.4 miles 404,5 kml day (10 days 12 hours)	1968
Fastest Crossing Sailing (monohull) (East–West)	Wilhelm Hirte & crew (Ger)	Kriter II 80 ft 24,38 m	Canary Is.	Barbados	13 days 8 hr	1977
Fastest Crossing (multihull) (West–East)	Loic Caradec (Fr) Philippe Facques	Royale 85 ft 25,9 m 8 m (Sloop-catamaran)	Sandy Hook, NJ	Lizard	7 days 21 hr 5 min (approx 39 mpd)	1986
Fastest Crossing (monohull) (West–East)	Richard Branson and crew	Virgin Atlantic Challenger II	Ambrose	Bishops Rock	3 days 8 hr 31 min	1986
Fastest Crossing Sailing Ship (West–East)	A. Eldridge (US) and crew	Red Jacket (Clipper) 260 ft 79,24 m	Sandy Hook, NJ	Liverpool Bar	12 days 00 hr 00 min 277.7 mpd	1854
Fastest Solo East–West (Northern) (monohull)	Kazimierz Jaworski (Poland)	Spaniel II 56 ft 17,06 m	Plymouth	Newport, R.I.	19 days 13 hr 25 min	1980
Fastest East–West (Northern) (monohull)	Bruno Bacileri (It) Marc Vallin	Faram Serenissima 66½ ft 20,27 m	Plymouth	Newport, R.I.	16 days 1 hr 25 min	1981
Fastest Solo East–West (Northern) (multihull)	Philip Weld (US)	Moxie 51 ft 15,54 m (Tri)	Plymouth	Newport, R.I.	17 days 23 hr 12 min	1980
Fastest Solo East–West (Southern) (monohull)	Sir Francis Chichester KBE (GB)	Gipsy Moth V 57 ft 17,37 m	Portuguese Guinea	Nicaragua	179.1 miles 288,2 kml day (22.4 days)	1970
Fastest Ever Yacht Sail (N. route) (East–West)	Loic Caradec (Fr) Oliver Despaigne	Royale 85 ft 25,9 m (Sloop-catamaran)	Plymouth	Newport, R.I.	13 days 6 hr 12 min (approx 235 mpd)	1986
Fastest 24-Hour Run	Michael Birch (Can) +8 crew	Formula Tag (BM Sloop—Cat)	Quebec	St Malo	512.3 miles in 23 hr 42 min on 27 Aug	1984
Fastest Solo Rowing East–West	Sidney Genders (51 years) (GB) (Oldest rower)	Khaggavisana 19¾ ft 6,02 m	Penzance, Cornwall	Miami, Florida via Antigua	37.8 miles 60,8 km/day 160 days 8 hr	1970
Youngest Rowers	Mike Nestor (23 yr 299 days) Sean Crowley (24 yr 146 days)	In Finnegans Wake 22 ft 6,7 m (GB)	Canaries (Pasito Blanco)	Guyana (Hague)	74 days	1986
Fastest Solo Rowing West–East	Gérard d'Aboville (Fr)	Capitaine Cook 5,60 m 18 ft 4 in	Chatham, Mass. 10 July	Ushant, France 20 Sept	71 days 23 hr 72 km 44.8 miles/day	1980
Earliest Solo Rowing East–West	John Fairfax (GB)	Britannia 22 ft 6,70 m	Las Palmas (20 Jan)	Ft Lauderdale, Florida (19 July)	180 days	1969
Earliest Solo Rowing West–East	Tom McClean (Ireland)	Super Silver 20 ft 6,90 m	St John's, Newfoundland	Black Sod Bay, Ireland (27 July)	70.7 days	1969
Youngest Solo Sailing	David Sandeman (17½ years) (GB)	Sea Raider 35 ft 10,67 m	Jersey, C.I.	Newport, R.I.	43 days	1976
Oldest Solo Sailing	Monk Farnham (74 years 276 days)	Seven Bells 28 ft 8,53 m	Shannon, Ireland	Rhode Is.	72 days (3 stops)	1983
Earliest by Sailboard	Christian M___ (F) (Escorted by yacht Assiduous)	_____ (type)	Dakar Senegal	Kourou Fr. Guiana	37 days 18 hr 4 min (slept on board)	1981–2

Fuchs (born 11 Feb 1908). The 2600 mile *4185 km* trans-Antarctic leg from Sanae to Scott Base of the 1980–82 Trans-Globe Expedition was achieved in 66 days from 26 Oct 1980 to 11 Jan 1981 having passed through the South Pole on 23 Dec 1980. The 3-man party on snowmobiles comprised Sir Ranulph Fiennes (b. 1944), Oliver Shepard and Charles Burton.

Polar circumnavigation

The first polar circumnavigation was achieved by Sir Ranulph Fiennes, Bt and Charles Burton of the British Trans-Globe Expedition who travelled south from Greenwich (2 Sept 1979), via the South Pole (17 Dec 1980) and the North Pole (11 Apr 1982), and back to Greenwich arriving after a 35,000 mile *56 325 km* trek on 29 Aug 1982.

Longest sledge journeys

The longest totally self-supporting Polar sledge journey ever made was one of 1080 miles *1738 km* from West to East across Greenland (now Kalaallit Nunaat) on 18 June to 5 Sept 1934 by Capt M. Lindsay (1905–1981) (later Sir Martin Lindsay of Dowhill, Bt, CBE, DSO), Lt Arthur S. T. Godfrey, RE (later Lt Col, k. 1942), Andrew N. C. Croft (later Col, DSO) and 49 dogs. The Ross Sea Party of 10 (3 died) sledged over 2000 miles *3220 km* in 300 days from 6 May 1975.

Greatest ocean descent

The record ocean descent was achieved in the Challenger Deep of the Marianas Trench, 250 miles *400 km* south-west of Guam, in the Pacific Ocean, when the Swiss-built US Navy bathyscaphe *Trieste*, manned by Dr Jacques Piccard (b. 1914) (Switzerland) and Lt Donald Walsh, USN, reached 35,820 ft (6.78 miles *10 917 m*) down, at 1.10 p.m. on 23 Jan 1960 (see page 53). The pressure of the water was 16,883 lbf/in^2 *1183 kgf/cm^2* and the temperature 37.4° F *3° C*. The descent took 4 hr 48 min and the ascent 3 hr 17 min.

Deep diving records

The record depth for the extremely dangerous activity of breath-held diving is 105 m *344 ft* by Jacques Mayol (France) off Elba, Italy, in December 1983 for men, and 147½ ft *45 m* by Giuliana Treleani (Italy) off Cuba in September 1967 for women. Mayol descended on a sled in 104 sec and ascended in 90 sec. The record dive with scuba (self-contained under-water breathing apparatus) is 437 ft *133 m* by John J. Gruener and R. Neal Watson (USA) off Freeport, Grand Bahama on 14 Oct 1968. The record dive utilising gas mixtures (nitrogen, oxygen and helium) is a simulated dive of 2250 ft *685,8 m* in a dry

chamber by Stephen Porter, Len Whitlock and Erik Kramer at Duke University Medical Center in Durham, North Carolina on 3 Feb 1981 in a 43-day trial in a sphere of 8 ft *2,43 m*. Patrick Raude and 5 Comex divers left and returned to the bell 'Petrel' at 501 m *1643 ft*, off Cavalaire, France, in 1982.

Deepest underwater escapes

The deepest underwater rescue achieved was of the *Pisces III* in which Roger R. Chapman, 28, and Roger Mallinson, 35, were trapped for 76 hr when it sank to 1575 ft *480 m* 150 miles *240 km* south-east of Cork, Ireland on 29 Aug 1973. She was hauled to the surface by the cable ship *John Cabot* after work by *Pisces V*, *Pisces II* and the remote control recovery vessel US CURV on 1 Sept. The greatest depth of an actual escape without any equipment has been from 225 ft *68,58 m* by Richard A. Slater from the rammed submersible *Nekton Beta* off Catalina Island, California on 28 Sept 1970.

Deepest salvage

The greatest depth at which salvage has been achieved is 16,500 ft *5029 m* by the bathyscaphe *Trieste II* (Lt Cdr Mel Bartels, USN) to attach cables to an 'electronic package' on the sea bed 400 miles *645 km* north of Hawaii on 20 May 1972.

Flexible dress divers

The deepest salvage operation ever achieved with divers was on the wreck of HM Cruiser *Edinburgh* sunk on 2 May 1942 in the Barents Sea off northern Norway inside the Arctic Circle in 803 ft *244,7 m* of water. Twelve divers dived on the wreck in pairs using a bell from the *Stephaniturm* (1423 tons) over 32 days under the direction of former RN officer Michael Stewart from 17 Sept to 7 Oct 1981.

A total of 460 gold ingots was recovered and was divided thus; £14.6 million to the USSR, £7.3 million to HM Government and some £22 million to the salvage contractors, Jessop Marine Recoveries Ltd (10 per cent) and Wharton Williams Ltd (90 per cent). John Rossier, 28, was the first to touch the gold. The longest decompression time was 7 days 10 hr 27 min. The £43.4 million is an all-time 100 per cent record.

Greatest penetration into the earth

The deepest penetration made into the ground by man is in the Western Deep Levels Mine at Carletonville, Transvaal, South Africa where a record depth of 12,391 ft *3777 m* (2.34 miles) was attained, the temperature being 131° F *55° C*.

Longest on a raft

The longest recorded survival alone on a raft is

133 days (4½ months) by Second Steward Poon Lim (b. Hong Kong) of the UK Merchant Navy, whose ship, the SS *Ben Lomond*, was torpedoed in the Atlantic 565 miles *910 km* west of St Paul's Rocks in Lat. 00° 30′ N Long. 38° 45′ W at 11.45 a.m. on 23 Nov 1942. He was picked up by a Brazilian fishing boat off Salinópolis, Brazil, on 5 Apr 1943 and could walk ashore. In July 1943 he was awarded the BEM and now lives in New York City.

Maurice and Maralyn Bailey of Derby survived 118¼ days in an inflatable dinghy 4½ ft *1,37 m* in diameter in the Pacific from 4 Mar to 30 June 1973.

Shaft sinking record

The one-month (31 days) world record is 1251 ft *381,3 m* for a standard shaft 26 ft *7,92 m* in diameter at Buffelsfontein Mine, Transvaal, South Africa, in March 1962. The British record of 131,2 m *430 ft* of 7,92 m *26 ft* diameter shaft was set in No 2 Shaft of the NCB's Whitemoor Mine near Selby, North Yorkshire in 31 days (15 Nov–16 Dec 1982).

Most marriages

The greatest number of marriages accumulated in the monogamous world is 27 by a former Baptist minister Glynn 'Scotty' Wolfe (b. 25 July 1908) of Blythe, California, who first married in 1927. His latest wife is Daisy Delgado (b. 29 Dec 1970), a Filipino from Liloan, Cebu. His previous oldest wife was 38. His total number of children is, he says, 41. He suffered only 25 mothers-in-law because two of his 25 wives were the subject of re-marriages.

Mrs Beverly Nina Avery, then aged 48, a barmaid from Los Angeles, California set a monogamous world record in October 1957 by obtaining her sixteenth divorce from her fourteenth husband, Gabriel Avery. She alleged outside the court that five of the 14 had broken her nose.

The record for bigamous marriages is 104 by Giovanni Vigliotto, one of some 50 aliases used by either Fred Jipp (b. New York City, 3 Apr 1936) or Nikolai Peruskov (b. Siracusa, Sicily, 3 Apr 1929) during 1949–1981 in 27 US states and 14 other countries. Four victims were aboard one ship in 1968 and two in London. On 28 Mar 1983 in Phoenix, Arizona he received 28 years for fraud, 6 for bigamy and fined $336,000.

The only monogamous citizen who married eight men is Olive Joyce Wilson of Marston Green, Birmingham. She has consecutively been Mrs John Bickley; Mrs Don Trethowan; Mrs George

TRANS-PACIFIC MARINE RECORDS

(Compiled by Sq Ldr D. H. Clarke, DFC, AFC)

CATEGORY	NAME	VESSEL	START	FINISH	DURATION	DATE
Fastest (Trans-Pac)	Bob Hanel (US) + 6 crew	*Double Bullet* (BM Sloop—Cat)	Los Angeles	Hawaii	7 days 7 hr 31 min 325.5 mpd	1983
Fastest Yacht (Australia–Horn)	O. K. Pennendreft (Fr) + 13 crew	*Kriter II* 80 ft *24,38 m*	Sydney	Cape Horn	21 days (275 mpd)	1975–6
Fastest Clipper (Australia–Horn)	Capt J. N. Forbes (GB) + crew	*Lightning* 244 ft *74,36 m*	Melbourne	Cape Horn	19 days 1 hr (315 mpd)	1854
Fastest Solo Monohull (Australia–Horn)	Philippe Jeantot (Fr)	*Crédit Agricole* 56 ft *17,07 m*	Sydney	Cape Horn	29 days 23 hr (5709 miles = 190.6 mpd)	1982–3
Earliest Solo (Woman)	Sharon Sites Adams (US)	*Sea Sharp II* 31 ft *9,45 m*	Yokohama, Japan	San Diego, Cal.	75 days (5911 miles)	1969
Earliest Rowing	John Fairfax (GB) Sylvia Cook (GB)	*Britannia II* 35 ft *10,66 m*	San Francisco 26 Apr 1971	Hayman I., Australia 22 Apr 1972	362 days	1971–2
Earliest Rowing Solo	Peter Bird (GB)	*Hele-on-Britannia* 32 ft *9,75 m*	San Francisco 23 Aug 1982	Gt Barrier Reef, Australia 14 June 1983	294 days 9000 miles *14 480 km*	1982–3
Fastest 2-crew Row	Curtis Saville (US) Kathleen (wife)	*Excalibur Pacific* 25 ft 5 in *7,75 m*	Callao, Peru	Australia	193 days rowing (approx 43 mpd)	1984–6
Earliest Solo (Totally Blind)	Hank Dekker (US)	*Dark Star* 25 ft 7 in *7,79 m* (BM Sloop)	San Francisco	Honolulu	23 days (Braille charts, compass and loran)	1983
Earliest Raft (shore to shore)	Vital Alsar (Sp) and 3 crew	*La Balsa* (Balsa logs) 42 ft *12,8 m*	Guayaquil Ecuador	Mooloolaba Australia	160 days	1970

N.B.—The earliest single-handed Pacific crossings were achieved East–West by Bernard Gilboy (US) in 1882 in the 18 ft *5,48 m* double-ender *Pacific* to Australia and West–East by Fred Rebel (Latvia) in the 18 ft *5,48 m* Elaine (from Australia) and Edward Miles (US) in the 36¾ ft *11,2 m* Sturdy II (from Japan) both in 1932, the latter via Hawaii.

Hundley; Mrs Raymond Ward; Mrs Harry Latrobe; Mrs Leslie Harris; Mrs Ray Richards and now Mrs John Grassick. All were divorced except Mr Hundley, who died.

Oldest bride and bridegroom

The oldest recorded bridegroom has been Harry Stevens, 103, who married Thelma Lucas, 84, at the Caravilla Retirement Home, Wisconsin on 3 Dec 1984.

The British record was set by Sir Robert Mayer CH, KCVO (1879–1985) who married Jacqueline Noble, 51, in London on 10 Nov 1980 when aged 101 years. Mrs Winifred Clark (b. 13 Nov 1871) became Britain's oldest recorded bride when she married Albert Smith, 80, at St Hugh's Church, Cantley, South Yorkshire the day before her 100th birthday.

Longest engagements

The longest engagement on record was between Octavio Guillen and Adriana Martinez. They finally took the plunge after 67 years in June 1969 in Mexico City. Both were then 82.

Longest marriage

The longest recorded marriages are of 86 years, one between Sir Temulji Bhicaji Nariman and Lady Nariman from 1853 to 1940 resulting from a cousin marriage when both were five. Sir Temulji (b. 3 Sept 1848) died, aged 91 years 11 months, in August 1940 at Bombay. Lazurus Rowe (b. Greenland, New Hampshire, 1725) and Molly Webber were recorded as marrying in 1743. He died first in 1829 after 86 years of marriage.

James Frederick Burgess (born 3 March 1861, died 27 Nov 1966) and his wife Sarah Ann, *née* Gregory (born 11 July 1865, died 22 June 1965) were married on 21 June 1883 at St James's, Bermondsey, London, and celebrated their 82nd anniversary.

Golden weddings

Despite the advent of the computer, records on golden (or 50-year-long) weddings remain largely uncollated. Unusual cases reported include that of Mrs Agnes Mary Amy Mynott (b. 25 May 1887) who attended the golden wedding of her daughter Mrs Violet Bangs of St Albans on 20 Dec 1980, 23 years after her own. The 3 sons and 4 daughters of Mr and Mrs J. Stredwick of East Sussex *all* celebrated golden weddings between May 1971 and April 1981. Triplets Lucille (Mrs Vogel), Marie (Mrs McNamara) and Alma (Mrs Prom) Pufpaff all celebrated their golden weddings on 12 Apr 1982 having all married in Cleveland, Minnesota in 1932.

Most married

Jack V. and Edna Moran of Seattle, Washington have married each other 40 times since the original and only really necessary occasion on 27 July 1937 in Seaside, Oregon. Subsequent ceremonies have included those at Banff, Canada (1952), Cairo (1966) and Westminster Abbey (1975).

Youngest married

It was reported in 1986 that an 11-month-old boy was married to a 3-month-old girl in Bangladesh to end a 20-year feud between two families over a disputed farm.

Mass ceremony

The largest mass wedding ceremony was one of 5837 couples from 83 countries officiated over by Sun Myung Moon (b. 1920) of the Holy Spirit Association for the Unification of World Christianity in the Chamsil Gymnasium, Seoul, South Korea on 14 Oct 1982. The response to the question 'Will you swear to love your spouse for ever?' is 'Ye'.

Most expensive wedding

The wedding of Mohammed, son of Shaik Rashid bin Saeed al Maktoum, to Princess Salama in Abu Dhabi in May 1981 lasted 7 days and cost an estimated £22 million in a purpose-built stadium for 20,000.

Oldest divorced

On 2 Feb 1984 a divorce was granted in Milwaukee, Wisconsin between Ida Stern, aged 91 and her husband Simon, 97. The British record age is 101 years by Harry Bidwell at Brighton, East Sussex. He divorced on 21 Nov 1980 from a younger wife.

Dining out

The world champion for eating out has been Fred E. Magel of Chicago, Illinois who since 1928 has dined out 46,000 times in 60 nations as a restaurant grader (to 21 June 1983). He asserts the one which served largest helpings was Zehnder's Hotel, Frankenmuth, Michigan. Mr Magel's favourite dishes were South African rock lobster and mousse of fresh English strawberries.

Party giving

The 'International Year of the Child' children's party in Hyde Park, London was attended by the Royal Family and 160,000 children on 30–31 May 1979. The longest street party ever staged was for 5500 children by the Oxford Street Association, to celebrate the Royal Wedding of TRH The Prince and Princess of Wales, on 25 July 1981 along the entire length from Park Street to St Giles Circus, London.

The largest Christmas Party ever staged was that thrown by The Boeing Company in the 65,000-seat Kingdome, Seattle, Washington, USA, in two shows totalling 103,152 people on 15 Dec 1979. During St Patrick's week of 11–17 Mar 1985, Houlihan's Old Place hosted St Pat's Parties at the 48 Kansas City, Missouri-based Gilbert/Robinson restaurants for a total of 206,854 documented guests.

Toastmasters

The Guild of Professional Toastmasters (founded 1962) has only 12 members. Its founder and President, Ivor Spencer, once had to listen to a speech in excess of 2 hr by the maudlin guest of honour of a retirement luncheon. The Guild also elects the most boring speaker of the year, but for professional reasons, will not publicise the winners' names until a decent interval has elapsed. Red coats were introduced by the pioneer professional, William Knight-Smith (d. 1932) *c.* 1900.

Lecture agency

In 1980 Bob Jones of Wellington, New Zealand addressed a seminar of 1048 people in Auckland on the subject of property. He received $NZ200,000 or $NZ16,666 per hour. In March 1981 it was reported that both Johnny Carson and Bob Hope commanded fees of $40,000 (*then £18,000*). The author Tom Peters of Palo Alto, California made 275 speeches in 1986 generating $1.5 million £930,000 in fees.

Working week

A case of a working week of 142 hours was recorded in June 1980 by Dr Paul Ashton, 32, the anaesthetics registrar at Birkenhead General Hospital, Merseyside. This left an average each day of 3 hr 42 min 51 sec for sleep. Some non-consultant doctors are contracted to work 110 hours a week or be available for 148 hours. Some contracts for fully salaried university lecturers call for a 3-hr week or a 72-hr year spread over 24 weeks.

Working career

The longest working life has been that of 98 years by Mr Izumi (see p. 11), who began work goading draft animals at a sugar mill at Isen, Tokunoshima, Japan in 1872. He retired as a sugar cane farmer in 1970 aged 105.

The longest working life recorded in the UK was that of Susan O'Hagan (1802–1909) who was in domestic service with 3 generations of the Hall family of Lisburn, near Belfast for 97 years from the age of 10 to light duties at 107.

The writer who has interviewed most heads of state and heads of government in the world is Brian Rossiter Crozier (GB) (b. 4 Aug 1918) with 58 from 36 countries in the period 1948–85.

The longest recorded industrial career in one job in Britain was that of Miss Polly Gadsby who started work with Archibald Turner & Co of Leicester aged 9. In 1932, after 86 years' service, she was still at her bench wrapping elastic, at the age of 95. Theodore C. Taylor (1850–1952) served 86 years with J. T. & T. Taylor of Batley, West Yorkshire including 56 years as chairman. The longest serving chairman (appointed July 1926) of any board of directors was Mrs Mary Henrietta Anne Moody (b. 7 Apr 1881) of Mark & Moody Ltd, printers and booksellers of Stourbridge, West Midlands. She had completed 59 years at the time of her death on 5 Aug 1985. Edward William Beard (1878–1982), a builder of Swindon, Wiltshire retired in October 1981 from the firm he founded in 1896 after 85 years. Commissioner Catherine Bramwell-Booth (b. 20 July 1883) has been serving the Salvation Army since 1903. Richard John Knight (b. 2 Apr 1881) was company secretary to 7 companies at the time of his death on 12 Nov 1984 aged 103 years.

Most durable coal miner

George Stephenson (b. 21 Apr 1833) worked at William Pit, a Whitehaven colliery, Cumbria from 1840 (aged 7) for 82 years until his retirement in 1922. He died on 18 Mar 1926 aged 92 years 10 months having received a testimonial of £54 12s.

Longest pension

Miss Millicent Barclay, daughter of Col William Barclay was born posthumously on 10 July 1872 and became eligible for a Madras Military Fund pension to continue until her marriage. She died unmarried on 26 Oct 1969 having drawn the pension for every day of her life of 97 years 3 months.

Medical families

The 4 sons and 5 daughters of Dr Antonio B. Vicencio of Los Angeles all qualified as doctors during 1964–82. Eight sons of John Robertson of Benview, Dumbarton graduated as medical doctors between 1892 and 1914. Henry Lewis Lutterloh and Elizabeth Grantham of Chatham County, North Carolina were the grandparents of 19 medical doctors. From 1850 to 1962 they practised a total of 704 man-years. The Maurice family of Marlborough, Wiltshire have had the same practice for 6 generations since 1792.

Miscellaneous Endeavours

ACCORDION PLAYING

Tom Luxton of Oldbury, West Midlands, played an accordion for 84 hr from 4–7 Aug 1982.

APPLE PEELING

The longest single unbroken apple peel on record is one of 172 ft 4 in *52,51 m* peeled by Kathy Wafler, of Wolcott, NY, USA in 11 hr 30 min at Long Ridge Mall, Rochester, NY on 16 Oct 1976. The apple weighed 20 oz *567 g*.

APPLE PICKING

The greatest recorded performance is 365¼ US bushels (354.1 imperial bushels *128,80 hecto-*

litres) picked in 8 hr by George Adrian, 32, of Indianapolis, Indiana on 23 Sept 1980.

AUCTIONEERING

The longest one-man auction on record is one of 53½ hr by Reg Coates at the Guinness World of Records Exhibition, Piccadilly, London from 3–5 July 1986.

BAG-CARRYING

The greatest non-stop bag-carrying feat carrying 1 cwt *50,8 kg* of household coal in an open bag is 34 miles *54,7 km* by Neil Sullivan, 37, of Small Heath, Birmingham in 12 hr 45 min on 24 May 1986.

The record for the 1012,5 m *1107.2 yd* course annual Gawthorpe, West Yorkshire race is 4 min 19 sec by Terry Lyons, 36, on 16 Apr 1979.

BAGPIPES

The duration record has been one of 100 hr by Neville Workman, Clive Higgins, Patrick Forth and Paul Harris, of Churchill School Pipe Band, Harare, Zimbabwe, playing two at a time in shifts, from 9–13 July 1976.

BALANCING ON ONE FOOT

The longest recorded duration for balancing on one foot is 34 hr by Shri N. Ravi in Sathyamangalam City, Tamil Nadu, India on 17–18 Apr 1982. The disengaged foot may not be rested on the standing foot nor may any object be used for support or balance.

BALLOON FLIGHTS

The longest reported toy balloon flight is one of 10,000 miles *16 090 km* from Dobbs Ferry, New York to Wagga Wagga, Australia. It was helium-filled and released by 11-year-old Justin Fiore on 19 Apr 1982. The longest recorded hydrogen-filled balloon flight from the geographical British Isles is one of 5880 miles *9460 km* from Jersey which was returned from Camps Bay, Cape Province, South Africa on 28 Apr 1974, 43 days after release by Gerard Wankling.

BALLOON RELEASE

The largest mass balloon release ever was one of 1,429,643 balloons at Public Square in Cleveland, Ohio on 27 Sept 1986.

BAND MARATHONS

The longest recorded 'blow-in' is 100 hr 2 min by the Du Val Senior High School, Lanham, Maryland from 13–17 May 1977. The minimum number of musicians is 10.

BAND, ONE-MAN

Rory Blackwell, aided by his left-footed perpendicular percussion-pounder and his right-footed horizontal four pronged differential beater, played 24 (4 melody, 20 percussion) instruments in Plymouth, Devon on 2 May 1985. He also played in a single rendition 314 instruments in 1 min 23.07 sec at Dawlish, Devon on 27 May 1985. Dave Sheriff of Rugby, Warwickshire played his one-man band (which must include at least 3 instruments played simultaneously) for 100 hr 20 min from 24–28 Mar 1986 at the Hotel Leofric, Coventry, West Midlands. Nicki Clarke of Chester, Cheshire created the women's record of the same time *at* the same time at the same place.

BARREL JUMPING *on Ice Skates*

The official distance record is 29 ft 5 in *8,99 m* over 18 barrels by Yvon Jolin at Terrebonne, Quebec, on 25 Jan 1981. The feminine record is 20 ft 4½ in *6,21 m* over 11 barrels by Janet Hainstock in Michigan, USA, on 15 Mar 1980.

BARREL ROLLING

The record for rolling a full 36-gallon metal beer barrel over a measured mile is 8 min 7.2 sec by Phillip Randle, Steve Hewitt, John Round, Trevor Bradley, Colin Barnes and Ray Glover of Haunchwood Collieries Institute and Social Club, Nuneaton, Warwickshire on 15 Aug 1982. A team of 10 rolled a 63½ kg *140 lb* barrel 240,35 km *150 miles* in 30 hr 31 min in Chlumcany, Czechoslovakia on 27–28 Oct 1982.

BARROW RACING

The fastest time attained in a 1 mile *1,609 km* wheelbarrow race is 4 min 50.29 sec by John Coates and Brian Roades of Richmond, BC, Canada on 9 July 1983 at the Ladner Sports Festival, Delta, BC. Brothers-in-law Malcolm Shipley and Adrian Freeburg pushed each other from John O'Groats to Land's End for charity in 30 days from 28 July–26 Aug 1981.

BARROW PUSHING

The heaviest loaded one-wheeled barrow pushed for a minimum 200 level feet *60,96 m* is one loaded with bricks weighing a gross 8275 lb *3,753 tonnes* through 243 ft *74,06 m* by John Sarich at London, Ontario, Canada on 19 Feb 1987.

BATH TUB RACING

The record for the annual international 36 mile *57,9 km* Nanaimo to Vancouver, British Columbia bath tub race is 1 hr 29 min 40 sec by Gary Deathbridge (Australia) on 30 July 1978. Tubs are limited to 75 in *1,90 m* and 6-hp motors. The greatest distance for paddling a hand-propelled bath tub in 24 hr is 90.5 miles *145,6 km* by 13 members of Aldington Prison Officers Social Club, nr Ashford, Kent on 28–29 May 1983.

BATON TWIRLING

Victor Cerda, Sol Lozano, Harry Little III (leader) and Manuel Rodriguez twirled batons for 122½ hours from 24–29 June 1984 in El Seveno, California.

BEARD OF BEES

The ultimate beard of bees was achieved by Max Beck, 21, of Arcola, Pennsylvania, USA with 70,000 bees weighing 20 lb *9 kg* reported in October 1985.

BED MAKING

The record time set under the rigorous rules of the Australian Bed Making Championships is 28.2 sec solo by Wendy Wall, 34, of Hebersham, Sydney, NSW on 30 Nov 1978. The British pair record with 1 blanket, 2 sheets, an undersheet, an uncased pillow, 1 counterpane and 'hospital' corners is 19.0 sec by Sisters Jill Bradbury and Chris Humpish of Hammersmith Hospital, London on 8 Oct 1985 on BBC TV *Record Breakers* programme.

BED OF NAILS

The Rev Ken Owen, 48, of Pontypridd, Mid-Glamorgan, lay on a bed of nails for a total of 300 hr, including 132 hr 30 min without a break, between 3–14 May 1986 starting at Bridgend Hotel, Pontygwaith, and concluding at the The Three Horse Shoes, Tonteg, Pontypridd. Much longer durations are claimed by uninvigilated *fakirs*—the most extreme case being *Silki* who claimed 111 days in São Paulo, Brazil ending on 24 Aug 1969.

BED PUSHING

The longest recorded push of a normally sessile object is of 3233 miles 1150 yd *5204 km* in the case of a wheeled hospital bed by a team of 9

Joan E. Herbert, 75, of Highgate, London displays a small part of the 41 ft × 42 ft 6 in *12,49 m × 12,95 m* blanket she crocheted to raise money for Cancer Research and the British Heart Foundation. The blanket took approximately 3850 oz *109,147 g* of wool and took her more than 6 months to complete.

employees of Bruntsfield Bedding Centre, Edinburgh from 21 June–26 July 1979.

BED RACE

The record time for the annual Knaresborough Bed Race (established 1966) in North Yorkshire is 12 min 36 sec for the 2 mile 63 yd *3,27 km* course crossing the River Nidd by the Beavers' Team on 9 June 1984. The course record for the 10 mile *16,09 km* Chew Valley Lake race (inst. 1977) in Avon, England is 50 min by the Westbury Harriers' 3-man bed team.

BEER MAT FLIPPING

Dean Gould, 22, of Felixstowe, Suffolk flipped and caught a pile of 90 mats (1.2 mm-thick 490 gsm wood pulp board) through 180 degrees at BBC TV Centre, London on 17 Sept 1986.

BEER STEIN CARRYING

Barmaid Rosie Schedelbauer covered 15 m *49 ft 2½ in* in 4.0 sec with 5 full steins in each hand in a televised contest at Königssee, West Germany on 29 June 1981.

BEST MAN

The world's champion 'best man' is Wally Gant, a bachelor fishmonger from Wakefield, West Yorkshire, who officiated for the 50th time since 1931 in December 1964.

BICYCLE *Most mounting simultaneously*

On 2 Apr 1984 at Mito, Ibaragi, Japan 16 members of the Mito-Itomi Unicycle Club mounted and rode a single bicycle a distance of 50 m *164 ft*.

BILLIARD TABLE JUMPING

Joe Darby (1861–1937) cleared a full-sized 12 ft *3,65 m* billiard table lengthwise, taking off from a 4 in *10 cm* high solid wooden block, at Wolverhampton, West Midlands on 5 Feb 1892.

BOOMERANG THROWING

The earliest mention of a word similar to *boomerang* is *wo-murrang* in Collins *Acct. N.S. Wales Vocab.* 1798. The earliest certain Australian account of a returning boomerang (term established, 1827) was in 1831 by Major (later Sir Thomas) Mitchell. Curved throwing sticks for wild fowl hunting were found in the tomb of Tutankhamun dating from the mid 14th century BC.

World championships and codified rules were not established until 1970. The Boomerang Association of Australia's championship record for distance reached before return is 111 m *364.1 ft* diameter by Bob Burwell in November 1981 at Albury, NSW. The longest unofficial out and return distance on record is one of 375 ft *114,3 m* by Peter Ruhf (US) at Randwick, Sydney, NSW on 28 June 1982. The longest flight duration (with self-catch) is one of 28.9 sec by Bob Burwell at Alberga, NSW on 7 Apr 1984. The greatest number of consecutive two-handed catches is 653 by Bob Croll (Victoria) on the same occasion.

BRICK CARRYING

The greatest distance achieved for carrying a brick 9 lb *4,08 kg* in a nominated ungloved hand in an uncradled downward pincher grip is 61¾ miles *99,37 km* by Reg Morris of Walsall, West Midlands on 16 July 1985.

The feminine record for a 9 lb 12 oz *4,422 kg* brick is 22½ miles *36,2 km* by Wendy Morris of Walsall, West Midlands, on 28 Apr 1986. The British feminine record for a 6 lb 9 oz *2,97 kg* smooth-sided brick is 6 miles *9,6 km* by Karen Stevenson of Wallasey, Merseyside on 17 Aug 1984.

BRICKLAYING

Robert Boll of Burbank, Illinois, USA laid 914 bricks in 60 min to win the first US Speed Bricklaying competition at Lansing, Michigan on 21 Feb 1987.

BRICK RACING

The record times recorded at the Annual NFBTE Young Builders Dry-brick Championship in Leicester are, for 100 metres: 1 min 7.0 sec + 11 penalty points giving a gross 1 min 18.0 sec by Ian Jones on 3 June 1979, and for 1 mile (team): 21 min 25 sec + 118 penalties giving an overall time of 23 min 23 sec by William Davis & Company (Leicester) Ltd, on 15 June 1980.

BRICK THROWING

The greatest reported distance for throwing a standard 5 lb *2,268 kg* building brick is 44.54 m *146 ft 1 in* by Geoff Capes at Braybrook School, Orton Goldhay, Cambridgeshire on 19 July 1978.

BUBBLE GUM BLOWING

The greatest reported diameter for a bubble gum bubble under the strict rules of this highly competitive activity is 22 in *55,8 cm* by Susan Montgomery Williams of Fresno, California in June 1985. The British record is 16½ in *42 cm* by Nigel Fell, 13, from Derriaghy, Northern Ireland in November 1979. This was equalled by John Smith of Willingham, Cambridgeshire on 25 Sept 1983.

BURIAL ALIVE

Voluntary burial alive claims (of which claims up to 217 days have been published) are inadmissible unless the depth of the coffin is a minimum 2 m *6 ft 6¾ in* below ground; the coffin has a maximum cubic capacity of 1,5 million cc *54 ft³* and the single aperture for communication and feeding has a maximum dimension of 10 cm *4 in*. 'Country' Bill White, 50, was so buried from 31 July to 19 Dec 1981 (141 days) in Killeen, Texas.

CAMPING OUT

The silent Indian *fakir* Mastram Bapu ('contented father') remained on the same spot by the roadside in the village of Chitra for 22 years from 1960–82.

CANAL JUMPING (DYKE VAULTING)

In the sport of Fierljeppen at Winsam, Friesland, Netherlands, the record is 18.61 m *61 ft 0¾ in* across the water with a 40 ft *12,2 m* aluminium pole set by Aarth de Wit in August 1983.

CARD THROWING

Kevin St Onge threw a standard playing card 185 ft 1 in *56,41 m* at the Henry Ford Community College Campus, Dearborn, Michigan on 12 June 1979.

CARRIAGE DRIVING

The only man to drive 48 horses in a single hitch is Dick Sparrow of Zearing, Iowa from 1972–77. The lead horses were on reins 135 ft *41 m* long.

CAR WRECKING

The greatest number of cars wrecked in a stunting career is 1912 to 1 May 1987 by Dick Sheppard of Gloucester, England.

CATAPULTING

The greatest recorded distance for a catapult shot is 1362 ft *415 m* by James M. Pfotenhauer using a patented 17 ft 1½ in *5,22 m* 'Monarch IV Supershot' and a 53-calibre lead musket ball on Ski Hill Road, Escanaba, Michigan on 10 Sept 1977.

CHAMPAGNE FOUNTAIN

The greatest number of storeys achieved in a champagne fountain, successfully filled from the top and using 10,404 traditional long-stem glasses, is 44 (height 24.7 ft *7,52 m*), achieved by Pascal Leclerc at the Biltmore Hotel, Los Angeles on 18 June 1984.

CLAPPING

The duration record for continuous clapping (sustaining an average of 160 claps per min audible at 120 yd *109,7 m*) is 54 hr by V. Jeyaraman of Tamil Nadu, India from 13–15 Dec 1985.

CLUB SWINGING

Albert Rayner set a world record of 17,512 revolutions (4.9 per sec) in 60 min at Wakefield, West Yorkshire on 27 July 1981. M. Dobrilla swung continuously for 144 hr at Cobar, NSW, Australia finishing on 15 Sept 1913.

COAL CUTTING

The individual record is 218 tons in a week of 5 shifts by Jim Marley (b. 1914) at East Walbottle Colliery, Tyne and Wear, England in 1949. This included 47½ tons in 6 hr. The NCB record for a week's production by a 48-man team is 32,333 tonnes at the biggest pit at Kellingley Colliery, Knottingley, West Yorkshire in the pre-Christmas 'Bull Week' in December 1982.

COAL SHOVELLING

The record for filling a ½-ton *508 kg* hopper with coal is 29.4 sec by Piet Groot at the Inangahua A and P Show, New Zealand on 1 Jan 1985.

COIN BALANCING

The tallest column of coins ever stacked on the edge of a coin is 205 Canadian 25-cent pieces on top of a Canadian Olympic commemorative coin which was freestanding vertically on the base of a coin flat on the surface, by Bruce McConachy (b. 1963) of West Vancouver, BC, Canada for Fuji-TV in Tokyo on 24 Feb 1985. Alex Chervinsky (b. 22 Feb 1908) of Lock Haven, Pennsylvania achieved a pyramid of 390 coins on his 75th birthday.

COIN SNATCHING

The greatest number of 10p pieces clean caught from being flipped from the back of a forearm into the same downward palm is 132 by Dean Gould at The Feathers public house in Walton, Suffolk on 8 Jan 1987.

COMPETITION WINNINGS

The largest individual competition prize win on record is $307,500 (*then £109,821*) by Herbert J. Idle, 55, of Chicago in an encyclopaedia contest run by Unicorn Press Inc, on 20 Aug 1953. The highest value first prize offered in Britain has been a £172,950 new house in a £491,000 competition run by the *London Evening Standard* in April and May 1987.

COW CHIP TOSSING

The record distances in the country sport of throwing dried cow chips depend on whether or not the projectile may be 'moulded into a spherical shape'. The greatest distance achieved under the 'non-sphericalisation and 100% organic' rule (established in 1970) is 266 ft *81,07 m* by Steve Urner at the Mountain Festival, Tehachapi, California on 14 Aug 1981.

CRAWLING

The longest continuous voluntary crawl (progression with one or other knee in unbroken contact with the ground) on record is 27 miles *43,45 km* by Chris Lock at Durdham Downs, Bristol, England on 18–19 Aug 1984. Over a space of 15 months ending on 9 Mar 1985 Jagdish Chander, 32, crawled 1400 km *870 miles* from Aligarh to Jamma, India to propitiate his favourite Hindu goddess, Mata.

CROCHET

Mrs Barbara Jean Sonntag (b. 1938) of Craig, Colorado, USA crocheted 330 shells plus 5 stitches (equivalent to 4412 stitches) in 30 min at a rate of 147 stitches a minute on 13 Jan 1981. Miss Ria van der Honing of Wormerveer, Netherlands, completed a crochet chain 62,50 km *38.83 miles* in length on 14 July 1986. Mrs Sybille Anthony completed a 100 hr crochet marathon at Toombul Shopping-town, Queensland, Australia on 7 Oct 1977.

Circus Records

The world's largest permanent circus is Circus Circus, Las Vegas, Nevada, USA opened on 18 Oct 1968 at a cost of $15,000,000 (then £6,250,000). It covers an area of 129,000 ft² *11 984 m²* capped by a tent-shaped flexiglass roof 90 ft *27,43 m* high. The largest travelling circus is the Circus Vargas in the USA which can accommodate 5000 people under its Big Top.

Flying trapeze
Downward circles or 'muscle grinding'—1350 by Sarah Denu (aged 14) (US) Madison, Wisconsin 21 May 1983. Single-heel hang on swinging bar, Angela Revelle (Angelique), Australia, 1977.

Triple twisting double somersault
Tom Robin Edelston to catcher John Zimmerman, Circus World, Florida, 20 Jan 1981.

Full twisting triple and the quadruple somersault
Vasquez Troupe. Miguel Vasquez to catcher Juan Vasquez at Ringling Bros, Amphitheater, Chicago, USA in November 1981. On 20 Sept 1984 he performed a triple somersault in a layout position (no turn) to catcher Juan Vasquez at the Sports Arena, Los Angeles, California.

Triple back somersault with 1½ twists
Terry Cavaretta Lemus (now Mrs St Jules). At Circus Circus, Las Vegas, Nevada in 1969.

Trampoline
Septuple twisting back somersault to bed and quintuple twisting back somersault to shoulders by Marco Canestrelli to Belmonte Canestrelli at Madison Square Garden, New York on 5 Jan and 28 Mar 1979. Richard Tison (France) performed a triple twisting triple back somersault for television near Berchtesgaden, West Germany on 30 June 1981.

Flexible pole
Double full twisting somersault to a 2 in *5,08 cm* diameter pole by Roberto Tabak (aged 11) in Sarasota, Florida in 1977. Triple full twisting somersault by Corina Colonelu Mosoianu (aged 13) at Madison Square Garden, New York on 17 Apr 1984.

Human pyramid (or tuckle)
Twelve (3 high) supported by a single understander. Weight 771 kg *1700 lb* or *121.4 stone* by Tahar Douis of the Hassani Troupe at BBC TV Pebble Mill Studio, Birmingham on 17 Dec 1979.

Nine high by top-mounter Josep-Joan Martínez Lozano, 10, of the Colla Vella dels Xiquets, 12 m *39 ft* tall on 25 Oct 1981 in Valls, Spain.

Oldest clown
Charlie Revel (b. Andrea Lassere, Spain, 24 Apr 1896) performed for 82 years (1899–1981).

JUGGLING RECORDS

7 clubs
Albert Petrovski (USSR), 1963; Sorin Munteanu (Romania), 1975; Jack Bremlov (Czechoslovakia), 1985; Albert Lucas (US) 1985.

8 plates
Enrico Rastelli (Italy), 1896–1931; Albert Lucas (US), 1984.

10 balls
Enrico Rastelli (Italy), 1896–1931; Albert Lucas (US), 1984.

12 rings
Albert Lucas (US), 1985.

Pirouettes with 3 cigar boxes
Kris Kremo (Switzerland) (quadruple turn with 3 boxes in mid-air), 1977.

Duration 5 clubs
37 min 10 sec, Albert Lucas (US), 1984.

3 clubs while running—joggling
Albert Lucas, USA, 100 m in 12.67 sec, 1984. Scott Damgaard, USA, 1 mile *1,6 km* in 4 min 37 sec, 1981. Marty Gardella, USA, 5 km *3.1 miles* in 18 min 47.95 sec, 1982.

5 ping-pong balls with mouth
Gran Picaso (Spain), 1971.

5 balls inverted
Bobby May (US), since 1953.

'Teeter-board' ● The seven-person high 'pyramid perch' set by the Bulgarian 'Kehaiovi Troupe' at the Tower Circus, Blackpool on 16 July 1986, was crowned by a leap from 13-year-old member Magdalena.

Below: Highest aerial act ● Ian Ashpole (b. 15 Jan 1956) of Ross-on-Wye, Hereford and Worcester performed a trapeze act suspended from a hot-air balloon between St Neots, Cambridgeshire and Newmarket, Suffolk at 16,420 ft *5004,8 m* on 16 May 1986.

CUCUMBER SLICING

Norman Johnson of Blackpool, Lancashire set a record of 13.4 sec for slicing a 12 in *30,48 cm* cucumber 1½ in *3,81 cm* in diameter at 22 slices to the inch (total 244 slices) on West Deutscher Rundfunk in Cologne on 3 Apr 1983.

CUSTARD PIE THROWING

The most times champion in the annual World Custard Pie Championships, now at Ditton, Maidstone, Kent (instituted 1968) have been 'The Birds' ('The Bashers') and the 'Coxheath Men' ('Custard Kings') each with 3 wins. The target (face) must be 8 ft 3¾ in *2,53 m* from the thrower who must throw a pie no more than 10¼ in *26,03 cm* in diameter. Six points are scored for a square hit full in the face.

DEBATING

The Oxford Union Society, Oxford University, debated the motion '. . . Heineken refreshes the parts' for 193 hr 49 min on 21–29 May 1986. The debate, with 175 formal speakers, included a 2½-hour joke and raised £2500 for charity.

DEMOLITION WORK

Fifteen members of the Black Leopard Karate Club demolished a 7-room wooden farmhouse west of Elnora, Alberta, Canada in 3 hr 18 min by foot and empty hand on 13 June 1982.

DOMINO STACKING

Leard Wayne Woedruff (76) of McFarland, California, USA successfully stacked 242 dominoes on a single supporting domino on 15 Sept 1986.

DRINK ROUND

The largest round of drinks ever recorded was one for 1501 people stood by Paul Deer at U-Zoo & Co, Atlanta, Georgia, USA on 14 July 1982.

DRUMMING

The world's duration drumming record is 44 days 1 hr by Trevor Mitchell at the Brown Cow Hotel, Scunthorpe, Humberside from 5 July–18 Aug 1986.

Four hundred separate drums were played in 58 seconds by rock star Cozy Powell on BBC TV's *Record Breakers* at TV Centre, London on 5 Nov 1985.

DUCKS AND DRAKES

The best is 29 skips (14 plinkers and 15 pitty-pats) by Arthur Ring, 69, at Midway Beach, California on 4 Aug 1984 and Jerdone 'Jerry' McGhee, 42, at Wimberley, Texas on 18 Nov 1986.

EGG HUNT

The greatest egg hunt on record involved 72,000 hard-boiled eggs and 40,000 candy eggs at the 26th annual Garrison Egg Hunt at Homer, Georgia on 7 Apr 1985.

EGG AND SPOON RACING

Chris Riggio of San Francisco, California completed a 28.5 mile *45,86 km* fresh egg and dessert spoon marathon in 4 hr 34 min on 7 Oct 1979.

EGG SHELLING

Two kitchen hands, Harold Witcomb and Gerald Harding, shelled 1050 dozen eggs in a 7¼-hr shift at Bowyers, Trowbridge, Wiltshire on 23 Apr 1971. Both were blind.

EGG THROWING

The longest authenticated distance for throwing a fresh hen's egg without breaking it is 96,90 m *317 ft 10 in* by Risto Antikainen to Jyrki Korhonen at Siilinjarvi, Finland on 6 Sept 1981.

ESCALATOR RIDING

Peter Baucher and Gordon Yuill, both 16, of the John Orr Technical High School, Johannesburg travelled a pair of 'up' and 'down' escalators at the Nedbank Cresta Centre in the city for 80 hrs from 20–23 June 1986. The total distance travelled was 143,04 km *88.88 miles*.

ESCAPOLOGY

The most renowned of all escape artists has been Ehrich Weiss *alias* Harry Houdini (1874–1926), who pioneered underwater escapes from locked, roped and weighted containers while handcuffed and shackled with irons.

A manufacturer of strait-jackets acknowledges that an escapologist 'skilled in the art of bone and muscle manipulation' could escape from a standard jacket in seconds. There are, however, methods by which such circumvention can itself be circumvented. Nick Janson of Benfleet, Essex can escape from handcuffs locked on him by more than 1000 different police officers.

FAMILY TREE

The farthest back the lineage of any family has been traced is that of K'ung Ch'iu or Confucius (551–479 BC). His 4 greats grandfather K'ung Chia is known from the eighth century BC. This man's 85th lineal descendants Wei-yi (b. 1939) and Wei-ning (b. 1947) live today in Taiwan (Formosa).

■ DANCING ■

Marathon dancing must be distinguished from dancing mania, or tarantism, which is a pathological condition. The worst outbreak of this was at Aachen, Germany, in July 1374, when hordes of men and women broke into a frenzied and compulsive choreomania in the streets. It lasted for many hours until injury or complete exhaustion ensued.

Largest and longest dances

An estimated 25,000 attended a 'Moonlight Serenade' outdoor evening of dancing to the music of the Glenn Miller Orchestra in Buffalo, New York on 20 July 1984. An estimated total of 20,000 dancers took part in the National Square Dance Convention at Louisville, Kentucky on 26 June 1983.

The most severe marathon dance staged as a public spectacle was one by Mike Ritof and Edith Boudreaux who logged 5148 hr 28½ min to win $2000 at Chicago's Merry Garden Ballroom, Belmont and Sheffield, Illinois, USA from 29 Aug 1930 to 1 Apr 1931. Rest periods were progressively cut from 20 to 10 to 5 to nil minutes per hour with 10-inch steps and a maximum of 15 seconds for closure of eyes.

Will Kemp in 1599 Morris-danced his way from London to Norwich in 9 days.

'Rosie Radiator' (Rose Marie Ostler) on 16 Aug 1986 claimed a mileage of 6 miles *9,6 km* in leading a column of 17 tap dancers across San Francisco.

Ballet

In the *entrechat* (a vertical spring from the fifth position with the legs extended criss-crossing at the lower calf), the starting and finishing position each count as one such that in an *entrechat douze* there are *five* crossings and uncrossings. This was performed by Wayne Sleep for the BBC *Record Breakers* programme on 7 Jan 1973. He was in the air for 0.71 sec.

Most turns

The greatest number of spins called for in classical ballet choreography is 32 *fouettés rond de jambe en tournant* in 'Swan Lake' by Pyotr Ilyich Chaykovskiy (Tschaikovsky) (1840–93). Miss Rowena Jackson (later Chatfield) MBE (b. Invercargill, NZ, 1925) achieved 121 such turns at her class in Melbourne, Victoria, Australia in 1940.

Most curtain calls

The greatest recorded number of curtain calls ever received is 89 by Dame Margaret Evelyn Arias DBE, *née* Hookham (born Reigate, Surrey, 18 May 1919) *alias* Margot Fonteyn, and Rudolf Hametovich Nureyev (born on a train near Irkutsk, USSR, 17 Mar 1938) after a performance of 'Swan Lake' at the Vienna Staatsoper, Austria, in October 1964.

Largest cast

The largest number of ballet dancers used in a production in Britain has been 2000 in the London Coster Ballet of 1962, directed by Lillian Rowley, at the Royal Albert Hall, London.

Ballroom *Marathon*

The individual continuous world record for ballroom dancing is 126 hr by Scott Michael, 31, a dancing instructor of Huntington Beach, California on 20–25 June 1986 at the Dance Masters Ballroom Studio, Stanton, California. 27 girls worked shifts as his partner.

Champions

The world's most successful professional ballroom dancing champions have been Bill Irvine, MBE and Bobbie Irvine MBE, who won 13 world titles between 1960 and 1972. The oldest competitive ballroom dancer is Albert J. Sylvester CBE, JP (b. 24 Nov 1889) of Corsham, Wiltshire, who retired aged 94. In 1977 he won the topmost amateur Alex Moore award for a 10-dance test with his partner Paula Smith in Bath on 26 Apr 1977. By 1981 he had won nearly 50 medals and trophies since he began dancing in 1964.

Belly dancing

The longest recorded example was one of 106 hr by Eileen Foucher at Rush Green Hospital, Romford, Essex from 30 July–3 Aug 1984.

Charleston

The charleston duration record is 110 hr 58 min by Sabra Starr of Lansdowne, Pennsylvania from 15–20 Jan 1979.

Conga

The longest recorded conga was one comprising a 'snake' of 8659 people from the South Eastern Region of the Camping and Caravanning Club of Great Britain and Ireland on 4 Sept 1982.

Disco

The longest recorded disco dancing marathon is one of 375 hours by Rémy Joseph Mercier in

Montreal, Quebec, Canada from 16 Sept to 6 Oct 1985.

Flamenco

The fastest flamenco dancer ever measured is Solero de Jerez, aged 17, who in Brisbane, Australia in September 1967 in an electrifying routine attained 16 heel taps per second.

High kicking

The world record for high kicks (heel to ear level) is 10,502 in 5 hr 30 min by Shawn Kovacich at Butte, Montana, on 27 Sept 1986. Johann Haywood (25) set a speed record of 98 kicks in 1 min at Kempton Park Village Shopping Centre, South Africa on 21 Mar 1987. Veronica Evans set a speed record for 50 in Manchester on 24 Dec 1931 at 25.0 sec.

Jiving

The duration record for non-stop jiving is 97 hr 42 min by Richard Rimmer (with a relay of partners) of Caterham, Surrey from 11–16 Nov 1979. Under the strict rules of the European Rock 'n' Roll Association the duration pair record is 22 hr by Mirco and Manuela Catalono in Munich on 6–7 Feb 1981.

Limbo

The lowest height for a bar (flaming) under which a limbo dancer has passed is 6¼ in *15,5 cm* off the floor by Marlene Raymond, 15, at the Port of Spain Pavilion, Toronto, Canada on 24 June 1973. Junior J. Renaud (b. 7 June 1954), Australia, became the first Official World Limbo Champion at the inaugural International Limbo Competition on 19 Feb 1974 at Port of Spain, Trinidad. The record on roller skates is 5¼ in *13,33 cm* by Tracey O'Callaghan on 2 June 1984 and Sandra Siviour on 30 Mar 1985, both at Bexley North, NSW, Australia to equal Denise Culp of Rock Hill, South Carolina on 22 Jan 1984.

Tap

The fastest *rate* ever measured for tap dancing is 1440 taps per min (24 per sec) by Roy Castle on BBC TV *Record Breakers* programme on 14 Jan 1973. On 31 Oct–1 Nov 1985 Roy achieved one million taps in 23 hr 44 min at the Guinness World of Records Exhibition, London, an average of 11.7 per second. The greatest ever assemblage of tap dancers in a single routine is 3783 outside Macy's Store in New York on 17 Aug 1986.

Tap dancing ● On tap . . . Record Breaker Roy Castle achieved one million taps in 23 hours 44 minutes at the Trocadero, London, 31 Oct–1 Nov 1985. With specially designed equipment counting taps by sound, and with just 5 minutes rest per hour, he maintained an average 11.7 taps per second over the entire period. (Photo: Julian Node)

FASHION SHOW

The longest distance covered by girl models is 71.1 miles *114,4 km* from 19–21 Sept 1983 by Roberta Brown and Lorraine McCourt at Parke's Hotel, Dublin. Male model Eddie Warke covered a further 11.9 miles *19,1 km* on the catwalk. The compère was Marty Whelan of Radio 2.

FAUX PAS

If measured by financial consequence, the greatest *faux pas* on record was that of the young multi-millionaire, James Gordon Bennett, committed on 1 Jan 1877 at the family mansion of his demure fiancée one Caroline May, in Fifth Avenue, New York. Bennett arrived in a two-horse cutter late and obviously in wine. By dint of intricate footwork, he gained the portals to enter the withdrawing room where he was the cynosure of all eyes. He mistook the fireplace for a plumbing fixture more usually reserved for another purpose. The May family broke the engagement and Bennett (1841–1918) was obliged to spend the rest of his foot-loose and fancy-free life based in Paris with the resultant non-collection of millions of tax dollars by the US Treasury.

FEMININE BEAUTY

Female pulchritude being qualitative rather than quantitative does not lend itself to records. It has been suggested that, if the face of Helen of Troy (*c.* 1200 BC) was capable of launching 1000 ships, a unit of beauty sufficient to launch one ship should be a millihelen.

The earliest international beauty contest was staged by P. T. Barnum (with the public to be the judges) in the United States in June 1855. The Miss America contest was staged at Atlantic City, New Jersey in 1921 and was won by a thin blue-eyed blonde with a 30 in *76,2 cm* chest, Margaret Gorman. The world's largest annual beauty pageants are the Miss World (inaugurated 1951) and Miss Universe (1952) contests. The most successful country in the latter contest

has been the USA with winners in 1954–56–60–67–70–80. The number of countries represented has reached 80. The United Kingdom is the only country to have produced five winners in the Miss World contest. They were Rosemarie Frankland (1961); Ann Sidney (1964); Lesley Langley (1965); Helen Morgan (1974), who resigned and Sarah-Jane Hutt (1983). The maximum number of contestants was 72 in November 1983. The shortest reign was 18 hours by Miss Germany (Gabriella Brum) in 1980.

FIRE PUMPING

The greatest gallonage stirrup-pumped by a team of 8 in an 80-hr charity pump is 17,570 gal *79 873 litres* by the York Fire Station team of the North Yorkshire Fire Brigade from 26–29 Mar 1986.

FIRE PUMP MANHANDLING

The longest unaided tow of a fire appliance in excess of 10 cwt *508 kg* in 24 hr on a closed circuit is 211 miles *339,5 km* by a 32-man team of the Dublin Fire Brigade with an 11 cwt *558,8 kg* fire pump on 18–19 June 1983.

FLUTE MARATHON

The longest recorded marathon by a flautist is 61 hr by Joseph Shury of the Sri Chinmoy Marathon Team, Toronto, Ontario, Canada from 21–23 Mar 1986.

FLYING DISC THROWING: FORMERLY FRISBEE

The World Flying Disc Federation indoor records are, men: 121,6 m *399 ft* by Van Miller at Flagstaff, Arizona on 18 Sept 1982; and women: 229.6 ft *69,9 m* by Suzanne Fields at Cedar Falls, Iowa on 26 Apr 1981. The outdoor records are, men: 166,42 m *546 ft* by Morten Sandorff, 21 May 1983, Farum, Denmark; and women: 401.5 ft *122,3 m* by Lizzie Reeve, 14 June 1980, Surrey, England. The throw, run and catch record is 83,10 m *272 ft 7 in* by Steve Bentley on 8 Apr 1982 at Sacramento, California. The group marathon record is 1198 hr by Prince George's Community College Flying High Club from 1 June–22 July 1983 (see Throwing p. 182).

FOOTBAG

The world record for keeping a footbag airborne is 36,230 consecutive kicks or hacks by Andy Linder (US) in Palatine, Illinois, USA on 24 Aug 1986. The feminine record is held by Tricia Sullivan with 12,838 on 31 July 1985 at Golden, Colorado, USA. The sport originated in Oregon, in 1972 and was invented by John Stalberger (US).

Domino toppling ● On 27 Dec 1986, 755,836 dominoes, set up to depict different parts of Holland, were toppled in Lisse. The thirty-day set-up was achieved by forty-five students from the Universities of Delft, Eindhoven and Twenty. The greatest number set up single-handed and toppled is 281,581 out of 320,236 by Klaus Friedrich, 22, in Bayern, West Germany on 27 Jan 1984. The dominoes fell within 12 min 57.3 sec having taken 31 days (10 hours daily) to set up.

GIRNING

The only girner to have won 6 national titles is Ron Looney of Egremont, Cumbria from 1979–84.

GLADIATORIAL COMBAT

Emperor Trajan of Rome (AD 98–117) staged a display involving 4941 pairs of gladiators over 117 days. Publius Ostorius, a freed-man, survived 51 combats in Pompeii.

GOLD PANNING

The fastest time for 'panning' 8 planted gold nuggets in a 10 in *25,4 cm* diameter pan is 9.23 sec by Bob Box of Ahwahnee, California, and the female record is 10.03 sec by Susan Bryeans of Fullerton, California, both in the 23rd World Gold Panning Championship on 6 Mar 1983 at Knotts Berry Farm, Buena Park, California.

GOLF BALL BALANCING

Lang Martin balanced 7 golf balls vertically without adhesive at Charlotte, North Carolina on 9 Feb 1980.

GRAPE CATCHING

The greatest distance at which a grape thrown from level ground has been caught in the mouth is 319 ft 8 in *97,43 m* by Arden Chapman at Northeast Louisiana University, Monroe on 18 July 1980.

GRAVE DIGGING

It is recorded that Johann Heinrich Karl Thieme, sexton of Aldenburg, Germany, dug 23,311 graves during a 50-year career. In 1826 his understudy dug *his* grave.

GUITAR PLAYING

The longest recorded solo guitar-playing marathon is one of 300 hours by Vincent Paxton at the Lord Nelson public house, Winterslow, Wiltshire from 23 Nov–6 Dec 1986.

GUM BOOT THROWING

The longest recorded distance for 'Wellie wanging' (size 8 Challenger Dunlop Boot) is 173 ft *52,73 m* by Tony Rodgers of Warminster, Wilts on 9 Sept 1978. Rosemary Payne established the feminine record at Cannon Hill Park, Birmingham on 21 June 1975 with 129 ft 11 in *39,60 m*.

GUN RUNNING

The record for the Royal Tournament Naval Field Gun Competition (instituted 1907, with present rules since 1913) is 2 min 40.6 sec by the Portsmouth Command Field Gun crew at Earl's Court, London on 19 July 1984. The barrel alone weighs 8 cwt *406 kg*. The wall is 5 ft *1,52 m* high and the chasm 28 ft *8,53 m* across.

HAGGIS HURLING

The longest recorded distance for throwing a haggis (min. weight 1 lb 8 oz *680 g*) is 180 ft 10 in *55,11 m* by Alan Pettigrew on Inchmurrin, Loch Lomond, Dumbartonshire on 24 May 1984.

HAIRDRESSING

Colin Watson and André Douglas each cut, set and styled hair continuously for 408 hours on 4–21 Aug 1986 in Northcliff, Transvaal, South Africa.

HAIR SPLITTING

The greatest reported achievement in hair splitting has been that of the former champion cyclist and craftsman Alfred West (1901–1985) who succeeded in splitting a human hair 17 times into 18 parts on eight occasions.

LARGEST DISH

The largest menu item in the world is roasted camel, prepared occasionally for Bedouin wedding feasts. Cooked eggs are stuffed into fish, the fish stuffed into cooked chickens, the chickens stuffed into a roasted sheep's carcass and the sheep stuffed into a whole camel.

MOST EXPENSIVE FOOD

The most expensively priced food (as opposed to spice) is First Choice Black Périgord truffle (*Tuber melanosporum*), retailed at £8.50 per 12.5 g *0.44 oz* tin. However, in January 1985 in the Hafr El-Baten market, Riyadh, Saudi Arabia local truffles sold for SR 5000 for 3 kg, equivalent to £50.16 for 12.5 g.

LONGEST BANANA SPLIT

The longest banana split ever made was one of 4.39 miles *7,06 km* in length made by the Princeton University Students, New Jersey, on 25 Apr 1987.

LARGEST BARBECUE

On 31 Jan 1981, 46,386 chicken halves supplied by Ernie Morgado were barbecued for 15,000 people at Iolani School, Honolulu, Hawaii.

At the Sertoma Club Barbecue, New Port Richey, Florida 21,112 lb *9576 kg* of beef was sold from 7–9 Mar 1986.

At the St Patrick's Irish Picnic, McEwan, Tennessee, 15,810 lb *7171 kg* of pork was sold on 25 July 1986.

LARGEST HAMBURGER

The largest hamburger on record is one of 2270,66 kg *5005 lb 13.8 oz* made on 13 Oct 1985 by Spur Steak Ranches (Pty) Ltd at Three Anchor Bay, Cape Town, South Africa. The burger had a diameter of 7,10 m *23 ft 3½ in* and was cut into over 15,750 portions after grilling.

LARGEST AND TALLEST CAKES

The largest cake ever created weighed 90,000 lb *40,82 tonnes*, included 30,000 lb *13,61 tonnes* of vanilla icing, was 110 × 80 ft *33,5 × 24,3 m* in size and was baked in 32 hours by Chef Franz Eichenauer at the City Coliseum, Austin, Texas on 20 Feb 1986. It was cut by HRH the Prince of Wales and the Governor of Texas, Mark White Jr. The tallest recorded free-standing cake is one of 71 tiers, 45 ft 5 in *13,84 m* completed by the management and staff of the Hyatt Central Plaza Bangkok Hotel, Thailand on 12 Sept 1985.

LARGEST CHEESE

The largest cheese ever made was a cheddar of 34,591 lb *15 190 kg* made in 43 hr from 20–22 Jan 1964 by the Wisconsin Cheese Foundation for exhibition at the New York World's Fair, USA. It was transported in a specially designed tractor trailer, 'Cheese Mobile', 45 ft *13,71 m* long.

LARGEST CHRISTMAS PUDDING

One of 617 lb *279,8 kg* was made for charity at Burton-on-Trent, Staffordshire on 14 Dec 1985.

LARGEST CHOCOLATE

The largest chocolate model was one measuring 10 × 5 m *32 ft 9½ in × 16 ft 4⅞ in* and 73 cm *28.7 in* high of the 1992 Olympic Centre, Barcelona by Gremi Provincial de Pastigeria i Confiteria School in November 1985.

HEAVIEST AND TALLEST EASTER EGGS

The heaviest Easter egg ever made was one weighing 3430 kg *7561 lb 13½ oz*, measuring 10 ft *3,04 m* high, by Siegfried Berndt at 'Macopa' Patisserie, Leicester and completed on 7 Apr 1982. An egg 5,78 m *18 ft 11½ in* tall was constructed by Tobler Suchard of Bedford, on 10 Apr 1987.

LARGEST HAGGIS

The largest haggis (encased in 8 ox stomach linings) on record was one weighing 603 lb *273,5 kg* made for the ASDA Superstore, Corby, Northants by David A. Hall Ltd. of Broxburn, Lothian, Scotland on 6 Nov 1986.

LARGEST JELLY

The world's largest jelly, a 35 000 litre *7700 gal* water melon flavoured pink jelly made by Paul Squires and Geoff Ross worth $14,000, was set at Roma Street Forum, Brisbane, Qld on 5 Feb 1981 in a tank by Pool Fab.

LONGEST LOAF

The longest loaf ever baked was a rosca de Reyes 649,90 m *2132 ft 2¾ ins* in length and 1173 kg *1.15 tons* in weight at the Exelaris Hyatt Regency Hotel, Acapulco, Mexico on 6 Jan 1985. If a consumer of the rosca (twisted loaf) finds the embedded bread doll he has to throw the next rosca party.

The longest pan loaf baked was one of 3051 lb 4 oz *138,46 kg* measuring 9 ft × 5 ft *2.7 m × 1.5 m* by the Calgary Italian Bakery and Southern Alberta Bakers' Association on 7 July 1986 at Calgary, Alberta.

LARGEST APPLE PIE

The largest apple pie ever baked was that by ITV chef Glynn Christian in a 40 ft × 23 ft *12 m × 7 m* dish at Hewitts Farm, Chelsfield, Kent from 25–27 Aug 1982. Over 600 bushels of apples were included in the pie which weighed 30,115 lb *13,66 tonnes*. It was cut by Rear Admiral Sir John Woodward.

LARGEST CUSTARD PIE

The largest custard pie made was one of 448 lb *203,2 kg* made in the kitchen of Jury's Hotel, Dublin under the supervision of Derek McLoughlin and John Clancy on 6 Feb 1987.

LARGEST CHERRY PIE

The largest cherry pie ever made was one weighing a total of 6¼ tons *6350 kg* and containing 4950 lb *2245 kg* of cherries. It measured 14 ft 4 in *4,36 m* in diameter, 24 in *60,96 cm* in depth, and was baked in the grounds of the Medusa Cement Corporation, Charlevoix, Michigan on 15 May 1976, as part of the town's contribution to America's Bicentennial celebrations.

LARGEST MEAT PIE

The largest ever made was 'The Chuck Wagon Gang's Chili Meat Pie', which weighed 13,362.9 lb *6061 kg*, on 17 Oct 1986 at Odessa, Texas. It was baked in a half cylinder 20 ft *6 m* long 4 ft *1,2 m* in diameter and had a 2000 lb *907 kg* crust.

Britain's largest meat pie weighed 5¾ tons and measured 18 × 6 ft 18 in deep *5,48 × 1,83 × 0,45 m*. Baked on 5 Sept 1964 to mark four royal births, it was the eighth in the series of Denby Dale, West Yorkshire pies. The first was in 1788 to celebrate King George III's return to sanity, but the fourth (Queen Victoria's Jubilee, 1887) went a bit 'off' and had to be buried in quick-lime.

LARGEST MINCE PIE

The largest mince pie recorded was one of 2260 lb *1025 kg* 20 × 5 ft *6,09 × 1,52 m*, baked at Ashby-de-la-Zouch, Leicestershire on 15 Oct 1932.

LARGEST OMELETTE

The largest omelette in the world was one made of 54,763 eggs with 531 lb *240 kg* cheese in a skillet 30 ft *9,1 m* in diameter cooked by Michael McGowan assisted by his staff and the Sunrise Jaycees of Las Vegas, Nevada on 25 Oct 1986.

LARGEST PANCAKE

The largest pancake, of 25 ft *7,62 m* diameter 1 in *25,4 mm* thick weighing 3727 lb *1690 kg* containing 5274 eggs, 92 gal *418 l* of milk, 165 lb *74,8 kg* of cornflour and 14 gal *636 l* of oil, was cooked by Derry Lynch and Dennis Thornton, assisted by Nick Cotterell at Cheltenham, Gloucs on 3 March 1987.

LONGEST PASTRY

The longest pastry in the world was the 'record' pastry 513,04 m *1683 ft 2½ in* in length made by chefs at the Hyatt Regency Ravinia, Atlanta, Georgia, USA on 26 July 1986.

LARGEST PIZZA PIE

The largest pizza ever baked was one measuring 26,4 m *86 ft 7 in* in diameter, hence 547 m² *5895 ft²* in area, completed by Marco Cagnazzo at Norwood Hypermarket, Johannesburg, South Africa on 31 Mar 1984.

LARGEST MILK SHAKE

The largest milk shake was one of 50 gal *227,3 l* containing 200 lb of vanilla ice cream, 25 gal of milk and 5 lb vanilla syrup, made by members of Uptown Mt Lebanon and Haagen Dazs-Pittsburg on 4 July 1986 at Mt Lebanon, Pennsylvania.

LARGEST POTATO CRISPS

Charles Chip Inc of Mountville, Pennsylvania, produced crisps 4 × 7 in *10 × 17,5 cm* from outsize potatoes in February 1977.

POTATO MASH

A single serving of 18,260 lb *8,26 tonnes* of potato mash was prepared in a concrete mixer for the 17th Annual Potato Bowl at Grand Forks, North Dakota, USA on 4 Sept 1982.

LARGEST ICED LOLLIPOP

The world's largest iced lollipop was one of 5750 lb *2608 kg* constructed for the Westside Assembly of God Church, Davenport, Iowa on 7 Sept 1975. The largest 'regular' lollipop was one of 2,052.5 lb *931 kg* (720 lb of sugar and 1,452 lb of corn syrup) made at the Hyatt Regency Memphis Hotel, Tennessee on 20 Feb 1986.

LARGEST PAELLA

The largest paella ever made was one with a diameter of 10 m *32 ft 9 in* and a depth of 45 cm *1 ft 5¾ in* cooked in the Plaza de Catalunya, Cornella de Llobregat, Barcelona, Spain on 24 June 1984 for 15,000 people. It included 750 kg *1650 lb* of meat and 300 kg *660 lb* of pimientos.

STICK OF ROCK

The mightiest piece was a stick weighing more than 673.5 lb *305,5 kg*, 12 ft *3,6 m* long and 16 in *40,6 cm* thick made by Carshalton Confectionery Company of Lancashire on 21 May 1987.

LONGEST SALAMI

The longest salami on record was one 17,9 m *58 ft 9 in* long with a circumference of 52,7 cm *20⅔ in*, weighing 391,6 kg *863.5 lb*, made by Kutztown Bologna Company, Pennsylvania on 21 August 1986.

LONGEST SAUSAGE

The longest continuous sausage ever made was one of 8.856 miles *14,25 km* weighing 17,484 lb *7930.62 kg* by M & M Meat Shops of Kitchener, Ontario on 23 Sept 1983.

LARGEST SMÖRGÅSTÅRTA

On 9 Mar 1985 in Köping, Sweden a *smör*-(butter) *gås*-(goose) *tårta*(cake) 510,69 m *1675 ft 6 in* long was set up by Hans Pettersson and a team. It was demolished in short order.

STRAWBERRY BOWL

The largest bowl of strawberries, with a net weight of 860 lb *390 kg*, was weighed on 29 Apr 1986 at Parkland High School, Sidney, British Columbia.

LARGEST SUNDAE

The largest ice cream sundae was one weighing 33,616.75 lb *15 248,32 kg* made by the Knudsen Corp of Los Angeles and Smucker's at Ohio at Disneyland Hotel in Anaheim, California, on 28 July 1985. It consisted of 26,020 lb of ice-cream, 7,521.75 lb of topping and 75 lb *34,02 kg* of whipped cream.

Largest Yorkshire pudding ● The largest was one measuring 166 ft² *15,42 m²* made by staff of the Guide Post Hotel, Bradford, Yorks with 50 dozen eggs, 140 lb *63,50 kg* of flour and 186 pints *105,7 l* of milk on 17 Aug 1986.

TOP-SELLING SWEET

The world's top-selling sweets (candies) are Life Savers with 33,431,236,300 rolls between 1913 and May 1987. A tunnel formed by the holes in the middle placed end to end would stretch to the Moon and back more than 3 times. Thomas Syta of Van Nuys, California made one last 7 hr 10 min (with hole intact) on 15 Jan 1983.

MOST EXPENSIVE SPICE

Prices for wild ginseng (root of *Panax quinquefolius*), from the Chan Pak Mountain area of China, thought to have aphrodisiac qualities, were reported in November 1977 to be as high as $23,000 (*then £10,454*) per ounce in Hong Kong. Total annual shipments from Jilin Province do not exceed 4 kg *140 oz* a year. A leading medical journal in the USA has likened its effects to 'corticosteroid poisoning'.

HOTTEST SPICE

The hottest of all spices is claimed to be Siling labuyo from the Philippines.

The chili pepper or capsicum known as Tepin, of south-west USA comes in pods ⅜ in *7 mm* in diameter. A single dried gram will produce detectable 'heat' in 68.3 lb *31 kg* of bland sauce.

MOST EXPENSIVE FRUIT

On 5 Apr 1977 John Synnott of Ashford, County Wicklow, Ireland sold 1 lb *453 g* of strawberries (a punnet of 30 berries) to the restaurateur Leslie Cooke, at auction by Walter L. Cole Ltd in the Dublin Fruit Market, for £530 or £17.70 a berry.

RAREST CONDIMENT

The world's most prized condiment is Cà Cuong, a secretion recovered in minute amounts from beetles in North Vietnam. Owing to war conditions, the price had risen to $100 (*now £57*) per ounce *28 g* before supplies virtually ceased in 1975.

LARGEST TRIFLE

The largest sherry trifle on record was one weighing 300 lb *136 kg* including 11 gallons *50 l* of sherry organised by Mrs Judy Fraser for St Andrew's Hospice, Cleethorpes, Humberside on 19 Aug 1984.

Gluttony Records

Records for eating and drinking by trenchermen do not match those suffering from the rare disease of bulimia (morbid desire to eat) and polydipsia (pathological thirst). Some bulimics exceed 20,000 calories a day and others eat all their waking hours. An extreme consumption of 384 lb 2 oz *174,236 kg* in six days by Matthew Daking, 12 (known as Mortimer's case), was reported in 1743. Fannie Meyer of Johannesburg, after a skull fracture, was stated in 1974 to be unsatisfied by less than 160 pints of water a day. By October 1978 he was down to 52 pints. Miss Helge Andersson (b. 1908) of Lindesberg, Sweden was reported in January 1971 to have drunk 40 pints *22,73 litres* of water a day since 1922—a total of 87,600 gal *3982 hectolitres*.

The world's greatest trencherman has been Edward Abraham ('Bozo') Miller (b. 1909) of Oakland, California. He consumes up to 25,000 calories per day or more than 11 times that recommended. He stands 5 ft 7½ in *1,71 m* tall but weighs from 20 to 21¼ st *127–139 kg* with a 57 in *144 cm* waist. He had been undefeated in eating contests since 1931 (see below). He ate 27 (2 lb *907 g*) pullets at a sitting in Trader Vic's, San Francisco in 1963. Phillip Yadzik (b. 1912) of Chicago in 1955 ate 77 large hamburgers in 2 hours and in 1957 101 bananas in 15 min. The bargees on the Rhine are reputed to be the world's heaviest eaters with 5200 calories a day. However, the New Zealand Sports Federation of Medicine reported in December 1972 that a long-distance road runner consumed 14,321 calories in 24 hr.

While no healthy person has been reported to have succumbed in any contest for eating non-toxic food or drinking non-alcoholic drinks, such attempts, from a medical point of view, must be regarded as *extremely* inadvisable, particularly among young people. Gluttony record attempts should aim at improving the *rate* of consumption rather than the volume. The *Guinness Book of Records* will not list any records involving the consumption of more than 2 litres *3.52 imperial pints* of beer nor any at all involving spirits. Nor will records for such potentially dangerous categories as live ants, chewing gum, marsh mallow or raw eggs with shells be published. The ultimate in stupidity—the eating of a bicycle—has however been recorded since it is unlikely to attract competition. (see Omnivore p. 175)

Liquidising, processing or puréeing foodstuffs is not permitted. However, drinking during attempts is permissible.

Records have been claimed as follows:

BAKED BEANS

2780 cold baked beans one by one with a cocktail stick in 30 min by Karen Stevenson, of Wallasey, Merseyside on 4 Apr 1981.

BANANAS

17 (edible weight minimum 4½ oz *128 g* each) in 2 min by Dr Ronald L. Alkana at the University of California, Irvine on 7 Dec 1973.

BEER

Steven Petrosino drank one litre of beer in 1.3 sec on 22 June 1977 at The Gingerbreadman, Carlisle, Pennsylvania. Peter G. Dowdeswell (b. London 29 July 1940) of Earls Barton, Northants holds the following records:
2 pints—2.3 sec Zetters Social Club, Wolverton, Bucks, 11 June 1975.
2 litres—6.0 sec Carriage Horse Hotel, Higham Ferrers, Northants, 7 Feb 1975.
Yards of Ale
2½ pints—5.0 sec RAF Upper Heyford, Oxfordshire, 4 May 1975.
3 pints—5.0 sec Royal Oak, Bishops Cleeve, Gloucestershire, 6 July 1985.
3½ pints—4.49 sec Silver Stadium, Rochester, New York, 19 June 1986.
Upside-down
2 pints—6.4 sec Top Rank Club, Northampton, 25 May 1975.

CHAMPAGNE

1000 bottles per annum by Bobby Acland of the Black Raven, Bishopsgate, City of London.

CHEESE

16 oz *453 g* of Cheddar in 1 min 13 sec by Peter Dowdeswell in Earls Barton, Northants on 14 July 1978.

CHICKEN

2.1 kg *4 lb 10 oz* in 10 min 37 sec by Valentin Florentino Muñoz Muñoz at Kortezubi, Vizcaya, Spain on 27 Apr 1986.
Sean Barry ate 3 lb 12 oz *1,7 kg* of chicken in 8 min 5 sec at the Royal Oak, Bishops Cleeve, Cheltenham, Gloucestershire on 5 July 1986.

CLAMS

424 (Littlenecks) in 8 min by Dave Barnes at Port Townsend Bay, Washington, USA on 3 May 1975.

COCKLES

2 pints *113,5 centilitres* in 60.8 sec by Tony Dowdeswell at Kilmarnock, Ayrshire on 1 June 1984.

DOUGHNUTS

12¾ (51 oz *1,445 kg*) in 5 min 46 sec by James Wirth, and 13 (52 oz *1,474 kg*) in 6 min 1.5 sec by John Haight, both at the Sheraton Inn, Canandaigua, New York on 3 Mar 1981.

EELS

1 lb *453 g* of elvers in 13.7 sec by Peter Dowdeswell at Reeves Club, Bristol on 20 Oct 1978.

EGGS

(Hard Boiled) 14 in 14.42 sec by John Kenmuir on Scottish Television's *Live at 1.30* programme on 17 Apr 1987.
(Soft Boiled) 38 in 75 sec by Peter Dowdeswell in Kilmarnock, Ayrshire on 28 May 1984.
(Raw) 13 in 1.0 sec by Peter Dowdeswell at Kilmarnock, Ayrshire on 16 May 1984.

FRANKFURTERS

23 (2 oz *56,6 g*) in 3 min 10 sec by Lynda Kuerth, 21, at the Veterans Stadium, Philadelphia, on 12 July 1977.

GHERKINS

1 lb *453 g* in 41.60 sec by Peter Dowdeswell at Ronelles Discotheque on 8 Feb 1986.

GRAPES

3 lb 1 oz of grapes in 34.6 sec by Jim Ellis of Montrose, Michigan on 30 May 1976.

HAGGIS

24 oz *680 g* in 31.94 sec by John Kenmuir at the Bully Inn, near Hamilton, Lanarkshire on 30 Nov 1986.

HAMBURGERS

21 hamburgers (each weighing 3½ oz *100 g* totalling *2,07 kg* of meat) and buns in 9 min 42 sec by Peter Dowdeswell at Cockshut Hill School, Yardley, Birmingham on 30 June 1984.

ICE CREAM

3 lb 6 oz *1,530 kg* in 31.67 sec by Tony Dowdeswell at the Guinness Museum of World Records, New York on 16 July 1986. The ice cream must be unmelted.

JELLY

20 fl oz *56,8 centilitres* in 8.25 sec by Peter Dowdeswell at the Royal Oak, Bishops Cleeve, Gloucestershire on 5 July 1986. The jelly must be gelatinous.

KIPPERS

27 (self-filleted) in 24 min 11 sec by Peter McPhee at Livingstone, West Lothian, Scotland on 12 July 1986.

LEMONS

12 quarters (3 lemons) whole (including skin and pips) in 15.3 sec by Bobby Kempf of Roanoke, Virginia on 2 May 1979.

MEAT

One whole roast ox in 42 days by Johann Ketzler of Munich, Germany in 1880.

MEAT PIES

22 (each weighing 5½ oz *156 g*) in 18 min 13 sec by Peter Dowdeswell at the Bell Inn, Ilmington on 9 Dec 1978.

MILK
2 pt (1 imperial quart or *113,5 centilitres*) in 3.2 sec by Peter Dowdeswell at Dudley Top Rank Club, West Midlands on 31 May 1975.

OYSTERS (*Eating, Opening*)
6 lb *2,72 kg* (edible mass of 288) in 1 min 33 sec by Tommy Greene in Annapolis, Maryland on 6 July 1985. The record for opening oysters is 100 in 2 min 42.74 sec by Mike Racz in Invercargill, New Zealand on 25 June 1986.

PANCAKES
(6 inch *15,2 cm* diameter buttered and with syrup) 62 in 6 min 58.5 sec by Peter Dowdeswell at The Drapery, Northampton on 9 Feb 1977.

PEANUTS
100 (whole unshelled) singly in 46 sec by Jim Kornitzer, 21, at Brighton, East Sussex on 1 Aug 1979.

PEAS
7175 petit pois one by one in 60 min using chopsticks by Mrs Janet Harris, Seal Hotel, Selsey, West Sussex on 16 Aug 1984.

PICKLED ONIONS
91 pickled onions (total weight 30 oz *850 g*) in 1 min 8 sec by Pat Donahue in Victoria, British Columbia on 9 Mar 1978.

PIZZA
825 g *1.8 lb* in 5 min 23 sec by Geir Storvann of Drammen, Norway on 24 Aug 1984 at Karl Johans Gate, Oslo.

POTATOES
3 lb *1,36 kg* in 1 min 22 sec by Peter Dowdeswell in Earls Barton, Northants on 25 Aug 1978.

POTATO CRISPS
Thirty 2 oz *56,6 g* bags in 24 min 33.6 sec, without a drink, by Paul G. Tully of Brisbane University in May 1969.

PRUNES
144 in 31.27 sec by Peter Dowdeswell at Silver Stadium, Rochester, New York, USA on 20 June 1986.

RAVIOLI
5 lb *2,25 kg* (170 squares) in 5 min 34 sec by Peter Dowdeswell at Pleasurewood Hills American Theme Park, Lowestoft, Suffolk on 25 Sept 1983.

SANDWICHES
40 in 17 min 53.9 sec (Jam 'butties' 6 × 3¾ × ½ in *15,2 × 9,5 × 1,2 cm*) by Peter Dowdeswell on 17 Oct 1977 at The Donut Shop, Reedley, California.

SAUSAGE MEAT
2630 g *5 lb 12¾ oz* (96 pieces) in 4 min 29 sec by Peter Dowdeswell on Fuji TV, Tokyo on 24 Feb 1985. No 'Hot Dog' contest results have been remotely comparable.

SHEEP'S BRAINS
1,16 kg *2.55 lb* by William Michael Burke at Balmain, NSW, Australia on 10 Nov 1986.

SHRIMPS
3 lb *1,36 kg* in 3 min 10 sec by Peter Dowdeswell at Weymouth, Dorset on 7 Aug 1985.

SNAILS
1,1 kg *38.8 oz* in 1 min 5.6 sec by Andoni Basterrechea Dominguez at Kortezubi, Vizcaya, Spain on 27 Apr 1986.

SPAGHETTI
100 yd *91,44 m* in 12.02 sec by Peter Dowdeswell at 42nd St Disco, Halesowen, West Midlands on 3 July 1986.

STRAWBERRIES
2 lb *907 g* in 12.95 sec by Peter Dowdeswell at Easby Street, Nottingham on 5 July 1985.

SUSHI
680 g *1½ lb* of nigiri-sushi in 1 min 13.5 sec in Tokyo, Japan by Peter Dowdeswell on 22 February 1985.

TORTILLA
74 (total weight 4 lb 1½ oz *1,85 kg*) in 30 min by Tom Nall in the 2nd World Championship at Mariano's Mexican Restaurant, Dallas, Texas on 16 Oct 1973.

WHELKS
100 (unshelled) in 5 min 17 sec by John Fletcher at The Apples and Pears public house, Liverpool Street Station, London on 18 Aug 1983.

WINKLING
50 shells picked (with a straight pin) in 3 min 15 sec by Mrs B. Charles at Eastbourne, East Sussex on 4 Aug 1982.

GREATEST OMNIVORE
Michel Lotito (b. 15 June 1950) of Grenoble, France, known as Monsieur Mangetout, has been eating metal and glass since 1959. Gastroenterologists have X-rayed his stomach and have described his ability to consume 2 lb *900 g* of metal per day as unique. His diet since 1966 has included 10 bicycles, a supermarket trolley in 4½ days, 7 TV sets, 6 chandeliers and a low-calorie Cessna light aircraft which he ate in Caracas, Venezuela. He is said to have provided the only example in history of a coffin (handles and all) ending up inside a man.

HANDBELL RINGING

The longest recorded handbell-ringing recital has been one of 56 hr 3 min by 12 handbell ringers of Ecclesfield School, Sheffield from 21–23 July 1985.

HANDSHAKING

A world record for handshaking was set up by President Theodore Roosevelt (1858–1919) when he shook hands with 8513 people at a New Year's Day White House presentation in Washington, DC, USA on 1 Jan 1907. Disc jockey Mike Butts of Ogden, Utah shook 16,615 different hands in 7 hr 25 min in the 'Shake a Hand, Help a Neighbor' campaign on 3 Oct 1986 in Salt Lake City.

Many record claims have been rendered meaningless because aspirants merely tend to arrange circular queues or wittingly or unwittingly shake the same hands repetitively.

HEDGE LAYING

John Williams of Sennybridge, Brecon and David James of Llanwern, Brecon hedged by the 'stake and pleach' method a total of 264 yd *241,4 m* in 11 hr 24 min.

HIGH DIVING

The highest regularly performed head first dives are those of professional divers from La Quebrada ('the break in the rocks') at Acapulco, Mexico, a height of 87½ ft *26,7 m*. The leader of the 27 divers in the Club de Clavadistas is Raul Garcia (b. 1928) with more than 35,000 dives. The first feminine accomplishment was by Mrs Barbara Winters (b. 12 Nov 1953), *née* Mayer, on 7 Dec 1976. The base rocks, 21 ft *6,40 m* out from the take-off, necessitate a leap of 27 ft *8,22 m* out. The water is 12 ft *3,65 m* deep.

The world record high dive is 174 ft 8 in *53,23 m* by Randal Dickison (US) at Ocean Park, Hong Kong on 6 Apr 1985. The feminine record is 120 ft *36,57 m* by Lucy Wardle (US) at the same exhibition. The highest witnessed in Britain is one of 108 ft *32,9 m* into 8 ft *2,43 m* of water at the Aqua Show at Earl's Court, London on 22 Feb 1946 by Roy Fransen (1915–85).

On 8 May 1885, Sarah Ann Henley, 24, jumped from the Clifton Suspension Bridge, which crosses the Avon, England. Her 250 ft *76 m* fall was slightly cushioned by her voluminous dress and petticoat acting as a parachute. She landed, bruised and bedraggled, in the mud on the north bank and was carried to hospital by four policemen. On 11 Feb 1968 Jeffrey Kramer, 24, leapt off the George Washington Bridge 250 ft *76 m* above the Hudson River, New York, and survived. Of the 696 (to 1 Jan 1980) identified people who have made 240 ft *73 m* suicide dives from the Golden Gate Bridge, San Francisco, California, USA since 1937, twelve survived of whom Todd Sharratt, 17, was the only one who managed to swim ashore unaided.

Col Harry A. Froboess (Switzerland) jumped 110 m *360 ft* into the Bodensee from the airship *Graf Hindenburg* on 22 June 1936.

The greatest height reported for a dive into an air bag is 326 ft *99,36 m* by stuntman Dan Koko from the top of Vegas World Hotel and Casino into a 20 × 40 × 14 ft *6,1 × 12,2 × 4,2 m* target on 13 Aug 1984. His impact speed was 88 mph *141 km/h*. Kitty O'Neill dived 180 ft *54,8 m* from a helicopter over Northridge, California on 9 Sept 1979 onto an air cushion measuring 30 × 60 ft *9,14 × 18,28 m* for a TV film stunt.

HIGHEST SHALLOW DIVE

Henri La Mothe (b. 1904) set a record diving 28 ft *8,53 m* into 12⅜ in *31,43 cm* of water in a child's paddling pool in Northridge, California, on 7 Apr 1979. He struck the water chest first at a speed of 28.4 mph *45,7 km/h*.

HIGH-WIRE ACT

The greatest height above street level of any high wire performance has been a 140 ft *42,6 m* long wire between the 1350 ft *411 m* tall twin towers of the World Trade Center, New York by Philippe Petit, 24, of Nemours, France on 7 Aug 1974. He was charged with criminal trespass after a 75 min display of at least 7 crossings. The police psychiatrist opined 'Anyone who does this 110 storeys up can't be entirely right.'

Tree eating ● In an 'Outrageous Contest' organised by WKQX Chicago from 11–15 Sept 1980, Jay Gwaltney, 19, ate a birch tree that was 11 ft *3,35 m* in length and had a 4.7 in *12 cm* diameter trunk. It took him 89 hours.

HITCH-HIKING

The title of world champion hitch-hiker is claimed by Bill Heid of Allen Park, Michigan who from 1964 to 1985 obtained free rides of 305,870 miles *492,248 km*. Stephen Burns of Melbourne, Australia hitched round all 48 co-terminuous states of the USA in 26 days 6 hr in an 11,438 mile *18,407 km* trip in 56 vehicles from 8 Sept–4 Oct 1984. The hitch-hiking record for the 874 miles *1406 km* from Land's End, Cornwall, to John O'Groats, Caithness, Scotland, is 17 hr 50 min by Andrew Markham of Brigg, South Humberside on 3–4 Sept 1979. The time before the first 'hitch' on the first day is excluded. The fastest time recorded for the round trip is 41 hr 42 min by Anthony D. Sproson of Wolverhampton on 17–19 Sept 1984.

HOD CARRYING

Jim Ford of Bury, Lancs carried bricks totalling 355 lb *161 kg* up the minimum 12 foot *3,65 m* ladder (17 rungs) on 28 June 1984 at Hever Castle, Kent on the International Guinness TV Show presented by David Frost. Eric Stenman of Jakobstad, Finland carried 74 bricks of 4 kg

8.8 lb each so totalling 651 lb *296 kg* in a 4 kg 8.8 lb hod 5 metres *16.4 ft* on the flat before ascending a runged ramp to a height of 7 ft *2,13 m* on 25 July 1939.

HOOP ROLLING

In 1968 it was reported that Zolilio Diaz (Spain) had rolled a hoop 600 miles *965 km* from Mieres to Madrid and back in 18 days.

HOP-SCOTCH

The longest recorded hop-scotch marathon is one of 101 hr 15 min by Mark Harrison and Tony Lunn at the Studio Night Club, Leicester from 30 Sept–4 Oct 1985.

HOUSE OF CARDS

The greatest number of storeys achieved in building freestanding houses of standard playing cards is 68 to a height of 12 ft 10 in *3,9 m* built by John Sain, 15, of South Bend, Indiana in May 1984.

HULA HOOPING

The highest claim for sustaining gyrating hoops between shoulders and hips is 81 by William Kleeman 'Chico' Johnson (b. 8 July 1939) on BBC TV's *Record Breakers* on 18 Sept 1983. Three complete gyrations are mandatory. The feminine record is 70 by Luisa Valencia (US) in Las Vegas, Nevada in May 1987. The longest marathon for a single hoop is 90 hours by Roxann Rose of Pullman, Washington from 2–6 Apr 1987.

HUMAN CANNONBALL

The first human cannonball was Emilio Onra *né* Maitrejean at Cirque d'Hiver, Paris on 21 Nov 1875. The record distance for firing a human from a cannon is 175 ft *53,3 m* in the case of Emanuel Zacchini, son of the pioneer Hugo Zacchini in the Ringling Bros and Barnum & Bailey Circus, Madison Square Gardens, New York in 1940. His muzzle velocity has been estimated at 54 mph *86,9 km/h.* On his retirement the management were fortunate in finding that his daughter Florinda was of the same calibre. An experiment on Yorkshire TV on 17 Aug 1978 showed that when Miss Sue Evans, 17, was fired she was ⅜ in *9,5 mm* shorter on landing.

HUMAN FLY

The longest climb achieved on the vertical face of a building occurred in August 1986 when Daniel Goodwin, 30, of California scaled the outside of the 1822 ft *555,33 m* CN Tower in Toronto using neither climbing aids nor safety equipment. Lead climber Jean-Claude Droyer (b. 8 May 1946) of Paris and Pierre Puiseux (b. 2 Dec 1953) of Pau, France climbed up the outside of the Eiffel Tower to a height of 300 m *984 ft* with no dynamic mechanical assistance on 21 July 1980. Jean-Claude took 2 hr 18 min 15 sec to complete the climb.

Jaromir Wagner (b. Czechoslovakia 1941) became the first man to fly the Atlantic standing on the wing of an aircraft. He took off from Aberdeen, Scotland on 28 Sept 1980.

JOKE CRACKING

T. R. (Tim) Benker of Chicago told jokes unremittingly for 48 hr 30 min in the window of the Marshall Field store, Chicago, Illinois, USA, from 17–19 Nov 1985. The duo record is 52 hr by Wayne Malton and Mike Hamilton at the Howard Johnson Motor Hotel, Toronto airport, Ontario, Canada on 13–16 Nov 1975.

JUMBLE SALE

Britain's largest jumble sale was 'Jumbly '79' organised by Woman's Own at Alexandra

Palace, London from 5–7 May 1979 in aid of the Save The Children Fund. The attendance was 60,000 and the gross takings in excess of £60,000. The Winnetka Congregational Church, Illinois raised $147,378.74 (*£98,253*) in their 54th one-day rummage sale on 8 May 1986.

The Cleveland Convention Center, Ohio, White Elephant Sale (inst. 1933) on 18–19 Oct 1983 raised $427,935.21 (*then £305,668*).

KISS OF LIFE

Five members of the St John Ambulance NSW District at Pier One, Sydney maintained a 'Kiss of Life' for 315 hr with 232,150 inflations from 27 Aug–9 Sept 1984. The 'patient' was a dummy. Robert Stanbary and Wyatt Pace completed a 53-hour CPR (cardiopulmonary resuscitation—15 compressions alternating with 2 breaths) between 27–29 Sept 1985 at Eastland Mall, Bloomington, Illinois.

KISSING

The most prolonged osculatory marathon in cinematic history is one of 185 sec by Regis Toomey and Jane Wyman (born Sarah Jane Faulks 4 Jan 1914, later Mrs Ronald Reagan) in *You're In the Army Now* released in 1940. Eddie Levin and Delphine Crha celebrated the breaking of the record for the longest ever kiss of 17 days 10¼ hr in Chicago on 24 Sept 1984 with a kiss. John McPherson kissed 4444 women in 8 hr in Eldon Square, Newcastle-upon-Tyne on 8 Mar 1985, a rate of 1 each 6.48 sec. The most protracted kiss underwater was one of 2 min 18 sec by Toshiaki Shirai and Yukiko Nagata on Channel 8, Fuji TV in Tokyo on 2 Apr 1980.

KITE FLYING

The largest kite flown was the Thai Snake flown by Herman van den Broek and Jan Pieter Kuil for 22 min 50 sec at Uithuizen, Netherlands on 11 Aug 1984. It measured 650 m *2133 ft* in length, with an area of 770 m² *8288ft².*

The most kites flown on a single line is 7150 by Sadao Harada, 69, at Kagoshima, Japan on 27 Apr 1987.

The classic record height is 9740 m *31,955 ft* by a chain of 8 kites over Lindenberg, Germany on 1 Aug 1919. The record for a single kite is 22,500 ft (min)–28,000 ft (max) *6860–8530 m* by Prof Philip R. and Jay P. Kunz of Laramie, Wyoming on 21 Nov 1967. *Kite Lines* magazine of Baltimore, Maryland does not accept triangulation by line angle and length but only range-finder sightings or radar.

The longest recorded flight is one of 180 hr 17 min by the Edmonds Community College team at Long Beach, Washington from 21–29 Aug 1982. Managing the flight of the J-25 parafoil was Harry N. Osborne.

KNITTING

The world's most prolific hand-knitter of all time has been Mrs Gwen Matthewman of Featherstone, West Yorkshire. She attained a speed of 111 stitches per min in a test at Phildar's Wool Shop, Central Street, Leeds on 29 Sept 1980. Her technique has been filmed by the world's only Professor of Knitting—a Japanese.

The Exeter Spinners—Audrey Felton, Christine Heap, Eileen Lancaster, Marjorie Mellis, Ann Sandercock and Maria Scott produced a jumper by hand from raw fleece in 1 hr 55 min 50.2 sec on 25 Sept 1983 at BBC Television Centre, London.

KNOT-TYING

The fastest recorded time for tying the six Boy Scout Handbook Knots (square knot, sheet bend, sheep shank, clove hitch, round turn and two

half hitches and bowline) on individual ropes is 8.1 sec by Clinton R. Bailey Sr, 52, of Pacific City, Oregon on 13 Apr 1977.

LEAP FROGGING

Fourteen members of the Phi Gamma Delta Club at the University of Washington, Seattle covered 602 miles *968,8 km* in 114 hr 46 min from 20–25 Mar 1983. (Total leaps 108,463—one every 9.77 yd.)

LIFE SAVING

In November 1974 the city of Galveston, Texas and the Noon Optimist Club unveiled a plaque to deaf-mute lifeguard Leroy Colombo (1905–74) who saved 907 people from drowning in the waters around Galveston Island from 1917 to his death.

LIGHTNING MOST TIMES STRUCK

The only man in the world to be struck by lightning 7 times is ex-park ranger Roy C. Sullivan (US) the human lightning conductor of Virginia. His attraction for lightning began in 1942 (lost big toe nail), and was resumed in July 1969 (lost eyebrows), in July 1970 (left shoulder seared), on 16 Apr 1972 (hair set on fire), on 7 Aug 1973 (new hair refired and legs seared), on 5 June 1976 (ankle injured), and sent to Waynesboro Hospital with chest and stomach burns on 25 June 1977 after being struck while fishing. In September 1983 he died by his own hand, reportedly rejected in love.

LION-TAMING

The greatest number of lions mastered and fed in a cage by an unaided lion-tamer was 40, by 'Captain' Alfred Schneider in 1925. Clyde Raymond Beatty handled more than 40 'cats' (mixed lions and tigers) simultaneously. Beatty (b. Bainbridge, Ohio, 10 June 1903, d. Ventura, California, USA, 19 July 1965) was the featured attraction at every show he appeared with for more than 40 years. He insisted upon being called a lion-trainer. More than 20 lion-tamers have died of injuries since 1900.

LOG ROLLING

The record number of International Championship wins is 10 by Jubiel Wickheim (of Shawnigan Lake, British Columbia, Canada) between 1956 and 1969. At Albany, Oregon on 4 July 1956 Wickheim rolled on a 14 in *35,5 cm* log against Chuck Harris of Kelso, Washington, USA for 2 hr 40 min before losing. The youngest international log-rolling champion is Cari Ann Hayer (b. 23 June 1977), who won her first championship on 15 July 1984 at Hayward, Wisconsin.

MAGICIAN MOST VERSATILE

Under the surveillance of four representatives of the International Brotherhood of Magicians, Paul Ricksecker performed 63 separate tricks in 4 min at the 56th Annual Magi-Fest, Columbus, Ohio on 5 Feb 1987.

MERRY-GO-ROUND

The longest merry-go-round marathon on record is one of 312 hr 43 min by Gary Mandau, Chris Lyons and Dana Dover in Portland, Oregon, USA from 20 Aug–2 Sept 1976.

MESSAGE IN A BOTTLE

The longest recorded interval between drop and pick-up is 72 years in the case of a message thrown from the SS *Arawatta* out of Cairns, Queensland on 9 June 1910 in a lotion bottle and reported to be found on Moreton Island on 6 June 1983.

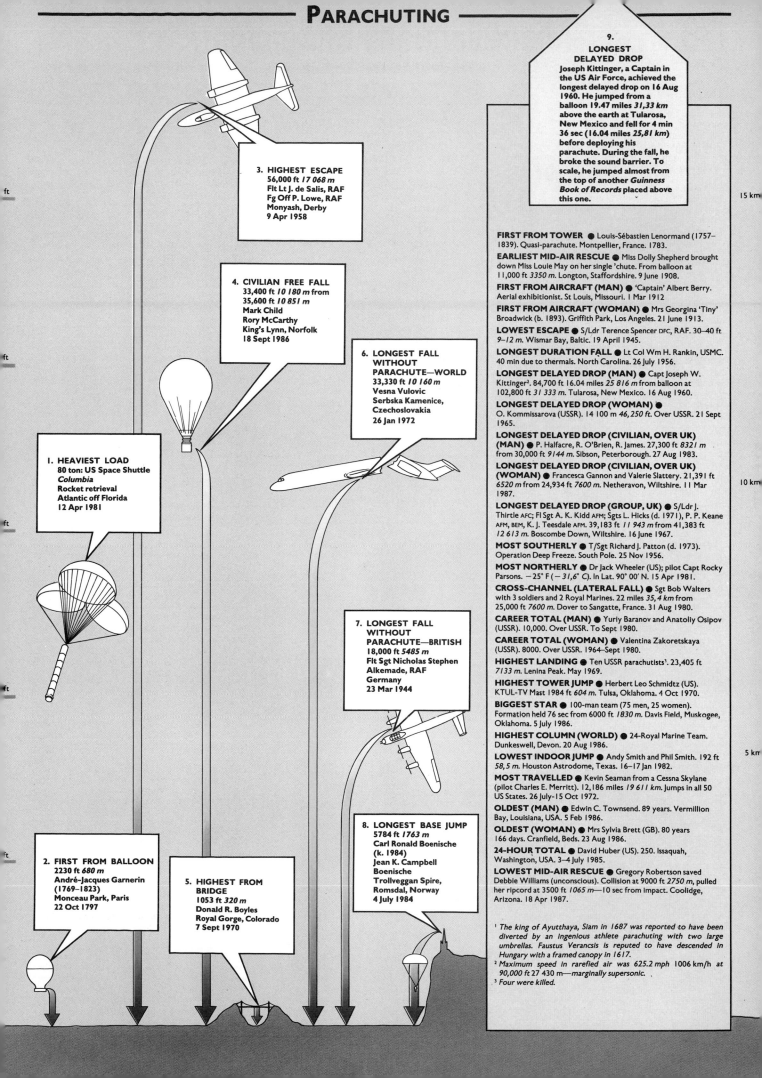

9. LONGEST DELAYED DROP
Joseph Kittinger, a Captain in the US Air Force, achieved the longest delayed drop on 16 Aug 1960. He jumped from a balloon 19.47 miles *31,33 km* above the earth at Tularosa, New Mexico and fell for 4 min 36 sec (16.04 miles *25,81 km*) before deploying his parachute. During the fall, he broke the sound barrier. To scale, he jumped almost from the top of another *Guinness Book of Records* placed above this one.

3. HIGHEST ESCAPE
56,000 ft *17 068 m*
Flt Lt J. de Salis, RAF
Fg Off P. Lowe, RAF
Monyash, Derby
9 Apr 1958

4. CIVILIAN FREE FALL
33,400 ft *10 180 m* from
35,600 ft *10 851 m*
Mark Child
Rory McCarthy
King's Lynn, Norfolk
18 Sept 1986

6. LONGEST FALL WITHOUT PARACHUTE—WORLD
33,330 ft *10 160 m*
Vesna Vulovic
Serbska Kamenice, Czechoslovakia
26 Jan 1972

1. HEAVIEST LOAD
80 ton: US Space Shuttle
Columbia
Rocket retrieval
Atlantic off Florida
12 Apr 1981

7. LONGEST FALL WITHOUT PARACHUTE—BRITISH
18,000 ft *5485 m*
Flt Sgt Nicholas Stephen Alkemade, RAF
Germany
23 Mar 1944

8. LONGEST BASE JUMP
5784 ft *1763 m*
Carl Ronald Boenische
(k. 1984)
Jean K. Campbell
Boenische
Trollveggan Spire,
Romsdal, Norway
4 July 1984

2. FIRST FROM BALLOON
2230 ft *680 m*
André-Jacques Garnerin
(1769–1823)
Monceau Park, Paris
22 Oct 1797

5. HIGHEST FROM BRIDGE
1053 ft *320 m*
Donald R. Boyles
Royal Gorge, Colorado
7 Sept 1970

ft

ft

ft

ft

ft

ft

15 km

10 km

5 km

FIRST FROM TOWER ● Louis-Sébastien Lenormand (1757–1839). Quasi-parachute. Montpellier, France. 1783.

EARLIEST MID-AIR RESCUE ● Miss Dolly Shepherd brought down Miss Louie May on her single 'chute. From balloon at 11,000 ft *3350 m*. Longton, Staffordshire. 9 June 1908.

FIRST FROM AIRCRAFT (MAN) ● 'Captain' Albert Berry. Aerial exhibitionist. St Louis, Missouri. 1 Mar 1912

FIRST FROM AIRCRAFT (WOMAN) ● Mrs Georgina 'Tiny' Broadwick (b. 1893). Griffith Park, Los Angeles. 21 June 1913.

LOWEST ESCAPE ● S/Ldr Terence Spencer DFC, RAF. 30–40 ft *9–12 m*. Wismar Bay, Baltic. 19 April 1945.

LONGEST DURATION FALL ● Lt Col Wm H. Rankin, USMC. 40 min due to thermals. North Carolina. 26 July 1956.

LONGEST DELAYED DROP (MAN) ● Capt Joseph W. Kittinger[2]. 84,700 ft 16.04 miles *25 816 m* from balloon at 102,800 ft *31 333 m*. Tularosa, New Mexico. 16 Aug 1960.

LONGEST DELAYED DROP (WOMAN) ● O. Kommissarova (USSR). 14 100 m *46,250 ft*. Over USSR. 21 Sept 1965.

LONGEST DELAYED DROP (CIVILIAN, OVER UK) (MAN) ● P. Halfacre, R. O'Brien, R. James. 27,300 ft *8321 m* from 30,000 ft *9144 m*. Sibson, Peterborough. 27 Aug 1983.

LONGEST DELAYED DROP (CIVILIAN, OVER UK) (WOMAN) ● Francesca Gannon and Valerie Slattery. 21,391 ft *6520 m* from 24,934 ft *7600 m*. Netheravon, Wiltshire. 11 Mar 1987.

LONGEST DELAYED DROP (GROUP, UK) ● S/Ldr J. Thirtle AFC; Flt Sgt A. K. Kidd AFM; Sgts L. Hicks (d. 1971), P. P. Keane AFM, BEM, K. J. Teesdale AFM. 39,183 ft *11 943 m* from 41,383 ft *12 613 m*. Boscombe Down, Wiltshire. 16 June 1967.

MOST SOUTHERLY ● T/Sgt Richard J. Patton (d. 1973). Operation Deep Freeze. South Pole. 25 Nov 1956.

MOST NORTHERLY ● Dr Jack Wheeler (US); pilot Capt Rocky Parsons. −25° F (−*31,6° C*). In Lat. 90° 00' N. 15 Apr 1981.

CROSS-CHANNEL (LATERAL FALL) ● Sgt Bob Walters with 3 soldiers and 2 Royal Marines. 22 miles *35,4 km* from 25,000 ft *7600 m*. Dover to Sangatte, France. 31 Aug 1980.

CAREER TOTAL (MAN) ● Yuriy Baranov and Anatoliy Osipov (USSR). 10,000. Over USSR. To Sept 1980.

CAREER TOTAL (WOMAN) ● Valentina Zakoretskaya (USSR). 8000. Over USSR. 1964–Sept 1980.

HIGHEST LANDING ● Ten USSR parachutists[3]. 23,405 ft *7133 m*. Lenina Peak. May 1969.

HIGHEST TOWER JUMP ● Herbert Leo Schmidtz (US). KTUL-TV Mast 1984 ft *604 m*. Tulsa, Oklahoma. 4 Oct 1970.

BIGGEST STAR ● 100-man team (75 men, 25 women). Formation held 76 sec from 6000 ft *1830 m*. Davis Field, Muskogee, Oklahoma. 5 July 1986.

HIGHEST COLUMN (WORLD) ● 24-Royal Marine Team. Dunkeswell, Devon. 20 Aug 1986.

LOWEST INDOOR JUMP ● Andy Smith and Phil Smith. 192 ft *58,5 m*. Houston Astrodome, Texas. 16–17 Jan 1982.

MOST TRAVELLED ● Kevin Seaman from a Cessna Skylane (pilot Charles E. Merritt). 12,186 miles *19 611 km*. Jumps in all 50 US States. 26 July–15 Oct 1972.

OLDEST (MAN) ● Edwin C. Townsend. 89 years. Vermillion Bay, Louisiana, USA. 5 Feb 1986.

OLDEST (WOMAN) ● Mrs Sylvia Brett (GB). 80 years 166 days. Cranfield, Beds. 23 Aug 1986.

24-HOUR TOTAL ● David Huber (US). 250. Issaquah, Washington, USA. 3–4 July 1985.

LOWEST MID-AIR RESCUE ● Gregory Robertson saved Debbie Williams (unconscious). Collision at 9000 ft *2750 m*, pulled her ripcord at 3500 ft *1065 m*—10 sec from impact. Coolidge, Arizona. 18 Apr 1987.

[1] The king of Ayutthaya, Siam in 1687 was reported to have been diverted by an ingenious athlete parachuting with two large umbrellas. Faustus Verancsis is reputed to have descended in Hungary with a framed canopy in 1617.

[2] Maximum speed in rarefied air was 625.2 mph *1006 km/h* at 90,000 ft *27 430 m*—marginally supersonic.

[3] Four were killed.

METEOROLOGICAL BALLOON INFLATION

The inflation of a standardised 1000-gramme meteorological balloon to a diameter of 8 ft *2,43 m* against time was achieved by Nicholas Berkeley Mason in 57 min 7 sec for a Fiji TV programme in Tokyo, Japan on 9 Mar 1986.

MILK BOTTLE BALANCING

The greatest distance walked by a person continuously balancing a full pint milk bottle on the head is 24 miles *38,6 km* by Ashrita Furman of Jamaica, NY, USA on 10 July 1983.

MORSE

The highest recorded speed at which anyone has received morse code is 75.2 words per minute—over 17 symbols per second. This was achieved by Ted R. McElroy of the United States in a tournament at Asheville, North Carolina, USA on 2 July 1939.

The highest speed recorded for hand key transmitting is 175 symbols a minute by Harry A. Turner of the US Army Signal Corps at Camp Crowder, Missouri on 9 Nov 1942. Thomas Morris, a GPO operator, is reputed to have been able to send at 39–40 wpm *c.* 1919 but this is not verifiable.

MUSICAL CHAIRS

The largest game on record was one starting with 5151 participants and ending with Bill Bronson on the last chair at University of Notre Dame, Indiana on 6 Sept 1985.

NEEDLE THREADING

The record number of times a strand of cotton has been threaded through a number 13 needle (eye $\frac{1}{2}$ in × $\frac{1}{16}$ in, *12,7 mm × 1,6 mm*) in 2 hr is 3795, set by Miss Brenda Robinson at the College of Further Education, Chippenham, Wiltshire on 20 Mar 1971.

NOODLE MAKING

Mark Pi of the China Gate Restaurant, Columbus, Ohio made 2048 noodle strings (over 5 ft *1,52 m*) in 34.5 sec on 12 Feb 1983.

OMELETTE MAKING

The greatest number of two-egg omelettes made in 30 min is 315 by John Elkhay at the City Lights Restaurant in Providence, Rhode Island on 29 June 1985.

ONION PEELING

The record for peeling 50 lb *22,67 kg* of onions is 3 min 18 sec by Alain St John in Plainfield, Connecticut on 6 July 1980. Under revised rules stipulating a minimum of 50 onions, Alfonso Salvo of York, Pennsylvania peeled 50 lb *22,67 kg* of onions (52 onions) in 5 min 23 sec on 28 Oct 1980.

ORGAN

The longest recorded electric organ marathon is one of 440 hr by Tony Peters at Sheppey Beach Social Club, Isle of Sheppey, Kent from 20 Apr–8 May 1987.

The longest church organ recital ever sustained has been 119 hours by Martin Stanley at St Mary the Virgin, Brixham, Devon from 25–30 Aug 1986.

PADDLE BOATING

The longest recorded voyage is 2226 miles *3582 km* in 103 days by the foot power of Mick Sigrist and Brad Rud down the Mississippi River from the headwaters in Minnesota to the Gulf of Mexico from 4 Aug–11 Nov 1979.

PARACHUTING

It is estimated that the human body reaches 99 per cent of its low-level terminal velocity after falling 1880 ft *573 m* which takes 13–14 secs. This is 117–125 mph *188–201 km/h* at normal atmospheric pressure in a random posture, but up to 185 mph *298 km/h* in a head down position.

The British record is 18,000 ft *5485 m* by Flt-Sgt Nicholas Stephen Alkemade, 21, who jumped from a blazing RAF Lancaster bomber over Germany on 23 Mar 1944. His headlong fall was broken by a fir tree near Oberkürchen and he landed without a broken bone in a snow bank 18 in *45 cm* deep.

Vesna Vulovic, 22, a Jugoslavenski Aerotransport hostess, survived when her DC-9 blew up at 33,330 ft *10 160 m* over the Czechoslovak village of Serbska Kamenice on 26 Jan 1972. She was in hospital for 16 months after emerging from a 27-day coma.

Joseph Kittinger, a Captain in the US Air Force achieved the longest delayed drop on 16 Aug 1960. He jumped from a balloon 19.47 miles *31,33 km* above the earth at Tularosa, New Mexico and fell for 4 min 36 sec (16.04 miles *25,81 km*) before deploying his parachute. During the fall, he broke the sound barrier.

PIANO PLAYING

The longest marathon has been one of 1218 hr (50 days 18 hr) playing 22 hr every day (with 5 min intervals each playing hour) from 7 May to 27 June 1982 by David Scott at Wagga Wagga League Football Club, NSW, Australia. *The non-stop category is now discontinued.*

PIANO SMASHING

The record time for demolishing an upright piano and passing the entire wreckage through a circle 9 in *22,8 cm* in diameter is 1 min 37 sec by six members of the Tinwald Rugby Football Club, Ashburton, New Zealand led by David Young on 6 Nov 1977. Messrs Anthony Fukes, Mike Newman and Terry Cullington smashed a piano with bare hands and feet in 2 min 53 sec in Nottingham on 25 Aug 1979. All wreckage was passed through the circle.

PIANO TUNING

The record time for pitch raising (one semi-tone or 100 cents) and then returning a piano to a musically acceptable quality is 4 min 20 sec by Steve Fairchild at the Piano Technicians Guild contest at the Dante Piano Co factory, NY, USA on 5 Feb 1980.

PILLAR BOX MOUNTING

The record number to pile on top of or hang from a standard double pillar box (oval top of 6 ft² *0,55 m²*) is 32, all students of Wentworth College, York University in Parliament St, York on 27 Feb 1985.

PIPE SMOKING

The duration record for keeping a pipe (3,3 g *0.1 oz* of tobacco) continuously alight with only an initial match under IAPSC (International Association of Pipe Smokers Clubs) rules is 126 min 39 sec by five-time champion William Vargo of Swartz Creek, Michigan at the 27th World Championships in 1975. The only other 5-time champion is Paul T. Spaniola (USA) (1951–66–70–73–77). On 18 Aug 1984 Joe Oetli achieved 130 min 11 sec at the 15th Iowa State Fair contest using *two* matches. Longer durations have been recorded in less rigorously invigilated contests in which the foul practices of 'tamping' and 'gardening' are not unknown.

PLANE PULLING

Dave Gauder, 30, frustrated the take-off of two Piper Cherokees by holding two tow ropes despite a pull of 612 kg *1349 lb* at Bobbington, Staffs on 16 July 1985.

A team of 60 pulled a British Caledonian McDonnell Douglas DC10/30 (170 tonnes) over 100 metres in 1 minute 17 seconds at London Gatwick Airport on 18 Nov 1986.

PLATE SPINNING

The greatest number of plates spun simultaneously is 84 by Dave Spathaky on BBC TV's *Record Breakers* on 21 Oct 1986.

POGO STICK JUMPING

The greatest number of jumps achieved is 130,077 by Gary Stewart in Reading, Ohio on 8–9 Mar 1985.

POLE-SQUATTING

Modern records do not, in fact, compare with that of St Simeon the Elder, (c. 390–459 AD), called 'Stylites', a monk who spent his last 39 years up a stone pillar on The Hill of Wonders, near Antioch, Syria. This is probably the longest-lasting example of record setting.

There being no international rules, the 'standards of living' atop poles vary widely. Mark Sutton finally descended from his pole on 1 July 1985 in Victoria, BC, Canada after 488 days.

Pat Bowen stayed in a barrel (max. capacity 150 gallons) atop a pole (18 ft *5,48 m*) outside the Bull Hotel, Ludlow, Shropshire for 40 days 1 hr from 28 May–7 July 1986.

POP GROUP

The duration record for a 4-man group is 147 hr by the 'Dekorators' at Becketts Bar, Bexhill-on-Sea, East Sussex from 8–14 Jan 1984.

POTATO PEELING

The greatest amount of potatoes peeled by 5 people to an institutional cookery standard with standard kitchen knives in 45 min is 266,5 kg *587 lb 8 oz* (net) by J. Mills, M. McDonald, P. Jennings, E. Gardiner and V. McNulty at Bourke Street Hall, Melbourne, Victoria on 17 Mar 1981.

PRAM PUSHING

The greatest distance covered in pushing a pram in 24 hr is 345.25 miles *555,62 km* by Runner's Factory of Los Gatos, California with an all-star team of 57 Californian runners on 23–24 June 1979. A 10-man Royal Marine team from the Commando Training Centre, Lympstone, Devon, with an adult 'baby', covered 252.65 miles *406,60 km* in 24 hr from 31 Mar–18 Apr 1984.

'PSYCHIATRIST' FASTEST

The world's fastest 'psychiatrist' was Dr Albert L. Weiner of Erlton, New Jersey, trained solely in osteopathy but who dealt with up to 50 psychiatric patients a day in four treatment rooms. He relied heavily on narcoanalysis, muscle relaxants and electro-shock treatments. In December 1961 he was found guilty on 12 counts of manslaughter from using unsterilised needles.

QUIZZES

The highest number of participants was 80,977 in the All-Japan High School Quiz Championship televised by NTV on 31 Dec 1983. The most protracted contest was that lasting 110 hrs in Long Hanborough, Oxfordshire from 27 Mar–1 Apr 1986. The two teams answered correctly 22,483 of the 37,310 questions.

QUOIT THROWING

The world record for rope quoit throwing is an unbroken sequence of 4002 pegs by Bill Irby, Sr of Australia in 1968.

RAMP JUMPING

The longest distance ever achieved for motorcycle long jumping is 241 ft *73,45 m* over 20 juggernauts by Chris Bromham at the Royal Victoria Dock on 31 Aug 1986. The take-off speed of his Yamaha was reported to be 128 mph *205 km/h.*

The pioneer of this form of exhibition—Evel Knievel (b. Robert Craig Knievel, 17 Oct 1938 at Butte, Montana) had suffered 433 bone fractures by his 1975 season. His abortive attempt to cross the 1600 ft *485 m* wide and 600 ft *180 m* deep Snake River Canyon, Idaho on 8 Sept 1974 in a rocket reputedly increased his lifetime earnings by $6 million (then £2½ million).

The longest ramp jump in a car by a professional stunt driver is 232 ft *70,73 m* by Jacqueline De Creed (*née* Creedy) in a 1967 Ford Mustang at Santa Pod Raceway, Bedfordshire on 3 Apr 1983.

RAPPELING (or Abseiling)

The west face of Thor Peak, Baffin Island, northern Canada allowed an abseiling or rappeling record of 3250 ft *990 m* by Steve Holmes (USA) in July 1982. The longest descent down the side of a skyscraper is one of 580 ft *176,7 m* (52 storeys) in Hong Kong by Capt Martin Fuller (1st Bn Cheshire Regt) on 1 Sept 1984.

Pogo stick jumping ● Ashrita Furman, 31, of New York, set a distance record of 11.53 miles *18,68 km* in 8 hours 21 minutes on 8 Jan 1986. His 'route' up and down the foothills of Mt Fuji, Japan, was from the Gotemba railroad station, west along the Gotembaguchi Tozando Road to an elevation of 90 metres, and return.

RIDING IN ARMOUR

The longest recorded ride in full armour (8 stone *50,8 kg*) is one of 167 miles *268,7 km* from Edinburgh to Dumfries in 3 days (riding time 28 hr 30 min) by Dick Brown, 48, from 13–15 June 1979.

RIVETING

The world's record for riveting is 11,209 in 9 hr by John Moir at the Workman Clark Ltd shipyard, Belfast, Northern Ireland, in June 1918. His peak hour was his seventh with 1409, an average of nearly 23½ per min.

ROCK BAND

A 6-piece band sponsored by WRQC, Cleveland, Ohio played continuously for 100 hr 25 min between 7–11 Apr 1986.

ROCKING CHAIR

The longest recorded 'Rockathon' is 453 hours 40 minutes by Robert McDonald at Mariposa, California from 14 Mar–2 Apr 1986.

ROLLING PIN

The record distance for a woman to throw a 2 lb *907 g* rolling pin is 175 ft 5 in *53,4 m* by Lori La

---

Deane Adams, 21, at Iowa State Fair, Iowa on 21 Aug 1979.

SAND SCULPTURING

The longest sand sculpture was a 10,760 ft *3279 m* long 'Millerpede' which meandered along South Padre Beach, Texas on 17 Mar 1987, organised by Louise Lowenthal.

SCOOTER RIDING

The greatest distance covered by a team of 25 in 24 hr is 336.11 miles *540,93 km* by Wimmera Young Farmers, Victoria, Australia on 22–23 Mar 1980.

SEARCH LONGEST

Walter Edwin Percy Zillwood (b. Deptford, London SE8, Dec 1900) traced his missing sister Lena (Mrs Elizabeth Eleanor Allen, b. Nov 1897, d. Jan 1982) after 79 years through the agency of the Salvation Army on 3 May 1980.

SEE-SAW

George Partridge and Tamara Marquez of Auburn High School, Washington, USA on a suspension see-saw completed 1101 hr 40 min (indoor) from 28 Mar–13 May 1977. Georgia Chaffin and Tammy Adams of Goodhope Junior High School, Cullman, Alabama, USA completed 730 hr 30 min (outdoor) from 25 June–25 July 1975.

SERMON

The longest sermon on record was delivered by the Rev Ronald Gallagher at the Baptist Temple,

Appomattox, Virginia for 120 hr from 26 June–1 July 1983. From 31 May to 10 June 1969 the 14th Dalai Lama (b. 6 July 1934 as Tenzin Gyalto), the exiled ruler of Tibet, completed a sermon on Tantric Buddhism for 5–7 hr per day to total 60 hr, in India.

SHAVING

The fastest demon barber on record is Gerry Harley, who shaved 987 men in 60 min with a safety razor in Gillingham, Kent on 28 Apr 1983 taking a perfunctory 3.64 sec per volunteer. On 13 Aug 1984 he shaved 235 even braver volunteers with a cut-throat razor in a less perfunctory 15.3 sec per face. He drew blood only once.

SHEEP TO SHOULDER

At the International Wool Secretariat Development Centre, Ilkley, Yorkshire, a team of 8 using commercial machinery produced a jumper from shearing sheep to the finished article in 2 hr 28 min 32 sec on 3 Sept 1986.

SHEAF TOSSING

The world's best performance for tossing a 3,63 kg *8 lb* sheaf for height is 19,77 m *64 ft 10¼ in* by Trond Ulleberg of Skolleborg, Norway on 11 Nov 1978. Such pitchfork contests date from 1914.

SHOESHINE BOYS

In this category (limited to a team of 4 teenagers; duration of 8 hr; shoes 'on the hoof') the record is 6780 pairs by the Sheffield Citadel Band of the Salvation Army, South Yorkshire, on 27 Feb 1982.

SHORTHAND FASTEST

The highest recorded speeds ever attained under championship conditions are: 300 words per min (99.64 per cent accuracy) for 5 minutes and 350 wpm (99.72 per cent accuracy, that is, two insignificant errors) for 2 minutes by Nathan Behrin (USA) in tests in New York in December 1922. Behrin (b. 1887) used the Pitman system invented in 1837. Morris I. Kligman, official court reporter of the US Court House, New York has taken 50,000 words in 5 hr (a sustained rate of 166.6 wpm). Rates are much dependent upon the nature, complexity and syllabic density of the material. Mr G. W. Bunbury of Dublin, Ireland

held the unique distinction of writing at 250 wpm for 10 minutes on 23 Jan 1894.

Mr Arnold Bradley achieved a speed of 309 wpm without error using the Sloan-Duployan system with 1545 words in 5 minutes in a test in Walsall, West Midlands on 9 Nov 1920.

SHOUTING

The greatest number of wins in the National Town Criers Contest is 11 (between 1939–73) by Ben Johnson of Fowey, Cornwall. The first national feminine champion has been town crier Mrs Henrietta Sargent, of The Three Horse Shoes, Cricklade, Wiltshire in 1980. On being told she had beaten the other 31 contestants she said 'I'm speechless.' (See also Longest-ranged voice, Chapter 1 page 18.)

SHOWERING

The most prolonged continuous shower bath on record is one of 340 hr 40 min by Kevin McCartney of State University College at Buffalo, New York from 29 Mar to 12 Apr 1985. The feminine record is 121 hr 1 min by Lisa D'Amato from 5–10 Nov 1981 at Harpur College, Binghamton, also New York. Desquamation can be a positive danger.

SINGING

The longest recorded solo-singing marathon is one of 200 hr 20 min by Jorge António Hidalgo Chamorro at the Piano Bar, Barcelona, Spain from 7–15 Nov 1985. The marathon record for a choir has been 74 hours 5 minutes by the Oriental Singers of Singapore at the Marina Square Exhibition Hall, Singapore from 21–26 Dec 1986. Acharya Prem Bhikuji (d. 18 Apr 1970) started chanting the Akhand Rama-Dhoon at Jamnagar,

Gujarat, India, on 31 July 1964 and devotees were continuing in April 1987.

SKATE BOARDING

'World' championships have been staged intermittently since 1966. David Frank, 25, covered 270.483 miles *435,3 km* in 36 hr 43 min 40 sec in Toronto, Canada on 11–12 Aug 1985.

The highest speed recorded on a skate board under USSA rules is 71.79 mph *115,53 km/h* on a course at Mt Baldy, California in a prone position by Richard K. Brown, 33, on 17 June 1979. The stand-up record is 53.45 mph *86,01 km/h* by John Hutson, 23, at Signal Hill, Long Beach, California on 11 June 1978. The high jump record is 5 ft 5.7 in *1,67 m* by Trevor Baxter (b. 1 Oct 1962) of Burgess Hill, East Sussex at Grenoble, France on 14 Sept 1982. At the 4th US Skateboard Association Championship, at Signal Hill on 25 Sept 1977, Tony Alva, 19, jumped 17 barrels (17 ft *5,18m*).

SLINGING

The greatest distance recorded for a sling-shot is 1434 ft 2 in *437,13 m* using a 51 in *129,5 cm* long sling and a 2 oz *56,5 g* stone by Lawrence L. Bray at Loa, Utah on 21 Aug 1981.

SMOKE RING BLOWING

The highest recorded number of smoke rings formed from the lips from a single pull of a cigarette (cheek-tapping is disallowed) is 355 by Jan van Deurs Formann of Copenhagen achieved in Switzerland in August 1979.

SNOW SHOEING

The USSA record for covering a mile *1609,34 m* is 7 min 56 sec by Mark Lessard at Corinth, New York in 1979.

SPEAR THROWING

The greatest distance achieved throwing a spear with the aid of a woomera is 326 ft 6 in *99,51 m* (or 16½ ft *5,29 m* less than the old-style javelin record) by Bailey Bush on 27 June 1982 at Camden, NSW, Australia.

SPIKE DRIVING

In the World Championship Professional Spike Driving Competition held at the Golden Spike

National Historic Site in Utah, Dale C. Jones, 49, of Lehi, drove six 7-inch railroad spikes in a time of 26.4 sec on 11 Aug 1984. He incurred no penalty points under the official rules.

SPINNING BY HAND

The duration record for spinning a clock-balance wheel by unaided hand is 5 min 26.8 sec by Philip Ashley, 16, of Leigh, Lancashire on 20 May 1968. The record using 36 in *91,4 cm* of string with a 7¼ oz *205,5 g* top is 58 min 20 sec by Peter Hodgson at Southend-on-Sea, Essex on 4 Feb 1985.

SPITTING

The greatest distance achieved at the Annual Tobacco Spitting Classic (instituted 1955) at Raleigh, Mississippi is 33 ft 7½ in *10,24 m* by Jeff Barber on 25 July 1981. (In 1980 he reached 45 ft *13,71 m* at Fulton, Missouri and on 29 June 1985 he won a record 13th National Spitting title at Raleigh). In the 3rd International Spittin', Belchin' and Cussin' Triathlon, Harold Fielden reached 34 ft 0¼ in *10,36 m* at Central City, Colorado on 13 July 1973. Distance is dependent on the quality of salivation, absence of cross wind, the two-finger pucker and coordination of the back arch and neck snap. Sprays or wads smaller than a dime are not measured. Randy Ober of Benton-ville, Arkansas spat a tobacco wad 47 ft 7 in *14,50 m* at the Calico 5th Annual Tobacco Chewing and Spitting Championships north of Barstow, California on 4 Apr 1982. The record for projecting a melon seed under WCWSSCA rules is 65 ft 4 in *19,91 m* by John Wilkinson in Luling, Texas on 28 June 1980. The furthest reported distance for a cherry stone is 65 ft 2 in *19,86 m* by Rick Krause, at Eau Claire, Michigan on 5 July 1980. Spitters who care about their image wear 12 in *30,4 cm* block-ended boots so practice spits can be measured without a tape.

SQUARE DANCE CALLING

Alan Covacic called continuously for 24 hr 2 min for the Wheelers and Dealers SDC at St John's Hospital, Stone, Bucks on 23–24 Nov 1984.

STAIR CLIMBING

The 100-storey record for stair climbing was set by Dennis W. Martz in the Detroit Plaza Hotel, Detroit, Michigan on 26 June 1978 at 11 min 23.8 sec. Dale Neil, 22, ran a vertical mile on the stairs of the Peachtree Plaza Hotel, Atlanta, Georgia in continuous action of 2 hr 1 min 24 sec on 9 Mar 1984. *These records can only be attempted in buildings with a minimum of 70 storeys.*

The record for the 1760 steps (vertical height 1122 ft *342 m*) in the world's tallest free-standing structure, Toronto's CN Tower, is 8 min 28 secs by George Kapenyes on 27 Oct 1985. Robert C. Jezequel ran 17 round trips in 11 hr 20 min on 18 Oct 1985 without use of the elevator for a vertical height of 15,708 ft *4787 m.*

Pete Squires raced up the 1575 steps of the Empire State Building, New York on 12 Feb 1981 in 10 min 59 sec.

In the line of duty Bill Stevenson mounted 334 of the 364 steps of the tower in the Houses of Parliament 4000 times in the 15 years 1968–83—equivalent to 24.9 ascents of Everest.

STAMP LICKING

Ian Thomas of Brisbane, Australia licked and affixed 204 stamps in 4 minutes at the Sunpex '85 Exhibition, Brisbane on 5 Oct 1985.

STANDING

The longest period on record that anyone has continuously stood is for more than 17 years in the case of Swami Maujgiri Maharij when performing the *Tapasya* or penance from 1955 to November 1973 in Shahjahanpur, Uttar Pradesh, India. When sleeping he would lean against a plank. He died aged 85 in Sept 1980.

STILT-WALKING

Hop stringers use stilts up to 15 ft *4,57 m*. In 1892 M. Garisoain of Bayonne stilt-walked 8 km *4.97 miles* into Biarritz in 42 min to average 11,42 km/h *7.10 mph*. In 1891 Sylvain Dornon stilt-walked from Paris to Moscow via Vilno in 50 stages for the 1830 miles *2945 km*. Another source gives his time as 58 days. Even with a safety or Kirby wire very high stilts are *extremely* dangerous—25 steps are deemed to constitute 'mastery'. Eddy Wolf ('Steady Eddy') of Loyal, Wisconsin mastered stilts measuring 40 ft 6½ in *12,36 m* from ground to ankle over a distance of 27 steps without touching his safety handrail wires, at Yokohama Dreamland Park, Yokohama on 9 Mar 1986. His aluminium stilts weighed 55 lb *25 kg* each. Joe Long (b. Kenneth Caesar), who has suffered 5 fractures, mastered 56 lb *25,4 kg* 24 ft *7,31 m* stilts at BBC TV Centre, London on 8 Dec 1978. The endurance record is 3008 miles *4804 km* from Los Angeles, California to Bowen, Kentucky, from 20 Feb to 26 July 1980 by Joe Bowen. Masaharu Tatsushiro, 28 (Japan), ran 100 m *328 ft* on 1 ft *30,48 cm* high stilts in 14.15 sec in Tokyo on 30 Mar 1980.

STOWAWAY

The most rugged stowaway was Socarras Rami-rez who escaped from Cuba on 4 June 1969 by stowing away in an unpressurised wheel well in the starboard wing of a Douglas DC8 from Havana to Madrid in a 5600 mile *9010 km* Iberian Airlines flight. He survived 8 hr at 30,000 ft *9145 m* where temperatures were −8°F *−22°C.*

> **Shouting** ● Donald H. Burns of St. George's, Bermuda won the Loudest Cry trophy in the Seventh International Town Criers Championship in Halifax, Nova Scotia, Canada on 15 Sept 1984 with a shout recorded at 113 decibels.

STRETCHER BEARING

The longest recorded carry of a stretcher case with a 10 st *63,5 kg* 'body' is 127 miles *204,34 km* in 45 hr 45 min by two four-man teams from the Sri Chinmoy marathon team of Jamaica, NY, USA, from 17–19 Apr 1981.

The record limited to Youth Organisations (un-der 20 years of age) and 8-hr carrying is 42.02 miles *67,62 km* by 8 members of the Henry Meoles School, Moreton, Wirral, Cheshire on 13 July 1980.

STRING BALL LARGEST

The largest ball of string on record is one of 12 ft 9 in *3,88 m* in diameter, 40 ft *12,19 m* in circum-ference and weighing 10 tons/*tonnes* amassed by Francis A. Johnson of Darwin, Minnesota between 1950–78.

SUBMERGENCE

The *continuous* duration record (*i.e.* no rest breaks) for 'scuba' (*i.e.* self-contained and with-out surface air hoses) is 212 hr 30 min by Michael Stevens of Birmingham in a Royal Navy tank at the National Exhibition Centre, Birmingham from 14–23 Feb 1986. Measures have to be taken to reduce the risk of severe desquamation in such endurance trials.

SUGGESTION BOXES

The most prolific example on record of the use of any suggestion box scheme is that of John Drayton (b. 18 Sept 1907) of Newport, Gwent who

has plied the British rail system with a total of 31,316 suggestions from 1924 to May 1987 of which over 100 have been accepted by London Transport. In 1983 he was presented with a chiming clock by British Rail to mark almost 60 years of suggestions.

SWINGING

The record duration for continuous swinging in a hammock is 240 hours by John David Joyce, 19, of Bryan, Texas, USA from 29 July–8 Aug 1986.

SWITCHBACK RIDING

The endurance record for rides on a roller coaster is 503 hr by M. M. Daniel Glada and Normand St-Pierre at Parc Belmont, Montreal, Canada from 18 July–10 Aug 1983. The minimum qualifying average speed required is 25 mph *40 km/h*.

TAILORING

The highest speed in which the manufacture of a 3-piece suit has been executed from sheep to finished article is 1 hr 34 min 33.42 sec by 65 members of the Melbourne College of Textiles, Pascoe Vale, Victoria, Australia on 24 June 1982. The catching and fleecing took 2 min 21 sec, and the carding, spinning, weaving and tailoring occupied the remaining time.

TALKING

The world record for non-stop talking has been 200 hours by S. E. Jayaraman (54) at the Agaram Gandhi Statue, Madras, India from 3–11 Feb 1987. A feminine non-stop talking record was set by Mrs Mary E. Davis, who on 2 Sept 1958 started at a radio station in Buffalo, New York, USA and did not draw breath until 110 hr 30 min 5 sec later on 7 Sept in Tulsa, Oklahoma, USA. (See also Filibusters, Chapter 11.)

Historically the longest recorded after-dinner speech with unsuspecting victims was one of 3 hr by the Rev Henry Whitehead (d. March 1896) at the Rainbow Tavern, Fleet Street, London on 16 Jan 1874. At a dinner at St George's Hotel, Lime Street, Liverpool Roger Cooper replied to the toast to the guests for 25 hours on 14–15 Nov 1986.

T-BONE DIVE

The so-called T-bone dives or Dive Bomber crashes by cars off ramps over and on to parked cars are often measured by the number of cars, but owing to their variable size and that their purpose is purely to cushion the shock, distance is more significant.

Jean-Pierre Vignan attained 59,86 m *196 ft 5 in* in a Ford Capri at Montlhéry, Paris on 20 July 1980.

TEETH-PULLING

The man with 'the strongest teeth in the world' is 'Hercules' John Massis (b. Wilfried Oscar Morbée, 4 June 1940) of Oostakker, Belgium, who raised a weight of 233 kg *513¾ lb* 15 cm *6 in* from the ground with a tooth bit at Evrey, France on 19 Mar 1977. Massis prevented a helicopter from taking off using only a tooth-bit harness in Los Angeles, California on 7 Apr 1979 for a *Guinness Spectacular* TV show.

THROWING

The greatest distance any inert object heavier than air has been thrown is 1298 ft *395,63 m* for a Skyro flying ring by Tom McRann, of Menlo Park, California on 21 May 1986 at Santa Clara, California. The ring made of plastic and rubber weighs 3,21 oz *91 g* and has a diameter of 11¼ in *29,21 cm*.

TIGHTROPE WALKING

The greatest 19th-century tightrope walker was Jean François Gravelet, *alias* Charles Blondin (1824–97), of France, who made the earliest crossing of the Niagara Falls on a 3 in *76 mm* rope, 110 ft *335 m* long, 160 ft *48,75 m* above the Falls on 30 June 1859. He also made a crossing with Harry Colcord pick-a-back on 15 Sept 1860. Though other artistes still find it difficult to believe, Colcord was his agent. The oldest wirewalker was 'Professor' William Ivy Baldwin (1866–1953), who crossed the South Boulder Canyon, Colorado on a 320 ft *97,5 m* wire with a 125 ft *38,1 m* drop on his 82nd birthday on 31 July 1948.

The world tightrope endurance record is 185 days by Henri Rochetain (b. 1926) of France on a wire 394 ft *120 m* long, 82 ft *25 m* above a supermarket in Saint Etienne, France, from 28 Mar–29 Sept 1973. His ability to sleep on the wire has left doctors puzzled. Steven G. Wallenda, 33, walked 2.36 miles *3,81 km* on a wire 250 ft *76,2 m* long 32 ft *9,75 m* high at North Port, Florida on 26 Mar 1983 in 3 hr 31 min.

Steve McPeak (b. 21 April 1945) of Las Vegas, Nevada, USA ascended the 46,6 mm *1.83 in* diameter Zugspitzbahn cable for a vertical height of 705 m *2313 ft* in 3 stints aggregating 5 hr 4 min on 24/25/28 June 1981. The maximum gradient over the stretch of 2282 m *7485 ft* was above 30 degrees. Earlier on 28 June 1981 he had walked on a thinner stayed cable 181 steps across a gorge at the top of the 2963 m *9721 ft* mountain with a sheer drop of 960 m *3150 ft* below him.

The first crossing of the River Thames was achieved by Charles Elleano (b. 1911) of Strasbourg, France on a 1050 ft *320 m* wire 60 ft *18,2 m* above the river in 25 min on 22 Sept 1951.

TOP SPINNING

A team of 25 from the Mizushima Plant of Kawasaki Steel Works in Okayama spun a giant top 2 m *6 ft 6¾ in* tall and 2.6 m *8 ft 6¼ in* in diameter weighing 360 kg *793.6 lb* for 1 hr 21 min 35 sec on 3 Nov 1986.

TREE CLIMBING

The fastest speed climb up a 100 ft *30,4 m* fir spar pole and return to the ground is one of 27.16 sec by Ed Johnson of Victoria, BC, Canada in July 1982 at the Lumberjack World Championships in Hayward, Wisconsin.

The fastest time up a 9 m *29.5 ft* coconut tree barefoot is 4.88 sec by Fuatai Solo, 17, in Sukuna Park, Fiji on 22 Aug 1980.

TREE SITTING

The duration record for sitting in a tree is 431 days by Timothy Roy at Golf N'Stuff Amusement Park, Norwalk, California, USA from 4 July 1982–8 Sept 1983.

TYPEWRITING

The world duration record for typewriting on an electric machine is 264 hr by Violet Gibson Burns at The Royal Easter Show, Sydney, Australia from 29 Mar–9 Apr 1985.

The longest duration in a typing marathon on a manual machine is 123 hours by Shambhoo Govind Anbhawane of Bombay, India from 18–23 Aug 1986 on a Godrej Prima manual machine in Bombay, aggregating 806,000 strokes. Les Stewart of Mudjimba Beach, Queensland, Australia has typed the numbers 1 to 467,000 in *words* on 9230 quarto sheets as of 12 Feb 1987. His target is to become a ''millionaire''.

The highest recorded speeds attained with a

ten-word penalty per error on a manual machine are:

Five Min: 176 wpm net Mrs Carole Forristall Waldschlager Bechen at Dixon, Illinois on 2 Apr 1959. One Hour: 147 wpm net Albert Tangora (US) (Underwood Standard), 22 Oct 1923.

The official hour record on an electric machine is 9316 words (40 errors) on an IBM machine, giving a net rate of 149 words per min, by Margaret Hamma, now Mrs Dilmore (US), in Brooklyn, New York on 20 June 1941. Mary Ann Morel (South Africa) set a numerical record at the CABEX '85 Exhibition in Johannesburg, South Africa on 6 Feb 1985 by typing spaced numbers from 1 to 781 in 5 min.

In an official test in 1946 Stella Pajunas, now Mrs Garnard, attained a rate of 216 words in a minute on an IBM machine.

TYRE SUPPORTING

The greatest number of motor tyres supported in a free-standing 'lift' is 96 by Gary Windebank of Romsey, Hants in Feb 1984. The total weight was 1440 lb *653 kg*. The tyres used were Michelin XZX 155 × 13.

UNSUPPORTED CIRCLE

The highest recorded number of people who have demonstrated the physical paradox of all being seated without a chair in an unsupported circle of 10,323 employees of the Nissan Motor Company at Komazawa Stadium, Tokyo on 23 Oct 1982.

The best British performance is one of 7402 participants at Goodwood Air Field, Sussex on 25 May 1986, as part of a Sport Aid event.

WAITER'S MARATHON

Beverly Hills restaurateur Roger Bourban, Switzerland, 'le garçon rapide', ran a full marathon in full uniform in London on 9 May 1982 carrying a free-standing open bottle of mineral water on a tray in the same hand (gross weight 3 lb 2 oz *1,42 kg*) in 2 hr 47 min.

WALKING ON HANDS

The duration record for walking on hands is 1400 km *871 miles* by Johann Hurlinger, of Austria, who in 55 daily 10-hr stints, averaged 1.58 mph *2,54 km/h* from Vienna to Paris in 1900. Shin Don-mok of South Korea completed a 50 m *54.68 yd* inverted sprint in 17.44 sec at the Toda Sports Centre, Saitama, Japan on 14 Nov 1986. Four men (Bob Sutton, Danny Scannell, Phil Johnson and John Hawkins) relayed a mile in Oak Ridge, Tennessee on 13 Mar 1983 in 31 min 15.8 sec.

WALKING ON WATER

Using outsize shoes-cum-floats Fritz Weber walked on the Main from Beyreuth over 300 km *185 miles* to Mainz, West Germany from 1 Sept to 15 Oct 1983.

WALL OF DEATH

The greatest endurance feat on a wall of death was 6 hr 7 min 38 sec by Hugo Dabbert (b. Hildesheim, 24 Sept 1938) at Rüsselsheim, West Germany on 14 Aug 1980. He rode 6841 laps on the 10 m *32.8 ft* diameter wall on a Honda CM 400T averaging 35,2 km/h *21.8 mph* for the 214,8 km *133.4 miles*.

WHIP CRACKING

The longest stock whip ever 'cracked' (*i.e. the end made to travel above the speed of sound—760 mph *1223 km/h*) is one of 140 ft *42,67 m* (excluding the handle) wielded by Garry Brophy at Adelaide, Australia on 31 Oct 1985.

WHISTLING

Roy Lomas achieved 122.5 decibels at 2½ metres in the Deadroom at the BBC studios in Manchester on 19 Dec 1983. The whistling marathon record is by David Frank of Toronto, Canada, who completed 30 hr 10 min non-stop at the Annapurna Vegetarian Restaurant, Toronto, on 23–24 Nov 1985.

WINDOW CLEANING

On 19 Oct 1984 at the Clearview Challenge Cup contest, Sydney, Australia Roy Ridley achieved 18.92 sec without a smear for three standard 40.94 × 45.39 in *1040 × 1153 mm* office windows with an *11.8 in* 300 mm long squeegee and 15.83 pts *9 l* of water.

WIRE SLIDE

The greatest distance recorded in a wire slide is from the London Weekend TV building to the barge 'Driftwood' 370 ft *112,7 m* below and 925 ft *281,9 m* distant on the Thames on 27 Oct 1986. This 'death slide' set up by the Royal Marines was traversed by Lady Nourse *née* Lavinia Malim for charity. The estimated run length was 1000 ft *305 m*.

WOOD CUTTING

The earliest competitions date from Tasmania in 1874. The records set at the Lumberjack World Championships at Hayward, Wisconsin, USA (founded 1960) are:

Power Saw		8.73 sec
Sven Johnson (US)		1983
One-Man Bucking		21.70 sec
Merv Jensen (NZ) (d. Apr 1983)		1982
Standing Block Chop		25.38 sec
Mel Lentz (US)		1982
Underhand Block Chop		18.66 sec
Mel Lentz (US)		1982
Two-Man Bucking		9.44 sec
Merv Jensen (NZ), Cliff Hughes (NZ)		1982
Hand Splitting a Cord into Quarters*	53 min 40 sec	
Richard Sawyer (US)		1982

White pine logs 14 in *35,5 cm* diameter are used for chopping and 20 in *50,8 cm* for sawing.
* Hardwood (white ash) cord of 128 ft³ *3,62 m³* using a quartering wedge at Sag Harbor, NY, on 2 July 1982.

WRITING MINUSCULE

In 1926 an account was published of Alfred McEwen's pantograph record in which the 56-word version of the Lord's Prayer was written by diamond point on glass in the space of 0.0016 × 0.0008 in *0,04 × 0,02 mm*. Frank C. Watts of Felmingham, Norfolk demonstrated for photographers on 24 Jan 1968 his ability, without mechanical or optical aid, to write the Lord's Prayer 34 times (9452 letters) within the size of a definitive UK postage stamp *viz* 0.84 × 0.71 in *21,33 × 18,03 mm*. Tsutomu Ishii of Tokyo demonstrated the ability to write the names of 44 countries (184 letters) on a single grain of rice and TOKYO JAPAN in Japanese on a human hair in April 1983.

WRITING UNDER HANDICAP

The ultimate feat in 'funny writing' appears to be the ability to write extemporaneously and decipherably backwards, upside down, laterally inverted (mirror-style), while blindfolded, with both hands simultaneously. Three claims to this ability with both hands and feet simultaneously, by Mrs Carolyn Webb of Thirlmere, NSW, Australia, Mrs Judy Hall of Chesterfield, Virginia, USA, and Robert Gray of Toronto, Ontario, Canada, are outstanding but have not been witnessed in the act by our staff.

YODELLING

The most protracted yodel on record was that of Errol Bird for 26 hr in Lisburn, Northern Ireland

---

Most expensive medals ● A medal group comprising a VC, DFC, 1939–45 Star (Battle of Britain bar), Air Crew Europe Star, Burma Star, Defense Medal and 1939–45 War Medal fetched a record £110,000 when it was sold at auction by Glendining & Co, London, on 27 Apr 1983.

---

on 27–28 Sept 1984. Yodelling has been defined as 'repeated rapid changes from the chest-voice to falsetto and back again'. The most rapid recorded is 5 tones (3 falsetto) in 1.9 sec by Donn Reynolds of Canada on 25 July 1984.

YO-YO

A yo-yo was a toy in Grecian times and is depicted on a bowl dated 450 BC. It was also a Filipino jungle fighting weapon recorded in the 16th century weighing 4 lb *1,81 kg* with a 20 ft *6 m* thong. The word means 'come-come'. Though illustrated in a book in 1891 as a bandalore the craze did not begin until it was started by Donald F. Duncan of Chicago in 1926. The most difficult modern yo-yo trick is the 'whirlwind' incorporating both inside and outside horizontal loop-the-loops. The individual continuous endurance record is 121 hr 10 min by Bob Brown of Boston, Mass, from 24–29 June 1985. Dr Allen Bussey in Waco, Texas on 23 Apr 1977 completed 20,302 loops in 3 hr (including 6886 in a single 60-min period). He used a Duncan Imperial with a 34½ in *87,6 cm* nylon string. Spins of 8000 rpm have been recorded.

The largest yo-yo ever constructed was one by Dr Tom Kuhn weighing 256 lb *116,11 kg* test launched from a 150 ft *52,2 m* crane in San Francisco, California on 13 Oct 1979.

Honours, Decorations and Awards

Oldest order

The earliest honour known was the 'Gold of Honour' for extraordinary valour awarded in the 18th dynasty *c.* 1440–1400 BC. A statuette was found at Qan-el-Kebri, Egypt. The order which can trace its origins furthest back is the Military Hospitaller Order of St Lazarus of Jerusalem founded by St Basil the Great in the 4th century AD. A date as early as AD 809 has been attributed to the Most Ancient Order of the Thistle, but is of doubtful provenance. The Order of St John in Scotland, founded in 1124, was suppressed in the 16th century but revived in 1947. The prototype of the princely Orders of Chivalry is the Most Noble Order of the Garter founded by King Edward III *c.* 1348.

Eponymous record

The largest object to which a human name is attached is the universe itself—in the case of three different cosmological models, known as Friedmanian models, devised in 1922 by the Russian mathematician Aleksandr Aleksandrovitch Friedman (1888–1925).

Most titles

The most titled person in the world is the 18th Duchess of Alba (Alba de Tormes), Doña Maria del Rosario Cayetana Fitz-James Stuart y Silva. She is 8 times a duchess, 15 times a marchioness, 21 times a countess and is 19 times a Spanish grandee.

Versatility

The only person to win a Victoria Cross and an Olympic Gold Medal has been Lt Gen Sir Philip Neame VC, KBE, CB, DSO (1888–1978). He won the VC in 1914 and was an Olympic gold medallist for Britain for rifle shooting in 1924 though under the illusion at the time that he was shooting for the British Empire. The only George Cross holder who was also a Fellow of the Royal Society was Prof Peter Victor Danckwerts GC, MBE, FRS F Eng (1916–1985) who defused 16 parachute mines in under 48 hr in the London docks during the Battle of Britain as a Sub Lt RNVR in August 1940.

Victoria Cross *Double awards*

The only three men ever to have been awarded a bar to the Victoria Cross (instituted 29 Jan 1856) are:

Surg-Capt (later Lt-Col) Arthur Martin-Leake VC', VD, RAMC (1874–1953) (1902 and bar 1915).
Capt Noel Godfrey Chavasse VC', MC, RAMC (1884–1917) (1916 and bar posthumously 14 Sept 1917).
Second Lt (later Capt) Charles Hazlitt Upham VC', NZMF (b. 21 Sept 1908) (1941 and bar 1942).

The most VCs awarded in a war were the 634 in World War I (1914–18). The greatest number won in a single action was 11 at Rorke's Drift in the Zulu War on 22–23 Jan 1879. The school with most recipients is Eton College, Col H. H. Jones being the 36th (in the Falklands campaign).

Youngest

The lowest established age for a VC is 15 years 100 days for hospital apprentice Andrew (wrongly gazetted as Arthur) Fitzgibbon (born at Peteragurh, northern India, 13 May 1845) of the Indian Medical Services for bravery at the Taku Forts in northern China on 21 Aug 1860. The youngest living VC is Capt Rambahadur Limbu (b. 1 Nov 1939, Chyangthapu, Nepal) of the 10th Princess Mary's Own Gurkha Rifles. The award was for his courage as a L/Cpl while fighting in the Bau district of Sarawak, east Malaysia, on 21 Nov 1965. He retired on 25 Mar 1985 as Lieutenant.

Longest lived

The longest lived of all the 1351 winners of the Victoria Cross has been Lt Col Harcus Strachan

VC. He was born in Bo'ness, West Lothian on 7 Nov 1884 and died in Vancouver, British Columbia on 1 May 1982 aged 97 years 175 days.

Most highly decorated

The six living persons to have been twice decorated with any of the United Kingdom's topmost decorations are Capt C. H. Upham VC and bar; the Viscount de l'Isle VC, KG; HM the Queen Mother CI, GCVO, GBE, who is a Lady of the Garter and a Lady of the Thistle; HRH the Duke of Edinburgh KG, KT, OM, GBE; HRH Prince Charles KG, KT, GCB and HM King Olaf V of Norway KG, KT, GCB, GCVO. Lord De L'Isle is the only person who has both the highest military and highest civil honour. Britain's most highly decorated woman is the World War II British agent Mrs Odette Hallowes GC, MBE, Légion d'Honneur, Ordre St George (Belge), who survived imprisonment and torture at the hands of the Gestapo from 1943–45. Violette Reine Elizabeth Szabo (*née* Bushnell) GC (1921–45) lost her husband in the French Legion at El Alamein in 1942. He was Etienne Szabo, Médaille Militaire, Légion d'Honneur and Croix de Guerre.

Top jet ace

The greatest number of kills in jet to jet battles is 16 by Capt Joseph Christopher McConnell, Jr, USAF (b. Dover, New Hampshire, 30 Jan 1922) in the Korean war (1950–3). He was killed on 25 Aug 1954. It is possible that an Israeli ace may have surpassed this total in the period 1967–70 but the identity of pilots is subject to strict security.

Top woman ace

The record score for any woman fighter pilot is 12 by Jnr Lt Lydia Litvak (USSR) (b. 1921) on the Eastern Front between 1941 and 1943. She was killed in action on 1 Aug 1943.

Top scoring air aces (World Wars I and II)

The 'scores' of air aces in both wars are *still* hotly disputed. The highest figures officially attributed have been:

World	United Kingdom
World War I	
75[1] Col René Paul Fonck (France) Gr Cordon Ld'H, C de G (26 palms), Méd. Mil., MC*, C de G (Belge) (d. 1953)	73 Major Edward Mannock VC, DSO**, MC*
World War II	
352 Major Erich Hartmann (Germany)	38 Wg Cdr (now AVM) James Edgar Johnson CB, CBE, DSO**, DFC*[2]

[1] A total of 80 was attributed to Rittmeister Manfred Freiherr (Baron) von Richthofen (Germany) but more than 20 of these are not fully verifiable from German records, leaving Col-Gen Ernst Udet (d. 1941) Ordre pour le Mérite, Iron Cross with the highest number of unquestioned victories at 62.

[2] The greatest number of successes against flying bombs (V.1s) was by Sqn Ldr Joseph Berry DFC** (b. Nottingham, 1920, killed 2 Oct 1944) who brought down 60 in 4 months. The most successful fighter pilot in the RAF was Sqn Ldr Marmaduke Thomas St John Pattle DFC*, of South Africa, with a known total of at least 40. In the Battle of Leyte Gulf, Cdr David McCampbell USN shot down 9 aircraft in one mission on 24 Oct 1944.

Youngest award

The youngest age at which an official gallantry award has ever been won is 8 years in the case of Anthony Farrer who was given the Albert Medal on 23 Sept 1916 for fighting off a cougar at Cowichan Lake, Vancouver Island, Canada to save Doreen Ashburnham. She was also awarded the AM, which, in 1971, was exchanged for the George Cross.

Most Lifeboat medals ● Manxman, Sir William Hilliary (1771–1847), founder of the Royal National Lifeboat Institution in 1824, who was personally and uniquely awarded four RNLI Gold Medals. The only triple award this century has been to Coxswain Henry Blogg GC, BEM (1876–1954) of Cromer, Norfolk.

Most mentions in despatches

The record number of 'mentions' is 24 by Field Marshal the Rt Hon. Sir Frederick Sleigh Roberts Bt, the Earl Roberts VC, KG, PC, KP, GCB, OM, GCSI, GCIE, VD (1832–1914).

Most post-nominal letters

Lord Roberts, who was also a privy counsellor, was the only non-royal holder of 8 sets of *official* post-nominal letters. Currently the record number is seven by Marshal of the RAF the Rt Hon. Lord Elworthy KG, GCB, CBE, DSO, LVO, DFC, AFC (b. 23 Mar 1911) of New Zealand. HRH the Duke of Windsor (1894–1972) when Prince of Wales had 10 sets and was also a privy counsellor *viz* KG, PC, KT, KP, GCB, GCSI, GCMG, GCIE, GCVO, GBE, MC. He later appended the ISO but never did so in the cases of the OM, CH or DSO of which orders he had also been sovereign.

— NOBEL PRIZES —

Earliest 1901 for Physics, Chemistry, Medicine and Physiology, Literature and Peace

Most Prizes USA outright or shared 120 including most for Medicine–Physiology (34); Physics (31); Peace (13); Economics (14); Chemistry (22). France has most for Literature (11). The United Kingdom total is 75 (all classes) comprising Physics (18); Chemistry (20); Medicine (16); Peace (9); Literature (7); Economics (5)

Oldest Laureate Prof Francis Peyton Rous (US) (1879–1970) in 1966 shared in Medicine prize aged 87

Youngest Laureates *At time of award:* Prof Sir William Bragg CH, OBE, MC (1890–1971) 1915 Physics prize at 25 *At time of work:* Bragg and Theodore W. Richards (US) (1868–1928) 1914 Chemistry prize at 23 *Literature:* Rudyard Kipling (UK) (1865–1936) 1907 prize at 41 *Peace:* Mrs Mairead Corrigan-Maguire (Northern Ireland) (b. 27 Jan 1944) 1976 prize (shared) at 32

Most Three Awards: International Committee for Red Cross (founded 1863) Peace 1917, 1944 and 1963 (shared); Two Awards: Dr Linus Carl Pauling (US) (b. 28 Feb 1901) Chemistry 1954 and Peace 1962; Mme Marja Sklodowska Curie (Polish-French) (1867–1934) Physics 1903 and Chemistry 1911; Prof John Bardeen (US) (b. 23 May 1908) Physics 1956 (shared) and 1972 (shared); Prof Frederick Sanger OM, CBE, FRS (b. 13 Aug 1918) Chemistry 1958 (shared) and 1980 (shared)

Highest Prize Sw Kr 1,650,000 (for 1984) equivalent to £152,800

Lowest Prize Sw Kr 115,000 (1923) equivalent to £6,620

Civilian gallantry

Reginald H. Blanchford of Guernsey received the MBE for gallantry in 1950; the Queen's Commendation in 1957; the George Medal in 1958; the OBE for gallantry in 1961 for saving life from cliff tops. He was also awarded the Life Saving Medal in Gold 1957 with golden bar 1963 and was made a Knight of Grace of the Order of St John in 1970.

USSR

The USSR's highest award for valour is the Gold Star of a Hero of the Soviet Union. Over 10,000 were awarded in World War II. Among the 109 awards of a second star were those to Marshal Iosif Vissarionovich Dzhugashvili, *alias* Stalin (1879–1953), and Lt-General Nikita Sergeyevich Khrushchyov (1894–1971). The only wartime triple awards were to Marshal Georgiy Konstantinovich Zhukov, Hon GCB (1896–1972) (subsequently awarded a fourth Gold Star) and to the leading air aces Guards Colonel (later Marshal of Aviation) the late Aleksandr Ivanovich Pokryshkin and Aviation Maj Gen Ivan Nikitovich Kozhedub Zhukov (b. 8 June 1920) (Order of the Red Banner, 7 times) who also uniquely had the Order of Victory (twice), the Order of Lenin (6 times) and the Order of the Red Banner (thrice). Leonid Brezhnev (1907–1982) was 4 times Hero of the Soviet Union, and Hero of Socialist Labour, Order of Victory, Order of Lenin (8 times) and Order of the Red Banner (twice).

Germany

The Knight's Cross of the Iron Cross with swords, diamonds and golden oak-leaves was uniquely awarded to Col Hans Ulrich Rudel (1916–1982) for 2530 operational flying missions on the Eastern Front in 1941–5. He destroyed 519 Soviet armoured vehicles.

USA

The highest US military decoration is the Medal of Honor. Five marines received both the Army and Navy Medals of Honor for the same acts in 1918 and 13 officers and men from 1863 to 1915 have received the medal on two occasions. Maj Audie Murphy (1924–1971) received in World War II the Medal of Honor, the Distinguished Service Cross, the Silver Star (thrice), the Legion of Merit, the Bronze Star Medal (twice) and the Purple Heart (thrice).

Record price

The highest price ever paid for a VC group has been £110,000 for the medals of the Battle of Britain fighter pilot Wing Cdr J. B. Nicholson VC, DFC, AFC (k. 1945), one of only 3 men ever to win the VC actually defending Britain. The auction was at Glendining & Co, London on 27 Apr 1983.

The record for a George Cross is £20,250 at Christie's on 14 Mar 1985 for that of Sgt Michael Willets (3rd Battalion Parachute Regiment), killed by an IRA bomb in Ulster in 1971.

Order of Merit

The Order of Merit (instituted on 23 June 1902) is limited to 24 members. The longest lived of the 154 holders has been the Rt Hon. Bertrand Arthur William Russell, 3rd Earl Russell, who died on 2 Feb 1970 aged 97 years 260 days. The oldest recipient was Admiral of the Fleet the Hon. Sir Henry Keppel GCB, OM (1809–1904), who received the Order aged 93 years 56 days on 9 Aug 1902. The youngest recipient has been HRH the Duke of Edinburgh KG, KT, OM, GBE, who was appointed on his 47th birthday on 10 June 1968.

Anti-submarine successes

The highest number of U-boat kills attributed to one ship in the 1939–45 War was 15 to HMS *Starling* (Capt Frederic John Walker CB, DSO***, RN). Captain Walker was in command at the sinking of a total of 25 U-boats between 1941 and the time of his death on 9 July 1944. The US Destroyer Escort *England* sank six Japanese submarines in the Pacific between 18 and 30 May 1944.

Most successful submarine captains
The most successful of all World War II submarine commanders was Leutnant Otto Kretschmer, captain of the U.23 and U.99 who up to March 1940 sank one destroyer and 44 allied merchantmen totalling 266,629 gross registered tons.

In World War I Kapitän-Leutnant (later Vizeadmiral) Lothar von Arnauld de la Périère, in the U.35 and U.139, sank 195 allied ships totalling 458,856 gross tons. The most successful boats were U.35, which in World War I sank 54 ships of 90,350 grt in a single voyage and 224 ships of 539,711 grt all told, and U.48 which sank 51 ships of 310,007 grt in World War II. The largest target ever sunk by a submarine was the Japanese aircraft carrier *Shinano* (59,000 tons) by USS *Archerfish* (Cdr Joseph F. Enright, USN) on 29 Nov 1944.

AWARDS
Most valuable annual prize
The Templeton Foundation Prize for Progress in Religion inaugurated in 1972 by John M. Templeton (b. 1912) rose in 1987 to a value of £220,000 and was awarded to the American theologian the Rev Stanley L. Jaki for work on the relation between science and faith.

Most statues
The world record for raising statues to oneself was set by Generalissimo Dr Rafael Leónidas Trujillo y Molina (1891–1961), former President of the Dominican Republic. In March 1960 a count showed that there were 'over 2000'. The country's highest mountain was named Pico Trujillo (later Pico Duarte). One province was called Trujillo and another Trujillo Valdez. The capital was named Ciudad Trujillo (Trujillo City) in 1936, but reverted to its old name of Santo Domingo de Guzmán on 23 Nov 1961. Trujillo was assassinated in a car ambush on 30 May 1961, and 30 May is now celebrated as a public holiday. The man to whom most statues have been raised is Buddha. The 20th-century champion is Vladimir Ilyich Ulyanov, *alias* Lenin (1870–1924), busts of whom have been mass-produced as also has been the case with Mao Tse-tung (1893–1976) and Ho Chi Minh (1890–1969).

PEERAGE
Most ancient
The oldest extant peerage is the premier Earldom of Scotland, held by the Rt Hon. Margaret of Mar, the Countess of Mar (b. 19 Sept 1940) and 31st holder of this Earldom, who is the heir-at-law of Roderick or Rothri, 1st Earl (or Mormaer) of Mar, who witnessed a charter in 1114 or 1115 as 'Rothri *comes*'.

Oldest creation
The greatest age at which any person has been raised to the peerage is 93 years 337 days in the case of Sir William Francis Kyffin Taylor GBE, KC (b. 9 July 1854), created Baron Maenan of Ellesmere, County Shropshire, on 10 June 1948, and died, aged 97, on 22 Sept 1951. The oldest elevation to a life peerage has been that of Emmanuel Shinwell PC, CH (b. 18 Oct 1884) on 2 June 1970 when aged 85 years 227 days. He died on 8 May 1986 aged 101.

Longest lived peer
The longest lived peer ever recorded was the Rt Hon. Emanuel Shinwell PC, CH (b. 18 Oct 1884), created a life baron in 1970. He died in London aged 101 years 202 days on 8 May 1986. The oldest peeress recorded was the Countess Desmond, who was alleged to be 140 when she

died in 1604. This claim is patently exaggerated but it is accepted that she may have been 104. Currently the oldest peer is the Rt Hon. Lord Brockway (b. Calcutta 1 Nov 1888).

Youngest peers
Twelve Dukes of Cornwall became (in accordance with the grant by the Crown in Parliament) peers at birth as the eldest sons of a sovereign; and the 9th Earl of Chichester inherited his earldom at his birth on 14 Apr 1944, 54 days after his father's death. The youngest age at which a person has had a peerage conferred on him is 7 days old in the case of the Earldom of Chester on HRH the Prince George (later George IV) on 19 Aug 1762. The youngest to be created a life peer or peeress is Baroness Masham of Ilton, Countess of Swinton (b. 19 Apr 1935) aged 34, in 1970.

Longest and shortest peerages
The longest tenure of a peerage has been 87 years 10 days in the case of Charles St Clair, Lord Sinclair, b. 30 July 1768, succeeded 16 Dec 1775 and died aged 94 years 243 days on 30 Mar 1863.

The shortest enjoyment of a peerage was the 'split second' by which the law assumes that the Hon. Wilfrid Carlyl Stamp (b. 28 Oct 1904), the 2nd Baron Stamp, survived his father, Sir Josiah Charles Stamp GCB, GBE, the 1st Baron Stamp, when both were killed as a result of German bombing of London on 16 Apr 1941. Apart from this legal fiction, the shortest recorded peerage was one of 30 min in the case of Sir Charles Brandon KB, the 3rd Duke of Suffolk, who died, aged 13 or 14, just after succeeding his brother, Henry, when both were suffering a fatal illness, at Buckden, Cambridgeshire, on 14 July 1551.

Highest numbering
The highest succession number borne by any peer is that of the present 35th Baron Kingsale (John de Courcy, b. 27 Jan 1941), who succeeded to the then 746-year-old Barony on 7 Nov 1969. His occupations have included barman, bingo-caller and plumber.

Most creations
The largest number of new hereditary peerages created in any year was the 54 in 1296. The record for all peerages (including 40 life peerages) is 55 in 1964. The greatest number of extinctions in a year was 16 in 1923 and the greatest number of deaths was 44 in 1935.

Most prolific
The most prolific peers of all time are believed to be the 1st Earl Ferrers (1650–1717) and the 3rd Earl of Winchilsea (c. 1627–89), each with 27 legitimate children. In addition, the former reputedly fathered 30 illegitimate children. Currently the peer with the largest family is the Rt Hon. Bryan Walter Guinness, 2nd Baron Moyne (b. 27 Oct 1905) with 6 sons (1 now deceased) and 5 daughters. The most prolific peeress is believed to be Mary Fitzgerald, wife of Patrick, 19th Baron Kingsale, who bore 23 children (no twins) who survived to baptism. She died in 1663.

Baronets
The greatest age to which a baronet has lived is 101 years 188 days, in the case of Sir Fitzroy Donald Maclean, 10th Bt KCB (1835–1936). He was the last survivor of the Crimean campaign of 1853–56. Capt Sir Trevor Wheler, 13th Baronet (b. 20 Sept 1889) entered his 83rd year as a baronet on 11 Aug 1984 but died aged 96 on 14 Jan 1986. The only baronetess is Dame Maureen Dunbar of Hempriggs, who succeeded in her own right as 8th in line of a 1706 baronetcy in 1965.

Knights *Youngest and oldest*
The youngest age for the conferment of a

knighthood is 29 days for HRH the Prince George (b. 12 Aug 1762) (later George IV) by virtue of his *ex officio* membership of the Order of the Garter (KG) consequent upon his creation as Prince of Wales on 17 or 19 Aug 1762. The greatest age for the conferment of a knighthood is on a 100th birthday, in the case of the Knight Bachelor Sir Robert Mayer CH (1879–1985), who was additionally made a KCVO by the Queen at the Royal Festival Hall, London on 5 June 1979.

Most brothers
George and Elizabeth Coles of Australia had 5 sons knighted—Sir George CBE (1885–1977); Sir Arthur (b. 1892); Sir Kenneth (b. 1896); Sir Edgar (b. 1899) and Sir Norman (b. 1907).

Most freedoms
Probably the greatest number of freedoms ever conferred on any man was 57 in the case of Andrew Carnegie (1835–1919), who was born in Dunfermline, Fife but emigrated to the United States in 1848. The most freedoms conferred upon any citizen of the United Kingdom is 42 for Sir Winston Churchill (1874–1965).

Most honorary degrees
The greatest number of honorary degrees awarded to any individual is 111, given to Rev Father Theodore M. Hesburgh (b. 1918), president of the University of Notre Dame, Indiana. These were accumulated from 1954 to June 1987.

Greatest vote
The largest monetary vote made by Parliament to a subject was the £400,000 given to the 1st Duke of Wellington (1769–1852) on 12 Apr 1814. He received in all £864,000. The total received by the 1st, 2nd and 3rd Dukes to January 1900 was £1,052,000.

The Royal Society (founded 1662)
The longest term as an FRS (Fellow of the Royal Society) has been 61 years in the case of Bertrand Russell, 3rd Earl (1872–1970), who had been elected in 1908. The longest lived FRS has been Sir Rickard Christophers CIE, OBE (1873–1978) aged 104 years 84 days. John Lubbock (1834–1913), later 1st Baron Avebury, was elected at the age of 23 in 1857.

Erasmus Darwin was elected on 9 Apr 1761 and was followed by his son Robert (1788 to 1848), *his* son Charles (1879 to 1881), his sons Sir George (1879 to 1912), Francis (1882–1925) and Horace (1903 to 1928) and Sir George's son Sir Charles (1922 to 1962) so spanning over 200 years with 5 generations.

Who's Who
The longest entry in *Who's Who* (founded 1848) was that of the Rt Hon. Sir Winston Leonard Spencer Churchill KG, OM, CH, TD (1874–1965), who appeared in 67 editions from 1899 (18 lines) and had 211 lines by the 1965 edition. Currently the longest entry in its wider format is that of Barbara Cartland, the romantic novelist, with 130 lines. Apart from those who qualify for inclusion by hereditary title, the youngest entry has been Sir Yehudi Menuhin OM, KBE (b. New York, 22 Apr 1916), the concert violinist, who first appeared in the 1932 edition aged 15. The longest entry of the 66,000 entries in *Who's Who in America* is that of Dr Glenn T. Seaborg (b. 19 Apr 1912) whose all-time record of 100 lines compares with the 9-line entry on President Reagan.

Oxford and Cambridge Unions
Four brothers were presidents of the Union in the case of the sons of the Rt Hon. Isaac Foot. Sir Dingle Foot (Balliol, 1927–8); John (Lord Foot) (Balliol, 1930–1) and the Rt Hon. Michael (Wadham, 1933–4) at Oxford and Hugh (Lord Caradon) (St John's, 1929) at Cambridge. The last named's son, the Hon. Paul, was president at Oxford (University College, 1960–1).

THE
HUMAN
WORLD

CHAPTER ELEVEN

Oldest chorister ● Vocal range . . . 97-year-old John Love Vokins (b. 19 June 1890) is the longest serving chorister, having joined the choir of Christ Church, Heeley, Sheffield in 1895 and that of St Michael's, Hathersage in 1930. To date that's 92 years' service at services. (Photo: Derbyshire Times)

Largest political division

The British Commonwealth of Nations, a free association of 49 sovereign independent states together with 27 non-sovereign states and dependencies administered by them, covers an area of 13,095,000 miles² *33 915 000 km²* with a population which in 1980 surpassed 1,000,000,000. The British Empire began to expand when Henry VII patented trade monopolies to John Cabot in March 1496 and when the East India Co was incorporated on 31 Dec 1600.

COUNTRIES

The world comprises 170 sovereign countries and 59 separately administered non-sovereign territories, making a total of 229.

The United Nations still lists the *de jure* territories of East Timor (now incorporated into Indonesia), Western Sahara (now in Morocco) and the uninhabited Canton and Enderbury Islands (now disputed between the US and Kiribati) but does not list the three Baltic states of Estonia, Latvia and Lithuania though their forcible incorporation into the USSR in 1940 has never been internationally recognised. Neither does it list the *de facto* territories of Taiwan, Mayotte or Spanish North Africa, the 4 Antarctic Territories or the Australian Territory of Coral Sea Islands and Heard and McDonald Islands.

Largest

The country with the greatest area is the Union of Soviet Socialist Republics (the Soviet Union), comprising 15 Union (constituent) Republics with a total area of 22 402 200 km² *8,648,500 miles²*, or 15.0 per cent of the world's total land area, and a total coastline (including islands) of 106 360 km *66,090 miles*. The country measures 8980 km *5580 miles* from east to west and 4490 km *2790 miles* from north to south and is 91.8 times the size of the United Kingdom. Its population on 1 Jan 1987 was 281,700,000.

The United Kingdom covers 94,221 miles² *244 030 km²* (including 1197 miles² *3100 km²* of inland water), or 0.16 per cent of the total land area of the world. Great Britain is the world's eighth largest island, with an area of 84,186 miles² *218 040 km²* and a coastline 4928 miles *7930 km* long, of which Scotland accounts for 2573 miles *4141 km*, Wales 426 miles *685 km* and England 1929 miles *3104 km*.

Smallest

The smallest independent country in the world is the State of the Vatican City or Holy See (Stato della Città del Vaticano), which was made an enclave within the city of Rome, Italy on 11 Feb 1929. The enclave has an area of 44 hectares *108.7 acres*. The maritime sovereign country with the shortest coastline is Monaco with 3.49 miles *5,61 km* excluding piers and breakwaters. The world's smallest republic is Nauru, less than 1 degree south of the equator in the western Pacific, which became independent on 31 Jan 1968. It has an area of 5263 acres *2129 ha* and a population of 8100 (latest estimate 1986).

The smallest colony in the world is Gibraltar (since 1969, the City of Gibraltar) with an area of 2½ miles² *5,8 km²*. However, Pitcairn Island, the only inhabited (55 people at 1 Jan 1986) island of a group of 4 (total area 18½ miles² *48 km²*), has an area of 1½ miles² or 960 acres *388 ha*.

The official residence, since 1834, of the Grand Master of the Order of the Knights of Malta, totalling 3 acres *1,2 ha* and comprising the Villa del Priorato di Malta on the lowest of Rome's seven hills, the 151 ft *46 m* Aventine, retains certain diplomatic privileges as does 68 via Condotti. The Order has accredited representatives to foreign governments and is hence sometimes cited as the world's smallest 'state'.

Flattest and most elevated

The country with the lowest highest point is the Republic of the Maldives which attains 8 ft *2,4 m*. The country with the highest lowest point is Lesotho. The egress of the Senqu (Orange) riverbed is 4530 ft *1381 m* above sea level.

Most impenetrable boundary

The 'Iron Curtain' (858 miles *1380 km*) dividing the Federal Republican (West) and the Democratic Republican (East) parts of Germany utilises 2,230,000 land mines and 50,000 miles *80 500 km* of barbed wire, much of it of British manufacture, in addition to many watch-towers containing detection devices. The whole strip of 270 yd *246 m* wide occupies 133 miles² *344 km²* of East German territory and cost an estimated $7000 million to build and maintain. It reduced the westward flow from more than 200,000 in 1961 to a trickle of 30 (including 8 guards) in 1985. The death toll has been 184 since 1962. Construction of the second wall began in East Berlin in March 1984.

Longest and shortest frontier

The longest *continuous* frontier in the world is that between Canada and the United States, which (including the Great Lakes boundaries) extends for 3987 miles *6416 km* (excluding 1538 miles *2547 km* with Alaska). The frontier which is crossed most frequently is that between the United States and Mexico. It extends for 1933 miles *3110 km* and there are more than 120,000,000 crossings every year. The Sino-Soviet frontier, broken by the Sino-Mongolian border, extends for 4500 miles *7240 km*, with no reported figure of crossings. The 'frontier' of the Holy See in Rome measures 2.53 miles *4,07 km*. The land frontier between Gibraltar and Spain at La Linea, closed in June 1969, measures 1672 yd *1,53 km*. It was opened again at midnight on 4–5 Feb 1985. Zambia, Zimbabwe, Botswana and Namibia (South West Africa) almost merge.

Most frontiers

China has the most land frontiers with 13—Mongolia, USSR, North Korea, Hong Kong, Macau, Vietnam, Laos, Burma, India, Bhutan, Nepal, Pakistan and Afghanistan. These extend for 24 000 km *14,900 miles*. France, if all her *départements d'outre-mer* are included, may, on extended territorial waters, have 20. The United Kingdom's frontier with the Republic of Ireland measures 223 miles *358 km*.

POPULATIONS
World

The daily increase in the world's population is 227,400, or 158 per minute. For past, present and future estimates see table.

Date	Millions	Date	Millions
8000 BC	c. 6	1960	3049
AD 1	c. 255	1970	3678
1000	c. 254	1975	4033
1250	416	1980	4415
1500	460	1981	4530
1600	579	1982	4607
1700	679	1983	4685
1750	770	1984	4763
1800	954	1985	4837
1900	1633	1986	4917
1920	1862	1987 (mid)	5000*
1930	2070	2000†	6122
1940	2295	2025	8206
1950	2513	2095	10,500

* Population Institute of Washington, DC declared this landmark was reached on 7 July 1986 whereas the UN nominated 11 July as 'Baby Five Billion Day'.
† The UN publication State of World Population, 1984 forecast that the world population will not stabilise until 2095 at c. 10,500 million.
Note The all-time peak annual increase of 2.0% c. 1958–1962 had declined to 1.73% by 1975–1980. By 1990 this should decline to 1.5%. This, however, now produces an annual increment of 83 million peaking to 90 million in the 1990s. On the estimates of the French demographer Biraben, A. R. Thatcher has calculated that 58,800 million people died between 40,000 BC and AD 1980. This indicates that there have thus been some 63,700 million specimens of Homo sapiens sapiens who ever lived, i.e. the present population is about 1/13th of those who have ever lived.

Most populous country

The largest population of any country is that of China, which in *pinyin* is written Zhongguo (meaning central land). The census of July 1982 was 1,008,175,288 while the 1984 population stood at 1,036,004,000. The rate of natural increase in the People's Republic of China is now estimated to be 38,700 a day or 14.1 million per year. The mid-year 1987 estimate is 1,053.7 million. The census required 5,100,000 enumerators to work for 10 days. India is set to overtake China in size of population during the next century.

Least populous

The independent state with the smallest population is the Vatican City or the Holy See (see Smallest country, above), with 750 inhabitants in 1986 and a nil return for births.

Most densely populated

The most densely populated territory in the world is the Portuguese province of Macau (or Macao), on the southern coast of China. It has an estimated population of 392,000 (mid-1985) in an area of 6.2 miles² *16,05 km²*, giving a density of 63,225 per mile² *24 423 per km²*.

Of territories with an area of more than 1000 km², Hong Kong (400.5 miles² *1037 km²*) contains 5,533,000 (1986), giving the territory a density of 13,390/mile² *5169/km²*. Hong Kong is now the most populous of all colonies. The transcription of the name is from a local pronunciation of the Peking dialect version of Xiang gang (a port for incense). The 1976 by-census showed that the west area of the urban district of Mong Kok on the Kowloon Peninsula had a density of 252,090/km² *652,910/mile²*. In 1959, at the peak of the housing crisis, it was reported that in one house designed for 12 people the number of occupants was 459, including 104 in one room and 4 living on the roof.

Of countries over 1000 miles² *2589 km²* the most densely populated is Bangladesh with a population of 103,200,000 (1986) living in 55,126 miles² *142 775 km²* at a density of 1882/mile² *727/km²*. The Indonesian island of Java (with an area of 48,763 miles² *126 295 km²*) had a population of 91,271,000 (1986), giving a density of 1871/mile² *722/km²*.

The United Kingdom (94,221 miles² *244 030 km²*) had an estimated population of 56,763,300 at mid-1986, giving a density of 602 persons/mile² *233/km²*. The population density for the Royal Borough of Kensington and Chelsea, London is 11 278.6/km² *29,211.4/mile²*.

Most sparsely populated

Antarctica became permanently occupied by relays of scientists from October 1956. The population varies seasonally and reaches 2000 at times.

The least populated territory, apart from Antarctica, is Kalaallit Nunaat (formerly Greenland), with a population of 53,406 (1986) in an area of 840,000 miles² *2 175 000 km²*, giving a density of one person to every 15.72 miles² *40,72 km²*. Some 84.3 per cent of the island comprises an ice-cap.

The lowest population densities in the United Kingdom are in the Scottish Highlands and Islands with 13,1/km² *33.9/mile²*. The most sparsely populated county in England is Northumberland with 154.15/mile² *59,51/km²*.

Emigration

More people emigrate from Mexico than from any other country. An estimated 800,000 emigrated illegally into the USA in 1980 alone. The Soviet invasion of Afghanistan in December 1979

caused an influx of 2,725,000 refugees mainly into Pakistan. A total of 108,000 emigrated from the UK in 1985. Her largest number of emigrants in any one year was 360,000 in 1852, mainly from Ireland.

Immigration
The country which regularly receives the most legal immigrants is the United States. It has been estimated that in the period 1820–1985 the USA has received 52,520,358 *official* immigrants. One in 24 of the US population is, however, an *illegal* immigrant. In 1986 629,000 aliens were arrested by US patrols on the Mexican border. The peak year for immigration into the United Kingdom was the 12 months from 1 July 1961 to 30 June 1962, when about 430,000 Commonwealth citizens arrived. The number of immigrants in the year 1985 was 23,640. The estimated total of 'nonwhites' for Great Britain was 2,376,000 or 4.3 per cent of the population in 1986.

Most patient 'Refusenik'
The USSR citizen who had waited longest for an exit visa is Benjamin Bogomolny (b. 7 Apr 1946) who first applied in 1966. He arrived in Vienna on 14 Oct 1986. Vladimir Slepak (b. 29 Oct 1927) is the new champion, having waited since June 1970.

Tourism
The record influx of tourists into the United Kingdom was 14,577,000 in 1985 and the record spending was £5,457 million in 1986. The projected figure for 1987 was £6000 million from 14.6 million tourists.

Birth rate
The rate for the whole world was 29.0 per 1000 in 1984. The highest estimated by the UN is 55.1 per 1000 for Kenya for 1980–85. A worldwide survey published in 1985 showed no country with a rising birth rate—the last being Nepal.

Excluding Vatican City, where the rate is negligible, the lowest recorded rate is 9.3 per 1000 (1985) for San Marino.

The 1986 rate in the United Kingdom was 13.5/1000 (13.2 in England and Wales, 12.9 in Scotland and 18.0 in Northern Ireland), while the 1986 rate for the Republic of Ireland was 17.5 registered births per 1000. The highest number of births in England and Wales (since the first full year of 463,787 in 1838) has been 957,782 in 1920 and the lowest this century 569,259 in 1977. After falling each year since 1964 (875,972) the figure started rising again at the end of 1977 with the 1986 figure being 666,000 or 1800 per day or 75 per hour.

Death rate
The death rate for the whole world was 11.0 per 1000 in 1984. The estimated death rate in Kampuchea of 40.0 per 1000 from 1975–80

subsided to 19.7 from 1980–85. The estimated figure for Sierra Leone from 1980–85 was 29.7.

The lowest of the latest available recorded rates is 3.5 deaths/1000 in Tonga in 1985.

The 1985 rate in the United Kingdom was 11.8/1000 (11.8 in England and Wales, 12.5 in Scotland and 10.2 in Northern Ireland). The highest SMR (Standard Mortality Ratio, where the national average is 100) is in Castle Morpeth, Northumberland, with a figure of 136. The 1985 rate for the Republic of Ireland was 9.1 registered deaths per 1000.

Natural increase
The rate of natural increase for the whole world is estimated to be 29.0–11.0 = 18.0 per 1000 in 1984 compared with a peak 22 per 1000 in 1965. The highest of the latest available recorded rates is 41.1 (55.1 – 14.0) in Kenya from 1980–85.

The 1985 rate for the United Kingdom was 1.5 (1.4 in England and Wales, 0.3 in Scotland and 7.6 in Northern Ireland). The rate for the first time in the first quarter of 1975 became one of natural decrease. The figure for the Republic of Ireland was 9.7/1000 in 1984.

The lowest rate of natural increase in any major independent country is in the Federal Republic of Germany with a negative figure of −1.9 per 1000 (9.6 births and 11.5 deaths) for 1985. On the Isle of Man the figure is −5.4 (11.2 births and 16.6 deaths).

Marriage ages
The lowest average age for marriage is India, with 20.0 years (males) and 14.5 years (females). At the other extreme is Ireland, with 26.8 (males) and 24.7 (females). In the mid-16th century the average age for first marriages by women in England was 26.7 years. In the People's Republic of China the *recommended* age for marriage for men has been 28 and for women 25. In England and Wales the peak (mode) ages for marriage in 1985 was 23 years (male) and 21 years (female). The average ages in 1985 were 27.5 (women) and 30.2 (men).

Divorces
The country with most divorces is the United States with a total of 1,187,000 in 1985—a rate of 48.94 per cent on the then current annual total of marriages. The all-time high rate was 49.75 per cent in 1981. In England and Wales the average age at divorce is 37.4 years for husbands, and 34.9 for wives.

Sex ratio
There were estimated in 1981 to be 1006.7 men in the world for every 1000 women. The country with the largest recorded shortage of males is the USSR, with 1132.1 females to every 1000 males (1985 census). The country with the largest recorded woman shortage is Pakistan, with 906 to every 1000 males in 1981. The figures are, however, probably under-enumerated due to *purdah*. The ratio in the United Kingdom was 1053 females to every 1000 males at mid-1986, and is expected to be 1034/1000 by AD 2000.

Infant mortality
The world rate in 1987 was 80 per 1000 live births. Based on deaths before one year of age, the lowest of the latest available recorded rates is 5.0 in Tonga in 1985.

In Ethiopia the infant mortality rate was unofficially estimated to be nearly 550/1000 live births in 1969. The highest rate recently estimated is *c.* 200/1000 for Djibouti.

The United Kingdom figure for 1985 was 9.4/1000 live births (England and Wales 9.2, Scotland 10.1, Northern Ireland 13). The Republic of Ireland figure for 1985 was 10.1.

Life expectation
World expectation of life is rising from 47.4 years (1950–55) towards 64.5 years (1995–2000). There is evidence that life expectation in Britain in the 5th century AD was 33 years for males and 27 years for females. In the decade 1890–1900 the expectation of life among the population of India was 23.7 years.

Based on the latest available data, the highest recorded expectation of life at age 12 months is 74.54 years in Japan for males and 80.18 years for females (1985).

The lowest recorded expectation of life at birth is 36.6 years for males and 37.3 years for females in Afghanistan.

The latest available figures for England and Wales (1982–84) are 71.8 years for males and 77.6 years for females, 70.0 and 75.8 in Scotland, 69.8 and 76.0 in Northern Ireland, and for the Republic of Ireland (1980) 69.5 years for males and 75 for females. The British figure for 1901–10 was 48.5 years (males) and 52.4 years (females).

Housing
For comparison, dwelling units are defined as a structurally separated room or rooms occupied by private households of one or more people and having separate access or a common passageway to the street.

The first country to surpass 100,000,000 housing units was India, in 1972. In 1981 the figure was 142,954,921.

Great Britain had a stock of 22,070,000 dwellings as at 1 Jan 1986, of which 63.0 per cent were owner-occupied. The record number of permanent houses built in a year has been 413,715 in 1968.

Physicians
The country with the most physicians is the USSR, with 831,300, or one to every 307 persons. China had an estimated 1.4 million para-medical personnel, known as 'barefoot doctors', by 1981. In the United Kingdom there were 129,299 doctors filling or provisionally registered in the list published by the General Medical Council, as at January 1987.

Dentists
The country with the most dentists is the United States, where there were 140,000 registered members of the American Dental Association in 1986. The number of dentists registered in the United Kingdom as at 1 Jan 1986 was 24,592.

Psychiatrists
The country with the most psychiatrists is the United States. The registered membership of the American Psychiatric Association (inst. 1894) was 32,000 in 1985. The membership of the American Psychological Association (inst. 1892) was 60,000 in 1986.

Hospital Largest *World*
The largest mental hospital in the world is the Pilgrim State Hospital, West Brentwood, Long Island, NY, USA, with 3618 beds. It formerly contained 14,200 beds. The largest psychiatric institute is at the University of California, Los Angeles.

The busiest maternity hospital in the world has been the Mama Yemo Hospital, Kinshasa, Zaïre with 41,930 deliveries in 1976. The record 'birthquake' occurred on a day in May 1976 with 175 babies born. The hospital had 599 beds.

Great Britain
The largest hospitals of any kind in Great Britain are Hartwood Hospital near Shotts, Lanarkshire with 1600 staffed beds for mentally ill patients.

The largest general hospital in Great Britain is the St James's University Hospital (which is also a teaching hospital), Leeds, West Yorkshire, with 1447 staffed beds.

The largest maternity hospital in Great Britain is the Simpson Memorial Maternity Pavilion, Edinburgh with 218 staffed beds.

The largest children's hospital in Great Britain is Queen Mary's Hospital for Children, at Carshalton, Sutton, Surrey, with 429 staffed beds.

Longest stay in hospital
Miss Martha Nelson was admitted to the Columbus State Institute for the Feeble-Minded in Ohio in 1875. She died in January 1975 aged 103 years 6 months in the Orient State Institution, Ohio after spending more than 99 years in institutions.

CITIES
Oldest
The oldest known walled town in the world is Arihā (Jericho). The latest radio-carbon dating on specimens from the lowest levels reached by archaeologists indicate habitation there by perhaps 3000 people as early as 7800 BC. The settlement of Dolní Věstonice, Czechoslovakia, has been dated to the Gravettian culture c. 27,000 BC. The oldest capital city in the world is Dimashq (Damascus), Syria. It has been continuously inhabited since c. 2500 BC.

The oldest town in Great Britain is often cited as Colchester, the old British Camulodunum, headquarters of Belgic chiefs in the 1st century BC. However, the name of the tin trading post Salakee, St Mary's, Isles of Scilly, is derived from pre-Celtic roots and hence *ante* 550 BC. The oldest borough in Britain is reputed to be Barnstaple, Devon whose charter was granted by King Athelstan (927–939) in AD 930.

The only one of the United Kingdom's 58 cities with a Saxon charter is Ripon, North Yorkshire which was a bishopric in 672 and had a charter dated 886.

Most populous
The most populous 'urban agglomeration' in the world is the 'Keihin Metropolitan Area' (Tokyo-Yokohama Metropolitan Area) of 1081 miles² 2800 km² containing an estimated 29,002,000 people in 1981. The municipal population of Tokyo in 1985 was 11,903,900. The population of the metropolitan area of Greater Mexico City in 1985 was published as 17,321,800 with the city proper at 10,499,000 in 1984.

The largest conurbation in Britain is London, with a population of 6,767,500 (mid-1985). The residential population of the City of London (677.3 acres *274 ha* plus 61.7 acres *24,9 ha* foreshore) is 5800 (1986 estimate) compared with 128,000 in 1801. The daytime figure is 285,000. The peak figure for London was 8,615,050 in 1939.

Largest in area
The world's largest town, in area, is Mount Isa, Queensland, Australia. The area administered by the City Council is 15,822 miles² *40 978 km²*. The largest conurbation in the United Kingdom is Greater London with an area of 609.8 miles² *1579,5 km²*.

Towns, villages and hamlets *Great Britain*
The smallest place with a town council is Llanwrtyd Wells, Powys (pop. 614 in 1979). The smallest town with a Royal Charter (granted in 1290) is Caerwys, Clwyd with a population of 801. The strongest claimant to be Britain's oldest village is Thatcham, Berkshire. The earliest Mesolithic settlement there has been dated to 7720 BC.

Highest
The highest capital in the world, before the domination of Tibet by China, was Lhasa, at an elevation of 12,087 ft *3684 m* above sea level. La Paz, administrative and *de facto* capital of Bolivia, stands at an altitude of 11,916 ft *3631 m* above sea level. El Alto airport is at 4080 m *13,385 ft.* The city was founded in 1548 by Capt Alonso de Mendoza on the site of an Indian village named Chuquiapu. It was originally called Ciudad de Nuestra Señora de La Paz (City of Our Lady of Peace), but in 1825 was renamed La Paz de Ayacucho, its present official name. Sucre, the legal capital of Bolivia, stands at 9301 ft *2834 m* above sea level. The new town of Wenchuan, founded in 1955 on the Chinghai–Tibet road, north of the Tangla range, is the highest in the world at 5100 m *16,732 ft* above sea level.

The highest village in Britain is Flash, in northern Staffordshire, at 1518 ft *462 m* above sea level. The highest in Scotland is Wanlockhead, in Dumfries and Galloway, at 1380 ft *420 m* above sea level.

Lowest
The settlement of Ein Bokek, which has a synagogue, on the shores of the Dead Sea is the lowest in the world at 1291 ft *393,5 m* below sea level.

Northernmost
The world's most northerly town with a population of more than 10,000 is the Arctic port of Dikson, USSR in 73° 32' N. The northernmost village is Ny Ålesund (78° 55' N), a coalmining settlement on King's Bay, Vest Spitsbergen, in the Norwegian territory of Svalbard, inhabited only during the winter season. The northernmost capital is Reykjavik, Iceland, in 64° 08' N. Its population was estimated to be 80,000 in 1985.

Southernmost
The world's southernmost village is Puerto Williams (population about 350), on the north coast of Isla Navarino, in Tierra del Fuego, Chile, 680 miles *1090 km* north of Antarctica. Wellington, North Island, New Zealand is the southernmost capital city on 41° 17' S. The world's southernmost administrative centre is Port Stanley (51° 43' S) in the Falkland Islands.

Most remote from the sea
The largest town most remote from the sea is Ürümqi in Xinjiang (formerly Tihwa, Sinkiang), capital of the Uighur autonomous region of China, at a distance of about 1400 miles *2250 km* from the nearest coastline. Its population was estimated to be 320,000 in 1974.

Royalty and Heads of State

Oldest ruling house and longest span
The Emperor of Japan, Hirohito (born 29 Apr 1901), is the 124th in line from the first Emperor, Jimmu Tenno or Zinmu, whose reign was traditionally from 660 to 581 BC, but more probably from c. 40 BC to c. 10 BC. The present Emperor, who succeeded on 25 Dec 1926, is currently the world's longest-reigning monarch.

Her Majesty Queen Elizabeth II (b. 21 Apr 1926) represents dynasties historically traceable back at least to the 4th century AD in the case of Tegid, great grandfather of Cunedda, founder of the House of Gwynedd in Wales; she is 54th in the line. If the historicity of some early Scoto-Irish and Pictish kings were acceptable, the lineage could be extended to about 70 generations.

Reigns *Longest all-time*
The longest recorded reign of any monarch is that of Phiops II or Neferkare, a Sixth Dynasty Pharaoh of ancient Egypt. His reign began c. 2281 BC, when he was aged 6, and is believed to have lasted c. 94 years. Minhti, King of Arakan (Burma) is reputed to have reigned for 95 years between 1279 and 1374. Musoma Kanijo, chief of the Nzega district of western Tanganyika (now part of Tanzania), reputedly reigned for more than 98 years from 1864, when aged 8, until his death on 2 Feb 1963. The longest reign of any European monarch was that of Afonso I Henriques of Portugal who ascended the throne on 30 Apr 1112 and died on 6 Dec 1185 after a reign of 73 years 220 days, first as a Count and then as King.

WORLD'S MOST POPULOUS URBAN SETTLEMENTS

Population	Name	Country	Date
> 100	Dolní Věstonice	Czechoslovakia	c.27000 BC
c. 150	Chemi Shanidar	Iraq	8900 BC
27,000	Jericho (Arihā)	Occupied Jordan	7800 BC
c. 5000	Çatal Huyuk, Anatolia	Turkey	c.6800 BC
> 5000	Hierakonopolis (Nekhen)	Egypt	c.3200 BC
50,000	Uruk (Erech) (now Warka) from 3800 BC	Iraq	3000 BC
250,000	Greater Ur (now Tell Muqayyar)	Iraq	2200 BC
350,000	Babylon (now al-Hillah)	Iraq	600 BC
500,000	Pataliputra (Patna) Bihār	India	400–185 BC
600,000	Seleukia (near Baghdad)	Iraq	300 BC–165 AD
1,100,000	Rome (founded c. 510 BC)	Italy	133 BC
1,500,000	Angkor	Cambodia	900 AD
1.0–1.5 million	Hangchow (now Hangzhou)	China	1279
707,000	Peking (Cambaluc) (now Beijing)	China	1578
1,117,290	London	United Kingdom	1801
8,615,050	London (peak)	United Kingdom	1939
11,903,900	Tokyo	Japan	1985

Note: The UN projection for AD 2000 for Greater Mexico City is 31,616,000.

Roman occupation

During the 369-year-long Roman occupation of England, Wales and parts of southern Scotland there were 40 sole and 27 co-emperors of Rome. Of these the longest reigning was Constantinus I (The Great) from 31 Mar 307 to 22 May 337—30 years 2 months.

Shortest

The Crown Prince Luis Filipe of Portugal was mortally wounded at the same time that his father was killed by a bullet which severed his carotid artery, in the streets of Lisbon on 1 Feb 1908. He was thus technically King of Portugal (Dom Luis III) for about 20 minutes.

Highest post-nominal numbers

The highest post-nominal number ever used to designate a member of a royal house was 75, briefly enjoyed by Count Heinrich LXXV Reuss (1800 to 1801). All male members of this branch of the German family are called Heinrich and are successively numbered from I upwards *each* century.

British regnal numbers date from the Norman Conquest. The highest is 8, used by Henry VIII (1509–1547) and Edward VIII (1936) who died as HRH the Duke of Windsor on 28 May 1972. Jacobites liked to style Henry Benedict, Cardinal York (b. 1725), the grandson of James II, as Henry IX in respect of his 'reign' from 1788 to 1807 when he died as last survivor in the male line of the House of Stuart.

Longest lived 'royals'

The longest life among the blood royal of Europe has been that of the Princess Pauline Marie Madeleine von Croy, who uniquely celebrated her 100th birthday in her birthplace of Le Roeulx, Belgium on 11 Jan 1887. The greatest age among European royal consorts is the 101 years 268 days of HSH Princess Leonilla Bariatinsky (b. Moscow, 9 July 1816), who married HSH Prince Louis of Sayn-Wittgenstein-Sayn and died in Ouchy, Switzerland on 1 Feb 1918. The longest lived queen on record has been the Queen Grandmother of Siam, Queen Sawang (b. 10 Sept 1862), 27th daughter of King Mongkut (Rama IV); she died on 17 Dec 1955 aged 93 years 3 months.

HRH Princess Alice Mary VA, GCVO, GBE, Countess of Athlone (b. 25 Feb 1883) became the longest ever lived British 'royal' on 15 July 1977 and died aged 97 years 313 days on 3 Jan 1981. She fulfilled 20,000 engagements, including the funerals of five British monarchs.

Youngest king and queen

Forty-six of the world's 170 sovereign states are not republics. They are led by one emperor, 14 kings, 3 queens, 4 princely rulers, 1 sultan, 3 amirs, the Pope, a shaik, a ruler and one elected monarch. Queen Elizabeth II is head of state of 16 other Commonwealth countries. That with the youngest king is Swaziland where King Mswati III was crowned on 25 Apr 1986 aged 18 years 6 days. He was born Makhosetive, the 67th son of King Subhusa II. That with the youngest queen is Denmark with Queen Margrethe II (b. 16 Apr 1940).

Heaviest monarch

The world's heaviest monarch is the 6 ft 3 in *1,90 m* tall King Taufa'ahau of Tonga who in Sept 1976 was weighed on the only adequate scales in the country at the airport, recording 33 st (462 lb) *209,5 kg*. By 1985 he was reported to have slimmed down to 22 st (308 lb) *139,7 kg*. His embassy car in London has the number plate '1 TON'.

Most prolific

The most prolific monogamous 'royals' have been Prince Hartmann of Liechtenstein (1613–86) who had 24 children, of whom 21 were live born, by Countess Elisabeth zu Salm-Reiffer-

scheidt (1623–88). HRH Duke Roberto I of Parma (1848–1907) also had 24 children but by two wives. One of his daughters, HIM Empress Zita of Austria (b. 9 May 1892), was exiled on 23 Mar 1919 but visited Vienna, her titles intact, on 17 Nov 1982 reminding republicans that her father succeeded to the throne of Parma in 1854.

Head of state *Oldest and youngest*

The oldest head of state in the world is the Emperor of Japan (b. 29 Apr 1901). The youngest is King Mswati III of Swaziland (b. 19 Apr 1968).

Earliest elected female

President Vigdis Finnbogadottir (b. 1930) of Iceland became the first democratically-elected female head of state on 30 June 1980.

Legislatures

PARLIAMENTS—WORLD

Earliest and oldest

The earliest known legislative assembly or *ukkim* was a bicameral one in Erech, Iraq c. 2800 BC. The oldest legislative body is the *Althing* of Iceland founded in AD 930. This body, which originally comprised 39 local chieftains at Thingvellir, was abolished in 1800, but restored by Denmark to a consultative status in 1843 and a legislative status in 1874. The legislative assembly with the oldest continuous history is the Court of Tynwald in the Isle of Man, which celebrated its millennium in 1979.

BRITISH MONARCHY RECORDS

LONGEST REIGN OR TENURE

Kings
59 years 96 days[1] George III 1760–1820

Queens Regnant
63 years 216 days Victoria 1837–1901

Queens Consort
57 years 70 days Charlotte 1761–1818 (Consort of George III)

SHORTEST REIGN OR TENURE

Kings
77 days[2] Edward V 1483

Queens Regnant
13 days[3] Jane 6–19 July 1553

Queens Consort
154 days Yoleta (1285–6) (Second Consort of Alexander III)

LONGEST LIVED

Kings
81 years 239 days[4] George III (b. 1738–d. 1820)

Queens Regnant
81 years 243 days Victoria (b. 1819–d. 1901)

Queens Consort
87 years Lady Elizabeth Bowes Lyon, Queen Elizabeth, the Queen Mother: (b. 4 Aug 1900)

MOST CHILDREN (LEGITIMATE)[5]

Kings
18 Edward I 1272–1307

Queens Regnant
9[6] Victoria (b. 1819–d. 1901)

Queens Consort
15 Eleanor (c. 1244–90) and Charlotte (b. 1744–d. 1818)

OLDEST TO START REIGN OR CONSORTSHIP

Kings
64 years 10 months William IV 1830–7

Queens Regnant
37 years 5 months Mary I 1553–8

Queens Consort
56 years 53 days Alexandra (b. 1844–d. 1925) (Consort of Edward VII)

YOUNGEST TO START REIGN OR CONSORTSHIP

Kings
269 days Henry VI in 1422

Queens Regnant
6 or 7 days Mary, Queen of Scots in 1542

Queens Consort
6 years 11 months Isabella (Second Consort of Richard II in 1396)

MOST MARRIED

Kings
6 times Henry VIII 1509–47

Queens Regnant
3 times Mary, Queen of Scots 1542–67 (Executed 1587)

Queens Consort
4 times Catherine Parr (b. c. 1512–d. 1548) (Sixth Consort of Henry VIII)

MOST ALIVE SIMULTANEOUSLY

Between 30 Oct 1683 (birth of George Augustus of Hanover, later George II) and 6 Feb 1685 (death of Charles II) there were 8 heads of state living simultaneously (Charles II, James II, William and Mary, Anne, George I and II) and also Richard Cromwell (d. 1712), the 2nd Lord Protector and *de facto* head of state in 1658–59.

Notes (Dates are of reigns or tenures unless otherwise indicated)
[1] *James Francis Edward, the Old Pretender, known to his supporters as James III, styled his reign from 16 Sept 1701 until his death 1 Jan 1766 (i.e. 64 years 109 days).*
[2] *There is the probability that in pre-Conquest times Sweyn 'Forkbeard', the Danish King of England, reigned for only 40 days in 1013–14.*
[3] *She accepted the allegiance of the Lords of the Council (9 July) and was proclaimed on 10 July so is often referred to as the '9 (or 10) day Queen'.*
[4] *Richard Cromwell (b. 4 Oct 1626), the 2nd Lord Protector from 3 Sept 1658 until his abdication on 24 May 1659, lived under the alias John Clarke until 12 July 1712 aged 85 years 9 months and was thus the longest lived head of state.*
[5] *Henry I (b. 1068–d. 1135) in addition to one (possibly two) legitimate sons and a daughter had at least 20 bastard children (9 sons, 11 daughters), and possibly 22, by six mistresses.*
[6] *Queen Anne (b. 1665–d. 1714) had 17 pregnancies, which produced only 5 live births.*

Largest
The largest legislative assembly in the world is the National People's Congress of the People's Republic of China. The sixth Congress, when convened in June 1983, had 2,978 members. Its standing committee has 197 members.

Smallest quorum
The House of Lords has the smallest quorum, expressed as a percentage of eligible voters, of any legislative body in the world, namely less than one-third of 1 per cent. To transact business there must be three peers present, including the Lord Chancellor or his deputy. The House of Commons' quorum of 40 MPs, including the Speaker or his deputy, is 20 times as exacting.

Highest-paid legislators
The most highly paid of all the world's legislators are members of the US Congress whose basic annual salary was raised on 1 Jan 1986 to $75,100 (*then £60,500*) and limited honoraria to $20,940 (*£17,550*). In addition, up to $1,021,167 (*£850,000*) per annum is allowed for office help, with a salary limit of $50,000 (*now £41,660*) for any one staff member (limited to 16 in number). Senators are allowed up to $143,000 (*£119,200*) per annum for an official office expense account from which official travel, telegram, long distance telephone, air mail, postage, stationery, subscriptions to newspapers, and office expenses in home state are paid. They also command very low rates for filming, speech and radio transcriptions and, in the case of women senators, beauty treatment. When abroad they have access to 'counterpart funds'. The President of the US has a salary of $200,000 taxable plus $170,000 non-taxable for travel or entertainment, and a lifetime pension of $69,630 per annum.

Longest membership
The longest span as a legislator was 83 years by József Madarász (1814–1915). He first attended the Hungarian Parliament in 1832–6 as *oblegatus absentium* (*i.e.* on behalf of an absent deputy). He was a full member in 1848–50 and from 1861 until his death on 31 Jan 1915.

Longest UN speech
The longest speech made in the United Nations has been one of 4 hr 29 min on 26 Sept 1960 by President Dr Fidel Castro Ruz (b. 13 Aug 1927) of Cuba.

Filibusters
The longest continuous speech in the history of the United States Senate was that of Senator Wayne Morse (1900–74) of Oregon on 24–25 Apr 1953, when he spoke on the Tidelands Oil Bill for 22 hr 26 min without resuming his seat. Interrupted only briefly by the swearing-in of a new senator, Senator Strom Thurmond (b. 1902) (South Carolina, Democrat) spoke against the Civil Rights Bill for 24 hr 19 min on 28–29 Aug 1957. The US national duration record is 43 hr by Texas State Senator Bill Meier against non-disclosure of industrial accidents in May 1977.

Oldest treaty
The Anglo-Portuguese Treaty of Alliance was signed in London over 614 years ago on 16 June 1373. The text was confirmed 'with my usual flourish' by John de Banketre, Clerk.

Constitutions
The world's oldest constitution is that of the United States of America ratified by the necessary Ninth State (New Hampshire) on 21 June 1788 and declared to be in effect on 4 Mar 1789. The only countries without one-document constitutions are Israel, Libya, New Zealand, Oman and the United Kingdom.

Women's suffrage
The earliest legislature with female voters was the Territory of Wyoming, USA in 1869, followed by the Isle of Man in 1881. The earliest country to have universal suffrage was New Zealand in 1893. The vote of Mrs Lily Maxwell in Manchester on 26 Nov 1867 was declared illegal on 9 Nov 1868.

PARLIAMENTS—UNITED KINGDOM

Earliest
The earliest known use of the term 'parliament' is in an official royal document, in the meaning of a summons to the King's (Henry III's) council, dating from 19 Dec 1241.

The Houses of Parliament of the United Kingdom in the Palace of Westminster, London, had 1826 members (House of Lords 1185, House of Commons 650) in May 1987.

Longest
The longest English Parliament was the 'Pensioners' Parliament of Charles II, which lasted from 8 May 1661 to 24 Jan 1679, a period of 17 years 8 months and 16 days. The longest United Kingdom Parliament was that of George V, Edward VIII and George VI, lasting from 26 Nov 1935 to 15 June 1945, a span of 9 years 6 months and 20 days.

Shortest
The parliament of Edward I, summoned to Westminster for 30 May 1306, lasted only one day. That of Charles II at Oxford lasted 7 days from 21–28 Mar 1681. The shortest United Kingdom Parliament was that of George III, lasting from 15 Dec 1806 to 29 Apr 1807, a period of only 4 months and 14 days.

Longest sittings
The longest sitting in the House of Commons was one of 41½ hr from 4 p.m. on 31 Jan 1881 to 9.30 a.m. on 2 Feb 1881, on the question of better Protection of Person and Property in Ireland. The longest sitting of the Lords has been 19 hr 16 min from 2.30 p.m. on 29 Feb to 9.46 a.m on 1 Mar 1968 on the Commonwealth Immigrants Bill (committee stage). The longest sitting of a standing committee occurred from 10.30 a.m. on 11 May to 12.08 p.m. on 13 May 1948 when Standing Committee D considered the Gas Bill through two nights for 49 hr 38 min.

Longest speeches
The longest recorded continuous speech in the Chamber of the House of Commons was that of Henry Peter Brougham (1778–1868) on 7 Feb 1828, when he spoke for 6 hr on Law Reform. He ended at 10.40 p.m. and the report of this speech occupied 12 columns of the next day's *Times*. Brougham, created the 1st Lord Brougham and Vaux on 22 Nov 1830, then set the House of Lords record, also with 6 hours, on 7 Oct 1831, when speaking on the second reading of the Reform Bill, 'fortified by 3 tumblers of spiced wine'.

The longest back-bench speech under present, much stricter, standing orders has been one of 4 hr 23 min by Ivan John Lawrence QC, MP (b. 24 Dec 1936), Conservative Member for Burton, opposing the Water (Fluoridation) Bill on 6 Mar 1985. John Golding MP (b. 9 Mar 1931) (then Labour, Newcastle-under-Lyme) spoke for 11 hr 15 min in committee on small amendments to the British Telecommunications Bill on 8–9 Feb 1983.

The longest speech in Stormont, Northern Ireland was one of 9 hr 26 min by Thomas Gibson Henderson MP (1887–1970) on the Appropriations Bill from 6.32 p.m. on 26 to 3.58 a.m. on 27 May 1936.

Greatest parliamentary petition
The greatest petition has been supposed to be the Great Chartist Petition of 1848 but of the 5,706,000 'signatures' only 1,975,496 were valid. The largest of all time was for the abolition of Entertainment Duty with 3,107,080 signatures, presented on 5 June 1951.

Most and least time-consuming legislation
The most profligate use of parliamentary time was on the Government of Ireland Bill of 1893–4, which required 82 days in the House of Commons of which 46 days were in committee. The record for a standing committee is 59 sessions for the Police and Criminal Evidence Bill from 17 Nov 1983 to 29 Mar 1984.

The Abdication Bill (of King Edward VIII) passed all its stages in the Commons (2 hr) and the Lords (8 min) on 11–12 Dec 1936 and received the Royal Assent at 1.52 a.m. on the latter date.

Private Members' Bills
Balloting by private members for parliamentary time was in being at least as early as 1844. The highest recorded number of public Bills introduced by private members was 226 in 1908 but the highest number to receive Royal Assent was 27 in the Commons and 7 in the Lords in 1963–64. The worst session was 1973–74 with nil from 42 presented in the Commons and nil from 10 in the Lords.

Divisions
The record number of divisions in the House of Commons is 64 on 23–24 Mar 1971 including 57 in succession between midnight and noon. The largest division was one of 350–310 on the vote of no confidence on 11 Aug 1892.

ELECTIONS—WORLD

Largest
The largest elections in the world were those beginning on 24 Dec 1984 for the Indian *Lok Sabha* (Lower House) which has 542 elective seats. The government of Rajiv Gandhi was returned in polls in which 379,000,000 electors were eligible to vote for 5,301 candidates at 480,000 polling stations manned by 2½ million staff. In Maduranthkam (electorate 120,021) there were 90 candidates.

Closest
The ultimate in close general elections occurred in Zanzibar (now part of Tanzania) on 18 Jan 1961, when the Afro-Shirazi Party won by a single seat, after the seat of Chake-Chake on Pemba Island had been gained by a single vote.

The narrowest recorded percentage win in an election would seem to be for the office of Southern District Highway Commissioner in Mississippi, USA on 7 Aug 1979. Robert E. Joiner was declared the winner over W. H. Pyron with 133,587 votes to 133,582. The loser got more than 49.9999 per cent of the votes.

Most decisive
North Korea recorded a 100 per cent turn-out of electors and a 100 per cent vote for the Workers' Party of Korea in the general election of 8 Oct 1962. The next closest approach was in Albania on 14 Nov 1982 when a single voter spoiled national unanimity for the official (and only) Communist candidates, who thus obtained only 99.99993 per cent of the poll in a 100 per cent turn-out of 1,627,968.

Most bent
In the Liberian presidential election of 1927 President Charles D. B. King (1875–1961) was returned with a majority over his opponent, Mr Thomas J. R. Faulkner of the People's Party, officially announced as 234,000. President King thus claimed a 'majority' more than 15½ times greater than the entire electorate.

Highest personal majority
The highest ever personal majority by any politician has been 424,545 by Ram Bilas Paswan, 30, the Janata candidate for Hajipur in Bihar, India in March 1977. The electorate was 625,179.

In 1956 W. R. D. Bandaranaike achieved 91.82% of the poll with 45,016 votes in Attanagalla constituency of Sri Lanka (then Ceylon).

Communist parties
The largest national Communist party outside the USSR (19,000,000 members in 1986) and communist states has been the Partito Comunista Italiano, with a membership of 2,300,000 in 1946. The total was 1,600,000 in 1986. The membership in mainland China was estimated to be 44,000,000 in 1987. The Communist Party of Great Britain, formed on 31 July 1920 in Cannon Street Station Hotel, London, attained its peak membership of 56,000 in December 1942, compared with 9,700 in 1986 of whom more than 7000 were claimed to have re-registered by the end of the year. The decline has been caused by divisions over relations with the USSR and doctrine leading to expulsions and the formation of new parties or groups within the Labour movement.

Largest ballot paper
On 5 Mar 1985 in the State Assembly (Vidha Sabha) elections in Karnataka, India there were 301 candidates for Belgaum City.

Voting age extremes
The eligibility for voting is 15 years of age in the Philippines and 25 years in Andorra.

Most coups
Statisticians contend that Bolivia, since it became a sovereign country in 1825, had its 191st coup on 30 June 1984 when President Hernan Siles Zuazo, 70, was kidnapped from his official residence by more than 60 armed men.

PRIME MINISTERS AND STATESMEN

Oldest
The longest lived prime minister of any country was Christopher Hornsrud, Prime Minister of Norway from 28 Jan to 15 Feb 1928. He was born on 15 Nov 1859 and died on 13 Dec 1960, aged 101 years 28 days. The Hon. Richard Gavin Reid (b. Glasgow 17 Jan 1879), Premier of Alberta, Canada in 1934–35, died on 17 Oct 1980 aged 101 years 274 days.

El Hadji Muhammad el Mokri, Grand Vizier of Morocco, died on 16 Sept 1957, at a reputed age of 116 Muslim (*Hijri*) years, equivalent to 112.5 Gregorian years. The oldest age of first appointment has been 81 by Morarji Ranchhodji Desai of India (b. 29 Feb 1896) in March 1977.

Longest term of office
The longest serving current prime minister is Lee Kuan Yew, Hon. GCMG, Hon. CH (b. 16 Sept 1923) of Singapore who has been 6 times re-elected and remains in office after 28 years.

Enver Hoxha (b. 16 Oct 1908), First Secretary of the Central Committee of the Albania Party of Labour, ruled from Oct 1944 to his death on 11 Apr 1985.

Andrey Andreyevich Gromyko (b. 6 July 1909) had been Minister of Foreign Affairs of the USSR since 15 Feb 1957, having been Deputy Foreign Minister since 1946, when he was elected President of the USSR on 2 July 1985. Pyotr Lomako (b. 1904) has served in the government of the USSR as Minister for Non-Ferrous Metallurgy from 1940. He was relieved of his post after 46 years on 1 Nov 1986, aged 82, having served on the Central Committee of the CPSU since 1952.

EUROPEAN ASSEMBLY ELECTION RECORDS

In the European Assembly elections of 14 June 1984 the highest majority in the 81 UK constituencies was 90,667 (T. Smith, Lab) in Wales South-East. Lowest was 2,625 (Sir Peter Vanneck, Con)

in Cleveland and Yorkshire North. Largest and smallest electorates were 574,022 in Essex North-East and 307,265 in Highlands and Islands. Highest turnout was 42.4 per cent in Wales North. Lowest was 25.2 per cent in London North-East. Northern Ireland voted by proportional representation.

MAJORITIES—UNITED KINGDOM

Party
The largest single party majority was that of the Liberals in 1832, of 307 seats, with a record 66.7 per cent of the vote. In 1931 the Coalition of Conservatives, Liberals and National Labour candidates had a majority of 491 seats and 60.5 per cent of the vote. The narrowest party majority was that of the Whigs in 1847, with a single seat. The highest popular vote for a single party was 13,948,883 for Labour in 1951.

The largest majority on a division was one of 463 (464 votes to 1), on a vote of confidence in the conduct of World War II, on 29 Jan 1942. Since the war the largest has been one of 461 (487 votes to 26) on 10 May 1967, during the debate on the Government's application for Britain to join the European Economic Community (the 'Common Market').

HOUSE OF LORDS

Oldest member
The oldest member ever was the Rt Hon. Lord Shinwell PC, CH (1884–1986) who first sat in the Lower House in November 1922 and lived to be 101 years 202 days. The oldest peer to make a maiden speech was Lord Maenan (1854–1951) aged 94 years 123 days (see Peerage, p. 185).

Youngest member
The youngest present member of the House of Lords has been HRH the Prince Charles Philip Arthur George KG, PC, KT, GCB, the Prince of Wales (b. 14 Nov 1948) because Dukes of Cornwall, of whom Prince Charles is the 24th, are technically eligible to sit, regardless of age—in his case from his succession on 6 Feb 1952, aged 3. The 20th and 21st holders, later King George IV (b. 1762) and King Edward VII (b. 1841), were technically entitled to sit from birth.

POLITICAL OFFICE HOLDERS

Chancellorship *Longest and shortest tenures*
The Rt Hon. Sir Robert Walpole KG, later the 1st Earl of Orford (1676–1745), served 22 years 5 months as Chancellor of the Exchequer, holding office continuously from 12 Oct 1715 to 12 Feb 1742, except for the period from 16 Apr 1717 to 2 Apr 1721. The briefest tenure of this office was 26 days in the case of the Baron (later the 1st Earl of) Mansfield (1705–93), from 11 Sept to 6 Oct 1767. The only man with four terms was the Rt Hon. William Ewart Gladstone (1809–98).

The longest budget speech was that of the Rt Hon. David (later Earl) Lloyd George PC, OM (1863–1945) on 29 Apr 1909 which lasted 4 hr 51 min but was interrupted by a 30-min laryngeal tea break. He announced *inter alia* the introduction of car tax and petroleum duty. Mr Gladstone spoke for 4¾ hours on 18 Apr 1853.

Foreign Secretaryship *Longest tenures*
The longest continuous term of office of any Foreign Secretary has been the 10 years 360 days of Sir Edward Grey KG, MP (later Viscount Grey of Fallodon) from 10 Dec 1905 to 5 Dec 1916. The Rt Hon. Sir Henry John Temple, 3rd Viscount Palmerston KG, PC, GCB, in three spells in 1830–34, 1835–41 and 1846–51 aggregated 15 years 296 days.

Speakership *Longest*
Arthur Onslow (1691–1768) was elected Mr Speaker on 23 Jan 1728, aged 36. He held the position for 33 years 43 days, until 18 Mar 1761 allowing for the 'lost' 11 days (3–13 Sept 1752).

MPs *Youngest*
The youngest ever woman MP has been Josephine Bernadette Devlin now Mrs Michael McAliskey (b. 23 Apr 1947) elected for Mid-Ulster (Ind. Unity) aged 21 years 359 days on 17 Apr 1969. Henry Long (1420–90) was returned for an Old Sarum seat also at the age of 15. His precise date of birth is unknown. Minors were debarred in law in 1695 and in fact in 1832.

Oldest
Sir Francis Knollys (c. 1550–1648), 'the ancientest Parliament man in England', was elected for Reading in 1640 when apparently aged 90 and was probably 97 or 98 at the time of his death.

The oldest of 20th-century members has been Samuel Young (b. 14 Feb 1822), Nationalist MP for East Cavan (1892 to 1918), who died on 18 Apr 1918, aged 96 years 63 days. The oldest 'Father of the House' in parliamentary history was the Rt Hon. Charles Pelham Villiers (b. 3 Jan 1802), member for Wolverhampton South when he died on 16 Jan 1898, aged 96 years 13 days. He was a member for 63 years 6 days, having been returned at 17 elections. The oldest member is Robert Edwards MP (Lab) for Wolverhampton South-East (b. 16 Jan 1905).

Longest span
Sir Francis Knollys (c. 1550–1648) was elected for Oxford in 1575 and died as sitting member for Reading 73 years later in 1648.

The longest span of service of any 20th-century MP is 63 years 11 months (1 Oct 1900 to 25 Sept 1964) by the Rt Hon. Sir Winston Leonard Spencer Churchill KG, OM, CH, TD (1874–1965), with breaks only in 1908 and 1922–24. The longest continuous span was that of C. P. Villiers (see above). The longest span in the Palace of Westminster (both Houses of Parliament) has been 72 years by the 10th Earl of Wemyss and March GCVO, who, as Sir Francis Wemyss-Charteris-Douglas, served as MP for East Gloucestershire (July 1841 to 1846) and Haddingtonshire (1847 to 1883) and then took his seat in the House of Lords, dying on 30 June 1914, aged 95 years 330 days. The longest living of all parliamentarians was Theodore Cooke Taylor (1850–1952), Liberal MP for Batley 1910 to 1918.

Briefest span
There are two 18th-century examples of posthumous elections. Capt the Hon. Edward Legge, RN (1710–47) was returned unopposed for Portsmouth on 15 Dec 1747. News came later that he had died in the West Indies 87 days before polling. In 1780 John Kirkman, standing for the City of London, expired before polling had ended but was nonetheless duly returned. A. J. Dobbs (Lab, Smethwick), elected on 5 July 1945, was killed on the way to take his seat.

Women
The first woman to be elected to the House of Commons was Mme Constance Georgine Markievicz (*née* Gore Booth). She was elected as member (Sinn Fein) for St Patrick's Dublin, on 28 December 1918. The first woman to take her seat was the Viscountess Astor CH (1879–1964) (*née* Nancy Witcher Langhorne at Danville, Virginia; formerly Mrs Robert Gould Shaw), who was elected Unionist member for the Sutton division of Plymouth, Devon on 28 Nov 1919, and took her seat three days later. The first woman to take her seat from the island of Ireland was Lady Fisher (*née* Patricia Smiles) as unopposed Ulster Unionist for North Down on 15 Apr 1953, as Mrs Patricia Ford.

UNITED KINGDOM
Electoral Records

1 **Lowest Electorate 1987** 23,507: Western Isles

2 **Largest Constituency by Area** 2,472,260 acres *954,680 ha* Ross, Cromarty & Skye

3 **Least votes since Universal Franchise** 5: Lt Cdr W. Boakes DSC RN (Public Safety Democratic Monarchist White Resident) Glasgow, Hillhead 25 Mar 1982

3 **Lowest Expenses** £54: James Maxton Glasgow, Bridgeton 1935

4 Longest Serving **Woman MP** Dame Irene Ward 1931–1974 Wallsend-Tynemouth

5 & **26** **Narrowest Majority** 1 vote Matthew Fowler (Lib) 1895 Durham and 1 vote by H. E. Duke (Unionist) Dec 1910 Exeter, Devon

6 **Lowest Vote** Nil: (Temperance Chartist) Ripon 1860 for F. R. Lees

7 **Heaviest Ever Poll (GB)** 92.7% Darwen (Lancs) 1924

8 **Dead-Heat** Returning Officer declared dead heat (1886) and gave casting vote to J. E. W. Addison (Con) Ashton-Under-Lyne (now Greater Manchester). Dead heat at Cirencester, Gloucester 13 Oct 1892 by-election. New by-election 23 Feb 1893 won by H. L. W. Lawson (Lib)

9 **Most By-Election Candidates** 17: Chesterfield 1 Mar 1984. Rt Hon A. N. Wedgewood-Benn contested for a current record 14th time (12 times returned)

10 & **12** **Narrowest Majority 1987** 56 votes: J. A. Meale (Lab) Mansfield: 56 votes R. Livsey (L/All) Brecon & Radnor

11 **Narrowest Majority Since Universal Franchise** 2 votes: By A. J. Flint (National Labour) Ilkeston (Derbyshire) in 1931

12 **Highest Poll 1987** 84.4%: Brecon & Radnor

13 **Oldest Father of the House** C. P. Villiers (Con) in 1898, 96 years of age, Wolverhampton South

14 & **29** **Most Recounts** 7: Peterborough 1966 and 7: Brighton (Kemptown) 1964

15 **Largest UK Majority 1987** 30,754: Allan Rogers (Lab) Rhondda

16 **Youngest Ever MP** Aged. 15/16 Edmund Waller (1606–87) in 1621 Amersham (Bucks)

17 **Longest Span** Sir Francis Knollys (c. 1550–1648) was elected for Oxford 1575 and died as sitting member for Reading 73 years later in 1648

18 **Greatest Swing: By-Election** 44.4%: Bermondsey 24 Feb 1983 Lab to L/All

18 **Largest Ever Electorate** 217,900: Hendon (Barnet) 1941

18 **Smallest Electorate Since Universal Franchise** 10,851: City of London 1945

18 **Lowest By-Election Poll** 9.3%: South Poplar (London) Aug 1942

18 **Lowest Ever General Election Poll** 29.7%: 1918 Kennington (London)

18 **Lowest General Election Vote** 13: B. C. Wedmore (Belgrano) Finchley 9 June 1983

18 **Most General Election Candidates** 11: Finchley 9 June 1983 in which the total 2579 candidates was a record

18 **Lowest Vote 1987** 30: Mrs M. Hughes (PIP) Kensington

19 **Fastest Ever Result** 57 min: Billericay (Essex) 1959

20 **Current Father of the House** Sir Bernard Braine (Con) elected 1950 Castle Point (Essex)

21 **Highest Majority by a Woman** 38,823: Countess of Iveagh (Con) 1931 Southend (Essex)

22 **Youngest MP for GB Seat since 1832** 21 years 183 days: Hon Esmond Harmsworth Isle of Thanet (Kent)

23 **Youngest MP in Current House** Mathew Taylor (L/All) (b. 3 Jan 1963) Truro

24 **First Woman MP to Take Seat** Nancy Astor 1919 Plymouth Sutton

25 **Fastest 1987 result** 61 min: Torbay (Devon)

27 **Most Rotten Borough** (8 Electors for 2 unopposed members) 1821 Old Sarum (Wiltshire) No elections contested 1295–1831

28 **Most Votes 1987** 43,093: Michael Mates (Con) Hampshire East

29 **Highest Ever Majority** 62,253: Sir Cooper Rawson (Con) Brighton 1931 and **Most Votes** 75,205

30 **Highest Electorate 1987** 98,694: Isle of Wight

31 **Last Unopposed Returns** 25 Oct 1951, Antrim N and S: R. W. H. O'Neill and D. L. Savory; Armagh: Major J. R. E. Horden and Londonderry: W. Wellwood (all Ulster Unionists)

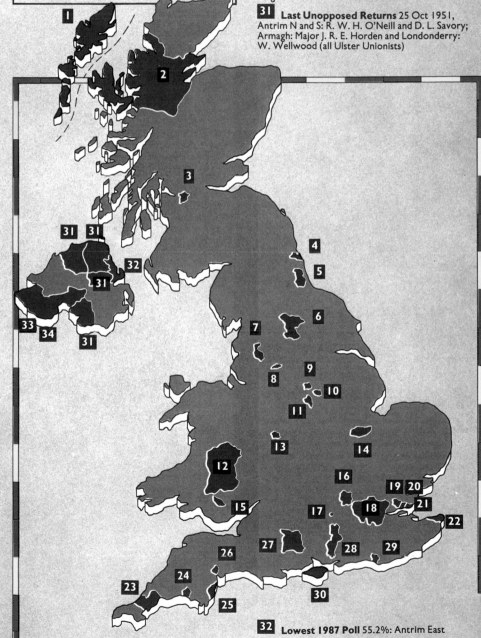

32 **Lowest 1987 Poll** 55.2%: Antrim East

33 **Youngest Member UK (since 1832)** 21 years 67 days James Dickson (Liberal) (1859–1941) returned for Dungannon Tyrone on 25 June 1880

34 **Heaviest Ever Poll (UK)** 93.42%: Fermanagh & S Tyrone in 1951

Artwork: Rhoda and Robert Burns

The first woman cabinet minister was the Rt Hon. Margaret Grace Bondfield PC, CH (1873–1953), appointed Minister of Labour in 1929.

Heaviest and tallest

The heaviest MP of all time is believed to be Cyril Smith MBE, Liberal member for Rochdale since October 1972, when in January 1976 his peak reported weight was 29 st 12 lb *189,60 kg*.

Sir Louis Gluckstein GBE, TD, QC (1897–1979), Conservative member for East Nottingham (1931–45), was an unrivalled 6 ft 7½ in *2,02 m*. Currently the tallest is the Hon. Archie Hamilton, Conservative member for Epsom and Ewell, at 6 ft 6 in *1,98 m*.

Mayoralties

The longest recorded mayoralty was that of Edmond Mathis (1852–1953), *maire* of Ehuns, Haute-Saône, France for 75 years (1878 to 1953). The mayoralty of the City of London dates from 1192 with the 20-year term of Henry Fitz Ailwyn until 1212. The most elections, since these became annual in 1215, has been 8 by Gregory de Rokesley (1274/5 to 1280/1). The earliest recorded mayor of the City of York, Nigel, dates from 1142. Alderman G. T. Paine served as Mayor

---

PRIME MINISTERIAL RECORDS

Though given legal warrant in the instrument of the Congress of Berlin in 1878 and an established place in the Orders of Precedence in England and Scotland in 1904, the office of Prime Minister was not statutorily recognised until 1917. All previous acknowledged First Ministers had tenure as First Lords of the Treasury with the exception of No 12, William Pitt, Earl of Chatham, who controlled his ministers as Secretary of State of the Southern Department or as Lord Privy Seal. The first to preside over his fellow King's ministers was Walpole from 1721, and undisputedly from 15 May 1730.

Record	Value	Position	Name	Details
LONGEST SERVING	20 years 326 days	1st	Sir Robert Walpole KG (1676–1745)	3 Apr 1721–12 Feb 1742
LONGEST SERVING (20th century)	8 years 243 days	38th	Earl of Oxford and Asquith KG (1852–1928)	8 Apr 1908–7 Dec 1916
MOST MINISTRIES	5 times	41st	Earl Baldwin KG (1867–1947)	22 May 1923–28 May 1937
SHORTEST SERVICE IN OFFICE	120 days	22nd	George Canning (1770–1827)	10 Apr–8 Aug 1827
YOUNGEST TO ASSUME OFFICE	24 years 205 days	17th	Hon. William Pitt (1759–1806)	19 Dec 1783 (declined when 23 yr 275 days)
OLDEST FIRST TO ASSUME OFFICE	70 years 109 days	31st	Viscount Palmerston KG, GCB (1784–1865)	6 Feb 1855
GREATEST AGE IN OFFICE	84 years 64 days	33rd	William Gladstone (1809–1898)	3 Mar 1894 (elected at 82 yr 171 days)
LONGEST LIVED	92 years 322 days	47th	Earl of Stockton OM (1894–1986)	from 6 Apr 1984 (so surpassing No 44)
LONGEST SURVIVAL AFTER OFFICE	41 years 45 days	13th	Duke of Grafton KG (1735–1811)	from 28 Jan 1770
SHORTEST LIVED	44 years	7th	Duke of Devonshire KG (1720–1764)	d. 2 Oct 1764 (exact birth date unknown)
SHORTEST MINISTRY	22 days	24th	Duke of Wellington KG, GCB, GCH (1769–1852)	17 Nov–9 Dec 1834
SHORTEST POSSESSION OF SEALS	c. 48 hours	4th	Earl of Bath (1684–1764)	10–12 Feb 1746
SHORTEST PRIOR SERVICE AS MP	2 years 11 months	17th	Hon. William Pitt (1759–1806)	–19 Dec 1783
LONGEST PRIOR SERVICE AS MP	47 years	31st	Viscount Palmerston KG, GCB (1784–1865)	1807–6 Feb 1855
LONGEST SUBSEQUENT SERVICE AS MP	22 years 156 days	39th	Earl Lloyd George OM (1863–1945)	22 Oct 1922–26 Mar 1945
LONGEST SPAN AS MP	63 years 360 days	44th	Sir Winston Churchill KG, OM, CH (1874–1965)	1 Oct 1900–25 Sept 1964
RICHEST	£7¼ million (now say £200 million)	29th	Earl of Derby KG, GCMG (1799–1869)	Annual rent roll in 1869 £170,000
POOREST	£40,000 (now > £1 million) in debt	17th	Hon. William Pitt (1759–1806)	Level of personal debt by 1800
TALLEST	6 ft 1½ in *1,83 m*	51st	Sir James Callaghan KG (b. 27 Mar 1912)	
SHORTEST	5 ft 4¾ in *1,64 m*	28th	Lord John Russell KG, GCMG (1792–1878)	Seven-month baby: max. wt. 8 stone *50,7 kg*
MOST CHILDREN (fathered)	15 or 16	13th	Duke of Grafton (1735–1811)	Twice married
MOST CHILDREN (uniquely mothered)	2	52nd	Margaret Thatcher (b. 13 Oct 1925)	Twins born 21 Aug 1953
MOST LIVING SIMULTANEOUSLY	18	9th–27th	Peel (b. 5 Feb 1788) to death of 9th Earl of Bute (d. 10 Mar 1792)	1788–1792
MOST LIVING EX PRIME MINISTERS	5	9th, 13–16th	Bute, Grafton, North, Shelburne, Portland (Pitt) till Bute died	19 Dec 1783–10 Mar 1792
	5	46–50th	Eden, Macmillan, Home, Wilson, Heath (Callaghan) till Eden died	5 Apr 1976–14 Jan 1977
	5	47–51st	Macmillan, Home, Wilson, Heath, Callaghan (Thatcher)	4 May 1979–29 Dec 1986
MOST PRINCIPAL OFFICES	4	51st	Sir James Callaghan KG uniquely served also as Foreign and Home	

of Lydd, Kent for 29 consecutive years from 1931 to 1961. Cllr Denis Martineau took office as Lord Mayor of Birmingham on 20 May 1986 following in office his father, grandfather, great grandfather and great great grandfather.

Local government service duration records

The oldest local office was that of reeve to supervise villeins. First mentioned in AD 787, it evolved to that of shire reeve, hence sheriff.

Major Sir Philip Barber Bt, DSO, TD, DL (1876–1961) served as county councillor for Nottinghamshire for 63 years 41 days from 8 Mar 1898 to 18 Apr 1961. Henry Winn (1816–1914) served as parish clerk for Fulletby near Horncastle, Lincolnshire for 76 years.

Clifford Tasker (1906–1980) of Pontefract, West Yorkshire was appointed as presiding officer for elections in 1921 when aged 15, and served for 59 years until March 1980.

Weight of legislation

The greatest amount of legislation in a year has been 11,453 pages (83 Public General Acts and 2251 Statutory Instruments) in 1975. This compares with 46 Acts and 1130 Instruments of 1998 pages in 1928. The most Acts were 123 in 1939 and the fewest 39 in 1929 and 1942. The peak for Statutory Instruments was 2916 in 1947.

Military and Defence

WAR

Earliest conflict

The oldest known offensive weapon is a broken wooden spear found in April 1911 at Clacton-on-Sea, Essex by S. Hazzledine Warren. This is much beyond the limit of carbon-dating but is estimated to have been fashioned before 200,000 BC.

Longest

The longest war was the 'Hundred Years War' between England and France, which lasted from 1338 to 1453 (115 years), although it may be said that the nine Crusades from the First (1096–1104) to the Ninth (1270–91), extending over 195 years, comprised a single holy war. The Swiss Jean Jacques Babel estimated that since c. 3500 BC there have been only 292 years in which warfare was unrecorded.

Shortest

The shortest war on record was that between the United Kingdom and Zanzibar (now part of Tanzania) from 9.02 to 9.40 a.m. on 27 Aug 1896. The UK battle fleet under Rear-Admiral (later Admiral Sir) Harry Rawson (1843–1910) delivered an ultimatum to the self-appointed Sultan Sa'īd Khalid to evacuate his palace and surrender. This was not forthcoming until after 38 minutes of bombardment. Admiral Rawson received the Brilliant Star of Zanzibar (first class) from Hamud ibn Muhammad, the new Sultan. It was proposed at one time that elements of the local populace should be compelled to defray the cost of the broadsides fired.

Bloodiest

By far the most costly war in terms of human life was World War II (1939–45), in which the total number of fatalities, including battle deaths and civilians of all countries, is estimated to have been 54,800,000 assuming 25 million USSR fatalities and 7,800,000 Chinese civilians killed. The country which suffered most was Poland with 6,028,000 or 22.2 per cent of her population of 27,007,000 killed. The total combatant death roll from World War I was 9,700,000 compared with the 15,600,000 of World War II.

In the case of the United Kingdom, however, the heavier armed forces fatalities occurred in World War I (1914–18), with 765,399 killed out of 5,500,000 engaged (13.9 per cent), compared with 265,000 out of 5,896,000 engaged (4.49 per cent) in World War II.

In the Paraguayan war of 1864–70 against Brazil, Argentina and Uruguay, their population was reduced from 1,400,000 down to 220,000 survivors of whom only 30,000 were adult males.

Surgeon Major William Brydon CB (1811–1873) was the sole survivor of the 7-day retreat of 16,000 soldiers and camp followers from Kabul, Afghanistan. His horse died two days after his arrival at Jellalabad, India on 13 Jan 1842.

Bloodiest civil

The bloodiest civil war in history was the T'ai-p'ing ('Great Peace') rebellion, in which peasant sympathisers of the southern Ming dynasty fought the Manchu government troops in China from 1851 to 1864. The rebellion was led by the deranged Hung Hsiu-ch'üan (executed) who imagined himself to be a younger brother of Jesus Christ. His force was named *T'ai-p'ing T'ien Kuo* (Heavenly Kingdom of Great Peace). According to the best estimates, the loss of life was between 20,000,000 and 30,000,000 including more than 100,000 killed by government forces in the sack of Nanking on 19–21 July 1864.

Most costly

The material cost of World War II far transcended that of the rest of history's wars put together and has been estimated at $1.5 million million. The total cost to the Soviet Union was estimated in May 1959 at 2,500,000,000,000 roubles (*£100,000 million*) while a figure of $530,000 million has been estimated for the USA. In the case of the United Kingdom the cost of £34,423 million was over five times as great as that of World War I (£6700 million) and 158.6 times that of the Boer War of 1899–1902 (£217 million).

Last battle on British soil

The last pitched land battle in Britain was at Culloden Field, Drummossie Moor, near Inverness on 16 Apr 1746. The last clan battle in Scotland was between Clan Mackintosh and Clan MacDonald at Mulroy, Inverness-shire in 1689. The last battle on English soil was the Battle of Sedgemoor, Somerset, on 6 July 1685, when the forces of James II defeated the supporters of Charles II's illegitimate son, James Scott (formerly called Fitzroy or Crofts), the Duke of Monmouth (1649–85). During the Jacobite rising of 1745-6, there was a skirmish at Clifton Moor, Cumbria, on 18 Dec 1745, when the English forces under Prince William, the Duke of Cumberland (1721–65), brushed with the rebels of Prince Charles Edward Stuart (1720–88) with about 12 killed on the King's side and 5 highlanders. This was a tactical victory for the Scots under Lord George Murray.

Bloodiest battle *Modern*

The battle with the greatest recorded number of *military* casualties was the first Battle of the Somme, France from 1 July to 19 Nov 1916, with 1,043,896—623,907 allied (of which 419,654 were British) and 419,989 German. The published German figure of c. 670,000 is not now accepted. Gunfire was heard on Hampstead Heath, London. The greatest death roll in a battle has been estimated at c. 2,100,000 in the Battle of Stalingrad ending with the German surrender on 31 Jan 1943 by Field Marshal Friedrich von Paulus (1890–1957). The Soviet garrison commander was Gen Vasiliy Chuikov. Additionally, only 1515 civilians from a pre-war population of more than 500,000 were found alive after the battle. The final investment of Berlin by the Red Army on 16 Apr–2 May 1945 involved 3,500,000 men; 52,000 guns and mortars; 7750 tanks and 11,000 aircraft on both sides.

Ancient

Modern historians give no credence, on logistic grounds, to the casualty figures attached to ancient battles, such as the 250,000 reputedly killed at Plataea (Greeks *v* Persians) in 479 BC or the 200,000 allegedly killed in a single day at Châlons, France (Huns *v* Romans) in AD 451.

British

The bloodiest battle fought on British soil was the battle of Towton, near Tadcaster, North Yorkshire, on 29 Mar 1461, when 36,000 Yorkists defeated 40,000 Lancastrians. The total loss has been estimated at between 28,000 and 38,000 killed. A figure of 80,000 British dead was attributed by Tacitus to the battle of AD 61 between Queen Boudicca (Boadicea) of the Iceni and the Roman Governor of Britain Suetonius Paulinus, for the reputed loss of only 400 Romans in an army of 10,000. The site of the battle is unknown but may have been near Borough Hill, Daventry, Northamptonshire, or more probably near Hampstead Heath, London. Prior to this battle the Romans had lost up to 70,000 in Colchester and London.

Greatest naval battle

The greatest number of ships and aircraft ever involved in a sea-air action was 231 ships and 1996 aircraft in the Battle of Leyte Gulf, in the Philippines. It raged from 22 to 27 Oct 1944, with 166 allied and 65 Japanese warships engaged, of which 26 Japanese and 6 US ships were sunk. In addition, 1280 US and 716 Japanese aircraft were engaged. The greatest purely naval battle of modern times was the Battle of Jutland on 31 May 1916, in which 151 Royal Navy warships were involved against 101 German warships. The Royal Navy lost 14 ships and 6097 men and the German fleet 11 ships and 2545 men. The greatest of ancient naval battles was the battle of Salamis, Greece on 23 Sept 480 BC. There were an estimated 800 vessels in the defeated Persian fleet and 310 in the victorious Greek fleet with a possible involvement of 190,000 men. The death roll at the Battle of Lepanto on 7 Oct 1571 has been estimated at 33,000.

Greatest invasion *Seaborne*

The greatest invasion in military history was the allied land, air and sea operation against the Normandy coasts of France on D-day, 6 June 1944. Thirty-eight convoys of 745 ships moved in on the first three days, supported by 4066 landing craft, carrying 185,000 men, 20,000 vehicles, and 347 minesweepers. The air assault comprised 18,000 paratroopers from 1087 aircraft. The 42 available divisions possessed an air support from 13,175 aircraft. Within a month 1,100,000 troops, 200,000 vehicles and 750,000 tons of stores were landed. The allied invasion of Sicily from 10–12 July 1943 involved the landing of 181,000 men in 3 days.

Airborne

The largest airborne invasion was the Anglo-American assault of three divisions (34,000 men), with 2800 aircraft and 1600 gliders, near Arnhem, in the Netherlands, on 17 Sept 1944.

Last on the soil of Great Britain

The last invasion of Great Britain occurred on 12 Feb 1797, when the Irish-American adventurer General Tate landed at Carreg Gwastad with 1400 French troops. They surrendered near Fishguard, Dyfed, to Lord Cawdor's force of the Castlemartin Yeomanry and some local inhabitants armed with pitchforks. The UK Crown Dependency of the Falkland Islands was invaded by Argentine troops on 2 Apr 1982. British troops re-landed at San Carlos on 21 May and accepted the surrender of Brig Gen Mario Menéndez 24 days later on 14 June 1982.

Most millionaires
The United States' total of millionaire families was estimated to have surpassed the million mark in 1987. The median example works 6 days a week for an average of $125,000 (£78,000) per annum. The last published Inland Revenue estimate for the United Kingdom was 11,000 in 1984. Most work 6 days a week for an average $121,000 (£79,000) per annum.

Richest women
The title of the world's wealthiest woman has been wrongly conferred upon the recluse Hioleko (b. 1930), widow since October 1986 of Kenji Osano. The US press first estimated her inherited wealth at $25,000 million. In fact much of her husband's wealth was diverted from her. HM The Queen is asserted by some to be the wealthiest woman but few of her assets under the perpetual succession of the Crown are either personal or disposable. The largest amount proved in the will of a woman in the United Kingdom has been the £7,607,168 of the Rt Hon. Countess of Sefton in 1981. Mrs Anna Dodge (later Mrs Hugh Dillman), who was born in Dundee and died on 3 June 1970 in the United States, aged 103, left an estate of £40,000,000 (equivalent to £235 million in 1987 £s).

The cosmetician Madame C. J. Walker née Sarah Breedlove (b. Delta, Louisiana 23 Dec 1867, d. 1919) is reputed to have become the first self-made millionairess. She was an uneducated Negro orphan scrub-woman whose fortune was founded on a hair straightener.

The youngest person ever to accumulate a million dollars was child film actor Jackie Coogan (b. Los Angeles, 26 Oct 1914), co-star with Sir Charles Chaplin (1889–1977) in The Kid, made in 1920. Shirley Temple (b. Santa Monica, California 23 Apr 1928), formerly Mrs John Agar, Jr, now Mrs Charles Black, accumulated wealth exceeding $1,000,000 (then £209,000) before she was 10. Her child acting career spanned the years 1934–9.

Richest families
It has been tentatively estimated that the combined value of the assets nominally controlled by the du Pont family of some 1600 members may be of the order of $150,000 million. The family arrived in the USA from France on 1 Jan 1800. Capital from Pierre du Pont (1730–1817) enabled his son Eleuthère Irénée du Pont to start his explosives company in the United States.

Largest dowry
The largest recorded dowry was that of Elena Patiño, daughter of Don Simón Iturbi Patiño (1861–1947), the Bolivian tin millionaire, who in 1929 bestowed £8,000,000 from a fortune at one time estimated to be worth £125,000,000.

Greatest miser
If meanness is measurable as a ratio between expendable assets and expenditure then Henrietta (Hetty) Howland Green (née Robinson) (1835–1916), who kept a balance of over $31,400,000 (then £6.2 million) in one bank alone, was the all-time world champion. Her son had to have his leg amputated because of her delays in finding a free medical clinic. She herself ate cold porridge because she was too thrifty to heat it. Her estate proved to be of $95 million (then £19 million [and now worth £270 million]).

Return of cash
The largest amount of cash ever found and returned to its owners was $500,000 (US) found by Lowell Elliott, 61, on his farm at Peru, Indiana. It had been dropped in June 1972 by a parachuting hijacker. Jim Priceman, 44, assistant cashier at Doft & Co Inc, returned an envelope containing $37.1 million (then £20.6 million) in negotiable bearer certificates found outside 110 Wall Street

to A G Becker Inc of New York on 6 April 1982. In announcing a reward of $250 (then £140) Beckers were acclaimed as 'being all heart'.

Greatest bequests
The greatest bequests in a lifetime of a millionaire were those of Ryoichi Sasakawa, chairman of the Japanese Shipbuilding Industry Foundation, who made total donations of 405,732,907,012 yen (£1,758,322,430) during the years 1962–84, and the late John Davison Rockefeller (1839–1937), who gave away sums totalling $750,000,000 (now £350 million). The greatest benefactions of a British millionaire were those of William Richard Morris, later the Viscount Nuffield GBE, CH (1877–1963), which totalled more than £30,000,000 between 1926 and his death on 22 Aug 1963. The Scottish-born US citizen Andrew Carnegie (1835–1919) is estimated to have made benefactions totalling £70 million during the last 18 years of his life. These included 7689 church organs and 2811 libraries. He had started life in a bobbin factory at $1.20 per week.

The largest bequest in the history of philanthropy was the $500,000,000 (then £178,570,000) gift, announced on 12 Dec 1955, to 4157 educational and other institutions by the Ford Foundation (established 1936) of New York.

Highest salary
The highest reported remuneration of any US businessman was $51,544,000 (£33¼ million) in salary, bonus and stock options received by Frederick W. Smith, board chairman of Federal Express, in 1982. The highest amount in salary in 1985 was $12.7 million (£8.8 million) paid to Victor Posner, chairman of DWG Corporation of Miami Beach, Florida.

Highest Fees
The highest-paid investment consultant in the world is Harry D. Schultz, who operates from western Europe. His standard consultation fee for 60 minutes is $2400 on weekdays and $3400 at weekends. His quarterly retainer permitting calls on a daily basis is $28,125. His 'International Newsletter', instituted in 1964, now sells at $50 (£35) per copy.

The highest salary ever paid by any public company has been £1,004,000 in 1986 to Sir Ralph Halpern, chairman of Burton Group PLC. Of this total some £800,000 related to a bonus on a £68-million increase in profits.

Golden handshake
In October 1986 it was confirmed that 'being fired well' in US industry can be more lucrative than working, with an alleged severance payment of $32 million to Michael C. Bergerac, former chairman of Revlon.

The highest-carat British handshake reported was one of 'nearly £700,000' on 20 Jan 1983 received by Bill Fieldhouse CBE (b. 1 Jan 1932) from Letraset of which he had been a director since 1969.

Lowest incomes
The poorest people in the world are the Tasaday tribe of cave-dwellers of central Mindanao, Philippines, who were 'discovered' in 1971 without any domesticated animals, agriculture, pottery, wheels or clothes.

PAPER MONEY
Earliest
Paper money is an invention of the Chinese, first tried in AD 812 and prevalent by AD 970. The world's earliest bank-notes (banco-sedler) were issued in Stockholm, Sweden, in July 1661, the oldest survivor being one of 5 dalers dated 6 Dec 1662. The oldest surviving printed Bank of England note is one for £555 to bearer, dated 19 Dec 1699 (4½ × 7½ in, 11,4 × 19,6 cm).

Largest and smallest
The largest paper money ever issued was the one-kwan note of the Chinese Ming dynasty issue of 1368–99, which measured 9 × 13 in 22,8 × 33,0 cm. In Oct 1983 one sold for £340. The smallest national note ever issued was the 10-bani note of the Ministry of Finance of Romania, in 1917. It measured (printed area) 27,5 × 38 mm 1.09 × 1.49 in. Of German notgeld the smallest are the 1–3 pfg of Passau (1920–21) measuring 18 × 18,5 mm 0.70 × 0.72 in.

Highest denominations
The highest denomination notes in circulation are US Federal Reserve bank-notes for $10,000 (£6580). They bear the head of Salmon Portland Chase (1808–73). None has been printed since July 1944 and the US Treasury announced in 1969 that no further notes higher than $100 would be issued. Only 348 $10,000 bills remain in circulation or unretired.

Two Bank of England notes for £1,000,000 still exist, dated before 1812 but these were used only for internal accounting. In November 1977 the existence of a Treasury £1-million note dated 30 Aug 1948 came to light and it was sold by private treaty for $A18,500 (then £11,300) in Australia. On 19 Feb 1987 a 50-tickal overprinted on a 1-tickal dark grey on grey Siamese note of 25 June 1918 was auctioned by Spinks in Singapore for $51,000 (£31,875).

The highest issued denominations have been £1000 notes, first printed in 1725, discontinued on 22 Apr 1943 and withdrawn on 30 Apr 1945. At least 16 of these notes were still unretired up to November 1979 (last data to be published). Of these perhaps 10 are in the hands of collectors or dealers.

Lowest denomination
The lowest denomination legal tender bank-note is the 1-sen (or 1/100th of a rupiah) Indonesian note. Its exchange value in mid-1984 was 140 to the new penny.

The lowest denomination Bank of England notes ever printed were the black on pale blue half-crown (now 12½p) notes in 1941, signed by the late Sir Kenneth Peppiatt. Very few examples have survived and they are now valued at from £750.

Highest circulation
The highest ever Bank of England note circulation in the United Kingdom was £14,400 million worth on 24 Dec 1986—equivalent to a pile 143.13 miles 230,34 km high in £5 notes.

CHEQUES AND COINS
Largest
The greatest amount paid by a single cheque in the history of banking has been one for Rs. 16,640,000,000, equivalent to £852,791,660, handed over by the Hon. Daniel P. Moynihan, US Ambassador to India in New Delhi, on 18 Feb 1974. An internal US Treasury cheque for $4,176,969,623.57 was drawn on 30 June 1954.

The largest cheque drawn in Britain was one for £604,604,115 drawn on 1 Sept 1982 by British Petroleum Oil Development Ltd, payable to the Inland Revenue against BP's North Sea oil tax bill. If converted to pound notes this would comprise a stack 36.84 miles 59,28 km high.

Greatest collection
The highest price paid for a coin collection has been $7,300,000 (then £3,550,000) for a 'hoard' of 407,000 US silver dollars from the La Vere Redfield estate in a courtroom auction in Reno, Nevada on 27 Jan 1976 by Steven C. Markoff of A-Mark Coin Co Inc of Beverley Hills, California.

Largest hoards

The largest hoard was one of about 80,000 aurei in Brescello near Modena, Italy in 1814, believed to have been deposited c. 37 BC. The numerically largest hoard ever found was the Brussels hoard of 1908 containing c. 150,000 coins. A hoard of 56,000 Roman coins was found at Cunetio near Marlborough, Wiltshire on 15 Oct 1978.

On 10 Dec 1986 the Irish High Court ruled that Michael Webb, farmer of Clonmel, Tipperary, have a hoard discovered by him in 1980 returned by the National Museum or be paid £5,225,000 in lieu. He had been offered £9,500 for the Christian Derrynaflan chalice and three other pieces.

On 20 July 1985 two sons of Mel Fisher found the main cargo of the Spanish *Nuestra Senhora de Atocha* sunk off Key West, Florida in 1622. The value of the cargo already recovered had been $80 million but is now expected to be close to $400 million, mainly in silver bars.

The greatest discovery of treasure is the estimated $2000 million of gold coins and platinum ingots from the sunken Tsarist battleship *Admiral Nakhimov* (8524 tons/tonnes) 200 ft *60 m* down off the Japanese island of Tsushima. She sank on 27 May 1905. A figure of $2000 million has also been ascribed to the *San Jose* which sank in 700–1200 ft *210–365 m* of water off Colombia in 1708. Diving began in August 1984.

Largest mint

The largest mint in the world is the US Treasury's mint built from 1965–9 on Independence Mall, Philadelphia, covering 11½ acres *4,65 ha* with an annual production capacity on a 3-shift 7-day week of 8000 million coins. A single stamping machine can produce coins at a rate of 10,000 per hour.

Charity fund raising

The globally televised 'Live Aid' concerts, organised by Bob Geldof and Bill Graham, with 60 rock acts in Philadelphia and London on 13 July 1985, raised £35 million within two weeks with an estimated further £60 million to come for famine relief. The estimated viewership, via a record 12 satellites, was 1.6 billion or one-third of the world's population. The 'Sport Aid' event, conceived by Chris Long and organised by Bob Geldof (Hon. KBE), took place in 277 cities in 78 countries on 25 May 1986 and raised a worldwide figure of over £67 million (*$100 million*).

The greatest recorded amount raised by a charity walk or run is (Can)$24.7 million by Terry Fox (1958–81) of Canada who ran, with an artifical leg, from St John's, Newfoundland to Thunder Bay, Ontario in 143 days from 12 Apr–2 Sept 1980. He covered 5373 km *3339 miles*.

Longest and most valuable line of coins

The most valuable column of coins amassed for charity was worth £13,628 and was knocked over by Frankie Vaughan at Mecca's Club, Bolton, Lancashire on 18 Aug 1984. The highest-valued line of coins was 10 miles, 5 feet, 7 inches (*16,12 km*) made up of 662,353 US quarters to a value of $165,788 (*£138,155*) on 16 Mar 1985 at Central City Park, Atlanta, Georgia and sponsored by the National Kidney Foundation of Georgia Inc. A line of 1,000,130 one-cent coins 19,782 km *12.29 miles* in length and totalling $10,001.30 was laid by pupils of Blacktown Girls' High School, Blacktown, NSW on 15 Nov 1985 at the local International Peace Park. The Copper Mountain, devised by Terry Pitts Fenby for the NSPCC at Selfridges, Oxford Street amassed over 3 million coins in 350 days (24 May 1984–7 May 1985), valued at £57,051.34.

LABOUR

Trade union *Oldest*

The oldest of the 105 trade unions affiliated to

COINS

OLDEST

World: c. 670 BC electrum staters of King Gyges of Lydia, Turkey[1]. *British: c.* 95 BC Westerham type gold stater (51 known)[2]

EARLIEST DATED

Samian silver tetradrachm struck in Zankle (now Messina), Sicily dated year 1 *viz.* 494 BC—shown as 'A'. *Christian Era:* MCCXXXIIII (1234) Bishop of Roskilde coins, Denmark (6 known)
British: 1539 James V of Scotland gold 'bonnet piece'. Earliest English 1551 Edward VI crown.

HEAVIEST

World: 19,71 kg *43 lb 7¼ oz* Swedish 10-daler copper plate 1644[3]. *British:* 39,94 g *1.4066 oz* gold £5 piece. The latest mintages are dated 1980, 1981, 1982, 1984 and 1985. (Legal tender record)[4]

LIGHTEST AND SMALLEST

World: 0,002 g or 14,000 to the oz Nepalese silver ¼ Jawa c. 1740. *British:* 7.27 grains or 61 to the oz Maundy silver one-penny piece since 1822

MOST EXPENSIVE

World: $1,000,000 for a set of 1804 US coins (including the rare silver dollar), once presented to the King of Spain by dealer Lester Merkin in 1979. *British:* £71,500 (including premium) bid for a Henry III gold 20 pence (6 known) at Spink's, London on 13 June 1985. 20th-century record: £40,000 bid for Edward VIII proof sovereign of 1937 at Spink's, London on 7 Dec 1984

RAREST

World: Many 'singletons' known, *e.g.* only 700 Axumite coins known of which only one of bronze and gold of Kaleb I c. AD 500. *British:* Unique: 1952 George VI half-crown; 1954 Elizabeth II 1d sold in March 1978 for £23,000

[1] Chinese uninscribed 'spade' money of the Chou dynasty has been dated to c. 770 BC.
[2] Bellovaci type gold staters circulated as early as c. 130 BC but were struck in northern France and not in Britain.
[3] The largest coin-like medallion was completed on 21 Mar 1986 for the World Exposition in Vancouver, BC, Canada, Expo 86—a $1,000,000 gold piece. Its dimensions were 37.5 in *95,25 cm* diameter and ¾ in *19,05 mm* thick and it weighed 166 kg *365 lb 15 oz* or 5337 oz (troy) of gold.
[4] The George III 'Cartwheel' copper 2d coin of 1797 weighed 2.04 oz *58,0 g*. The 5-guinea gold pieces introduced by Charles II weighed 41,75 g *1.472 oz*.

---

the Trades Union Congress (founded 1868) is the National Society of Brushmakers and General Workers (current membership 725), founded in 1747. The oldest union currently affiliated to the TUC under its original name is the Educational Institute of Scotland (EIS), founded in 1847, with 43,282 members.

Largest

The world's largest union has been Solidarność (Solidarity), founded in Poland in November 1980 which by October 1981 was reported to have 8,000,000 members at the time it was outlawed.

The largest union in the United Kingdom is the Transport and General Workers' Union, with 1,377,944 members at 1 Jan 1987. Its peak membership was 2,086,281 in 1979.

Smallest

The ultimate in small unions was the Jewelcase and Jewellery Display Makers Union (JJDMU) founded in 1894. It was dissolved on 31 Dec 1986 by its General Secretary, Charles Evans. The motion was seconded by Fergus McCormack, its only surviving member.

Longest name

The union with the longest name is the International Association of Marble, Slate and Stone Polishers, Rubbers and Sawyers, Tile and Marble Setters' Helpers and Marble Mosaic and Terrazzo Workers' Helpers, or the IAMSSPRSTMSHMMTWH of Washington, DC, USA.

Labour dispute *Earliest*

A labour dispute concerning monotony of diet and working conditions was recorded in 1153 BC in Thebes, Egypt. The earliest recorded strike was one by an orchestra leader named Aristos from Greece, in Rome c. 309 BC. The cause was meal breaks.

Largest

The most serious single labour dispute in the United Kingdom was the General Strike of 4–12 May 1926, called by the Trades Union Congress in support of the Miners' Federation. During the nine days of the strike 1,580,000 people were involved and 14,500,000 working days were lost.

During the year 1926 a total of 2,750,000 people were involved in 323 different labour disputes and the working days lost during the year amounted to 162,300,000, the highest figure ever recorded. The figures for 1986 were 1,923,000 working days involving 1071 stoppages with 681,000 workers involved.

Longest

The world's longest recorded strike ended on 4 Jan 1961, after 33 years. It concerned the employment of barbers' assistants in Copenhagen, Denmark. The longest recorded major strike was that at the plumbing fixtures factory of the Kohler Co in Sheboygan, Wisconsin between April 1954 and October 1962. The strike is alleged to have cost the United Automobile Workers' Union about $12,000,000 (*then £4.8 million*) to sustain.

Britain's most protracted national strike was called by the National Union of Mineworkers from 8 Mar 1984 to 5 Mar 1985. HM Treasury estimated the cost to be £2625 million or £118.93 per household.

Unemployment *Highest*

The highest recorded percentage unemployment in Great Britain was on 23 Jan 1933, when the total of unemployed persons on the Employment Exchange registers was 2,903,065, representing 22.8 per cent of the insured working population. The peak figure for the post-war period has been 14.1 per cent (3,407,729) in Jan 1986.

Lowest

In Switzerland in December 1973 (pop. 6.6 million), the total number of unemployed was reported to be 81. The lowest recorded peacetime level of unemployment in Britain was 0.9 per cent on 11 July 1955, when 184,929 persons were registered. The peak figure for the employed labour force in the United Kingdom has been 25,520,000 in December 1979.

ASSOCIATION

Oldest club

Britain's oldest gentleman's club is White's, St James's, London, opened c. 1697 by Francis White (d. 1711) as a Chocolate House, and moved to its present site in 37 St James's in 1755. This has been described as an 'oasis in a desert of democracy'. Britain's oldest known dining club is the Charterhouse School Founder's Day Dinner held each twelfth of December. The 1984 dinner to commemorate Old Etonian coal-owner Thomas Sutton (1532–1611) was the 358th.

London clubland's two most senior members are believed to be Major Leonard M. E. Dent DSO and Sir Walter Howard MBE who joined the United Oxford and Cambridge University Club in 1912 and who were both born in 1888.

This compares with the British Telecom figure of 22,072,799 (20 Mar 1987) (sixth largest in the world to the USA, Japan, USSR, West Germany and France), or 390 per 1000 people. The territory with fewest reported telephone lines is Pitcairn Island with 24.

The city with most telephones is New York with 5,808,145 (821 per 1000 people) at 1 Jan 1985. In 1983 Washington, DC reached the level of 1730 telephones per 1000 people.

Longest telephone cable

The world's longest submarine telephone cable is the Commonwealth Pacific Cable (COMPAC), which runs for 9340 miles *15 032 km* from Sydney, Australia, via Norfolk Island, Fiji and the Hawaiian Islands to Port Alberni, Canada. It cost about £35,000,000 and was inaugurated on 2 Dec 1963. The final splice was made on 24 Mar 1984.

> **Shortest street** ● The world title is claimed by Bacup in Lancashire where 'Elgin Street', situated by the old market ground, measures just 17 ft 0 in *5,18 m*. It is not a carriageway but a railed close. (Photo: John Davidson)

Longest call

A telephone call around the world, over an estimated 98,700 miles *158 845 km* was made on 28 Dec 1985 from, and back to, the Royal Institution, London, during one of the Christmas lectures given by David Pye, Professor of Zoology, Queen Mary College, London. The international telecommunications 'rule', that only one communication satellite be used at a time, was suspended for the demonstration so that both geostationary Intelsats, one over the Indian Ocean and one over the Pacific, could be employed. The two 'telephonists', Anieka Russell and Alison Risk experienced a delay in their conversation of 530 milliseconds.

Telephone directories

The world's most difficult directory to tear in half would be that for Houston, Texas which runs to 2889 pages for 939,640 listings. It is now issued in 2 sections. The easiest would be that for Knippa, Texas—221 listings on 2 pages. The directory for Anguilla in 1972 was of 26 numbers in typescript.

Largest switchboard

The world's biggest switchboard is that in the Pentagon, Washington, DC with 25,000 lines and an annual phone bill of $8.7 million.

Optical fibre

The longest distance at which signals have been transmitted without repeaters is 251,6 km *156.3 miles* at the British Telecom research laboratory at Martlesham Heath, Suffolk in February 1985. The laser wavelength was 1525 nm and the rate was 35 megabits/sec.

POSTAGE STAMPS

EARLIEST
Put on sale at GPO 1 May 1840. 1d Penny Black of Great Britain, Queen Victoria, 68,158,080 printed. Available for prepayment of postage on 6 May 1840.

HIGHEST PRICE (TENDER) (WORLD)
$1 million (then £495,000). 5-cent Blue Alexandria USA cover, Nov 25 1846 by George Normann via David Feldmans of Geneva on 9 May 1981.

HIGHEST PRICE (AUCTION) (WORLD)
£615,000 (incl. buyer's premium). Baden 9-kr black on blue-green, colour error 1851 from the John R. Boker collection sold by Heinrich Köhler in Weisbaden, West Germany on 16 Mar 1985.

HIGHEST PRICE (AUCTION) (UK)
£105,000. Norwegian 4-skilling Blue, 1855 block of 39 used—found in Trondheim railway station *c.* 1923 sold by Phillips, London on 5 Mar 1981.

LARGEST PHILATELIC PURCHASE
$11,000,000 (then £4,945,000). Marc Haas collection of 3000 US postal and pre-postal covers to 1869 by Stanley Gibbons International Ltd of London in August 1979.

LARGEST (SPECIAL PURPOSE)
9¾ × 2¾ in 247,5 × 69,8 mm. Express Delivery of China, 1913.

(STANDARD POSTAGE)
6.3 × 4.33 in 160 × 110 mm. Marshall Islands 75-cent issued 30 Oct 1979.

SMALLEST
0.31 × 0.37 in 8 × 9,5 mm. 10-cent and 1-peso Colombian State of Bolivar, 1863–6.

HIGHEST DENOMINATION (WORLD)
£100. Red and black, George V of Kenya, 1925–7.
(UK)
£5. Orange, Victoria, issued 21 Mar 1882. Pink and blue Elizabeth II definitive 2 Feb 1977.

LOWEST DENOMINATION
3000 pengö of Hungary. Issued 1946 when 150 million million pengö = 1p.

RAREST (WORLD)
Unique examples include: British Guiana (now Guyana) 1-cent black on magenta of 1856 (see above); Swedish 3-skilling banco yellow colour error of 1855. Gold Coast provisional of 1885 and the US post-master stamp from Boscowen, New Hampshire and Lockport, NY.

RAREST (UK) (Issued for postal use)
11 or 12. 6d dull purple Inland Revenue Edward VII, issued on 14 Mar and withdrawn on 14 May 1904. Only one specimen in private hands from W. H. Harrison-Cripps sold by Stanley Gibbons for £10,000 on 27 Oct 1972.

Postal services

The country with the largest mail in the world is the United States, whose population posted 140.1 billion letters and packages in 1985 when the US Postal Service employed 744,490 people, with the world's largest civilian vehicle fleet of 200,811 cars and trucks. The United Kingdom total was 11,700 million letters and 209 million parcels in the year ending 31 Mar 1986. The record day was 15 Dec 1986 with 120 million items when Christmas cards coincided with the British Gas flotation.

The United States also takes first place in the average number of letters which each person posts during one year. The figure was 589 in 1985. The United Kingdom figure was 209 per head in 1986.

Postal address *Highest numbering*

The practice of numbering houses began on the Pont Nôtre Dame, Paris, France in 1463. The highest-numbered house in Britain is No 2679 Stratford Road, Hockley Heath, West Midlands, owned since 1964 by Mr and Mrs Howard Hughes. The highest-numbered house in Scotland is No 2629 London Road, Mount Vernon, Glasgow, which is part of the local police station.

Oldest pillar-boxes

The oldest pillar-box still in service in the British Isles is one dating from 8 Feb 1853 in Union Street, St Peter Port, Guernsey. It was cast by John Vaudin in Jersey and was restored to its original maroon livery in October 1981. The oldest box in mainland Britain is at Barnes Cross, Holwell (postally in Bishop's Caundle), Dorset, dating from probably later in 1853. The hexagonal-roofed pillar box in Kent Railway Station, Glanmere, Cork dates from 1857.

Post offices

The Post Office's northernmost post office is at Haroldswick, Unst, Shetland Islands. The most southerly in the British Isles is at Samarès, Jersey. The oldest is at Sanquhar, Dumfries and Galloway which was first referred to in 1763. In England the post office at Shipton-under-Wychwood, Oxon dates back to April 1845. The highest post office in England is at Flash, Staffordshire at 1518 ft *462,6 m.*

The longest counter in Britain was one of 185 ft *56,38 m* with 33 positions when opened in 1962 at Trafalgar Square, London. The longest in 1985 is at George Square, Glasgow, being 157 ft *47,8 m* long with 27 positions.

Education

Compulsory education was first introduced in 1819 in Prussia. It became compulsory in the United Kingdom in 1870.

University *Oldest*

The Sumerians had scribal schools or *É-Dub-ba* soon after 3500 BC. The oldest existing educational institution in the world is the University of Karueein, founded in AD 859 in Fez, Morocco. The University of Bologna was founded in 1088.

The oldest university in the United Kingdom is the University of Oxford, which came into being *c.* 1167. The oldest of the existing colleges is probably University College (1249), though its foundation is less well documented than that of Merton in 1264. The earliest college at Cambridge University is Peterhouse, founded in 1284. The largest at either university is Trinity College, Cambridge, founded in 1546. The oldest university in Scotland is the University of St Andrews, Fife. Established as a university in 1411, theology and medicine may have been taught there since *c.* 900 AD.

Greatest enrolment

The university with the greatest enrolment in the world is the State University of New York, USA, with 156,175 students enrolled in 1984–1985. Its oldest college at Potsdam, New York was founded in 1816. Britain's largest university is the University of London with 63,504 internal students and 24,498 external students (in 1985–86) so totalling 88,002. The Open University, first called the University of the Air (Royal Charter 30 May 1969), at Walton Hall near Milton Keynes has 5209 part-time tutors and 133,198 students.

Largest

Tenders for the $3.4 billion (*£1790 million*) University of Riyadh, Saudi Arabia closed in June 1978. The University will house 15,000 families and have its own mass transport system.

The largest existing university building in the world is the M. V. Lomonosov State University on the Lenin Hills, south of Moscow, USSR. It stands 240 m *787.4 ft* tall, has 32 storeys and 40,000 rooms. It was constructed from 1949–53.

Most northerly

The world's most northerly university is Inupiat University of the Arctic Barrow, Alaska in Lat. 71° 16′ N. Eskimo subjects feature in the curricula.

Largest court or quadrangle

The largest college quadrangle at any Oxford or Cambridge college is the Great Court, Trinity College, Cambridge, completed in 1605. It averages 325 ft × 273 ft *99,06 m × 83,2 m.*

Professor *Youngest*

The youngest at which anybody has been elected to a chair in a university is 19 years in the case of Colin MacLaurin (1698–1746), who was elected to Marischal College, Aberdeen as Professor of Mathematics on 30 Sept 1717. In 1725 he was made Professor of Mathematics at Edinburgh University on the recommendation of Sir Isaac Newton, who was a professor at Cambridge aged 26.

Most durable

Dr Joel Hildebrand (1881–1983), Professor Emeritus of Physical Chemistry at the University of California, Berkeley, first became an Assistant Professor in 1913 and published his 275th research paper 68 years later in 1981. The longest period for which any professorship has been held in Britain is 63 years in the case of Thomas Martyn (1735–1825), Professor of Botany at Cambridge University from 1762 until his death. The last professor-for-life was the pathologist Professor Henry Roy Dean (1879–1961) for his last 39 years at Cambridge.

Senior Wranglers

Since 1910, the Wranglers (first class honours students in the Cambridge University mathematical Tripos, part 2) have been placed in alphabetical order only. In 1890 Miss Philippa Garrett Fawcett (d. 1948) in Newnham was placed 'above the Senior Wrangler'.

Most graduates in family

Mr & Mrs Albert Kunz of Bloomington, Indiana saw all their 8 daughters and 5 sons graduate from Indiana University between 1932 and 1956.

Youngest undergraduate and graduate

The most extreme recorded case of undergraduate juvenility was that of William Thomson (1824–1907), later Lord Kelvin OM, GCVO, who entered Glasgow University aged 10 years 4 months in October 1834 and matriculated on 14 Nov the same year. Dr Merrill Kenneth Wolf (b. 28 Aug 1931) of Cleveland, Ohio took his BA in music from Yale University in September 1945 in the month of his 14th birthday. Ruth Lawrence (b. 1971) of Huddersfield, West Yorkshire passed Pure Mathematics O level at the age of 9 and Pure Mathematics A level and Grade 1 S level in June 1981, aged 10. She was accepted for

entrance to Oxford at the age of 12 and graduated from St Hugh's with a first class degree, top of 191 entrants, on 4 July 1985.

Youngest doctorate

On 13 Apr 1814 the mathematician Carl Witte of Lochau was made a Doctor of Philosophy of the University of Giessen, Germany when aged 12.

School *Oldest in Britain*

The title of the oldest existing school in Britain is contested. It is claimed that King's School in Canterbury, Kent, was a foundation of Saint Augustine, some time between his arrival in Kent in AD 597 and his death *c.* 604. Cor Tewdws (College of Theodosius) at Llantwit Major, South Glamorgan, reputedly burnt down in AD 446, was refounded, after an elapse of 62 years, by St Illtyd in 508, and it flourished into the 13th century. Winchester College was founded in 1382. Lanark Grammar School claims to have been referred to in a papal bull drawn up in 1183 by Lucius III.

Largest

In 1983/84 South Point High School, Calcutta (founded 1954) had an enrolment of 12,350 regular students.

The school with the most pupils in Great Britain was Exmouth Comprehensive, Devon with 2599 (1983/84). The highest enrolment in Scotland has been at Our Lady's Roman Catholic High School, Motherwell, Lanarkshire with a peak of 2325 in August 1977. The total in Holy Child School, Belfast, Northern Ireland reached 2752 in 1973 before being split up. The highest enrolment in 1986/87 is 2212 at the Methodist College, Belfast.

Most expensive

The annual cost of keeping a boy at the Oxford Academy (founded 1906), Westbrook, Connecticut, USA for 1987/88 was $23,500.

In the academic year 1987/88 St Andrew's Private Tutorial Centre, Cambridge, England (Co-founders W. A. Duncombe and C. T. Easterbrook) charged £13,359 for full-time science students (tuition and accommodation). The most expensive school in Great Britain is Millfield (founded 1935) in Street, Somerset (headmaster C. R. M. Atkinson). The annual fee for boarding entries in 1987/88 was £7365. The most expensive girls' school in 1985 was Cobham Hall, near Gravesend, Kent (founded 1960) (headmistress Miss Susan Cameron), with annual fees of £5820.

Earliest comprehensive school

Lakes School, Cumbria, formed from an intake from Windermere Grammar School and other Westmorland schools, adopted the non-selective comprehensive principle as early as 1945. Calder High School was established after formal rejection of the 11-plus examinations from two West Riding schools in 1950. The earliest purpose built was Kidbrooke Comprehensive for Girls in south-east London, opened in 1954.

Oldest old school tie

The practice of wearing distinctive neckties bearing the colours of registered designs of schools, universities, sports clubs, regiments, etc., appears to date from *c.* 1880. It originated in Oxford University, where boater bands were converted into use as 'ribbon ties'. The earliest definitive evidence stems from an order from Exeter College for college ties, dated 25 June 1880.

Oldest PTA

The parent-teacher association with the earliest known foundation date in Britain is that for Lawrence Sheriff School, Rugby, Warwickshire, formed in 1908.

Most schools

The greatest documented number of schools attended by a pupil is 265 by Wilma Williams, now Mrs R. J. Horton, from 1933–43 when her parents were in show business in the USA.

Most O and A levels
Dr Francis L. Thomason of Hammersmith, London, had by August 1986 accumulated 70 O and O/A, 16 A and 1 S levels making a total of 87, of which 36 were in the top grade. A. F. Prime, a prisoner in HM Open Prison Sudbury, accumulated a total of 1 S, 14 As and 34 Os between 1968 and 1982. Environmental difficulties tend to make study harder in prison than elsewhere.

Stephen Murrell of Crown Woods School, Eltham passed 8 A levels at one sitting in June 1978 achieving 7 at grade A. Robert Pidgeon (b. 7 Feb 1959) of St Peter's School, Bournemouth, secured 13 O level passes at grade A at one sitting in the summer of 1975. Subsequently he passed 3 A levels at grade A and 2 S levels with firsts.

Andrew Maclaren (b. 1963) of Chelmsford, Essex passed 14 O levels, 5 A levels, all at grade A and 3 S levels at grade one—making 22 top grades. At Queens' College, Cambridge he obtained first class honours in 1983.

Youngest headmaster
The youngest headmaster of a major public school was Henry Montagu Butler (b. 2 July 1833), appointed Headmaster of Harrow School on 16 Nov 1859, when aged 26 years 137 days. His first term in office began in January 1860.

Largest Mormon temple ● The Salt Lake Temple, Utah, USA was dedicated on 6 Apr 1893. It has a floor area covering 253,015 ft² or 5.80 acres *23,505 m²*. (Photo: Graham Ling)

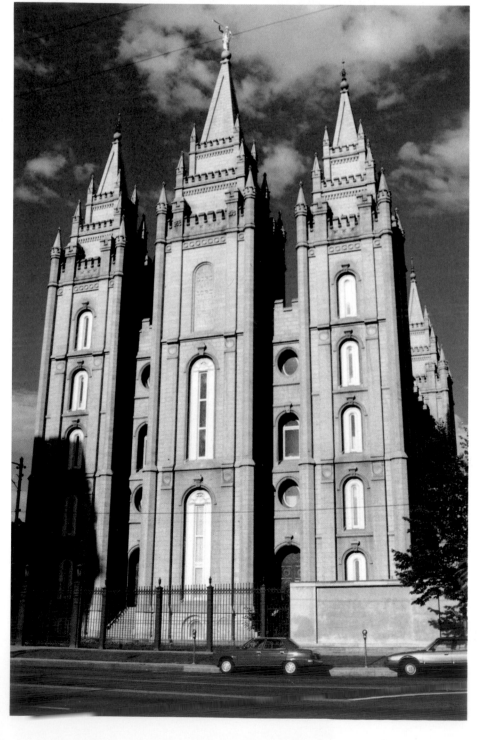

Most durable don
Dr Martin Joseph Routh (b. Sept 1755) was President of Magdalen College, Oxford, from April 1791 for 63 years 8 months, until his death in his 100th year on 22 Dec 1854. He had previously been a fellow for 16 years and was thus a don for a span of 79 years.

Most durable teachers
David Rhys Davies (1835–1928) taught as a pupil teacher and latterly as teacher and headmaster of Dame Anna Child's School, Whitton, Powys for a total of 76 years 2 months. Col Ernest Achey Loftus CBE, TD, DL (b. 11 Jan 1884) served as a teacher over a span of 73 years from May 1901 in York, England until 18 Feb 1975 in Zambia, retiring as the world's oldest civil servant aged 91 years 38 days. His father William was born in Hull in the reign of William IV in 1832.

Elsie Marguerite Touzel (1889–1984) of Jersey began her teaching career aged 16 in 1905 and was teaching at Les Alpes School, Faldonet until her retirement 75 years later on 30 Sept 1980.

Highest endowment
The greatest single gift in the history of higher education has been $125 million to Louisiana State University by C. B. Pennington in 1983.

Religions

Oldest
Human burial, which has religious connotations, is known from *c.* 60,000 BC among *Homo sapiens neanderthalensis* in the Shanidar cave, northern Iraq. The earliest named prophet was Zoroaster (Zarathustra) dated to *c.* 1600 BC. He has 250,000 followers today.

Largest
Religious statistics are necessarily only approximate. The test of adherence to a religion varies widely in rigour, while many individuals, particularly in the East, belong to two or more religions.

Christianity is the world's prevailing religion, with some 1,620,000,000 adherents in 1986. The Vatican statistics office reported that in 1986 there were 900,545,000 Roman Catholics.

The largest non-Christian religion is Islam (Muslim) with some 560,000,000 followers.

In the United Kingdom the Anglicans comprise members of the Established Church of England, the Dis-established Church in Wales, the Episcopal Church in Scotland and the Church of Ireland. The Church of England has two provinces (Canterbury and York), 44 dioceses, 10,649 full-time diocesan clergymen and 13,369 parishes (mid-1987).

In Scotland the most numerous group is the Church of Scotland (12 synods, 47 presbyteries), which had 854,311 members as at 1 Jan 1987.

Jews
The total of world Jewry was estimated to be 16 million in 1987. The highest concentration is in the USA with 5,834,650 of whom 1,742,500 are in the New York area. The total in Israel is 3,537,000. The total of British Jewry is 330,000 of whom 201,000 are in London, and 11,000 in Glasgow, the largest concentration in Scotland. The total in Tokyo is only 750.

PLACES OF WORSHIP

Earliest
A sculpted stone face, half primate/half feline, discovered by Dr Leslie Freeman of the University of Chicago in the El Juyo cave shrine, northern Spain, is claimed to be the oldest known religious shrine and is dated to *c.* 12,000 BC. The oldest surviving Christian church in the world is

a converted house in Douro-Europos (now Qal'at es Salihiye) in eastern Syria, dating from AD 232.

Oldest *Great Britain*

The oldest ecclesiastical building in the United Kingdom is a 6th-century cell built by St Brendan in AD 542 on Eileachan Naoimh (pronounced Noo), Garvelloch Islands, Argyllshire. The church in Great Britain with the oldest origins is St Martin's Church in Canterbury, Kent. It was built in AD 560 on the foundations of a 1st-century Roman church. The chapel of St Peter on the Wall, Bradwell-on-Sea, Essex was built from AD 654–660. The oldest church in Ireland is the Gallerus Oratory, built *c.* 750 at Ballyferriter, near Kilmalkedar, County Kerry. Britain's oldest nunnery is St Peter and Paul Minster, on the Isle of Thanet, Kent. It was founded *c.* 748 by the Abbess Eadburga of Bugga. The oldest Catholic church is St Etheldreda, Ely Place, Holborn, London, founded in 1251. The oldest non-conformist chapel is the thatched chapel at Horningsham, Wiltshire, dated 1566.

Largest temple

The largest religious structure ever built is Angkor Wat (City Temple), enclosing 402 acres *162,6 ha* in Kampuchea, south-east Asia. It was built to the Hindu god Vishnu by the Khmer King Suryavarman II in the period 1113–50. Its curtain wall measures 1400 × 1400 yd *1280 × 1280 m* and its population, before it was abandoned in 1432, was 80,000. The whole complex of 72 major monuments, begun *c.* AD 900, extends over 15 × 5 miles *24 × 8 km*. The largest Buddhist temple in the world is Borobudur, near Jogjakarta, Indonesia, built in the 8th century. It is 103 ft *31,5 m* tall and 403 ft *123 m* square.

Largest cathedral

The world's largest cathedral is the cathedral church of the Diocese of New York, St John the Divine, with a floor area of 121,000 ft² *11 240 m²* and a volume of 16,822,000 ft³ *476 350 m³*. The cornerstone was laid on 27 Dec 1892, and work on the Gothic building was stopped in 1941. Work re-started in earnest in July 1979. In New York it is referred to as 'Saint John the Unfinished'. The nave is the longest in the world at 601 ft *183,18 m* in length, with a vaulting 124 ft *37,79 m* in height.

The cathedral covering the largest area is that of Santa Mariá de la Sede in Sevilla (Seville), Spain. It was built in Spanish Gothic style between 1402 and 1519 and is 414 ft *126,18 m* long, 271 ft *82,60 m* wide and 100 ft *30,48 m* high to the vault of the nave.

The largest cathedral in the British Isles is the Cathedral Church of Christ in Liverpool. Built in modernised Gothic style, work was begun on 18 July 1904, and it was finally consecrated on 25 Oct 1978 after 74 years (*cf.* Exeter 95 years) using ¼ million stone blocks and 12 million bricks at an actual cost of some £6 million. The building encloses 104,275 ft² *9687 m²* and has an overall length of 636 ft *193,85 m*. The Vestey Tower is 331 ft *100,88 m* high. It contains the highest vaulting in the world—175 ft *53,34 m* maximum at undertower, and the highest Gothic arches ever built, being 107 ft *32,61 m* at apices.

Smallest

The smallest church in the world designated as a cathedral is that of the Christ Catholic Church,

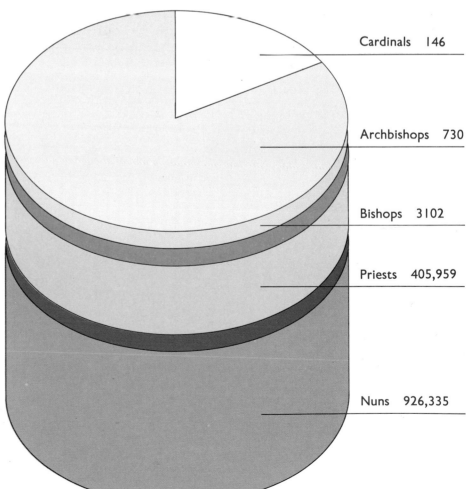

LARGEST RELIGIOUS ORGANISATION
— THE ROMAN CATHOLIC CHURCH —

Cardinals 146

Archbishops 730

Bishops 3102

Priests 405,959

Nuns 926,335

Highlandville, Missouri. Consecrated in July 1983 it measures 14 × 17 ft *4,26 × 5,18 m* and has seating for 18 people. The smallest cathedral in use in the United Kingdom (of old foundation) is St Asaph in Clwyd. It is 182 ft *55,47 m* long, 68 ft *20,72 m* wide and has a tower 100 ft *30,48 m* high. Oxford Cathedral in Christ Church (College) is 155 ft *47,24 m* long. The nave of the Cathedral of the Isles on the Isle of Cumbrae, Bute measures only 40 × 20 ft *12,19 × 6,09 m*. The total floor area is 2124 ft² *197,3 m²*.

Largest church

The largest church in the world is the basilica of St Peter, built between 1492 and 1612 in the Vatican City, Rome. Its length, measured from the apse, is 611 ft 4 in *186,33 m*. The area is 162,990 ft² *15 142 m²*. The inner diameter of the famous dome is 137 ft 9 in *41,98 m* and its centre is 119 m *390 ft 5 in* high. The external height is 457 ft 9 in *139,52 m*.

The elliptical Basilique of St Pie X at Lourdes, France, completed in 1957 at a cost of £2,000,000, has a capacity of 20,000 under its giant span arches and a length of 200 m *656 ft*.

The crypt of the underground Civil War Memorial Church in the Guadarrama Mountains, 45 km *28 miles* from Madrid, Spain, is 260 m *853 ft* in length. It took 21 years (1937–58) to build, at a reported cost of £140,000,000, and is surmounted by a cross 150 m *492 ft* tall.

The largest Church in the United Kingdom is the Collegiate Church of St Peter at Westminster built AD 1050–1745. Its maximum dimensions are overall: length 530 ft *161,5 m*; breadth across

Tallest minaret ● The tallest minarets in the world are the four of 137,4 m *450 ft 9 in* being built for a new mosque in Shah Alam, Selangor, Malaysia.

transept 203 ft *61,87 m* and internal height 101 ft 8 in *30,98 m*. The largest parish church is the Parish Church of the Most Holy and Undivided Trinity at Kingston-upon-Hull, covering 27,235 ft² *2530 m²* and with an external length and width of 288 ft × 124 ft *87,7 × 37,7 m*. It is also believed to be the country's oldest brick building serving its original purpose, dating from c. 1285. Both the former Cathedral of St Mungo, Glasgow and Beverley Minster, Humberside are now used as parish churches. The largest school chapel is that of the 150 ft *45,7 m* high Lancing College, West Sussex with a capacity of 600.

Smallest church

The world's smallest church is the Union Church at Wiscasset, Maine with a floor area of 31½ ft² *2,92 m²* (7 × 4½ ft *2,13 × 1,37 m*). St Gobban's Church, Portbradden, County Antrim, Northern Ireland measures 12 ft 1½ in by 6 ft 6 in *3,7 × 2,0 m*.

The smallest church in use in England is Bremilham Church, Cowage Farm, Foxley near Malmesbury, Wiltshire which measures 12 × 12 ft *3,65 × 3,65 m* and is used for service once a year. The smallest completed mediaeval English church in regular use is that at Culbone, Somerset, which measures 35 × 12 ft *10,66 × 3,65 m*. The smallest Welsh chapel is St Trillo's

Chapel, Rhôs-on-Sea (Llandrillo-yn-Rhos), Clwyd, measuring only 12 × 6 ft *3,65 × 1,83 m*. The smallest chapel in Scotland is St Margaret's, Edinburgh, measuring 16½ × 10½ ft *5,02 × 3,20 m*, giving a floor area of 173½ ft² *16,09 m²*.

Largest synagogue

The largest synagogue in the world is the Temple Emanu-El on Fifth Avenue at 65th Street, New York. The temple, completed in September 1929, has a frontage of 150 ft *45,72 m* on Fifth Avenue and 253 ft *77,11 m* on 65th Street. The sanctuary proper can accommodate 2500 people, and the adjoining Beth-El Chapel seats 350. When all the facilities are in use, more than 6000 people can be accommodated.

The largest synagogue in Great Britain is the Edgware Synagogue, Barnet, London, completed in 1959, with a capacity of 1630 seats. That with the highest registered membership is Ilford Synagogue with 2492 at 1 Jan 1983.

Largest mosque

The largest mosque ever built was the now ruinous al-Malawiya mosque of al-Mutawakil in Samarra, Iraq built from AD 842–52 and measuring 9.21 acres *3,72 ha* with dimensions of 784 × 512 ft *238,9 × 156,0 m*. The world's largest mosque in use is the Umayyad Mosque in Damascus, Syria built on a 2000-year-old religious site measuring 157 × 97 m *515 × 318 ft* thus covering an area of 3.76 acres *1,52 ha*. The largest mosque is the Merdeka Mosque in Djakarta, Indonesia, which was begun in 1962. The cupola spans 45 m *147,6 ft* in diameter and the capacity is in excess of 50,000 people.

Tallest and oldest pagoda

The world's tallest pagoda is the Phra Pathom Chedi at Nakhon Pathom, Thailand, which was built for King Mongkut from 1853–70. It rises to 115 m *377 ft*. The oldest pagoda in China is Sung-Yo Ssu in Honan built with 15 12-sided storeys in AD 523, though the 326 ft *99,3 m* tall Shwedagon Pagoda, Rangoon, Burma is built on the site of a 27 ft *8,2 m* tall pagoda of 585 BC.

Sacred object

The sacred object with the highest intrinsic value is the 15th-century gold Buddah in Wat Trimitr Temple in Bangkok, Thailand. It is 10 ft *3,04 m* tall and weighs an estimated 5¼ tonnes. At $500 per fine ounce its intrinsic worth has been put at £28¼ million. The gold under the plaster exterior was found only in 1954.

Longest nave

The longest nave in the United Kingdom is that of St Albans Cathedral, which is 285 ft *86,86 m* long. The central tower of Liverpool's Anglican Cathedral (internal overall length 636 ft *193,85 m*) interrupts the nave with an undertower space.

Tallest spire

The tallest cathedral spire in the world is that of the Protestant Cathedral of Ulm in West Germany. The building is early Gothic and was begun in 1377. The tower, in the centre of the west façade, was not finally completed until 1890 and is 160,90 m *528 ft* high. The world's tallest church spire is that of the Chicago Temple of the First Methodist Church on Clark Street, Chicago, Illinois. The building consists of a 22-storey skyscraper (erected in 1924) surmounted by a parsonage at 330 ft *100,5 m*, a 'Sky Chapel' at 400 ft *121,92 m* and a steeple cross at 568 ft *173,12 m* above street level.

The highest spire in Great Britain is that of the church of St Mary, called Salisbury Cathedral. The Lady Chapel was built in the years 1220–5 and the main fabric of the cathedral was finished and consecrated in 1258. The spire was added later, *ante* 1305, and reaches a height of 404 ft *123,13 m*. The central spire of Lincoln Cathedral, completed *c.* 1307 and which fell in 1548, was 525 ft *160,02 m* tall.

Stained glass *Oldest*

Pieces of stained glass dated before AD 850, some possibly even to the 7th century, excavated by Prof Rosemary Cramp, were placed into a window of that date in the nearby St Paul's Church, Jarrow, County Durham. The oldest complete stained glass in the world represents the Prophets in a window of the Cathedral of Augsburg, Bavaria, West Germany, dating from the second half of the 11th century. The oldest datable stained glass in the United Kingdom has been represented by a figure of St Michael in All Saints Church, Dalbury, Derbyshire of the late 11th century.

Largest

The largest stained-glass window is the complete mural of the Resurrection Mausoleum in Justice, Illinois, measuring 22,381 ft² *2079 m²* in 2448 panels, completed in 1971. The back-lit glass mural installed in 1979 in the atrium of the Ramada Hotel, Dubai is 135 ft *41,14 m* high. The largest single stained-glass window in Great Britain is the East Window in Gloucester Cathedral measuring 72 × 38 ft *21,94 × 11,58 m*, set up to commemorate the Battle of Crécy (1346), while the largest area of stained glass comprises the 128 lights, totalling 25,000 ft² *2322 m²* in York Minster.

Brasses

The world's oldest monumental brass is that commemorating Bishop Yso von Wölpe in Andreaskirche, Verden, near Hanover, West Ger-

many, dating from 1231. An engraved coffin plate of St Ulrich (d. 973), laid in 1187, was found buried in the Church of SS Ulrich and Afra, Augsburg, West Germany in 1979. The oldest brass in Great Britain is of Sir John D'Abernon (d. 1277) at Stoke D'Abernon, near Leatherhead, Surrey, dating from *c.* 1320.

A dedication brass dated 24 Apr 1241 in Ashbourne Church, Derbyshire has been cited as the earliest arabic writing extant in Britain.

CHURCH PERSONNEL

Saints

There are 1848 'registered' saints (including 60 St Johns) of whom 628 are Italians, 576 French and 271 from the United Kingdom and Ireland. Of these, 8 came from Cambridge and 7 from Oxford between 1535 and 1645, but none from the House of Commons. Britain's first Christian martyr was St Alban, executed *c.* AD 209. The first US-born saint is Mother Elizabeth Ann Bayley Seton (1774–1821), canonised 14 Sept 1975. The total includes 79 popes.

Most rapidly canonised

The shortest interval that has elapsed between the death of a saint and his canonisation was in the case of St Anthony of Padua, Italy, who died on 13 June 1231 and was canonised 352 days later on 30 May 1232. For the other extreme of 857 years see papal table.

Bishopric *Longest tenure*

The longest tenure of any Church of England bishopric is 57 years in the case of the Rt Rev Thomas Wilson, who was consecrated Bishop of Sodar and Man on 16 Jan 1698 and died in office on 7 Mar 1755. Of English bishoprics the longest tenures, if one excludes the unsubstantiated case of Aethelwulf, reputedly Bishop of Hereford from 937 to 1012, are those of 47 years by Jocelin de Bohun (Salisbury) 1142–89 and Nathaniel Crew or Crewe (Durham) 1674–1721.

Bishop *Oldest*

The oldest serving bishop (excluding suffragans and assistants) in the Church of England as at June 1987 was the Right Reverend Richard David Say, Bishop of Rochester, who was born on 4 Oct 1914.

The oldest Roman Catholic bishop in recent years has been Bishop Angelo Teutonico, formerly Bishop of Aversa (b. 28 Aug 1874), who died aged 103 years 276 days on 31 May 1978. He had celebrated mass about 24,800 times. Bishop Herbert Welch of the United Methodist Church, who was elected a Bishop for Japan and Korea in 1916, died on 4 Apr 1969 aged 106.

Youngest

The youngest bishop of all time was HRH The Duke of York and Albany KG, GCB, GCH, the second son of George III, who was elected Bishop of Osnabrück, through his father's influence as Elector of Hanover, at the age of 196 days on 27 Feb 1764. He resigned after 39 years' enjoyment. The youngest serving bishop (excluding suffragans and assistants) in the Church of England is the Rev Dr David Hope (b. 14 Apr 1940) whose appointment to the See of Wakefield was announced on 2 July 1985. When suffragans and assistants are counted, the youngest is Canon Michael Scott-Joynt, Bishop of Stafford who was appointed on 21 Apr 1987 aged 44.

Oldest parish priest

Father Alvaro Fernandez (b. 8 Dec 1880) served as a parish priest at Santiago de Abres, Spain from 1919 continuing into his 105th year. The oldest Anglican clergyman, the Rev Clement Williams (b. 30 Oct 1879), died aged 106 years 3 months on 3 Feb 1986. He lined the route at Queen Victoria's funeral and was ordained in 1904.

Longest incumbency

The longest Church of England incumbency on record is one of 75 years 357 days by the Rev Bartholomew Edwards, Rector of St Nicholas, Ashill, Norfolk from 1813 to 1889. There appears to be some doubt as to whether the Rev Richard Sherinton was installed at Folkestone from 1524 or 1529 to 1601. If the former is correct it would surpass the Norfolk record. The parish of Farrington, Hampshire had only two incumbents in a 122-year period *viz.* Rev J. Benn (28 Mar 1797 to 1857) and Rev T. H. Massey (1857 to 5 Apr 1919). From 1675 to 1948 the incumbents of Rose Ash, Devon were from 8 generations of the family of Southcomb.

Longest serving chorister

John Love Vokins (b. 9 June 1890) has been a chorister for 91 years. He joined the choir of Christ Church, Heeley, Sheffield in 1895 and that of St Michael's, Hathersage 35 years later. Having become a chorister in 1876 at the age of 9, Thomas Rogers was appointed vicar's warden in 1966 at Montacute, Somerset aged 99.

Sunday school

Sunday schools were established by Congregationalists in Neath and Tirdwyncyn, Wales in 1697. Roland E. Daab (b. 25 Mar 1914) now of St Paul United Church of Christ, Columbia, Illinois has attended for 3540 consecutive Sundays without a miss for 68 years to 28 Sept 1986.

Largest and smallest parishes

The smallest parish in the United Kingdom is The Scares, which consists of rocky islets in Luce Bay with an area of 1.10 acres *0,44 ha* and is included in Wigtown, Dumfries and Galloway. In 1982 the parish of Dallinghoo Wield, Suffolk boasted a population of nil and an area of 38 acres *14,6 ha*. The largest parish is Kilmonivaig in Inverness with an area of 267,233.03 acres *108 145,46 ha*.

Oldest parish register

The oldest part of any parish register surviving in England contains entries from the summer of 1538. There is a sheet from that of Alfriston, East Sussex recording a marriage on 10 July 1504 but this is amid entries from 1547. Scotland's oldest surviving register is that for Anstruther-Wester, Fife, with burial entries from 1549.

Largest crowds

The greatest recorded number of human beings assembled with a common purpose was an estimated 12,700,000 at the Hindu festival of Kumbh-Mela, which was held at the confluence of the Yamuna (formerly called the Jumna), the Ganges and the invisible 'Sarasvati' at Allahabad, Uttar Pradesh, India, on 19 Jan 1977. The holiest time during this holiest day since 1833 was during the planetary alignment between 9.28 and 9.40 a.m. during which only 200,000 achieved immersion to wash away the sins of a lifetime.

Largest funerals

The funeral of the charismatic C. N. Annadurai (died 3 Feb 1969), Madras Chief Minister, was, according to a police estimate, attended by 15 million. The longest funeral in Britain was probably that of Vice Admiral Viscount Nelson on 9 Jan 1806. Ticket-holders were seated in St Paul's Cathedral by 8.30 a.m. Many were unable to leave until after 9 p.m.

The queue at the grave of the chansonnier and guitarist Vladimir Visotsky (died 28 July 1980), stretched 10 km *6.2 miles*.

Biggest demonstrations

A figure of 2.7 million was published from China for the demonstration against the USSR in Shanghai on 3–4 Apr 1969 following the border clashes, and one of 10 million for the May Day celebrations of 1963 in Peking.

WORST IN THE WORLD

DISASTER	NUMBER KILLED	LOCATION	DATE
Pandemic	75,000,000	Eurasia: The Black Death (bubonic, pneumonic and septicaemic plague)	1347–51
Genocide	c. 35,000,000	Mongol extermination of Chinese peasantry	1311–40
Famine	c. 30,000,000[1]	Northern China	1959–61
Influenza	21,640,000	Worldwide: Influenza	April–Nov 1918
Earthquake	1,100,000	Near East and E. Mediterranean (see p. 62)	c. July 1201
Circular Storm[2]	1,000,000	Ganges Delta Islands, Bangladesh	12–13 Nov 1970
Flood	900,000	Hwang-ho River, China	Oct 1887
Landslide	180,000	Kansu Province, China	16 Dec 1920
Atomic Bomb	141,000	Hiroshima, Japan	6 Aug 1945
Conventional Bombing[3]	c. 140,000	Tokyo, Japan	10 Mar 1945
Volcanic Eruption	92,000	Tambora Sumbawa, Indonesia	5–7 April 1815
Avalanches	c. 18,000[4]	Yungay, Huascarán, Peru	31 May 1970
Marine (Single Ship)	c. 7700	Wilhelm Gustloff (25,484 tons) German Liner torpedoed off Danzig by USSR submarine S-13	30 Jan 1945
Dam Burst	c. 5000[5]	Manchhu River Dam, Morvi, Gujaret, India	11 Aug 1979
Panic	c. 4000[6]	Chungking (Zhong qing) China, air raid shelter	c. 8 June 1941
Smog	2850	London fog, England (excess deaths)	5–13 Dec 1951
Tunnelling (Silicosis)	c. 2500	Hawk's Nest hydroelectric tunnel, W. Virginia, USA	1931–35
Industrial (Chemical)	2352[7]	Union Carbide methylisocyanate plant, Bhopal, India	2–3 Dec 1984
Explosion	1963[8]	Halifax, Nova Scotia, Canada	6 Dec 1917
Fire[9] (Single Building)	1670	The Theatre, Canton, China	May 1845
Mining[10]	1572	Hinkeiko Colliery, China (coal dust explosion)	26 April 1942
Riot	c. 1200	New York anti-conscription riots	13–16 July 1863
Road[11]	c. 1100	Petrol tanker explosion inside Salang Tunnel, Afghanistan	2 or 3 Nov 1982
Mass Suicide	913	People's Temple cult by cyanide, Jonestown, Guyana	18 Nov 1978
Crocodiles	c. 900	Japanese soldiers, Ramree I., Burma (disputed)	19–20 Feb 1945
Railway	>800	Bagmati River, Bihar state, India	6 June 1981
Fireworks	>800	Dauphin's Wedding, Seine, Paris	16 May 1770
Tornado	689	South Central States, USA (3 hours)	18 Mar 1925
Aircraft (Civil)[12]	583	KLM-Pan Am Boeing 747 ground crash, Tenerife	27 Mar 1977
Man-eating Animal	436	Champawat district, India, tigress shot by Col Jim Corbet (d. 1955)	1907
Terrorism	329	Bomb aboard Air-India Boeing 747, crashed into Atlantic south-west of Ireland. Sikh extremists suspected	23 June 1985
Bacteriological & Chemical Warfare	c. 300	Novosibirsk B & CW plant, USSR	April-May 1979
Hail	246	Moredabad, Uttar Pradesh, India	20 April 1888
Off-Shore Oil Plant	123	Alexander L. Kielland 'Flotel' (10,105 tons), North Sea	27 Mar 1980
Submarine	130	Le Surcouf rammed by US merchantman Thomas Lykes in Caribbean	18 Feb 1942
Helicopter	54	Israel, military 'Sea Stallion', West Bank	10 May 1977
Ski Lift (Cable Car)	42	Cavalese resort, Northern Italy	9 Mar 1976
Mountaineering	40[13]	USSR expedition on Mount Everest	Dec 1952
Nuclear Reactor	31[14]	Chernobyl No 4, Ukraine, USSR	7 Aug 1986
Elevator (Lift)	23	Vaal Reefs gold mine lift fell 1.2 miles 1,93 km	27 Mar 1980
Lightning	21	Hut in Chinamasa Krael nr Matari, Zimbabwe (single bolt)	23 Dec 1975
Yacht Racing	19	28th Fastnet Race—23 boats sank or abandoned in Force 11 gale	13–15 Aug 1979
Space Exploration	7	US Challenger 51L Shuttle, Cape Canaveral, Florida	28 Jan 1986
Nuclear Waste Accident	high but undis-[15] closed	Venting of plutonium extraction wastes, Kyshtym, USSR	c. Dec 1957

--- WORST IN WORLD FOOTNOTES ---

[1] It has been estimated that more than 5 million died in the post-World War I famine of 1920–1 in the USSR. The USSR Government in July 1923 informed Mr (later President) Herbert Hoover that the ARA (American Relief Administration) had since August 1921 saved 20 million lives from famine and famine-related diseases.

[2] This figure published in 1972 for the Bangladeshi disaster was from Dr Afzal, Principal Scientific Officer of the Atomic Energy Authority Centre, Dacca. One report asserted that less than half of the population of the 4 islands of Bhola, Charjabbar, Hatia and Ramagati (1961 Census 1.4 million) survived. The most damaging hurricane recorded was Hurricane Gloria from 26-28 Sept 1985 with estimated insurance losses of £3,500 million.

[3] The number of civilians killed by the bombing of Germany has been put variously as 593,000 and 'over 635,000' including 550,000 deaths in the raids on Dresden, Germany from 13–15 Feb 1945. Total Japanese fatalities were 600,000 (conventional) and 220,000 (nuclear).

[4] A total of 18,000 Austrian and Italian troops was reported to have been lost in the Dolomite valleys of northern Italy on 13 Dec 1916 in more than 100 snow avalanches. Some of the avalanches were triggered by gun-fire.

[5] The dynamiting of a Yangtze Kiang dam at Huayuan Kow by the KMT during the Sino-Japanese war in 1938 is reputed to have resulted in 900,000 deaths.

[6] It was estimated that some 5000 people were trampled to death in the stampede for free beer at the coronation celebration of Czar Nicholas II in Moscow in May 1896.

[7] Certified total true figure obscured by litigation.

[8] Some sources maintain that the final death roll was over 3000 on 6–7 Dec. Published estimates of the 11,000 killed at the BASF chemical plant explosion at Oppau, West Germany on 21 Sept 1921 were exaggerated. The best estimate is 561 killed.

[9] > 200,000 killed in the sack of Moscow, freed by the Tartars in May 1571. Worst ever hotel fire 162 killed, Hotel Daeyungak, Seoul, South Korea 25 Dec 1971. Worst circus fire 168 killed Hartford, Conn., USA 6 July 1944.

[10] The worst gold mining disaster in South Africa was when 182 were killed in Kinross gold mine on 16 Sept 1986.

[11] Some estimates ran as high as 2700 victims from carbon monoxide asphyxiation after Soviet military sealed both ends of the 1.7 mile 2,7 km long tunnel. The worst ever years for road deaths in the USA and the UK have been respectively

1969 (56,400) and 1941 (9169). The global aggregate death roll was put at 25 million by September 1975. The world's highest death rate is 29 per 100,000 in 1978 in Luxembourg and Portugal. The greatest pile-up on British roads was on the M6 near Lymm Interchange, near Thelwell, involving 200 vehicles on 13 Sept 1971 with 11 dead and 60 injured.

[12] The crash of JAL's Boeing 747, flight 123, near Tokyo on 12 Aug 1985, in which 520 passengers and crew perished, was the worst single plane crash in aviation history.

[13] According to Polish sources, not confirmed by the USSR. Also

23 died on Mount Fuji, Japan, in blizzard and avalanche on 20 Mar 1972.

[14] Explosion at 0123 hrs Soviet European time 26 Apr 1986. The estimates for the eventual death roll vary between 200 to 600 by AD 2026 (per Nikolay Romanenko, Ukrainian Health Minister on 4 Apr 1987) and 75,000 (per Dr Robert Gale, US bone transplant specialist).

[15] More than 30 small communities in a 1200 km² 460 mile² area eliminated from USSR maps since 1958. Possibly an ammonium nitrate-hexone explosion.

WORST IN THE UNITED KINGDOM

DISASTER	NUMBER KILLED	LOCATION	DATE
Famine	1,500,000[1]	Ireland (famine and typhus)	1846–51
Pandemic	800,000	The Black Death (bubonic, pneumonic and septicaemic plague)	1347–50
Influenza	225,000	Influenza ....Sept–Nov	1918
Circular Storm	c. 8000	'The Channel Storm' ....26 Nov	1703
Smog	2850	London fog (excess deaths) ....5–13 Dec	1951
Flood	c. 2000[2]	Severn Estuary ....20 Jan	1606
Conventional bombing	1436	London ....10–11 May	1941
Marine (Single Ship)	c. 800[3]	HMS Royal George, off Spithead ....29 Aug	1782
Riot	565 (min)	London anti-Catholic Gordon riots ....2–13 June	1780
Mining	439	Universal Colliery, Senghenydd, Mid-Glamorgan ....14 Oct	1913
Dam Burst	250	Bradfield Reservoir, Dale Dyke, near Sheffield, South Yorkshire (embankment burst) ....12 Mar	1864
Railway	227[4]	Triple collision, Quintins Hill, Dumfries & Galloway ....22 May	1915
Fire (Single Building)	188[5]	Theatre Royal, Exeter ....5 Sept	1887
Panic	183	Victoria Hall, Sunderland, Tyne and Wear ....16 June	1883
Landslide	144	Pantglas coal tip No 7, Aberfan, Mid-Glamorgan ....21 Oct	1966
Explosion	134[6]	Chilwell, Notts. (explosives factory) ....1 July	1918
Aircraft (Civil)	118[7]	BEA Trident 1C, Staines, Surrey ....18 June	1972
Submarine	99	HMS Thetis, during trials, Liverpool Bay ....1 June	1939
Tornado	75	Tay Bridge collapsed under impact of two tornadic vortices ....28 Dec	1879
Helicopter	45	Chinook, off Sumburgh, Shetland ....6 Nov	1986
Nuclear Reactor	39	Excess cancer deaths to 1977 Windscale (now Sellafield), Cumbria ....10 Oct	1957
Road	33	Coach crash, River Dibb, nr Grassington, North Yorks ....27 May	1975
Lightning	31	(Annual total) Worst year on record (annual av. 12)	1914
Off-Shore Oil Plant	24[8]	Alexander L. Kielland 'Flotel' (10,105 tons), North Sea ....27 Mar	1980
Terrorism	21	Birmingham pub bombs (IRA) ....21 Nov	1974
Yacht Racing	19	28th Fastnet Race—23 boats sank or abandoned in Force 11 gale. Of 316 starters only 128 finished ....13–15 Aug	1979
Avalanches	8	Lewes, East Sussex ....27 Dec	1836
Mountaineering	6	On Cairngorm, Scotland (4084 ft) ....21 Nov	1971
Earthquake	2	London earthquake, Christ's Hospital (Newgate) ....6 April	1580

— WORST IN UK FOOTNOTES —

[1] Based on the net rate of natural increase between 1841 and 1851, a supportable case for a loss of population of 3 million can be made out if rates of under-enumeration of 25 per cent (1841) and 10 per cent (1851) are accepted. Potato rot (Phytophthora infestans) was first reported on 13 Sept 1845.

[2] Death rolls of 100,000 were reputed in England and Holland in the floods of 1099, 1421 and 1446.

[3] c. 2800 were lost on HM Troopship Lancastria 16,243 tons, off St Nazaire on 17 June 1940. The Princess Alice collision in the Thames with the Bywell Castle off Woolwich on 3 Sept 1878 killed 786.

[4] The 213 yd 194,7 m long troop train was telescoped to 67 yd 61,2 m. Signalmen Meakin and Tinsley were sentenced for manslaughter. Britain's worst underground train disaster was the Moorgate Tube disaster of 28 Feb 1975 when 43 were killed.

[5] In July 1212, 3000 were killed in the crush, burned or drowned when London Bridge caught fire at both ends. The death roll in the Great Fire of London of 1666 was only 8. History's first 'fire storm' occurred in the Quebec Yard, Surrey Docks, Southwark, London during the 300-pump fire in the Blitz on 7–8 Sept 1940. Dockland casualties were 306 killed. Britain's most destructive fire was that leading to a £165-million loss at the Army Ordnance depot, Donnington, Shropshire in June 1982.

[6] HM armed cruiser Natal blew up off Invergordon killing 428 on 30 Dec 1915.

[7] The worst crash by a UK operated aircraft was that of the Dan-Air Boeing 727 from Manchester which crashed into a mountain on the Canary Islands on 25 Apr 1980 killing 146 people. There were no survivors.

[8] 24 Britons of a total death roll of 123.

SPORTS
GAMES AND
PASTIMES
CHAPTER TWELVE

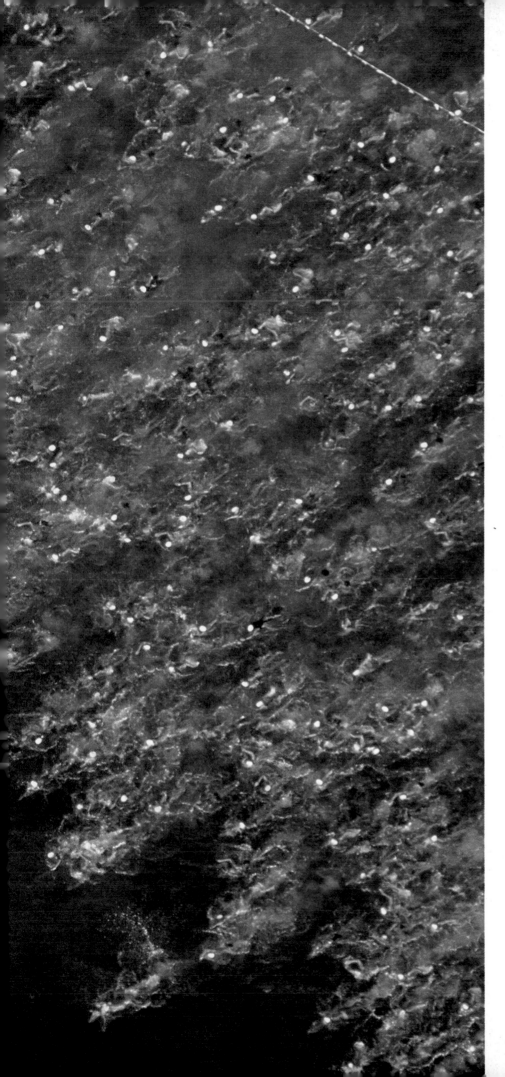

General Records

The origins of sport stem from the time when self-preservation ceased to be the all-consuming human preoccupation. Archery, although a hunting skill in Mesolithic times (by *c.* 8000 BC), did not become an organised sport until later, possibly as early as *c.* 1150 BC, as an archery competition is described in Homer's Iliad, and certainly by *c.* AD 300, among the Genoese. The earliest dated evidence is *c.* 2750–2600 BC for wrestling. Ball games by girls depicted on Middle-Kingdom murals at Beni Hasan, Egypt have been dated to *c.* 2050 BC.

Fastest

The highest speed reached in a non-mechanical sport is in sky-diving, in which a speed of 185 mph *298 km/h* is attained in a head-down free-falling position, even in the lower atmosphere. In delayed drops speeds of 625 mph *1005 km/h* have been recorded at high, rarefied altitudes. The highest projectile speed in any moving ball game is *c.* 188 mph *302 km/h* in pelota. This compares with 170 mph *273 km/h* (electronically timed) for a golf ball driven off a tee.

Slowest

In wrestling, before the rules were modified towards 'brighter wrestling', contestants could be locked in holds for so long that a single bout once lasted for 11 hr 40 min. In the extreme case of the 2 hr 41 min pull in the regimental tug o' war in Jubbulpore, India, on 12 Aug 1889, the winning team moved a net distance of 12 ft *3,6 m* at an average speed of 0.00084 mph *0,00135 km/h*.

Longest

The most protracted sporting contest was an 'Earth-Moon' automobile duration test of 222,621 miles *358 273 km* (equivalent to 8.93 times around the equator) by Appaurchaux and others in a Ford Taunus 12M at the Miranas circuit, France, over 142 days from July–November 1963. The car averaged 65.33 mph *106 km/h.*

The most protracted human-powered sporting event is the *Tour de France* cycling race. In 1926 this was over 3569 miles *5743 km*, lasting 29 days, but the duration is now reduced to 23 days.

Largest pitch

The largest pitch of any ball game is that of polo, with 12.4 acres *5,0 ha*, or a maximum length of 300 yd *274 m* and a width, without side boards, of 200 yd *182 m*. With boards the width is 160 yd *146 m*. Twice a year in the Parish of St Columb Major, Cornwall, a game called hurling (not to be confused with the Irish game) is played on a 'pitch' which consists of the entire parish, approximately 25 square miles *64,7 km²*.

Youngest and oldest world record breakers

The youngest at which anybody has broken a non-mechanical world record is 12 yr 298 days for Gertrude Caroline Ederle (USA) (b. 23 Oct 1906) with 13 min 19.0 sec for women's 880 yd freestyle swimming at Indianapolis, USA, on 17 Aug 1919. Gerhard Weidner (West Germany) (b. 15 Mar 1933) set a 20-mile walk record on 25 May 1974, aged 41 yr 71 days.

The most gruelling sporting contest ● The Hawaiian Iron Man is the best established triathlon event. Competitors first swim 2.4 miles *3.8 km* then cycle 112 miles *180 km* and finally run a full marathon. (Photo: Robert Beck/Focus).

General Records

Youngest and oldest champions

The youngest successful competitor in a world title event was a French boy, whose name is not recorded, who coxed the Netherlands' Olympic pair at Paris on 26 Aug 1900. He was not more than ten and may have been as young as seven. The youngest individual Olympic winner was Marjorie Gestring (USA) (b. 18 Nov 1922), who took the springboard diving title at the age of 13 yr 268 days at the Berlin Games on 12 Aug 1936. Oscar Gomer Swahn (Sweden) (1847–1927) was aged 64 yr 258 days when he won a gold medal in the 1912 Olympic Running Deer team shooting competition.

Youngest internationals

The youngest age at which any person has won international honours is eight years in the case of Joy Foster, the Jamaican singles and mixed doubles table tennis champion in 1958. The youngest British international has been diver Beverley Williams (b. 5 Jan 1957), who was 10 yr 268 days old when she competed against the USA at Crystal Palace, London, on 30 Sept 1967.

Oldest competitor at major games

William Edward Pattimore (b. 1 Mar 1892) competed for Wales at bowls at the 1970 Commonwealth Games in Edinburgh at the age of 78, the oldest competitor at such an international event open to competitors of all ages. Britain's oldest Olympian was Hilda Lorna Johnstone (b. 4 Sept 1902) who was 70 yr 5 days when she was placed twelfth in the dressage competition at the 1972 Olympic Games.

Most versatile

Charlotte 'Lottie' Dod (1871–1960) won the Wimbledon singles tennis title five times between 1887 and 1893, the British Ladies' Golf Championship in 1904, an Olympic silver medal for archery in 1908, and represented England at hockey in 1899. She also excelled at skating and tobogganing.

Mildred 'Babe' Zaharias (née Didrikson) (1914–56) (USA) won two gold medals (80 m hurdles and javelin) and a silver (high jump) at the 1932 Olympic Games. She set world records at those three events in 1930–32. She was an All-American basketball player for three years and set the world record for throwing the baseball 296 ft *90,22 m*. Switching to golf she won the US Women's Amateur title in 1946 and the US Women's Open in 1948, 1950 and 1954. She also excelled at several other sports.

Charles Burgess Fry (GB) (1872–1956) was probably the most versatile male sportsman at the highest level. On 4 Mar 1893 he equalled the world long jump record of 23 ft 6½ in *7,17 m*. He represented England v. Ireland at soccer (1901) and played first-class rugby for the Barbarians. His greatest achievements, however, were at cricket, where he headed the English batting averages in six seasons and captained England in 1912. He was also an excellent angler and tennis player.

Most prolific record breaker

Between 24 Jan 1970 and 1 Nov 1977 Vasiliy Alekseyev (USSR) (b. 7 Jan 1942) broke 80 official world records in weightlifting.

Longest reign

The longest reign as a world champion is 33 years (1829–62) by Jacques Edmond Barre (France) (1802–73) at real tennis. The longest reign as a British champion is 41 years by the archer Alice Blanche Legh (1855–1948) who won 23 national titles between 1881 and 1922, the last when she was aged 67.

Shortest reign

Olga Rukavishnikova (USSR) (b. 13 Mar 1955) held the pentathlon world record for 0.4 sec at

Moscow on 24 July 1980. That is the difference between her second-place time of 2 min 04.8 sec in the final 800 m event of the Olympic five-event competition, and that of third-placed Nadyezhda Tkachenko (USSR), whose overall points were better, 5083 to 4937.

Heaviest sportsman

The heaviest sportsman of all time was the professional wrestler William J. Cobb of Macon, Georgia, USA, who in 1962 was billed as the 802 lb (57 st 4 lb *363 kg*) 'Happy Humphrey'. The heaviest player of a ball-game was Bob Pointer, the 487 lb *221 kg* US football tackle formerly on the 1967 Santa Barbara High School Team, California, USA.

Greatest earnings

The greatest fortune amassed by an individual in sport is an estimated $69 million by the boxer Muhammad Ali (USA) from 1960–81. The highest-paid woman athlete in the world is tennis player Martina Navratilova (b. 18 Oct 1956) (USA, formerly Czechoslovakia) whose official career earnings passed $12 million in 1987. (See Tennis section.)

Biggest sports contract

In March 1982, the National Football League concluded a deal worth $2000 million for five years' coverage of American football by the three major TV networks, ABC, CBS and NBC. This represented $14.2 million for each league team.

Largest crowd

The greatest number of live spectators for any sporting spectacle is the estimated 2,500,000 who annually line the route of the New York Marathon. However, spread over 23 days, it is estimated that more than 10,000,000 see the annual *Tour de France* cycling race along the route.

The total attendance at the 1984 summer Olympic Games was given as 5,797,923 for all sports, including 1,421,627 for soccer and 1,129,465 for track and field athletics.

The largest crowd travelling to any single sporting venue is 'more than 400,000' for the annual *Grand Prix d'Endurance* motor race on the Sarthe circuit near Le Mans, France. The record stadium crowd was one of 199,854 for the Brazil v. Uruguay soccer match in the Maracaña Municipal Stadium, Rio de Janeiro, Brazil, on 16 July 1950.

Most participants

An estimated 104,000 runners contested the 77th annual Examiner Bay to Breakers 7.6-mile race in San Francisco in 1986. The 1983 Women's International Bowling Congress Championship tournament attracted 75,480 bowlers for the 83-day event held 7 Apr—1 July at Showboat Lanes, Las Vegas, Nevada, USA.

Gymnastics/aerobics display

The annual Czechoslovak Sportakiad features gymnastics displays by about 180,000 participants. Held at the Strahov Stadium, Prague, there are 200,000 spectators for each of the four days. On the six-hectare infield there are markers for 13,824 gymnasts at a time.

Worst disasters

The worst sports disaster in recent history was when an estimated 604 were killed after stands at the Hong Kong Jockey Club racecourse collapsed and caught fire on 26 Feb 1918. During the reign of Antoninus Pius (AD 138–161) the upper wooden tiers in the Circus Maximus, Rome, collapsed during a gladiatorial combat killing some 1112 spectators. Britain's worst sports disaster was when 66 were killed and 145 injured at the Rangers v. Celtic football match at Exit 13 of Ibrox Park Stadium, Glasgow on 2 Jan 1971.

American Football

American football, a direct descendant of the British games of soccer and rugby, evolved at American Universities in the 19th century. The first match under the Harvard Rules was played by Harvard against McGill University of Montreal at Cambridge, Mass., in 1874. The Intercollegiate Football Association was founded in 1876. The professional game dates from August 1895 when Latrobe played Jeanette at Latrobe, Pennsylvania. The American Professional Football Association was formed in 1919. This became the National Football League (NFL) in 1922. The American Football League (AFL) was formed in 1960; the NFL and AFL merged in 1970.

PROFESSIONAL RECORDS
(NFL 1920–87, AFL 1960–9)

MOST POINTS .... career **2002**
George Blanda (Chicago Bears, Baltimore, Houston,
  Oakland) 1949–75
  season **176**
Paul Hornung (Green Bay) 1960
  game **40**
Ernie Nevers (Chicago Cardinals) .... 28 Nov 1929

MOST TOUCHDOWNS .... career **126**
Jim Brown (Cleveland) 1957–65
  season **24**
John Riggins (Washington Redskins) 1983
  game **6**
Ernie Nevers (Chicago Cardinals) .... 28 Nov 1929
  6
William 'Dub' Jones (Cleveland) .... 25 Nov 1951
  6
Gale Sayers (Chicago) .... 12 Dec 1965

**MOST YARDS GAINED
RUSHING** .... career **16,193**
Walter Payton (Chicago Bears) 1975–87
  season **2105**
Eric Dickerson (Los Angeles Rams) 1984
  game **275**
Walter Payton (Chicago Bears) .... 20 Nov 1977

**MOST YARDS GAINED
PASSING** .... career **47,003**
Fran Tarkentin (Minnesota, New York Giants) 1961–78
  season **5084**
Dan Marino (Miami Dolphins) 1984
  game **554**
Norm Van Brocklin (Los Angeles Rams) ...... 28 Sept 1951

**MOST PASSES
COMPLETED** .... career **3686**
Fran Tarkenton (Minnesota, New York Giants) ... 1961–78
  season **378**
Dan Marino (Miami Dolphins) 1986
  game **42**
Richard Todd (New York Jets) .... 21 Sept 1980

PASS RECEPTIONS .... career **716**
Charley Joiner (Houston, Cincinnati, San Diego) ... 1969–85
  season **106**
Art Monk (Washington Redskins) 1984
  game **18**
Tom Fears (Los Angeles Rams) .... 3 Dec 1950

FIELD GOALS .... career **373**
Jan Stenerud (Kansas City, Green Bay, Minnesota) 1967–85
  season **35**
Ali Haji-Sheikh (New York Giants) 1983
  game **7**
Jim Bakken (St Louis Cardinals) .... 24 Sept 1967

Super Bowl

First held in 1967 between the winners of the NFL and the AFL. Since 1970 it has been contested by the winners of the National and American Conferences of the NFL. Pittsburgh Steelers have most wins, four, 1975–6 and 1979–80. The highest aggregate score was in 1979 when Pittsburgh beat Dallas Cowboys 35–31. The highest team score and record victory margin was when the Chicago Bears beat the New England Patriots 46–10 at New Orleans, Louisiana on 26 Jan 1986. The Green Bay Packers won a record 11 NFL titles between 1929 and 1967.

College football *Highest team score*

Georgia Tech, Atlanta, Georgia scored 222 points, including a record 32 touchdowns, against Cumberland University, Lebanon, Tennessee (nil) on 7 Oct 1916.

Record completion percentage in the Super Bowl ● Voted Most Valuable Player of Super Bowl XXI, quarterback Phil Simms achieved an 88 per cent completion rate for the New York Giants, winners over Denver Broncos 39–20 in Pasadena on 25 Jan 1987.
American football in Britain ● The London Ravens beat Streatham Olympians 20–12 in the final of the inaugural Budweiser Bowl, contested by 72 teams in 1986, and below, Taylor celebrates the first touchdown. (Photos: All-Sport)

SUPER BOWL INDIVIDUAL GAME RECORDS

POINTS	18	Roger Craig (San Francisco 49ers)	1985
TOUCHDOWNS	3	Roger Craig (San Francisco 49ers)	1985
YARDS GAINED RUSHING	191	Marcus Allen (Los Angeles Raiders)	1984
YARDS GAINED PASSING	331	Joe Montana (San Francisco 49ers)	1985
PASSES COMPLETED	29	Dan Marino (Miami Dolphins)	1985
PASS RECEPTIONS	11	Dan Ross (Cincinnati Bengals)	1982
FIELD GOALS	4	Don Chandler (Green Bay Packers)	1968
	4	Ray Wersching (San Francisco 49ers)	1982

Angling

Oldest existing club

The Ellem fishing club was formed by a number of Edinburgh and Berwickshire gentlemen in 1829. Its first annual general meeting was held on 29 April 1830.

Largest single catch

The largest officially ratified fish ever caught on a rod is a man-eating Great white shark (*Carcharodon carcharias*) weighing 2664 lb *1208 kg* and measuring 16 ft 10 in *5,13 m* long, caught on a 130 lb *58 kg* test line by Alf Dean at Denial Bay, near Ceduna, South Australia, on 21 Apr 1959. A

and Robert Tesse (France) took the individual title uniquely three times, in 1959–60 and 1965. The record weight (team) is 34,71 kg *76.52 lb* in 3 hr by West Germany on the Neckar at Mannheim, West Germany on 21 Sept 1980. The individual record is 16,99 kg *37.45 lb* by Wolf-Rüdiger Kremkus (West Germany) at Mannheim on 20 Sept 1980. The most fish caught were 652 by Jacques Isenbaert (Belgium) at Dunajvaros, Yugoslavia on 27 Aug 1967.

Fly Fishing

World fly fishing championships were inaugurated by the CIPS in 1981. The first British winner was Henry Anthony 'Tony' Pawson (b. 22 Aug 1921) at Salamanca, Spain in 1984. He also played amateur soccer for England and captained Oxford University at cricket.

British championship

The National Angling Championship (instituted 1906) has been won seven times by Leeds (1909–10, 1914, 1928, 1948–9, 1952). James H. R. Bazley (Leeds) won the individual title twice (1909, 1927). Since 1972 the event has been split into divisions. Eddie Townsin (Cambridge) won the national title in 1967 and Div. 4 in 1982; Charlie Hibbs (Leigh) won Div. 2 in 1974 and 1984. The record catch is 76 lb 9 oz *34,72 kg* by David Burr (Rugby) in the Huntspill, Somerset in 1965. The largest single fish caught in the Championships is a carp of 14 lb 2 oz *6,41 kg* by John C. Essex on 13 Sept 1975 on the River Nene, Peterborough. The heaviest total produced by Division 1 team champions is 63,99 kg *141.07 lbs* by the 12-angler team from Nottingham Federation.

Match fishing

In a sweepstake on the Sillees River, a tributary of the Erne, Co. Fermanagh, Ulster, on 14 May 1981, Peter Burrell weighed in 258 lb 9¼ oz *117,29 kg* of fish in the five-hour open event.

Casting

The longest freshwater cast ratified under ICF (International Casting Federation) rules is 175,01 m *574 ft 2 in* by Walter Kummerow (West Germany), for the Bait Distance Double-handed 30 g event held at Lenzerheide, Switzerland in the 1968 Championships. The British National record is 148,78 m *488 ft 1 in* by Andy Dickison on the same occasion. The longest Fly Distance Double-handed cast is 78,38 m *257 ft 2 in* by Sverne Scheen (Norway), also at Lenzerheide in September 1968. Peter Anderson set a British national professional record of 70,50 m *231 ft 3 in* on water at Scarborough on 11 Sept 1977, and Hugh Newton cast 80,47 m *264 ft* on land at Stockholm, Sweden on 20 Sept 1978. The UK Surfcasting Federation record (150 gr *5¼ oz* weight) is 248 m *815 ft* by Neil Mackellow on 4 Sept 1983 at Norwich.

IGFA WORLD RECORDS

The International Game Fish Association (IGFA) recognise world records for game fish—both freshwater and saltwater—for a large number of species of fish. Their thousands of categories include all-tackle, various line classes and tippet classes for fly fishing. The IGFA recognised 1074 new world records in 1984, 694 in 1985 and 619 in 1986.

The heaviest category recognised by the IGFA is for the sturgeon—468 lb *212,28 kg* by Joey Pallotta on 9 July 1983 off Benicia, California, USA.

Longest fight

The longest recorded individual fight with a fish is 32 hr 5 min by Donal Heatley (b. 1938) (New Zealand) with a Black marlin (estimated length 20 ft *6,09 m* and weight 1500 lb *680 kg*) off Mayor Island off Tauranga, North Island on 21–22 Jan 1968. It towed the 12 tonne/tonne launch 50 miles *80 km* before breaking the line.

Great white shark weighing 3388 lb *1537 kg* was caught by Clive Green off Albany, Western Australia, on 26 Apr 1976 but will remain unratified as whale meat was used as bait. The biggest ever rod-caught fish by a British angler is a 1260 lb *571,5 kg* Black marlin, by Edward A. Crutch off Cairns, Queensland, Australia on 19 Oct 1973.

In June 1978 a Great white shark measuring 29 ft 6 in *9,00 m* in length and weighing over 10,000 lb *4536 kg* was harpooned and landed by fishermen in the harbour of San Miguel, Azores.

The largest marine animal killed by *hand* harpoon was a Blue whale 97 ft *29,56 m* in length, by Archer Davidson in Twofold Bay, New South Wales, Australia, in 1910. Its tail flukes measured 20 ft *6,09 m* across and its jaw bone 23 ft 4 in *7,11 m*.

The largest officially ratified fish ever caught in a British river was a 388 lb *176 kg* sturgeon (9 ft 2 in *2,79 m* long) landed by Alec Allen (1895–1972), helped by David Price, from the River Towy between Llandeilo and Carmarthen, Wales, on 25 July 1933.

> **'Big Fish'** ● Don Mann uniquely caught all nine of the IGFA-recognised billfish within a year. This is the broadbill swordfish.

Smallest catch

The smallest fish to win a competition has been a Smelt, weighing 1/16 oz *1 dram*, caught by Peter Christian at Buckenham Ferry, Norfolk, England on 9 Jan 1977, in defeating 107 other competitors.

Spear fishing

The largest fish ever taken underwater was an 804 lb *364 kg* Giant black grouper or jewfish by Don Pinder of the Miami Triton Club, Florida, USA, in 1955. The British spear-fishing record is 89 lb *40,36 kg* for an Angler fish by James Brown (Weymouth Association Divers) in 1969.

World freshwater championship

The *Confédération Internationale de la Pêche Sportive* (CIPS) championships were inaugurated as European championships in 1953 and recognised as World Championships in 1957. France won twelve times between 1956 and 1981

WORLD RECORDS—FRESHWATER AND SALTWATER

A selection of all-tackle records ratified by the International Game Fish Association as at June 1986

Species	Weight lb oz	kg/g	Name of Angler	Location	Date
BARRACUDA, GREAT	83 0	37,64	K. J. W. Hackett	Lagos, Nigeria	13 Jan 1952
BASS, EUROPEAN	20 11	9,40	Jean Baptiste Bayle	Stes Maries de la Mer, France	6 May 1986
BASS, LARGEMOUTH	22 4	10,09	George W. Perry	Montgomery Lake, Georgia, USA	2 June 1932
BASS, SMALLMOUTH	11 15	5,41	David L. Hayes	Dale Hollow Lake, Kentucky, USA	9 July 1955
BASS, STRIPED	78 8	35,60	Albert R. McReynolds	Atlantic City, New Jersey, USA	21 Sept 1982
BLUEFISH	31 12	14,40	James M. Hussey	Hatteras, North Carolina, USA	30 Jan 1972
BONEFISH	19 0	8,61	Brian W. Batchelor	Zululand, South Africa	26 May 1962
CATFISH, FLATHEAD	98 0	44,45	William D. Stephens	Lewisville, Texas, USA	2 June 1986
COD, ATLANTIC	98 12	44,79	Alphonse J. Bielevich	Isle of Shoals, New Hampshire, USA	8 June 1969
DOLPHIN	87 0	39,46	Manuel Salazar	Papagalio Gulf, Costa Rica	25 Sept 1976
HALIBUT (Pacific)	350 0	158,76	Vern S. Foster	Homer, Alaska, USA	30 June 1982
JACK, CREVALLE	54 7	24,69	Thomas F. Gibson, Jr	Port Michel, Gabon	15 Jan 1982
JEWFISH	680 0	308,44	Lynn Joyner	Fernandina Beach, Florida, USA	20 May 1961
MACKEREL, KING	90 0	40,82	Norton I. Thornton	Key West, Florida, USA	16 Feb 1976
MARLIN, BLACK	1560 0	707,61	Alfred C. Glassell, Jr	Cabo Blanco, Peru	4 Aug 1953
MARLIN, BLUE (Atlantic)	1282 0	581,51	Larry Martin	St Thomas, Virgin Islands	6 Aug 1977
MARLIN, BLUE (Pacific)	1376 0	624,14	Jay Wm. de Beaubien	Kaaiwi Point, Kona Coast, Hawaii, USA	31 May 1982
MARLIN, STRIPED	494 0	224,10	Bill Boniface	Tutukaka, New Zealand	16 Jan 1986
MARLIN, WHITE	181 14	82,49	Evando Luiz Coser	Vitoria, Brazil	8 Dec 1979
MUSKELLUNGE	69 15	31,72	Arthur Lawton	St Lawrence River, New York, USA	22 Sept 1957
PIKE, NORTHERN	46 2	20,92	Peter Dubuc	Sacandaga Reservoir, New York, USA	15 Sept 1940
SAILFISH (Atlantic)	128 1	58,10	Harm Steyn	Luanda, Angola	27 Mar 1974
SAILFISH (Pacific)	221 0	100,24	C. W. Stewart	Santa Cruz Island, Ecuador	12 Feb 1947
SALMON, ATLANTIC	79 2	35,89	Harm Steyn	Luanda, Angola	27 Mar 1974
SALMON, CHINOOK	97 4	44,11	Les Anderson	Kenia River, Alaska, USA	17 May 1985
SALMON, COHO	31 0	14,06	Mrs Lee Halberg	Cowichan Bay, BC, Canada	11 Oct 1947
SHARK, HAMMERHEAD	991 0	449,50	Allen Ogle	Sarasota, Florida, USA	30 May 1982
SHARK, MAKO	1080 0	489,88	James L. Melanson	Montauk, New York, USA	26 Aug 1979
SHARK, PORBEAGLE	465 0	210,92	Jorge Potier	Padstow, Cornwall, England	23 July 1976
SHARK, THRESHER	802 0	363,80	Dianne North	Tutukaka, New Zealand	8 Feb 1981
SHARK, TIGER	1780 0	807,40	Walter Maxwell	Cherry Grove, S. Carolina, USA	14 June 1964
SHARK, WHITE	2664 0	1208,38	Alfred Dean	Ceduna, South Australia	21 Apr 1959
SNAPPER, CUBERA	121 8	55,11	Mike Hebert	Cameron, Louisiana, USA	5 July 1982
SNOOK	53 10	24,32	Gilbert Ponzi	Rio de Parasmina, Costa Rica	18 Oct 1978
STURGEON	468 0	212,28	Joey Pallotta, III	Benicia, California, USA	9 July 1983
SWORDFISH	1182 0	536,15	L. Marron	Iquique, Chile	17 May 1953
TARPON	283 0	128,36	M. Salazar	Lake Maracaibo, Venezuela	19 Mar 1956
TROUT, BROOK	14 8	6,57	Dr W. J. Cook	Nipigon River, Ontario, Canada	July 1916
TROUT, BROWN	35 15	16,30	Eugenio Cavaglia	Nahuel Huapi, Argentina	16 Dec 1952
TROUT, LAKE	65 0	29,48	Larry Daunis	Great Bear Lake, NWT, Canada	8 Aug 1970
TROUT, RAINBOW	42 2	19,10	David Robert White	Bell Island, Alaska, USA	22 June 1970
TUNA, BIGEYE (Pacific)	435 0	197,31	Dr Russel V. A. Lee	Cabo Blanco, Peru	17 Apr 1957
TUNA, BLUEFIN	1496 0	679,00	Ken Fraser	Aulds Cove, Nova Scotia, Canada	26 Oct 1979
TUNA, YELLOWFIN	388 12	176,35	Curt Wiesenhutter	San Benedicto I., Mexico	1 Apr 1977
WAHOO	149 0	67,58	John Pirovano	Cat Cay, Bahamas	15 June 1962
WALLEYE	25 0	11,34	Mabry Harper	Old Hickory Lake, Tennessee, USA	1 Apr 1960

BRITISH RECORDS—NATIONAL COARSE FISH

A selection of those recognised by the National Association of Specialist Anglers

Species	Weight lb oz dr	kg	Name of Angler	Location	Date
BARBEL	14 6 –	6,52	A. D. Tryon	Royalty Fishery, Hampshire Avon	1934
BLEAK	4 4	0,120	B. Derrington	River Monnow, Wye Mouth	1982
BREAM, COMMON	16 6 –	7,43	Anthony Bromley	Private water, Staffordshire	1986
CARP	51 8 –	23,36	C. Yates	Redmire Pool	1980
CARP, CRUCIAN	5 10 8	2,56	G. Halls	Lake near Kings Lynn, Norfolk	1976
CARP, GRASS	16 – –	7,26	K. Crow	Lake near Canterbury, Kent	1986
CATFISH (WELS)	43 8 –	19,73	R. J. Bray	Wilstone Reservoir, Tring, Hertfordshire	1970
CHUB	8 4 –	3,74	G. F. Smith	Royalty Fishery, Hampshire Avon	1913
DACE	1 4 4	0,57	J. L. Gasson	Little Ouse, Thetford, Norfolk	1960
EEL	11 2 –	5,04	S. Terry	Kingfisher Lake, Ringwood, Hampshire	1978
GUDGEON	4 4	0,120	M. J. Brown	Fish Pond, Ebbw Vale, Gwent	1977
ORFE, GOLDEN	5 6 –	2,44	M. Foot	Kingsley, Hampshire	1978
PERCH	5 9 –	2,52	J. Shayler	Private water, Kent	1985
PIKE	44 14 –	20,35	Michael Linton	Ardleigh Reservoir	1987
ROACH	4 1 –	1,84	R. G. Jones	Gravel pit, Nottinghamshire	1975
RUDD	4 8 –	2,04	Rev. E. C. Alston	Thetford, Norfolk	1933
RUFFE	5 4	0,148	R. J. Jenkins	West View Farm, Cumbria	1980
TENCH	12 8 11	5,69	A. Wilson	Wilstone Reservoir, Tring, Herts	1985
WALLEYE	11 12 –	5,33	F. A. Adams	The Delph, Welney, Norfolk	1934
ZANDER	17 12 –	8,05	D. Litton	Great Ouse, Relief Channel, Norfolk	1977

Highest women's archery team score ●
The South Korean team of Kim Mi-Ja, Kim Jin-Ho and Park Jung-Ah scored 3935 out of a possible 4320 to win the 1986 Asian Games title in Seoul. (Photo: David Cannon/All-Sport)

Archery

Though the earliest pictoral evidence of bows is seen in the Mesolithic cave paintings in Spain, archery as an organised sport appears to have developed in the 3rd century AD. Competi-tive archery may, however, date back to the 12th century BC. The oldest archery body in the British Isles is the Society of Archers in Yorkshire, formed on 14 May 1673, though the Society of Kilwinning Archers, in Scotland, has contested the Pa-pingo Shoot since 1488. The world governing body is the *Fédération Internationale de Tir à l'Arc* (FITA), founded in 1931.

World Records   *Single FITA rounds*

Event	Points	Name and Country	Pos-sible	Year
MEN				
FITA	1341	Darrell Pace (USA)	1440	1979
90 m	322	Vladimir Yesheyev (USSR)	360	1980
70 m	342	Richard McKinney (USA)	360	1985
50 m	345	Richard McKinney (USA)	360	1982
30 m	357	Takayoshi Matsushita (Jap)	360	1986
Team	3912	USA (Richard McKinney, Darrell Pace, Jerry Pylpchuk)	4320	1985
WOMEN				
FITA	1331	Lyudmila Arzhanikova (USSR)	1440	1986
70 m	328	Natalya Butuzova (USSR)	360	1979
60 m	338	Lyudmila Arzhanikova (USSR)	360	1984
	338	Kim Jin-Ho (S. Korea)	360	1986
50 m	335	Yanzhina Tsyrenzhapova (USSR)	360	1985
30 m	354	Kim Mi-Ja (S. Korea)	360	1986
Team	3935	S. Korea (Kim Mi-Ja, Kim Jin-Ho, Park Jung-Ah)	4320	1986

Indoor Double FITA rounds at 25 m

MEN	589	Darrell Pace (USA)	600	1984
WOMEN	588	Elena Marfel (USSR)	600	1985

Indoor FITA round at 18 m

MEN	590	Thierry Venant (France)	600	1987
WOMEN	583	Natalya Butuzova (USSR)	600	1983

Highest championship scores

The highest scores achieved in either a World or Olympic championship for Double FITA rounds are: men, 2617 points (possible 2880) by Darrell Pace (b. 23 Oct 1956) (USA) and Richard McKinney (b. 20 Oct 1963) (USA); and women, 2616 points by Kim Jin-Ho (S. Korea), all at Long Beach, California, USA on 21-22 Oct 1983. Park Jung-Ah (S. Korea) set a women's record of 2634 points at the 1986 Asian Games at Seoul, S. Korea.

British records

York round—possible 1296 pts: Single Round, 1160 Steven Hallard at Meriden on 26 June 1983; Double Round, 2240 Steven Hallard at Stoneleigh on 14 Aug 1983.

Hereford (Women)—possible 1296 pts: Single round, 1182 Elaine Tomkinson at Bingley on 10 Aug 1980; Double Round, 2331 Sue Willcox at Oxford on 27-28 June 1979.

FITA round (Men): Steven Hallard, 1300 Single round and 2566 double round, both at Castle Ashby, Nottinghamshire on 20 May 1983.

FITA round (Women): Single round, 1273 Pauline Edwards at Worcester on 23 July 1983; double round, 2520 Rachel Fenwick at Brussels, Belgium on 12-13 Aug 1978.

Most titles *World*

The greatest number of world titles (instituted 1931) ever won by a man is four by Hans Deutgen (b. 28 Feb 1917) (Sweden) from 1947-50. The greatest number won by a woman is seven by Janina Spychajowa-Kurkowska (b. 8 Feb 1901) (Poland) from 1931-4 and in 1936, 1939 and 1947. Oscar Kessels (Belgium) (1904-68) participated in 21 world championships.

Olympic

Hubert van Innis (1866-1961) (Belgium) won six gold and three silver medals at the 1900 and 1920 Olympic Games.

British

The greatest number of British Championships is 12 by Horace Alfred Ford (1822-80) in 1849-59 and 1867, and 23 by Alice Blanche Legh (1855-1948) in 1881, 1886-92, 1895, 1898-1900, 1902-9, 1913 and 1921-2. Miss Legh was inhibited from winning from 1882 to 1885 because her mother was champion, and for four further years 1915-

18 because there were no championships during World War I.

Flight shooting

The longest recorded distance ever shot is 1 mile 268 yd *1854,40 m* in the unlimited footbow class by Harry Drake (b. 7 May 1915) (USA) at 3000 ft *915 m* altitude at Ivanpah Dry Lake, California, USA on 24 Oct 1971. The female footbow record is 1113 yd 2 ft 6 in *1018,48 m* by Arlyne Rhode (b. 4 May 1936) at Wendover, Utah, USA on 10 Sept 1978. Alan Webster (England) set the flight record for the handbow with 1231 yd 1 ft 10 in *1126,19 m* on 2 Oct 1982 and April Moon (USA) set a women's record of 1039 yd 1 ft 1 in *950,39 m* on 13 Sept 1981, both at Ivanpah Dry Lake. Drake holds the crossbow flight record with 1359 yd 2 ft 5 in *1243,4 m* on 14 Oct 1967 and the conventional footbow record with 1542 yd 2 ft 10 ins *1410,87 m* on 6 Oct 1979, both at Ivanpah Dry Lake. Compound bow world records are: (men) 1030 yd 2 ft 11 in *942,72 m* by Arlan Reynolds (USA); and (women) 704 yd 1 ft 9 in *644,27 m* by his wife Sherrie Reynolds, both at the Bonneville Flight Range, Wendover, Utah, USA in 1986.

Greatest draw

Gary Sentman, of Roseberg, Oregon, USA drew a longbow weighing a record 176 lb *79,83 kg* to the maximum draw on the arrow of 28¼ in *72 cm* at Forksville, Penn., on 20 Sept 1975.

24 hours—target archery

The highest recorded score over 24 hours by a pair of archers is 52,008 during 48 Portsmouth Rounds (40 arrows per round at 20 yards at 60 cm FITA targets) by Mick Brown and Les Powici of Guildford Archery Club on 14-15 Mar 1987.

Phyllis Griffiths, aged 64, achieved a score of 31,000 in 76 Portsmouth rounds in 24 hours at Holsworthey, Devon on 30-31 Mar 1986.

Badminton

A similar game was played in China in the 2nd millennium BC. The modern game may have evolved *c.* 1870 at Badminton Hall in Avon, the seat of the Dukes of Beaufort, or from a game played in India. The first modern rules were codified in Poona in 1876.

World team championships

The most wins at the men's International Championship for the Thomas Cup (instituted 1948) is eight by Indonesia (1958, 1961, 1964, 1970, 1973, 1976, 1979 and 1984). The most wins at the ladies' International Championship for the Uber Cup (instituted 1956) is five by Japan (1966, 1969, 1972, 1978 and 1981).

Most titles

The All-England Championships were instituted in 1899. The men's singles have been won eight times by Rudy Hartono Kurniawan (Indonesia) (b. 18 Aug 1948) from 1968-74 and 1976. The greatest number of titles won (including doubles) is 21 by George Alan Thomas (1881-1972) between 1903 and 1928. The women's singles were won ten times by Judy Hashman (*née* Devlin) (USA) (b. 22 Oct 1935) in 1954, 1957-8, 1960-4, 1966-7. She also equalled the greatest number of titles won of 17 by Meriel Lucas (later Mrs King Adams) from 1899 to 1910.

Shortest game

In the 1969 Uber Cup in Tokyo, Japan, Noriko Takagi (later Mrs Nakayama) (Japan) beat Poppy Tumengkol (Indonesia) in 9 min.

Longest hit

Frank Rugani drove a shuttlecock 79 ft 8¼ in *24,29 m* in indoor tests at San José, California, USA, on 29 Feb 1964.

Longest rallies

In the men's singles final of the 1987 All-England Championships between Morten Frost (Denmark) and Icuk Sugiarto (Indonesia) there were two successive rallies of over 90 strokes.

Most shuttles

In the final of the Indian National Badminton Championships 1986, when Syed Modi beat Vimal Kunar 15–12, 15–12, 182 shuttles were used in the 66-minute period.

Baseball

The Rev Thomas Wilson, of Maidstone, Kent, England, wrote disapprovingly, in 1700, of baseball being played on Sundays. The earliest baseball game under the Cartwright (Alexander Joy Cartwright, Jr 1820–92) rules was at Hoboken, New Jersey, USA, on 19 June 1846, with the New York Nine beating the Knickerbockers 23–1 in four innings.

There are two major leagues in the USA: the National League (NL), formed on 2 Feb 1876 at the Grand Central Hotel, New York, and the American League (AL), on 28 Jan 1901.

Most home runs

Henry Louis 'Hank' Aaron (Milwaukee and Atlanta Braves) (b. 5 Feb 1934) holds the major

Most All-England badminton titles ● Rudy Hartono Kurniawan (Indonesia) (b. 18 Aug 1948) won a record eight men's singles titles, 1968–74 and 1976. (Photo: Tommy Hindley)

league career home run record of 755, from 1954 to 1976. George Herman 'Babe' Ruth (1895–1948) had the highest home run percentage, 8.5 per cent for 714 home runs from 8399 times at bat, 1914–38. Joshua Gibson (1911–47) of Homestead Grays and Pittsburgh Crawfords Negro League clubs, achieved a career total of nearly 800 homers including an unofficial total of 75 in 1931.

The US major league record for home runs in a season is 61 by Roger Eugene Maris (1934–85) for New York Yankees in 162 games in 1961. 'Babe' Ruth hit 60 in 154 games in 1927 for the New York Yankees. The most official home runs in minor leagues is 72 by Joe Bauman of Rosewell, New Mexico in 1954.

US MAJOR LEAGUE RECORDS
AL American League, NL National League

BATTING

Batting av., career	.367	Tyrus Raymond Cobb (Detroit AL, Philadelphia AL)	1905–28
Batting av., season	.438	Hugh Duffy (Boston, NL)	1894
Runs, career	2245	Tyrus Raymond Cobb (Detroit AL, Philadelphia AL)	1905–28
RBIs, career	2297	Henry 'Hank' Aaron (Milwaukee NL, Atlanta NL, Milwaukee AL)	1954–76
„ season	190	Lewis Rober 'Hack' Wilson (Chicago NL)	1930
„ game	12	James LeRoy Bottomley (St Louis NL)	16 Sept 1924
„ innings	7	Edward Cartwright (St Louis AA)	23 Sept 1890
Base hits, career	4256	Peter Edward Rose (Cincinnati NL, Philadelphia NL)	1963–86
„ season	257	George Harold Sisler (St Louis AL)	1920
Total bases, career	6856	Henry 'Hank' Aaron	1954–76
„ season	457	George Herman 'Babe' Ruth (New York AL)	1921
Hits, consecutive	12	Michael Franklin 'Pinky' Higgins (Boston AL)	19–21 June 1938
„ „	12	Walter 'Moose' Dropo (Detroit AL)	14–15 July 1952
Consecutive games batted safely	56	Joseph Paul DiMaggio (New York AL)	15 May–16 July 1941
Stolen bases, career	938	Louis Clark Brock (Chicago NL, St Louis NL)	1961–79
„ „ season	130	Rickey Henley Henderson (Oakland AL)	1982
Consecutive games played	2130	Henry Louis 'Lou' Gehrig (New York AL)	1 June 1925–30 Apr 1939

PITCHING

Games won, career	511	Denton True 'Cy' Young	1890–1911
„ „ season	60	Charles Gardner Radbourn (Providence NL)	1884
Consecutive games won	24	Carl Owen Hubbell (New York NL)	1936–37
Shutouts, career	110	Walter Perry Johnson (Washington AL)	1907–27
„ season	16	George Washington Bradley (St Louis NL)	1876
	16	Grover Cleveland Alexander (Philadelphia NL)	1916
Strikeouts, career	4373	Lynn Nolan Ryan (New York NL, California AL, Houston NL)	1968–87
„ season	383	Lynn Nolan Ryan (California AL)	1973
„ game (9 innings)	20	Roger Clemens (Boston AL) v. Seattle	29 Apr 1986
No-hit games, career	5	Lynn Nolan Ryan	1966–81
Earned run av., season	0.90	Ferdinand Schupp (140 inn) (New York NL)	1916
„ „	1.01	Hubert 'Dutch' Leonard (222 inn) (Boston AL)	1914
„ „	1.12	Robert Gibson (305 inn) (St Louis NL)	1968
Complete games, career	751	Denton True 'Cy' Young (Cleveland NL, St Louis NL, Boston AL, Cleveland AL)	1890–1911

WORLD SERIES RECORDS
AL American League, NL National League

Most wins	22	New York Yankees (AL)	1923–78
Most series played	14	Lawrence Peter 'Yogi' Berra (New York AL) (10 wins/75 games)	1947–63
Most home runs in a game	3	George Herman 'Babe' Ruth (New York AL)	6 Oct 1926
	3	Reginald Martinez Jackson (New York AL)	18 Oct 1977
Only perfect pitch (in 9 innings)		Donald James Larson (New York AL) v. Brooklyn	8 Oct 1956

JAPANESE LEAGUE RECORDS Superior to those in US major leagues:

Home runs, career	868	Sadaharu Oh (Yomuiri)	1959–80
Stolen bases, career	939	Yutaka Fukumoto (Hankyu)	1969–83
Consecutive games played	2131	Sachio Kinugasa	1970–87

Longest home run

The longest home run ever measured was one of 618 ft *188,4 m* by Roy Edward 'Dizzy' Carlyle (1900–56) in a minor league game at Emeryville Ball Park, California, USA, on 4 July 1929. In 1919 Babe Ruth hit a 587 ft *178,9 m* homer in a Boston Red Sox v. New York Giants exhibition match at Tampa, Florida.

Longest throw

The longest throw (ball weighs 5–5¼ oz *141–148 g*) is 445 ft 10 in *135,88 m* by Glen Edward Gorbous (b. Canada 8 July 1930) on 1 Aug 1957. The longest throw by a woman is 296 ft *90,2 m* by Mildred Ella 'Babe' Didrikson (later Mrs Zaharias) (US) (1914–56) at Jersey City, New Jersey, USA on 25 July 1931.

Fastest base runner

The fastest time for circling bases is 13.3 sec by Ernest Evar Swanson (1902–73) at Columbus, Ohio, in 1932, averaging 18.45 mph *29,70 km/h*.

Fastest pitcher

The fastest recorded pitcher was Lynn Nolan Ryan (then of the California Angels) (b. 31 Jan 1947) who, on 20 Aug 1974 at Anaheim Stadium, California, USA, was measured to pitch at 100.9 mph *162,3 km/h*.

Youngest player

The youngest major league player of all time

Most strikeouts in a game ● Roger Clemens
(b. 4 Aug 1962) threw 20 strikeouts in a
9-innings game for Boston v. Seattle in the
American League on 29 Apr 1986. (Photo:
T. G. Higgins/All-Sport)

was the Cincinnati pitcher Joseph Henry Nuxhall
(b. 30 July 1928) who played one game in June
1944, aged 15 yr 314 days. He did not play again
in the NL until 1952.

Record attendances and receipts
The World Series record attendance is 420,784
(six games) when the Los Angeles Dodgers beat
the Chicago White Sox 4–2 from 1–8 Oct 1959.
The single game record is 92,706 for the fifth
game at the Memorial Coliseum, Los Angeles,
California, on 6 Oct 1959. The highest seating
capacity in a baseball stadium is now 74,208 in
the Cleveland Municipal Stadium, Ohio, USA.
The all-time season record for attendances for
both leagues has been over 47 million in 1985/
86, an average of 23,103 per match.

An estimated 114,000 spectators watched a game
between Australia and an American Services
team in a demonstration event during the
Olympic Games at Melbourne, 1 Dec 1956.

Basketball

The game of 'Pok-ta-Pok' was played in the 10th
century BC, by the Olmecs in Mexico, and closely
resembled basketball in its concept. 'Ollamalit-
zli' was a variation of this game played by the
Aztecs in Mexico as late as the 16th century. If
the solid rubber ball was put through a fixed
stone ring the player was entitled to the clothing
of all the spectators. Modern basketball (which
may have been based on the German game
Korbball) was devised by Canadian-born Dr
James A. Naismith (1861–1939) at the Training
School of the International YMCA College at
Springfield, Massachusetts, USA, in mid-Decem-
ber 1891. The first game played under modified
rules was on 20 Jan 1892. The International
Amateur Basketball Federation (FIBA) was
founded in 1932; it has now dropped the word
Amateur from its title.

Most titles *Olympic*
The USA have won nine men's Olympic titles.
From the time the sport was introduced to the

The highest paid baseball player ● Mike Schmidt of Philadelphia was reported to have the highest
salary in major leagues in 1987—$2,127,333 plus bonuses. He has led the National League for home runs
on a record eight occasions. (Mike Powell/All-Sport)

Games in 1936 until 1972 they won 63 consecutive
matches in the Olympic Games until they lost
50–51 to the USSR in the disputed Final match in
Munich. They won eighth and ninth titles in 1976
and 1984. The women's title was won by the
USSR in 1976 and 1980 and by the USA in 1984.

World
The USSR has won most titles at both the men's
World Championships (inst. 1950) with three
(1967, 1974 and 1982) and the women's (inst.
1953) with six (1959, 1964, 1967, 1971, 1975 and
1983).

American professional
The most National Basketball Association (NBA)
titles (instituted 1947), played for between the
leading professional teams in the United States,
have been won by the Boston Celtics with 16
victories between 1957 and 1986.

English
The most English National Championship titles
(instituted 1936) have been won by London
Central YMCA with eight wins in 1957–8, 1960,

1962–4, 1967 and 1969. The English National
League title has been won seven times by
Crystal Palace in 1974, 1976–8, 1980 and 1982–3.
Most English Women's Cup titles (instituted
1965) have been won by the Tigers with eight
wins, 1972–3, 1976–80 and 1982.

Highest score *International*
The highest score recorded in a senior interna-
tional match is 251 by Iraq against Yemen (33) at
New Delhi in November 1982 at the Asian Games.
The highest in a British championship is 125 by
England *v.* Wales (54) on 1 Sept 1978. England
beat Gibraltar 130–45 on 31 Aug 1978.

Match
The highest aggregate score in an NBA match is
370 when the Detroit Pistons (186) beat the
Denver Nuggets (184) in Denver on 13 Dec 1983.
Overtime was played after a 145–145 tie in
regulation time. The highest score in a US college
match is 210 when Essex County (Community)
College beat Englewood Cliffs College (67) on
20 Jan 1979.

United Kingdom

The highest score recorded in a match is 250 by the Nottingham YMCA Falcons v. Mansfield Pirates at Nottingham, on 18 June 1974. It was a handicap competition and Mansfield received 120 points towards their total of 145. The highest score in a senior National League match is 167 by West Bromwich Kestrels v. Milton Keynes (69) on 13 Feb 1983. The highest in the National Cup is 146 by Doncaster v. Cleveland (109) on 11 Feb 1976.

Individual

Mats Wermelin, 13 (Sweden), scored all 272 points in a 272-0 win in a regional boys' tournament in Stockholm, Sweden on 5 Feb 1974. The highest single game score in an NBA game is 100 points by Wilton Norman Chamberlain (b. 21 Aug 1936) for Philadelphia v. New York on 2 Mar 1962. The record score by a woman is 156 points by Marie Boyd (now Eichler) of Central HS, Lonaconing, Maryland, USA in the 163-3 defeat of Ursaline Academy, Cumberland on 25 Feb 1924.

The highest score by a British player is 124 points by Paul Ogden for St Albans School, Oldham (226) v. South Chadderton (82) on 9 Mar 1982. The highest individual score in a league match in Britain is 108 by Lewis Young for Forth Steel in his team's 154-74 win over Stirling in the Scottish League Division One at Stirling on 2 Mar 1985. The record in an English National League (Div. One) or Cup match is 73 points by Terry Crosby (USA) for Home Spare Bolton in his team's 120-106 defeat by Cottrills Manchester Giants at Altrincham, Cheshire on 26 Jan 1985.

Most points

Kareem Abdul-Jabbar (formerly Lewis Ferdinand Alcindor) (b. 16 Apr 1947) has scored a career record 36,000 points from 1969 to 1987 for the Milwaukee Bucks and Los Angeles Lakers. The previous record holder, Wilt Chamberlain, had a record average of 30.1 points per game for his total of 31,419. He set a season's record 4029 for Philadelphia in 1962. The records for the most points scored in a college career are: (women) 4061, Pearl Moore of Francis Marion College, Florence, S. Carolina, 1975-9; (men) 4045 by Travis Grant for Kentucky State, 1969-72. In the English National League, Ian Day (b. 16 May 1953) scored 3456 points in 203 games, 1973-84.

Tallest players

The tallest player of all time is reputed to be Suleiman Ali Nashnush (b. 1943) who played for the Libyan team in 1962 when measuring 2,45 m 8 ft. Aleksandr Sizonenko of Kuibyshev Stroitel and USSR is 2,39 m 7 ft 10 in tall. The tallest woman player was Iuliana Semenova (USSR) (b. 9 Mar 1952) at a reported 2,18 m 7 ft 2 in and weighing 127 kg 281 lb. The tallest British player has been the 2,29 m 7 ft 6¼ in tall Christopher Greener of London Latvians whose international debut for England was v. France on 17 Dec 1969.

Shooting speed

The greatest goal-shooting demonstration has been by Ted St Martin of Jacksonville, Florida, who, on 25 June 1977, scored with 2036 consecutive free throws.

In 24 hours Jeff Liles scored 15,138 free throws from a total of 17,862 taken (84.75 per cent) at Lakeland Christian School, Lakeland, Florida, USA on 11-12 Apr 1986.

Steve Bontrager (USA) of Polycell Kingston scored 21 points in one minute from seven positions in a demonstration for BBC TV's Record Breakers on 29 Oct 1986.

Longest goal

The longest recorded field goal in a match is a measured 92 ft 5¼ in 28,17 m by Bruce Morris for

Most three-cushion billiards titles ●
Raymond Ceulemans (Belgium) (b. 12 July 1935) won a record 19 UIMB titles, 1963-6, 1968-73, 1975-81, 1983 and 1985. (Photo: All-Sport/ Vandystadt)

Most English Amateur billiards titles ●
Norman Dagley (b. 27 June 1930) won a record 15 English Amateur titles, 1965-6, 1970-5, 1978-84. He won the world professional title in 1987. (Photo: Eric Whitehead)·

Marshall University v. Appalachian State University at Huntington, West Virginia, USA on 8 Feb 1985. A British record of 75 ft 9½ in 23,10 m is claimed by David Tarbatt (b. 23 Jan 1949) of Altofts Aces v. Harrogate Demons at Featherstone, West Yorkshire on 27 Jan 1980.

Billiards

The earliest recorded mention of billiards was in France in 1429, while Louis XI, King of France 1461-83, is reported to have had a billiard table. The first recorded public billiards room in England was the Piazza, Covent Garden, London, in the early part of the 19th century. Rubber cushions were introduced in 1835 and slate beds in 1836.

Most titles *Professional*

The greatest number of world championships (instituted 1870) won by one player is eight by John Roberts, Jr (1847-1919) (England) in 1870 (twice), 1871, 1875 (twice), 1877 and 1885 (twice). The greatest number of United Kingdom titles (instituted 1934) won is seven (1934-39 and 1947)

by Joe Davis (1901-78) (England), who also won four world titles (1928-30 and 1932).

Amateur

The record for world amateur titles is four by Robert James Percival Marshall (Australia) (b. 10 Apr 1910) in 1936, 1938, 1951 and 1962. The greatest number of English Amateur Championships (instituted 1888) won is 15 by Norman Dagley (b. 27 June 1930) in 1965-66, 1970-75, 1978-84. The record number of women's titles is eight by Vera Selby (b. 13 Mar 1930), 1970-8.

Highest breaks

Tom Reece (1873-1953) made an unfinished break of 499,135, including 249,152 cradle cannons (two points each) in 85 hr 49 min against Joe Chapman at Burroughes' Hall, Soho Square, London, between 3 June and 6 July 1907. This was not recognised because press and public were not continuously present. The highest certified break made by the anchor cannon is 42,746 by William Cook (England) from 29 May to 7 June 1907. The official world record under the then baulk-line rule is 1784 by Joe Davis in the United Kingdom Championship on 29 May 1936. Walter Albert Lindrum (Australia) (1898-1960) made an official break of 4137 in 2 hr 55 min against Joe Davis at Thurston's on 19-20 Jan 1932, before the baulk-line rule was in force. Davis had an unofficial personal best of 2502 (mostly pendulum cannons) in a match against Tom Newman (1894-1943) (England) in Manchester in 1930. The highest break recorded in amateur competition is 1149 by Michael Ferreira (India) at Calcutta, India on 15 Dec 1978. Under the more stringent 'two pot' rule, restored on 1 Jan 1983, the highest break is Ferreira's 962 unfinished in a tournament at Bombay, India on 29 Apr 1986.

Fastest century

Walter Lindrum made an unofficial 100 break in 27.5 sec in Australia on 10 Oct 1952. His official record is 100 in 46.0 sec set in Sydney in 1941.

3 CUSHION

This pocketless variation dates back to 1878. The world governing body, the *Union Mondiale de Billiard* (UMB), was formed in 1928. The most successful exponent spanning the pre and post international era from 1906 to 1952 was William F. Hoppe (USA) (1887-1959) who won 51 billiards championships in all forms. Most UMB titles have been won by Raymond Ceulemans (Belgium) (b. 12 July 1935) with 19 (1963-6, 1968-73, 1975-81, 1983, 1985).

BAR BILLIARDS

The record scoring rate in a league game has been 28,530 in 19 min 5 sec by Keith Sheard at the Crown and Thistle, Headington, Oxford on 9 July 1984. Sheard scored 1500 points in one minute on BBC TV's *Record Breakers* on 23 Sept 1986.

The highest bar billiards score in 24 hours by a team of five is 1,506,570 by John Burrows, Kent Murray, Ray Hussey, Roy Buckle and Brian Ray of The Hour Glass, Sands, High Wycombe, Buckinghamshire on 26-27 Nov 1983.

Board Games

BACKGAMMON

Forerunners of the game have been traced back to a dice and a board game found in excavations at Ur, dated to 3000 BC. Later the Romans played a game remarkably similar to the modern one. The name 'backgammon' is variously ascribed to the Welsh 'little battle', or the Saxon 'back game'.

Alan Malcolm Beckerson (b. 21 Feb 1938) devised the shortest game of 16 throws in 1982.

CHESS

The game originated in ancient India under the name Chaturanga (literally 'four-corps'—an army game). The name chess is derived from the Persian word *shah* (a king or ruler). The earliest reference is from the Middle Persian *Karnamak* (*c.* AD 590–628), though in December 1972 two ivory chessmen were found in the Uzbek Soviet Republic datable to *c.* AD 200. The game reached Britain *c.* 1255. The *Fédération Internationale des Echecs* (FIDE) was established in 1924.

Most world titles

World champions have been generally recognised since 1886. The longest undisputed tenure was 26 yr 337 days by Dr Emanuel Lasker (1868–1941) of Germany, from 1894 to 1921. The women's world championship title was held by Vera Francevna Menchik-Stevenson (1906–44) (USSR, later GB) from 1927 until her death, and was successfully defended a record seven times. Nona Terentievna Gaprindashvili (USSR) (b. 3 May 1941) held the title from 1962 to 1978 and defended successfully four times. Robert James 'Bobby' Fischer (USA) (b. 9 March 1943) is reckoned on the officially adopted Elo System to be the greatest Grand Master of all time with a 2785 rating. Gary Kimovich Kasparov (USSR) (b. 13 Apr 1963) at 2735 is currently the highest-ranked player. The highest rated woman player is Maya Chiburdanidze (USSR) (b. 17 Jan 1961) at 2530. The USSR has won the men's team title (Olympiad) a record 16 times and the women's title 11 times (every time entered) to 1986.

The most active world champion has been Anatoliy Yevgenyevich Karpov (USSR) (b. 23 May 1951), who in his tenure as champion, 1975–85, averaged 45.2 competitive games per year, played in 32 tournaments and finished first in 26.

Youngest and oldest world champions

The youngest world champion is Gary Kasparov, who won the title on 9 Nov 1985 at 22 yr 210 days. The oldest was Wilhelm Steinitz (Czechoslovakia) (1836–1900), who was 58 yr 10 days when he lost his title to Lasker on 26 May 1894. Maya Chiburdanidze won the women's title in 1978 when only 17.

Most British titles

The most British titles have been won by Dr Jonathan Penrose (b. 7 Oct 1933) with ten titles in 1958–63 and 1966–9. Rowena Mary Bruce (*née* Dew) (b. 15 May 1919) won 11 women's titles between 1937 and 1969. The first British player to attain official International Grand Master status was Anthony John Miles (b. 23 Apr 1955), on 24 Feb 1976. The top British player on the Elo list of 1 Jan 1987 is Nigel David Short (b. 1 June 1965), on 2615. The top British woman is Jana Miles (b. 9 Dec 1947) (*née* Malypetrova, formerly Hartston), on 2340.

Least games lost by a world champion

José Raúl Capablanca (Cuba) (1888–1942) lost only 34 games in his adult career, 1909–39. He was unbeaten from 10 Feb 1916 to 21 Mar 1924 and was world champion 1921–7.

Most opponents

Vlastimil Hort (b. 12 Jan 1944) (Czechoslovakia), in Seltjarnes, Iceland on 23–24 Apr 1977, played 550 opponents (on a replacement basis) including 201 simultaneously; he lost only ten games. Eric G. J. Knoppert (Netherlands) (b. 20 Sept 1959) played 500 games of 10-minute chess against opponents averaging 2002 on the Elo scale on 13–16 Sept 1985. He scored 413 points (1 for win, ½ for draw), a success rate of 82.6 per cent. The record for most consecutive games played is 663 by Vlastimil Hort over 32½ hours at Porz, West Germany on 5–6 Oct 1984. He played 60–100 opponents at a time, scoring over 80 per cent wins and averaging 30 moves per game.

Slowest and longest games

The slowest reported moving (before modern rules) in an official event is reputed to have been by Louis Paulsen (Germany) (1833–91) against Paul Charles Morphy (USA) (1837–84) on 29 Oct 1857. The game ended in a draw on move 56 after 15 hours of play of which Paulsen used most of the allotted time. Grand Master Friedrich Sämisch (1896–1975) (Germany) ran out of the allotted time (2 hr 30 min for 45 moves) after only 12 moves, in Prague, Czechoslovakia, in 1938.

The slowest move played, since time clocks were introduced, was at Vigo, Spain in 1980 when Francisco Trois (b. 3 Sept 1946) took 2 hrs 20 mins for his seventh move v. Luis M. C. P. Santos (b. 30 June 1955).

The Master game with most moves on record was when Yedael Stepak (Israel) (b. 21 Aug 1940) beat Yaakov Mashian (Iran, later Israel) (b. 17 Dec 1943) in 193 moves in Tel Aviv, Israel from 23 Mar–16 Apr 1980. The total playing time was a record 24 hr 30 min.

DRAUGHTS

Draughts, known as checkers in North America, has origins earlier than chess. It was played in Egypt in the second millennium BC. The earliest book on the game was by Antonio Torquemada of Valencia, Spain in 1547.

Walter Hellman (USA) (1916–75) won a record six world championships, 1948–67. Melvin Pomeroy (USA) was internationally undefeated from 1914 until his death in 1933.

The British Championship (biennial) was inaugurated in 1886. A record six titles were won by Samuel Cohen (London), 1924, 1927, 1929, 1933, 1937 and 1939. John McGill (Kilbride) won six Scottish titles between 1959 and 1974. William Edwards of Abercynon, Wales won the English open title on a record four successive occasions—1979, 1981, 1983 and 1985. In 1987 Andrew Knapp, on his first attempt, became at age 19 the youngest ever winner of the English Amateur Championship (inst. 1910).

Most opponents

Con McCarrick (Ireland) was reported as having played a record 154 games simultaneously, winning 136, drawing 17 and losing one, in 4 hr 30 min at Dundalk, Co. Louth, Ireland on 14 Mar 1982. Newell W. Banks (b. Detroit, USA, 10 Oct 1887) played 140 games simultaneously, winning 133 and drawing seven, in Chicago, Illinois in 1933. His playing time was 145 min, so averaging about one move per sec. In 1947 he played blindfold for 4 hr per day for 45 consecutive days, winning 1331 games, drawing 54 and losing only two, while playing six games at a time.

Longest and shortest games

In competition the prescribed rate of play is not less than 30 moves per hour with the average game lasting about 90 min. In 1958 a match between Dr Marion Tinsley (USA) and Derek Oldbury (GB) lasted 7 hr 30 min. The shortest possible game is one of 20 moves composed by Alan Malcolm Beckerson (GB) in 1977.

MAH-JONG

The tile game of Mah-Jong is of 19th century Chinese origin, where it was played in varying forms according to province and dialect. The name derives from various transliterations signifying 'sparrow' or 'bird of 100 intelligences', and a bird appears on one of the tiles, the 'one-bamboo'. Mah-Jong is the western version, the name having been coined and copyrighted by Joseph P. Babcock, a US resident in Shanghai, shortly after World War I. The National Mah-Jong League was founded in the United States in 1937 and today has over 150,000 members.

The highest scoring hand obtainable as the game is played in the western world is 'Heavenly Paradise'. A Pung/Kong of Red, White and Green Dragons, plus a Pung/Kong of own Wind when it is also Wind of the round, a pair of any other Wind and a Bouquet of Flowers make up the hand which clears the table and ends the game.

SCRABBLE ® Crossword Game

The crossword game was invented by Alfred M. Butts in 1931 and was developed, refined and trademarked as Scrabble ® Crossword Game by James Brunot in 1948.

Highest scores

The highest competitive league game score is 849 by Maurice Rocker (GB) at Sheffield on 6 July 1985. The highest competitive single-turn score recorded is 392 by Dr Saladin Karl Khoshnaw (of Kurdish origin) in Manchester in April 1982. He laid down 'CAZIQUES', which means 'native chiefs of West Indian aborigines'.

The greatest margin of victory in a league game was achieved by Ron Hendra when he beat Amber Sturdy 730–180 in a London League match in 1983.

Most titles

British National Championships were instituted in 1971. Olive Behan, 1972 and 1975, and Philip Nelkon, 1978 and 1981, have both won twice. The highest score in the Championship has been 1843 (three-game total) by Viraf Mehta in 1986.

SOLITAIRE

The shortest time taken to complete the game is 17.8 secs by Caroline Harrison, 16, at Sittingbourne, Kent on 25 Mar 1987.

BIGGEST BOARD GAME

The world's biggest board game, called Heartopoly, involved 4317 participants and stretched around the ¼ mile *403 m* Flagler Dog Track in Miami, Florida, USA on 14–15 Sept 1985.

Bobsleigh and Tobogganing

BOBSLEDDING

The oldest known sledge is dated *c.* 6500 BC and came from Heinola, Finland. The first known bobsleigh race took place at Davos, Switzerland in 1889. The International Federation of Bobsleigh and Tobogganing was formed in 1923, followed by the International Bobsleigh Federation in 1957.

Most titles *Olympic*

The Olympic four-man bob title (inst. 1924) has been won four times by Switzerland (1924, 1936, 1956 and 1972). The USA (1932, 1936), Switzerland (1948, 1980), Italy (1956, 1968), West Germany (1952, 1972) and GDR (1976, 1984) have won the Olympic two-man bob (inst. 1932) event twice. The most gold medals won by an individual is three by Meinhard Nehmer (GDR) (b. 13 June 1941) and Bernhard Germeshausen (GDR) (b. 21 Aug 1951) in the 1976 two-man, 1976 and 1980 four-man events. The most medals won is six (two gold, two silver, two bronze) by Eugenio Monti (Italy) (b. 23 Jan 1928), 1956 to 1968. The only British victory was at two-man bob in 1964 by the Hon. Robin Thomas Valerian Dixon (b. 21 Apr 1935) and Anthony James Dillon Nash (b. 18 Mar 1936).

World (including Olympics)

The world four-man bob title (inst. 1924) has been won 16 times by Switzerland (1924, 1936,

1939, 1947, 1954–7, 1971–3, 1975, 1982–3, 1986–7). Italy won the two-man title 14 times (1954, 1956–63, 1966, 1968–9, 1971 and 1975). Eugenio Monti was a member of eleven world championship crews, eight two-man and three four-man from 1957–68.

TOBOGGANING

The word toboggan comes from the Micmac American Indian word *tobaakan.* The St Moritz Tobogganing Club, Switzerland, founded in 1887 is the oldest toboggan club in the world. It is unique in being the home of the Cresta Run, which dates from 1884, and for the introduction of the one-man skeleton racing toboggan. The course is 1212,25 m *3977 ft* long with a drop of 157 m *514 ft* and the record is 50.91 sec (av. 85,72 km/h *53.27 mph*) by Franco Gansser of Switzerland on 16 Feb 1986. On 21 Feb 1986 Nico Baracchi (Switzerland) set a record from Junction (890,2 m *2920 ft*) of 41.58 sec.

The greatest number of wins in the Grand National (inst. 1885) is eight by the 1948 Olympic champion Nino Bibbia (Italy) (b. 9 Sept 1924) in 1960–4, 1966, 1968 and 1973. The greatest number of wins in the Curzon Cup (inst. 1910) is eight by Bibbia in 1950, 1957–8, 1960, 1962–4, and 1969, who hence won the double in 1960 and 1962–4.

LUGEING

In lugeing the rider adopts a sitting, as opposed to a prone, position. Official international competition began at Klosters, Switzerland, in 1881. The first European Championships were at Reichenberg, Germany, in 1914 and the first World Championships at Oslo, Norway, in 1953. The International Luge Federation was formed in 1957. Lugeing became an Olympic sport in 1964.

Fastest speed

The highest recorded, photo-timed speed is 137,4 km/h *85.38 mph* by Asle Strand (Norway) at Tandådalens Linbane, Sälen, Sweden on 1 May 1982.

Most titles *World and Olympic*

The most successful riders in the World Championships are Thomas Köhler (GDR) (b. 25 June 1940), who won the single-seater title in 1962, 1964 (Olympic), 1966 and 1967 and shared the two-seater title in 1967 and 1968 (Olympic), and Hans Rinn (GDR) (b. 19 Mar 1953), Olympic champion two-seater 1976 and 1980 and world champion at single-seater 1973 and 1977, two-seater 1977 and 1980. Margit Schumann (GDR) (b. 14 Sept 1952) has won five women's titles, 1973–5, 1976 (Olympic) and 1977.

Bowling (Tenpin)

The ancient German game of nine-pins (*Heidenwerfen*—knock down pagans) was exported to the United States in the early 17th century. In 1841 the Connecticut state legislature prohibited the game and other states followed. Eventually a tenth pin was added to evade the ban; but there is some evidence of ten pins being used in Suffolk, UK about 300 years ago. The first body to standardise rules was the American Bowling Congress (ABC), established in New York on 9 Sept 1895.

The world's largest bowling centre is the Fukuyama Bowl, Osaka, Japan which has 144 lanes. The Tokyo World Lanes Centre, Japan, now closed, had 252 lanes.

World Championships

The World (*Fédération Internationale des Quilleurs*) Championships were instituted for men in 1954 and for women in 1963. The highest pinfall in the individual men's event is 5963 (in 28 games) by Ed Luther (USA) at Milwaukee, Wisconsin, on 28 Aug 1971. For the current schedule of 24 games the men's record is 5261 by Rick Steelsmith (USA) and the women's is 4894 by Sandra Jo Shiery (USA), both at Helsinki, Finland in June 1987.

Highest scores *World*

The highest individual score for three sanctioned games (possible 900) is 886 by Albert 'Allie' Brandt of Lockport, New York, USA, on 25 Oct 1939. The record for consecutive strikes in sanctioned match play is 33, first achieved by John Pezzin (b. 1930) at Toledo, Ohio, USA on 4 Mar 1976. The highest number of sanctioned 300 games is 27 (to 1986) by Elvin Mesger (b. 24 Mar 1916) of Sullivan, Missouri, USA; the women's record is eleven by Jeanne Maiden.

The maximum 900 for a three-game series was achieved by Glenn Allison (b. 1930) at the La Habra Bowl in Los Angeles, California on 1 July 1982, but this was not recognised by the ABC due to the oiling patterns on the boards. It has been recorded four times in unsanctioned games—by Leo Bentley at Lorain, Ohio, USA, on 26 Mar 1931; by Joe Sargent at Rochester, New York State, USA, in 1934; by Jim Murgie in Philadelphia, Pennsylvania, USA, on 4 Feb 1937 and by Bob Brown at Roseville Bowl, California, USA on 12 Apr 1980. Such series must have consisted of 36 consecutive strikes (*i.e.* all pins down with one ball).

The highest average for a season attained in sanctioned competition is 242 by John Ragard (b. 5 Feb 1954) of Susquehanna, Pennsylvania, USA for 66 games in 1981–82. The women's record is 232 by Patty Ann of Bloomington, Illinois, USA in 1983–84.

Great Britain

The British record for a three-game series is 802 by Simon Brown (b. 22 Oct 1963) of Havant, Hampshire in April 1986. Army Sergeant Michael Langley scored 835 at S.H.A.P.E., Belgium on 15 Apr 1985. The maximum score for a single game of 300 has been achieved on several occasions. The first man to do so was Albert Kirkham (b. 1931) of Burslem, Staffordshire, on 5 Dec 1965. The first woman was Georgina Wardle at the Sheffield Bowl, South Yorkshire on 20 Jan 1985. The first person to achieve the feat twice was Patrick Duggan, in 1972 and 1986, both at

Women's record score at bowling ● Jeanne Maiden (b. 10 Nov 1957) of Solon, Ohio set a WIBC three-game record of 864 on 23 Nov 1986. (Photo: WIBC)

Bexleyheath Bowl, Kent. The three-game series record for a woman player is 740 by Elizabeth Cullen at the Astra Bowl, RAF Brize Norton, Oxfordshire on 15 Mar 1983.

Highest earnings

Earl Anthony (b. 1938) won a record $1,265,171 in Professional Bowlers Association (PBA) competition including a record 41 PBA titles to 1986. The season's record is $201,200 by Mike Aulby in 1985.

Highest score—24 hours

The Dragons team of six scored 54,407 in 24 hours at Nowra Tenpin Bowl and Leisure Centre, Nowra, NSW, Australia on 7–8 Mar 1987.

Bowls

Whilst bowling games date back some 7000 years, the game of bowls in recognisable form can be traced back to the 13th century in England. The Southampton Town Bowling was

World indoor pairs bowls ● David Bryant and Tony Allcock won the pairs titles on the first two occasions that the pairs event was staged, 1986–7. (Eric Whitehead)

formed in 1299. A green dating back to 1294 is claimed by the Chesterfield Bowling Club. After falling into disrepute, the game was rescued by the bowlers of Scotland who, headed by William W. Mitchell (1803–84), framed the modern rules in 1848–9.

Most titles *World*
The only man to win two singles titles is David John Bryant (b. 27 Oct 1931) (England) in 1966 and 1980. At Johannesburg, South Africa, in February 1976, the South African team achieved an unprecedented clean sweep of all four titles plus the team competition (Leonard Trophy).

Elsie Wilke (New Zealand) won two women's singles titles, 1969 and 1974. Merle Richardson (Australia) has won three women's gold medals: fours 1977, singles and pairs 1985.

English & British
The record number of English Bowls Association (founded 8 June 1903) Championships won or shared is 16 by David Bryant, comprising six singles (1960, 1966, 1971–3, 1975), three pairs (1965, 1969, 1974), three triples (1966, 1977, 1985) and four fours championships (1957, 1968, 1969 and 1971). He has also won seven British Isles titles (four singles, one pairs, one triples, one fours) in the period 1957–86.

Highest score
The highest score achieved in an international bowls match is the 63–1 victory by Swaziland v. Japan during the World Championships at Melbourne, Australia on 16 Jan 1980.

Most eights
Freda Ehlers and Linda Bertram uniquely scored three consecutive eights in the Southern Transvaal pairs event at Johannesburg, South Africa on 30 Jan 1978.

International appearances
The greatest number of international appearances outdoors by any bowler is 78 by Syd Thompson (b. 29 Aug 1912) for Ireland 1947–73. He also had 50 indoor caps. The youngest bowler to represent England was Gerard Anthony Smyth (b. 29 Dec 1960) at 20 yr 196 days on 13 July 1981. The youngest ever EBA singles champion was David J. Cutler (b. 1 Aug 1954) at 25 yr 16 days in 1979. He had been a member of the winning triples team at 18 yr 18 days in 1972.

INDOOR
The English Indoor Bowling Association became an autonomous body in 1971. Prior to that it was part of the English Bowling Association.

Championships
The four-corner international championship was first held in 1936. England has won a record 23 titles. The National Singles title (inst. 1960) has been won most often by David Bryant with nine wins between 1964 and 1983. David Bryant has won the World Indoor singles (inst. 1979) three times, 1979–81 and with Tony Allcock has won the doubles (inst. 1986) twice 1986–7.

The youngest EIBA singles champion, John Dunn (b. 6 Oct 1963), was 17 yr 117 days when he won in 1981.

Highest score
The highest score in a British international match is 52 by Scotland v. Wales (3) at Tees-side in March 1972.

C. Hammond and B. Funnell of The Angel, Tonbridge beat A. Wise and C. Lock 55–0 over 21 ends in the second round of the EIBA National Pairs Championship on 17 Oct 1983 at The Angel, Tonbridge, Kent.

Boxing with gloves was depicted on a fresco from the Isle of Thera, Greece which has been dated to 1520 BC. The earliest prize-ring code of rules was formulated in England on 16 Aug 1743 by the champion pugilist Jack Broughton (1704–89), who reigned from 1734 to 1750. Boxing, which had in 1867 come under the Queensberry Rules formulated for John Sholto Douglas, 8th Marquess of Queensberry (1844–1900), was not established as a legal sport in Britain until after the ruling, *R. v. Roberts and Others*, of Mr Justice Grantham, following the death of Billy Smith (Murray Livingstone) due to a fight on 24 Apr 1901.

Longest fights
The longest recorded fight with gloves was between Andy Bowen of New Orleans (1867–94) and Jack Burke in New Orleans, Louisiana, USA, on 6–7 Apr 1893. It lasted 110 rounds, 7 hr 19 min (9.15 p.m.–4.34 a.m.), and was declared a no contest (later changed to a draw). Bowen won an 85-round bout on 31 May 1893. The longest bare-knuckle fight was 6 hr 15 min between James Kelly and Jack Smith at Fiery Creek, Dalesford, Victoria, Australia on 3 Dec 1855. The greatest number of rounds was 276 in 4 hr 30 min when Jack Jones beat Patsy Tunney in Cheshire in 1825.

Shortest fights
There is a distinction between the quickest knock-out and the shortest fight. A knock-out in 10½ sec (including a 10-sec count) occurred on 23 Sept 1946, when Al Couture struck Ralph Walton while the latter was adjusting a gum shield in his corner at Lewiston, Maine, USA. If the time was accurately taken it is clear that Couture must have been more than half way across the ring from his own corner at the opening bell. The shortest fight on record appears to be one in a Golden Gloves tournament at Minneapolis, Minnesota, USA, on 4 Nov 1947 when Mike Collins floored Pat Brownson with the first punch and the contest was stopped, without a count, 4 sec after the bell.

The fastest officially timed knock-out in British boxing is 11 sec (including a doubtless fast 10-sec count) when Jack Cain beat Harry Deamer, both of Notting Hill, London, at the National Sporting Club on 20 Feb 1922. More recently, Hugh Kelly knocked out Steve Cook with the first punch of their contest at the Normandy Hotel, Glasgow on 14 May 1984, again in 11 sec, including the 10-sec count.

The shortest world-title fight was the James J. Jeffries (1875–1953)–Jack Finnegan heavyweight bout on 6 Apr 1900, won by Jeffries in 55 sec. The shortest ever British title fight was one of 40 sec (including the count), when Dave Charnley knocked out David 'Darkie' Hughes in a lightweight championship defence in Nottingham on 20 Nov 1961.

Most British titles
The most defences of a British heavyweight title is 14 by 'Bombardier' Billy Wells (1889–1967) from 1911 to 1919. The only British boxer to win three Lonsdale Belts outright was Henry William Cooper (b. 3 May 1934), heavyweight champion. He retired after losing to Joe Bugner (b. Hungary, 13 Mar 1950), having held the British heavyweight title from 12 Jan 1959 to 28 May 1969 and from 24 Mar 1970 to 16 Mar 1971.

The fastest time to win a Lonsdale Belt, for three successive championship wins, is 203 days by Robert Dickie (b. 23 June 1964) at featherweight, 9 Apr–29 Oct 1986.

Tallest
The tallest boxer to fight professionally was Gogea Mitu (b. 1914) of Romania in 1935. He was 233 cm *7 ft 4 in* and weighed 148 kg *327 lb*. John

Rankin, who won a fight in New Orleans, Louisiana, USA, in November 1967, was reputedly also 233 cm *7 ft 4 in*.

Most fights without loss
Edward Henry (Harry) Greb (USA) (1894–1926) was unbeaten in a sequence of 178 bouts, but these included 117 'no decision', of which five were unofficial losses, in 1916–23. Of boxers with complete records, Packey McFarland (USA) (1888–1936) had 97 fights (five draws) from 1905–15 without a defeat. Pedro Carrasco (Spain) (b. 7 Nov 1943) won 83 consecutive fights from 22 Apr 1964 to 3 Sept 1970, drew once and had a further nine wins before his loss to Armando Ramos in a WBC lightweight contest on 18 Feb 1972.

Most knock-outs
The greatest number of finishes classed as 'knock-outs' in a career (1936–63) is 145 (129 in professional bouts) by Archie Moore (USA) (b. Archibald Lee Wright, 13 Dec 1913 or 1916). The record for consecutive KOs is 44 by Lamar Clark (b. 1 Dec 1934) (USA) from 1958 to 11 Jan 1960. He knocked out six in one night (five in the first round) at Bingham, Utah, on 1 Dec 1958.

Largest purse
The total purse for the world middleweight fight between 'Marvelous' Marvin Hagler (b. 23 May 1954) and 'Sugar' Ray Leonard (b. 17 May 1956) (USA) at Caesar's Palace car park, Las Vegas on 6 Apr 1987, was estimated as at least $28 million, $17 m for Hagler and $11 m for Leonard, who won on points in a split decision. Gross takings were estimated as $100 million.

Highest earnings in career
The largest fortune made in a fighting career is an estimated $69 million (including exhibitions) by Muhammad Ali from October 1960 to December 1981 in 61 fights comprising 549 rounds.

Attendances *Highest*
The greatest paid attendance at any boxing fight has been 120,757 (with a ringside price of $27.50) for the Tunney v. Dempsey world heavyweight title fight at the Sesquicentennial Stadium, Philadelphia, Pennsylvania, USA, on 23 Sept 1926. The indoor record is 63,350 at the Ali v. Leon Spinks fight in the Superdrome, New Orleans, Louisiana, on 15 Sept 1978. The British attendance record is 82,000 at the Len Harvey v. Jock McAvoy fight at White City, London, on 10 July 1939.

The highest non-paying attendance is 135,132 at the Tony Zale v. Billy Pryor fight at Juneau Park, Milwaukee, Wisconsin, USA, on 16 Aug 1941.

Lowest
The smallest attendance at a world heavyweight title fight was 2434 at the Clay v. Liston fight at Lewiston, Maine, USA, on 25 May 1965.

WORLD HEAVYWEIGHT CHAMPIONS

Earliest title fight
The first world heavyweight title fight, with gloves and 3-min rounds, was that between John Lawrence Sullivan (1858–1918) and 'Gentleman' James John Corbett (1866–1933) in New Orleans, Louisiana, USA, on 7 Sept 1892. Corbett won in 21 rounds.

Longest and shortest reigns
The longest reign of any world heavyweight champion is 11 years 252 days by Joe Louis (USA) (b. Joseph Louis Barrow, 1914–81), from 22 June 1937, when he knocked out James Joseph Braddock in the eighth round at Chicago, Illinois, USA, until announcing his retirement on 1 Mar 1949. During his reign Louis made a record 25 defences of his title. The shortest reign was 83 days for James 'Bonecrusher' Smith (USA) (b. 3

Apr 1955), WBA champion 13 Dec 1986 to 7 Mar 1987, and for Ken Norton (USA) (b. 9 Aug 1945), recognised by the WBC as champion from 18 Mar to 9 June 1978. The longest lived world heavyweight champion was Jack Dempsey, who died on 31 May 1983 aged 87 yr 341 days.

Most recaptures

Muhammad Ali (b. Cassius Marcellus Clay, Jr, 17 Jan 1942) is the only man to regain the heavyweight championship twice. Ali first won the title on 25 Feb 1964 defeating Sonny Liston. He defeated George Foreman on 30 Oct 1974 having been stripped of the title by the world boxing authorities on 28 Apr 1967. He won the WBA title from Leon Spinks on 15 Sept 1978 having previously lost to him on 15 Feb 1978.

Undefeated

Rocky Marciano (b. Rocco Francis Marchegiano) (1923–69) is the only world heavyweight champion to have been undefeated during his entire professional career (1947–56). He won all his 49 fights, 43 by knock-outs or stoppages.

Oldest and youngest

The oldest man to win the heavyweight crown was Jersey Joe Walcott (USA) (b. Arnold Raymond Cream, 31 Jan 1914), who knocked out Ezzard Mack Charles (1921–75) on 18 July 1951 in Pittsburgh, Pennsylvania, when aged 37 yr 168 days. Walcott was the oldest holder at 38 yr 236 days, losing his title to Rocky Marciano (1923–69) on 23 Sept 1952.

Heaviest and lightest

The heaviest world champion was Primo Carnera (Italy) (1906–67), the 'Ambling Alp', who won the title from Jack Sharkey in New York City, NY, USA, on 29 June 1933. He then scaled 267 lb *121 kg* but his peak weight was 270 lb *122 kg*. He had an expanded chest measurement of 53 in *134 cm* and the longest reach at 85½ in *217 cm* (finger tip to finger tip). The lightest champion was Robert James 'Bob' Fitzsimmons (1863–1917), from Helston, Cornwall, who at 167 lb *75 kg* won the title by knocking out James Corbett at Carson City, Nevada, USA, on 17 Mar 1897. The greatest differential in a world title fight was 86 lb *39 kg* between Carnera (270 lb *122 kg*) and Tommy Loughran (184 lb *83 kg*) of the USA, when the former won on points at Miami, Florida, USA, on 1 Mar 1934.

Tallest and shortest

The tallest world champion according to measurements by the physical education director of the Hemingway Gymnasium, Harvard University, was Carnera at 6 ft 5.4 in *196,6 cm*, although he was widely reported and believed to be up to 6 ft 8½ in *204 cm*. Jess Willard (1881–1968), who won the title in 1915, often stated to be 6 ft 6¼ in *199 cm* was in fact 6 ft 5¼ in *196 cm*. The shortest was Tommy Burns, world champion from 23 Feb 1906 to 26 Dec 1908, who stood 5 ft 7 in *170 cm* and weighed between 168 and 180 lb *76–81 kg*.

WORLD CHAMPIONS *Any weight*

Longest reign

Joe Louis's heavyweight duration record of 11 years 252 days stands for all divisions.

Youngest and oldest

The youngest age at which any world championship has been won is 17 yr 176 days by Wilfred Benitez (b. New York, 12 Sept 1958) of Puerto Rico, who won the WBA light welterweight title in San Juan, PR, on 6 Mar 1976. The oldest world champion was Archie Moore, who was recognised as a light heavyweight champion up to 10 Feb 1962 when his title was removed. He was then believed to be between 45 and 48.

Longest career

Bob Fitzsimmons had the longest career of any

Youngest heavyweight world champion ●
Mike Tyson (b. 30 June 1966) became the youngest ever heavyweight champion at the age of 20 yr 145 days when he defeated Trevor Berbick on 22 Nov 1986 in Las Vegas to gain the WBC title. He added the WBA title on 7 Mar 1987, outpointing James 'Bonecrusher' Smith. (Photo: Sporting Pictures)

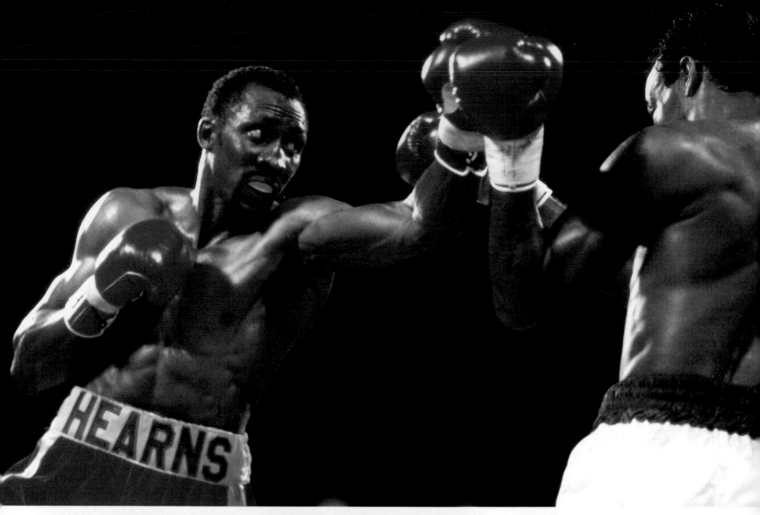

official world titleholder with over 31 years from 1883 to 1914. He had his last world title bout on 20 Dec 1905 at the age of 42 yr 208 days.

Longest fight

The longest world title fight (under Queensberry Rules) was that between the lightweights Joe Gans (1874–1910), of the USA, and Oscar Matthew 'Battling' Nelson (1882–1954), the 'Durable Dane', at Goldfield, Nevada, USA, on 3 Sept 1906. It was terminated in the 42nd round when Gans was declared the winner on a foul.

Most recaptures

The only boxer to win a world title five times at one weight is 'Sugar' Ray Robinson (USA) (b. Walker Smith, Jr, 3 May 1921), who beat Carmen Basilio (USA) in the Chicago Stadium on 25 Mar 1958, to regain the world middleweight title for the fourth time. The record number of title bouts in a career is 37, of which 18 ended in 'no decision' by Jack Britton, three-time world welterweight champion (USA) (1885–1962) from 1915–22.

Greatest weight span

The only man to hold world titles at three weights *simultaneously* was Henry 'Homicide Hank' Armstrong (b. 12 Dec 1912), now the Rev Henry Jackson, of the USA, at featherweight, lightweight and welterweight from August to December 1938.

Greatest 'tonnage'

The greatest 'tonnage' recorded in any fight has been 700 lb *317 kg* when Claude 'Humphrey' McBride (Oklahoma), 340 lb *154 kg*, knocked out Jimmy Black (Houston), who weighed 360 lb *163 kg*, in the third round at Oklahoma City on 1 June 1971. The greatest 'tonnage' in a world title fight was 488¾ lb *221¼ kg*, when Carnera, then 259¼ lb *117¼ kg*, fought Paolino Uzcudun (Spain), 229¼ lb *104 kg*, in Rome on 22 Oct 1933.

Most knock-downs in title fights

Vic Toweel (South Africa) (b. 12 Jan 1929) knocked down Danny O'Sullivan of London 14

'Hitman' Hearns ● Thomas Hearns (b. 8 Oct 1958) is one of 10 men to be world champion at three different weights and is currently bidding to be the first to win in four different categories. (Photo: All Sport)

times in ten rounds in their world bantamweight fight at Johannesburg on 2 Dec 1950, before the latter retired.

AMATEUR

Most Olympic titles

Only two boxers have won three Olympic gold medals: southpaw László Papp (b. 25 Mar 1926) (Hungary), middleweight 1948, light-middleweight 1952 and 1956; and Teofilo Stevenson (b. 23 Mar 1952) (Cuba), heavyweight 1972, 1976 and 1980. The only man to win two titles in one celebration was Oliver L. Kirk (USA), who won both bantam and featherweight titles in St Louis, Missouri, USA in 1904, but he needed only one bout in each class.

Oldest gold medallist

Richard Kenneth Gunn (1871–1961) (GB) won the Olympic featherweight gold medal on 27 Oct 1908 in London aged 37 yr 254 days.

World Championships

Two boxers have won three World Championships (inst. 1974): Teofilo Stevenson (Cuba), heavyweight 1974, 1978 and super-heavyweight 1986, and Adolfo Horta (b. 3 Oct 1957) (Cuba) bantam 1978, feather 1982 and lightweight 1986.

Most titles *Great Britain*

The greatest number of ABA titles won by any boxer is six by Joseph Steers at middleweight and heavyweight between 1890 and 1893 and by John Lyon (b. 9 Mar 1962) at light-flyweight 1981–4 and at flyweight 1986–7. Alex 'Bud' Watson (b. 27 May 1914) of Leith, Scotland won the Scottish heavyweight title in 1938, 1942?–3 and the light-heavyweight championship 1937–9, 1943–5 and

1947, making ten in all. He also won the ABA light-heavyweight title in 1945 and 1947.

Longest span

The greatest span of ABA title-winning performances is that of the heavyweight Hugh 'Pat' Floyd (b. 23 Aug 1910), who won in 1929 and gained his fourth title 17 years later in 1946.

Canoeing

The acknowledged pioneer of canoeing as a modern sport was John Macgregor (1825–92), a British barrister, in 1865. The Canoe Club was formed on 26 July 1866.

Most titles *Olympic*

Gert Fredriksson (b. 21 Nov 1919) of Sweden won a record six Olympic gold medals, 1948–60. He added a silver and a bronze for a record eight medals. The most by a woman is three, by Lyudmila Pinayeva (*née* Khvedosyuk) (b. 14 Jan 1936) (USSR), 1964–72. The most gold medals at one Games is three by Vladimir Parfenovich (b. 2 Dec 1958) (USSR) in 1980 and by Ian Ferguson (b. 20 July 1952) (New Zealand) in 1984.

World

Including the Olympic Games, a men's record thirteen titles have been won by Gert Fredriksson, 1948–60, Rüdiger Helm (GDR) (b. 6 Oct 1956), 1976–83, and Ivan Patzaichin (Romania) (b. 26 Nov 1949), 1968–84. The women's record is 17, by Birgit Schmidt (née Fischer) (b. 25 Feb 1962), 1978–85.

The most individual titles by a British canoeist is three by Alan Emus, canoe sailing 1961, 1965 and 1969 and by Richard Fox at K1 slalom in 1981, 1983 and 1985.

Highest speed

The Olympic 1000 m best performance of 3 min 02.70 sec, set in a heat by the USSR K4 at Moscow on 31 July 1980, represents an average speed of

19,70 km/h *12.24 mph*. They achieved 21,15 km/h *13.14 mph* for the first 250 m.

Longest journey

The longest journey ever made by canoe is 12,181 miles *19 603 km* by father and son Dana and Donald Starkell from Winnipeg, Manitoba, Canada by ocean and river to Belem, Brazil from 1 June 1980 to 1 May 1982. All portages were human powered.

The longest journey without portages or aid of any kind is one of 6102 miles *9820 km* by Richard H. Grant and Ernest 'Moose' Lassy circumnavigating the eastern USA via Chicago, New Orleans, Miami, New York and the Great Lakes from 22 Sept 1930 to 15 Aug 1931.

Longest open sea voyage

Beatrice and John Dowd, Ken Beard and Steve Denson (Richard Gillett replaced him mid-journey) paddled 2170 miles *3491 km* (of a total 2192 miles *3527 km*) from Venezuela to Miami, Florida, USA, via the West Indies, 11 Aug 1977–29 Apr 1978 in two Klepper Aerius 20 kayaks.

Cross-Channel

The singles record across the English Channel is 3 hr 33 min 47 sec by Andrew William Dougall Samuel (b. 12 July 1937) of Glasgow, from Shakespeare Bay, Dover, to Wissant, France, on 5 Sept 1976. The doubles record is 2 hr 28 min 18 sec by Shaun Rice (Ireland) and Colin Simpkins (South Africa) in a K2 on 19 July 1986 from Shakespeare Bay, Dover to Cap Gris Nez, France.

North Sea

On 22–23 June 1986, a team of five in the 'Canadian Club Challenge' paddled K1s from Zeebrugge, Belgium to Felixstowe, England, over 110 miles *177 km* across open sea, in 28 hr 56 min 12 sec.

Loch Ness

The fastest time for a K1 from Fort Augustus to Lochend (22.7 miles *36,5 km*) is 3 hr 13 min 47 sec by Flt Lt John David Anderson (RAF) in a Jaguar K1 on 22 Oct 1985.

Highest altitude

In September 1976 Dr Michael Leslie Jones (1951–78) and Michael Hopkinson of the British Everest Canoe Expedition canoed down the River Dudh Kosi, Nepal from an altitude of 17,500 ft *5334 m*.

Longest race

The longest race ever staged was 3283 miles *5283 km* from Rocky Mountain House, Alberta to the Expo 67 site at Montreal, Quebec as the Canadian Government Centennial Voyageur Canoe Pageant and Race. Ten canoes represented Canadian provinces and territories. The winner of the race, which took from 24 May to 4 Sept 1967, was the Province of Manitoba canoe *Radisson*.

24 hours

The solo 24-hour canoe record is 230,65 km *143.32 miles* by Dr Chris L. Greeff (South Africa) in a Jaguar K1 canoe on the Breede River, Robertson to Cape Infanta, Cape Province, South Africa on 11–12 Aug 1985. The women's record was set at 156,4 km *97.2 miles* by Lydia Formentin on the Swan River, Western Australia in 1979.

The record in flat water, without benefit of current, is 199,53 km *123.98 miles* by Thomas J. Mazuzan on the Barge Canal, New York State on 24–5 Sept 1986. The record in open sea is 194,1 km *120.6 miles* by Randy Fine (USA) along the Florida coast on 26–7 June 1986.

Greatest lifetime distance

Fritz Lindner of Berlin, West Germany, totalled 91 486 km *56,847 miles* from 1928 to 1983.

Eskimo rolls

Ray Hudspith (b. 18 Apr 1960) achieved 1000 eskimo rolls in 34 min 43 sec at the Elswick Pool, Newcastle-upon-Tyne, on 20 Mar 1987. Julian Dean achieved 1555 continuous rolls at Casterton Swimming Pool, Cumbria, taking 1 hr 49 min 45 sec on 6 Dec 1983. Colin Brian Hill (b. 16 Aug 1970) set a 'hand-rolling' record of 1000 rolls in 31 min 55.62 sec at Consett, Co. Durham on 12 Mar 1987. He achieved 100 rolls in 2 min 39.2 sec at Crystal Palace, London on 22 Feb 1987.

Card Games

CONTRACT BRIDGE

Bridge (a corruption of Biritch, a now-obsolete Russian word whose meanings include 'declarer') is thought either to be of Levantine origin, similar games having been played there in the early 1870s, or to have come from India.

Auction bridge (highest bidder names trump) was invented *c.* 1902. The contract principle, present in several games (notably the French game *Plafond, c.* 1917) was introduced to bridge by Harold Sterling Vanderbilt (USA) on 1 Nov 1925 during a Caribbean voyage aboard the SS *Finland*. It became a worldwide craze after the USA *v.* Great Britain challenge match between Romanian-born Ely Culbertson (1891–1955) and Lt-Col Walter Thomas More Buller (1887–1938) at Almack's Club, London, in September 1930. The USA won the 200-hand match by 4845 points.

Most world titles

The World Championship (Bermuda Bowl) has been won most often by Italy's Blue Team (*Squadra Azzura*), 1957–9, 1961–3, 1965–7, 1969, 1973–5. Italy also won the Olympiad in 1964, 1968 and 1972. Giorgio Belladonna (b. 7 June 1923) was in all these winning teams.

Most master points

In the latest ranking list based on master points awarded by the World Bridge Federation, the leading male player in the world was Giorgio Belladonna (Italy) with 1821¼ points. The world's leading woman player is Jacqui Mitchell (USA) with 347 points.

Barry Crane of Los Angeles led the American Contract Bridge League rankings from 1968 to his murder in 1985. He amassed a record total of 35,137.6 master points. The current leader is Paul Soloway with 27,435 to May 1987. The most master points scored in a year is 3270 by Grant Baze (USA) in 1984.

The first man to win 10,000 master points was Oswald Jacoby (USA) (1902–84) in October 1967. He had been a member of the winning world championship team in 1935 and on 4 Dec 1983 became the oldest member of a winning team of a major open team championship, in the Curtis Reisinger Trophy.

Youngest Life Master

Dougie Hsieh (b. 23 Nov 1969) of New York City became the world's youngest ever Life Master in 1981 at 11 yr 306 days. The youngest ever female Master is Patricia Thomas (b. 10 Oct 1968) at 14 yr 28 days in 1982.

Perfect deals

The mathematical odds against dealing 13 cards of one suit are 158,753,389,899 to 1, while the odds against a named player receiving a 'perfect hand' consisting of all 13 spades are 635,013,559,599 to 1. The odds against each of the four players receiving a complete suit ('perfect deal') are 2,235,197,406,895,366,368,301,559,999 to 1.

Possible auctions

The number of possible auctions with North as dealer is 128,745,650,347,030,683,120,231,926,111, 609,371,363,122,697,557.

Caving

The world depth record was set by the Groupe Vulcain in the Gouffre Jean Bernard, France at 1535 m *5035 ft* in October 1983. However, this cave, explored via multiple entrances, has never been entirely descended, so the 'sporting' record for the greatest descent into a cave is recognised as 1370 m *4495 ft* in the Snezhnaya–Mezhonnogo, USSR by a team led by A. Morozov in 1984. The deepest cave explored through a single entrance is the 1338 m *4391 ft* Sima de la Puerta de Illamina in Spain by F. Vergier in August 1981.

Cricket

The earliest evidence of a game similar to cricket is from a drawing depicting two men playing with a bat and ball dated *c.* 1250. The game was played in Guildford, Surrey, at least as early as 1550. The earliest major match of which the full score survives was one in which a team representing England (40 and 70) was beaten by Kent (53 and 58 for 9) by one wicket at the Artillery Ground in Finsbury, London, on 18 June 1744.

Biggest tournament ● The Epson World Bridge Championship, held on 16 May 1987, was contested by 73,256 players playing the same hands at more than 1537 centres. Britain's Rixi Markus, the first woman World Grand Master, is seen here with Seiko Epson Managing Director, Takao Sakuma.

Cricket

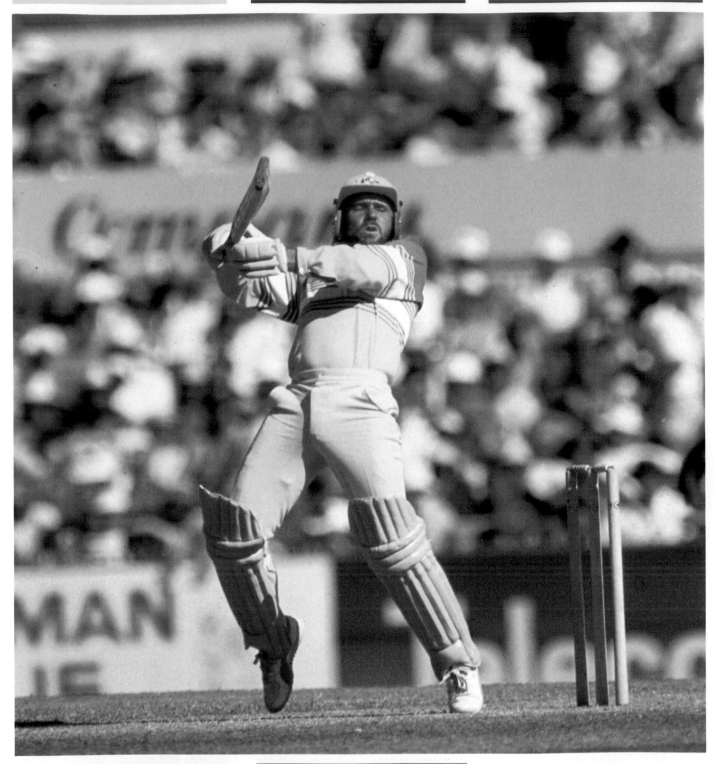

Cricket was played in Australia as early as 1803. The first international match was played between Canada and the USA in 1844. Fifteen years later those countries were host to the first English touring team. The first touring team to visit England was an Australian Aborigine XI in 1868.

FIRST-CLASS CRICKET (1815 to 1987)

BATTING RECORDS *Teams*

Highest innings

The highest recorded innings by a team was 1107 runs in 10 hr 30 min by Victoria *v.* New South Wales in an Australian Sheffield Shield match at Melbourne on 27–28 Dec 1926.

The highest innings in Test cricket and the highest made in England is 903 runs for 7 wickets

Most one-day Internationals ● Australia's captain Allan Robert Border (b. 27 July 1955) has played in a record 151 one-day international matches, 1978–87, scoring 3952 runs, the most by an Australian. (Photo: Adrian Murrell/All-Sport)

declared in 15 hr 17 min, by England *v.* Australia at Kennington Oval, London, on 20, 22 and 23 Aug 1938. The highest innings in a county championship match is 887 in 10 hr 50 min by Yorkshire *v.* Warwickshire at Edgbaston, Birmingham on 7–8 May 1896.

Lowest innings

The lowest recorded innings is 12 by Oxford University *v.* the Marylebone Cricket Club

(MCC) at Cowley Marsh, Oxford on 24 May 1877, and by Northamptonshire *v.* Gloucestershire at Gloucester on 11 June 1907. On the occasion of the Oxford match, however, the University batted a man short. The lowest score in a Test innings is 26 by New Zealand *v.* England at Auckland on 28 Mar 1955.

The lowest aggregate for two innings is 34 (16 and 18) by Border *v.* Natal in the South African Currie Cup at east London on 19 and 21 Dec 1959.

Greatest victory

The greatest recorded margin of victory is an innings and 851 runs, when Pakistan Railways (910 for 6 wickets declared) beat Dera Ismail Khan (32 and 27) at Lahore from 2–4 Dec 1964.

The largest margin in England is an innings and 579 runs by England over Australia at The Oval from 20–24 Aug 1938 when Australia scored 201 and 123 with two men short in both innings. The most one-sided county match was when Surrey (698) defeated Sussex (114 and 99) by an innings and 485 runs at The Oval from 9–11 Aug 1888.

Most runs in a day

The greatest number of runs scored in a day is 721 all out (ten wickets) by the Australians v. Essex at Southchurch Park, Southend-on-Sea on 15 May 1948. The Test record for runs in a day is 588 at Old Trafford, Manchester, on 27 July 1936 when England added 398 and India were 190 for 0 in their second innings by the close.

BATTING RECORDS *Individuals*

Highest innings

The highest individual innings is 499 in 10 hr 35 min by Hanif Mohammad (b. 21 Dec 1934) for Karachi v. Bahawalpur at Karachi, Pakistan, on 8, 9 and 11 Jan 1959. The highest in England is 424 in 7 hr 50 min by Archibald Campbell MacLaren (1871–1944) for Lancashire v. Somerset at Taunton on 15–16 July 1895. The record for a Test match is 365 not out in 10 hr 14 min by Sir Garfield St Aubrun Sobers (b. 28 July 1936) for the West Indies v. Pakistan at Sabina Park, Kingston, Jamaica, from 27 Feb–1 Mar 1958. The England Test record is 364 by Sir Leonard Hutton (b. 23 June 1916) v. Australia at The Oval on 20, 22 and 23 Aug 1938.

Longest innings

The longest innings is one of 16 hr 10 min for 337 runs by Hanif Mohammad (Pakistan) v. West Indies at Bridgetown, Barbados, from 20–23 Jan 1958. The record in England is 13 hr 17 min by Len Hutton in his record Test score of 364.

Most runs *Off an over*

The first batsman to score 36 runs off a six-ball over was Sir Garfield Sobers (Nottinghamshire) off Malcolm Andrew Nash (b. 9 May 1945) (Glamorgan) at Swansea on 31 Aug 1968. His feat was emulated by Ravishankar Jayadritha Shastri (b. 27 May 1962) for Bombay v. Baroda at Bombay, India on 10 Jan 1985 off the bowling of Tilak Raj.

Off a ball

The most runs scored off a single hit is ten by Albert Neilson Hornby (1847–1925) off James Street (1839–1906) for Lancashire v. Surrey at The Oval on 14 July 1873, and by Samuel Hill Wood (later Sir Samuel Hill Hill-Wood (1872–1949) off Cuthbert James Burnup (1875–1960) for Derbyshire v. MCC at Lord's, London, on 26 May 1900.

Most sixes *In an innings*

The most sixes hit in an innings is 15 by John Richard Reid (b. 3 June 1928), in an innings of 296, lasting 3 hr 40 min, for Wellington v. Northern Districts in a Plunket Shield match at Wellington, New Zealand, on 14–15 Jan 1963. The Test record is ten by Walter Hammond in an innings of 336 not out for England v. New Zealand at Auckland on 31 Mar and 1 Apr 1933.

Double hundreds

The only batsman to score double hundreds in both innings is Arthur Edward Fagg (1915–77), who made 244 and 202 not out for Kent v. Essex at Colchester from 13–15 July 1938. Sir Donald Bradman scored a career record 37 double hundreds from 1927–49.

Fastest scoring

The fastest 50 was completed off 13 balls in 8 min (1.22 to 1.30 p.m.) in 11 scoring strokes by Clive Clay Inman (b. 29 Jan 1936) in an innings of 57 not out for Leicestershire v. Nottinghamshire at Trent Bridge, Nottingham on 20 Aug 1965. Full tosses were bowled to expedite a declaration.

INDIVIDUAL CAREER RECORDS
All First-Class Cricket (FC) and Test Cricket (Test)

			Name	Team	Year
BATTING					
Most runs	FC	61,237	Sir John Berry 'Jack' Hobbs (1882–1963) (av 50.65)	Surrey/England	1905–34
	Test	10,122	Sunil Manohar Gavaskar (b. 10 July 1949) (av 51.12)	India (125 Tests)	1971–87
Most centuries	FC	197	Sir Jack Hobbs (in 1315 innings)	Surrey/England	1905–34
	Test	34	Sunil Gavaskar	India	1971–87
Highest average	FC	95.14	Sir Donald George Bradman (b. 27 Aug 1908) (28,067 runs in 338 innings)	NSW/South Australia/Australia	1927–49
	Test	99.94	Sir Don Bradman (6996 runs in 80 innings)	Australia (52 Tests)	1928–48
BOWLING					
Most wickets	FC	4187	Wilfred Rhodes (1877–1973) (av 16.71)	Yorkshire/England	1898–1930
	Test	366	Ian Terrence Botham (b. 24 Nov 1955) (av 27.21)	England (89 Tests)	1977–87
Lowest average (min 15 wkts)	Test	10.75	George Alfred Lohmann (1865–1901) (112 wkts)	England (18 Tests)	1886–96
WICKET-KEEPING					
Most dismissals	FC	1648	Robert William Taylor (b. 17 July 1941)	Derbyshire/England	1960–86
	Test	355	Rodney William Marsh (b. 11 Nov 1947)	Australia (96 Tests)	1970–84
Most catches	FC	1473	Robert Taylor	Derbyshire/England	1960–86
	Test	343	Rodney Marsh	Australia	1970–84
Most stumpings	FC	415	Leslie Ethelbert George Ames (b. 3 Dec 1905)	Kent/England	1926–51
	Test	52	William Albert Stanley Oldfield (1894–1976)	Australia (54 Tests)	1920–37
FIELDING					
Most catches	FC	1018	Frank Edward Woolley (1887–1978)	Kent/England	1906–38
	Test	122	Gregory Stephen Chappell (b. 7 Aug 1948)	Australia (87 Tests)	1970–84

INDIVIDUAL SEASON'S RECORDS
All First-Class Cricket in England

		Name	Team	Year
BATTING				
Most runs	3816	Denis Charles Scott Compton (b. 23 May 1918) (av 90.85)	Middlesex/England	1947
Most centuries	18	Denis Compton (in 50 innings with 8 not outs)	Middlesex/England	1947
Highest average	115.66	Sir Donald Bradman (2429 runs in 26 innings, with 5 not outs)	Australians	1938
BOWLING				
Most wickets	304	Alfred Percy 'Tich' Freeman (1888–1965) (1976.1 overs) (av 18.05)	Kent	1928
Lowest average (min 100 wkts)	8.54	Alfred Shaw (1842–1907) (186 wkts)	Nottinghamshire	1880
WICKET-KEEPING				
Most dismissals	127	Leslie Ames (79 caught, 48 stumped)	Kent	1929
Most catches	96	James Graham Binks (b. 5 Oct 1935)	Yorkshire	1960
Most stumpings	64	Leslie Ames	Kent	1932
FIELDING				
Most catches	78	Walter Reginald Hammond (1903–65)	Gloucestershire	1928

INDIVIDUAL RECORDS IN A TEST SERIES

		Name	Team	Year
BATTING				
Most runs	974	Sir Donald Bradman (av 139.14)	Australia v. England (5 T)	1930
Most centuries	5	Clyde Leopold Walcott (b. 17 Jan 1926)	West Indies v. Australia (5 T)	1954–55
Highest average	563.00	Walter Reginald Hammond (563 runs, 2 inns, 1 n.o.)	England v. New Zealand (2 T)	1932–33
BOWLING				
Most wickets	49	Sydney Francis Barnes (1873–1967) (av 10.93)	England v. South Africa (4 T)	1913–14
Lowest average (min 20 wkts)	5.80	George Alfred Lohmann (35 wkts)	England v. South Africa (3 T)	1895–96
WICKET-KEEPING				
Most dismissals	28	Rodney Marsh (all caught)	Australia v. England (5 T)	1982–83
Most stumpings	9	Percy William Sherwell (1880–1948)	South Africa v. Australia (5 T)	1910–11
FIELDING				
Most catches	15	Jack Morrison Gregory (1895–1973)	Australia v. England (5 T)	1920–21
ALL-ROUND				
400 runs/ 30 wickets	475/34	George Giffen (1859–1927)	Australia v. England (5 T)	1894–95

Cricket

The fastest hundred was completed in 35 min off between 40 and 46 balls by Percy George Herbert Fender (b. 22 Aug 1892), when scoring 113 not out for Surrey *v.* Northamptonshire at Northampton on 26 Aug 1920. Steven Joseph O'Shaughnessy (b. 9 Sept 1961) also scored a hundred in 35 minutes for Lancashire *v.* Leicestershire at Old Trafford, Manchester off 54 balls on 13 Sept 1983. In all he scored 105 and with Graeme Fowler (b. 20 Apr 1957) put on 201 runs for the first wicket in 45 mins. The match was 'dead' and irregular bowlers were used.

The hundred in fewest recorded deliveries was by David William Hookes (b. 3 May 1955) in 34 balls, in 43 min, for South Australia *v.* Victoria at Adelaide on 25 Oct 1982. In all he scored 107 from 40 balls in this, the second, innings, following 137 in the first innings. The most prolific scorer of hundreds in an hour or less was Gilbert Laird Jessop (1874–1955), with 11 between 1897 and 1913. The fastest Test hundred was one off 56 balls by Isaac Vivian Alexander Richards (b. 7 Mar 1952) for the West Indies *v.* England at St John's, Antigua on 15 Apr 1986. His final score was 110 in 81 balls. Edwin Boaler Alletson (1884–1963) scored 189 runs in 90 min for Nottinghamshire *v.* Sussex at Hove on 20 May 1911.

A double hundred in 113 min was scored by Ravi Shastri off 123 balls for Bombay *v.* Baroda at Bombay on 10 Jan 1985 (see most runs off an over). Clive Hubert Lloyd (b. 31 Aug 1944), for the West Indians *v.* Glamorgan at Swansea on 9 Aug 1976, and Gilbert Jessop (286), for Gloucestershire *v.* Sussex at Hove on 1 June 1903, both scored 200 in 120 min. Lloyd received 121 balls but the figure for Jessop is not known.

The fastest treble hundred was completed in 181 min by Denis Compton, who scored 300 for the MCC *v.* North-Eastern Transvaal at Benoni on 3–4 Dec 1948.

Slowest scoring

The longest time a batsman has ever taken to score his first run is 1 hr 37 min by Thomas Godfrey Evans (b. 18 Aug 1920), who scored 10 not out for England *v.* Australia at Adelaide on 5–6 Feb 1947. The longest innings without scoring is 87 minutes by Vincent Richard Hogg (b. 3 July 1952) for Zimbabwe–Rhodesia 'B' *v.* Natal 'B' at Pietermaritzburg in the South African Castle Bowl competition on 20 Jan 1980.

The slowest hundred on record is by Mudassar Nazar (b. 6 Apr 1956) of Pakistan *v.* England at Lahore on 14–15 Dec 1977. He required 9 hr 51 min for 114, reaching the 100 in 9 hr 17 min. The slowest double hundred is one of 10 hr 52 min (426 balls) by Anshuman Dattajirao Gaekwad (b. 23 Sept 1952) during an innings of 201 for India *v.* Pakistan at Jullundur on 25–29 Sept 1983.

Highest partnership

The record partnership for any wicket is the fourth wicket stand of 577 by Gul Mahomed (b. 15 Oct 1921) (319) and Vijay Samuel Hazare (b. 11 Mar 1915) (288) for Baroda *v.* Holkar at Baroda, India, from 8–10 Mar 1947. The highest in England is the first-wicket partnership of 555 by Percy Holmes (1886–1971) (224 not out) and Herbert Sutcliffe (1894–1978) (313) for Yorkshire *v.* Essex at Leyton on 15–16 June 1932.

The highest Test partnership is 451 for the second wicket by William Harold Ponsford (b. 19 Oct 1900) (266) and Sir Donald Bradman (244) for Australia *v.* England at the Oval on 18 Aug 1934, and for the third wicket by Mudassar Nazar (231) and Javed Miandad Khan (b. 12 Jun 1957) (280 not out) for Pakistan *v.* India at Hyderabad, Pakistan on 14–15 Jan 1983.

BOWLING

Most wickets *In an innings*

Only one bowler has taken all ten wickets in an innings on three occasions—Alfred 'Tich' Freeman of Kent, 1929–31. The fewest runs scored off a bowler taking all ten wickets is ten, off Hedley Verity (1905–43) for Yorkshire *v.* Nottinghamshire at Leeds on 12 July 1932. The only bowler to bowl out all ten was John Wisden (1826–84) for North *v.* South at Lord's in 1850.

In a match

James Charles Laker (1922–86) took 19 wickets for 90 runs (9–37 and 10–53) for England *v.* Australia at Old Trafford from 27–31 July 1956. No other bowler has taken more than 17 wickets in a first-class match.

Most consecutive wickets

No bowler in first-class cricket has yet achieved five wickets with five consecutive balls. The nearest approach was that of Charles Warrington Leonard Parker (1882–1959) (Gloucestershire) in his own benefit match against Yorkshire at Bristol on 10 Aug 1922, when he struck the stumps with five successive balls but the second was called as a no-ball. The only man to have taken four wickets with consecutive balls more than once is Robert James Crisp (b. 28 May 1911) for Western Province *v.* Griqualand West at Johannesburg on 24 Dec 1931 and against Natal at Durban, South Africa on 3 Mar 1934.

Patrick Ian Pocock (b. 24 Sep 1946) took five wickets in six balls, six in nine balls and seven in eleven balls for Surrey *v.* Sussex at Eastbourne on 15 Aug 1972. In his own benefit match at Lord's on 22 May 1907, Albert Edwin Trott (1873–1914) of Middlesex took four Somerset wickets with four consecutive balls and then later in the same innings achieved a 'hat trick'.

Most consecutive maidens

Hugh Joseph Tayfield (b. 30 Jan 1929) bowled 16 consecutive eight-ball maiden overs (137 balls without conceding a run) for South Africa *v.* England at Durban on 25–26 Jan 1957. The greatest number of consecutive six-ball maiden overs bowled is 21 (131 balls) by Rameshchandra Gangaram 'Bapu' Nadkarni (b. 4 Apr 1932) for India *v.* England at Madras on 12 Jan 1964.

Most balls

The most balls bowled in a match is 917 by Cottari Subbanna Nayudu (b. 18 Apr 1914), 6–153 and 5–275, for Holkar *v.* Bombay at Bombay from 4–9 Mar 1945. The most balls bowled in a Test match is 774 by Sonny Ramadhin (b. 1 May 1929) for the West Indies *v.* England, 7–49 and 2–179, at Edgbaston from 29 May–4 June 1957. In the second innings he bowled a world record 588 balls (98 overs).

Most expensive bowling

The greatest number of runs hit off one bowler in an innings is 362 off Arthur Alfred Mailey (1886–1967) of New South Wales by Victoria at Melbourne from 24–28 Dec 1926. The most runs conceded by a bowler in a match is 428 by Cottari Subbanna Nayudu in the Holkar *v.* Bombay match above. The most runs conceded in a Test innings is 298 by Leslie O'Brien 'Chuck' Fleetwood-Smith (1910–71) for Australia *v.* England at The Oval from 20–23 Aug 1938.

Fastest

The highest electronically measured speed for a ball bowled by any bowler is 99.7 mph *160,45 km/h* by Jeffrey Robert Thomson (b. 16 Aug 1950) (Australia) against the West Indies in December 1975.

ALL-ROUNDERS

The double

The 'double' of 1000 runs and 100 wickets in the same season was performed a record number of 16 times by Wilfred Rhodes between 1903 and 1926. The greatest number of consecutive seasons in which a player has performed the double is 11 (1903–13) by George Herbert Hirst (1871–1954), of Yorkshire and England. Hirst is also the only player to score 2000 runs (2385) and take 200 wickets (208) in the same season (1906).

Test cricket

The best all-round Test career record is that of Ian Terrence Botham (b. 24 Nov 1955) with 4825 runs (av. 34.96), 366 wickets (av. 27.21) and 106 catches in 89 matches to 1 June 1987. Botham is the only player to score a hundred and take eight wickets in an innings in the same Test, with 108 and eight for 34 for England *v.* Pakistan at Lord's, 15–19 June 1978. He scored a hundred (114) and took more than ten wickets (6–58 and 7–48) in a Test for England *v.* India in the Golden Jubilee Test at Bombay, 15–19 Feb 1980. This feat was emulated by Imran Khan Niazi (b. 25 Nov 1952) with 117, 6–98 and 5–82 for Pakistan *v.* India at Faisalabad, 3–8 Jan 1983. Botham completed the double of 1000 runs and 100 wickets in the fewest Test matches (21) on 30 Aug 1979. Kapil Dev Nikhanj (India) (b. 6 Jan 1959) achieved this double in the shortest time, 1 year 107 days, and at the youngest age, 21 yr 27 days, in his 25th Test. The double of 2000 runs and 200 wickets was achieved in fewest matches (42) by Botham and at the youngest age by Kapil Dev at 24 yr 68 days. Botham completed 3000 runs and 300 wickets in 71 Tests at 28 yr 259 days.

Test bowling records ● Richard John Hadlee (New Zealand) (b. 3 July 1951) has taken 5 wickets in a Test innings on a record 28 occasions, 1973–87. With 351 wickets in 69 Tests he is challenging Ian Botham and Dennis Lillee for the overall wickets record. (Photo: Adrian Murrell/All Sport)

WICKET-KEEPING

Most dismissals *Innings*

The most dismissals by a wicket-keeper in an innings is eight (all caught) by Arthur Theodore Wallace 'Wally' Grout (1927–68) for Queensland *v.* Western Australia at Brisbane on 15 Feb 1960 and by David Edward East (b. 27 July 1959) for Essex *v.* Somerset at Taunton on 27 July 1985. The most stumpings in an innings is six by Henry 'Hugo' Yarnold (1917–74) for Worcestershire *v.* Scotland at Broughty Ferry, Tayside, on 2 July 1951. The Test record is seven (all caught) by Wasim Bari (b. 23 Mar 1948) for Pakistan *v.* New Zealand at Auckland on 23 Feb 1979, and by Bob Taylor for England *v.* India at Bombay on 15 Feb 1980.

Match

The most dismissals by a wicket-keeper in a match is 12 by: Edward Pooley (1838–1907), eight caught, four stumped, for Surrey *v.* Sussex at The Oval on 6–7 July 1868; nine caught, three stumped by both Donald Tallon (1916–84) for Queensland *v.* New South Wales at Sydney, Australia on 2–4 Jan 1939, and by Hedley Brian Taber (b. 29 Apr 1940) for New South Wales *v.* South Australia at Adelaide, 13–17 Dec 1968. The record for catches is 11 by: Arnold Long (b. 18 Dec 1940), for Surrey *v.* Sussex at Hove on 18 and 21 July 1964; by Rodney Marsh for Western Australia *v.* Victoria at Perth, 15–17 Nov 1975; and by David Leslie Bairstow (b. 1 Sept 1951) for Yorkshire *v.* Derbyshire at Scarborough, 8–10 Sept 1982. The most stumpings in a match is nine by Frederick Henry Huish (1869–1957) for Kent *v.* Surrey at The Oval, 21–23 Aug 1911. The Test record for dismissals is ten, all caught, by Robert Taylor for England *v.* India at Bombay, 15–19 Feb 1980.

FIELDING

Most catches *Innings and Match*

The greatest number of catches in an innings is seven, by: Michael James Stewart (b. 16 Sept 1932) for Surrey *v.* Northamptonshire at Northampton on 7 June 1957; and by Anthony Stephen Brown (b. 24 June 1936) for Gloucestershire *v.* Nottinghamshire at Trent Bridge on 26 July 1966.

The most catches in a Test match is seven, by: Greg Chappell for Australia *v.* England at Perth, 13–17 Dec 1974; and by Yajurvindra Singh (b. 1 Aug 1952) for India *v.* England at Bangalore on 28 Jan–2 Feb 1977.

Walter Hammond held a match record total of ten catches (four in the first innings, six in the second) for Gloucestershire *v.* Surrey at Cheltenham on 16–17 Aug 1928.

Longest throw

A cricket ball (5½ oz *155 g*) was reputedly thrown 140 yd 2 ft *128,6 m* by Robert Percival, a left-hander, on Durham Sands racecourse on Easter Monday, 18 Apr 1881.

OTHER TEST RECORDS

Test appearances

Sunil Gavaskar has played in a record 125 Tests, 1971–87, including a record 106 consecutive Tests, 1975–87. The English record for consecutive Tests is 65 by: Alan Philip Eric Knott (b. 9 Apr 1946), 1971–77; and by Ian Botham, 1978–84.

Longest match

The lengthiest recorded cricket match was the 'timeless' Test between England and South Africa at Durban, 3–14 Mar 1939. It was abandoned after ten days (eighth day rained off) because the boat taking the England team home was due to leave. The total playing time was 43 hr 16 min and a record Test match aggregate of 1981 runs was scored.

Largest crowds

The greatest attendance at a cricket match is about 394,000 for the Test between India and England at Eden Gardens, Calcutta, 1–6 Jan 1982. The record for a Test series is 933,513 for Australia *v.* England (5 matches) in 1936–37. The greatest recorded attendance at a cricket match on one day was 90,800 on the second day of the Test between Australia and the West Indies at Melbourne on 11 Feb 1961. The English record is 159,000 for the Test between England and Australia at Headingley, Leeds, 22–27 July 1948, and the record for one day probably a capacity of 46,000 for Lancashire *v.* Yorkshire at Old Trafford on 2 Aug 1926. The English record for a Test series is 549,650 for the series against Australia in 1953. The highest attendance for a limited-overs game is 84,153 at the Benson & Hedges World Series Cup match between Australia and England at Melbourne on 20 Jan 1985.

Most successful Test captain

Clive Hubert Lloyd (b. 31 Aug 1944) led the West Indies in a record 74 Test matches from 22 November 1974 to 2 January 1985. Of these, 36 were won, 12 lost and 26 drawn. His team set records for most successive Test wins, 11 in 1984, and most Tests without defeat, 27, between losses to Australia in December 1981 and January 1985 (through injury Lloyd missed one of those matches, when the West Indies were captained by Vivian Richards).

ENGLISH COUNTY CHAMPIONSHIP

The greatest number of victories since 1890, when the championship was officially constituted, has been by Yorkshire with 29 outright wins (the last in 1968), and one shared (1949). The record number of consecutive title wins is seven by Surrey from 1952 to 1958. The greatest number of appearances in county championship matches is 763 by Wilfred Rhodes for Yorkshire between 1898 and 1930, and the greatest number of consecutive appearances is 423 by Kenneth George Suttle (b. 25 Aug 1928) of Sussex between 1954 and 1969. James Graham 'Jimmy' Binks (b. 5 Oct 1935) played in every county championship match for Yorkshire between his debut in 1955 and his retirement in 1969—412 matches. The seven sons of the Rev Henry Foster, of Malvern, uniquely all played county cricket for Worcestershire between 1899 and 1934.

OLDEST AND YOUNGEST

The oldest man to play in a Test match was Wilfred Rhodes, aged 52 yr 165 days, for England *v.* West Indies at Kingston, Jamaica on 12 April 1930. Rhodes made his Test debut in the last Test of William Gilbert Grace (1848–1915), who at 50 yr 320 days at Nottingham on 3 June 1899 was the oldest ever Test captain. The youngest Test captain was the Nawab of Pataudi (later Mansur Ali Khan) at 21 yr 77 days on 23 Mar 1962 of India *v.* West Indies at Bridgetown, Barbados. The youngest Test player was Mushtaq Mohammad (b. 22 Nov 1943), aged 15 yr 124 days, for Pakistan *v.* West Indies at Lahore on 26 Mar 1959. England's youngest player was Dennis Brian Close (b. 24 Feb 1931), aged 18 yr 149 days *v.* New Zealand at Old Trafford on 23 July 1949.

The oldest player in first-class cricket was Col Cottari Kanakaiya Nayudu (1895–1967) (India), aged 68 yr 4 days, for the Maharashtra Governor's XI *v.* Chief Minister's XI at Nagpur, India on 4 Nov 1963. The youngest is reputed to be Qasim Feroze (Pakistan) (b. 21 Jan 1958) for Bahawalpur *v.* Karachi Whites on 19 Jan 1971, aged 12 yr 363 days. The oldest Englishman was George Robert Canning, the 4th Lord Harris (1851–1932)

for Kent *v.* All India at Catford on 4 July 1911, aged 60 yr 151 days. The youngest English first-class player was Charles Robertson Young for Hampshire *v.* Kent at Gravesend on 13 June 1867, aged 15 yr 131 days.

WOMEN'S CRICKET

Earliest

The first recorded women's match took place at Gosden Common, Surrey, England on 26 June 1745. *Circa* 1807 Christina Willes is said to have introduced the roundarm bowling style. The first Test match was Australia *v.* England at Brisbane, 28–31 Dec 1934. The International Women's Cricket Council was formed in 1958.

Batting *Individual*

The highest individual innings recorded is 224 not out by Mabel Bryant for Visitors *v.* Residents at Eastbourne, East Sussex, in August 1901. The highest innings in a Test match is 190 by Sandhya Aggarwal, in 563 minutes, for India *v.* England at Worcester on 14 July 1986 in a four-day Test. The highest in a three-day Test is 189 (in 222 minutes) by Elizabeth Alexandra 'Betty' Snowball for England *v.* New Zealand at Christchurch, NZ on 16 Feb 1935. Rachel Flint (*née* Heyhoe) (b. 11 June 1939) scored the most runs in Test cricket with 1814 (av. 49.02) in 25 matches from December 1960 to July 1979.

Team

The highest innings score by any team is 567 by Tarana *v.* Rockley, at Rockley, NSW, Australia in 1896. The highest Test innings is 503 for five

Most wickets in the Sunday League ● To the start of the 1987 season Derek Leslie Underwood (b. 8 June 1945) has a record 344 wickets (av. 16.79) in his career in the John Player League. He also has taken the most wickets (2420, including 297 in Tests) in first-class cricket of any current player. (Photo: Adrian Murrell/All-Sport)

ONE-DAY INTERNATIONALS

The first 'limited overs' international was played at Melbourne Cricket Ground on 5 Jan 1971 between Australia and England. The Prudential Trophy series of one-day internationals began in England in 1972, matches being of 55 overs per side. The Benson and Hedges World Cup Series has been held annually in Australia since 1979–80.

World Cup

The World Cup was first held in England in 1975. It was held again in 1979 and 1983, and in 1987 will be staged in India and Pakistan. The West Indies won in 1975 and 1979, India in 1983. Matches are played at 60 overs per side.

One-day international records

Highest score: 338–5 (60 overs) Pakistan v. Sri Lanka, Swansea 9 June 1983
Lowest completed innings: 45 Canada v. England, Old Trafford 14 June 1979
Victory margin: 232 Australia v. Sri Lanka (323–2 to 91), Adelaide 28 Jan 1985

Individual match records

Highest score: 189* Isaac Vivian Alexander Richards (b. 7 Mar 1952), West Indies v. England, Old Trafford 31 May 1984
Best bowling: 7–51 Winston Walter Davis (b. 18 Sept 1958), West Indies v. Australia, Headingley 12 June 1983
Best partnership: 224* Dean Mervyn Jones (b. 24 Mar 1961) and Allan Robert Border (b. 27 July 1955), Australia v. Sri Lanka, Adelaide 28 Jan 1985.
(* not out)

Career records

Most matches: 151 Allan Border (Australia) 1979–87
Most runs: 5095 Vivian Richards (West Indies) 128 matches 1975–87
Most wickets: 146 Joel Garner (West Indies) (b. 16 Dec 1952) 98 matches 1977–87

Most dismissals in one-day internationals
● Peter Jeffrey Leroy Dujon (West Indies) (b. 28 May 1956) has captured a record 127 dismissals (114 catches, 13 stumpings) in 97 one-day internationals. (Photo: Adrian Murrell/All-Sport)

wickets declared by England v. New Zealand at Christchurch, NZ on 16 and 18 Feb 1935. The most in a Test in England is 379 by Australia v. England at The Oval, London on 26–27 July 1976. The highest innings total in England is 410 for two wickets declared by the South v. East at Oakham, Leicestershire on 29 May 1982.

The lowest innings in a Test is 35 by England v. Australia at St Kilda, Melbourne, Australia on 22 Feb 1958. The lowest in a Test in England is 63 by New Zealand at Worcester on 5 July 1954.

Bowling

Mary Beatrice Duggan (England) (1925–73) took a record 77 wickets (av. 13.49) in 17 Tests from 1949 to 1963. She recorded the best Test analysis with seven wickets for six runs for England v. Australia at St Kilda, Melbourne on 22 Feb 1958.

On 26 June 1931 Rubina Winifred Humphries (b. 19 Aug 1915), for Dalton Ladies v. Woodfield SC, took all ten wickets for no runs. (She also scored all her team's runs.) This bowling feat was equalled by Rosemary White (b. 22 Jan 1938) for Wallington LCC v. Beaconsfield LCC in July 1962.

World Cup

Three women's World Cups have been staged. Australia won in 1978 and 1982 and England in 1973. The highest individual score in this series is 138 not out by Janette Ann Brittin (b. 4 July 1959) for England v. International XI at Hamilton, New Zealand on 14 Jan 1982.

MINOR CRICKET RECORDS

(where excelling those in First-class Cricket)

Highest individual innings

In a Junior House match between Clarke's House (now Poole's) and North Town, at Clifton College, Bristol, 22–23, 26–28 June 1899, Arthur Edward Jeune Collins (1885–1914) scored an unprecedented 628 not out in 6 hr 50 min, over five afternoons' batting, carrying his bat through the innings of 836. The scorer, E. W. Pegler, gave the score as '628—plus or minus 20, shall we say'.

Fastest individual scoring

Stanley Keppel 'Shunter' Coen (South Africa) (1902–67) scored 50 runs (11 fours and one six) in 7 min for Gezira v. the RAF in 1942. The fastest hundred by a prominent player in a minor match was by Vivian Frank Shergold Crawford (1879–

ENGLISH ONE-DAY CRICKET RECORDS

GC/NWT—Gillette Cup (inst. 1963)/Nat West Bank Trophy (from 1981)—60 overs matches
SL—Sunday League—John Player (1969–86), Refuge Assurance (1987)—40 overs matches
B & H—Benson & Hedges Cup (inst. 1972)—55 overs matches

MOST WINS
GC/NWT—4 Lancashire 1970–2, 1975; Sussex 1963–4, 1978, 1986
SL —3 Kent 1972–3, 1976; Essex 1981, 1984–5
B & H —3 Kent 1973, 1976, 1978; Leicestershire 1972, 1975, 1985; Hampshire 1975, 1978, 1986

HIGHEST INDIVIDUAL INNINGS
GC/NWT—206 Alvin Isaac Kallicharan (b. 21 Mar 1949) Warwickshire v. Oxfordshire, Edgbaston, 1984
SL —176 Graham Alan Gooch (b. 23 July 1953) Essex v. Glamorgan, Southend, 1983
B & H —198* Graham Gooch, Essex v. Sussex, Hove, 1982

BEST INDIVIDUAL BOWLING
GC/NWT—8–31 Derek Leslie Underwood (b. 8 June 1945) Kent v. Scotland, Edinburgh, 1987
SL —8–26 Keith David Boyce (b. 11 Oct 1943) Essex v. Lancashire, Old Trafford, 1971;
Alan Ward (b. 10 Aug 1947) took 4 wickets in 4 balls, Derbyshire v. Sussex, Derby, 1970
B & H —7–12 Wayne Wendell Daniel (b. 16 Jan 1956) Middlesex v. Minor Counties (East), Ipswich, 1978

MOST DISMISSALS IN INNINGS
GC/NWT—6 Robert William Taylor (b. 17 July 1941) Derbyshire v. Essex, Derby, 1981
6 Terry Davies (b. 25 Oct 1960), Glamorgan v. Staffordshire, Stone, 1986
SL —7 Bob Taylor, Derbyshire v. Lancashire, Old Trafford, 1975
B & H —8 Derek John Somerset Taylor (b. 12 Nov 1942) Somerset v. Combined Universities, Taunton, 1982

HIGHEST INNINGS TOTAL
GC/NWT—404–3 Worcestershire v. Devon, Worcester, 1987
SL —310–5 Essex v. Glamorgan, Southend, 1983
B & H —350–3 Essex v. Oxford & Cambridge Universities, Chelmsford, 1979

LOWEST COMPLETED INNINGS TOTAL
GC/NWT—39 Ireland v. Sussex, Hove, 1985
SL —23 Middlesex v. Yorkshire, Headingley, 1974
B & H —56 Leicestershire v. Minor Counties, Wellington, 1982

RUNS IN CAREER
GC/NWT—1920 Clive Hubert Lloyd (b. 31 Aug 1944) Lancashire 1969–86
SL —6861 Dennis Leslie Amiss (b. 7 Apr 1943) Warwickshire 1969–86
B & H —2938 Graham Gooch, Essex 1973–86

WICKETS IN CAREER
GC/NWT—81 Geoffrey Graham Arnold (b. 3 Sept 1944) Surrey, Sussex 1963–80
SL —344 John Kenneth Lever (b. 24 Feb 1949) Essex 1969–86
344 Derek Leslie Underwood (b. 8 June 1945) Kent 1969–87
B & H —132 John Lever, Essex 1972–86

DISMISSALS IN CAREER
GC/NWT—66 Bob Taylor, Derbyshire 1963–84
SL —236 Bob Taylor, Derbyshire 1969–84
B & H —100 David Leslie Bairstow (b. 1 Sept 1951), Yorkshire 1972–86

* Not out

1922) in 19 min at Cane Hill, Surrey on 16 Sept 1899. David Michael Roberts Whatmore (b. 6 Apr 1949) scored 210 (including 25 sixes and 12 fours) off 61 balls for Alderney v. Sun Alliance at Alderney on 19 June 1983. His first 100 came off 33 balls and his second off 25 balls.

Successive sixes

Cedric Ivan James Smith (1906–79) hit nine successive sixes for a Middlesex XI v. Harrow and District at Rayner's Lane, Harrow in 1935. This feat was repeated by Arthur Dudley Nourse (1910–81) in a South African XI v. Military Police match at Cairo, Egypt in 1942–3. Nourse's feat included six sixes in one over.

Fastest scoring rates

In the match Royal Naval College, Dartmouth v. Seale Hayne Agricultural College in 1923, Kenneth Anderson Sellar (b. 11 Aug 1906) and Leslie Kenneth Allen Block (1906–80) were set to score 174 runs in 105 min but achieved this total in 33 min, so averaging 5.27 runs per min.

Most runs off a ball

A scoring stroke of 11 (all run, with no overthrows) was achieved by Lt (later Lt-Col) Philip Mitford (1879–1946), QO Cameron Highlanders, in a Malta Governor's Cup match on 28 May 1903.

Most runs off an over

H. Morely scored 62, nine sixes and two fours, off an eight-ball over from R. Grubb which had four no-balls, in a Queensland country match in 1968–9.

Bowling

Nine wickets with nine consecutive balls were taken by: Stephen Fleming, for Marlborough College 'A' XI v. Bohally Intermediate at Blenheim, New Zealand in December 1967; and by Paul Hugo for Smithfield School v. Aliwal North, South Africa in February 1931. In the Inter-Divisional Ships Shield at Purfleet, Essex, on 17 May 1924, Joseph William Brockley (b. 9 Apr 1907) took all ten wickets, clean bowled, for two runs in 11 balls—including a triple hat trick. Jennings Tune took all ten wickets, all bowled, for 0 runs in five overs for Cliffe v. Eastrington in the Howden and District League at Cliffe, Yorkshire on 6 May 1922.

In 1881 Frederick Robert Spofforth (1835–1926) at Bendigo, Victoria, Australia clean bowled all ten wickets in *both* innings. J. Bryant for Erskine v. Deaf Mutes in Melbourne on 15 and 22 Oct 1887, and Albert Rimmer for Linwood School v. Cathedral GS at Canterbury, New Zealand in December 1925, repeated the feat. In the 1910 season, H. Hopkinson, of Mildmay CC London, took 99 wickets for 147 runs.

Maurice Hanes bowled 107 consecutive balls (17 overs and five balls) for Bedworth II v. A P Leamington II at Bedworth, Warwickshire on 16 June 1979, without conceding a run.

Wicket-keeping

Welihinda Badalge Bennett (b. 25 Jan 1933) caught four and stumped six batsmen in one innings, on 1 March 1953, for Mahinda College v. Galle CC, at the Galle Esplanade, Sri Lanka.

Fielding

In a Wellington, New Zealand secondary schools 11-a-side match on 16 Mar 1974, Stephen Lane, 13, held 14 catches in the field (seven in each innings) for St Patrick's College, Silverstream v. St Bernard's College, Lower Hutt.

Croquet

Croquet was probably derived from the French game *Jeu de Mail* first mentioned in the 12th century. A game resembling croquet, possibly of foreign origin, was played in Ireland in the

Most wins ● G. Nigel Aspinall (b. 1946) has won croquet's President's Cup (an invitation event for the best eight players) a record 11 times, 1969–1970, 1973–6, 1978, 1980, 1982, 1984–5. (Sporting Pictures)

1830s and was introduced to Hampshire 20 years later. The first club was formed in the Steyne Gardens, Worthing, West Sussex in 1865.

Most championships

The greatest number of victories in the Open Croquet Championships (instituted at Evesham, Worcestershire, 1867) is ten by John William Solomon (b. 1931) (1953, 1956, 1959, 1961, 1963–8). He also won ten Men's Championships (1951, 1953, 1958–60, 1962, 1964–5, 1971–2), ten open doubles (with Edmond Patrick Charles Cotter) (1954–5, 1958–9, 1961–5 and 1969) and one mixed doubles (with Freda Oddie) in 1954, making a total of 31 titles. Solomon has also won the President's Cup (inst. 1934) on nine occasions (1955, 1957–9, 1962–4, 1968 and 1971), and was Champion of Champions on all four occasions that this competition has been run (1967–70).

Dorothy Dyne Steel (1884–1965), fifteen times winner of the Women's Championship (1919–39), won the Open Croquet Championship four times (1925, 1933, 1935–36). She had also five doubles and seven mixed doubles for a total of 31 titles.

International trophy

The MacRobertson International Shield (instituted 1925) has been won a record seven times by Great Britain (1925, 1937, 1956, 1963, 1969, 1974 and 1982). A record six appearances have been made by John G. Prince (New Zealand), in 1963, 1969, 1974, 1979, 1982 and 1986; on his debut he was the youngest ever international at 17 yr 190 days.

Cross-country Running

WORLD CHAMPIONSHIPS

The earliest recorded international cross-country race took place over 14,5 km *9 miles 18 yd* from Ville d'Avray, outside Paris, on 20 Mar 1898 between England and France (England won by 21 points to 69). The inaugural International Cross-Country Championships took place at the Hamilton Park Racecourse, Scotland, on 28 Mar 1903. The greatest margin of victory is 56 sec or 390 yd *356 m* by John 'Jack' Thomas Holden (England) (b. 13 Mar 1907) at Ayr Racecourse, Scotland, on 24 Mar 1934. Since 1973 the events have been official world championships under the auspices of the International Amateur Athletic Federation.

Most wins

The greatest number of team victories has been by England with 45 for men, 11 for junior men and 7 for women. The USA have a record eight women's team victories.

The greatest number of men's individual victories is four by: Jack Holden (England) in 1933–5 and 1939; Alain Mimoun-o-Kacha (France) (b. 1 Jan 1921) in 1949, 1952, 1954 and 1956; and Gaston Roelants (Belgium) (b. 5 Feb 1937) in 1962, 1967, 1969 and 1972. The women's race has been won five times by: Doris Brown-Heritage (USA) (b. 17 Sept 1942) from 1967–71; and Grete Waitz (*née* Andersen) (Norway) (b. 1 Oct 1953), in 1978–81 and 1983.

Most appearances

Marcel van de Wattyne (Belgium) (b. 7 July 1924) ran in a record 20 races, 1946–65. The women's record is 16 by Jean Lochhead (Wales) (b. 24 Dec 1946), 1967–79, 1981, 1983–4.

English Championship

The English Cross-Country Championship was inaugurated at Roehampton, Wandsworth, London, in 1877. The most individual titles won is four by Percy H. Stenning (1854–92) (Thames Hare and Hounds) from 1877–80 and Alfred E. Shrubb (1878–1964) (South London Harriers) from 1901–4. The most successful club in the team race has been Birchfield Harriers from Birmingham with 27 wins and one tie between 1880 and 1953. The largest field was the 2006 finishers in the senior race in 1987 at Luton, Bedfordshire.

Largest field

The largest recorded field in any cross-country race was 11,763 starters (10,810 finished) in the 30 km *18.6 miles* Lidingöloppet, near Stockholm, Sweden, on 3 Oct 1982.

Curling

Although a 15th-century bronze figure in the Florence Museum appears to be holding a curling stone, the earliest illustration of the sport was in one of the Flemish painter Pieter Bruegel's winter scenes *c.* 1560. The game was probably introduced into Scotland by Flemings in the 15th century. The earliest documented club in Muthill, Tayside, Scotland, formed in 1739. Organised administration began in 1838 with the formation in Edinburgh of the Grand (later Royal) Caledonian Curling Club, the international legislative body until the foundation of the International Curling Federation in 1966. The first indoor ice rink to introduce curling was in Montreal, Canada in 1807, and the first in Britain was at Southport, Merseyside in 1878.

The USA won the first Gordon International Medal series of matches, between Canada and the USA, at Montreal in 1884. Curling has been a demonstration sport at the Olympic Games of 1924, 1932 and 1964 and will be again in 1988.

Most titles

Canada has won the Men's World Championships (inst. 1959) 18 times, 1959–64, 1966, 1968–72, 1980, 1982–3, 1985–7. The most Strathcona Cup (inst. 1903) wins is seven by Canada (1903, 1909, 1912, 1923, 1938, 1957, 1965) against Scotland. The most Women's World Championships (inst. 1979) wins is five by Canada (1980, 1984–7).

'Perfect' games

Stu Beagle, of Calgary, Alberta, Canada, played a perfect game (48 points) against Nova Scotia in the Canadian Championships (Brier) at Fort William (now Thunder Bay), Ontario, on 8 Mar 1960. Bernice Fekete, of Edmonton, Alberta, Canada, skipped her rink to two consecutive eight-enders on the same ice at the Derrick Club, Edmonton, on 10 Jan and 6 Feb 1973. Two eight-enders in one bonspiel were scored at the Parry Sound Curling Club, Ontario, Canada from 6–8 Jan 1983.

Fastest game

Eight curlers from the Burlington Golf & Country Club curled an eight-end game in 47 min 24 sec at Burlington, Ontario, Canada on 4 Apr 1986. The time is taken from when the first rock crosses the near hogline until the game's last rock comes to a complete stop.

Largest bonspiel

The largest bonspiel in the world is the Manitoba Curling Association Bonspiel held annually in Winnipeg, Canada. In 1985, there were 848 teams of four men, a total of 3392 curlers, using 171 sheets of curling ice.

Largest rink

The world's largest curling rink is the Big Four Curling Rink, Calgary, Alberta, Canada, opened in 1959. Ninety-six teams and 384 players are accommodated on two floors each with 24 sheets of ice.

Cycling

The earliest recorded bicycle race was a velocipede race over 2 km *1.24 miles* at the Parc de St Cloud, Paris, on 31 May 1868, won by Dr James Moore (GB) (1847–1935) (later Chevalier de la Légion d'Honneur).

Highest speed

The highest speed ever achieved on a bicycle is 152.284 mph *245,077 km/h* by John Howard (USA) behind a wind-shield at Bonneville Salt Flats, Utah, USA on 20 July 1985. It should be noted that considerable help is provided by the slipstreaming effect of the lead vehicle. The British speed record is 98.21 mph *158,05 km/h* over 200 metres by David Le Grys on a closed section of the M42 at Alvechurch, Warwickshire on 28 Aug 1985. Fred Markham, 29, recorded an official unpaced 6.832 sec for 200 m (65.484 mph *105,386 km/h*) on a streamlined bicycle on Highway 120, California, USA, on 11 May 1986.

The greatest distance ever covered in one hour is 122,771 km *76 miles 504 yd* by Leon Vanderstuyft (Belgium) (1890–1964) on the Montlhéry Motor Circuit, France, on 30 Sept 1928, achieved from a standing start paced by a motorcycle. The 24-hr record behind pace is 860 miles 367 yd *1384,367 km* by Hubert Ferdinand Opperman (later the Hon. Sir) (b. 29 May 1904) in Melbourne, Australia on 23 May 1932.

Most titles *Olympic*

The most gold medals won is three by: Paul Masson (France) (1874–1945) in 1896; Francisco Verri (Italy) (1885–1945) in 1906; and Robert Charpentier (France) (1916–66) in 1936. Daniel Morelon (France) won two in 1968, and a third in 1972; he also won a silver in 1976 and a bronze medal in 1964. In the 'unofficial' 1904 cycling programme, Marcus Hurley (USA) (1884–1950) won four events.

World

World championships are contested annually. They were first staged for amateurs in 1893 and for professionals in 1895. The most wins at a particular event is ten by Koichi Nakano (Japan) (b. 14 Nov 1955), professional sprint 1977–86. The most wins at a men's amateur event is seven by: Daniel Morelon (France) (b. 28 July 1944), sprint 1966–7, 1969–71, 1973, 1975; and Leon Meredith (UK) (1882–1930), 100-km motor-paced 1904–5, 1907–9, 1911, 1913. The most women's titles is seven by: Beryl Burton (UK) (b. 12 May 1937), pursuit 1959–60, 1962–3, 1966 and road 1960, 1967; and Yvonne Reynders (Belgium), pursuit 1961, 1964–5 and road 1959, 1961, 1963, 1966.

British

Beryl Burton (b. 12 May 1937), 25 times British all-round time trial champion (1959–83), has won 72 individual road TT titles, 14 track pursuit titles and 12 road race titles to 1986. Ian Hallam (b. 24 Nov 1948) won a record 25 men's titles, 1969–82.

Tour de France

The greatest number of wins in the Tour de France (inaugurated 1903) is five by: Jacques Anquetil (France) (b. 8 Jan 1934), 1957, 1961–4; Eddy Merckx (Belgium) (b. 17 June 1945), 1969–72 and 1974; and Bernard Hinault (France) (b. 14 Nov 1954) 1978–9, 1981–2 and 1985. The closest race ever was in 1968 when after 4665 km *2898.7 miles* over 25 days (27 June–21 July) Jan Janssen (Netherlands) (b. 19 May 1940) beat Herman van Springel (Belgium) in Paris by 38 sec. The fastest average speed was 37,84 km/h *23.51 mph* by Bernard Hinault in 1981. The longest race was 5745 km *3569 miles* in 1926, and the most participants were 170 starters in 1982 and 1984. The longest ever stage was the 486 km from Les Sables d'Olonne to Bayonne in 1919. The longest in 1984 was 338 km from Nantes to Bordeaux.

Tour of Britain (Milk Race)

Four riders have won the Tour of Britain twice each—Bill Bradley (GB) (1959–60), Les West (GB) (1965, 1967), Fedor den Hertog (Netherlands) (1969, 1971) and Yuríy Kashurin (USSR) (1979, 1982). The closest race ever was in 1976 when after 1035 miles *1665,67 km* over 14 days (30 May–12 June) Bill Nickson (GB) (b. 30 Jan 1953) beat Joe Waugh (GB) by 5 sec. The fastest average speed is 26.213 mph *42,185 km/h* by Joey McLoughlin (GB) (b. 3 Dec 1964) in the 1986 race (1065 miles *1714 km*). Malcolm Elliott (b. 1 July 1961) won a record six stages in 1983 and had taken his total to 17 by 1987, when he gained overall victory. The longest Milk Race was in 1969 (1515 miles *2438,16 km*) although the longest ever Tour of Britain was in 1953 (1631 miles *2624,84 km* starting and finishing in London).

Six-day races

The most wins in 6-day races is 88 out of 233 events by Patrick Sercu (b. 27 June 1944), of Belgium, 1964–83.

Longest one-day race

The longest single-day 'massed start' road race is the 551–620 km *342–385 mile* Bordeaux–Paris, France, event. Paced over all or part of the route, the highest average speed was in 1981 with 47,186 km/h *29.32 mph* by Herman van Springel (Belgium) (b. 14 Aug 1943) for 584,5 km *363.1 miles* in 13 hr 35 min 18 sec.

Land's End to John o' Groats

The 'end to end' record for the 847 miles *1363 km* is 1 day 21 hr 3 min 16 sec (average speed 18.80 mph *30,25 km/h*) by John Woodburn (b. 22 Dec 1936) on 14–15 Aug 1982. The women's record is 2 days 11 hr 7 min by Eileen Sheridan (b. 18 Oct 1923) from 9–11 July 1954. She completed 1000 miles *1609 km* in 3 days 1 hr.

Cross-America

The trans-America solo records recognised by the Ultra-Marathon Cycling Association are: men, Pete Penseyres 8 days 9 hr 47 min; women, Elaine Mariolle 10 days 2 hr 4 min, both in the McDonald's Race Across America, Huntington Beach, California to Atlantic City, NJ, 3107 miles *5000 km*, starting on 6 July 1986.

The trans-Canada record is 14 days 22 hr 47 min by Wayne Phillips of Richmond, BC, 3800 miles *6115 km* from Vancouver, BC to Halifax, Nova Scotia, from 13–28 June 1982.

Endurance

Thomas Edward Godwin (1912–75) (GB) in the 365 days of 1939 covered 75,065 miles *120 805 km* or an average of 205.65 miles *330,96 km* per day. He then completed 100,000 miles *160 934 km* in 500 days to 14 May 1940.

Jay Aldous and Matt DeWaal cycled 14,290 miles *22 997 km* on a round-the-world trip from Place Monument, Salt Lake City, Utah, USA in 106 days from 2 Apr–16 July 1984.

Nicholas Mark Sanders (b. 26 Nov 1957) of Glossop, Derbyshire, circumnavigated the world (13,035 road miles *20 977,8 km*) in 78 days 3 hr 30 min between 5 July and 21 Sept 1985. He cycled 4802 miles *7728 km* around Britain in 22 days from 10 June–1 July 1984.

One-legged cycling

Hugh G. E. Culverhouse (GB), who has an immobile left leg, completed the trans-America race in 13 days 11 hr 1 min from 20 Sept–4 Oct 1986. He took 77 hr 53 min 17 sec for Land's End to John O'Groats, 1363 km *847 miles*, from 21–24 Aug 1986.

Cycle touring

The greatest mileage amassed in a cycle tour was more than 402,000 miles *643 700 km* by the itinerant lecturer Walter Stolle (b. Sudetenland, 1926) from 24 Jan 1959 to 12 Dec 1976. He visited 159 countries starting from Romford, Essex, England. From 1922 to 25 Dec 1973 Tommy Chambers (1903–84) of Glasgow rode a verified total of 799,405 miles *1 286 517 km*.

Visiting every continent, John W. Hathaway (b. England, 13 Jan 1925) of Vancouver, Canada covered 50,600 miles *81 300 km* from 10 Nov 1974 to 6 Oct 1976. Veronica and Colin Scargill, of Bedford, travelled 18,020 miles *29 000 km* around

> **Most popular sporting spectacle ●** The world's greatest cycle race, the Tour de France, is watched annually by an estimated 10,000,000 people. (Photo: All-Sport/Vandytstadt)

the world, on a tandem, from 25 Feb 1974–27 Aug 1975.

The most participants in a bicycle tour were 27,300 in the 56 mile *90 km* London to Brighton Bike Ride on 15 June 1986.

Non-stop

Carlos Vieira cycled for 191 hr 'non-stop' at Leira, Portugal from 8–16 June 1983. The distance covered was 2407,64 km *1496.04 miles* and he was moving 98.7 per cent of the time.

Highest altitude

Adrian Crane (UK) cycled from the lower summit of Mount Chimborazo, an altitude of 6267 m *20,561 ft*, to the town of Riobamba, Ecuador at *c*. 2750 m *9022 ft* on 11 May 1986. His brothers Nicholas and Richard Crane held the previous record, from Mount Kilimanjaro, Tanzania at 5894 m *19,340 ft*.

CYCLO-CROSS

The greatest number of world championships (inst. 1950) has been won by Eric de Vlaeminck (Belgium) (b. 23 Aug 1945) with the Amateur and Open in 1966 and six Professional titles from 1968–73. British titles (inst. 1955) have been won most often by John Atkins (b. 7 Apr 1942) with five Amateur (1961–2, 1966–8), seven Professional (1969–75) and one Open title in 1977.

Pennine Way

John North (b. 18 Aug 1943) of Rawtenstall, Lancashire, cycled or carried his machine along the 271 miles *436 km* Pennine Way from Edale, Derbyshire to Kirk Yetholm, Borders in 2 days 8 hr 45 min from 9–11 June 1978.

Cycling

WORLD RECORDS

Records are recognised by the Union Cycliste Internationale (UCI) *for both professionals and amateurs on open-air and indoor tracks for a variety of distances at unpaced flying and standing starts and for motor-paced. In this list only the best are shown, with AM to indicate an amateur record and PR a professional record.*

━━ OPEN-AIR TRACKS ━━

MEN

Distance	hr min sec	Name and country	Venue	Date	
Unpaced standing start					
1 km	1:02.547	Maic Malchow (GDR)	Mexico City	14 Oct 1980	AM
4 km	4:37.614	Steve Hegg (USA)	Colorado Springs, USA	16 Aug 1986	AM
5 km	5:44.700	Gregor Braun (W. Germany)	La Paz, Bolivia	12 Jan 1986	PR
10 km	11:39.720	Francesco Moser (Italy)	Mexico City	19 Jan 1984	PR
20 km	23:21.592	Francesco Moser (Italy)	Mexico City	23 Jan 1984	PR
100 km	2:11:21.428	Beat Meister (Switzerland)	Zürich, Switzerland	14 July 1986	AM
1 hour	51,15135 km	Francesco Moser (Italy)	Mexico City	23 Jan 1984	PR
Unpaced flying start					
200 metres	10.190	Lutz Hesslich (GDR)	Colorado Springs, USA	4 July 1985	AM
500 metres	26.993	Rory O'Reilly (USA)	La Paz, Bolivia	23 Nov 1985	AM
1 km	58.269	Dominguez Rueda Efrain (Colombia)	La Paz, Bolivia	13 Dec 1986	PR
Motor-paced					
50 km	35:35.248	Aleksandr Romanov (USSR)	Tbilisi, USSR	11 May 1984	AM
100 km	1:10:57.11	Bruno Vicino (Italy)	Bassano del Grappa, Italy	11 July 1986	PR
1 hour	84,489 km	Bruno Vicino (Italy)	Bassano del Grappa, Italy	11 July 1986	PR

WOMEN

Distance	hr min sec	Name and country	Venue	Date	
Unpaced standing start					
1 km	1:14.249	Erika Salumyae (USSR)	Tashkent, USSR	17 May 1984	
3 km	3:49.780	Rebecca Twigg (USA)	Barcelona, Spain	29 Aug 1984	
5 km	6:41.75	Amanda Jones (GB)	Leicester, England	31 July 1982	
10 km	13:30.055	Jeannie Longo (France)	Colorado Springs, USA	20 Sept 1986	
20 km	26:55.611	Jeannie Longo (France)	Colorado Springs, USA	20 Sept 1986	
100 km	2:31:28.374	Francesco Galli (Italy)	Milan, Italy	8 Aug 1985	
1 hour	44,77028 km	Jeannie Longo (France)	Colorado Springs, USA	20 Sept 1986	
Unpaced flying start					
200 metres	11.383	Isabelle Gautheron (France)	Colorado Springs, USA	16 Aug 1986	
500 metres	30.59	Isabelle Gautheron (France)	Cali, Colombia	14 Sept 1986	
1 km	1:10.463	Erika Salumyae (USSR)	Tashkent, USSR	15 May 1984	

Many of the above venues, such as La Paz, Colorado Springs, Cali and Mexico City, are at high altitude. The UCI recognises separate world records for the classic one-hour event at venues below 600 metres. These are: MEN 49,80193 km Francesco Moser on 3 Oct 1986, WOMEN 43,58789 km Jeannie Longo on 30 Sept 1986, both at Milan.

━━ INDOOR TRACKS ━━

MEN

Distance	hr min sec	Name and country	Venue	Date	
Unpaced standing start					
1 km	1:02.955	Lothar Thoms (GDR)	Moscow, USSR	22 July 1980	AM
4 km	4:28.900	Vyacheslav Yekimov (USSR)	Moscow, USSR	20 Sept 1986	AM
5 km	5:48.256	Ginautas Umaras (USSR)	Moscow, USSR	3 Aug 1984	AM
10 km	11:51.493	Vyacheslav Yekimov (USSR)	Moscow, USSR	27 Oct 1986	AM
20 km	23:52.098	Vyacheslav Yekimov (USSR)	Moscow, USSR	27 Oct 1986	AM
100 km	2:17:43.923	Aleksandr Vasekin (USSR)	Moscow, USSR	14 May 1986	AM
4 km team	4:12.830	USSR	Moscow, USSR	9 July 1986	AM
1 hour	49,672 km	Vyacheslav Yekimov (USSR)	Moscow, USSR	27 Oct 1986	AM
Unpaced flying start					
200 metres	10.224	Michael Hubner (GDR)	Moscow, USSR	8 July 1986	AM
500 metres	27.469	Aleksandr Panfilov (USSR)	Moscow, USSR	5 Aug 1984	AM
1 km	58.718	Vladimir Sultanov (USSR)	Moscow, USSR	19 Aug 1986	AM
Motor-paced					
50 km	32:56.746	Aleksandr Romanov (USSR)	Moscow, USSR	21 Feb 1987	AM
100 km	1:05:58.031	Aleksandr Romanov (USSR)	Moscow, USSR	21 Feb 1987	AM
1 hour	91,131 km	Aleksandr Romanov (USSR)	Moscow, USSR	21 Feb 1987	AM

WOMEN

Distance	hr min sec	Name and country	Venue	Date	
Unpaced standing start					
1 km	1:13.377	Erika Salumyae (USSR)	Moscow, USSR	21 Sept 1983	
3 km	3:43.490	Jeannie Longo (France)	Paris (Bercy), France	14 Nov 1986	
5 km	6:22.713	Jeannie Longo (France)	Grenoble, France	2 Nov 1986	
10 km	13:29.395	Jeannie Longo (France)	Grenoble, France	7 Nov 1986	
20 km	26:58.152	Jeannie Longo (France)	Grenoble, France	7 Nov 1986	
100 km	2:31:30.043	Mieke Havik (Netherlands)	Rotterdam, Netherlands	19 Sept 1983	
1 hour	44,718 km	Jeannie Longo (France)	Grenoble, France	7 Nov 1986	
Unpaced flying start					
200 metres	11.373	Erika Salumyae (USSR)	Moscow, USSR	28 May 1987	
500 metres	30.484	Natalya Krushelnitskaya (USSR)	Moscow, USSR	4 Feb 1987	
1 km	1:05.232	Erika Salumyae (USSR)	Moscow, USSR	30 May 1987	

LONG-DISTANCE BESTS (unpaced)

		Name and country	Venue	Date	
24 hr	830,79 km *516.24 miles*	Michael L. Secrest (USA)	Montreal, Canada	13–14 Mar 1985	
1000 km	32 hr 4 min	Herman de Munck (Belgium)	Keerbergen, Belgium	23–24 Sept 1983	
1000 miles	51 hr 12 min 32 sec	Herman de Munck (Belgium)	Keerbergen, Belgium	23–25 Sept 1983	

CYCLE SPEEDWAY

First mention of the sport is at Coventry in 1920 and it was first organised in 1945. The sport's governing body, the Cycle Speedway Council, was formed in 1973. The most British Senior Team Championships (inst. 1950) is six by: Wednesfield, Wolverhampton (1974, 1976–8, 1981 and 1983); and Offerton, Cheshire (1962, 1964–5, 1969, 1972–3). The most individual titles is four, by Derek Garnett (b. 16 July 1937) (1963, 1965, 1968 and 1972).

ROLLER CYCLING

Dave Le Grys (GB) (b. 10 Aug 1955) achieved a record speed of 203,7 km/h *126.6 mph* on BBC TV's *Record Breakers* on 11 Nov 1986.

STATIONARY CYCLING

Rudi Jan Jozef de Greef (b. 28 Dec 1955) stayed stationary without support for 10 hr at Meensel-Kiezegem, Belgium on 19 Nov 1982.

Darts

The origins of darts date from the use by archers of heavily weighted ten-inch throwing arrows for self-defence in close quarters fighting. The 'dartes' were used in Ireland in the 16th century and darts was played on the *Mayflower* by the Plymouth pilgrims in 1620. The modern game dates from at least 1896 when Brian Gamlin of Bury, Lancashire, is credited with inventing the present numbering system on the board. The first recorded score of 180 was by John Reader at the Highbury Tavern in Sussex in 1902.

DARTS SCORING RECORDS

━━ 24-HOUR SCORES ━━

Men (8 players)	1,722,249 by Broken Hill Darts Club at Broken Hill, New South Wales, Australia on 28–29 Sept 1985.
Women (8 players)	562,012 by a team from the Ring O' Bells, St Columb Major, Cornwall on 21–22 Nov 1986.
Individual	486,470 by Duncan Swift at Felixstowe, Suffolk on 7–8 Apr 1987 (averaging 26.6 per dart).
Bulls and 25s (8 players)	487,175 by a team from the Queen's Head, Bishopsworth, Bristol on 12–13 Dec 1986.

━━ TEN-HOUR SCORES ━━

Most trebles	3056 (from 7992 darts) by Paul Taylor at the Woodhouse Tavern, Leytonstone, London on 19 Oct 1985.
Most doubles	3085 (from 9945 darts) by David Broad at Blantyre Sports Club, Malawi on 17 Mar 1984.
Highest score (retrieving own darts)	394,165 by Alan Clacey and Allan Jopling at The Rifle Volunteer, Wokingham, Berkshire on 27 Dec 1986.
Bulls (individual)	855 by Fred Carter (GB) at Accrington, 11 Jan 1987.

━━ SIX-HOUR HIGHEST SCORES ━━

Men	189,153 by Daniel Tryner at St Joseph's Catholic Club, Nottingham on 9 Feb 1986.
Women	89,697 by Karen Heavey at the Rose Inn, Gillingham, Kent on 25 Apr 1986.

━━ MILLION AND ONE UP ━━

Men (8 players)	37,809 darts by a team from the Gardener's Arms, Ipswich from 28 Feb–2 Mar 1986 (their attempt included 180 180s).
Women (8 players)	70,066 darts by the Delinquents darts team at the Top George, Combe Martin, Devon from 18–20 Apr 1986.

Most titles

Eric Bristow (b. 25 Apr 1957) has most wins in the World Masters Championship (inst. 1974) with five, 1977, 1979, 1981 and 1983–4, the World Professional Championship (inst. 1978) with five, 1980–1 and 1984–6, and the World Cup Singles (inst. 1977) with two, 1983 and 1985. Six men have won the annual *News of the World* Individual Championship twice; most recently Eric Bristow in 1983 and 1984 and Bobby George in 1978 and 1986. John Lowe (b. 21 July 1945) is the only other man to have won each of the four major titles: World Masters, 1976 and 1980; World Professional, 1979 and 1987; World Cup Singles, 1981; and *News of the World*, 1981.

World Cup

The first World Cup was held at the Wembley Conference Centre, London in 1977. England have a record four wins at this biennial tournament. A World Cup for women was instituted in 1983 and has been won twice by England.

Record prize

John Lowe won £102,000 for achieving the first 501 scored with the minimum nine darts in a major event on 13 Oct 1984 at Slough in the quarter-finals of the World Match-play Championships. His darts were six successive treble 20s, treble 17, treble 18 and double 18.

Speed records

The fastest time taken to complete three games of 301, finishing on doubles, is 1 min 47 sec by Keith Deller on BBC TV's *Record Breakers* on 22 Oct 1985.

The record time for going round the board clockwise in 'doubles' at arm's length is 9.2 sec by Dennis Gower at the Millers Arms, Hastings, East Sussex on 12 Oct 1975 and 14.5 sec in numerical order by Jim Pike (1903–60) at the Craven Club, Newmarket in March 1944. The record for this feat at the 9 ft *2,7 m* throwing distance, retrieving own darts, is 2 min 13 sec by Bill Duddy (b. 29 Sept 1932) at The Plough, Haringey, London on 29 Oct 1972.

Least darts

Scores of 201 in four darts, 301 in six darts, 401 in seven darts and 501 in nine darts have been achieved on various occasions. The lowest number of darts thrown for a score of 1001 is 19 by Cliff Inglis (b. 27 May 1935) (160, 180, 140, 180, 121, 180, 40) at the Bromfield Men's Club, Devon on 11 Nov 1975. A score of 2001 in 52 darts was achieved by Alan Evans (b. 14 June 1949) at Ferndale, Glamorgan on 3 Sept 1976. 3001 in 73 darts was thrown by Tony Benson at the Plough

Inn, Gorton, Manchester on 12 July 1986. Linda Batten (b. 26 Nov 1954) set a women's 3001 record of 117 darts at The Old Wheatsheaf, Enfield, Middlesex on 2 Apr 1986.

100,001 was achieved in 3732 darts by Alan Downie of Stornoway on 21 Nov 1986.

Equestrian Sports

Evidence of horse-riding dates from a Persian engraving dated c. 3,000 BC. Pignatelli's academy of horsemanship at Naples dates from the 16th century. The earliest jumping competition was at the Agricultural Hall, Islington, London, in 1869. Equestrian events have been included in the Olympic Games since 1912.

SHOW JUMPING

Olympic Games

The greatest number of Olympic gold medals is five by Hans-Günter Winkler (b. 24 July 1926) (West Germany), four team in 1956, 1960, 1964 and 1972 and the individual Grand Prix in 1956. The most team wins in the Prix des Nations is five by Germany in 1936, 1956, 1960, 1964 and 1972. The lowest score obtained by a winner is no faults by: Frantisek Ventura (1895–1969) (Czechoslovakia) on *Eliot*, 1928; and Alwin Schockemöhle (b. 29 May 1937) (West Germany) on *Warwick Rex*, 1976. Pierre Jonquères d'Oriola (b. 1 Feb 1920) (France) uniquely won the individual gold medal twice, 1952 and 1964.

World Championships

The Men's World Championships (inst. 1953) have been won twice by Hans-Günter Winkler (West Germany) (1954–5) and Raimondo d'Inzeo (Italy) (1956 and 1960). The women's title (1965–74) was won twice by Jane 'Janou' Tissot (née Lefebvre) (France) (b. Saigon, 14 May 1945) on *Rocket* (1970 and 1974).

President's Cup

The world team championships (inst. 1965) has been won a record twelve times by Great Britain, 1965, 1967, 1970, 1972–4, 1977–9, 1983, 1985–6.

World Cup

Instituted in 1969, the only double winner is Conrad Homfeld (USA) (b. 25 Dec 1951), 1980 and 1985.

King George V Gold Cup and Queen Elizabeth II Cup

David Broome (b. 1 Mar 1940) has won the King George V Gold Cup (first held 1911) a record five times, 1960 on *Sunsalve*, 1966 on *Mister Softee*, 1972 on *Sportsman*, 1977 on *Philco* and 1981 on *Mr Ross*. The Queen Elizabeth II Cup (first held 1949), for women, has been won five times by his sister Elizabeth Edgar (b. 28 Apr 1943), 1977 on *Everest Wallaby*, 1979 on *Forever*, 1981 and 1982 on *Everest Forever*, 1986 on *Everest Rapier*. The only horse to win both these trophies is *Sunsalve* in 1957 (with Elisabeth Anderson) and 1960.

Jumping records

The official *Fédération Equestre Internationale* records are: high jump 8 ft 1¼ in *2,47 m* by *Huasó*, ridden by Capt Alberto Larraguibel Morales (Chile) at Viña del Mar, Santiago, Chile, on 5 Feb

---

Most dressage world titles ● Dr Reiner Klimke (West Germany) (b. 14 Jan 1936) is the only rider to win two world titles, on *Mehmed* in 1974 and *Ahlerich* in 1982.

1949; long jump over water 27 ft 6¾ in *8,40 m* by *Something*, ridden by André Ferreira (S. Africa) at Johannesburg on 26 Apr 1975.

The British high jump record is 7 ft 7⁵⁄₁₆ in *2,32 m* by the 16.2 hands *167 cm* grey gelding *Lastic* ridden by Nick Skelton (b. 30 Dec 1957) at Olympia, London, on 16 Dec 1978. On 25 June 1937, at Olympia, the Lady Wright (née Margery Avis Bullows) set the best recorded height for a British equestrienne on her liver chestnut *Jimmy Brown* at 7 ft 4 in *2,23 m*.

The greatest recorded height reached bareback is 7 ft *2,13 m* by Michael Whitaker (b. 17 Mar 1960) on *Red Flight* at Dublin on 14 Nov 1982.

THREE-DAY EVENT

Olympic Games and World Championships

Charles Ferdinand Pahud de Mortanges (Netherlands) (1896–1971) won a record four Olympic gold medals, team 1924 and 1928, individual (riding *Marcroix*) 1928 and 1932, when he also won a team silver medal. Richard John Hannay Meade (b. 4 Dec 1938) is the only British rider to win three gold medals, individual 1972 and team 1968 and 1972.

Badminton

The Badminton Three-Day Event (inst. 1949) has been won six times by Lucinda Green (née Prior-Palmer) (b. 7 Nov 1953) in 1973 (on *Be Fair*), 1976 (*Wide Awake*), 1977 (*George*), 1979 (*Killaire*), 1983 (*Regal Realm*) and 1984 (*Beagle Bay*).

DRESSAGE

Henri St Cyr (Sweden) (1904–79) won a record four Olympic gold medals, both team and individual in 1952 and 1956. Germany (West Germany post-war) has won a record six team gold medals, 1928, 1936, 1964, 1968, 1976 and 1984, and has most team wins, five, at the World Championships.

CARRIAGE DRIVING

World Championships were first held in 1972. Three team titles have been won by Great Britain, 1972, 1974 and 1980 and Hungary, 1976, 1978 and 1986. Two individual titles have been won by György Bárdos (Hungary), 1978 and 1980 and by Tjeerd Velstra (Netherlands), 1982 and 1986.

Longest ride

Henry G. Perry, a stockman from Mollongghip, Victoria, Australia, rode 22 565 km *14,021 miles* around Australia in 157 days, 1 May to 4 Oct 1985, with six horses.

Fencing

'Fencing' (fighting with single sticks) was practised as a sport, or as a part of a religious ceremony, in Egypt as early as c. 1360 BC. The first governing body for fencing in Britain was the Corporation of Masters of Defence founded by Henry VIII before 1540, and fencing has been practised as sport, notably in prize fights, since that time. The modern foil was introduced in France as a practice weapon for the short court sword in the mid-17th century. In the late 19th century the épée was developed in France and the light fencing sabre in Italy.

Most titles *World*

The greatest number of individual world titles won is five by Aleksandr Romankov (USSR) (b. 7 Nov 1953), at foil 1974, 1977, 1979, 1982 and 1983, but Christian d'Oriola (France) won four world foil titles, 1947, 1949, 1953–4, as well as two individual Olympic titles. Four women foilists have won three world titles: Hélène Mayer

(Germany) (1910–53) 1929, 1931, 1937; Ilona Schacherer-Elek (Hungary) (b. 17 May 1907) 1934–5, 1951; Ellen Müller-Preis (Austria) (b. 6 May 1912) 1947, 1949–50; and Cornelia Hanisch (West Germany) (b. 12 June 1952) 1979, 1981, 1985. Of these only Ilona Schacherer-Elek also won two individual Olympic titles (1936 and 1948).

Olympic

The most individual Olympic gold medals won is three by Ramón Fonst (Cuba) (1883–1959) in 1900 and 1904 (two) and by Nedo Nadi (Italy) (1894–1952) in 1912 and 1920 (two). Nadi also won

> **Most three-day event world titles ●** Bruce Davidson (USA) (b. 13 Dec 1949) won on *Irish Cap* in 1974 and *Might Tango* in 1978. Here he rides *J J Babu* at Badminton in 1986. (Sporting Pictures)

three team gold medals in 1920 making a then unprecedented total of five gold medals at one celebration. Edoardo Mangiarotti (Italy) (b. 7 Apr 1919) with six gold, five silver and two bronze holds the record of 13 Olympic medals. He won them for foil and épée from 1936 to 1960. The most gold medals by a woman is four (one

individual, three team) by Elena Novikova (*née* Byelova) (USSR) (b. 28 July 1947) from 1968 to 1976, and the record for all medals is seven (two gold, three silver, two bronze) by Ildikó Sagi-Retjö (formerly Ujlaki-Retjö) (Hungary) (b. 11 May 1937) from 1960 to 1976.

British Olympic records

The only British fencer to win a gold medal is Gillian Mary Sheen (b. 21 Aug 1928) in the 1956 foil. A record three Olympic medals were won by Edgar Seligman (1867–1958) with silver medals in the épée team event in 1906, 1908 and 1912. Henry William Furse Hoskyns (b. 19 Mar

1931) has competed most often for Great Britain with six Olympic appearances, 1956–76.

Amateur Fencing Association titles

The most won at one weapon is ten at women's foil by Gillian Sheen (now Donaldson), 1949, 1951–8, 1960.

> Fencing is one of the five disciplines of the Modern Pentathlon ● Anatoliy Starostin was Olympic champion in 1980 and World Champion in 1983. (All-Sport)

Field Sports

FOXHUNTING

Earliest references

Hunting the fox in Britain became popular from the second half of the 18th century, though it is mentioned very much earlier. Prior to that time hunting was confined principally to the deer and the hare.

Pack *Earliest*

The Old Charlton Hunt (later the Goodwood) in West Sussex (now extinct), the Duke of Monmouth and Lord Grey of Werke at Charlton, Sussex, and the Duke of Buckingham in north Yorkshire, owned packs which were entered to fox only during the reign (1660–85) of Charles II.

Largest

The pack with the greatest number of hounds has been the Duke of Beaufort's hounds maintained at Badminton, Avon, since 1786. At times hunting six days a week, this pack once had 120 couples at hounds. It now meets four days a week.

Longest hunt

The longest recorded hunt was one held by Squire Sandys which ran from Holmbank, northern Lancashire to Ulpha, Cumbria, a total of nearly 80 miles *128 km* in reputedly only 6 hr, in January or February 1743. The longest duration hunt was one of 10 hr 5 min by Charlton Hunt of West Sussex, which ran from East Dean Wood at 7.45 a.m. to a kill over 57¼ miles *92 km* away at 5.50 p.m. on 26 Jan 1738.

Most widespread hunting

Between 1969 and 1987, J. N. P. Watson, hunting correspondent to *Country Life*, has hunted with 243 different packs of foxhounds, staghounds and harehounds in Britain, Ireland, USA and Europe.

GAME SHOOTING

Record heads

The world's finest head is the 23-pointer stag in the Maritzburg collection, East Germany. The outside span is 75½ in *191 cm*, the length 47½ in *120 cm* and the weight 41½ lb *18,824 kg*. The greatest number of points is probably 33 (plus 29) on the stag shot in 1696 by Frederick III (1657–1713), the Elector of Brandenburg, later King Frederick I of Prussia.

Largest tally to a single sportsman

556,813 head of game fell to the guns of the 2nd Marquess of Ripon between 1867 and the morning of 22 Sept 1923 when he dropped dead on a grouse moor after shooting his 52nd bird. This figure included 241,234 pheasants, 124,193 partridges and 31,900 hares. (His game books are held by the gunmakers, James Purdey and Sons.)

Thomas, 6th Baron Walsingham bagged 1070 grouse, a one-day record for a single gun, in Yorkshire on 30 Aug 1888.

Fives

ETON FIVES

A handball game against the buttress of Eton College Chapel was first recorded in 1825. New courts were built at Eton in 1840, the rules were codified in 1877, and rewritten laws were introduced three times, last amended in 1981.

Most titles

One pair has won the amateur championship (Kinnaird Cup) eight times—Anthony Hughes and Arthur James Gordon Campbell (1958, 1965–8, 1971, 1973 and 1975). Hughes was also in the winning pair in 1963 and has played in 16 finals. Brian C. Matthews and John P. Reynolds won a record six successive titles, 1981–6.

RUGBY FIVES

As now known, this game dates from *c.* 1850 with the first inter-public school matches recorded in the early 1870s. The Oxford *v.* Cambridge contest was inaugurated in 1925 and the Rugby Fives Association was founded in the home of Dr Edgar Cyriax (1874–1954), in Welbeck Street, London, on 29 Oct 1927. The dimensions of the Standard Rugby Fives court were approved by the Association in 1931.

Most titles

The greatest number of Amateur Singles Championships (instituted 1932) ever won is 13 by Wayne Enstone in 1973–8 and 1980–6. The record for the Amateur Doubles Championship (instituted 1925) is seven, shared by John Frederick Pretlove (1952, 1954, 1956–9, 1961) and David E. Gardner (1960, 1965–6, 1970–2, 1974).

The invitation World Championships was first held in 1983. On the first three occasions Wayne Enstone won the singles and Enstone and Steve Ashton the doubles.

Football (Association)

A game with some similarities, termed *Tsu-chu*, was played in China in the 4th and 3rd centuries BC. One of the earliest references to the game in England is a Royal Proclamation by Edward II in 1314 banning the game in the City of London. The earliest clear representation of football is an Edinburgh print dated 1672–3. The game was standardised with the formation of the Football Association in England on 26 Oct 1863. The oldest club is Sheffield FC, formed on 24 Oct 1857. The oldest in the Football League is Notts County, founded in 1862. Eleven per side became standard in 1870.

PROFESSIONAL

Longest match

The duration record for first-class fixtures is 3 hr 30 min (with interruptions), in the Copa Libertadores in Santos, Brazil, on 2–3 Aug 1962, when Santos drew 3–3 with Penarol FC of Montevideo, Uruguay.

The longest British match on record was one of 3 hr 23 min between Stockport County and Doncaster Rovers in the second leg of the Third Division (North) Cup at Edgeley Park, Stockport, Greater Manchester on 30 Mar 1946.

Longest unbeaten run

Nottingham Forest were undefeated in 42 consecutive Division I matches from 20 Nov 1977 to 9 Dec 1978. In Scottish football, Glasgow Celtic were undefeated in 62 matches (49 won, 13 drawn), 13 Nov 1915–21 April 1917.

— LARGEST BRITISH BAGS —

Hare	1215	*11 guns*	Holkham, Norfolk, 19 Dec 1877
Rabbit	6943	*5 guns*	Blenheim, Oxfordshire, 17 Oct 1898
Goose (Brent)	704[1]	*32 punt-guns*	Colonel Russell l/c, River Blackwater, Essex, c. 1860
Grouse	1070	*1 gun*[1]	Thomas, 6th Baron Walsingham in Yorkshire, 30 Aug 1888
Grouse	2929	*8 guns*	Littledale and Abbeystead, Lancashire, 12 Aug 1915
Partridge (Wild)	2015[2]	*6 guns*	Rothwell, Lincolnshire, 3 Oct 1952
Pheasant	3937	*7 guns*[3]	Hall Barn, Beaconsfield, Buckinghamshire, 18 Dec 1913
Pigeon	561	*1 gun*	K. Ransford, Salop-Powys, 22 July 1970
Snipe	1108	*2 guns*	Tiree, Inner Hebrides, 25 Oct–3 Nov 1906
Woodcock	228	*6 guns*	Ashford, County Galway, Ireland, 28 Jan 1910
Woodpigeon	550	*1 gun*	Major A. J. Coates, near Winchester, Hampshire, 10 Jan 1962

[1] *Plus about 250 later picked up.*   [2] *Plus 104 later picked up.*
[3] *Including HM King George V.*

Most postponements

The Scottish Cup tie between Inverness Thistle and Falkirk during the winter of 1978-9 was postponed a record 29 times due to weather conditions. Finally, Falkirk won the game 4-0.

GOAL SCORING

Teams

The highest score recorded in a first-class match is 36. This occurred in the Scottish Cup match between Arbroath and Bon Accord on 5 Sept 1885, when Arbroath won 36-0 on their home ground. But for the lack of nets and the consequent waste of retrieval time, the score must have been even higher. Seven further goals were disallowed for offside.

The highest margin recorded in an international match is 17, when England beat Australia 17-0 at Sydney on 30 June 1951. This match is not listed by England as a *full* international. The highest in the British Isles was when England beat Ireland 13-0 at Belfast on 18 Feb 1882.

The highest score between English clubs in any major competition is 26, when Preston North End beat Hyde 26-0 in an FA Cup tie at Deepdale, Lancashire on 15 Oct 1887. The biggest victory in an FA Cup Final is six when Bury beat Derby County 6-0 at Crystal Palace on 18 Apr 1903, in which year Bury did not concede a single goal in the five Cup matches.

The highest score by one side in a Football League (Division I) match is 12 goals, when West Bromwich Albion beat Darwen 12-0 at West Bromwich, West Midlands on 4 Apr 1892; when Nottingham Forest beat Leicester Fosse by the same score at Nottingham on 21 Apr 1909; and when Aston Villa beat Accrington 12-2 at Perry Barr, West Midlands on 12 Mar 1892.

The highest aggregate in League Football was 17 goals when Tranmere Rovers beat Oldham Athletic 13-4 in a Third Division (North) match at Prenton Park, Merseyside, on Boxing Day, 1935. The record margin in a League match has been 13 in the Newcastle United 13, Newport County 0 (Division II) match on 5 Oct 1946 and in the Stockport County 13, Halifax 0 (Division III (North)) match on 6 Jan 1934.

The highest number of goals by any British team in a professional league in a season is 142 in 34 matches by Raith Rovers (Scottish Division II) in the 1937-8 season. The English League record is 134 in 46 matches by Peterborough United (Division IV) in 1960-1.

Individual

The most scored by one player in a first-class match is 16 by Stephan Stanis (né Stanikowski, b. Poland, 15 July 1913) for Racing Club de Lens v. Aubry-Asturies, in Lens, France, in a wartime French Cup game on 13 Dec 1942.

The record number of goals scored by one player in an international match is ten by Sofus Nielsen (1888-1963) for Denmark v. France (17-1) in the 1908 Olympics; and by Gottfried Fuchs (1889-1972) for Germany who beat Russia 16-0 in the 1912 Olympic tournament (consolation event) in Sweden.

Career

Artur Friedenreich (1892-1969) (Brazil) scored an undocumented 1329 goals in a 43-year first-class football career. The most goals scored in a specified period is 1216 by Edson Arantes do Nascimento (Brazil) (b. 23 Oct 1940), known as Pelé, from 7 Sept 1956 to 2 Oct 1974 in 1254 games. His best year was 1959 with 126, and the *milesimo* (1000th) came in a penalty for his club Santos in the Maracaña Stadium, Rio de Janeiro on 19 Nov 1969 when playing his 909th first-class match. He later played for New York Cosmos

and on his retirement on 1 Oct 1977 his total had reached 1281, in 1363 games. He added two more goals later in special appearances. Franz 'Bimbo' Binder (b. 1 Dec 1911) scored 1006 goals in 756 games in Austria and Germany between 1930 and 1950.

The international career record for England is 49 goals by Robert 'Bobby' Charlton (b. 11 Oct 1937). His first was v. Scotland on 19 Apr 1958 and his last on 20 May 1970 v. Colombia.

The greatest number of goals scored in British first-class football is 550 (410 in Scottish League matches) by James McGrory of Glasgow Celtic (1922-38). The most scored in League matches is 434, for West Bromwich Albion, Fulham, Leicester City and Shrewsbury Town, by George Arthur Rowley (b. 21 Apr 1926) between 1946 and April 1965. Rowley also scored 32 goals in the FA Cup and one for England 'B'.

Fastest goals

The fastest Football League goals on record were scored in 6 sec by: Albert E. Mundy (b. 12 May 1926) (Aldershot) in a Division IV match v. Hartlepool United at Victoria Ground, Hartlepool, Cleveland on 25 Oct 1958; Barrie Jones (b. 31 Oct 1938) (Notts Co.) in a Division III match v. Torquay United on 31 Mar 1962; Keith Smith (b. 15 Sept 1940) (Crystal Palace) in a Division II match v. Derby County at the Baseball Ground, Derby on 12 Dec 1964; and Tommy W. Langley (b. 8 Feb 1958) (Queen's Park Rangers) in a Division II match v. Bolton Wanderers on 11 Oct 1980.

The fastest confirmed hat-trick is in 2½ minutes by: Ephraim 'Jock' Dodds (b. 7 Sept 1915) for Blackpool v. Tranmere Rovers on 28 Feb 1942; and Jimmy Scarth (b. 26 Aug 1920) for Gillingham v. Leyton Orient in Div III (Southern) on 1 Nov 1952. A hat-trick in 1 min 50 sec is claimed for Maglioni of Independiente v. Gimnasia y Escrima de la Plata in Argentina on 18 Mar 1973. John

---

> # BRITISH GOAL-SCORING RECORDS
>
> ### SCOTTISH CUP
> 13 John Petrie for Arbroath v. Bon Accord on 5 Sept 1885
>
> ### FOOTBALL LEAGUE
> 10 Joe Payne (1914-77) for Luton Town v. Bristol Rovers (Div 3S) at Luton on 13 Apr 1936
>
> ### F. LEAGUE DIVISION ONE
> 7 Ted Drake (b. 16 Aug 1912) for Arsenal v. Aston Villa at Birmingham on 14 Dec 1935; James David Ross for Preston NE v. Stoke at Preston on 6 Oct 1888
>
> ### FA CUP (PRELIMINARY ROUND)
> 10 Chris Marron for South Shields v. Radcliffe at South Shields on 20 Sept 1947
>
> ### FA CUP
> 9 Edward 'Ted' MacDougall (b. 8 Jan 1947) for Bournemouth v. Margate at Bournemouth on 20 Nov 1971
>
> ### SCOTTISH LEAGUE
> 8 James Edward McGrory (1904-82) for Celtic v. Dunfermline (Div 1) at Celtic Park, Glasgow on 14 Jan 1928
>
> ### HOME INTERNATIONAL
> 6 Joe Bambrick (b. 3 Nov 1905) for Ireland v. Wales at Belfast on 1 Feb 1930
>
> ### AMATEUR INTERNATIONAL
> 6 William Charles Jordan (1885-1949) for England v. France at Park Royal, London on 23 Mar 1908; Vivian John Woodward (1879-1954) for England v. Holland at Stamford Bridge, London on 11 Dec 1909; Harold A. Walden for Great Britain v. Hungary at Stockholm, Sweden on 1 July 1912

McIntyre (Blackburn Rovers) scored four goals in 5 min v. Everton at Ewood Park, Blackburn, Lancashire on 16 Sept 1922. William 'Ginger' Richardson (West Bromwich Albion) scored four goals in 5 min from the kick-off against West Ham United at Upton Park on 7 Nov 1931. Frank Keetley scored six goals in 21 min in the second half of the Lincoln City v. Halifax Town league match on 16 Jan 1932. The international record is three goals in 3½ min by Willie Hall (Tottenham Hotspur) for England v. Ireland on 16 Nov 1938 at Old Trafford, Greater Manchester.

Fastest own goal

Torquay United's Pat Kruse (b. 30 Nov 1953) equalled the fastest goal on record when he headed the ball into his own net only 6 sec after kick-off v. Cambridge United on 3 Jan 1977.

GOALKEEPING

Individual record

The longest that any goalkeeper has succeeded in preventing any goals being scored past him in international matches is 1142 min for Dino Zoff (Italy), from September 1972 to June 1974.

The British club record in all competitive matches is 1196 min by Chris Woods (b. 14 Nov 1959) for Glasgow Rangers from 26 Nov 1986 to 31 Jan 1987.

FA CHALLENGE CUP AND SCOTTISH FA CUP

Most wins

The greatest number of FA Cup wins is seven by: Aston Villa, 1887, 1895, 1897, 1905, 1913, 1920 and 1957 (nine final appearances); and Tottenham Hotspur, 1901, 1921, 1961, 1962, 1967, 1981 and 1982 (eight appearances). Newcastle United and Arsenal have been in the Final 11 times. The highest aggregate scores have been 6-1 in 1890 and 4-3 in 1953.

The greatest number of Scottish FA Cup wins is 27 by Celtic in 1892, 1899, 1900, 1904, 1907-8, 1911-12, 1914, 1923, 1925, 1927, 1931, 1933, 1937, 1951, 1954, 1965, 1967, 1969, 1971, 1972, 1974, 1975, 1977, 1980 and 1985.

Youngest player

The youngest player in an FA Cup Final was Paul Allen (b. 28 Aug 1962) for West Ham United v. Arsenal on 10 May 1980, aged 17 years 256 days. Derek Johnstone (Rangers) (b. 4 Nov 1953) was 16 years 11 months old when he played in the Scottish League Cup Final against Celtic on 24 Oct 1970. The youngest goal scorer in the FA Cup Final was Norman Whiteside (b. 7 May 1965) for Manchester United v. Brighton at 18 yr 19 days on 26 May 1983. The youngest player ever in the FA Cup competition was goalkeeper Scott Endersby (b. 20 Feb 1962) at 15 years 288 days for Kettering v. Tilbury on 26 Nov 1977.

Most medals

Three players have won five FA Cupwinners' medals: James Forrest (Blackburn Rovers) (1884-6, 1890-1); the Hon. Sir Arthur Fitzgerald Kinnaird KT (Wanderers) (1873, 1877-8) and Old Etonians (1879, 1882); and Charles H. R. Wollaston (Wanderers) (1872-3, 1876-8). The most Scottish Cupwinners' medals won is eight by Charles Campbell (Queen's Park) in 1874-6, 1880-2, 1884 and 1886.

Longest tie

The most protracted FA Cup tie in the competition proper was that between Stoke City and Bury in the third round, with Stoke winning 3-2 in the fifth meeting after 9 hr 22 min of play in January 1955. The matches were at Bury (1-1) on 8 Jan; Stoke-on-Trent on 12 Jan (abandoned after 22 min of extra time with the score 1-1); Goodison Park (3-3) on 17 Jan; Anfield (2-2) on 19 Jan; and finally at Old Trafford on 24 Jan. In the 1972 final qualifying round Alvechurch beat Oxford City after five previous drawn games (total playing time 11 hours).

FOOTBALL LEAGUE/MILK CUP/ LITTLEWOODS CUP

Instituted in 1960–1, the most wins is four by Liverpool, 1981–4.

SCOTTISH LEAGUE SKOL CUP

Instituted in 1946–7, the most wins is 13 by Rangers between 1947 and 1985.

LEAGUE CHAMPIONSHIPS

The record number of successive National League Championships is nine by: Celtic (Scotland) 1966–74; CSKA, Sofia (Bulgaria) 1954–62; and MTK Budapest (Hungary) 1917–25. The Sofia club holds a European postwar record of 23 league titles.

English

The greatest number of League Championships (Division I) is 16 by Liverpool in 1901, 1906, 1922–23, 1947, 1964, 1966, 1973, 1976–7, 1979–80, 1982–84, and 1986. The record number of wins in a season is 33 from 42 matches by Doncaster Rovers in Division III (North) in 1946–7. The Division I record is 31 wins from 42 matches by Tottenham Hotspur in 1960–1. In 1893–4 Liverpool won 22 and drew 6 in 28 Division II games. They

also won the promotion match. The most points in a season under the current scoring system is 102 by Swindon in Division IV in 1985–6. In 1985–6 Wimbledon gained promotion to the First Division only nine seasons after entering the league.

'Double'

The only FA Cup and League Championship 'doubles' are those of Preston North End in 1889, Aston Villa in 1897, Tottenham Hotspur in 1961, Arsenal in 1971 and Liverpool in 1986. Preston won the League without losing a match and the Cup without having a goal scored against them throughout the whole competition.

Scottish

Glasgow Rangers have won the Scottish League Championship 37 times between 1899 and 1987 and were joint champions in 1891. Their 76 points in the Scottish Division I in 1920–1 represent a record in any division.

EVERTON v. LIVERPOOL
Dixie Dean v. Ian Rush

The most goals in a League season is 60 in 39 games by William Ralph 'Dixie' Dean (1907–80) for Everton (Division I) in 1927–8 and 66 in 38 games by James Smith (1902–76) for Ayr United (Scottish Division II) in the same season. With three more in Cup ties and 19 in representative matches, Dean's total was 82.

Ian Rush equalled Dixie Dean's record of 19 goals in Mersey derby matches by scoring twice in the 136th League encounter between Liverpool and Everton on 25 April 1987 at Anfield. Liverpool won 3–1. But Rush's total was made up of 10 League goals, 5 Screen Sport Super Cup, 2 FA Cup, one Littlewoods Cup and one in the Charity Shield from 1981–82. In contrast, Dean achieved 18 League goals and one in the FA Cup from 1925–26 to 1936–37.

Artwork: Ashley Hamilton Lloyd

Closest win

In 1923-4 Huddersfield won the Division I Championship over Cardiff by 0.02 of a goal with a goal average of 1.81.

THE FIFA WORLD CUP

The Fédération Internationale de Football Association (FIFA), which was founded on 21 May 1904, instituted the first World Cup on 13 July 1930, in Montevideo, Uruguay. It is now held quadrennially. Three wins have been achieved by: Brazil 1958, 1962 and 1970; and Italy 1934, 1938 and 1982. Brazil, uniquely, have taken part in all 13 finals tournaments.

Goal scoring and appearances

Antonio Carbajal (b. 1923) (Mexico) is the only player to have appeared in five World Cup final tournaments, keeping goal for Mexico in 1950, 1954, 1958, 1962 and 1966, playing 11 games in all. The most appearances in finals tournaments is 21 by: Uwe Seeler (b. 5 Nov 1936) (West Germany), 1958-70; and Władysław Zmuda (Poland) (b. 6 June 1954), 1974-86. Pelé is the only player to have been with three World Cup winning teams, in 1958, 1962 and 1970. The youngest ever to play in the World Cup is Norman Whiteside, who played for Northern Ireland *v.* Yugoslavia aged 17 yr 42 days on 17 June 1982.

Just Fontaine (b. Marrakesh, Morocco, 18 Aug 1933) of France scored 13 goals in six matches in the final stages of the 1958 competition in Sweden. Gerd Müller (b. 3 Nov 1945) (West Germany) scored 10 goals in 1970 and four in 1974 for the highest aggregate of 14 goals. Fontaine and Jairzinho (Brazil) are the only two players to have scored in every match in a final series, as Jairzinho scored seven in six games in 1970.

The most goals scored in a final is three by Geoff Hurst (b. 8 Dec 1941) for England *v.* West Germany on 30 July 1966. Three players have scored in two finals: Vava (real name Edwaldo

Most World Cup appearances ● The record of 21 games in World Cup finals tournaments was equalled by Władysław Zmuda. (Photo: All Sport)

Izito Neto) (Brazil) in 1958 and 1962; Pelé in 1958 and 1970; and Paul Breitner (West Germany) in 1974 and 1982. The fastest goal in World Cup competition was one in 27 sec by Bryan Robson (b. 11 Jan 1957) for England *v.* France in Bilbao on 16 June 1982.

Leading goal scorer 1986 World Cup finals ● Gary Lineker (b. 11 Nov 1960), scorer of 6 goals in Mexico, fails to find target this time in England's victory against Paraguay. (Photo: Sporting Pictures)

The highest score in a World Cup match occurred in a qualifying match in Auckland on 15 Aug 1981 when New Zealand beat Fiji 13-0. The highest score during the final stages is 10, scored by Hungary in a 10-1 win over El Salvador at Elche, Spain on 15 June 1982. The highest match aggregate in the finals tournament is 12, when Austria beat Switzerland in 1954.

The highest scoring team in a final tournament has been West Germany, who scored 25 in six matches in 1954, for the highest average of 4.17 goals per game.

The best defensive record belongs to England, who in six matches in 1966 conceded only three goals. Curiously, no team has ever failed to score in a World Cup Final.

TOURNAMENT RECORDS

World Club Championship

This club tournament was started in 1960 between the winners of the European Cup and the Copa Libertadores, the South American equivalent. The most wins is three by Penarol, Uruguay in 1961, 1966 and 1982. Independiente, Argentina won in 1973 and 1984 and reached the final in 1975, but couldn't agree dates for the matches with Bayern Munich.

European Championship *(Nations Cup)*

Held every four years from 1958. West Germany is the only country to have won twice, in 1972 and 1980. They also lost in the 1976 final, to Czechoslovakia.

European Champion Clubs Cup

The European Cup for the league champions of the respective nations was approved by FIFA on 8 May 1955 and is run by the European governing body UEFA (Union of European Football Associations), which came into being in the previous year. Real Madrid won the first final, and have won a record six times, 1956-60, 1966. The highest score in a final was Real Madrid's 7-3 win over Eintracht Frankfurt at Hampden Park, Glasgow on 18 May 1960.

Glasgow Celtic became the first British club to win the Cup, beating Inter-Milan 2–1 in Lisbon, Portugal on 25 May 1967. They also became the first British club to win the European Cup and the two senior domestic tournaments (League and Cup) in the same season. Liverpool, winners in 1977, 1978, 1981 and 1984, have been the most successful British club and in the 1983–4 season emulated Celtic by also winning two domestic competitions—League and Milk Cup.

European Cup Winners Cup

A tournament for national cup winners started in 1960–1. Clubs to win twice have been: AC Milan 1968 and 1973; Anderlecht 1976 and 1978; Barcelona 1979 and 1982; and Dynamo Kiev 1975 and 1986. Tottenham Hotspur was the first British club to win the trophy, when they set a record score for the final beating Atlético Madrid 5–1 in Rotterdam on 15 May 1963.

UEFA Cup

Originally known as the International Inter-City Industrial Fairs Cup, this club tournament began in 1955. The first competition lasted three years, the second two years. In 1960–1 it became an annual tournament and since 1971–2 has been replaced by the UEFA Cup. The most wins is three by Barcelona in 1958, 1960 and 1966. The first British club to win the trophy was Leeds United in 1968.

PLAYERS

Most durable

The most durable player in League history has been Terence Lionel Paine (b. 23 Mar 1939) who made 824 league appearances from 1957 to 1977 playing for Southampton and Hereford Utd. Norman John Trollope (b. 14 June 1943) made 770 League appearances for one club, Swindon Town, between 1960 and 1980.

Transfer fees

The greatest transfer fee quoted for a player is 15,895 million lire (£6.9 million) by Napoli in 1984 for Diego Maradona (Argentina) (b. 30 Oct 1960) from Barcelona. This exceeded the c. £5 million that Barcelona paid for Maradona in 1982. The record fee between British clubs was £1,500,000 (including VAT and other levies) paid by Manchester United to West Bromwich Albion for Bryan Robson on 3 Oct 1981. The highest transfer fee for a British player is the estimated £3.2 million paid by Juventus of Italy to Liverpool for Ian Rush (b. 20 Oct 1961) in June 1986. He was loaned to remain with Liverpool for the 1986–7 season.

Heaviest goalkeeper

The biggest goalkeeper in representative football was the England international Willie J. 'Fatty' Foulke (1874–1916), who stood 6 ft 3 in *1,90 m* and weighed 22 st 3 lb *141 kg*. His last games were for Bradford City, by which time he was 26 st *165 kg*. He once stopped a game by snapping the cross bar.

INTERNATIONAL CAPS

Oldest and youngest

The oldest international has been William Henry 'Billy' Meredith (1874–1958) (Manchester City and United) who played outside right for Wales v. England at Highbury, London, on 15 Mar 1920 when aged 45 yr 229 days. He played internationally for a record span of 26 years (1895–1920).

The youngest British international was Norman Whiteside, who played for Northern Ireland v. Yugoslavia at 17 yr 42 days on 17 June 1982.

England's youngest international was Duncan Edwards (1936–58) (Manchester United) v. Scotland at Wembley on 2 Apr 1955, at 18 yr 183 days. The youngest Welsh cap was John Charles (b. 27 Dec 1931) (Leeds United) v. Ireland at Wrexham on 8 Mar 1950, aged 18 yr 71 days. Scotland's youngest international has been Johnny Lambie (Queen's Park), at 17 yr 92 days v. Ireland on 20 Mar 1886. The youngest for the Republic of Ireland was James Holmes (b. 11 Nov 1953) (Coventry City), at 17 yr 200 days v. Austria in Dublin on 30 May 1971.

Most international appearances

The greatest number of appearances for a national team is 150 by Hector Chumpitaz (b. 12 Apr 1943) (Peru) from 1963 to 1982. This includes all matches played by the national team. The record for full internationals against other national teams is 119 by Pat Jennings of Northern Ireland (as below).

The most women's international appearances is 56 (49 as captain) by Carol Thomas (b. 5 June 1955) for England, 1974–86.

ATTENDANCES

Greatest crowds

The greatest recorded crowd at any football match was 205,000 (199,589 paid) for the Brazil v. Uruguay World Cup match in the Maracaña Municipal Stadium, Rio de Janeiro, Brazil on 16 July 1950. The record attendance for a European Cup match is 136,505 at the semi-final between Glasgow Celtic and Leeds United at Hampden Park, Glasgow on 15 Apr 1970.

The British record paid attendance is 149,547 at the Scotland v. England international at Hampden Park, Glasgow, on 17 Apr 1937. It is, however, probable that this total was exceeded (estimated 160,000) at the FA Cup Final between Bolton Wanderers and West Ham United at Wembley Stadium on 28 Apr 1923, when the crowd broke in on the pitch and the start was delayed 40 minutes until the pitch was cleared. The counted admissions were 126,047.

The Scottish Cup record attendance is 146,433 when Celtic played Aberdeen at Hampden Park on 24 Apr 1937. The record attendance for a League match in Britain is 118,567 for Rangers v. Celtic at Ibrox Park, Glasgow on 2 Jan 1939.

The highest attendance at an amateur match has been 120,000 in Senayan Stadium, Jakarta, Indo-

nesia, on 26 Feb 1976 for the Pre-Olympic Group II Final, North Korea v. Indonesia.

Smallest crowd

The smallest crowd at a full home international was 2315 for Wales v. Northern Ireland on 27 May 1982 at the Racecourse Ground, Wrexham, Clwyd. The smallest paying attendance at a Football League fixture was for the Stockport County v. Leicester City match at Old Trafford, Greater Manchester, on 7 May 1921. Stockport's own ground was under suspension and the 'crowd' numbered 13, but an estimated 2000 gained free admission. When West Ham beat Castilla of Spain (5–1) in the European Cup Winners Cup at Upton Park, Greater London, on 1 Oct 1980 and when Aston Villa beat Besiktas of Turkey (3–1) in the European Cup at Villa Park on 15 Sept 1982, there were no paying spectators due to disciplinary action by the European Football Union.

PENALTIES

The greatest number of penalty kicks taken to decide a cup game under the jurisdiction of the Football League occurred in a Freight Rover Trophy, Southern Section quarter-final between Aldershot and Fulham on 10 February 1987, at the Recreation Ground, Aldershot, Hampshire. After 90 minutes play the score was 1–1. A further 30 minutes of extra time produced no further scoring. It needed 28 penalty kicks, of which only seven were missed, before Aldershot won 11–10.

In the Cyprus First-Division match in which Omonia beat Olympiakos 6–4 in Nicosia on 15 February 1987, FIFA referee Stefanos Hadjiste-fanou awarded six penalties, three to each side, all of which were converted by George Savvides (Omonia) and Sylvester Vernon (Olympiakos).

OLYMPIC GAMES

The only country to have won the Olympic football title three times is Hungary in 1952, 1964 and 1968. The United Kingdom won the unofficial tournament in 1900 and the official tournaments of 1908 and 1912. The highest Olympic score is 17, by Denmark v. France 'A' (1) in 1908.

OTHER MATCHES

Highest scores *Teams*

In a Felixstowe Sunday League match on 11 Mar 1984, Ipswich Exiles beat Seaton Rovers 45–0.

In an Under-14 League match between Midas FC and Courage Colts, in Kent, on 11 Apr 1976, the full-time score after 70 minutes play was 59–1. Top scorer for Midas was Kevin Graham with 17 goals. Courage had scored the first goal.

Needing to improve their goal 'difference' to gain promotion in 1979, Ilinden FC of Yugoslavia, with the collusion of the opposition, Mladost, and the referee, won their final game of the season by 134–1. Their rivals in the promotion race won their match, under similar circumstances, by 88–0.

Individual

Dean Goodliff scored 26 goals for Deleford Colts v. Iver Minors in the Slough Boys Soccer Combination Under-14 League at Iver, Buckinghamshire in his team's 33–0 win on 22 Dec 1985. The women's record is 22 goals by Linda Curl of Norwich Ladies in a 40–0 league victory over Milton Keynes Reserves at Norwich on 25 Sept 1983.

Season

The greatest number of goals in a season reported for an individual player in junior professional league football is 96 by Tom Duffy (b. 7 Jan 1937) for Ardeer Thistle FC, Strathclyde

—— BRITISH INTERNATIONAL APPEARANCES ——

NORTHERN IRELAND....119
Patrick A. Jennings (b. 12 June 1945) ....Watford/Tottenham H/Arsenal 1964–86

ENGLAND....108
Robert Frederick 'Bobby' Moore (b. 12 Apr 1941) ....West Ham U/Fulham 1962–73

SCOTLAND....102
Kenneth M. Dalglish (b. 4 Mar 1951) ....Celtic/Liverpool 1971–86

WALES....72
Joseph P. 'Joey' Jones (b. 4 Mar 1955) ....Wrexham, Liverpool, Chelsea, Huddersfield T 1972–86

REPUBLIC OF IRELAND....65
William John Brady (b. 13 Feb 1956) ....Arsenal/Juventus/Sampdoria/Internazionale
.....................................Arsenal/West Ham U 1974–87

in 1960–1. Paul Anthony Moulden (b. 6 Sept 1967) scored 289 goals in 40 games for Bolton Lads Club in Bolton Boys Federation intermediate league and cup matches in 1981–2. An additional 51 goals scored in other tournaments brought his total to 340, the highest season figure reported in any class of competitive football for an individual. He made his Football League debut for Manchester City on 1 Jan 1986 and has played for the England Youth team.

Fastest goals

Wind-aided goals in 3 sec after kick-off have been scored by a number of players. Damian Corcoran (b. 25 Nov 1976) scored three goals for 7th Fulwood Cubs v. 4th Fulwood Cubs on 1 Feb 1987.

Fastest own goal

The fastest own goals on record have been 5 sec after kick-off, 'scored' by Peter Johnson of Chesham United v. Wycombe Wanderers on 21 Feb 1976 and by John Smythe of Vernon Carus v. Duke Williams Reserves in March 1986.

Longest ties

In the Hertfordshire Intermediate Cup, London Colney beat Leavesden Hospital after 12 hr 41 min play and seven ties from 6 Nov to 17 Dec 1971.

Largest tournament

The Metropolitan Police 5-a-side Youth Competition in 1981 attracted an entry of 7008 teams, a record for an FA-sanctioned competition.

Most and least successful teams

Winlaton West End FC, Tyne and Wear, completed a run of 95 league games without defeat between 1976 and 1980. Stockport United FC, of the Stockport Football League, lost 39 consecutive league and cup matches, September 1976 to 18 Feb 1978.

Most indisciplined

In the local cup match between Tongham Youth Club, Surrey and Hawley, Hampshire, on 3 Nov 1969, the referee booked all 22 players including one who went to hospital, and one of the linesmen. The match, won by Tongham 2–0, was described by a player as 'a good, hard game'.

Longest unbeaten ● Penlake Junior Football Club remained unbeaten for 153 games (winning 152 including 85 in succession) in the Warrington Hilden Friendly League from 1981 until 1986.

In a Gancia Cup match at Waltham Abbey, Essex on 23 Dec 1973, the referee, Michael J. Woodhams, sent off the entire Juventus-Cross team and some club officials. Glencraig United, Faifley, nr Clydebank, had all 11 team members and two substitutes for their 2–2 draw against Goldenhill Boys' Club on 2 Feb 1975 booked in the dressing room before a ball was kicked. The referee, Mr Tarbet of Bearsden, took exception to the chant which greeted his arrival. It was not his first meeting with Glencraig.

Ball control

Mikael Palmquist (Sweden) juggled a regulation soccer ball for 14 hr 14 min non-stop with feet, legs and head without the ball ever touching the ground at Göteborg, Sweden on 6 Apr 1986. Allan Abuto Nyanjong (Kenya) also headed a regulation football non-stop for 5 hr at Coronado High School Gym, El Paso, Texas, USA on 25 Apr 1987. Uno Lindström of Boden, Sweden kept a football up while he travelled a distance of 21,097 km *13.110 miles* in 2 hr 55 min 49 sec on 10 Aug 1985.

Gaelic Football

The game developed from inter-parish 'free for all' with no time limit, specific playing area or rules. The earliest reported match was Meath v. Louth, at Slane in 1712. Standardisation came with the formation of the Gaelic Athletic Association in Thurles, Ireland, on 1 Nov 1884.

All-Ireland Championships

The greatest number of All-Ireland Championships won by one team is 30 by Ciarraidhe (Kerry) between 1903 and 1986. The greatest number of successive wins is four by: Wexford (1915–18); and Kerry, twice (1929–32, 1978–81). The most finals contested is eleven, including eight wins by the Kerry players Pat Spillane, Michael Sheehy, Paudie O'Shea, Ger Power and Denis Moran, 1975–86.

The highest team score in a final was when Dublin, 27 (5 goals, 12 points) beat Armagh, 15 (3 goals, 6 points) on 25 Sept 1977. The highest combined score was 45 points when Cork (26) beat Galway (19) in 1973. A goal equals three points. The highest individual score in an All-Ireland Final has been 2 goals, 6 points by Jimmy Keaveney (Dublin) v. Armagh in 1977, and by Michael Sheehy (Kerry) v. Dublin in 1979.

Largest crowd

The record crowd is 90,556 for the Down v. Offaly Final at Croke Park, Dublin, in 1961.

Gaelic Football stronghold ● Ambrose O'Donovan collects the All-Ireland trophy when Kerry won in 1984. (All-Sport)

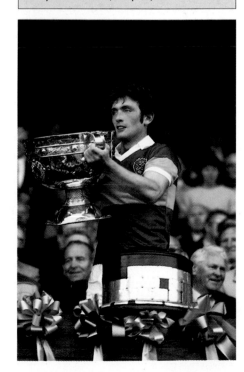

Gambling

Gambling

World's biggest win
The world's biggest individual gambling win is $40 million by Mike Wittkowski in the Illinois State Lottery, announced on 3 Sept 1984. From $35 worth of 'Lotto' tickets bought by his family, the winning six numbers bring him $2 million annually for 20 years.

Largest casino
The largest casino in the world is the Burswood Island Casino, Perth, Western Australia, opened on 30 Dec 1985. In an area of 7500 sq m *80,729 sq ft* it has 200 video games and 142 gaming tables.

BINGO
Bingo is a lottery game which, as keno, was developed in the 1880s from lotto, whose origin is thought to be the 17th-century Italian game *tumbule*. It has long been known in the British Army (called Housey-Housey) and the Royal Navy (called Tombola). The winner was the first to complete a random selection of numbers from 1 to 90. The USA version, called Bingo, differs in that the selection is from 1 to 75. There are an estimated six million players in the United Kingdom.

Largest house
The largest 'house' in Bingo sessions was 15,756 at the Canadian National Exhibition, Toronto on 19 Aug 1983. Staged by the Variety Club of Ontario Tent #28, there was total prize money of $C250,000 with a record one-game payout of $C100,000.

Earliest and latest Full House
A 'Full House' call occurred on the 15th number by: Norman A. Wilson at Guide Post Working Men's Club, Bedlington, Northumberland on 22 June 1978; Anne Wintle of Brynrethin, Mid-Glamorgan, on a coach trip to Bath on 17 Aug 1982; and Shirley Lord at Kahibah Bowling Club, New South Wales, Australia on 24 Oct 1983. 'House' was not called until the 86th number at the Hillsborough Working Men's Club, Sheffield, South Yorkshire on 11 Jan 1982. There were 32 winners.

ELECTIONS
The highest ever individual bet was £90,000 to win £20,000 for the Conservative party to return the most MPs in the 1983 General Election, by an unnamed man. A bet of £5000 at 200-1 was placed by Frank Egerton in April 1975 that his Centre Party would win the next (1979) General Election. It didn't.

FOOTBALL POOLS
Two unnamed punters won *c.* £1.5 million each in November 1972 on the state-run Italian pools. The winning dividend paid out by Littlewoods Pools in their first week in February 1923 was £2 12s 0d (£2.60). In 1985–6 the three British Pools companies which comprise the Pool Promoters Association (Littlewoods, Vernons and Zetters) had a total record turnover of £550,434,000 of which Littlewoods contributed over 70 per cent.

Biggest win
The record payout from the British Pools—which is also the biggest ever prize paid in any British competition—is £1,032,088.40 paid by Littlewoods Pools to a housewife from Bexley, south London from a £1.20 stake on 25 Apr 1987.

The record double payout is £1,773,775 by Littlewoods on 26 Nov 1986 to Bill Anderson of Alexandria, Glasgow (£879,147) and Eric Coleman of Tonbridge, Kent (£894,628). On 27 Mar 1985, Littlewoods paid a record treble—the first time three people each won over £½ million each. They were: Patricia Samways, of Dorchester, Dorset, with £574,847.55; Kevin Adams and seven friends, of Sunderland, Tyne & Wear, with £513,805.23; and George Pinnock, of Colchester, Essex, who received £512,138.19—a record total of £1,600,790.97. Littlewoods' record total payout in one week is £2,758,088 on 18 Mar 1987.

The odds for selecting 8 draws (if there are only 8 draws) from 55 matches for an all-correct line are 1,217,566.350 to 1 against. (In practice, the approximate odds of winning a dividend of any size on Littlewoods Pools are 80 to 1.)

HORSE RACING

Highest ever odds
The highest secured odds were 1,670,759 to 1 by George Rhodes of Aldershot, Hampshire. For a 5p bet, with a 10% bonus for the ITV Seven, less tax, he was paid £86,056.42 by the William Hill Organisation on 30 Sept 1984. Edward Hodson of Wolverhampton landed a 3,956,748 to 1 bet for a 55p stake on 11 Feb 1984, but his bookmaker had a £3000 payout limit. The world record odds on a 'double' are 31,793 to 1 paid by the New Zealand Totalisator Agency Board on a five-shilling tote ticket on *Red Emperor* and *Maida Dillon* at Addington, Christchurch, in 1951.

Greatest payout
Anthony A. Speelman and Nicholas John Cowan (both Great Britain) won $1,627,084.40, after federal income tax of $406,768.00 was withheld, on a $64 nine-horse accumulator at Santa Anita racecourse, California, USA on 19 April 1987. Their first seven selections won and the payout was for a jackpot, accumulated over 24 days. The largest payout by a British bookmaker has been £185,640 by Corals, paid to Ernie Platt for a £10 Ante-Post Accumulator (tax paid) placed on 14 Dec 1984 and collected on 4 May 1985.

Biggest tote win
The best recorded tote win was one of £341 2s 6d to 2s (£341.12½ to 10p) representing odds of 3410¼ to 1, by Catharine Unsworth of Blundellsands, Liverpool at Haydock Park on a race won by *Coole* on 30 Nov 1929. The highest odds in Irish tote history were £289.64 for a 10p unit on *Gene's Rogue* at Limerick on 28 Dec 1981.

Largest bookmaker
The world's largest bookmaker is Ladbrokes with a turnover from gambling in 1986 of £940 million. The largest chain of betting shops is that of Ladbrokes with 1660 shops in the United Kingdom at the end of 1986, as well as 820 in Belgium.

Topmost tipster
The only recorded instance of a racing correspondent forecasting ten out of ten winners on a race card was at Delaware Park, Wilmington, Delaware, USA on 28 July 1974 by Charles Lamb of the *Baltimore News American*.

SLOT MACHINES
The biggest beating handed to a 'one-armed bandit' was $2,478,716.15 by Rocco Dinubilo from Fresno, California at Harrah's Tahoe Casino, Nevada, USA on 31 Dec 1983.

Gliding

Isadore William Deiches has researched evidence of the use of gliders in ancient Egypt *c.* 2500–1500 BC. Emanuel Swedenborg (1688–1772)

GLIDING—WORLD RECORDS
(Single-seaters)

BRITISH RECORDS
(Single-seaters)

STRAIGHT DISTANCE	1460,8 km *907.7 miles*	Hans-Werner Grosse (W. Germany) in an ASW-12 on 25 Apr 1972 from Lübeck to Biarritz	949,7 km *589.9 miles*	Karla Karel in an LS-3 over Australia on 20 Jan 1980
DECLARED GOAL DISTANCE	1254,26 km *779.4 miles*	Bruce Drake, David Speight, S. H. 'Dick' Georgeson (all NZ) all in Nimbus 2s, Te Anau to Te Araroa, 14 Jan 1978	859,20 km *534 miles*	M. T. Alan Sands in a Nimbus 3, Ridge Soaring to Chilhowee, USA, 23 Apr 1986
GOAL AND RETURN	1646,68 km *1023.2 miles*	Tom Knauff (USA) in a Nimbus 3 from Williamsport, Pennsylvania to Knoxville, Tennessee on 25 April 1983	1127,68 km *700.72 miles*	M. T. Alan Sands in a Nimbus 3, Lock Haven, Pa. to Bluefield, Va., USA on 7 May 1985
ABSOLUTE ALTITUDE	14 938 m *49,009 ft*	Robert R. Harris (USA) in a Grob G102 over California on 17 Feb 1986	11 500 m *37,729 ft*	H. C. N. Goodhart in a Schweizer 1-23 over California, USA on 12 May 1955
HEIGHT GAIN	12 894 m *42,303 ft*	Paul Bikle in a Schweizer SGS1-23E over Mojave, California on 25 Feb 1961	10 065 m *33,022 ft*	D. Benton in a Nimbus 2 on 18 Apr 1980

SPEED OVER TRIANGULAR COURSE				
100 km	195,30 km/h *121.35 mph*	Ingo Renner (Australia) in a Nimbus 3 on 14 Dec 1982	143,3 km/h *88.99 mph*	E. Paul Hodge in a Standard Cirrus over Rhodesia on 30 Oct 1976
300 km	169,49 km/h *105.32 mph*	Jean-Paul Castel (France) in a Nimbus 3 over South Africa on 15 Nov 1986	146,8 km/h *91.2 mph*	Edward Pearson in a Nimbus 2 over S.W. Africa on 30 Nov 1976
500 km	164,11 km/h *101.97 mph*	Jean-Paul Castel (France) in an Nimbus 3 over South Africa on 10 Dec 1986	141,3 km/h *87.8 mph*	Bradley James Grant Pearson in an ASW-20 over South Africa on 28 Dec 1982
750 km	158,40 km/h *98.43 mph*	Hans-Werner Grosse (W. Germany) in an ASW-22 over Australia on 8 Jan 1985	109,8 km/h *68.2 mph*	Michael R. Carlton in a Kestrel 19 over South Africa on 5 Jan 1975
1000 km	145,32 km/h *90.29 mph*	Hans-Werner Grosse (W. Germany) in an ASW-17 over Australia on 3 Jan 1979		
1250 km	133,24 km/h *82.79 mph*	Hans-Werner Grosse (W. Germany) in an ASW-17 over Australia on 9 Dec 1980	109,01 km/h *67.73 mph*	Robert L. Robertson in a Ventus A in the USA on 2 May 1986

of Sweden made sketches of gliders *c.* 1714. The earliest man-carrying glider was designed by Sir George Cayley (1773–1857) and carried his coachman (possibly John Appleby) about 500 yd *457 m* across a valley in Brompton Dale, North Yorkshire in the summer of 1853.

Most titles *World*

The most World Individual Championships (inst. 1948) won is four by Ingo Renner (Australia) in 1976 (Standard class), 1983, 1985 and 1987 (Open).

British

The British National Championship (inst. 1939) has been won six times by Ralph Jones (b. 29 Mar 1936). The first woman to win this title was Anne Burns (b. 23 Nov 1915) of Farnham, Surrey on 30 May 1966.

Altitude records *Women*

The women's single-seater world record for absolute altitude is 12 637 m *41,449 ft* by Sabrina Jackintell (USA) in an Astir GS on 14 Feb 1979. The British single-seater record is 10 550 m *34,612 ft* by Anne Burns in a Skylark 3B over South Africa on 13 Jan 1961, when she set a women's world record for height gain of 9119 m *29,918 ft.*

HANG GLIDING

In the eleventh century the monk, Eilmer, is reported to have flown from the 60 ft *18,3 m* tower of Malmesbury Abbey, Wiltshire. The earliest modern pioneer was Otto Lilienthal (1848–96) (Germany) with about 2500 flights in gliders of his own construction between 1891

——— WORLD RECORDS ———

As officially recognised by the *Fédération Aéronautique Internationale.*

MEN

Greatest distance: (Flexwing) 321,47 km *199.76 miles* Randy Haney (Canada), Golden, Canada to Trego, USA, 2 June 1986; (Rigid Wing) 161,904 km *100.607 miles* Larry Tudor (USA), Owens Valley, California, USA, 12 July 1985.
Height gain: (Flexwing) 4343,4 m *14,250 ft* Larry Tudor (USA) at Owens Valley, 4 Aug 1985; (Rigid Wing) 3820 m *12,532 ft* Rainer Scholl (West Germany) at Owens Valley, 5 Aug 1985.
Declared goal distance: 272,19 km *169.13 miles* Geoffrey R. Loyns (GB) at Owens Valley, 11 June 1986.
Out and return distance: 172,6 km *107.25 miles* Klaus Kohmstedt (West Germany), 15 July 1985.
Triangular course distance: (Flexwing) 80,83 km *50.22 miles* Denis Cummings (Australia), Parks, NSW, 29 Dec 1985.

WOMEN

Greatest distance: (Flexwing) 233,9 km *145.34 miles* Judy Leden (GB), Owens Valley, 13 July 1983.
Height gain: (Flexwing) 3291,84 km *2045.51 miles* Page Pfieffer (USA), Owens Valley, 12 July 1979.
Out and return distance: 118,09 km *73.38 miles* Valerie Wallington (Australia), Australia, 4 Jan 1985.
Declared goal distance: 124,52 km *77.37 miles* Judy Lori (USA), Owens Valley, 15 July 1983.

British records

The British record for distance is held by John Pendry, 300,62 km *186.80 miles*, flying an Airwave Magic 3 from Horseshoe Meadows, Owens Valley, California to Summit Mountain, Nevada, USA on 13 July 1983. The best in Britain is 217,07 km *134.88 miles* by Patrick Laverty, Cemmaes Mountain, Wales on 31 Aug 1986. In 1987 Pendry became the first hang-glider pilot to receive the Royal Aero Club's gold medal.

The British height gain record is 3230 m *10,600 ft* by John Stirk at Wether Fell, North Yorkshire on 6 July 1984.

and 1896. In the 1950s Professor Francis Rogallo of the National Space Agency, USA, developed a flexible 'wing' from his space capsule re-entry researches.

World Championships

The World Team Championships have been won most often by Great Britain (1981 and 1985).

Greatest descent

John Bird piloted a hang glider from a height of 39,000 ft *11 887.2 m* when he was released from a hot-air balloon, to the ground, landing in Edmonton, Alberta, Canada on 29 Aug 1982. He touched down 50 miles *80,4 km* from his point of departure.

Golf

Although a stained glass window in Gloucester Cathedral, dating from 1350, portrays a golfer-like figure, the earliest mention of golf occurs in a prohibiting law passed by the Scottish Parliament in March 1457 under which 'goff be utterly cryit doune and not usit'. The Romans had a cognate game called *paganica* which may have been carried to Britain before AD 400. The Chinese Nationalist Golf Association claim the game is of Chinese origin (*Ch'ui Wan*—the ball hitting game) in the 3rd or 2nd century BC. There were official ordinances prohibiting a ball game with clubs in Belgium and Holland from 1360. Gutta percha balls succeeded feather balls in 1848 and by 1902 were in turn succeeded by rubber-cored balls, invented in 1899 by Coburn Haskell (USA). Steel shafts were authorised in the USA in 1925 and in Britain in 1929.

Oldest club

The oldest club of which there is written evidence is the Gentlemen Golfers (now the Honourable Company of Edinburgh Golfers) formed in March 1744—ten years prior to the institution of the Royal and Ancient Club of St Andrews, Fife. However, the Royal Burgess Golfing Society of Edinburgh claims to have been founded in 1735.

Highest course

The highest golf course in the world is the Tuctu Golf Club in Morococha, Peru, which is 4369 m *14,335 ft* above sea level at its lowest point. Golf has, however, been played in Tibet at an altitude of over 4875 m *16,000 ft.*

The highest golf course in Great Britain is one of nine holes at Leadhills, Strathclyde, 1500 ft *457 m* above sea level.

The highest recorded golf shot played on Earth was at 6194 m *20,320 ft* from the summit of Mt McKinley, Alaska, USA by Timothy J. Ayers (USA) on 23 May 1984.

Longest hole

The longest hole in the world is the 7th hole (par-7) of the Sano Course, Satsuki GC, Japan, which measures 831 m *909 yd.* The longest hole on a championship course in Great Britain is the sixth at Troon, Strathclyde, which stretches 577 yd *528 m.*

Largest green

Probably the largest green in the world is that of the par-6 695 yd *635 m* fifth hole at International GC, Bolton, Massachusetts, USA, with an area greater than 28,000 ft² *2600 m².*

Biggest bunker

The world's biggest bunker (called a trap in the USA) is Hell's Half Acre on the 585 yd *535 m* seventh hole of the Pine Valley course, Clementon, New Jersey, USA, built in 1912 and generally regarded as the world's most trying course.

Longest course

The world's longest course is the par-77 8325 yd *7612 m* International GC (*see also above*), from the 'Tiger' tees, remodelled in 1969 by Robert Trent Jones.

Floyd Satterlee Rood used the United States as a course, when he played from the Pacific surf to the Atlantic surf from 14 Sept 1963 to 3 Oct 1964 in 114,737 strokes. He lost 3511 balls on the 3397.7 mile *5468 km* trail.

Longest drives

In officially regulated long driving contests over level ground the greatest distance recorded is 392 yd *358 m* by William Thomas 'Tommie' Campbell (b. 24 July 1927) (Foxrock Golf Club) at Dun Laoghaire, Co. Dublin, in July 1964.

On an airport runway Liam Higgins (Ireland) drove a Spalding Top Flite ball 579,8 m *634.1 yd* at Baldonnel military airport, Dublin, Ireland on 25 Sept 1984. The greatest recorded drive on an ordinary course is one of 515 yd *471 m* by Michael Hoke Austin (b. 17 Feb 1910) of Los Angeles, California, USA, in the US National Seniors Open Championship at Las Vegas, Nevada, on 25 Sept 1974. Austin, 6 ft 2 in *1,88 m* tall and weighing 210 lb *92 kg* drove the ball to within a yard of the green on the par-4 450 yd *412 m* fifth hole of the Winterwood Course and it rolled 65 yd *59 m* past the flagstick. He was aided by an estimated 35 mph *56 km/h* tailwind.

A drive of 2640 yd (1½ miles) *2414 m* across ice was achieved by an Australian meteorologist named Nils Lied at Mawson Base, Antarctica, in 1962. Arthur Lynskey claimed a drive of 200 yd *182 m* horizontal and 2 miles *3200 m* vertical off Pikes Peak, Colorado (14,110 ft *4300 m*) on 28 June 1968. On the Moon the energy expended on a mundane 300 yd *274 m* drive would achieve, craters permitting, a distance of 1 mile *1,6 km*.

Longest putt

The longest recorded holed putt in a major tournament was one of 86 ft *26 m* on the vast 13th green at the Augusta National, Georgia by Cary Middlecoff (b. 6 Jan 1921) (USA) in the 1955 Masters' Tournament. Robert Tyre 'Bobby' Jones, Jr (1902–71) was reputed to have holed a putt in excess of 100 ft *30 m* at the fifth green in the first round of the 1927 Open at St Andrews. Bob Cook (USA) sank a putt measured at 140 ft 2¾ in *42,74 m* on the 18th at St Andrew's in the International Fourball Pro Am Tournament on 1 Oct 1976.

SCORES

Lowest 9 holes

Nine holes in 25 (4, 3, 3, 2, 3, 3, 1, 4, 2) was recorded by A. J. 'Bill' Burke in a round in 57 (32 + 25) on the 6389 yd *5842 m* par-71 Normandie course at St Louis, Missouri, USA on 20 May 1970. The tournament record is 27 by: Mike Souchak (USA) (b. 10 May 1927) for the second nine (par-35), first round of the 1955 Texas Open (*see 72 holes*); Andy North (USA) (b. 9 Mar 1950), second nine (par-34), first round, 1975 BC Open at En-Joie GC, Endicott, NY; José Maria Canizares (Spain) (b. 18 Feb 1947), first nine, third round, in the 1978 Swiss Open on the 6811 yd *6228 m* Crans-Sur course; and Robert Lee (GB) (b. 12 Oct 1961), first nine, first round, in the Monte Carlo Open on the 5714 m *6249 yd* Mont Agel course on 28 June 1985.

Lowest 18 holes *Men*

At least four players have played a long course (over 6000 m *6561 yd*) in a score of 58, most recently Monte Carlo Money (USA) (b. 3 Dec 1954), the par-72, 6607 yd *6041 m* Las Vegas Municipal GC, Nevada, USA on 11 Mar 1981. Alfred Edward Smith (1903–85) achieved an 18-hole score of 55 (15 under bogey 70) on his home course on 1 Jan 1936. The course measured 4248 yd *3884 m*. The detail was 4, 2, 3, 4, 2, 4, 3, 4, 3 = 29 out, and 2, 3, 3, 3, 3, 2, 5, 4, 1 = 26 in.

The United States PGA tournament record for 18 holes is 59 (30 + 29) by Al Geiberger (b. 1 Sept 1937) in the second round of the Danny Thomas Classic, on the 72-par 7249 yd *6628 m* Colonial GC course, Memphis, Tennessee on 10 June 1977. Other golfers to have recorded 59 over 18 holes in major non-PGA tournaments include: Samuel Jackson Snead (b. 27 May 1912) in the third round of the Sam Snead Festival at White Sulphur Springs, West Virginia, USA on 16 May 1959; Gary Player (South Africa) (b. 1 Nov 1935) in the second round of the Brazilian Open in Rio de Janeiro on 29 Nov 1974; David Jagger (GB) (b. 9 June 1949) in a Pro-Am tournament prior to the 1973 Nigerian Open at Ikoyi Golf Club, Lagos; and Miguel Martin (Spain) in the Argentine Southern Championship at Mar de Plata on 27 Feb 1987.

Women

The lowest recorded score on an 18-hole course (over 6000 yd *5486 m*) for a woman is 62 (30 + 32) by Mary 'Mickey' Kathryn Wright (b. 14 Feb 1935) (USA) on the Hogan Park Course (par-71, 6286 yd *5747 m*) at Midland, Texas, USA, in November 1964. Wanda Morgan (b. 22 Mar 1910) recorded a score of 60 (31 + 29) on the Westgate and Birchington Golf Club course, Kent, over 18 holes (5002 yd *4573 m*) on 11 July 1929.

Great Britain

The lowest score recorded in a first-class professional tournament on a course of more than 6000 yd *5486 m* in Great Britain is 61 (29 + 32), by Thomas Bruce Haliburton (1915–75) of Wentworth GC in the Spalding Tournament at Worthing, West Sussex, in June 1952, and 61 (32 + 29) by Peter J. Butler (b. 25 Mar 1932) in the Bowmaker Tournament at Sunningdale, Berkshire, on 4 July 1967.

Lowest 36 holes

The record for 36 holes is 122 (59 + 63) by Sam Snead in the 1959 Sam Snead Festival on 16–17 May 1959. Horton Smith (1908–1963), twice US Masters Champion, scored 121 (63 + 58) on a short course on 21 Dec 1928 (*see 72 holes*). The lowest score by a British golfer has been 124 (61 + 63) by Alexander Walter Barr 'Sandy' Lyle (b. 9 Feb 1958) in the Nigerian Open at the 6024 yd *5508 m* (par-71) Ikoyi Golf Club, Lagos in 1978.

Lowest 72 holes

The lowest recorded score on a first-class course is 255 (29 under par) by Leonard Peter Tupling (b. 6 Apr 1950) (GB) in the Nigerian Open at Ikoyi Golf Club, Lagos in February 1981, made up of 63, 66, 62 and 64 (average 63.75 per round).

The lowest 72 holes in a US professional event is 257 (60, 68, 64, 65) by Mike Souchak in the 1955 Texas Open at San Antonio.

The lowest 72 holes in an open championship in Europe is 262 (67, 66, 66, 63) by Percy Alliss (GB) (1897–1975) in the 1932 Italian Open at San Remo, and by Lu Liang Huan (Taiwan) (b. 10 Dec 1935) in the 1971 French Open at Biarritz. Kelvin D. G. Nagle (b. 21 Dec 1920) of Australia shot 261 in the Hong Kong Open in 1961. The lowest for four rounds in a British first-class tournament is 262 (66, 63, 66 and 67) by Bernard Hunt in the Piccadilly tournament on the par-68 6184 yd *5655 m* Wentworth East course, Virginia Water, Surrey on 4–5 Oct 1966.

Horton Smith scored 245 (63, 58, 61 and 63) for 72 holes on the 4700 yd *4297 m* course (par-64) at Catalina Country Club, California, USA, to win the Catalina Open on 21–23 Dec 1928.

World one-club record

Thad Daber (USA), with a 6-iron, played the 6037 yd *5520 m* Lochmore GC, Cary, N. Carolina,

---

MOST TITLES *World's major championships:*

The Open	Harry Vardon (1870–1937)	6	1896, 1898–9, 1903, 11,14
The Amateur	John Ball (1861–1940)	8	1888, 90, 92, 94, 99, 1907, 10, 1912
US Open	Willie Anderson (1880–1910)	4	1901, 03–5
	Robert Tyre Jones, Jr. (1902–71)	4	1923, 26, 29–30
	William Ben Hogan (b. 13 Aug 1912)	4	1948, 50–1, 53
	Jack William Nicklaus (b. 21 Jan 1940)	4	1962, 67, 72, 80
US Amateur	Robert Tyre Jones, Jr. (1902–71)	5	1924–25, 27–8, 30
PGA Championship (USA)	Walter Charles Hagen (1892–1969)	5	1921, 24–7
	Jack William Nicklaus (b. 21 Jan 1940)	5	1963, 71, 73, 75, 80
Masters' Championship (USA)	Jack William Nicklaus (b. 21 Jan 1940)	6	1963, 65–6, 72, 75, 86
US Women's Open	Elizabeth 'Betsy' Earle-Rawls (b. 4 May 1928)	4	1951, 53, 57, 60
	'Mickey' Wright (b. 14 Feb 1935)	4	1958–59, 61, 64
US Women's Amateur	Glenna C. Vare (*née* Collett) (b. 20 June 1903)	6	1922, 25, 28–30, 35
British Women's	Charlotte Cecilia Pitcairn Leitch (1891–1977)	4	1914, 20–1, 26
	Joyce Wethered (b. 17 Nov 1901) (Now Lady Heathcoat-Amory)	4	1922, 24–5, 29

Note: Nicklaus is the only golfer to have won five different major titles (The Open, US Open, Masters, PGA and US Amateur titles) twice and a record 20 all told (1959–86). His remarkable record in The US Open is four firsts, eight seconds and two thirds. In 1930 Bobby Jones achieved a unique 'Grand Slam' of the US and British Open and Amateur titles.

Highest earnings ● Greg Norman (Australia) known as "The Great White Shark", who in 1986 earned over $1 million in prize money including $653,296 on the US P.G.A. circuit. In all four major 1986 tournaments, he led after three rounds, but won only the British Open.

Highest earnings ● Pat Bradley (US) who is the first woman in golf history to earn prize money of more than $2 million in a career.
Curtis Cup ● The Great Britain and Ireland winning team in 1986 included Mary McKenna (back row, far left) who was in the team for a record ninth time.

USA in 73 on 10 Nov 1985 to win the world one-club championship.

Highest score

It is recorded that Chevalier von Cittern went round 18 holes in 316, averaging 17.55 per hole, at Biarritz, France in 1888. Steven Ward took 222 strokes for the 6212 yd *5680 m* Pecos course, Reeves County, Texas, USA, on 18 June 1976—but he was aged only 3 years 286 days.

Most shots for one hole

A woman player in the qualifying round of the Shawnee Invitational for Ladies at Shawnee-on-Delaware, Pennsylvania, USA, *c.* 1912, took 166 strokes for the short 130 yd *118 m* 16th hole. Her tee shot went into the Binniekill River and the ball floated. She put out in a boat with her exemplary but statistically-minded husband at the oars. She eventually beached the ball 1½ miles *2,4 km* downstream but was not yet out of the wood. She had to play through one on the home run. In a competition at Peacehaven, Sussex, England in 1890, A. J. Lewis had 156 putts on one green without holing out.

The highest score for a single hole in the British Open is 21 by a player in the inaugural meeting at Prestwick in 1860. Double figures have been recorded on the card of the winner only once, when Willie Fernie (1851–1924) scored a ten at Musselburgh, Lothian, in 1883. Ray Ainsley of Ojai, California, took 19 strokes for the par-4 16th hole during the second round of the US Open at Cherry Hills Country Club, Denver, Colorado, on 10 June 1938. Most of the strokes were used in trying to extricate the ball from a brook. Hans Merell of Mogadore, Ohio, took 19 strokes on the par-3 16th (222 yd *203 m*) during the third round of the Bing Crosby National Tournament at Cypress Point Club, Del Monte, California, USA, on 17 Jan 1959.

Fastest rounds *Individual*

With such variations in lengths of courses, speed records, even for rounds under par, are of little comparative value. The fastest round played when the golf ball comes to rest before each new stroke is 28 min 9 sec by Gary Shane Wright (b. 27 Nov 1946) at Tewantin-Noosa Golf Club, Queensland (18 holes, 6039 yd *5522 m*) on 9 Dec 1980. The British record is 30 min 28 sec by Sydney M. Webb at West Derby GC, Liverpool (6083 yd *5562 m*) on 30 Aug 1986.

Team

Seventy-seven players completed the 18-hole 6502 yd *5945 m* Kern City course, California, USA in 10 min 30 sec on 24 Aug 1984 using only one ball. They scored 80!

Slowest rounds

The slowest stroke-play tournament round was one of 6 hr 45 min taken by South Africa in the first round of the 1972 World Cup at the Royal Melbourne GC, Australia. This was a four-ball medal round; everything holed out.

Most holes in 24 hours/1 week

The greatest number of rounds played on foot in 24 hr is 22 rounds and five holes (401 holes) by Ian Colston, 35, at Bendigo GC, Victoria (par-73, 6061 yd *5542 m*) on 27–28 Nov 1971. The British record is 360 holes by Antony J. Clark at Childwall GC, Liverpool on 18 July 1983. Using golf carts for transport Mark Rick Matthews played 724 holes in 24 hr at Rockwood Municipal GC, Fort Worth, Texas (6048 yd *5530 m*) on 27–28 June 1986. Terry Zachary played 391 holes in 12 hours on the 6706 yd *6132 m* course at Connaught Golf Club, Alberta, Canada on 16 June 1986. The most holes played on foot in a week (168 hr) is 1128 by Steve Hylton at the Mason Rudolph Golf Club (6060 yd *5541m*), Clarkesville, Tennessee, USA from 25–31 Aug 1980.

Throwing the golf ball

The lowest recorded score for throwing a golf ball round 18 holes (over 6000 yd *5500 m*) is 82 by Joe Flynn (USA), 21, at the 6228 yd *5694 m* Port Royal course, Bermuda, on 27 Mar 1975.

CHAMPIONSHIP RECORDS

The Open

The Open Championship was inaugurated in 1860 at Prestwick, Strathclyde, Scotland. The lowest score for 9 holes is 28 by Denis Durnian (b. 30 June 1950), at Royal Birkdale, Southport, Lancashire in the second round on 15 July 1983.

The lowest round in The Open is 63 by: Mark Stephen Hayes (b. 12 July 1949) (USA) at Turnberry, Strathclyde, on 7 July 1977; Isao Aoki (b. 31 Aug 1942) (Japan) at Muirfield, East Lothian, on 19 July 1980; and Gregory John Norman (b. 10 Feb 1955) (Australia) at Turnberry on 18 July 1986. Thomas Henry Cotton (b. 26 Jan 1907) at Royal St George's, Sandwich, Kent completed the first 36 holes in 132 (67 + 65) on 27 June 1934. The lowest 72-hole aggregate is 268 (68, 70, 65, 65) by Thomas Sturges Watson (b. 4 Sept 1949) (USA) at Turnberry, in July 1977.

US Open

The United States Open Championship was inaugurated in 1895. The lowest 72-hole aggregate is 272 (63, 71, 70, 68) by Jack Nicklaus (b. 21 Jan 1940) on the lower course (7015 yd *6414 m*) at Baltusrol Country Club, Springfield, New Jersey, from 12–15 June 1980. The lowest score for 18 holes is 63 by: Johnny Miller (b. 29 Apr 1947) on the 6921 yd *6328 m* par-71 Oakmont Country Club course, Pennsylvania on 17 June 1973; Jack Nicklaus (*see above*); and Tom Weiskopf (USA) (b. 9 Nov 1942), both on 12 June 1980.

US Masters

The lowest score in the US Masters (instituted on the par-72 6980 yd *6382 m* Augusta National Golf Course, Georgia, in 1934) is 271 by Jack Nicklaus in 1965 and Raymond Loran Floyd (b. 4 Sept 1942) in 1976. The lowest round is 63 by Nicholas Raymond Leige Price (b. 28 Jan 1957) (Zimbabwe) in 1986.

World Cup (formerly Canada Cup)

The World Cup (instituted as the Canada Cup in 1953) has been won most often by the USA with 16 victories between 1955 and 1983. The only men to have been on six winning teams have been Arnold Palmer (b. 10 Sept 1929) (1960, 1962–4, 1966–7) and Jack Nicklaus (1963–4, 1966–7, 1971 and 1973). Only Nicklaus has taken the individual title three times (1963–4, 1971). The lowest aggregate score for 144 holes is 544 by Australia, Bruce Devlin (b. 10 Oct 1937) and Anthony David Graham (b. 23 May 1946), at San Isidro, Buenos Aires, Argentina from 12–15 Nov 1970. The lowest individual score has been 269 by Roberto de Vicenzo (Argentina) (b. 14 Apr 1923), also in 1970.

Ryder Cup

The biennial Ryder Cup professional match between the USA and Europe (British Isles or Great Britain prior to 1979) was instituted in 1927. The USA have won 21½ to 4½ to date. William Earl 'Billy' Casper (b. San Diego, California, USA, 24 June 1931) has the record of winning most matches in the Trophy with 20 in 1961–75. Christy O'Connor, Sr (b. 21 Dec 1924) (Ireland) played in ten matches, 1955–73.

Walker Cup

The USA *v.* GB & Ireland series was instituted in 1921 (for the Walker Cup since 1922 and now held biennially). The USA have won 27, GB&I 2 (in 1938 and 1971) and the 1965 match was tied. Joseph Boynton Carr (GB&I) (b. 18 Feb 1922) played in ten contests, 1947–67.

HOLES IN ONE

Longest

The longest straight hole ever holed in one shot was, appropriately, at the tenth (447 yd *408 m*) at Miracle Hills Golf Club, Omaha, Nebraska, USA by Robert Mitera (b. 1944) on 7 Oct 1965. Mitera stood 5 ft 6 in *1,68 m* tall and weighed 165 lb *75 kg* (11 st 11 lb). He was a two handicap player who normally drove 245 yd *224 m*. A 50 mph *80 km/h* gust carried his shot over a 290 yd *265 m* drop-off. The longest 'dog-leg' hole achieved in one is the 480 yd *439 m* fifth at Hope Country Club, Arkansas by L. Bruce on 15 Nov 1962. The women's record is 393 yd *359 m* by Marie Robie on the first hole of the Furnace Brook Golf Club, Wollaston, Mass., USA, on 4 Sept 1949. The longest hole in one performed in the British Isles is the seventh (par-4, 393 yd *359 m*) at West Lancashire GC by Peter Richard Parkinson (b. 26 Aug 1947) on 6 June 1972.

Consecutive

There are at least 16 cases of 'aces' being achieved in two consecutive holes, of which the greatest was Norman L. Manley's unique 'double albatross' on the par-4 330 yd *301 m* seventh and par-4 290 yd *265 m* eighth holes on the Del Valle Country Club course, Saugus, California, on 2 Sept 1964. The first woman to record consecutive 'aces' was Sue Prell, on the 13th and 14th holes at Chatswood Golf Club, Sydney, Australia on 29 May 1977.

The closest to achieving three consecutive holes in one were the late Dr Joseph Boydstone on the 3rd, 4th and 9th at Bakersfield GC, California, USA, on 10 Oct 1962 and the Rev Harold Snider (b. 4 July 1900) who aced the 8th, 13th and 14th holes of the par-3 Ironwood course, Arizona, USA on 9 June 1976.

Youngest and oldest

The youngest golfer recorded to have shot a hole-in-one was Coby Orr (5 years) of Littleton, Colorado on the 103 yd *94 m* fifth at the Riverside Golf Course, San Antonio, Texas in 1975. The oldest golfers to have performed this feat are: (men) 99 yr 244 days Otto Bucher (Switzerland) (b. 12 May 1885) on the 130 yd *100 m* 12th at La Manga GC, Spain on 13 Jan 1985; (women) 95 yr 257 days Erna Ross (b. 9 Sept 1890) on the 112 yd *102 m* 17th at The Everglades Club, Palm Beach, Florida, USA on 25 May 1986. The British record was set by Samuel Richard Walker (b. 6 Jan 1892) at the 156 yd *143 m* 8th at West Hove GC, East Sussex at the age of 92 yr 169 days on 23 June 1984.

The oldest player to score his age is C. Arthur Thompson (1869–1975) of Victoria, British Columbia, Canada, who scored 103 on the Uplands course of 6215 yd *5682 m* aged 103 in 1973.

Curtis Cup

The biennial ladies' Curtis Cup match between the USA and Great Britain and Ireland was first held in 1932. The USA have won 19, GB&I three (1952, 1956 and 1986) and two matches have been tied. Mary McKenna (GB&I) (b. 29 Apr 1949) played in a record ninth match in 1986, when for the first time she was on the winning team.

Richest prizes

The greatest first place prize money was $500,000 (total purse $1,100,000) won by Johnny Miller in 1982 and Raymond Floyd in 1983, at Sun City, Bophuthatswana, South Africa. Both won in play-offs, from Severiano Ballesteros and Craig Stadler respectively.

Highest earnings *US PGA and LPGA circuits*

The all-time professional money-winner is Jack Nicklaus, with $4,957,173 to May 1987. The record for a year was set by Greg Norman in 1986 with $653,296 on the US PGA circuit and over $1 million in total worldwide prize money. The record career earnings for a woman is by Pat Bradley (b. 24 Mar 1951) with $2,414,694 to 2 June 1987, including a season's record $492,021 in 1986.

European circuit

Severiano Ballesteros (Spain) (b. 9 Apr 1957) won a European record £242,208.70 in European Order of Merit tournaments in 1986.

Most tournament wins

John Byron Nelson (b. 4 Feb 1912) (USA) won a record 18 tournaments (plus one unofficial) including a record 11 consecutively from 8 Mar to 4 Aug 1945. Sam Snead won 84 official US PGA tour events 1936–65, and has been credited with a total 134 tournament victories since 1934. The Ladies' PGA record is 88 by Kathy Whitworth (b. 27 Sept 1939) from 1962 to 1985.

The Open lowest round ● Isao Aoki of Japan, one of only four golfers in the history of The Open to achieve a round of 63. (Photo: David Cannon/All-Sport)

Biggest winning margin
The greatest margin of victory in a major tournament is 21 strokes by Jerry Pate (b. 16 Sept 1953) (USA), who won the Colombian Open with 262 from 10–13 Dec 1981. Cecilia Leitch won the Canadian Ladies' Open Championship in 1921 by the biggest margin for a major title, 17 up and 15 to play.

Youngest and oldest champions
The youngest winner of The Open was Tom Morris, Jr (1851–75) at Prestwick, Strathclyde in 1868 aged 17 yr 249 days. The oldest Open Champion was 'Old Tom' Morris (1821–1908), aged 46 yr 99 days when he won at Prestwick in 1867. In recent times the 1967 champion, Roberto de Vicenzo, was aged 44 yr 93 days. The oldest US Open Champion was Raymond Floyd (b. 4 Sept 1942) at 43 yr 284 days on 15 June 1986. Isabella 'Belle' Robertson (b. 11 Apr 1936) won the 1986 Scottish Women's Championship aged 50 yr 43 days.

Most club championships
Marjorie Edey (1913–1981) was ladies champion at Charleswood Golf Club, Winnipeg, Manitoba, Canada 36 times between 1937 and 1980. The men's record is 34 by Bernard Charles Cusack (b. 24 Jan 1920), including 33 consecutively, at the Narembeen GC, Western Australia, between 1943 and 1982. The British record is 32 by Helen Gray at Todmorden GC, Lancashire between 1951 and 1986.

Largest tournament
The Volkswagen Grand Prix Open Amateur Championship in the United Kingdom attracted a record 321,779 (206,820 men and 114,958 women) competitors in 1984.

Greyhound Racing

The first greyhound meeting was staged at Hendon, north London with a railed hare operated by a windlass, in September 1876. Modern greyhound racing originated with the perfecting of the mechanical hare by Owen Patrick Smith at Emeryville, California, USA, in 1919. St Petersburg Kennel Club, located in St Petersburg, Florida, USA, which opened on 3 Jan 1925, is the oldest greyhound track in the world still in operation on its original site. The earliest greyhound race behind a mechanical hare in the British Isles was at Belle Vue, Manchester, opened on 24 July 1926.

Derby
The only two greyhounds to have won the English Greyhound Derby twice (instituted 1927, now over 500 m *546 yd*) are *Mick the Miller* (1926–39) on 25 July 1929, when owned by Albert H. Williams, and on 28 June 1930, when owned by Mrs Arundel H. Kempton, and *Patricia's Hope* on 24 June 1972, when owned by Gordon and Basil Marks and Brian Stanley, and 23 June 1973, when owned by G. & B. Marks and J. O'Connor. The highest prize was £35,000 to *Indian Joe* for the Derby on 28 June 1980. The only greyhounds to win the English, Scottish and Welsh Derby 'triple' are *Trev's Perfection*, owned by Fred Trevillion,

> **Most consecutive wins** ● *Ballyregan Bob*, owned by Cliff Kevern and trained by George Curtis, won 32 successive races from 1985 to 8 Dec 1986, including 16 track record times. His wins were by an average of more than nine lengths. (Photo: Alf Baker)

in 1947, *Mile Bush Pride*, owned by Noel W. Purvis, in 1959, and *Patricia's Hope* in 1972. The only two greyhounds to have twice won the American Derby, at Taunton, Mass., are *Real Huntsman* in 1950–51 and *Dutch Bahama* in 1984–5.

Grand National
The only greyhound to have won the Grand National (inst. 1927 over 525 yd *480 m*, now 500 m *546 yd*, and five flights) three times is *Sherry's Prince* (1967–78) owned by Mrs Joyce Mathews of Sanderstead, Surrey, in 1970–72.

Fastest greyhound
The highest speed at which any greyhound has been timed is 41.72 mph *67,14 km/h* (410 yd *374 m* in 20.1 sec) by *The Shoe* on the then straightaway track at Richmond, NSW, Australia on 25 Apr 1968. It is estimated that he covered the last 100 yd *91,44 m* in 4.5 sec or at 45.45 mph *73,14 km/h*. The highest speed recorded for a greyhound in Great Britain is 39.13 mph *62,97 km/h* by *Beef Cutlet*, when covering a straight course of 500 yd *457 m* in 26.13 sec at Blackpool, Lancashire, on 13 May 1933.

Fastest speeds for four-bend tracks
The fastest automatically timed speed recorded for a full 4-bend race is 38.89 mph *62,59 km/h* at Brighton, East Sussex by *Glen Miner* on 4 May 1982 with a time of a 29.62 sec for 515 m *563 yd*. The fastest over hurdles is 37.64 mph *60,58 km/h* at Brighton by *Wotchit Buster* on 22 Aug 1978.

Most wins
The most career wins is 143 by the American greyhound *JR's Ripper* in 1982–6.

Highest earnings
The career earnings record is held by *My Tipper* with $240,262.67 in the USA, 1984–6 from 133 starts of which he won 61. The richest first prize for a greyhound race is $125,000 won by *Ben G. Speedboat* in the Greyhound Race of Champions at Leabrook, Texas, USA in 1986.

Longest odds
Apollo Prince won at odds of 250–1 at Sandown GRC, Springvale, Victoria, Australia on 14 Nov 1968.

Gymnastics

A primitive form of gymnastics was practised in ancient Greece and Rome during the period of the ancient Olympic Games (776 BC to AD 393) but Johann Friedrich Simon was the first teacher of modern gymnastics at Basedow's School, Dessau, Germany in 1776.

Most titles *World*
The greatest number of individual titles won by a man in the World Championships (including Olympic Games) is ten by Boris Shakhlin (b. 27 Jan 1932) (USSR) between 1954 and 1964. He also had three team wins. The female record is 12 individual wins and five team titles by Larissa Semyonovna Latynina (b. 27 Dec 1934) of the USSR, between 1956 and 1964. Japan has won the men's team title a record ten times between 1960 and 1978, and the USSR the women's team title on 17 occasions (out of 20 titles since 1952).

The most overall individual titles in Modern Rhythmic Gymnastics is three by Maria Gigova (Bulgaria) in 1969, 1971 and 1973 (shared). Bulgaria has a record five team titles, 1969, 1971, 1973, 1983 and 1985.

Olympic
Japan (1960, 1964, 1968, 1972 and 1976) has won the men's team title most often. The USSR has won the women's title eight times (1952–80). The most men's individual gold medals is six by: Boris Shakhlin (USSR), one in 1956, four (two

shared) in 1960 and one in 1964; and Nikolay Andrianov (USSR) (b. 14 Oct 1952), one in 1972, four in 1976 and one in 1980.

Vera Caslavska-Odlozil (b. 3 May 1942) (Czechoslovakia) has won most individual gold medals with seven, three in 1964 and four (one shared) in 1968. Larissa Latynina won six individual gold medals and was in three winning teams from 1956–64, making nine gold medals. She also won five silver and four bronze making 18 in all—an Olympic record. The most medals for a male gymnast is 15 by Nikolay Andrianov (USSR), 7 gold, 5 silver and 3 bronze from 1972–80.

Greatest success at Modern Rhythmic Gymnastics ● Bulgaria has won a record five team titles at this type of gymnastics, characterised by the handling of light portable objects. Lilia Ignatova, who has won both the individual World Cup titles that have been held, in 1983 and 1986, demonstrates her skill with the ribbons. (Photo: Eileen Langsley)

Press-ups champion ● Paul Lynch of Balham, south London holds the one-arm record, and the previous record, 29,753 for push-ups in 24 hours. (Photo: Jon Arno)

EXERCISES
SPEED AND STAMINA

Records are accepted for the most repetitions of the following activities within the given time span.

CHINS (FROM DEAD-HANG POSITION)—**CONSECUTIVE** 170 Lee Chin-yong (b. 15 Aug 1925) at Backyon Gymnasium, Seoul, South Korea on 10 May 1983.

CHINS ONE ARM (FROM A RING)—**CONSECUTIVE** 22 Robert Chisnall (b. 9 Dec 1952) at Queen's University, Kingston, Ontario, Canada on 3 Dec 1982. (Also 18 two-finger chins, 12 one-finger chins.)

PARALLEL BAR DIPS—1 HOUR 1320 Vince Manson at HM Prison, Gartree, Leicestershire on 17 April 1987.

PRESS-UPS (PUSH-UPS)—24 HOURS 32,251 Jeffrey Warwick (USA) at the YMCA, Buffalo, USA on 16 June 1987.

PRESS-UPS (ONE ARM)—5 HOURS 3857 Paul Lynch (GB) at the Guinness World of Records, London on 6 June 1987.

PRESS-UPS (FINGER-TIP)—5 HOURS 5010 John Decker (GB) at Kendal's Department Store, Manchester on 19 June 1987.

PUSH-UPS (ONE FINGER)—CONSECUTIVE 100 Harry Lee Welch, Jr at Durham, N. Carolina, USA on 31 Mar 1985.

HAND-STAND PUSH-UPS—1 HOUR 1985 by Chung Kwun Ying (Hong Kong) at Government City Hall, Hong Kong on 18 May 1986. Against a wall the record is 3300 by Chung Man Wah, aged 4, at the Chung Ize Kung Fu (HK) Association, Hong Kong on 4 Jan 1987.

SIT-UPS—24 HOURS 43,418 Louis Scripa, Jr (USA) at Jack La Lanne's American Health & Fitness Spa, Sacramento, Cal., USA on 6–7 Oct 1984.

LEG RAISES—12 HOURS 21,598 Louis Scripa, Jr in 6 hours at Fairfield, Cal., USA on 8 Dec 1983.

SQUATS—1 HOUR 1509 Tonie Felix (GB) at Ashwell Prison, Leicestershire on 17 May 1987.

JUMPING JACKS—24 HOURS 45,027 Ashrita Furman at Civic Park, San Francisco, Cal., USA on 4 Dec 1986.

PUMMEL HORSE DOUBLE CIRCLES—CONSECUTIVE 75 by Lee Thomas (GB) on BBC television on 12 Dec 1985.

PRESS-UPS IN A YEAR Adam Parsons, a retired Lieutenant Colonel in the US Air Force, achieved a documented 1,293,850 press-ups in Akron, Ohio, USA in the calendar year of 1985.

Aleksandr Ditiatin (USSR) (b. 7 Aug 1957) is the only man to win a medal in all eight categories in the same Games, with 3 gold, 4 silver and 1 bronze at Moscow in 1980.

Highest score *Olympics*
Nadia Comaneci (Romania) (b. 12 Nov 1961) was the first to achieve a perfect score (10.00), and achieved seven in all at the Montreal Olympics in July 1976.

Youngest international and world champion
Pasakevi 'Voula' Kouna (b. 6 Dec 1971) was aged 9 yr 299 days at the start of the Balkan Games at Serres, Greece on 1 Oct 1981, when she represented Greece. Olga Bicherova (USSR) (b. 26 Oct 1966) won the women's world title at 15 yr 33 days on 28 Nov 1981. The youngest male world champion was Dmitriy Belozerchev (USSR) (b. 17 Dec 1966) at 16 years 315 days at Budapest, Hungary on 28 Oct 1983.

Most titles *British*
The British Gymnastic Championship was won ten times by Arthur John Whitford (b. 2 July 1908) in 1928–36 and 1939. He was also in four winning teams. Wray 'Nik' Stuart (b. 20 July 1927) equalled the record of nine successive wins, 1956–64. The women's record is eight by Mary Patricia Hirst (b. 18 Nov 1918) (1947, 1949–50 and 1952–6). The most overall titles in Modern Rhythmic Gymnastics is by Sharon Taylor with five successive, 1977–81.

World Cup
Gymnasts to have won two World Cup (inst. 1975) overall titles are three men, Nikolay Andrianov (USSR), Aleksandr Ditiatin (USSR) and Li Ning (China) (b. 8 Sept 1963), and one woman, Maria Filatova (USSR) (b. 19 July 1961).

Somersaults
Ashrita Furman performed 7400 forward rolls over 12 miles 390 yards *19.67 km* from Boston to Lexington in April 1986. Shigeru Iwasaki (b. 1960)

backwards somersaulted over 50 m *54.68 yd* in 10.8 sec at Tokyo, Japan on 30 Mar 1980.

Static wall 'sit' (or Samson's Chair)
Kevin DeWitt stayed in an unsupported sitting position against a wall for 76 min 12 sec in Kennewick, Washington, USA on 31 July 1986.

Handball

Handball was first played c. 1895 in Germany. It was introduced into the Olympic Games at Berlin in 1936 as an 11-a-side outdoor game, with Germany winning, but when re-introduced in 1972 it was an indoor game with seven-a-side, the standard size of team since 1952.

The International Handball Federation was founded in 1946. The first international match was held at Halle/Saale on 3 Sept 1925 when Austria beat Germany 6–3.

Most championships
Three Olympic titles have been won by the USSR—men 1976, women 1976 and 1980, and by Yugoslavia—men 1972 and 1984, women 1984. The most victories won in world championship (inst. 1938) competition are by Romania with four men's and three women's titles from 1956 to 1974.

The most European Cup titles is twelve in the women's event by Spartak Kiev, USSR between 1970 and 1987. FC Barcelona became the first men's team to win the European Cup three times in succession, 1984–6.

The only club team to win all possible major competitions in one season is V f L Gummers-bach, West Germany, in 1983: national champions and cup-winners, European Champions Cup and Super Cup.

Highest score
The highest score in an international match was recorded when the USSR beat Afghanistan 86–2 in the 'Friendly Army Tournament' at Miskolc, Hungary in August 1981.

Harness Racing

Trotting races were held in Valkenburg, Netherlands in 1554. In England the trotting gait (the simultaneous use of the diagonally opposite legs) was known in the 16th century. The sulky first appeared in 1829. Pacers thrust out their fore and hind legs simultaneously on one side.

Most successful driver
The most successful sulky driver in North American harness racing history has been Herve Filion (b. 1 Feb 1940) of Quebec, Canada, who achieved his 10,000th win on 24 May 1987. His career earnings (1953–87) at that time exceeded $52 million. The most wins in a year is 770 by Mike Lachance in 1986. The greatest earnings in a year is $10,207,372 by William O'Donnell (b. 4 May 1948) when he won 419 races in 1985.

Highest price
The highest price ever paid for a pacer is $19.2 million for *Nihilator* who was syndicated by Wall Street Stable and Almahurst Stud Farm in 1984. The highest price paid for a trotter is $5.25 million for *Mystic Park* by Lana Lobell Farms from Gerald and Irving Wechter of New York and Robert Lester of Florida, announced on 13 July 1982.

Greatest winnings
The greatest winnings for any harness horse is $3,225,653 by the pacer *Nihilator*, who won 35 of 38 races in 1984–5. The greatest amount won by

a trotting horse is $2,753,666 by *Idéal du Gazeau* (France) to July 1983. The single season record is $1,864,286 by *Nihilator* in 1985.

The largest ever purse was $2,161,000 for the Woodrow Wilson two-year-old race over 1 mile at the Meadowlands, New Jersey on 16 Aug 1984. Of this sum a record $1,080,500 went to the winner *Nihilator*, driven by William O'Donnell.

HARNESS RACING MILE RECORDS

TROTTING

World race record	1:53.4	*Prakas* (driver, William O'Donnell) at Du Quoin, Illinois, USA	31 Aug 1985
British record	2:06.2	*Silver Glorie* (driver, M. A. Strutter) at York	5 Aug 1986

PACING

World	1:49.2	*Niatross* (driver, Clint Galbraith) at Lexington, Kentucky, USA	1 Oct 1980
World race record	1:49.6	*Nihilator* (driver, William O'Donnell) at East Rutherford, New Jersey, USA	3 Aug 1985
British record	2:02.1	*Lydia M* (driver, James Pickard) at York	10 July 1982

Hockey

A representation of two players with curved snagging sticks apparently in an orthodox 'bully' position was found in Tomb No 17 at Beni Hasan, Egypt and has been dated to *c.* 2050 BC. There is a British reference to the game in Lincolnshire in 1277. The modern game evolved in south London in the 1870s. An English Hockey Association was founded in 1875, but the current English men's governing body, the Hockey Association, was formed on 18 Jan 1886. The All-England Women's Hockey Association was founded in 1895. The *Fédération Internationale de Hockey* was formed on 7 Jan 1924.

The first organised club was the Blackheath Rugby and Hockey Club founded in 1861. The oldest club with a continuous history is Teddington HC formed in the autumn of 1871. They played Richmond on 24 Oct 1874 and used the first recorded circle *versus* Surbiton at Bushey Park on 9 Dec 1876. The first international match was the Wales *v.* Ireland match at Rhyl on 26 Jan 1895. Ireland won 3–0.

Most Olympic medals

The Indians were Olympic champions from the re-introduction of Olympic hockey in 1928 until 1960, when Pakistan beat them 1–0 at Rome. They had their eighth win in 1980. Of the seven Indians who have won three Olympic team gold medals two have also won a silver medal—Leslie Walter Claudius (b. 25 Mar 1927) in 1948, 1952, 1956 and 1960 (silver) and Udham Singh (b. 4 Aug 1928) in 1952, 1956, 1964 and 1960 (silver). A women's tournament was added in 1980 when Zimbabwe were the winners. The Netherlands won in 1984.

World Cup

The World Cup for men was first held in 1971, and for women in 1974. The most wins are: (men) three by Pakistan, 1971, 1978 and 1982; (women) four by the Netherlands, 1974, 1978, 1983 and 1986.

MEN

Highest international score

The highest score in international hockey was when India defeated the USA 24–1 at Los Angeles, California, USA, in the 1932 Olympic

> **Most successful women's World Cup team**
> ● The Netherlands captained here by Marjolein Bolhuis in 1986, have won four of the six competitions for the women's World Cup at hockey. (Photo: Eileen Langsley)

Games. The greatest number of goals in a home international match was when England defeated France 16–0 at Beckenham on 25 Mar 1922.

Most international appearances

Michael Peter (b. 7 May 1949) represented West Germany over 250 times between 1969 and 1984, indoors and out. The most by a player from the British Isles is 144 by Terry Gregg (b. 23 Nov 1950), 102 for Ireland and 42 for Great Britain, 1970–80. H. David Judge (b. 19 Jan 1936) played a record 124 times for Ireland, 1957–78. The first player to achieve 100 international appearances for England is Norman Hughes (b. 30 Sept 1952) on 21 Sept 1986.

Greatest scoring feats

The greatest number of goals scored in international hockey is 267 by Paul Litjens (Netherlands) (b. 9 Nov 1947) in 177 games. M. C. Marckx (Bowden 2nd XI) scored 19 goals against Brooklands 2nd XI (score 23–0) on 31 Dec 1910. He was selected for England in March 1912 but declined due to business priorities. Between 1923 and 1958, Fred H. Wagner scored 1832 goals for Beeston HC, Nottingham Casuals and the Nottinghamshire county side. David Ashman has scored 1537 goals for one club, Hamble Old Boys, Southampton, from 1958 to 1987.

The fastest goal in an international was 7 sec after the bully-off by John French for England v. West Germany at Nottingham, on 25 Apr 1971.

Greatest goalkeeping

Richard James Allen (b. 4 June 1902) (India) did not concede a goal during the 1928 Olympic tournament and a total of only three in the following two Olympics of 1932 and 1936. In these three Games India scored a total of 102 goals.

Longest game

The longest international game on record was one of 145 min (into the sixth period of extra time), when the Netherlands beat Spain 1–0 in the Olympic tournament at Mexico City on 25 Oct 1968. Club matches of 205 min have twice been recorded: the Hong Kong Football Club beat Prison Sports Dept as the first to score in a 'sudden death' play-off after 2–2 at full time on 11 Mar 1979 and Gore Court beat Hampstead in the first round of the English Club Championships in 1983.

WOMEN

The earliest women's club was East Molesey in Surrey, England formed c. 1887. Two ladies' hockey clubs, Wimbledon and Ealing, each founded one year later, are still in existence. The first national association was the Irish Ladies' Hockey Union founded in 1894. The All England Women's Hockey Association held its first formal meeting in Westminster Town Hall, London, on 23 Nov 1895. The first international match was an England v. Ireland game in Dublin in 1896. Ireland won 2–0.

Most international appearances

Valerie Robinson made a record 144 appearances for England, 1963–84.

Highest scores

The highest score in a women's international match was when England beat France 23–0 at Merton, Greater London, on 3 Feb 1923. In club hockey, Ross Ladies beat Wyeside, at Ross-on-Wye, Herefordshire, 40–0 on 24 Jan 1929, when Edna Mary Blakelock (b. 22 Oct 1904) scored a record 21 goals.

Highest attendance

The highest attendance at a women's hockey match was 65,165 for the match between England and the USA at Wembley, London, on 11 Mar 1978.

Horse Racing

Horsemanship was an important part of the Hittite culture of Anatolia, Turkey dating from 1400 BC. The 33rd ancient Olympic Games of 648 BC in Greece featured horse racing. The earliest races recorded in England were those held in about AD 200 at Netherby, Cumbria, between Arab horses imported by the Romans.

Largest prizes

The highest prize money for a day's racing is $10 million for the Breeders' Cup series of seven races staged at Hollywood Park, Los Angeles on 10 Nov 1984, at Aqueduct, New York, on 2 Nov 1985 and at Santa Anita Park, California, on 1 Nov 1986. Included was a record $3 million for the Breeders' Cup Classic.

A record $2.6 million for one race was won by *Spend A Buck* in the Jersey Derby, Garden State Park, NJ, USA on 27 May 1985. This included a $2-million bonus for having previously won the Kentucky Derby and two preparatory races at Garden State Park.

Most runners

The most horses in a race has been 66 in the Grand National on 22 Mar 1929. The record for the Flat is 58 in the Lincolnshire Handicap at Lincoln on 13 Mar 1948.

Most successful horses

The horse with the best win-loss record was *Kincsem*, a Hungarian mare foaled in 1874, who was unbeaten in 54 races (1876–9) throughout Europe, including the Goodwood Cup of 1878. The longest winning sequence is 56 races by *Camarero*, foaled in 1951, in Puerto Rico from 19 Apr 1953 to his first defeat on 17 Aug 1955. (In his career to 1956 he won 73 of 77 races.) The most wins in a career is 137 from 159 starts by *Galgo Jr* (foaled 1928) in Puerto Rico between 1930 and 1936; in 1931 he won a record 30 races in one year.

The only horse to win the same race in seven successive years was *Doctor Syntax* (foaled 1811) in the Preston Gold Cup,1815–21.

Triple Crown winners

The English Triple Crown (2000 Guineas, Derby, St Leger) has been won 15 times, most recently by *Nijinsky* in 1970. The fillies' equivalent (1000 Guineas, Oaks, St Leger) has been won 9 times, most recently by *Oh So Sharp* in 1985. Two of these fillies also won the 2000 Guineas: *Formosa* (in a dead heat) in 1868 and *Sceptre* in 1902. The American Triple Crown (Kentucky Derby, Preakness Stakes, Belmont Stakes) has been achieved 11 times, most recently by *Affirmed* in 1978.

Horses *Highest price*

Enormous valuations placed on potential stallions may be determined from sales of a minority holding, but such valuations would, perhaps, not be reached on the open market. The highest price so quoted has been $40 million for *Shareef Dancer*, syndicated in August 1983 by his owner Sheikh Mohammed bin Rashid al Maktoum. Forty shares were issued at $1 million each. The most paid for a yearling is $13.1 m on 23 July 1985 at Keeneland, Kentucky, by Robert Sangster and partners for *Seattle Dancer*.

Greatest winnings

The career earnings record is $6,597,947 by the gelding *John Henry* (foaled 1975) with 39 wins from 83 races, 1977–84. The leading money-winning mare is *All Along* (foaled 1979) with $3,018,420 in France and the USA, 1981–4.

The greatest amount earned in a year is $3,552,704 by *Spend A Buck* (USA) in 1985.

Biggest weight

The biggest weight ever carried is 30 stone *190 kg* by both Mr Maynard's mare and Mr Baker's horse in a match won by the former over a mile at York on 21 May 1788.

Oldest winners

The oldest horses to win on the Flat have been the 18-year-olds *Revenge* at Shrewsbury in September 1790, *Marksman* at Ashford, Kent in September 1826 and *Jorrocks* at Bathurst, Australia in February 1851. At the same age *Wild Aster* won three hurdle races in six days in March 1919 and *Sonny Somers* won two steeplechases in February 1980.

World speed records

The highest race speed recorded is 69,62 km/h *43.26 mph* by *Big Racket*, 20.8 sec for ¼ mile *409,26 m*, at Mexico City, Mexico on 5 Feb 1945. The 4-year-old carried 114 lb *51,7 kg*. The record for 1½ miles *2414 m* is 60,76 km/h *37.76 mph* by *Fiddle Isle* (carrying 124 lb *56,2 kg*) on 21 Mar 1970 and by *John Henry* (carrying 126 lb *57,1 kg*) on 16 Mar 1980, both at Santa Anita Park, Arcadia, California, USA in a time of 2 min 23 sec.

Jockeys *Most successful*

William Lee 'Bill' Shoemaker (USA) (b. weighing 2½ lb *1,1 kg*, 19 Aug 1931), now weighing 95 lb *43 kg* and standing 4 ft 11 in *1,50 m*, has ridden a record 8621 winners from 38,853 mounts from his first ride on 19 Mar 1949 and first winner on 20 Apr 1949 to the start of the 1987 season. Laffit Pincay (b. 29 Dec 1946, Panama City) has earned a career record $116,222,655 from 1966 to the start of the 1987 season.

Wins on one card

The most winners ridden on one card is eight by: Hubert S. Jones, 17, from 13 rides at Caliente, Cal., USA on 11 June 1944; Oscar Barattuci, at Rosario City, Argentina, on 15 Dec 1957; Dave Gall, from ten rides at Cahokia Downs, East St Louis, Illinois, USA on 18 Oct 1978; Chris Loseth, from ten rides at Exhibition Park, Vancouver, BC, Canada on 9 Apr 1984; and Robert Williams from ten rides at Lincoln, Nebraska, USA on 29 Sept 1984. The longest winning streak is 12 by: Sir Gordon Richards (1904–86) (one race at Nottingham on 3 Oct, six out of six at Chepstow on 4 Oct and the first five races next day at Chepstow) in 1933; and by Pieter Aroebel at Bulawayo, southern Rhodesia (now Zimbabwe), 7 June–7 July 1958.

Trainers

Jack Van Berg (USA) has the greatest number of wins in a year, 496 in 1976, and in a career, over 4800 to 1987. The greatest amount won in a year is $13,344,595 by D. Wayne Lukas (USA) in 1986 from 1510 mounts, 259 winners.

The only trainer to saddle the first five finishers in a championship race is Michael Dickinson in the 1983 Cheltenham Gold Cup; on 27 Dec 1982 he won a record 12 races in one day.

Owners

The most lifetime wins by an owner is 4775 by Marion Van Berg in North America in the 35 years up to his death in 1971. The most winners in a year is 494 by Dan R. Lasater (USA) in 1974. The greatest amount won in a year is $5,451,201 by Eugene Klein (USA) in 1985.

BRITISH TURF RECORDS

Most successful horses

Eclipse (foaled 1764) still has the best win-loss record, being unbeaten in a career of 18 races between May 1769 and October 1770. The longest winning sequence is 21 races by *Meteor* (foaled 1783) between 1786 and 1788. The most races won in a season is 23 by three-year-old *Fisherman* in 1856. *Catherina* (foaled 1830) won a career record 79 out of 176 races, 1832–41. The most successful sire was *Stockwell* (foaled 1849) whose progeny won 1153 races (1858–76) and who in 1866 set a record of 132 races won. The greatest amount ever won by an English-trained horse is $1,182,140 by the filly *Pebbles* (foaled 1981) in 1983–5. In 1985 she won a record $1,012,611 in one season, including the Breeders' Cup Turf in New York. The biggest winning margin in a Classic is 20 lengths by *Mayonaise* in the 1000 Guineas in 1859.

Most successful jockeys

Sir Gordon Richards won 4870 races from 21,834 mounts from his first mount at Lingfield Park on 16 Oct 1920 to his last at Sandown Park on 10 July 1954. His first win was on 31 Mar 1921. In 1953, at his 28th and final attempt, he won the Derby, six days after his knighthood. He was champion jockey 26 times between 1925 and 1953 and won a record 269 races in 1947. Lester Piggott (b. 5 Nov 1935) won 4349 races in Great Britain, 1948–85, but his global total exceeded 5200.

The most Classic races won by a jockey is 29 by Lester Piggott from his first on *Never Say Die* in the 1954 Derby to the 1985 2000 Guineas on *Shadeed*. (Derby—9, St Leger—8, Oaks—6, 2000 Guineas—4, 1000 Guineas—2).

Champion trainer ● Left: Michael Ronald Stoute (b. 22 Oct 1945) set a British record for first-place prize money earned in a season: £1,269,933 from 76 winners in 1986. (Photo: Sporting Pictures)

Champion jockey ● Above: Laffit Pincay, USA, won $13,415,049 In 1985, the greatest amount ever by a jockey in one season. (Photo: All-Sport)

MAJOR RACE RECORDS

RACE	RECORD TIME	MOST WINS Jockey	Trainer	Owner	LARGEST FIELD
FLAT					
Derby (1780) 1½ miles *2414 m* Epsom	2 min 33.8 sec *Mahmoud* 1936	9—Lester Piggott 1954, 57, 60, 68, 70, 72, 76, 77, 83	7—Robert Robson 1793, 1802, 09, 10, 15, 17, 23 7—John Porter 1868, 82, 83, 86, 90, 91, 99 7—Fred Darling 1922, 25, 26, 31, 38, 40, 41	5—3rd Earl of Egremont 1782, 1804, 05, 07, 26 5—HH Aga Khan III 1930, 35, 36, 48, 52	34 (1862)
2000 Guineas (1809) I mile *1609 m* Newmarket	1 min 35.8 sec *My Babu* 1948	9—Jem Robinson 1825, 28, 31, 33, 34, 35, 36, 47, 48	7—John Scott 1842, 43, 49, 53, 56, 60, 62	5—4th Duke of Grafton 1820, 21, 22, 26, 27 5—5th Earl of Jersey 1831, 34, 35, 36, 37	28 (1930)
1000 Guineas (1814) I mile *1609 m* Newmarket	1 min 36.85 sec *Oh So Sharp* 1985	7—George Fordham 1859, 61, 65, 68, 69, 81, 83	9—Robert Robson 1818, 19, 20, 21, 22, 23, 25, 26, 27	8—4th Duke of Grafton 1819, 20, 21, 22, 23, 25, 26, 27	29 (1926)
Oaks (1779) 1½ miles *2414 m* Epsom	2 min 34.21 sec *Time Charter* 1982	9—Frank Buckle 1797, 98, 99, 1802, 03, 05, 17, 18, 23	12—Robert Robson 1802, 04, 05, 07, 08, 09, 13, 15, 18, 22, 23, 25	6—4th Duke of Grafton 1813, 15, 22, 23, 28, 31	26 (1848)
St Leger (1776) I m 6 f 127 yd *2932 m* Doncaster	3 min 01.6 sec *Coronach* 1926 *Windsor Lad* 1934	9—Bill Scott 1821, 25, 28, 29, 38, 39, 40, 41, 46	16—John Scott 1827, 28, 29, 32, 34, 38, 39, 40, 41, 45, 51, 53, 56, 57, 59, 62	7—9th Duke of Hamilton 1786, 87, 88, 92, 1808, 09, 14	30 (1825)
King George VI and Queen Elizabeth Diamond Stakes (1951) 1½ miles *2414 m* Ascot	2 min 26.98 sec *Grundy* 1975	7—Lester Piggott 1965, 66, 69, 70, 74, 77, 84	4—Dick Hern 1972, 79, 80, 85	2—Nelson Bunker Hunt 1973, 74	19 (1951)
Prix de l'Arc de Triomphe (1920) 2400 metres *I mile 864 yd* Longchamp, France	2 min 27.7 sec *Dancing Brave* 1986	4—Jacques Doyasbère 1942, 44, 50, 51 4—Frédéric 'Freddy' Head 1966, 72, 76, 79 4—Yves Saint-Martin 1970, 74, 82, 84	4—Charles Semblat 1942, 44, 46, 49 4—Alec Head 1952, 59, 76, 81 4—François Mathet 1950, 51, 70, 82	6—Marcel Boussac 1936, 37, 42, 44, 46, 49	30 (1967)
VRC Melbourne Cup (1861) 3200 metres *I mile 1739 yd* Flemington, Victoria, Australia	3 min 19.1 sec *Rain Lover* 1968	4—Bobby Lewis 1902, 15, 19, 27 4—Harry White 1974, 75, 78, 79	7—Bart Cummings 1965, 66, 67, 74, 75, 77, 79	4—Etienne de Mestre 1861, 62, 67, 78	39 (1890)
Kentucky Derby (1875) 1¼ miles *2012 m* Churchill Downs, USA	1 min 59.4 sec *Secretariat* 1973	5—Eddie Arcaro 1938, 41, 45, 48, 52 5—Bill Hartack 1957, 60, 62, 64, 69	6—Ben Jones 1938, 41, 44, 48, 49, 52	8—Calumet Farm 1941, 44, 48, 49, 52, 57, 58, 68	23 (1974)
Irish Derby (1866) 1½ miles *2414 m* The Curragh	2 min 28.8 sec *Tambourine* 1962	6—Morny Wing 1921, 23, 30, 38, 42, 46	6—Vincent O'Brien 1953, 57, 70, 77, 84, 85	5—HH Aga Khan III 1925, 32, 40, 48, 49	24 (1962)

Major Race Records

RACE	RECORD TIME	MOST WINS Jockey	Trainer	Owner	LARGEST FIELD
— JUMPING —					
Grand National (1839) 4½ miles *7242 m* Aintree, Liverpool	9 min 01.9 sec *Red Rum* 1973	5—George Stevens 1856, 63, 64, 69, 70	4—Fred Rimell 1956, 61, 70, 76	3—James Machell 1873, 74, 76 3—Sir Charles Assheton-Smith 1893, 1912, 13 3—Noel Le Mare 1973, 74, 77	66 (1929)
Cheltenham Gold Cup (1924) 3¼ miles *5230 m* Cheltenham	6 min 23.4 sec *Silver Fame* 1951	4—Pat Taaffe 1964, 65, 66, 68	5—Tom Dreaper 1946, 64, 65, 66, 68	7—Dorothy Paget 1932, 33, 34, 35, 36, 40, 52	22 (1982)
Champion Hurdle (1927) 2 miles *3218 m* Cheltenham	3 min 51.7 sec *See You Then* 1985	4—Tim Molony 1951, 52, 53, 54	5—Peter Easterby 1967, 76, 77, 80, 81	4—Dorothy Paget 1932, 33, 40, 46	24 (1964)

Most successful trainers

The most Classics won by a trainer is 40 by John Scott (1794–1871) of Malton, Yorkshire between 1827 and 1863. James Croft of Middleham, Yorkshire trained the first four horses in the 1822 St Leger. Alec Taylor of Manton, Wiltshire headed the trainers' list for a record 12 seasons between 1907 and 1925. In 1867 John Day, Jr of Danebury, Hampshire won 146 races.

Most successful owners

HH Aga Khan III (1877–1957) was leading owner a record 13 times between 1924 and 1952. The record first-prize money won in a season is £1,082,502 by Sheikh Mohammed bin Rashid al

Prix de l'Arc de Triomphe record ●
Dancing Brave, here ridden by Pat Eddery, set the race record in 1986, following the British season when he won the 2000 Guineas, Eclipse Stakes and the King George VI and Queen Elizabeth Stakes. (Photo: Sporting Pictures)

Maktoum in 1985; in 1986 his horses won a record 119 races. The most Classics won is 20 by the 4th Duke of Grafton (1760–1844) between 1813 and 1831 and by the 17th Earl of Derby (1865–1948) between 1910 and 1945.

THE DERBY

The greatest of England's five Classics is the Derby Stakes, inaugurated on 4 May 1780, and named after the 12th Earl of Derby (1752–1834). The distance was increased in 1784 from a mile to 1½ miles *2414 km*. The race has been run at Epsom Downs, Surrey, except for the two war periods, when it was run at Newmarket, and is for three-year-olds only. Since 1884 the weights have been: colts 9 st *57 kg*, fillies 8 st 9 lb *55 kg*. Geldings were eligible until 1904.

Largest and smallest winning margins

Shergar, ridden by Walter R. Swinburn, won the Derby by a record ten lengths in 1981. There have been two dead heats: in 1828 when *Cadland*

beat *The Colonel* in the run-off, and in 1884 between *St Gatien* and *Harvester* (stakes divided).

Longest and shortest odds

Three winners have been returned at odds of 100–1: *Jeddah* (1898), *Signorinetta* (1908) and *Aboyeur* (1913). The shortest-priced winner was *Ladas* (1894) at 2–9 and the hottest losing favourite was *Surefoot*, fourth at 40–95 in 1890.

Largest prize

The richest prize on the British Turf was £267,000 in the 208th Derby on 2 June 1987, won by Mr Louis Freedman's *Reference Point*.

JUMPING

Most successful horses

Triple champion hurdler *Sir Ken* (foaled 1947) won a record 16 hurdle races in succession, April 1951 to March 1953.

The greatest amount earned by a British- or Irish-trained jumper is £247,344 in 1982–86 by the mare *Dawn Run* (k. 1986), the first horse ever to win both Champion Hurdle (1984) and Cheltenham Gold Cup (1986).

Most successful jockeys

John Francome (b. 13 Dec 1952) won a career record 1138 races over jumps (from 5061 mounts), from 1970 to 1985.

The record number of wins in a season is 149 by Jonjo O'Neill (b. 13 Apr 1952) in 1977–8. The most wins in a day is six by amateur Charlie Cunningham at Rugby on 29 Mar 1881. The record number of successive wins is ten by: John Alnam 'Johnny' Gilbert (b. 26 July 1920), 8–30 Sept 1959; and by Phil Tuck (b. 10 July 1956), 23 Aug–8 Sept 1986. The record number of championships is seven by: Gerald 'Gerry' Wilson (1903–68) 1933–8 and 1941; and by John Francome (one shared) in 1976, 1979, 1981–5.

Most successful trainers

The most first-prize money earned in a season is £358,837 from a record 120 winners by Michael Dickinson in 1982–3. Fred Winter won a record eight trainers' championships, 1971–5, 1977–8 and 1985.

GRAND NATIONAL

The first Grand National Steeple Chase may be regarded as the Grand Liverpool Steeple Chase of 26 Feb 1839 though the race was not given its present name until 1847. It became a handicap in 1843. Except for 1916–18, and 1941–5, the race has been run at Aintree, near Liverpool, over 30 fences.

Most wins

The only horse to win three times is *Red Rum* (foaled 1965) in 1973, 1974 and 1977, from five runs. He came second in 1975 and 1976. *Manifesto* ran a record eight times (1895–1904). He won in 1897 and 1899, came third three times and fourth once.

Highest prize

The highest prize and the richest ever over jumps in Great Britain was £64,710 won by *Maori Venture* on 4 Apr 1987.

Highest weight

The highest weight ever carried to victory is 12 st 7 lb *79,4 kg* by *Cloister* (1893), *Manifesto* (1899), *Jerry M.* (1912) and *Poethlyn* (1919).

Hurling

A game of very ancient origin, hurling was included in the Tailteann Games (inst. 1829 BC). It only became standardised with the formation of the Gaelic Athletic Association in Thurles, Ireland, on 1 Nov 1884. The Irish Hurling Union was formed on 24 Jan 1879.

Most titles *All-Ireland*

The greatest number of All-Ireland Championships won by one team is 26 by Cork between 1890 and 1986. The greatest number of successive wins is four by Cork (1941–4).

Inter-provincials

Munster holds the greatest number of interprovincial (Railway Cup) championships with 34 (1928–77).

Most appearances

The most appearances in All-Ireland finals is ten shared by Christy Ring (Cork and Munster) and John Doyle (Tipperary). They also share the record of All-Ireland medals won with eight each. Ring's appearances on the winning side were in 1941–4, 1946 and 1952–4, while Doyle's were in 1949–51, 1958, 1961–2 and 1964–5. Ring also played in a record 22 inter-provincial finals (1942–63) and was on the winning side 18 times.

Highest and lowest scores

The highest score in an All-Ireland final (60 min) was in 1896 when Tipperary (8 goals, 14 points) beat Dublin (no goals, 4 points). The record aggregate score was when Cork (6 goals, 21 points) defeated Wexford (5 goals, 10 points) in the 80-minute final of 1970. A goal equals three points. The highest recorded individual score was by Nick Rackard (Wexford), who scored 7 goals and 7 points against Antrim in the 1954 All-Ireland semi-final. The lowest score in an All-Ireland final was when Tipperary (1 goal, 1 point) beat Galway (nil) in the first championship at Birr in 1887.

Longest stroke

The greatest distance for a 'lift and stroke' is one of 129 yd *117 m* credited to Tom Murphy of Three Castles, Kilkenny, in a 'long puck' contest in 1906.

Largest crowd

The largest crowd was 84,865 for the All-Ireland final between Cork and Wexford at Croke Park, Dublin, in 1954.

Ice Hockey

There is pictorial evidence that a hockey-like game (*kalv*) was played on ice in the early 16th century in The Netherlands. The game was probably first played in North America on 25 Dec 1855 at Kingston, Ontario, Canada, but Halifax also lays claim to priority. The International Ice Hockey Federation was founded in 1908. The National Hockey League (NHL) of North America was inaugurated in 1917.

World Championships and Olympic Games

World Championships were first held for amateurs in 1920 in conjunction with the Olympic Games, which were also considered as world championships up to 1968. From 1977 World Championships have been open to professionals. The USSR won 20 world titles between 1954 and 1986, including the Olympic titles of 1956, 1964 and 1968. They won three further Olympic titles in 1972, 1976 and 1984. Canada won 19 titles between 1920 and 1961, including six Olympic titles (1920, 1924, 1928, 1932, 1948 and 1952). The longest Olympic career is that of Richard Torriani (b. 1 Oct 1911) (Switzerland) from 1928 to 1948. The most gold medals won by any player is three, achieved by USSR players Vitaliy Davidov, Anatoliy Firssov, Viktor Kuzkin and Aleksandr Ragulin in 1964, 1968 and 1972, and by Vladislav Tretyak in 1972, 1976 and 1984.

Stanley Cup

The Stanley Cup, presented by the Governor-General, Lord Stanley (original cost $48.67), became emblematic of National Hockey League supremacy 33 years after the first contest at Montreal in 1893. It has been won most often by the Montreal Canadiens with 23 wins in 1916, 1924, 1930–1, 1944, 1946, 1953, 1956–60, 1965–6, 1968–9, 1971, 1973, 1976–9, 1986.

British competitions

The English National (later British) League Championship (inst. 1935) has been won by the Wembley Lions four times, in 1936–7, 1952 and 1957 and by Streatham (now Redskins) in 1950, 1953, 1960 and 1982. Murrayfield Racers have won the Northern League (inst. 1966) seven times, 1970–2, 1976, 1979–80 and 1985. The Icy Smith Cup (first held 1966), the premier British club competition until 1981, was won by Murrayfield Racers nine times, 1966, 1969–72, 1975 and 1979–81. The British club championship (inst. 1982) was won by Dundee Rockets in 1982, 1983 and 1984.

Most goals *Team*

The greatest number of goals recorded in a world championship match was when Australia beat New Zealand 58–0 at Perth on 15 Mar 1987. The NHL record is 21 goals when Montreal Canadiens beat Toronto St Patrick's, at Montreal, 14–7 on 10 Jan 1920.

Most goals and points *Individual*

The most goals scored in a season in the NHL is 92 in the 1981–2 season by Wayne Gretzky (b. 26 Jan 1961) (Edmonton Oilers). He scored a record 215 points, including a record 163 assists in 1985–6. In 1981–2 in all games, adding Stanley Cup play-offs and for Canada in the World Championship, he scored 238 points (103 goals, 135 assists). The North American career record for goals is 1071 (a record 801 in the NHL) by Gordie Howe (b. 31 Mar 1928) (Detroit Red Wings, Houston Aeros, New England Whalers and Hartford Whalers) from 16 Oct 1946 in 32 seasons ending in 1979–80. He took 2204 games to achieve the 1000th goal, but Robert Marvin 'Bobby' Hull (b. 3 Jan 1939) (Chicago Black Hawks and Winnipeg Jets) scored his 1000th in 1600 games on 12 Mar 1978. Wayne Gretzky is establishing a much faster rate: 612 goals in 733 NHL and Stanley Cup play-off games to June 1987. With 1117 assists in these games his points total is 1729. The NHL points record is 1850 by Gordie Howe, 1946–71. Gretzky has reached 1695 points.

British

The highest score and aggregate in a British League match was set when Medway Bears beat Richmond Raiders 48–1 at Gillingham in a Second Division fixture on 1 Dec 1985, when Kevin McNaught scored a record 25 points from seven goals and 18 assists.

The most individual goals scored in a senior game is 14 by Ron Halpin (Canada) (b. 18 Oct 1955) for Dundee Rockets in a 24–1 win over Durham Wasps at Dundee on 4 April 1982. Steve Moria (Canada) (b. 1960) achieved the highest number of assists, 13, for Fife Flyers at Cleveland on 28 Mar 1987. Rick Fern (Canada) (b. 1964) set British season's records of 165 goals and 318 points for Murrayfield Racers in 48 games in 1986–87. Tim Salmon (Canada) (b. 27 Nov 1964) achieved a season's record 183 assists in 47 games for Ayr Bruins in 1985–6.

Most points one game

The North American major league record for most points scored in one game is ten (3 goals, 7 assists) by Jim Harrison (b. 9 July 1947) (for Alberta, later Edmonton Oilers) in a World Hockey Association match at Edmonton on 30 Jan 1973, and by Darryl Sittler (b. 18 Sept 1950)

Ice Skating

(6 goals, 4 assists) for Toronto Maple Leafs in an NHL match at Toronto on 7 Feb 1976.

Fastest scoring *World*
In the NHL the fastest goal was after 4 seconds in the second period by Joseph Antoine Claude Provost (b. 17 Sept 1933) (Montreal Canadiens) *v.* Boston Bruins at Montreal on 9 Nov 1957. Doug Smail of the Winnipeg Jets scored 5 seconds from the opening whistle against St Louis on 20 Dec 1981. Canadian Bill Mosienko (Chicago Black Hawks) (b. 2 Nov 1921) scored three goals in 21 sec *v.* New York Rangers on 23 Mar 1952. Toronto scored eight goals in 4 min 52 sec *v.* New York Americans on 19 Mar 1938.

In minor leagues, Kim D. Miles scored in 3 seconds for University of Guelph *v.* University of W Ontario on 11 Feb 1975. Three goals in 12 seconds was achieved by Steve D'Innocenzo for Holliston *v.* Westwood in a high school match in Massachusetts, USA on 9 Jan 1982. The Skara Ishockeyclubb, Sweden, scored three goals in 11 seconds against Örebro IK at Skara on 18 Oct 1981. The Vernon Cougars scored five goals in 56 seconds against Salmon Arm Aces at Vernon, BC, Canada on 6 Aug 1982. The Kamloops Knights of Columbus scored seven goals in 2 min 22 sec *v.* Prince George Vikings on 25 Jan 1980.

Great Britain
The fastest goal in the Heineken League was scored by Steve Johnson for Durham Wasps after four seconds *v.* Ayr Bruins at Ayr, Scotland on 6 Nov 1983. Kenny Westman (Nottingham Panthers) scored a hat trick in 30 seconds *v.* Brighton Tigers on 3 Mar 1955.

In an English Junior League (under-16) game Jonathan Lumbis scored a hat-trick in 13 seconds for Nottingham Cougars *v.* Peterborough Jets on 4 Nov 1984.

Most successful goaltending
The most matches played by a goaltender in an NHL career without conceding a goal is 103 by Terrance 'Terry' Gordon Sawchuck (1929–70) of Detroit, Boston, Toronto, Los Angeles and New York Rangers, between 1950 and 1967. Gerry Cheevers (b. 2 Dec 1940), Boston Bruins, went a record 33 successive games without a defeat in 1971–2.

Longest match
The longest match was 2 hr 56 min 30 sec (playing time) when Detroit Red Wings beat Montreal Maroons 1–0 in the sixth period of overtime at the Forum, Montreal, at 2.25 a.m. on 25 Mar 1936. Norm Smith, the Red Wings goaltender, turned aside 92 shots for the NHL's longest single shutout.

Ice Skating

The earliest reference to ice skating is in early Scandinavian literature referring to the 2nd century though its origins are believed, on archaeological evidence, to be ten centuries earlier still. The earliest English account of 1180 refers to skates made of bone. The earliest skating club was the Edinburgh Skating Club formed in about 1742.

The first recorded race was from Wisbech to Whittlesea, East Anglia, in 1763. The earliest artificial rink in the world was opened at the Baker Street Bazaar, Portman Square, London, on 7 Dec 1842, although the surface was not of ice. The first artificial ice rink was opened in the King's Road, Chelsea, London on 7 Jan 1876.

The National Skating Association of Great Britain was founded in 1879. The International Skating Union was founded at Scheveningen, Netherlands in 1892.

FIGURE SKATING

Most titles *Olympic*
The most Olympic gold medals won by a figure skater is three by: Gillis Grafström (1893–1938) of Sweden in 1920, 1924 and 1928 (also silver medal in 1932); by Sonja Henie (1912–69) of Norway in 1928, 1932 and 1936; and by Irina Rodnina (b. 12 Sept 1949) (USSR) with two different partners in the pairs event in 1972, 1976 and 1980.

World
The greatest number of individual world figure skating titles (instituted 1896) is ten by Ulrich Salchow (1877–1949) of Sweden, in 1901–5 and 1907–11. The women's record (inst. 1906) is also ten individual titles by Sonja Henie between 1927 and 1936. Irina Rodnina has won ten pairs titles (inst. 1908), four with Aleksey Ulanov (b. 4 Nov 1947), 1969–72, and six with her husband Aleksandr Zaitsev (b. 16 June 1952), 1973–8. The most ice dance titles (inst. 1952) won is six by Lyudmila Pakhomova (1946–86) and her husband Aleksandr Gorshkov (b. 8 Oct 1946) (USSR), 1970–4 and 1976. They also won the first ever Olympic ice dance title in 1976.

British
The most individual British titles is: (men) 11 by Jack Ferguson Page (1900–47) (Manchester SC) in 1922–31 and 1933; and (women) six by Cecilia Colledge (b. 28 Nov 1920) (Park Lane FSC, London) in 1935–6, 1937 (two), 1938 and 1946. Page and Ethel M. Muckelt (1885–1953) won nine pairs titles, 1923–31. The most by an ice dance couple is six by Jayne Torvill (b. 7 Oct 1957) and Christopher Dean (b. 27 July 1958), 1978–83.

Triple Crown
The only British skaters to win the 'Grand Slam' of World, Olympic and European titles in the same year are John Anthony Curry (b. 9 Sept 1949) in 1976 and the ice dancers Jayne Torvill and Christopher Dean in 1984. Karl Schäfer (Austria) (1909–76) and Sonja Henie achieved double 'Grand Slams', both in the years 1932 and 1936.

Highest marks
The highest tally of maximum six marks awarded in an international championship was 29 to Jayne Torvill and Christopher Dean (GB) in the World Ice Dance Championships at Ottawa, Canada on 22–24 Mar 1984. This comprised seven in the compulsory dances, a perfect set of nine for presentation in the set pattern dance and 13 in the free dance, including another perfect set from all nine judges for artistic presentation. They previously gained a perfect set of nine

sixes for artistic presentation in the free dance at the 1983 World Championships in Helsinki, Finland and at the 1984 winter Olympic Games in Sarajevo, Yugoslavia. In their career Torvill and Dean received a record total of 136 sixes.

The most by a soloist was seven to Donald Jackson (b. 2 Apr 1940) (Canada) in the World Men's Championship at Prague, Czechoslovakia, in 1962.

Distance
Robin Cousins (GB) (b. 17 Mar 1957) achieved 19 ft 1 in *5,81 m* in an axel jump and 18 ft *5,48 m* with a back flip at Richmond Ice Rink, Surrey on 16 Nov 1983.

Largest rink
The world's largest indoor ice rink is in the Moscow Olympic arena which has an ice area of 8064 m² *86,800 ft²*. The five rinks at Fujikyu Highland Skating Centre, Japan total 26 500 m² *285,243 ft²*.

SPEED SKATING

Most titles *Olympic*
The most Olympic gold medals won in speed skating is six by Lidia Skoblikova (b. 8 Mar 1939) of Chelyabinsk, USSR, in 1960 (two) and 1964 (four). The male record is by Clas Thunberg (1893–1973) (Finland) with five gold (including one tied), and also one silver and one tied bronze, in 1924 and 1928. Eric Heiden (USA) (b. 14 June 1958) also won five gold medals, uniquely at one Games at Lake Placid, NY, USA, in 1980.

World
The greatest number of world overall titles (inst. 1893) won by any skater is five by: Oscar Mathisen (Norway) (1888–1954) in 1908–9 and 1912–14; and Clas Thunberg in 1923, 1925, 1928–9 and 1931. The most titles won in the women's events (inst. 1936) is four by: Inga Voronina (*née* Artomonova) (1936–66) (USSR) in 1957, 1958, 1962 and 1964; Atje Keulen–Deelstra (b. 31 Dec 1938) (Netherlands) 1970, 1972–4; and Karin Kania (*née* Enke) (b. 20 June 1961) (GDR) 1982, 1984, 1986–7. Kania has also won a record six overall titles at the World Sprint Championships 1980–1, 1983–4, 1986–7.

The record score achieved in the world overall title is 159.356 points by Nikolay Gulyayev (USSR) at Heerenveen, Netherlands on 14–15 Feb 1987. The record women's score is 171.760 points by Andrea Schöne (GDR) (b. 1 Dec 1960) at Medeo, 23–24 Mar 1984.

SPEED SKATING WORLD RECORDS

MEN

Metres	min sec	Name (Country)	Place	Date
500	36.23*	Nick Thometz (USA)	Medeo, USSR	26 Mar 1987
1000	1.12.05	Nick Thometz (USA)	Medeo, USSR	27 Mar 1987
1500	1.52.48	Andrey Bobrov (USSR)	Medeo, USSR	27 Mar 1987
3000	3.59.27	Leo Visser (Netherlands)	Heerenveen, Netherlands	19 Mar 1987
5000	6.47.01	Lee Visser (Netherlands)	Heerenveen, Netherlands	14 Feb 1987
10 000	14.03.92	Geir Karlstad (Nor)	Heerenveen, Netherlands	15 Feb 1987

WOMEN

Metres	min sec	Name (Country)	Place	Date
500	39.28	Bonnie Blair (USA)	Medeo, USSR	26 Mar 1987
1000	1.18.84	Karin Kania (née Enke) (GDR)	Karuizawa, Japan	23 Feb 1986
1500	1.59.30	Karin Kania (GDR)	Medeo, USSR	22 Mar 1986
3000	4.16.85	Yvonne van Gennip (Netherlands)	Heerenveen, Netherlands	19 Mar 1987
5000	7.20.36	Yvonne van Gennip (Netherlands)	Heerenveen, Netherlands	20 Mar 1987

* represents an average speed of 49,68 km/hr *30.87 mph*.
Note that Medeo, Alma Ata, USSR is situated at an altitude of 1691 m above sea level.

Fastest woman speed skater ● Bonnie Blair (USA) skated 500 metres in 39.28 sec at Medeo in 1987; this represents an average speed of 45,82 km/h *28.27 mph*. (Photo: Bob Martin/All-Sport)

WORLD SHORT TRACK SPEED SKATING RECORDS

MEN

Metres	min sec	Name (Country)	Place	Date
500	45.08	Louis Grenier (Canada)	Amsterdam, Netherlands	16 Mar 1985
1000	1.34.79	Guy Daignealt (Canada)	Chamonix, France	6 Apr 1986
1500	2.27.27	Tatsuyoshi Ishihara (Japan)	Den Haag, Netherlands	28 Mar 1981
3000	5.04.24	Tatsuyoshi Ishihara (Japan)	Amsterdam, Netherlands	17 Mar 1985

WOMEN

Metres	min sec	Name (Country)	Place	Date
500	48.12	Bonnie Blair (USA)	Chamonix, France	5 Apr 1986
1000	1.41.80	Marie Perrault (Canada)	Chamonix, France	6 Apr 1986
1500	2.36.92	Eiko Shishii (Japan)	Montreal, Canada	3 Apr 1987
3000	5.31.65	Nathalie Lambert (Canada)	Montreal, Canada	5 Apr 1987

BRITISH SHORT TRACK SPEED SKATING RECORDS

MEN

Distance	min sec	Name	Place	Date
500 metres	45.61	Wilfred O'Reilly	Amsterdam, Netherlands	16 Mar 1985
1000 metres	1.35.25	Wilfred O'Reilly	Chamonix, France	6 Apr 1986
1500 metres	2.32.84	Wilfred O'Reilly	Amsterdam, Netherlands	15 Mar 1985
3000 metres	5.17.47	Wilfred O'Reilly	Chamonix, France	6 Apr 1986

WOMEN

Distance	min sec	Name	Place	Date
500 metres	51.78	Kim Ferran	Brugge, Belgium	18 Mar 1984
1000 metres	1.46.63	Nicky Bell	Chamonix, France	5 Apr 1986
1500 metres	2.46.88	Amanda Worth	Tokyo, Japan	8 Apr 1983
3000 metres	5.59.08	Amanda Worth	Richmond, England	1 Mar 1985

Longest race

The 'Elfstedentocht' ('Tour of the Eleven Towns') was held in the Netherlands from the 1800s to 1963 and again in 1985, covering 200 km *124 miles 483 yd*. It was transferred first to Lake Vesijärvi, near Lahti, Finland and in 1984 to Canada as the International Race of 11 Cities on the Ottawa River. The record time for 200 km is 6 hr 5 min 12 sec by Jan-Roelof Kruithof (Netherlands) (b. 1936) on 25 Feb 1979 at Oulu, Finland. Kruithof won the race eight times, 1974, 1976–7, 1979–83. An estimated 16,000 skaters took part in 1986.

24 hours

Ton Smits (Netherlands) skated 506,375 km *314.65 miles* in 24 hours in Eindhoven, Netherlands on 15–16 Dec 1984.

Ice and Sand Yachting

The sport originated in the Low Countries from the year 1600 (earliest patent granted) and along the Baltic coast. The earliest authentic record is Dutch, dating from 1768. Land or sand yachts of Dutch construction were first reported on beaches (now in Belgium) in 1595. The earliest International Championship was staged in 1914.

Largest yacht

The largest ice yacht was *Icicle*, built for Commodore John E. Roosevelt for racing on the Hudson River, New York, in 1869. It was 68 ft 11 in *21 m* long and carried 1070 ft² *99 m²* of canvas.

Highest speeds *Ice*

The highest speed officially recorded is 143 mph *230 km/h* by John D. Buckstaff in a Class A stern-steerer on Lake Winnebago, Wisconsin, USA, in 1938. Such a speed is possible in a wind of 72 mph *115 km/h*.

Sand

The official world record for a sand yacht is 107 km/h *66.48 mph* set by Christian-Yves Nau (b. 1944) (France) in *Mobil* at Le Touquet, France on 22 Mar 1981, when the wind speed reached 120 km/h *75 mph*. A speed of 88.4 mph *142,26 km/h* was attained by Nord Embroden (USA) in *Midnight at the Oasis* at Superior Dry Lake, California, USA on 15 Apr 1976.

Judo

Judo is a modern combat sport which developed out of an amalgam of several old Japanese fighting arts, the most popular of which was ju-jitsu (jiu-jitsu), which is thought to be of Chinese origin. Judo has greatly developed since 1882, when it was first devised by Dr Jigoro Kano (1860–1938). The International Judo Federation was founded in 1951.

Most titles *World and Olympic*

World Championships were inaugurated in Tokyo in 1956. Women's championships were first held in 1980 in New York. Yashiro Yamashita won nine consecutive Japanese titles 1977–85, four world titles; Over 95 kg 1979, 1981 and 1983, Open 1981, and the Olympic Open category in 1984. He retired undefeated after 203 successive wins, 1977–85. Two other men have won four world titles, Wilhelm Ruska (b. 29 Aug 1940) (Netherlands), Over 93 kg 1967, 1971 and the 1972 Olympic Over 93 kg and Open titles, and Shozo Fujii (Japan) (b. 12 May 1950). Ingrid Berghmans (Belgium) has won a record five women's world titles (first held 1980): Open 1980, 1982, 1984 and 1986 and Under 72 kg in 1984.

Karen Briggs (b. 11 Apr 1963) is the most successful British player, with three world titles, Under 48 kg in 1982, 1984 and 1986.

British

The greatest number of titles (inst. 1966) won is nine by David Colin Starbrook (b. 9 Aug 1945) (6th dan): Middleweight 1969–70, Light-heavyweight 1971–5 and the Open division 1970–1. A record six titles in the women's events (inst. 1971) were won by Christine Child (now Mrs Gallie) (b. 1946) (6th dan): Heavyweight in 1971–5 and the Open division in 1973. Neil Adams (b. 27 Sept 1958) has the most successful international record of any British player. He has won two junior (1974 and 1977) and five senior (1979–80, 1983–5) European titles, four World Championships medals (one gold, one silver, two bronze) and two Olympic silver medals. He has won eight British senior titles.

Highest grades

The efficiency grades in Judo are divided into pupil (*kyu*) and master (*dan*) grades. The highest awarded is the extremely rare red belt *Judan* (10th dan), given to only 13 men so far. The Judo protocol provides for an 11th dan (*Juichidan*) who also would wear a red belt, a 12th dan (*Junidan*) who would wear a white belt twice as wide as an ordinary belt and the highest of all, *Shihan* (doctor), but these have never been bestowed, save for the 12th dan to the founder of the sport Dr Jigoro Kano. The highest British native Judo grade is 8th dan by Charles Stuart Palmer (b. 1930). Christine Gallie (née Child) was awarded her 6th Dan in 1983.

10 hours

The brothers Steven (b. 8 Dec 1967) and Alan (b. 21 Aug 1963) McManus from the East Side Judo Club completed 10,123 judo throwing techniques in a ten-hour period at Crystal Palace National Sports Centre, London on 11 Apr 1987.

Jiu-Jitsu

The World Council of Jiu-Jitsu Organizations have staged two World Championships, in 1984 and 1986. The Canadian team were the team winners on each occasion.

Karate

Based on techniques devised from the 6th-century Chinese art of Shaolin boxing (Kempo), Karate was developed by an unarmed populace in Okinawa as a weapon against armed Japanese oppressors c. 1500. Transmitted to Japan in the 1920s by Funakoshi Gichin, this method of combat was refined into karate and organised into a sport with competitive rules. The five major styles of karate in Japan are: *Shotokan, Wado-ryu, Goju-ryu, Shito-ryu* and *Kyokushinkai*, each of which places different emphasis on speed and power, etc. Other styles include *Sankukai, Shotokai* and *Shukokai. Wu shu* is a comprehensive term embracing all Chinese martial arts. *Kung fu* is one aspect of these arts popularised by the cinema.

The governing body for the sport in Britain is the Martial Arts Commission upon which all the martial arts are represented.

World Championships

Great Britain has won a record four world titles (inst. 1970) at the Kumite team event, 1975, 1982, 1984 and 1986. Pat McKay (GB) is the only man to win two individual kumite titles, at Under 80 kg, 1982 and 1984.

Top exponents

The leading exponents among karatekas are a

number of 10th dans in Japan. The leading exponents in the United Kingdom are Tatsuo Suzuki (8th dan, *Wado-ryu*) (b. 27 Apr 1928), chief instructor to the European Karatedo Wadokai; Keinosuke Enoeda (8th dan, *Shotokan*), resident instructor to the Karate Union of Great Britain; Steve Arneil (7th dan, *Kyokushinkai*), British national born in South Africa; and national coach David Donovan (7th dan, *Ishinryu*).

Women's karate champions ● Mie Nakayama (**right**) of Japan, won three world titles at individual kata in 1982, 1984 and 1986. In the same three championships, Guus van Mourik (**far right**) of the Netherlands won the Over 60 kg title. (Photos: World Karate-Do Federation, van Moorik)

Most successful British judo competitor at World Championships ● Karen Briggs (**below**) (b. 11 Apr 1963) has won three titles: Under 48 kg in 1982, 1984 and 1986. (Photo: John Gichigi/All-Sport)

Lacrosse

MEN'S LACROSSE

The game is of American Indian origin, derived from the inter-tribal game *baggataway*, and was played before 1492 by Iroquois Indians in lower Ontario, Canada and upper New York State, USA. The French named it after their game of *chouler à la crosse*, known in 1381. It was introduced into Great Britain in 1867. The English Lacrosse Union was formed in 1892. Lacrosse was included in the Olympic Games of 1904 and 1908 and featured as an exhibition sport in the 1928, 1932 and 1948 Games.

Most titles *World*

The United States have won four of the five World Championships, in 1967, 1974, 1982 and 1986, and also won the pre-Olympic tournament in 1984. Canada won the other world title in 1978 beating the USA 17–16 after extra time—this was the first drawn international match.

English

The English Club Championship (Iroquois Cup—inst. 1890) has been won most often by Stockport with 16 wins between 1897 and 1987. The record score in a final is 33 by Stockport *v*. London University (4) on 9 May 1987.

Most international appearances

The record number of international representations is 33 for England by James Michael 'Mike' Roberts (Urmston) (b. 22 Feb 1946), to 1982. He is the only Englishman to play in five World Championships.

Highest scores

The highest score in an international match was the United States' 32–8 win over England at Toronto, Canada in 1986. England's highest score was their 19–11 win over Canada at Melbourne in 1974.

Fastest scoring

Rod Burns scored only 4 seconds into the game for South Manchester and Wythenshawe *v*. Sheffield University on 6 Dec 1975.

WOMEN'S LACROSSE

The first reported playing of lacrosse by women was in 1886. The All-England Women's Lacrosse Association was formed in 1912. The game has evolved from the men's game so that the rules now differ considerably.

World Championships/World Cup

Three World Championships were held, being replaced by the World Cup in 1978. The only double winner at these quadrennial events is the USA, 1974 and 1982.

Most international appearances

Caro Macintosh (b. 18 Feb 1932) played in 56 internationals (52 for Scotland and 4 for Great Britain), 1952–69, and Barbara Dootson (b. 24 Aug 1955) in 54 (41 England, 13 Great Britain), 1974–86.

Highest score

The highest score by an international team was by Great Britain and Ireland with their 40–0 defeat of Long Island during their 1967 tour of the USA.

Marbles

Marbles may have been a children's game in ancient Egypt, and was introduced into Britain by the Romans in the 1st century AD. It became a competitive sport under the British Marbles Board of Control at the Greyhound Hotel, Tinsley Green, Crawley, West Sussex in 1926.

Most championships

The British Championship (established 1926) has been won most often by the Toucan Terribles with 20 consecutive titles (1956-75). Three founder members, Len Smith, Jack and Charlie Dempsey played in every title win. They were finally beaten in 1976 by the Pernod Rams, captained by Len Smith's son, Paul. Len Smith (b. 13 Oct 1917) won the individual title 15 times (1957-64, 1966, 1968-73) but lost in 1974 to his son Alan.

Speed record

The record for clearing the ring (between 5¾ and 6¼ ft *1,75-1,90 m* in diameter) of 49 marbles is 2 min 57 sec by the Toucan Terribles at Worthing, West Sussex in 1971.

Microlighting

Altitude

The highest recognised altitude is 7906,5 m *25,939.64 ft* by Richard J. Rowley (USA) on 17 Sept 1983. Bob Calvert set a British record of 5791,27 m *19,000 ft* on 19 Feb 1983 at Middleton Sands, Lancashire.

Distance

Alfred Clark (Australia) set a distance record of 789,5 km *490.59 miles* at Phoenix Park, Australia on 2 Aug 1986. Peter Davies set a British record of 545,52 km *338.98 miles* from Parham, Sussex to St Just, Cornwall on 3 Mar 1984.

Speed

Dave Cook (GB) set an FAI world speed record (3 km *1.86 mile* course, restricted altitude) of 126,356 km/h *78.51 mph* at Bungay, Suffolk on 4 Aug 1982.

Modern Pentathlon & Biathlon

Points scores in riding, fencing, cross country and hence overall scores have no comparative value between one competition and another. In shooting and swimming (300 m) the scores are of record significance and the best achievements are shown.

The Modern Pentathlon (Riding, Fencing, Swimming, Shooting and Running) was inaugurated into the Olympic Games at Stockholm in 1912. The Modern Pentathlon Association of Great Britain was formed in 1922. *L'Union Internationale de Pentathlon Moderne et Biathlon* (UIPMB) was founded in 1948. Originally the UIPM, the administration of Biathlon (cross-country skiing and shooting) was added in 1957, and the name modified accordingly.

MODERN PENTATHLON

Most titles *World*

András Balczó (Hungary) (b. 16 Aug 1938) won the record number of world titles (inst. 1949), six individual and seven team. He won the world individual title in 1963, 1965-7 and 1969 and the Olympic title in 1972. His seven team titles (1960-70) comprised five world and two Olympic. The USSR has won a record 12 world and three Olympic team titles.

Women's World Championships were first held in 1981. Great Britain won three team titles 1981-83, with Sarah Parker (b. 16 July 1956) a member of each of those teams. Wendy Johana Norman (b. 20 Feb 1965) won the individual title in 1982 and team golds in 1981-2. She also won the individual World Cup title in 1980 and Great Britain won three World Cup team titles, 1978-80.

Olympic

The greatest number of Olympic gold medals won is three by András Balczó, a member of the winning team in 1960 and 1968 and the 1972 individual champion. Lars Hall (b. 30 Apr 1927) (Sweden) has uniquely won two individual Championships (1952 and 1956). Pavel Lednyev (USSR) (b. 25 Mar 1943) won a record seven medals (two gold, two silver, three bronze), 1968-80. The best British performance is the team gold medal in 1976 by Jim Fox, Adrian Philip Parker and Daniel Nightingale. The best individual placing is fourth by Jeremy Robert 'Jim' Fox (b. 19 Sept 1941) in 1972.

Probably the greatest margin of victory was by William Oscar Guernsey Grut (b. 17 Sept 1914) (Sweden) in the 1948 Games, when he won three events and was placed fifth and eighth in the other two.

British

The pentathlete with most British titles is Jim Fox, with ten (1963, 1965-8, 1970-4). Wendy Norman won a record four women's titles, 1978-80 and 1982.

BIATHLON

The biathlon, which combines cross-country skiing and rifle shooting, was first included in the Olympic Games in 1960, and World Championships were first held in 1958.

Most titles *Olympic Games*

Magnar Solberg (Norway) (b. 4 Feb 1937), in 1968 and 1972, is the only man to have won two Olympic individual titles. The USSR has won all five 4 × 7,5 km relay titles, 1968-84. Aleksandr Tikhonov (b. 2 Jan 1947) who was a member of the first four teams also won a silver in the 1968 20 km.

World Championship

Frank Ullrich (GDR) (b. 24 Jan 1958) has won a record six individual world titles, four at 10 km, 1978-81, including the 1980 Olympics, and two at 20 km, 1982-3. Aleksandr Tikhonov was in ten winning USSR relay teams, 1968-80 and won four individual titles.

The Biathlon World Cup (inst. 1979) was won three times by Frank Ullrich, 1980-2. He was second in 1979 and third in 1983.

Motorcycle Racing

Earliest race

The first motorcycle race was held over a mile *1,6 km* on an oval track at Sheen House, Richmond, Surrey, on 29 Nov 1897, won by Charles Jarrott (1877-1944) on a Fournier. The oldest motorcycle races in the world are the Auto-Cycle Union Tourist Trophy (TT) series, first held on the 15.81 mile *25,44 km* 'Peel' (St John's) course in the Isle of Man on 28 May 1907, and still run on the island on the 'Mountain' circuit.

Fastest circuits

The highest average lap speed attained on any closed circuit is 160.288 mph *257,958 km/h* by Yvon du Hamel (Canada) (b. 1941) on a modified 903-cc four-cylinder Kawasaki Z1 at the 31-degree banked 2.5 mile *4,02 km* Daytona International Speedway, Florida, USA, in March 1973. His lap time was 56.149 sec.

The fastest road circuit was the Francorchamps circuit near Spa, Belgium, then 8.74 miles *14,12 km* in length. It was lapped in 3 min 50.3 sec (average speed 137.150 mph *220,721 km/h*) by Barry Stephen Frank Sheene (GB) (b. 11 Sept 1950) on a 495-cc four-cylinder Suzuki during the Belgian Grand Prix on 3 July 1977. The world's fastest now is the Portstewart-Coleraine-Portrush circuit in Londonderry, Northern Ireland. The lap record (10.1 mile *16,26 km* lap) is 4 min 53.2 sec (average speed 124.060 mph *199,655 km/h*) by John Glyn Williams (1946-78) on a 747-cc four-cylinder Yamaha on lap five of the 750-cc event of the North-West 200, on 21 May 1977. Minor circuit changes prior to 1986 have resulted in slower times.

The lap record for the outer circuit (2.767 miles *4,453 km*) at the Brooklands Motor Course, near Weybridge, Surrey (open between 1907 and 1939) was 80.0 sec (average speed 124.51 mph *200,37 km/h*) by Noel Baddow 'Bill' Pope (later Major) (1909-71) of the United Kingdom on a Brough Superior powered by a supercharged 996-cc V-twin '8-80' JAP engine developing 110 bhp, on 4 July 1939.

Fastest race *World*

The fastest road race is the 500-cc Belgian Grand Prix held on the Francorchamps circuit (*see above*). The record time for this ten-lap (87.74 mile *141,20 km*) race is 38 min 58.5 sec (average

MODERN PENTATHLON HIGHEST SCORES

In major competition

	Performance	Points	Name and Place	Date and Venue
WORLD				
Shooting	200/200	—[1]	Charles Leonard (USA) (b. 23 Feb 1913)	3 Aug 1936, Berlin, Germany
	200/200	1132	Daniele Masala (Italy) (b. 12 Feb 1955)	21 Aug 1978, Jönköping, Sweden
	200/200	1132	George Horvath (Sweden) (b. 14 Mar 1960)	22 July 1980, Moscow, USSR
Swimming	3 min 08.22 sec	1368	John Scott (USA) (b. 14 Apr 1962)	27 Aug 1982, London, England
BRITISH				
Shooting	198/200	1088	Timothy Kenealy (b. 3 Mar 1950)	4 June 1979, Helsinki, Finland
Swimming	3 min 14 sec	1320	Richard Lawson Phelps (b. 19 Apr 1961)	5 July 1986, Milton Keynes, England

[1] *points not given in 1936 Olympic Games.*

speed 135.068 mph *217,370 km/h*) by Barry Sheene, on a 495-cc four-cylinder Suzuki, on 3 July 1977.

United Kingdom

The fastest race in the United Kingdom is the 750-cc event of the North-West 200 held on the Londonderry circuit (*see above*). The record lap speed is 127.63 mph *205,395 km/h* by Tom Herron (1949–79) on a 747-cc Yamaha in 1978.

Longest race

The longest race was the Liège 24 hr, run on the old Francorchamps circuit. The greatest distance ever covered is 2761.9 miles *4444,8 km* (average speed 115.08 mph *185,20 km/h*) by Jean-Claude Chemarin and Christian Leon, both of France, on a 941-cc four-cylinder Honda on the Francorchamps circuit on 14–15 Aug 1976.

Longest circuit

The 37.73 mile *60,72 km* 'Mountain' circuit on the Isle of Man, over which the principal TT races have been run since 1911 (with minor amendments in 1920), has 264 curves and corners and is the longest used for any motorcycle race.

Most successful riders *Tourist Trophy*

The record number of victories in the Isle of Man TT races is 14 by Stanley Michael Bailey Hailwood (1940–81) between 1961 and 1979. The first man to win three consecutive TT titles in two events was James A. Redman (Rhodesia) (b. 8 Nov 1931). He won the 250-cc and 350-cc events in 1963–5. Mike Hailwood won three events in one year, in 1961 and 1967, and this feat was emulated by Joey Dunlop (Ireland) in 1985.

The TT circuit speed record is 118.47 mph *190,66 km/h* by Joey Dunlop on a Honda on 4 June 1984.

World championships

The most World Championship titles (instituted by the *Fédération Internationale Motocycliste* in 1949) won is 15 by Giacomo Agostini (Italy) (b. 16 June 1942), seven at 350 cc in 1968–74, and eight at 500 cc in 1966–72, 1975. He is the only man to win two World Championships in five consecutive years (350- and 500-cc titles 1968–72).

Agostini won 122 races (68 at 500 cc, 54 at 350 cc) in the World Championship series between 24 Apr 1965 and 29 Aug 1976, including a record 19 in 1970, also achieved by Mike Hailwood in 1966. Angel Roldan Nieto (Spain) (b. 25 Jan 1947) won a record seven 125-cc titles, 1971–2, 1979, 1981–4, and Klaus Enders (West Germany) (b. 1937) won six world side-car titles, 1967, 1969–70, 1972–4.

In 1985 Freddie Spencer (USA), riding for Honda, became the first man ever to win the 250-cc and 500-cc titles in the same year.

Trials

A record three World Trials Championships have been won by Yrjö Vesterinen (Finland), 1976–8 and by Eddie Lejeune (Belgium), 1982–4.

Moto-cross

Joël Robert (Belgium) (b. 11 Nov 1943) won six 250-cc Moto-cross World Championships (1964, 1968–72). Between 25 Apr 1964 and 18 June 1972 he won a record fifty 250-cc Grands Prix. He became the youngest moto-cross world champion on 12 July 1964 when he won the 250-cc title aged 20 yr 244 days.

Most successful machines

Italian MV-Agusta machines won 37 World Championships between 1952 and 1973, and 276 World Championship races between 1952 and 1976.

Youngest and oldest world champions

Alberto 'Johnny' Cecotto (Venezuela) (b. 25 Jan 1956) is the youngest to win a World Champion-

ship. He was 19 yr 211 days when he won the 350-cc title on 24 Aug 1975. The oldest was Hermann-Peter Müller (1909–76) of West Germany, who won the 250-cc title in 1955 aged 46.

Highest speeds

Official world speed records must be set with two runs over a measured distance made in opposite directions within a time limit—1 hr for FIM records and 2 hr for AMA records.

Donald A. Vesco (USA) (b. 8 Apr 1939), riding his 21 ft *6,4 m* long *Lightning Bolt* streamliner, powered by two 1016-cc Kawasaki engines on Bonneville Salt Flats, Utah, USA on 28 Aug 1978 set AMA and FIM absolute records with an overall average of 318.598 mph *512,733 km/h* and had a fastest run at an average of 318.66 mph *513,165 km/h*.

The highest speed achieved over two runs in the UK is 191.897 mph *308,82 km/h* by Roy Francis Daniel (b. 7 Dec 1938) on his 998-cc supercharged twin-engined RDS Triumph at Elvington, North Yorkshire on 29 July 1978. His average time for the flying 440 yd *402 m* was 4.69 sec.

The world record for 1 km *1093.6 yd* from a standing start is 16.68 sec by Henk Vink (b. 24 July 1939) (Netherlands) on his supercharged 984-cc four-cylinder Kawasaki, at Elvington Airfield, North Yorkshire on 24 July 1977. The faster run was made in 16.09 sec.

The world record for 440 yd *402 m* from a standing start is 8.805 sec by Henk Vink on his supercharged 1132-cc four-cylinder Kawasaki at Elvington Airfield, North Yorkshire on 23 July 1977. The faster run was made in 8.55 sec.

The fastest time for a single run over 440 yd *402 m* from a standing start is 7.08 sec by Bo O'Brechta (USA) riding a supercharged 1200-cc Kawasaki-based machine at Ontario, California, in 1980. The highest terminal velocity recorded at the end of a 440 yd *402 m* run from a standing start is 199.55 mph *321,14 km/h* by Russ Collins (USA) at Ontario on 7 Oct 1978.

Motor Racing

Earliest races

There are various conflicting claims, but the first automobile race was the 201 mile *323 km* Green Bay to Madison, Wisconsin, USA run in 1878 won by an Oshkosh steamer. In 1887 Count Jules Félix Philippe Albert de Dion de Malfiance (1856–1946) won the *La Vélocipède* 19.3 miles *31 km* race in Paris in a De Dion steam quadricycle in which he is reputed to have exceeded 37 mph *59 km/h*. The first 'real' race was from Paris to Bordeaux and back (732 miles *1178 km*) on 11–13 June 1895. The first to finish was Emile Levassor (1844–97) of France, in a Panhard-Levassor two-seater, with a 1.2-litre Daimler engine developing 3½ hp. His time was 48 hr 47 min (average speed 15.01 mph *24,15 km/h*). The first closed circuit race was held over five laps of a mile *1,6 km* dirt track at Narragansett Park, Cranston, Rhode Island, USA, on 7 Sept 1896, won by A. H. Whiting, driving a Riker electric.

The oldest race in the world still regularly run, is the RAC Tourist Trophy, first staged on 14 Sept 1905, in the Isle of Man. The oldest continental race is the French Grand Prix, first held on 26–27 June 1906. The Coppa Florio, in Sicily, has been irregularly held since 1900.

Fastest circuits

The highest average lap speed attained on any

GUINNESS HAVE PUBLISHED *MOTOR RACING: THE RECORDS* AT £8.95

closed circuit is 403,878 km/h *250.958 mph* in a trial by Dr Hans Liebold (b. 12 Oct 1926) (Germany) who lapped the 12,64 km *7.85 mile* high-speed track at Nardo, Italy in 1 min 52.67 sec in a Mercedes-Benz C111-IV experimental coupé on 5 May 1979. It was powered by a V8 engine with two KKK turbochargers with an output of 500 hp at 6200 rpm.

The fastest road circuit was the Francorchamps circuit near Spa, Belgium, then 8.761 miles *14,10 km* in length which was lapped in 3 min 13.4 sec (average speed 262,461 km/h *163.086 mph*) on 6 May 1973, by Henri Pescarolo (France) (b. 25 Sept 1942) driving a 2993-cc V12 Matra-Simca MS670 Group 5 sports car. The race lap average speed record at Berlin's AVUS track was 276,38 km/h *171.75 mph* by Bernd Rosemeyer (Germany) (1909–38) in a 6-litre V16 Auto Union in 1937.

The General Motors' High Speed Circuit (3,27 km *2.07 mile* with a 21.4 degree banking all round), at Millbrook, Bedfordshire, was lapped in 41.48 secs (average speed 283,49 km/h *176.16 mph*) by Tom Walkinshaw (b. 1947), partnered by Michael Scarlett, driving a 5343-cc V12 Jaguar XJS Group A racing saloon in June 1985.

Fastest pit stop
Robert William 'Bobby' Unser (USA) (b. 20 Feb 1934) took 4 seconds to take on fuel on lap 10 of the Indianapolis 500 on 30 May 1976.

Fastest race
The fastest race is the Busch Clash at Daytona, Florida over 125 miles *201 km* on a 2½ mile *4 km* 31-degree banked track. In 1979 Elzie Wylie 'Buddy' Baker (b. 25 Jan 1941) averaged 194.384 mph *312,831 km/h* in an Oldsmobile. Bill Elliott set the world record for a 500 mile *805 km* race in 1985 when he won at Talladega, Alabama at an average speed of 186.288 mph *299,793 km/h*. The NASCAR (National Association for Stock Car Automobile Racing) qualifying record is 212.809 mph *342,482 km/h* by Bill Elliott (b. 8

Most successful Grand Prix drivers ● John Young 'Jackie' Stewart (GB) (b. 11 June 1939) won a record 27 Grand Prix victories between 12 Sept 1965 and 5 Aug 1973. This tally was equalled on 17 May 1987 by Alain Prost (France) (b. 24 Feb 1955) driving a McLaren TAG Porsche **(above)**. (Photo: All-Sport/Vandystadt)

Oct 1955) in a Ford Thunderbird at Alabama International Motor Speedway, Talladega, Alabama, USA, a 2.66 mile *4,28 km* oval speedway with 33-degree banked turns, on 30 Apr 1987.

NASCAR records
Richard Lee Petty (USA) (b. 2 July 1937) won 200 NASCAR Winston Cup races in 1024 starts from 1958 to 3 May 1987. His best season was 1967 with 27 wins. Petty, on 1 Aug 1971, was the first driver to pass $1 million career earnings. The NASCAR career money record is $7,542,785 to 21 May 1987 by Darrell Waltrip (b. 5 Feb 1949). Bill Elliott won a year's record $2,044,468 in NASCAR events in 1985. Geoff Bodine (b. 18 Apr 1949) won 55 races in NASCAR Modified racing in 1978.

WORLD CHAMPIONSHIP GRAND PRIX MOTOR RACING
Most successful drivers
The World Drivers' Championship, inaugurated in 1950, has been won a record five times by Juan-Manuel Fangio (Argentina) (b. 24 June 1911) in 1951 and 1954–7. He retired in 1958, after having won 24 Grand Prix races (two shared) from 51 starts.

The most Grand Prix points in a career is 420½ by Niki Lauda (Austria) (b. 22 Feb 1949) in 171 Grands Prix, with 25 wins from 1971 to 1985. The most Grand Prix victories in a year is seven by James 'Jim' Clark (GB) (1936–68) in 1963 and by Alain Prost in 1984. The most Grand Prix starts is 176 (out of a possible 184) between 18 May 1958 and 26 Jan 1975 by Norman Graham Hill (GB) (1929–75) and by Jacques Laffite (France) (b. 21 Nov 1943), 1974–86. Between 20 Nov 1960 and 5 Oct 1969 Hill took part in 90 consecutive Grands Prix.

Oldest and youngest
The youngest world champion was Emerson Fittipaldi (Brazil) (b. 12 Dec 1946) who won his first World Championship on 10 Sept 1972 aged 25 yr 273 days. The oldest world champion was Juan-Manuel Fangio who won his last World Championship on 18 Aug 1957 aged 46 yr 55 days.

The youngest Grand Prix winner was Bruce Leslie McLaren (1937–70) of New Zealand, who won the United States Grand Prix at Sebring, Florida, on 12 Dec 1959 aged 22 yr 104 days. The oldest Grand Prix winner (in pre-World Championship days) was Tazio Giorgio Nuvolari (Italy) (1892–1953), who won the Albi Grand Prix at Albi, France on 14 July 1946 aged 53 yr 240 days. The oldest Grand Prix driver was Louis Alexandre Chiron (Monaco) (1899–1979), who finished 6th in the Monaco Grand Prix on 22 May 1955 aged 55 yr 292 days. The youngest driver to qualify for a Grand Prix was Michael Christopher Thackwell (New Zealand) (b. 30 Mar 1961) at the Canadian GP on 28 Sept 1980, aged 19 yr 182 days.

Manufacturers

Ferrari have won a record eight Manufacturers' World Championships, 1961, 1964, 1975-7, 1979, 1982-3. Ferrari have 91 race wins in 392 Grands Prix, 1950-85.

Fastest race

The fastest overall average speed for a Grand Prix race on a circuit in current use is 235,405 km/h *146.274 mph* by Alain Prost (France) in a McLaren at Silverstone in the British Grand Prix on 21 July 1985. The qualifying lap record was set on this occasion by Keke Rosberg (Finland) at 1 min 05.59 sec, an average speed of 258,803 km/h *160.817 mph*, in a Williams-Honda on 20 July 1985.

Closest finish

The closest finish to a World Championship race was when Ayrton Senna (Brazil) in a Lotus beat Nigel Mansell (GB) in a Williams by 0.014 sec in the Spanish Grand Prix at Jerez de la Frontera on 13 Apr 1986. In the Italian Grand Prix at Monza on 5 Sept 1971, 0.61 sec separated winner Peter Gethin (GB) from the fifth-placed driver.

BRITISH GRAND PRIX

First held in 1926 as the RAC Grand Prix, and held annually with the above name since 1949, the venue has alternated between Brands Hatch, Kent and Silverstone, Northamptonshire.

Fastest speed

The fastest race time is 1 hr 18 min 10.436 sec, when Alain Prost won in 1985. See Fastest race (above).

Most wins

The most wins by a driver is five by Jim Clark, 1962-65 and 1967, all in Lotus cars. Ferrari have most wins with ten, 1951-4, 1956, 1958, 1961, 1976, 1978 and 1983.

LE MANS

The greatest distance ever covered in the 24-hour *Grand Prix d'Endurance* (first held on 26-27 May 1923) on the old Sarthe circuit at Le Mans, France is 5333,724 km *3314.222 miles* by Dr Helmut Marko (Austria) (b. 27 Apr 1943) and Gijs van Lennep (Netherlands) (b. 16 Mar 1942) in a 4907-cc flat-12 Porsche 917K Group 5 sports car, on 12-13 June 1971. The record for the current circuit is 5088,507 km *3161.938 miles* (av. speed 212,021 km/h *131.747 mph*) by Klaus Ludwig (West Germany), Paulo Barillo (Italy) and John Winter (West Germany) in a Porsche 956 on 15-16 June 1985.

The race lap record (13,64 km *8.475 mile* lap) is 3 min 25.1 sec (average speed 239,16 km/h *148.61 mph* by Jacky Ickx (Belgium) in a Porsche 962C in 1985. The practice lap record is 3 min 14.8 sec (av. speed 252,05 km/h *156.62 mph*) by Hans Stück (West Germany) in a Porsche 962C on 14 June 1985.

Most wins

The race has been won by Porsche cars twelve times, in 1970-1, 1976-7, 1979, 1981-7. The most wins by one man is six by Jacques Bernard 'Jacky' Ickx (Belgium) (b. 1 Jan 1945), 1969, 1975-7 and 1981-2.

INDIANAPOLIS 500

The Indianapolis 500 mile *804 km* race (200 laps) was inaugurated in the USA on 30 May 1911. Two drivers have four wins: Anthony Joseph 'A.J.' Foyt, Jr (USA) (b. 16 Jan 1935) in 1961, 1964, 1967 and 1977; and Al Unser, Snr (USA) (b. 29 May 1939) in 1970-1, 1978 and 1987. The record time is 2 hr 55 min 42.48 sec (average speed 170.722 mph *274,743 km/h*) by Bobby Rahal (USA) driving a Penske March-Cosworth on 31 May 1986. The qualifying record average speed

is 216.828 mph *348,951 km/h* for four laps, by Rick Mears (USA) in a March-Cosworth on 10 May 1986. The one-lap record is 218.204 mph *351,155 km/h* by Mario Gabriele Andretti (USA) (b. 28 Feb. 1940) on 6 May 1987. The record prize fund is $4,001,450 and the individual prize record $581,062 by Bobby Rahal, both in 1986.

RALLYING

The earliest long rally was promoted by the Parisian daily *Le Matin* in 1907 from Peking, China to Paris over about 7500 miles *12 000 km* on 10 June. The winner, Prince Scipione Borghese (1872-1927) of Italy, arrived in Paris on 10 Aug 1907 in his 40-hp Itala accompanied by his chauffeur, Ettore, and Luigi Barzini.

Longest

The longest ever rally was the *Singapore Airlines* London–Sydney Rally over 19,329 miles *31 107 km* from Covent Garden, London on 14 Aug 1977 to Sydney Opera House, won on 28 Sept 1977 by Andrew Cowan, Colin Malkin and Michael Broad in a Mercedes 280E. The longest held annually is the Safari Rally (first run 1953 through East Africa (now only Kenya)), which has been up to 3874 miles *6234 km* long, as in the 17th Safari held between 8 and 12 Apr 1971. It has been won a record five times by Shekhar Mehta (b. Uganda 1945) in 1973, 1979-82.

Monte Carlo

The Monte Carlo Rally (first run 1911) has been won a record four times by: Sandro Munari (b. 1940) (Italy) in 1972, 1975, 1976 and 1977; and Walter Röhrl (b. 7 Mar 1947) (with co-driver Christian Geistdorfer) in 1980, 1982-84, each time in a different car. The smallest car to win was an 851-cc Saab driven by Erik Carlsson (Sweden) (b. 5 Mar 1929) and Gunnar Häggbom (Sweden) on 25 Jan 1962, and by Carlsson and Gunnar Palm on 24 Jan 1963.

Britain

The RAC Rally (first held 1932) has been recognised by the FIA since 1957. Hannu Mikkola (Finland) (b. 24 May 1942) (with co-driver Arne Hertz) has a record four wins, in a Ford Escort, 1978-9 and an Audi Quatro, 1981-2.

DRAGGING

Piston engined

The lowest elapsed time recorded by a piston-engined dragster is 5.176 sec from a standing start for 440 yd *402 m* by Darrell Gwynn (USA) at Dallas, Texas on 15 Apr 1987. The highest terminal velocity recorded at the end of a 440-yd run is 279.24 mph *449,38 km/h* by Joe Amato (USA) at Commerce, Georgia on 26 Apr 1987.

The world record for two runs in opposite directions over 440 yd *402 m* from a standing start is 6.70 sec by Dennis Victor Priddle (b. 1945) of Yeovil, Somerset, driving his 6424-cc supercharged Chrysler dragster developing 1700 bhp using nitromethane and methanol, at Elvington Airfield, North Yorkshire on 7 Oct 1972. The faster run was made in 6.65 sec.

Rocket or jet engined

The highest terminal velocity recorded by any dragster is 392.54 mph *631,732 km/h* by Kitty O'Neil (USA) at El Mirage Dry Lake, California, USA on 7 July 1977. The lowest elapsed time is 3.58 sec by Sammy Miller in a Pontiac 'Funny Car' in 1986.

Highest speeds *See also pp. 160-1*

The most successful land speed record breaker was Sir Malcolm Campbell (1885-1948). He broke the official record nine times between 25 Sept 1924, with 146.157 mph *235,216 km/h* in a Sunbeam, and 3 Sept 1935, when he achieved 301.129 mph *480,620 km/h* in the Rolls-Royce-engined *Bluebird*.

Duration record

The greatest distance ever covered in one year is 400 000 km *248,548.5 miles* by François Lecot (1879-1949), an innkeeper from Rochetaillée, near Lyon, France, in a 1900-cc 66-bhp Citroën 11 sedan, mainly between Paris and Monte Carlo, from 22 July 1935 to 26 July 1936. He drove on 363 of the 370 days allowed.

Mountaineering

Although bronze-age artifacts have been found on the summit of the Riffelhorn, Switzerland (2927 m *9605 ft*), mountaineering as a sport has a continuous history dating back only to 1854. Isolated instances of climbing for its own sake exist back to the 13th century. The Atacamenans built sacrificial platforms near the summit of Llullaillaco (6723 m *22,058 ft*) in late pre-Columbian times *c.* 1490. The earliest recorded rock climb in the British Isles was of Stac na Biorrach, St Kilda (71,9 m *236 ft*) by Sir Robert Moray in 1698.

Mount Everest

Mount Everest (8848 m *29,028 ft*) was first climbed at 11.30 a.m. on 29 May 1953, when the summit was reached by Edmund Percival Hillary (b. 20 July 1919), created KBE, of New Zealand, and the Sherpa, Tenzing Norgay (1914-86, formerly called Tenzing Khumjung Bhutia), who was awarded the GM. The successful expedition was led by Col (later Hon. Brigadier) Henry Cecil John Hunt CBE, DSO (b. 22 June 1910), who was created a Knight Bachelor in 1953, a life Baron on 11 June 1966 and KG on 23 Apr 1979.

The Sherpa, Sundare (or Sungdare) has climbed Everest a record four times in 1979, 1981, 1982 and 1985. Ang Rita Sherpa, with ascents in 1983, 1984 and 1985, is the first person to scale Everest three times without the use of bottled oxygen. Reinhold Messner (b. 17 Sept 1944) (Italy) was the first to make the entire climb solo on 20 Aug 1980. Messner and Peter Habeler (b. 22 July 1942) (Austria) made the first entirely oxygenless ascent on 8 May 1978.

The first Britons to reach the summit were Douglas Scott (b. 29 May 1941) and Dougal Haston (1940-77) on 24 Sept 1975. The first woman to reach the summit was Junko Tabei (b. 22 Sept 1939) (Japan) on 16 May 1975. The oldest person was Richard Daniel Bass (b. 21 Dec 1929) aged 55 yr 130 days on 30 Apr 1985.

Ace climber ● Reinhold Messner (b. 17 Sept 1944) is the first man to climb all 14 of the world's mountains over 8000 m *26,250 ft* in height. He achieved this feat without oxygen. With his ascent of Kanchenjunga in 1982 he also became the first to climb the world's three highest mountains, having earlier reached the peaks of Everest and K2.

face of the Eiger had been climbed on 20 Aug 1932 by Hans Lauper, Alfred Zurcher, Alexander Graven and Josef Knubel. The greatest alpine solo climb was that of Walter Bonatti (b. 22 June 1930) (Italy) of the South-West Pillar of the Dru, Montenvers, now called the Bonatti Pillar, with five bivouacs in 126 hr 7 min from 17–22 Aug 1955.

The most demanding free climbs in the world are those rated at 5.13, the premier location for these being in the Yosemite Valley, California, USA. The top routes in Britain are graded E7.7b, which relates closely to 5.13.

Highest bivouac
Douglas Scott and Dougal Haston bivouacked in a snow hole at 8747 m *28,700 ft* on the south summit of Everest on the night of 24 Sept 1975. Two Japanese, Hironobu Kamuro (1951–83) and Hiroshi Yoshino (1950–83), bivouacked at 8800 m *28,870 ft* on Everest on the night of 8/9 Oct 1983, but neither survived beyond the following day.

Oldest
Teiichi Igarashi (b. 21 Sept 1886) (Japan) climbed Mount Fuji (3776 m *12,388 ft*) at the age of 99 years 30 days on 20 July 1986.

MOUNTAIN RACING

Mount Cameroun
Timothy Leku Lekunze (Cameroun) descended from the summit 4095 m *13,435 ft* to Buea at 915 m *3002 ft* in 1 hr 9 min 26 sec on 26 Jan 1986, achieving a vertical rate of 45 m *150 ft* per min. He also set the record for the race to the summit and back of 3 hr 46 min 34 sec on 25 Jan 1987, when the temperature varied from 35°C at the start to 0°C at the summit. The record time for the ascent is 2 hr 34 min 27 sec by Michael Short (GB) in 1985.

Ben Nevis
The record time for the race from Fort William Town Park to the cairn on the summit of Ben Nevis (4418 ft *1346,6 m*) and return is 1 hr 25 min 34 sec by Kenneth Stuart (b. 25 Feb 1957), and the feminine record is 1 hr 43 min 25 sec by Pauline Haworth (b. 1 Aug 1956), both on 1 Sept 1984. The full course by the bridle path is about 14 miles *22 km* but distance is saved by crossing the open hillside. The mountain was first climbed *c.* 1720 and the earliest run, by William Swan in 2 hr 41 min, was in 1895.

Snowdon
The Snowdon Race (Ras Yr Wyddfa) has been run annually since 1976 from Llanberis to the summit of Snowdon and back. The fastest time is 1 hr 3 min 46 sec by Fausto Bonzi (Italy) on 21 July 1984. On the same date Pauline Haworth set a women's record of 1 hr 24 min 3 sec.

FELL RUNNING

In the 1972 Skiddaw Fell Race (3053 ft to 250 ft *930 to 107m*) a vertical descent rate of 128 ft *39m* per min was achieved by George Jeffrey Norman (b. 6 Feb 1945) (Altrincham AC).

Joss Naylor (b. 10 Feb 1936) won the Ennerdale mountain race (23 miles *37 km*) nine times, 1968–1977. The fastest time is 3 hr 20 min 57 sec by Kenny Stuart (b. 25 Feb 1957) of Keswick AC in 1985.

The Yorkshire three-peak record for the current 24-mile course is 2 hr 49 min 13 sec by Hugh Symonds of Kendal AC in 1985. The record for the former 23-mile course was 2 hr 37 min 30 sec by John Wild on 25 Apr 1982.

The Lakeland 24-hr record is 72 peaks achieved by Joss Naylor on 22–23 June 1975. He covered 105 miles *168 km* with 37,000 ft *11,227 m* of ascents and descents in 23 hr 11 min.

Greatest walls
The highest final stage in any wall climb is that on the south face of Annapurna I (8091 m *26,545 ft*). It was climbed by the British expedition led by Christian John Storey Bonington (b. 6 Aug 1934) when from 2 Apr to 27 May 1970, using 5500 m *18,000 ft* of rope, Donald Whillans and Dougal Haston scaled to the summit. The longest wall climb is on the Rupal-Flank from the base camp at 3560 m *11,680 ft* to the South Point 8042 m *26,384 ft* of Nanga Parbat—a vertical ascent of 4482 m *14,704 ft*. This was scaled by the Austro-German-Italian expedition led by Dr Karl Maria Herrligkoffer in April 1970.

Munro mounter ● Craig Caldwell took 377 days to cycle, walk and climb to the top of the 277 Munros (mountains over 3000 ft *914 m*) and the 222 Corbetts (2500–3000 ft *762–914 m*) in Scotland. In all he cycled 4152 miles *6682 km*, walked 3030 miles *4876 km*, and climbed 828,491 ft *252 542 m*.

Europe's greatest wall is the 2000 m *6600 ft* north face of the Eigerwand (Ogre wall) first climbed by Heinrich Harrer and Fritz Kasparek of Austria and Anderl Heckmair and Wiggerl Vörg of Germany from 21–24 July 1938. The north-east

The record for the Bob Graham Round of 42 lakeland peaks covering a total distance of 72 miles *116 km* and 27,000 ft *8230 m* of ascent and descent, is 13 hr 54 min by Billy Bland, 34, on 19 June 1982. Ernest Roger Baumeister (b. 17 Dec 1941) (Dark Peak Fell Runners Club) ran the double Bob Graham Round in 46 hr 34½ min on 30 June–1 July 1979.

The record for traversing the 85 mile *136,79 km* cross-country route of the nine 4000 ft *1219,2 m* Scottish peaks is 22 hr 33 min by J. S. 'Stan' Bradshaw (Clayton-le-Moors Harriers) on 30 May 1982.

The 'Three Thousander' record over the 14 Welsh peaks of over 3000 ft *914 m* is 4 hr 46 min 22 sec, by Joss Naylor on 17 June 1973.

The Ten Peaks run is from Burnthwaite Farm, Wasdale Head, Cumbria to the top of Skiddaw via England's nine other highest mountains and tops. The record time is 6 hr 56 min by Joss Naylor, wholly on foot, in May 1975.

Three Peaks record
The Three Peaks route from sea level at Fort William, Inverness-shire, to sea level at Caernarvon, via the summits of Ben Nevis, Scafell Pike and Snowdon, was walked by Arthur Eddleston (1939–84) (Cambridge H) in 5 days 23 hr 37 min from 11–17 May 1980. Peter and David Ford, David Robinson, Kevin Duggan and John O'Callaghan, of Luton and Dunstable, ran the distance in relay in 54 hr 39 min 14 sec from 7–9 Aug 1981. The fastest individual total time for climbing the three mountains is 4 hr 16 min by Joss Naylor on 8–9 July 1971.

On 23 June 1984 a team of three from the Greater Manchester Police Tactical Aid Group covered the distance in 8 hrs 22 min, being transported between the peaks by helicopter. Their running time was 5 hr 4 min.

A total climbing time of 7 hr 47 min was achieved by Brian Stadden from 13–15 Aug 1982 for Five Peaks, adding the highest points in Northern Ireland—Slieve Donard (2796 ft *852 m*) and in the Republic of Ireland—Carrauntaul (3414 ft *1041 m*) to the Three Peaks.

Pennine Way
The record for traversing the 271 mile *436 km* long Pennine Way is 2 days 21 hr 55 min by Michael Cudahy, 43, from 1–3 June 1984. The club relay record for a team of 24 is 29 hr 7 min 58 sec by Holmfirth Harriers on 28–9 June 1986.

Multiple peaks
Three members of the 'Climathon' team, Mick Cottam, Matthew Beresford and Andrew Curson, completed a climb of all 349 peaks in England over 2000 ft *609,6 m* (walking a distance of 402.5 miles *647,76 km*) from 21 July–11 Aug 1985.

Top to bottom
Clive Johnson and Les Heaton of 'Mountain Adventure' climbed the highest peaks and descended the deepest caves in each of England, Scotland and Wales in 44 hr 50 min from 16–18 Sept 1986.

Netball

The game was invented in the USA in 1891 and introduced into England in 1895 by Dr Toles. The All England Women's Netball Association was formed in 1926. The oldest club in continuous existence is the Polytechnic Netball Club of London founded in 1907.

Most titles *World*
Australia has won the World Championships (inst. 1963) a record five times, 1963, 1971, 1975, 1979 and 1983.

English
The National Club's Championships (inst. 1966) have been won eight times by Sudbury Netball Club, 1968–70, 1971 (shared), 1973, 1983–5). Surrey has won the County Championships (inst. 1932) a record 19 times (1949–64, 1966, 1981; 1969 and 1986 (both shared)).

Most international appearances
The record number of internationals is 90 by June Wightman (b. 28 June 1946) for Northern Ireland, 1964–85. The record for England is 83 by Jillean Hipsey, 1978–86.

Highest scores
The World Tournament record score was in Auckland, New Zealand in 1975 when England beat Papua New Guinea 114 goals to 16. The record number of goals in the World Tournament is 402 by Judith Heath (England) (b. 1942) in 1971.

Olympic Games

These records include the Games held at Athens in 1906.

The earliest celebration of the ancient Olympic Games of which there is a certain record is that of July 776 BC, when Coroibos, a cook from Elis, won the foot race, though their origin dates from perhaps as early as *c.* 1370 BC. The ancient Games were terminated by an order issued in Milan in AD 393 by Theodosius I, 'the Great' (*c.* 346–95), Emperor of Rome. At the instigation of Pierre de Fredi, Baron de Coubertin (1863–1937), the Olympic Games of the modern era were inaugurated in Athens on 6 Apr 1896.

Ever present
Five countries have never failed to be represented at the 21 celebrations of the Summer Games: Australia, France, Greece, Great Britain and Switzerland. Of these only Great Britain has been present at all Winter celebrations as well.

Largest crowd
The largest crowd at any Olympic site was 150,000 at the 1952 ski-jumping at the Holmenkøllen, outside Oslo, Norway. Estimates of the number of spectators at the marathon race through Tokyo, Japan on 21 Oct 1964 ranged from 500,000 to 1,500,000. The total spectator attendance at Los Angeles in 1984 was given as 5,797,923 (see All Sports).

Most medals *Individual gold*
In the ancient Olympic Games victors were given a chaplet of wild olive leaves. Leonidas of Rhodos won 12 running titles 164–152 BC. The most individual gold medals won by a male competitor in the modern Games is ten by Raymond Clarence Ewry (USA) (1874–1937) (see Track and Field Athletics). The female record is seven by Vera Caslavska-Odlozil (Czechoslova-kia) (see Gymnastics). The most gold medals won by a British competitor is four by: Paul Radmilovic (1886–1968) in water polo, 1908, 1912 and 1920 and the 4 × 200 m freestyle relay in 1908; and swimmer Henry Taylor (1885–1951) in 1906 and 1908. The Australian swimmer Iain Murray Rose, who won four gold medals, was born in Birmingham, England on 6 Jan 1939. The only Olympian to win four consecutive individual titles in the same event has been Alfred A. Oerter (USA) (b. 19 Sept 1936), who won the discus, 1956–68.

Swimmer Mark Andrew Spitz (USA) (b. 10 Feb 1950) won a record seven golds at one celebration, at Munich in 1972, including three in relays. The most won in individual events at one celebration is five by speed skater Eric Heiden (USA) (b. 14 June 1958) at Lake Placid, USA, in 1980.

The only man to win a gold medal in both the Summer and Winter Games was Edward F. Eagan (USA) (1898–1967) who won the 1920 light-heavyweight boxing title and was a member of the winning four-man bob in 1932.

Individual
Gymnast Larissa Latynina (USSR) (b. 27 Dec 1934) won a record 18 medals (see Gymnastics). The record at one celebration is eight by gymnast Aleksandr Ditiatin (USSR) (b. 7 Aug 1957) in 1980.

Youngest and oldest gold medallists
The youngest ever winner was a French boy (whose name is not recorded) who coxed the Netherlands pair in 1900. He was 7–10 years old and he substituted for Dr Hermanus Brockmann, who coxed in the heats but proved too heavy. The youngest ever female champion is Marjorie Gestring (USA) (b. 18 Nov 1922, now Mrs Bowman), aged 13 yr 267 days, in the 1936 women's springboard event. Oscar Swahn (*see p. 220*) was in the winning running deer shooting team in 1912 aged 64 yr 258 days.

Youngest and oldest *Great Britain*
The youngest competitor to represent Britain in the Olympic Games was Magdalena Cecilia Colledge (b. 28 Nov 1920), aged 11 yr 73 days when she skated in the 1932 Games. The oldest was Hilda Lorna Johnstone (b. 4 Sept 1902), aged 70 yr 5 days, in the equestrian dressage in the 1972 Games.

Longest span
The longest span of an Olympic competitor is 40 years by: Dr Ivan Osiier (Denmark) (1888–1965) in fencing, 1908–32 and 1948; and Magnus Konow

GUINNESS HAVE PUBLISHED *OLYMPIC GAMES RECORDS* AT £8.95

MOST MEDALS
NATIONAL
The total figures for medals for all Olympic events (including those now discontinued) for the Summer (1896–1984) and Winter Games (1924–84)

	Gold	Silver	Bronze	Total
1. **USA**	750	575	478	1803
2. **USSR** (formerly Russia)	408	340	303	1051
3. **GB** (including Ireland to 1920)	175	216	207	598
4. **Germany** (Germany 1896–1964, West Germany from 1968)	170	215	213	598

Excludes medals won in official art competitions 1912–48.

(Norway) (1887–1972) in yachting, 1908–20 and 1936–48. The longest feminine span is 24 years (1932–56) by the Austrian fencer Ellen Müller-Preis (b. 6 May 1912). Raimondo d'Inzeo (b. 8 Feb 1925) competed for Italy in equestrian events at a record eight celebrations from 1948 to 1976, gaining one gold, two silver and three bronze medals. Janice Lee York Romary (b. 6 Aug 1928), the US fencer, competed in all six Games from 1948 to 1968, and Lia Manoliu (Romania) (b. 25 Apr 1932) competed from 1952 to 1972, winning the discus in 1968.

The longest span of any British competitor is 28 years by Enoch Jenkins (b. 6 Nov 1892) who appeared in the 1924 and the 1952 Games in the clay pigeon shooting event, and the longest feminine span 20 years by Dorothy Jennifer Beatrice Tyler (née Odam) (b. 14 Mar 1920) who high-jumped from 1936 to 1956. The record number of appearances for Great Britain is six by fencer Bill Hoskyns from 1956 to 1976. Durward Randolph Knowles (b. 2 Nov 1917) competed in yachting for Britain in 1948 and in the following six Games for the Bahamas.

Orienteering

Orienteering as now known was invented by Major Ernst Killander in Sweden in 1918. It was based on military exercises of the 1890s. The term was first used for an event at Oslo, Norway on 7 Oct 1900. World Championships were instituted in 1966. Annual British Championships were instituted in 1967 following the formation of the British Orienteering Federation.

Most titles *World*
Sweden has won the men's relay six times between 1966 and 1979 and the women's relay seven times, 1966, 1970, 1974, 1976, 1981, 1983 and 1985. Three women's individual titles have been won by Annichen Kringstad-Svensson (Sweden) (b. 15 July 1960), 1981, 1983 and 1985. The men's title has been won twice by: Åge Hadler (Norway) (b. 14 Aug 1944) in 1966 and 1972; Egil Johansen (Norway) (b. 18 Aug 1954), 1976 and 1978; and Öyvin Thon (Norway) (b. 25 Mar 1958) in 1979 and 1981.

British
Geoffrey Peck (b. 27 Sept 1949) won the men's individual title a record five times, 1971, 1973, 1976–7 and 1979 as well as the over-35s title in 1985–6. Carol McNeill (b. 20 Feb 1944) won the women's title six times, 1967, 1969, 1972–76. She also won the over-35s title in 1984 and 1985.

Lorna Collett (b. 2 Sept 1922) of South Ribble OC and Terry Dooris (b. 22 Sept 1926) of Southern Navigators have both competed in all 20 British individual championships 1967–86.

Most competitors
The most competitors at an event in one day is 22,510 on the first day of the Swedish O-Ringen at Småland on 18 July 1983.

Parachuting

See also page 177

Parachuting became a regulated sport with the institution of World Championships in 1951. A team title was introduced in 1954 and women's events were included in 1956.

Most titles *World*
The USSR won the men's team title in 1954, 1958, 1960, 1966, 1972, 1976 and 1980, and the women's team title in 1956, 1958, 1966, 1968, 1972 and 1976. Nikolay Ushamyev (USSR) has won the individual title twice, 1974 and 1980.

British
Sgt Ronald Alan 'Scotty' Milne (b. 5 Mar 1952) of the Parachute Regiment won the British title five times in 1976–7, 1979–81. Rob Colpus and Geoff Sanders have each shared ten British titles for Relative Work parachuting, the 4-Way and 8-Way titles won by their team 'Symbiosis' in 1976–7, 1979, 1981–2.

Greatest accuracy
Jacqueline Smith (GB) (b. 29 Mar 1951) scored ten consecutive dead centre strikes (10 cm *4 in* disc) in the World Championships at Zagreb, Yugoslavia, 1 Sept 1978. At Yuma, Arizona, USA, in March 1978, Dwight Reynolds scored a record 105 daytime dead centres, and Bill Wenger and Phil Munden tied with 43 night-time DCs, competing as members of the US Army team, the Golden Knights. With electronic measuring the official FAI record is 50 DCs by Aleksandr Aasmiae (USSR) at Ferghana, USSR, Oct 1979.

The Men's Night Accuracy Landing record on an electronic score pad is 27 consecutive dead centres by Cliff Jones (USA) in 1981.

Parascending
Andrew Wakelin (UK) at Artesia Airport, New Mexico, USA on a Sorcerer 33 canopy on a 1600 ft *488 m* line on 1 Aug 1985 set records for distance: 7300 m *23,950 ft*, and height gain: 400 m *1312 ft*. The duration record is 21 min 8 sec by Pat Sugrue on a Paramount 9 in South Wales on 12 Apr 1986.

Nigel Horder scored four successive dead centres at the Dutch Open, Flevhof, Netherlands on 22 May 1983.

Pelota Vasca *(Jaï Alaï)*

The game, which originated in Italy as *longue paume* and was introduced into France in the 13th century, is said to be the fastest of all ball games. The glove or *gant* was introduced *c.* 1840 and the *chistera* was invented by Jean 'Gantchiki' Dithurbide of Ste Pée, France. The *grand chistera* was invented by Melchior Curuchague of Buenos Aires, Argentina in 1888. The world's largest *frontón* (enclosed stadium) is the World Jaï Alaï at Miami, Florida, USA, which had a record attendance of 15,052 on 27 Dec 1975.

World Championships
The Federacion Internacional de Pelota Vasca stage World Championships every four years (first in 1952). The most successful pair have been Roberto Elias and Juan Labat (Argentina), who won the *Trinquete Share* four times, 1952, 1958, 1962 and 1966. Labat won a record seven world titles in all. The most wins in the long court game *Cesta Punta* is three by Hamuy of Mexico, with two different partners, 1958, 1962 and 1966.

Highest speed
An electronically-measured ball velocity of 302 km/h *188 mph* was recorded by José Ramon Areitio at the Newport Jai Alai, Rhode Island, USA on 3 Aug 1979.

Longest domination
The longest domination as the world's No 1 player was enjoyed by Chiquito de Cambo (*né* Joseph Apesteguy) (France) (1881–1955) from the beginning of the century until succeeded in 1938 by Jean Urruty (France) (b. 19 Oct 1913).

Pétanque

The origins of pétanque or boules can be traced back over 2000 years, but it was not until 1945 that the *Fédération Français de Pétanque et Jeu*

Provençal was formed, and subsequently the *Fédération Internationale* (FIPJP). The first recognised British club was formed on 30 Mar 1966 as the Chingford Club de Pétanque and the British Pétanque Association was founded in 1974.

World Championships
Winner of the most World Championships (inst. 1959) has been France with eight titles to 1985.

Highest score in 24 hours
David Gyton, Paul Gyton and Michael Morris scored a record 1767 points in 24 hours (159 games) at the Gin Trap, Ringstead, Norfolk on 27–8 June 1986.

Pigeon Racing

Pigeon racing developed from the use of homing pigeons for carrying messages. The sport originated in Belgium from commercial services and the earliest long-distance race was from London to Antwerp in 1819, involving 36 pigeons.

Longest flights
The greatest recorded homing flight by a pigeon was made by one owned by the 1st Duke of Wellington (1769–1852). Released from a sailing ship off the Ichabo Islands, West Africa, on 8 April, it dropped dead a mile from its loft at Nine Elms, Wandsworth, London on 1 June 1845, 55 days later, having flown an airline route of 5400 miles *8700 km*, but an actual distance of possibly 7000 miles *11 250 km* to avoid the Sahara Desert. The official British duration record (into Great Britain) is 1173 miles *1887 km* in 15 days by *C.S.O.*, owned by Rosie and Bruce of Wick, in the 1976 Palamos Race. In the 1975 Palamos Race, *The Conqueror*, owned by Alan Raeside, homed to Irvine, Strathclyde, 1010 miles *1625 km*, in 43 hr 56 min. The greatest number of flights over 1000 miles flown by one pigeon is that of *Dunning Independence*, owned by D. Smith, which annually flew from Palamos to Dunning, Perthshire, Scotland 1039 miles *1662 km* between 1978 and 1981.

Highest speeds
In level flight in windless conditions it is very doubtful if any pigeon can exceed 60 mph *96 km/h*. The highest race speed recorded is one of 3229 yd *2952 m* per min (110.07 mph *177,14 km/h*) in the East Anglian Federation race from East Croydon on 8 May 1965 when the 1428 birds were backed by a powerful south south-west wind. The winner was owned by A. Vigeon & Son, Wickford, Essex.

The highest race speed recorded over a distance of more than 1000 km *621.37 miles* is 2432.7 yd *2224,5 m* per min (82.93 mph *133,46 km/h*) by a hen in the Central Cumberland Combine race over 683 miles 147 yd *1099,316 km* from Murray Bridge, South Australia to North Ryde, Sydney on 2 Oct 1971.

24-hr records
The world's longest reputed distance in 24 hr is 803 miles *1292 km* (velocity 1525 yd *1394 m* per min) by E. S. Petersen's winner of the 1941 San Antonio R.C. event in Texas, USA.

The best 24-hr performance into the United Kingdom is 724 miles 219 yd *1165,3 km* by E. Cardno's *Mormond Lad*, on 2 July 1977, from Nantes, France to Fraserburgh, Grampian. Average speed was 1648 yd *1507 m* per min (56.18 mph *90,41 km/h*).

Career records
Owned by R. Green, of Walsall Wood, West Midlands, *Champion Breakaway* won 59 first prizes from 1972 to May 1979.

The greatest competitive distance flown is 20,082 miles *32 318 km* by *Nunnies*, a chequer cock owned by Terry Haley of Abbot's Langley, Hertfordshire, England.

Highest priced bird

The highest recorded price paid for a pigeon is £41,000 by Louis Massarella of Loughborough, England for *Peter Pan* in November 1986. The bird was thus worth about ten times its weight in gold. In February 1986 André van Bruaene (Belgium) turned down an offer of £55,000 for his champion *Barcelona II*.

Polo

Polo is usually regarded as being of Persian origin, having been played as *Pulu c.* 525 BC. Other claims have come from Tibet and the Tang Dynasty of China AD 250. The earliest polo club of modern times was the Cachar Club (founded in 1859) in Assam, India. The oldest club still existing is the Calcutta Polo Club (1862). The game was introduced into England from India in 1869 by the 10th Hussars at Aldershot, Hampshire and the earliest match was one between the 9th Lancers and the 10th Hussars on Hounslow Heath, Greater London, in July 1871. The earliest international match between England and the USA was in 1886.

The game's governing body is the Hurlingham Polo Association, which drew up the first English rules in 1875.

Most titles

The British Open Championship for the Cowdray Park Gold Cup (inst. 1956) has been won five times by Stowell Park, 1973–4, 1976, 1978 and 1980.

Highest handicap

The highest handicap based on eight 7½-min 'chukkas' is ten goals introduced in the USA in 1891 and in the United Kingdom and in Argentina in 1910. A total of 55 players have received ten-goal handicaps. The only two currently playing in Britain are the Mexicans Guillermo and Carlos Gracida. The latter, with Ernesto Trotz (Argentina) in 1985 is the most recent recipient of this handicap. The last (of six) ten-goal handicap players from Great Britain was Gerald Balding in 1939. A match of two 40-goal teams was staged, for the only time, at Palermo, Buenos Aires, Argentina in 1975.

The highest handicaps of current United Kingdom players are nine by: Julian Hipwood (b. 23 June 1946); and by Howard Hipwood (b. 24 Mar 1950). Claire J. Tomlinson of Gloucestershire attained a handicap of five, the highest ever by a woman, in 1986.

Highest score

The highest aggregate number of goals scored in an international match is 30, when Argentina beat the USA 21–9 at Meadow Brook, Long Island, New York, USA, in September 1936.

Pool

Pool or championship pocket billiards with numbered balls began to become standardised *c.* 1890. The greatest exponents were Ralph Greenleaf (USA) (1899–1950), who won the 'world' professional title 19 times (1919–37), and William Mosconi (USA) (b. 27 June 1913), who dominated the game from 1941 to 1957.

The longest consecutive run in an American straight pool match is 625 balls by Michael Eufemia at Logan's Billiard Academy, Brooklyn, NY, on 2 Feb 1960. The greatest number of balls pocketed in 24 hr is 15,780 by Vic Elliott at the Royal George, Lincoln on 2–3 Apr 1985.

The record time for potting all 15 balls in a speed

Cowes–Torquay powerboating ● Renato della Valle (Italy) drove *Ego Rothman* to a record four consecutive wins, 1982–5, in the 320,4 km *199 mile* Cowes–Torquay offshore powerboating classic race. (Photo: Steve Powell/All-Sport)

competition is 40.06 sec by Ross McInnes (b. 19 Jan 1955) at Clacton, Essex on 11 Sept 1983.

A record break of 132 for 14–1 pool was set by Ross McInnes at Pontin's, Heysham, Lancashire on 3 Oct 1984.

Powerboat Racing

A petrol engine was first installed in a boat by Jean Joseph Etienne Lenoir (1822–1900) on the River Seine, Paris in 1865. Actual powerboat racing started in about 1900, the first prominent race being from Calais to Dover in 1903. International racing was largely established by the presentation of a Challenge Trophy by Sir Alfred Harmsworth in 1903. Thereafter, racing developed mainly as a 'circuit' or short, sheltered course type competition. Offshore or sea-passage races also developed, initially for displacement (non-planing) cruisers. Offshore events for fast (planing) cruisers began in 1958 with a 170 mile *273 km* passage race from Miami, USA to Nassau, Bahamas. Outboard motor, *i.e.* the combined motor/transmission detachable propulsion unit type racing began in the USA in about 1920. Both inboard and outboard motor boat engines are mainly petrol fuelled, but since 1950 diesel (compression ignition) engines have appeared and are widely used in offshore sport.

Highest speeds *(For the world water speed record see page 161.)*

The highest speed recorded by a propeller-driven boat is 229.00 mph *368,54 km/h* by *The Texan*, a Kurtis Top Fuel Hydro Drag boat, driven by Eddie Hill on 5 Sept 1982 at Chowchilla, California, USA. He also set a 440 yd *402 m* elapsed time record of 5.16 seconds in this boat at Firebird Lake, Arizona, USA on 13 Nov 1983. The official American Drag Boat Association record is 223.88 mph *360,29 km/h* by *Final Effort*, a Blown Fuel Hydro boat driven by Robert T. Burns at Creve Coeur Lake, St Louis, Missouri, USA on 15 July 1985 over a ¼ mile *402 m* course.

The fastest speed recognised by the *Union Internationale Motonautique* for an outboard-powered boat is in Class (e): *285,83 km/h* 177.61 mph by P. R. Knight in a Chevrolet-engined Lauterbach hull on Lake Ruataniwha, New Zealand in 1986. Robert F. Hering (USA) set the world Formula One record at 165.338 mph *266,085 km/h*, at Parker, Arizona on 21 Apr 1986.

The fastest speed recognised for an offshore boat is 154.438 mph *248,537 km/h* for one way and 148.238 mph *238,559 km/h* for two runs by Tom Gentry (USA) in his 49 ft *15 m* catamaran, powered by four Gentry Turbo Eagle V8 Chevrolets.

The fastest speed recorded for a diesel (compression ignition) boat is 218,26 km/h *135.62 mph* by the hydroplane *Iveco World Leader*, powered by an Aifo-Fiat engine, driven by Carlo Bonomi at Venice, Italy in 1985.

Highest race speeds

The highest speed recorded in an offshore race is 103.29 mph *166,22 km/h* by Tony Garcia (USA) in a Class I powerboat at Key West, Florida, USA in November 1983.

Longest races

The longest offshore race has been the Port Richborough London to Monte Carlo Marathon Offshore international event. The race extended over 2947 miles *4742 km* in 14 stages from 10–25 June 1972. It was won by *H.T.S.* (GB) driven by Mike Bellamy, Eddie Chater and Jim Brooker in 71 hr 35 min 56 sec for an average of 41.15 mph *66,24 km/h*. The longest circuit race is the 24-hour race held annually since 1962 on the River Seine at Rouen, France. The 1983 winners François Greens, Jan van Brockels and Roger Robin of Belgium drove a Johnson outboard-engined Piranha boat at an average speed of 75,02 km/h *46.63 mph*.

Longest jetboat jumps

The longest ramp jump achieved by a jetboat has been 120 ft *36,57 m* by Peter Horak (USA) in a Glastron Carlson CVX 20 Jet Deluxe with a 460 Ford V8 engine (take-off speed 55 mph *88 km/h*) for a documentary TV film, at Salton Sea, California, USA on 26 Apr 1980. The longest leap on to land is 172 ft *38,7 m* by Norm Bagrie (NZ) from the Shotover River on 1 July 1982 in the 1½-ton jetboat *Valvolene*.

Rackets

There is record of the sale of a racket court at Southernhay, Exeter, Devon dated 12 Jan 1798. The game which is of 17th-century origin was played by debtors in the Fleet Prison, London in the middle of the 18th century, and an inmate, Robert Mackay, claimed the first 'world' title in 1820. The first closed court champion was Francis Erwood at Woolwich in 1860.

World Championships

Of the 22 world champions since 1820 the longest reign is by Geoffrey Willoughby Thomas Atkins (b. 20 Jan 1927) who held the title, after beating the professional James Dear (1910–81) in 1954, until retiring, after defending it four times, in April 1972.

Most Amateur titles

Since the Amateur Singles Championship was instituted in 1888 the most titles won by an individual is nine by Edgar Maximilian Baerlein (1879–1971) between 1903 and 1923. Since the institution of the Amateur Doubles Championship in 1890 the most shares in titles has been eleven by: David Sumner Milford (1905–84), between 1938 and 1959; and John Ross Thompson (b. 10 May 1918), between 1948 and 1966; they won ten titles together. Milford also won seven Amateur Singles titles (1930–51), an Open title (1936) and held the World title from 1937 to 1946. Thompson has additionally won an Open Singles title and five Amateur Singles titles.

Racketball

Racquetball using a 40 ft by 20 ft court was invented in 1950 by Joe Sobek at the Greenwich YMCA, Connecticut, USA, originally as Paddle Rackets. The International Racquetball Association was founded in 1968 by Bob Kendler (USA). John Treharne won three British titles, 1981–83.

Racketball using a 32 ft by 21 ft court (as for squash) was introduced to Britain by Ian Wright in 1976. The British Racketball Association was formed and staged inaugural British National Championships in 1984. Two titles have been won at the women's event by Bett Dryhurst, 1985–6.

Rodeo

Rodeo, which developed from 18th-century *fiestas*, came into being in the early days of the North American cattle industry. The sport originated in Mexico and spread from there into the cattle regions of the USA. Steer wrestling came in with Bill Pickett (1870–1932) of Texas, in 1900.

The largest rodeo in the world is the Calgary Exhibition and Stampede at Calgary, Alberta, Canada. In 1981 the total paid attendance for the rodeo events over ten days was 122,268. The National Finals Rodeo is organised annually by the Professional Rodeo Cowboys Association (PRCA). In 1985 a record $1,790,000 prize money was offered for the event, staged in Las Vegas, Nevada, USA.

Most world titles

The record number of all-around titles in the PRCA World Championships is six by Larry Mahan (USA) (b. 21 Nov 1943) in 1966–70 and 1973 and, consecutively, 1974–9 by Tom Ferguson (b. 20 Dec 1950). Tom Ferguson had record career earnings of $1,049,744 to 1986. Jim Shoulders (b. 1928) of Henryetta, Oklahoma, USA has won a record 16 World Championships between 1949 and 1959. The record figure for prize money in a single season is $166,042 by Lewis Feild in 1986. The record for one rodeo is $30,677 by Dee Pickett at the National Finals Rodeo, Oklahoma City in December 1984.

Youngest champions

The youngest winner of a world title is Metha Brorsen, of Oklahoma, USA, who won the International Rodeo Association cowgirls barrel-racing event in 1975 at 11 years old. The youngest champion in Professional Rodeo Cowboys Association/Women's Professional Rodeo Association competition is Jackie Jo Perrin of Antlers, Oklahoma, USA, who won the barrel-racing title in 1977 at age 13.

Time records

Records for PRCA timed events, such as calf-roping and steer-wrestling, are not always comparable, because of the widely varying conditions due to the sizes of arenas and amount of start given the stock. The fastest time recorded for roping a calf is 5.7 sec by Lee Phillips at Assiniboia, Saskatchewan, Canada in 1978, and the fastest time for overcoming a steer is 2.4 sec by: James Bynum, at Marietta, Oklahoma, USA, in 1955; Carl Deaton at Tulsa, Oklahoma, USA in 1976; and Gene Melton at Pecatonica, Illinois, USA, in 1976.

The highest score in bull riding was 98 points out of a possible 100 by Denny Flynn on *Red Lightning* at Palestine, Illinois, USA in 1979.

Champion bull

The top bucking bull was probably *Tornado*, who bucked out of the chute 220 times before Freckles Brown, in 1967, became the first cowboy to ride him to the eight-second bell. *Tornado* retired a year later after a 14-year career.

Champion bronc

Traditionally, a bronc called *Midnight* owned by Jim McNab of Alberta, Canada was never ridden in 12 appearances at the Calgary Stampede.

Roller Skating

The first roller skate was devised by Jean Joseph Merlin (1735–1803) of Huy, Belgium, in 1760 and demonstrated by him in London but with disastrous results. James L. Plimpton of New York produced the present four-wheeled type and patented it in January 1863. The first indoor rink was opened in the Haymarket, London, in about 1824.

Most titles *Speed*

The most world speed titles won is 18 by two women: Alberta Vianello (Italy), eight track and ten road 1953–65; and Annie Lambrechts (Belgium), one track and 17 road 1964–81, at distances from 500 m to 10 000 m. Most British national individual men's titles have been won by Michael Colin McGeogh (b. 30 Mar 1946) with 19 in 1966–85. Chloe Ronaldson (b. 30 Nov 1939) won 40 individual and 14 team ladies' senior titles from 1958 to 1985.

Figure

The records for figure titles are: five by Karl Heinz Losch in 1958–9, 1961–2 and 1966; and four by Astrid Bader in 1965–8, both of West Germany. The most world pair titles is four by Dieter Fingerle (West Germany), 1959, 1965–7 with two different partners.

Speed skating

The fastest speed put up in an official world record is 43,05 km/h *26.75 mph* when Patrizio Sarto (b. 19 Jan 1964) (Italy) recorded 25.088 sec for 300 m on a road at Bogota, Colombia in 1984. The world records on a rink for 10 000 m are: (men) 15 min 49.7 sec, Roberto Marotta (b. 6 Mar 1948) (Italy) at Inzell, West Germany 1968; (women) 16 min 30.484 sec, Annie Lambrechts (Belgium) at Louvain, Belgium on 1 July 1985. Lambrechts went on to skate 37,097 km *23.051 miles* in 1 hr and 50 km in 1 hr 21 min 25 sec. The men's 1-hour record on a track is 37,230 km *23.133 miles* by Alberto Civolani (Italy) (b. 16 Mar 1933) at Inzell, West Germany on 28 Sept 1968. He went on to skate 50 miles *80,46 km* in 2 hr 20 min 33.1 sec.

Largest rink

The greatest indoor rink ever to operate was located in the Grand Hall, Olympia, London. Opened in 1890 and closed in 1912, it had an actual skating area of 68,000 ft² *6 300 m²*. The current largest is the main arena of 34,981 ft² *3250 m²* at Guptill Roll-Arena, Boght Corner, New York, USA. The total rink area is 41,380 ft² *3844 m²*.

Endurance

Theodore James Coombs (b. 1954) of Hermosa Beach, California, skated 5193 miles *8357 km* from Los Angeles to New York and back to Yates Center, Kansas from 30 May to 14 Sept 1979.

Land's End to John o'Groats

Steve Fagan, 20, roller skated the distance, 925 miles *1488 km*, in 9 days 10 hr 25 min from 1–10 May 1984, averaging 157 km *98 miles* a day.

ROLLER HOCKEY

Roller hockey (previously known as rink hockey in Europe) was introduced to Britain as rink polo, at the old Lava rink, Denmark Hill, London in the late 1870s. The Amateur Rink Hockey Association was formed in 1908, and in 1913 became the National Rink Hockey (now Roller Hockey) Association. England won the first four World Championships, 1936–9, since when Portugal has won most titles with 12 between 1947 and 1982. Portugal also won a record 16 European (inst. 1926) titles between 1947 and 1987.

Rowing

The Sphinx stela of Amenhotep II (1450–1425 BC) records that he *stroked* a boat for some three miles. The earliest established sculling race is the Doggett's Coat and Badge, which was first rowed on 1 Aug 1716 from London Bridge to Chelsea as a race for apprentices, and is still contested annually. Although rowing regattas were held in Venice in 1300 the first English regatta probably took place on the Thames by the Ranelagh Gardens, near Putney in 1775.

Most Olympic medals

Six oarsmen have won three gold medals: John B. Kelly (USA) (1889–1960), father of the late HSH Princess Grace of Monaco, single sculls (1920) and double sculls (1920 and 1924); his cousin Paul Vincent Costello (USA) (b. 27 Dec 1899), double sculls (1920, 1924 and 1928); Jack Beresford, Jr (GB) (1899–1977), single sculls (1924), coxless fours (1932) and double sculls (1936); Vyacheslav Ivanov (USSR) (b. 30 July 1938), single sculls (1956, 1960 and 1964); Siegfried Brietzke (GDR) (b. 12 June 1952), coxless pairs (1972) and coxless fours (1976, 1980); and Pertti Karpinen (Finland) (b. 17 Feb 1953), single sculls 1976, 1980 and 1984.

World Championships

World rowing championships distinct from the Olympic Games were first held in 1962, at first four yearly, but from 1974 annually, except in Olympic years.

The most gold medals won at World Championships and Olympic Games is six by the GDR oarsmen: the twins Bernd and Jörg Landvoigt (b. 23 Mar 1951); Joachim Dreifke (b. 26 Dec 1952); Karl-Heinz Bussert (b. 8 Jan 1955); Ulrich Diessner (b. 27 Dec 1954); Siegfried Brietzke (b. 12 June 1952); and Wolfgang Mager (b. 24 Aug 1952);

and at lightweight events by Ruggero Verroca (Italy) (b. 3 Jan 1961).

The most wins at single sculls is five, by Peter-Michael Kolbe (West Germany) (b. 2 Aug 1953), 1975, 1978, 1981, 1983 and 1986, and by Pertti Karpinen, 1979 and 1985 with his three Olympic wins (above), and in the women's events by Christine Hahn (née Schieblich) (GDR) (b. 31 Dec 1954), 1974–5, 1977–8 (and the 1976 Olympic title).

Boat Race

The earliest University Boat Race, which Oxford won, was from Hambledon Lock to Henley Bridge on 10 June 1829. Outrigged eights were first used in 1846. In the 133 races to 1987, Cambridge won 69 times, Oxford 63 times and there was a dead heat on 24 Mar 1877.

The race record time for the course of 4 miles 374 yd *6,779 km* (Putney to Mortlake) is 16 min 45 sec by Oxford on 18 Mar 1984. This represents an average speed of 15.09 mph *24,28 km/h*. The smallest winning margin has been by a canvas by Oxford in 1952 and 1980. The greatest margin (apart from sinking) was Cambridge's win by 20 lengths in 1900.

Boris Rankov (Oxford, 1978–83) rowed in a record six winning boats. Susan Brown (b. 29 June 1958), the first woman to take part, coxed the winning Oxford boats in 1981 and 1982. Daniel Topolski coached Oxford to ten successive victories 1976–85.

The heaviest man ever to row in a University boat has been Gavin Stewart (Wadham) at 231 lb *105 kg* for Oxford in 1987. The 1983 Oxford crew averaged a record 204.3 lb *92,5 kg*. The lightest oarsman was the 1882 Oxford stroke, Alfred Herbert Higgins, at 9 st 6½ lb *60 kg*. The lightest coxes, Francis Henry Archer (Cambridge) (1843–89) in 1862 and Hart Parker Vincent Massey (Oxford) (b. Canada, 30 Mar 1918) in 1939, were both 5 st 2 lb *32,6 kg*.

The youngest 'blue' ever was Matthew John Brittin (Cambridge) (b. 1 Sept 1968) at 18 yr 208 days, in 1986.

Head of the River

A processional race for eights instituted in 1926, the Head has an entry limit of 420 crews (3780 competitors). The record for the course Mortlake–Putney (the reverse of the Boat Race) is 16 min 37 sec by the ARA National Squad in 1987.

Henley Royal Regatta

The annual regatta at Henley-on-Thames, Oxfordshire, was inaugurated on 26 Mar 1839. Since then the course, except in 1923, has been about 1 mile 550 yd *2112 m* varying slightly according to the length of boat. In 1967 the shorter craft were 'drawn up' so all bows start level.

The most wins in the Diamond Challenge Sculls (inst. 1844) is six consecutively by Stuart A. Mackenzie (b. 5 Apr 1937) (Australia and GB) 1957–62. The record time is 7 min 40 sec by Sean Drea (Neptune RC, Ireland) on 5 July 1975. The Grand Challenge Cup (inst. 1839) for eights has been won 27 times by Leander crews between 1840 and 1953. The record time for the event is 6 min 13 sec by Harvard University, USA, and a combined Leander/Thames Tradesmen crew, both on 5 July 1975.

Sculling

The record number of wins in the Wingfield Sculls (Putney to Mortlake) (instituted 1830) is seven by Jack Beresford, Jr from 1920 to 1926. The fastest time for the course has been 21 min 11 sec by Leslie Frank 'Dick' Southwood (b. 18 Jan 1906) in winning the Wingfield Sculls on 12 Aug 1933.

Highest speed

The highest recorded speed on non-tidal water for 2000 m *2187 yd* is by an American eight in 5 min 27.14 sec (22,01 km/h *13.68 mph*) at Lucerne, Switzerland on 17 June 1984. A crew from Penn AC, USA, was timed in 5 min 18.8 sec (14.03 mph *22,58 km/h*) in the FISA Championships on the River Meuse, Liège, Belgium, on 17 Aug 1930.

24 hours

The greatest distance rowed in 24 hours (upstream and downstream) by an eight is 130 miles *209 km* by members of the Renmark Rowing Club, South Australia, on 20–1 Apr 1984.

Cross Channel

Ivor Lloyd sculled across the English Channel in a record 3 hr 35 min 1 sec on 4 May 1983.

River Thames

A crew of five from Poplar Fire Station, London Fire Brigade rowed the navigable length of the Thames, 185.88 miles *299,14 km*, from Lechlade Bridge, Gloucestershire to Southend Pier, Essex in 45 hr 32 min in a 22 ft 10 in *6,96 m* skiff from 16–18 Apr 1984.

The fastest time from Folly Bridge, Oxford to Westminster Bridge, London (112 miles *180 km*) is 14 hr 25 min 15 sec by an eight from Kingston Rowing Club on 1 Feb 1986.

Longest race

The longest annual rowing race is the annual Tour du Lac Leman, Geneva, Switzerland for coxed fours (the five-man crew taking turns as cox) over 160 km *99 miles*. The record winning time is 12 hr 52 min by LAGA Delft, Netherlands on 3 Oct 1982.

International Dragon Boat Races

Instituted in 1975 and held annually in Hong Kong, the fastest time achieved for the 640 metres *700 yd* course is 2 min 27.45 sec by the Chinese Shun De team on 30 June 1985. The best time for a British team was 2 min 51.8 sec by an Amateur Rowing Association team in 1984. Teams have 28 members—26 rowers, one steersman and one drummer.

Rugby League

There have been four different scoring systems in rugby league football. For the purpose of these records all points totals remain as they were under the system in operation at the time they were made.

The Northern Rugby Football Union was formed on 29 Aug 1895 at the George Hotel, Huddersfield, West Yorkshire. Twenty-one clubs from Yorkshire and Lancashire were present and all but one agreed to resign from the Rugby Union. Payment for loss of wages was the major cause of the breakaway and full professionalism was allowed in 1898. A reduction in the number of players from 15 to 13 took place in 1906. The title 'Rugby Football League' was adopted in 1922.

Most titles

There have been seven World Cup Competitions. Australia have most wins, with four, 1957, 1968, 1970 and 1977 as well as a win in the International Championship of 1975.

The Northern Rugby League was formed in 1901. The word 'Northern' was dropped in 1980. Wigan has won the League Championship a record ten times (1909, 1922, 1926, 1934, 1946, 1947, 1950, 1952, 1960 and 1987).

In the Rugby League Challenge Cup (inaugurated 1896–7 season) Leeds have most wins with ten, 1910, 1923, 1932, 1936, 1941–2 (wartime), 1957, 1968, 1977–8. Oldham is the only club to appear in four consecutive Cup Finals (1924–7).

Since 1974 there have been five major competitions for RL clubs: Challenge Cup, League Championship, Premiership, John Player Special Trophy and County Cups. Wigan has a record 40 wins in these competitions, and won four, the League Championship, John Player Special Trophy, Lancashire Cup and Premiership in 1986–7.

Three clubs have won all possible major Rugby League trophies in one season: Hunslet, 1907–8 season, Huddersfield, 1914–15 and Swinton, 1927–8, all won the Challenge Cup, League Championship, County Cup and County League (now defunct).

HIGHEST SCORES
Senior match
The highest aggregate score in a game where a senior club has been concerned was 121 points,

Gold medals at the Commonwealth Games
● Steven Redgrave (England) (b. 23 Mar 1962) won a unique three gold medals for rowing at the 1986 Commonwealth Games in Edinburgh—single sculls, coxless pairs and coxed fours. (Photo: Michael King/All-Sport)

Rugby League

when Huddersfield beat Swinton Park Rangers by 119 (19 goals, 27 tries) to 2 (one goal) in the first round of the Northern Union Cup on 28 Feb 1914. The highest score in League football is 112 points by Leeds v. Coventry (nil) on 12 Apr 1913. St Helens beat Carlisle 112–0 in the Lancashire Cup on 14 Sept 1986.

Challenge Cup Final
The highest score in a Challenge Cup Final is 38 points (8 tries, 7 goals) by Wakefield Trinity v. Hull (5) at Wembley on 14 May 1960. The record aggregate is 52 points when Wigan beat Hull 28–24 at Wembley on 4 May 1985. The greatest winning margin was 34 points when Huddersfield beat St Helens 37–3 at Oldham on 1 May 1915.

International match
The highest score in an international match is Australia's 63–13 defeat of England at Paris, France on 31 Dec 1933. The highest score in a World Cup match is the 53–19 win by Great Britain over New Zealand at Hameau, Paris on 4 Nov 1972.

Touring teams
The record score for a British team touring Australasia is 101 points by England v. South Australia (nil) at Adelaide in May 1914. The record for a touring team in Britain is 92 (10 goals, 24 tries) by Australia against Bramley (7, 2 goals and 1 try) at the Barley Mow Ground, Bramley, near Leeds, on 9 Nov 1921.

Most points *Season*
Leigh scored a record 1436 points (258 tries, 199 goals, 6 drop goals) in the 1985–6 season, playing in 43 Cup and League games.

HIGHEST INDIVIDUAL SCORES

Most points, goals and tries in a game
George Henry 'Tich' West (1882–1927) scored 53 points (10 goals and 11 tries) for Hull Kingston Rovers (73) in a Challenge Cup tie v. Brookland Rovers (5) on 4 Mar 1905.

The record for a League match is 39 (5 tries, 12 goals) by Jimmy Lomas in Salford's 78–0 win over Liverpool City on 2 Feb 1907.

The most goals in a Cup match is 22 kicked by Jim Sullivan (1903–77) for Wigan v. Flimby and Fothergill on 14 Feb 1925. The most goals in a League match is 15 by Mick Stacey for Leigh v. Doncaster on 28 Mar 1976. The most tries in a League match is 10 by Lionel Cooper (b. Australia, 1922) for Huddersfield v. Keighley on 17 Nov 1951.

Most points *Season & career*
The record number of points in a season was 496 by Benjamin Lewis Jones (Leeds) (b. 11 Apr 1931), 194 goals, 36 tries, in 1956–7.

Neil Fox (b. May 1939) scored 6220 points (2575 goals, 358 tries, 4 drop goals) in a senior Rugby League career from 10 Apr 1956 to the end of the 1979–80 season.

Most tries *Season & career*
Albert Aaron Rosenfeld (1885–1970) (Huddersfield), an Australian-born wing-threequarter, scored 80 tries in 42 matches in the 1913–14 season.

Brian Bevan (b. Australia, 24 Apr 1924), a wing-threequarter, scored 796 tries in 18 seasons (16 with Warrington, two with Blackpool Borough) from 1946 to 1964. He scored 740 for Warrington, 17 for Blackpool and 39 in representative matches.

Most goals *Season & career*
The record number of goals in a season is 221 by David Watkins (b. 5 Mar 1942) (Salford) in the 1972–3 season.

Jim Sullivan (Wigan) kicked 2859 goals in his club and representative career, 1921–46.

Most consecutive scores
David Watkins (Salford) played and scored in every club game during seasons 1972–3 and 1973–4, contributing 41 tries and 403 goals—a total of 929 points, in 92 games.

Individual international records
Jim Sullivan (Wigan) played in most internationals (60 for Wales and Great Britain), kicked most goals (160) and scored most points (329).

Mick Sullivan (no kin) (b. 12 Jan 1934) of Huddersfield, Wigan, St Helens and York played in 51 international games for England and Great Britain and scored a record 45 tries.

John Holmes scored a record 26 points for Great Britain v. New Zealand at Pau, France on 4 Nov 1972.

Most Challenge Cup Finals
Eric Batten (Leeds, Bradford Northern and Featherstone Rovers) played in a record eight Challenge Cup Finals including war-time guest appearances between 1941 and 1952 and was on four winning sides.

Seven players have been in four Challenge Cup winning sides—Alan Edwards, Eric Batten, Alex Murphy, Brian Lockwood, Mick Adams, Keith Elwell and Eric Hughes. Alan Edwards (b. 15 May 1916) was the only one to do so with four different clubs, Salford 1938, Leeds 1942, Dewsbury 1943, Bradford Northern 1949.

Youngest and oldest players
Harold Wagstaff (1891–1939) played his first League game for Huddersfield at 15 yr 175 days, for Yorkshire at 17 yr 141 days, and for England at 17 yr 228 days.

The youngest player in a Cup Final was Shaun Edwards (b. 17 Oct 1966) at 17 yr 201 days for Wigan when they lost 6–19 to Widnes at Wembley on 5 May 1984. He became the youngest Great Britain international when he played against France at Headingley, Leeds on 1 Mar 1985 at 18 yr 135 days.

The oldest player for Great Britain was Jeff Grayshon (b. 4 Mar 1949) at 36 yr 243 days v. New Zealand at Wigan on 2 Nov 1985.

Most durable player
The most appearances for one club is 769 by Jim Sullivan for Wigan, 1921–46. He played a record 921 first-class games in all. The longest continuous playing career is that of Augustus John 'Gus' Risman (b. 21 Mar 1911), who played his first game for Salford on 31 August 1929 and his last for Batley on 27 December 1954.

Keith Elwell (b. 12 Feb 1950) played in 239 consecutive games for Widnes from 5 May 1977 to 5 September 1982. In his career, 1972–85, he received a record 28 winners' or runners-up medals in major competitions.

Most and least successful teams
Wigan won 31 consecutive league games from February 1970 to February 1971. Hull is the only club to win all League games in a season, 26 in Division II 1978–9. Doncaster holds the record of losing 40 consecutive League games from 16 Nov 1975 to 21 Apr 1977.

Record transfer fee
The highest RL transfer fee has been £172,500 paid by Leeds to Hull for forward Lee Crooks (b. 18 Sept 1963) on 2 June 1987.

Greatest crowds
The greatest attendance at any Rugby League match is 102,569 for the Warrington v. Halifax Challenge Cup Final replay at Odsal Stadium, Bradford, on 5 May 1954.

The record attendance for any international match is 70,204 for the Test between Australia and England on the Sydney Cricket Ground on 6 June 1932. The highest international attendance in Britain is 50,583 for the Test between Great Britain and Australia at Old Trafford, Manchester on 25 Oct 1986.

AMATEUR RUGBY LEAGUE
The British Amateur Rugby League Association (BARLA) was formed in 1973 'to foster, develop, extend and control amateur rugby league football in Great Britain'. Prior to that year the ultimate control of amateurs as well as professionals rested with the Rugby Football League. A National League was formed in 1986–7.

National Cup
Pilkington Recreation (St Helens, Merseyside) have won the National Cup four times (1975, 1979, 1980, 1982).

Highest score *Major competition*
Humberside beat Carlisle by 138 points to nil in the second round of the National Inter-league Competition on 20 Oct 1984.

Rugby Union

Records are determined in terms of present-day scoring values, *i.e.* a try at 4 points; a dropped goal, penalty or goal from a mark at 3 points; and a conversion at 2 points. The *actual* score, in accordance with whichever of the eight earlier systems was in force at the time, is also given, in brackets.

Although there are records of a game with many similarities to rugby dating back to the Roman occupation, the game is traditionally said to have originated from a breach of the rules of the football played in November 1823 at Rugby School by William Webb Ellis (later the Rev) (c. 1807–72). This handling code of football evolved gradually and was known to have been played at Cambridge University by 1839. The Rugby Football Union was founded on 26 Jan 1871. The International Rugby Football Board (IRFB) was founded in 1886.

INTERNATIONAL CHAMPIONSHIP
The International Championship was first contested by England, Ireland, Scotland and Wales in 1884. France first played in 1910.

Wales has won a record 21 times outright and tied for first a further ten times. Since 1910 Wales has 15 wins and 9 ties and England 15 wins and 7 ties.

Highest team score
The highest score in an International Championship match was set at Swansea on 1 Jan 1910 when Wales beat France 49–14 or 59–16 on present-day scoring values (8 goals, 1 penalty goal, 2 tries, to 1 goal, 2 penalty goals, 1 try).

Season's scoring
Jean-Patrick Lescarboura (France) (b. 12 Mar 1961) scored a record 54 points (10 penalty goals, 6 conversions, 4 dropped goals) in 1984.

Individual match records
William John 'Billy' Bancroft (1871–1959) kicked a record 9 goals (8 conversions and 1 penalty goal) for Wales v. France at Swansea in 1910.

HIGHEST TEAM SCORES

Internationals
The highest score in any full international was when France beat Spain by 92 points (including 19 tries) to nil at Oléron, France on 4 Mar 1979.

The highest aggregate score for any international match between the Four Home Unions is

69 when England beat Wales by 69 points (7 goals, 1 drop goal and 6 tries) to nil at Blackheath, London in 1881. (Note: there was no point scoring in 1881.) The highest score under the modern points system between IRFB members is the 60–0 by which Ireland beat Romania at Dublin on 1 Nov 1986.

The highest score by any overseas side in an international in the British Isles is 53 points (7 goals, 1 drop goal and 2 tries) to nil when South Africa beat Scotland at Murrayfield, Edinburgh, on 24 Nov 1951 (44–0).

Tour match

The record score for any international tour match is 125–0 (17 goals, 5 tries and 1 penalty goal) (103–0) when New Zealand beat Northern New South Wales at Quirindi, Australia, on 30 May 1962. The highest under scoring in use for the game is 117–6 for New Zealand's defeat of South Australia on 1 May 1974.

Match

In Denmark, Comet beat Lindo by 194–0 on 17 Nov 1973. The highest British score is 174–0 by 7th Signal Regiment v. 4th Armoured Workshop, REME, on 5 Nov 1980 at Herford, West Germany. Scores of over 200 points have been recorded in school matches; for example Radford School beat Hills Court 214 points (31 goals and 7 tries) to nil (200–0) on 20 Nov 1886.

Season

The highest number of points accumulated in a season by a club is 1607 points by Pontypool, Gwent in 1983–4. The record number of tries is 269 by Bridgend, Mid-Glamorgan, 1983–4.

HIGHEST INDIVIDUAL SCORES

Internationals

Phil Bennett (Wales) scored 34 points (2 tries, 10 conversions, 2 penalty goals) for Wales v. Japan at Tokyo on 24 Sept 1975, when Wales won 82–6. This total was equalled by Didier Camberabero in the 1987 World Cup (see above). The highest individual points score in any match between members of the International Board is 26 by Alan Hewson (b. 1953) (1 try, 2 conversions, 5 penalty goals and a drop goal) for New Zealand against Australia at Auckland on 11 Sept 1982.

The most tries in an international match is five by George Campbell Lindsay (1863–1905) for Scotland v. Wales, 1887, and by Douglas 'Daniel' Lambert (1883–1915) for England v. France, 1907. Ian Scott Smith (Scotland) (1903–72) scored a record six consecutive international tries in 1925, comprising the last three v. France and, two weeks later, the first three v. Wales. The most tries in an international career is 25 by David Campese (b. 21 Oct 1962) for Australia to 18 June 1987.

In all internationals Hugo Porta (b. 1951) scored a record 441 points in 46 matches for Argentina, 1973–87, including 338 in 37 against IRB teams. Andrew Robertson Irvine (Heriots) (b. 16 Sept 1951) scored 301 points in his career, 273 for Scotland (including 12 v. Romania) and 28 for the British Lions, from 1973 to 1982.

Season

The first-class season scoring record is 581 points by Samuel Arthur Doble (1944–77) of Moseley, in 52 matches in 1971–2. He also scored 47 points for England in South Africa out of season.

Andy Higgins (b. 4 Mar 1963) scored a record 28 drop goals in a season in first-class rugby, for the Vale of Lune in 1986–7.

Career

William Henry 'Dusty' Hare (b. 29 Nov 1952) scored 6319 points in first-class games from 1971–86, comprising 1800 for Nottingham, 3548 for Leicester, 240 for England, 88 for the British Lions and 643 in other representative matches.

THE 1987 WORLD CUP

The inaugural World Cup was contested in Australia and New Zealand by 16 national teams in 1987. The final in Auckland on 20 June 1987 was won by New Zealand, who beat France 29–9. The highest team score was New Zealand's 74–13 victory over Fiji at Christchurch on 27 May 1987; they scored ten goals, two tries and two penalty goals. The individual match record was 30 points (3 tries, 9 conversions) by Didier Camberabero (France) v. Zimbabwe at Auckland on 2 June 1987.

**Winning captain ●
Right:** David Kirk with the William Webb Ellis trophy, won by New Zealand.

Goal kicking ● Below: The leading scorer in the tournament was Grant Fox of New Zealand with 126 points in six matches. (Photos: All-Sport)

GUINNESS HAVE PUBLISHED *RUGBY: THE RECORDS* AT £8.95

MOST INTERNATIONAL APPEARANCES

IRELAND	69	Cameron Michael Henderson Gibson (b. 3 Dec 1942)	1964–79
NEW ZEALAND	55	Colin Earl Meads (b. 3 June 1936)	1957–71
WALES	55	John Peter Rhys 'JPR' Williams (b. 2 Mar 1949)	1969–81
FRANCE	52	Roland Bertranne (b. 6 Dec 1949) (in all matches—69)	1971–81
SCOTLAND	51	Andrew Robertson Irvine (b. 16 Sept 1951)	1973–82
	51	James Menzies 'Jim' Renwick (b. 12 Feb 1952)	1972–83
AUSTRALIA	45	Simon Paul Poidevin (b. 31 Oct 1958)	1980–87
ENGLAND	43	Anthony Neary (b. 25 Nov 1948)	1971–80
SOUTH AFRICA	38	Frederick Christoffel Hendrick Du Preez (b. 28 Nov 1935)	1960–71
	38	Jan Hendrik Ellis (b. 5 Jan 1943)	1965–76

Rugby Union

Match

Jannie van der Westhuizen scored 80 points (14 tries, 9 conversions, 1 dropped goal, 1 penalty goal) for Carnarvon (88) v. Williston (12) at North West Cape, South Africa on 11 March 1972.

In a junior house match in February 1967 at William Ellis School, Edgware, Greater London, between Cumberland and Nunn, Thanos Morphitis, 12, contributed 90 points (13 tries and 19 conversions) (77) to Cumberland's winning score.

All-rounder

Canadian international Barrie Burnham scored all possible ways—try, conversion, penalty goal, drop goal, goal from mark—for Meralomas v. Georgians (20–11) at Vancouver, BC, on 26 Feb 1966.

Most international appearances

Cameron Michael Henderson Gibson (b. 3 Dec 1942) played in 69 internationals for Ireland, 1964–79, a record for matches between the seven member countries of the 'International Rugby Football Board' and France. Including 12 appearances for the British Lions, he played in a total of 81 international matches. Willie John McBride (b. 6 June 1940) made a record 17 appearances for the British Lions, as well as 63 for Ireland.

Youngest international

Edinburgh Academy pupils Ninian Jamieson Finlay (1858–1936) and Charles Reid (1864–1909) were both 17 yr 36 days old when they played for Scotland v. England in 1875 and 1881 respectively. However, as Finlay had one less leap year in his lifetime up to his first cap, the outright record must be credited to him. Daniel Brendan Carroll (b. 17 Feb 1892) was aged only 16 yr 149 days when he played for Australia in the 1908 Olympic Games rugby tournament —not considered to be a 'full' international.

County Championships

The County Championships (inst. 1889) have been won most often by Gloucestershire with 15 titles (1910, 1913, 1920–2, 1930–2, 1937, 1972, 1974–6 and 1983–4). The most individual appearances is 104 by Richard Trickey (Sale) (b. 6 Mar 1945) for Lancashire between 1964 and 1978.

Club Championships

The most outright wins in the RFU Club Competition (John Player Cup, inst. 1971–2) is four by Bath, 1984–7.

The most wins in the Welsh Rugby Union Challenge Cup (Schweppes Welsh Cup, inst. 1971–2) is five, by Llanelli, 1973–6 and 1985 and by Cardiff, 1981–2, 1984 and 1986–7. The most wins in the Scottish League Division One (inst. 1973–4) is ten by Hawick between 1973 and 1987.

Seven-a-sides *Origins*

Seven-a-side rugby dates from 28 Apr 1883 when Melrose RFC Borders, in order to alleviate the poverty of a club in such a small town, staged a seven-a-side tournament. The idea was that of Ned Haig, the town's butcher.

Hong Kong Sevens

This, the world's most prestigious international tournament for seven-a-side teams, was first held in 1979. The record of four wins is held by Fiji, 1977–8, 1980 and 1984, and by Australia, 1979, 1982–3 and 1985.

Middlesex Seven-a-sides

The Middlesex Seven-a-sides were inaugurated in 1926. The most wins is ten by Harlequins, 1926–9, 1933, 1935, 1967, 1978, 1986–7.

Greatest crowd

The record paying attendance is 104,000 for Scotland 3 18–18 win over Wales at Murrayfield, Edinburgh, on 1 Mar 1975.

Highest posts

The world's highest rugby union goal posts are 110 ft ½ in *33,54 m* high at the Roan Antelope Rugby Union Club, Luanshya, Zambia. The posts at Brixham RFC, Devonshire, are 57 ft *17,37 m* high with an additional 1 ft *0,30 m* spike.

Longest kicks

The longest recorded successful drop-goal is 90 yd *82 m* by Gerald Hamilton 'Gerry' Brand (b. 8 Oct 1906) for South Africa v. England at Twickenham, Greater London, on 2 Jan 1932. This was taken 7 yd *6 m* inside the England 'half', 55 yd *50 m* from the posts, and dropped over the dead ball line.

The place kick record is reputed to be 100 yd *91 m* at Richmond Athletic Ground, London, by Douglas Francis Theodore Morkel (b. 1886) in an unsuccessful penalty for South Africa v. Surrey on 19 Dec 1906. This was not measured until 1932. In the match Bridlington School 1st XV v. an Army XV at Bridlington, Humberside on 29 Jan 1944, Ernie Cooper (b. 21 May 1926), captaining the school, landed a penalty from a measured 81 yd *74 m* from the post with a kick which carried over the dead ball line. The record in an international was set at 70 yd 8½ in *21,55 m* by Paul Thorburn (b. 24 Nov 1962) for Wales v. Scotland on 1 Feb 1986.

Fastest try

The fastest try in an international game was when H. L. 'Bart' Price scored for England v. Wales at Twickenham on 20 Jan 1923 less than 10 sec after kick off.

Most tries

Alan Morley (b. 25 June 1950) has scored 473 tries in senior rugby in 1968–86 including 378 for Bristol, a record for one club. John Huins scored 85 tries in 1953–4, 73 for St Luke's College, Exeter and 12 more for Neath and in trial games.

Longest try

The longest 'try' ever executed was by a team of 15, from Power-House RUFC, Victoria, Australia, who ran a try of 1470.6 miles *2366,7 km* from 4–13 Mar 1983 around Albert Park Lake, Victoria. There were no forward passes or knock-ons, and the ball was touched down between the posts in the prescribed manner (Law 12).

Most successful team

The Leamington Spa junior team played 92 successive games without defeat from 6 Oct 1980 to 13 Apr 1984.

Shinty

Shinty (from the Gaelic *sinteag*, a bound) has roots reaching back more than 2000 years to the ancient game of *camanachd*, the sport of the curved stick, the diversion of the heroes of Celtic history and legend. It was effective battle training, exercising speed and co-ordination of eye and arm along with aggression and cool self-control. In spite of the break-up of the clan system in the Highlands of Scotland, the 'ball plays', involving whole parishes, without limit in number or time except the fall of night, continued in areas such as Lochaber, Badenoch and Strathglass. Whisky and the inspiration of the bagpipes were important ingredients of these occasions. The ruling body of this apparently ungovernable game was established in 1893 when the Camanachd Association was set up at Kingussie, Highland.

Most titles

Newtonmore, Highland has won the Camanachd Association Challenge Cup (instituted 1896) a record 28 times, 1907–86. Johnnie Campbell, David Ritchie and Hugh Chisholm, all of Newton-

more, have won a record 11 winners' medals. In 1923 the Furnace Club, Argyll won the cup without conceding a goal throughout the competition.

In 1984 Kingussie Camanachd Club won all five senior competitions, including the Camanachd Cup Final. This feat was equalled by Newtonmore in 1985.

Highest scores

The highest Scottish Cup Final score was in 1909 when Newtonmore beat Furnace 11–3 at Glasgow, Dr Johnnie Cattanach scoring eight hails or goals. In 1938 John Macmillan Mactaggart scored ten hails for Mid-Argyll in a Camanachd Cup match.

Shooting

The Lucerne Shooting Guild (Switzerland) was formed c.1466 and the first recorded shooting match was at Zurich in 1472.

Most Olympic medals

The record number of medals won is 11 by Carl Townsend Osburn (USA) (1884–1966) in 1912, 1920 and 1924, consisting of five gold, four silver and two bronze. Six other marksmen have won five gold medals. The only marksman to win three individual gold medals has been Gudbrand Gudbrandsönn Skatteboe (Norway) (1875–1965), in 1906. Separate events for women were first held in 1984.

Bisley

The National Rifle Assocation was instituted in 1859. The Queen's (King's) Prize has been shot since 1860 and has only once been won by a woman—Marjorie Elaine Foster (1894–1974) (score 280) on 19 July 1930. Arthur George Fulton (1887–1972) won three times (1912, 1926, 1931). Both his father and his son also won the Prize.

The highest score (possible 300) for the final of the Queen's Prize is 295 by Lindsay Peden (Scotland) on 24 July 1982. The record for the Silver Medals is 150 (possible 150) by Martin John Brister (City Rifle Club) (b. 1951) and (Lord) John Swansea (b. 1 Jan 1925) on 24 July 1971. This was equalled by John Henry Carmichael (WRA Bromsgrave RC) on 28 July 1979 and Robert Stafford on 26 July 1980, with the size of the bullseyes reduced.

Small-bore

The National Small-Bore Rifle Association, of Britain, was formed in 1901. The British team record (1966 target) is 1988 × 2000 by Lancashire in 1968–9 and London in 1980–1. The British individual small-bore rifle record for 60 shots prone is 600 × 600, first achieved by John Palin (b. 16 July 1934) in Switzerland in 1972. Richard Hansen shot 5000 bullseyes in 24 hr at Fresno, Cal., USA on 13 June 1929.

Clay pigeon

Most world titles have been won by Susan Nattrass (Canada) (b. 5 Nov 1950) with six, 1974–5, 1977–9, 1981. The record number of clay birds shot in an hour is 2215 by Joseph Kreckman at the Paradise Shooting Center, Cresco, Pennsylvania, USA on 28 Aug 1983 (from 3176 shots from the hip). Graham Douglas Geater (b. 21 July 1947) shot 2264 targets in an hour on a trapshooting range at the NILO Gun Club, Papamoa, New Zealand on 17 Jan 1981.

The maximum 200/200 was achieved by Ricardo Ruiz Rumoroso at the Spanish Clay Pigeon Championships at Zaragossa on 12 June 1983.

Noel D. Townend achieved the maximum 200 consecutive down-the-line targets at Nottingham on 21 Aug 1983.

Bench rest shooting
The smallest group on record at 1000 yd *914 m* is 5.093 in *12,94 cm* by Rick Taylor with a 300 Weatherby at Williamsport, Penn., USA on 24 Aug 1980.

Highest score in 24 hr
The Easingwold Rifle and Pistol Club team of John Smith, Edward Kendall, Phillip Kendall and Paul Duffield scored 120,242 points (averaging 95.66 per card) on 6–7 Aug 1983.

Skiing

The most ancient ski in existence was found well preserved in a peat bog at Hoting, Sweden, dating from *c.* 2500 BC. The earliest recorded military use of skiing was at the Battle of Isen, near Oslo, Norway in 1200. The Trysil Shooting and Skiing Club, founded in Norway in 1861, claims it is the world's oldest. The oldest ski competitions are the Holmenkøllen Nordic events which were first held in 1866. The first downhill races were staged in Australia in the 1850s. The International Ski Federation (FIS) was founded on 2 Feb 1924, succeeding the International Skiing Commission, founded at Christiania (Oslo), Norway on 18 Feb 1910. The Ski Club of Great Britain was founded on 6 May 1903. The National Ski Federation of Great Britain was formed in 1964 and changed its name to the British Ski Federation in 1981.

Most titles *World Championships—Alpine*
The World Alpine Championships were inaugurated at Mürren, Switzerland, in 1931. The greatest number of titles won has been by Christel Cranz (b. 1 July 1914) of Germany, with seven individual—four slalom (1934, 1937–9) and three downhill (1935, 1937, 1939), and five combined (1934–5, 1937–9). She also won the gold medal for the combined in the 1936 Olympics. The most won by a man is seven by Anton 'Toni' Sailer (b. 17 Nov 1935) (Austria), who won all four in 1956 (giant slalom, slalom, downhill and the non-Olympic Alpine combination) and the downhill, giant slalom and combined in 1958.

World Championships—Nordic
The first World Nordic Championships were those of the 1924 Winter Olympics in Chamonix, France. The greatest number of titles won is nine by Galina Kulakova (b. 29 Apr 1942) (USSR) in 1970–78. She also won four silver and four bronze medals for a record 17 in total. The most won by a man is eight, including relays, by Sixten Jernberg (b. 6 Feb 1929) (Sweden) in 1956–64. Johan Grøttumsbraaten (1899–1942) of Norway won six individual titles (two 18 km cross-country, four Nordic combined) in 1926–32. The record for a jumper is five by Birger Ruud (b. 23 Aug 1911) of Norway, in 1931–2 and 1935–7. Ruud is the only person to win Olympic events in each of the dissimilar Alpine and Nordic disciplines. In 1936 he won the ski-jumping and the Alpine downhill (which was not then a separate event, but only a segment of the combined event).

WORLD CUP

The World Cup was introduced for Alpine events in 1967 and for Nordic events in 1981. The most

SHOOTING—INDIVIDUAL WORLD RECORDS

World records are accepted only when set at major international championships.

MEN

Event	Score	Name	Place	Date
FREE RIFLE				
Three positions 3 × 40 shots at 300 m	1166/1200	Malcolm Cooper (GB)	Zürich, Switzerland	7 June 1987
Prone 60 shots at 300 m	599/600	Malcolm Cooper (GB)	Skouder, Sweden	28 Aug 1986
STANDARD RIFLE				
Three positions 3 × 20 shots at 300 m	583/600	Malcolm Cooper (GB)	Zürich, Switzerland	8 June 1985
SMALL-BORE RIFLE				
Three positions 3 × 40 shots at 50 m	1175/1200	Kiril Ivanov (USSR)	Osijek, Yugoslavia	11 Sept 1985
Prone 60 shots at 50 m	600/600	Alistair Allan (GB)	Titograd, Yugoslavia	21 Sept 1981
	600/600	Ernest van de Zande (USA)	Rio de Janeiro, Brazil	10 Nov 1981
	600/600	Five men at	Suhl, GDR	10 Sept 1986
FREE PISTOL 60 shots at 50 m	581/600	Aleksandr Melentev (USSR)	Moscow, USSR	20 July 1980
RAPID-FIRE PISTOL 60 shots at 25 m	599/600	Igor Puzryev (USSR)	Titograd, Yugoslavia	21 Sept 1981
CENTRE-FIRE PISTOL 60 shots at 25 m	597/600	Thomas D. Smith (USA)	Sao Paulo, Brazil	20 Apr 1963
STANDARD PISTOL 60 shots at 25 m	584/600	Eric Buljong (USA)	Caracas, Venezuela	20 Aug 1983
RUNNING GAME TARGET				
60 shots at 50 m with small-bore rifle	595/600	Igor Sokolov (USSR)	Miskulc, Hungary	9 Aug 1981
OLYMPIC TRAP 200 birds	200/200	Danny Carlisle (USA)	Caracas, Venezuela	21 Aug 1983
OLYMPIC SKEET 200 birds	200/200	Matthew Dryke (USA)	Sao Paulo, Brazil	11 Nov 1981
	200/200	Jan Hula (Czechoslovakia)	Zaragossa, Spain	16 June 1984
AIR RIFLE 60 shots at 10 m	596/600	Jean-Pierre Amat (France)	Zürich, Switzerland	5 June 1987
AIR PISTOL 60 shots at 10 m	591/600	Vladas Tourla (USSR)	Caracas, Venezuela	20 Aug 1983

WOMEN

Event	Score	Name	Place	Date
STANDARD RIFLE				
Three positions 3 × 20 shots at 50 m	592/600	Marlies Helbig (GDR)	Titograd, Yugoslavia	17 Sept 1981
Prone 60 shots at 50 m	598/600	Eulalia Rolinska (Poland)	Suhl, GDR	28 Aug 1971
	598/600	Margaret Murdock (USA)	Thun, Austria	21 Sept 1974
	598/600	Nonka Matova (Bulgaria)	Osijek, Yugoslavia	8 Sept 1985
	598/600	Eva Forian (Hungary)	Suhl, GDR	9 Sept 1986
SMALL-BORE SPORT PISTOL				
60 shots at 25 m	594/600	Silvia Kaposztai (Romania)	Osijek, Yugoslavia	6 Sept 1985
OLYMPIC TRAP 200 birds	195/200	Susan Nattrass (Canada)	Seoul, S. Korea	4 Oct 1978
OLYMPIC SKEET 200 birds	197/200	Svetlana Yakimova (USSR)	Zaragossa, Spain	16 June 1984
AIR RIFLE 40 shots at 10 m	395/400	Anna Malekhova (USSR)	The Hague, Netherlands	18 Mar 1982
	395/400	Marlies Helbig (GDR)	Innsbruck, Austria	22 Sept 1983
AIR PISTOL 40 shots at 10 m	387/400	Nina Stolyarova (USSR)	Enschede, Netherlands	23 Feb 1974
	387/400	Marina Dobrancheva (USSR)	Varna, Bulgaria	2 Mar 1985
	387/400	Anke Völker (GDR)	Suhl, GDR	9 Sept 1986

119.30 mph, and Patrick Knauff (France) set a one-legged record of 185,089 km/h *115.012 mph*. The highest average speed in the Olympic downhill race was 104,53 km/h *64.95 mph* by William D. Johnson (USA) (b. 30 Mar 1960) at Sarajevo, Yugoslavia on 16 Feb 1984. The fastest in a World Cup downhill is 107,82 km/h *67.00 mph* by Harti Weirather (Austria) (b. 25 Jan 1958) at Kitzbühl, Austria on 15 Jan 1982.

Highest speed—cross-country
Bill Koch (USA) (b. 13 Apr 1943) on 26 Mar 1981 skied ten times round a 5 km *3.11 mile* loop on Marlborough Pond, near Putney, Vermont, USA. He completed the 50 km in 1 hr 59 min 47 sec, an average speed of 25,045 km/h *15.57 mph*. A race includes uphill and downhill sections; the record time for a 50 km race in World Championships or Olympic Games is 2 hr 10 min 49.9 sec by Gunde Svan (Sweden) (b. 12 Jan 1962) in 1985, an average speed of 22,93 km/h *14.25 mph*. The record for a 15-km Olympic or World Championship race is 38 min 52.5 sec by Oddvar Braa (Norway) (b. 16 Mar 1951) at the 1982 World Championships, an average speed of 23,15 km/h *14.38 mph*.

Closest verdict
The narrowest winning margin in a championship ski race was one hundredth of a second by Thomas Wassberg (Sweden) over Juha Mieto (Finland) (b. 20 Nov 1949) in the Olympic 15-km cross-country race at Lake Placid, USA on 17 Feb 1980. His winning time was 41 min 57.63 sec.

Highest altitude
Jean Afanassieff and Nicolas Jaeger skied from 8200 m *26,900 ft* to 6200 m *20,340 ft* on the 1978 French expedition on Mt Everest.

Steepest descent
The steepest descents in alpine skiing history have been by Sylvain Saudan. At the start of his descent from Mont Blanc on the north-east side down the Couloir Gervasutti from 4248 m *13,937 ft* on 17 Oct 1967 he skied to gradients of *c.* 60°.

Longest run
The longest all-downhill ski run in the world is the Weissfluhjoch-Küblis Parsenn course, near Davos, Switzerland, which measures 12,23 km *7.6 miles*. The run from the Aiguille du Midi top of the Chamonix lift (vertical lift 2759 m *9052 ft*) across the Vallée Blanche is 20,9 km *13 miles*.

Most competitors—*Alpine*
1700 downhill skiers competed at Åre, Jämtland, Sweden, on 30 Apr 1984. The most competitors in a skiing competition in Britain are the 425 who took part in the Army Ski Association (Scotland) Championships at Aviemore, Grampian from 2–7 Mar 1987.

Longest races—*Nordic*
The world's greatest Nordic ski race is the Vasaloppet, which commemorates an event of 1521 when Gustav Vasa (1496–1560), later King Gustavus Eriksson, fled 85,8 km *53.3 miles* from Mora to Sälen, Sweden. He was overtaken by loyal, speedy scouts on skis, who persuaded him to return eastwards to Mora to lead a rebellion and become the king of Sweden. The re-enactment of this return journey is now an annual event at 89 km *55.3 miles*, contested by about 12,000 skiers. The fastest time is 3 hr 48 min 55 sec by Bengt Hassis (Sweden) on 2 Mar 1986.

The Finlandia Ski Race, 73 km *45 miles* from Homeenlinna to Lahti, on 26 Feb 1984 had a record 13,226 starters and 12,909 finishers.

The longest downhill race is the *Inferno* in Switzerland, 15,8 km *9.8 miles* from the top of the Schilthorn to Lauterbrunnen. The record entry was 1401 in 1981 and the record time 15 min 26.44 sec by Ueli Grossniklaus (Switzerland) in 1987.

---

individual event wins is 85 by Ingemar Stenmark (Sweden) (b. 18 Mar 1956) in 1974–87, including a record 13 in one season in 1979. Franz Klammer (Austria) (b. 3 Dec 1953) won a record 35 downhill races, 1974–85. Annemarie Moser (née Pröll) (Austria) (b. 27 Mar 1953) won a women's record 62 individual event wins, 1970–9. She had a record 11 consecutive downhill wins from Dec 1972 to Jan 1974.

Ski-jumping
The longest ski-jump ever recorded is one of 194 m *636 ft* by Piotr Fijas (Poland) at Planica, Yugoslavia on 14 Mar 1987. The female record is 110 m *361 ft* by Tiina Lehtola (b. 3 Aug 1962) (Finland) at Ruka, Finland on 29 Mar 1981. The longest dry ski-jump is 92 m *302 ft* by Hubert Schwarz (West Germany) at Berchtesgarten, West Germany on 30 June 1981.

> **Four World Cup skiing titles in one year ●**
> Pirmin Zurbriggen (Switzerland) (b. 4 Feb 1963) won the 1987 World Cup downhill, giant slalom, super-giant slalom and overall titles. The only man previously to win four titles in one year was Jean-Claude Killy (France) (b. 30 Aug 1943) in 1967. (Photo: Steve Powell/All Sport)

Highest speed
The highest speed claimed for a skier is 212,514 km/h *132.053 mph* by Graham Wilkie (GB) (b. 21 Sept 1951) on 17 Apr 1987 and the fastest by a woman is 201,005 km/h *124.902 mph* by Jacqueline Blanc (France) on 19 Apr 1987, both at Les Arcs, France. At the same venue on 18 Apr 1987 a British women's record was set by Divina Galica (b. 13 Aug 1944) at 191,99 km/h

Most World Cup Titles

ALPINE

MEN

OVERALL	4	Gustavo Thoeni (Italy)	1971–3, 1975
DOWNHILL	5	Franz Klammer (Austria)	1975–8, 1983
SLALOM	8	Ingemar Stenmark (Sweden)	1975–81, 1983
GIANT SLALOM	7	Ingemar Stenmark	1975–6, 1978–81, 1984

Two men have won four titles in one year—downhill, slalom, giant slalom and overall: Jean-Claude Killy (France) (b. 30 Aug 1943) in 1967 and Pirmin Zurbriggen (Switzerland) (b. 4 Feb 1963) in 1987.

WOMEN

OVERALL	6	Annemarie Moser (Austria)	1971–5, 1979
DOWNHILL	7	Annemarie Moser	1971–5, 1978–9
SLALOM	4	Erika Hess (Switzerland)	1981–3, 1985
GIANT SLALOM	3	Annemarie Moser	1971–2, 1975

NORDIC

MEN

JUMPING	3	Matti Nykänen (Finland)	1983, 1985–6
CROSS-COUNTRY	3	Gunde Svan (Sweden)	1984–6

WOMEN

CROSS-COUNTRY	2	Marja-Liisa Kirvesniemi (née Hämäläinen) (Finland)	1983–4
	2	Margo Matikainen (Finland)	1986–7

MOST OLYMPIC TITLES

MEN ALPINE	3	Anton 'Toni' Sailer (Austria) (b. 17 Nov 1935)	Downhill, slalom, giant slalom, 1956
	3	Jean-Claude Killy (France) (b. 30 Aug 1943)	Downhill, slalom, giant slalom, 1968
MEN NORDIC	4[1]	Sixten Jernberg (Sweden) (b. 6 Feb 1929)	50 km, 1956; 30 km, 1960; 50 km and 4 × 10 km, 1964
WOMEN ALPINE	2	Andrea Mead-Lawrence (USA) (b. 19 Apr 1932)	Slalom, giant slalom, 1952
	2	Marielle Goitschel (France) (b. 28 Sept 1945)	Giant slalom, 1964; slalom, 1968
	2	Marie-Thérèse Nadig (Switz) (b. 8 Mar 1954)	Downhill, giant slalom, 1972
	2[2]	Rosi Mittermaier (now Neureuther) (W. Germany) (b. 5 Aug 1950)	Downhill, slalom, 1976
	2[3]	Hanni Wenzel (Liechtenstein) (b. 14 Dec 1956)	Giant slalom, slalom 1980
WOMEN NORDIC	4[4]	Galina Kulakova (USSR) (b. 29 Apr 1942)	5 km, 10 km and 3 × 5 km relay, 1972; 4 × 5 km relay, 1976
	(individual) 3	Marja-Liisa Hämäläinen (Finland) (b. 10 Aug 1955)	5 km, 10 km and 20 km 1984

[1] Jernberg also won three silver and two bronze for a record nine Olympic medals.
[2] Also won silver medal in giant slalom in 1976.
[3] Wenzel won a silver in the 1980 downhill and a bronze in the 1976 slalom.
[4] Kulakova also won two silver and two bronze medals in 1968, 1976 and 1980.

Long-distance Nordic

In 24 hours Teuvo Rantanen covered 315 km *195 miles* at Jyväskylä, Finland on 24–25 Mar 1984. The women's record is 197,83 km *122.9 miles* by Marlene Severs at East Burke, Vermont, USA on 7–8 Mar 1985.

In 48 hours Bjørn Løkken (Norway) (b. 27 Nov 1937) covered 513,568 km *319 miles 205 yd* from 11–13 Mar 1982.

Longest lift

The longest gondola ski lift is 6239 m *3.88 miles* long at Grindelwald-Männlichen, Switzerland (in two sections, but one gondola). The longest chair lift in the world was the Alpine Way to Kosciusko Chalet lift above Thredbo, near the Snowy Mountains, New South Wales, Australia. It took from 45 to 75 min to ascend the 3.5 miles *5,6 km*, according to the weather. It has now collapsed. The highest is at Chacaltaya, Bolivia, rising to 5029 m *16,500 ft*.

Ski-bob *Origins*

The ski-bob was invented by J. C. Stevenson of Hartford, Connecticut, USA in 1891, and patented (No 47334) on 19 Apr 1892 as a 'bicycle with ski-runners'. The *Fédération Internationale de Skibob* was founded on 14 Jan 1961 in Innsbruck, Austria and the first World Championships were held at Bad Hofgastein, Austria in 1967. The Ski-Bob Association of Great Britain was registered on 23 Aug 1967. The highest speed attained is 166 km/h *103.4 mph* by Erich Brenter (b. 1940) (Austria) at Cervinia, Italy, in 1964.

World Championships

The only ski-bobbers to retain a World Championship are: men—Alois Fischbauer (Austria) (b. 6 Oct 1951), 1973 and 1975, Robert Mühlberger (West Germany), 1979 and 1981; women— Gerhilde Schiffkorn (Austria) (b. 22 Mar 1950), 1967 and 1969, Gertrude Geberth (Austria) (b. 18 Oct 1951), 1971 and 1973.

Snowmobile

A record speed of 148.6 mph *239,1 km/h* was set by Tom Earhart (USA) in a Budweiser-Polaris snowmobile designed and owned by Bob Gaudreau at Lake Mille Lacs, Minnesota, USA on 25 Feb 1982. (*See also p. 131*).

GRASS SKIING

Grass skis were first manufactured by Josef Kaiser (West Germany) in 1963. World Championships (awarded for giant slalom, slalom and combined) were first held in 1979. The most titles won is seven by Ingrid Hirschhofer (Austria) to 1985. The most by a man is four by Erwin Gansner (Switzerland), two each in 1981 and 1983.

The speed record is 86,88 km/h *53.99 mph* by Erwin Gansner on 5 Sept 1982; the British record is 79,49 km/h *43.39 mph* by Laurence Beck on 8 Sept 1985, both at Owen, West Germany.

Skittles

24 hours

The highest score at West Country skittles by a team of eight is 90,202 by the Torquay Blues at Torquay, Devon on 26–27 Sept 1986; they reset the skittles after every ball. The highest hood skittle score in 24 hr is 118,951 pins by 12 players from the White Hart, Grafton Regis, Northamptonshire on 9–10 April 1986. The highest long alley score is 59,140 by a team of eight from the British Institute for Brain Injured Children in Bridgwater, Somerset on 28 Feb–1 Mar 1986. The highest table skittle score in 24 hr is 90,446 skittles by 12 players at the Finney Gardens Hotel, Hanley, Staffs on 27–28 Dec 1980.

Snooker

Origins

Research shows that snooker was originated by Colonel Sir Neville Francis Fitzgerald Chamberlain (1856–1944) as a hybrid of 'black pool', 'pyramids' and billiards, in Jubbulpore, India in 1875. It did not reach England until 1885, where the modern scoring system was adopted in 1891. Championships were not instituted until 1916. The World Professional Championship was instituted in 1927.

Most titles *World*

The world professional title (inst. 1927) was won a record 15 times by Joe Davis, 1927–40 and 1946. The most wins in the Amateur Championships (inst. 1963) have been two by: Gary Owen (England) in 1963 and 1966; Ray Edmonds (England) 1972 and 1974; and Paul Mifsud (Malta), 1985–6.

Women

Maureen Baynton (*née* Barrett) won a record eight Women's Amateur Championships between 1954 and 1968, as well as seven at billiards.

World Championships *Youngest*

White (GB) (b. 2 May 1962) who was 18 yr 191 days when he won the World Amateur Snooker Championship in Launceston, Tasmania, Australia on 9 Nov 1980. Stacey Hillyard (GB) won the Women's World Amateur Championship in October 1984 at the age of 15.

Highest breaks

Over 100 players have achieved the 'maximum' break of 147. The first to do so was E. J. 'Murt' O'Donoghue (b. New Zealand 1901) at Griffiths, NSW, Australia on 26 Sept 1934. The first officially ratified 147 was by Joe Davis against Willie Smith at Leicester Square Hall, London on 22 Jan 1955. The first maximum achieved in a major tournament was by John Spencer (b. 18 Sept 1935) at Slough, Berkshire on 13 Jan 1979, but the table had oversized pockets. Steve Davis (b. 22 Aug 1957) had a ratified break of 147 against John Spencer in the Lada Classic at Oldham on 11 Jan 1982. The first 147 scored in the World Championships was by Cliff Thorburn (Canada) (b. 16 Jan 1948) against Terry Griffiths at the Crucible Theatre, Sheffield on 23 April 1983, thereby winning a £10,000 jackpot prize. The other 147 in tournament play was by Kirk Stevens (Canada) (b. 17 Aug 1958) in the Benson & Hedges Masters at Wembley, London on 28 Jan 1984.

The world amateur record break is 141 by Martin Clark (England) (b. 27 Oct 1968) at Heysham, Lancashire in September 1986. David Taylor (b. 29 July 1943) made three consecutive frame clearances of 130, 140, and 139 at Minehead, Somerset, on 1 June 1978. Jim Meadowcroft (b. 15

SKIPPING

MARATHON
The longest recorded skipping marathon (5 min per hour breaks) was one of 13 hr 30 min 49 sec by Edwin Lagerwij (b. 19 Jan 1967) at Riesmalen, the Netherlands on 16 May 1987.

DURATION 1264 miles *2034 km* by Tom Morris, Brisbane-Cairns, Queensland, 1963.

Other records made without a break:

MOST TURNS IN 10 SEC 128 by Albert Rayner (b. 19 Apr 1923), Stanford Sports, Birmingham, England, 19 Nov 1982.

MOST TURNS IN 1 MIN 334 by Albert Rayner at Wakefield Karate College, West Yorkshire on 9 Aug 1986.

MOST DOUBLES (WITH CROSS) 2110 by Sean Birch at the Four Seasons, Tralee, Co. Kerry, Ireland, 19 Oct 1986.

DOUBLE TURNS 10,133 by Katsumi Suzuki, Saitama, Japan, 27 Sept 1979.

TREBLE TURNS 381 by Katsumi Suzuki, Saitama, Japan, 29 May 1975.

QUADRUPLE TURNS 51 by Katsumi Suzuki, Saitama, Japan, 29 May 1975.

QUINTUPLE TURNS 6 by Hideyuki Tateda (b. 1968), Aomori, Japan, 19 June 1982.

MOST ON SINGLE ROPE (minimum 12 turns obligatory) 160 (50 m rope) by Shimizu Iida Junior High School, Shizuoka-ken, Japan, 10 Dec 1982.

MOST TURNS ON SINGLE ROPE (team of 90) 160 by students from Nishigoshi Higashi Elementary School, Kumamoto, Japan on 27 Feb 1987.

ON A TIGHTROPE 58 (consecutive) by Bryan Andro (*né* Dewhurst) TROS TV, the Netherlands, 6 Aug 1981.

MOST TURNS IN 1 HOUR 12,496 Matt Davis and Shelly Nelson, Douglas Elementary School, Boulder, Colorado, 19 Dec 1986.

Dec 1946) made four consecutive frame clearances of 105, 115, 117 and 125 at Connaught Leisure Centre, Worthing on 27 Jan 1982.

The first century break by a woman in competitive play was 114 by Stacey Hillyard in a league match at Bournemouth on 15 Jan 1985.

Softball

Softball, the indoor derivative of baseball, was invented by George Hancock at the Farragut Boat Club of Chicago, Illinois in 1887. Rules were first codified in Minneapolis, Minnesota, USA in 1895 as Kitten Ball. The name Softball was introduced by Walter Hakanson at a meeting of the National Recreation Congress in 1926. The name was adopted throughout the USA in 1930. Rules were formalised in 1933 by the International Joint Rules Committee for Softball and adopted by the Amateur Softball Association of America. The International Softball Federation was formed in 1950 as governing body for both fast pitch and slow pitch. It was re-organised in 1965.

Most titles

The USA have won the men's World Championship (inst. 1966) four times, 1966, 1968, 1976 (shared), and 1980. The USA won the women's title (inst. 1965) in 1974, 1978 and 1986.

Speedway

Motorcycle racing on large dirt track surfaces has been traced back to 1902 in the United States. The first organised 'short track' races were at the West Maitland (New South Wales, Australia) Agricultural Show on 22 Dec 1923, promoted by Johnnie Hoskins (NZ) (1892–1987), who brought the sport to Britain, where it evolved with small diameter track racing at Droylsden, Manchester on 25 June 1927 and a cinder track event at High Beech, Essex, on 19 Feb 1928.

British championships

The National League was contested from 1932 to 1964. The Wembley Lions, who won in 1932, 1946–7 and 1949–53, had a record eight victories. In 1965 it was replaced by the British League which Belle Vue have won four times, including three times in succession (1970–2). Wimbledon

Snooker superstars ● The Matchroom team: (left to right) Terry Griffiths, Neal Foulds, Tony Meo, Dennis Taylor and Steve Davis. In the 1980s Steve Davis has dominated the world of snooker, winning to date 33 of the 75 major titles. (Photo: All-Sport)

is the only club to have competed every year since 1929 in Southern, National and British Leagues. Belle Vue (Manchester) had a record nine victories (1933–7, 1946–7, 1949 and 1958) in the National Trophy Knock-out Competition (held 1931–64). This was replaced in 1965 by the Knock-Out Cup, which has been won four times by Cradley Heath and Ipswich. Oxford set a record of 28 successive wins in the British League in 1986.

World championships

The World Speedway Championship was inaugurated at Wembley, London on 10 Sept 1936. The most wins have been six by Ivan Gerald Mauger (New Zealand) (b. 4 Oct 1939) in 1968–70, 1972, 1977 and 1979. Barry Briggs (New Zealand) (b. 30 Dec 1934) made a record 17 consecutive appearances in the finals (1954–70) and won the world title in 1957–8, 1964 and 1966. He also scored a record 201 points in world championship competition from 87 races.

England has most wins in the World Team Cup (inst. 1960) with eight, and the World Pairs Championship (inst. 1968) with seven. Poland uniquely competed in 21 successive World Team Cup Finals, 1960–80 and in a 22nd in 1984. The maximum 30 points were scored in the World Pairs Championship by: Jerzy Szczakiel (b. 28 Jan 1949) and Andrzej Wyglenda (Poland) at Rybnik, Poland in 1971; and Arthur Dennis Sigalos (b. 16 Aug 1959) and Robert Benjamin 'Bobby' Schwartz (b. 10 Aug 1956) (USA) at Liverpool, New South Wales, Australia on 11 Dec 1982.

Ivan Mauger also won four World Team Cup, two World Pairs (including an unofficial win in 1969) and two world long track titles. Ove Fundin (Sweden) (b. 23 May 1933) won twelve world titles: five individual, one Pairs, and six World Team Cup medals in 1956–70. Erik Gundersen (Denmark) (b. 8 Oct 1959) became in 1985 the first man to hold simultaneously world titles at individual, pairs, team and long-track events.

League racing

League racing was introduced to British speedway in 1929. The highest score recorded was when Crayford beat Milton Keynes 76–20 in the then 16-heat formula for the National League on 26 Oct 1982. A maximum possible score was achieved by Bristol when they defeated Glasgow (White City) 70–14 on 7 Oct 1949 in the National League Division Two. The highest number of League points scored by an individual in a season was 516 by Stephen Faulder Lawson (b. 11 Dec 1957) for Glasgow in the National League in 1982. The League career record is 6471 points by Nigel Boocock (b. 17 Sept 1937), 1955–80.

Tests—*maximum points*

The only rider to have scored maximum points in every match of a Test series was Arthur 'Bluey' Wilkinson (b. 27 Aug 1911) in five matches for Australia v. England in Sydney in 1937–8.

Squash Rackets

Although rackets (US spelling racquets) with a soft ball was played in 1817 at Harrow School, Harrow, London, there was no recognised champion of any country until John A. Miskey of Philadelphia won the American Amateur Singles Championship in 1907.

World Championships

Jahangir Khan (b. 10 Dec 1963) (Pakistan) won five World Open (inst. 1976) titles, 1981–5, and the ISRF world individual title (formerly World Amateur, inst. 1967) in 1979, 1983 and 1985. Geoffrey B. Hunt (b. 11 Mar 1947) (Australia) won four World Open titles, 1976–7 and 1979–80 and three World Amateur, 1967, 1969 and 1971.

Australia, 1967, 1969, 1971 and 1973, and Pakistan, 1977, 1981, 1983 and 1985 have each won four men's team titles and Australia have won three women's, 1976, 1981 and 1983.

Most titles *Open Championship*

The most wins in the Open Championship (amateurs or professionals), held annually in Britain, is eight by Geoffrey Hunt in 1969, 1974 and 1976–81. Hashim Khan (Pakistan) (b. 1915) won seven times, 1950–5 and 1957, and also won the Vintage title six times in 1978–83.

The most British Open women's titles is 16 by Heather Pamela McKay (*née* Blundell) (Australia) (b. 31 July 1941) from 1961 to 1977. She also won the World Open title in 1976 and 1979.

Amateur Championship
The most wins in the Amateur Championship is six by Abdelfattah Amr Bey (Egypt) (b. 14 Feb 1910), who won in 1931-3 and 1935-7.

Unbeaten sequences
Heather McKay was unbeaten from 1962 to 1980. Jahangir Khan was unbeaten from his loss to Geoff Hunt at the British Open on 10 April 1981 until Ross Norman (New Zealand) beat him in the World Open final on 11 Nov 1986.

Longest and shortest championship matches
The longest recorded competitive match was one of 2 hr 45 min when Jahangir Khan beat Gamal Awad (Egypt) (b. 8 Sept 1955) 9-10, 9-5, 9-7, 9-2, the first game lasting a record 1 hr 11 min, in the final of the Patrick International Festival at Chichester, West Sussex, England on 30 Mar 1983. Suzanne Burgess beat Carolyn Mett in just 8 min (9-2, 9-0, 9-0) in the British Under-23 Open Championship at The Oasis Club, Marlow, Buckinghamshire on 20 Jan 1986.

Most international appearances
The men's record is 110 by David Gotto for Ireland. The women's record is 71 by Geraldine Barniville for Ireland, 1973-83.

Largest crowd and tournament
The finals of the Hi-Tec British Open Squash Championships at the Wembley Conference Centre, London had a record attendance for squash of 3026 on 14 Apr 1987.

The InterCity National Squash Challenge was contested by 8916 players in 1986-7, a knock-out tournament record.

Surfing

The traditional Polynesian sport of surfing in a canoe (*ehorooe*) was first recorded by Captain James Cook, RN, FRS (1728-79) on his first voyage at Tahiti in December 1771. Surfing on a board (*Amo Amo iluna ka lau oka nalu*) was first described as 'most perilous and extraordinary . . . altogether astonishing and is scarcely to be credited' by Lt (later Capt) James King, RN, FRS in March 1779 at Kealakekua Bay, Hawaii Island. A surfer was first depicted by this voyage's official artist, John Webber. The sport was revived at Waikiki by 1900. Hollow boards were introduced in 1929 and the light plastic foam type in 1956.

Most titles
World Amateur Championships were inaugurated in May 1964 at Sydney, Australia. The most titles is three by Michael Novakov (Australia) who won the Kneeboard event in 1982, 1984 and 1986. A World Professional series was started in 1975 and Mark Richards (Australia) has won the men's title five times, 1975 and 1979-82.

Highest waves ridden
Makaha Beach, Hawaii provides the reputedly highest consistently high waves often reaching the ridable limit of 30-35 ft *9-10 m*. The highest wave ever ridden was the *tsunami* of 'perhaps 50 ft *15,24 m*', which struck Minole, Hawaii on 3 Apr 1868, and was ridden to save his life by a Hawaiian named Holua.

Longest ride *Sea wave*
About four to six times each year ridable surfing waves break in Matanchen Bay near San Blas, Nayarit, Mexico, which makes rides of c. 5700 ft *1700 m* possible.

Longest ride *River bore*
The longest recorded rides on a river bore have been set on the Severn bore, England. The official British Surfing Association record for riding a surfboard in a standing position is 0.8 mile *1,3 km* by Nick Hart (b. 11 Dec 1958) from Lower Rea to Hempsted on 26 Oct 1984. The longest ride on a surfboard standing or lying down is 2.94 miles *4,73 km* by Colin Kerr Wilson (b. 23 June 1954) on 23 May 1982.

Swimming

In Japan, swimming in schools was ordered by imperial edict of Emperor Go-Yozei (1586-1611) in 1603 but competition was known from 36 BC. Sea-water bathing was fashionable at Scarborough, North Yorkshire as early as 1660. The earliest pool was Pearless Pool, north London, opened in 1743. In Great Britain competitive swimming originated from at least 1791. Swimming races were particularly popular in the 1820s in Liverpool, where the first pool opened at St George's Pier Head in 1828.

Largest pools
The largest swimming pool in the world is the sea-water Orthlieb Pool in Casablanca, Morocco. It is 480 m *1574 ft* long and 75 m *246 ft* wide, and has an area of 3.6 ha *8.9 acres*. The largest land-locked swimming pool with heated water was the Fleishhacker Pool on Sloat Boulevard, near Great Highway, San Francisco, California, USA. It measured 1000 × 150 ft *304,8 × 45,7 m* and up to 14 ft *4,26 m* deep and contained 7,500,000 US gal *28 390 hectolitres* of heated water. It was opened on 2 May 1925 but has now been abandoned. The greatest spectator accommodation is 13,614 at Osaka, Japan. The largest in use in the United Kingdom is the Royal Commonwealth Pool, Edinburgh, completed in 1970 with 2000 permanent seats, but the covered over and unused pool at Earls Court, London (opened 1937) could seat some 12,000 spectators.

Fastest swimmer
The fastest speed measured in a 50 m pool is by the world record holders for 50 metres (see table): *men*: Matthew Biondi 8,06 km/h *5.01 mph*, and *women*: Tamara Costache 7,12 km/h *4.42 mph*.

Most world records
Men: 32, Arne Borg (Sweden) (b. 18 Aug 1901), 1921-9. Women: 42, Ragnhild Hveger (Denmark) (b. 10 Dec 1920), 1936-42. Under modern conditions (only metric distances in 50 m pools) the most are 26 by Mark Andrew Spitz (USA) (b. 10 Feb 1950), 1967-72, and 23 by Kornelia Ender (GDR) (b. 25 Oct 1958), 1973-6.

Most world titles
In the World Championships (inst. 1973) the most medals won is ten by Kornelia Ender with eight gold and two silver in 1973 and 1975. The most by a man is eight by Ambrose 'Rowdy' Gaines (USA) (b. 17 Feb 1959), five gold and three silver, in 1978 and 1982. The most gold medals is six by James Montgomery (USA) (b. 24 Jan 1955) in 1973 and 1975. The most medals at a single championship is seven by Matthew Biondi (USA) (b. 8 Oct 1965), three gold, one silver, three bronze, in 1986.

OLYMPIC RECORDS

Most medals *Men*
The greatest number of Olympic gold medals won is nine by Mark Spitz (USA): 100 m and 200 m freestyle 1972; 100 m and 200 m butterfly 1972; 4 × 100 m freestyle 1968 and 1972; 4 × 200 m freestyle 1968 and 1972; 4 × 100 m medley 1972. *All but one of these performances (the 4 × 200 m freestyle of 1968) were also new world records.* He also won a silver (100 m butterfly) and a bronze (100 m freestyle) in 1968 for a record eleven medals.

Women
The record number of gold medals won by a woman is four, shared by: Patricia McCormick (*née* Keller) (USA) (b. 12 May 1930), the high and springboard diving double in 1952 and 1956 (also the female record for individual golds); Dawn Fraser (Australia) (b. 4 Sept 1937), the 100 m freestyle (1956, 1960 and 1964) and the 4 × 100 m freestyle (1956); and Kornelia Ender (GDR), the 100 and 200 m freestyle, 100 m butterfly and 4 × 100 m medley in 1976. Dawn Fraser is the only swimmer to win the same event on three successive occasions.

The most medals won by a woman is eight, by: Dawn Fraser, who in addition to her four golds won four silvers (400 m freestyle 1956, 4 × 100 m freestyle 1960 and 1964, 4 × 100 m medley 1960); Kornelia Ender, who in addition to her four golds won four silvers (200 m individual medley 1972, 4 × 100 m medley 1972, 4 × 100 m freestyle 1972 and 1976); and Shirley Babashoff (USA) (b. 3 Jan 1957), who won two golds (4 × 100 m freestyle 1972 and 1976) and six silvers (100 m freestyle 1972, 200 m freestyle 1972 and 1976, 400 m and 800 m freestyle 1976, 4 × 100 m medley 1976).

Most individual gold medals
The record number of individual gold medals won is four, by: Charles M. Daniels (USA) (1884-1973) (100 m freestyle 1906 and 1908, 220 yd freestyle 1904, 440 yd freestyle 1904); Roland Matthes (GDR) (b. 17 Nov 1950) with 100 m and 200 m backstroke 1968 and 1972; Mark Spitz; and Pat McCormick. The most individual golds by a British swimmer is three by Henry Taylor.

Most medals *British*
The record number of gold medals won by a British swimmer (excluding water polo, *q.v.*) is four by Henry Taylor (1885-1951) in the mile freestyle (1906), 400 m freestyle (1908), 1500 m freestyle (1908) and 4 × 200 m freestyle (1908).

Henry Taylor won a record eight medals in all with a silver (400 m freestyle 1906) and three bronzes (4 × 200 m freestyle 1906, 1912, 1920). The most medals by a British woman is four by

SWIMMING—WORLD RECORDS (set in 50-m pools)

MEN

FREESTYLE	Min Sec	Name, country and date of birth	Place	Date	
50 metres	22.33	Matthew Biondi (USA) (b. 8 Oct 1965)	Orlando, Florida, USA	26 June	1986
100 metres	48.74	Matthew Biondi (USA)	Orlando, Florida, USA	24 June	1986
200 metres	1:47.44	Michael Gross (W. Germany) (b. 17 June 1964)	Los Angeles, USA	29 July	1984
400 metres	3:47.80	Michael Gross (W. Germany)	Remscheid, W. Germany	27 June	1985
800 metres	7:50.64	Vladimir Salnikov (USSR) (b. 21 May 1960)	Moscow, USSR	4 July	1986
1500 metres	14:54.76	Vladimir Salnikov (USSR)	Moscow, USSR	22 Feb	1983
4 × 100 metres relay	3:17.08	United States (Scott McAdam, Michael Heath, Paul Wallace, Matthew Biondi)	Tokyo, Japan	17 Aug	1985
4 × 200 metres relay	7:15.69	United States (Michael Heath, David Larson, Jeffrey Float, Lawrence Bruce Hayes)	Los Angeles, USA	30 July	1984

BREASTSTROKE	Min Sec				
100 metres	1:01.65	Steven Lundquist (USA) (b. 20 Feb 1961)	Los Angeles, USA	29 July	1984
200 metres	2:13.34	Victor Davis (Canada) (b. 19 Feb 1964)	Los Angeles, USA	2 Aug	1984

BUTTERFLY	Min Sec				
100 metres	52.84	Pedro Pablo Morales (USA) (b. 5 Dec 1964)	Orlando, Florida, USA	23 June	1986
200 metres	1:56.24	Michael Gross (W. Germany)	Hannover, W. Germany	28 June	1986

BACKSTROKE	Min Sec				
100 metres	55.19	Richard 'Rick' Carey (USA) (b. 13 Mar 1963)	Caracas, Venezuela	21 Aug	1983
200 metres	1:58.14	Igor Polyanskiy (USSR) (b. 20 Mar 1967)	Erfurt, GDR	3 Mar	1985

MEDLEY	Min Sec				
200 metres	2:01.42	Alex Baumann (Canada) (b. Prague 21 Apr 1964)	Los Angeles, USA	4 Aug	1984
	2:01.42	Alex Baumann (Canada)	Montreal, Canada	4 Mar	1986
400 metres	4:17.41	Alex Baumann (Canada)	Los Angeles, USA	30 July	1984
4 × 100 metres relay	3:38.28	United States (Richard Carey, John Moffet, Pedro Pablo Morales, Matthew Biondi)	Tokyo, Japan	18 Aug	1985

WOMEN

FREESTYLE	Min Sec	Name, country and date of birth	Place	Date	
50 metres	25.28	Tamara Costache (Romania) (b. 1970)	Madrid, Spain	23 Aug	1986
100 metres	54.73	Kristin Otto (GDR) (b. 7 Feb 1965)	Madrid, Spain (relay first leg)	19 Aug	1986
200 metres	1:57.55	Heike Friedrich (GDR) (b. 1970)	East Berlin, GDR	18 June	1986
400 metres	4:06.28	Tracey Wickham (Australia) (b. 24 Nov 1962)	West Berlin, W. Germany	24 Aug	1978
800 metres	8:24.62	Tracey Wickham (Australia)	Edmonton, Canada	5 Aug	1978
1500 metres	16:04.49	Kim Lineham (USA) (b. 11 Dec 1962)	Fort Lauderdale, Florida, USA	19 Aug	1979
4 × 100 metres relay	3:40.57	GDR (Kristin Otto, Manuela Stellmach, Sabine Schulze, Heike Friedrich)	Madrid, Spain	19 Aug	1986
4 × 200 metres relay	7:59.33	GDR (Manuela Stellmach, Astrid Strauss, Nadja Bergknecht, Heike Friedrich)	Madrid, Spain	17 Aug	1986

BREASTSTROKE	Min Sec				
100 metres	1:08.11	Sylvia Gerasch (GDR) (b. 16 Mar 1969)	Madrid, Spain	21 Aug	1986
200 metres	2:27.40	Silke Hörner (GDR) (b. 12 Sept 1965)	Madrid, Spain	18 Aug	1986

BUTTERFLY	Min Sec				
100 metres	57.93	Mary T. Meagher (USA) (b. 27 Oct 1964)	Milwaukee, Wisconsin, USA	16 Aug	1981
200 metres	2:05.96	Mary T. Meagher (USA)	Milwaukee, Wisconsin, USA	13 Aug	1981

BACKSTROKE	Min Sec				
100 metres	1:00.59	Ina Kleber (GDR) (b. 29 Sept 1964)	Moscow, USSR	24 Aug	1984
200 metres	2:08.60	Betsy Mitchell (USA) (b. 15 Jan 1966)	Orlando, Florida, USA	27 June	1986

MEDLEY	Min Sec				
200 metres	2:11.73	Ute Geweniger (GDR) (b. 24 Feb 1964)	East Berlin, GDR	4 July	1981
400 metres	4:36.10	Petra Schneider (GDR) (b. 11 Jan 1963)	Guayaquil, Ecuador	1 Aug	1982
4 × 100 metres relay	4:03.69	GDR (Ina Kleber, Sylvia Gerasch, Ines Geissler, Birgit Meineke)	Moscow, USSR	24 Aug	1984

M. Joyce Cooper (now Badcock) (b. 18 Apr 1909) with one silver (4 × 100 m freestyle 1928) and three bronze (100 m freestyle 1928, 100 m backstroke 1928, 4 × 100 m freestyle 1932).

Most short-course world records ● In addition to his three long-course records, Michael Gross holds the world record in 25-m pools for 200, 400 and 800 metres freestyle and 100 and 200 metres butterfly. (Photo: All-Sport)

Closest verdict

The closest verdict in the Olympic Games was in Los Angeles on 29 July 1984, when Nancy Hogshead (b. 17 Apr 1962) and Carrie Steinseifer (b. 12 Feb 1968) (both USA) dead-heated for the women's 100 m freestyle gold medal in 55.92 sec. In the 1972 men's 400 m individual medley Gunnar Larsson (Sweden) (b. 12 May 1951) beat Tim McKee (USA) (b. 14 Mar 1953) by just 2/1000 of a second, just 3 mm. Timings are now determined only to hundredths.

DIVING

Most Olympic medals *World*

The most medals won by a diver are five (three gold, two silver) by Klaus Dibiasi (b. Austria, 6 Oct 1947) (Italy) in the four Games from 1964 to 1976. He is also the only diver to win the same event (highboard) at three successive Games (1968, 1972 and 1976). Pat McCormick (*see above*) won four gold medals.

British

The highest placing by a Briton has been the silver medal by Beatrice Eileen Armstrong (later Purdy) (1894–1981) in the 1920 highboard event. The best placings by male divers are the bronze medals by Harold Clarke (b. 1888) (plain high diving, 1924) and Brian Phelps (b. 21 Apr 1944) (highboard, 1960).

Most world titles

Greg Louganis (USA) (b. 29 Jan 1960) won a record five world titles, highboard in 1978, and both highboard and springboard in 1982 and 1986, as well as two Olympic gold medals in 1984. Three gold medals at one event have also been won by Phil Boggs (USA) (b. 29 Dec 1949), springboard 1973, 1975 and 1978.

Highest scores

Greg Louganis achieved record scores at the 1984 Olympic Games in Los Angeles, with 754.41 points for the 11-dive springboard event and 710.91 for the highboard. At the World Championships in Guayaquil, Ecuador in 1984 he was awarded a perfect score of 10.0 by all seven judges for his highboard inward 1½ somersault in the pike position.

The first diver to be awarded a score of 10.0 by all seven judges was Michael Finneran (b. 21 Sept 1948) in the 1972 US Olympic Trials, in Chicago, Illinois, for a backward 1½ somersault, 2½ twist, from the 10 m board.

CHANNEL SWIMMING

The first to swim the English Channel from shore to shore (without a life jacket) was the Merchant Navy captain Matthew Webb (1848–83), who swam from Dover, England to Calais Sands, France, in 21 hr 45 min from 12.56 p.m. to 10.41 a.m., 24–25 Aug 1875. He swam an estimated 38 miles *61 km* to make the 21 mile *33 km* crossing. Paul Boyton (USA) had swum from Cap

World record: women's 200 metres breaststroke ● 2:27.40 long-course and 2:25.71 short-course, set in 1986 and 1987 respectively by Silke Hörner (GDR) (b. 12 Sept 1965). (Photo: Tony Duffy/All-Sport)

Gris-Nez to the South Foreland in his patent life-saving suit in 23 hr 30 min on 28–29 May 1875. There is good evidence that Jean-Marie Saletti, a French soldier, escaped from a British prison hulk off Dover by swimming to Boulogne in July or August 1815. The first crossing from France to England was made by Enrico Tiraboschi, a wealthy Italian living in Argentina, in 16 hr 33 min on 12 Aug 1923, to win the *Daily Sketch* prize of £1000.

The first woman to succeed was Gertrude Caroline Ederle (b. 23 Oct 1906) (USA) who swam from Cap Gris-Nez, France to Deal, England on 6 Aug 1926, in the then overall record time of 14 hr 39 min. The first woman to swim from England to France was Florence Chadwick (b. 1918) (USA) in 16 hr 19 min on 11 Sept 1951. The first Englishwoman to succeed was Mercedes Gleitze (later Carey) (1900–81) who swam from France to England in 15 hr 15 min on 7 Oct 1927.

Fastest

The official Channel Swimming Association (founded 1927) record is 7 hr 40 min by Penny Dean (b. 21 Mar 1955) of California, USA, from Shakespeare Beach, Dover to Cap Gris-Nez, France, on 29 July 1978.

The fastest crossing by a relay team is 7 hr 17 min, by six Dover lifeguards, from England to France on 9 Aug 1981.

BRITISH NATIONAL RECORDS

MEN

Event	Time Min Sec	Name and date of birth	Place	Date
FREESTYLE				
50 metres	23.41	David Lowe (b. 28 Feb 1960)	Los Angeles, USA	16 July 1983
100 metres	50.91	Andrew Jameson (b. 19 Feb 1965)	Madrid, Spain	19 Aug 1986
200 metres	1:51.52	Andrew Astbury (b. 29 Nov 1960)	Brisbane, Australia	2 Oct 1982
400 metres	3:51.93	Kevin Boyd (b. 23 June 1966)	Madrid, Spain	21 Aug 1986
800 metres	8:09.83	Tony Day (b. 14 April 1965)	Edinburgh, Scotland	30 July 1986
1500 metres	15:22.76	Tony Day	Edinburgh, Scotland	30 July 1986
4 × 100 metres relay	3:23.61	GB (David Lowe, Roland Lee, Paul Easter, Richard Burrell)	Los Angeles, USA	2 Aug 1984
4 × 200 metres relay	7:24.78	GB (Neil Cochran, Paul Easter, Paul Howe, Andrew Astbury)	Los Angeles, USA	30 July 1984
BREASTSTROKE				
100 metres	1:02.28	Adrian Moorhouse (b. 24 May 1964)	Madrid, Spain	19 Aug 1986
200 metres	2:15.11	David Andrew Wilkie (b. 8 Mar 1954)	Montreal, Canada	24 July 1976
BUTTERFLY				
100 metres	53.67	Andrew Jameson	Madrid, Spain	18 Aug 1986
200 metres	2:00.21	Philip Hubble (b. 19 July 1960)	Split, Yugoslavia	11 Sept 1981
BACKSTROKE				
100 metres	57.72	Gary Abraham (b. 8 Jan 1959)	Moscow, USSR	24 July 1980
200 metres	2:04.23	Douglas Campbell (b. 30 Sept 1960)	Moscow, USSR	26 July 1980
MEDLEY				
200 metres	2:03.76	Neil Cochran (b. 12 Apr 1965)	Austin, Texas, USA	6 Dec 1985
400 metres	4:24.70	John Davey (b. 29 Dec 1964)	Coventry, England	30 May 1986
4 × 100 metres relay	3:44.85	England (Neil Harper, Adrian Moorhouse, Andrew Jameson, Roland Lee)	Edinburgh, Scotland	30 July 1986

WOMEN

Event	Time Min Sec	Name and date of birth	Place	Date
FREESTYLE				
50 metres	26.39	Caroline Cooper (b. 26 May 1966)	Austin, Texas	12 June 1985
100 metres	56.60	June Croft (b. 17 June 1963)	Amersfoort, Netherlands	31 Jan 1982
200 metres	1:59.74	June Croft	Brisbane, Australia	4 Oct 1982
400 metres	4:07.68	Sarah Hardcastle (b. 9 April 1969)	Edinburgh, Scotland	27 July 1986
800 metres	8:24.77	Sarah Hardcastle	Edinburgh, Scotland	29 July 1986
1500 metres	16:43.95	Sarah Hardcastle	Montreal, Canada	18 Apr 1985
4 × 100 metres relay	3:49.65	England (Caroline Cooper, Nicola Fibbens, Zara Long, Annabelle Cripps)	Edinburgh, Scotland	27 July 1986
4 × 200 metres relay	8:13.70	England (Annabelle Cripps, Sarah Hardcastle, Karen Mellor, Zara Long)	Edinburgh, Scotland	25 July 1986
BREASTSTROKE				
100 metres	1.11.05	Susannah 'Suki' Brownsdon (b. 16 Oct 1965)	Split, Yugoslavia	8 Sept 1981
200 metres	2:33.16	Susannah 'Suki' Brownsdon	Cardiff, Wales	4 May 1985
BUTTERFLY				
100 metres	1:01.48	Nicola Fibbens (b. 29 Apr 1964)	Los Angeles, USA	2 Aug 1984
200 metres	2:11.97	Samantha Purvis (b. 24 June 1967)	Los Angeles, USA	4 Aug 1984
BACKSTROKE				
100 metres	1:03.61	Beverley Rose (b. 21 Jan 1964)	Los Angeles, USA	31 July 1984
200 metres	2:14.87	Katharine Read (b. 30 June 1969)	Coventry, England	30 May 1986
MEDLEY				
200 metres	2:17.21	Jean Hill (b. 15 July 1964)	Edinburgh, Scotland	26 July 1986
400 metres	4:46.83	Sharron Davies (b. 1 Nov 1962)	Moscow, USSR	26 July 1980
4 × 100 metres relay	4:12.24	GB (Helen Jameson, Margaret Kelly, Ann Osgerby, June Croft)	Moscow, USSR	20 July 1980

Earliest and latest

The earliest date in the year on which the Channel has been swum is 6 June by Dorothy Perkins (England) (b. 1942) in 1961, and the latest is 28 Oct by Michael Peter Read (GB) (b. 9 June 1941) in 1979.

Youngest and oldest

The youngest conqueror is Marcus Hooper (GB) (b. 14 June 1967) who swam from Dover to Sangatte, France in 14 hr 37 min on 5–6 Aug 1979, when he was aged 12 yr 53 days. The youngest girl is Samantha Claire Druce (GB) (b. 21 Apr 1971) who was 12 yr 119 days on 18 Aug 1983 when she swam from Dover to Cap Gris-Nez in 15 hr 27 min.

The oldest has been Ashby Harper (b. 1 Oct 1916) of Albuquerque, USA at 65 years 332 days when he swam from Dover to Cap Blanc-Nez in 13 hr 52 min on 28 Aug 1982. The oldest woman was Stella Ada Rosina Taylor (b. 20 Dec 1929) aged 45 yr 350 days when she did the swim in 18 hr 15 min on 26 Aug 1975.

Double crossing

The first double crossing was by Antonio Abertondo (Argentina) (b. 1919) in 43 hr 10 min from 20–22 Sept 1961. Kevin Murphy (b. 1949) completed the first double crossing by a Briton in 35 hr 10 min on 6 Aug 1970. The first swimmer to achieve a crossing both ways was Edward Harry Temme (1904–78) on 5 Aug 1927 and 19 Aug 1934.

The fastest double crossing was in 17 hr 56 min by Philip Rush (New Zealand) (b. 6 Nov 1963) on 9 Sept 1985. The women's record is 18 hr 15 min by Irene van der Laan (Netherlands) (b. 27 Dec 1960) on 18 Aug 1983. The first British woman to achieve the double crossing was Alison Streeter (b. 29 Aug 1964) in 21 hr 16 min on 4 Aug 1983. The fastest by a relay team is 15 hr 36½ min by the six-man West One International Team (GB) on 24 Sept 1985.

Triple crossing

The first triple crossing was by Jon Erikson (USA) (b. 6 Sept 1954) in 38 hr 27 min on 11–12 Aug 1981.

Most conquests

The greatest number of Channel conquests is 31 by Michael Read (GB) from 24 Aug 1969 to 19 Aug 1984, including a record six in one year. The most by a woman is 19 (including five two-way) by Cynthia Cindy M. Nicholas (Canada) (b. 20 Aug 1957) from 29 July 1975 to 14 Sept 1982.

World record: men's 200 metres breaststroke ● Victor Davis (Canada) (b. 19 Feb 1964), Olympic champion in 1984, holds world records at 200m breaststroke, 2:13.34 long-course in 1984, and 2:08.82 short-course (25m pool) in 1987. (Photo: Tony Duffy/All-Sport)

LONG-DISTANCE SWIMMING

Longest swims

The greatest recorded distance ever swum is 1826 miles *2938 km* down the Mississippi, USA between Ford Dam near Minneapolis and Carrollton Ave, New Orleans, Louisiana, by Fred P. Newton, (b. 1903) of Clinton, Oklahoma from 6 July to 29 Dec 1930. He was 742 hr in the water.

The greatest distance covered in a continuous swim is 299 miles *481,5 km* by Ricardo Hoffmann (b. 5 Oct 1941) from Corrientes to Santa Elena, Argentina in the River Parana in 84 hr 37 min on 3–6 Mar 1981.

The longest ocean swim is one of 128.8 miles *207,3 km* by Walter Poenisch, Snr (USA) (b. 1914), who started from Havana, Cuba, and arrived at Little Duck Key, Florida, USA (in a shark cage and wearing flippers) 34 hr 15 min later from 11–13 July 1978.

In 1966 Mihir Sen of Calcutta, India uniquely swam the Palk Strait from Sri Lanka to India (in 25 hr 36 min on 5–6 Apr); the Straits of Gibraltar (in 8 hr 1 min on 24 Aug); the length of the Dardanelles (in 13 hr 55 min on 12 Sept), the Bosphorus (in 4 hr on 21 Sept) and the length of the Panama Canal (in 34 hr 15 min from 29–31 Oct).

Irish Channel

The swimming of the 23 mile *37 km* wide North Channel from Donaghadee, Northern Ireland to Portpatrick, Scotland was first accomplished by Tom Blower of Nottingham in 15 hr 26 min in 1947. A record time of 11 hr 21 min was set by Kevin Murphy on 11 Sept 1970. The first Irish-born swimmer to achieve the crossing was Ted Keenan on 11 Aug 1973 in 52–56°F *11–13°C* water in 18 hr 27 min.

Bristol Channel

The first person to achieve a crossing of the Bristol Channel was Kathleen Thomas (now Mrs Day) (b. April 1906), who swam from Penarth, South Glamorgan to Weston-super-Mare, Avon in 7 hr 20 min on 5 Sept 1927. The record for the longer swim from Glenthorne Cove, Devon to Porthcawl, Mid-Glamorgan is 10 hr 46 min by

---

Jane Luscombe (b. 13 Jan 1961) of Jersey, CI, on 19 Aug 1976.

Lake swims

The fastest time for swimming the 22.7 mile *36,5 km* long Loch Ness is 9 hr 57 min by David Trevor Morgan (b. 25 Sept 1963) on 31 July 1983. The first successful swim was by Brenda Sherratt (b. 1948) of West Bollington, Cheshire on 26–27 July 1966. David Morgan achieved a unique double crossing of Loch Ness in 23 hr 4 min on 1 Aug 1983. The fastest time for swimming Lake Windermere, 10.5 miles *16,9 km* is 3 hr 49 min 56 sec by Karen Toole, 17, of Darlington on 5 Sept 1981. The fastest time for the Lake Windermere International Championship, 16.5 miles *26,5 km*, is 6 hr 10 min 33 sec by Mary Beth Colpo (USA) (b. 1961) on 5 Aug 1978.

Longest duration

The longest duration swim ever achieved was one of 168 continuous hours, ending on 24 Feb 1941, by the legless Charles Zibbelman, *alias* Zimmy (b. 1894) in a pool in Honolulu, Hawaii, USA. The longest duration swim by a woman was 87 hr 27 min in a salt-water pool by Myrtle Huddleston (USA) at Raven Hall, Coney Island, NY, USA, in 1931.

24 hours

David Goch (USA) swam 55.682 miles *89,611 km* in a 25 yd *22,86 m* pool at the University of Michigan, USA on 17–18 May 1986. The record in a 50-m pool is 87,528 km *54.39* miles by Bertrand Malègue at St Etienne, France on 31 May–1 June 1980.

The women's record is 42.05 miles *67,67 km* by Alyson Gibbons (Sutton Coldfield) in the 25-m Aston Newtown Baths, Birmingham on 7–8 Sept 1985.

Greatest lifetime distance

Gustave Brickner (b. 10 Feb 1912) of Charleroi, Pennsylvania, USA in 59 years to November 1986 had recorded 38,512 miles *61 977 km*.

Long-distance relays

The New Zealand national relay team of 20 swimmers swam a record 182,807 km *113.59 miles* in Lower Hutt, NZ in 24 hours, passing 160 km *100 miles* in 20 hr 47 min 13 sec on 9–10 Dec 1983. The most participants in a one-day swim relay is 2135, each swimming a length, organised by Syracuse YMCA in Syracuse, New York, USA on 11 Apr 1986.

The longest duration swim relay was 216 hr 50 min 16 sec for 601,180 km by a team of 20 at Katowice, Poland from 17–26 Feb 1987.

Underwater swimming

Paul Cryne (UK) and Samir Sawan al Awami of Qatar swam 49.04 miles *78,92 km* in a 24-hour period from Doha, Qatar to Umm Said and back on 21–22 Feb 1985 using sub-aqua equipment. They were swimming underwater for 95.5 per cent of the time.

Tony Boyle, Eddie McGettigan, Laurence Thermes and Gearoid Murphy swam a relay of 332.88 miles *535,71 km* underwater in 168 hr using sub-aqua equipment at the Mosney Holiday Centre, Co. Meath, Ireland, 22–29 June 1985.

The first underwater cross-Channel swim was achieved by Fred Baldasare (b. 1924) (USA), who completed a 42 mile *67,5 km* distance from France to England with scuba equipment in 18 hr 1 min on 10–11 July 1962.

Sponsored swimming

The greatest amount of money collected in a charity swim was £91,552.05 in 'Splash '86' organised by the Royal Bank of Scotland Swimming Club for the 1986 Commonwealth Games Appeal. Held at the Royal Commonwealth Pool, Edinburgh, Scotland on 11 18 Jan 1986, 6000 swimmers took part.

Table Tennis

The earliest evidence relating to a game resembling table tennis has been found in the catalogues of London sports goods manufacturers in the 1880s. The old Ping Pong Association was formed in 1902 but the game proved only a temporary craze until resuscitated in 1921. The International Table Tennis Federation was founded in 1926 and the English Table Tennis Association was formed on 24 Apr 1927. Table tennis is to be included at the Olympic Games for the first time in 1988.

Most English titles
The highest total of English men's titles (instituted 1921) is 20 by G. Viktor Barna (1911–72) (b. Hungary, Gyözö Braun). The women's record is 17 by Diane Rowe (b. 14 Apr 1933), now Mrs Eberhard Scholer. Her twin Rosalind (now Mrs Cornett) has won nine (two in singles).

The most titles won in the English Closed Championships is 23 by Desmond Douglas (b. 20 July 1955), a record ten men's singles, 1976 and 1979–87, nine men's doubles and four mixed doubles. A record seven women's singles were won by Jill Patricia Hammersley (now Parker née Shirley) (b. 6 Dec 1951) in 1973–6, 1978–9 and 1981.

Internationals
The youngest ever international was Joy Foster, aged 8, when she represented Jamaica in the West Indies Championships at Port of Spain, Trinidad in Aug 1958. The youngest ever to play for England was Carl Prean (b. 20 Aug 1967), aged 14 yr 191 days, against Portugal at Lisbon on 27 Feb 1982.

Jill Parker played for England on a record 413 occasions, 1967–83.

Counter hitting
The record number of hits in 60 sec is 170 by English internationals Alan Cooke (b. 23 Mar 1966) and Desmond Douglas at Scotswood Sports Centre, Newcastle-upon-Tyne on 28 Feb 1986. The women's record is 163 by the sisters Lisa (b.

9 Mar 1967) and Jackie (b. 9 Sept 1964) Bellinger at Stopsley Sports Centre, Luton, Bedfordshire on 23 June 1985. With a bat in each hand, Gary D. Fisher of Olympia, Washington, USA, completed 5000 consecutive volleys over the net in 44 min 28 sec on 25 June 1979.

Highest speed
No conclusive measurements have been published but in a lecture M. Sklorz (West Germany) stated that a smashed ball had been measured at speeds up to 170 km/h *105.6 mph*.

Taekwon-Do

The founder and father of this martial art is General Choi Hong Hi 9th Dan, the highest Dan awarded. Taekwon-Do was officially recognised as part of Korean tradition and culture on 11 Apr 1955. The International Taekwon-Do Federation was formed in 1966 and has staged World Championships from 1974. Taekwon-Do is being staged as a demonstration sport at the 1988 Olympic Games.

The highest Dan in Britain is Master Rhee Ki Ha 8th Dan, the Chief Instructor of the United Kingdom Taekwon-Do Association.

Tennis (Lawn)

The modern game is generally agreed to have evolved as an outdoor form of the indoor game of tennis (see separate entry). 'Field tennis' is mentioned in an English magazine—*Sporting Magazine*—of 29 Sept 1793. The earliest club for such a game, variously called Pelota or Lawn Rackets, was the Leamington Club, founded in 1872 by Major Harry Gem. The earliest attempt to commercialise the game was by Major Walter Clopton Wingfield (1833–1912) who patented a form called 'sphairistike' on 23 Feb 1874. It soon became called lawn tennis. Amateur players were permitted to play with and against professionals in 'open' tournaments in 1968.

Grand slam
To achieve the grand slam is to hold at the same time all four of the world's major championship singles: Wimbledon, the United States, Australian and French championships. The first man to have won all four was Frederick John Perry (GB) (b. 18 May 1909) when he won the French title in 1935. The first man to hold all four championships simultaneously was John Donald Budge (USA) (b. 13 June 1915) in 1938. The first man to achieve the grand slam twice was Rodney George Laver (Australia) (b. 9 Aug 1938) as an amateur in 1962, and again in 1969 when the titles were open to professionals.

Three women have achieved the grand slam: Maureen Catherine Connolly (USA) (1934–69) in 1953; Margaret Jean Court (*née* Smith) (Australia) (b. 16 July 1942) in 1970, and Martina Navratilova (USA) (b. 18 Oct 1956) in 1983–4. Miss Navratilova won six successive grand slam singles titles in 1983–4 and with Pamela Howard Shriver (USA) (b. 4 July 1962) won eight successive grand slam tournament women's doubles titles and 109 successive matches in all events from April 1983 to July 1985.

The most singles championships won in grand slam tournaments is 24 by Margaret Court (eleven Australian, five French, five USA, three Wimbledon), 1960–73. The men's record is 12 by Roy Emerson (Australia) (b. 3 Nov 1936) (six Australian, two each French, USA, Wimbledon), 1961–7.

Fastest service
The fastest service timed with modern equipment is 138 mph *222 km/h* by Steve Denton (USA) (b. 5 Sept 1956) at Beaver Creek, Colorado, USA on 29 July 1984. The fastest *ever* measured was one of 163.6 mph *263 km/h* by William Tatem Tilden (1893–1953) (USA) in 1931.

Longest game
The longest known singles game was one of 37 deuces (80 points) between Anthony Fawcett (Rhodesia) and Keith Glass (GB) in the first round of the Surrey Championships at Surbiton, Surrey, on 26 May 1975. It lasted 31 minutes. Noëlle van Lottum and Sandra Begijn played a game lasting 52 minutes in the semi-finals of the Dutch Indoor Championships at Ede, Gederland on 12 Feb 1984.

The longest rally in tournament play was one of 643 times over the net between Vicky Nelson and Jean Hepner at Richmond, Virginia, USA in October 1984. The 6 hr 22 min match was won by Nelson 6–4, 7–6. It concluded with a 1 hr 47 min tiebreak, 13–11, of which one point took 29 minutes.

The longest tiebreak was 26–24 for the fourth and decisive set of a first round men's doubles at the Wimbledon Championships on 1 July 1985. Jan Gunnarsson (Sweden) and Michael Mortensen (Denmark) defeated John Frawley (Australia) and Victor Pecci (Paraguay) 6–3, 6–4, 3–6, 7–6.

Greatest crowd
A record 30,472 people were at the Astrodome, Houston, Texas on 20 Sept 1973, when Billie-Jean King (*née* Moffitt) (b. 22 Nov 1943) (USA) beat Robert Larimore Riggs (b. 25 Feb 1918) (USA). The record for an orthodox tennis match is 25,578 at Sydney, NSW, Australia on 27 Dec 1954 in the Davis Cup Challenge Round (first day) Australia *v.* USA.

Highest earnings
Ivan Lendl (Czechoslovakia) (b. 7 Mar 1960) won a men's season's record $2,028,850 in 1982. The record for a woman is $2,173,556 in 1984 (including a $1-million grand slam bonus) by Martina Navratilova. Earnings from special restricted events and team tennis are not included. Navratilova's lifetime earnings by 19 July 1987 reached

TEAM AND INDIVIDUAL TABLE TENNIS CHAMPIONSHIPS

MOST WINS IN WORLD CHAMPIONSHIPS
(Instituted 1926–7)

Event	Name and Nationality	Times	Years
Men's Singles (St Bride's Vase)	G. Viktor Barna (Hungary) (1911–72)	5	1930, 1932–5
Women's Singles (G. Geist Prize)	Angelica Rozeanu (Romania) (b. 15 Oct 1921)	6	1950–5
Men's Doubles	G. Viktor Barna (Hungary)	8	1929–35, 1939
Women's Doubles	Maria Mednyanszky (Hungary) (1901–79)	7	1928, 1930–5
Mixed Doubles (Men)	Ferenc Sido (Hungary) (b. 1923)	4	1949–50, 1952–3
Mixed Doubles (Women)	Maria Mednyanszky (Hungary)	6	1927–8, 1930–1, 1933–4

G. Viktor Barna gained a personal total of 15 world titles, while 18 have been won by Maria Mednyanszky.

MOST TEAM TITLES

Event	Team	Times	Years
Men's Team (Swaythling Cup)	Hungary	12	1927–31, 1933–5, 1938, 1949, 1952, 1979
Women's Team (Marcel Corbillon Cup)	Japan	8	1952, 1954, 1957, 1959, 1961, 1963, 1967, 1971
	China	8	1965, 1975, 1977, 1979, 1981, 1983, 1985, 1987

MOST WINS IN ENGLISH OPEN CHAMPIONSHIPS
(Instituted 1921)

Event	Name and Nationality	Times	Years
Men's Singles	Richard Bergmann (Austria, then GB) (1920–70)	6	1939–40, 1948, 1950, 1952, 1954
Women's Singles	Maria Alexandru (Romania) (b. 1941)	6	1963–4, 1970–2, 1974
Men's Doubles	G. Viktor Barna (Hungary, then GB)	7	1931, 1933–5, 1938–9, 1949
Women's Doubles	Diane Rowe (GB) (now Scholer) (b. 14 Apr 1933)	12	1950–6, 1960, 1962–5
Mixed Doubles (Men)	G. Viktor Barna (Hungary, then GB)	8	1933–6, 1938, 1940, 1951, 1953
Mixed Doubles (Women)	Diane Rowe (GB) (now Scholer)	4	1952, 1954, 1956, 1960

$12,282,753. The men's record is $10,753,215 by Ivan Lendl.

The one-match record is $500,000 by James Scott Connors (USA) (b. 2 Sept 1952) when he beat John David Newcombe (Australia) (b. 23 May 1944) in a challenge match at Caesar's Palace, Las Vegas, USA on 26 Apr 1975. The highest total prize money was $3,450,800 for the 1986 US Championships.

Longest span as national champion
Walter Westbrook (b. June 1898) won the US National Clay Court men's doubles with Harvey Snodgrass in 1925. Fifty-eight years later he won the US National 85-and-over Clay Court Men's Singles Championship. In the final he defeated Kirk Reid, whom he had first defeated to win the Western Clay Court Championships in 1925.

Dorothy May Bundy-Cheney (USA) (b. Sept 1916) won 151 US titles in various age groups from 1941 to 1986.

International contest *Longest span*
Jean Borotra (France) (b. 13 Aug 1898) played in every one of the twice-yearly contests between the International Club of France and the I.C. of Great Britain from the first in 1929 to his 100th match at Wimbledon, 1–3 Nov 1985. On that occasion he played in a mixed doubles against Kitty Godfree (GB) (b. 7 May 1896). Both were former Wimbledon singles champions, and aged 87 and 89 respectively.

INTERNATIONAL TEAM COMPETITIONS

Davis Cup
The most wins in the Davis Cup (inst. 1900), the men's international team championship, has been 28 by the USA. The most appearances for Cup winners is eight by Roy Emerson (Australia), 1959–62, 1964–7. The British Isles/Great Britain have won nine times, 1903–6, 1912 and 1933–6.

Nicola Pietrangeli (b. 11 Sept 1933) (Italy) played a record 163 rubbers (66 ties), 1954 to 1972, winning 120. He played 109 singles (winning 78) and 54 doubles (winning 42). The record number of rubbers by a British player is 65 (winning 43) by Michael J. Sangster (b. 9 Sept 1940), 1960–8; the most wins is 45 from 52 rubbers by Fred Perry, including 34 of 38 singles, 1931–6.

Wightman Cup
The Wightman Cup (inst. 1923) has been won 48 times by the United States and 10 times by Great Britain. Virginia Wade (GB) (b. 10 July 1945) played in a record 21 ties and 56 rubbers, 1965–85. Christine Marie Evert (USA) (b. 21 Dec 1954) won all 26 of her singles matches, 1971 to 1985.

Federation Cup
The most wins in the Federation Cup (inst. 1963), the women's international team championship, is 12 by the USA. Virginia Wade (GB) played each year from 1967 to 1983, in a record 57 ties, playing 100 rubbers, including 56 singles (winning 36) and 44 doubles (winning 30). Chris Evert won her first 29 singles matches, 1977–86. Her overall record, 1977–86, is 31 wins in 32 singles and 14 wins in 15 doubles matches.

UNITED STATES CHAMPIONSHIPS

Most wins
Margaret Evelyn du Pont (*née* Osborne) won a record 25 titles between 1941 and 1960. She won a record 13 women's doubles (12 with Althea Louise Brough), nine mixed doubles and three singles. The men's record is 16 by William Tatem Tilden, including seven men's singles, 1920–25, 1929—a record for singles shared with: Richard Dudley Sears (1861–1943), 1881–7; William A. Larned (1872–1926), 1901–2, 1907–11; and at women's singles by: Molla Mallory (*née* Bjurstedt) (1892–1959), 1915–6, 1918, 1920–2, 1926; and Helen Moody (*née* Wills), 1923–5, 1927–9, 1931.

Youngest and oldest
The youngest champion was Vincent Richards (1903–59), who was 15 yr 139 days when he won the men's doubles with Bill Tilden in 1918. The youngest singles champion was Tracy Ann Austin (b. 12 Dec 1962), who was 16 yr 271 days when she won the women's singles in 1979. The oldest champion was Margaret du Pont who won the mixed doubles at 42 yr 166 days in 1960. The oldest singles champion was William Larned at 38 yr 242 days in 1911.

WIMBLEDON CHAMPIONSHIPS

Pictured below is the world's most famous tennis court, the Wimbledon Centre Court photographed by record breaker Bob Paluzzi (see Longest negative, page 74)

MOST WINS *Women*
Billie-Jean King (*née* Moffit) (USA) (b. 22 Nov 1943) won a record 20 titles between 1961 and 1979, six singles, ten women's doubles and four mixed doubles. Elizabeth Montague Ryan (USA) (1892–1979) won a record 19 doubles (12 women's, 7 mixed) titles from 1914 to 1934.

MOST WINS *Men*
Hugh Laurence Doherty (GB) (1875–1919) won 13 with five singles (1902–6) and eight men's doubles (1897–1901, 1903–5) partnered by his brother Reginald Frank (1872–1910).

MOST WINS *Singles*
Helen Newington Moody (*née* Wills) (USA) (b. 6 Oct 1905), won 8 (1927–30, 1932–3, 1935 and 1938), a record shared with Martina Navratilova, 1978–9, 1982–7. The most men's singles wins since the Challenge Round was abolished in 1922 is five consecutively, by Bjørn Borg (Sweden), 1976–80. William Charles Renshaw (GB) (1861–1904) won seven singles titles, 1881–6 and 1889.

MOST WINS *Mixed doubles*
Elias Victor Seixas (USA) (b. 30 Aug 1923) in 1953–6; Kenneth Norman Fletcher (Australia) (b.

Most 'grand slam' titles ● Margaret Jean Court (*née* Smith) (Australia) (b. 16 July 1942) won a record 24 singles titles: eleven Australian, five French, five USA and three Wimbledon, between 1960 and 1973, and a record 62 titles overall, including doubles. (Photo: All-Sport)

FRENCH CHAMPIONSHIPS

Most wins (from international status 1925)

Margaret Court won a record 13 titles—five singles, four women's doubles and four mixed doubles, 1962–73. The men's record is nine by Henri Cochet (France) (1901–87)—four singles, three men's doubles and two mixed doubles, 1926–30. The singles record is seven by Chris Evert, 1974–5, 1979–80, 1983, 1985–6. Bjørn Borg won a record six men's singles, 1974–5, 1978–81.

Youngest and oldest

The youngest champions were the 1981 mixed doubles winners, Andrea Jaeger (b. 4 June 1965) at 15 yr 339 days, and Jimmy Arias (b. 16 Aug 1964) at 16 yr 296 days. The youngest singles winner was Mats Wilander (Sweden) (b. 22 Aug 1964) at 17 yr 288 days in 1982. The oldest champion was Elizabeth Ryan who won the 1934 women's doubles with Simone Mathieu (France) at 42 yr 88 days. The oldest singles champion was Andres Gimeno in 1972 at 34 yr 301 days.

15 June 1940) in 1963, 1965–6, 1968; and Owen Keir Davidson (Australia) (b. 4 Oct 1943) in 1967, 1971, 1973–4 each won 4. Elizabeth Ryan (USA) won seven (1919 to 1932).

MOST APPEARANCES

Arthur William Charles 'Wentworth' Gore (1868–1928) (GB) made a record 36 appearances at Wimbledon between 1888 and 1927. In 1964, Jean Borotra (b. 13 Aug 1898) of France made his 35th appearance since 1922. In 1977 he appeared in the veterans' doubles aged 78.

YOUNGEST CHAMPIONS

The youngest champion was Charlotte 'Lottie' Dod (1871–1960), who was 15 yr 285 days when she won the women's singles in 1887. The youngest male champion was Boris Becker (West Germany) (b. 22 Nov 1967), who won the men's singles title in 1985 at 17 yr 227 days. The youngest ever player at Wimbledon was reputedly Mita Klima (Austria), who was 13 yr in the 1907 singles competition. The youngest player to win a match at Wimbledon was Kathy Rinaldi (b. 24 Mar 1967) (USA), at 14 yr 91 days on 23 June 1981.

OLDEST CHAMPIONS

The oldest champion was Margaret Evelyn du Pont (*née* Osborne) (USA) (b. 4 Mar 1918) at 44 yr 125 days when she won the mixed doubles in 1962 with Neale Fraser (Australia). The oldest singles champion was Arthur Gore (GB) in 1909 at 41 yr 182 days.

GREATEST CROWD

The record crowd for one day was 39,813 on 26 June 1986. The record for the whole Championship was 400,032 in 1986.

GRAND PRIX MASTERS

The first Grand Prix Masters Championships were staged in Tokyo, Japan in 1970. They have been held in New York annually from 1977. Qualification to this annual event is by relative success in the preceding year's Grand Prix tournaments. A record four titles have been won by: Ilie Nastase (Romania) (b. 19 Aug 1946), 1971–3, 1975; and by Ivan Lendl, 1982–3 and two in 1986 (January and December). James Scott Connors (USA) (b. 7 Sept 1952) uniquely qualified for 14 consecutive years, 1972–85. He chose not to play in 1975, 1976 and 1985, and won in 1977.

A record seven doubles titles were won by John Patrick McEnroe (b. 16 Feb 1959) and Peter Fleming (b. 21 Jan 1955) (both USA), 1979–85.

OLYMPIC GAMES

Tennis is being reintroduced to the Olympic Games in 1988, having originally been included at the Games from 1896 to 1924. It was also a demonstration sport in 1984.

A record four gold medals as well as a silver and a bronze were won by Max Decugis (France) (1882–1978), 1900–20. A women's record five medals (one gold, two silver, two bronze) were achieved by Kitty McKane (later Mrs Godfree) (GB) (b. 7 May 1897) in 1920 and 1924.

Tennis (Real/Royal)

The game originated as *jeu de paume* in French monasteries *c.* 1050. A tennis court is mentioned in the sale of the Hôtel de Nesle, Paris, bought by King Philippe IV of France in 1308. The oldest of the surviving active courts in Great Britain is that at Falkland Palace, Fife, Scotland, built by King James V of Scotland in 1539.

Most titles *World*

The first recorded world tennis champion was Clerge (France) *c.* 1740. Jacques Edmond Barre (France) (1802–73) held the title for a record 33 yr from 1829 to 1862. Pierre Etchebaster (1893–1980), a Basque, holds the record for the greatest number of successful defences of the title with eight between 1928 and 1952.

The first two Women's World Championships in 1985 and 1987 were won by Judy Clarke (Australia).

British

The Amateur Championship of the British Isles (instituted 1888) has been won 16 times by Howard Rea Angus (b. 25 June 1944), 1966–80 and 1982. He also won eight Amateur Doubles Championships with David Warburg, 1967–70, 1972–74 and 1976, and was world champion 1976–81.

Tiddlywinks

National Championships

Alan Dean (Edwinstowe, Notts) (b. 22 July 1949) has won the singles title six times, 1971–3, 1976, 1978 and 1986, and the pairs title five times. Jonathan Mapley (b. 1947) has won the pairs title six times, 1972, 1975, 1977, 1980 and 1983–4.

Potting records

The record for potting 24 winks from 18 in *45 cm* is 21.8 sec by Stephen Williams (Altrincham Grammar School) in May 1966. Allen R. Astles (University of Wales) potted 10,000 winks in 3 hr 51 min 46 sec at Aberystwyth, Cardiganshire in February 1966.

A record 35 winks were potted in relay in three minutes (24 in two minutes) by Duncan Budd, Tim Hedger, Alex Satchell and Nick Inglis of the Cambridge University Tiddlywinkers Club at Queen's College, Cambridge on 20 May 1987.

Track and Field Athletics

The earliest evidence of organised running was at Memphis, Egypt *c.* 3800 BC. The earliest accurately dated Olympic Games were in July 776 BC, at which celebration Coroibos won the foot race. The oldest surviving measurements are a long jump of 7,05 m *23 ft 1½ in* by Chionis of Sparta *c.* 656 BC and a discus throw of 100 cubits (about 46,30 m *152 ft*) by Protesilaus.

Fastest speed

The fastest speed recorded in an individual world record is 36,51 km/h *22.69 mph*, but this does not allow for the effects of the delay in reaching peak speed from a standing start. Maximum speeds exceeding 40 km/h *25 mph* for men and 36,5 km/h *22.5 mph* for women have been measured, for instance for Carl Lewis (8.94 sec) and Evelyn Ashford (9.97 sec) respectively for their final 100 metres in the 1984 Olympic sprint relays.

Highest jump above own head

The greatest height cleared above an athlete's own head is 23¼ in *59 cm* by Franklin Jacobs (USA) (b. 31 Dec 1957), who cleared 7 ft 7¼ in *2,32 m* at New York, USA, on 27 Jan 1978. He is 5 ft 8 in *1,73 m* tall. The greatest height cleared by a woman above her own head is 30,5 cm *12 in* by Cindy John Holmes (USA) (b. 29 Aug 1960), 5 ft *1,525 m* tall, who jumped 6 ft *1,83 m* at Provo, Utah, USA on 1 June 1982.

Most Olympic titles *Men*

The most Olympic gold medals won is ten (an absolute Olympic record) by Ray C. Ewry (USA) (1874–1937) in the standing high, long and triple jumps in 1900, 1904, 1906 and 1908.

Women

The most gold medals won by a woman is four, shared by: Francina 'Fanny' E. Blankers-Koen (Netherlands) (b. 26 Apr 1918) with 100 m, 200 m, 80 m hurdles and 4 × 100 m relay, 1948; Betty Cuthbert (Australia) (b. 20 Apr 1938) with 100 m, 200 m, 4 × 100 m relay, 1956, and 400 m, 1964; and Bärbel Wöckel (*née* Eckert) (b. 21 Mar 1955) (GDR) with 200 m and 4 × 100 m relay in 1976 and 1980.

Most wins at one Games

The most gold medals at one celebration is five by Paavo Johannes Nurmi (Finland) (1897–1973) in 1924: 1500 m, 5000 m, 10 000 m cross-country, 3000 m team and cross-country team. The most at individual events is four by Alvin C. Kraenzlein (USA) (1876–1928) in 1900: 60 m, 110 m hurdles, 200 m hurdles and long jump.

Most Olympic medals *Men*

The most medals won is 12 (nine gold and three silver) by Paavo Nurmi (Finland) in the Games of 1920, 1924 and 1928.

Women

The most medals won by a woman athlete is seven by Shirley de la Hunty (*née* Strickland) (Australia) (b. 18 July 1925), with three gold, one silver and three bronze in the 1948, 1952 and 1956 Games. A recently discovered photo-finish indicates that she finished third, not fourth, in the 1948 200 metres event, thus unofficially increasing her medal haul to eight. Irena Szewinska (*née* Kirszenstein) (Poland) (b. 24 May 1946) won three gold, two silver and two bronze in 1964, 1968, 1972 and 1976, and is the only woman athlete to win a medal in four successive games.

Most Olympic titles *British*

The most gold medals won by a British athlete (excluding tug of war and walking, *q.v.*) is two by: Charles Bennett (1871–1949) (1500 m and 5000 m team, 1900); Alfred Tysoe (1874–1901) (800 m and 5000 m team, 1900); John Rimmer (1879–1962) (4000 m steeplechase and 5000 m team, 1900); Albert G. Hill (1889–1969) (800 m and 1500 m, 1920); Douglas Gordon Arthur Lowe (1902–81) (800 m, 1924 and 1928); Sebastian Newbold Coe (b. 29 Sept 1956) (1500 m, 1980 and 1984) and Francis Morgan 'Daley' Thompson (b. 30 July 1958) (decathlon, 1980 and 1984). Daley Thompson was also world champion at the decathlon in 1983.

Most Olympic medals *British*

The most medals won by a British athlete is four by: Guy M. Butler (1899–1981), gold for the 4 × 400 m relay and silver for 400 m in 1920, and bronze for each of these events in 1924; and by Sebastian Coe, who also won silver medals at 800 m in 1980 and 1984. Three British women athletes have won three medals: Dorothy Hyman (b. 9 May 1941) with a silver (100 m, 1960) and two bronze (200 m, 1960 and 4 × 100 m relay, 1964); Mary Denise Rand (now Toomey, *née* Bignal) (b. 10 Feb 1940) with a gold (long jump), a silver (pentathlon) and a bronze (4 × 100 m relay), all in 1964; and Kathryn Jane Cook (*née* Smallwood) (b. 3 May 1960), all bronze—at 4 × 100 m relay 1980 and 1984, and at 400 m in 1984.

Olympic champions *Oldest and youngest*

The oldest athlete to win an Olympic title was Irish-born Patrick J. 'Babe' McDonald (USA) (1878–1954), who was aged 42 yr 26 days when he won the 56 lb *25,4 kg* weight throw at Antwerp, Belgium on 21 Aug 1920. The oldest female champion was Lia Manoliu (Romania) (b. 25 Apr 1932), aged 36 yr 176 days when she won the discus at Mexico City on 18 Oct 1968. The youngest gold medallist was Barbara Pearl Jones (USA) (b. 26 Mar 1937), who at 15 yr 123 days was a member of the winning 4 × 100 m relay team at Helsinki, Finland on 27 July 1952. The youngest male champion was Robert Bruce Mathias (USA) (b. 17 Nov 1930), aged 17 yr 263 days when he won the decathlon at the London Games on 5–6 Aug 1948.

The oldest Olympic medallist was Tebbs Lloyd Johnson (1900–84), aged 48 yr 115 days when he was third in the 1948 50 000 m walk. The oldest woman medallist was Dana Zátopkova, aged 37 yr 348 days when she was second in the javelin in 1960.

World record breakers *Oldest and youngest*

For the greatest age at which anyone has broken a world record under IAAF jurisdiction see p. 219. The female record is 36 yr 139 days for Marina Styepanova (*née* Makeyeva) (USSR) (b. 1 May 1950) with 52.94 sec for the 400 m hurdles at Tashkent, USSR on 17 Sept 1986. The youngest individual record breaker is Wang Yang (b. 9 Apr 1971) (China) who set a women's 3000 m walk record at age 14 yr 334 days with 21 min 33.8 sec at Jian, China on 9 Mar 1986. The male record is 17 yr 198 days for Thomas Ray (1862–1904) when he pole-vaulted 3.42 m *11 ft 2¾ in* on 19 Sept 1879 (prior to IAAF ratification).

Most records in a day

Jesse Owens (1913–80) (USA) set six world records in 45 min at Ann Arbor, Michigan on 25 May 1935 with a 9.4 sec 100 yd at 3.15 p.m., a 26 ft 8¼ in *8,13 m* long jump at 3.25 p.m., a 20.3 sec *220 yd* (and 200 m) at 3.45 p.m. and a 22.6 sec 220 yd (and 200 m) low hurdles at 4.00 p.m.

Most national titles *Great Britain*

The greatest number of senior AAA titles (excluding those in tug-of-war events) won by one athlete is 14 individual and one relay title by Emmanuel McDonald Bailey (Trinidad) (b. 8 Dec 1920), between 1946 and 1953. The most won outdoors in a single event is 13 by Denis Horgan (Ireland) (1871–1922) in the shot put between

1893 and 1912. 13 senior titles were also won by: Michael Anthony Bull (b. 11 Sept 1946) at pole vault, eight indoor and five out; and by Geoffrey Lewis Capes (b. 23 Aug 1949) at shot, six indoor and seven out.

The greatest number of WAAA titles won by one athlete is 14 by Suzanne Allday (née Farmer) (b. 26 Nov 1934), with seven each at shot and discus between 1952 and 1962. She also won two WAAA indoor shot titles. Judith Miriam Oakes (b. 14 Feb 1958) at the shot has won seven WAAA outdoor, nine WAAA indoor and six UK titles, 1977–87.

Most international appearances

The greatest number of international matches contested for any nation is 89 by Bjørn Bang Andersen (b. 14 Nov 1937) for Norway, 1960–81.

The greatest number of full Great Britain international appearances (outdoors and indoors) is 73 by Verona Marolin Elder (née Bernard) (b. 5 Apr 1953), mostly at 400 metres, from 1971 to 1983. The men's record is 67 by shot putter Geoff Capes, 1969–80. At pole vault or decathlon Mike Bull had 66 full internationals, or 69 including the European Indoor Games before these were official internationals. The most outdoors is 61 at the hammer by Andrew Howard Payne (b. South Africa, 17 Apr 1931) from 1960 to 1974.

Oldest and youngest internationals

The oldest full Great Britain international was Hector Harold Whitlock (1903–85) at 50 km walk at the 1952 Olympic Games, aged 48 yr 218 days. The oldest woman was Christine Rosemary Payne (née Charters) (b. 19 May 1933) at discus in the Great Britain v. Finland match on 26 Sept 1974, aged 41 yr 130 days. The youngest man was high jumper Ross Hepburn (b. 14 Oct 1961) v. the USSR on 26 Aug 1977, aged 15 yr 316 days, and the youngest woman was Janis Walsh (b. 28 Mar 1960) v. Belgium (indoor) at 60 m and 4 × 200 m relay on 15 Feb 1975, aged 14 yr 324 days.

Longest career

Duncan McLean (1884–1980) of Scotland set a world age (92) record of 100 m in 21.7 sec in August 1977, over 73 years after his best ever sprint of 100 yd in 9.9 sec in South Africa in February 1904.

Longest winning sequence

Iolanda Balas (Romania) (b. 12 Dec 1936) won a record 140 consecutive competitions at high jump from 1956 to 1967. The record at a track event is 122 at 400 m hurdles by Edwin Corley Moses (USA) (b. 31 July 1955), between his loss to Harold Schmid (West Germany) (b. 29 Sept 1957) at Berlin on 26 Aug 1977 and that to Danny Harris (USA) (b. 7 Sept 1965) at Madrid on 4 June 1987.

London to Brighton race

Ian Thompson (b. 16 Oct 1949) (Luton United H) won the 54.3 mile 87,4 km race (inst. 1951) in 5 hr 15 min 15 sec on 28 Sept 1980, averaging 10.33 mph 16,62 km/h. The most wins is four by Bernard Gomersall (b. 28 Aug 1932), 1963–6. The women's record is 6 hr 37 min 8 sec by Ann Franklin (b. 26 Apr 1951) on 25 Sept 1983.

'End to end'

The fastest confirmed run from John o'Groats to Land's End is 12 days 1 hr 59 min by Kenneth John Craig (S. Africa) (b. 27 Nov 1935) from 29 Aug–10 Sept 1984. A faster 10 days 3 hr 30 min was claimed by Fred Hicks (GB) for 876 miles 1410 km from 20–30 May 1977.

Longest non-stop run

Bertil Järlåker (Sweden) (b. 1936) ran 352.9 miles 568 km in 121 hr 54 min at Norrköping, Sweden, 26–31 May 1980. He was moving for 95.04 per cent of the time.

Longest running race

The longest races ever staged were the 1928

(3422 miles 5507 km) and 1929 (3665 miles 5898 km) trans-continental races from New York City, NY, to Los Angeles, California, USA. The Finnish-born Johnny Salo (1893–1931) was the winner in 1929 in 79 days, from 31 Mar to 18 June. His elapsed time of 525 hr 57 min 20 sec (averaging 6.97 mph 11,21 km/h) left him only 2 min 47 sec ahead of Englishman Pietro 'Peter' Gavuzzi (1905–81).

The longest race staged annually is Australia's Westfield Run from Paramatta, New South Wales to Doncaster, Victoria (Sydney to Melbourne). The distance run in 1987 was 1060 km 658 miles, and the record for this course is 5 days 14 hr 47 min by Yiannis Kouros (Greece) (b. 13 Feb 1956) in 1987.

Longest runs

The longest ever solo run is 10,608 miles 17 072 km by Robert J. Sweetgall (USA) (b. 8 Dec 1947) around the perimeter of the USA starting and finishing in Washington, DC, 9 Oct 1982–15 July 1983. Ron Grant (Australia) (b. 15 Feb 1943) ran around Australia, 13 383 km 8316 miles in 217 days 3 hr 45 min, running every day from 28 Mar to 31 Oct 1983. Max Telford (NZ) (b. Hawick, Scotland, 2 Feb 1935) ran 5110 miles 8224 km from Anchorage, Alaska to Halifax, Nova Scotia, in 106 days 18 hr 45 min from 25 July to 9 Nov 1977.

The fastest time for the cross-America run is 46 days 8 hr 36 min by Frank Giannino, Jr (USA) (b. 1952) for the 3100 miles 4989 km from San Francisco to New York from 1 Sept–17 Oct 1980. The women's trans-America record is 69 days 2 hours 40 min by Mavis Hutchison (South Africa) (b. 25 Nov 1924) from 12 Mar–21 May 1978.

Dedicated running

Dr Ron Hill (b. 21 Sept 1938), the 1969 European and 1970 Commonwealth marathon champion, has run twice a day (once only on Sundays) every day from 24 Dec 1964. His meticulously compiled training log shows a total of 113,768 miles 183 091 km from 3 Sept 1956 to 25 June 1987.

Marathon—oldest female finisher ● left: Thelma Pitt-Turner completed the Hastings, New Zealand marathon at the age of 82 in August 1985. A running and swimming competitor since 1920, Mrs Pitt-Turner has overcome a heart ailment in 1947, two major abdominal operations and a rheumatic condition which semi-paralysed her for 6 months. She completed the marathon in 7 hr 58 min.

MARATHON

The marathon is run over a distance of 26 miles 385 yd 42,195 m. This distance was that used for the race at the 1908 Olympic Games, run from Windsor to the White City stadium, and which became standard from 1924.

The marathon (of 40 km) was introduced to the 1896 Olympic Games to commemorate the legendary run of Pheidippides (or Philippides) from the battlefield of Marathon to Athens in 490 BC. The 1896 Olympic marathon was preceded by trial races that year.

The first Boston marathon, the world's longest-lasting major marathon, was held on 19 Apr 1897 at 39 km 24 miles 1232 yd, and the first national marathon championship was that of Norway in 1897.

It is only in the past decade that marathon running by women has become widespread, following the pioneering efforts, particularly in the USA, of some determined women who had quite a struggle to overcome prejudices against their participation. The first championship marathon for women was organised by the Road Runners Club of America on 27 Sept 1970.

Records

There are as yet no official records for the marathon, and it should be noted that courses may vary in severity. The following are the best times recorded, all on courses whose distance has been verified.

World

Men: 2:07:12 Carlos Alberto Sousa Lopes (Portugal) (b. 18 Feb 1947) Rotterdam, Netherlands 20 Apr 1985.

Women: 2:21:06 Ingrid Kristiansen (née Christensen) (Norway) (b. 21 Mar 1956) London 21 Apr 1985.

British

Men: 2:07:13 Stephen Henry Jones (b. 4 Aug 1955) Chicago, USA 20 Oct 1985.

Women: 2:26:51 Priscilla Welch (b. 22 Nov 1944) London 10 May 1987.

Most competitors

The largest field for a marathon has been about 23,000 starters in the Mexico City marathon on 28 Sept 1986. The record number of finishers is 19,710 in the London marathon on 10 May 1987. A record 93 men ran under 2 hr 20 min, 29 under 2:15, at London in 1983, and a record 6 men ran under 2:10 at Fukuoka, Japan on 4 Dec 1983. A record 9 women ran under 2:30 in the first Olympic marathon for women at Los Angeles, USA on 5 Aug 1984.

Oldest finishers

The oldest man to complete a marathon was Dimitrion Yordanidis (Greece), aged 98, in Athens, Greece on 10 Oct 1976. He finished in 7 hr 33 min.

WORLD RECORDS MEN

World records for the men's events scheduled by the International Amateur Athletic Federation. Fully automatic electric timing is mandatory for events up to 400 metres.

RUNNING	Min Sec	Name and country	Place	Date
100 metres	9.93A	Calvin Smith (USA) (b. 8 Jan 1961)	Colorado Springs, Colorado, USA ... 3 July	1983
200 metres	19.72A	Pietro Mennea (Italy) (b. 28 June 1952)	Mexico City, Mexico	12 Sept 1979
400 metres	43.86A	Lee Edward Evans (USA) (b. 25 Feb 1947)	Mexico City, Mexico	18 Oct 1968
800 metres	1:41.73	Sebastian Newbold Coe (GB) (b. 29 Sept 1956)	Florence, Italy	10 June 1981
1000 metres	2:12.18	Sebastian Newbold Coe (GB)	Oslo, Norway	11 July 1981
1500 metres	3:29.46	Saïd Aouita (Morocco) (b. 2 Nov 1960)	W. Berlin, W. Germany	23 Aug 1985
1 mile	3:46.32	Steven Cram (GB) (b. 14 Oct 1960)	Oslo, Norway	27 July 1985
2000 metres	4:50.81	Saïd Aouita (Morocco)	Paris, France	16 July 1987
3000 metres	7:32.1	Henry Rono (Kenya) (b. 12 Feb 1952)	Oslo, Norway	27 June 1978
5000 metres	12:58.39	Saïd Aouita (Morocco)	Rome, Italy	22 July 1987
10 000 metres	27:13.81	Fernando Mamede (Portugal) (b. 1 Nov 1951)	Stockholm, Sweden	2 July 1984
20 000 metres	57:24.2	Josephus Hermens (Netherlands) (b. 8 Jan 1950)	Papendal, Netherlands	1 May 1976
25 000 metres	1 hr 13:55.8	Toshihiko Seko (Japan) (b. 15 July 1956)	Christchurch, New Zealand	22 Mar 1981
30 000 metres	1 hr 29:18.8	Toshihiko Seko (Japan)	Christchurch, New Zealand	22 Mar 1981
1 hour	20 944 m 13 miles 24 yd 2 ft	Josephus Hermens (Netherlands)	Papendal, Netherlands	1 May 1976

A *These records were set at high altitude—Mexico City 2240 m 7349 ft, Colorado Springs 2195 m 7201 ft. Best results at low altitude have been: 100 m: 9.95 sec, Ben Johnson (Can) (b. 30 Dec 1961), Moscow, USSR, 9 July 1986. 200 m: 19.75 sec, Frederick Carlton 'Carl' Lewis (USA) (b. 1 July 1961), Indianapolis, Indiana, USA, 19 June 1983. 400 m: 44.10 sec, Harry 'Butch' Reynolds (USA) (b. 8 Aug 1964), Columbus, Ohio, USA, 3 May 1987.*

DECATHLON
8847 points
Francis Morgan 'Daley' Thompson (GB)
(b. 30 July 1958), Los Angeles, USA... 8–9 Aug 1984

1st day: 100 m 10.44 sec, Long Jump 8,01 m *26' 3½"*,
Shot Put 15,72 m *51' 7"*, High Jump 2,03 m *6' 8"*,
400 m 46.97 sec

2nd day: 110 m Hurdles 14.33 sec,
Discus 46,56 m *152' 9"*, Pole Vault 5,00 m *16' 4¾"*,
Javelin 65,24 m *214' 0"*, 1500 m 4:35.00 sec

MEN'S —LONG JUMP—

Carl Lewis is currently the leading jumper with a low-altitude

William DeHart Hubbard USA 1925

Silvio Cator Haiti 1928

Peter O'Connor Ireland 1901

From William Newburn to Bob Beamon ● The long jump record is indicated, from the first jump to exceed 24 ft, in 1898, up the rising sand-coloured area to reach the world and Olympic record mark of 8,90 metres *29 ft 2 in* at the high altitude of Mexico City in 1968.

Artwork: Rob Burns and Ashley Hamilton Lloyd

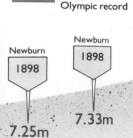

World and Olympic record

Gourdin 1921

Prinstein 1900

Kraenzlein 1899

O'Connor 1900

LeGendre 1924

Hamm 1928

Namb 193

Newburn 1898

Newburn 1898

7.98

7.69m

7.76m

7.90m

7.93m

7.43m

7.50m

7.51m

7.61m

7.89m

7.25m

7.33m

HURDLING

110 metres (3' 6" 106 cm)	12.93	Renaldo Nehemiah (USA) (b. 24 Mar 1959)	Zürich, Switzerland	19 Aug 1981
400 metres (3' 0" 91,4 cm)	47.02	Edwin Corley Moses (USA) (b. 31 Aug 1955)	Koblenz, W. Germany	31 Aug 1983
3000 metres steeplechase	8:05.4	Henry Rono (Kenya)	Seattle, Washington, USA	13 May 1978

RELAYS

4 × 100 metres	37.83	United States national team: Sam Graddy, Ronald James Brown, Calvin Smith, Frederick Carlton Lewis	Los Angeles, USA	11 Aug 1984
4 × 200 metres	1:20.26†	University of Southern California, USA: Joel Andrews, James Sanford, William Mullins, Clancy Edwards	Tempe, Arizona, USA	27 May 1978
4 × 400 metres	2:56.16A	United States national team: Vincent Edward Matthews, Ronald J. Freeman, George Lawrence James, Lee Edward Evans	Mexico City, Mexico	20 Oct 1968
4 × 800 metres	7:03.89	Great Britain: Peter Elliott, Garry Peter Cook, Steven Cram, Sebastian Newbold Coe	Crystal Palace, London	30 Aug 1982
4 × 1500 metres	14:38.8	West Germany: Thomas Wessinghage, Harald Hudak, Michael Lederer, Karl Fleschen	Cologne, W. Germany	17 Aug 1977

† Texas Christian University ran 1:20.20 at Philadelphia, Pa, USA on 26 Apr 1986. This time could not be ratified as their team was composed of different nationalities: Roscoe Tatum (USA), Andrew Smith (Jamaica), Leroy Reid (Jamaica), Greg Sholars (USA).
A Best result at low altitude: 2:57.91 USA (Sunder Nix, Ray Armstead, Alonzo Babers, Antonio McKay) Los Angeles, USA, 11 Aug 1984.

Men's Field Events World Records continued over page

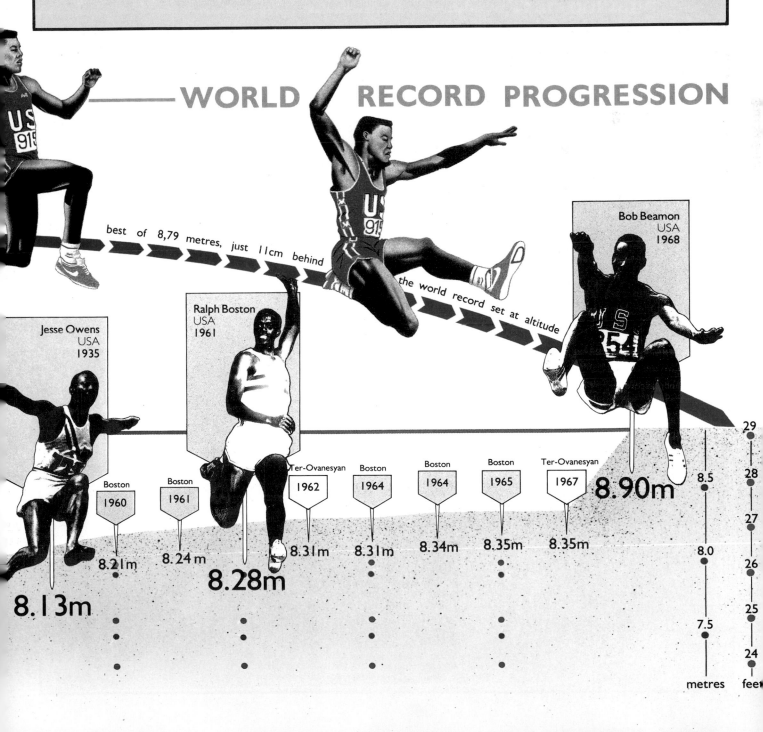

WORLD RECORD PROGRESSION

best of 8,79 metres, just 11cm behind the world record set at altitude

Bob Beamon
USA
1968

Ralph Boston
USA
1961

Jesse Owens
USA
1935

Boston 1960 — 8.21m

Boston 1961 — 8.24m

Ter-Ovanesyan 1962 — 8.31m

Boston 1964 — 8.31m

Boston 1964 — 8.34m

Boston 1965 — 8.35m

Ter-Ovanesyan 1967 — 8.35m

8.90m

8.28m

8.13m

29
28
27
26
25
24

8.5
8.0
7.5

metres feet

Men's World Records continued

FIELD EVENTS	m	ft	in	Name	Place	Date
High Jump	2,42	7	11¼	Jan Niklas Patrik Sjöberg (Sweden) (b. 5 Jan 1965)	Stockholm, Sweden	30 June 1987
Pole Vault	6,03	19	9½	Sergey Bubka (USSR) (b. 4 Dec 1963)	Prague, Czechoslovakia	23 June 1987
Long Jump	8,90A	29	2½	Robert Beamon (USA) (b. 29 Aug 1946)	Mexico City, Mexico	18 Oct 1968
Triple Jump	17,97	58	11½	William Augustus 'Willie' Banks (USA) (b. 11 Mar 1956)	Indianapolis, USA	16 June 1985
Shot 7,26 kg *16 lb*	22,64*	74	3¼	Udo Beyer (GDR) (b. 9 Aug 1955)	East Berlin, GDR	20 Aug 1986
Discus 2 kg *4 lb 6.55 oz*	74,08	243	0	Jürgen Schult (GDR) (b. 11 May 1960)	Neubrandenburg, GDR	6 June 1986
Hammer 7,26 kg *16 lb*	86,74	284	7	Yuriy Georgiyevich Sedykh (USSR) (b. 11 Jun 1955)	Stuttgart, W. Germany	30 Aug 1986
Javelin 800 g *28.22 oz*	104,80†	343	10	Uwe Hohn (GDR) (b. 16 July 1962)	East Berlin, GDR	20 July 1984

* *One professional performance is superior to the IAAF figure, but the same highly rigorous rules as to measuring and weighing were not necessarily applied.*
22,86 ... 75 0 ....*Brian Ray Oldfield (USA) (b. 1 Jan 1945)* ....*El Paso, Texas, USA* ....*10 May 1975*

† *Old javelin. A new javelin, with the centre of gravity moved forward, was introduced in 1986. The best performance is 87,66 m* 287 ft 7 in *by Jan Zelezný (Czechoslvakia) (b. 16 June 1966) at Nitra, Czechoslovakia on 31 May 1987.*

A *Set at high altitude; the low altitude best: 8,79 m* 28 ft 10¼ in, *Carl Lewis, Indianapolis, Indiana, USA, 19 June 1983.*

Most miles in a year

The greatest competitive distance run in a year is 8855 km *5502 miles* by Malcolm Campbell (GB) (b. 17 Nov 1934) in 1985.

Mass relay records

The record for 100 miles *160,9 km* by 100 runners from one club is 7 hr 53 min 52.1 sec by Baltimore Road Runners Club, Towson, Maryland, USA, on 17 May 1981. The women's record is 10 hr 47 min 9.3 sec on 3 Apr 1977 by the San Francisco Dolphins Southend Running Club, USA.

The longest relay ever run was 16 936 km *10,524 miles* by 2660 runners at Trondheim, Norway from 26 Aug–20 Oct 1985. Twenty members of the Melbourne Fire Brigade ran 15 059 km *9357 miles* around Australia on Highway No 1 in 43 days 23 hr 58 min, 10 July–23 Aug 1983. The most participants is 4800, 192 teams of 25, in the Batavierenrace, 167,2 km *103.89 miles* from Nijmegan to Enschede, Netherlands on 23 Apr 1983.

Highland Games

The weight and height of cabers (Gaelic *cabar*) vary considerably. Extreme values are 25 ft *7,62 m* and 280 lb *127 kg*. The Braemar caber (19 ft 3 in *5,86 m* and 120 lb *54,4 kg*) in Grampian, Scotland, was untossed from 1891 until 1951 when it was tossed by George Clark (1907-86). The best authentic mark recorded for throwing the

World Records *Women*

World records for the women's events scheduled by the International Amateur Athletic Federation. The same stipulation about automatically timed events as in the men's list applies in the six events up to 400 metres.

RUNNING	Min Sec	Name and country	Place	Date
100 metres	10.76	Evelyn Ashford (USA) (b. 15 Apr 1957)	Zürich, Switzerland	22 Aug 1984
200 metres	21.71	Marita Koch (GDR) (b. 18 Feb 1957)	Karl Marx Stadt, GDR	10 June 1979
		Marita Koch (GDR)	Potsdam, GDR	21 July 1984
		Heike Drechsler [*née* Daute] (GDR) (b. 16 Dec 1964)	Jena, GDR	29 June 1986
		Heike Drechsler (GDR)	Stuttgart, W.Germany	29 Aug 1986
400 metres	47.60	Marita Koch (GDR)	Canberra, Australia	6 Oct 1985
800 metres	1:53.28	Jarmila Kratochvilova (Czechoslovakia)	Munich, W. Germany	26 July 1983
1000 metres	2:30.6	Tatyana Providokhina (USSR) (b. 26 Mar 1953)	Podolsk, USSR	20 Aug 1978
1500 metres	3:52.47	Tatyana Kazankina (USSR) (b. 17 Dec 1951)	Zürich, Switzerland	13 Aug 1980
1 mile	4:16.71	Mary Slaney [*née* Decker] (USA) (b. 4 Aug 1958)	Zürich, Switzerland	21 Aug 1985
2000 metres	5:28.69	Maricica Puica (Rumania) (b. 29 July 1950)	Crystal Palace, London	11 July 1986
3000 metres	8:22.62	Tatyana Kazankina (USSR)	Leningrad, USSR	26 Aug 1984
5000 metres	14:37.33	Ingrid Kristiansen [*née* Christensen] (Norway) (b. 21 Mar 1956)	Stockholm, Sweden	5 Aug 1986
10 000 metres	30:13.74	Ingrid Kristiansen (Norway)	Oslo, Norway	5 July 1986

HURDLING				
100 metres (2' 9" *84 cm*)	12.26	Yordanka Donkova (Bulgaria) (b. 28 Sept 1961)	Ljubljiana, Yugoslavia	7 Sept 1986
400 metres (2' 6" *76 cm*)	52.94	Marina Styepanova [*née* Makeyeva] (USSR) (b. 1 May 1950)	Tashkent, USSR	17 Sept 1986

RELAYS				
4 × 100 metres	41.37	GDR: Silke Gladisch, Sabine Rieger, Ingrid Auerswald [*née* Brestrich], Marlies Göhr [*née* Oelsner]	Canberra, Australia	6 Oct 1985
4 × 200 metres	1:28.15	GDR: Marlies Göhr [*née* Oelsner], Romy Müller [*née* Schneider], Bärbel Wöckel [*née* Eckert], Marita Koch	Jena, GDR	9 Aug 1980
4 × 400 metres	3:15.92	GDR: Gesine Walther, Sabine Busch, Dagmar Rübsam, Marita Koch	Erfurt, GDR	3 June 1984
4 × 800 metres	7:50.17	USSR: Nadezhda Olizarenko, Lyubov Gurina, Lyudmila Borisova, Irina Podyalovskaya	Moscow, USSR	4 Aug 1984

FIELD EVENTS	m	ft	in	Name	Place	Date
High Jump	2,08	6	9¾	Stefka Kostadinova (Bulgaria) (b. 25 Mar 1965)	Sofia, Bulgaria	31 May 1986
Long Jump	7,45	24	5½	Heike Drechsler (GDR)	Tallinn, USSR	21 June 1986
				Heike Drechsler (GDR)	Dresden, GDR	3 July 1986
Shot 4 kg *8 lb 13 oz*	22,63	74	3	Natalya Lisovskaya (USSR) (b. 16 July 1962)	Moscow, USSR	7 June 1987
Discus 1 kg *2 lb 3.27 oz*	74,56	244	7	Zdenka Silhava (Czechoslovakia) (b. 15 June 1954)	Nitra, Czechoslovakia	26 Aug 1984
Javelin 600 g *24.74 oz*	77,44	254	1	Fatima Whitbread (GB) (b. 3 Mar 1961)	Stuttgart, W. Germany	28 Aug 1986

HEPTATHLON			
7158 points	Jacqueline Joyner (USA) (b. 3 Mar 1962) (100 m Hurdles 13.18 sec; High Jump 1,88 m *6 ft 2 in*; Shot 15,20 m *49 ft 0¼ in*; 200 m 22.85 sec; Long Jump 7,03 m *23 ft 0¾ in*; Javelin 50,12 m *164 ft 5 in*; 800 m 2 min 09.69 sec	Houston, USA	1–2 Aug 1986

56 lb weight for height, using one hand only, is 17 ft 2 in *5,23 m* by Geoffrey Lewis Capes (GB) (b. 23 Aug 1949) at Lagos, Nigeria on 5 Dec 1982. The best throw recorded for the Scots hammer is 151 ft 2 in *46,08 m* by William Anderson (b. 6 Oct 1938) at Lochearnhead on 26 July 1969.

Highest one-legged jump

One-legged Arnie Boldt (b. 1958), of Saskatchewan, Canada, cleared 2,04 m *6 ft 8¼ in* in Rome, Italy on 3 Apr 1981.

Backwards running

Anthony 'Scott' Weiland, 27, ran the Detroit marathon backwards in 4 hr 7 min 54 sec on 3 Oct 1982. Donald Davis (b. 10 Feb 1960) (USA) ran 1 mile backwards in 6 min 7.1 sec at the University of Hawaii on 21 Feb 1983. Ferdie Adoboe (USA) ran 100 yd backwards in 12.8 sec (100 m in 14.0 sec) at Amherst, Mass. on 28 July 1983.

Arvind Pandya of India ran backwards across America, Los Angeles to New York, in 107 days, 18 Aug-3 Dec 1984. He also ran backwards from John O'Groats to Land's End, 880 miles *1416,2 km* in 29 days 5 hr 39 min, 2-31 Oct 1985.

Fastest blind sprinting

Graham Henry Salmon (GB) (b. 5 Sept 1952) ran 100 m *109 yd* in 11.4 sec at Grangemouth, Scotland on 2 Sept 1978.

WALKING

Most Olympic medals

Walking races have been included in the Olympic events since 1906. The only walker to win three gold medals has been Ugo Frigerio (Italy) (1901-68), with the 3000 m in 1920, and 10 000 m in 1920 and 1924. He also holds the record for most medals, with four (he won the bronze medal at 50 000 m in 1932), a total shared with Vladimir Golubnichiy (USSR) (b. 2 June 1936), who won gold medals for the 20 000 m in 1960 and 1968, the silver in 1972 and the bronze in 1964.

The best British performance has been two gold medals by George Edward Larner (1875-1949) for the 3500 m and the 10 miles in 1908, but Ernest J. Webb (1872-1937) won three medals, being twice 'walker up' to Larner and finishing second in the 10 000 m in 1912.

Most titles

Four-time Olympian, Ronald Owen Laird (b. 31 May 1938) of the New York AC, USA, won a total of 65 US national titles from 1958 to 1976, plus four Canadian Championships. The greatest number of UK national titles won by a British walker is 27 by Vincent Paul Nihill (b. 5 Sept 1939) from 1963 to 1975.

Longest race

The Paris–Colmar, until 1980 Strasbourg–Paris, event (inst. 1926 in the reverse direction), now about 518 km *322 miles*, is the world's longest annual race walk.

The fastest performance is by Robert Pietquin (Belgium) (b. 1938) who walked 507 km *315 miles* in the 1980 race in 60 hr 1 min 10 sec (after deducting 4 hr compulsory stops). This represents an average speed of 8,45 km/h *5.25 mph*. Gilbert Roger (France) (b. 1914) won six times (1949, 1953-4, 1956-8). The first woman to complete the race was Annie van der Meer (Netherlands) (b. 24 Feb 1947), who was 10th in 1983 in 82 hr 10 min.

Dumitru Dan (1890-1978) of Romania was the only man of 200 entrants to succeed in a contest in walking 100 000 km *62,137 miles*, organised by the *Touring Club de France* on 1 Apr 1910. He covered 96 000 km *59,651 miles* up to 24 Mar 1916, so averaging 43,85 km *27.24 miles* a day.

Double world indoor champion and record breaker ● Heike Drechsler (GDR) (b. 16 Dec 1964) set a world indoor record of 22.27 sec to win the 200m title at the inaugural World Indoor Championships at Indianapolis on 7 Mar 1987. She also won the long jump, at which she set the world indoor record of 7,32 m *24 ft 0¼ in* in New York on 27 Feb 1987. (Photo: Tony Duffy/All-Sport)

UNITED KINGDOM (NATIONAL) RECORDS MEN

RUNNING	Min Sec	Name	Place	Date
100 metres	10.03	Linford Christie (b. 10 Apr 1960)	Budapest, Hungary	6 July 1987
200 metres	20.21	Allan Wipper Wells (b. 3 May 1952)	Moscow, USSR	28 July 1980
400 metres	44.59	Roger Anthony Black (b. 31 Mar 1966)	Stuttgart, W. Germany	29 Aug 1986
800 metres	1:41.73	Sebastian Newbold Coe (b. 29 Sept 1956)	Florence, Italy	10 June 1981
1000 metres	2:12.18	Sebastian Newbold Coe	Oslo, Norway	11 July 1981
1500 metres	3:29.67	Steven Cram (b. 14 Oct 1960)	Nice, France	16 July 1985
1 mile	3:46.32	Steven Cram	Oslo, Norway	27 July 1985
2000 metres	4:51.39	Steven Cram	Budapest, Hungary	4 Aug 1985
3000 metres	7:32.79	David Robert Moorcroft (b. 10 Apr 1953)	London (Crystal Palace)	17 July 1982
5000 metres	13:00.41	David Robert Moorcroft	Oslo, Norway	7 July 1982
10 000 metres	27:30.3 *	Brendan Foster (b. 12 Jan 1948)	London (Crystal Palace)	23 June 1978
20 000 metres	58:39.0	Ronald Hill (b. 25 Sept 1938)	Leicester	9 Nov 1968
25 000 metres	1 hr 15:22.6	Ronald Hill	Bolton, Lancashire	21 July 1965
30 000 metres	1 hr 31:30.4	James Noel Carroll Alder (b. 10 June 1940)	London (Crystal Palace)	5 Sept 1970
1 hour	12 miles 1268 yd *20 472m*	Ronald Hill	Leicester	9 Nov 1968

* Ratified at 27:30.6

HURDLING

	Min Sec	Name	Place	Date
110 metres	13.29	Jonathan Peter Ridgeon (b. 14 Feb 1967)	Zagreb, Yugoslavia	15 July 1987
400 metres	48.12	David Peter Hemery (b. 18 July 1944)	Mexico City, Mexico	15 Oct 1968
3000 metres steeplechase	8:12.11	Colin Robert Reitz (b. 5 April 1960)	Brussels, Belgium	5 Sept 1986

RELAYS

	Min Sec	Name	Place	Date
4 × 100 metres	38.62	United Kingdom: Michael Anthony McFarlane, Allan Wipper Wells, Robert Cameron Sharp, Andrew Emlyn McMaster	Moscow, USSR	1 Aug 1980
4 × 200 metres	1:23.5	Team Solent: Paul Anthony Harmsworth, Roger Anthony Black, Kriss Kezie Uche Chukwu Akabusi, Todd Anthony Bennett	Southampton	19 July 1987
4 × 400 metres	2:59.13	United Kingdom: Kriss Akabusi, Garry Peter Cook, Todd Bennett, Phil Brown	Los Angeles, USA	11 Aug 1984
4 × 800 metres	7:03.89	United Kingdom: Peter Elliott, Garry Peter Cook, Steven Cram, Sebastian Newbold Coe	London (Crystal Palace)	30 Aug 1982
4 × 1500 metres	14:56.8	United Kingdom: Alan David Mottershead, Geoffrey Michael Cooper, Stephen John Emson, Roy Wood	Bourges, France	24 June 1979

FIELD EVENTS

	m	ft in	Name	Place	Date
High Jump	2,28*	7 5¾	Geoffrey Peter Parsons (b. 14 Aug 1964)	London (Crystal Palace)	17 May 1986
	2,28	7 5¾	Geoffrey Parsons	Edinburgh	31 July 1986
Pole Vault	5,65	18 6½	Keith Frank Stock (b. 18 Mar 1957)	Oslo, Norway	7 July 1981
Long Jump	8,23	27 0	Lynn Davies (b. 20 May 1942)	Bern, Switzerland	30 June 1968
Triple Jump	17,57	57 7¾	Keith Leroy Connor (b. 16 Sept 1957)	Provo, Utah, USA	5 June 1982
Shot 7,26 kg 16 lb	21,68	71 1½	Geoffrey Lewis Capes (b. 23 Aug 1949)	Cwmbran, Gwent	18 May 1980
Discus 2 kg 4 lb 6.55 oz	64,32†	211 0	William Raymond Tancred (b. 6 Aug 1942)	Woodford, Essex	10 Aug 1974
Hammer 7,26 kg 16 lb	77,54	254 5	Martin Girvan (b. 17 Apr 1960)	Wolverhampton, West Midlands	12 May 1984
Javelin 800 g 28.22 oz	91,40‡	299 10	Arne-Roald Bradstock (b. 24 Apr 1962)	Arlington, Texas, USA	4 May 1985

* Also 2,30 m 7 ft 6½ in indoors by Geoff Parsons at Cosford, Shropshire on 25 Jan 1986.

† William Raymond Tancred threw 64.94 m 213 ft 1in at Loughborough on 21 July 1974 and Richard Charles Slaney (b. 16 May 1956) threw 65,16 m 213 ft 9 in at Eugene, Oregon, USA on 1 July 1985 but these were not ratified.

‡ Old javelin; best with new javelin is 85,24 m 279 ft 8 in by Michael Christopher Hill (b. 22 Oct 1964) at Stockholm, Sweden on 30 June 1987.

DECATHLON

	Name	Place	Date
8847 points	Francis Morgan 'Daley' Thompson (b. 30 July 1958)	Los Angeles, USA	8–9 Aug 1984

(1st day: 100 m 10.44 sec, Long Jump 8,01 m 26′ 3½″, Shot Put 15,72m 51′ 7″, High Jump 2,03 m 6′ 8″, 400 m 46.97 sec)

(2nd day: 110 m Hurdles 14.33 sec, Discus 46,56 m 152′ 9″, Pole Vault 5,00 m 16′ 4¾″, Javelin 65,24 m 214′ 0″, 1500 m 4:35.00 sec)

UNITED KINGDOM (NATIONAL) RECORDS WOMEN

RUNNING

	Min Sec	Name	Place	Date
100 metres	11.10	Kathryn Jane Smallwood [now Cook] (b. 3 May 1960)	Rome, Italy	5 Sept 1981
200 metres	22.10	Kathryn Jane Cook [née Smallwood]	Los Angeles, USA	9 Aug 1984
400 metres	49.43	Kathryn Jane Cook [née Smallwood]	Los Angeles, USA	6 Aug 1984
800 metres	1:57.42	Kirsty Margaret McDermott [now Wade] (b. 6 Aug 1962)	Belfast, N. Ireland	24 June 1985
1000 metres	2:33.70	Kirsty Margaret McDermott [now Wade]	Gateshead, Tyne and Wear	9 Aug 1985
1500 metres	3:59.96	Zola Budd (b. 26 May 1966)	Brussels, Belgium	30 Aug 1985
1 mile	4:17.57	Zola Budd	Zürich, Switzerland	21 Aug 1985
2000 metres	5:29.58	Yvonne Carol Grace Murray (b. 4 Oct 1964)	London (Crystal Palace)	11 July 1986
3000 metres	8:28.83	Zola Budd	Rome, Italy	7 Sept 1985
5000 metres	14:48.07	Zola Budd	Crystal Palace, London	26 Aug 1985
10 000 metres	31:41.42	Elizabeth Lynch (b. 24 May 1964)	Edinburgh	28 July 1986

RELAYS

	Min Sec	Name	Place	Date
4 × 100 metres	42.43	United Kingdom: Heather Regina Hunte [now Oakes], Kathryn Jane Smallwood [now Cook], Beverley Lanita Goddard [now Callender], Sonia May Lannaman	Moscow, USSR	1 Aug 1980
4 × 200 metres	1:31.57	United Kingdom: Donna-Marie Louise Hartley [née Murray], Verona Marolin Elder [née Bernard], Sharon Colyear [now Danville], Sonia May Lannaman	London (Crystal Palace)	20 Aug 1977
4 × 400 metres	3:25.51	United Kingdom: Michelle Scutt (née Probert), Helen Catherine Barnett (now Burkart), Gladys Taylor, Joslyn Yvonne Hoyte-Smith	Los Angeles, USA	11 Aug 1984
4 × 800 metres	8:23.8	Great Britain: Joan Florence Allison [née Page], Sheila Janet Carey [née Taylor], Patricia Barbara Lowe [now Cropper], Rosemary Olivia Stirling [now Wright]	Paris, France	2 Oct 1971

HURDLING

	Min Sec	Name	Place	Date
100 metres	12.87	Shirley Elaine Strong (b. 18 Nov 1958)	Zürich, Switzerland	24 Aug 1983
400 metres	56.04	Susan Anita Jayne Morley [now Chick] (b. 6 Jan 1960)	Helsinki, Finland	10 Aug 1983

FIELD EVENTS

	m	ft in	Name	Place	Date
High Jump	1,95	6 4¾	Diana Clare Elliot (now Davies) (b. 7 May 1961)	Oslo, Norway	26 June 1982
Long Jump	6,90	22 7¾	Beverley Kinch (b. 14 Jan 1964)	Helsinki, Finland	14 Aug 1983
Shot 4 kg 8 lb 13 oz	19,00*	62 4	Judith Miriam Oakes (b. 14 Feb 1958)	Cwmbran, Gwent	26 May 1986
Discus 1 kg 2 lb 3.27 oz	67,48	221 5	Margaret Elizabeth Ritchie	Walnut, California, USA	26 April 1981
Javelin 600 g 21.16 oz	77,44	254 1	Fatima Whitbread (b. 3 Mar 1961)	Stuttgart, W. Germany	28 Aug 1986

HEPTATHLON

	Name	Place	Date
6623 points	Judy Earline Veronica Livermore (b. 14 Nov 1960)	Stuttgart, W. Germany	29–30 Aug 1986

(100 m Hurdles 13.05 sec; High Jump 1,92 m 6′ 3½″; Shot 14,75 m 48′ 4″; 200 m 25.09 sec; Long Jump 6,56 m 21′ 6¼″; Javelin 40,92 m 134′ 3″; 800 m 2 min 11.70 sec)

* Venissa Anne Head (b. 1 Sept 1956) achieved 19,06 m 62 ft 6½ in indoors at St Athan, Gwent on 7 Apr 1984.

'End to end'

The fastest Land's End to John o'Groats walk is 12 days 3 hr 45 min for 886.3 miles *1426,4 km* by WO2 Malcolm Barnish of the 19th Regiment, Royal Artillery from 9–21 June 1986. The women's record is 13 days 17 hr 42 min by Ann Sayer (b. 16 Oct 1936) from 20 Sept–3 Oct 1980. The Irish 'end to end' record over the 400.2 miles *644 km* from Malin Head, Donegal to Mizen Head, Cork is 5 days 22 hr 30 min, set by John 'Paddy' Dowling (b. 15 June 1929) from 18–24 Mar 1982.

London to Brighton

The record time for the 53 mile *85 km* walk is 7 hr 35 min 12 sec by Donald James Thompson (b. 20 Jan 1933) on 14 Sept 1957. Richard Esmond Green (b. 22 Apr 1924) completed the course a record 44 times from 1950 to 1980.

Longest non-stop walk

Georges Holtyzer (Belgium) walked 673,48 km *418.49 miles* in 6 days 10 hr 58 min, 452 laps of a 1,49-km circuit, at Ninove, Belgium from 19–27 July 1986. He was not permitted any stops for rest and was moving 98.78 per cent of the time.

24 hours

The greatest distance walked in 24 hr is 226,432 km *140 miles 1229 yd* by Paul Forthomme (Belgium) on a road course at Woluwé, Belgium on 13–14 Oct 1984. The best by a woman is 202,3 km *125.7 miles* by Annie van der Meer at Rouen, France on 30 Apr–1 May 1984 over a 1,185-km lap road course.

Backwards walking

The greatest ever exponent of reverse pedestrianism has been Plennie L. Wingo (b. 24 Jan 1895), then of Abilene, Texas, who completed his 8000 mile *12 875 km* trans-continental walk from Santa Monica, California to Istanbul, Turkey, from 15 Apr 1931 to 24 Oct 1932. The longest distance recorded for walking backwards in 24 hr is 84.0 miles *135,18 km* by Anthony Thornton (USA) in Minneapolis, Ma., USA on 31 Dec 1985–1 Jan 1986.

TRACK WALKING WORLD RECORDS

The International Amateur Athletic Federation recognises men's records at 20 km, 30 km, 50 km and 2 hours, and women's at 5 km and 10 km. This table also includes world bests for other standard distances.

Event	Time hr min sec	Name, country and date of birth	Place	Date
MEN				
3 km	10 54.6	Carlo Mattioli (Italy) (23 Oct 1954)	Milan, Italy	6 Feb 1980
10 km	38 02.6	Jozef Pribilinec (Czechoslovakia) (6 July 1960)	Banska Bystrica, Czechoslovakia	30 Aug 1985
20 km	1 18 40.0	Ernesto Canto (Mexico) (18 Oct 1959)	Fana, Norway	5 May 1984
30 km	2 06 07.3†	Maurizio Damilano (Italy) (6 Apr 1957)	San Donato Milanese	5 May 1985
50 km	3 41 38.4	Raul Gonzalez (Mexico) (29 Feb 1952)	Fana, Norway	25 May 1979
1 hour	15 547 metres	Jozef Pribilinec (Czechoslovakia)	Hildesheim, W. Germany	6 Sept 1986
2 hours	28 565 metres†	Maurizio Damilano (Italy)	San Donato Milanese	5 May 1985
WOMEN				
3 km	12 05.49	Olga Krishtop (USSR) (23 June 1957)	Indianapolis, USA*	6 Mar 1987
5 km	21 20.2	Yan Hong (China) (23 Oct 1966)	Xinglong, China	29 Mar 1987
10 km	44 26.5	Xu Yongjiu (China) (29 Oct 1984)	Xinglong, China	31 Mar 1987

* indoors.   † Unratified.

In a mixed race Kerry Ann Saxby (Australia) (b. 2 June 1961) achieved 21 min 16 sec at Sydney, Australia on 4 Apr 1987.

ULTRA LONG DISTANCE TRACK WORLD RECORDS

WORLD BESTS—LONG-DISTANCE TRACK EVENTS

Event	hr:min:sec	Name	Place	Date
50 km	2:48:06	Jeff Norman (UK)	Timperley, Manchester	7 June 1980
50 miles	4:51:49	Don Ritchie (UK)	Hendon, London	12 Mar 1983
100 km	6:10:20	Don Ritchie (UK)	Crystal Palace	28 Oct 1978
100 miles	11:30:51	Don Ritchie (UK)	Crystal Palace	15 Oct 1977
200 km	15:11:10†	Yiannis Kouros (Greece)	Montauban, France	15–16 Mar 1985
200 miles	27:48:35	Yiannis Kouros (Greece)	Montauban, France	15–16 Mar 1985
500 km	60:23:00	Yiannis Kouros (Greece)	Colac, Australia	26–29 Nov 1984
500 miles	105:42:09	Yiannis Kouros (Greece)	Colac, Australia	26–30 Nov 1984
1000 km	136:17:00	Yiannis Kouros (Greece)	Colac, Australia	26–31 Nov 1984
	kilometres			
24 hours	283,600	Yiannis Kouros (Greece)	Montauban, France	15–16 Mar 1985
48 hours	452,270	Yiannis Kouros (Greece)	Montauban, France	15–17 Mar 1985
6 days	1023,200	Yiannis Kouros (Greece)	Colac, Australia	26 Nov–1 Dec 1984

LONG-DISTANCE ROAD BESTS

Where superior to track bests and run on properly measured road courses.

	hr:min:sec			
50 miles	4:50:21	Bruce Fordyce (South Africa)	London–Brighton	25 Sept 1983
1000 miles	11 d 20 hr 36 min	Stu Mittleman (USA)	Queens, New York, USA	26 Apr–8 May 1986
	kilometres			
24 hours	286,463	Yiannis Kouros (Greece)	New York, USA	28–29 Sept 1985

WORLD BESTS—WOMEN'S LONG-DISTANCE TRACK EVENTS

	hr:min:sec			
15 km	49:44.0	Silvana Cruciata (Italy)	Rome	4 May 1981
20 km	1:06:55.5	Rosa Mota (Portugal)	Lisbon	14 May 1983
25 km	1:31:04.3	Chantal Langlacé (France)	Amiens	3 Sep 1983
30 km	1:49:55.7	Chantal Langlacé (France)	Amiens	3 Sep 1983
50 km	3:36:58	Ann Franklin (UK)	Barry, Wales	9 Mar 1986
50 miles	6:17:30†	Monika Kuno (W. Germany)	Vogt, W. Germany	8–9 July 1983
100 km	8:01:01	Monika Kuno (W. Germany)	Vogt, W. Germany	8–9 July 1983
100 miles	15:25:46	Eleanor Adams (UK)	Honefoss, Norway	12–13 July 1986
200 km	20:09:28†	Eleanor Adams (UK)	Honefoss, Norway	12–13 July 1986
200 miles	44:44:08	Eleanor Adams (UK)	Montauban, France	15–17 Mar 1986
500 km	86:31:21	Eleanor Adams (UK)	Colac, Australia	24–28 Feb 1986
500 miles	143:38:55	Eleanor Adams (UK)	Colac, Australia	24 Feb–2 Mar 1986
	kilometres			
1 hour	18,084	Silvana Cruciata (Italy)	Rome	4 May 1981
24 hours	222,800	Eleanor Adams (UK)	Nottingham	4–5 Aug 1985
48 hours	347,420	Arlette Touchard (France)	Montauban, France	14–16 Mar 1986
6 days	808,000	Eleanor Adams (UK)	Colac, Australia	24 Feb–2 Mar 1986

† Timed on one running watch only.

WOMEN'S LONG-DISTANCE ROAD BESTS

Where superior to track bests and run on properly measured road courses.

	hr:min:sec			
50 km	3:13:51	Janis Klecker (USA)	Tallahassee, USA	17 Dec 1983
40 miles	4:43:22	Marcy Schwam (USA)	Chicago, USA	3 Oct 1982
50 miles	5:59:26	Marcy Schwam (USA)	Chicago, USA	3 Oct 1982
100 km	7:47:28	Marcy Schwam (USA)	Santander, Spain	19 Sept 1981
100 miles	15:07:45	Christine Barrett (UK)	Forthampton, Gloucestershire	14 Apr 1984
500 km (actually 518 km)	82:10	Annie van der Meer (Holland)	Paris–Colmar	8–11 Jun 1983
24 hours	227,261 km	Eleanor Adams (UK)	Milton Keynes, England	14–15 Feb 1987

It should be noted that road times must be assessed with care as course conditions can vary considerably.

ROAD WALKING WORLD BEST PERFORMANCES

It should be noted that the severity of road race courses and the accuracy of their measurement may vary, sometimes making comparisons of times unreliable.

MEN

20 km in 1 hr 19 min 24 sec, Carlos Mercenario (Mexico) (b. 3 May 1967) at New York, USA on 3 May 1987.
30 km in 2 hr 03 min 06 sec, Daniel Bautista (Mexico) (b. 4 Aug 1952) at Cherkassy, USSR on 27 Apr 1980.
50 km in 3 hr 38 min 17 sec, Ronald Weigel (GDR) (b. 8 Aug 1950) at Potsdam, GDR on 25 May 1986.

WOMEN

10 km in 43 min 22 sec, Olga Krishtop (USSR) (b. 23 June 1957) at New York, USA on 2 May 1987.
20 km in 1 hr 33 min 29 sec, Kerry Ann Saxby (Australia) (b. 2 June 1961) at Canberra, Australia on 13 Sept 1985.
50 km in 5 hr 01 min 52 sec, Lillian Millen (GB) (b. 5 Mar 1945) at York, GB on 16 Apr 1983.

BRITISH BEST PERFORMANCES

MEN

20 km in 1 hr 22 min 37 sec, Ian Peter McCombie (b. 11 Jan 1961) at Thamesmead, London on 11 May 1985.
30 km in 2 hr 7 min 56 sec, Ian Peter McCombie at Edinburgh on 27 Apr 1986.
50 km in 4 hr 00 min 47 sec, Leslie Morton (b. 1 July 1958) at Madrid, Spain on 16 Mar 1986.

WOMEN

10 km in 45 min 42 sec, Lisa Martine Langford (b. 15 Mar 1967) at New York, USA on 3 May 1987.
20 km in 1 hr 40 min 45 sec, Irene Lillian Bateman at Basildon, Essex on 9 Apr 1983.

Trampolining

Trampolines were used in show business at least as early as 'The Walloons' of the period 1910–12. The sport of trampolining (from the Spanish word *trampolin*, a springboard) dates from 1936, when the prototype 'T' model trampoline was developed by George Nissen (USA).

Most titles

World Championships were instituted in 1964. A record five titles were won by Judy Wills (USA) (b. 1948) in the women's event 1964-8. Five men have won two men's titles.

A record seven United Kingdom titles have been won by Wendy Wright (1969-70, 1972-5, 1977). The most by a man has been five by Stewart Matthews (b. 19 Feb 1962) (1976-80).

Youngest international *Great Britain*

Andrea Holmes (b. 2 Jan 1970) competed for Britain at 12 yr 131 days in the World Championships at Montana, USA on 13 May 1982.

Somersaults

Richard Cobbing of Gateshead Metro Trampoline Club performed 1610 consecutive somersaults at Gateshead, Tyne and Wear, on 22 July 1984.

The most somersaults completed in one minute is 73 by Zoe Finn at Lordwood Sports & Social Centre, Chatham, Kent on 21 Nov 1986.

Triathlon

The Triathlon combines long-distance swimming, cycling and running. Distances for each of the phases can vary, but for the best established event, the Hawaii Ironman (inst. 1978), competitors first swim 3,8 km *2.4 miles*, then cycle 180 km *112 miles*, and finally run a full marathon of 42 195 m *26 miles 385 yards*. Record times for the Hawaii Ironman are: (men) 8 hr 28 min 37 sec Dave Scott (USA); (women) 9 hr 49 min 14 sec Paula Newby-Fraser (USA), both on 19 Oct 1986. Dave Scott has won a record five races, 1980, 1982-4 and 1986.

For the same distances as in the Ironman, Scott Tinley (USA) (b. 1956), at 8 hr 27 min 46 sec, and Erin Baker (New Zealand) (b. 23 May 1961), at 9 hr 27 min 36 sec, set records for men and women respectively in the 1986 European Championships at Sofia, Bulgaria.

World Championships

This race has been held annually in Nice, France from 1982, the distances being 3200 m, 120 km and 32 km respectively. Mark Allen (USA) won all five titles 1982-6, setting a record time of 5 hr 46 min 10 sec in 1986. The women's record is 6 hr 37 min 21 sec by Erin Baker in 1985.

Largest field

The largest field in a triathlon race has been 2363 finishers in the Bud Light US Triathlon series race at Chicago in 1986. This series encompasses races over 1500 m, 40 km and 10 km for the three phases.

Tug of War

Though ancient China and Egypt have been suggested as the originating countries of the sport, it is known that Neolithic flint miners in Norfolk, England practised 'rope-pulling'. The first rules were those framed by the New York AC in 1879. Tug of War was an Olympic sport from 1900 until 1920. In 1958 the Tug-of-War Association was formed to administer Britain's 600 clubs. World Championships have been held annually from 1975, with a women's event introduced in 1986.

Most titles

The most successful team at the World Championships has been the Sheen Farmers, competing for England, who won at 640 kg in 1975-6 and at 720 kg in 1977-8 and 1980. The Wood Treatment team (formerly the Bosley Farmers) of Cheshire won 20 consecutive AAA Catchweight Championships 1959-78, two world titles (1975-6) and ten European titles at 720 kg. Hilary Brown (b. 13 Apr 1934) was in every team.

Longest pulls

The longest recorded pull (prior to the introduction of AAA rules) is one of 2 hr 41 min when 'H' Company beat 'E' Company of the 2nd Battalion of the Sherwood Foresters (Derbyshire Regiment) at Jubbulpore, India, on 12 Aug 1889. The longest recorded pull under AAA Rules (in which lying on the ground or entrenching the feet is not permitted) is one of 11 min 23 sec for the first pull between the Isle of Oxney and St Claret's at Chertsey, Surrey on 26 May 1979. The record time for 'The Pull' (inst. 1898), across the Black River, between freshman and sophomore teams at Hope College, Holland, Mich., USA, is 3 hr 51 min on 23 Sept 1977, but the method of bracing the feet precludes this replacing preceding records.

Volleyball

The game was invented as *mintonette* in 1895 by William G. Morgan at the YMCA gymnasium at Holyoke, Massachusetts, USA. The International Volleyball Association was formed in Paris in April 1947. The Amateur (now English) Volleyball Association of Great Britain was formed in May 1955.

Most world titles

World Championships were instituted in 1949 for men and 1952 for women. The USSR has won six men's titles (1949, 1952, 1960, 1962, 1978 and 1982) and four women's (1952, 1956, 1960 and 1970).

Most Olympic titles

The sport was introduced to the Olympic Games for both men and women in 1964. The USSR has won a record three men's (1964, 1968 and 1980) and three women's (1968, 1972 and 1980) titles. The only player to win four medals is Inna Ryskal (USSR) (b. 15 June 1944), who won women's silver medals in 1964 and 1976 and golds in 1968 and

1972. The record for men is held by: Yuriy Poyarkov (USSR) (b. 10 Feb 1937), who won gold medals in 1964 and 1968 and a bronze in 1972; and by Katsutoshi Nekoda (Japan) (b. 1 Feb 1944), who won gold in 1972, silver in 1968 and bronze in 1964.

Most internationals *Great Britain*

Ucal Ashman (b. 10 Nov 1957) made a record 153 men's international appearances for England, 1976-86. The women's record is 171 by Ann Jarvis (b. 3 June 1955) for England, 1974-87.

Water Polo

Water polo was developed in England as 'water soccer' in 1869 and first included in the Olympic Games in Paris in 1900.

Most Olympic titles

Hungary has won the Olympic tournament most often with six wins in 1932, 1936, 1952, 1956, 1964 and 1976. Great Britain won in 1900, 1908, 1912 and 1920.

Five players share the record of three gold medals: Britons George Wilkinson (1879-1946) in 1900, 1908, 1912, Paulo 'Paul' Radmilovic (1886-1968), and Charles Sidney Smith (1879-1951) in 1908, 1912, 1920; and Hungarians Deszo Gyarmati (b. 23 Oct 1927) and György Kárpáti (b. 23 June 1935) in 1952, 1956, 1964. Paul Radmilovic also won a gold medal for the 4 × 200 m freestyle swimming in 1908.

World Championships

First held at the World Swimming Championships in 1973. The USSR is the only double winner, 1975 and 1982. A women's competition was introduced in 1986, when it was won by Australia.

Most goals

The greatest number of goals scored by an individual in an international is 13 by Debbie Handley for Australia (16) *v.* Canada (10) at the World Championships in Guayaquil, Ecuador in 1982.

Most international appearances

The greatest number of international appearances is 412 by Aleksey Barkalov (USSR) (b. 18 Feb 1946), 1965-80. The British record is 126 by Martyn Thomas, of Cheltenham, 1964-78.

Water Skiing

The origins of water skiing derive from walking on planks and aquaplaning. A 19th-century treatise on sorcerers refers to Eliseo of Tarentum who, in the 14th century, 'walks and dances' on the water. The first report of aquaplaning was on America's Pacific coast in the early 1900s. At Scarborough, Yorkshire, on 15 July 1914, a single plank-gliding contest was won by H. Storry.

The present-day sport of water skiing was pioneered by Ralph W. Samuelson (1904-77) on Lake Pepin, Minnesota, USA, on two curved pine boards in the summer of 1922, although claims have been made for the birth of the sport on Lake Annecy (Haute Savoie), France at about the same time. The first world organisation, the *Union Internationale de Ski Nautique*, was formed in Geneva on 27 July 1946.

Most titles

World Overall Championships (inst. 1949) have been won three times by one man, Sammy Duvall (USA) in 1981, 1983 and 1985, and by two women: Willa McGuire (*née* Worthington) of the USA in 1949-50 and 1955; and Elizabeth 'Liz' Allan-Shetter (USA) in 1965, 1969 and 1975. Liz Allan-Shetter has won a record eight individual championship events and is the only person to

Water Skiing Records

WORLD RECORDS MEN

Slalom	5 buoys on a 10,75 m line	Bob LaPoint (USA)	Shreveport, Florida, USA	1984
	5 buoys on a 10,75 m line	Andy Mapple (GB)	USA	Sept 1985
Tricks	10,550 points	Patrice Martin (France)	Lac Cadeuil, Royan, France	28 Sept 1986
Jumping	61,9 m *203 ft*	Michael Hazelwood (GB)	Birmingham, Alabama, USA	30 June 1986

WORLD RECORDS WOMEN

Slalom	4 buoys on a 11,25 m line	Deena Brush (USA)	Palm Beach, Florida, USA	2 Oct 1983
	4 buoys on a 11,25 m line	Jennifer Leachman (USA)		Aug 1985
Tricks	8350 points	Ana Maria Carasco (Venezuela)		Sept 1984
Jumping	46,0 m *150 ft 11 in*	Deena Brush (USA)	Houston, USA	30 May 1987

BRITISH RECORDS MEN

Slalom	5 buoys on a 10,75 m line	Andy Mapple (b. 3 Nov 1962)	USA	Sept 1985
Tricks	8650 points	John Battleday (b. 1 Feb 1957)	Lyon, France	5 Aug 1984
Jumping	61,9 m *203 ft*	Michael Hazelwood (b. 14 Apr 1958)	Birmingham, Alabama, USA	30 June 1986

BRITISH RECORDS WOMEN

Slalom	4½ buoys at 12 m	Karen Jane Morse (b. 14 Aug 1956)	France	1982
Tricks	6820 points	Nicola Rasey (b. 6 June 1966)	Martigues, France	27 Oct 1984
Jumping	44,9 m *147 ft*	Kathy Hulme (b. 11 Feb 1959)	Kirtons Farm, Reading, Berkshire	1 Aug 1982

Most world water skiing titles ● Sammy Duvall (USA) has won three overall World Water Skiing Championships, contested bienially, at slalom, tricks and jumping. (Photo: Sporting Pictures Ltd)

win all four titles—slalom, jumping, tricks and overall in one year, at Copenhagen, Denmark in 1969. The USA has won the team championship on 15 successive occasions, 1957–85.

The most British Overall titles (inst. 1953) won by a man is seven by Michael Hazelwood (b. 14 Apr 1958) in 1974, 1976–9, 1981 and 1983; the most by a woman is nine by Karen Jane Morse (b. 1956) in 1971–6, 1978, 1981 and 1984.

Highest speed

The fastest water skiing speed recorded is 230,26 km/h *143.08 mph* by Christopher Michael Massey (Australia) on the Hawkesbury River, Windsor, New South Wales, Australia on 6 Mar 1983. His drag boat driver was Stanley Charles Sainty. Donna Patterson Brice (b. 1953) set a feminine record of 178,81 km/h *111.11 mph* at Long Beach, California on 21 Aug 1977. The fastest recorded speed by a British skier over a measured kilometre is 131,217 km/h *81.535 mph* (average) by Billy Rixon on Lake Windermere, Cumbria on 18 Oct 1973. The fastest by a British woman is 122,187 km/h *75.92 mph* by Elizabeth Hobbs on Windermere, 14 Oct 1982.

Longest run

The greatest distance travelled is 2099,7 km *1304.6 miles* by Will Coughey on 18–19 Feb 1984 on Lake Tikitapu, New Zealand.

Most skiers towed by one boat

A record 100 water skiers were towed on double skis over a nautical mile by the cruiser *Reef Cat* at Cairns, Queensland, Australia on 18 Oct 1986. This feat, organised by the Cairns and District Powerboat and Ski Club, was then replicated by 100 skiers on single skis.

Barefoot

The first person to water ski barefoot is reported to be Dick Pope, Jr at Lake Eloise, Florida, on 6 Mar 1947. The barefoot duration record is 2 hr 42 min 39 sec by Billy Nichols (USA) (b. 1964) on Lake Weir, Florida, on 19 Nov 1978. The backwards barefoot record is 39 min by Paul McManus (Australia). The British duration record is 67 min 5 sec by John Doherty on 1 Oct 1974. The official barefoot speed record is 192,08 km/h *119.36 mph* by Scott Michael Pellaton (b. 8 Oct 1956) over a quarter-mile course at Chowchilla, California, USA on 4 Sept 1983. The fastest by a woman is 118,56 km/h *73.67 mph* by Karen Toms (Australia) on the Hawkesbury River, Windsor, New South Wales on 31 Mar 1984. The British records are: (men) 114,86 km/h *71.37 mph* by Richard Mainwaring at Holme Pierrepont, Nottinghamshire on 2 Dec 1978; (women) 80,25 km/h *49.86 mph* by Michele Doherty (b. 28 May 1964) (also 71,54 km/h *44.45 mph* backwards), both at Witney, Oxfordshire on 18 Oct 1986. The fastest official speed backwards barefoot is 100 km/h *62 mph* by Robert Wing (Australia) (b. 13 Aug 1957) on 3 Apr 1982.

The barefoot jump record is 20,10 m *65 ft 11¼ in* by Mike Siepel (USA) in 1984. The British record is 18,00 m *59 ft 0¾ in* by Chris Harris in Italy in 1985.

Weightlifting

Competitions for lifting weights of stone were held in the ancient Olympic Games. The first championships entitled 'world' were staged at the Café Monico, Piccadilly, London, on 28 Mar 1891 and then in Vienna, Austria on 19–20 July 1898, subsequently recognised by the IWF. Prior to that time, weightlifting consisted of professional exhibitions in which some of the advertised poundages were open to doubt.

The International Weightlifting Federation (IWF) was established in 1920, and its first official

World Weightlifting Records

Bodyweight class	Lift	kg	lb	Name and Country	Place	Date
52 kg *114½ lb* FLYWEIGHT	Snatch	116,5	256¾	He Zhuqiang (China)	Ageo, Japan	17 Apr 1987
	Jerk	152,5	336	Neno Terziyski (Bulgaria)	Vitoria, Spain	27 Apr 1984
	Total	262,5	578½	Neno Terziyski (Bulgaria)	Vitoria, Spain	27 Apr 1984
56 kg *123¼ lb* BANTAMWEIGHT	Snatch	133	293	Oksen Mirzoyan (USSR)	Varna, Bulgaria	12 Sept 1984
	Jerk	170,5	375¾	Neum Shalamanov (Bulgaria)	Belgrade	12 Sept 1984
	Total	300	661¼	Neum Shalamanov (Bulgaria)	Varna, Bulgaria	11 May 1984
60 kg *132¼ lb* FEATHERWEIGHT	Snatch	148	326¼	Neum Shalamanov (Bulgaria)	Melbourne, Australia	7 Dec 1986
	Jerk	188	414¼	Neum Shalamanov (Bulgaria)	Melbourne, Australia	7 Dec 1986
	Total	335	738½	Neum Shalamanov (Bulgaria)	Melbourne, Australia	7 Dec 1986
67,5 kg *148¾ lb* LIGHTWEIGHT	Snatch	157,5	347	Mikhail Petrov (Bulgaria)	Reims, France	4 May 1987
	Jerk	200	440¾	Alexander Varbanov (Bulgaria)	Varna, Bulgaria	13 Sept 1984
	Total	352,5	777	Andreas Behm (GDR)	Schwedt, GDR	20 July 1984
75 kg *165¼ lb* MIDDLEWEIGHT	Snatch	168,5	371¼	Borislav Gydikov (Bulgaria)	Sofia, Bulgaria	11 Nov 1986
	Jerk	215	474	Alexander Varbanov (Bulgaria)	Sofia, Bulgaria	11 Nov 1986
	Total	377,5	832	Zdravko Stoichkov (Bulgaria)	Varna, Bulgaria	14 Sept 1984
82,5 kg *181¾ lb* LIGHT-HEAVYWEIGHT	Snatch	183	403¼	Asen Zlatev (Bulgaria)	Melbourne, Australia	7 Dec 1986
	Jerk	225	496	Asen Zlatev (Bulgaria)	Sofia, Bulgaria	12 Nov 1986
	Total	405	892½	Yurik Vardanyan (USSR)	Varna, Bulgaria	14 Sept 1984
90 kg *198¼ lb* MIDDLE-HEAVYWEIGHT	Snatch	195,5	431	Blagoi Blagoyev (Bulgaria)	Varna, Bulgaria	1 May 1983
	Jerk	233,5	514¾	Anatoliy Khrapatiy (USSR)	Lvov, USSR	5 Mar 1987
	Total	422,5	931¼	Viktor Solodov (USSR)	Varna, Bulgaria	15 Sept 1984
100 kg *220¼ lb*	Snatch	200,5	442	Nicu Vlad (Romania)	Sofia, Bulgaria	14 Nov 1986
	Jerk	242,5	532¼	Pavel Kuznyetsov (USSR)	Arkhangelsk, USSR	4 July 1987
	Total	440	970	Yuriy Zakharevich (USSR)	Odessa, USSR	4 Mar 1983
110 kg *242½ lb* HEAVYWEIGHT	Snatch	202,5	446¼	Yuriy Zakharevich (USSR)	Reims, France	9 May 1987
	Jerk	248	546¾	Yuriy Zakharevich (USSR)	Sofia, Bulgaria	15 Nov 1986
	Total	447.5	986½	Yuriy Zakharevich (USSR)	Sofia, Bulgaria	15 Nov 1986
Over 110 kg *242½ lb* SUPER-HEAVYWEIGHT	Snatch	215	474	Antonio Krastev (Bulgaria)	Sofia, Bulgaria	16 Nov 1986
	Jerk	265,5	585¼	Leonid Taranenko (USSR)	Arkhangelsk, USSR	5 July 1987
	Total	472,5	1,041½	Leonid Taranenko (USSR)	Arkhangelsk, USSR	5 July 1987

* unratified

championships were held in Tallinn, Estonia on 29–30 Apr 1922. The first Women's World Championships were held in Miami, USA in October 1987.

There are two standard lifts: the 'snatch' and the 'clean and jerk' (or 'jerk'). Totals of the two lifts determine competition results. The 'press', which was a standard lift, was abolished in 1972.

Most Olympic medals
Norbert Schemansky (USA) (b. 30 May 1924) won a record four Olympic medals: gold, middle-heavyweight 1952; silver, heavyweight 1948; bronze, heavyweight 1960 and 1964.

Most titles *World*
The most world title wins, including Olympic Games, is eight by: John Davis (USA) (1921–84) in 1938, 1946–52; Tommy Kono (USA) (b. 27 June 1930) in 1952–9; and Vasiliy Alekseyev (USSR) (b. 7 Jan 1942), 1970–7.

Youngest world record holder
Naim Suleimanov (now Neum Shalamanov) (Bulgaria) (b. 23 Nov 1967) set 56-kg world records for clean and jerk (160 kg) and total (285 kg) at 15 yr 123 days at Allentown, New Jersey, USA on 26 Mar 1983.

Most successful British lifter
The only British lifter to win an Olympic title has been Launceston Elliot (1874–1930), the open one-handed lift champion in 1896 at Athens. Louis George Martin (b. Jamaica, 11 Nov 1936)

won four world and European mid-heavyweight titles in 1959, 1962–3 and 1965. He won an Olympic silver medal in 1964 and a bronze in 1960 and three Commonwealth gold medals in 1962, 1966 and 1970. His total of British titles was 12.

Heaviest lift to body weight
The first man to clean and jerk more than three times his body weight was Stefan Topurov (Bulgaria), who lifted 180 kg *396¾ lb* in Moscow, USSR on 24 Oct 1983.

POWERLIFTING
The sport of powerlifting was first contested at national level in Great Britain in 1958. The first US Championships were held in 1964. The International Powerlifting Federation was founded in 1972, a year after the first, unofficial world championships were held. Official championships have been held annually for men from 1973 and for women from 1980. The three standard lifts are: squat, bench press and dead lift, the totals from the three lifts determining competition results.

Most world titles
The winner of the most world titles is Hideaki Inaba (Japan) with 12, at 52 kg 1974–83 and 1985–6. The most by a British lifter is seven by Ron Collins: 75 kg 1972–4, 82 kg 1975–7 and 1979. The most by a woman is six by Beverley Francis (Australia) (b. 15 Feb 1955) at 75 kg 1980 and 1982, 82.5 kg 1981 and 1983–5.

BRITISH WEIGHTLIFTING RECORDS (in kg)

Class	Snatch		Date
52 kg	92,5	Precious McKenzie	25 Jan 1974
56 kg	105	Dean Willey	15 June 1981
60 kg	122,5	Dean Willey	26 Feb 1983
67,5 kg	145	Dean Willey	26 July 1986
75 kg	155	David Morgan	11 Nov 1986
82,5 kg	161	David Morgan	13 June 1987
90 kg	160	Gary Langford	13 Apr 1980
100 kg	160,5	Gary Langford	7 Mar 1982
110 kg	180	Gary Taylor	30 Mar 1985
Super	162,5	John Burns	5 Sept 1982

Class	Jerk		Date
52 kg	122,5	Precious McKenzie	25 Jan 1974
56 kg	132,5	Geoff Laws	1982
60 kg	152,5	Dean Willey	26 Mar 1983
67,5 kg	170	Dean Willey	1 Aug 1984
75 kg	190	David Morgan	11 Nov 1986
82,5 kg	205	David Morgan	13 June 1987
90 kg	201	David Mercer	26 May 1984
100 kg	202,5	Peter Pinsent	17 Sept 1983
110 kg	200	Brian Strange	28 Feb 1976
Super	200	Andrew Kerr	9 Nov 1974

Class	Total		Date
52 kg	215	Precious McKenzie	25 Jan 1974
56 kg	235	Geoff Laws	1982
60 kg	272,5	Dean Willey	26 Feb 1983
67,5 kg	315	Dean Willey	1985
75 kg	345	David Morgan	11 Nov 1986
82,5 kg	365	David Morgan	13 June 1987
90 kg	352,5	David Mercer	5 Aug 1984
100 kg	362,5	Peter Pinsent	17 Sept 1983
110 kg	375	Gary Taylor	30 Mar 1985
Super	350	Brian Strange	4 Mar 1978

WORLD POWERLIFTING RECORDS (All weights in kilograms)

Class	Squat		Bench Press		Deadlift		Total	
MEN								
52 kg	243	Hideaki Inaba (Japan) 1986	146,5	Joe Cunha (USA) 1982	235	Hideaki Inaba 1986	577,5	Hideaki Inaba 1986
56 kg	237,5	Hideaki Inaba 1982	155	Hiroyaki Isagawa (Jap) 1986	289,5	Lamar Gant (USA) 1982	625	Lamar Gant 1982
60 kg	295	Joe Bradley (USA) 1980	180	Joe Bradley 1980	300,5	Lamar Gant 1986	707,5	Joe Bradley 1982
67,5 kg	297	Robert Wahl (USA) 1982	200	Kristoffer Hulecki (Swe) 1985	312,5	Raimo Valineva (Fin) 1981	732,5	Joe Bradley 1981
75 kg	327,5	Mike Bridges (USA) 1980	217,5	James Rouse (USA) 1980	325,5	Eric Coppin (Bel) 1985	850	Rick Gaugler (USA) 1982
82,5 kg	379,5	Mike Bridges 1982	240	Mike Bridges 1981	357,5	Veli Kumpuniemi (Fin) 1980	952,5	Mike Bridges 1982
90 kg	375	Fred Hatfield (USA) 1980	255	Mike MacDonald (USA) 1980	372,5	Walter Thomas (USA) 1982	937,5	Mike Bridges 1980
100 kg	400	Fred Hatfield 1982	261.5	Mike MacDonald 1977	377,5	James Cash (USA) 1982	952,5	James Cash 1982
110 kg	393,5	Dan Wohleber (USA) 1981	270	Jeffrey Magruder (USA) 1982	395	John Kuc (USA) 1980	1000	John Kuc 1980
125 kg	412,5	David Waddington (USA) 1982	278,5	Tom Hardman (USA) 1982	385	Terry McCormick (USA) 1982	1005	Ernie Hackett (USA) 1980
125 + kg	445	Dwayne Fely (USA) 1982	300	Bill Kazmaier (USA) 1981	403,5	Lars Noren (Swe) 1987	1100	Bill Kazmaier 1981
WOMEN								
44 kg	140	Anna-Liisa Prinkkala (Fin) 1984	75	Teri Hoyt (USA) 1982	165	Nancy Belliveau (USA) 1985	352,5	Marie Vassart (Bel) 1985
48 kg	147,5	Keiko Nishio (Japan) 1987	82,5	Michelle Evris (USA) 1981	182,5	Majik Jones (USA) 1984	390	Majik Jones 1984
52 kg	173	Sisi Dolman (Hol) 1986	95	Mary Ryan (USA) 1984	197	Diana Rowell (USA) 1984	427,5	Diana Rowell 1984
56 kg	190	Vicki Steenrod (USA) 1984	112	Vicki Steenrod 1984	200	Diana Rowell 1984	482,5	Vicky Steenrod 1984
60 kg	200,5	Ruthi Shafer (USA) 1983	105	Vicki Steenrod 1985	213	Ruthi Shafer 1983	502,5	Vicki Steenrod 1985
67,5 kg	230	Ruthi Shafer 1984	107,5	Heidi Wittesch (Aus) 1986	244	Ruthi Shafer 1984	565	Ruthi Shafer 1984
75 kg	214,5	Terry Byland (USA) 1987	140	Beverley Francis (Aus) 1981	210	Pam Mathews (Aus) 1982	550	Beverley Francis 1981
82,5 kg	230	Juanita Trujillo (USA) 1986	150	Beverley Francis 1981	227,5	Vicky Gagne (USA) 1981	577,5	Beverley Francis 1983
90 kg	237,5	Lorraine Constanzo (USA) 1986	120,5	Gael Martin (Aus) 1983	212	Lorraine Constanzo 1987	550	Lorraine Constanzo 1986
90 + kg	247,5	Jan Todd (USA) 1983	130	Gael Martin 1982	230	Wanda Sander (USA) 1983	567,5	Gael Martin 1982

BRITISH POWERLIFTING RECORDS (All weights in kilograms)

Class	Squat		Bench Press		Deadlift		Total	
MEN								
52 kg	217,5	Phil Stringer 1980	130	Phil Stringer 1981	222,5	Precious McKenzie 1975	530	Phil Stringer 1982
56 kg	235	Phil Stringer 1982	137,5	Phil Stringer 1983	229	Precious McKenzie 1973	567,5	Narendra Bhairo 1982
60 kg	247,5	Tony Galvez 1981	142,5	Clint Lewis 1985	275	Eddy Pengelly 1977	645	Eddy Pengelly 1979
67,5 kg	275	Eddy Pengelly 1981	165	Hassan Salih 1979	295	Eddy Pengelly 1982	710	Eddy Pengelly 1982
75 kg	302,5	John Howells 1979	185	Peter Fiore 1981	310	Robert Limerick 1984	760	Steve Alexander 1983
82,5 kg	337,5	Mike Duffy 1984	210	Mike Duffy 1981	355	Ron Collins 1980	855	Ron Collins 1980
90 kg	347,5	David Caldwell 1985	227,5	Jeff Chandler 1985	350,5	Ron Collins 1980	870	David Caldwell 1985
100 kg	380	Tony Stevens 1984	225	Tony Stevens 1985	362,5	Tony Stevens 1984	955	Tony Stevens 1984
110 kg	372,5	Tony Stevens 1984	235	John Neighbour 1987	380	Arthur White 1982	940	John Neighbour 1987
125 kg	385	Sean Spillane 1985	240	Sean Spillane 1985	365	Steven Zetolofsky 1984	957,5	Steven Zetolofsky 1984
125 + kg	380	Steven Zetolofsky 1979	258	Terry Purdue 1971	377,5	Andy Kerr 1982	982,5	Andy Kerr 1983
WOMEN								
44 kg	112,5	Helen Wolsey 1987	57,5	Jane White 1983	130	Ann Brown 1982	300	Helen Wolsey 1987
48 kg	125	Suzanne Smith 1985	75	Suzanne Smith 1985	133,5	Sheila Stapleton 1987	325	Suzanne Smith 1985
52 kg	142,5	Jenny Hunter 1985	81	Jenny Hunter 1986	172,5	Jenny Hunter 1986	390	Jenny Hunter 1986
56 kg	152,5	Jenny Hunter 1987	87,5	Jenny Hunter 1986	180	Jenny Hunter 1986	412,5	Jenny Hunter 1986
60 kg	160	Rita Bass 1985	85	Rita Bass 1986	177,5	Donna Webb 1984	420	Rita Bass 1986
67,5 kg	170	Tracy Roberts 1986	85	Tracy Roberts 1986	177,5	Joanne Nicholls 1987	425	Tracy Roberts 1986
75 kg	195	Patricia Morgan 1984	95	Judith Oakes 1981	202,5	Judith Oakes 1984	492,5	Judith Oakes 1984
82,5 kg	210	Judith Oakes 1986	112,5	Judith Oakes 1983	210	Judith Oakes 1986	532,5	Judith Oakes 1986
90 kg	177,5	Jackie Pepper 1987	100	Janis Kerr 1983	192,5	Jackie Pepper 1987	462,5	Jackie Pepper 1987
90 + kg	162,5	Janis Kerr 1981	112,5	Venissa Head 1982	185	Janis Kerr 1981	440	Janis Kerr 1980

Heaviest weight

The greatest weight ever raised by a human being is 6270 lb *2844 kg* (2.80 tons *2,84 tonnes*) in a back lift (weight raised off trestles) by the 26 stone *165 kg* Paul Anderson (USA) (b. 17 Oct 1932), at Toccoa, Georgia, USA, on 12 June 1957. The greatest lift by a woman is 3564 lb *1616 kg* with a hip and harness lift by Josephine Blatt (*née* Schauer) (1869–1923) at the Bijou Theater, Hoboken, New Jersey, USA, on 15 Apr 1895.

Powerlifting feats

Paul Anderson, as a professional, reportedly achieved 1200 lb *544 kg* in a squat, thus aggregating, with a 627 lb *284 kg* press and an 820 lb *371 kg* dead lift, a career total of 2647 lb *1200 kg*. Lamar Gant (USA) was the first man to deadlift five times his own body weight, lifting 299,5 kg *661 lb* when 59,5 kg *132 lb* in 1985.

The greatest power lift by a woman is a squat of 545½ lb *247,5 kg* by Jan Suffolk Todd (b. 22 May 1952) (USA) (weighing 88,5 kg *195 lb*) at Columbus, Georgia, USA in Jan 1981. Cammie Lynn Lusko (b. 5 Apr 1958) (USA) became the first woman to lift more than her body weight with one arm, with 59,5 kg *131 lbs* at a body weight of 58,3 kg *128.5 lb*, at Milwaukee, Wisconsin, USA on 21 May 1983.

24-hr and 1-hr lifts

A deadlifting record of 2 392 150 kg *5,273,781 lb* in 24 hr was set by a team of ten from Finchale Weightlifting Club, Co Durham on 18–19 May 1987.

A bench press record of 3 869 011 kg *8,529,700 lb* was set by a nine-man team from the Hogarth Barbell Club, Chiswick, London on 18–19 July 1987. A squat record of 2 168 625 kg *4,780,994 lb* was set by a ten-man team from St Albans Weightlifting Club and Ware Boys Club, Hertfordshire on 20–21 July 1986. A record 54,421 arm-curling repetitions using three 22 kg *48¼ lb* weightlifting bars and dumb-bells were achieved by a team of nine from HMS *Osprey*, Portland, Dorset on 9–10 Apr 1987.

Vincent Manson (b. 5 Nov 1943) achieved 940 repetitions of his bodyweight (57,6 kg *127 lb*) in one hour by bench presses on 3 May 1987 at H.M. Prison, Gartree, Leicestershire.

Strandpulling

The International Steel Strandpullers' Association was founded by Gavin Pearson (Scotland) in 1940. The greatest ratified poundage to date is a super-heavyweight right-arm push of 815 lb *369,5 kg* by Malcolm Bartlett (b. 9 June 1955) of Oldham, Lancashire. The record for the back press anyhow is 645 lb *292,5 kg* by Barry Anderson, of Leeds, in 1975. A record 20 British Open titles have been won by Ian Storton (b. 2 Feb 1951), of Morecambe, 1974–86.

Wrestling

The earliest depictions of wrestling holds and falls on wall plaques and a statue indicate that organised wrestling dates from *c.* 2750–2600 BC. It was the most popular sport in the ancient Olympic Games and victors were recorded from 708 BC. The Greco-Roman style is of French origin and arose about 1860. The International Amateur Wrestling Federation (FILA) was founded in 1912.

Most titles *Olympic*

Three Olympic titles have been won by: Carl Westergren (1895–1958) (Sweden) in 1920, 1924 and 1932; Ivar Johansson (1903–79) (Sweden) in 1932 (two) and 1936; and Aleksandr Medved (b. 16 Sept 1937) (USSR) in 1964, 1968 and 1972. Four Olympic medals were won by: Eino Leino (b. 7 Apr 1891) at freestyle, 1920–32; and by Imre

Polyák (Hungary) (b. 16 Apr 1932) at Greco-Roman, 1952–64.

World

The freestyler Aleksandr Medved (USSR) (b. 16 Sept 1937) won a record ten World Championships, 1962–4 and 1966–72 at three weight categories. The only wrestler to win the same title in seven successive years has been Valeriy Rezantsev (b. 2 Feb 1947) (USSR), in the Greco-Roman 90 kg class 1970–6, including the Olympic Games of 1972 and 1976.

Heaviest sumo wrestler ● Samoan-American Salevaa Fuali Atisnoe of Hawaii, *alias* Konishiki, who in 1987 had a peak weight of 527 lb *239 kg*. He also became the first *sumoturi* to gain promotion to the second-highest rank of ozeki (champion) on 27 May 1987. Weight is amassed by over-alimentation with a high-protein stew called *chankonabe*.

Most titles and longest span *British*

The most British titles won in one weight class is ten by heavyweight Kenneth Alan Richmond (b. 10 July 1926) between 1949 and 1960. The longest span for BAWA titles is 24 years by George Mackenzie (1890–1957) between 1909 and 1933. He represented Great Britain in five successive Olympiads, 1908 to 1928.

Most wins

In international competition, Osamu Watanabe (b. 21 Oct 1940), of Japan, the 1964 Olympic Freestyle 63 kg Champion, was unbeaten and unscored-upon in 187 consecutive matches. Outside of FILA sanctioned competition, Wade Schalles (USA) won 821 bouts from 1964 to 1984, with 530 of these victories by pin.

Longest bout

The longest recorded bout was one of 11 hr 40 min when Martin Klein (1885–1947) (Estonia, representing Russia) beat Alfred Asikáinen

The successful high-school students after their volleyball endurance marathon

En route to 316 hours of snooker

SCRABBLE .... 2 .... 153 hr
Peter Finan and Neil Smith at St Anselm's College, Wirral, Merseyside, 18–25 Aug 1984. (Ken Cardozo played for 155 hr 48 min against various opponents at Perfect Pizza, Fulham, 5–11 Dec 1984.)

SKIING (Alpine) ... 1 .... 138 hr
Luc Labrie at Daie Comeau, Quebec, Canada, 20–5 Feb 1984.

SKIING (Alpine) ... 2 .... 83 hr 17 min
With no waiting for lifts—Dave Phillips spnd Gerry O'Neil at Grouse Mountain, North Vancouver, Canada, 20–3 Feb 1986.

SKITTLES .... 6 .... 168 hr
Gloucester & Dinmino Irish Society at Gloucester, 15–22 Aug 1981.

SNAKES & LADDERS .... 4 .... 260 hr
Team from Essex Young Farmers Club, West Mersea, Essex, 29 Jan–2 Feb 1982.

SNOOKER .... 2 .... 316 hr
Xavier van Huyssteen and Gerhaan Swert at the Kine Center, Johannesburg, South Africa, 10–23 Feb 1987.

SOFTBALL (fast pitch) .... 18 .... 60 hr
Two teams from the Campbelltown District Association at Ingleburn, New South Wales, Australia, 6–8 Dec 1985.

SOFTBALL (slow pitch) .... 20 .... 111 hr 2 min
Brigade Service Support Group-1 and Marine Aircraft Group-24 at Kareohe Marine Corps Air Station, Hawaii, USA, 3–8 Sept 1986.

SQUASH .... 2 ...... 122 hr 44 min
Amir Shaikh and Phillip Marlowe at Wembley Squash Centre, Wembley, Middlesex, 8–13 Nov 1985.

SUBBUTEO TABLE FOOTBALL .... 5 .... 68 hr
Paul Andrews, Patrick Comer, Brian McIver, Stephen Monoghan and Eddie Fitzpatrick at Malvern, South Australia, 1977.

TABLE FOOTBALL 2 .... 91 hr 20 min
Shaun Unterslak and Jay Boccia in South Africa, 5–9 Apr 1987.

TABLE TENNIS ... 2 ...... 147 hr 47 min
Shaun Unterslak and Jay Boccia at Dewaal Hotel, Cape Town, South Africa, 12–18 Nov 1983.

TABLE TENNIS (doubles) .... 4 .... 101 hr 1 min
Lance, Phil and Mark Warren and Bill Weir at Sacramento, Cal., USA, 9–13 Apr 1979.

TENNIS (Lawn) ... 2 .... 117 hr
Mark and Jim Pinchoff at the Fitness Resort, Lafayette, Louisiana, USA, 14–19 May 1985.

TENNIS (doubles) .... 4 .... 96 hr 25 min
Ann Wilkinson, Peter Allsopp, John Thorpe and David Dicks at Mansfield Lawn Tennis Club, Nottinghamshire, 17–21 Aug 1983.

TIDDLYWINKS ...... 6 .... 300 hr
Southampton University Tiddlywinks Club, 20 Feb–5 Mar 1981.

TRAMPOLINING ... 1 .... 266 hr 9 min
Jeff Schwartz at Glenview, Illinois, USA, 14–25 Aug 1981.

TRIVIAL PURSUIT 4–6 ... 108 hr 52 min
Six sixth formers at Richmond School, North Yorkshire, 25–9 Oct 1986.

VOLLEYBALL ...... 12 .... 100 hr 3 min
High-school students for the Daddy Bruce Randolph Foundation, Denver, Colorado, USA, 29 June–3 July 1986.

WATER POLO ...... 14 .... 25 hr 34 min
Two teams of seven from Shrewsbury School, Shropshire at Shrewsbury Baths, 29–30 Nov 1986.

IMPORTANT

Rest breaks of five minutes for each completed hour played (not calculated according to a running total) are permitted in these endurance marathons. Such breaks are aggregable but at no time can the earned rest period be exceeded. The number of participants in team events is shown in the table; all must be in action throughout the attempt, except that a drop-out rate of up to 20 per cent of the people is permitted. No substitutes are allowed. Claims for new records must be accompanied by full authentication.

Stop Press

Living dwarfs ● (p. 8) Nelson de la Rosa has since been diagnosed to be suffering from Seckel's syndrome.
Oldest man ● (p. 12) John Evans was 110 on 19 Aug 1987.
Twins oldest living ● (p. 13) Edith Marjorie Chavasse died in Windsor aged 100 years 332 days on 27 July 1987.
Siamese twins ● (p. 14) Fonda and Shannon Beaver were successfully separated in February 1981;
Hassan and Hussein (Sudan) were separated at Great Ormond Street Hospital, London, on 29 Apr 1987
Quintuplets ● (p. 14) The world's first test-tube quintuplets Alan, Brett, Connor, Douglas and Edward were born to Linda and Bruce Jacobssen at University College Hospital, London on 26 Apr 1985.
Multiple Births – UK ● (p. 14) 7 (septuplets (4 female 3 male) to Mrs Susan Halton, 27, at Oxford St. Maternity Hospital, Liverpool on 15 Aug 1987. Two boys and three girls had died within 5 days.
Fire breathing ● (p. 20) Reg Morris achieved 31 ft *9,4 m* from his mouth at the Miner's Rest, Chasetown, Staffs on 29 Oct 1986.
Isolation ● (p. 21) Maurrizio Montalbini lived for 210 days in a cave from 14 Dec 1986 to 13 July 1987 near Ancona, Italy watched only by TV monitors. On resurfacing he thought it was March.
Largest British rodent ● (p. 28) It was reported in June 1987 that the Coypu was now on the verge of extinction after 3000 had been hunted down since 1981.
Dogs: strength and endurance ● (p. 30) At the American Dog Breeders' Association 'Weight Pull' at Conroe, Texas on 7 Dec 1985 an American Pit Bull Terrier bitch named 'Crazy II', owned by Bill Grimsley of Choctaw, Oklahoma, pulled 3050 lb (70.98 lb per lb of body weight).
Birds rarest ● (p. 33) The last known Dusky seaside sparrow was found dead on 16 June 1987 at the Walt Disney World's Discovery Island, Orlando, Florida.
'Igor', the last Californian condor still living in the wild was captured in April 1987. No condor has bred in captivity.
Crocodile largest ● (p. 33) An estuarine specimen at the Bhitarkanika Wild Life Sanctuary, Orissa, India, exceeded 7 m *23 ft.*
Chicken flying ● (p. 35) 'Sheena', a barnyard bantam, owned by Bill and Bob Knox flew 630 ft 2 in *192,07 m* at Parkesburg, Penn. on 31 May 1985.
Shortest venomous snake ● (p. 36) The average adult length of the Namaqua dwarf adder (*Bitis schneideri*) of Namibia, Southern Africa, is 20 cm *8 in.*
Butterfly farm largest ● (p. 40) The enclosed flight space of The Australian Butterfly Sanctuary at Kurunda is 3660 m³ *129,250 ft³*.
Vineyards most southerly ● (p. 46) Renton Burgess Vineyard south of Alexandra, S. Island, New Zealand, is in Lat. 44° 36″ S.
Bouquet largest ● (p. 46) Thirty six people took 335 hr to make a 11,23 m *36 ft 10 in* high bouquet of 9299 flowers at Annecy, France on 19 Sept 1986.
Kale tallest ● (p. 47) Gosse Haisma of Bunbury, Western Australia grew a stalk to 4.77 m *15 ft 7¾ in.*
Cucumber largest ● (p. 48) Mrs Chappel grew one of 24 kg *52 lb 14¾ oz* on 25 June 1987.
Highest Mountains ● (p. 55) The Chinese on 13 Aug 1987 reaffirmed their heights of 29,029 ft *8848 m* for Everest and 28,250 ft *8620 m* for K2 (Qogir) respectively.
Supernovae ● (p. 68) Now designated as – 69 202.
Age of the universe ● (pp. 68 & 69) Prof Harvey Butcher of the Kapteyn Astronomical Institute, Netherlands published in *Nature* on 9 July 1987 a reassessment based on the ratio of the decay rate of thorium against the stability of neodymium. His low figure of only 10,000 million years is not yet internationally accepted.
People in Space ● (p. 70) On 22 July 1987 Mohommad Faris (b. 26 May 1951) (Syria) raised the number of persons in space to 201 and the number of space flights to 320.
Element 110 ● (p. 72) was synthesized by bombarding Th and U isotopes with Ca and A nuclei at Dubna, USSR—announced 18 Aug 1987.
Spirits most expensive ● (p. 74) Ian Boasman (see Bottle collections) paid £5000 for a 1789 Cognac Grande Champagne at Sotheby's London on 8 Apr 1987. Première Wine Merchants of New York, USA, paid £5000 for a bottle of the malt whisky 'The Macallan Highland Malt' on 22 July 1987.

Eight foot barrier threatened ● On 30 June 1987 Sweden's Patrik Sjöberg cleared 2,42m *7 ft 11¼ in* in the Olympic Stadium, Stockholm. Here he demonstrates his ability to drape himself mid-air around the bar such that his centre of gravity passes beneath it. (All-Sport)

Bottle collections ● (p. 74) George E. Terren of Southboro, Massachusetts, USA has a collection of 26,702 miniature distilled spirit and liquor bottles as at 12 June 1987. Ian Boasman's collection of unduplicated labels in May 1987 reached 1843.
Photograph most expensive ● (p. 74) One taken on 9 Feb 1864 of Abraham Lincoln and his son Tad sold at Sotheby's, New York in May 1985 to Malcolm Forbes Jr for $104,500 (*then £87,000*).
Painter most prolific ● (p. 80) Morris Katz's sales reached 170,000 by 1 May 1987.
Sculpture most expensive ● (p. 81) Jean-Antoine Houdon's 1787 portrait sculpture of Thomas Jefferson, used as a model for the 5-cent coin, was sold for $2,860,000 (£1,787,500) at Christie's, New York on 29 May 1987.
Longest word ● (p. 84) The German 39-letter Rechtsschutzversicherungsgesellschaften means 'insurance companies which provide legal protection'.
Musical manuscript (including buyer's premium) ● (p. 86) London dealer James Kirkman paid £2,585,0000 for a 508 page 8½ × 6½ in *21,6 × 16,5 cm* bound volume of 9 complete symphonies in Mozart's hand at Sotheby's, London on 22 May 1987. The seller was an anonymous European.
Letters in *The Times* ● (p. 86) David Green's total reached 116 by 4 Aug 1987.
Most durable feature ● (p. 90) Eric Hardy of Liverpool is now in his 60th year as a regular natural history contributor to the *Daily Post* of Liverpool.
Largest Circulation ● (p. 90) *Parade* attained 32,022,000 in September 1987. *Trud* attained 18,000,000 by March 1987.
Advertising Rates ● (p. 91) The four-colour inside page rate for *Parade* rose to $315,400 in summer 1987.

Crosswords ● (p. 91) Roger Squires surpassed 29,000 by August 1987.
Largest drum ● (p. 93) A £5000 drum 13 ft *3,96 m* in diameter, built by the Supreme Drum Co, was played at the Royal Festival Hall, London on 31 May 1987.
Broadway-longest run ● (p. 97) *A Chorus Line* entered its 13th year in August 1987. It was created by Michael Bennett (b. 1943) who died of AIDS, aged 44, in Arizona on 2 July 1987.
Most successful singer ● (p. 98) In August 1987, *Who's That Girl?* gave Madonna (Madonna Louise Veronica Ciccone, Mrs Sean Penn, b. 16 Aug 1959) her fifth No 1 single increasing her lead over her nearest female rival, Sandie Shaw, who has three. She is now level with Police and Blondie.
Radio most durable programme ● (p. 102) The Mormon Tabernacle Choir made its 3000th broadcast (from Salt Lake City, Utah) on 15 Feb 1987.
Tallest Building ● (p. 106) Demolition on the Central Place site in Brisbane, Queensland, began on 9 Aug 1987 for the erection of the 120 storey world's tallest building of 445 m *1460 ft* for completion at a cost of $A800 million (*£360 million*) by late 1990.
Largest hotel lobby ● (p. 108) The lobby at the Hyatt Regency, San Francisco, is 350 ft *106,6 m* long 160 ft *48,7 m* wide and at 170 ft *51,8 m* is the height of a 17 storey building.
Flats tallest ● (p. 110) The 716 ft *218 m* tall Metropolitan Tower on W 57 St, New York, is of 78 storeys of which the upper 48 are residential.
Largest illuminated sign ● (p. 117) The letter 'M' installed on the Great Mississippi River Bridge is 1800 ft *548,6 m* long and comprises 200 high intensity lamps.
Marquee largest ● (p. 118) Manor Marquees Ltd, of Maidstone, Kent erected a 470 ft *143 m* long marquee in one lift on 16 May 1987.

Snow construction ● (p. 120) A snow palace 26.5 m *87 ft* high and one of four structures which spanned 214.2 m *702.7 ft* wide was unveiled on 7 Feb 1987 at Asahikawa City, Hokkaido, Japan.
Fastest car ● (p. 128) The Porsche 959 has a road-tested speed of 197 mph 317 km. Ferrari asserted a speed of 201 mph *323,5 km/h* for their £140,000 F40 in July 1987.
Oldest driver ● (p. 129) Benjamin Kagan (father of Lord Kagan) was still driving in 1983 at 102.
Two-side-wheel driving ● (p. 129) Göran Eliason achieved 143,027 km/hr *88.87 mph* in a standard Volvo 760 on two wheels at Anderstrop, Sweden on 24 May 1987.
Round Britain driving ● (p. 129) From 4–10 June 1987 the Bevercotes Team of Newark, Notts covered 3658 mile *5886,8 km* in a Diahatsu diesel turbo *Charade* at 69.66 mpg *24,66 km/litre*.
Battery-powered vehicle ● (p. 129) The 'end-to-end record' (John O'Groats to Lands End) for a Sinclair C5 is 80 hr 47 min from 18–21 May 1987 by Robert Dodds and Ian Pridding with the support of the Pontllanfraith Rotary Club.
Rail travel ● (p.135) Martyn Tebbutt and Ian Buttery of Leeds travelled 1729 miles *2782,4 km* in 24 hours from 16–17 June 1987. Reg Wright of Hartlepool, Cleveland completed 2021 miles in 23 hr 59 min on 11 Nov 1982, reported in July 1987.
Oldest passenger ● (p. 141) Charlotte Hughes (b. 1 Aug 1877) of Marske, Cleveland flew by Concorde to New York on 4 Aug 1987 as a 110th birthday present. She returned 4 days later.
Paper Aircraft ● (p. 141) Duration 17–20 sec G. Blackburn in Milwaukee, Wisconsin on 28 July 1987. Felch attained 196 ft 2 in *59,59 m.*
Windmill ● (p. 143) The Orkney aerogenerator is due to become operational in October 1987.
Largest clock ● (p. 146) The digital, electronic, two-sided clock which revolves on top of the Texas Building in Fort Worth, Texas, USA is 44 × 44 × 28 ft *13,4 × 13,4 × 8,5 m.*
Art auctioneering ● (p. 148) A single session record of $63.6 million (*then £39,750,000*) was set at Sotheby's, New York on 11 May 1987.
Longest wait for a sale ● (p. 149) Kevin Mellish (b. 2 Aug 1948) queued for a carpet reduced in price by more than 86 per cent for 20 days outside Arding and Hobbs, Clapham, London, from 7 to 27 Dec 1986.
Property rentals ● (p. 150) In May 1987 prime offices in Tokyo reached £87.54 per ft² *£942.30 per m²*.
Stock exchange records ● (p. 151) An all-time record for the Dow Jones of 2706.79 was reached on 20 Aug 1987. The FT-SE 100 share index reached a peak of 2371.0 and the FT-SE 30 share index 1846.0 on 9 July 1987.
Largest flotation ● (p. 152) The Government's remaining 32 per cent stake in BP, together with the proceeds of a simultaneous 'rights issue', is expected to make £8500 million in autumn 1987.
Guns ● (p. 152) The prototype .45 Colt of 1873 was sold at auction in the USA for $242,000 (£151,250) on 15 May 1987.
Jigsaw ● (p. 155) The Stave puzzles are made by Steve Richardson of Norwich, Vermont, USA.
In July 1986 'L'asociation l'Arbre aux Mille Sources' constructed a jigsaw consisting of 150,000 pieces and measuring 25 × 14,64 m *82 × 48 ft.*
Toy construction ● (p. 157) The tallest Lego tower, 49 ft 2⅞ in *15,01 m*, was built in the forecourt of Waterloo Station, London on 29–30 Oct 1985.
Highest priced goat ● (p. 158) An angora goat was sold for £14,700 at a sale at Longhope, Gloucestershire on 23 May 1987.
Altitude records ● (p. 160) By FAI definition 'space' starts at an altitude of 100 km *62.137 miles* or *328,083 ft.*
Trans-Atlantic Records ● (p. 164) Fast-test Solo West–East Crossing, Tom McClean (N. Ireland) in his 20 ft *6,10 m* boat from St. John's, Newfoundland to Bishop Rock (11 Aug 1987) in 54 days 23 hrs but rowed less miles/day over a shorter route than Gérard d'Aboville.
Deep diving ● (p. 165) Rossana Majorca (Italy) reached 75 m *246 ft ¾ in* without equipment off Syracuse, Sicily on 31 July 1987, being underwater for 2 min 7 sec.
Mantle of Bees ● (p. 167) Max Beck on 19 Aug 1987 was covered overall by a mantle of 160,000 swarming bees weighing 50 lb *22,5 kg.*

Stop Press

Baton Twirling ● (p. 167) Horizontal 'Head Roll' 7 min 29 sec Annetta Lucero; Elbow Pop-up 1 min 32 sec Angie Gifford at Milwaukee, Wisconsin 28 July 1987.
Longest Bubble ● (p. 168) Garry Thomas created a bubble 35 ft *10,66 m* in length in San Antonio, Texas on 31 July 1987.
Joggling ● (p. 169) Owen Morse at Akron, Ohio on 15 July 1987 ran 100 metres in 12.12 sec and 15.25 sec with 5 balls.
Cigar Box Balancing ● (p. 169) 134 King Edward boxes for 15 sec on chin by Bruce Bloch in Hilton Hotel, Akron, Ohio on 15 July 1987.
Round of drinks ● (p. 170) Liam Fallon treated 1613 people to a free drink at a charity fund-raising gathering on 4 July 1987 at Lord Byron's Wine Bar, Solihull, Warwickshire.
Conga ● (p. 170) A 'snake' of 10,442 people was recorded at the Edmonton Heritage Festival, Alberta, Canada on 3 Aug 1987.
Roller limbo ● (p. 171) Kelly Foley, 12, also achieved $5\frac{1}{4}$ in *13,33 cm* on 23 May 1987 at Parramatta, NSW, Australia
Tallest cake ● (p. 173) A team of 20 chefs at Collins Hotel, Melbourne, Australia completed 83 tiers, standing 70 ft $4\frac{1}{2}$ in *21.43 m* on 18 June 1987
Spanish omelette ● (p. 173) An omelette weighing 300 kg *660 lb* was made by Jose Antinio Rivera Casal at Caracacia, Padron, Spain on 17 May 1987 and consisting of 5000 eggs, 500 kg *1102 lb* of potatoes, 80 kg 176 lb of red peppers, 10 kg *22 lb* of salt and 150 litres *33 gallons* of oil.
Paella ● (p. 173) Andres Esteban Hernandez made a paella in Getafe, Madrid, Spain for 25,000 on 28 June 1987 12,2 m *40 ft* in diameter with 4.7 tonnes of fish and rice and 400 litres *88 gal* of oil.
Sausage ● (p. 173) The longest continuous sausage was 9.89 miles *15,91 km* prepared by Messrs Dewhurst in 21 hr 17 min on 17–18 June 1987 and transported to Hyde Park, and cooked by scouts on 20 June 1987. Nearly 100,000 portions weighing $4\frac{1}{2}$ tons were served as part of the St John Ambulance Brigade Centenary.
Longest Gum Wrapper Chain ● (p. 173) Fastened by Robert Wooley of San Antonio, Texas. Measured on 31 July 1987 to be 3731 ft 3 in *1137,28 m* with 93,000 wrappers.
Strawberry bowl ● (p. 174) Children from Hazelrigg School picked 1256 lb *569,72 kg* of strawberries at Hewitts Farm, Chelsfield, Kent on 2 July 1987.
Frankfurters ● (p. 174) Reg Morris of Brownhills, West Midlands ate thirty 2 oz *56,6 g* frankfurters in 64 sec at the Miners Rest, Burntwood, Staffs on 10 Dec 1986.
Jam butties ● (p. 174) Reg Morris ate 40 jam butties measuring $6 \times 4 \times \frac{1}{2}$ in *15,2 × 10, 16 × 1,27 cm* in a time of 17 min 20 sec at the Miners Rest, Burntwood, Staffs on 25 Nov 1986.
Pizza ● (p. 175) John Kenmuir ate a pizza weighing 2 lb *907 g* at Pizzaland, Glasgow in 55.28 sec on 26 June 1987.
Sausage Meat ● (p. 175) 96 1 oz pieces (6 lb *2,72 kg*) by Reg Morris at Spring Cottage, Shelfield, Walsall, West Midlands on 28 Dec 1986.
Log Rolling ● (p. 176) Julie Janke (*aka* Hughes) was champion at Albany, Oregon for 1987.
Kiss of life ● (p. 176) Geoff Law and Frank Smith of the West Midlands Ambulance Service completed a 73 hr CPR between 25–8 May 1987 at the National Exhibition Centre, Birmingham.
Leap frogging ● (p. 176) The Phi Gamma Delta Club covered 602 miles *968,8 km* in 105 hr 44 min from 16–21 May 1986 (Total leaps 106,406—one every 9.957 yd *9,104 m*.)
Most versatile magician ● (p. 176) Topper Martyn of Uppsala, Sweden performed 69 separate tricks within 4 min on the Swedish TV's 'Fantasktisk' on 17 Oct 1986.
Hula hooping ● (p. 176) Miss Desai of the Kehaiovi Troupe of Bulgaria gyrated 75 hoops on Wellington Pier, Great Yarmouth on 12 July 1987.
Parachute records ● (p. 177) Nicholas Alkemade died in Cornwall on 22 June 1987 aged 64. Biggest Star: 126 over Koksijde, Belgium 11 July 1987.
Sand sculpting ● (p. 179) A sand sculpture of a snake 3.53 miles *5,68 km* long was made by 90 teams at Great Yarmouth, Norfolk on 12 July 1987.
Quail Eggs ● (p. 179) 27 in 60 sec by Lester Tucker at Grand Prairie, Texas on 31 July 1987.
Jalapeno Peppers ● (p. 179) 29 (no coolants permitted) in 2 min by John Espinoza in San Antonio, Texas on 30 July 1987.
Soap Box Derby ● (p. 181) Chris Wade (b. 1934) set a record of 27.36 sec for the $953\frac{3}{4}$ ft *290,7 m* course at Akron, Ohio on 15 Aug 1987.
Spitting ● (p. 181) Rick Krause achieved 66 ft 6 in *20,26 m* at the 14th Annual Championship on 4 July 1987 at Eau Claire, Michigan, USA.
Stair climbing ● (p. 181) A team of 200 ran up the 1336 stairs of the world's tallest hotel, the Westin Stamford, Singapore on 3 May 1987. The fastest time was recorded by Kenneth Keng at 7 min 20 sec.
Largest boat trot ● (p. 181) The 'City of Dublin' Appeal Committee of the Royal National Lifeboat Institution organised 329 sailing boats belonging to members of Dublin sailing clubs to be moored into a double ring pattern in the shape of a sunflower.
T-bone dive ● (p. 182) Joe Delaney drove a Rover SDI for a leap of exactly 200 ft *60,98 m* on 18 July 1987 at Long Marston Raceway, Warwickshire.
Tightrope walking ● (p. 182) Ashley Brophy, Australia, covered 11,566 km *7.18 miles* in 3 hr 30 min in November 1985 at the Adelaide Grand Prix.
Versatility ● (p. 182) Ashrita Furman of Jamaica, N.Y. was presented in Aug 1987 with a Special Award on the *David Frost presents the Guinness Book of World Records TV Show* for participating in 10 unrelated stamina records.
Walking on hands ● (p. 182) A four-man team of David Lutterman, Brendan Price, Philip Savage and Danny Scannel covered 1 mile *1,609 km* in 24 min 48 sec on 15 Mar 1987 at Knoxville, Tennessee, USA. This compares with the record of 3 min 2 sec the right way up.
Tree Topping ● (p. 182) World champion Guy German climbed 100 ft *30,5 m* spar and sawed off the top in record time of 70.87 sec at Albany, Oregon July 1987.
Whittling ● (p. 183) A wooden chain comprising 69 links 10 ft $2\frac{1}{4}$ in *3,11 m* in length was completed by Charles Paulin in December 1985.
World population ● (p. 187) Matej Gaspar born 11 July 1987 in Yugoslavia was symbolically named the world's 5 billionth inhabitant by the United Nations Secretary-General.
Divorce ● (p. 188) In 1986 some 2 per cent of all *existing* marriages in the US broke up.
Immigration ● (p. 188) The number accepted by the Home Office for settlement in 1986–87 was 45,700.
Prime Ministerial records ● (p. 194) Tallest and Most offices: for Sir James read Lord Callaghan; add Winner of Most General Election Victories Lord Liverpool (4th win in July 1826).
Drill ● (p. 196) On 8–9 July 1987 a 90-man squad of the Queen's Colour Squadron, RAF, performed a total of 2,722,662 dril movements (2,001,384 rifle and 721,278 foot) at RAF Uxbridge from memory and without a word of command in 23 hr 55 min.
Marching ● (p. 196) Lima Company of 42 Commando Royal Marines each man carrying 40 lb *18,14 kg* packs, including a rifle covered the Plymouth Marathon in 4 hr 48 min 9.71 sec on 7 Dec 1986.
Bail ● (p. 198) Shabtai Kalmanowitch, charged with dishonestly procuring $2,030,000, was allowed £500,000 bail at Bow Street Magistrates Court, London on 3 July 1987.
Damages—world ● (p. 199) An unnamed eight-year-old boy born with deformed limbs attributed to his mother's anti-nausea drugs was awarded $95 million *£59.3 million* by a federal jury in Washington, DC, on 14 July 1987.
Damages—Great Britain ● (p. 199) Samir Aboul-Hosn, 23, was awarded £1,032,000 by Mr Justice Hirst in the High Court, London on 10 July 1987 against the Italian Hospital, Bloomsbury, for post-operative negligence resulting in 'catastrophic and irreversible brain damage'.
Defamation ● (p. 199) Author and politician, Jeffrey Archer (b. 15 Apr 1940), was awarded £500,000 by a High Court jury in London against the *Star* newspaper on 24 July 1987. An appeal was lodged.
Most prolific murderers—UK ● (p. 201) The worst armed rampage in Britain was at Hungerford, Berkshire on 19 Aug 1987 as a result of which Michael Ryan, 27, shot dead 15 people and wounded 15 others before shooting himself.
Prolific Murder Charges ● (p. 201) The Court of Appeal is expected to complete a review of evidence on the Birmingham pub case in November 1987.
Robbery ● (p. 201) The robbery in the Knightsbridge Safety Deposit Centre, London on 12 July 1987 was estimated at £30 million for 80 of the 126 boxes robbed. The managing director Parvez Latiff, 30 was among those charged on 17 Aug 1987.
Death Row ● (p. 203) From the reinstatement of the death penalty in the US in 1977 to mid-June 1987, 78 murderers were executed.
Most Expensive Prison ● (p. 204) 'Prisoner Hess' committed suicide on 17 Aug 1987, aged 93. Spandau prison is to be demolished.
'Multiest' multi-billionaire ● (p. 205) Forbes Magazine estimated on 13 July 1987 that Yoshiaki Tsutsumi, 53, Chairman of the Seiba Group, is the world's richest man from 70 real estate and transport companies with assets of $21,000 million *£13,125 million.* Japan is said to have 22 billionaires—one more than the USA.
Longest line of coins ● (p. 207) Residents and visitors to Boulder City, Nevada, laid 34,425 km *21.391 miles* of one-cent coins (worth $19,784.14) on 21 Sept 1985.
University highest enrollment ● (p. 211) The University of Rome (founded 1930) reported 180,000 students in June 1987.
School largest ● (p. 211) Shiu Lang primary school, Taipei, Taiwan has 12,000 students aged 5 to 12 with 292 staff members in 4 ha *9.9 acres.*
Youngest 'A' level Pass ● (p. 211) John Adams, (b. Dec 1977) of Asfordby, Leicestershire achieved a grade C in 'A' level mathematics on 1 June 1987 (announced on 13 August 1987).
Most durable teacher ● (p. 212) Col Loftus died in Harare, Zimbabwe on 7 July 1987 aged 103 years 178 days.
Archery ● (p. 224) World Records: Men's Team 3948 USA 1987; Women 30 m 356 Kim Su Nyong 1987.
Baseball ● (p. 225) Japanese league career records; stolen bases 1059 Yubaka Kukomoto. Consecutive career games, 2154, Sachio Kinugasa.
Basketball ● (p. 227) Most points: Kareem Abdul-Jabbar's career total reached 36,474 by the end of the 1987 season.
Board games ● (p. 228) Draughts: Most games simultaneously—177 by Gary Davis at Marketown, Mt District. NSW, Australia on 4 July 1987.
Scrabble: Highest score in the British Championship is 1863 by Nigel Ingham in 1987.
Ten-pin bowling ● (p. 229) Highest 24-hr scores: 65,584 by a team of six at Goulburn Ten Pin Bowl, Goulburn, NSW, Australia, on 11–12 July 1987.
Cricket ● (p. 236) Ian Botham Test Record: 5057 runs (av. 34.88), 373 wickets (av. 27.86), 109 catches in 94 tests to 11 Aug 1987.
Cycling ● (p. 242) World indoor unpaced flying start records, men 200 m: 10.123 Nikolay Kovch in Moscow 2 Aug 1987; women 200 m: 11.232 Erika Salumyae, Moscow 2 Aug 1987; 500 m; 30.384 Krushelnitskaya.
Darts ● (p. 242) Million and one: 36,750 by the Jobby Crossan select team at St Eugene's Parish Hall, Derry, Northern Ireland on 12–13 June 1987.
24-hr women: 586,111 by a team from the Jeffrey's Arms, Ystradgynlais, Powys, on 6–7 July.
Football (Association) ● (p. 250) Record transfer fee between British clubs: £1.9 million paid by Liverpool to Newcastle United for Peter Beardsley (b. 18 Jan 1961) on 14 July 1987.
Gambling ● (p. 252) Biggest pools win: £1,339,358.30 by Jim Anderson, 51 of Aderton, Northants for matches on 11 July 1987.
Slot machines: The biggest win was $3,041,864.40 by an unidentified teacher at Harrah's Lake Tahoe Casino, Nevada on 11 July 1987.
Golf ● (p. 254) Lowest 72 holes, women: Trish Johnson scored 242 (64,60,60,58) (21 under par) in the Bloor Homes Eastleigh Classic at the Flemming Park Course (4402 yd) at Eastleigh, Hants on 22–25 July 1987.
● (p. 256) Fastest rounds: James Carvill (b. 13 Oct 1965) played 18 holes at the Warrenpoint GC, Co Down, Northern Ireland (5628 m) in 27 min 9 sec on 18 June 1987.
Gymnastics ● (p. 259) Leg raises: Geoffrey Meyers completed 22,071 in 12 hr at the Hyde Park Health Club, Johannesburg, South Africa on 20 June 1987.
Judo Black Belts ● (p. 268) Great grandmother Lucille 'Killer' Thompson of Danville, Illinois (b. 16 Mar 1896) qualified in 1986 age 90. Westley Ciaranella (b. 29 June 1979) of Staten Island, New York qualified in 1983 aged 4.
Motor racing ● (p. 273) Fastest race: 235,421 km/h *146.284 mph* by Nigel Mansell (GB) in a Williams at Zaltweg, Austria on 16 Aug 1987.
Mountaineering ● (p. 274) Charles Cole executed the longest ever Tyrolean Traverse of 870 ft *265 m* in 2 hr 15 min in Yosemite Valley, California.
Skipping ● (p. 285) Most turns on a single rope: 163 at the International Rope Skipping Competition, Greeley, Colorado on 2 July 1987.
Skittles ● (p. 285) 24 hours: 99,051 pins by the 'Alkies' Skittles team at Courtlands Holiday Inn, Torquay on 4–5 Apr 1987.
Swimming ● (p. 288) Men's world record: 50 m freestyle: 22.32 Tom Jager (USA) at Brisbane, Australia on 13 Aug 1987. Women's world records: Janet Evans (USA) (b. 28 Aug 1971). 800 m freestyle: 8:22.44 on 28 July 1987 and 1500 m freestyle: 16:00.73 on 1 Aug 1987 both at Clovis, California, USA.
● (p. 289) British records. Men: 50 m freestyle: 23.30 Mark Foster (b. 12 May 1970) 1 Aug 1987; 100 m freestyle: 50.91 Roland Lee (b. 30 July 1964) 2 Aug 1987; 200 m backstroke: 2:04.16 John Davey (b. 29 Dec 1964) 30 July 1987; 400 m medley: 4:24.20 John Davey 31 July 1987, all at Crystal Palace, London.
Swimming ● (p. 290) Philip Rush, 23, (NZ) completed the triple Channel Crossing in 28 hr 21 min on 17–18 Aug 1987. Oldest: Clifford Batt, 68 of Australia swam the Channel on 20 Aug 1987.
Table tennis ● (p. 291) Counter hitting in 60 sec—women: 168 by Jackie and Lisa Bellinger at the Crest Hotel, Luton, Bedfordshire, on 23 June 1985.
Track and field ● (p. 298) Women's world record: Javelin 78.90 m *258 ft 10 in* Petra Felke (GDR) at Leipzig, GDR on 29 July 1987.
Women's 100 m hurdles: 12.25 sec, Ginka Zagorcheva (BUL) at Dŕama, Greece on 8 Aug 1987.
Women's joint world record: Long Jump 7,45 m *24 ft $5\frac{1}{2}$ in* Jackie Joyner-Kersee (USA) at Indianapolis, USA on 14 Aug 1987.
Water Skiing ● (p. 303) 'Banana' George Blair barefoot pioneer of Florida, USA became the only skier to have skied in every continent (including Antartica).
Weightlifting ● (p. 304) Karen Marshall of New York City clean and jerked 303 lb *137,4 kg* in 1987.
Boardsailing endurance ● (p. 307) 107 hr by Neil Marlow (GB) in Braye Bay, Alderney and Pembroke Bay, Guernsey, Channel Islands from 4–8 Aug 1987.
Endurance marathons ● (pp. 307–8)
Badminton (singles) 80 hr 20 min 2 sec, Gordon D Nel and Jannie Vosloo at Komga Town Hall, Komga, South Africa on 26–29 June 1987.
Badminton (doubles) 86 hr 22 min 44 sec, Cameron McMullen, Michael Pattison, Stephen Breuer and Michael Bain at Rhyl, Clywd, Wales on 18–21 July 1987.
Racquetball endurance 43 hr by Phillip Simons and Chris Cornish in Neubreucke, West Germany, from 12–14 July 1987.
Squash endurance 126 hr 1 min, P Etherton, L Davies at Tanuum Sands, Queensland, Australia on 7–12 July 1987.

An asterisk indicates a further reference in the Stop Press

313

heaviest sub-nuclear, newest, shortest lived nuclear 72
PARTICLE ACCELERATOR, *most powerful 78*
PARTY GIVING, *most expensive, largest 166*
PASS, *highest 209*
PASSENGER, *oldest*, youngest air 141*
PASSENGER LIFT, *fastest world, longest UK 144*
PASSENGER LINER, *largest, longest 124*
PASTRY, *longest 173*
PATENT, *earliest radio 101, television 102, earliest H Bomb 197, earliest English, most applications, shortest, longest 198, greatest infringement damages 199*
PEACH, *largest 47*
PEANUTS, *eating record 175*
PEAPOD, *longest 47*
PEAR, *heaviest 47*
PEARL, *largest, most expensive 77*
PEAS, *eating record 175*
PEDIGREE, *longest 84*
PEELING, *records, onion, potato 178*
PEER, *most ancient peerage, oldest creation, longest lived, youngest, longest and shortest, highest succession number, most creations, most prolific 185*
PEERAGE, *most ancient, oldest creation, longest, shortest, highest numbering, most creations, most prolific 185*
PEERESS, *most prolific 185*
PELOTA VASCA, *276*
PENAL CAMPS, *largest 203*
PENAL SETTLEMENT, *largest French 203*
PENDULUM, *longest 146*
PENINSULA, *largest 54*
PENKNIFE, *most blades 156*
PENNINE WAY, *cycling 241, fell running 274–5*
PENNY-FARTHING, *records 133*
PENPALS, *most durable 87*
PENS, *most expensive 156*
PENSION, *longest 166*
PEPPERS, JALAPENO, *eating record**
PERFECT DEALS, *(bridge) 233*
PERFECT NUMBERS, *lowest, highest 77*
PERFORMER, *biggest audience 94, highest-paid TV 103, 104*
PERFUME, *most expensive 73*
PERIODICAL, *oldest world, GB, largest circulation, world, GB, annual 90, highest advertising rates 91*
PERMAFROST, *deepest 61*
PERSONAL INJURY, *highest damages world, GB 198–9*
PERSONAL NAMES, *earliest, longest pedigree, longest single Christian name, surname, world, UK, most Christian names, shortest, commonest surname, most 'Macs', most versions of, most changed 84, most contrived 85*
PETANQUE, *276*
PETITION, *greatest parliamentary 191*
PETROL, *consumption 128, first unleaded 130*
PETUNIA, *tallest 47*
PHARMACEUTICALS, *biggest sales 150*
PHILODENDRON, *largest 46*
PHONE, see **Telephone**
PHONOGRAPH, *see* **Gramophone**
PHOTOGRAPHIC STORE, *largest 150*
PHOTOGRAPHY, *earliest world, UK, earliest aerial, largest negative 74*
PHYSICAL EXTREMES, *77–8*
PHYSICIANS, *most, highest, lowest proportion 188*
PHYSIOLOGY, *15–21*
Pi, *number of places memorised 17, most accurate, inaccurate version 77*
PIANIST, *highest-paid, greatest span 95*
PIANO, *earliest, grandest, most expensive, smallest 91, highest notes 93*
PIANO COMPOSITION, *longest 94*
PIANO PLAYING, *world, UK 178*
PIANO SMASHING, *record 178*
PIANO TUNING, *record 178*
PICKLED ONIONS, *eating record 175*
PIE, *largest apple, cherry, custard, meat, mince, pizza 173*
PIER, *oldest, longest, most, pleasure, world, GB 111, longest world, GB 119–20*
PIG, *highest price 158, heaviest, prolificacy record 159*
PIGEON RACING, *276–7*
PIGGERY, *largest 157*
PILLAR BOX, *oldest 211*
PILLAR BOX STANDING, *record number of people 178*
PILLAR OF COINS, *207*
PILL TAKER, *greatest 21*
PILOT, *most flying hours, most take offs and landings, oldest and youngest, human-powered flight 141, ace 184*
PINEAPPLE, *largest 47*
PINNIPEDS, *largest world, GB, smallest, most abundant, rarest, fastest, deepest dive, longest lived 27*
PIPELINE, *longest oil, submarine, natural gas, water, most expensive 144*
PIPE SMOKING, *duration record 178*
PISTOLS, *most expensive 156, highest auction price 153*
PITCH, *(sound) highest detectable 18, bat 27, (sport) largest 219*
PIZZA PIE, *largest 173, eating record 175**
PLACE NAMES, *earliest, longest world, GB, shortest world, GB, most spellings 85*
PLAGUE, *most infectious disease 19*
PLANE PULLING, *178*
PLANET, *largest, shortest 'day' 66, smallest, coldest, outermost 66, 67, highest orbital speed, hottest, nearest, surface features, brightest and faintest, densest and least dense, conjunctions, most dramatic, next conjunction, largest scale model 66*
PLANETARIUM, *first, largest, earliest world, GB 75*
PLANT KINGDOM, *45–50, oldest, rarest, northernmost, southernmost, highest, roots, depth, length, worst weeds, most spreading, smallest flowering, fruiting, fastest growth, slowest flowering, oldest pot plant, biggest collection, earliest flower 45, largest leaves world, GB 48*
PLATEAU, *greatest 56*
PLATE SPINNING, *record 178*
PLATFORM, Railway, *longest 135*
PLATINUM, *largest refinery 122*
PLATINUM DISC, *unique award 98*
PLAY, *longest runs 96–7, shortest runs, longest, Shakespeare 97*
PLAYING CARDS, *rarest and most expensive 153*
PLEASURE BEACH, *biggest 111*
PLEASURE PIER, *earliest, longest, most 111*
PLOUGHING, *championship, greatest acreage ploughed, fastest 158*
PLUCKING, *chicken, turkey record 159*
POEM, *longest, most successful 88*
POET LAUREATE, *youngest, oldest 88*
POGO-STICK JUMPING, *178, 179*
POISON, *most potent 73 (also most poisonous snake, most active frog venom 37, most venomous fish 38, most poisonous spider 39), mass poisoning 201*
POLAR CONQUESTS, *first North, South, first at both poles, first circumnavigation 162–3*
POLAR LIGHT, see **Aurora**
POLDER, *largest 116*
POLE SQUATTING, *records 178*
POLICY, Life assurance, *largest, highest pay out 149–50*
POLITICAL DIVISION, *largest 187*
POLITICAL SPEECH, *longest on record 191*
POLLEN COUNT, *highest 50*
POLO, *277*
POOL, *277, 307*
POPE, *longest, shortest reign, longest lived, oldest, youngest, last non-Italian, last ex-Cardinalate, English, last married, quickest and slowest election 213*
POP FESTIVAL, *greatest attendance 94*
POP GROUP, *most successful 99, non-stop playing 178*
POPULATION, *world*, progressive mid-year estimates, largest, smallest, densest, UK, sparsest 187, cities 189*
PORCELAIN, *highest price 153*
PORT, *largest, busiest 208*
PORTRAIT, *most expensive miniature 81*
PORTRAITIST, *most prolific 80*
POST OFFICE, *northernmost UK, and southernmost, oldest, longest counter 211*
POSTAGE STAMPS, *see* **Stamps**
POSTAL SERVICE, *largest and highest average letter mail, highest-numbered address, oldest pillar boxes, northernmost and southernmost, oldest post office, longest counter 211*
POSTCARDS, *156*
POSTER, *largest, highest priced 81*
POTATO, *record display 48, dimension, weight 47, record yield 158, peeling record 178, eating record 175*
POTATO CRISPS, *eating record 175, largest 173*
POTATO MASH, *largest serving 173*
POT LID, *highest price 153*
POT PLANT, *largest, oldest 45*
POTTERY, *highest price 153*
POWDER, *finest 73*
POWERBOAT RACING, *277*
POWER FAILURE, *greatest 143*
POWERLIFTING, *303–305*
POWER PRODUCERS, *141–3*
POWER STATION, *largest world, non-hydro-electric, largest GB, atomic, solar, tidal 142*
PRAM PUSHING, *record distance 178*
PREDATOR, *largest 43*
PREGNANCY, *longest, shortest 15*
PREHISTORIC ANIMALS, *see* **Extinct Animals**
PREHISTORIC MONUMENT, *largest 119*
PREMIER, see **Prime Minister**
PREMIUM, Insurance, *largest 149–50*
PRESS, *largest 144*
PRESS-UPS, *259*
PRESSURE, *highest, lowest barometric 61, laboratory 77*
PRIMATE, *largest, heaviest, smallest 27, rarest 27–8, longest lived, strongest 28, earliest 10, 44, largest extinct 44*
PRIME MINISTER, *oldest, longest term of office 192, UK, records, shortest, most times, youngest, other records 194**
PRIME NUMBERS, *lowest, highest 76–7*
PRINT, *record price 81*
PRINTER, *largest 89, fastest 144*
PRINTING, *earliest, earliest books, largest, smallest 85, most valuable books 86, highest print order 88, 89*
PRISON, *longest sentences, world, GB, longest time served, longest detention, escapes from Broadmoor, largest GB 203, highest population 203–4, most secure, most expensive*, longest escape, greatest break 204*
PRISONER, *oldest, most convictions 203*
PRIZE, *largest radio 102, TV 104, competition 168, most valuable annual 185*
PROCARYOTA, *50*
PRODUCER, *youngest Broadway 97, most prolific TV 103, 104*
PROFESSOR, *youngest, most durable 211*
PROFIT AND LOSS, *greatest 148*
PROMISE, Breach of, *highest damages 199*
PROPELLER, *largest ship 125, largest aircraft 138*
PROPERTY, *most valuable 150*
PROSECUTION, *rarest 203*
PROTEIN, *most and least proteinous fruit 47*
PROTISTA, *largest, smallest, fastest-moving, fastest reproduction 49–50*
PROTOPHYTE, *smallest 50*
PROTOZOAN, *largest, smallest, fastest-moving, fastest reproduction 50*
PRUNES, *eating record 175*
PSALM, *longest, shortest 86*
PSYCHIATRIST, *most 189, fastest 178*
PSYCHIC FORCES, *22*
PUBLICATION, *largest 85–6*
PUBLIC HOUSE, *oldest UK, largest world, GB, smallest, longest bars world, UK, Ireland, longest tenure, longest name, shortest name, commonest name, highest, most visits 112*
PUBLIC RELATIONS, *largest firm 150*
PUBLISHERS, *fastest 88, oldest 88–9, most prolific 89*
PUBLISHING, *largest enterprise 150*
PULSARS, *first, fastest 69*
PULSE RATES, *highest, lowest 19*
PUMPING, *(fire) greatest gallonage 171*
PUMPKIN, *heaviest 47*
PUMP-TURBINE, *largest 143*
PURGE, *greatest 200*
PYGMIES, *smallest 8*
PYRAMID, *tallest (progressive records), oldest 114, largest, work force 120*

Q.C., see **Queen's Counsel**
QUADRUPLETS, *oldest 12, heaviest, most sets 14*
QUARRY, *deepest, largest world, England 122*
QUASAR, *69*
QUAY, *longest 119–20*
QUEEN, *longest lived 189–90, youngest, British records 190*
QUEEN'S COUNSEL, *youngest, most successful 200*
QUIETEST PLACE, *78*
QUILT, *world's largest 156*
QUINDECAPLETS, *15*
QUINTUPLETS, *heaviest 14, test tube**
QUIZ, *largest TV prize 104, most participants, most protracted 178*
QUOIT THROWING, *record 179*
QUORUM, *smallest parliamentary 191*

RABBITS, *largest litter 32, largest breed, heaviest specimen, smallest, most prolific, longest ears, oldest 32*
RACE, *(ethnology) poorest 206*
RACQETBALL, *278, 307**
RACKETS, *278*
RADAR INSTALLATION, *largest 144*
RADIO, *origins, earliest patent 101, earliest broadcast world, GB, earliest trans-Atlantic, longest broadcast, topmost prize, most durable programmes*, most heard broadcaster, earliest antipodal reception, most assiduous ham, most stations, highest listenership, highest response, smallest set 102, tallest masts 112*
RADIO-MICROPHONES, *earliest 102*
RADIO TELESCOPE, *first fully steerable, largest 74*
RADISH, *heaviest 47*
RAFT, *longest survival 165*
RAILWAY, *longest bridge, highest bridge 113, tunnel, subway tunnel 116, earliest, fastest, longest non-stop 133, most powerful engine 133–4, greatest load, longest freight train, longest run, longest straight, widest, narrowest gauge world, GB, highest, lowest 134, steepest (world, GB) 134–5, shallowest gradients, busiest rail system, calling all stations*, most countries, railroad handcar pumping, longest journey, stations, largest world, GB, oldest, busiest, highest, largest waiting rooms, longest platform, underground: most extensive, greatest depth, longest, quickest journey, most stations, busiest subway, model railway: duration record, longest run, most miniature 135, country with greatest length, furthest place from in GB, number of journeys on British Rail 208, disasters 216–17*
RAILWAY DISASTERS, *worst world, U.K. 216–17*
RAILWAY ENGINE, *see* **Engine** *(Railway)*
RAINBOW, *longest lasting 60*
RAINFALL, *most intense, greatest, least 60–61*
RAINY DAYS, *most in years 60–61*
RALLY, *(motor) earliest, longest 273*
RAMP JUMPING, *longest 179*
RANSOM, *highest 202*
RAPPELING, *longest descent 179*
RAT, *oldest 32*
RATTING, *record by dog 31*
RAVIOLI, *eating record 175*
REACTION, *fastest human 19*
REACTOR, *largest single atomic 142*
REAL ESTATE, *most valuable 150*
REAL TENNIS, *294*
RECORD, Gramophone, *see* **Gramophone Record**
RECORD BREAKERS, *(sport) youngest and oldest 219, most prolific 220*
RECORDED SOUND *98–100, earliest, oldest, smallest, jazz records, earliest tape, most successful artist 98, group: earliest, most golden discs, most recordings, biggest sales, fastest-selling album, top ten singles 99, greatest advance sales 99–100, compact discs, Grammy awards 100*
RECORDING ARTIST, *most successful* 98, earliest golden disc, most golden discs, most recordings, best-selling, charts, fastest sellers 99, greatest advance sales 99–100, Grammy awards 100*
RED CABBAGE, *heaviest 47*
REED, *tallest 48*
REEF, *longest 55–6*
REFINERY, *(oil) largest 150*
REFLECTING TELESCOPE, *largest and most powerful 74*
REFLEXES, *fastest 19*
REFRACTING TELESCOPE, *largest 74*
'REFUSENIK', *most patient 188*
REGIMENT, *British, oldest, most senior 196*
REGISTRATION PLATE, *earliest, most expensive 127*
REIGN, *number lived through 12, longest 189–90, shortest, highest post-nominal numbers, longest lived 'royals', British records 190*
RELIGION, *oldest, largest, Christian, largest non-Christian, total world Jewry 212, Roman Catholic records 213, earliest 212–13, oldest buildings, largest temple, largest 213, smallest cathedral 213–14, largest church world, GB, smallest church, synagogue, mosque 214*
RENT, *highest, land 150*
REPTILE, *crocodilians: largest*, longest, smallest, oldest, rarest 35,*

Indexing by

Anna Pavord

World Copyright Reserved   Copyright © 1987   Guinness Publishing Ltd

This book is sold subject to the Standard Conditions of Sale of Net Books and may not be resold in the United Kingdom below the net price fixed by the publishers and ascertainable from their 1987 Catalogue.

British Library Cataloguing in Publication Data

Guinness book of records.—34th ed.
1. World records—Periodicals
032'.02   AG240

ISBN 0-85112-868-8

Standard Book Number ISBN: 0-85112-868-8
Standard Book Number ISBN: 0-85112-873-4 (Australian Edition)

'Guinness' is a registered trade mark of Guinness Publishing Ltd.

Printed in England. Produced by Jarrold Printing, Norwich, Norfolk, and William Clowes Limited, Beccles, Suffolk.

The Editors of the
GUINNESS BOOK OF RECORDS
wish to thank
David F. Hoy

Deputy Editors
Stewart Newport
Alex E Reid
Sarah Shaps
Ian R Smith
Sheelagh Thomas

Sports Editor
Peter J Matthews

Art Editor
David L Roberts

Picture Editor
Alex P Goldberg

Assistants
Ann Collins
Sheila Goldsmith
Muriel Ling
Anna Nicholas

Contributors
Andrew Adams; C V Appleton; John W Arblaster AIM; Moira Banks; Howard Bass; Pat Beresford;
Robin Bradford; Henry G Button; Sq Ldr D H Clarke DFC, AFC; Colin Dyson; Clive Everton;
Julian Farino; Victoria Fisher; Frank L Forster; Bill Frindall; Tim Furniss; Ian Goold; Steven Goldberg;
Stan Greenberg; J C Greetham; Albert Herbert; Sir Peter Johnson; Alan Jones (Gallup); Peter Lunn;
John Marshall; Andy Milroy; Alan Mitchell BA, BAg(For); John Moody; Ian Morrison; Susann Palmer; Tessa Pocock;
John Randall; Jack Rollin; Irving Saxton; Robert Shopland; Colin C Smith; Graham Snowdon; Donald Steel;
Lance Tingay; Nicholas Todd (GRR Books); Juhani Virola; Dr A C Waltham; Rick Wilson; Gerald L Wood FZS

Grateful acknowledgement is made to the governing bodies and organisations who have helped in our researches

Overseas Editors
Denmark—Per Theil Hansen; *Finland*—Synnöve Takala; *France*—Philippe Scali;
Germany—Hans Heinrich Kummel; *Greece*—Athanasios Rigas; *Hindi*—Ashok Gupta;
Hungary—Paul Satinoff; *Iceland*—Orlygur Halfdanarson; *India*—Desu Subrahmanyam;
Israel—Daphne Hausman; *Italy*—Maurizio Orlandi; *Japan*—H Nishio; *Middle East*—Antoine Naufal;
Netherlands—Klaas de Boer; *Norway*—Anne Fjeldberg; *Spain*—Margarita Jordan;
Sweden—Lisbet Ekberg; *Thailand*—Aphai Prakobpol; *USA*—David A Boehm
and to
Josie Ashworth (New Zealand); D Richard Bowen (Europe); Bob Burton (Australia); Ben Matsumoto (Far East)

Production/Printing
Laurie Hammond; David Browne; John Catchpole;
Alan Berryman; John Barnard; Malcolm Debenham;
Basil Forder; Des Palmer; Eddy Thurston; Ted Tuffen

Cover Design
By Pocknell & Co.
Photographs by Virgin; London Features International Ltd; Rex Features; All-Sport and Colorific

Artwork, Maps and Diagrams
Robert and Rhoda Burns—Drawing Attention; Peter Harper; Eddie Botchway;
Matthew Hillier; Ashley Hamilton-Lloyd; Peter Harris; Top Draw; Tobasco and Pocknell & Co

FACTS
FIGUR
FEATS

GREATEST

SMALLEST

FASTEST

VISIT THE GUINNESS WORLD
...IT'S A FASCINATING

THE TROCADERO · PICCADILLY CIRCUS · LONDON W1V 7FD